SOCIOLOGICAL THEORY

ORIGIN 1897

FOUNDERS Émile Durkheim, Robert Ezra Park, Ernest Burgess, Clifford Shaw, Walter Reckless, Frederic Thrasher

MOST IMPORTANT WORKS Durkheim, *The Division of Labor in Society* (1893), and *Suicide: A Study in Sociology* (1897); Park, Burgess, and John McKenzie, *The City* (1925); Thrasher, *The Gang* (1926); Shaw et al., *Delinquency Areas* (1925); Edwin Sutherland, *Criminology* (1924)

CORE IDEAS A person's place in the social structure determines his or her behavior. Disorganized urban areas are the breeding ground of crime. A lack of legitimate opportunities produces criminal subcultures. Socialization within the family, the school, and the peer group controls behavior.

MODERN OUTGROWTHS Strain Theory, Cultural Deviance Theory, Social Learning Theory, Social Control Theory, Social Reaction Theory, Labeling

Émile Durkheim

Corbis/Bettmann

Sheldon and Eleanor Glueck

Harvard Law School Library

Karl Marx

Stock Montage, Inc.

MULTIFACTOR THEORY

ORIGIN About 1930

FOUNDERS Sheldon and Eleanor Glueck

MOST IMPORTANT WORKS Sheldon and Eleanor Glueck: *Five Hundred Delinquent Women* (1934); *Later Criminal Careers* (1937); *Criminal Careers in Retrospect* (1943); *Juvenile Delinquents Grown Up* (1940); *Unraveling Juvenile Delinquency* (1950)

CORE IDEAS Crime is a function of environmental, socialization, physical, and psychological factors. Each makes an independent contribution to shaping and directing behavior patterns. Deficits in these areas of human development increase the risk of crime. People at risk for crime can resist anti-social behaviors if these traits and conditions can be strengthened.

MODERN OUTGROWTHS Developmental Theory, Life Course Theory, Latent Trait Theory

Just what you need to know NOW!

Your portal to more effective studying!

A web-based, intelligent study system, ThomsonNOW™ enables you to save time, learn more, and succeed in your criminology course! ThomsonNOW™ is students' number-one pick to get the grade, and it offers you everything you need for success, from an assessment tool that gauges your unique study needs to a *Personalized Study Plan* that focuses your study time on the concepts you most need to master to a *Post-Test* that enables you to assess your progress. If access is not packaged with your book, visit **http://www.thomson edu.com** to purchase an access code.

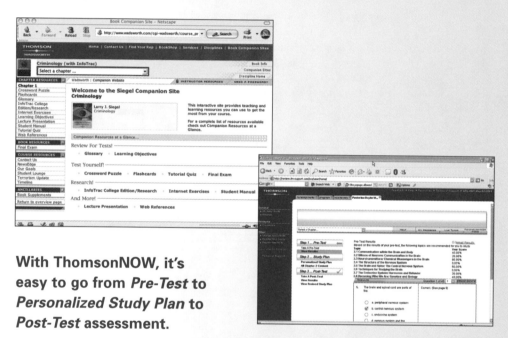

With ThomsonNOW, it's easy to go from *Pre-Test* to *Personalized Study Plan* to *Post-Test* assessment.

At the Book Companion Website—**www.thomsonedu.com/criminaljustice**—you'll log onto ThomsonNOW™ by using your access code. After you take a *Pre-Test* covering the chapter you've just read, ThomsonNOW™ calculates the results and generates your *Personalized Study Plan* based on your answers to the *Pre-Test*. The plan outlines those topics that require review (noted by section title and page number) and guides you to media activities—including interactive learning modules, visual overviews, simulations, video clips, and much more—all of which clarify the most essential concepts you must master. A follow-up *Post-Test* helps you assess final mastery of the material.

Many of our online resources are available through 1pass™.
To learn more, please visit http://www.thomsonedu.com

NINTH EDITION

CRIMINOLOGY

Theories, Patterns, and Typologies

Larry J. Siegel
UNIVERSITY OF MASSACHUSETTS, LOWELL

THOMSON

WADSWORTH ™   Australia • Brazil • Canada • Mexico • Singapore • Spain • United Kingdom • United States

Criminology: Theories, Patterns, and Typologies, Ninth Edition
Larry J. Siegel

Senior Acquisitions Editor, Criminal Justice: Carolyn Henderson Meier
Development Editor: Shelley Murphy
Assistant Editor: Jana Davis
Editorial Assistant: Rebecca Johnson
Technology Project Manager: Susan DeVanna
Marketing Manager: Terra Schultz
Marketing Assistant: Jaren Boland
Marketing Communications Manager: Linda Yip
Project Manager, Editorial Production: Jennie Redwitz
Creative Director: Rob Hugel
Art Director: Vernon Boes

Print Buyer: Karen Hunt
Permissions Editor: Bobbie Broyer
Production Service: Robin C. Hood
Text Designer: Jeanne Calabrese
Photo Researcher: Billie Porter
Copy Editor: Jennifer Gordon
Cover Designer: Yvo
Cover Image: © Margaret Carsello/Images.com
Compositor: Pre-Press Co., Inc.
Text and Cover Printer: Transcontinental Printing/Interglobe

Library of Congress Control Number: 2005937991

ISBN 0-495-00572-X

Thomson Higher Education
10 Davis Drive
Belmont, CA 94002-3098
USA

For more information about our products, contact us at:
Thomson Learning Academic Resource Center
1-800-423-0563
For permission to use material from this text or product, submit a request online at **http://www.thomsonrights.com**.
Any additional questions about permissions can be submitted by email to **thomsonrights@thomson.com**.

This book is dedicated to my children,
Rachel, Eric, Andrew, and Julie,
and to Therese J. Libby (my wife,
lawyer, and best friend).

ABOUT THE AUTHOR

LARRY J. SIEGEL was born in the Bronx in 1947. While attending City College of New York in the 1960s, he was swept up in the social and political currents of the time. He became intrigued with the influence contemporary culture had on individual behavior: Did people shape society or did society shape people? He applied his interest in social forces and human behavior to the study of crime and justice. After graduating CCNY, he attended the newly opened program in criminal justice at the State University of New York at Albany, earning both his M.A. and Ph.D. degrees there. After completing his graduate work, Dr. Siegel began his teaching career at Northeastern University, where he was a faculty member for nine years. He has also held teaching positions at the University of Nebraska–Omaha and Saint Anselm College in New Hampshire. He is currently a professor at the University of Massachusetts–Lowell.

Dr. Siegel has written extensively in the area of crime and justice, including books on juvenile law, delinquency, criminology, and criminal procedure. He is a court certified expert on police conduct and has testified in numerous legal cases. The father of four and grandfather of two, Larry Siegel and his wife, Terry, now reside in Bedford, New Hampshire, with their two cockapoos, Watson and Cody.

BRIEF CONTENTS

v

CONTENTS

Chapter 11 ▎ Property Crime 366

Chapter 12 ▎ Enterprise Crime: White-Collar and Organized Crime 394

In July 2004, Troy Victorino and some friends were illegally squatting in a Florida home while the owners were spending the summer in Maine. When the owners' granddaughter, Erin Belanger, found them, she called the police to have them removed from the premises. The squatters were kicked out, but they left behind an Xbox game system that Erin took back to her home, which she was sharing with friends. Over the next few days, Troy and his friends threatened Belanger and slashed the tires on her car. They warned her that they were going to come back and beat her with a baseball bat while she was sleeping. Then on August 6, 2004, Victorino and three accomplices armed with aluminum bats kicked in the locked front door. The invaders, wearing black clothes and with scarves over their faces, grabbed knives inside and attacked victims in different rooms of the three-bedroom house as some of them slept. All six victims, including Erin Belanger, were beaten and stabbed beyond recognition. All six died.

Victorino was a career criminal. He had spent eight of the last eleven years before the killings serving prison sentences for a variety of crimes including auto theft, battery, arson, theft, and burglary. In 1996, he beat a man so severely that doctors needed fifteen titanium plates to rebuild the victim's face. The week before the attack Victorino was arrested for punching a 28-year-old man in the face and charged with felony battery; he was released on a $2,500 bond and visited his probation officer for his regular check-in the day before the murders. Although he should have been arrested then for violating his probation, his case supervisor failed to take action; in the aftermath of the murders, Victorino's probation officer and three of his supervisors were dismissed. On October 27, 2005, one of the attackers, Robert Cannon, pleaded guilty to fourteen charges and agreed to give evidence against the other three defendants—Victorino (28), Michael Salas (19), and Jerome Hunter (19). The prosecution is asking for the death penalty.

The Xbox murder case, while particularly senseless and brutal, is certainly not unique: More than 10,000 Americans are murdered each year. It is not surprising then that many of us are concerned about crime and are worried about becoming the victims of violent crime, having our houses broken into, our cars stolen, and our pension funds misappropriated. We alter our behavior to limit the risk of victimization and question whether legal punishment alone can control criminal offenders. We watch movies about law firms, clients, fugitives, and stone-cold killers. We are shocked by the news media when they give graphic accounts of school shootings, police brutality, and sexual assaults.

I, too, have had a life-long interest in crime, law, and justice. Why do people behave the way they do? What causes one person like Troy Victorino to become violent and antisocial, while another person channels his or her energy into work, school, and family? Why are some adolescents able to resist the "temptation of the streets" and become law-abiding citizens, while others join gangs and enter into criminal careers? Conversely, what accounts for the behavior of the multimillionaire who cheats on his taxes or engages in fraudulent schemes? The former has nothing yet is able to resist crime; the latter has everything and falls prey to its lure. And what should be done with convicted criminals? After the murders, Troy Victorino's mother claimed that his problems stemmed from being sexually abused as a child. Should such abuse mitigate his guilt? Or should he be given the death penalty for his horrible crimes? Conversely, should Robert Cannon escape death because he was willing to testify against his co-conspirators?

GOALS OF THIS TEXT

For the past 35 years I have been able to channel this interest into a career as a teacher of criminology. My goal in writing this text is to help engender in students the same fascination in the twists and turns of human behavior. This goal is directed toward answering the question that is the ultimate objective of criminology: Why do people behave the way they do? And from my perspective, there can be no more important or intriguing field of study than one that deals with such wide-ranging topics as the motivation for mass murder, the effects of violent media on young people, drug abuse, and organized crime. Criminology is a dynamic field, changing constantly with the release of major research studies, Supreme Court rulings, and governmental policy. This dynamism and diversity make it an engrossing and rewarding area of study.

One reason that the study of criminology is so important is that debates continue over the nature and extent of crime and the causes and prevention of criminality. Some view criminals as society's victims who are forced to violate the law because they live in poverty and lack meaningful legitimate opportunities for success. Another view is that aggressive or antisocial behavior is a product of mental and physical abnormalities, present at birth or soon after, that make people prone to commit crime. It is also possible that criminals are greedy people who choose to commit crime because they believe it will return large profits with small risks. There is no single explanation for the cause of crime, and criminologists spend their careers searching for answers to two basic questions: Why do some people engage in antisocial acts? And what can be done to prevent or deter their behavior?

Because interest in crime and justice is so timely, this text is designed to review these ongoing issues and cover the field of criminology in an organized and comprehensive manner. It is meant as a broad overview of the field, designed to whet the reader's appetite and encourage further and more in-depth exploration. Several major themes recur throughout the book.

Competing Viewpoints

In every chapter an effort is made to introduce students to the diversity of thought that characterizes the discipline. Lively debates swirl over the nature and extent of crime and the causes and prevention of criminality. As noted, some experts view criminal offenders as society's victims—unfortunate people who are forced to violate the law because they lack hope of legitimate opportunity. Others view aggressive, antisocial behavior as a product of mental and physical abnormalities, present at birth or soon after, which are stable over the life course. Still another view is that crime is a function of the rational choice of greedy, selfish people who can only be deterred though the threat of harsh punishments. I try to cover all the bases and present every side of the various arguments. Students are helped in this regard by Concept Summary features that set out the central theme of each viewpoint.

Critical Thinking

It is important for students to think critically about law and justice and to develop a critical perspective toward the social and legal institutions entrusted with crime control. Throughout the book, students are asked to think outside the box. To aid in this task, each chapter ends with a "Thinking Like a Criminologist" feature that presents a scenario that can be analyzed with the help of material found in the chapter.

Diversity

Diversity is a key issue in criminology because crime data tell us that the poor and minority group members are overrepresented both as criminal offenders and as the victims of crime and may suffer disparate treatment in the criminal justice system. The text attempts to focus on issues of racial, ethnic, gender, and cultural diversity to understand these important aspects of racial disparity. Comparative information is also essential to the study of criminology, for it helps us think outside of American norms, so I have included in the text material on international issues, such as the use of the death penalty abroad. To help with the coverage of diversity issues, Race, Culture, Gender, and Criminology features cover topics such as "Capitalism and Patriarchy" (Chapter 8) and "The Code of the Streets" (Chapter 6).

Current Research and Policy

Throughout the book, every effort is made to use the most current research to show students the major trends in criminological research and policy. Most people who use the book have told me that this is one of its strongest features. The Criminological Enterprise features review important current research in criminology and show how it is used to shape policy.

Use of Technology

The text focuses on technology and its impact on criminology. The new chapter on cyber crime and technology represents a clear indication that the use of technology is now shaping both criminal behavior and law enforcement responses to crime. The chapter includes a number of boxed inserts that focus on these emerging uses of technology. One boxed feature entitled "Crime Scene Investigation Goes High Tech" discusses how through a combination of laser/computer technology and high-definition surveying (HDS) criminal investigators are able to virtually maneuver every piece of evidence at a crime scene in order to increase an investigation's effectiveness. Another feature on biometric technology shows how recording and accessing facial recognition patterns have reshaped the way homeland security agencies combat terrorism.

Not only does the book focus on the influence of technology in criminology, but it also uses it as a learning tool. Woven throughout the manuscript are links that direct students to websites that further discuss the material presented in the chapter. In addition, the text makes extensive use of InfoTrac College Edition, an online research site that contains hundreds of thousands of full-text articles. There are InfoTrac College Edition exercises included in every chapter. In sum, the primary goals in writing this text are:

1. To provide students with a thorough knowledge of criminology and show its diversity and intellectual content

2. To be as thorough and up-to-date as possible

3. To be objective and unbiased

4. To describe current theories, crime types, and methods of social control and analyze their strengths and weaknesses

5. To show how criminological thought has influenced social policy

ORGANIZATION

Criminology: Theories, Patterns, and Typologies is a thorough introduction to this fascinating field and intended for students in introductory level courses in criminology. It is divided into three main sections or topic areas.

Part One provides a framework for studying criminology. The first chapter defines the field and discusses its most basic concepts: the definition of crime, the component areas of criminology, the history of criminology, the concept of criminal law, and the ethical issues that confront the field. Chapter 2 covers criminological research methods, and the nature, extent, and patterns of crime. Chapter 3 is devoted to the concept of victimization, including the nature of victims, theories of victimization, and programs designed to help crime victims.

Part Two contains six chapters that cover criminological theory: Why do people behave the way they do? Why do they commit crimes? These views focus on choice (Chapter 4), biological and psychological traits (Chapter 5), social structure and culture (Chapter 6), social process and socialization (Chapter 7), social conflict (Chapter 8), and human development (Chapter 9).

Part Three is devoted to the major forms of criminal behavior. The chapters in this section cover violent crime (Chapter 10), common theft offenses (Chapter 11), white-collar and organized crime (Chapter12), public order crimes (Chapter 13), and cyber crime (Chapter 14).

WHAT IS NEW IN THE NINTH EDITION

- Chapter 1 now begins with the story of Kobe Bryant, the star athlete arrested on rape charges, and how publicity may have influenced his trial. A Comparative Criminology feature entitled "International Crime Trends" looks at crime trends around the world. A number of new cases are analyzed, including the 2003 case *Smith v. Doe,* which concerned the Alaska Sex Offender Registration Act, and an important 2003 case, *Lawrence v. Texas,* in which the Supreme Court declared that laws banning sodomy are unconstitutional. The chapter now covers the topic of criminal law in a concise yet thorough presentation. Topics such as the history of the law, the purpose of the law, the legal definition of a crime, and criminal defenses are included.

- Chapter 2 begins with a discussion of the case of Eric Rudolph, who was arrested and charged with the deadly bombing of an Atlanta abortion clinic. It has a new discussion of the NIBRS data, which is the future of the Uniform Crime Report. There is a new analysis of criminological methods, including surveys, cohort studies, and meta-analysis and systematic review. There is an analysis of important research, including work on understanding why crime rates fell during the past decade, as well as new research explaining neighborhood drug arrest rates and the reporting of sexual victimization to the police. There is also the latest data from the Monitoring the Future study, the National Crime Victimization Survey, and the Uniform Crime Reports. These reports are the focus of a new Concept Summary on data collection methods. A Policy and Practice in Criminology feature on gun control has been updated.

- Chapter 3 starts with the story of Philip Giordano, the mayor of Waterbury, Connecticut, a married father of three, who was convicted of engaging in sexual relations with minors as young as 9 years old. The chapter also contains material on criminal justice system costs as part of the economic loss due to the victimization. The Criminological Enterprise feature explores the problems faced by adolescent victims of violence. The book *Aftermath: Violence and the Remaking of a Self,* by rape victim Susan Brison, tells of her experiences following a sexual assault. Among the research studies now integrated within the chapter are ones covering the effect of victimization on hostility and risk factors for the sexual victimization of women. There is expanded coverage of the victims' rights movement, including a Comparative Criminology feature discussing victims' rights in Europe.

- Chapter 4 reviews a number of important new research studies, including Bruce Jacobs's research on robbers who target drug dealers. There is also analysis of data on the association between the level of police and crime rates as well as the effects of deterrent measures on crime prevention, the success of a breath-analyzed ignition interlock device to prevent drunk driving, the effects of closed-circuit television on crime, and whether the police can prevent homicide. A new Concept Summary compares crime control methods.

- Chapter 5 includes the latest findings from the Minnesota Study of Twins Reared Apart. It contains updated research on such topics as the effects of prenatal exposure to mercury and data from a national assessment of Americans' exposure to environmental chemicals. It covers the intergenerational transmission of antisocial behavior, the effects of a depressed mood on delinquency, cognitive ability and delinquent behavior, and research on juvenile sex offenders.

- Chapter 6 has a new Race, Culture, Gender, and Criminology feature, "The Code of the Streets," and a new Criminological Enterprise feature, "Random Family." Data from the most recent World Wealth Report show how the poor now receive the smallest share ever of all income, while the top 20 percent of households receive more than 50 percent of all income, a record high. What effect does income inequality have on crime? To find out, the chapter reviews recent research on the effects of poverty concentration, inferior housing on mental health, the role of culture in a socially disorganized area, perceptions of police in minority communities, and the structural correlates of homicide rates. It expands coverage of community cohesion and collective efficacy and shows how they influence victimization risk. There is new information on the neighborhood context of policing, as well as the association of neighborhood structure and parenting processes. The latest NCVS and census data are presented. Neighborhood ecology and victimization are explored.

■ Chapter 7 reviews a number of new research studies examining the effects of socialization on criminality. It covers the importance of family and school in shaping adolescent deviance. There are new studies examining the influence of early work experiences on adolescent deviance and substance abuse. Other new research studies look at the effects of pairing aggressive and non-aggressive children in social relations and the influence of parental monitoring on adolescents' delinquent behavior. The sections on stigma, labeling, and delinquency have all been updated.

■ Chapter 8 now includes a major section on the effects of globalization on crime and well-being. It contains research on a wide variety of conflict theory topics including the effects of racial profiling and whether human empathy can transform the justice system. A gendered theory of crime is analyzed. The chapter now includes extensive coverage of the restorative justice movement.

■ Chapter 9 contains a new Criminological Enterprise feature, "Shared Beginnings, Divergent Lives," and new material on how marriage helps reduce the likelihood of chronic offending. New research covers such topics as childhood predictors of offense trajectories, stability and change in antisocial behavior, the relationship of childhood and adolescent factors to offending trajectories, the intergenerational transmission of antisocial behavior, and the relationship among race, life circumstances, and criminal activity. The concept of social capital is analyzed. And the chapter has been thoroughly revised and simplified to make it more student-friendly. There is a new section on the policy implications of developmental theory, including a feature on the Fast Track Project.

■ Chapter 10 has been revised and reorganized to provide more balanced coverage between the different types of violence. There is a new section discussing sexual assault allegations at U.S. service academies, expanded coverage of the USA Patriot Act, and more in-depth treatment of domestic terrorism, including responses to terrorism by the FBI and the Department of Homeland Security and the creation of new offices such as National Counterterrorism Center (NCTC) and the Director of National Intelligence (DNI). There is also a new Criminological Enterprise feature, "Masculinity and Sexual Violence among the Urban Poor," as well as new sections on psychological and social learning views of rape causation. Changes in rape law have been updated with a new section on consent. There has been an expansion of the sections on murder and homicide, including material on who is at risk to become a school shooter and the effects of being exposed to

violence. There are also new materials on causes of child abuse, parental abuse, and hate crime.

■ Chapter 11 contains new material on shoplifting control, including the use of electronic tagging of products. It lists the cars and car parts crooks love best. There is more information on credit card theft and what is being done to control the problem. There is new material on burglary, including repeat burglary and infectious burglary. The section on arson has been expanded.

■ Chapter 12 has been reorganized to reflect its expanded coverage of white-collar crime. An updated Comparative Criminology feature covers Russian organized crime, while a Criminological Enterprise feature, "Tyco, Enron, and WorldCom: Enterprise Crime at the Highest Levels," reviews these critical cases of corporate crime. A number of new cases involving white-collar crime are covered, including the case of TV personality Martha Stewart, the Securities and Exchange Commission investigation of leading Wall Street brokerage firms, and Operation Bullpen, a 2005 effort to control fraud in the sports memorabilia industry.

■ Chapter 13 now has material on changes in the distribution of pornography via the Internet. There is more on the international trade in prostitution, including a new feature on the "Natasha Trade," the coercion of women from the former Soviet Union into prostitution. A number of important legal cases are summarized, including *Dale v. Boy Scouts of America,* which upheld the Boy Scouts' right to ban gay men from becoming scout masters, and *Ashcroft, Attorney General v. Free Speech Coalition,* which dealt with the government's right to control Internet pornography. There is a new section on cyber prostitution. The latest data on drug use and the association between substance abuse and crime are included in the chapter.

■ Chapter 14 is an entirely new chapter, created to reflect the growing importance of cyber crimes and cyber criminals in American society. Cyber crimes involve people using the instruments of modern technology for criminal purpose. Among the topics now covered are computer fraud, distribution of illegal sexual material over the Internet, denial of service attacks, Internet securities fraud, identity theft, and e-tailing fraud. Data from the most recent Computer Crime and Security Survey by the Computer Security Institute are analyzed. There are sections on cyber vandalism, the use of the Internet to commit cyber crime with malicious intent. Topics covered include the use of worms, viruses, Trojan horses, logic bombs, and spam, as well as web defacement, cyber stalking, and cyber spying. Cyber terrorism and the control of cyber crime are covered. The chapter also includes sections that trace the growing importance of information technology in law enforcement, since criminals are not the only ones using technology today. Finally, there is a section on technology and civil liberties that directly addresses whether the use of technology by law enforcement agents presents a threat to privacy and freedom.

FEATURES

This text contains many different learning aids to help students understand and analyze material and also link it to other material in the book:

- *The Criminological Enterprise* features review important issues in criminology. For example, in Chapter 2 "Explaining Crime Trends" discusses the social and political factors that cause crime rates to rise and fall. The Criminological Enterprise boxes new to this edition are:

  - The Elements of Criminal Law (Chapter 1)
  - Adolescent Victims of Violence (Chapter 3)
  - Rape on Campus: Lifestyle and Risk (Chapter 3)
  - Hector Vega: A Life in the Drug Trade (Chapter 4)
  - Does Capital Punishment Deter Murder? (Chapter 4)
  - Random Family (Chapter 6)
  - Shared Beginnings, Divergent Lives (Chapter 9)
  - Masculinity and Sexual Violence among the Urban Poor (Chapter 10)
  - Credit Card Fraud (Chapter 11)
  - Tyco, Enron, and WorldCom: Enterprise Crime at the Highest Levels (Chapter 12)

- *Policy and Practice in Criminology* features show how criminological ideas and research can be put into action. In Chapter 2, "Should Guns be Controlled?" examines the pros and cons of the gun control debate. The Policy and Practice in Criminology features that are new to this edition include:

  - The Fast Track Project (Chapter 9)
  - Crime Scene Investigation Goes High Tech (Chapter 14)

- *Race, Culture, Gender, and Criminology* features cover issues of racial, sexual, and cultural diversity. For example, in Chapter 6, "Bridging the Racial Divide" discusses the work and thoughts of William Julius Wilson, one of the nation's leading sociologists. Race, Culture, Gender, and Criminology features new to this edition include:

  - The Code of the Streets (Chapter 6)
  - Are There Gender Differences in Burglary? (Chapter 11)

- *Comparative Criminology* features, which are new to this edition, compare criminological policies, trends, and practices in the United States and abroad. All of

these boxes are accompanied by critical thinking questions and links to articles in the InfoTrac College Edition online database. Comparative Criminology topics include:

- International Crime Trends (Chapter 1)
- Victims' Rights in Europe (Chapter 3)
- CCTV or Not CCTV? Comparing Situational Crime Prevention Efforts in Great Britain and the United States (Chapter 4)
- Diet and Crime: An International Perspective (Chapter 5)
- Practicing Restorative Justice Abroad (Chapter 8)
- Russian Organized Crime (Chapter 12)
- The Natasha Trade: International Trafficking in Prostitution (Chapter 13)

- *Concept Summary* features, new to this edition, provide students with concise summaries of some of the key concepts introduced in each chapter.

- *Connections* are short boxed inserts that help link the material to related topics covered elsewhere in the book. For example, a Connections box in Chapter 11 shows how efforts to control theft offenses are linked to the choice theory of crime discussed in Chapter 4.

- *InfoTrac College Edition* features provide links throughout the text suggesting key terms and articles related to the content that can be searched in the InfoTrac College Edition database.

- *Chapter Outlines* provide a roadmap to coverage and serve as a useful review tool.

- *Chapter Learning Objectives,* which are new to this edition, help students get the most out of the chapter coverage.

- *Thinking Like a Criminologist* sections at the end of each chapter present challenging questions or issues that students must use their criminological knowledge to answer or confront. For example, in Chapter 14 students are asked to respond to a request to evaluate the pros and cons of implanting a chip under a person's skin that allows the individual to be monitored and tracked in order to improve antiterrorism surveillance. Applying the information learned in the text will help students begin to "think like criminologists."

- *Doing Research on the Web,* which is new to this edition, guides students to web pages that will help them answer the criminological questions posed by the Thinking Like a Criminologist sections.

- *Critical Thinking Questions* at the end of each chapter will help develop students' critical thinking skills.

- *Key Terms* at the end of each chapter list the terms and page numbers where the terms are discussed in the chapter.

ANCILLARIES

A number of supplements provided by Thomson Wadsworth help instructors use *Criminology: Theories, Patterns, and Typologies,* Ninth Edition, in their courses and aid students in preparing for exams. *Available to qualified adopters. Please consult your local sales representative for details.*

For the Instructor

- **Instructor's Resource Manual with Test Bank** by Joanne Ziembo-Vogl of Grand Valley State University. Prepare for class more quickly and effectively with such resources as Detailed Chapter Outlines, Chapter Objectives, Key Terms, Discussion Questions, Lecture Suggestions, and a Resource Integration Guide. A Test Bank with more than 1000 questions in multiple choice, true/false, fill-in-the-blank, and essay formats, coded according to Bloom's taxonomy, saves you time creating tests.

- **Instructor's Edition** The Instructor's Edition previews the features that save you time and help students learn, and demonstrates how to integrate our powerful supplements into your curriculum.

- **JoinIn™ on TurningPoint®** Our exclusive agreement to offer TurningPoint® software lets you pose book-specific questions and display students' answers seamlessly within the Microsoft® PowerPoint® slides of your own lecture, in conjunction with the "clicker" hardware of your choice. Enhance how your students interact with you, your lecture, and each other. *For college and university adopters only. Contact your local Thomson representative to learn more.*

- **Multimedia Manager: A Microsoft® PowerPoint® Tool** This one-stop lecture tool makes it easy for you to assemble, edit, publish, and present custom lectures for your course, using Microsoft PowerPoint. The Multimedia Manager lets you bring together text-specific lecture outlines and art from Thomson Wadsworth texts with video and animations from the web or your own materials—culminating in a powerful, personalized, media-enhanced presentation.

- **ThomsonNOW™** Empower your students with the first assessment-centered student tutorial system for criminology. Seamlessly tied to the new edition of this text, this powerful and interactive web-based learning tool helps students gauge their unique study needs, then gives them a Personalized Learning Plan that focuses their study time on the concepts they most need to master. By providing students with a better understanding of exactly what they need to focus on, ThomsonNOW helps students make the optimum use of their study time, bringing them closer to success!

- **ABC Videos: Criminology, Vol. 1** ABC videos feature short, high-interest clips from current news events as well as historic raw footage going back 40 years. Perfect for discussion starters or to enrich your lectures and spark interest in the material in the text, these brief videos provide students with a new lens through which to view the past and present, one that will greatly enhance their knowledge and understanding of significant events and open up to them new dimensions in learning. Clips are drawn from such programs as *World News Tonight, Good Morning America, This Week, PrimeTime Live, 20/20,* and *Nightline,* as well as numerous ABC News specials and material from the Associated Press Television News and British Movietone News collections.

- **The Wadsworth Criminal Justice Video Library** Visit cj.wadsworth.com/videos to view all of Wadsworth's rich video offerings. View video suggestions for a particular course, see publication dates and running times, download clip descriptions, and learn about Wadsworth's video policy. Videos are available from sources such as CNN, ABC, *Films for the Humanities and Social Sciences,* CourtTV, the *A&E American Justice* series, and more. Many selections are available in either DVD or VHS formats. Your Thomson Wadsworth representative will be happy to provide a complete listing of videos and policies.

- **ExamView® Computerized Testing** Quickly create customized tests that can be delivered in print or online. ExamView's simple "what you see is what you get" interface allows you to easily generate tests of up to 250 items. (Contains all the Test Bank questions electronically.)

- **WebTutor™ ToolBox for WebCT® and Blackboard®** Combines easy-to-use course management tools with content from this text's rich companion website. Ready to use as soon as you log on—or, customize WebTutor ToolBox with web links, images, and other resources.

- **Thomson InSite for Writing and Research™** This all-in-one, online writing and research tool includes electronic peer review, an originality checker, an assignment library, help with common errors, and access to InfoTrac College Edition. InSite makes course management practically automatic!

- **Opposing Viewpoints Resource Center** NOT SOLD SEPARATELY. Boost the power of your course by bringing students the meat of today's most compelling social and scientific issues—from genetic engineering to environmental policy, prejudice, abortion, health care reform, violence in the media, and much more!

- **Current Perspectives: Readings from InfoTrac College Edition: Terrorism and Homeland Security, Second Edition** This reader features articles from both popular and academic sources on key issues in terrorism. Edited and introduced by Sabina Burton, University of California, Irvine, this reader will provide students with the most current information on terrorism today. Along with the reader, students are given FREE access to InfoTrac College Edition and can create their own online reader in InfoTrac College Edition using InfoMarks. FREE when packaged with this text!

- **Current Perspectives: Readings from InfoTrac College Edition: Juvenile Justice** This reader features articles from both popular and academic sources on current issues in the juvenile justice system. Edited and introduced by James Chriss, Cleveland State University, this reader will provide students with the most current information on juvenile justice today. Along with the reader, students are given FREE access to InfoTrac College Edition and can create their own online reader in InfoTrac College Edition using InfoMarks. FREE when packaged with this text!

- **Current Perspectives: Readings from InfoTrac College Edition: Public Policy and Criminal Justice** This reader features articles from both popular and academic sources on new challenges in shaping policy. Edited and introduced by Sabina Burton, University of California, Irvine, this reader will provide students with the most current information on policy today. Along with the reader, students are given FREE access to InfoTrac College Edition and can create their own online reader in InfoTrac College Edition using InfoMarks. FREE when packaged with this text!

For the Student

- **Study Guide** by Joanne Ziembo-Vogl of Grand Valley State University. Thoroughly updated, the *Study Guide* includes the following elements to help students get the most out of their classroom experience: learning objectives, a chapter summary, key terms and concepts, and a self-test. The self-test consists of multiple choice, fill-in-the-blank, true/false, and essay questions.

- **ThomsonNOW™** Save time, learn more, and succeed in the course with ThomsonNOW! ThomsonNOW is students' #1 pick to get the grade, and offers you everything you need for success. Just follow these simple steps. (1) Take a pre-test before or after you read a chapter of the text, to generate a Personalized Study Plan with exactly what you need to learn to be prepared for class and for exams. (2) Follow the Personalized Study Plan links to find fun and interactive visual and audio resources that will help you master what you need to know. (3) Use the integrated online text just like a printed textbook; or read the text pages when your study plan sends you there. (4) Take the Post-Test Assessments before exams to make sure you're ready.

- **Book Companion Website** http://cj.wadsworth.com/siegel_crimtpt9e Rich teaching and learning resources, including chapter-by-chapter online tutorial quizzes, a final exam, ABC videos with questions, chapter outlines, chapter review, chapter-by-chapter web links, flash cards, and more!

- **InfoTrac® College Edition with InfoMarks®** Save time, save money—and eliminate the trek to the library and long waits for reserved readings. Do in-depth research for class right from your desktop or catch up on the latest news online—using your four-month access to InfoTrac College Edition. With InfoTrac College Edition, completing research papers has never been so easy! Search this virtual university library's more than 18 million reliable, full-length articles from 5000 academic and popular periodicals (including *The New York Times, Newsweek, Science, Forbes,* and *USA Today*) and retrieve results almost instantly. You also have access to InfoMarks—stable URLs that you can link to articles, journals, and searches to save you time when doing research—AND to the InfoWrite online resource center, where you can access guides to writing research papers, grammar help, "critical thinking" guidelines, and much more.

- **InfoTrac College Edition Student Guide for Criminal Justice** Features a "cheat sheet" of search terms for your course, plus quick help guides for getting the most from InfoTrac College Edition.

- **InfoTrac College Edition Exercises for Criminal Justice** A Wadsworth exclusive! This 60-page booklet, written by Dale Mooso, provides exercises for further research using InfoTrac College Edition. FREE when packaged with this text!

- **Crime and Evidence in Action CD-ROM** The tools to practice investigation techniques are all here! This CD-ROM, with its accompanying website, places you in the center of the action as you make decisions as patrol officer, detective, prosecutor, defense attorney, judge, corrections officer, and parole officer. As you interact with one of the three realistic in-depth simulations, you are guided through each stage of the case—from crime scene investigation to arrest, trial, incarceration, and parole or probation.

- **Crime Scenes 2.0: An Interactive Criminal Justice CD-ROM** Newly updated for today's operating systems, this interactive CD-ROM, written by Bruce Berg (California State University, Long Beach), features six vignettes that allow you to play various roles as you explore all aspects of the criminal justice system such as policing, investigation, courts, sentencing, and corrections. Awarded the gold medal in higher education and silver medal for video interface by *New Media* magazine's Invision Awards.

- **Careers in Criminal Justice 3.0 Interactive CD-ROM** The Careers in Criminal Justice 3.0 Interactive CD-ROM provides you with extensive career profiling information and links to self-assessment testing, and is designed to help you investigate and focus on the criminal justice career choices that are right for you. With links and tools to assist you in finding a professional position, this new version includes ten new Career Profiles and two new Video Interviews, bringing the total number of careers covered to 58.

- **Internet Activities for Criminal Justice, Second Edition** This 77-page booklet, written by Carolyn Dennis and Tere Chipman, shows you how to best utilize the Internet for research through searches and activities. FREE when packaged with this text!

- **Wadsworth's Guide to Careers in Criminal Justice, Third Edition** This concise 60-page booklet by Carol Mathews of Century College provides a brief introduction to the exciting and diverse field of criminal justice. Learn about opportunities in law enforcement, courts, and corrections—and how to get those jobs. FREE when packaged with this text!

- **Six Steps to Effective Writing in Criminal Justice** This compact resource, written by Judy Schmidt (Pennsylvania State University) and Mike Hooper (California Department of Justice), is intended to embed strong writing skills and prepare you for your academic and professional pursuits. Includes sample writing, topics, examples, formats, and papers that reflect the criminal justice discipline. FREE when packaged with this text!

- **Writing for Criminal Justice** This handy guide pulls together various articles and excerpts on writing skills to give you an introduction to academic, professional, and research writing, along with a basic grammar review and a survey of verbal communication on the job. The voices of practitioners and people who use these techniques every day will help you to see the relevance of these skills to their future careers.

ACKNOWLEDGMENTS

The preparation of this text would not have been possible without the aid of my colleagues who helped by reviewing the previous editions and gave me important suggestions for improvement.

REVIEWERS OF THE NINTH EDITION

Wanda Foglia, Rowan University
Farrukh Hakeem, Shaw University
Jim Hawdon, Virginia Tech University
Kathryn Morgan, University of Alabama at Birmingham
Joanne Ziembo-Vogl, Grand Valley State University

Reviewers of previous editions include M. H. Alsikafi, Alexander Alvarez, Thomas Arvanites, Patricia Atchison, Timothy Austin, Agnes Baro, Bonnie Berry, James Black, Joseph Blake, David Bordua, Susan Brinkley, Stephen Brodt, Thomas Calhoun, Mike Carlie, Mae Conley, Thomas Courtless, Mary Dietz, Edna Erez, Stephen Gibbons, Dorothy Goldsborough, Edward Green, Julia Hall, Marie Henry, Denny Hill, Alfred Himelson, Dennis Hoffman, Gerrold Hotaling, Joseph Jacoby, Casey Jordan, John Martin, Pamela Mayhall, Cynthia Perez McCluskey, James McKenna, Steven Messner, Linda O'Daniel, Hugh O'Rourke, Nikos Passos, Gary Perlstein, William Pridemore, Xin Ren, Jim Ruiz, Louis San Marco, Kip Schlegel, Theodore Skotnick, Mark Stetler, Kathleen Sweet, Gregory Talley, Kevin Thompson, Charles Tittle, Paul Tracy, Glenna Van Metre, Charles Vedder, Joseph Vielbig, Ed Wells, Angela West, Michael Wiatkowski, Cecil Willis, Janet Wilson, and Joanne Ziembo-Vogl.

My colleagues at Thomson Wadsworth did their typically outstanding job in the preparation of the text. They are all really terrific. My new editor Carolyn Henderson Meier is professional, thorough, dedicated, and also a lot of fun to work with. My good friend Shelley Murphy is a wonderful development editor; I would simply be lost without her. I have worked with Robin Hood, the book's production editor many times, and she is talented, kind, and very patient. Billie Porter did a great job on the photo research, and Jennifer Gordon was terrific at copyediting the manuscript. The astonishing Jennie Redwitz somehow pulls everything together as production manager and then turns things over to Terra Schultz, the magnificent marketing manager (how's that for alliteration?). I also wish to thank Assistant Editor Jana Davis and Technology Project Manager Susan Devanna, who do a wonderful job developing the print and media supplements for this book.

Larry Siegel
Bedford, New Hampshire

CONCEPTS OF CRIME, LAW, AND CRIMINOLOGY

IIIIIIIIIIIIIIIIIIIIIIIIIIIIIIIIIIIIIIII

How is crime defined? How much crime is there, and what are the trends and patterns in the crime rate? How many people fall victim to crime, and who is likely to become a crime victim? How did our system of criminal law develop, and what are the basic elements of crimes? What is the science of criminology all about?

Concern about crime and justice has been an important part of the human condition for more than 5,000 years, since the first criminal codes were set down in the Middle East. Although criminology—the scientific study of crime—is considered a modern science, it has existed for more than two centuries. These are some of the core issues that will be addressed in the first three chapters of this text. Chapter 1 introduces the field of criminology: its nature, areas of study, methodologies, and historical development. It also introduces one of the key components of criminology—the development of criminal law. It discusses the social history of law, the purpose of law, and how law defines crime. Chapter 2 focuses on the acquisition of crime data, crime rate trends, and observable patterns within the crime rate. Chapter 3 focuses on victimization; topics include the effects of victimization, the cause of victimization, and efforts to help crime victims.

CHAPTER 1

Ed Andrieski/EPA/Landov

When basketball idol Kobe Bryant was arrested in Eagle, Colorado, on July 4, 2003, and charged with felony sexual assault on July 18, a strong ripple went through all levels of American society. Bryant was alleged to have assaulted a 19-year-old girl who worked at a luxury hotel in which he was staying when he was in Colorado for knee surgery.

The case dominated the media for months. ESPN told viewers that a hotel bellman saw the woman leaving Bryant's room with marks on her face and neck. People magazine reported that Kobe Bryant bought his wife a $4 million, 8-carat pink diamond ring. Other reports said that Bryant's accuser overdosed on pills two months before the alleged incident and that she was sexually promiscuous. Bryant, a married man with an infant daughter, used the media to announce that he had committed adultery with the woman but insisted the sex was consensual. On July 23, 2004, before the trial began, a Colorado judge ruled that the defense had met the burden required under the state's rape victim law of proving that evidence about the woman's sex life was relevant for the jury to hear. Bowing to the pressure (which included death threats), Bryant's accuser refused to testify. On September 1, 2004, prosecutors were forced to drop the case. Bryant issued a statement that said, in part:

> Although I truly believe this encounter between us was consensual, I recognize now that she did not and does not view this incident the same way I did. . . . After months of reviewing discovery, listening to her attorney, and even her testimony in person, I now understand how she feels that she did not consent to this encounter.

CRIME AND CRIMINOLOGY

| | | | | | | **CONNECTIONS** | | | | | |

For the criminological view on the relationship between media and violence, see Chapter 5. For more on the relationship between pornography and crime, see Chapter 13. And for the concept of rape shield laws go to Chapter 10.

To read numerous news reports on the **Bryant case,** go to the CourtTV website at http://www.courttv.com/trials/bryant.

The Bryant case certainly raises questions about justice in the United States. It illustrates the media's role in high-profile criminal trials. How is it possible to select a fair and impartial jury and carry out an objective trial if the case has already been tried in the press? Is it fair for the media to expose the victim's sexual and medical history? How do details from her past contribute to deciding the truth of a criminal matter? If Kobe Bryant had been accused of robbing a store, would it be fair to reveal the owner's financial background and/or sexual orientation? How relevant are such details to proving guilt in the case at hand?

The case also illustrates that the definition of crime is not always obvious. Bryant admitted having a sexual relationship with the woman but denied it was rape. In his statement he concedes that she may have viewed the act as nonconsensual and therefore a sexual assault. Can a clear line be drawn between legal and illegal behavior, and if so who gets to draw it? Is the definition of crime open to subjective interpretation?

Although a suspect's race or ethnic background should not be relevant in a criminal matter, the fact that Bryant was a famous black athlete facing an accusation from a white woman was not lost on the public. Was Kobe Bryant another O.J. Simpson? Are African American men routinely and falsely accused by the justice system? And if he did indeed attack the young girl, what factors could have motivated a wealthy and famous athlete to commit a violent act? Could he possess an impulsive personality that limited his ability to exercise self-control over his actions?

The questions about crime and its control raised by the Bryant case and other similar criminal trials have spurred continued and intense interest in **criminology,** an academic discipline that makes use of scientific methods to study the nature, extent, cause, and control of criminal behavior. Using these methods, **criminologists** are devoted to the design and collection of valid and reliable data that address the causes of crime as well as crime patterns and trends. Unlike media commentators, whose opinions about crime may be colored by personal experiences, biases, and values, criminologists remain objective as they study crime and its consequences.

This text analyzes criminology and its major subareas of inquiry. It focuses on the nature and extent of crime, the causes of crime, and patterns of criminal behavior. This chapter introduces and defines criminology: What are its goals? What is its history? How do criminologists define crime? How do they conduct research? What ethical issues face those wishing to conduct criminological research?

WHAT IS CRIMINOLOGY?

Criminology is the scientific approach to studying criminal behavior. In their classic definition, criminologists Edwin Sutherland and Donald Cressey state:

> Criminology is the body of knowledge regarding crime as a social phenomenon. It includes within its scope the processes of making laws, of breaking laws, and of reacting toward the breaking of laws. . . . The objective of criminology is the development of a body of general and verified principles and of other types of knowledge regarding this process of law, crime, and treatment.[1]

Sutherland and Cressey's definition includes some of the most important areas of interest to criminologists: (1) the development of criminal law and its use to define crime, (2) the cause of law violation, and (3) the methods used to control criminal behavior. This definition also makes reference to the term *verified principles,* which underscores the fact that criminologists use the **scientific method** when conducting their research. They gather data, create theories to explain the patterns found in the data, and test the theories' validity by posing research questions (hypotheses), which they answer empirically. In conducting their research and testing their theories, criminologists employ established methods of social science inquiry, including experimental designs and sophisticated data analysis. Because criminology is essentially an **interdisciplinary science** and criminologists have been trained in diverse fields—most commonly sociology but also criminal justice, political science, psychology, economics, and the natural sciences—they are able to employ a wide range of methods and techniques to conduct research and test hypotheses.

Criminology and Criminal Justice

Although the terms *criminology* and *criminal justice* may seem similar, and people often confuse the two or lump them together, there are major differences between these fields of study. Criminology explains the etiology (origin), extent, and nature of crime in society, whereas criminal justice refers to the study of the agencies of social control—police, courts, and corrections. Criminologists are mainly concerned with identifying the suspected causes of crime, while criminal justice scholars strive to identify effective methods of crime control.

Because both fields are crime related, they do overlap. Criminologists must be aware of how the agencies of justice operate, how they influence crime and criminals, and how justice policies shape crime rates and trends. Criminal justice experts cannot begin to design programs of crime prevention or rehabilitation without first understanding something of the nature of crime. It is common, therefore, for criminal justice programs to feature courses on criminology and for criminology courses to evaluate the agencies of justice.

Criminology and Deviance

Criminology is also sometimes confused with the study of deviant behavior. However, significant distinctions can be made between these areas of scholarship. **Deviant behavior** is behavior that departs from social norms. Included within the broad spectrum of deviant acts are behaviors ranging from violent crimes to joining a nudist colony.

Crime and deviance are often confused because not all crimes are deviant or unusual acts, and not all deviant acts are illegal or criminal. For example, using recreational drugs, such as marijuana, may be illegal, but is it deviant? A significant percentage of the population have used or are using drugs.[2] Therefore, it is erroneous to argue that all crimes are deviant behaviors that depart from the norms of society. Similarly, many deviant acts are not criminal even though they may be both disturbing and shocking to the conscience. Suppose a passerby witnesses someone floundering in the ocean and makes no rescue attempt. Most people would condemn the onlooker's coldhearted behavior as callous, immoral, and deviant. However, no legal action could be taken since private citizens are not required by law to effect rescues. There is no legal requirement that a person rush into a burning building, brave a flood, or jump into the ocean to save another from harm. In sum, many criminal acts, but not all, fall within the concept of deviance. Similarly, some deviant acts, but not all, are considered crimes.

The principal purpose of the **Office on National Drug Control Policy (ONDCP)** is to establish policies, priorities, and objectives for the nation's drug control program, the goals of which are to reduce illicit drug use, manufacturing, and trafficking; reduce drug-related crime and violence; and reduce drug-related health consequences. To read more about their efforts, go to their website at http://www.whitehousedrugpolicy.gov. For an up-to-date list of web links, go to http://cj.wadsworth.com/siegel_crimtpt9e.

Becoming Deviant

To understand the nature and purpose of law, criminologists study both the process by which deviant acts are criminalized (become crimes) and, conversely, how criminal acts are **decriminalized** and/or legalized. In some instances, individuals, institutions, or government agencies mount a campaign aimed at convincing both the public and lawmakers that what was considered merely deviant behavior is actually dangerous and must be outlawed. During the 1930s, Harry Anslinger, then head of the Federal Bureau of Narcotics, used magazine articles, public appearances, and public testimony to sway public opinion about the dangers of marijuana, which up until that time had been legal to use and possess.[3]

In testimony before the House Ways and Means Committee considering passage of the Marijuana Tax Act of 1938, Anslinger stated:

> In Florida a 21-year-old boy under the influence of this drug killed his parents and his brothers and sisters. The evidence showed that he had smoked marihuana. In Chicago recently two boys murdered a policeman while under the influence of marihuana. Not long ago we found a 15-year-old boy going insane because, the doctor told the enforcement officers, he thought the boy was smoking marihuana cigarettes. They traced the sale to some man who had been growing marihuana and selling it to these boys all under 15 years of age, on a playground there.[4]

As a result of Anslinger's efforts, a deviant behavior, marijuana use, became a criminal behavior, and previously law-abiding citizens were defined as criminal offenders. Today, some national organizations, such as the Drug Policy Alliance, are committed to repealing draconian drug laws and undoing Anslinger's "moral crusade." They call for an end to the "war against drugs," which they believe has become overzealous in its effort to punish drug traffickers. In 2004, the alliance issued this statement:

> Many of the problems the drug war purports to resolve are in fact caused by the drug war itself. So-called "drug-related" crime is a direct result of drug prohibition's distortion of immutable laws of supply and demand. Public health problems like HIV and Hepatitis C are all exacerbated by zero tolerance laws that restrict access to clean needles. The drug war is not the promoter of family values that some would have us believe. Children of inmates are at risk of educational failure, joblessness, addiction and delinquency. Drug abuse is bad, but the drug war is worse.[5]

| | | | | | | | CONNECTIONS | | | | | | |

It is interesting that some of the drugs considered highly dangerous today were once sold openly and considered medically beneficial. For example, the narcotic drug heroin, now considered extremely addicting and dangerous, was originally named in the mistaken belief that its pain-killing properties would prove "heroic" to medical patients. The history of drug and alcohol abuse and legalization efforts will be discussed further in Chapter 13.

Moral crusades designed to draw a clear line between behavior that is deviant but legal and behavior that is outlawed and criminal did not end in the 1930s. In 2004, radio host Howard Stern was fined by the Federal Communication Commission (FCC) for "repeated, graphic and explicit sexual descriptions that were pandering, titillating or used to shock the audience."[6] The government action prompted Clear Channel Communications to drop Stern's show from their stations. In retaliation, Stern posted on his website transcripts from the *Oprah* TV show that used very similar language but was deemed nonoffensive by government regulators.[7] Stern was so outraged by the campaign to censor his program that he left public broadcasting for unregulated satellite radio; Stern abandoned free commercial radio for satelite radio in 2005.

In sum, criminologists are concerned with the concept of deviance and its relationship to criminality. The shifting definition of deviant behavior is closely associated with our concept of crime. The relationship among criminology, criminal justice, and deviance is illustrated in Concept Summary 1.1.

A BRIEF HISTORY OF CRIMINOLOGY

The scientific study of crime and criminality is relatively recent. Although written criminal codes have existed for thousands of years, these were restricted to defining crime and setting punishments. What motivated people to violate the law remained a matter for conjecture.

During the Middle Ages (1200–1600), superstition and fear of satanic possession dominated thinking. People who violated social norms or religious practices were believed to be witches or possessed by demons. The prescribed method for dealing with the possessed was burning at the stake, a practice that survived into the seventeenth century. Between 1581 and 1590, Nicholas Remy, head of the Inquisition in the French province of Lorraine, ordered 900 sorcerers and witches burned to death; likewise, Peter Binsfield, the bishop of the German city of Trier, ordered 6,500 people to death. An estimated 100,000 people were prosecuted throughout Europe for witchcraft during the sixteenth and seventeenth centuries. It was also commonly believed that some families produced offspring who were unsound or unstable and that social misfits were inherently damaged by reason of their "inferior blood."[8] It was common practice to use cruel tortures to extract confessions, and those convicted of violent or theft

During the Middle Ages, superstition and fear of satanic possession dominated thinking. People who violated social norms or religious practices were believed to be witches or possessed by demons. The prescribed method for dealing with the possessed was burning at the stake, a practice that survived into the seventeenth century. This painting, *The Trial of George Jacobs, August 5, 1692* by T. H. Matteson (1855), depicts the ordeal of Jacobs, a patriarch of Salem, Massachusetts. During the witch craze, he had ridiculed the trials, only to find himself being accused, tried, and executed.

T.H. Matteson, © The Trail of George Jacobs, August 5, 1692. Oil on canvas 39 × 53 inches. #1.246 Peabody Essex Museum, Salem, MA

crimes suffered extremely harsh penalties including whipping, branding, maiming, and execution.

Classical Criminology

During the eighteenth century, social philosophers such as Jeremy Bentham began to embrace the view that human behavior was a result of rational thought processes. According to Bentham's **utilitarianism,** people choose to act when, after weighing costs and benefits, they believe that their actions will bring them an increase in pleasure and a reduction of pain. It stands to reason that criminal behavior could be eliminated or controlled if would-be law violators could be convinced that the pain of punishment exceeds the benefits of crime.

Cesare Beccaria (1738–1794) applied these principles to criminal behavior in his famous treatise "On Crimes and Punishment." Because he believed that people want to achieve pleasure and avoid pain, Beccaria suggested that harsh punishments and routine use of torture were inappropriate and excessive. If every felon were punished with death, he reasoned, there would be little incentive for criminals not to escalate the severity of their crimes. To deter crime, the pain of punishment must be administered in a fair, balanced, and proportionate amount to counterbalance the pleasure obtained from crime. Beccaria stated his famous theorem:

> In order for punishment not to be in every instance, an act of violence of one or many against a private citizen, it must be essentially public, prompt, necessary, the least possible in the given circumstances, proportionate to the crimes, and dictated by the laws.[9]

The writings of Beccaria and his followers form the core of what today is referred to as **classical criminology.** As originally conceived in the eighteenth century, classical criminology theory had several basic elements:

- In every society people have free will to choose criminal or lawful solutions to meet their needs or settle their problems.

- Criminal solutions may be more attractive because they usually require less work for a greater payoff.

- A person's choice of crime may be controlled by his or her fear of punishment.

- To be an effective crime deterrent, punishment must be severe, certain, and swift.

This classical perspective influenced penal practices for more than two centuries. The law was made proportionate to the crime so that the most serious offenses earned the harshest punishments. Executions were still widely used but gradually were reserved for only the most serious crimes. The catch phrase was "let the punishment fit the crime."

During the nineteenth century, a new perspective challenged the validity of classical theory and presented an innovative way of looking at the causes of crime.

Nineteenth-Century Positivism

During the late nineteenth century the scientific method was beginning to take hold in Europe. Rather than rely on pure thought and reason, people began using careful observation and analysis of natural phenomena to understand the way the world worked. This movement inspired new discoveries in biology, astronomy, and chemistry. Work on the evolution of man by Charles Darwin (1809–1882) encouraged a nineteenth-century "cult of science" that mandated that all human activity could be verified by scientific principles. If the scientific method could be applied to natural phenomena, then why not use it to study human behavior?

Auguste Comte (1798–1857), considered the founder of sociology, applied scientific methods to the study of society. According to Comte, societies pass through stages that can be grouped on the basis of how people try to understand the world in which they live. People in primitive societies consider inanimate objects as having life (for example, the sun is a god); in later social stages, people embrace a rational, scientific view of the world. Comte called this final stage the positive stage, and those who followed his writings became known as positivists.

As we understand it today, **positivism** has two main elements. The first is the belief that human behavior is a function of forces beyond a person's control. Some of these forces

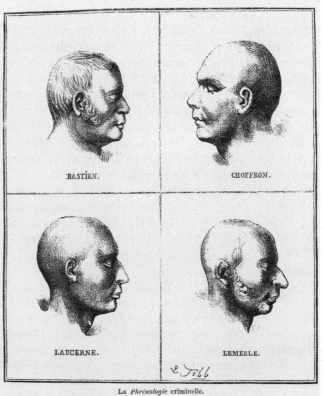

Early positivists believed the shape of the skull was a key determinant of behavior. These drawings from the nineteenth century illustrate "typical" criminally shaped heads.

are social, such as the effect of wealth and class, and some are political and historical, such as war and famine. Other forces are more personal and psychological, such as an individual's brain structure and his or her biological makeup or mental ability. Each of these forces influences and shapes human behavior.

> Positivism can be used as an orientation in shaping the content of the law. To learn about this perspective, use InfoTrac College Edition to read: Claire Finkelstein, "Positivism and the Notion of an Offense," *California Law Review* 88 (March 2000): 335.

The second aspect of positivism is the use of the scientific method to conduct research. Positivists rely on the strict use of empirical methods to test hypotheses. That is, they believe in the factual, firsthand observation and measurement of conditions and events. Positivists would agree that an abstract concept such as intelligence exists because it can be measured by an IQ test. They might question the concept of the soul because it is a condition that cannot be verified by the scientific method. These principles began to be applied to the study of criminal behaviors.

BIOLOGICAL POSITIVISM The earliest "scientific" studies applying the positivist model to criminology were conducted by **physiognomists,** such as J. K. Lavater (1741–1801), who studied the facial features of criminals to determine whether the shape of ears, nose, and eyes and the distance between them were associated with antisocial behavior. **Phrenologists,** such as Franz Joseph Gall (1758–1828) and Johann K. Spurzheim (1776–1832), studied the shape of the skull and bumps on the head to determine whether these physical attributes were linked to criminal behavior. Phrenologists believed that external cranial characteristics dictate which areas of the brain control physical activity. Other beliefs are that the brain has thirty different areas or faculties that control behavior, that the larger the area the more active it is, that the size of a brain area could be determined by inspecting the contours of the skull, and that the relative size of brain areas could be increased or decreased through exercise and self-discipline.[10] Though their techniques and methods are no longer practiced or taken seriously, these efforts were an early attempt to use a scientific method to study crime.

By the early nineteenth century, abnormality in the human mind was being linked to criminal behavior patterns.[11] Philippe Pinel (1745–1826), one of the founders of French psychiatry, claimed that some people behave abnormally even without being mentally ill. He coined the phrase *manie sans delire* to denote what today is referred to as a **psychopathic personality.** In 1812, an American, Benjamin Rush, described patients with an "innate preternatural moral depravity."[12] Another early criminological pioneer, English physician Henry Maudsley (1835–1918), believed that insanity and criminal behavior were strongly linked. He stated: "Crime is a sort of outlet in which their unsound tendencies are discharged; they would go mad if they were not criminals,

and they do not go mad because they are criminals."[13] These early research efforts shifted attention to brain functioning and personality as the keys to criminal behavior. When Sigmund Freud's (1856–1939) work on the unconscious gained worldwide attention, the psychological basis of behavior was forever established.

In Italy, Cesare Lombroso (1835–1909), a physician who served much of his career in the Italian army, was studying the cadavers of executed criminals in an effort to scientifically determine whether law violators were physically different from people of conventional values and behavior.[14] Lombroso believed that serious offenders—those who engaged in repeated assault- or theft-related activities—inherited criminal traits. These "born criminals" inherited physical problems that impelled them into a life of crime. Lombroso held that born criminals suffer from **atavistic anomalies**—physically, they are throwbacks to more primitive times when people were savages. Criminals were believed to have the enormous jaws and strong canine teeth common to carnivores and savages who devour raw flesh. These criminogenic traits can be acquired through indirect heredity, from a degenerate family whose members suffered from such ills as insanity, syphilis, and alcoholism. He believed that direct heredity—being related to a family of criminals—is the second primary cause of crime.

Lombroso's version of **criminal anthropology** was brought to the United States via articles and textbooks that adopted his ideas. He attracted a circle of followers who expanded on his vision of **biological determinism**, and his scholarship helped stimulate interest in a criminal anthropology.[15] His work was actually more popular in the United States than it was in Europe. By the turn of the century, American authors were discussing "the science of penology" and "the science of criminology."[16]

Lombroso's version of strict biological determinism is no longer taken seriously. Later in his career even he recognized that not all criminals are biological throwbacks. Today, those criminologists who suggest that crime has some biological basis also believe that environmental conditions influence human behavior. Hence, the term **biosocial theory** has been coined to reflect the assumed link among physical and mental traits, the social environment, and behavior.

SOCIAL POSITIVISM At the same time that biological views were dominating criminology, social positivists were developing the field of sociology to scientifically study the major social changes that were taking place in nineteenth-century society.

Sociology seemed an ideal perspective from which to study society. After thousands of years of stability, the world was undergoing a population explosion: The population estimated at 600 million in 1700 had risen to 900 million by 1800. People were flocking to cities in ever-increasing numbers. Manchester, England, had 12,000 inhabitants in 1760 and 400,000 in 1850; during the same period, the population of Glasgow, Scotland, rose from 30,000 to 300,000.

The development of machinery such as power looms had doomed cottage industries and given rise to a factory system in which large numbers of people toiled for extremely low wages. The spread of agricultural machines increased the food supply while reducing the need for a large rural workforce; these excess laborers further swelled city populations. At the same time, political, religious, and social traditions continued to be challenged by the scientific method.

The Foundations of Sociological Criminology

The foundations of sociological criminology can be traced to the works of pioneering sociologists L. A. J. (Adolphe) Quetelet (1796–1874) and (David) Émile Durkheim (1858–1917). Quetelet instigated the use of data and statistics in performing criminological research. Durkheim, considered one of the founders of sociology, defined crime as a normal and necessary social event.[17] These two perspectives have been extremely influential on modern criminology.

L. A. J. (ADOLPHE) QUETELET A Belgian mathematician, Quetelet began (along with a Frenchman, Andre-Michel Guerry) what is known as the **cartographic school of criminology.**[18] This approach made use of social statistics that were being developed in Europe in the early nineteenth century. Statistical data provided important demographic information on the population, including density, gender, religious affiliations, and wealth.

Quetelet studied data gathered in France (called the *Comptes generaux de l'administration de la justice*) to investigate the effect of social factors on the propensity to commit crime. In addition to finding a strong influence of age and sex on crime, Quetelet also uncovered evidence that season, climate, population composition, and poverty were related to criminality. More specifically, he found that crime rates were greatest in the summer, in southern areas, among heterogeneous populations, and among the poor and uneducated. He also found crime rates to be influenced by drinking habits.[19] Quetelet identified many of the relationships between crime and social phenomena that still serve as a basis for criminology today. His findings that crime has a social basis directly challenged Lombrosian biological determinism.

ÉMILE DURKHEIM According to Durkheim's vision of social positivism, crime is part of human nature because it exists during periods of both poverty and prosperity.[20] Crime is normal because it is virtually impossible to imagine a society in which criminal behavior is totally absent. Such a society would almost demand that all people be and act exactly alike. Durkheim believed that the inevitability of crime is linked to the differences (heterogeneity) within society. Since people are so different from one another and employ such a variety of methods and forms of behavior to meet their needs, it is not surprising that some will resort to criminality. Even if "real" crimes were eliminated, human weaknesses and petty vices would be elevated to the status of crimes. As long as human differences exist, then,

crime is inevitable and one of the fundamental conditions of social life.

Durkheim argued that crime can be useful and, on occasion, even healthy for society. He held that the existence of crime paves the way for social change and means that the social structure is not rigid or inflexible. Put another way, if crime did not exist, it would mean that everyone behaved the same way and agreed on what is right and wrong. Such universal conformity would stifle creativity and independent thinking. To illustrate this concept, Durkheim offered the example of the Greek philosopher Socrates, who was considered a criminal and put to death for corrupting the morals of youth simply because he expressed ideas that were different from what people believed at that time.

Durkheim reasoned that another benefit of crime is that it calls attention to social ills. A rising crime rate can signal the need for social change and promote a variety of programs designed to relieve the human suffering that may have caused crime in the first place. In his influential book, *The Division of Labor in Society,* Durkheim described the consequences of the shift from a small, rural society, which he labeled "mechanical," to the more modern "organic" society with a large urban population, division of labor, and personal isolation.[21] From this shift flowed **anomie,** or norm and role confusion, a powerful sociological concept that helps describe the chaos and disarray accompanying the loss of traditional values in modern society. Durkheim's research on suicide indicated that anomic societies maintain high suicide rates; by implication, anomie might cause other forms of deviance as well.

|||||| **CONNECTIONS** ||||||

Durkheim's writing and research has had a profound effect on criminology. His vision of anomie and its influence on contemporary criminological theory will be discussed further in Chapter 6.

The Development of Sociological Criminology

The primacy of sociological positivism was secured by research begun in the early twentieth century by Robert Ezra Park (1864–1944), Ernest W. Burgess (1886–1966), Louis Wirth (1897–1952), and their colleagues in the sociology department at the University of Chicago. The scholars who taught at this program created what is still referred to as the **Chicago School,** in honor of their unique style of doing research.

These urban sociologists pioneered research on the **social ecology** of the city. Their work inspired a generation of scholars to conclude that social forces operating in urban areas create criminal interactions; some neighborhoods become "natural areas" for crime.[22] These urban neighborhoods maintain such a high level of poverty that critical social institutions, such as the school and the family, break down. The resulting social disorganization reduces the ability of social institutions to control behavior, and the outcome is a high crime rate. Criminal behavior, they argued, was not a function of personal traits or characteristics but rather a reaction to an environment that was inadequate for proper human relations and development. They initiated the ecological study of crime by examining how neighborhood conditions, such as poverty levels, influenced crime rates. Their findings substantiated their belief that crime is a function of where one lives rather than individual pathologies.

The Development of Social Process Theories

During the 1930s and 1940s, another group of sociologists added a social-psychological link to criminological behavior. They concluded that the individual's relationship to important social processes—such as education, family life, and peer relations—is the key to understanding human behavior. Some concluded that poverty and social disorganization alone are not sufficient to cause criminal activity. After all, many people living in the most deteriorated areas never commit criminal offenses. Something else is needed. Their research indicated that children who grow up in homes wracked by conflict, attend inadequate schools, and/or associate with deviant peers become exposed to pro-crime forces. Edwin Sutherland, the preeminent American criminologist, suggested that people learn criminal attitudes from older, more experienced law violators. Crime is a learned behavior similar to any other such as driving and playing sports. Another view, developed by Walter Reckless, is that crime occurs when children develop an inadequate self-image, which renders them incapable of controlling their own misbehavior.

Criminologists seized upon this concept of control and suggested that it is a key element in a criminal career: People become crime prone when social forces prove inadequate to control their behavior. Both of these views—learning and control—link criminality to the failure of **socialization,** the interactions people have with the various individuals, organizations, institutions, and processes of society that help them mature and develop.

Use InfoTrac College Edition to learn more about how socialization affects human development. Use "socialization" as a key word. You might also want to look at this article to learn how TV affects socialization: Susan D. Witt, "The Influence of Television on Children's Gender Role Socialization," *Childhood Education* 76 (mid-summer 2000): 322.

By mid-century, most criminologists had embraced either the **ecological view** or the **socialization view** of crime. However, these were not the only views of how social institutions influence human behavior. In Europe, the writings of another social thinker, Karl Marx (1818–1883), had pushed the understanding of social interaction in another direction and sowed the seeds for a new approach in criminology.[23]

The Roots of Conflict Criminology

In his *Communist Manifesto* and other writings, Marx described the oppressive labor conditions prevalent during the rise of industrial capitalism. Observations of the economic structure convinced Marx that the character of every civilization is determined by its mode of production—the way its people develop and produce material goods (materialism). The most important relationship in industrial culture is between the owners of the means of production, the capitalist **bourgeoisie,** and the people who do the actual labor, the **proletariat.** The economic system controls all facets of human life; consequently, people's lives revolve around the means of production. The exploitation of the working class, he believed, would eventually lead to class conflict and the end of the capitalist system.

Though these writings laid the foundation for a Marxist criminology, decades passed before the impact of Marxist theory was realized. In the United States during the 1960s, social and political upheaval was fueled by the Vietnam War, the development of an anti-establishment counterculture movement, the civil rights movement, and the women's movement. Young sociologists interested in applying Marxist principles to the study of crime began to analyze the social conditions in the United States that promoted class conflict and crime. What emerged from this intellectual ferment was a Marxist-based critical criminology that indicted the economic system as producing the conditions that support a high crime rate. The critical tradition has played a significant role in criminology ever since.

| | | | | | | | CONNECTIONS | | | | | | | |

The modern versions of the various schools of criminological thought will be discussed in greater detail throughout the book. Choice theories, the modern offshoot of Beccaria, are reviewed in Chapter 4. Current biological and psychological theories are the topic of Chapter 5. Contemporary theories based on Durkheim's views as well as theories based on the writings of the Chicago School are contained in Chapter 6. The social process view will be discussed in Chapter 7, and Marxist views are contained in Chapter 8. Developmental views are discussed in Chapter 9.

Contemporary Criminology

The various schools of criminology developed throughout the past two centuries. Though they have evolved, each continues to have an impact on the field. For example, classical theory has evolved into rational choice and deterrence theories. Choice theorists today argue that criminals are rational and use available information to decide if crime is a worthwhile undertaking; an offshoot of choice theory, deterrence theory holds that this choice is structured by the fear of punishment. Biological positivism has undergone a similar transformation. Although criminologists no longer believe that a single trait or inherited characteristic can explain crime, some are convinced that biological and psychological traits interact with environmental factors to influence all human behavior, including criminality. Biological and psychological theorists study the association between criminal behavior and such traits as diet, hormonal makeup, personality, and intelligence.

Sociological theories, tracing back to Quetelet and Durkheim, maintain that individuals' lifestyles and living conditions directly control their criminal behavior. Contemporary social ecological theory holds that those at the bottom of the social structure cannot achieve success and thus experience anomie, strain, failure, and frustration.

Learning and control theories are still popular with contemporary criminologists. In their modern incarnation, they suggest that individuals' learning experiences and socialization directly control their behavior. In some cases, children learn to commit crime by interacting with and modeling their behavior on those they admire, whereas other criminal offenders are people whose life experiences have shattered their social bonds to society. Current social process theories will be discussed in Chapter 7.

The writings of Marx and his followers continue to be influential. Many criminologists view social and political conflict as the root cause of crime. The inherently unfair economic structure of the United States and other advanced capitalist countries is the engine that drives the high crime rate. Critical criminology, the contemporary form of Marxist/conflict theory will be discussed further in Chapter 8.

Some criminologists are now integrating each of these concepts into more complex theories that link personal, situational, and social factors. These developmental theories of crime are analyzed in Chapter 9. Each of the major perspectives is summarized in Concept Summary 1.2.

 CONCEPT SUMMARY 1.2

Criminological Perspectives

The major perspectives of criminology focus on individual (biological, psychological, and choice theories); social (structural and process theories); political and economic (conflict theory); and multiple (developmental theory) factors.

Classical/Choice Perspective

- *Situational forces:* Crime is a function of free will and personal choice. Punishment is a deterrent to crime.

Biological/Psychological Perspective

- *Internal forces:* Crime is a function of chemical, neurological, genetic, personality, intelligence, or mental traits.

Structural Perspective

- *Ecological forces:* Crime rates are a function of neighborhood conditions, cultural forces, and norm conflict.

Process Perspective

- *Socialization forces:* Crime is a function of upbringing, learning, and control. Peers, parents, and teachers influence behavior.

Conflict Perspective

- *Economic and political forces:* Crime is a function of competition for limited resources and power. Class conflict produces crime.

Developmental Perspective

- *Multiple forces:* Biological, social-psychological, economic, and political forces may combine to produce crime.

WHAT CRIMINOLOGISTS DO: THE CRIMINOLOGICAL ENTERPRISE

Regardless of their theoretical orientation, criminologists are devoted to the study of crime and criminal behavior. As two noted criminologists, Marvin Wolfgang and Franco Ferracuti, put it: "A criminologist is one whose professional training, occupational role, and pecuniary reward are primarily concentrated on a scientific approach to, and study and analysis of, the phenomenon of crime and criminal behavior."[24]

Several subareas of criminology exist within the broader arena of criminology. Taken together, these subareas make up the **criminological enterprise.** Criminologists may specialize in a subarea in the same way that psychologists might specialize in a subfield of psychology, such as child development, perception, personality, psychopathology, or sexuality. Some of the more important criminological specialties are described next and summarized in Concept Summary 1.3.

Criminal Statistics

The subarea of criminal statistics involves measuring the amount and trends of criminal activity. How much crime occurs annually? Who commits it? When and where does it occur? Which crimes are the most serious?

Criminologists interested in criminal statistics try to create valid and reliable measurements of criminal behavior. They create techniques to access the records of police and court agencies and use sophisticated statistical methods to understand underlying patterns and trends. They develop survey instruments and then use them with large samples to determine the actual number of crimes being committed and the number of victims who suffer criminal violations: How many people are victims of crime, and what percentage reports crime to police?

The development of valid methods to measure crime is a crucial aspect of the criminological enterprise, because without valid and reliable data sources, efforts to conduct research on crime and create criminological theories would be futile. It is also important to determine why crime rates vary across and within regions in order to gauge the association between social and economic forces and criminal activity. Criminal statistics can also be used to make international comparisons to understand why some countries are crime free while others are beset by antisocial activities. This is the topic of the Comparative Criminology feature on pages 14–15.

The Sociology of Law

The sociology of law is a subarea of criminology concerned with the role social forces play in shaping criminal law and, concomitantly, the role of criminal law in shaping society. These criminologists study the history of legal thought, how social forces shape the law, and the effectiveness of legal change.

The law is constantly evolving. Computer fraud, airplane hijacking, ATM theft, and cyber stalking did not exist when the nation was founded. Consequently, the law must be revised to reflect cultural, societal, and technological changes. Criminologists are often asked to determine whether legal change is required and, if so, what shape it should take. In fact, the Supreme Court often considers empirical research supplied by criminologists on such topics as racial discrimination in death penalty cases before it renders an opinion.[25] The research conducted by criminologists then helps form the direction of their legal decision making.

Theory Construction

Social theory is typically viewed as a systematic set of interrelated statements or principles that explain some aspect of social life; it serves as a model or framework for understanding human behavior. Theories are aimed at trying to explain the structure of criminal behavior and the forces that change or alter its content and direction.

Ideally, criminological theories are based on *social facts*—readily observed phenomenon that can be consistently quantified and measured. Once constructed, theories are tested by constructing hypotheses—expectations of behavior that can be derived from the theory and then assessing them using valid empirical research. If, for example, a theory states that the greater the number of police on the street the lower the crime

It might be possible to test the theory "increasing the number of police officers on patrol will reduce crime rates" by first measuring crime rate trends in cities that have added large numbers of officers to their force, and then comparing the results with those tallied in nearby cities that have reduced the size of their police force because of budget cuts or fiscal policies.

© Getty Images

rate, the hypothesis that could be used to support the theory might include:

1. Cities with the most police officers per capita will also have the lowest crime rates.

2. Adding more police officers to the local force will cause the crime rate to decline.

3. Cities that reduce the size of their police force will experience an upsurge in criminal activity.

If adding police officers had little or no effect on the crime rate, then the validity of the theory would be damaged. In contrast, if research shows that adding police reduces crime and this effect is observed at different times in a number of different locales, then the theory might eventually become an accepted element of social thought.

Sometimes criminologists use innovative methods to test theory. For example, when Dennis Wilson sought to determine whether adding police would deter crime, he used data from the National Hockey League to test the hypothesis that adding an enforcement agent (in this case, an additional referee) would deter law violations (penalties). His analysis of game data supported the theory that adding police would bring the crime rate down: As the number of refs increases, serious penalties that are potentially harmful decline![26]

Criminal Behavior Systems

The criminal behavior systems subarea of criminology involves research on specific criminal types and patterns: violent crime, theft crime, public order crime, and organized crime. Numerous attempts have been made to describe and understand particular crime types. For example, Marvin Wolfgang's famous 1958 study, *Patterns in Criminal Homicide,* is considered a landmark analysis of the nature of homicide and the relationship between victim and offender.[27] Edwin Sutherland's analysis of business-related offenses helped coin a new phrase—**white-collar crime**—to describe economic crime activities. The study of criminal behavior also involves research on the links between different types of crime and criminals. This is known as **crime typology.** Some typologies focus on the criminal, suggesting the existence of offender groups such as professional criminals, psychotic criminals, occasional criminals, and so on. Others focus on the crimes, clustering them into categories such as property crimes, sex crimes, and so on.

Penology

The study of **penology** involves the correction and control of known criminal offenders; it is the segment of criminology that most resembles criminal justice. Criminologists conduct research designed to evaluate justice initiatives in order to determine their efficiency, effectiveness, and impact. For example, should capital punishment continue to be employed or is its use simply too risky?

Recent research by Samuel Gross and his colleagues helps answer this critical question. Gross looked at the number of death row inmates who were later found to be innocent. During the period he studied, 1989–2003, 340 people (327 men and 13 women) were exonerated after having served years in prison. Almost half (144 people) were cleared by DNA evidence. Collectively, they had spent more than 3,400 years in prison for crimes they did not commit—an average of more than 10 years each. Gross and his colleagues found that exonerations for death row prisoners are more than 25 times more frequent than exonerations for other prisoners convicted of murder and more than 100 times more frequent than for all imprisoned felons.[28] The Gross research illustrates how important it is to evaluate penal measures in order to determine their effectiveness and reliability.

Victimology

In two classic criminological studies, one by Hans von Hentig and another by Stephen Schafer, the critical role of the victim in the criminal process was identified. These authors were among the first to suggest that victim behavior is often a key determinant of crime and that victims' actions may actually precipitate crime. Both men believe that the study of crime is not complete unless the victim's role is considered.[29]

For those studying the role of the victim in crime, these areas are of particular interest:

- Using victim surveys to measure the nature and extent of criminal behavior not reported to the police

- Calculating the actual costs of crime to victims

- Measuring the factors that increase the likelihood of becoming a victim of crime

- Studying the role of the victim in causing or precipitating crime

- Designing services for the victims of crime, such as counseling and compensation programs

The study of victims and victimization has uncovered some startling results. For one thing, criminals have been found to be at greater risk for victimization than noncriminals.[30] Rather than being the passive targets of criminal acts and simply being in the wrong place at the wrong time, victims may engage in high-risk lifestyles that increase their chances of victimization and make them vulnerable to crime.

||||||| CONNECTIONS |||||||

In recent years, criminologists have devoted ever-increasing attention to the victim's role in the criminal process. A person's lifestyle and behavior may actually increase the risk that he or she will become a victim of crime. Some have suggested that living in a high-crime neighborhood increases risk; others point to the problems caused by associating with dangerous peers and companions. For a discussion of victimization risk, see Chapter 3.

International Crime Trends

India has experienced a shocking form of violence against women known as bride burning. A woman may be burned to death if her family fails to provide the expected dowry to the groom's family or if she is suspected of premarital infidelity; many Indian women commit suicide to escape the brutality of their situation.

The danger from various forms of violent behavior, such as bride burning in India, has become a worldwide epidemic. While crime rates are trending downward in the United States, they seem to be increasing abroad. The United States in 1980 clearly led the Western world in overall crime, but there has been a marked decline in U.S. crime rates, a trend that has now ranked crime prevalence in the United States below other industrialized nations, including England and Wales, Denmark, and Finland. And, contrary to the common assumption that the United States is the most heavily armed nation on earth, there is new evidence that people around the world are arming themselves in record numbers: Residents in the fifteen countries of the European Union have an estimated 84 million firearms. Of that, 67 million (80 percent) are in civilian hands. With a total population of 375 million people, this amounts to 17.4 guns for every 100 people.

Though these trends are alarming, making international comparisons is often difficult because the legal definitions of crime vary from country to country. There are also differences in the way crime is measured. For example, in the United States, crime may be measured by counting criminal acts reported to the police or by using victim surveys, while in many European countries crime is measured by the number of cases solved by the police. Despite these problems, valid comparisons can still be made about crime across different countries using a number of reliable data sources. For example, the United Nations Survey of Crime Trends and Operations of Criminal Justice Systems (UNCJS) is the most well-known source of information on cross-national data. The International Crime Victims Survey (ICVS) is conducted in sixty countries and managed by the Ministry of Justice of the Netherlands, the Home Office of the United Kingdom, and the United Nations Interregional Crime and Justice Research Institute. There is also the United Nations International Study on the Regulation of Firearms. INTERPOL, the international police agency, collects data from police agencies in 179 countries. The World Health Organization (WHO) has conducted surveys on global violence. The *European Sourcebook of Crime and Criminal Justice Statistics* provides data from police agencies in thirty-six European nations.

What do these various sources tell us about international crime rates?

- *Homicide:* Many nations, especially those experiencing social or economic upheaval, have murder rates much higher than the United States. Colombia has about 63 homicides per 100,000 people, and South Africa 51, compared to less than 6 in the United States. During the 1990s there were more homicides in Brazil than in the United States, Canada, Italy, Japan, Australia, Portugal, Britain, Austria, and Germany combined. Why are murder rates so high in nations like Brazil? Law enforcement officials link the upsurge in violence to drug trafficking, gang feuds, vigilantism, and disputes over trivial matters, in which young, unmarried, uneducated males are involved.

- *Rape:* Until 1990, U.S. rape rates were higher than those of any Western nation, but by 2000, Canada took the lead. Violence against women is related to economic hardship and the social status of women. Rates are high in poor nations in which women are oppressed. Where women are more emancipated, the rates of violence against women are lower.

  For many women, sexual violence starts in childhood and adolescence and may occur in the home, school, and community. Studies conducted in a wide variety of nations, ranging from Cameroon to New Zealand, found high rates of reported forced sexual initiation. In some nations, as many as 46 percent of adolescent women and 20 percent of adolescent men report sexual coercion at the hands of family members, teachers, boyfriends, or strangers.

HOW CRIMINOLOGISTS VIEW CRIME

Professional criminologists usually align themselves with one of several schools of thought or perspectives in their field. Each perspective maintains its own view of what constitutes criminal behavior and what causes people to engage in criminality. This diversity of thought is not unique to criminology; biologists, psychologists, sociologists, historians, economists, and natural scientists disagree among themselves about critical issues in their fields. Considering the multidisciplinary nature of the field of criminology, fundamental issues—such as the

Sexual violence has significant health consequences, including suicide, stress, mental illnesses, unwanted pregnancy, sexually transmitted diseases, HIV/AIDS, self-inflicted injuries, and, in the case of child sexual abuse, adoption of high-risk behaviors such as multiple sexual partners and drug use.

- *Robbery:* Countries with more reported robberies than the United States included England and Wales, Portugal, and Spain. Countries with fewer reported robberies included Germany, Italy, and France, as well as Middle Eastern and Asian nations.

- *Burglary:* The United States had lower burglary rates than Australia, Denmark, Finland, England and Wales, and Canada. It had higher reported burglary rates than Spain, Korea, and Saudi Arabia.

- *Vehicle theft:* Australia, England and Wales, Denmark, Norway, Canada, France, and Italy now have higher rates of vehicle theft than the United States.

- *Child abuse:* A World Health Organization report found that child physical and sexual abuse takes a significant toll around the world. In a single year about 57,000 children under 15 years of age are murdered. The homicide rates for children aged 0 to 4 years were over twice as high as rates among children aged 5 to 14 years. Many more children are subjected to nonfatal abuse and neglect; 8 percent of male and 25 percent of female children up to age 18 experience sexual abuse of some kind.

Why the Change?

Why are crime rates increasing around the world while leveling off in the United States? In some developing nations, crime rates may be spiraling upward because they are undergoing rapid changes in their social and economic makeup. In eastern Europe, the fall of communism has brought about a transformation of the family, religion, education, and economy. These changes increase social pressures and result in crime rate increases. Some Asian societies, such as China, are undergoing rapid industrialization, urbanization, and social change. The shift from agricultural to industrial and service economies has produced political turmoil and a surge in crime rates. For example, the island of Hong Kong, long a British possession but now part of the People's Republic of China, is experiencing an upsurge in club drugs. Tied to the local dance scene, ecstasy and ketamine use has skyrocketed along with the traditional drug of choice, heroin. The crime problems we experience in the United States are not unique.

Critical Thinking

1. While risk factors at all levels of social and personal life contribute to youth violence, kids in all nations who experience change in societal-level factors—such as economic inequalities; rapid social change; and the availability of firearms, alcohol, and drugs—seem the most likely to get involved in violence. Can anything be done to help alleviate these social problems?

2. The United States is well known for employing much tougher penal measures than Europe. Do you believe our tougher measures explain why crime is declining in the United States while increasing abroad?

InfoTrac College Edition Research

To find out more about violence around the world, use "violence Europe," "violence Asia," and "violence Africa" as key words in InfoTrac College Edition.

Sources: Karen Joe Laidler, "The Rise of Club Drugs in a Heroin Society: The Case of Hong Kong," *Substance Use & Misuse* 40 (2005): 1,257–1,279; Virendra Kumar and Sarita Kanth, "Bride Burning," *Lancet* 364 (2004): 18–19; Etienne Krug, Linda Dahlberg, James Mercy, Anthony Zwi, and Rafael Lozano, *World Report on Violence and Health* (Geneva: World Health Organization, 2002); Gene Stephens, "Global Trends in Crime: Crime Varies Greatly around the World, Statistics Show, but New Tactics Have Proved Effective in the United States. To Keep Crime in Check in the Twenty-First Century, We'll All Need to Get Smarter, Not Just Tougher," *The Futurist* 37 (2003): 40–47; Graeme Newman, *Global Report on Crime and Justice* (New York: Oxford University Press, 1999); Gary Lafree and Kriss Drass, "Counting Crime Booms among Nations: Evidence for Homicide Victimization Rates, 1956–1998," *Criminology* 40 (2002): 769–801; "The Small Arms Survey, 2004." http://www.smallarmssurvey.org/publications/yb_2004.htm. Accessed July 10, 2005; Pedro Scuro, *World Factbook of Criminal Justice Systems: Brazil* (Washington, DC: Bureau of Justice Statistics, 2003).

nature and definition of crime itself—are cause for disagreement among criminologists.

A criminologist's choice of orientation or perspective depends, in part, on his or her definition of crime: The beliefs and research orientations of most criminologists are related to this definition. This section discusses the three most common concepts of crime used by criminologists.

The Consensus View of Crime

According to the **consensus view,** crimes are behaviors believed to be repugnant to all elements of society. The term *consensus* is used because it implies that there is general agreement among a majority of citizens on what behaviors should be outlawed by the criminal law and viewed as crimes. The **substantive criminal law**, which is the written code that defines crimes and their punishments, reflects the values, beliefs, and opinions of society's mainstream. As stated by eminent criminologists Sutherland and Cressey:

> Criminal behavior is behavior in violation of the criminal law. . . . [I]t is not a crime unless it is prohibited by the criminal law [which] is defined conventionally as a body of specific rules regarding human conduct which have been promulgated by political authority, which apply uniformly to all members of the classes to which the rules refer, and which are enforced by punishment administered by the state.[31]

This approach to crime implies that it is a function of existing beliefs, morality, and rules administered by elected and or appointed government officials. According to Sutherland and Cressey's statement, criminal law is applied "uniformly to all members of the classes to which the rules refer." This statement reveals the authors' faith in the concept of an ideal legal system that deals fairly with all classes and types of people. Laws outlawing theft and violence may be directed at the neediest members of society, whereas laws banning insider trading, embezzlement, and corporate price-fixing are aimed at controlling the wealthiest. The reach of the criminal law is not restricted to any single element of society.

SOCIAL HARM The consensus view of crime links illegal behavior to the concept of **social harm**. Though people generally enjoy a great deal of latitude in their behavior, it is agreed that behaviors that are harmful to others and to society in general must be controlled. Social harm is what sets strange, unusual, or deviant behavior—or any other action that departs from social norms—apart from criminal behaviors.[32]

||||||| CONNECTIONS |||||||

Recall how earlier we covered the efforts by Harry Anslinger to show the social harm caused by smoking marijuana. His efforts resulted in a merely deviant act being transformed into a criminal act; previously law-abiding citizens were now defined as criminal offenders. To read more about crime, morality, and social harm, see Chapter 13.

This position is not without controversy. Although it is clear that rape, robbery, and murder are inherently harmful and their control justified, behaviors such as drug use and prostitution are more problematic because the harm they inflict is primarily on those who are willing participants. According to the consensus view, society is justified in controlling these so-called victimless crimes because public opinion holds that they undermine the social fabric and threaten the general well-being of society. Society has a duty to protect all its members—even those who choose to engage in high-risk behaviors.

The Conflict View of Crime

The **conflict view** depicts society as a collection of diverse groups—owners, workers, professionals, students—who are in constant and continuing conflict. Groups able to assert their political power use the law and the criminal justice system to advance their economic and social position. Criminal laws, therefore, are viewed as acts created to protect the haves from the have-nots. Critical criminologists often contrast the harsh penalties exacted on the poor for their "street crimes" (burglary, robbery, and larceny) with the minor penalties the wealthy receive for their white-collar crimes (securities violations and other illegal business practices), though the latter may cause considerably more social harm. While the poor go to prison for minor law violations, the wealthy are given lenient sentences for even the most serious breaches of law. Rather than being class neutral, criminal law reflects and protects established economic, racial, gendered, and political power and privilege.[33]

Crime, according to this definition, is a political concept designed to protect the power and position of the upper classes at the expense of the poor. Even crimes prohibiting violent acts—such as armed robbery, rape, and murder—may have political undertones. Banning violent acts ensures domestic tranquility and guarantees that the anger of the poor and disenfranchised classes will not be directed at their wealthy capitalist exploiters. According to this conflict view of crime, "real" crimes would include the following acts:

- Violations of human rights due to racism, sexism, and imperialism
- Unsafe working conditions
- Inadequate child care
- Inadequate opportunities for employment and education and substandard housing and medical care
- Crimes of economic and political domination
- Pollution of the environment
- Price-fixing
- Police brutality
- Assassinations and war-making
- Violations of human dignity
- Denial of physical needs and necessities and impediments to self-determination
- Deprivation of adequate food and blocked opportunities to participate in political decision making[34]

The Interactionist View of Crime

The **interactionist view** of crime traces its antecedents to the symbolic interaction school of sociology, first popularized by pioneering sociologists George Herbert Mead, Charles Horton Cooley, and W. I. Thomas.[35] This position holds that (1) people act according to their own interpretations of reality, through which they assign meaning to things; (2) they observe

According to the interactionist view of crime, moral entrepreneurs try to shape the definition of crime to reflect their own preferences and opinions. Some may go on crusades to legalize activities that are currently criminal, such as using marijuana for medical reasons, while others seek to criminalize behaviors that are currently legal, such as abortion.

the way others react, either positively or negatively; and (3) they reevaluate and interpret their own behavior according to the meaning and symbols they have learned from others.

According to this perspective, there is no objective reality. People, institutions, and events are viewed subjectively and labeled either good or evil according to the interpretation of the evaluator. For example, some people might consider the film *Pulp Fiction* obscene, foul-mouthed, and degrading, but another observer may consider the same film an imposing work of art. When an argument results in the death of one of the participants, a jury may be asked to decide whether it was murder, self-defense, or merely an accidental fatality. Each person on the jury may have his or her own interpretation of what took place.

According to the interactionist view, the definition of crime reflects the preferences and opinions of people who hold social power in a particular legal jurisdiction. These people use their influence to impose their definition of right and wrong on the rest of the population. Criminals are individuals society has **stigmatized,** or chosen to label as outcasts or deviants, because they have violated social rules. In a classic statement, sociologist Howard Becker argued, "The deviant is one to whom that label has successfully been applied; deviant behavior is behavior people so label."[36] Crimes are outlawed behaviors because society defines them that way and not because they are inherently evil or immoral acts.

The interactionist view of crime is similar to the conflict perspective; both suggest that behavior should be outlawed when it offends people who maintain the social, economic, and political power necessary to have the law conform to their interests or needs. However, unlike the conflict view, the interactionist perspective does not attribute capitalist

economic and political motives to the process of defining crime. Instead, interactionists see the criminal law as conforming to the beliefs of moral crusaders or **moral entrepreneurs,** who use their influence to shape the legal process in the way they see fit.[37] Laws against pornography, prostitution, and drugs are believed to be motivated more by moral crusades than by economic values.

The three main views of crime are summarized in Concept Summary 1.4.

CONCEPT SUMMARY 1.4

The Definition of Crime

The definition of crime affects how criminologists view the cause and control of illegal behavior and shapes their research orientation.

Consensus View

- The law defines crime.
- Agreement exists on outlawed behavior.
- Laws apply to all citizens equally.

Conflict View

- The law is a tool of the ruling class.
- Crime is a politically defined concept.
- "Real crimes" are not outlawed.
- The law is used to control the underclass.

Interactionist View

- Moral entrepreneurs define crime.
- Acts become crimes because society defines them that way.
- Criminal labels are life-transforming events.

Defining Crime

Today, each definition of crime has its own followers. This is important because criminologists' personal definitions of crime dominate their thinking, research, and attitudes toward their profession. Because of their diverse perspectives, criminologists have taken a variety of approaches in explaining the causes of crime and suggesting methods for its control. Considering these differences, it is possible to take elements from each school of thought to formulate an integrated definition of **crime:**

> Crime is a violation of societal rules of behavior as interpreted and expressed by a criminal legal code created by people holding social and political power. Individuals who violate these rules are subject to sanctions by state authority, social stigma, and loss of status.

This definition combines the consensus position that the criminal law defines crimes with the conflict perspective's emphasis on political power and control and the interactionist concept of labeling and stigma. Thus crime, as defined here, is a political, social, and economic function of modern life.

CRIME AND THE CRIMINAL LAW

No matter which definition of crime we embrace, criminal behavior is tied to the criminal law. It is therefore important for all criminologists to have some understanding of the development of criminal law, its objectives, its elements, and how it evolves.

The concept of criminal law has been recognized for more than 3,000 years. Hammurabi (1792–1750 BCE), the sixth king of Babylon, created the most famous set of written laws of the ancient world, known today as the **Code of Hammurabi.** Preserved on basalt rock columns, the code established a system of crime and punishment based on physical retaliation ("an eye for an eye"). The severity of punishment depended on class standing: If convicted of an unprovoked assault, a slave would be killed, whereas a free man might lose a limb.

More familiar is the **Mosaic Code** of the Israelites (1200 BCE). According to tradition, God entered into a covenant or contract with the tribes of Israel in which they agreed to obey his law (the 613 laws of the Old Testament, including the Ten Commandments), as presented to them by Moses, in return for God's special care and protection. The

Mosaic Code is not only the foundation of Judeo-Christian moral teachings but is also a basis for the U.S. legal system. Prohibitions against murder, theft, perjury, and adultery preceded by several thousand years the same laws found in the modern United States.

> Did you know that the ancient Romans had laws governing the behavior of women at parties? To learn more about these and other ancient laws, use "Greek law" and "Roman law" as subject guides with InfoTrac College Edition.

Though ancient formal **legal codes** were lost during the Dark Ages, early German and Anglo-Saxon societies developed legal systems featuring monetary compensation for criminal violations. Guilt was determined by two methods. One was **compurgation,** in which the accused person swore an oath of innocence with the backing of twelve to twenty-five oathhelpers, who would attest to his or her character and claims of innocence. The second was trial by **ordeal,** which was based on the principle that divine forces would not allow an innocent person to be harmed. It involved such measures as having the accused place his or her hand in boiling water or hold a hot iron. If the wound healed, the person was found innocent; if the wound did not heal, the accused was deemed guilty. Another version of the ordeal was trial by combat, which allowed the accused to challenge his accuser to a duel, with the outcome determining the legitimacy of the accusation. Punishments included public flogging, branding, beheading, and burning.

Common Law

After the Norman conquest of England in 1066, royal judges began to travel throughout the land, holding court in each county several times a year. When court was in session, the royal administrator, or judge, would summon a number of citizens who would, on their oath, tell of the crimes and serious breaches of the peace that had occurred since the judge's last visit. The royal judge would then decide what to do in each case, using local custom and rules of conduct as his guide. Courts were bound to follow the law established in previous cases unless a higher authority, such as the king or the pope, overruled the law.

The present English system of law came into existence during the reign of Henry II (1154–1189), when royal judges began to publish their decisions in local cases. Judges began to use these written decisions as a basis for their decision making, and eventually a fixed body of legal rules and principles was established. If a new rule was successfully applied in a number of different cases, it would become a precedent. These precedents would then be commonly applied in all similar cases—hence the term **common law.** Crimes such as murder, burglary, arson, and rape are common-law crimes whose elements were initially defined by judges. They are referred to as *mala in se,* or inherently evil and depraved. When the situation required, the English Parliament enacted legislation to supplement the judge-made common law. Crimes defined by

Parliament, which reflected existing social conditions, were referred to as *mala prohibitum,* or **statutory crimes.**

Before the American Revolution, the colonies, then under British rule, were subject to the common law. After the colonies acquired their independence, state legislatures standardized common-law crimes such as murder, burglary, arson, and rape by putting them into statutory form in criminal codes. As in England, whenever common law proved inadequate to deal with changing social and moral issues, the states and Congress supplemented it with legislative statutes, creating new elements in the various state and federal legal codes. Concept Summary 1.5 lists a number of crimes that were first defined in common law.

Contemporary Criminal Law

Criminal laws are now divided into felonies and misdemeanors. The distinction is based on seriousness: A **felony** is a serious offense; a misdemeanor is a minor or petty crime. Crimes such as murder, rape, and burglary are felonies; they are punished with long prison sentences or even death. Crimes such as unarmed assault and battery, petty larceny, and disturbing the peace are misdemeanors; they are punished with a fine or a period of incarceration in a county jail.

Regardless of their classification, acts prohibited by the criminal law constitute behaviors considered unacceptable and impermissible by those in power. People who engage in these acts are eligible for severe sanctions. By outlawing these behaviors, the government expects to achieve a number of social goals:

- *Enforce social control:* Those who hold political power rely on criminal law to formally prohibit behaviors believed to threaten societal well-being or to challenge their authority. For example, U.S. criminal law incorporates centuries-old prohibitions against the following behaviors harmful to others: taking another person's possessions, physically harming another person,

---

(◉) CONCEPT SUMMARY 1.5

Common-Law Crimes

Crimes against the Person

- *First-degree murder:* **First-degree murder** is unlawful killing of another human being with malice aforethought and with premeditation and deliberation. Example: A woman buys poison and pours it into a cup of coffee her husband is drinking, intending to kill him for the insurance benefits.

- *Voluntary manslaughter:* **Voluntary manslaughter** is intentional killing committed under extenuating circumstances that mitigate the killing, such as killing in the heat of passion after being provoked. Example: A husband coming home early from work finds his wife in bed with another man. The husband goes into a rage and shoots and kills both lovers with a gun he keeps by his bedside.

- *Battery:* **Battery** is the unlawful touching of another with intent to cause injury. Example: A man sees a stranger sitting in his favorite seat in a cafeteria and goes up to that person and pushes him out of the seat.

- *Assault:* **Assault** is intentional placing of another in fear of receiving an immediate battery. Example: A student aims an unloaded gun at her professor and threatens to shoot. The professor believes the gun is loaded.

- *Rape:* **Rape** is unlawful sexual intercourse with a female without her consent. Example: After a party, a man offers to drive a young female acquaintance home. He takes her to a wooded area and, despite her protests, forces her to have sexual relations with him.

- *Robbery:* **Robbery** is wrongful taking and carrying away of personal property from a person by violence or intimidation. Example: A man armed with a loaded gun approaches another man on a deserted street and demands his wallet.

Inchoate (Incomplete) Offenses

- *Attempt:* An intentional act for the purpose of committing a crime that is more than mere preparation or planning of the crime. The crime is not completed, however. Example: A person places a bomb in the intended victim's car so that it will detonate when the ignition key is used. The bomb is discovered before the car is started. Attempted murder has been committed.

- *Conspiracy:* Voluntary agreement between two or more people to achieve an unlawful object or to achieve a lawful object using means forbidden by law. Example: A doctor conspires with a con man to fake accidents and then bring the false "victims" to his office so he can collect medical fees from an insurance company.

- *Solicitation:* With the intent that another person engage in conduct constituting a felony, a person solicits, requests, commands, or otherwise attempts to cause that person to engage in such conduct. Example: A terrorist approaches a person he believes is sympathetic to his cause and begs him to join in a plot to blow up a government building.

Crimes against Property

- *Burglary:* **Burglary** is breaking and entering of a dwelling house of another in the nighttime with the intent to commit a felony. Example: Intending to steal some jewelry and silver, a young man breaks a window and enters another's house at 10 P.M.

- *Arson:* **Arson** is the intentional burning of a dwelling house of another. Example: A worker, angry that her boss did not give her a raise, goes to his house and sets it on fire.

- *Larceny:* **Larceny** is taking and carrying away the personal property of another with the intent to keep and possess the property. Example: While shopping, a woman sees a diamond ring displayed at the jewelry counter. When no one is looking, the woman takes the ring, places it in her pocket, and walks out of the store without paying.

Source: Developed by Therese J. Libby, J.D.

damaging another person's property, and cheating another person out of his or her possessions. Similarly, the law prevents actions that challenge the legitimacy of the government, such as planning its overthrow, collaborating with its enemies, and so on.

■ *Discourage revenge:* By punishing people who infringe on the rights, property, and freedom of others, the law shifts the burden of revenge from the individual to the state. As Oliver Wendell Holmes stated, this prevents "the greater evil of private retribution."[38] Although state retaliation may offend the sensibilities of many citizens, it is greatly preferable to a system in which people would have to seek justice for themselves.

■ *Express public opinion and morality:* Criminal law reflects constantly changing public opinions and moral values. *Mala in se* crimes, such as murder and forcible rape, are almost universally prohibited; however, the prohibition of legislatively created *mala prohibitum* crimes, such as traffic offenses and gambling violations, changes according to social conditions and attitudes. Criminal law is used to codify these changes.

■ *Deter criminal behavior:* Criminal law has a **social control function.** It can control, restrain, and direct human behavior through its sanctioning power. The threat of punishment associated with violating the law is designed to prevent crimes before they occur. During the Middle Ages, public executions drove this point home. Today criminal law's impact is felt through news accounts of long prison sentences and an occasional execution.

■ *Punish wrongdoing:* The deterrent power of criminal law is tied to the authority it gives the state to sanction or punish offenders. Those who violate criminal law are subject to physical coercion and punishment.

■ *Maintain social order:* All legal systems are designed to support and maintain the boundaries of the social system they serve. In medieval England, the law protected the feudal system by defining an orderly method of property transfer and ownership. Laws in some socialist nations protect the primacy of the state by strictly curtailing profiteering and individual enterprise. Our own capitalist system is also supported and sustained by criminal law. In a sense, the content of criminal law is more a reflection of the needs of those who control the existing economic and political system than a representation of some idealized moral code.

Some of the elements of the contemporary criminal law are discussed in The Criminological Enterprise feature "The Elements of Criminal Law" on pages 22–23.

The Evolution of Criminal Law

Criminal law is constantly evolving in an effort to reflect social and economic conditions. Sometimes legal changes are prompted by highly publicized cases that generate fear and concern. For example, a number of notorious cases of celebrity stalking, including Robert John Bardo's fatal shooting of actress Rebecca Schaeffer on July 18, 1989, prompted more than twenty-five states to enact **stalking** statutes. Such laws prohibit "the willful, malicious, and repeated following and harassing of another person."[39] Similarly, after 7-year-old Megan Kanka of Hamilton Township, New Jersey, was killed in 1994 by a repeat sexual offender who had moved into her neighborhood, the federal government passed legislation requiring that the general public be notified of local **pedophiles** (sexual offenders who target children).[40] California's sexual predator law, which took effect on January 1, 1996, allows people convicted of sexually violent crimes against two or more victims to be committed to a mental institution after their prison terms have been served.[41]

The criminal law is constantly evolving to reflect social, economic, and cultural shifts. Changes in the law may be a sign of toleration for behavior considered socially unacceptable and harmful only a few years before. Here Boston City Registrar Judith McCarthy goes over the application for a marriage license submitted by successful same-sex marriage lawsuit plaintiffs Julie and Hillary Goodridge at City Hall in Boston May 17, 2004. Massachusetts became the first state in the United States to legally sanction same-sex marriage based on the ruling of the Massachusetts Supreme Judicial Court that required the state to issue marriage licenses to gay and lesbian couples. Does Massachusetts' same-sex marriage law reflect changing national values or is it merely a reflection of the beliefs of a few liberal judges in an open-minded state?

The criminal law may also change because of shifts in the culture and in social conventions, reflecting a newfound tolerance of behavior condemned only a few years before. For example, in an important 2003 case, *Lawrence v. Texas*, the Supreme Court declared that laws banning sodomy were unconstitutional because they violated the due process rights of citizens based on their sexual orientation. In its decision, the court said

> Although the laws involved . . . here . . . do not more than prohibit a particular sexual act, their penalties and purposes have more far-reaching consequences, touching upon the most private human conduct, sexual behavior, and in the most private of places, the home. They seek to control a personal relationship that, whether or not entitled to formal recognition in the law, is within the liberty of persons to choose without being punished as criminals. The liberty protected by the Constitution allows homosexual persons the right to choose to enter upon relationships in the confines of their homes and their own private lives and still retain their dignity as free persons.

As a result of the decision, all sodomy laws in the United States are now unconstitutional and therefore not enforceable.[42]

The future direction of U.S. criminal law remains unclear. Certain actions, such as crimes by corporations and political corruption, will be labeled as criminal and given more attention. Other offenses, such as recreational drug use, may diminish in importance or be removed entirely from the criminal law system. In addition, changing technology and its ever-increasing global and local roles in our lives will require modifications in criminal law. For example, technologies such as automatic teller machines and cellular phones have already spawned a new generation of criminal acts including identity theft and software piracy.

| | | | | | | CONNECTIONS | | | | | | |

As the information highway sprawls toward new expanses, the nation's computer network advances, and biotechnology produces new substances, criminal law will be forced to address threats to the public safety that today are unknown. These new forms of Internet-related technocrimes will be discussed in more detail in Chapter 14.

ETHICAL ISSUES IN CRIMINOLOGY

A critical issue facing students of criminology involves recognizing the field's political and social consequences. All too often, criminologists forget the social responsibility they bear as experts in the area of crime and justice. When government agencies request their views of issues, their pronouncements and opinions become the basis for sweeping social policy. The lives of millions of people can be influenced by criminological research data.

Debates over gun control, capital punishment, and mandatory sentences are ongoing and contentious. Some criminologists have successfully argued for social service, treatment, and rehabilitation programs to reduce the crime rate, but others consider them a waste of time, suggesting instead that a massive prison construction program coupled with tough criminal sentences can bring the crime rate down. By accepting their roles as experts on law-violating behavior, criminologists place themselves in a position of power; the potential consequences of their actions are enormous. Therefore, they must be aware of the ethics of their profession and be prepared to defend their work in the light of public scrutiny. Major ethical issues include these:

- What is to be studied?
- Who is to be studied?
- How are studies to be conducted?

WHAT TO STUDY? Under ideal circumstances, when criminologists choose a subject for study, they are guided by their own scholarly interests, pressing social needs, the availability of accurate data, and other similar concerns. Nonetheless, in recent years, a great influx of government and institutional funding has influenced the direction of criminological inquiry. Major sources of monetary support include the Justice Department's National Institute of Justice and the Office of Juvenile Justice and Delinquency Prevention. Both the National Science Foundation and the National Institute of Mental Health have been prominent sources of government funding. Private foundations, such as the Edna McConnell Clark Foundation, have also played an important role in supporting criminological research.

Though the availability of research money has spurred criminological inquiry, it has also influenced the direction of the research. State and federal governments provide a significant percentage of available research funds, and they may also dictate the areas that can be studied. In recent years, for example, the federal government has spent millions of dollars funding long-term cohort studies of criminal careers. Consequently, academic research has recently focused on criminal careers. Other areas of inquiry may be ignored because there is simply not enough funding to pay for or sponsor the research.

A potential conflict of interest may arise when the institution funding research is itself one of the principal subjects of the research project. For example, the government may be reluctant to fund research on fraud and abuse of power by government officials. It may also exert a not-so-subtle influence on the criminologists seeking research funding: If criminologists are too critical of the government's efforts to reduce or counteract crime, perhaps they will be barred from receiving further financial help. This situation is even more acute when we consider that criminologists typically work for universities or public agencies and are under pressure to bring in a steady flow of research funds or to maintain the continued viability of their agency.

Even when criminologists maintain discretion of choice, the direction of their efforts may not be truly objective. The objectivity of research may be questioned if studies are

The Elements of Criminal Law

While each state and the federal government have unique methods of defining crime, there are significant uniformities and similarities that shape the essence of almost all criminal law codes. While the laws of California, Texas, and Maine may be somewhat different, the underlying concepts that guide and shape their legal systems are universal. The question remains: Regardless of jurisdictional boundaries, what is the legal definition of a crime, and how does the criminal law deal with it?

Legal Definition of a Crime

Today, in all jurisdictions, the legal definition of a crime involves the elements of the criminal acts that must be proven in a court of law if the defendant is to be found guilty. For the most part, common criminal acts have both mental and physical elements, both of which must be present if the act is to be considered a legal crime. In order for a crime to occur, the state must show that the accused committed the guilty act, or *actus reus,* and had the *mens rea,* or criminal intent, to commit the act. The *actus reus* may be an aggressive act, such as taking someone's money, burning a building, or shooting someone; or it may be a failure to act when there is a legal duty to do so, such as a parent's neglecting to seek medical attention for a sick child. The *mens rea* (guilty mind) refers to an individual's state of mind at the time of the act or, more specifically, the person's intent to commit the crime.

Actus Reus

To satisfy the requirements of *actus reus,* guilty actions must be voluntary. Even though an act may cause harm or damage, it is not considered a crime if it was done by accident or was an involuntary act. For example, it would not be a crime if a motorist obeying all the traffic laws hit a child who had run into the street. If the same motorist were drinking or speeding, then his action would be considered a vehicular crime because it was a product of negligence. Similarly, it would not be considered a crime if a baby-sitter accidentally dropped a child and the child died. However, it would be considered manslaughter if the sitter threw the child down in anger or frustration, and the blow caused the child's death. In some circumstances of *actus reus,* the use of words is considered criminal. In the crime of sedition, the words of disloyalty constitute the *actus reus.* If a person falsely yells "fire" in a crowded theater and people are injured in the rush to exit, that person is held responsible for the injuries, because the use of the word in that situation constitutes an illegal act.

Typically, the law does not require people to aid people in distress, such as entering a burning building to rescue people trapped by a fire. However, failure to act is considered a crime in certain instances:

- *Relationship of the parties based on status:* Some people are bound by relationship to give aid. These relationships include parent–child and husband–wife. If a husband finds his wife unconscious because she took an overdose of sleeping pills, he is obligated to save her life by seeking medical aid. If he fails to do so and she dies, he can be held responsible for her death.

- *Imposition by statute:* Some states have passed laws requiring people to give aid. For example, a person who observes a broken-down automobile in the desert but fails to stop and help the other parties involved may be committing a crime.

- *Contractual relationships:* These relationships include lifeguard and swimmer, doctor and patient, and baby-sitter or au pair and child. Because lifeguards have been hired to ensure the safety of swimmers, they have a legal duty to come to the aid of drowning persons. If a lifeguard knows a swimmer is in danger and does nothing about it and the swimmer drowns, the lifeguard is legally responsible for the swimmer's death.

Mens Rea

In most situations, for an act to constitute a crime, it must be done with criminal intent, or *mens rea.* Intent, in the legal sense, can mean carrying out an act intentionally, knowingly, and willingly. However, the definition also

---

funded by organizations that have a vested interest in the outcome of the research. For example, a study on the effectiveness of the defensive use of handguns to stop crime may be tainted if the funding for the project comes from a gun manufacturer whose sales may be affected by the research findings. Efforts to show that private prisons are more effective than state correctional facilities might be tainted if the researchers received a research grant from a corporation that maintains private prisons.

WHOM TO STUDY? A second major ethical issue in criminology concerns who is the subject of the inquiries and study. Too often, criminologists focus their attention on the poor and minorities while ignoring the middle-class criminal who may be committing white-collar crime, organized crime, or government crime. Critics have charged that by "unmasking" the poor and desperate, criminologists have justified any harsh measures taken against them. For example, a few social scientists have suggested that criminals

encompasses situations in which recklessness or negligence establishes the required criminal intent.

Criminal intent also exists if the results of an action, although originally unintended, are certain to occur. For example, when Timothy McVeigh planted a bomb in front of the Murrah Federal Building in Oklahoma City, he did not intend to kill any particular person in the building. Yet the law would hold that McVeigh or any other person would be substantially certain that people in the building would be killed in the blast, and McVeigh therefore had the criminal intent to commit murder.

Strict Liability

Though common-law crimes require that both the *actus reus* and the *mens rea* must be present before a person can be convicted of a crime, several crimes defined by statute do not require *mens rea*. In these cases, the person accused is guilty simply by doing what the statute prohibits; intent does not enter the picture. These **strict liability crimes,** or public welfare offenses, include violations of health and safety regulations, traffic laws, and narcotics control laws. For example, a person stopped for speeding is guilty of breaking the traffic laws regardless of whether he or she intended to go over the speed limit or did it by accident. The underlying purpose of these laws is to protect the public; therefore, intent is not required.

Criminal Defenses

When people defend themselves against criminal charges, they must refute one or more of the elements of the crime of which they have been accused. A number of different approaches can be taken to create this defense.

First, defendants may deny the *actus reus* by arguing that they were falsely accused and that the real culprit has yet to be identified. Second, defendants may claim that although they engaged in the criminal act of which they are accused, they lacked the *mens rea* (intent) needed to be found guilty of the crime.

If a person whose mental state is impaired commits a criminal act, it is possible for the person to excuse his or her criminal actions by claiming that he or she lacked the capacity to form sufficient intent to be held criminally responsible. Insanity, intoxication, and ignorance are types of excuse defenses. A defendant might argue that because he suffered from a mental impairment that prevented him from understanding the harmfulness of his acts, he lacked sufficient *mens rea* to be found guilty as charged.

Another type of defense is justification. Here the individual usually admits committing the criminal act but maintains that he or she should not be held criminally liable because the act was justified. Among the justification defenses are necessity, duress, self-defense, and entrapment. A battered wife who kills her mate might argue that she acted out of duress; her crime was committed to save her own life.

People standing trial for criminal offenses may thus defend themselves by claiming that they did not commit the act in question, that their actions were justified under the circumstances, or that their behavior can be excused by their lack of *mens rea*. If either the physical or mental elements of a crime cannot be proven, then the defendant cannot be convicted.

Critical Thinking

1. Should the concept of the guilty mind be eliminated from the criminal law and replaced with a strict liability standard? If you do the crime, you do the time?

2. Some critics believe that current criminal defenses, such as the battered wife defense or the insanity defense, allow the guilty to go free even though they committed serious criminal acts. Do you agree?

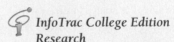
InfoTrac College Edition Research

To find out more about the "insanity defense" use the term as a key word search with InfoTrac College Edition.

Sources: Joshua Dressler, *Cases and Materials on Criminal Law* (American Casebook Series) (Eagan, MN: West, 2003); Joel Samaha, *Criminal Law* (Belmont, CA: Wadsworth, 2001).

have lower intelligence quotients than the average citizen, and that because minority group members have lower than average IQ scores, their crime rates are high.[43] This was the conclusion reached in the *The Bell Curve,* a popular though highly controversial book written by Richard Herrnstein and Charles Murray.[44] Although such research is often methodologically unsound, it brings to light the tendency of criminologists to focus on one element of the community while ignoring others. The question that remains is whether

or not it is ethical for criminologists to publish biased or subjective research findings, paving the way for injustice.

HOW TO STUDY? Ethics are once again questioned in cases where subjects are misled about the purpose of the research. When white and African American youngsters are asked to participate in a survey of their behavior or to take an IQ test, they are rarely told in advance that the data they provide may later be used to prove the existence of significant racial differences in their self-reported crime rates. Should subjects be told about the true purpose of a survey? Would such disclosures make meaningful research impossible? How far should criminologists go when collecting data? Is it ever permissible to deceive subjects to collect data? Criminologists must take extreme care when they select subjects for their research studies to ensure that they are selected in an unbiased and random manner.[45]

When criminological research efforts involve experimentation and treatment, care must be taken to protect those subjects who have been chosen for experimental and control groups. For example, it may be unethical to provide a special treatment program for one group while depriving others of the same opportunity. Conversely, criminologists must be careful to protect subjects from experiments that may actually cause them harm. For example, an examination of the highly publicized Scared Straight program, which brought youngsters into contact with hardcore prison inmates to scare them out of a life of crime, discovered that the young subjects may have been harmed by their experience. Rather than being frightened into conformity, subjects actually increased their criminal behavior.[46]

SUMMARY

- Criminology is the scientific approach to the study of criminal behavior and society's reaction to law violations and violators. It is essentially an interdisciplinary field; many of its practitioners were originally trained as sociologists, psychologists, economists, political scientists, historians, and natural scientists.

- Criminology has a rich history, with roots in the utilitarian philosophy of Beccaria, the biological positivism of Lombroso, the social theory of Durkheim, and the political philosophy of Marx.

- The criminological enterprise includes subareas such as criminal statistics, the sociology of law, theory construction, criminal behavior systems, penology, and victimology.

- When they define crime, criminologists typically hold one of three perspectives: the consensus view, the conflict view, or the interactionist view.

- The consensus view holds that criminal behavior is defined by laws that reflect the values and morals of a majority of citizens.

- The conflict view states that criminal behavior is defined in such a way that economically powerful groups can retain their control over society.

- The interactionist view portrays criminal behavior as a relativistic, constantly changing concept that reflects society's current moral values. According to the interactionist view, behavior is labeled as criminal by those in power; criminals are people society chooses to label as outsiders or deviants.

- The criminal law is a set of rules that specify the behaviors society has outlawed.

- The criminal law serves several important purposes: It represents public opinion and moral values, it enforces social controls, it deters criminal behavior and wrongdoing, it punishes transgressors, and it banishes private retribution.

- The criminal law used in U.S. jurisdictions traces its origin to the English common law. In the U.S. legal system, lawmakers have codified common-law crimes into state and federal penal codes.

- Every crime has specific elements. In most instances, these elements include both the *actus reus* (guilty act) and the *mens rea* (guilty mind)—the person's state of mind or criminal intent.

- At trial, a defendant may claim to have lacked *mens rea* and, therefore, not be responsible for a criminal action. One type of defense is excuse for mental reasons, such as insanity, intoxication, necessity, or duress. Another type of defense is justification by reason of self-defense or entrapment.

- The criminal law is undergoing constant reform. Some acts are being decriminalized—their penalties are being reduced—while penalties for others are becoming more severe.

- Ethical issues arise when information-gathering methods appear biased or exclusionary. These issues may cause serious consequences because research findings can significantly impact individuals and groups.

ThomsonNOW

Thinking Like a Criminologist

You have been experimenting with various techniques to identify a sure-fire method to predict violence-prone behavior in delinquents. Your procedure involves brain scans, DNA testing, and blood analysis. Used with samples of incarcerated adolescents, your procedure has been able to distinguish with 80 percent accuracy between youths with a history of violence and those who are exclusively property offenders.

Your research indicates that if any youth were tested with your techniques, potentially violence-prone career criminals easily could be identified for special treatment. For example, children in the local school system could be tested, and those who are identified as violence prone carefully monitored by teachers. Those at risk to future violence could be put into special programs as a precaution.

Some of your colleagues argue that this type of testing is unconstitutional because it violates the subjects' Fifth Amendment right against self-incrimination. There is also the problem of error: Some kids may be falsely labeled as violence prone. How would you answer your critics? Is it fair and/or ethical to label people as potentially criminal and violent even though they have not yet exhibited any antisocial behaviors? Do the risks of such a procedure outweigh its benefits?

Doing Research on the Web

Read more on the history of criminology by going to criminological historian Nicole Rafter's take on biological theories of crime: http://www.albany.edu/museum/wwwmuseum/criminal/curator/nicole.html.

Stigma is a key element of the social interactionist view of crime. To see how it pertains to mental health, go to: http://www.cmha-tb.on.ca/stigma.htm#what.

If you are interested in a career in forensics, go to: http://www.wcupa.edu/_ACADEMICS/sch_cas.psy/Career_Paths/Forensic/Career08.htm

BOOK COMPANION WEBSITE

http://cj.wadsworth.com/siegel_crimtpt9e To quiz yourself on the material in this chapter, go to the companion website, where you'll find chapter-by-chapter online tutorial quizzes, a final exam, ABC videos with questions, chapter outlines, chapter review, chapter-by-chapter web links, flash cards, and more!

KEY TERMS

criminology (4)
criminologists (4)
scientific method (4)
interdisciplinary science (4)
deviant behavior (5)
decriminalized (5)
utilitarianism (7)
classical criminology (7)
positivism (7)
physiognomist (8)
phrenologist (8)
psychopathic personality (8)
atavistic anomalies (8)
criminal anthropology (8)
biological determinism (8)
biosocial theory (8)
cartographic school of criminology (9)
anomie (9)
Chicago School (9)
social ecology (9)
socialization (10)

ecological view (10)
socialization view (10)
bourgeoisie (10)
proletariat (10)
criminological enterprise (11)
white-collar crime (13)
crime typology (13)
penology (13)
consensus view (15)
substantive criminal law (16)
social harm (16)
conflict view (16)
interactionist view (17)
stigmatize (17)
moral entrepreneurs (17)
crime (18)
Code of Hammurabi (18)
Mosaic Code (18)
legal code (18)
compurgation (18)
ordeal (18)

common law (18)
mala in se crimes (18)
mala prohibitum crimes (19)
statutory crimes (19)
first-degree murder (19)
voluntary manslaughter (19)
battery (19)
assault (19)
rape (19)
robbery (19)
burglary (19)
arson (19)
larceny (19)
felony (19)
social control function (20)
stalking (20)
pedophile (20)
actus reus (22)
mens rea (22)
strict liability crimes (23)

CRITICAL THINKING QUESTIONS

1. Beccaria argued that the threat of punishment controls crime. Are there other forms of social control? Aside from the threat of legal punishments, what else controls your own behavior?

2. What research method would you employ if you wanted to study drug and alcohol abuse at your own school? What are the ethical implications of this type of research?

3. Would it be ethical for a criminologist to observe a teenage gang by "hanging" with them, drinking, and watching as they steal cars? Should he report that behavior to the police?

4. Can you identify behaviors that are deviant but not criminal? What about crimes that are not deviant?

5. Do you agree with conflict theorists that some of the most damaging acts in society are not punished as crimes? If so, what are they?

6. Under common law a person must have *mens rea* to be guilty of a crime. Would society be better off if criminal intent were not considered? After all, aren't we merely guessing about a person's actual motivation for committing crime?

NOTES

1. Edwin Sutherland and Donald Cressey, *Principles of Criminology*, 6th ed. (Philadelphia: Lippincott, 1960), p. 3.

2. Monitoring the Future, *National Survey Results on Drug Use, 1975–2004*, vols. 1 and 2. http://www.monitoringthefuture.org/pubs/monographs/vol1_2004.pdf. Accessed October 20, 2005.

3. Edward Brecher, *Licit and Illicit Drugs* (Boston: Little, Brown, 1972), pp. 413–416.

4. Hearings on H.R. 6385 April 27, 28, 29, 30, and May 4, 1937. http://www.druglibrary.org/schaffer/hemp/taxact/anslng1.htm. Accessed April 10, 2004.

5. http://www.dpf.org/drugwar. Accessed April 12, 2004.

6. Federal Communications Commission, In the Matter of Clear Channel Broadcasting File No. EB-03-IH-0159, Washington, DC, April 7, 2004. http://www.fcc.gov/eb/Orders/2004/FCC-04-88A1.html.

7. http://www.howardstern.com/oprah.html. Accessed April 7, 2004.

8. Eugen Weber, *A Modern History of Europe* (New York: Norton, 1971), p. 398.

9. Marvin Wolfgang, *Patterns in Criminal Homicide* (Philadelphia: University of Pennsylvania Press, 1958).

10. Nicole Rafter, "The Murderous Dutch Fiddler: Criminology, History, and the Problem of Phrenology," *Theoretical Criminology* 9 (2005): 65–97.

11. Nicole Rafter, "The Unrepentant Horse-Slasher: Moral Insanity and the Origins of Criminological Thought," *Criminology* 42(2004): 979–1,008.

12. Described in David Lykken, "Psychopathy, Sociopathy, and Crime," *Society* 34 (1996): 29–38.

13. See Peter Scott, "Henry Maudsley," in *Pioneers in Criminology*, ed. Hermann Mannheim (Montclair, NJ: Prentice-Hall, 1981).

14. Gina Lombroso-Ferrero, *Criminal Man, According to the Classification of Cesare Lombroso* (Patterson Smith reprint series in criminology, law enforcement, and social problems, publication no. 134) (Montclair, NJ: Patterson Smith, 1972).

15. Nicole Hahn Rafter, "Criminal Anthropology in the United States," *Criminology* 30 (1992): 525–547.

16. Ibid., p. 535.

17. See, generally, Robert Nisbet, *The Sociology of Émile Durkheim* (New York: Oxford University Press, 1974).

18. L. A. J. Quetelet, *A Treatise on Man and the Development of His Faculties* (Gainesville, FL: Scholars' Facsimilies and Reprints, 1969), pp. 82–96.

19. Ibid., p. 85.

20. Émile Durkheim, *Rules of the Sociological Method,* reprint ed., trans. W. D. Halls (New York: Free Press, 1982).

21. Émile Durkheim, *The Division of Labor in Society,* reprint ed. (New York: Free Press, 1997).

22. Robert Park and Ernest Burgess, *The City* (Chicago: University of Chicago Press, 1925).

23. Karl Marx and Friedrich Engels, *Capital: A Critique of Political Economy,* trans. E. Aveling (Chicago: Charles Kern, 1906); Karl Marx, *Selected Writings in Sociology and Social Philosophy,* trans. P. B. Bottomore (New York: McGraw-Hill, 1956). For a general discussion of Marxist thought, see Michael Lynch and W. Byron Groves, *A Primer in Radical Criminology* (New York: Harrow and Heston, 1986), pp. 6–26.

24. Marvin Wolfgang and Franco Ferracuti, *The Subculture of Violence* (London: Social Science Paperbacks, 1967), p. 20.

25. Rosemary Erickson and Rita Simon, *The Use of Social Science Data in Supreme Court Decisions* (Champaign: University of Illinois Press, 1998).

26. Dennis Wilson, "Additional Law Enforcement as a Deterrent to Criminal Behavior: Empirical Evidence from the National Hockey League," *Journal of Socio-Economics* 34 (2005): 319–330.

27. Marvin Wolfgang, *Patterns in Criminal Homicide* (Philadelphia: University of Pennsylvania Press, 1958).

28. Samuel Gross, Kristen Jacoby, Daniel Matheson, Nicholas Montgomery, and Sujata. Patil, "Exonerations in the United States 1989 Through 2003," *Journal of Criminal Law & Criminology* 95 (2005): 523–559.

29. Hans von Hentig, *The Criminal and His Victim* (New Haven: Yale University Press, 1948); Stephen Schafer, *The Victim and His Criminal* (New York: Random House, 1968).

30. Linda Teplin, Gary McClelland, Karen Abram, and Darinka Mileusnic, "Early Violent Death among Delinquent Youth: A Prospective Longitudinal Study," *Pediatrics* 115 (2005): 1,586–1,593.

31. Sutherland and Cressey, p. 8.

32. Charles McCaghy, *Deviant Behavior* (New York: MacMillan, 1976), pp. 2–3.

33. Michael Lynch, Raymond Michalowski, and W. Byron Groves, *The New Primer in Radical Criminology: Critical Perspectives on Crime, Power and Identity,* 3rd ed. (Monsey, NY: Criminal Justice Press, 2000), p. 59.

34. ibid.

35. See Herbert Blumer, *Symbolic Interactionism* (Englewood Cliffs, NJ: Prentice-Hall, 1969).

36. Howard Becker, *Outsiders: Studies in the Sociology of Deviance* (New York: Free Press, 1963), p. 9.

37. Ibid.

38. Oliver Wendell Holmes, *The Common Law,* ed. Mark De Wolf (Boston: Little, Brown, 1881), p. 36.

39. National Institute of Justice, *Project to Develop a Model Anti-Stalking Statute* (Washington, DC: National Institute of Justice, 1994).

40. "Clinton Signs Tougher 'Megan's Law,'" *CNN News Service,* 17 May 1996.

41. Associated Press, "Judge Upholds State's Sexual Predator Law," *Bakersfield Californian,* 2 October 1996.

42. *Lawrence et al v. Texas* 02-102 (2003).

43. See, for example, Michael Hindelang and Travis Hirschi, "Intelligence and Delinquency: A Revisionist Review," *American Sociological Review* 42 (1977): 471–486.

44. Richard Herrnstein and Charles Murray, *The Bell Curve* (New York: Free Press, 1994).

45. Victor Boruch, Timothy Victor, and Joe Cecil, "Resolving Ethical and Legal Problems in Randomized Experiments," *Crime and Delinquency* 46 (2000): 330–353.

46. Anthony Petrosino, Carolyn Turpin-Petrosino, and James Finckenauer, "Well-Meaning Programs Can Have Harmful Effects! Lessons from Experiments of Programs Such as Scared Straight," *Crime and Delinquency* 46 (2000): 354–379.

CHAPTER 2

FBI TEN MOST WANTED FUGITIVE

MALICIOUSLY DAMAGED, BY MEANS OF AN EXPLOSIVE DEVICE, BUILDINGS AND PROPERTY AFFECTING INTERSTATE COMMERCE WHICH RESULTED IN DEATH AND INJURY

ERIC ROBERT RUDOLPH

Date of photograph unknown Date of photograph unknown Date of Sketch July 1998

© Reuters / Landov

On May 31, 2003, Eric Rudolph was arrested behind a grocery store in rural western North Carolina after five years on the run. Rudolph had detonated a bomb that exploded outside a Birmingham abortion clinic on January 29, 1998, killing a police officer and critically injuring a clinic nurse. He also set off a bomb that killed one person and injured 150 others in a park in downtown Atlanta during the 1996 Olympics and was involved in the 1997 bombings of a gay nightclub and a building that housed an abortion clinic.

Rudolph's crime spree is believed to have been motivated by his extreme political beliefs. He was a member of a white supremacist group called the Army of God. Rudolph was also an ardent anti-Semite who claimed that the Holocaust never happened and that the Jews now control the media and the government. Ironically, soon after he was arrested, the court appointed Richard S. Jaffe, a practicing Jew, to lead Rudolph's defense team.[1] On April 8, 2005, Rudolph agreed to plead guilty in all the attacks he was accused of executing in order to avoid the death penalty; he was sentenced to four consecutive life terms. On April 13, 2005, he issued the following statement:

> *In the summer of 1996, the world converged upon Atlanta for the Olympic Games. Under the protection and auspices of the regime in Washington millions of people came to celebrate the ideals of global socialism. Multinational corporations spent billions of dollars, and Washington organized an army of security to protect these best of all games. Even though the conception and purpose of the so-called Olympic movement is to promote the values of global socialism, as perfectly expressed in the song "Imagine" by John Lennon, which was the theme of the 1996 Games even though the purpose of the Olympics is to promote these despicable ideals, the purpose of the attack on 27 July was to confound, anger and embarrass the Washington government in the eyes of the world for its abominable sanctioning of abortion on demand. The plan was to force the cancellation of the Games, or at least create a state of insecurity to empty the streets around the venues and thereby eat into the vast amounts of money invested.[2]*

THE NATURE AND EXTENT OF CRIME

CHAPTER OBJECTIVES

1. Be familiar with the various forms of crime data
2. Know the problems associated with collecting data
3. Be able to discuss the recent trends in the crime rate
4. Be familiar with the factors that influence crime rates
5. Be able to discuss the patterns in the crime rate
6. Be able to discuss the association between social class and crime
7. Recognize that there are age, gender, and racial patterns in crime
8. Describe the various positions on gun control
9. Be familiar with Wolfgang's pioneering research on chronic offending
10. Be able to discuss the influence the discovery of the chronic offender has had on criminology

Stories such as Rudolph's help convince most Americans that we live in a violent society. Are Americans justified in their fear of violent crime? Should they barricade themselves behind armed guards? Are crime rates actually rising or falling? And where do most crimes occur and who commits them? To answer these and similar questions, criminologists have devised elaborate methods of crime data collection and analysis. Without accurate data on the nature and extent of crime, it would not be possible to formulate theories that explain the onset of crime or to devise social policies that facilitate its control or elimination. Accurate data collection is also critical in order to assess the nature and extent of crime, track changes in the crime rate, and measure the individual and social factors that may influence criminality.

In this chapter, we review how crime data are collected on criminal offenders and offenses and what this information tells us about crime patterns and trends. We also examine the concept of criminal careers and discover what available crime data can tell us about the onset, continuation, and termination of criminality. We begin with a discussion of the most important sources of crime data.

PRIMARY SOURCES OF CRIME DATA

The primary sources of crime data are surveys and official records. Criminologists use these techniques to measure the nature and extent of criminal behavior and the personality, attitudes, and background of criminal offenders. It is important to understand how these data are collected to gain insight into how professional criminologists approach various problems and questions in their field.

Official Record Research

In order to understand more about the nature and extent of crime, criminologists use the records of government agencies such as police departments, prisons, and courts. In some instances these records are collected, compiled, and analyzed by government agencies such as the federal government's Bureau of Justice Statistics or the Federal Bureau of Investigation (FBI).

Official record data can be used to examine crime rates and trends. It can also be analyzed to uncover the individual and social forces that affect crime. For example, to study the relationship between crime and poverty, criminologists might use income and family data from the U.S. Census Bureau and then cross-reference this information with crime data collected by local police departments.

The **Bureau of Justice Statistics** web page may be accessed at http://www.ojp.usdoj.gov/bjs. For an up-to-date list of web links, go to http://cj.wadsworth.com/siegel_crimtpt9e.

THE UNIFORM CRIME REPORT The most important crime record data is collected from local law enforcement agencies by the Federal Bureau of Investigation and published yearly in their **Uniform Crime Report (UCR).** The UCR includes both crimes reported to local law enforcement departments and the number of arrests made by police agencies. The UCR is the best-known and most widely cited source of official criminal statistics.[3] The FBI receives and compiles records from more than 17,000 police departments serving a majority of the U.S. population. Its major unit of analysis involves **index crimes,** or **Part I crimes:** murder and nonnegligent

Because they get a lot of media attention, high-profile criminal cases may give the impression that crime rates are skyrocketing. One such incident was the murder of Bonny Lee Bakley, the wife of actor Robert Blake, on May 4, 2001. Blake was acquitted of Bakley's murder in a 2005 criminal trial. Rather than relying on media accounts, criminologists employ a variety of data to measure the true trends and patterns in the crime rate.

© Axel Koester/Corbis

manslaughter, forcible rape, robbery, aggravated assault, burglary, larceny, arson, and motor vehicle theft. Exhibit 2.1 defines these crimes.

The FBI tallies and annually publishes the number of reported offenses by city, county, standard metropolitan statistical area, and geographical divisions of the United States. In addition to these statistics, the UCR shows the number and characteristics (age, race, and gender) of individuals who have been arrested for these and all other crimes, except traffic violations (**Part II crimes**).

EXHIBIT 2.1

Part I Index Crime Offenses

Criminal Homicide

MURDER AND NONNEGLIGENT MANSLAUGHTER The willful (nonnegligent) killing of one human being by another. Deaths caused by negligence, attempts to kill, assaults to kill, suicides, accidental deaths, and justifiable homicides are excluded. Justifiable homicides are limited to (1) the killing of a felon by a law enforcement officer in the line of duty and (2) the killing of a felon, during the commission of a felony, by a private citizen.

MANSLAUGHTER BY NEGLIGENCE The killing of another person through gross negligence. Traffic fatalities are excluded. Although manslaughter by negligence is a Part I crime, it is not included in the Crime Index.

Forcible Rape

The carnal knowledge of a female forcibly and against her will. Included are rapes by force and attempts or assaults to rape. Statutory offenses (no force used—victim under age of consent) are excluded.

Robbery

The taking or attempting to take anything of value from the care, custody, or control of a person or persons by force or threat of force or violence and/or by putting the victim in fear.

Aggravated Assault

An unlawful attack by one person upon another for the purpose of inflicting severe or aggravated bodily injury. This type of assault usually is accompanied by the use of a weapon or by means likely to produce death or great bodily harm. Simple assaults are excluded.

Burglary/Breaking or Entering

The unlawful entry of a structure to commit a felony or a theft. Attempted forcible entry is included.

Larceny/Theft (except motor vehicle theft)

The unlawful taking, carrying, leading, or riding away of property from the possession or constructive possession of another. Examples are thefts of bicycles or automobile accessories, shoplifting, pocket picking, or the stealing of any property or article that is not taken by force and violence or by fraud. Attempted larcenies are included. Embezzlement, con games, forgery, worthless checks, and so on are excluded.

Motor Vehicle Theft

The theft or attempted theft of a motor vehicle. A motor vehicle is self-propelled and runs on the surface and not on rails. Specifically excluded from this category are motorboats, construction equipment, airplanes, and farming equipment.

Arson

Any willful or malicious burning or attempt to burn, with or without intent to defraud, a dwelling house, public building, motor vehicle, or aircraft, personal property of another, or the like.

Source: FBI, Uniform Crime Report, 2005.

COMPILING THE UNIFORM CRIME REPORT The methods used to compile the UCR are quite complex. Each month law enforcement agencies report the number of index crimes known to them. These data are collected from records of all crime complaints that victims, officers who discovered the infractions, or other sources reported to these agencies.

Whenever criminal complaints are found through investigation to be unfounded or false, they are eliminated from the actual count. However, the number of actual offenses known is reported to the FBI whether or not anyone is arrested for the crime, the stolen property is recovered, or prosecution ensues.

In addition, each month law enforcement agencies also report how many crimes were **cleared.** Crimes are cleared in two ways: (1) when at least one person is arrested, charged, and turned over to the court for prosecution; or (2) by exceptional means, when some element beyond police control precludes the physical arrest of an offender (for example, the offender leaves the country). Data on the number of clearances involving the arrest of only juvenile offenders, data on the value of property stolen and recovered in connection with Part I offenses, and detailed information pertaining to criminal homicide are also reported. Traditionally, slightly more than 20 percent of all reported index crimes are cleared by arrest each year (Figure 2.1).

Violent crimes are more likely to be solved than property crimes because police devote more resources to these more serious acts. For these types of crime, witnesses (including the victim) are frequently available to identify offenders, and in many instances the victim and offender were previously acquainted. The UCR uses three methods to express crime data. First, the number of crimes reported to the police and arrests made are expressed as raw figures (for instance, 16,137 murders occurred in 2004). Second, crime rates per 100,000 people are computed. That is, when the UCR indicates that the murder rate was 5.5 in 2004, it means that almost 6 people in every 100,000 were murdered between January 1 and December 31 of 2004. This is the equation used:

$$\frac{\text{Number of Reported Crimes}}{\text{Total U.S. Population}} \times 100,000 = \text{Rate per 100,000}$$

Third, the FBI computes changes in the number and rate of crime over time. Murder rates declined 3.3 percent between 2003 and 2004, and the number of murders decreased 2.4 percent.

VALIDITY OF THE UNIFORM CRIME REPORT Despite criminologists' continued reliance on the UCR, its accuracy has been suspect. The three main areas of concern are reporting

FIGURE 2.1

Percentage of Index Crimes Cleared by Arrest, 2004

More serious crimes such as murder and rape are cleared at much higher rates than less serious crimes such as larceny. Factors may include the fact that police spend more re-sources solving serious crimes and that there is more often an associa-tion between victim and offender in serious crimes. Arson is not included in most calculations because it is not reported by all police departments.

Source: http://www.fbi.gov/ucr/cius_04/ offenses_cleared/index.html.

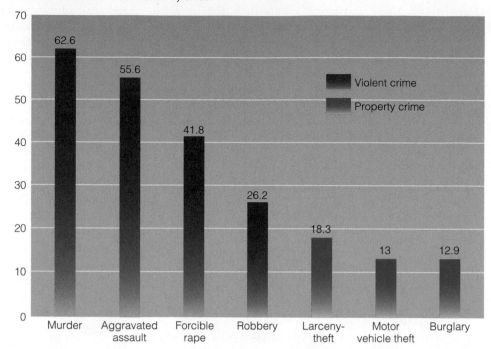

Percent of index crimes cleared by arrest

practices, law enforcement practices, and methodological problems.

1. *Reporting practices:* Some criminologists claim that victims of many serious crimes do not report these incidents to police; therefore, these crimes do not become part of the UCR. The reasons for not reporting vary. Some victims do not trust the police or have confidence in their ability to solve crimes. Others do not have property insurance and therefore believe it is useless to report theft. In other cases, victims fear reprisals from an offender's friends or family or, in the case of family violence, from their spouse, boyfriend, and/or girlfriend.[4]

   According to surveys of crime victims, less than 40 percent of all criminal incidents are reported to the police. Some of these victims justify nonreporting by stating that the incident was "a private matter," that "nothing could be done," or that the victimization was "not important enough."[5] These findings indicate that the UCR data may significantly underreport the total number of annual criminal events.

2. *Law enforcement practices:* The way police departments record and report criminal and delinquent activity also affects the validity of UCR statistics. Some police departments define crimes loosely—reporting a trespass as a burglary or an assault on a woman as an attempted rape—whereas others pay strict attention to FBI guidelines. These reporting practices may help explain interjurisdictional differences in crime.[6] Arson may be seriously underreported because many fire departments do not report to the FBI, and those that

do define many fires that may well have been set by arsonists as "accidental" or "spontaneous."[7]

   Some local police departments make systematic errors in UCR reporting. They may count an arrest only after a formal booking procedure, although the UCR requires arrests to be counted if the suspect is re-leased without a formal charge. One survey of arrests found an error rate of about 10 percent in every Part I offense category.[8] More serious allegations claim that in some cases police officials may deliberately alter re-ported crimes to improve their department's public image. Police administrators interested in lowering the crime rate may falsify crime reports by classifying a burglary as a nonreportable trespass.[9] In 2004 an audit of the Atlanta Police Department, which included confidential interviews with police officers, concluded that the department consistently underreported crimes for years. The reason? To improve the city's image for tourism.[10]

   Ironically, boosting police efficiency and profes-sionalism may actually help increase crime rates: As people develop confidence in the police, they may be more motivated to report crime. A New York City po-lice program provided special services (such as follow-up visits and education) to a select sample of domestic violence victims.[11] Evaluation of the program showed that households that received the extra attention were more likely to report new incidences of violence than those that received no special services. Although it is possible that the follow-ups encouraged violence, a more realistic assessment is that the interventions increased citizens' confidence in the ability of the police to handle domestic assaults and encouraged greater crime reporting.

Higher crime rates may occur as departments adopt more sophisticated computer technology and hire better-educated, better-trained employees. Crime rates also may be altered based on the way law enforcement agencies process UCR data. As the number of employees assigned to dispatching, record keeping, and criminal incident reporting increases, so too will national crime rates. What appears to be a rising crime rate may be simply an artifact of improved police record-keeping ability.[12]

3. *Methodological issues*: Methodological issues also contribute to questions pertaining to the UCR's validity. The most frequent issues include the following:
   - No federal crimes are reported.
   - Reports are voluntary and vary in accuracy and completeness.
   - Not all police departments submit reports.
   - The FBI uses estimates in its total crime projections.
   - If an offender commits multiple crimes, only the most serious is recorded.
     Thus, if a narcotics addict rapes, robs, and murders a victim, only the murder is recorded. Consequently, many lesser crimes go unreported.
   - Each act is listed as a single offense for some crimes but not for others. If a man robbed six people in a bar, the offense is listed as one robbery; but if he assaulted or murdered them, it would be listed as six assaults or six murders.
   - Incomplete acts are lumped together with completed ones.
   - Important differences exist between the FBI's definition of certain crimes and those used in a number of states.[13]

In addition to these issues, the complex scoring procedure used in the UCR program means that many serious crimes are not counted. If during an armed bank robbery, the robber strikes a teller with the butt of a handgun, runs from the bank, and steals an automobile at the curb, he has technically committed robbery, aggravated assault, and motor vehicle theft, which are three separate Part I offenses. However, the UCR only records robbery, the most serious crime.[14]

NIBRS: THE FUTURE OF THE UNIFORM CRIME REPORT

Clearly there must be a more reliable source for crime statistics than the UCR as it stands today. Beginning in 1982, a five-year redesign effort was undertaken to provide more comprehensive and detailed crime statistics. The effort resulted in the **National Incident-Based Reporting System (NIBRS)**, a program that collects data on each reported crime incident. Instead of submitting statements of the kinds of crime that individual citizens report to the police and summary statements of resulting arrests, the new program requires local police agencies to provide at least a brief account of each incident and arrest, including the incident, victim, and offender information.

Under NIBRS, law enforcement authorities provide information to the FBI on each criminal incident involving forty-six specific offenses, including the eight Part I crimes, that occur in their jurisdiction; arrest information on the forty-six offenses plus eleven lesser offenses is also provided in NIBRS. These expanded crime categories include numerous additional crimes, such as blackmail, embezzlement, drug offenses, and bribery; this allows a national database on the nature of crime, victims, and criminals to be developed. Other collected information includes statistics gathered by federal law enforcement agencies, as well as data on hate or bias crimes. Thus far more than twenty states have implemented their NIBRS program, and twelve others are in the process of finalizing their data collections. When this program is fully implemented and adopted across the nation, it should bring about greater uniformity in cross-jurisdictional reporting and improve the accuracy of official crime data. Whether it can capture cases missing in the UCR remains to be seen.[15]

> To read more about **NIBRS,** go to http://www.ojp .usdoj.gov/bjs/nibrs.htm. For an up-to-date list of web links, go to http://cj.wadsworth.com/ siegel_crimtpt9e.

Survey Research

Another important method of measuring crime is through surveys in which people are asked about their attitudes, beliefs, values, and characteristics, as well as their experiences with crime and victimization. Surveys typically involve **sampling,** which refers to the process of selecting for study a limited number of subjects who are representative of entire groups sharing similar characteristics, called the **population.** To understand the social forces that produce crime, a criminologist might interview a sample of 3,000 prison inmates drawn from the population of more than 2 million inmates in the United States; in this case, the sample represents the entire population of U.S. inmates. It is assumed that the characteristics of people or events in a carefully selected sample will be similar to those of the population at large. If the sampling is done correctly, the responses of the 3,000 inmates should represent the entire population of inmates.

In some circumstances criminologists may want the survey to be representative of all members of society; this is referred to as a **cross-sectional survey.** A survey of all students who attend the local public high school would be considered a cross-sectional survey since all members of the community, both rich and poor, male and female, go to high school. For a number of reasons, cross-sectional surveys are a useful and cost-effective technique for measuring the characteristics of large numbers of people:

- Because questions and methods are standardized for all subjects, uniformity is unaffected by the perceptions or biases of the person gathering the data.

- Carefully drawn samples enable researchers to generalize their findings from small groups to large populations.

- Though surveys measure subjects at a single point in their life span, questions can elicit information on subjects' past behavior as well as expectations of future behaviors.[16]

A number of academic institutes are devoted to **survey research.** Here is the link to the Princeton University Survey Research Center (SRC): http://www.wws .princeton.edu/~psrc. For an up-to-date list of web links, go to http://cj.wadsworth.com/siegel_crimtpt9e.

SELF-REPORT SURVEYS Participants in **self-report surveys** are asked to describe, in detail, their recent and lifetime participation in criminal activity. Self-reports are given in groups, and the respondents are promised anonymity in order to ensure the validity and honesty of the responses. Most self-report studies have focused on juvenile delinquency and youth crime.[17] However, self-reports can also be used to examine the offense histories of prison inmates, drug users, and other segments of the population.[18]

Most self-report surveys also contain questions about attitudes, values, and behaviors. There may be questions about a participant's substance abuse history (for instance, How many times have you used marijuana?) and the participant's family history (Did your parents ever strike you with a stick or a belt?). By correlating the responses, criminologists are able to analyze the relationship between personal factors and criminal behaviors. Statistical analysis of the responses can be used to determine whether people who report being abused as children are also more likely to use drugs as adults. When psychologist Christiane Brems and her associates used this approach to collect data from 274 women and 556 men

receiving drug detoxification services, they found that 20 percent of men and more than 50 percent of women reported childhood physical or sexual abuse. Individuals who reported an abuse history also reported earlier onset age of drinking, more problems associated with use of alcohol/drugs, more severe psychopathology, and more lifetime arrests.[19] Figure 2.2 illustrates some typical self-report items.

SELF-REPORT PATTERNS One important source of self-report data is the Monitoring the Future (MTF) study, which researchers at the University of Michigan Institute for Social Research (ISR) have been conducting annually since 1978. This national survey typically involves more than 2,500 high school seniors.[20] The MTF is considered the national standard by which to measure substance abuse trends among American teens.

||||||| CONNECTIONS |||||||

MTF data on patterns and trends in teenage substance abuse is analyzed in Chapter 13. Despite public perception to the contrary, teen drug use seems to be on the decline.

You can reach the **Monitoring the Future** website at http://monitoringthefuture.org. For an up-to-date list of web links, go to http://cj.wadsworth.com/siegel_ crimtpt9e.

The MTF data indicate that the number of people who break the law is far greater than the number projected by official statistics. Almost everyone questioned is found to have violated a law at some time including truancy, alcohol abuse, false ID use, shoplifting or larceny under $50, fighting, marijuana use, and damage to the property of others. Furthermore, self-reports dispute the notion that criminals and delinquents specialize in one type of crime

FIGURE 2.2

Self-Report Survey Questions

Please indicate how often in the past 12 months you did each act (check the best answer).

	Never did act	One time	2–5 times	6–9 times	10+ times
Stole something worth less than $50					
Stole something worth more than $50					
Used cocaine					
Been in a fistfight					
Carried a weapon such as a gun or knife					
Fought someone using a weapon					

or another; offenders seem to engage in a mixed bag of crime and deviance.[21]

VALIDITY OF SELF-REPORTS Critics of self-report studies frequently suggest that it is unreasonable to expect people to candidly admit illegal acts. This is especially true of those with official records, who may be engaging in the most criminality. At the same time, some people may exaggerate their criminal acts, forget some of them, or be confused about what is being asked. Some surveys contain an overabundance of trivial offenses, such as shoplifting small items or using false identification to obtain alcohol, often lumped together with serious crimes to form a total crime index. Consequently, comparisons between groups can be highly misleading.

The "missing cases" phenomenon is also a concern. Even if 90 percent of a school population voluntarily participate in a self-report study, researchers can never be sure whether the few who refuse to participate or are absent that day comprise a significant portion of the school's population of persistent high-rate offenders. Research indicates that offenders with the most extensive prior criminality are also the most likely "to be poor historians of their own crime commission rates."[22] It is also unlikely that the most serious chronic offenders in the teenage population are willing to cooperate with criminologists administering self-report tests.[23] Institutionalized youths, who are not generally represented in the self-report surveys, are not only more delinquent than the general youth population but are also considerably more misbehaving than the most delinquent youths identified in the typical self-report survey.[24] Consequently, self-reports may measure only nonserious, occasional delinquents while ignoring hardcore chronic offenders who may be institutionalized and unavailable for self-reports.

| | | | | | | | **CONNECTIONS** | | | | | | | |

Criminologists suspect that a few high-rate offenders are responsible for a disproportionate share of all serious crime. Results would be badly skewed if even a few of these chronic offenders were absent or refused to participate in schoolwide self-report surveys. For more on chronic offenders, see the sections at the end of this chapter.

Finally, there is evidence that reporting accuracy differs among racial, ethnic, and gender groups. One recent study found that while girls were more willing than boys to disclose drug use, Latino girls underreport their drug usage. Such differences might provide a skewed and inaccurate portrait of criminal and or delinquent activity—in this case, the self-report data would falsely show that Latino girls use fewer drugs than other females.[25]

To address these criticisms, various techniques have been used to verify self-report data.[26] The "known group" method compares youths who are known to be offenders with those who are not to see whether the former report more delinquency. Research shows that when kids are asked if they have ever been arrested or sent to court, their responses accurately reflect their true life experiences.[27]

While these studies are supportive, self-report data must be interpreted with some caution. Asking subjects about their past behavior may capture more serious crimes but miss minor criminal acts; that is, people remember armed robberies and rapes better than they do minor assaults and altercations.[28] In addition, some classes of offenders (for example, substance abusers) may have a tough time accounting for their prior misbehavior.[29]

The National Crime Victimization Survey (NCVS)

Because many victims do not report their experiences to the police, the UCR cannot measure all the annual criminal activity. To address the nonreporting issue, the federal government sponsors the **National Crime Victimization Survey (NCVS),** a comprehensive, nationwide survey of victimization in the United States.

| | | | | | | | **CONNECTIONS** | | | | | | | |

Victim surveys provide information not only about criminal incidents that have occurred but also about the individuals who are most at risk of falling victim to crime and where and when they are most likely to become victimized. Data from recent NCVS surveys are used in Chapter 3 to draw a portrait of the nature and extent of victimization in the United States.

Each year data are obtained from a large nationally representative sample; in 2004, more than 84,000 households with more than 149,000 people age 12 or older were interviewed.[30] In **victimization surveys,** people are asked to report their experiences with such crimes as rape, sexual assault, robbery, assault, theft, household burglary, and motor vehicle theft. Due to the care with which the samples are drawn and the high completion rate, NCVS data are considered a relatively unbiased, valid estimate of all victimizations for the target crimes included in the survey.

The NCVS finds that many crimes go unreported to police. The UCR shows that slightly more than 94,000 rapes or attempted rapes occur each year, but the NCVS estimates that about 210,000 actually occur. The reason for such discrepancies is that fewer than half of violent crimes, fewer than one-third of personal theft crimes (such as pocket picking), and fewer than half of household thefts are reported to police. Victims seem to report to the police only crimes that involve considerable loss or injury. If we are to believe NCVS findings, the official UCR statistics do not provide an accurate picture of the crime problem because many crimes go unreported to the police.

To read the results on an international victimization study, use InfoTrac College Edition to read: Martin Killias, John van Kesteren, and Martin Rindlisbacher, "Guns, Violent Crime, and Suicide in 21 Countries," *Canadian Journal of Criminology* 43 (October 2001): 429–446.

VALIDITY OF THE NCVS The NCVS may also suffer from some methodological problems. As a result, its findings must be interpreted with caution. Among the potential problems are the following:

- Overreporting due to victims' misinterpretation of events. A lost wallet may be reported as stolen, or an open door may be viewed as a burglary attempt.

- Underreporting due to the embarrassment of reporting crime to interviewers, fear of getting in trouble, or simply forgetting an incident.

- Inability to record the personal criminal activity of those interviewed, such as drug use or gambling; murder is also not included, for obvious reasons.

- Sampling errors, which produce a group of respondents who do not represent the nation as a whole.

- Inadequate question format that invalidates responses. Some groups, such as adolescents, may be particularly susceptible to error because of question format.[31]

Evaluating Primary Crime Data Sources

The UCR, NCVS, and self-reports are the standard sources of data used by criminologists to track trends and patterns in the crime rate, and each has its own strengths and weaknesses. The UCR contains information on the number and characteristics of people arrested, information that the other data sources lack. Some recent research indicates that for serious crimes, such as drug trafficking, arrest data can provide a meaningful measure of the level of criminal activity in a particular neighborhood environment, which the other data sources cannot provide. It is also the source of information on particular crimes such as murder, which no other data source can provide.[32] It remains the standard unit of analysis upon which most criminological research is based. However, UCR data omits many criminal incidents victims choose not to report to police, and it is subject to the reporting caprices of individual police departments.

The NCVS includes unreported crime and important information on the personal characteristics of victims. However, the data consist of estimates made from relatively limited samples of the total U.S. population, so that even narrow fluctuations in the rates of some crimes can have a major impact on findings. It also relies on personal recollections that may be inaccurate. In addition, the NCVS does not include data on important crime patterns, including murder and drug abuse.

Self-report surveys can provide information on the personal characteristics of offenders—such as their attitudes, values, beliefs, and psychological profiles—that is unavailable from any other source. Yet, at their core, self-reports rely on the honesty of criminal offenders and drug abusers, a population not generally known for accuracy and integrity.

Although their tallies of crimes are certainly not in sync, the crime patterns and trends they record are often quite similar (see Concept Summary 2.1).[33] Each of the sources of crime data agree about the personal characteristics of serious criminals (such as age and gender) and where and when crime occurs (such as urban areas, nighttime, and summer months). In addition, the problems inherent in each source are consistent over time. Therefore, even if the data sources are incapable of providing a precise and valid count of crime at any given time, they are reliable indicators of changes and fluctuations in yearly crime rates.

⊙ CONCEPT SUMMARY 2.1

Data Collection Methods

Uniform Crime Report

- Data is collected from records from police departments across the nation.
- Strengths of the UCR are that it measures homicides and arrests. It is a consistent, national sample.
- Weaknesses of the UCR are that it omits crimes not reported to police, omits most drug usage, and contains reporting errors.

National Crime Victimization Survey

- Data is collected from a national survey of victims.
- Strengths of the NCVS are that it includes crimes not reported to the police, uses careful sampling techniques, and is a yearly survey.
- Weaknesses of the NCVS are that it relies on victims' memory and honesty, and it omits substance abuse.

Self-Report Surveys

- Data is collected from surveys of students.
- Strengths of self-report surveys are that they include nonreported crimes, substance abuse, and offenders' personal information.
- Weaknesses of self-report surveys are that they rely on the honesty of offenders and that they omit offenders who refuse to or who are unable to participate and who may be the most deviant.

▌ SECONDARY SOURCES OF CRIME DATA

In addition to these main sources of crime data, a number of other techniques are used by criminologists to gather data on specific crime problems and trends, to examine the lives of criminal offenders, and to assess the effectiveness of crime control efforts.

Cohort Research

Cohort research involves observing a group of people who share a like characteristic over time. Researchers might select all girls born in Albany, New York, in 1970 and then follow their behavior patterns for twenty years. The research data might include their school experiences, arrests, hospitalizations, and information about their family life (divorces, parental relations). The subjects might be given repeated intelligence and physical exams, and their diets might be monitored. Data may be collected directly from the subjects during interviews and meetings with family members. Criminologists might also examine records of social organizations, such as hospitals, schools, welfare departments, courts, police departments, and prisons. School records contain data on students' academic performance, attendance, intelligence, disciplinary problems, and teacher ratings. Hospitals record incidents of drug use and suspicious wounds, which may be indicative of child abuse. Police files contain reports of criminal activity, arrest data, personal information on suspects, victim reports, and actions taken by police officers. Court records enable researchers to compare the personal characteristics of offenders with the outcomes of their court appearances, conviction rates, and types of sentence. Prison records contain information on inmates' personal characteristics, adjustment problems, disciplinary records, rehabilitation efforts, and length of sentence served. If the cohort is carefully drawn, it may be possible to determine which life experiences produce criminal careers.

Because it is extremely difficult, expensive, and time-consuming to follow a cohort over time, another approach is to take an intact cohort from the past and collect data from educational, family, police, and hospital records. This format is known as a **retrospective cohort study**.[34] For example, a cohort of girls who were in grade school in 1980 could be selected from school attendance records. A criminologist might then acquire their police and court records over the proceeding two decades to determine (a) which ones developed a criminal record and (b) whether school achievement predicts adult criminality.

| | | | | | | CONNECTIONS | | | | | | |

Some critical criminological research has been based on cohort studies, such as the important research conducted by University of Pennsylvania criminologist Marvin Wolfgang and his colleagues. Their findings have been instrumental in developing an understanding about the onset and development of a criminal career. Wolfgang's cohort research, which is discussed later in this chapter, helped identify the chronic criminal offender.

Experimental Research

Sometimes criminologists are able to conduct controlled experiments to collect data on the cause of crime. They may wish to directly test whether (a) watching a violent TV show will (b) cause viewers to act aggressively. This test requires experimental research. To conduct experimental research, criminologists manipulate or intervene in the lives of their subjects to see the outcome or the effect of the intervention. True experiments usually have three elements: (1) random selection of subjects, (2) a control or comparison group, and (3) an experimental condition. To find out the effects of viewing violent media content, a criminologist might have one group of randomly chosen subjects watch an extremely violent and gory film (*Kill Bill*) while another randomly selected group views something more mellow (*Princess Diaries*). The behavior of both groups would be monitored; if the subjects who had watched the violent film were significantly more aggressive than those who had watched the nonviolent film, an association between media content and behavior would be supported. The fact that both groups were randomly selected would prevent some preexisting condition from invalidating the results of the experiment.

Because it is sometimes impossible to randomly select subjects or manipulate conditions, criminologists may be forced to rely on what is known as a *quasi-experimental design*. A criminologist may want to measure whether kids who were abused as children are more likely to become violent as teens. Of course, it is impossible to randomly select youth, assign them to two independent groups, and then purposely abuse members of one group in order to gauge their reactions. To get around this dilemma, a criminologist may follow a group of kids who were abused and compare them with a matched group who though similar in every other respect were never abused in order to discover if the battered kids were more likely to become violent teens.

Criminological experiments are relatively rare because they are difficult and expensive to conduct; they involve manipulating subjects' lives, which can cause ethical and legal roadblocks; and they require long follow-up periods to verify results. Nonetheless, they have been an important source of criminological data.

Observational and Interview Research

Sometimes criminologists focus their research on relatively few subjects, interviewing them in depth or observing them as they go about their activities. This research often results in the kind of in-depth data absent in large-scale surveys. In one such effort Claire Sterk-Elifson focused on the lives of middle-class female drug abusers.[35] The thirty-four interviews she conducted provide insight into a group whose behavior might not be captured in a large-scale survey. Sterk-Elifson found that these women were introduced to cocaine at first "just for fun": "I do drugs," one 34-year-old lawyer told her, "because I like the feeling. I would never let drugs take over my life."[36] Unfortunately, many of these subjects succumbed to the power of drugs and suffered both emotional and financial stress.

Another common criminological method is to observe criminals firsthand to gain insight into their motives and activities. This may involve going into the field and participating in group activities; this was done in sociologist William

Whyte's famous study of a Boston gang, *Street Corner Society.*[37] Other observers conduct field studies but remain in the background, observing but not being part of the ongoing activity.[38]

Meta-Analysis and Systematic Review

Meta-analysis involves gathering data from a number of previous studies. Compatible information and data are extracted and pooled together. When analyzed, the grouped data from several different studies provide a more powerful and valid indicator of relationships than the results provided from a single study. A **systematic review** is another widely accepted means of evaluating the effectiveness of public policy interventions. It involves collecting the findings from previously conducted scientific studies that address a particular problem, appraising and synthesizing the evidence, and using the collective evidence to address a particular scientific question.

Through these well-proven techniques, criminologists can identify what is known and what is not known about a particular problem and use the findings as a first step for carrying out new research. Criminologists David Farrington and Brandon Welsh used a systematic review and a meta-analysis in order to study the effects of street lighting on crime.[39] After identifying and analyzing thirteen relevant studies, Farrington and Welsh found evidence showing that neighborhoods that improve their street lighting do in fact experience a reduction in crime rates. Their findings should come as no great surprise: It seems logical that well-lit streets would have fewer robberies and thefts because (1) criminals could not conceal their efforts under the cover of darkness, and (2) potential victims could take evasive action if they saw a suspicious-looking person lurking about. However, their analysis produced an unusual finding: Improving lighting caused the crime rate to go down during the day just as much as it did during the night! Obviously, the crime-reducing effect of street lights had little to do with illuminating the streets. Farrington and Welsh speculate that improved street lighting increases community pride and solidarity, and the result of this newfound community solidarity is a lowered crime rate, both during the day and evening.

Data Mining

A relatively new criminological technique, **data mining** uses multiple advanced computational methods, including artificial intelligence (the use of computers to perform logical functions), to analyze large data sets usually involving one or more data sources. The goal is to identify significant and recognizable patterns, trends, and relationships that are not easily detected through traditional analytical techniques.[40] Criminologists use this information for various purposes, such as the prediction of future events or behaviors.

Data mining might be employed to help a police department determine if burglaries in their jurisdiction have a particular pattern. To determine if such a pattern exists, a criminologist might employ data mining techniques with a variety of sources including calls for service data, crime or incident reports, witness statements, suspect interviews, tip information, telephone toll analysis, or Internet activity. The data mining might uncover a strong relationship between the time of day and place of occurrence. The police could use the findings to plan an effective burglary elimination strategy.

Crime Mapping

Criminologists now use **crime mapping** to create graphic representations of the spatial geography of crime. Computerized crime maps allow criminologists to analyze and correlate a wide array of data to create immediate, detailed visuals of crime patterns.

The simplest maps display crime locations or concentrations and can be used, for example, to help law enforcement agencies increase the effectiveness of their patrol efforts. More complex maps can be used to chart trends in criminal activity. For example, criminologists might be able to determine if certain neighborhoods in a city have significantly higher crime rates than others, whether they are so-called hot spots of crime.[41]

CRIME TRENDS

Crime is not new.[42] Studies have indicated that a gradual increase in the crime rate, especially in violent crime, occurred from 1830 to 1860. Following the Civil War, this rate increased significantly for about fifteen years. Then, from 1880 up to the time of the First World War, with the possible exception of the years immediately preceding and following the war, the number of reported crimes decreased. After a period of readjustment, the crime rate steadily declined until the Depression (about 1930), when another crime wave was recorded. As measured by the UCR, crime rates increased gradually following the 1930s until the 1960s, when the growth rate became much greater. The homicide rate, which had actually declined from the 1930s to the 1960s, also began a sharp increase that continued through the 1970s.

In 1981 the number of index crimes rose to about 13.4 million and then began a consistent decline until 1984, when police recorded 11.1 million crimes. By the following year, however, the number of crimes once again began an upward trend, so that by 1991 police recorded about 14.6 million crimes. Since then the number of crimes has been in decline; in 2003 about 11.8 million crimes were reported to the police. Figure 2.3 illustrates crime rate trends between 1960 and 2004, the last data available. As the figure shows, there has been a significant downward trend in the rate of crime for more than a decade. Even teenage criminality, a source of

Rate per 1,000 population

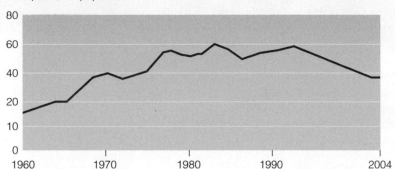

FIGURE 2.3

Crime Rate Trends

Source: FBI, *Crime in the United States*, 2004.

Rate per 100,000 population

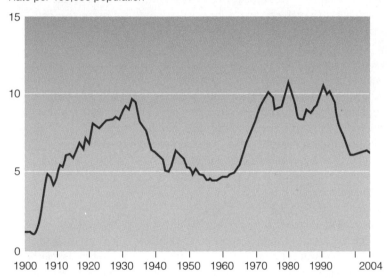

FIGURE 2.4

Homicide Rate Trends, 1900–2004

Sources: Bureau of Justice Statistics, *Violent Crime in the United States* (Washington, DC: 1992); Updated with data from FBI, *Crime in the Untied States,* 2004.

national concern, has been in decline during this period, decreasing by about one-third over the past twenty years. The teen murder rate, which had remained stubbornly high, has also declined during the past few years.[43] The factors that help explain the upward and downward movement in crime rates are discussed in The Criminological Enterprise feature "Explaining Crime Trends."

 To read more about crime trends, use the term as a subject guide with InfoTrac College Edition.

Trends in Violent Crime

The violent crimes reported by the FBI include murder, rape, assault, and robbery. In 2004, about 1.4 million violent crimes were reported to police, a rate of around 465 per 100,000 Americans. According to the UCR, violence in the United States has decreased 24 percent since 1995 when the violence rate was 684 per 100,000 and about 1.8 million violent crimes took place.

Particularly encouraging has been the decrease in the number and rate of murders. Murder statistics are generally regarded as the most accurate aspect of the UCR. Figure 2.4 illustrates homicide rate trends since 1900. Note that the rate peaked around 1930, then held relatively steady at about 4 to 5 per 100,000 population from 1950 through the mid-1960s, at which point they started rising to a peak of 10.2 per 100,000 population in 1980. From 1980 to 1991, the homicide rate fluctuated between 8 to 10 per 100,000 population; in 1991 the number of murders topped 24,000 for the first time in the nation's history. Between 1991 and 2004, homicide rates dropped more than 40 percent; about 16,000 murders now occur each year.

Trends in Property Crime

The property crimes reported in the UCR include larceny, motor vehicle theft, and arson. In 2004, about 10.3 million property crimes were reported, a rate of about 3,517 per 100,000 population. Property crime rates have declined in

Explaining Crime Trends

Crime experts have identified a variety of social, economic, personal, and demographic factors that influence crime rate trends. Although crime experts are still uncertain about how these factors impact these trends, directional change seems to be associated with changes in crime rates.

Age

Because teenagers have extremely high crime rates, crime experts view change in the population age distribution as having the greatest influence on crime trends: As a general rule, the crime rate follows the proportion of young males in the population. Kids who commit a lot of crime early in childhood are also likely to continue to commit crime in their adolescence and into adulthood. The more children in the population, the greater the likelihood of having a significant number of persistent offenders.

With the "graying" of society in the 1980s and a decline in the birthrate, it is not surprising that the overall crime rate has been in decline. The number of juveniles should be increasing over the next decade, and some crime experts fear that this will signal a return to escalating crime rates. However, the number of senior citizens is also expanding, and their presence in the population may have a moderating effect on crime rates (seniors do not commit much crime), offsetting the effect of teens.

Economy/Jobs

There is debate over the effect the economy has on crime rates. It seems logical that when the economy turns down, people (especially those who are unemployed) will become more motivated to commit theft crimes. However, some crime experts believe a poor economy actually helps lower crime rates because unemployed parents are at home to supervise children and guard their possessions. Because there is less to spend, a poor economy reduces the number of valuables worth stealing. Also, it seems unlikely that law-abiding, middle-aged workers will suddenly turn to a life of crime if they are laid off during an economic downturn. Not surprisingly, most research efforts fail to find a definitive relationship between unemployment and crime. Research conducted by Gary Kleck and Ted Chiricos shows that the relationship between unemployment and crime rates is insignificant. Unemployed people are neither likely to stick up gas stations, banks, and drug stores, nor are they more likely to engage in non-violent property crimes including shoplifting, residential burglary, theft of motor vehicle parts, and theft of automobiles, trucks, and motorcycles.

It is possible that over the long haul, a strong economy will help lower crime rates, while long periods of sustained economic weakness and unemployment may eventually lead to increased rates: Crime skyrocketed in the 1930s during the Great Depression; crime rates fell when the economy surged for almost a decade during the 1990s.

One reason for this confusion may simply be methodological: Measuring the association among variables such as jobs, the economy, and crime is quite difficult. There are significant economic differences at the state, county, community, and neighborhood level. While people in one area of the city are doing well, their neighbors living in another part of town may be suffering unemployment. Crime rates may vary by street, an association that is difficult to detect. Fahui Wang's research in Chicago, which employed highly sophisticated multiple geographic mapping techniques, shows that homicide rates are lowest in areas with the highest accessibility to new jobs.

Social Malaise

As the level of social problems increases—such as single-parent families, dropout rates, racial conflict, and teen pregnancies—so too do crime rates. Crime rates are correlated with the number of unwed mothers in the population. It is possible that children of unwed mothers need more social services than children in two-parent families. As the number of kids born to single mothers increases, the child welfare system will be taxed and services depleted. The teenage birthrate has trended downward in recent years, and so too have crime rates.

Racial conflict may also increase crime rates. Areas undergoing racial change, especially those experiencing an in-migration of minorities into predominantly white neighborhoods, seem prone to significant increases in their crime rate. Whites in these areas may be using violence to protect what they view as their home turf. Racially motivated crimes actually diminish as neighborhoods become more integrated and power struggles are resolved.

Abortion

In a controversial work, John J. Donohue III and Steven D. Levitt found empirical evidence that the recent drop in the crime rate can be attributed to the availability of legalized abortion. In 1973, *Roe v. Wade* legalized abortion nationwide. Within a few years of *Roe v. Wade*, more than 1 million abortions were being performed annually, or roughly one abortion for every three live births. Donohue and Levitt suggest that the crime rate drop, which began approximately eighteen years later in 1991, can be tied to the fact that at that point the first groups of potential offenders affected by the abortion decision began reaching the peak age of criminal activity. They find that states that legalized abortion before the rest of the nation were the first to experience decreasing crime rates and that states with high abortion rates have seen a greater fall in crime since 1985.

It is possible that the link between crime rates and abortion is the result of two mechanisms: (1) selective abortion on the part of women most at risk to have children who would engage in criminal activity, and (2) improved childrearing or environmental circumstances caused by better maternal, familial, or fetal care because women are having fewer children. According to Donohue and Levitt, if abortion were illegal, crime rates might increase by 10 to 20 percent. If these estimates are correct, legalized abortion can explain about half of the recent fall in crime. All else equal, the researchers predict that crime rates will continue to fall slowly for an additional fifteen to twenty years as the full effects of legalized abortion are gradually felt.

Guns

The availability of firearms may influence the crime rate, especially the proliferation of weapons in the hands of teens. There is evidence that more guns than ever before are finding their way into the hands of young people. Surveys of high school students indicate that between 6 and 10 percent carry guns at least some of the time. Guns also cause escalation in the seriousness of crime. As the number of gun-toting students increases, so too does the seriousness of violent crime as, for example, a schoolyard fight turns into murder.

Gangs

Another factor that affects crime rates is the explosive growth in teenage gangs. Surveys indicate that there are about 750,000 gang members in the United States. Boys who are members of gangs are far more likely to possess guns than

non-gang members; criminal activity increases when kids join gangs. According to Alfred Blumstein, gangs involved in the urban drug trade recruit juveniles because they work cheaply, are immune from heavy criminal penalties, and are daring and willing to take risks. Arming themselves for protection, these drug-dealing children present a menace to their community, which persuades non–gang-affiliated neighborhood adolescents to arm themselves for protection. The result is an arms race that produces an increasing spiral of violence.

The decade-long decline in the crime rate may be tied to changing gang values. Some streetwise kids have told researchers that they now avoid gangs because of the "younger brother syndrome"—they have watched their older siblings or parents caught in gangs or drugs and want to avoid the same fate. However, there has been a recent upswing in gang violence, a phenomenon that may herald an overall increase in violent crime.

Drug Use

Some experts tie increases in the violent crime rate between 1980 and 1990 to the crack epidemic, which swept the nation's largest cities, and to drug-trafficking gangs that fought over drug turf. These well-armed gangs did not hesitate to use violence to control territory, intimidate rivals, and increase market share. As the crack epidemic has subsided, so too has the violence in New York City and other metropolitan areas where crack use was rampant. A sudden increase in drug use on the other hand may be a harbinger of future increases in the crime rate.

Media

Some experts argue that violent media can influence the direction of crime rates. As the availability of media with a violent theme skyrocketed with the

introduction of home video players, DVDs, cable TV, computer and video games, and so on, so too did teen violence rates. According to a recent analysis of all available scientific data conducted by Brad Bushman and Craig Anderson, watching violence on TV is correlated to aggressive behaviors especially for people with a preexisting tendency toward crime and violence. This conclusion is bolstered by research showing that the more kids watch TV, the more often they get into violent encounters. Jeffrey Johnson and his associates at Columbia University found that 14-year-old boys who watched less than 1 hour of TV per day later got into an average of 9 fights resulting in injury. In contrast, adolescent males watching 1 to 3 hours of TV per day got into an average of 28 fights; those watching more than 3 hours of TV got into an average of 42 fights. Of those watching 1 to 3 hours per day, 22.5 percent later engaged in violence, such as assaults or robbery, in their adulthood; 28.8 percent of kids who regularly watched more than 3 hours of TV in a 24-hour period engaged in violent acts as adults.

Medical Technology

Some crime experts believe that the presence and quality of healthcare can have a significant impact on murder rates. According to research conducted by Anthony Harris and his associates, murder rates would be up to five times higher than they are today without medical breakthroughs in treating victims of violence developed over the past forty years. They estimate that the United States would suffer between 50,000 to 115,000 homicides per year as opposed to the current number, which has fluctuated at around 15,000. Looking back more than forty years, they found that the aggravated assault rate has increased at a far higher pace than the murder rate, a

(continued)

fact they attribute to the decrease in mortality of violence victims in hospital emergency rooms. The big breakthrough occurred in the 1970s when technology developed to treat injured soldiers in Vietnam was applied to trauma care in the nation's hospitals. Since then, fluctuations in the murder rate can be linked to the level and availability of emergency medical services.

Justice Policy

Some law enforcement experts have suggested that a reduction in crime rates may be attributed to adding large numbers of police officers and using them in aggressive police practices that target "quality of life" crimes such as panhandling, graffiti, petty drug dealing, and loitering. By showing that even the smallest infractions will be dealt with seriously, aggressive police departments may be able to discourage potential criminals from committing more serious crimes. Michael White and his associates have recently shown that cities employing aggressive, focused police work may be able to lower homicide rates in the area.

It is also possible that tough laws imposing lengthy prison terms on drug dealers and repeat offenders can affect crime rates. The fear of punishment may inhibit some would-be criminals and place a significant number of potentially high-rate offenders behind bars, lowering crime rates. As the nation's prison population expanded, the crime rate has fallen.

Crime Opportunities

Crime rates may drop when market conditions change or when an alternative criminal opportunity develops. The decline in the burglary rate over the past decade may be explained in part by the abundance and subsequent decline in price of commonly stolen merchandise such as VCRs, DVD players, cell phones, TVs, and digital cameras. Improving home and commercial security devices may also discourage would-be burglars, convincing them to turn to other forms of crime such as theft from motor vehicles. On the other hand, new targets may increase crime rates: Subway crime increased in New York when thieves began targeting people carrying iPods.

Critical Thinking

While crime rates have been declining in the United States, they have been increasing in Europe. Is it possible that factors that correlate with crime-rate changes in the United States have little utility in predicting changes in other cultures? What other factors may increase or reduce crime rates?

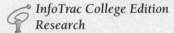

InfoTrac College Edition Research

Gang activity may have a big impact on crime rates. To read about the effect, see: John M. Hagedorn, Jose Torres, and Greg Giglio, "Cocaine, Kicks, and Strain: Patterns of Substance Use in Milwaukee Gangs," *Contemporary Drug Problems* 25 (spring 1998): 113–145; Mary E. Pattillo, "Sweet Mothers and Gangbangers: Managing Crime in a Black Middle-Class Neighborhood," *Social Forces* 76 (March 1998): 747.

Sources: David Fergusson, L. John Horwood, Elizabeth Ridder, "Show Me the Child at Seven: The Consequences of Conduct Problems in Childhood for Psychosocial Functioning in Adulthood," *Journal of Child Psychology & Psychiatry & Allied Disciplines* 46 (2005): 837–849; Fahui Wang, "Job Access and Homicide Patterns in Chicago: An Analysis at Multiple Geographic Levels Based on Scale-Space Theory," *Journal of Quantitative Criminology* 21 (2005): 195–217; Gary Kleck and Ted Chiricos, "Unemployment and Property Crime: A Target-Specific Assessment of Opportunity and Motivation as Mediating Factors," *Criminology* 40 (2002): 649–680; Michael Brick, "An IPod Crime Wave? How Terrible. On Second Thought," *New York Times,* 2 May 2005; Steven Levitt, "Understanding Why Crime Fell in the 1990s: Four Factors that Explain the Decline and Six that Do Not," *Journal of Economic Perspectives* 18 (2004): 163–190; Michael White, James Fyfe, Suzanne Campbell, and John Goldkamp, "The Police Role in Preventing Homicide: Considering the Impact of Problem-Oriented Policing on the Prevalence of Murder," *Journal of Research in Crime and Delinquency* 40 (2003): 194–226; Jeffrey Johnson, Patricia Cohen, Elizabeth Smailes, Stephanie Kasen, and Judith Brook, "Television Viewing and Aggressive Behavior During Adolescence and Adulthood," *Science* 295 (2002): 2,468–2,471; Brad Bushman and Craig Anderson, "Media Violence and the American Public," *American Psychologist* 56 (2001): 477–489; Anthony Harris, Stephen Thomas, Gene Fisher, and David Hirsch, "Murder and Medicine: The Lethality of Criminal Assault 1960–1999," *Homicide Studies* 6 (2002): 128–167; Steven Messner, Lawrence Raffalovich, and Richard McMillan, "Economic Deprivation and Changes in Homicide Arrest Rates for White and Black Youths, 1967–1998: A National Time-Series Analysis," *Criminology* 39 (2001): 591–614; John Laub, "Review of the Crime Drop in America," *American Journal of Sociology* 106 (2001): 1,820–1,822; John J. Donohue and Steven D. Levitt, "The Impact of Legalized Abortion on Crime," *Quarterly Journal of Economics* 116 (2001): 379–420; Robert O'Brien, Jean Stockard, and Lynne Isaacson, "The Enduring Effects of Cohort Characteristics on Age-Specific Homicide Rates, 1960–1995," *American Journal of Sociology* 104 (1999): 1,061–1,095; Darrell Steffensmeier and Miles Harer, "Making Sense of Recent U.S. Crime Trends, 1980 to 1996/1998: Age Composition Effects and Other Explanations," *Journal of Research in Crime and Delinquency* 36 (1999): 235–274

recent years, though the drop has not been as dramatic as that experienced by the violent crime rate. Between 1995 and 2004, the total number of property crimes declined about 14 percent, and the property crime rate declined about 23 percent; property crime rates declined an additional 2.1 percent between 2003 and 2004.

For the results of an international victimization study, use InfoTrac College Edition to read: Martin Killias, John van Kesteren, and Martin Rindlisbacher, "Guns, Violent Crime, and Suicide in 21 Countries," *Canadian Journal of Criminology* 43 (2001): 429–446.

While property crime rates have trended downward it is possible that valuable new commodities such as the iPod may encourage more theft activity. Thefts on New York City subway trains have risen as thieves target music-playing devices such as the iPod, game-playing cell phones, and other popular mobile electronic devices.

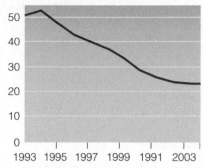

FIGURE 2.5

Violent Crime Trends, 1993–2004

Violent victimization rates have declined significantly between 1993 and 2004.

Violent victimizations per 1,000 population age 12 or over

Source: http://www.ojp.usdoj.gov/bjs/pub/pdf/cv04.pdf.

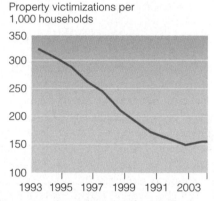

FIGURE 2.6

Property Crime Trends, 1993–2004

Property victimization rates have declined between 1993 and 2004.

Property victimizations per 1,000 households

Source: http://www.ojp.usdoj.gov/bjs/pub/pdf/cv04.pdf.

Trends in Victimization Data (NCVS Findings)

According to the National Crime Victimization Survey (NCVS), the UCR's view of a declining crime rate is accurate. In 2004 U.S. residents age 12 or older experienced about 24 million violent and property victimizations. This represents a significant downward trend in reported victimization that began in 1994 and has resulted in a significant decline in the number of criminal victimizations since 1973, when an estimated 44 million victimizations were recorded. Between 1993 and 2004 the violent crime rate decreased more than 50 percent, from 50 to 21 victimizations per 1,000 persons age 12 or older, and the property crime rate declined at about the same rate(from 319 to 161 crimes per 1,000 households). In 2004 the rate for rape and attempted rape was down almost 70 percent from the1993 rate; the rate for robbery was down about 60 percent. Figure 2.5 shows the recent trends in violent crime, and Figure 2.6 tracks property victimizations.

To access the most recent **NCVS data,** go to http://www.ojp.usdoj.gov/bjs/cvict.htm. For an up-to-date list of web links, go to http://cj.wadsworth.com/siegel_crimtpt9e.

Trends in Self-Reporting

Self-report results appear to be more stable than the UCR and the NCVS. When the results of recent self-report surveys are compared with various studies conducted over a twenty-year period, a uniform pattern emerges: The use of drugs and alcohol increased markedly in the 1970s, leveled off in the 1980s, and then began to increase in the mid-1990s until 1997, when the use of most drugs began to decline. Theft, violence, and damage-related crimes seem more stable. Although

TABLE 2.1

Survey of Criminal Activity of High School Seniors, 2004

Crime	Total	Percentage Engaging in Offenses Committed More than Once
Set fire on purpose	4	2
Damaged school property	13	7
Damaged work property	7	4
Auto theft	5	3
Auto part theft	6	3
Break and enter	23	13
Theft, less than $50	27	14
Theft, more than $50	9	5
Shoplift	28	15
Gang fight	19	9
Hurt someone bad enough to require medical care	13	7
Used force to steal	4	2
Hit teacher or supervisor	3	2
Gotten into serious fight	14	7

Source: Monitoring the Future, 2004 (Ann Arbor, MI: Institute for Social Research, 2004).

a self-reported crime wave has not occurred, neither has there been any visible reduction in self-reported criminality. Table 2.1 contains data from the most recent (2004) Monitoring the Future survey. A surprising number of these *typical* teenagers reported involvement in serious criminal behavior: About 13 percent reported hurting someone badly enough that the victim needed medical care (7 percent said they did it more than once); about 27 percent reported stealing something worth less than $50, and another 9 percent stole something worth more than $50; 28 percent reported shoplifting; 13 percent had damaged school property.

If the MTF data are accurate, the crime problem is much greater than FBI data would lead us to believe. There are approximately 40 million youths between the ages of 10 and 18. Extrapolating from the MTF findings, this group accounts for more than 100 percent of all theft offenses reported in the UCR. More than 3 percent of the students said they used a knife or a gun in a robbery. At this rate, high school students commit 1.2 million armed robberies per year. In comparison, the UCR tallied about 230,000 armed robberies for all age groups in 2004. Over the past decade, the MTF surveys indicate that, with a few exceptions, self-reported participation in theft, violence, and damage-related crimes seems to be more stable than the trends reported in the UCR arrest data.

How is the data collected from the Monitoring the Future study used in research? Read the following paper: Patrick M. O'Malley and Lloyd D. Johnston, "Unsafe Driving by High School Seniors: National Trends from 1976 to 2001 in Tickets and Accidents after Use of Alcohol, Marijuana, and Other Illegal Drugs," *Journal of Studies on Alcohol* 64 (2003): 305–312.

WHAT THE FUTURE HOLDS

It is risky to speculate about the future of crime trends because current conditions can change rapidly, but some criminologists have tried to predict future patterns. Criminologist James A. Fox predicts a significant increase in teen violence if current trends persist. There are approximately 50 million school-age children in the United States, and many are under age 10; this is a greater number than we have had for decades. Many come from stable homes, but some lack stable families and adequate supervision. These children will soon enter their prime crime years. As a result, Fox predicts, the number of juvenile homicides should begin to grow in the coming years.[44] Such predictions are based on population trends and other factors discussed previously.

Fox's predictions are persuasive, but not all criminologists believe we are in for an age-driven crime wave. Some, such as Steven Levitt, dispute the fact that the population's age makeup contributes as much to the crime rate as suggested by Fox and others.[45] Even if teens commit more crime in the future, he finds that their contribution may be offset by the aging of the

© AP/Louis Lazane/Wide World Photos

In the future, crime rates may be influenced by new forms of criminal activity that are just beginning to have an impact on American society. The Internet may provide one source of new criminal activity. Philip Cummings, shown here, was a 33-year-old former customer service representative at a Long Island, New York, tech company who helped orchestrate a vast credit card/identity theft fraud scheme that claimed more than 30,000 victims and resulted in losses of between $50–100 million dollars. Cummings' company provided software and hardware that allowed banks and lending companies to get commercial credit information. He used his position at his company to get access codes that other companies use to check consumer credit and sold them, along with other information such as Social Security numbers and credit card numbers. The buyers then used the information to defraud victims across the country. Cummings pled guilty to fraud charges on September 15, 2004.

population, which will produce a large number of senior citizens and elderly, a group with a relatively low crime rate.

Criminologists Darrell Steffensmeier and Miles Harer predict a much more moderate increase in crime than previously believed possible.[46] Steffensmeier and Harer agree that the age structure of society is one of the most important determinants of crime rates, but they believe the economy, technological change, and social factors help moderate the crime rate.[47] They note that American culture is being transformed because baby boomers, now in their late 50s and 60s, are exerting a significant influence on the nation's values and morals. As a result, the narcissistic youth culture that stresses materialism is being replaced by more moralistic cultural values.[48] Positive social values have a "contagion effect"; those held by the baby boomers will have an important influence on the behavior of all citizens, even crime-prone teens. The result may be a moderation in the potential growth of the crime rate.

Such prognostication is reassuring, but there is, of course, no telling what changes are in store that may influence crime rates either up or down. Technological developments such as e-commerce on the Internet have created new classes of crime. Concern about the environment in rural areas may produce a rapid upswing in environmental crimes ranging from vandalism to violence.[49] Although crime rates have trended downward, it is too early to predict that this trend will continue into the foreseeable future.

CRIME PATTERNS

Criminologists look for stable crime-rate patterns to gain insight into the nature of crime. The cause of crime may be better understood by examining the rate. If, for example, criminal statistics consistently show that crime rates are higher in poor neighborhoods in large urban areas, then the cause of crime may be related to poverty and neighborhood decline. If, in contrast, crime rates are spread evenly across society, and rates are equal in poor and affluent neighborhoods, this would provide little evidence that crime has an economic basis. Instead, crime might be linked to socialization, personality, intelligence, or some other trait unrelated to class position or income. In this section we examine traits and patterns that may influence the crime rate.

The Ecology of Crime

Patterns in the crime rate seem to be linked to temporal and ecological factors. Some of the most important of these are discussed here.

DAY, SEASON, AND CLIMATE Most reported crimes occur during the warm summer months of July and August. During the summer, teenagers, who usually have the highest crime levels, are out of school and have greater opportunity to commit crime. People spend more time outdoors during warm weather, making themselves easier targets. Similarly, homes are left vacant more often during the summer, making them more vulnerable to property crimes. Two exceptions to this trend are murders and robberies, which occur frequently in December and January (although rates are also high during the summer).

Crime rates also may be higher on the first day of the month than at any other time. Government welfare and Social Security checks arrive at this time, and with them come increases in such activities as breaking into mailboxes and accosting recipients on the streets. Also, people may have more disposable income at this time, and the availability of extra money may relate to behaviors associated with crime such as drinking, partying, gambling, and so on.[50]

TEMPERATURE Weather effects (such as temperature swings) may have an impact on violent crime rates. Traditionally, the association between temperature and crime was thought to resemble an inverted U-shaped curve: Crime rates increase with rising temperatures and then begin to decline at some point (85 degrees) when it may be too hot for any physical exertion[51](Figure 2.7). However, criminologists continue to debate this issue:

- Some believe that crime rates rise with temperature (the hotter the day, the higher the crime rate).[52]

- Others have found evidence that the curvilinear model is correct.[53]

- Some research shows that a rising temperature will cause some crimes to continually increase (for example, domestic assault), while others (such as rape) will decline after temperatures rise to an extremely high level.[54]

If, in fact, there is an association between temperature and crime, can it be explained? The relationship may be due to the stress and tension caused by extreme temperature. The human body generates stress hormones (adrenaline and

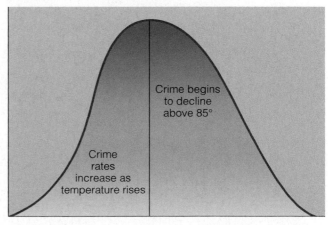

FIGURE 2.7

The Relationship between Temperature and Crime

Crime rate

Crime begins to decline above 85°

Crime rates increase as temperature rises

Temperature   85°

testosterone) in response to excessive heat; hormonal activity has been linked to aggression.[55]

One way to combat the temperature–crime association is to turn off the air conditioner! James Rotton and Ellen Cohn found that assaults in air-conditioned settings increased as the temperature rose; assaults in non–air-conditioned settings declined after peaking at moderately high temperatures.[56]

REGIONAL DIFFERENCES Large urban areas have by far the highest violence rates; rural areas have the lowest per capita crime rates. Exceptions to this trend are low population resort areas with large transient or seasonal populations—such as Atlantic City, New Jersey. Typically, the western and southern states have had consistently higher crime rates than the Midwest and Northeast (Figure 2.8). This pattern has convinced some criminologists that regional cultural values

---

FIGURE 2.8

Regional Crime Rates, 2004: Violent and Property Crimes per 100,000 Inhabitants

Source: http://www.fbi.gov/ucr/cius_04/summary/crime_map/index.html.

influence crime rates; others believe that regional differences can be explained by economic differences.

Use of Firearms

Firearms play a dominant role in criminal activity. According to the NCVS, firearms are typically involved in about 20 percent of robberies, 10 percent of assaults, and more than 5 percent of rapes. According to the UCR, about two-thirds of all murders involved firearms; most of these weapons were handguns.

Because of these findings, there is an ongoing debate over gun control. International criminologists Franklin Zimring and Gordon Hawkins believe the proliferation of handguns and the high rate of lethal violence they cause is the single most significant factor separating the crime problem in the United States from the rest of the developed world.[57] Differences between the United States and Europe in nonlethal crimes are only modest at best and getting smaller over time.[58]

In contrast, some criminologists believe that personal gun use can actually be a deterrent to crime. Gary Kleck and Marc Gertz have found that as many as 400,000 people per year use guns in situations in which they later claim that the guns almost "certainly" saved lives. Even if these estimates are off by a factor of 10, it means that armed citizens may save 40,000 lives annually. Although Kleck and Gertz recognize that guns are involved in murders, suicides, and accidents, which claim more than 30,000 lives per year, they believe their benefit as a crime prevention device should not be overlooked.[59] Because this is so important, the Policy and Practice in Criminology feature "Should Guns Be Controlled?" discusses this issue in some detail.

Social Class, Socioeconomic Conditions, and Crime

It makes logical sense that crime is a lower-class phenomenon. After all, people at the lowest rungs of the social structure have the greatest incentive to commit crimes. Those unable to obtain desired goods and services through conventional means may consequently resort to theft and other illegal activities—such as selling narcotics—to obtain them. These activities are referred to as **instrumental crimes.** Those living in poverty are also believed to engage in disproportionate amounts of **expressive crimes,** such as rape and assault, as a result of their rage, frustration, and anger against society. Alcohol and drug abuse, common in impoverished areas, help fuel violent episodes.[60]

When measured with UCR data, official statistics indicate that crime rates in inner-city, high-poverty areas are generally higher than those in suburban or wealthier areas.[61] Surveys of prison inmates consistently show that prisoners were members of the lower class and unemployed or underemployed in the years before their incarceration.

An alternative explanation for these findings is that the relationship between official crime and social class is a function of law enforcement practices, not actual criminal behavior patterns. Police may devote more resources to poor areas, and consequently apprehension rates may be higher there. Similarly, police may be more likely to formally arrest and prosecute lower-class citizens than those in the middle and upper classes, which may account for the lower-class's overrepresentation in official statistics and the prison population.

CLASS AND SELF-REPORTS Self-report data have been used extensively to test the class–crime relationship. If people in all social classes self-report similar crime patterns, but only those in the lower class are formally arrested, that would explain higher crime rates in lower-class neighborhoods. However, if lower-class people report greater criminal activity than their middle- and upper-class peers, it would indicate that official statistics accurately represent the crime problem.

Surprisingly, early self-report studies conducted in the 1950s, specifically those conducted by James Short and F. Ivan Nye, did not find a direct relationship between social class and youth crime.[62] They found that socioeconomic class was related to official processing by police, courts, and correctional agencies but not to the actual commission of crimes. In other words, although lower- and middle-class youth self-reported equal amounts of crime, the lower-class youths had a greater chance of being arrested, convicted, and incarcerated and becoming official delinquents. In addition, factors generally associated with lower-class membership, such as broken homes, were found to be related to institutionalization but not to admissions of delinquency. Other studies of this period reached similar conclusions.[63]

For more than twenty years after the use of self-reports became widespread, a majority of self-report studies concluded that a class–crime relationship did not exist: If the poor possessed more extensive criminal records than the wealthy, this difference was attributable to differential law enforcement and not to class-based behavior differences. That is, police may be more likely to arrest lower-class offenders and treat the affluent more leniently.

Almost thirty years ago, Charles Tittle, Wayne Villemez, and Douglas Smith published what is still considered the definitive review of the relationship between class and crime.[64] They concluded that little if any support exists for the contention that crime is primarily a lower-class phenomenon. Consequently, Tittle and his associates argued that official statistics probably reflect class bias in processing lower-class offenders. In a subsequent article written with Robert Meier, Tittle once again reviewed existing data on the class–crime relationship and found little evidence of a consistent association between class and crime.[65] More recent self-report studies generally support Tittle's conclusions: There is no direct relationship between social class and crime.[66]

Should Guns be Controlled?

The 2002 sniper killings in the Washington, DC, area focused a spotlight on a long-running policy debate in the United States: Should guns be controlled? According to the 2003 Small Arms Survey, the United States has by far the largest number of publicly owned firearms in the world and is approaching the point where there is one gun for every American, about 280 million firearms. An estimated 50 million of these guns are illegal. Handguns are linked to many violent crimes, including 20 percent of all injury deaths (second to autos) and 60 percent of all murders and suicides. They are also responsible for the deaths of about two-thirds of all police officers killed in the line of duty.

To some critics the deadly sniper attacks that paralyzed the Virginia-Maryland area in October 2002 were a sad result of the widespread availability of deadly rifles and handguns. This perception is supported by research showing a significant association between firearm ownership and crime. Cross-national research conducted by Anthony Hoskin found that nations, including the United States, that have high levels of privately owned firearms also have the highest levels of murder. Similarly, Matthew Miller and his associates show that in areas where household firearm ownership rates were high, a disproportionately large number of people died from homicide. And in a recent meta-analysis, Lisa Hepburn and David Hemenway found that (a) households with firearms are at higher risk for homicide, (b) there is no beneficial effect of firearm ownership, (c) both men and women are at higher risk for homicide in nations with high rates of gun ownership, and (d) gun prevalence is related to homicide rates.

The association between guns and crime has spurred many Americans to advocate controlling the sale of handguns and banning the cheap mass-produced handguns known as Saturday night specials. In contrast, gun advocates view control as a threat to personal liberty and call for severe punishment of criminals rather than control of handguns. They argue that the Second Amendment of the U.S. Constitution protects the right to bear arms. A survey by Robert Jiobu and Timothy Curry found that the typical gun owner has a deep mistrust of the federal government; to this individual, a gun is an "icon for democracy and personal empowerment" (p. 87).

Gun Control Efforts

Efforts to control handguns have come from many different sources. States and many local jurisdictions have laws banning or restricting sales or possession of guns; some regulate dealers who sell guns. The Federal Gun Control Act of 1968, which is still in effect, requires that all dealers be licensed, fill out forms detailing each trade, and avoid selling to people prohibited from owning guns such as minors, ex-felons, and drug users. Dealers must record the source and properties of all guns they sell and carefully account for their purchase. Gun buyers must provide identification and sign waivers attesting to their ability to possess guns. Unfortunately, the resources available to enforce this law are meager.

On November 30, 1993, the Brady Handgun Violence Prevention Act was enacted, amending the Gun Control Act of 1968. The bill was named after former Press Secretary James Brady, who was severely wounded in the attempted assassination of President Ronald Reagan by John Hinckley in 1981. The Brady Law imposes a waiting period of five days before a licensed importer, manufacturer, or dealer may sell, deliver, or transfer a handgun to an unlicensed individual. The waiting period applies only in states without an acceptable alternate system of conducting background checks on handgun purchasers. Beginning November 30, 1998, the Brady Law changed, providing an instant check on whether a prospective buyer is prohibited from purchasing a weapon. Federal law bans gun purchases by people convicted of or under indictment for felony charges, fugitives, the mentally ill, those with dishonorable military discharges, those who have renounced U.S. citizenship, illegal aliens, illegal drug users, and those convicted of domestic violence misdemeanors or who are under domestic violence restraining orders (individual state laws may create other restrictions). The Brady Law now requires background approval not just for handgun buyers but also for those who buy long guns and shotguns. In addition, the Federal Violent Crime Control and Law Enforcement Act of 1994 banned a group of military-style semiautomatic firearms (that is, assault weapons). However, this ban on assault weapons was allowed to lapse in 2004.

Although gun control advocates see this legislation as a good first step, some question whether such measures will ultimately curb gun violence. When Jens Ludwig and Philip Cook compared two sets of states—thirty-two that installed the Brady Law in 1994 and eighteen states plus the District of Columbia, which already had similar types of laws prior to 1994—they found that there was no evidence that implementing the Brady Law contributed to a reduction in homicide.

Another approach is to severely punish people caught with unregistered handguns. The most famous attempt to regulate handguns using this method is the Massachusetts Bartley-Fox Law, which provides a mandatory one-year prison term for possessing a handgun (outside the home) without a permit. A detailed analysis of violent crime in Boston after the law's passage found that the use of handguns in robberies and murders did decline substantially (in robberies by 35 percent and in murders by 55 percent in a two-year period). However, these optimistic results must be tempered by two facts: Rates for similar crimes dropped significantly in comparable cities that did not have gun control laws, and the use of other weapons, such as knives, increased in Boston.

Some jurisdictions have tried to reduce gun violence by adding extra punishment, such as a mandatory prison sentence for any crime involving a handgun. California's "10-20-life" law requires an additional ten years in prison for carrying a gun while committing a violent felony, twenty years if the gun is fired, and from twenty-five years to life in prison if someone is injured.

Can Guns Be Outlawed?

Even if outlawed or severely restricted, the government's ability to control guns is problematic. If legitimate gun stores were strictly regulated, private citizens could still sell, barter, or trade handguns. Unregulated gun fairs and auctions are common throughout the United States; many gun deals are made at gun shows with few questions asked. People obtain firearms illegally through a multitude of unauthorized sources including unlicensed dealers, corrupt licensed dealers, and "straw" purchasers (people who buy guns for those who cannot purchase them legally).

If handguns were banned or outlawed, they would become more valuable; illegal importation of guns might increase as it has for other controlled substances (for instance, narcotics). Increasing penalties for gun-related crimes has also met with limited

success because judges may be reluctant to alter their sentencing policies to accommodate legislators. Regulating dealers is difficult, and tighter controls on them would only encourage private sales and bartering. Relatively few guns are stolen in burglaries, but many are sold to licensed gun dealers who circumvent the law by ignoring state registration requirements or making unrecorded or mis-recorded sales to individuals and unlicensed dealers. Even a few corrupt dealers can supply tens of thousands of illegal handguns.

Is There a Benefit to Having Guns?

Not all experts are convinced that strict gun control is a good thing. Gary Kleck, a leading advocate of gun ownership, argues that guns may actually inhibit violence. Along with Marc Gertz, Kleck conducted a national survey that indicates that Americans use guns for defensive purposes up to 2.5 million times a year. While this figure seems huge, it must be viewed in the context of gun ownership: About 47.6 million households own a gun; more than 90 million, or 49 percent of the adult U.S. population, live in households with guns; and about 59 million adults personally own guns. Considering these numbers it is not implausible that 3 percent of the people (or 2.5 million people) with access to guns could have used one defensively in a given year.

Guns have other uses. In many assaults, Kleck reasons, the aggressor does not wish to kill but only scare the victim. Possessing a gun gives aggressors enough killing power so that they may actually be inhibited from attacking. Research by Kleck and Karen McElrath found that during a robbery, guns can control the situation without the need for illegal force. Guns may also enable victims to escape serious

injury. Victims may be inhibited from fighting back without losing face; it is socially acceptable to back down from a challenge if the opponent is armed with a gun. Guns then can de-escalate a potentially violent situation. Kleck, along with Michael Hogan, finds that people who own guns are only slightly more likely to commit homicide than nonowners. The benefits of gun ownership, he concludes, outweigh the costs.

John Lott has evaluated the passage of right-to-carry laws across the United States. He, along with David Mustard, found that jurisdictions that allow citizens to carry concealed weapons also have lower violent crime rates. If all states allowed citizens to carry concealed weapons, their analysis indicates that 1,500 murders, 4,000 rapes, 11,000 robberies, and 60,000 aggravated assaults would be avoided yearly. The annual social benefit from each additional concealed handgun permit is as high as $5,000, saving society more than $6 billion per year.

Does Defensive Gun Use Really Work?

While this research is persuasive many criminologists are still skeptical about the benefits of carrying a handgun. Tomislav Kovandzic and Thomas Marvell examined right-to-carry laws in Florida and found that they have little effect on local crime rates. And while Kleck's research shows that carrying a gun can thwart crimes, other research shows that defensive gun use may be more limited than he believes. Even people with a history of violence and mental disease are less likely to kill when they use a knife or other weapon than when they employ a gun. Do guns kill people or do people kill people? Research indicates that even the most dangerous people are less likely to resort to lethal violence if the gun is taken out of their hands.

(continued)

Critical Thinking

1. Should the sale and possession of handguns be banned?

2. Which of the gun control methods discussed do you feel would be most effective in deterring crime?

InfoTrac College Edition Research

One method of reducing gun violence may be to make guns safer. Read more about this plan in: Krista D. Robinson, Stephen P. Teret, Susan DeFrancesco, and Stephen W. Hargarten, "Making Guns Safer," *Issues in Science and Technology* 14 (1998): 37–41.

Sources: Donald Kennedy, "Research Fraud and Public Policy," *Science* 300 (April 18, 2003): 393; Tomislav Kovandzic and Thomas Marvell, "Right-to-Carry Concealed Handguns and Violent Crime: Crime Control through Gun Control?" *Criminology & Public Policy* 2 (2003): 363–396;

Lisa Hepburn and David Hemenway, "Firearm Availability and Homicide: A Review of the Literature," *Aggression & Violent Behavior* 9 (2004): 417–440; "The Small Arms Survey, 2003." http://www.smallarmssurvey.org. Accessed July 10, 2003; Matthew Miller, Deborah Azrael, and David Hemenway, "Rates of Household Firearm Ownership and Homicide across US Regions and States, 1988-1997," *American Journal of Public Health* 92 (2002): 1,988–1,993; Stephen Schnebly, "An Examination of the Impact of Victim, Offender, and Situational Attributes on the Deterrent Effect of Gun Use: A Research Note," *Justice Quarterly* 19 (2002): 377–399; William Wells and Julie Horney, "Weapon Effects and Individual Intent to Do Harm: Influences on the Escalation of Violence," *Criminology* 40 (2002): 265–296; John Lott, Jr., "More Guns, Less Crime: Understanding Crime and Gun-Control Laws," *Studies in Law and Economics*, 2nd ed. (Chicago: University of Chicago Press, 2001); John Lott, Jr., and David Mustard, "Crime, Deterrence, and Right-to-Carry Concealed Handguns," *Journal of Legal Studies* 26 (1997): 1–68; Anthony A. Braga and David M. Kennedy, "The Illicit Acquisition of Firearms by Youth and Juveniles," *Journal of Criminal Justice* 29 (2001): 379–388; Anthony Hoskin, "Armed Americans: The Impact of Firearm Availability on National Homicide Rates," *Justice Quarterly* 18

(2001): 569–592; J. Robert Jiobu and Timothy Curry, "Lack of Confidence in the Federal Government and the Ownership of Firearms," *Social Science Quarterly* 82 (2001): 77–87; Jens Ludwig and Philip Cook, "Homicide and Suicide Rates Associated with the Implementation of the Brady Violence Prevention Act," *Journal of the American Medical Association* 284 (2000): 585–591; Julius Wachtel, "Sources of Crime Guns in Los Angeles, California," *Policing* 21 (1998): 220–239; Gary Kleck and Michael Hogan, "National Case-Control Study of Homicide Offending and Gun Ownership," *Social Problems* 46 (1999): 275–293; Garen Wintemute, Mora Wright, Carrie Parham, Christina Drake, and James Beaumont, "Denial of Handgun Purchase: A Description of the Affected Population and a Controlled Study of Their Handgun Preferences," *Journal of Criminal Justice* 27 (1999): 21–31; Shawn Schwaner, L. Allen Furr, Cynthia Negrey, and Rachelle Seger, "Who Wants a Gun License?" *Journal of Criminal Justice* 27 (1999): 1–10; Gary Kleck and Marc Gertz, "Armed Resistance to Crime: The Prevalence and Nature of Self-Defense with a Gun," *Journal of Criminal Law and Criminology* 86 (1995): 150–187; Colin Loftin, David McDowall, Brian Wiersma, and Talbert Cottey, "Effects of Restrictive Licensing of Handguns on Homicide and Suicide in the District of Columbia," *New England Journal of Medicine* 325 (1991): 1,615–1,620.

Tittle's findings have sparked significant debate in the criminological community. Many self-report instruments include trivial offenses such as using a false ID or drinking alcohol, which may invalidate findings. It is possible that affluent youths frequently engage in trivial offenses such as petty larceny, using drugs, and simple assault but rarely escalate their criminal involvement. Those who support a class–crime relationship suggest that if only serious felony offenses are considered, a significant association can be observed.[67] Some studies find that when only serious crimes, such as burglary and assault, are considered, lower-class youths are significantly more delinquent than their more affluent peers.[68]

THE CLASS–CRIME CONTROVERSY The relationship between class and crime is an important one for criminological theory. If crime is related to social class, then it follows that economic and social factors, such as poverty and neighborhood disorganization, cause criminal behavior. If class and economic conditions are not related to crime rates, than the cause of crime may be found at an individual level, related more to a person's psychological and biological makeup than their economic predicament.

One reason that a true measure of the class–crime relationship has so far eluded criminologists is that the methods now employed to measure social class vary widely. Some commonly used measures of social class, such as father's occupation and education, are only weakly related to self-reported crime, but others, such as unemployment or receiving welfare, are more significant predictors of criminality.[69]

It is also possible that the association between class and crime is difficult to calculate because it is quite complex and cannot be explained with a simple linear relationship (that is, the poorer you are, the more crime you commit).[70] Class and economic conditions may affect some crimes and some people differently than it affects others. Some subgroups in the population (for example, women or African Americans) seem more deeply influenced by economic factors than others (males, whites).[71] Job loss seems to affect young adults more than it does teens. Younger adults are affected not only when they experience job loss but when only low-wage jobs are available.[72]

These findings show why the true relationship between class and crime is difficult to determine. The effect may be obscured because its impact varies within and between groups.

DOES CLASS MATTER? Like so many other criminological controversies, the debate over the true relationship between class and crime will most likely persist. The weight of recent evidence seems to suggest that serious, official crime is more prevalent among the lower classes, whereas less serious and self-reported crime is spread more evenly throughout the social structure.[73] Income inequality, poverty, and resource deprivation are all associated with the most serious violent crimes, including homicide and assault.[74] Members of the lower class are more likely to suffer psychological abnormality including high rates of anxiety and conduct disorders, conditions that may promote criminality.[75]

Communities that lack economic and social opportunities also produce high levels of frustration; their residents believe they are relatively more deprived than residents in more affluent areas and may then turn to criminal behavior to relieve their frustration.[76] Family life is disrupted, and law-violating youth groups thrive in a climate that undermines adult supervision.[77] Conversely, when the poor are provided with economic opportunities via welfare and public assistance, crime rates drop.[78] The debate is far from over. Although crime rates may be higher in lower-class areas, poverty alone cannot explain why a particular individual becomes a chronic violent criminal; if it could, the crime problem would be much worse than it is now.[79]

||||||| CONNECTIONS |||||||

If class and crime are unrelated, then the causes of crime must be found in factors experienced by members of all social classes—psychological impairment, family conflict, peer pressure, school failure, and so on. Theories that view crime as a function of problems experienced by members of all social classes are reviewed in Chapter 7.

Age and Crime

There is general agreement that age is inversely related to criminality. Criminologists Travis Hirschi and Michael Gottfredson state, "Age is everywhere correlated with crime. Its effects on crime do not depend on other demographic correlates of crime."[80]

||||||| CONNECTIONS |||||||

Hirschi and Gottfredson have used their views on the age–crime relationship as a basis for their General Theory of Crime. This important theory holds that the factors that produce crime change little after birth and that the association between crime and age is constant. For more on this view, see the section on the General Theory of Crime in Chapter 9.

Regardless of economic status, marital status, race, sex, and so on, younger people commit crime more often than their older peers; research indicates this relationship has been stable across time periods ranging from 1935 to the present.[81] Official statistics tell us that young people are arrested at a disproportionate rate to their numbers in the population; victim surveys generate similar findings for crimes in which assailant age can be determined. Whereas youths ages 13 to 17 collectively make up about 6 percent of the total U.S. population, they account for about 25 percent of index crime arrests and 17 percent of arrests for all crimes. As a general rule, the peak age for property crime is believed to be 16, and for violence 18 (Figure 2.9). In contrast, adults 45 and over, who make up 32 percent of the population, account for only 7 percent of index crime arrests. The elderly are particularly resistant to the temptations of crime; they make up more than 12 percent of the population and less than 1 percent of arrests. Elderly males 65 and over are predominantly arrested for alcohol-related matters (such as public drunkenness and drunk driving) and elderly females for larceny (for example, shoplifting). The elderly crime rate has remained stable for the past twenty years.[82]

AGING OUT OF CRIME Most criminologists agree that people commit less crime as they age.[83] Crime peaks in adolescence and then declines rapidly thereafter. According to criminologist Robert Agnew, this peak in criminal activity can be linked to essential features of adolescence in modern, industrial societies. Because adolescents are given most of the privileges and responsibilities of adults in these cultures, they also experience:

- A reduction in supervision

- An increase in social and academic demands

FIGURE 2.9

Relationship between Age and Serious Crime Arrests

Arrest rate per 100,000 persons

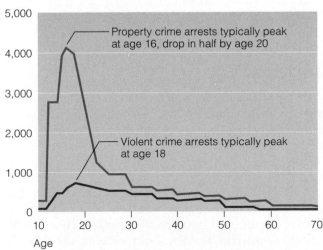

Source: FBI, *Uniform Crime Report*, 2003, p. 280.

- Participation in a larger, more diverse, peer-oriented social world

- An increased desire for adult privileges

- A reduced ability to cope in a legitimate manner and increased incentive to solve problems in a criminal manner[84]

Adding to these incentives is the fact that young people, especially the indigent and antisocial, tend to discount the future.[85] They are impatient, and because their future is uncertain, they are unwilling or unable to delay gratification. As they mature, troubled youths are able to develop a long-term life view and resist the need for immediate gratification.[86] **Aging out** of crime may be a function of the natural history of the human life cycle.[87] Deviance in adolescence is fueled by the need for money and sex and reinforced by close relationships with peers who defy conventional morality. At the same time, teenagers are becoming independent from parents and other adults who enforce conventional standards of morality and behavior. They have a new sense of energy and strength and are involved with peers who are similarly vigorous and frustrated. Adults, on the other hand, develop the ability to delay gratification and forgo the immediate gains that law violations bring. They also start wanting to take responsibility for their behavior and to adhere to conventional mores, such as establishing long-term relationships and starting a family.[88] Research does show that people who maintain successful marriages are more likely to desist from antisocial behaviors than those whose marriages fail.[89]

| | | | | | | CONNECTIONS | | | | | | |

Those who oppose the Hirschi and Gottfredson view argue that although most people age out of crime, a small group continues into old age as chronic or persistent offenders. It is possible that the population may contain different sets of criminal offenders: one group whose criminality declines with age; another whose criminal behavior remains constant through maturity. This issue will be discussed in greater detail in Chapter 9.

Gender and Crime

Male crime rates are much higher than those of females. Victims report that their assailant was male in more than 80 percent of all violent personal crimes. The Uniform Crime Report arrest statistics indicate that the overall male–female arrest ratio is almost 4 male offenders to 1 female offender; for serious violent crimes, the ratio is almost 5 males to 1 female; murder arrests are 8 males to 1 female. MTF data also show that males commit more serious crimes, such as robbery, assault, and burglary, than females. However, although the patterns in self-reports parallel official data, the ratios are smaller. In other words, males self-report more

TABLE 2.2

Percentage of High School Seniors Admitting to at Least One Offense during the Past 12 Months, by Gender

Delinquent Acts	Males	Females
Serious fight	19	9
Gang fight	25	15
Hurt someone badly	19	5
Used a weapon to steal	6	1
Stole less than $50	34	21
Stole more than $50	14	5
Shoplift	31	23
Breaking and entering	29	17
Arson	7	1
Damaged school property	20	6

Source: Monitoring the Future, 2004 (Ann Arbor, MI: Institute for Social Research, 2004).

criminal behavior than females—but not to the degree suggested by official data (Table 2.2). How can these differences be explained?

TRAITS AND TEMPERAMENT Early criminologists pointed to emotional, physical, and psychological differences between males and females to explain the differences in crime rates. Cesare Lombroso's 1895 book *The Female Offender* argued that a small group of female criminals lacked "typical" female traits of "piety, maternity, undeveloped intelligence, and weakness."[90] In physical appearance as well as in their emotional makeup, delinquent females appeared closer to men than to other women. Lombroso's theory became known as the **masculinity hypothesis**; in essence, a few "masculine" females were responsible for the handful of crimes women commit.

Another early view of female crime focused on the supposed dynamics of sexual relationships. Female criminals were viewed as either sexually controlling or sexually naive, either manipulating men for profit or being manipulated by them. The female's criminality was often masked because criminal justice authorities were reluctant to take action against a woman.[91] This perspective is known as the **chivalry hypothesis,** which holds that much female criminality is hidden because of the culture's generally protective and benevolent attitude toward women.[92] In other words, police are less likely to arrest, juries are less likely to convict, and judges are less likely to incarcerate female offenders.

Although these early writings are no longer taken seriously, some criminologists still believe that gender-based traits are a key determinant of crime rate differences. Suspected differences include physical strength and hormonal influences. According to this view, male sex hormones (androgens) account for more aggressive male behavior, and gender-related hormonal differences explain the gender gap in the crime rate.[93]

| | | | | | | CONNECTIONS | | | | | |

Gender differences in the crime rate may be a function of androgen levels because these hormones cause areas of the brain to become less sensitive to environmental stimuli, making males more likely to seek high levels of stimulation and to tolerate more pain in the process. Chapter 5 discusses the biosocial causes of crime and reviews this issue in greater detail.

While women still commit less crime than men, the gender gap is closing. Women are now getting involved in some high-profile violent crimes. American Nancy Kissel, 41, is seen arriving at Hong Kong's High Court during her lengthy murder trial. Kissel was found guilty on September 1, 2005, of murdering her husband, a Merrill Lynch investment banker, and sentenced to life imprisonment. Kissel served her husband a milkshake laced with sedatives and then battered him to death with a lead ornament. She then wrapped him up in a carpet and tried to conceal the corpse for several days.

SOCIALIZATION AND DEVELOPMENT Although there are few gender-based differences in aggression during the first few years of life, girls are socialized to be less aggressive than boys and are supervised more closely by parents.[94] Differences in aggression become noticeable between the ages of 3 and 6 when children are first socialized into organized peer groups such as the daycare center or school. Males are more likely then to display physical aggression while girls display relational aggression—excluding disliked peers from play groups, gossiping, and interfering with social relationships.

Males are taught to be more aggressive and assertive and less likely to form attachments to others. They often view their aggression as a gender-appropriate means to gain status and power, either by joining deviant groups and gangs or engaging in sports. Even in the middle-class suburbs, they may seek approval by knocking down or running through peers on the playing field, while females literally cheer them on. The male search for social approval through aggressive behavior may make them more susceptible to criminality, especially when the chosen form of aggression is antisocial or illegal. Recent research by Jean Bottcher found that young boys perceive their roles as being more dominant than young girls.[95] Male perceptions of power, their ability to have freedom and hang with their friends, helped explain the gender differences in crime and delinquency.

In contrast, girls are encouraged to care about other people and avoid harming them; their need for sensitivity and understanding may help counterbalance the effects of poverty and family problems. And because they are more verbally proficient, many females may develop social skills that help them deal with conflict without resorting to violence. Females are taught to be less aggressive and to view belligerence as a lack of self-control—a conclusion that is unlikely to be reached by a male.

Girls are usually taught—directly or indirectly—to respond to provocation by feeling anxious and depressed, whereas boys are encouraged to retaliate. Overall, when they are provoked, females are much more likely to feel distressed than males—experiencing sadness, anxiety, and uneasiness. Although females may get angry as often as males, many have been taught to blame themselves for harboring such negative feelings. Females are therefore much more likely than males to respond to anger with feelings of depression, anxiety, fear,

and shame. Although females are socialized to fear that their anger will harm valued relationships, males react with "moral outrage," looking to blame others for their discomfort.[96]

COGNITIVE DIFFERENCES Psychologists note significant cognitive differences between boys and girls that may impact on their antisocial behaviors. Girls have been found to be superior to boys in verbal ability, while boys test higher in visual-spatial performance. Girls acquire language faster, learning to speak earlier and with better pronunciation. Girls are far less likely to have reading problems than boys, while boys do much better on standardized math tests. (This difference is attributed by some experts to boys receiving more attention from math teachers.) In most cases these cognitive differences are small, narrowing, and usually attributed to cultural expectations. When given training, girls demonstrate an ability to increase their visual-spatial skills to the point that their abilities become indistinguishable from the ability of boys.

Cognitive differences may contribute to behavioral variations. Even at an early age, girls are found to be more empathic than boys, that is, more capable of understanding and relating to the feelings of others.[97] Empathy for others may help shield girls from antisocial acts because they are more likely to understand a victim's suffering. Girls are more concerned with relationship and feeling issues, and they are less interested than boys in competing for material success. Boys who are not tough and aggressive are labeled sissies and cry babies. In contrast, girls are given different messages; they are expected to form closer bonds with their friends and to share feelings.

FEMINIST VIEWS In the 1970s **liberal feminist theory** focused attention on the social and economic role of women in society and its relationship to female crime rates.[98] This view suggested that the traditionally lower crime rate for women could be explained by their "second-class" economic and social position. As women's social roles changed and their lifestyles became more like men's, it was believed that their crime rates would converge.

> To read about the history and nature of the women's movement in the United States, go to InfoTrac College Edition and use "liberal feminism" as a subject guide.

Criminologists, responding to this research, began to refer to the "new female criminal." The rapid increase in the female crime rate, especially in what had traditionally been male-oriented crimes (such as burglary and larceny), supports the feminist view. In addition, self-report studies seem to indicate that (1) the pattern of female criminality, if not its frequency, is similar to that of male criminality; and (2) the factors that predispose male criminals to crime have an equal impact on female criminals.[99]

| | | | | | | CONNECTIONS | | | | | | |

Critical criminologists view gender inequality as stemming from the unequal power of men and women in a capitalist society and the exploitation of females by fathers and husbands. This perspective is considered more fully in Chapter 8.

IS CONVERGENCE LIKELY? Although male arrest rates are still considerably higher than female rates, female arrest rates seem to be increasing at a faster pace; it is possible that they may eventually converge. Between 1993 and 2003 the male arrest rate actually declined by about 6 percent while the female rate actually increased by 14 percent. Women are getting involved in serious violent crimes.[100] Young girls are joining gangs in record numbers.[101]

While these trends indicate that gender differences in the crime rate may be eroding, some criminologists remain skeptical about the data. They find that gender-based crime rate differences are still significant; the "emancipation of women" may have had relatively little influence on female crime rates.[102] For one thing, many female criminals come from the socioeconomic class least affected by the women's movement; their crimes seem more a function of economic inequality than women's rights. For another, the offense patterns of women are still quite different from those of men. While males commit a disproportionate share of serious crimes such as robbery, burglary, murder, and assault, most female criminals are engaging in petty property crimes such as welfare and credit card fraud and public order crimes such as prostitution.[103] How then can increases in female arrest rates be explained? According to Darrell Steffensmeier and his associates, these arrest trends may be explained more by changes in police activity than in criminal activity: Police today may be more willing to arrest girls for minor crimes; they are making more arrests for crimes that occur at school and in the home; and they are responding more vigorously to public demands for action and therefore are less likely to use their discretion to help females.[104] Police may also be abandoning their traditional deference toward women in an effort to be "gender neutral." In addition, changing laws such as dual arrest laws in domestic cases, which mandate both parties be taken into custody, result in more women suffering arrest in domestic incidents.[105]

Race and Crime

Official crime data indicate that minority group members are involved in a disproportionate share of criminal activity. African Americans make up about 12 percent of the general population, yet they account for about 38 percent of Part I violent crime arrests and 30 percent of property crime arrests. They also are responsible for a disproportionate number of Part II arrests (except for alcohol-related arrests, which detain primarily white offenders).

It is possible that these data reflect true racial differences in the crime rate, but it is also likely that they reflect bias in the justice process. We can evaluate this issue by comparing racial differences in self-report data with those found in official delinquency records. Charges of racial discrimination in the justice process would be substantiated if whites and blacks self-reported equal numbers of crimes, but minorities were arrested and prosecuted far more often.

Early efforts by noted criminologists Leroy Gould in Seattle, Harwin Voss in Honolulu, and Ronald Akers in seven midwestern states found virtually no relationship between race and self-reported delinquency.[106] These research efforts supported a case for police bias in the arrest decision. Other, more recent self-report studies that use large national samples of youths have also found little evidence of racial disparity in crimes committed. One effort conducted by the Institute for Social Research at the University of Michigan found that, if anything, black youths self-report less delinquent behavior and substance abuse than whites.[107] Another nationwide study of youth, conducted by social scientists at the Behavioral Science Institute at Boulder, Colorado, found few interracial differences in crime rates, although black youths were much more likely to be arrested and taken into custody.[108] These and other self-report studies seem to indicate that the delinquent behavior rates of black and white teenagers are generally similar and that differences in arrest statistics may indicate a differential selection policy by police.[109] Suspects who are poor, minority, and male are more likely to be formally arrested than suspects who are white, affluent, and female.[110]

Racial differences in the crime rate remain an extremely sensitive issue. Although official arrest records indicate that African Americans are arrested at a higher rate than members of other racial groups, self-report data suggest that these differences are an artifact of justice system bias.[111] Some critics charge that police officers routinely use racial profiling to stop African Americans and search their cars without probable cause or reasonable suspicion. Police officers, they glibly suggest, have created a new form of traffic offense called DWB, "driving while black."[112] Findings from a national survey of driving practices show that young black and Latino males are more likely to be stopped by police and suffer citations, searches, and arrests, as well as be the target of force even though they are no more likely to be in the possession of illegal contraband than white drivers.[113] This view is not lost on the minority community.

Although the official statistics, such as UCR arrest data, may reflect discriminatory justice system practices, African Americans are arrested for a disproportionate amount of serious violent crime, such as robbery and murder. It is improbable that police discretion and/or bias alone could account for these proportions. It is doubtful that police routinely release white killers, robbers, and rapists while arresting violent black offenders who commit the same offenses.[114] How can these racial differences in serious crimes be explained?

RACISM AND DISCRIMINATION To explain racial and ethnic differences in the violent crime rate, criminologists focus on the impact of economic deprivation and the legacy of racism discrimination on personality and behavior.[115] The fact that U.S. culture influences African American crime rates is underscored by the fact that black violence rates are much lower in other nations—both those that are predominantly white, such as Canada, and those that are predominantly black, such as Nigeria.[116]

Some criminologists view black crime as a function of socialization in a society where the black family was torn apart and black culture destroyed in such a way that recovery has proven impossible. Early experiences, beginning with slavery, have left a wound that has been deepened by racism and lack of opportunity.[117] Children of the slave society were thrust into a system of forced dependency and ambivalence and antagonism toward one's self and group.

In an important work, *All God's Children: The Bosket Family and the American Tradition of Violence,* crime reporter Fox Butterfield chronicles the history of the Boskets, a black family, through five generations.[118] He focuses on Willie Bosket, who is charming, captivating, and brilliant. He is also one of the worst criminals in the New York State penal system. By the time he was in his teens, he had committed more than 200 armed robberies and 25 stabbings. Butterfield shows how early struggles in the South, with its violent slave culture, led directly to Willie Bosket's rage and violence on the streets of New York City. Beginning in South Carolina in the 1700s, the southern slave society was a place where white notions of honor demanded immediate retaliation for the smallest slight. According to Butterfield, contemporary black violence is a tradition inherited from white southern violence. The need for respect has turned into a cultural mandate that can provoke retaliation at the slightest hint of insult.

INSTITUTIONAL RACISM Racism is still an element of daily life in the African American community, a factor that undermines faith in social and political institutions and weakens confidence in the justice system. Such fears are supported by empirical evidence that, at least in some jurisdictions, young African American males are treated more harshly by the criminal and juvenile justice systems than are members of any other group.[119]

Empirical evidence shows that, in at least some jurisdictions, young African American males are treated more harshly by the criminal and juvenile justice systems than are members of any other group. Elements of institutional racism have become so endemic that terms such as "DWB" (Driving While Black) are now part of the vernacular, used to signify the fact that young African American motorists are routinely stopped by police.

Research shows that blacks and Latinos are less likely to receive bail in violent crime cases than whites.[120] There is also evidence that African Americans, especially those who are indigent or unemployed, receive longer prison sentences than whites with the same employment status. It is possible that judges impose harsher punishments on unemployed African Americans because they view them as "social dynamite," considering them more dangerous and more likely to recidivate than white offenders.[121] Yet when African Americans are victims of crime, their predicaments receive less public concern and media attention than that afforded white victims.[122] Murders involving whites (and females) are much more likely to be punished with death than those whose victims are black males, a fact not lost on the minority population.[123]

In his book *Search and Destroy*, correctional reformer Jerome Miller spells out how millions of young African Americans acquire a criminal record each year because police officers abuse their authority. Miller argues that conservative politicians complain about providing welfare because they believe government should stay out of people's lives, but they do not mind the traumatic intrusion to the black community being made by agents of the criminal justice system who seem bent on "identifying and managing unruly groups."[124] Differential enforcement practices take their toll on the black community. A national survey found that more that 13 percent of all African American males have lost the right to vote, that in seven states 25 percent have been disenfranchised, and in two states, Florida and Alabama, 33 percent of black males have lost their voting privileges.[125] It is not surprising then that African Americans of all social classes hold negative attitudes toward the justice system and view it as an arbitrary and unfair institution.[126]

ECONOMIC AND SOCIAL DISPARITY Racial and ethnic differentials in crime rates may also be tied to economic and social disparity. Racial and ethnic minorities are often forced to live in high crime areas where the risk of victimization is significant. People who witness violent crime and are victimized may themselves engage in violence.[127]

Racial and ethnic minorities face a greater degree of social isolation and economic deprivation than the white majority, a condition that has been linked by empirical research to high violence rates.[128] Not helping the situation is the fact that during tough economic times, whites may find themselves competing against minorities for shrinking job opportunities. As economic competition between the races grows, interracial homicides do likewise; economic and political rivalries lead to greater levels of interracial violence.[129]

Even during times of economic growth, lower-class African Americans are left out of the economic mainstream, a fact that meets with a growing sense of frustration and failure.[130] As a result of being shut out of educational and economic opportunities enjoyed by the rest of society, this population may be vulnerable to the lure of illegitimate gain and criminality. African Americans living in lower-class inner-city areas may be disproportionately violent because they are exposed to more violence in their daily lives than other racial and economic groups. This exposure is a significant risk factor for violent behavior.[131]

| | | | | | | CONNECTIONS | | | | | | |

The concept of relative deprivation refers to the fact that people compare their success to those with whom they are in immediate contact. Even if conditions improve, they still may feel as if they are falling behind. A sense of relative deprivation, discussed in Chapter 6, may lead to criminal activity.

FAMILY DISSOLUTION Family dissolution in the minority community may be tied to low employment rates among African American males, which places a strain on marriages. The relatively large number of single, female-headed households in these communities may also be a result of the high mortality rate among African American males due in part to their increased risk of early death by disease and violence.[132] When families are weakened or disrupted, their social control is compromised. It is not surprising, then, that divorce and separation rates are significantly associated with homicide rates in the African American community.[133]

| | | | | | | CONNECTIONS | | | | | | |

According to some criminologists, racism has created isolated subcultures that espouse violence as a way of coping with conflict situations. Exasperation and frustration among minority group members who feel powerless to fit into middle-class society are manifested in aggression. This view is discussed further in Chapter 10, which reviews the subculture of violence theory.

IS CONVERGENCE POSSIBLE? Considering these overwhelming social problems, is it possible that racial crime rates will soon converge? One argument is that if economic conditions improve in the minority community, then differences in crime rates will eventually disappear.[134] A trend toward residential integration, underway since 1980, may also help reduce crime rate differentials.[135] Convergence in crime rates will occur if economic and social obstacles can be removed.

In sum, the weight of the evidence shows that although there is little difference in the self-reported crime rates of racial groups, Latinos and African Americans are more likely to be arrested for serious violent crimes. The causes of minority crime have been linked to poverty, racism, hopelessness, lack of opportunity, and urban problems experienced by all too many minority citizens.

Chronic Offenders/Criminal Careers

Crime data show that most offenders commit a single criminal act and upon arrest discontinue their antisocial activity. Others commit a few less serious crimes. A small group of criminal offenders, however, account for a majority of all criminal offenses. These persistent offenders are referred to as **career criminals** or **chronic offenders.** The concept of the chronic or career offender is most closely associated with the research efforts of Marvin Wolfgang, Robert Figlio, and Thorsten Sellin.[136] In their landmark 1972 study, *Delinquency in a Birth Cohort,* they used official records to follow the criminal careers of a cohort of 9,945 boys born in Philadelphia in 1945 from the time of their birth until they reached 18 years of age in 1963. Official police records were used to identify delinquents. About one-third of the boys (3,475) had some police contact. The remaining two-thirds (6,470) had none. Each delinquent was given a seriousness weight score for every delinquent act.[137] The weighting of delinquent acts allowed the researchers to differentiate, between a simple assault requiring no medical attention for the victim and serious battery in which the victim needed hospitalization. The best-known discovery of Wolfgang and his associates was that of the so-called chronic offender. The cohort data indicated that 54 percent (1,862) of the sample's delinquent youths were repeat offenders, whereas the remaining 46 percent (1,613) were one-time offenders. The repeaters could be further categorized as nonchronic recidivists and chronic recidivists. The former consisted of 1,235 youths who had been arrested more than once but fewer than five times and who made up 35.6 percent of all delinquents. The latter were a group of 627 boys arrested five times or more, who accounted for 18 percent of the delinquents and 6 percent of the total sample of 9,945.

The chronic offenders (known today as "the chronic 6 percent") were involved in the most dramatic amounts of delinquent behavior: They were responsible for 5,305 offenses, or 51.9 percent of all the offenses committed by the cohort. Even more striking was the involvement of chronic offenders in serious criminal acts. Of the entire sample, the chronic 6 percent committed 71 percent of the homicides, 73 percent of the rapes, 82 percent of the robberies, and 69 percent of the aggravated assaults.

Wolfgang and his associates found that arrests and court experience did little to deter the chronic offender. In fact, punishment was inversely related to chronic offending: The more stringent the sanction chronic offenders received, the more likely they would be to engage in repeated criminal behavior.

In a second cohort study, Wolfgang and his associates selected a new, larger birth cohort, born in Philadelphia in 1958, which contained both male and female subjects.[138] Although the proportion of delinquent youths was about the same as that in the 1945 cohort, they again found a similar pattern of chronic offending. Chronic female delinquency was relatively rare—only 1 percent of the females in the survey were chronic offenders. Wolfgang's pioneering effort to identify the chronic career offender has been replicated by a number of other researchers in a variety of locations in the United States.[139] The chronic offender has also been found abroad.[140]

WHAT CAUSES CHRONICITY?

As might be expected, kids who have been exposed to a variety of personal and social problems at an early age are the most at risk to repeat

---

EXHIBIT 2.2

Characteristics that Predict Chronic Offending

School Behavior/Performance Factor

- Attendance problems (truancy or a pattern of skipping school)
- Behavior problems (recent suspensions or expulsion)
- Poor grades (failing two or more classes)

Family Problem Factor

- Poor parental supervision and control
- Significant family problems (illness, substance abuse, discord)
- Criminal family members
- Documented child abuse, neglect, or family violence

Substance Abuse Factor

- Alcohol or drug use (by minors in any way but experimentation)

Delinquency Factor

- Stealing pattern of behavior
- Runaway pattern of behavior
- Gang member or associate

Source: Michael Schumacher and Gwen Kurz, *The 8% Solution: Preventing Serious Repeat Juvenile Crime* (Thousand Oaks, CA: Sage, 1999).

---

offending; a concept referred to as **early onset.** One important study of delinquent offenders in Orange County, California, conducted by Michael Schumacher and Gwen Kurz, found several factors (see Exhibit 2.2) that characterized the chronic offender, including problems in the home and at school.[141] Other research studies have found that involvement in criminal activity (getting arrested before age 15), relatively low intellectual development, and parental drug involvement were key predictive factors for chronicity.[142]

IIIIIII CONNECTIONS IIIIIII

It is evident that chronic offenders suffer from a profusion of social problems. Some criminologists believe that accumulating a significant variety of these social deficits is the key to understanding criminal development. For more on this topic, see the discussion on problem behavior syndrome in Chapter 9.

PERSISTENCE: THE CONTINUITY OF CRIME One of the most important findings from the cohort studies is that persistent juvenile offenders are the ones most likely to continue their criminal careers into adulthood.[143] Paul Tracy and Kimberly Kempf-Leonard followed up all subjects in the second 1958 cohort and found that two-thirds of delinquent offenders desisted from crime, but those who started their delinquent careers early and who committed serious violent crimes throughout adolescence were the most likely to persist as adults.[144] This phenomenon is referred to as **persistence** or the **continuity of crime**.[145]

Children who are found to be disruptive and antisocial as early as age 5 or 6 are the most likely to exhibit stable, long-term patterns of disruptive behavior throughout adolescence.[146] They have measurable behavior problems in areas such as learning and motor skills, cognitive abilities, family relations, and other areas of social, psychological, and physical functioning.[147] Youthful offenders who persist are more likely to abuse alcohol, get into trouble while in military service, become economically dependent, have lower aspirations, get divorced or separated, and have a weak employment record.[148] They do not specialize in one type of crime; rather, they engage in a variety of criminal acts, including theft, use of drugs, and violent offenses.

IMPLICATIONS OF THE CHRONIC OFFENDER CONCEPT

The findings of the cohort studies are quite important for criminological theory. If relatively few offenders become chronic, persistent criminals, then perhaps they possess some individual trait that is responsible for their behavior. Most people, even those who commit crime, exposed to troublesome social conditions, such as poverty, do not become chronic offenders, so it is unlikely that social conditions alone can cause chronic offending. Traditional theories of criminal behavior have failed to distinguish between chronic and occasional offenders. They concentrate more on explaining why people begin to commit crime and pay scant attention to why people stop offending. The discovery of the chronic offender thirty years ago forced criminologists to consider such issues as persistence and desistance in their explanations of crime; more recent theories account for not only the onset of criminality but also its termination.

The chronic offender has become a central focus of crime control policy. Apprehension and punishment seems to have little effect on the offending behavior of chronic offenders, and most repeat their criminal acts after their correctional release.[149] Because chronic offenders rarely learn from their mistakes, sentencing policies designed to incapacitate chronic offenders for long periods of time without hope of probation or parole have been established. Incapacitation rather than rehabilitation is the goal. Among the policies spurred by the chronic offender concept are mandatory sentences for violent or drug-related crimes; **"three strikes"** policies, which require people convicted of a third felony offense to serve a mandatory life sentence; and "truth in sentencing" polices, which require that convicted felons spend a significant portion of their sentence behind bars. Whether such policies can reduce crime rates or are merely "get tough" measures designed to placate voters concerned about crime remains to be seen.

SUMMARY

- Criminologists use various research methods to gather information that will shed light on criminal behavior. These include official record studies, surveys, cohort studies, experiments, observations, meta-analysis and systematic reviews.

- The FBI's Uniform Crime Report is an annual tally of crime reported to local police departments. It is the nation's official crime database.

- The National Crime Victimization Survey (NCVS) samples more than 50,000 people annually in order to estimate the total number of criminal incidents, including those not reported to police.

- Self-report surveys ask respondents about their own criminal activity. They are useful in measuring crimes rarely reported to police, such as drug usage.

- Each data source has its strengths and weaknesses, and although different from one another, they actually agree on the nature of criminal behavior.

- Crime rates peaked in the early 1990s and have been in sharp decline ever since. The murder rate has undergone a particularly steep decline.

- A number of factors are believed to influence the crime rate, including the economy, drug use, gun availability, and crime control policies like adding police and putting more criminals in prison.

- It is difficult to gauge future trends. Some experts forecast an increase in crime, while others foresee a long-term decline in the crime rate.

- Data sources show stable patterns in the crime rate.

- Ecological patterns show that some areas of the country are more crime prone than others, that there are seasons and times for crime, and that these patterns are quite stable.

- There is also evidence of gender and age gaps in the crime rate: Men commit more crime than women, and young people commit more crime than the elderly. Crime data show that people commit less crime as they age, but the significance and cause of this pattern is not completely understood.

- Similarly, racial and class patterns appear in the crime rate. However, it is unclear whether these are true differences or a function of discriminatory law enforcement. Some criminologists suggest that institutional racism, such as police profiling, accounts for the racial differences in the crime rate. Others believe that high African American crime rates are a function of living in a racially segregated and/or biased society.

- One of the most important findings in the crime statistics is the existence of the chronic offender, a repeat criminal responsible for a significant amount of all law violations. Chronic offenders begin their careers early in life and, rather than aging out of crime, persistently offend into adulthood. The discovery of the chronic offender has led to the study of why people persist, desist, terminate, or escalate their deviant behavior.

Thinking Like a Criminologist

The planning director for the State Department of Juvenile Justice has asked for your advice on how to reduce the threat of chronic offenders. Some of the more conservative members of her staff seem to believe that these kids need a strict dose of rough justice if they are to be turned away from a life of crime. They believe juvenile delinquents who are punished harshly are less likely to recidivate than youths who receive lesser punishments, such as community corrections or probation. In addition, they believe that hardcore, violent offenders deserve to be punished; excessive concern for offenders and not their acts ignores the rights of victims and society in general.

The planning director is unsure whether such an approach can reduce the threat of chronic offending. Can tough punishment produce deviant identities that lock kids into a criminal way of life? She is concerned that a strategy stressing punishment will have relatively little impact on chronic offenders and, if anything, may cause escalation in serious criminal behaviors.

She has asked you for your professional advice. On one hand, the system must be sensitive to the adverse effects of stigma and labeling. On the other hand, the need for control and deterrence must not be ignored. Is it possible to reconcile these two opposing views?

Doing Research on the Web

To help formulate your answer to the question above, you might want to review some of these web-based resources: Eric B. Schnurer and Charles R. Lyons, "Turning Chronic Juvenile Offenders into Productive Citizens: Comprehensive Model Emerging": http://www.cnponline.org/Issue% 20Briefs/Statelines/statelin0101.htm.

For an international view, see "Juvenile Offending: Predicting Persistence and Determining the Cost-Effectiveness of Intervention": http://www.lawlink.nsw.gov.au/bocsar1.nsf/pages/r33textsection1.

Also, go to InfoTrac College Edition and use "chronic offender" in a key word search.

Uniform Crime Report (UCR) (30)
index crimes (30)
Part I crimes (30)
Part II crimes (31)
cleared crimes (31)
National Incident-Based Reporting
    System (NIBRS) (33)
sampling (33)
population (33)
cross-sectional survey (33)
self-report survey (34)

National Crime Victimization Survey
    (NCVS) (35)
victimization surveys (35)
cohort (36)
retrospective cohort study (37)
meta-analysis (38)
systematic review (38)
data mining (38)
crime mapping (38)
instrumental crimes (47)
expressive crimes (47)

aging out (52)
masculinity hypothesis (52)
chivalry hypothesis (52)
liberal feminist theory (54)
career criminals (57)
chronic offenders (57)
early onset (57)
persistence (58)
continuity of crime (58)
three strikes (58)

CRITICAL THINKING QUESTIONS

1. Would you answer honestly if a national crime survey asked you about your criminal behavior, including drinking and drug use? If not, why not? If you would not answer honestly, do you question the accuracy of self-report surveys?

2. How would you explain gender differences in the crime rate? Why do you think males are more violent than females?

3. Assuming that males are more violent than females, does that mean crime has a biological rather than a social basis (because males and females share a similar environment)?

4. The UCR reports that crime rates are higher in large cities than in small towns. What does that tell us about the effects of TV, films, and music on teenage behavior?

5. What social and environmental factors do you believe influence the crime rate? Do you think a national emergency would increase or decrease crime rights?

NOTES

1. Information on the Rudolph case can be obtained at http://www.cnn.com/2003/US/05/31/rudolph.arrest.

2. Cited on http://en.wikipedia.org/wiki/Eric_Rudolph. Accessed August 17, 2005.

3. Federal Bureau of Investigation, *Crime in the United States, 2004* (Washington, DC: U.S. Government Printing Office, 2005).

4. Richard Felson, Steven Messner, Anthony Hoskin, and Glenn Deane, "Reasons for Reporting and Not Reporting Domestic Violence to the Police," *Criminology* 40 (2002): 617–648.

5. Shannan Catalano, *Criminal Victimization: 2004* (Washington, DC: Bureau of Justice Statistics, 2005). Herein cited as NCVS, 2004.

6. Duncan Chappell, Gilbert Geis, Stephen Schafer, and Larry Siegel, "Forcible Rape: A Comparative Study of Offenses Known to the Police in Boston and Los Angeles," in *Studies in the Sociology of Sex,* ed. James Henslin (New York: Appleton Century Crofts, 1971), pp. 169–193.

7. Patrick Jackson, "Assessing the Validity of Official Data on Arson," *Criminology* 26 (1988): 181–195.

8. Lawrence Sherman and Barry Glick, "The Quality of Arrest Statistics," *Police Foundation Reports* 2 (1984): 1–8.

9. David Seidman and Michael Couzens, "Getting the Crime Rate Down: Political Pressure and Crime Reporting," *Law and Society Review* 8 (1974): 457.

10. Ariel Hart, "Report Finds Atlanta Police Cut Figures on Crimes," *New York Times,* 21 February 2004, p. A3.

11. Robert Davis and Bruce Taylor, "A Proactive Response to Family Violence: The Results of a Randomized Experiment," *Criminology* 35 (1997): 307–333.

12. Robert O'Brien, "Police Productivity and Crime Rates: 1973–1992," *Criminology* 34 (1996): 183–207.

13. Leonard Savitz, "Official Statistics," in *Contemporary Criminology,* eds. Leonard Savitz and Norman Johnston (New York: Wiley, 1982), pp. 3–15.

14. FBI, *UCR Handbook* (Washington, DC: U.S. Government Printing Office, 1998), p. 33.

15. Lynn Addington, "The Effect of NIBRS Reporting on item Missing Data in Murder Cases," *Homicide Studies* 8 (2004): 193–213.

16. Michael Gottfredson and Travis Hirschi, "The Methodological Adequacy of Longitudinal Research on Crime," *Criminology* 25 (1987): 581–614.

17. A pioneering effort in self-report research is A. L. Porterfield, *Youth in Trouble* (Fort Worth, TX: Leo Potishman Foundation, 1946); for a review, see Robert Hardt and George Bodine, *Development of Self-Report Instruments in Delinquency Research: A Conference Report* (Syracuse, NY: Syracuse University Youth Development Center, 1965). See also Fred Murphy, Mary Shirley, and Helen Witner, "The Incidence of Hidden Delinquency," *American Journal of Orthopsychology* 16 (1946): 686–696.

18. See John Paul Wright and Francis Cullen, "Juvenile Involvement in Occupational Delinquency," *Criminology* 38 (2000): 863–896.

19. Christiane Brems, Mark Johnson, David Neal, and Melinda Freemon, "Childhood Abuse History and Substance Use among Men and Women Receiving Detoxification Services," *American Journal of Drug & Alcohol Abuse* 30 (2004): 799–821.

20. Lloyd Johnston, Patrick O'Malley, and Jerald Bachman, *Monitoring the Future, 1990* (Ann Arbor, MI: Institute for Social Research, 1991); Timothy Flanagan and Kathleen Maguire, *Sourcebook of Criminal Justice Statistics, 1989* (Washington, DC: U.S. Government Printing Office, 1990), pp. 290–291.

21. D. Wayne Osgood, Lloyd Johnston, Patrick O'Malley, and Jerald Bachman, "The Generality of Deviance in Late Adolescence and Early Adulthood," *American Sociological Review* 53 (1988): 81–93.

22. Leonore Simon, "Validity and Reliability of Violent Juveniles: A Comparison of Juvenile Self-Reports with Adult Self-Reports Incarcerated in Adult Prisons." Paper presented at the annual meeting of the American Society of Criminology, Boston, November 1995, p. 26.

23. Stephen Cernkovich, Peggy Giordano, and Meredith Pugh, "Chronic Offenders: The Missing Cases in Self-Report Delinquency Research," *Journal of Criminal Law and Criminology* 76 (1985): 705–732.

24. Terence Thornberry, Beth Bjerregaard, and William Miles, "The Consequences of Respondent Attrition in Panel Studies: A Simulation Based on the Rochester Youth Development Study," *Journal of Quantitative Criminology* 9 (1993): 127–158.

25. Julia Yun Soo Kim, Michael Fendrich, and Joseph S. Wislar, "The Validity of Juvenile Arrestees' Drug Use Reporting: A Gender Comparison," *Journal of Research in Crime and Delinquency* 37 (2000): 419–432.

26. See Spencer Rathus and Larry Siegel, "Crime and Personality Revisited: Effects of MMPI Sets on Self-Report Studies," *Criminology* 18 (1980): 245–251; John Clark and Larry Tifft, "Polygraph and Interview Validation of Self-Reported Deviant Behavior," *American Sociological Review* 31 (1966): 516–523.

27. Mallie Paschall, Miriam Ornstein, and Robert Flewelling, "African-American Male Adolescents' Involvement in the Criminal Justice System: The Criterion Validity of Self-Report Measures in Prospective Study," *Journal of Research in Crime and Delinquency* 38 (2001): 174–187.

28. Jennifer Roberts, Edward Mulvey, Julie Horney, John Lewis, and Michael Arter, "A Test of Two Methods of Recall for Violent Events," *Journal of Quantitative Criminology* 21 (2005): 175–193.

29. Lila Kazemian and David Farrington, "Comparing the Validity of Prospective, Retrospective, and Official Onset for Different Offending Categories," *Journal of Quantitative Criminology* 21 (2005): 127–147.

30. Shannan Catalano, *Criminal Victimization 2004* (Washington, DC: Bureau of Justice Statistics, 2005). Data in this section come from this report.

31. L. Edward Wells and Joseph Rankin, "Juvenile Victimization: Convergent Validation of Alternative Measurements," *Journal of Research in Crime and Delinquency* 32 (1995): 287–307.

32. Barbara Warner and Brandi Wilson Coomer, "Neighborhood Drug Arrest Rates: Are They a Meaningful Indicator of Drug Activity? A Research Note," *Journal of Research in Crime and Delinquency* 40 (2003): 123–139.

33. Alfred Blumstein, Jacqueline Cohen, and Richard Rosenfeld, "Trend and Deviation in Crime Rates: A Comparison of UCR and NCVS Data for Burglary and Robbery," *Criminology* 29 (1991): 237–248. See also Michael Hindelang, Travis Hirschi, and Joseph Weis, *Measuring Delinquency* (Beverly Hills: Sage, 1981).

34. See, generally, David Farrington, Lloyd Ohlin, and James Q. Wilson, *Understanding and Controlling Crime* (New York: Springer-Verlag, 1986), pp. 11–18.

35. Claire Sterk-Elifson, "Just for Fun? Cocaine Use among Middle-Class Women," *Journal of Drug Issues* 26 (1996): 63–76.

36. Ibid., p. 63.

37. William F. Whyte, *Street Corner Society* (Chicago: University of Chicago Press, 1955).

38. Herman Schwendinger and Julia Schwendinger, *Adolescent Subcultures and Delinquency* (New York: Praeger, 1985).

39. David Farrington and Brandon Welsh, "Improved Street Lighting and Crime Prevention," *Justice Quarterly* 19 (2002): 313–343.

40. Colleen McCue, Emily Stone, and Teresa Gooch, "Data Mining and Value-Added Analysis," *FBI Law Enforcement Bulletin* 72 (2003): 1–6.

41. Jerry Ratcliffe, "Aoristic Signatures and the Spatio-Temporal Analysis of High Volume Crime Patterns," *Journal of Quantitative Criminology* 18 (2002): 23–43.

42. Clarence Schrag, *Crime and Justice: American Style* (Washington, DC: U.S. Government Printing Office, 1971), p. 17.

43. Thomas Bernard, "Juvenile Crime and the Transformation of Juvenile Justice: Is There a Juvenile Crime Wave?" *Justice Quarterly* 16 (1999): 336–356.

44. James A. Fox, *Trends in Juvenile Violence: A Report to the United States Attorney General on Current and Future Rates of Juvenile Offending* (Boston: Northeastern University, 1996).

45. Steven Levitt, "The Limited Role of Changing Age Structure in Explaining Aggregate Crime Rates," *Criminology* 37 (1999): 581–599.

46. Darrell Steffensmeier and Miles Harer, "Did Crime Rise or Fall during the Reagan Presidency? The Effects of an 'Aging' U.S. Population on the Nation's Crime Rate," *Journal of Research in Crime and Delinquency* 28 (1991): 330–339.

47. Darrell Steffensmeier and Miles Harer, "Making Sense of Recent U.S. Crime Trends, 1980 to 1996/1998: Age Composition Effects and Other Explanations," *Journal of Research in Crime and Delinquency* 36 (1999): 235–274.

48. Ibid., p. 265.

49. Ralph Weisheit and L. Edward Wells, "The Future of Crime in Rural America," *Journal of Crime and Justice* 22 (1999): 1–22.

50. Ellen Cohn, "The Effect of Weather and Temporal Variations on Calls for Police Service," *American Journal of Police* 15 (1996): 23–43.

51. R. A. Baron, "Aggression as a Function of Ambient Temperature and Prior Anger Arousal," *Journal of Personality and Social Psychology* 21 (1972): 183–189.

52. Brad Bushman, Morgan Wang, and Craig Anderson, "Is the Curve Relating

Temperature to Aggression Linear or Curvilinear? Assaults and Temperature in Minneapolis Reexamined," *Journal of Personality & Social Psychology* 89 (2005): 62–66.

53. Paul Bell, "Reanalysis and Perspective in the Heat-Aggression Debate," *Journal of Personality & Social Psychology* 89 (2005): 71–73.

54. Ellen Cohn, "The Prediction of Police Calls for Service: The Influence of Weather and Temporal Variables on Rape and Domestic Violence," *Journal of Environmental Psychology* 13 (1993): 71–83.

55. John Simister and Cary Cooper, "Thermal Stress in the U.S.A.: Effects on Violence and on Employee Behaviour," *Stress and Health* 21 (2005): 3–15.

56. James Rotton and Ellen Cohn, "Outdoor Temperature, Climate Control, and Criminal Assault," *Environment & Behavior* 36 (2004): 276–306.

57. See generally Franklin Zimring and Gordon Hawkins, *Crime Is Not the Problem: Lethal Violence in America* (New York Oxford University Press, 1997).

58. Ibid., p. 36.

59. Gary Kleck and Marc Gertz, "Armed Resistance to Crime: The Prevalence and Nature of Self-Defense with a Gun," *Journal of Criminal Law and Criminology* 86 (1995): 219–249.

60. Robert Nash Parker, "Bringing 'Booze' Back In: The Relationship between Alcohol and Homicide," *Journal of Research in Crime and Delinquency* 32 (1995): 3–38.

61. Victoria Brewer and M. Dwayne Smith, "Gender Inequality and Rates of Female Homicide Victimization across U.S. Cities," *Journal of Research in Crime and Delinquency* 32 (1995): 175–190.

62. James Short and F. Ivan Nye, "Extent of Unrecorded Juvenile Delinquency, Tentative Conclusions," *Journal of Criminal Law, Criminology, and Police Science* 49 (1958): 296–302.

63. Ivan Nye, James Short, and Virgil Olsen, "Socio-Economic Status and Delinquent Behavior," *American Journal of Sociology* 63 (1958): 381–389; Robert Dentler and Lawrence Monroe, "Social Correlates of Early Adolescent Theft," *American Sociological Review* 63 (1961): 733–743. See also Terence Thornberry and Margaret Farnworth, "Social Correlates of Criminal Involvement: Further Evidence of the Relationship between Social Status and Criminal Behavior," *American Sociological Review* 47 (1982): 505–518.

64. Charles Tittle, Wayne Villemez, and Douglas Smith, "The Myth of Social Class and Criminality: An Empirical Assessment of the Empirical Evidence," *American Sociological Review* 43 (1978): 643–656.

65. Charles Tittle and Robert Meier, "Specifying the SES/Delinquency Relationship," *Criminology* 28 (1990): 271–301.

66. R. Gregory Dunaway, Francis Cullen, Velmer Burton, and T. David Evans, "The Myth of Social Class and Crime Revisited: An Examination of Class and Adult Criminality," *Criminology* 38 (2000): 589–632.

67. Delbert Elliott and Suzanne Ageton, "Reconciling Race and Class Differences in Self-Reported and Official Estimates of Delinquency," *American Sociological Review* 45 (1980): 95–110.

68. See also Delbert Elliott and David Huizinga, "Social Class and Delinquent Behavior in a National Youth Panel: 1976–1980," *Criminology* 21 (1983): 149–177. For a similar view, see John Braithwaite, "The Myth of Social Class and Criminality Reconsidered," *American Sociological Review* 46 (1981): 35–58; Hindelang, Hirschi, and Weis, *Measuring Delinquency,* p. 196.

69. David Brownfield, "Social Class and Violent Behavior," *Criminology* 24 (1986): 421–439.

70. Douglas Smith and Laura Davidson, "Interfacing Indicators and Constructs in Criminological Research: A Note on the Comparability of Self-Report Violence Data for Race and Sex Groups," *Criminology* 24 (1986): 473–488.

71. Dunaway, Cullen, Burton, and Evans, "The Myth of Social Class and Crime Revisited."

72. Lauren Krivo and Ruth D. Peterson, "Labor Market Conditions and Violent Crime among Youth and Adults," *Sociological Perspectives* 47 (2004): 485–505.

73. Judith Blau and Peter Blau, "The Cost of Inequality: Metropolitan Structure and Violent Crime," *American Sociological Review* 147 (1982): 114–129; Richard Block, "Community Environment and Violent Crime," *Criminology* 17 (1979): 46–57; Robert Sampson, "Structural Sources of Variation in Race-Age-Specific Rates of Offending across Major U.S. Cities," *Criminology* 23 (1985): 647–673.

74. Chin-Chi Hsieh and M. D. Pugh, "Poverty, Income Inequality, and Violent Crime: A Meta-Analysis of Recent Aggregate Data Studies," *Criminal Justice Review* 18 (1993): 182–199.

75. Richard Miech, Avshalom Caspi, Terrie Moffitt, Bradley Entner Wright, and Phil Silva, "Low Socioeconomic Status and Mental Disorders: A Longitudinal Study of Selection and Causation during Young Adulthood," *American Journal of Sociology* 104 (1999): 1,096–1,131; Marvin Krohn, Alan Lizotte, and Cynthia Perez, "The Interrelationship between Substance Use and Precocious Transitions to Adult Sexuality," *Journal of Health and Social Behavior* 38 (1997): 87–103, at 88; Richard Jessor, "Risk Behavior in Adolescence: A Psychosocial Framework for Understanding and Action," in *Adolescents at Risk: Medical and Social Perspectives,* eds. D. E. Rogers and E. Ginzburg (Boulder, CO: Westview, 1992).

76. Robert Agnew, "A General Strain Theory of Community Differences in Crime Rates," *Journal of Research in Crime and Delinquency* 36 (1999): 123–155.

77. Bonita Veysey and Steven Messner, "Further Testing of Social Disorganization Theory: An Elaboration of Sampson and Groves's Community Structure and Crime," *Journal of Research in Crime and Delinquency* 36 (1999): 156–174.

78. Lance Hannon and James DeFronzo, "Welfare and Property Crime," *Justice Quarterly* 15 (1998): 273–288.

79. Alan Lizotte, Terence Thornberry, Marvin Krohn, Deborah Chard-Wierschem, and David McDowall, "Neighborhood Context and Delinquency: A Longitudinal Analysis," in *Cross National Longitudinal Research on Human Development and Criminal Behavior,* eds. E. M. Weitekamp and H. J. Kerner (Stavernstr, Netherlands: Kluwer, 1994), pp. 217–227.

80. Travis Hirschi and Michael Gottfredson, "Age and the Explanation of Crime," *American Journal of Sociology* 89 (1983): 552–584, at 581.

81. Darrell Steffensmeier and Cathy Streifel, "Age, Gender, and Crime across Three Historical Periods: 1935, 1960 and 1985," *Social Forces* 69 (1991): 869–894.

82. For a comprehensive review of crime and the elderly, see Kyle Kercher,

"Causes and Correlates of Crime Committed by the Elderly," in *Critical Issues in Aging Policy,* eds. E. Borgatta and R. Montgomery (Beverly Hills: Sage, 1987), pp. 254–306; Darrell Steffensmeier, "The Invention of the 'New' Senior Citizen Criminal," *Research on Aging* 9 (1987): 281–311.

83. Hirschi and Gottfredson, "Age and the Explanation of Crime."

84. Robert Agnew, "An Integrated Theory of the Adolescent Peak in Offending," *Youth & Society* 34 (2003): 263–302.

85. Margo Wilson and Martin Daly, "Life Expectancy, Economic Inequality, Homicide, and Reproductive Timing in Chicago Neighbourhoods," *British Journal of Medicine* 314 (1997): 1,271–1,274.

86. Edward Mulvey and John LaRosa, "Delinquency Cessation and Adolescent Development: Preliminary Data," *American Journal of Orthopsychiatry* 56 (1986): 212–224.

87. James Q. Wilson and Richard Herrnstein, *Crime and Human Nature* (New York: Simon & Schuster, 1985): 126–147.

88. Ibid., p. 219.

89. Erich Labouvie, "Maturing Out of Substance Use: Selection and Self-Correction," *Journal of Drug Issues* 26 (1996): 457–474.

90. Cesare Lombroso, *The Female Offender* (New York: Appleton, 1920), p. 122.

91. Otto Pollack, *The Criminality of Women* (Philadelphia: University of Pennsylvania, 1950).

92. For a review of this issue, see Darrell Steffensmeier, "Assessing the Impact of the Women's Movement on Sex-Based Differences in the Handling of Adult Criminal Defendants," *Crime and Delinquency* 26 (1980): 344–357.

93. Alan Booth and D. Wayne Osgood, "The Influence of Testosterone on Deviance in Adulthood: Assessing and Explaining the Relationship," *Criminology* 31 (1993): 93–118.

94. This section relies on the following sources: Kristen Kling, Janet Shibley Hyde, Carolin Showers, and Brenda Buswell, "Gender Differences in Self-Esteem: A Meta Analysis," *Psychological Bulletin* 125 (1999): 470–500; Rolf Loeber and Dale Hay, "Key Issues in the Development of Aggression and Violence from Childhood to Early Adulthood," *Annual Review of Psychology* 48 (1997): 371–410; Darcy Miller, Catherine Trapani, Kathy Fejes-Mendoza, Carolyn Eggleston, and Donna Dwiggins, "Adolescent Female Offenders: Unique Considerations," *Adolescence* 30 (1995): 429–435; John Mirowsky and Catherine Ross, "Sex Differences in Distress: Real or Artifact?" *American Sociological Review* 60 (1995): 449–468; Anne Campbell, *Men, Women and Aggression* (New York: Basic Books, 1993); Ann Beutel and Margaret Mooney Marini, "Gender and Values," *American Sociological Review* 60 (1995): 436–448; John Gibbs, Velmer Burton, Francis Cullen, T. David Evans, Leanne Fiftal Alarid, and R. Gregory Dunaway, "Gender, Self-Control, and Crime," *Journal of Research in Crime and Delinquency* 35 (1998): 123–147; David Rowe, Alexander Vazsonyi, and Daniel Flannery, "Sex Differences in Crime: Do Means and Within-Sex Variation Have Similar Causes?" *Journal of Research in Crime and Delinquency* 32 (1995): 84–100.

95. Jean Bottcher, "Social Practices of Gender: How Gender Relates to Delinquency in the Everyday Lives of High-Risk Youths," *Criminology* 39 (2001): 893–932

96. Daniel Mears, Matthew Ploeger, and Mark Warr, "Explaining the Gender Gap in Delinquency: Peer Influence and Moral Evaluations of Behavior," *Journal of Research in Crime and Delinquency* 35 (1998): 251–266.

97. Lisa Broidy, Elizabeth Cauffman, and Dorothy Espelage,"Sex Differences in Empathy and Its Relation to Juvenile Offending," *Violence and Victims* 18 (2003): 503–516.

98. Freda Adler, *Sisters in Crime* (New York: McGraw-Hill, 1975); Rita James Simon, *The Contemporary Woman and Crime* (Washington, DC: U.S. Government Printing Office, 1975).

99. David Rowe, Alexander Vazsonyi, and Daniel Flannery, "Sex Differences in Crime: Do Mean and Within-Sex Variation Have Similar Causes?" *Journal of Research in Crime and Delinquency* 32 (1995): 84–100; Michael Hindelang, "Age, Sex, and the Versatility of Delinquency Involvements," *Social Forces* 14 (1971): 525–534; Martin Gold, *Delinquent Behavior in an American City* (Belmont, CA: Brooks/Cole, 1970); Gary Jensen and Raymond Eve, "Sex Differences in Delinquency: An Examination of Popular Sociological Explanations," *Criminology* 13 (1976): 427–448.

100. Knut Steen and Steinar Hunskaar, "Gender and Physical Violence," *Social Science & Medicine* 59 (2004): 567–571.

101. Finn-Aage Esbensen and Elizabeth Piper Deschenes, "A Multisite Examination of Youth Gang Membership: Does Gender Matter?" *Criminology* 36 (1998): 799–828.

102. Darrell Steffensmeier and Renee Hoffman Steffensmeier, "Trends in Female Delinquency," *Criminology* 18 (1980): 62–85; see also Darrell Steffensmeier and Renee Hoffman Steffensmeier, "Crime and the Contemporary Woman: An Analysis of Changing Levels of Female Property Crime, 1960–1975," *Social Forces* 57 (1978): 566–584; Joseph Weis, "Liberation and Crime: The Invention of the New Female Criminal," *Crime and Social Justice* 1 (1976): 17–27; Carol Smart, "The New Female Offender: Reality or Myth," *British Journal of Criminology* 19 (1979): 50–59; Steven Box and Chris Hale, "Liberation/Emancipation, Economic Marginalization or Less Chivalry," *Criminology* 22 (1984): 473–478.

103. Anne Campbell, Steven Muncer, and Daniel Bibel, "Female–Female Criminal Assault: An Evolutionary Perspective," *Journal of Research in Crime and Delinquency* 35 (1998): 413–428.

104. Darrell Steffensmeier Jennifer Schwartz, Hua Zhong, and Jeff Ackerman, "An Assessment of Recent Trends in Girls' Violence Using Diverse Longitudinal Sources: Is the Gender Gap Closing," *Criminology* 43 (2005): 355–406.

105. Susan Miller, Carol Gregory, and Leeann Iovanni, "One Size Fits All? A Gender-Neutral Approach to a Gender-Specific Problem: Contrasting Batterer Treatment Programs for Male and Female Offenders," *Criminal Justice Policy Review* 16 (2005): 336–359.

106. Leroy Gould, "Who Defines Delinquency: A Comparison of Self-Report and Officially Reported Indices of Delinquency for Three Racial Groups," *Social Problems* 16 (1969): 325–336; Harwin Voss, "Ethnic Differentials in Delinquency in Honolulu," *Journal of Criminal Law, Criminology, and Police Science* 54 (1963): 322–327; Ronald Akers, Marvin Krohn, Marcia Radosevich, and Lonn Lanza-Kaduce, "Social Characteristics

and Self-Reported Delinquency," in *Sociology of Delinquency,* ed. Gary Jensen (Beverly Hills: Sage, 1981), pp. 48–62.

107. Institute for Social Research, *Monitoring the Future* (Ann Arbor, MI: Author, 2001).

108. David Huizinga and Delbert Elliott, "Juvenile Offenders: Prevalence, Offender Incidence, and Arrest Rates by Race," *Crime and Delinquency* 33 (1987): 206–223. See also Dale Dannefer and Russell Schutt, "Race and Juvenile Justice Processing in Court and Police Agencies," *American Journal of Sociology* 87 (1982): 1,113–1,132.

109. Paul Tracy, "Race and Class Differences in Official and Self-Reported Delinquency," in *From Boy to Man, from Delinquency to Crime,* eds. Marvin Wolfgang, Terence Thornberry, and Robert Figlio (Chicago: University of Chicago Press, 1987), p. 120.

110. Miriam Sealock and Sally Simpson, "Unraveling Bias in Arrest Decisions: The Role of Juvenile Offender Type-Scripts," *Justice Quarterly* 15 (1998): 427–457.

111. Phillipe Rushton, "Race and Crime: An International Dilemma," *Society* 32 (1995): 37–42; for a rebuttal, see Jerome Neapolitan, "Cross-National Variation in Homicides: Is Race a Factor?" *Criminology* 36 (1998): 139–156.

112. "Law Enforcement Seeks Answers to 'Racial Profiling' Complaints," *Criminal Justice Newsletter* 29 (1998): 5.

113. Robin Shepard Engel and Jennifer Calnon, "Examining the Influence of Drivers' Characteristics during Traffic Stops with Police: Results from a National Survey," *Justice Quarterly* 21 (2004): 49–90.

114. Daniel Georges-Abeyie, "Definitional Issues: Race, Ethnicity and Official Crime/Victimization Rates," in *The Criminal Justice System and Blacks,* ed. D. Georges-Abeyie (New York: Clark Boardman, 1984), p. 12; Robert Sampson, "Race and Criminal Violence: A Demographically Disaggregated Analysis of Urban Homicide," *Crime and Delinquency* 31 (1985): 47–82.

115. Barry Sample and Michael Philip, "Perspectives on Race and Crime in Research and Planning," in *The Criminal Justice System and Blacks,* ed. Georges-Abeyie, pp. 21–36.

116. Candace Kruttschnitt, "Violence by and against Women: A Comparative and Cross-National Analysis," *Violence and Victims* 8 (1994): 4.

117. James Comer, "Black Violence and Public Policy," in *American Violence and Public Policy,* ed. Lynn Curtis (New Haven: Yale University Press, 1985), pp. 63–86.

118. Fox Butterfield, *All God's Children: The Bosket Family and the American Tradition of Violence* (New York: Avon, 1996).

119. Michael Leiber and Jayne Stairs, "Race, Contexts and the Use of Intake Diversion," *Journal of Research in Crime and Delinquency* 36 (1999): 56–86; Darrell Steffensmeier, Jeffery Ulmer, and John Kramer, "The Interaction of Race, Gender, and Age in Criminal Sentencing: The Punishment Cost of Being Young, Black, and Male," *Criminology* 36 (1998): 763–798.

120. Traci Schlesinger, "Racial and Ethnic Disparity in Pretrial Criminal Processing," *Justice Quarterly* 22 (2005): 170–192.

121. Tracy Nobiling, Cassia Spohn, and Miriam DeLone, "A Tale of Two Counties: Unemployment and Sentence Severity," *Justice Quarterly* 15 (1998): 459–486.

122. Alexander Weiss and Steven Chermak, "The News Value of African-American Victims: An Examination of the Media's Presentation of Homicide," *Journal of Crime and Justice* 21 (1998): 71–84.

123. Jefferson Holcomb,. Marian Williams, and Stephen Demuth, "White Female Victims and Death Penalty Disparity Research," *Justice Quarterly* 21 (2004): 877–902.

124. Jerome Miller, *Search and Destroy: African American Males in the Criminal Justice System* (New York: Cambridge University Press, 1996), p. 226.

125. *The Sentencing Project, Losing the Vote: The Impact of Felony Disenfranchisement Laws in the United States* (Washington, DC: Sentencing Project, 1998).

126. Ronald Weitzer and Steven Tuch, "Race, Class, and Perceptions of Discrimination by the Police," *Crime and Delinquency* 45 (1999): 494–507.

127. Joanne Kaufman, "Explaining the Race/Ethnicity–Violence Relationship: Neighborhood Context and Social Psychological Processes," *Justice Quarterly* 22 (2005): 224–251.

128. Karen Parker and Patricia McCall, "Structural Conditions and Racial Homicide Patterns: A Look at the Multiple Disadvantages in Urban Areas," *Criminology* 37 (1999): 447–469.

129. David Jacobs and Katherine Woods, "Interracial Conflict and Interracial Homicide: Do Political and Economic Rivalries Explain White Killings of Blacks or Black Killings of Whites?" *American Journal of Sociology* 105 (1999): 157–190.

130. Melvin Thomas, "Race, Class and Personal Income: An Empirical Test of the Declining Significance of Race Thesis, 1968–1988," *Social Problems* 40 (1993): 328–339.

131. Mallie Paschall, Robert Flewelling, and Susan Ennett, "Racial Differences in Violent Behavior among Young Adults: Moderating and Confounding Effects," *Journal of Research in Crime and Delinquency* 35 (1998): 148–165.

132. R. Kelly Raley, "A Shortage of Marriageable Men? A Note on the Role of Cohabitation in Black-White Differences in Marriage Rates," *American Sociological Review* 61 (1996): 973–983.

133. Julie Phillips, "Variation in African-American Homicide Rates: An Assessment of Potential Explanations," *Criminology* 35 (1997): 527–559.

134. Roy Austin, "Progress toward Racial Equality and Reduction of Black Criminal Violence," *Journal of Criminal Justice* 15 (1987): 437–459.

135. Reynolds Farley and William Frey, "Changes in the Segregation of Whites from Blacks during the 1980s: Small Steps toward a More Integrated Society," *American Sociological Review* 59 (1994): 23–45.

136. Marvin Wolfgang, Robert Figlio, and Thorsten Sellin, *Delinquency in a Birth Cohort* (Chicago: University of Chicago Press, 1972).

137. See Thorsten Sellin and Marvin Wolfgang, *The Measurement of Delinquency* (New York: Wiley, 1964), p. 120.

138. Paul Tracy and Robert Figlio, "Chronic Recidivism in the 1958 Birth Cohort." Paper presented at the American Society of Criminology meeting, Toronto, October 1982; Marvin Wolfgang, "Delinquency in Two Birth Cohorts," in *Perspective Studies of Crime and Delinquency,* eds. Katherine Teilmann Van Dusen and Sarnoff Mednick (Boston: Kluwer-

Nijhoff, 1983), pp. 7–17. The following sections rely heavily on these sources.

139. Lyle Shannon, *Criminal Career Opportunity* (New York: Human Sciences Press, 1988).

140. D. J. West and David P. Farrington, *The Delinquent Way of Life* (London: Hienemann, 1977).

141. Michael Schumacher and Gwen Kurz, *The 8% Solution: Preventing Serious Repeat Juvenile Crime* (Thousand Oaks, CA: Sage, 1999).

142. Peter Jones, Philip Harris, James Fader, and Lori Grubstein, "Identifying Chronic Juvenile Offenders," *Justice Quarterly* 18 (2001): 478–507.

143. See, generally, Wolfgang, Thornberry, and Figlio, eds., *From Boy to Man, from Delinquency to Crime.*

144. Paul Tracy and Kimberly Kempf-Leonard, *Continuity and Discontinuity in Criminal Careers* (New York: Plenum Press, 1996).

145. Kimberly Kempf-Leonard, Paul Tracy, and James Howell, "Serious, Violent, and Chronic Juvenile Offenders: The Relationship of Delinquency Career Types to Adult Criminality," *Justice Quarterly* 18 (2001): 449–478.

146. R. Tremblay, R. Loeber, C. Gagnon, P. Charlebois, S. Larivee, and M. LeBlanc, "Disruptive Boys with Stable and Unstable High Fighting Behavior Patterns during Junior Elementary School," *Journal of Abnormal Child Psychology* 19 (1991): 285–300.

147. Jennifer White, Terrie Moffitt, Felton Earls, Lee Robins, and Phil Silva, "How Early Can We Tell? Predictors of Childhood Conduct Disorder and Adolescent Delinquency," *Criminology* 28 (1990): 507–535.

148. John Laub and Robert Sampson, "Unemployment, Marital Discord, and Deviant Behavior: The Long-Term Correlates of Childhood Misbehavior." Paper presented at the annual meeting of the American Society of Criminology, Baltimore, November 1990; rev. version.

149. Michael Ezell and Amy D'Unger, "Offense Specialization among Serious Youthful Offenders: A Longitudinal Analysis of a California Youth Authority Sample" (Durham, NC: Duke University, 1998, unpublished report).

CHAPTER 3

© AP/Steve Miller/Wide World Images

In 2001, the state of Connecticut was rocked when Waterbury Mayor Philip Giordano, a married father of three, was arrested for engaging in sexual relations with minors as young as 9 years old. Giordano was a highly respected officeholder who had been the Republican candidate for the U.S. Senate in the 2000 campaign (he lost to incumbent Joseph Lieberman). During an FBI investigation into city corruption, a 17-year-old girl came forward and charged that Giordano had paid her to have sex with him in his private law office and to watch him have sex with her aunt, known in the case as "Jane Doe." The teenager told state officials that from the time she was 12, Jane Doe arranged for her to have paid sexual encounters with men (including the mayor); Doe's own daughter, only 8 years old, was also involved.[1] On March 25, 2003, a federal jury convicted Giordano of violating the civil rights of the two young girls. He was also found guilty of conspiracy and of using an interstate device—a cell phone—to arrange the meetings with the girls and received a sentence of thirty-seven years in federal prison.[2]

The Giordano case is shocking because it involves a high public official. And although it is unusual for its sordidness, it is not unique or uncommon. A recent multinational survey concluded that each year in the United States 325,000 children are subjected to some form of sexual exploitation, which includes sexual abuse, prostitution, use in pornography, and molestation by adults.[3]

VICTIMS AND VICTIMIZATION

These incidents illustrate the importance of understanding the victim's role in the crime process. Criminologists who focus their attention on crime victims refer to themselves as **victimologists.** This chapter examines victims and their relationship to the criminal process. First, using available victim data, we analyze the nature and extent of victimization. We then discuss the relationship between victims and criminal offenders. During this discussion, we look at the various theories of victimization that attempt to explain the victim's role in the crime problem. Finally, we examine how society has responded to the needs of victims and discuss the special problems they still face.

PROBLEMS OF CRIME VICTIMS

The National Crime Victimization Survey (NCVS) indicates that the annual number of victimizations in the United States is about 24 million.[4] Being the target or victim of a rape, robbery, or assault is a terrible burden that can have considerable long-term consequences.[5] The costs of victimization can include such things as damaged property, pain and suffering to victims, and the involvement of the police and other agencies of the justice system. In this section we explore some of the effects of these incidents.

The mission of the **National Center for Victims of Crime** is to help victims of crime rebuild their lives: "We are dedicated to serving individuals, families, and communities harmed by crime." Visit their website at http://www.ncvc.org/ncvc/Main.aspx. For an up-to-date list of web links, go to http://cj.wadsworth.com/siegel_crimtpt9e.

Use InfoTrac College Edition to read: Julie Brienza, "Crime Victim Laws Sometimes Ignored," *Trial* 35 (May 1999): 103.

Economic Loss

When the costs of goods taken during property crimes is added to productivity losses caused by injury, pain, and emotional trauma, the cost of victimization is estimated to be in the hundreds of billions of dollars.

SYSTEM COSTS Part of the economic loss due to victimization is the cost to American taxpayers of maintaining the justice system. For example, violent crime by juveniles alone costs the United States $158 billion each year.[6] This estimate includes some of the costs incurred by federal, state, and local governments to assist victims of juvenile violence, such as medical treatment for injuries and services for victims, which amounts to about $30 billion. The remaining $128 billion is due to losses suffered by victims, such as lost wages, pain,

suffering, and reduced quality of life. Not included in these figures are the costs incurred trying to reduce juvenile violence, which include early prevention programs, services for juveniles, and the juvenile justice system.

Juvenile violence is only one part of the crime picture. If the cost of the justice system, legal costs, treatment costs, and so on are included, the total loss due to crime amounts to $450 billion annually, or about $1,800 per U.S. citizen. Crime produces social costs that must be paid by nonvictims as well. For example, each heroin addict is estimated to cost society more than $135,000 per year; an estimated half-million addicts cost society about $68 billion per year.[7]

INDIVIDUAL COSTS In addition to these societal costs, victims may suffer long-term losses in earnings and occupational attainment. Victim costs resulting from an assault are as high as $9,400, and costs are even higher for rape and arson; the average murder costs around $3 million.[8] Research by Ross Macmillan shows that Americans who suffer a violent victimization during adolescence earn about $82,000 less than nonvictims; Canadian victims earn $237,000 less. Macmillan reasons that victims bear psychological and physical ills that inhibit first their academic achievement and later their economic and professional success.[9]

System Abuse

The suffering endured by crime victims does not end when their attacker leaves the scene of the crime. They may suffer more **victimization** by the justice system.

While the crime is still fresh in their minds, victims may find that the police interrogation following the crime is handled callously, with innuendos or insinuations that they were somehow at fault. Victims have difficulty learning what is going on in the case; property is often kept for a long time as evidence and may never be returned. Some rape victims report that the treatment they receive from legal, medical, and mental health services is so destructive that they cannot help feeling "re-raped."[10] Victims may also suffer economic hardship because of wages lost while they testify in court and find that authorities are indifferent to their fear of retaliation if they cooperate in the offenders' prosecution.[11]

Long-Term Stress

Victims may suffer stress and anxiety long after the incident is over and the justice process has been forgotten. Experiencing abuse is particularly traumatic for adolescents who often suffer hostility and posttraumatic stress disorders.[12] For example, girls who were psychologically, sexually, or physically abused as children are more likely to have lower self-esteem and be more suicidal as adults than those who were not abused.[13] They are also placed at greater risk to be re-abused as adults than those who escaped childhood victimization.[14] Children who are victimized in the home are more likely to run away to escape their environment, which puts them at risk for juvenile arrest and involvement with the justice system.[15] Many who undergo traumatic sexual experiences later suffer psychological deficits such as eating disorders and mental illness and social problems such as homelessness and repeat victimization.[16] For example, a recent study of homeless women found that they were much more likely than other women to report childhood physical abuse, childhood sexual abuse, adult physical assault, previous sexual assault in adulthood, and a history of mental health problems.[17]

Stress does not end in childhood. Spousal abuse victims suffer a high prevalence of depression, **posttraumatic stress disorder** (**PTSD**—an emotional disturbance following exposure to stresses outside the range of normal human experience), anxiety disorder, and **obsessive-compulsive disorder** (an extreme preoccupation with certain thoughts and compulsive performance of certain behaviors).[18] One reason may be that abusive spouses are as likely to abuse their victims psychologically with threats and intimidation as they are to use physical force; psychological abuse can lead to depression and other long-term disabilities.[19]

Some victims are physically disabled as a result of serious wounds sustained during episodes of random violence, including a growing number who suffer paralyzing spinal cord injuries. And if victims have no insurance, the long-term effects of the crime may have devastating financial as well as emotional and physical consequences.[20] The Criminological Enterprise feature discusses the long-term effects violence has on adolescent victims.

Did you know that Australia, the United States, and other developed countries offer elementary school programs that heighten children's awareness about the possibility of abduction? To read about these and other programs on InfoTrac College Edition, use "crime victims" as a subject guide and look for the subcategory "youth—crimes against."

Fear

Many people fear crime, especially the elderly, the poor, and minority group members.[21] However, people who have suffered crime victimization remain fearful long after their wounds have healed. Even if they have escaped attack themselves, hearing about another's victimization may make people timid and cautious. For example, a recent effort to reduce gang crime and drug dealing in some of Chicago's most troubled housing projects failed to meet its objectives because residents feared retaliation from gang boys and possible loss of relationships; joining an effort to organize against crime placed them at extreme risk.[22]

Victims of violent crime are the most deeply affected, fearing a repeat of their attack. There may be a spillover effect in which victims become fearful of other forms of crime they have not yet experienced; people who have been assaulted develop fears that their house will be burglarized.[23]

Victims experience fear and suffer psychological pain long after their physical injuries have healed. Teacher Jose Rodriguez reads T-shirts designed by survivors of sexual abuse at the Denim Day in L.A. Speak-out and Rally on April 21, 2004, at the Civic Center in Los Angeles, California. The event, part of Sexual Assault Awareness Month, encourages sexual assault victims to break their silence and speak out about their experiences. Do you believe that going public about a sexual assault can assist the healing process?

Many go through a fundamental life change, viewing the world more suspiciously and as a less safe, controllable, and meaningful place. These people are more likely to suffer psychological stress for extended periods of time.[24] Crime can have devastating effects on its victims, who may take years to recover from the incident. In a moving book, *Aftermath: Violence and the Remaking of a Self,* rape victim Susan Brison recounts the difficult time she had recovering from her ordeal. The trauma disrupted her memory, cutting off events that happened before the rape from those that occurred afterward, and eliminated her ability to conceive of a happy or productive future. Although sympathizers encouraged her to forget the past, she found that confronting it could be therapeutic.[25]

Adolescent Victims of Violence

How many adolescents experience extreme physical and sexual violence, and what effect does the experience have on their lives? To answer these critical questions, Dean Kilpatrick, Benjamin Saunders, and Daniel Smith conducted interviews with 4,023 adolescents ages 12 to 17 to obtain information on their substance use, abuse, delinquency, and posttraumatic stress disorder (PTSD), as well as their experiences with sexual assault, physical assault, physically abusive punishment, and witnessing acts of violence.

Kilpatrick and his colleagues found that rates of interpersonal violence and victimization among adolescents in the United States are extremely high. Approximately 1.8 million adolescents age 12 to 17 have been sexually assaulted, and 3.9 million have been severely physically assaulted. Another 2.1 million have been punished by physical abuse. The most common form of youth victimization was witnessing violence, with approximately 8.8 million youths indicating that they had seen someone else being shot, stabbed, sexually assaulted, physically assaulted, or threatened with a weapon.

There were distinct racial and ethnic patterns in youth victimization. There is a much higher incidence of all types of victimization among black and Native American adolescents; more than half of black, Latino, and Native American adolescents had witnessed violence in their lifetime. Native American adolescents had the largest rate for sexual assault victimizations; whites and Asians reported the lowest. Native Americans, blacks, and Latinos also reported the highest rate of physical assault victimization—20 to 25 percent of each group reported experiencing at least one physical assault.

Gender also played a role in increasing the exposure to violence.

Girls were at greater risk of sexual assault than boys (13.0 percent versus 3.4 percent). Boys were at significantly greater risk of physical assault than girls (21.3 percent versus 13.4 percent). A substantial number of all adolescents (43.6 percent of boys and 35 percent of girls) reported having witnessed violence. Physically abusive punishment was similar for boys (8.5 percent) and girls (10.2 percent).

What Are the Outcomes of Abuse and Violence?

The research discovered a clear relationship between youth victimization and mental health problems and delinquent behavior. For example:

- Negative outcomes in victims of sexual assault were three to five times the rates observed in nonvictims.

- The lifetime prevalence of posttraumatic stress disorder is 8.1 percent, indicating that approximately 1.8 million adolescents had met the criteria for PTSD at some point during their lifetime.

- Girls were significantly more likely than boys to have lifetime PTSD (10.1 percent versus 6.2 percent).

- Among boys who had experienced sexual assault, 28.2 percent had PTSD at some point in their lives. The rate of lifetime PTSD among boys who had not been sexually assaulted was 5.4 percent.

- Sexually assaulted girls had a lifetime PTSD rate of 29.8 percent, compared with 7.1 percent of girls with no sexual assault history.

- Experiencing either a physical assault or physically abusive punishment was associated with a lifetime PTSD rate of 15.2 percent for boys. The rate of lifetime PTSD in boys who had not been physically assaulted or abusively punished was 3.1 percent.

- Approximately 25 percent of physically assaulted or abused adolescents reported lifetime substance abuse or dependence. Rates of substance problems among non-physically assaulted or abused adolescents were roughly 6 percent.

- The percentage of boys who were physically assaulted and had committed an index offense was 46.7 percent, compared with 9.8 percent of boys who were not assaulted. Similarly, 29.4 percent of physically assaulted girls reported having engaged in serious delinquent acts at some point in their lives, compared with 3.2 percent of nonassaulted girls.

The Kilpatrick research shows that youth between 12 and 17 are at the greatest risk of victimization by violent acts and that those who experience violent victimizations suffer significant social problems. Protecting adolescents must become a significant national priority.

Critical Thinking

1. Should people who abuse or harm adolescent children be punished more severely than those who harm adults?

2. Would you advocate the death penalty for someone who rapes an adolescent female?

 InfoTrac College Edition Research

To read more about this topic, go to InfoTrac College Edition and read the following article: Arthur H. Green, "Child Sexual Abuse: Immediate and Long-Term Effects and Intervention," *Journal of the American Academy of Child and Adolescent Psychiatry* 32 (1993): 890–902.

Source: Dean Kilpatrick, Benjamin Saunders, and Daniel Smith, *Youth Victimization: Prevalence and Implications* (Washington, DC: National Institute of Justice, 2003).

Antisocial Behavior

There is growing evidence that crime victims are more likely to commit crimes themselves. Being abused or neglected as a child increases the odds of being arrested, both as a juvenile and as an adult.[26] People, especially young males, who were physically or sexually abused are much more likely to smoke, drink, and take drugs than are nonabused youth. Incarcerated offenders report significant amounts of posttraumatic stress disorder as a result of prior victimization, which may in part explain their violent and criminal behaviors.[27]

The abuse–crime phenomenon is referred to as the **cycle of violence.**[28] Research shows that both boys and girls are more likely to engage in violent behavior if they were the target of physical abuse and were exposed to violent behavior among adults they know or live with or were exposed to weapons.[29]

 To quiz yourself on this material, go to the Criminology TPT 9e website.

THE NATURE OF VICTIMIZATION

How many crime victims are there in the United States, and what are the trends and patterns in victimization? According to the NCVS, an estimated 24 million criminal events occurred during 2003.[30]

| | | | | | | CONNECTIONS | | | | | | |

As discussed in Chapter 2, the NCVS is currently the leading source of information about the nature and extent of victimization. It employs a highly sophisticated and complex sampling methodology to collect data annually from thousands of citizens. Statistical techniques then estimate victimization rates, trends, and patterns that occur in the entire U.S. population.

The National Crime Victimization Survey (NCVS), like the Uniform Crime Report, shows that crime rates have been declining (Figure 3.1). All told, between 1993 and 2003 the violent crime victimization rate decreased 55 percent (from 50 to about 23 personal victimizations per 1,000 persons age 12 or older), and the property crime victimization rate declined 50 percent (from 319 to 163 crimes per 1,000 households). Figure 3.2 and Figure 3.3 show these decreases.

Patterns in the victimization survey findings are stable and repetitive, suggesting that victimization is not random but is a function of personal and ecological factors. The stability of these patterns allows us to make judgments about the nature of victimization; policies can then be created in an effort to reduce the victimization rate. Who are victims? Where does victimization take place? What is the

FIGURE 3.1

Declining Crime Rates, 1973–2003

On four measures of serious violent crime, the NCVS data show declines that are similar to the UCR data.

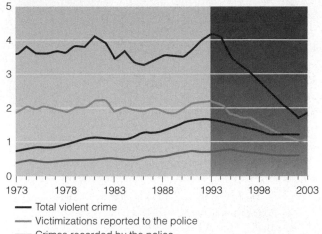

Offenses in millions

— Total violent crime
— Victimizations reported to the police
— Crimes recorded by the police
— Arrests for violent crime

Note: The NCVS redesign was implemented in 1993; the area with the lighter shading is before the redesign and the darker area after the redesign.

Source: Shannan Catalano, *Criminal Victimization 2003* (Washington, DC: Bureau of Justice Statistics, 2004).

FIGURE 3.2

Violent Crime Victimization Rates, 1973–2003

The NCVS reveals long-term declines in victimization to the lowest per capita rates in thirty years.

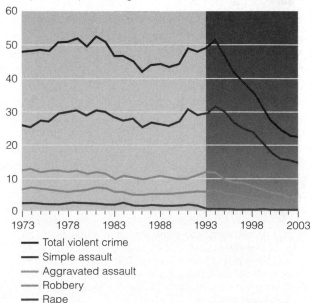

Rate per 1,000 persons age 12 or older

— Total violent crime
— Simple assault
— Aggravated assault
— Robbery
— Rape

Note: The violent crimes included are rape, robbery, aggravated and simple assault, and homicide. The NCVS redesign was implemented in 1993; the area with the lighter shading is before the redesign and the darker area after the redesign.

Source: Shannan Catalano, *Criminal Victimization 2003* (Washington, DC: Bureau of Justice Statistics, 2004).

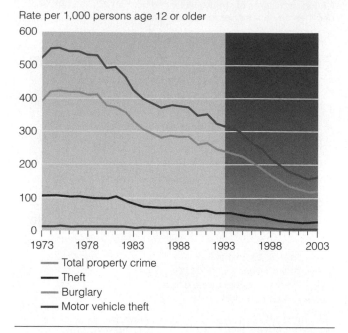

FIGURE 3.3

Property Crime Victimization Rates, 1973–2003

Rate per 1,000 persons age 12 or older

- Total property crime
- Theft
- Burglary
- Motor vehicle theft

Note: Property crimes include burglary, theft, and motor vehicle theft. The NCVS redesign was implemented in 1993; the area with the lighter shading is before the redesign and the darker area after the redesign.

Source: Shannan Catalano, *Criminal Victimization 2003* (Washington, DC: Bureau of Justice Statistics, 2004).

relationship between victims and criminals? The following sections discuss some of the most important victimization patterns and trends.

The Social Ecology of Victimization

The NCVS shows that violent crimes are slightly more likely to take place in an open, public area—such as a street, a park, or a field); in a school building; or at a commercial establishment such as a tavern during the daytime or early evening hours than in a private home during the morning or late evening hours. The more serious violent crimes, such as rape and aggravated assault, typically take place after 6 P.M. Approximately two-thirds of rapes and sexual assaults occur at night—6 P.M. to 6 A.M. Less serious forms of violence, such as unarmed robberies and personal larcenies like purse snatching, are more likely to occur during the daytime.

> Did you know that a great deal of victimization occurs in school buildings? Although school violence may be declining, about one-third of all students are injured in a physical altercation each year. To learn more about this phenomenon, use InfoTrac College Edition to read: "Violence Decreasing in U.S. High Schools," *The Brown University Child and Adolescent Behavior Letter* 15 (December 1999): 3.

Neighborhood characteristics affect the chances of victimization. Those living in the central city have significantly higher rates of theft and violence than suburbanites; people living in rural areas have a victimization rate almost half that of city dwellers. The risk of murder for both men and women is significantly higher in disorganized inner-city areas where gangs flourish and drug trafficking is commonplace.

The Victim's Household

The NCVS tells us that within the United States, larger, African American, western, and urban homes are the most vulnerable to crime. In contrast, rural, white homes in the Northeast are the least likely to contain crime victims or be the target of theft offenses, such as burglary or larceny. People who own their homes are less vulnerable than renters.

Recent population movement and changes may account for decreases in crime victimization. U.S. residents have become extremely mobile, moving from urban areas to suburban and rural areas. In addition, family size has been reduced; more people than ever before are living in single-person homes (about 26 percent of households). It is possible that the decline in household victimization rates during the past decades can be explained by the fact that smaller households in less populated areas have a lower victimization risk.

Victim Characteristics

Social and demographic characteristics also distinguish victims and nonvictims. The most important of these factors are gender, age, social status, and race.

GENDER Gender affects victimization risk. Males are more likely than females to be the victims of violent crime. Men are almost twice as likely as women to experience robbery and 50 percent more likely to be the victim of assault; women are much more likely than men to be victims of rape or sexual assault. For all crimes, males are more likely to be victimized than females.

However, the gender differences in the victimization rate appear to be narrowing.

Females are most often victimized by someone they know, whereas males are more likely to be victimized by a stranger. Of those offenders victimizing females, about two-thirds are described as someone the victim knows or is related to. In contrast, only about half of male victims are attacked by a friend, relative, or acquaintance.

AGE Victim data reveal that young people face a much greater victimization risk than do older people. As Figure 3.4 shows, victim risk diminishes rapidly after age 25.

The elderly, who are thought of as the helpless targets of predatory criminals, are actually much safer than their grandchildren. People over 65, who make up about 15 percent of the population, account for only 1 percent of violent victimizations; teens 12 to 19, who also make up 15 percent of the population, typically account for more than 30 percent of victimizations. For example, teens 16 to 19 suffer more than 50 personal victimizations per 1,000, whereas people over 65 experience only 2.

SUSPECT DATABASE
Name: CARR
       JASON
DOB: 12 / 30 / 74
Race: MALE
Sex: WHITE
Hgt/Wgt: 6' 02"   160 lbs.
Eyes: BLUE   Hair: BROWN
Image#: 1070245
Type: BOOKING RECORD
Picture Date/Time:
       10 / 10 / 00   20 : 05

Men are typically attacked by strangers, but about two-thirds of all attacks against women are committed by a husband, boyfriend, family member, or an acquaintance. Jason Carr, shown here in his booking photograph in Pinellas County, Florida, was placed under house arrest after his tenth felony conviction. He was then arrested and charged with domestic violence and child abuse—committed while serving his sentence at home!

FIGURE 3.4

Violent Crime Rates by Age of Victim

Young people are much more likely to become victims than are the elderly.

Rate per 1,000 persons age 12 and over

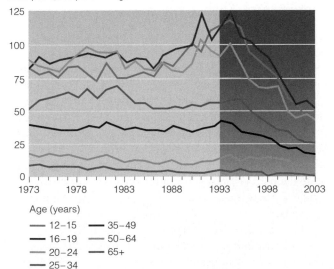

Age (years)

— 12–15   — 35–49
— 16–19   — 50–64
— 20–24   — 65+
— 25–34

Note: Violent crimes included are homicide, rape, robbery, and both simple and aggravated assault. The NCVS redesign was implemented in 1993; the area with the lighter shading is before the redesign and the darker area after the redesign.

Source: Shannan Catalano, *Criminal Victimization 2003* (Washington, DC: Bureau of Justice Statistics, 2004).

Although the elderly are less likely to become crime victims than the young, they are most often the victims of a narrow band of criminal activities from which the young are more immune. Frauds and scams, purse snatching, pocket picking, stealing checks from the mail, and crimes committed in long-term care settings claim predominantly elderly victims. The elderly are especially susceptible to fraud schemes because they have insurance, pension plans, proceeds from the sale of homes, and money from Social Security and savings that make them attractive financial targets. Because many elderly live by themselves and are lonely, they remain more susceptible to telephone and mail fraud. Unfortunately, once victimized the elderly have less opportunity to either recover their lost money or to earn enough to replace it.[31] Elder abuse is a particularly important issue because of shifts in the U.S. population; the Bureau of the Census predicts that by 2030 the population over age 65 will nearly triple to more than 70 million people, and older people will make up more than 20 percent of the population (up from 12.3 percent in 1990). The saliency of **elder abuse** is underscored by reports from the National Center on Elder Abuse, which show an increase of 150 percent in reported cases of elder abuse nationwide since 1986.[32]

||||||| CONNECTIONS |||||||

The association between age and victimization is undoubtedly tied to lifestyle: Adolescents often stay out late at night, go to public places, and hang out with other kids who have a high risk of criminal involvement. Teens also face a high victimization risk because they spend a great deal of time in the most dangerous building in the community—the local school. As Chapter 2 indicated, adolescents have the highest crime rates. It is not surprising that people who associate with these high-crime-rate individuals (other adolescents) have the greatest victimization risk.

SOCIAL STATUS The poorest Americans are also the most likely victims of violent and property crime. This association occurs across all gender, age, and racial groups. Although the poor are more likely to suffer violent crimes, the wealthy are more likely targets of personal theft crimes such as pocket picking and purse snatching. Perhaps the affluent—sporting more expensive attire and driving better cars—attract the attention of thieves.

MARITAL STATUS Marital status also influences victimization risk. Never-married males and females are victimized more often than married people. Widows and widowers have the lowest victimization risk. This association between marital status and victimization is probably influenced by age, gender, and lifestyle:

■ Many young people, who have the highest victimization risk, are too young to have been married.

■ Young single people go out in public more often and sometimes interact with high-risk peers, increasing their exposure to victimization.

■ Widows and widowers suffer much lower victimization rates because they are older, interact with older people, and are more likely to stay home at night and to avoid public places.

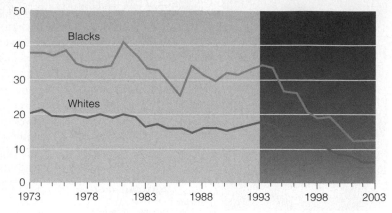

FIGURE 3.5

Violent Crime Rates by Race of Victim

Blacks are more likely than whites to be victims of violent crime.

Note: Serious violent crimes included are homicide, rape, robbery, and aggravated and simple assault. The NCVS redesign was implemented in 1993; the area with the lighter shading is before the redesign and the darker area after the redesign.

Source: Shannan Catalano, *Criminal Victimization 2003* (Washington, DC: Bureau of Justice Statistics, 2004).

RACE AND ETHNICITY As Figure 3.5 shows, blacks are more likely than whites to be victims of violent crime, and serious violent crime rates declined in recent years for both blacks and whites.

Why do these discrepancies exist? Because of income inequality, racial and minority group members are often forced to live in deteriorated urban areas beset by alcohol and drug abuse, poverty, racial discrimination, and violence. Consequently, their lifestyle places them in the most at-risk population group. However, as Figure 3.5 shows, the rate of black victimization has been in steep decline, and the racial gap seems to be narrowing.

REPEAT VICTIMIZATION Does prior victimization enhance or reduce the chances of future victimization? Individuals who have been crime victims have a significantly higher chance of future victimization than people who have not been victims.[33] Households that have experienced victimization in the past are the ones most likely to experience it again in the future.[34]

What factors predict **chronic victimization**? Most repeat victimizations occur soon after a previous crime has occurred, suggesting that repeat victims share some personal characteristic that makes them a magnet for predators.[35] For example, children who are shy, physically weak, or socially isolated may be prone to being bullied in the schoolyard.[36] David Finkelhor and Nancy Asigian have found that three specific types of characteristics increase the potential for victimization:

1. *Target vulnerability:* The victims' physical weakness or psychological distress renders them incapable of resisting or deterring crime and makes them easy targets.

2. *Target gratifiability:* Some victims have some quality, possession, skill, or attribute that an offender wants to obtain, use, have access to, or manipulate. Having attractive possessions such as a leather coat may make one vulnerable to predatory crime.

3. *Target antagonism:* Some characteristics increase risk because they arouse anger, jealousy, or destructive impulses in potential offenders. Being gay or effeminate, for example, may bring on undeserved attacks in the street; being argumentative and alcoholic may provoke barroom assaults.[37]

Repeat victimization may occur when the victim does not take defensive action. For example, if an abusive husband finds out that his battered wife will not call the police, he repeatedly victimizes her; or if a hate crime is committed and the police do not respond to reported offenses, the perpetrators learn they have little to fear from the law.[38]

Victims and Their Criminals

The victim data also tell us something about the relationship between victims and criminals. Males are more likely to be violently victimized by a stranger, and females are more likely to be victimized by a friend, an acquaintance, or an intimate.

Victims report that most crimes are committed by a single offender over age 20. Crime tends to be intraracial: Black offenders victimize blacks, and whites victimize whites. However, because the country's population is predominantly white, it stands to reason that criminals of all races will be more likely to target white victims. Victims report that substance abuse is involved in about one-third of violent crime incidents.[39]

On April 15, 2002, the body of Jackson Carr, a 6-year-old boy, was found buried in mud in Lewisville, Texas; he had been stabbed to death. Later that day, Jackson's 15-year-old sister and 10-year-old brother confessed to the crime and were charged with murder.[40] (Sibling homicide is called **siblicide**.) Although many violent crimes are committed by strangers, a surprising number of violent crimes are committed by relatives or acquaintances of the victims. In fact, more than half of all nonfatal personal crimes are committed by people who are described as being known to the victim. Women are especially vulnerable to people they know. More than six in ten rape or sexual assault victims state the offender was an intimate, a relative, a friend, or an acquaintance. Women are more likely than men to be robbed by a friend or acquaintance; 74 percent of males and 43 per-

the volume of easily transportable wealth increased, creating a greater number of available targets.[75] These structural changes in society led to thirty years of increasing crime rates. To counteract these forces, some communities became better organized, restricted traffic, changed street patterns, and limited neighborhood entrances to control the opportunity to commit crime and reduce the chances of residents' victimization.[76]

Skyrocketing drug use in the 1980s created an excess of motivated offenders, and the rates of some crimes, such as robbery, increased dramatically. Crime rates may have fallen in the 1990s because a robust economy decreased the pool of motivated offenders, and the growing number of police officers increased guardianship.[77] If crime is rational, criminal motivation should be reduced if potential offenders perceive alternatives to crime; in contrast, the perception of opportunities for crime should increase criminal motivation. The Criminological Enterprise feature on crime in everyday life shows how these relationships can be influenced by cultural and structural change.

The various theories of victimization are summarized in Concept Summary 3.1.

 To quiz yourself on this material, go to the Criminology TPT 9e website.

CARING FOR THE VICTIM

National victim surveys indicate that almost every American age 12 and over will one day become the victim of a common-law crime, such as larceny or burglary, and in the aftermath suffer financial problems, mental stress, and physical hardship.[78] Surveys show that more than 75 percent of the general public has been victimized by crime at least once in their life; as many as 25 percent of the victims develop posttraumatic stress syndrome, and their symptoms last for more than a decade after the crime occurred.[79] The long-term effects of sexual victimization can include years of problem avoidance, social withdrawal, and self-criticism.[80]

Helping the victim to cope is the responsibility of all of society. Law enforcement agencies, courts, and correctional and human service systems have come to realize that due process and human rights exist for both the defendant and the victim of criminal behavior.

The Government's Response

Because of public concern over violent personal crime, President Ronald Reagan created a Task Force on Victims of Crime in 1982.[81] This group suggested that a balance be achieved between recognizing the victim's rights and providing the defendant with due process. Recommendations included providing witnesses and victims with protection from intimidation, requiring restitution in criminal cases, developing guidelines for fair treatment of crime victims and witnesses, and expanding programs of victim compensation.[82] Consequently, the Omnibus Victim and Witness Protection Act was passed, which required the use of victim impact statements at sentencing in federal criminal cases, greater protection for witnesses, more stringent bail laws, and the use of restitution in criminal cases.

It is the mission of the **Crime Victims Board of New York** to provide compensation to innocent victims of crime in a timely, efficient, and compassionate manner; to fund direct services to crime victims via a network of community-based programs; and to advocate for the rights and benefits of all innocent victims of crime. You can learn more about this program at http://www.cvb.state.ny.us/. For an up-to-date list of web links, go to http://cj.wadsworth.com/siegel_crimtpt9e.

In 1984 the Comprehensive Crime Control Act and the Victims of Crime Act authorized federal funding for state victim compensation and assistance projects.[83] With these acts, the federal government began to aid the plight of the victim and make victim assistance an even greater concern of the public and the justice system.

The **Office for Victims of Crime (OVC)** was established by the 1984 Victims of Crime Act (VOCA) to oversee diverse programs that benefit victims of crime. OVC provides substantial funding to state victim assistance and compensation programs and supports training designed to educate criminal justice and allied professionals regarding the rights and needs of crime victims. For more information on this topic, go to http://www.ojp.usdoj.gov/ovc/. For an up-to-date list of web links, go to http://cj.wadsworth.com/siegel_crimtpt9e.

Victim Service Programs

An estimated 2,000 **victim-witness assistance programs** have developed around the United States.[84] Victim-witness assistance programs are organized on a variety of governmental levels and serve a variety of clients. We will look at the most prominent forms of victim services operating in the United States.[85]

VICTIM COMPENSATION One of the primary goals of victim advocates has been to lobby for legislation creating crime **victim compensation** programs.[86] As a result of such legislation, the victim ordinarily receives compensation from the state to pay for damages associated with the crime. Rarely are two compensation schemes alike, however, and many state programs suffer from lack of both adequate funding and proper organization within the criminal justice system. Compensation may be made for medical bills, loss of wages, loss of future earnings, and counseling. In the case of death, the victim's survivors can receive burial expenses and aid for loss of support.[87] Awards are typically in the $100 to $15,000 range. Occasionally programs will provide emergency assistance to indigent victims until compensation is available. Emergency assistance may come in the form of food vouchers or replacement of prescription medicines.

In 1984, the federal government created the Victim of Crime Act (VOCA), which grants money to state compensation boards derived from fines and penalties imposed on federal offenders. The money is distributed each year to the states to fund both their crime victim compensation programs and their victim assistance programs, such as rape crisis centers and domestic violence shelters. VOCA payments have increased by more than $200 million (or 82.5 percent) in the past five years. Victims of child abuse comprised 23 percent of the recipients of crime victim compensation, while domestic violence victims were 26 percent of all adult victims compensated. What did the payments go for? Medical expenses were 41 percent of all payments; economic support for lost wages and lost support in homicides comprised 26 percent of the total; and 15 percent went toward mental health counseling. Victims of violent crime will receive an estimated $625 million in fiscal year 2004.[88]

Patti Stafford, of Benton, Arkansas, holds a picture of her murdered daughter, Sarah, during a Parents of Murdered Children rally on July 27, 2004, in Little Rock, Arkansas. Stafford urged the state's governor to consider victims' rights when deciding whether to grant clemency to convicted murderers. A national organization, Parents of Murdered Children is dedicated to providing emotional support for parents and other survivors, facilitating the reconstruction of a "new life," and helping parents not only to deal with their acute grief, but also with the criminal justice system.

To read about how **healthcare providers can help the victims of domestic violence,** read this article by Nancy E. Isaac and V. Pualani Enos, "Documenting Domestic Violence: How Health Care Providers Can Help Victims" at http://www.ncjrs.org/pdffiles1/nij/188564.pdf. For an up-to-date list of web links, go to http://cj.wadsworth.com/siegel_crimtpt9e.

COURT SERVICES A common victim service helps victims deal with the criminal justice system. One approach is to prepare victims and witnesses by explaining court procedures: how to be a witness, how bail works, and what to do if the defendant makes a threat. Lack of such knowledge can cause confusion and fear, making some victims reluctant to testify in court proceedings. Many victim programs also provide transportation to and from court and counselors, who remain in the courtroom during hearings to explain procedures and provide support. Court escorts are particularly important for elderly and disabled victims, victims of child abuse and assault, and victims who have been intimidated by friends or relatives of the defendant. These types of services may be having a positive effect since recent research (2004) shows that victims may be now less traumatized by a court hearing with their attacker present than previously believed.[89]

PUBLIC EDUCATION More than half of all victim programs include public education programs that help familiarize the general public with their services and with other agencies that assist crime victims. In some instances, these are primary education programs, which teach methods of dealing with conflict without resorting to violence. For example, school-based programs present information on spousal and dating abuse followed by discussions of how to reduce violent incidents.[90]

CRISIS INTERVENTION Most victim programs refer victims to specific services to help them recover from their ordeal. Clients are commonly referred to the local network of public and private social service agencies that can provide emergency and long-term assistance with transportation, medical care, shelter, food, and clothing. In addition, more than half of victim programs provide **crisis intervention** to victims, many of whom feel isolated, vulnerable, and in need of immediate services. Some programs counsel at their offices, and others visit victims' homes, the crime scene, or a hospital.

VICTIM–OFFENDER RECONCILIATION PROGRAMS Victim–offender reconciliation programs (VORPs) use mediators to facilitate face-to-face encounters between victims and their attackers. The aim is to engage in direct negotiations that lead to **restitution agreements** and, possibly, reconciliation between the two parties involved.[91] More than 120 reconciliation programs are currently in operation, and they handle an estimated 16,000 cases per year. Designed at first to address routine misdemeanors such as petty theft and vandalism, programs now commonly hammer out restitution agreements in more serious incidents such as residential burglary and even attempted murder.

||||||| CONNECTIONS |||||||

Reconciliation programs are based on the concept of restorative justice, which rejects punitive correctional measures in favor of viewing crimes of violence and theft as interpersonal conflicts that need to be settled in the community through noncoercive means. See Chapter 8 for more on this approach.

VICTIM IMPACT STATEMENTS Most jurisdictions allow victims to make an impact statement before the sentencing judge. This gives the victim an opportunity to tell of his or her experiences and describe the ordeal; in the case of a murder trial, the surviving family can recount the effect the crime has had on their lives and well-being.[92] The effect of victim/witness statements on sentencing has been the topic of some debate. Some research finds that victim statements result in a higher rate of incarceration, but others find that the statements are insignificant.[93] Those who favor the use of impact statements argue that because the victim is harmed by the crime, the victim has a right to influence the outcome of the case. After all, the public prosecutor is allowed to make sentencing recommendations because the public has been harmed by the crime. Logically the harm suffered by the victim legitimizes his or her right to make sentencing recommendations.[94]

The **National Organization for Victim Assistance** is a private, nonprofit organization of victim and witness assistance programs and practitioners, criminal justice agencies and professionals, mental health professionals, researchers, former victims and survivors, and others committed to the recognition and implementation of victim rights and services. To learn more about these services, go to http://www.try-nova.org/. For an up-to-date list of web links, go to http://cj.wadsworth.com/siegel_crimtpt9e.

Victims' Rights

More than twenty years ago, legal scholar Frank Carrington suggests that crime victims have legal rights that should assure them of basic services from the government.[95] According to Carrington, just as the defendant has the right to counsel and a fair trial, society is also obliged to ensure basic rights for law-abiding citizens. These rights range from adequate protection from violent crimes to victim compensation and assistance from the criminal justice system.

Because of the influence of victims' rights advocates, every state now has some form of legal rights for crime victims in its code of laws, often called a victims' Bill of Rights; thirty-three states have added victims' rights amendments to their state constitutions.[96] A national constitutional

Victims' Rights in Europe

While the United States has taken steps to improve the rights of victims, the European Union has also moved toward increasing the role of victims in the justice process. The Council of the European Union has been at the forefront of this effort. The Council is the main decision-making body of the European Union. Its duties include:

- Passing laws, usually legislating jointly with the European Parliament
- Co-ordinating the broad economic policies of the member states
- Defining and implementing the EU's common foreign and security policy, based on guidelines set by the European Council
- Concluding, on behalf of the Community and the Union, international agreements between the EU and one or more states or international organizations
- Coordinating the actions of member states and adopting measures in the area of police and judicial cooperation in criminal matters
- With the Council and the European Parliament, constituting the budgetary authority that adopts the Community's budget.

Recently, the Council agreed to implement the Framework Decision on the standing of victims in criminal proceedings. The Framework Decision is groundbreaking in that it sets out minimum standards for the treatment of victims of crime (and their families) and that it applies throughout the European Union. The Framework Decision is binding on EU Member States. It highlights issues of concern, sets out principles that must be taken into consideration, and then lists a series of rights to which victims of crime are entitled in the course of criminal proceedings. European states are expected to modify their laws to conform to the Framework Decision.

Framework Principles

The Framework Decision stipulates that minimum standards must be drawn up for the protection of victims of crime—in particular, to secure access to justice and to compensate for damages, including legal costs. A series of principles underpinning these entitlements state that:

- Victims of crime are entitled to a high level of protection.
- The laws and regulations of Member States should be approximated [brought closer] to achieve the main rights set out in the Framework Decision.
- The needs of crime victims should be addressed in a comprehensive and coordinated manner to avoid secondary victimization; thus provisions are not confined to criminal proceedings.
- Cooperation between Member States should be strengthened through networks of victims' organizations.

---

amendment to enhance the rights of victims has been debated for years but has not passed Congress. In 2004 the Senate passed a bill to provide new rights to victims of federal crimes that does not require changing the Constitution (S. 2329). A House version of the bill is now in committee. The elements of this legislation are shown in Exhibit 3.1. The United States is not alone in mandating victim's rights. As the Comparative Criminology feature describes, this is also a priority of the European Union.

Victim Advocacy

Assuring victims' rights can involve an eclectic group of advocacy groups, some independent, others government sponsored, and some self-help. Advocates can be especially helpful when victims need to interact with the agencies of justice. For example, advocates can lobby police departments to keep investigations open as well as request the return of recovered stolen property. They can demand from prosecutors

EXHIBIT 3.1
Crime Victims' Bill of Rights

1. The right to be reasonably protected from the accused
2. The right to reasonable, accurate, and timely notice of any public proceeding involving the crime or of any release or escape of the accused
3. The right not to be excluded from any such public proceeding
4. The right to be reasonably heard at any public proceeding involving release, plea, or sentencing
5. The right to confer with the attorney for the government in the case
6. The right to full and timely restitution as provided in law
7. The right to proceedings free from unreasonable delay
8. The right to be treated with fairness and with respect for the victim's dignity and privacy

Source: S.2329, a Senate bill to protect crime victims' rights, introduced April 21, 2004.

- Suitable and adequate training should be given to people who come into contact with victims of crime.

Framework Provisions: Minimum Standards of Treatment

All victims of crime should:

- Be treated with respect
- Have their entitlement to a real and appropriate role in criminal proceedings recognized
- Have ther right to be heard during proceedings, and to supply evidence, safeguarded
- Receive information on: the type of support available; where and how to report an offense; criminal proceedings and their role in them; access to protection and advice; entitlement to compensation; and, if they wish, the outcomes of their complaints including sentencing and release of the offender
- Have communication safeguards: that is, Member States should take measures to minimize communication difficulties in criminal proceedings
- Have access to free legal advice concerning their role in the proceedings and, where appropriate, legal aid
- Receive payment of expenses incurred as a result of participation in criminal proceedings
- Receive reasonable protection, including protection of privacy
- Receive compensation in the course of criminal proceedings
- Receive penal mediation in the course of criminal proceedings where appropriate
- Benefit from various measures to minimize the difficulties faced where victims are resident in another Member State, especially when organizing criminal proceedings

In addition, cooperation between Member States is to be encouraged; specialist services and victims' organizations should be promoted; training for personnel who come into contact with victims should be encouraged; and steps should be taken to prevent secondary victimization and to avoid placing victims under unnecessary pressure.

In addition to the Framework Decision, on April 29, 2004, the EU Council adopted another directive which mandates that by July 1, 2005, each Member State has a national scheme in place that guarantees fair and appropriate compensation to victims of crime. The directive ensures that compensation is easily accessible in practice regardless of where in the EU a person becomes the victim of a crime. All Member States are required to guarantee fair and appropriate compensation to victims.

Sources: Council Framework Decision of 15 March 15, 2001, on the standing of victims in criminal proceedings: http://europa.eu.int/ eurlex/pri/en/oj/dat/2001/l_082/ l_08220010322en00010004.pdf; Proposal for a Council Directive on compensation to crime victims: http:// europa.eu.int/eur-lex/en/com/ pdf/2002/com2002_0562en01.pdf.

---

and judges protection from harassment and reprisals by, for example, making "no contact" a condition of bail. They can help victims make statements during sentencing hearings as well as probation and parole revocation procedures. Victim advocates can also interact with news media, making sure that reporting is accurate and that victim privacy is not violated. Victim advocates can be part of an independent agency similar to a legal aid society. If successful, top-notch advocates may eventually open private offices, similar to attorneys, private investigators, or jury consultants.[97]

Self-Protection

Although the general public mostly approves of the police, fear of crime and concern about community safety have prompted some to become their own "police force," taking an active role in community protection and citizen crime control groups.[98] The more crime in an area, the greater the amount of fear and the more likely residents will be to engage in self-protective measures.[99]

Research indicates that a significant number of crimes may not be reported to police simply because victims prefer to take matters into their own hands.[100] One manifestation of this trend is the concept of **target hardening,** or making one's home and business crime proof through locks, bars, alarms, and other devices.[101] Other commonly used crime prevention techniques include a fence or barricade at the entrance; a doorkeeper, guard, or receptionist in an apartment building; an intercom or phone to gain access to the building; surveillance cameras; window bars; warning signs; and dogs chosen for their ability to guard the house. The use of these measures is inversely proportional to perception of neighborhood safety: People who feared crime are more likely to use crime prevention techniques. Although the true relationship is still unclear, there is mounting evidence that people who protect their homes are less likely to be victimized by property crimes.[102] One study conducted in the Philadelphia area found that people who install burglar alarms are less likely to suffer burglary than those who forgo similar preventive measures.[103]

Some people take self-protection to its ultimate end by preparing to fight back when criminals attack them. How successful are victims when they resist? Research indicates that victims who fight back often frustrate their attackers but also face increased odds of being physically harmed during the attack.[104] In some cases, fighting back decreases the odds of a crime being completed but increases the victim's chances of injury.[105] Resistance may draw the attention of bystanders and make a violent crime physically difficult to complete, but it can also cause offenders to escalate their violence.[106]

What about the use of firearms? Each year, 2.5 million times, victims use guns for defensive purposes, a number that is not surprising considering that about one-third of U.S. households contain guns.[107] Gary Kleck has estimated that armed victims kill between 1,500 and 2,800 potential felons each year and wound between 8,700 and 16,000. Kleck's research shows, ironically, that by fighting back victims kill far more criminals than the estimated 250 to 1,000 killed annually by police.[108] Kleck has found that the risk of collateral injury is relatively rare and that potential victims should be encouraged to fight back.[109] According to Kleck, empirical research studies unanimously show that defensive gun use is associated with both lower rates of crime completion and lower rates of injury to the victim.[110]

Community Organization

Not everyone is capable of buying a handgun or semiautomatic weapon and doing battle with predatory criminals. An alternative approach has been for communities to organize on the neighborhood level against crime. Citizens have been working independently and in cooperation with local police agencies in neighborhood patrol and block watch programs. These programs organize local citizens in urban areas to patrol neighborhoods, watch for suspicious people, help secure the neighborhood, lobby for improvements (such as increased lighting), report crime to police, put out community newsletters, conduct home security surveys, and serve as a source for crime information or tips.[111] Although such programs are welcome additions to police services, there is little evidence that they appreciably affect the crime rate. There is also concern that their effectiveness is spottier in low-income, high-crime areas, which need the most crime pre-

People in the community may band together to fight crime and prevent victimization. An alternative approach has been for communities to organize on the neighborhood level against crime. As the nation's largest grassroots, non-partisan, chapter-based organization leading the fight to prevent gun violence, the Million Mom March united with the Brady Campaign is dedicated to creating an America free from gun violence, where all Americans are safe at home, at school, at work, and in their communities.

vention assistance.[112] Block watches and neighborhood patrols seem more successful when they are part of general-purpose or multi-issue community groups rather than when they focus directly on crime problems.[113]

 To quiz yourself on this material, go to the Criminology TPT 9e website.

SUMMARY

- Criminologists now consider victims and victimization a major focus of study. About 24 million U.S. citizens are victims of crime each year. Like the crime rate, the victimization rate has been in sharp decline.

- The social and economic costs of crime are in the billions of dollars.

Victims suffer long-term consequences such as experiencing fear and posttraumatic stress disorder.

- Research shows that victims are more likely to engage in antisocial behavior than nonvictims.

- Like crime, victimization has stable patterns and trends. Violent crime

victims tend to be young, poor, single males living in large cities, although victims come in all ages, sizes, races, and genders.

- Females are more likely to be victimized by someone they know than are males.

- Adolescents maintain a high risk of being physically and sexually victimized. Their victimization has been linked to a multitude of subsequent social problems.

- Many victimizations occur in the home, and many victims are the target of relatives and loved ones.

- Victim precipitation theory holds that victims provoke criminals, either through active or passive precipitation.

- Lifestyle theory suggests that victims put themselves in danger by engaging in high-risk activities, such as going out late at night, living in a high-crime area, and associating with high-risk peers.

- Deviant place theory argues that victimization risk is related to neighborhood crime rates.

- The routine activities theory maintains that a pool of motivated offenders exists and that these offenders will take advantage of unguarded, suitable targets.

- Numerous programs help victims by providing court services, economic compensation, public education, and crisis intervention. Most states have created a victims' Bill of Rights.

- Rather than depend on the justice system, some victims have attempted to help themselves through community organization for self-protection.

ThomsonNOW

Thomson NOW! Optimize your study time and master key chapter concepts with **ThomsonNOW™**—the first web-based assessment-centered study tool for Criminology. This powerful resource helps you determine your unique study needs and provides you with a *Personalized Study Plan,* guiding you to interactive media that includes that Learning Modules, Topic Reviews, ABC Video Clips with Questions, Animations, an integrated E-book, and more!

Thinking Like a Criminologist

The director of the state's department of human services has asked you to evaluate a self-report survey of adolescents ages 10 to 18. She has provided you with the following information on physical abuse:

Adolescents experiencing abuse or violence are at high risk of immediate and lasting negative effects on health and well-being. Of the high school students surveyed, an alarming one in five (21 percent) said they had been physically abused.

Of the older students, ages 15 to 18, 29 percent said they had been physically abused. Younger students also reported significant rates of abuse: 17 percent responded "yes" when asked whether they had been physically abused. Although girls were far less likely to report abuse than boys, 12 percent said they had been physically abused. Most abuse occurs at home, occurs more than once, and the abuser is usually a family member. More than half of those physically abused had tried alcohol and drugs, and 60 percent had admitted to a violent act. Nonabused children were significantly less likely to abuse substances, and only 30 percent indicated they had committed a violent act.

How would you interpret these data? What factors might influence their validity? What is your interpretation of the association between abuse and delinquency?

 # Doing Research on the Web

The National Council on Child Abuse and Family Violence (NCCAFV) maintains a website with links to documents on child abuse and violence: http://www.nccafv.org/.

In Canada, the National Clearinghouse on Family Violence maintains information on abuse and violence: http://www.hc-sc.gc.ca/hppb/familyviolence/nfntsnegl_e.html. Read the following article on InfoTrac College Edition to learn more about the effects of abuse and harsh parenting on antisocial behavior: Kimberly Becker, Jeffrey Stuewig, Veronica Herrera, and Laura McCloskey, "A Study of Firesetting and Animal Cruelty in Children: Family Influences and Adolescent Outcomes," *Journal of the American Academy of Child and Adolescent Psychiatry* 43 (2004): 905–912.

KEY TERMS

victimologists (68)
victimization (68)
posttraumatic stress disorder (PTSD) (69)
obsessive-compulsive disorder (69)
cycle of violence (71)
elder abuse (73)
chronic victimization (74)
siblicide (74)

victim precipitation theory (75)
active precipitation (75)
passive precipitation (75)
lifestyle theory (75)
deviant place theory (77)
routine activities theory (78)
suitable targets (78)
capable guardians (78)
motivated offenders (78)

date rape (78)
victim-witness assistance programs (82)
victim compensation (82)
crisis intervention (83)
restitution agreements (83)
target hardening (85)

CRITICAL THINKING QUESTIONS

1. Considering what we learned in this chapter about crime victimization, what measures can you take to better protect yourself from crime?

2. Do you agree with the assessment that schools are some of the most dangerous locations in the community? Did you find your high school to be a dangerous environment?

3. Does a person bear some of the responsibility for his or her victimization if the person maintains a lifestyle that contributes to the chances of becoming a crime victim? That is, should we "blame the victim"?

4. Have you ever experienced someone "precipitating" crime? If so, did you do anything to help the situation?

NOTES

1. Mark Pazniokas, "Mayor Again Denied Bail, Giordano Remains Flight Risk, Judge Says," *Hartford Courant,* 9 November 2001, p. A1; Associated Press, "Waterbury Mayor Paid Teenager for Sex, Reports Say," *New York Times,* 16 August 2001, p.1.

2. Associated Press, "Giordano Guilty in Federal Trial Involving Child Sex Abuse," *Hartford Courant,* 25 March 2003, p. 1

3. Richard Estes and Neil Alan Weiner, *The Commercial Sexual Exploitation of Children in the U.S., Canada, and Mexico* (Philadelphia: University of Pennsylvania Press, 2001).

4. Shannan Catalano, *Criminal Victimization 2003* (Washington, DC: Bureau of Justice Statistics, 2004).

5. Arthur Lurigio, "Are All Victims Alike? The Adverse, Generalized, and Differential Impact of Crime," *Crime and Delinquency* 33 (1987): 452–467.

6. Children's Safety Network Economics and Insurance Resource Center, "State Costs of Violence Perpetrated by Youth." http://www.csneirc.org/pubs/tables/youth-viol.htm. Accessed July 12, 2000.

7. George Rengert, *The Geography of Illegal Drugs* (Boulder, CO: Westview, 1996), p. 5.

8. Ted R. Miller, Mark A. Cohen, and Brian Wiersema, *Victim Costs and Consequences: A New Look* (Washington, DC: National Institute of Justice, 1996), p. 9, table 2.

9. Ross Macmillan, "Adolescent Victimization and Income Deficits in Adulthood: Rethinking the Costs of Criminal Violence from a Life-Course Perspective," *Criminology* 38 (2000): 553–588.

10. Rebecca Campbell and Sheela Raja, "Secondary Victimization of Rape Victims: Insights from Mental Health Professionals Who Treat Survivors of Violence," *Violence and Victims* 14 (1999): 261–274.

11. Peter Finn, *Victims* (Washington, DC: Bureau of Justice Statistics, 1988), p. 1.

12. Catherine Grus, "Child Abuse: Correlations with Hostile Attributions," *Journal of Developmental & Behavioral Pediatrics* 24 (2003): 296–298.

13. Michael Wiederman, Randy Sansone, and Lori Sansone, "History of Trauma and Attempted Suicide among Women in a Primary Care Setting," *Violence and Victims* 13 (1998): 3–11; Susan Leslie Bryant and Lillian Range, "Suicidality in College Women Who Were Sexually and Physically Abused and Physically Punished by Parents," *Violence and Victims* 10 (1995): 195–215; William Downs and Brenda Miller, "Relationships between Experiences of Parental Violence During Childhood and Women's Self-Esteem," *Violence and Victims* 13 (1998):

63–78; Sally Davies-Netley, Michael Hurlburt, and Richard Hough, "Childhood Abuse as a Precursor to Homelessness for Homeless Women with Severe Mental Illness," *Violence and Victims* 11 (1996): 129–142.

14. Jane Siegel and Linda Williams, "Risk Factors for Sexual Victimization of Women," *Violence Against Women* 9 (2003): 902–930.

15. Jeanne Kaufman and Cathy Spatz Widom, "Childhood Victimization, Running Away, and Delinquency," *Journal of Research in Crime and Delinquency* 36 (1999): 347–370.

16. Kim Logio, "Gender, Race, Childhood Abuse, and Body Image among Adolescents," *Violence Against Women* 9 (2003): 931–955.

17. Lana Stermac and Emily Paradis, "Homeless Women and Victimization: Abuse and Mental Health History among Homeless Rape Survivors," *Resources for Feminist Research* 28 (2001): 65–81.

18. Dina Vivian and Jean Malone, "Relationship Factors and Depressive Symptomology Associated with Mild and Severe Husband-to-Wife Physical Aggression," *Violence and Victims* 12 (1997): 19–37; Walter Gleason, "Mental Disorders in Battered Women," *Violence and Victims* 8 (1993): 53–66; Daniel Saunders, "Posttraumatic Stress Symptom Profiles of Battered Women: A Comparison of Survivors in Two Settings," *Violence and Victims* 9 (1994): 31–43.

19. K. Daniel O'Leary, "Psychological Abuse: A Variable Deserving Critical Attention in Domestic Violence," *Violence and Victims* 14 (1999): 1–21.

20. James Anderson, Terry Grandison, and Laronistine Dyson, "Victims of Random Violence and the Public Health Implication: A Health Care of Criminal Justice Issue," *Journal of Criminal Justice* 24 (1996): 379–393.

21. Ron Acierno, Alyssa Rheingold, Heidi Resnick, and Dean Kilpatrick, "Predictors of Fear of Crime in Older Adults," *Journal of Anxiety Disorders* 18 (2004): 385–396.

22. Susan Popkin, Victoria Gwlasda, Dennis Rosenbaum, Jean Amendolla, Wendell Johnson, and Lynn Olson, "Combating Crime in Public Housing: A Qualitative and Quantitative Longitudinal Analysis of the Chicago Housing Authority's Anti-Drug Initiative," *Justice Quarterly* 16 (1999): 519–557.

23. Pamela Wilcox Rountree, "A Reexamination of the Crime–Fear Linkage," *Journal of Research in Crime and Delinquency* 35 (1998): 341–372.

24. Robert Davis, Bruce Taylor, and Arthur Lurigio, "Adjusting to Criminal Victimization: The Correlates of Postcrime Distress," *Violence and Victimization* 11 (1996): 21–34.

25. Susan Brison, *Aftermath: Violence and the Remaking of a Self* (Princeton, NJ: Princeton University Press, 2001).

26. Timothy Ireland and Cathy Spatz Widom, *Childhood Victimization and Risk for Alcohol and Drug Arrests* (Washington, DC: National Institute of Justice, 1995).

27. Brigette Erwin, Elana Newman, Robert McMackin, Carlo Morrissey, and Danny Kaloupek, "PTSD, Malevolent Environment, and Criminality among Criminally Involved Male Adolescents," *Criminal Justice and Behavior* 27 (2000): 196–215.

28. Cathy Spatz Widom, *The Cycle of Violence* (Washington, DC: National Institute of Justice, 1992), p. 1.

29. Steve Spaccarelli, J. Douglas Coatsworth, and Blake Sperry Bowden, "Exposure to Serious Family Violence among Incarcerated Boys: Its Association with Violent Offending and Potential Mediating Variables," *Violence and Victims* 10 (1995): 163–180; Jerome Kolbo, "Risk and Resilience among Children Exposed to Family Violence," *Violence and Victims* 11 (1996): 113–127.

30. Victim data used in these sections are from Catalano, *Criminal Victimization 2003*.

31. Lamar Jordan, "Law Enforcement and the Elderly: A Concern for the 21st Century," *FBI Law Enforcement Bulletin* 71 (2002): 20–24.

32. Robert C. Davis and Juanjo Medina-Ariza, *Results from an Elder Abuse Prevention Experiment in New York* (Washington, DC: National Institute of Justice, September 2001).

33. Karin Wittebrood and Paul Nieuwbeerta, "Criminal Victimization during One's Life Course: The Effects of Previous Victimization and Patterns of Routine Activities," *Journal of Research in Crime and Delinquency* 37 (2000): 91–122; Janet Lauritsen and Kenna Davis Quinet, "Repeat Victimizations among Adolescents and Young Adults," *Journal of Quantitative Criminology* 11 (1995): 143–163.

34. Denise Osborn, Dan Ellingworth, Tim Hope, and Alan Trickett, "Are Repeatedly Victimized Households Different?" *Journal of Quantitative Criminology* 12 (1996): 223–245.

35. Graham Farrell, "Predicting and Preventing Revictimization," in *Crime and Justice: An Annual Review of Research,* eds. Michael Tonry and David Farrington, vol. 20 (Chicago: University of Chicago Press, 1995), pp. 61–126.

36. Ibid., p. 61.

37. David Finkelhor and Nancy Asigian, "Risk Factors for Youth Victimization: Beyond a Lifestyles/Routine Activities Theory Approach," *Violence and Victimization* 11 (1996): 3–19.

38. Graham Farrell, Coretta Phillips, and Ken Pease, "Like Taking Candy: Why Does Repeat Victimization Occur?" *British Journal of Criminology* 35 (1995): 384–399.

39. Christopher Innes and Lawrence Greenfeld, *Violent State Prisoners and Their Victims* (Washington, DC: Bureau of Justice Statistics, 1990).

40. Associated Press, "Texas Siblings Accused of Killing 6-Year-Old Brother," *New York Times,* 16 April 2002.

41. Hans Von Hentig, *The Criminal and His Victim: Studies in the Sociobiology of Crime* (New Haven: Yale University Press, 1948), p. 384.

42. Marvin Wolfgang, *Patterns of Criminal Homicide* (Philadelphia: University of Pennsylvania Press, 1958).

43. Menachem Amir, *Patterns in Forcible Rape* (Chicago: University of Chicago Press, 1971).

44. Susan Estrich, *Real Rape* (Cambridge, MA: Harvard University Press, 1987).

45. Edem Avakame, "Female's Labor Force Participation and Intimate Femicide: An Empirical Assessment of the Backlash Hypothesis," *Violence and Victim* 14 (1999): 277–283.

46. Martin Daly and Margo Wilson, *Homicide* (New York: Aldine de Gruyter, 1988).

47. Rosemary Gartner and Bill McCarthy, "The Social Distribution of Femicide in Urban Canada, 1921–1988," *Law and Society Review* 25 (1991): 287–311.

48. Lening Zhang, John W. Welte, and William F. Wieczorek, "Deviant Lifestyle and Crime Victimization," *Journal of Criminal Justice* 29 (2001): 133–143.

49. Dan Hoyt, Kimberly Ryan, and Mari Cauce, "Personal Victimizaton in a High-Risk Environment: Homeless and Runaway Adolescents," *Journal of Research in Crime and Delinquency* 36 (1999): 371–392.

50. See, generally, Gary Gottfredson and Denise Gottfredson, *Victimization in Schools* (New York: Plenum Press, 1985).

51. Gary Jensen and David Brownfield, "Gender, Lifestyles, and Victimization: Beyond Routine Activity Theory," *Violence and Victims* 1 (1986): 85–99.

52. Rolf Loeber, Mary DeLamatre, George Tita, Jacqueline Cohen, Magda Stouthamer-Loeber, and David Farrington, "Gun Injury and Mortality: The Delinquent Backgrounds of Juvenile Offenders," *Violence and Victims* 14 (1999): 339–351.

53. Bonnie Fisher, John Sloan, Francis Cullen, and Chunmeng Lu, "Crime in the Ivory Tower: The Level and Sources of Student Victimization," *Criminology* 36 (1998): 671–710.

54. Adam Dobrin, "The Risk of Offending on Homicide Victimization: A Case Control Study," *Journal of Research in Crime and Delinquency* 38 (2001): 154–173.

55. Rolf Loeber, Larry Kalb, and David Huizinga, *Juvenile Delinquency and Serious Injury Victimization* (Washington, DC: Office of Juvenile Justice and Delinquency Prevention, 2001).

56. James Garofalo, "Reassessing the Lifestyle Model of Criminal Victimization," in *Positive Criminology,* eds. Michael Gottfredson and Travis Hirschi (Newbury Park, CA: Sage, 1987), pp. 23–42.

57. Maryse Richards, Reed Larson, and Bobbi-Viegas Miller, "Risky and Protective Contexts and Exposure to Violence in Urban African American Young Adolescents," *Journal of Clinical Child and Adolescent Psychology* 33 (2004): 138–148.

58. Terance Miethe and David McDowall, "Contextual Effects in Models of Criminal Victimization," *Social Forces* 71 (1993): 741–759.

59. Rodney Stark, "Deviant Places: A Theory of the Ecology of Crime," *Criminology* 25 (1987): 893–911.

60. Ibid., p. 902.

61. Pamela Wilcox Rountree, Kenneth Land, and Terance Miethe, "Macro–Micro Integration in the Study of Victimization: A Hierarchical Logistic Model Analysis across Seattle Neighborhoods." Paper presented at the annual meeting of the American Society of Criminology, Phoenix, November 1993.

62. William Julius Wilson, *The Truly Disadvantaged* (Chicago: University of Chicago Press, 1990); see also, Allen Liska and Paul Bellair, "Violent-Crime Rates and Racial Composition: Convergence over Time," *American Journal of Sociology* 101 (1995): 578–610.

63. Lawrence Cohen and Marcus Felson, "Social Change and Crime Rate Trends: A Routine Activities Approach," *American Sociological Review* 44 (1979): 588–608.

64. Teresa LaGrange, "The Impact of Neighborhoods, Schools, and Malls on the Spatial Distribution of Property Damage," *Journal of Research in Crime and Delinquency* 36 (1999): 393–422.

65. Georgina Hammock and Deborah Richardson, "Perceptions of Rape: The Influence of Closeness of Relationship, Intoxication, and Sex of Participant," *Violence and Victimization* 12 (1997): 237–247.

66. Wittebrood and Nieuwbeerta, "Criminal Victimization during One's Life Course," pp. 112–113.

67. Don Weatherburn, Bronwyn Lind, and Simon Ku, "'Hotbeds of Crime?' Crime and Public Housing in Urban Sydney," *Crime and Delinquency* 45 (1999): 256–271.

68. Andy Hochstetler, "Opportunities and Decisions: Interactional Dynamics in Robbery and Burglary Groups," *Criminology* 39 (2001): 737–763.

69. Richard Felson, "Routine Activities and Involvement in Violence as Actor, Witness, or Target," *Violence and Victimization* 12 (1997): 209–223.

70. Jon Gunnar Bernburg and Thorolfur Thorlindsson, "Routine Activities in Social Context: A Closer Look at the Role of Opportunity in Deviant Behavior," *Justice Quarterly* 18 (2001): 543–568.

71. Martin Schwartz, Walter DeKeseredy, David Tait, and Shahid Alvi, "Male Peer Support and a Feminist Routine Activities Theory: Understanding Sexual Assault on the College Campus," *Justice Quarterly* 18 (2001): 623–650.

72. Terance Miethe and Robert Meier, *Crime and Its Social Context: Toward an Integrated Theory of Offenders, Victims, and Situations* (Albany: State University of New York Press, 1994).

73. Ronald Clarke, "Situational Crime Prevention," in *Building a Safer Society, Strategic Approaches to Crime Prevention,* vol. 19 of *Crime and Justice, A Review of Research,* eds. Michael Tonry and David Farrington (Chicago: University of Chicago Press, 1995), pp. 91–151.

74. Steven Messner, Lawrence Raffalovich and Richard McMillan, "Economic Deprivation and Changes in Homicide Arrest Rates for White and Black Youths, 1967–1998: A National Time-Series Analysis," *Criminology* 39 (2001): 591–614.

75. Lawrence Cohen, Marcus Felson, and Kenneth Land, "Property Crime Rates in the United States: A Macrodynamic Analysis, 1947–1977, with Ex-Ante Forecasts for the Mid-1980s," *American Journal of Sociology* 86 (1980): 90–118.

76. Patrick Donnelly and Charles Kimble, "Community Organizing, Environmental Change, and Neighborhood Crime," *Crime and Delinquency* 43 (1997): 493–511.

77. Simha Landau and Daniel Fridman, "The Seasonality of Violent Crime: The Case of Robbery and Homicide in Israel," *Journal of Research in Crime and Delinquency* 30 (1993): 163–191.

78. Patricia Resnick, "Psychological Effects of Victimization: Implications for the Criminal Justice System," *Crime and Delinquency* 33 (1987): 468–478.

79. Dean Kilpatrick, Benjamin Saunders, Lois Veronen, Connie Best, and Judith Von, "Criminal Victimization: Lifetime Prevalence, Reporting to Police, and Psychological Impact," *Crime and Delinquency* 33 (1987): 479–489.

80. Mark Santello and Harold Leitenberg, "Sexual Aggression by an Acquaintance: Methods of Coping and Later Psychological Adjustment," *Violence and Victims* 8 (1993): 91–103.

81. U.S. Department of Justice, *Report of the President's Task Force on Victims of Crime* (Washington, DC: U.S. Government Printing Office, 1983).

82. Ibid., pp. 2–10; and "Review on Victims—Witnesses of Crime," *Massachusetts Lawyers Weekly,* 25 April 1983, p. 26.

83. Robert Davis, *Crime Victims: Learning How to Help Them* (Washington, DC: National Institute of Justice, 1987).

84. Peter Finn and Beverly Lee, *Establishing a Victim-Witness Assistance Program* (Washington, DC: U.S. Government Printing Office, 1988).

85. This section leans heavily on Albert Roberts, "Delivery of Services to Crime Victims: A National Survey," *American Journal of Orthopsychiatry* 6 (1991): 128–137; see also Albert Roberts, *Helping Crime Victims: Research, Policy, and Practice* (Newbury Park, CA: Sage, 1990).

86. Randall Schmidt, "Crime Victim Compensation Legislation: A Comparative Study," *Victimology* 5 (1980): 428–437.

87. Ibid.

88. National Association of Crime Victim Compensation Boards. http://nacvcb.org/. Accessed September 24, 2003.

89. Ulrich Orth and Andreas Maercker, "Do Trials of Perpetrators Retraumatize Crime Victims?" *Journal of Interpersonal Violence* 19 (2004): 212–228.

90. Pater Jaffe, Marlies Sudermann, Deborah Reitzel, and Steve Killip, "An Evaluation of a Secondary School Primary Prevention Program on Violence in Intimate Relationships," *Violence and Victims* 7 (1992): 129–145.

91. Andrew Karmen, "Victim–Offender Reconciliation Programs: Pro and Con," *Perspectives of the American Probation and Parole Association* 20 (1996): 11–14.

92. Rachelle Hong, "Nothing to Fear: Establishing an Equality of Rights for Crime Victims through the Victims' Rights Amendment," *Notre Dame Journal of Legal Ethics and Public Policy* (2002): 207–225; see also, *Payne v. Tennessee,* 111 S.Ct. 2597, 115 L.Ed.2d 720 (1991).

93. Robert Davis and Barbara Smith, "The Effects of Victim Impact Statements on Sentencing Decisions: A Test in an Urban Setting," *Justice Quarterly* 11 (1994): 453–469; Edna Erez and Pamela Tontodonato, "The Effect of Victim Participation in Sentencing on Sentence Outcome," *Criminology* 28 (1990): 451–474.

94. Douglas E. Beloof, "Constitutional Implications of Crime Victims as Participants," *Cornell Law Review* 88 (2003): 282–305.

95. See Frank Carrington, "Victim's Rights Litigation: A Wave of the Future," in *Perspectives on Crime Victims,* eds. Burt Galaway and Joe Hudson (St. Louis: Mosby, 1981).

96. National Center for Victims of Crime. http://www.ncvc.org/policy/issues/rights/. Accessed September 24, 2003.

97. Ibid., pp. 9–10.

98. Sara Flaherty and Austin Flaherty, *Victims and Victims' Risk* (New York: Chelsea House, 1998).

99. Pamela Wilcox Rountree and Kenneth Land, "Burglary Victimization, Perceptions of Crime Risk, and Routine Activities: A Multilevel Analysis across Seattle Neighborhoods and Census Tracts," *Journal of Research in Crime and Delinquency* 33 (1996): 1,147–1,180.

100. Leslie Kennedy, "Going It Alone: Unreported Crime and Individual Self-Help," *Journal of Criminal Justice* 16 (1988): 403–413.

101. Ronald Clarke, "Situational Crime Prevention: Its Theoretical Basis and Practical Scope," in *Annual Review of Criminal Justice Research,* eds. Michael Tonry and Norval Morris (Chicago: University of Chicago Press, 1983).

102. See generally, Dennis P. Rosenbaum, Arthur J. Lurigio, and Robert C. Davis, *The Prevention of Crime: Social and Situational Strategies* (Belmont, CA: Wadsworth, 1998).

103. Andrew Buck, Simon Hakim, and George Rengert, "Burglar Alarms and the Choice Behavior of Burglars," *Journal of Criminal Justice* 21 (1993): 497–507; for an opposing view, see James Lynch and David Cantor, "Ecological and Behavioral Influences on Property Victimization at Home: Implications for Opportunity Theory," *Journal of Research in Crime and Delinquency* 29 (1992): 335–362.

104. Alan Lizotte, "Determinants of Completing Rape and Assault," *Journal of Quantitative Criminology* 2 (1986): 213–217.

105. Polly Marchbanks, Kung-Jong Lui, and James Mercy, "Risk of Injury from Resisting Rape," *American Journal of Epidemiology* 132 (1990): 540–549.

106. Caroline Wolf Harlow, *Robbery Victims* (Washington, DC: Bureau of Justice Statistics, 1987).

107. Gary Kleck, "Guns and Violence: An Interpretive Review of the Field," *Social Pathology* 1 (1995): 12–45, at 17.

108. Ibid.

109. Gary Kleck, "Rape and Resistance," *Social Problems* 37 (1990): 149–162.

110. Personal communication with Gary Kleck, January 10, 1997; see also Kleck, "Guns and Violence: An Interpretive Review of the Field."

111. James Garofalo and Maureen McLeod, *Improving the Use and Effectiveness of Neighborhood Watch Programs* (Washington, DC: National Institute of Justice, 1988).

112. Peter Finn, *Block Watches Help Crime Victims in Philadelphia* (Washington, DC: National Institute of Justice, 1986).

113. Ibid.

PART Two

THEORIES OF CRIME CAUSATION

IIIIIIIIIIIIIIIIIIIIIIIIIIIII

An important goal of the criminological enterprise is to create valid and accurate theories of crime causation. A theory can be defined as an abstract statement that explains why certain things do (or do not) happen. To be called a theory, this statement must have empirical (observable) implications—that is, it must make predictions that something observable will (or will not) happen under certain specified circumstances. *

Criminologists have sought to collect vital facts about crime and interpret them in a scientifically meaningful fashion. By developing empirically verifiable statements, or hypotheses, and organizing them into theories of crime causation, they hope to identify the causes of crime.

Since the late nineteenth century, criminological theory has pointed to various underlying causes of crime. The earliest theories generally attributed crime to a single underlying cause: atypical body build, genetic abnormality, insanity, physical anomalies, or poverty. Later theories attributed crime causation to multiple factors: poverty, peer influence, school problems, and family dysfunction.

In this section, theories of crime causation are grouped into six chapters. Chapters 4 and 5 focus on theories that view crime as based on individual traits. They hold that crime is either a free will choice made by an individual, a function of personal psychological or biological abnormality, or both. Chapters 6, 7, and 8 investigate theories based in sociology and political economy. These theories portray crime as a function of the structure, process, and conflicts of social living. Chapter 9 is devoted to theories that combine or integrate these various concepts into a cohesive, complex, developmental view of crime.

* Rodney Stark, *Sociology*, 8th ed. (Belmont, CA: Wadsworth, 2001), p. 2.

CHAPTER 4

© Getty Images

Johnny Ray Gasca was a native New Yorker with a track record of petty crime when he moved to Hollywood in 2002 to seek his fortune in the movie business. Given his criminal leanings, Gasca was less interested in making movies than in stealing them!

Gasca began to pose as a movie industry insider and hang around theaters where advance screenings of feature films were scheduled. Once in the theater he would rig his camera to an armrest for stability and start filming when the lights went down. He used high-end sound and recording equipment that produced extraordinary quality master recordings. He then would mass produce the recordings on 11 interlinked VCRs and sell them over the Internet. By beating the public release of blockbuster films, he cleared as much as $4,500 a week from his illegal pirating scheme.

Though he was known as the Prince of Pirates, Gasca had a bad habit of getting caught in the act. Police in Burbank, California, arrested him when he was filming the science fiction film The Core. He was also arrested when he began filming Anger Management and 8 Mile. When Gasca's apartment was searched, federal agents found two videocameras, a micro-camera built onto a trouser belt, two DVD recorders, the 11 linked VCRs, a stolen Social Security card, and two diaries chronicling his exploits.[1] While he was out on bail, Gasca threatened to sell up to 20 more unreleased movies online unless the Motion Picture Association of America (MPAA) helped him get his equipment back. In 2003, Gasca became the first person ever indicted on federal charges of movie piracy. Placed in his lawyer's custody, he disappeared without a trace until he was located two years later in Kissimmee, Florida, where, not surprisingly, he was supporting himself by illegally copying movies. On June 29, 2005, Gasca was found guilty of eight federal criminal charges, including three counts of copyright infringement.

CHOICE THEORIES

CHAPTER OBJECTIVES

1. Be familiar with the concept of rational choice
2. Know the work of Beccaria
3. Be familiar with the concept of offense-specific crime
4. Be familiar with the concept of offender-specific crime
5. Be able to discuss why violent and drug crimes are rational
6. Know the various techniques of situational crime prevention
7. Be able to discuss the association between punishment and crime
8. Be familiar with the concepts of certainty, severity, and speed of punishment
9. Know what is meant by specific deterrence
10. Be able to discuss the issues involving the use of incapacitation
11. Understand the concept of just desert

Johnny Ray Gasca's criminal enterprise was certainly well thought out and planned. His method of operation involved both the learning of criminal techniques and the development of methods to use them for criminal gain.

While we can easily assume that international drug dealers, white-collar criminals, and organized crime figures use planning, organization, and rational decision making to commit their crimes, can we also assume that such common crimes as theft, fraud, and even murder are a function of detailed planning and decision making? Are these random senseless acts or a matter of personal choice, designed to maximize gain and minimize loss?

The view that crime is a matter of **rational choice** is held by a number of criminologists who believe the decision to violate any law—commit a robbery, sell drugs, attack a rival, fill out a false tax return—is made for a variety of personal reasons, including greed, revenge, need, anger, lust, jealousy, thrill-seeking, or vanity. Regardless of the motive, criminal actions occur only after individuals carefully weigh the potential benefits and consequences of crime. The jealous suitor, for example, concludes that the risk of punishment is worth the satisfaction of punching a rival. The greedy shopper considers the chance of apprehension by store detectives so small that she takes a "five-finger discount" on a new sweater. The drug dealer concludes that the huge profit from a single shipment of cocaine far outweighs the possible costs of apprehension.

This chapter reviews the philosophical underpinnings of choice theory, tracing it back to the classical school of criminology. We then turn to more recent theoretical models that flow from the concept of choice. These models hold that because criminals are rational, their behavior can be controlled or deterred by the fear of punishment; desistance can then be explained by a growing and intense fear of criminal sanctions. These views include situational crime control, general deterrence theory, specific deterrence theory, and incapacitation. Finally, the chapter briefly reviews how choice theory has influenced criminal justice policy.

THE DEVELOPMENT OF RATIONAL CHOICE THEORY

Rational choice theory has its roots in the classical school of criminology developed by the Italian social thinker Cesare Beccaria.[2] In keeping with his utilitarian views, Beccaria called for fair and certain punishment to deter crime. He believed people are egotistical and self-centered, and therefore they must be motivated by the fear of punishment, which provides a tangible motive for them to obey the law and suppress the "despotic spirit" that resides in every person.[3]

To read about **Beccaria's life history and the formulation of his ideas,** go to http://www.criminology.fsu.edu/crimtheory/beccaria.htm. For an up-to-date list of web links, go to http://cj.wadsworth.com/siegel_crimtpt9e.

| | | | | | | **CONNECTIONS** | | | | | |

As you may recall from Chapter 1, classical criminology is based on the work of Cesare Beccaria and other utilitarian philosophers. Its core concepts are that (1) people choose all behavior, including criminal behavior; (2) their choices can be controlled by fear of punishment; and (3) the more severe, certain, and swift the punishment, the greater its ability to control criminal behavior.

To deter people from committing more serious offenses, Beccaria believed crime and punishment must be proportional; if not, people would be encouraged to commit more serious offenses. For example, if robbery, rape, and murder were all punished by death, robbers or rapists would have little reason to refrain from killing their victims to eliminate them as witnesses to the crime. Today, this is referred to as the concept of **marginal deterrence**—if petty offenses were subject to the same punishment as more serious crimes, offenders would choose the worse crime because the resulting punishment would be about the same.[4]

To learn more about the influence of Beccaria's views, go to InfoTrac College Edition and read: Richard Bellamy, "Crime and Punishment," *History Review* (September 1997): 24.

The Classical Theory of Crime

Beccaria's ideas and writings inspired social thinkers to believe that criminals choose to commit crime and that crime can be controlled by judicious punishment. His vision was widely accepted throughout Europe and the United States.[5]

In Britain, philosopher Jeremy Bentham (1748–1833) helped popularize Beccaria's views in his writings on utilitarianism. Bentham believed that people choose actions on the basis of whether they produce pleasure and happiness and help them avoid pain or unhappiness.[6] The purpose of law is to produce and support the total happiness of the community it serves. Because punishment is in itself harmful, its existence is justified only if it promises to prevent greater evil than it creates. Punishment, therefore, has four main objectives:

1. To prevent all criminal offenses

2. When it cannot prevent a crime, to convince the offender to commit a less serious crime

3. To ensure that a criminal uses no more force than is necessary

4. To prevent crime as cheaply as possible[7]

To read more about the life of **Jeremy Bentham,** go to http://www.blupete.com/Literature/Biographies/Philosophy/Bentham.htm. For an up-to-date list of web links, go to http://cj.wadsworth.com/siegel_crimtpt9e.

This vision was embraced by France's postrevolutionary Constituent Assembly (1789) in its Declaration of the Rights of Man:

> [T]he law has the right to prohibit only actions harmful to society. . . . The law shall inflict only such punishments as are strictly and clearly necessary . . . no person shall be punished except by virtue of a law enacted and promulgated previous to the crime and applicable to its terms.

Similarly, a prohibition against cruel and unusual punishment was incorporated in the Eighth Amendment to the U.S. Constitution.

Beccaria's writings have been credited as the basis of the elimination of torture and severe punishment in the nineteenth century. The practice of incarcerating criminals and structuring prison sentences to fit the severity of crime was a reflection of his classical criminology.

By the end of the nineteenth century, the popularity of the classical approach began to decline, and by the middle of the twentieth century, this perspective was neglected by mainstream criminologists. During this period, positivist criminologists focused on internal and external factors—poverty, IQ, education, home life—which were believed to be the true causes of criminality. Because these conditions could not be easily manipulated, the concept of punishing people for behaviors beyond their control seemed both foolish and cruel. Although classical principles still controlled the way police, courts, and correctional agencies operate, most criminologists rejected classical criminology as an explanation of criminal behavior.

I I I I I I I CONNECTIONS I I I I I I I

The rise of positivist criminology is discussed in Chapter 1. Positivist theories of criminology, which stress that people are influenced by internal and external forces beyond their control, are analyzed in Chapters 4 though Chapter 9.

Choice Theory Emerges

Beginning in the mid-1970s, the classical approach began to enjoy resurging popularity. First, the rehabilitation of known criminals—considered a cornerstone of positivist policy—came under attack. According to positivist criminology, if crime was caused by some social or psychological problem, such as poverty, then crime rates could be reduced by providing good jobs and economic opportunities. Despite some notable efforts to provide such opportunities, a number of national surveys (the best known being Robert Martinson's "What Works?") failed to find examples of rehabilitation programs that prevented future criminal activity.[8] A well-publicized book, *Beyond Probation*, by Charles Murray and Louis Cox, went as far as suggesting that punishment-oriented programs could suppress future criminality much more effectively than those that relied on rehabilitation and treatment efforts.[9]

Was Martinson right? To find out more about the effectiveness of correctional treatment, use "correctional treatment" as a subject guide with InfoTrac College Edition.

A significant increase in the reported crime rate, as well as serious disturbances in the nation's prisons, frightened the general public. The media depicted criminals as callous and dangerous rather than as needy people deserving of public sympathy. Some criminologists began to suggest that it made more sense to frighten these cold calculators with severe punishments than to waste public funds by futilely trying to improve entrenched social conditions linked to crime such as poverty.[10]

THINKING ABOUT CRIME Beginning in the late 1970s, a number of criminologists began producing books and monographs expounding the theme that criminals are rational actors who plan their crimes, fear punishment, and deserve to be penalized for their misdeeds. In a 1975 book that came to symbolize renewed interest in classical views, *Thinking about Crime,* political scientist James Q. Wilson debunked the positivist view that crime was a function of external forces, such as poverty, that could be altered by government programs. Instead, he argued, efforts should be made to reduce criminal opportunity by deterring would-be offenders and incarcerating known criminals. People who are likely to commit crime, he maintained, lack inhibition against misconduct, value the excitement and thrills of breaking the law, have a low stake in conformity, and are willing to take greater chances than the average person. If they could be convinced that their actions will bring severe punishment, only the totally irrational would be willing to engage in crime.[11] Wilson made this famous observation:

> Wicked people exist. Nothing avails except to set them apart from innocent people. And many people, neither wicked nor innocent, but watchful, dissembling, and calculating of their chances, ponder our reaction to wickedness as a clue to what they might profitably do.[12]

Here Wilson is saying that unless we react forcefully to crime, those "sitting on the fence" will get a clear message—crime pays.

To read a famous talk given by **James Wilson, "Two Nations,"** the 1997 Francis Boyer lecture delivered at the annual dinner of the American Enterprise Institute, go to http://www.aei.org/boyer/jwilson.htm. For an up-to-date list of web links, go to http://cj.wadsworth.com/siegel_crimtpt9e.

IMPACT ON CRIME CONTROL Coinciding with the publication of Wilson's book was a conservative shift in U.S. public policy, which resulted in Ronald Reagan's election to the presidency in 1980. Political decision makers embraced Wilson's ideas as a means to bring the crime rate down. Tough new laws were passed, creating mandatory prison sentences for drug offenders; the nation's prison population skyrocketed. Critics decried the disproportionate number of young minority men being locked up for drug law violations.[13] Despite liberal anguish, conservative views of crime control have helped shape criminal justice policy for the past two decades.[14] Many Americans, some of whom are passionate opponents of abortion on the grounds that it takes human life, became, ironically, ardent supporters of the death penalty![15] This "get tough" attitude was supported by the fact that while the prison population has grown to new heights, the crime rate has been in a steep decline.

 Even if the **death penalty** were an effective deterrent, some critics believe it presents ethical problems that make its use morally dubious. Read what the American Civil Liberties Union has to say at http://www.aclu.org/death-penalty/. For an up-to-date list of web links, go to http://cj.wadsworth.com/siegel_crimtpt9e.

From these roots, a more contemporary version of classical theory evolved that is based on intelligent thought processes and criminal decision making; today this is referred to as the *rational choice* approach to crime causation.[16]

 To quiz yourself on this material, go to the Criminology TPT 9e website.

THE CONCEPTS OF RATIONAL CHOICE

According to the rational choice approach, law-violating behavior occurs when an offender decides to risk breaking the law after considering both personal factors (such as the need for money, revenge, thrills, and entertainment) and situational factors (how well a target is protected and the efficiency of the local police force). Before choosing to commit a crime, the **reasoning criminal** evaluates the risk of apprehension, the seriousness of expected punishment, the potential value of the criminal enterprise, and his or her immediate need for criminal gain. Conversely, the decision to forgo crime may be based on the criminal's perception that the economic benefits are no longer there or that the risk of apprehension is too great.[17]

Criminals then are people who share the same ambitions as conventional citizens but have decided to cut corners and use illegal means to achieve their goals. Many criminal offenders retain conventional American values of striving for success, material attainment, and hard work.[18] When Philippe Bourgois studied crack dealers in East Harlem in New York City, he found that their motivations were not dissimilar from the "average citizen": They were upwardly mobile, scrambling around to obtain their "piece of the pie."[19] If they commit crime, it is because they have chosen an illegal path to obtain the goals that might otherwise have been out of reach.

According to choice theory, crime occurs when an individual believes he or she will successfully profit from an act even if it results in a law violation. Shown here is Susan Almgren, a first-grade teacher, after she pled guilty in a Lexington, Kentucky, court to charges of prostitution and running an illegal escort service. Almgren, a first-time offender, was fined $300. Could greed alone cause an educated woman such as Almgren to engage in such a risky scheme as running a shady escort service?

| | | | | | CONNECTIONS | | | | | | |

Lack of conventional opportunity is a persistent theme in sociological theories of crime. The frustration caused by a perceived lack of opportunity explains the high crime rates in lower-class areas. Chapter 6 discusses strain and cultural deviance theories, which provide alternative explanations of how lack of opportunity is associated with crime.

Offense- and Offender-Specific Crimes

Rational choice theorists view crime as both offense and offender specific.[20] An **offense-specific crime** means that offenders will react selectively to the characteristics of particular offenses. The decision of whether to commit burglary, for example, might involve evaluating the target's likely cash yield, the availability of resources such as a getaway car, and the probability of capture by police.[21] An **offender-specific crime** means that criminals are not simply automatons who, for one reason or another, engage in random acts of antisocial behavior. Before deciding to commit crime, individuals must decide whether they have the prerequisites to commit a successful criminal act, including the proper skills, motives, needs, and fears. Criminal acts might be ruled out if potential offenders perceive that they can reach a desired personal goal through legitimate means or if they are too afraid of getting caught.[22]

Note the distinction made here between crime and **criminality**.[23] *Crime* is an event; *criminality* is a personal trait. Professional criminals do not commit crime all the time, and even ordinary citizens may, on occasion, violate the law. Some people considered "high risk" because they are indigent or disturbed may never violate the law, whereas others who are seemingly affluent and well adjusted may risk criminal behavior given enough provocation and/or opportunity. What conditions promote crime and enhance criminality?

Structuring Criminality

A number of personal factors condition people to choose crime. Among the more important factors are economic opportunity, learning and experience, and knowledge of criminal techniques.

ECONOMIC OPPORTUNITY In the August 2004 issue of *Boston Magazine*, a university lecturer with a master's degree from Yale and a doctorate in cultural anthropology wrote a first-person account of how she took another job to pay the bills: call girl.[24] Rather than living on the meager teaching salary she was offered, she *chose* to take the tax-free $140 per hour for her services (she charged $200, handing over $60 to the escort service that arranged her dates). She left the "business" when she became financially self-sufficient.

The Ivy League hooker is not alone. Perceptions of economic opportunity influence the decision to commit crime. Increases in criminal activity may flow from economic necessity. For example, Christopher Uggen and Melissa Thompson found that people who begin taking hard drugs also increase their involvement in crime, illegally taking in from $500 to $700 per month. Once they become cocaine and heroin users, the benefits of criminal enterprise become overwhelmingly attractive.[25]

Crime also becomes attractive when an individual becomes convinced that it will result in excessive profits with few costs. Research shows that criminals may be motivated to commit crime when they know others who have made "big scores" and are quite successful at crime. Although the prevailing wisdom is that crime does not pay, a small but significant subset of criminals actually enjoy earnings of close to $50,000 per year from crime, and their success may help motivate other would-be offenders.[26] However, offenders are likely to desist from crime if they believe that their future criminal earnings will be relatively low and that attractive and legal opportunities to generate income are available.[27] In this sense, rational choice is a function of a person's perception of conventional alternatives and opportunities.

| | | | | | CONNECTIONS | | | | | |

The role of economic needs in the motivation of white-collar criminals is discussed in Chapter 12. Research shows that even consistently law-abiding people may turn to criminal solutions when faced with overwhelming economic needs. They make the rational decision to commit crimes to solve some economic crisis.

LEARNING AND EXPERIENCE Learning and experience may be important elements in structuring the choice of crime.[28] Career criminals may learn the limitations of their powers; they know when to take a chance and when to be cautious. Experienced criminals may turn from a life of crime when they develop a belief that the risk of crime is greater than its potential profit.[29] Patricia Morgan and Karen Ann Joe's three-city study (San Francisco, San Diego, and Honolulu) of female drug abusers found that experience helped dealers avoid detection. One dealer, earning $50,000 per year, explained her strategy this way:

> I stayed within my goals, basically . . . I don't go around doing stupid things. I don't walk around telling people I have drugs for sale. I don't have people sitting out in front of my house. I don't have traffic in and out of my house . . . I control the people I sell to.[30]

Morgan and Joe found that these female dealers consider drug distribution a positive experience that gives them economic independence, self-esteem, increased ability to function, professional pride, and the ability to maintain control over their lives. These women often seemed more like yuppies opening a boutique than out-of-control addicts:

> I'm a good dealer. I don't cut my drugs, I have high-quality drugs insofar as it's possible to get high-quality drugs. I want to be known as somebody who sells good drugs, but doesn't always have them, as opposed to someone who always has them and sometimes the drugs are good.[31]

Here we see how experience in the profession shapes criminal decision making.

KNOWLEDGE OF CRIMINAL TECHNIQUES Criminals report learning techniques that help them avoid detection, a sure sign of rational thinking and planning. In his studies of drug dealers, criminologist Bruce Jacobs found that crack dealers learn how to stash crack cocaine in some undisclosed location so that they are not forced to carry large amounts of product on their persons. Dealers carefully evaluate the security of their sales area before setting up shop.[32] Most consider the middle of a long block the best place for drug deals because they can see everything in both directions; police raids can be spotted before they develop.[33] If a buyer seems dangerous or unreliable, the dealer would require that they do business in spaces between apartment buildings or in back lots. Although dealers lose the tactical edge of being on a public street, they gain a measure of protection because their associates can watch over the deal and come to the rescue if the buyer tries to "pull something." [34] Similar detection avoidance schemes were found by Gordon Knowles in his study of crack dealers in Honolulu, Hawaii. Knowles found that drug dealers often use pornographic film houses as their base of operations because they offer both privacy and convenience. [35]

When Jacobs, along with Jody Miller, studied female crack dealers, they discovered a variety of defensive moves used by the dealers to avoid detection; these are set out in Exhibit 4.1. [36]

Criminals who learn the proper techniques may be able to prolong their criminal careers. Jacobs found that these offenders use specific techniques to avoid being apprehended by police. They play what they call the "peep game" before dealing drugs, scoping out the territory to make sure the turf is free from anything out of place that could be a potential threat (such as police officers or rival gang members). [37] One crack dealer told Jacobs:

> There was this red Pontiac sittin' on the corner one day with two white guys inside. They was just sittin' there for an hour, not doin' nothin'. Another day, diff'rent people be walkin' up and down the street you don't really recognize. You think they might be kin of someone but then you be askin' around and they [neighbors] ain't never seen them before neither. When ya' see strange things like that, you think somethin' be goin' on [and you don't deal]. [38]

Drug dealers told Jacobs that they also carefully consider whether they should deal alone or in groups; large groups draw more attention from police but can offer more protection. Drug-dealing gangs and groups can help divert the attention of police: If their drug dealing is noticed by detectives, a dealer can slyly walk away or dispose of evidence while confederates distract the cops. [39]

Do drug dealers make rational decisions? Use "drug dealing" as a subject guide on InfoTrac College Edition to find out.

||||||| CONNECTIONS |||||||

Rational choice theory dovetails with routine activities theory, which you learned about in Chapter 3. Although not identical, these approaches both claim that crime rates are a normal product of criminal opportunity. Both suggest that criminals consider such elements as guardianship and target attractiveness before they decide to commit crimes.

The routine activities and rational choice views also agree that criminal opportunity is a key element in the criminal process. The overlap between these two viewpoints may help criminologists suggest means for effective crime control.

Structuring Crime

Not only do criminals structure their careers, but they rationally choose where and when to commit crime and whom to target. According to the rational choice approach, the decision to commit crime is structured by analysis of (1) the type of crime, (2) the time and place of crime, and (3) the target of crime.

CHOOSING THE TYPE OF CRIME Some criminals are specialists, for example, professional car thieves. Others are generalists who sell drugs one day and commit burglaries the next. Their choice of crime may be dictated by a rational analysis of market conditions. For example, they may rob the elderly on the first of the month when they know that Social Security checks have been cashed.

Sometimes the choice of crime is structured by the immediacy of the need for funds. Eric Baumer and his associates found that cities with greater levels of crack cocaine often experience an increase in robbery and a corresponding decrease in burglary rates. Baumer reasons that crack users need a quick influx of cash to purchase drugs and are in no position to plan a burglary and take the time to sell their loot; street robberies are designed to provide a quick influx of cash that meets their lifestyle needs.[40]

CHOOSING THE TIME AND PLACE OF CRIME There is evidence of rationality in the way criminals choose the time and place of their crimes. Burglars seem to prefer "working" between 9 A.M. and 11 A.M. and in mid-afternoon, when parents are either working or dropping off or picking up kids at school.[41] Burglars avoid Saturdays because most families are at home; Sunday morning during church hours is considered a prime time for weekend burglaries.[42] Some find out which families have star high school athletes because those that do are sure to be at the weekend game, leaving their houses unguarded.[43]

Evidence of rational choice may also be found in the way criminals choose target locations. Thieves seem to avoid freestanding buildings because they can more easily be surrounded by police; they like to select targets that are known to do a primarily cash business, such as bars, supermarkets, and restaurants.[44] Burglars appear to monitor car and pedestrian traffic and avoid selecting targets on heavily traveled streets.[45] Corner homes, usually near traffic lights or stop signs, are the ones most likely to be burglarized: Stop signs give criminals a legitimate reason to stop their cars and look for an attractive target.[46] Secluded homes, such as those at the end of a cul-de-sac or surrounded by wooded areas, make suitable targets.[47] Thieves also report being concerned about target convenience. They are more apt to choose familiar burglary sites that are located in easily accessible and open areas.[48]

Because criminals often go on foot or use public transportation, they are unlikely to travel long distances to commit crimes and are more likely to drift toward the center of a city than move toward outlying areas.[49] Some may occasionally commute to distant locations to commit crimes, but most prefer to stay in their own neighborhood where they are familiar with the terrain. They will only travel to unfamiliar areas if they believe the new location contains a worthy target and lax law enforcement. They may be encouraged to travel when the police are cracking down in their own neighborhood and the "heat is on."[50] Evidence is accumulating that predatory criminals are in fact aware of law enforcement capabilities and consider them closely before deciding to commit crimes. Communities with the reputation of employing aggressive "crime-fighting" cops are less likely to attract potential offenders than areas perceived to have passive law enforcers.[51]

CHOOSING THE TARGET OF CRIME Criminals may also be well aware of target vulnerability. For example, there is evidence that people engaging in deviant or antisocial behaviors

It is not difficult to spot the sophisticated planning, preparation, and design in some crimes. Here Christopher Harn is led into Federal Court in White Plains, New York, on November 12, 2002. Harn, who worked for the bet-taking company Autotote, and two of his former college classmates, Derrick Davis and Glen DaSilva, were charged with wire fraud and conspiracy in a plot to rig bets for a million-dollar payout at the Breeders Cup in Arlington Park near Chicago. The men placed bets, then hacked into a computer system that tracked the wagers to change them after the races were completed. Harn placed the bets through an off-track betting parlor using the accounts of Davis and DaSilva. He then altered the tickets to make them winners using the touch-tone betting system that he himself designed. He also printed fake tickets with the serial numbers of uncashed tickets that he found in the Autotote system and gave them to Davis and DaSilva to cash at various race tracks. The winning amounts were small enough to not require IRS reporting but together amounted to thousands of dollars. Harn pled guilty to conspiracy to commit fraud and conspiracy to launder money (and agreed to testify against his friends!).

are also the most likely to become crime victims.[52] Perhaps predatory criminals sense that people with "dirty hands" make suitable targets because they are unlikely to want to call police or get entangled with the law.

Criminals tend to shy away from victims who are perceived to be armed and potentially dangerous.[53] In a series of interviews with career property offenders, Kenneth Tunnell found that burglars avoid targets if they feel there are police in the area or if "nosy neighbors" might be suspicious and cause trouble.[54]

 To quiz yourself on this material, go to the Criminology TPT 9e website.

IS CRIME RATIONAL?

It is relatively easy to show that some crimes are the product of rational, objective thought, especially when they involve an ongoing criminal conspiracy centered on economic gain. When prominent bankers in the savings and loan industry were indicted for criminal fraud, their elaborate financial schemes not only exhibited signs of rationality but brilliant, though flawed, financial expertise.[55] The stock market manipulations of executives at Enron and Worldcom, the drug dealings of international cartels, and the gambling operations of organized crime bosses all demonstrate a reasoned analysis of market conditions, interests, and risks. Even small-time wheeler-dealers, such as the female drug dealers discussed earlier in the chapter, are guided by their rational assessment of the likelihood of apprehension and take pains to avoid detection. But what about common crimes of theft and violence? Are these rational acts or unplanned, haphazard, and spontaneous?

Is Theft Rational?

Common theft-related crimes—burglaries, larcenies, shoplifting, purse snatchings—seem more likely to be random acts of criminal opportunity than well-thought-out conspiracies. However, there is evidence that even these seemingly unplanned events may be the product of careful risk assessment, including environmental, social, and structural factors. For example, there are professional shoplifters, referred to as **boosters,** who use complex methods in order to avoid detection. They steal with the intention of reselling stolen merchandise to professional fences, another group of criminals who use cunning and rational decision making in their daily activities.

Burglars also seem to use skill and knowledge when choosing targets. Experienced burglars report having to learn detection avoidance techniques. Some check to make sure that no one is home, either by calling ahead or ringing the doorbell, preparing to claim they had the wrong address if someone answers. Others seek unlocked doors and avoid the ones with deadbolts; houses with dogs are usually considered off limits.[56] Most burglars prefer to commit crimes in **permeable neighborhoods** with a greater than usual number of access streets from traffic arteries into the neighborhood.[57] These areas are chosen for theft and break-ins because they are familiar and well traveled, they appear more open and vulnerable, and they offer more potential escape routes.[58]

American burglars are not alone in using rational choice. English authorities report that carefully planned burglaries seem to be on the decline presumably because goods that were the target a few years back—video recorders and DVD players—are now so cheap that they are not worth stealing; in English terms, they are barely worth nicking. Televisions may be valuable but those that are the most valuable have become so large that they are impractical to steal.[59] As a result, the planned professional burglary is on a decline in Britain at the same time that street muggings are on the rise.

Is Drug Use Rational?

Did actor Robert Downey, Jr., make an objective, rational choice to abuse drugs and potentially sabotage his career? Did comedian Chris Farley make a rational choice when he abused alcohol and other drugs to the point that it killed him? Is it possible that drug users and dealers, a group not usually associated with clear thinking, make rational choices? Research does in fact show that from its onset drug use is controlled by rational decision making. Users report that they begin taking drugs when they believe that the benefits of substance abuse outweigh its costs (for example, they believe that drugs will provide a fun, exciting, thrilling experience). Their entry into substance abuse is facilitated by their perception that valued friends and family members endorse and encourage drug use and abuse substances themselves.[60]

In adulthood, heavy drug users and dealers show signs of rationality and cunning in their daily activity, approaching drug dealing as a business proposition. Research conducted by Leanne Fiftal Alarid and her partners provides a good illustration of this phenomenon because it focused on how women drawn into dealing drugs learn the trade in a businesslike manner. One young dealer told them how she learned the techniques of the trade from an older male partner:

> He taught me how to "recon" [reconstitute] cocaine, cutting and repacking a brick from 91 proof to 50 proof, just like a business. He treats me like an equal partner, and many of the friends are business associates. I am a catalyst. . . . I even get guys turned on to drugs.[61]

Note the business terminology used. This coke dealer could be talking about taking a computer training course at a major corporation! If criminal acts are treated as business decisions, in which profit and loss potential must be carefully calculated, then crime must indeed be a rational event. The Criminological Enterprise feature, "Hector Vega: A Life in the Drug Trade," discusses the rational aspects of drug dealing.

Is Violence Rational?

In 1998, Brandon Wilson, 21, slashed the throat of Matthew Cecchi, a 9-year-old California boy, then stabbed him in the back and left him to bleed to death. After his conviction on murder charges, Wilson told the jury that he would "do it again in a second if I had the chance." When the jury later

Hector Vega: A Life in the Drug Trade

In summer 2004, a dramatic murder trial took place in New York City that aptly illustrates the concept of rational choice. Two Bronx men, Alan Quiñones and Diego Rodriguez, were accused of heroin trafficking and killing a police informant. The trial hinged on the testimony of one of their confederates—Hector Vega, a key government witness who had previously pleaded guilty to taking part in the murder. He described in vivid detail how he watched the defendants beat the victim, Edwin Santiago, as he lay handcuffed on the floor of a Bronx apartment. He told the jury how the defendants Quiñones and Rodriguez spit in Santiago's face to show what they thought of police informants. Santiago's body was found mutilated and burned beyond recognition on June 28, 1999.

During the trial, Vega gave the jury a detailed lesson in retail drug operations. In the Bronx, beatings, slashings, and shootings are routinely used to enforce what he called "the drug law": "If people deserved it, I beat them up." He showed them a tattoo on his upper right arm that meant "Money, Power, Respect." Vega, 31, also told the jury that he headed a group of heroin vendors who did business from his "spot," his sales area, between Daly and Honeywell Avenues in the Bronx. He said he had learned the trade from a stepfather, a building superintendent who he said had a second job as a narcotics entrepreneur: "I always knew about the drug business. I was raised around it."

As a mid-level drug dealer, Vega received heroin on consignment from big-time drug wholesalers and turned it over in $100 packages to people he called his "managers," who in turn found "runners" to sell it on the street. His job was to "make sure everybody is working, and I will make sure everything is running correctly." Vega received a "commission" of about 35 percent of all sales in his organization; he estimated that he made a total of at least $500,000 in the five years before his arrest.

Vega told how he used strict rules to run his organization. He did not sell between 1 and 3 P.M. because of "school hours." He did not allow anyone to sell at his spot without his approval, or steal drugs from him, or pass him a counterfeit bill, or taint the quality of drugs sold under his name. If that happened, he said, "I'd be looking like a fool. The drug spot will go down." When Manny, one of his workers, stole one package of heroin, Vega slashed his face with a box cutter. When the wound did not immediately bleed, "I didn't see nothing cut, I didn't see anything I did, so I did it a second time," he said, until he saw blood. Angered by a counterfeit bill he received from a crack addict, "I punched him in the face, I kicked him, I threw him on the floor and kicked him again." He disciplined one stranger who cheated him by hitting the man in the back of the head with a three-foot tree branch. Police informants were given special treatment. "In the drug world, in the drug law, we say that snitches get stitches," he said. "In jail you cut their face. In the street, you beat them. You kill them."

Vega testified that the defendants Quiñones and Rodriguez were heroin wholesalers and that he began buying drugs from them a few months before Santiago's death. After he learned that Quiñones suspected Santiago of working undercover for the police, he helped him lure Santiago to the apartment of a girlfriend where the beatings and murder took place. For his cooperation, Vega faced a fifteen-year sentence rather than the death penalty.

The Vega case illustrates the concept that rational choice is a key element in crime. Drug dealing is a business with rules that have to be obeyed and roles that must be faithfully carried out. Drug deals are not spontaneous acts motivated by rage, mental illness, or economic desperation but rational albeit illegal business enterprise engaged in by highly motivated players. Those who violate corporate policy are dealt with ruthlessly.

Critical Thinking

Do you agree that drug dealing is a business in the traditional sense, or are dealers forced into a life of crime by social forces beyond their control? Can an analogy be made between drug dealing and legitimate business enterprise?

 InfoTrac College Edition Research

Is drug dealing and smuggling a type of business enterprise? Use InfoTrac College Edition to read: Terrance G. Lichtenwald, "Drug Smuggling Behavior: A Development Smuggling Model (Part 2)," *The Forensic Examiner* 13 (2004): 14–23.

Source: Julia Preston, "Witness Gives Details of Life as Drug Dealer," *New York Times*, 12 July 2004.

---

met to consider the death penalty, Wilson told them, "My whole purpose in life is to help destroy your society. You people are here as representatives of that society. As such, you should do everything in your power to rid the world of me, execute me." Granting his wish, the jury foreman told reporters, "If there was ever a case that deserved the death penalty, this one fits."[62]

Though seemingly a demented child killer, Brandon Wilson's statements indicate that he is a rational and calculating killer who may have carefully chosen his victim. Is it possible that violent acts, through which the offender gains little material benefit, are the product of reasoned decision making?

RATIONAL ROBBERS Street robbers also are likely to choose victims who are vulnerable, have low coercive power, and do not pose any threat.[63] In their survey of violent felons, James Wright and Peter Rossi found that robbers avoid victims who may be armed and dangerous. About three-fifths of all felons interviewed were more afraid of armed victims than police; about two-fifths had avoided a victim because they believed the victim was armed; and almost one-third reported that they had been scared off, wounded, or captured by armed victims.[64] It comes as no surprise that cities with higher than average gun-carrying rates generally have lower rates of unarmed robbery.[65]

Robbers also tend to pick the time and day of crimes carefully. When they rob a commercial establishment, they choose the time when there is the most cash on hand to increase their take from the crime. For example, robbery rates increase in the winter partly because the Christmas shopping season means more money in the cash registers of potential targets.[66] Targets are generally found close to robbers' homes or in areas in which they routinely travel. Familiarity with the area gives them ready knowledge of escape routes; this is referred to as their "awareness space."[67] Robbers may be wary of people who are watching the community for signs of trouble: Research by Paul Bellair shows that robbery levels are relatively low in neighborhoods where residents keep a watchful eye on their neighbors' property.[68] Robbers avoid buildings that can be easily surrounded by police; they also prefer to rob businesses that deal primarily with cash.[69] Their activities show clear signs of rational choice.

RATIONAL KILLERS? Hollywood likes to portray deranged people killing innocent victims at random, but people who carry guns and are ready to use them typically do so for more rational reasons. They may perceive that they live in a dangerous environment and carry a weapon for self-protection.[70] Some are involved in dangerous illegal activities such as drug dealing and carry weapons as part of the job.[71] Even in apparently senseless killings among strangers, the conscious motive is typically revenge for a prior dispute or disagreement among the parties involved or their families.[72] Many homicides are motivated by offenders' desire to avoid retaliation from a victim they assaulted or to avoid future prosecutions by getting rid of witnesses.[73] Although some killings are the result of anger and aggression, others are the result of rational planning.

Even serial murderers, outwardly the most irrational of all offenders, tend to pick their targets with care. Most choose victims who are either defenseless or who cannot count on police protection: prostitutes, gay men, hitchhikers, children, hospital patients, the elderly, and the homeless. Rarely do serial killers target weightlifters, martial arts experts, or any other potentially powerful group.[74]

Even killers can be rational, educated people. Harvard University graduate student Alexander Pring-Wilson, 25, stands during his arraignment in the stabbing death of Michael Colono, 18, April 14, 2003, in Cambridge, Massachusetts. Pring-Wilson and Colono got into an altercation the night of April 12, 2004, that resulted in Colono's death. Pring-Wilson claimed he acted in self-defense but a Massachusetts jury found him guilty of manslaughter because he stabbed Colono five times, which seemed excessive considering the fact that the victim was unarmed.

RATIONAL RAPISTS? Serial rapists also show rationality in their choice of targets. They travel, on average, 3 miles from their homes to commit their crimes. This indicates that they are careful, for the most part, to avoid victims who might recognize them later.

The desire to avoid detection supersedes the wish to obtain a victim with little effort. Older, more experienced rapists who have extensive criminal histories are willing to travel further; younger rapists who have less experience committing crimes travel less and are therefore more at risk of detection.[75]

ATTRACTION OF CRIME For many people, then, crime is attractive; it brings rewards, excitement, prestige, or other desirable outcomes without lengthy work or effort.[76] Whether it is violent or profit oriented, crime has an allure that some people cannot resist. Crime may produce a natural high and other positive sensations that are instrumental in maintaining and reinforcing criminal behavior.[77] Some law violators describe the adrenaline rush that comes from successfully executing illegal activities in dangerous situations. This has been described as **edgework**, the "exhilarating, momentary integration of danger, risk, and skill" that motivates people to try a variety of dangerous criminal and noncriminal behaviors.[78] Crime is not some random act but a means that can provide both pleasure and solutions to vexing personal problems.

 To quiz yourself on this material, go to the Criminology TPT 9e website.

ELIMINATING CRIME

If crime is rational and people choose to commit crime, then it follows that crime can be controlled or eradicated by convincing potential offenders that crime is a poor choice that will not bring them rewards but pain, hardship, and deprivation instead. Evidence shows that jurisdictions with relatively low incarceration rates also experience the highest crime rates.[79] As we have seen, according to rational choice theory, street-smart offenders know which areas offer the least threat and plan their crimes accordingly. Strategies for crime control based on this premise are illustrated in Concept Summary 4.1. The following sections discuss each of these crime reduction or control strategies.

Situational Crime Prevention

Because criminal activity is offense specific, rational choice theory suggests that crime prevention, or at least crime reduction, should be achieved through policies that convince potential criminals to desist from criminal activities, delay their actions, or avoid a particular target. Criminal acts will be avoided if (1) potential targets are guarded securely, (2) the means to commit crime are controlled, and (3) potential offenders are carefully monitored. Desperate people may contemplate crime, but only the truly irrational would attack a well-defended, inaccessible target and risk strict punishment. Crime prevention can be achieved by reducing the opportunities people have to commit particular crimes, a practice known as **situational crime prevention**.

Situational crime prevention was first popularized in the United States in the early 1970s by Oscar Newman, who coined the term **defensible space**. This term signifies that crime can be prevented or displaced through the use of residential architectural designs that reduce criminal opportunity, such as well-lit housing projects that maximize surveillance.[80] C. Ray Jeffery wrote *Crime Prevention through Environmental Design,* which extended Newman's concepts and applied them to nonresidential areas, such as schools and factories.[81] According to this view, mechanisms such as security systems, deadbolt locks, high-intensity street lighting, and neighborhood watch patrols should reduce criminal

---

CONCEPT SUMMARY 4.1

Crime Control Strategies Based on Rational Choice

Situational Crime Prevention

- This strategy is aimed at convincing would-be criminals to avoid specific targets. It relies on the doctrine that crime can be avoided if motivated offenders are denied access to suitable targets.

- Operationalizations of this strategy are home security systems or guards, which broadcast the message that guardianship is great here, stay away; the potential reward is not worth the risk of apprehension.

- Problems with the strategy are the extinction of the effect and displacement of crime.

General Deterrence Strategies

- These strategies are aimed at making potential criminals fear the consequences of crime. The threat of punishment is meant to convince rational criminals that crime does not pay.

- Operationalizations of these strategies are the death penalty, mandatory sentences, and aggressive policing.

- Problems with these strategies are that criminals do not fear punishment and the certainty of arrest and punishment is low.

Specific Deterrence Strategy

- This strategy refers to punishing known criminals so severely that they will never be tempted to repeat their offenses. If crime is rational, then painful punishment should reduce its future allure.

- Operationalizations of this strategy are harsh prisons and stiff fines.

- A problem of this strategy is that punishment may increase re-offending rates rather than deter crime.

Incapacitation Strategies

- These strategies attempt to reduce crime rates by denying motivated offenders the opportunity to commit crime. If, despite the threat of law and punishment, some people still find crime attractive, then the only way to control their behavior is to incarcerate them for extended periods.

- Operationalizations of these strategies are long prison sentences, placing more people behind bars.

- Problems of these strategies are people are kept in prison beyond the years they may commit crime. Minor, nondangerous offenders are locked up; and this is a very costly strategy.

---

opportunity.[82] The subway system in Washington, DC, has used some of these environmental crime reduction techniques to control crime since it began operations in 1976. Some of these strategies are set out in Exhibit 4.2.

In 1992 Ronald Clarke published *Situational Crime Prevention,* which compiled the best-known strategies and

Using Environmental Design to Control Crime in the Washington, DC, Subway System

- High, arched ceilings not only are architecturally sound and aesthetically pleasing but also create a feeling of openness that reduces passenger fears and provides an open view of the station. Long, winding corridors and corners were avoided to reduce shadows and nooks that criminals and panhandlers could occupy.

- Passengers buy multiple-use fare cards in any dollar amount, reducing the time money is exposed to pickpockets and robbers. Fare cards also must be used on entry and exit from the system, reducing the likelihood of fare evasion.

- Metro trains are equipped with graffiti- and vandal-resistant materials to discourage potential offenders. When graffiti artists or vandals do cause damage, maintenance workers clean and repair damaged property promptly.

- No public restrooms, lockers, or excess seats allow potential offenders to loiter. Fast-food establishments are prohibited because customers generate litter, and they provide victims for robbers and pickpockets.

- Rules prohibiting "quality of life" violations, such as smoking or eating on trains, are enforced, and all vandalism and graffiti are promptly reported to maintenance personnel to ensure a safe and clean environment.

- Entrance kiosks are continuously staffed while Metro is open. Station attendants are aided by closed-circuit televisions at all unattended entrances, tunnels, and platforms, and they carry two-way radios to report crime and maintenance problems.

Source: Nancy LaVigne, *Visibility and Vigilance: Metro's Situational Approach to Preventing Subway Crime* (Washington, DC: National Institute of Justice, 1997).

A Total Community Situational Crime Prevention Model

- Schedule school release uniformly so that there is no doubt when kids belong in school and when they are truant.

- Control truancy.

- Organize after-school activities to keep kids under adult supervision.

- Organize weekend activities with adult supervision.

- Offer school lunches to keep kids in school and away from shopping areas.

- Prohibit cash in schools to reduce kids' opportunity either to be a target or to consume drugs or alcohol.

- Keep shopping areas and schools separate.

- Construct housing to maximize guardianship and minimize illegal behavior.

- Encourage neighborhood stability so that residents will be acquainted with one another.

- Encourage privatization of parks and recreation facilities so that people will be responsible for their area's security.

Source: Marcus Felson, "Routine Activities and Crime Prevention," in *National Council for Crime Prevention, Studies on Crime and Crime Prevention, Annual Review,* vol. 1 (Stockholm: Scandinavian University Press, 1992), pp. 30–34.

tactics to reduce criminal incidents.[83] Criminologists have suggested using a number of situational crime prevention efforts that might reduce crime rates. One approach is not to target a specific crime but to create an environment that can reduce the overall crime rate by limiting the access to tempting targets for a highly motivated offender group (such as high school students). Notice that this approach is designed not to eliminate a specific crime but to reduce the overall crime rate. Such a strategy might include some or all of the elements contained in Exhibit 4.3.[84]

TARGETING SPECIFIC CRIMES Situational crime prevention can also involve developing tactics to reduce or eliminate a specific crime problem (such as shoplifting in an urban mall or street-level drug dealing). According to criminologists Ronald Clarke and Ross Homel, crime prevention tactics used today generally fall in one of four categories:

- Increase the effort needed to commit crime

- Increase the risks of committing crime

- Reduce the rewards for committing crime

- Induce guilt or shame for committing crime

Exhibit 4.4 lists sixteen strategies to limit opportunities for crime based on these categories of prevention.

INCREASE EFFORTS Some of the tactics to increase efforts include target-hardening techniques such as putting unbreakable glass on storefronts, locking gates, and fencing yards. Technological advances can make it more difficult to commit crimes; for example, having an owner's photo on credit cards should reduce the use of stolen cards. The development of new products, such as steering locks on cars, can make it more difficult to commit crimes. Empirical evidence indicates that steering locks have helped reduce car theft in the United States, Britain, and Germany.[85] Installing a locking device on cars that prevents inebriated drivers from starting the vehicle significantly reduces drunk-driving rates.[86] Similarly, installing a locking device on cars that prevents drunk drivers from starting the vehicle (breath-analyzed ignition interlock device) significantly reduces drunk-driving rates among people with a history of driving while intoxicated.[87] Removing signs from store windows, installing brighter lights, and instituting a pay-first policy can help reduce thefts from gas stations and convenience stores.[88]

Another way to increase effort is to reduce opportunities for criminal activity. For example, many cities have established curfew laws in an effort to limit the opportunity juveniles have to engage in antisocial behavior. In some jurisdictions, such as Dallas, Texas, these laws have limited criminal

EXHIBIT 4.4

Sixteen Situational Prevention Techniques

Increasing Perceived Effort

1. *Target hardening*
   Slug rejector devices
   Steering locks
   Bandit screens

2. *Access control*
   Parking lot barriers
   Fenced yards
   Entry phones

3. *Deflecting offenders*
   Bus stop placement
   Tavern location
   Street closures

4. *Controlling facilitators*
   Credit card photo
   Caller ID
   Gun controls

Increasing Perceived Risks

5. *Entry/exit screening*
   Automatic ticket gates
   Baggage screening
   Merchandise tags

6. *Formal surveillance*
   Burglar alarms
   Speed cameras
   Security guards

7. *Surveillance by employees*
   Pay phone location
   Park attendants
   CCTV systems

8. *Natural surveillance*
   Defensible space
   Street lighting
   Cab driver ID

Reducing Anticipated Rewards

9. *Target removal*
   Removable car radio
   Women's refuges
   Phone card

10. *Identifying property*
    Property marking
    Vehicle licensing
    Cattle branding

11. *Reducing temptation*
    Gender-neutral phone lists
    Off-street parking

12. *Denying benefits*
    Ink merchandise tags
    PIN for car radios
    Graffiti cleaning

Inducing Guilt or Shame

13. *Rule setting*
    Harassment codes
    Customs declaration
    Hotel registrations

14. *Strengthening moral condemnation*
    "Shoplifting is stealing"
    Roadside speedometers
    "Bloody idiots drink and drive"

15. *Controlling disinhibitors*
    Drinking age laws
    Ignition interlock
    Server intervention

16. *Facilitating compliance*
    Improved library checkout
    Public lavatories
    Trash bins

Source: Ronald Clarke and Ross Homel, "A Revised Classification of Situation Crime Prevention Techniques," in *Crime Prevention at a Crossroads,* ed. Steven Lab (Cincinnati: Anderson, 1997), p. 4.

---

activity including violent gang crimes.[89] However, curfew laws have not met with universal success. In a comprehensive systematic review of the existing literature on curfews, criminologist Ken Adams found little evidence that juvenile crime and victimization were influenced in any way by the implementation of curfew laws.[90] Similarly, efforts to reduce DWI cases by instituting a countywide ban on the sale of alcohol have not proven successful.[91]

Environmental design is a branch of situational crime prevention that has as its basic premise that the physical environment can be changed or managed to produce behavioral effects that will reduce the incidence and fear of crime. To read more about the concept, go to http://www.cpted.com.au/. For an up-to-date list of web links, go to http://cj.wadsworth.com/siegel_crimtpt9e.

REDUCE REWARDS Target reduction strategies are designed to reduce the value of crime to the potential criminal. These include making car radios removable so they can be kept in the home at night, marking property so that it is more difficult to sell when stolen, and having gender-neutral phone listings to discourage obscene phone calls. Tracking systems, such as those made by the Lojack Corporation, help police locate and return stolen vehicles.

INCREASE RISK If criminals believe that committing crime is very risky, only the most foolhardy would attempt to commit criminal acts. Managing crime falls into the hands of people Marcus Felson calls **crime discouragers**.[92] These guardians can be grouped into three categories: guardians, who monitor targets (such as store security guards); handlers, who monitor potential offenders (such as parole officers and parents); and managers, who monitor places (such as homeowners and doorway attendants). If they do their job correctly, the potential criminal will be convinced that the risk of crime outweighs any potential gains.[93]

Crime discouragers have different levels of responsibility, ranging from highly personal involvement, such as the

Crime discouragers are people whose actions directly influence crime prevention. Here, School Resource Officer (SRO) Joe Hoffar adjusts the controls of a television monitor that displays images from several security cameras placed at Atwater High School in Atwater, California, June 14, 2001. Following the 1999 shootings at Colorado's Columbine High School, the legislature passed a law aimed at limiting school violence by providing additional funds for safety-related items, such as security cameras, and for police officers on campus, known as school resource officers. Hoffar is supervisor of the SROs for the Merced Union High School District.

© AP/Wide World Photos

TABLE 4.1
Crime Discouragers

Types of Supervisors and Objects of Supervision

Level of Responsibility	Guardians (monitoring suitable targets)	Handlers (monitoring likely offenders)	Managers (monitoring amenable places)
Personal (owners, family, friends)	Student keeps eye on own bookbag	Parent makes sure child gets home	Homeowner monitors area near home
Assigned (employees with specific assignment)	Store clerk monitors jewelry	Principal sends kids back to school	Doorman protects building
Diffuse (employees with general assignment)	Accountant notes shoplifting	School clerk discourages truancy	Hotel maid impairs trespasser
General (strangers, other citizens)	Bystander inhibits shoplifting	Stranger questions boys at mall	Customer observes parking structure

Source: Marcus Felson, "Those Who Discourage Crime," in John Eck and David Weisburd, *Crime and Place* (Monsey, NY: Criminal Justice Press, 1995), p. 59. Reprinted by permission.

homeowner protecting her house and the parent controlling his children, to the most impersonal general involvement, such as a stranger who stops someone from shoplifting in the mall (Table 4.1).

Research indicates that crime discouragers can have an impact on crime rates. An evaluation of a police initiative in Oakland, California, found that an active working partnership with residents and businesspeople who have a stake in maintaining order in their places of work or residences can reduce levels of drug dealing while at the same time increasing civil behavior. Collective action and cooperation in solving problems were effective in controlling crime,

whereas individual action (such as calling 911) seemed to have little effect.[94]

In addition to crime discouragers, it may be possible to raise the risks of committing crime by creating mechanical devices that increase the likelihood that a criminal will be observed and captured. The Comparative Criminology feature, "CCTV or Not CCTV?" discusses a recent evaluation of such methods in Great Britain and the United States.

INCREASE GUILT Inducing guilt or shame might include such techniques as setting strict rules to embarrass offenders. For example, publishing "John lists" in the newspaper punishes those arrested for soliciting prostitutes. Facilitating compliance by providing trash bins might shame chronic litterers into using them. Ronald Clarke shows how caller ID in New Jersey resulted in significant reductions in the number of obscene phone calls. Caller ID displays the telephone number of the party placing the call; the threat of exposure had a deterrent effect on the number of obscene calls reported to police.[95]

SITUATIONAL CRIME PREVENTION: COSTS AND BENEFITS
Some attempts at situational crime prevention have proven highly successful while others have not met their goals. However, it is now apparent that the approach brings with it certain nontransparent or hidden costs and benefits that can either increase effectiveness or undermine success. Before the overall success of this approach can be evaluated, these costs and benefits must be considered.

Among the hidden benefits of situational crime prevention are those that arise from not targeting a specific crime. For example, **diffusion** occurs when efforts to prevent one crime unintentionally prevent another and when crime control efforts in one locale reduce crime in other nontarget areas.[96] Diffusion may be produced by two independent effects. Crime control efforts may deter criminals by causing them to fear apprehension. For example, video cameras set

Comparative Criminology

CCTV or Not CCTV? Comparing Situational Crime Prevention Efforts in Great Britain and the United States

As you may recall from Chapter 2, international criminologists Brandon Welsh and David Farrington have been using systematic review and meta-analysis as a technique to assess the comparative effectiveness of situational crime prevention techniques. In their most recent study (2004), they evaluated the effectiveness of closed-circuit television (CCTV) surveillance cameras and improved street lighting, techniques that are currently being used both in England and the United States.

Welsh and Farrington found significant differences in the use of these methods in the United States and Great Britain. For example, CCTV is quite popular in Great Britain where it is the single most heavily funded crime prevention measure: Between 1999 to 2001, the British government spent approximately $320 million for CCTV schemes in town and city centers, parking lots, crime hot spots, and residential areas; CCTV accounted for more than three-quarters of total spending on crime prevention by the British Home Office; there are more than 40,000 surveillance cameras currently in use! In contrast, CCTV is less popular in America, perhaps because it raises the specter of a Big Brother society that is constantly watching (and recording) every person's behavior and activities.

There are also cross-national differences in the use of street lighting

to prevent criminal activity. Improving street lighting to reduce crime is not a popular crime control mechanism in Great Britain. In contrast, many U.S. towns and cities have embarked upon major street lighting programs as a means of reducing crime.

After an exhaustive search of the existing research Welsh and Farrington found thirty-two relevant studies that met their standards for inclusion (nineteen for CCTV and thirteen for street lighting). Of the nineteen CCTV studies, fourteen were from England, and the other five were from North America (four from the United States and one from Canada). Of the thirteen improved street-lighting evaluations, eight were from the United States, and the other five were from England. All of these evaluations were carried out in one of four settings: city center, residential or public housing, parking lots, or public transportation.

Based on their analysis of the existing data, they concluded that CCTV and street lighting are equally effective in reducing crime: Improved street lighting seemed to be a more effective method of reducing crime in city centers; both techniques were more effective in reducing property crimes than violent crimes; and there were additional benefits when both techniques were used together.

Welsh and Farrington also found that both measures were far more effective in reducing crime in Great Britain than in America. Though there may be a number of possible reasons for this puzzling cross-national difference, Welsh and Farrington suspect there may be a cultural explanation: In Great Britain, there is a high level of

public support for the use of CCTV cameras in public settings to prevent crime, while the American public seems more wary of sophisticated surveillance technology. Public resistance can sometimes take a legal form, resulting in lawsuits charging that surveillance undermines the U.S. Constitution's Fourth Amendment prohibition against unreasonable searches and seizures. While the British Home Office embraces CCTV, American caution has resulted in cuts in program funding, the police assigning lower priority to the schemes, and attempts to discourage desirable media coverage. In contrast, improving street lighting has engendered little public enmity in the United States. Nonetheless, while Americans may be cautious about the installation of CCTV, the terrorist attack of September 11, 2001, has resulted in increased use of CCTV surveillance cameras around the nation.

Critical Thinking

Would you be willing to have a surveillance camera set up in your home or dorm in order to prevent crime, knowing that your every move was being watched and recorded?

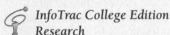

InfoTrac College Edition Research

Use "situational crime prevention" as a subject search on InfoTrac College Edition.

Source: Brandon Welsh and David Farrington," Surveillance for Crime Prevention in Public Space: Results and Policy Choices in Britain and America," *Criminology and Public Policy* 3 (2004): 701–730.

---

up in a mall to reduce shoplifting can also reduce property damage because would-be vandals fear they will be caught on camera. One recent police program targeting drugs in areas of Jersey City, New Jersey, also reduced public morals crimes.[97]

Discouragement occurs when crime control efforts targeting a particular locale help reduce crime in surrounding areas and populations. In her study of the effects of the SMART program (a drug enforcement program in Oakland, California, that enforces municipal codes and nuisance abatement laws), criminologist Lorraine Green found that not only did drug dealing decrease in targeted areas but improvement was found in adjacent areas as well. She suggests that the program most likely discouraged buyers and sellers who saw familiar hangouts closed. This sign that drug dealing would not be tolerated probably decreased the total number of people involved in drug activity even though they did not operate in the targeted areas.[98]

Another example of this effect can be found in evaluations of the Lojack auto protection system. Lojack uses a hidden radio transmitter to track stolen cars. As the number of Lojack installations rises, police notice that the sale of stolen auto parts declines. It appears that people in the illegal auto parts business (that is, chop shops) close down because they fear that the stolen cars they buy might contain Lojack.[99] A device designed to protect cars from theft also has the benefit of disrupting the sale of stolen car parts.

Although situational crime prevention appears to work in some situations, there are also hidden problems that limit its success. One primary issue is **crime displacement**: A program that seems successful because its helps lower crime rates at specific locations or neighborhoods may simply be re-directing offenders to alternative targets; crime is not prevented but deflected or displaced.[100] For example, beefed-up police patrols in one area may shift crimes to a more vulnerable neighborhood.[101] Although crime displacement undercuts the effectiveness of situational crime prevention, under some circumstances deflection seems to reduce the frequency of crime and may produce less serious offense patterns.[102]

Extinction refers to the phenomenon in which crime reduction programs may produce a short-term positive effect, but benefits dissipate as criminals adjust to new conditions. They learn to dismantle alarms or avoid patrols; they may try new offenses they had previously avoided. For example, if every residence in a neighborhood has a foolproof burglar alarm system, motivated offenders may turn to armed robbery, a riskier and more violent crime.

Before the effectiveness of situational crime prevention can be accepted, these hidden costs and benefits must be weighed and balanced.

General Deterrence

According to the rational choice view, motivated, rational people will violate the law if left free and unrestricted. The concept of **general deterrence** holds that crime rates are influenced and controlled by the threat of criminal punishment. If people fear being apprehended and punished, they will not risk breaking the law. An inverse relationship should then exist between crime rates and the *severity, certainty,* and *speed* of legal sanctions. If, for example, the punishment for a crime is increased and the effectiveness and efficiency of the criminal justice system are improved, then the number of people engaging in that crime should decline. The factors of severity, certainty, and speed of punishment may also influence one another. For example, if a crime—say,

robbery—is punished severely, but few robbers are ever caught or punished, the severity of punishment for robbery will probably not deter people from robbing. However, if the certainty of apprehension and conviction is increased by modern technology, more efficient police work, or some other factor, then even minor punishment might deter the potential robber.

Deterrence theorists tend to believe that the certainty of punishment seems to have a greater impact than its severity or speed. In other words, people will more likely be deterred from crime if they believe that they will get caught; what happens to them after apprehension seems to have less impact.[103] Nonetheless, all three elements of the deterrence equation are important, and it would be a mistake to emphasize one at the expense of the others. For example, if all resources were given to police agencies to increase the probability of arrest, crime rates might increase because there were insufficient funds for swift prosecution and effective correction.[104]

Do these factors actually affect the decision to commit crime and, consequently, general crime rates?

CERTAINTY OF PUNISHMENT According to **deterrence theory**, if the probability of arrest, conviction, and sanctioning could be increased, crime rates should decline. As criminals become more certain they will be punished, they may desist from crime because they realize that the risks of crime outweigh its rewards.[105] If people believe that their criminal transgressions will result in apprehension and punishment, then only the truly irrational will commit crime.[106]

Certainty of punishment is often linked to a concept referred to as the "tipping point": The certainty of punishment will only have a deterrent effect if the likelihood of getting caught reaches a critical level. For example, research shows that the crime rate would significantly decline if police could increase their effectiveness and make an arrest in at least 30 percent of all reported crimes.[107] Crime persists because we have not reached the tipping point, and most criminals believe (a) that there is only a small chance they will be arrested for committing a particular crime, (b) that police officers are sometimes reluctant to make arrests even when they are aware of crime, and (c) that even if apprehended there is a good chance of receiving a lenient punishment.[108] The likelihood of being arrested or imprisoned will have little effect on crime rates if criminals believe that they have only a small chance of suffering apprehension and punishment.[109] A central theme of deterrence theory is that people who believe they will be punished for future crimes will avoid doing those crimes.[110] Crime may occur, despite the threat of punishment, because seasoned criminals act impulsively and are indifferent to the threat of future punishment. Yet, research shows that experienced criminals are in fact the ones most likely to fear the deterrent power of the law.[111] Perhaps if punishment levels reach a yet-undetermined tipping point, those who are most crime prone will be the first to be deterred.

DOES INCREASING POLICE ACTIVITY DETER CRIME? If certainty of apprehension and punishment deters criminal behavior, then increasing the number of police officers on the street should cut the crime rate. Moreover, if these police officers are active, aggressive crime fighters, would-be criminals should be convinced that the risk of apprehension outweighs the benefits they can gain from crime.[112]

In the past, criminologists questioned whether simply increasing the number of police officers in a community could lower crime rates. There was little evidence that adding additional officers could produce a deterrent effect.[113] One problem is that as crime rates increase, communities add police officers. Consequently, the number of officers increases along with the crime rate, making it appear that adding police actually increases crime rates rather than lowering them. However, recent research using sophisticated methodological tools has found evidence that increasing levels of crime only cause small increases in the number of police officers, whereas increased police levels cause substantial reductions in crime over time.[114] It is therefore possible that the presence of police officers does in fact have a substantial deterrent effect.

Some police departments have conducted experiments to determine whether increasing police activities or allocation of services can influence crime rates. Perhaps the most famous experiment was conducted by the Kansas City, Missouri, police department.[115] To evaluate the effectiveness of police patrols, fifteen independent police beats or districts were divided into three groups: The first retained a normal police patrol; the second (proactive) was supplied with two to three times the normal amount of patrol forces; the third (reactive) eliminated its preventive patrol entirely, and police officers responded only when summoned by citizens to the scene of a crime.

Surprisingly, these variations in patrol techniques had little effect on the crime patterns. The presence or absence of patrol forces did not seem to affect residential or business burglaries, auto thefts, larcenies involving auto accessories, robberies, vandalism, or other criminal behavior. Variations in police patrol techniques appeared to have little effect on citizens' attitudes toward the police, their satisfaction with police, or their fear of future criminal behavior. It is possible that as people traveled around the city they noticed a large number of police officers in one area and relatively few in another; the two effects may have cancelled each other out!

The Kansas City study convinced criminologists that the mere presence of patrol officers on the street did not have a deterrent effect. But what if the officers were engaging in aggressive, focused crime fighting initiatives, targeting specific crimes such as murder and/or robbery? Would such activities result in more arrests and a greater deterrent effect?[116] For example, the UCR data show that murder is the index crime most often cleared by arrest. There is evidence that the visibility of homicide in the media and the importance police agencies place on homicide clearances cause homicide detectives to work aggressively to clear all homicides regardless of where they occur or the personal characteristics of homicide victims.[117] It is possible that this aggressive approach to

solving crime spurred on by media attention to high-profile cases has helped lower the homicide rate.

To lower crime rates and increase the certainty of punishment, some police departments have instituted **crackdowns**—sudden changes in police activity designed to increase the communicated threat or actual certainty of punishment. For example, a police task force might target street-level narcotics dealers by using undercover agents and surveillance cameras in known drug-dealing locales. Crackdown efforts have met with mixed reviews.[118] In one well-known study Lawrence Sherman found that while crackdowns initially deterred crime, crime rates returned to earlier levels once the crackdown ended.[119] A more recent study by Jacqueline Cohen and her colleagues found that drug dealing in bars and taverns could be suppressed and controlled by significant levels of police intervention—that is, drug raids—and that the longer the duration of the intervention, the greater the impact on crime. However, Cohen also found that the initial effect of the crackdown soon wore off after high intensity police activity ended.[120]

Although these results are troubling, there is some evidence that when police combine crackdowns with the use of aggressive problem-solving and community improvement techniques, such as increasing lighting and cleaning vacant lots, crackdowns may be successful in reducing some forms of crime.[121] For example, a recent initiative by the Dallas Police Department to aggressively pursue truancy and curfew enforcement resulted in lower rates of gang violence.[122] A month-long crackdown and cleanup initiative in Richmond, Virginia, in seven city neighborhoods found that crime rates declined by 92 percent; the effects persisted up to 6 months after the crackdown ended, and no displacement was observed.[123] Police seem to have more luck deterring crime when they use more focused approaches, such as aggressive problem-solving and community improvement techniques.[124] Merely saturating an area with police may not deter crime, but focusing efforts at a particular problem area may have a deterrent effect.

Another form of crackdown occurs when a particular crime becomes the focus of public concern, and the government acts swiftly to pass legislation designed to reduce or eliminate the hazardous behavior. For example, when the teenage drunk-driving death rate became a national concern, the minimum legal drinking age (MLDA) was established in most jurisdictions as well as a zero tolerance (0.02% blood alcohol concentration) limit for drivers younger than 21. Analysis of these legal crackdowns finds they were in fact effective at reducing the proportion of fatal crashes involving teens who drink and drive.[125]

SEVERITY OF PUNISHMENT AND DETERRENCE According to deterrence theory, the severity of punishment is inversely proportional to the level of crime rates. Increasing punishments should lower crime rates. Some studies have in fact found that increasing sanction levels can control common criminal behaviors. For example, the National Center for Policy Analysis uncovered evidence of a direct correlation

A newspaper ad sponsored by the Motion Picture Association of America gives a chilling reminder of the consequences for illegally downloading copyrighted material such as films or DVDs. According to deterrence theory, severe punishments should convince would-be law violators to think twice before committing crimes. Would you download copyrighted music after viewing this ad? I didn't think so!

between the probability of imprisonment for a particular crime and a subsequent decline in the rate of that crime.[126] The probability of going to prison for murder increased 17 percent between 1993 and 1997, and the murder rate dropped 23 percent during that time period; robbery declined 21 percent as the probability of prison increased 14 percent.

These data seem persuasive, but there is little consensus that the severity of criminal sanctions alone can reduce criminal activities.[127] While there is some evidence that the severity of punishment may have the effect hypothesized by deterrence theorists, other data seem to contradict its importance in the deterrence equation.[128] One way to evaluate this is to determine which factor potential offenders fear most— severity or certainty—and then calculate whether their fear prevents them from committing crime. When criminologist Greg Pogarsky used this technique with college students, he found that some people are more "deterrable" than others and that those who are seem to respond to the severity of sanctions more than previously thought possible.[129]

Another method of testing the effect of sanction severity is to evaluate the impact increasing criminal penalties have on crime rates. Recent research out of Australia shows that the rate of road accidents per 100,000 vehicles actually increased after the statutory penalties for drunk-driving offenses were doubled in New South Wales, Australia.[130]

These contradictory findings illustrate how difficult it is for criminologists to identify the factors that produce a deterrent effect. Because the likelihood of getting caught for some crimes is relatively low, the impact of deterrent measures is negligible over the long term.[131] Thus, it becomes difficult to determine whether severity and/or certainty of punishment have the effect assumed by deterrence theories. In summary, it has not been proven that just increasing the punishment for specific crimes can reduce their occurrence.

CAPITAL PUNISHMENT It stands to reason that if severity of punishment can deter crime, then fear of the death penalty, the ultimate legal deterrent, should significantly reduce murder rates. Because no one denies its emotional impact, failure of the death penalty to deter violent crime would jeopardize the validity of the entire deterrence concept. Because this topic is so important, it is featured in The Criminological Enterprise.

IIIIIII **CONNECTIONS** IIIIIII

Even if capital punishment proves to be a deterrent, many experts still question its morality, fairness, and legality. Chapter 14 provides further discussion that can help you decide whether the death penalty is an appropriate response to murder.

INFORMAL SANCTIONS Evidence is mounting that the fear of **informal sanctions** may have a greater crime-reducing impact than the fear of formal legal punishment.[132] Informal sanctions occur when significant others—such as parents, peers, neighbors, and teachers—direct their disapproval, stigma, anger, and indignation toward an offender. If this happens, law violators run the risk of feeling shame, being embarrassed, and suffering a loss of respect.[133] Can the fear of public humiliation deter crime?

Research efforts have in fact established that the threat of informal sanctions can be a more effective deterrent than the threat of formal sanctions.[134] The reason for this is that social control is influenced by the way people perceive negative reactions from interpersonal acquaintances. Legal sanctions may act as a supplement to informal control processes. In other words, a combination of informal and formal social control may have a greater impact on the decision to commit crime than either deterrent measure alone.[135] Other studies have found that people who are committed to conventional moral values or believe crime to be sinful are unlikely to violate the law.[136] For example, British efforts to control drunk driving by shaming offenders produced a moral climate that helped reduce its incidence.[137]

SHAME AND HUMILIATION Fear of shame and embarrassment can be a powerful deterrent to crime. Those who fear being rejected by family and peers are reluctant to engage in deviant behavior.[138] These factors manifest themselves in two ways: (1) personal shame over violating the law and (2) the fear of public humiliation if the deviant behavior becomes public knowledge. People who say that their involvement in crime will cause them to feel ashamed are less likely to commit theft, fraud, motor vehicular, and other offenses than people who report they will not feel ashamed.[139]

Anticrime campaigns have been designed to play on this fear of shame; they are most effective when they convince the general public that being accused of crime will make them feel ashamed or embarrassed.[140] For example, spouse abusers report they are more afraid of the social costs of crime (like loss of friends and family disapproval) than they are of legal punishment (such as going to jail). Women are more likely to fear shame and embarrassment than men, a finding that may help explain gender differences in the crime rate.[141]

The effect of informal sanctions may vary according to the cohesiveness of community structure and the type of crime. Informal sanctions may be most effective in highly unified areas where everyone knows one another and the crime cannot be hidden from public view. The threat of informal sanctions seems to have the greatest influence on instrumental crimes, which involve planning, and not on impulsive or expressive criminal behaviors or those associated with substance abuse.[142]

CRITIQUE OF GENERAL DETERRENCE Some experts believe that the purpose of the law and justice system is to create a "threat system."[143] That is, the threat of legal punishment should, on the face of it, deter lawbreakers through

fear. Nonetheless, as we have already discussed, the relationship between crime rates and deterrent measures is far less clear than choice theorists might expect. Despite efforts to punish criminals and make them fear crime, there is little evidence that the fear of apprehension and punishment can reduce crime rates. How can this discrepancy be explained?

1. *Rationality:* Deterrence theory assumes a rational offender who weighs the costs and benefits of a criminal act before deciding on a course of action. In many instances, criminals are desperate people who suffer from personality disorders that impair their judgment and render them incapable of making truly rational decisions. As we saw in Chapter 3, a relatively small group of chronic offenders commits a significant percentage of all serious crimes. Some psychologists believe this select group suffers from an innate or inherited emotional state that renders them both incapable of fearing punishment and less likely to appreciate the consequences of crime.[144] For example, people who are easily aroused sexually also say that they will be more likely to act in a sexually aggressive fashion and not consider the legal consequences of their actions.[145] Their heightened emotional state negates the deterrent effect of the law.

2. *Need:* Many offenders are members of what is referred to as the underclass—people cut off from society, lacking the education and skills they need to be in demand in the modern economy.[146] Such desperate people may not be deterred from crime by fear of punishment because, in reality, they perceive few other options for success. Among poor, high-risk groups, such as teens living in economically depressed neighborhoods, the threat of formal sanctions is irrelevant.[147] Young people in these areas have less to lose because their opportunities are few, and they have little attachment to social institutions such as school or family. In their environment, they see many people who appear relatively well-off (the neighborhood drug dealer) committing crimes without getting caught or punished.[148]

3. *Greed:* Some may be immune to deterrent effects because they believe the profits from crime are worth the risk of punishment; it may be their only significant chance for gain and profit. When criminologists Alex Piquero and George Rengert studied active burglars, they found that the lure of criminal profits outweighed their fears of capture and subsequent punishment. Perceived risk of punishment may deter some potential and active criminal offenders, but only if they doubt that they can make a "big score" from committing a crime.[149]

4. *Severity and speed:* As Beccaria's famous equation tells us, the threat of punishment involves not only its severity but its certainty and speed. Our legal system

Does Capital Punishment Deter Murder?

According to deterrence theory, the death penalty—the ultimate deterrent—should deter murder—the ultimate crime. Most Americans approve of the death penalty, including, as Norma Wilcox and Tracey Steele found, convicted criminals who are currently behind bars. But is the public's approval warranted? Does the death penalty actually deter murder?

Empirical research on the association between capital punishment and murder can be divided into three types: immediate impact studies, comparative research, and time-series analysis.

Immediate Impact

If capital punishment is a deterrent, the reasoning goes, then its impact should be greatest after a well-publicized execution. Robert Dann began testing this assumption in 1935 when he chose five highly publicized executions of convicted murderers in different years and determined the number of homicides in the 60 days before and after each execution. Each 120-day period had approximately the same number of homicides, as well as the same number of days on which homicides occurred. Dann's study revealed that an average of 4.4 more homicides occurred during the 60 days following an execution than during those preceding it, suggesting that the overall impact of executions might actually be an increase in the incidence of homicide.

Recently (2004), Lisa Stolzenberg and Stewart D'Alessio examined the effect of the death penalty on the murder rate in Houston, Texas. They found that even when executions were highly publicized in the local press, an execution had little influence on the murder rate.

Comparative Research

Another type of research compares the murder rates in jurisdictions that have abolished the death penalty with the rates of those that employ the death penalty. Studies using this approach have found little difference in the murder rates of adjacent states, regardless of their use of the death penalty; capital punishment did not appear to influence the reported rate of homicide. Research conducted in fourteen nations around the world found little evidence that countries with a death penalty have lower violence rates than those without; homicide rates actually decline after capital punishment is abolished, a direct contradiction to its supposed deterrent effect.

Time-Series Studies

Time-series studies look at the long-term association between capital sentencing and murder. If capital punishment is a deterrent, then periods that have an upswing in executions should also experience a downturn in violent crime and murder. Most research efforts have failed to show such a relationship. For example, a recent test of the deterrent effect of the death penalty in Texas by Jon Sorenson and his colleagues found no association between the frequency of execution during the years 1984 to 1997 and murder rates.

These findings seem to indicate that the threat and/or reality of execution has relatively little influence on murder rates. Although it is still uncertain why the threat of capital punishment fails as a deterrent, the cause may lie in the nature of homicide itself. Murder is often an expressive "crime of passion" involving people who know each other and who may be under the influence of drugs and alcohol. Those who choose to take a life may be less influenced by the threat of punishment, even death, than those who commit crime for economic gain.

Rethinking the Deterrent Effect of Capital Punishment

Despite this lack of empirical verification, some recent studies have

---

is not very effective. Only 10 percent of all serious offenses result in apprehension (half go unreported, and police make arrests in about 20 percent of reported crimes). Police routinely do not arrest suspects in personal disputes even when they lead to violence.[150] As apprehended offenders are processed through all the stages of the criminal justice system, the odds of their receiving serious punishment diminish. As a result, some offenders believe they will not be severely punished for their acts and consequently have little regard for the law's deterrent power.

Criminologist Raymond Paternoster found that adolescents, a group responsible for a disproportionate amount of crime, may be well aware that the juvenile court is generally lenient about imposing meaningful sanctions on even the most serious juvenile offenders.[151] Even those accused of murder are often convicted of lesser offenses and spend relatively short amounts of time behind bars.[152] In making their "rational choice," offenders may be aware that the deterrent effect of the law is minimal.

Specific Deterrence

The general deterrence model focuses on future or potential criminals. In contrast, the theory of **specific deterrence** (also called *special* or *particular deterrence*) holds that criminal sanctions should be so powerful that known criminals

concluded that executing criminals may, in fact, bring the murder rate down. Those who still maintain that an association exists between capital punishment and murder rate believe that the relationship has been masked or obscured by faulty research methods. Newer studies, using sophisticated data analysis, have been able to uncover a more significant association. For example, criminologist Steven Stack has conducted a number of research studies that show that the immediate impact of a well-publicized execution can lower the murder rate during the following month. James Yunker, using a national data set, has found evidence that there is a deterrent effect of capital punishment now that the pace of executions has accelerated. Economists Hashem Dezhbakhsh, Paul H. Rubin, and Joanna M. Shepherd performed an advanced statistical analysis on county-level homicide data in order to calculate the effect of each execution on the number of homicides that would otherwise have occurred. Using a variety of models (for example, the effect of an execution conducted today on reducing homicides in five years, and so on), they found that each execution leads to an average of eighteen fewer murders.

These efforts contradict findings that capital punishment fails as a deterrent. They instead suggest that

now that the death penalty is being used more frequently, it is possible that the *tipping point* has been reached, after which it may become an effective deterrent measure. After years of study, the death penalty remains a topic of considerable criminological debate.

Critical Thinking

Even if effective, there is no question the death penalty still carries with it tremendous baggage. For example, when Geoffrey Rapp studied the effect of the death penalty on the safety of police officers, he found that the introduction of capital punishment actually created an extremely dangerous environment for law enforcement officers. Because the death penalty does not have a deterrent effect, criminals are more likely to kill police officers when the death penalty is in place. Tragically, the death penalty may lull officers into a false sense of security, causing them to let down their guard—killing fewer citizens but getting killed more often themselves Given Rapp's findings, should we still maintain the death penalty?

 InfoTrac College Edition Research

Use "capital punishment" and the "death penalty" as subject searches on InfoTrac College Edition.

Sources: Lisa Stolzenberg and Stewart D'Alessio, "Capital Punishment, Execution Publicity, and Murder in Houston, Texas," *Journal of Criminal Law & Criminology* 94 (2004): 351–380; Geoffrey Rapp "The Economics of Shootouts: Does the Passage of Capital Punishment Laws Protect or Endanger Police Officers?" *Albany Law Review* 65 (2002): 1051–1084; Robert Dann, "The Deterrent Effect of Capital Punishment," *Friends Social Service Series* 29 (1935); Thorsten Sellin, *The Death Penalty* (Philadelphia: American Law Institute, 1959); Walter Reckless, "Use of the Death Penalty," *Crime and Delinquency* 15 (1969): 43–51; Dane Archer, Rosemary Gartner, and Marc Beittel, "Homicide and the Death Penalty: A Cross-National Test of a Deterrence Hypothesis," *Journal of Criminal Law and Criminology* 74 (1983): 991–1014; Jon Sorenson, Robert Wrinkle, Victoria Brewer, and James Marquart, "Capital Punishment and Deterrence: Examining the Effect of Executions on Murder in Texas," *Crime and Delinquency* 45 (1999): 481–931; Norma Wilcox and Tracey Steele, "Just the Facts: A Descriptive Analysis of Inmate Attitudes toward Capital Punishment," *Prison Journal* 83 (2003): 464–483; Zhiqiang Liu, "Capital Punishment and the Deterrence Hypothesis: Some New Insights and Empirical Evidence," *Eastern Economic Journal* (in press); Steven Stack, "The Effect of Well-Publicized Executions on Homicide in California," *Journal of Crime and Justice* 21 (1998): 1–12; James Yunker, "A New Statistical Analysis of Capital Punishment Incorporating U.S. Postmoratorium Data," *Social Science Quarterly* 82 (2001): 297–312; Hashem Dezhbakhsh, Paul H. Rubin, and Joanna M. Shepherd, "Does Capital Punishment Have a Deterrent Effect? New Evidence from Postmoratorium Panel Data," *American Law and Economics Review* 5(2003): 344–376.

will never repeat their criminal acts. For example, the drunk driver whose sentence is a substantial fine and a week in the county jail should, according to this theory, be convinced that the price to be paid for drinking and driving is too great to consider future violations. Similarly, burglars who spend five years in a tough maximum security prison should find their enthusiasm for theft dampened.[153] In principle, punishment works if a connection can be established between the planned action and memories of its consequence; if these recollections are adequately intense, the action will be unlikely to occur again.[154]

At first glance, specific deterrence does not seem to work because a majority of known criminals are not deterred by their punishment. As you have already seen, arrest and

punishment seem to have little effect on experienced criminals and may even increase the likelihood that first-time offenders will commit new crimes.[155] A sentence to a juvenile justice facility does little to deter a persistent delinquent from becoming an adult criminal.[156] Most prison inmates had prior records of arrest and conviction before their current offenses.[157] About two-thirds of all convicted felons are rearrested within three years of their release from prison, and those who have been punished in the past are the most likely to recidivate.[158] Incarceration may sometimes slow down or delay recidivism in the short term, but the overall probability of re-arrest does not change following incarceration.[159]

According to the theory of specific deterrence, the harsher the punishment, the less likely the chances of

Deterring Domestic Violence

Is it possible to use a specific deterrence strategy to control domestic violence? Would the memory of a formal police arrest reduce the incidence of spousal abuse? Despite the fact that domestic violence is a prevalent, serious crime, police departments have been accused of rarely arresting suspected perpetrators. Lack of forceful action may contribute to chronic episodes of violence, which obviously is of great concern to women's advocacy groups. Is it possible that prompt, formal action by police agencies might prevent the reoccurrence of this serious crime that threatens and even kills so many women?

In the famous Minneapolis domestic violence study, Lawrence Sherman and Richard Berk had police officers randomly assign treatments to the domestic assault cases they encountered on their beats. One approach was to give some sort of advice and mediation; another was to send the assailant from the home for a period of 8 hours; and the third was to arrest the assailant. They found that when police took formal action (arrest), the chance of recidivism was substantially less than with less punitive measures, such as warning offenders or ordering offenders out of the house for a cooling-off period.

A 6-month followup found that only 10 percent of those who were arrested repeated their violent behavior, while 19 percent of those advised and 24 percent of those sent away repeated their offenses. Sherman and Berk's interviews of 205 victims demonstrated that arrests were somewhat effective in controlling domestic assaults: 19 percent of the women whose attackers had been arrested reported their mates had assaulted them again; in contrast, 37 percent of those whose mates were advised and 33 percent of those whose mates were sent away reported further assaults. Sherman and Berk concluded that a formal arrest was the most effective means of controlling domestic violence, regardless of what happened to the offender in court.

The Minneapolis experiment deeply affected police operations around the nation. Atlanta, Chicago, Dallas, Denver, Detroit, New York, Miami, San Francisco, and Seattle, among other large cities, adopted policies encouraging arrests in domestic violence cases. A number of states adopted legislation mandating that police either take formal action in domestic abuse cases or explain in writing their failure to act.

Although the findings of the Minneapolis experiment received quick acceptance, government-funded research replicating the experimental design in five other locales—including Omaha, Nebraska, and Charlotte, North Carolina—failed to duplicate the original results. In these locales, formal arrest was not a greater deterrent to domestic abuse than warning or advising the assailant. Christopher Maxwell and his associates recently pooled the findings from all the replication cites in order to provide an overall picture of the arrest–deterrence relationship. While positive, the effect of arrest on re-offending was at best modest. What seemed more important predictors of repeat offending were the batterers' prior criminal record and/or his age.

Why Is the Deterrent Effect Minimal?

There are a number of reasons why arrest does not deter domestic violence. Sherman and his associates found that in some instances the effect of arrest quickly decays and, in the long run, may escalate the frequency of repeat domestic violence.

Explaining why the initial deterrent effect of arrest decays over time is difficult. It is possible that offenders who are arrested initially fear punishment but eventually replace fear with anger and violent intent toward their mates when their cases do not result in severe punishment. Many repeat abusers do not fear arrest, believing

recidivism. But research shows that this is not always the case. Offenders sentenced to prison do not have lower rates of recidivism than those receiving more lenient community sentences for similar crimes. For example, white-collar offenders who receive prison sentences are as likely to recidivate as a matched group of offenders who receive community-based sanctions.[160] Rather than reducing the frequency of crime, some research efforts have shown that severe punishments may actually increase re-offending rates.[161] Punishment may bring defiance rather than deterrence, or perhaps the stigma of apprehension may help lock offenders into a criminal career instead of convincing them to avoid one. In fact, some research efforts have shown

that, rather than reducing the frequency of crime, severe punishment may backfire and actually increase re-offending rates.[162] For example, even the criminals who receive probation are less likely to recidivate than those who are sent to prison for committing similar crimes; specific deterrence theory would predict that those punished severely (prison sentences) should have lower recidivism rates than those treated leniently (probation).[163] It is possible that punishment may bring defiance rather than deterrence, while the stigma of apprehension may help lock offenders into a criminal career. Criminals who are punished may also believe that the likelihood of getting caught twice for the same type of crime is remote: "Lightning never strikes

that formal police action will not cause them harm. They may be aware that police are reluctant to make arrests in domestic violence cases unless there is a significant chance of injury to the victim—for example, when a weapon is used.

It is also possible that the threat of future punishment may have little impact on repeat offenders who have already become involved in the justice system. For example, when they surveyed men in an abuse prevention program, D. Alex Heckert and Edward Gondolf found that while the subjects were aware of potential punishment, it was unlikely they were sufficiently harsh to deter their spousal abuse. Similarly, Robert Davis and his associates also found little association between severity of punishment for past spousal abuse and re-arrest on subsequent charges. Men were just as likely to recidivate if their case was dismissed, if they were given probation, or even if they were sent to jail. It is possible that people who have already experienced arrest and been punished on spouse abuse charges perceive the law as less severe than they had imagined, encouraging rather than deterring future violations.

These studies indicate that there is little reason to believe that domestic violence can be controlled through the administration of harsh punishments.

Treating offenders within a rehabilitative setting using counseling and other techniques may be more effective methods, especially if, as Jill Gordon and Laura Moriarty found, the abuser takes the program seriously and completes all treatment sessions.

Critical Thinking

1. Why do arrests seem to have little effect on future domestic violence? Could it be that getting arrested increases feelings of strain and hostility and does little to reduce the problems that led to domestic conflict in the first place? Explain how you think this works.

2. What policies would you suggest to reduce the reoccurrence of domestic violence?

 InfoTrac College Edition Research

Would police be more efficient in combating domestic violence if they feared lawsuits from victims? To find out, read: Lisa Gelhaus, "Civil Suits against Police Change Domestic Violence Response," *Trial* 35 (September 1999): 103.

Sources: Jill Gordon and Laura Moriarty, "The Effects of Domestic Violence Batterer Treatment on Domestic Violence Recidivism: The Chesterfield County Experience," *Criminal Justice and Behavior* 30 (2003): 118–135; Christopher Maxwell, Joel H. Garner, and Jeffrey A. Fagan,

The Effects of Arrest in Intimate Partner Violence: New Evidence from the Spouse Assault Replication Program (Washington, DC: National Institute of Justice, 2001); D. Alex Heckert and Edward Gondolf, "The Effect of Perceptions of Sanctions on Batterer Program Outcomes," *Journal of Research in Crime and Delinquency* 37 (2000): 369-391; Robert Kane, "Patterns of Arrest in Domestic Violence Encounters: Identifying a Police Decision-Making Model," *Journal of Criminal Justice* 27 (1999): 65–79; Dana Jones and Joanne Belknap, "Police Responses to Battering in a Progressive Pro-Arrest Jurisdiction," *Justice Quarterly* 16 (1999): 249–273; Robert Davis, Barbara Smith, and Laura Nickles, "The Deterrent Effect of Prosecuting Domestic Violence Misdemeanors," *Crime and Delinquency* 44 (1998): 434–442; Amy Thistlethwaite, John Wooldredge, and David Gibbs, "Severity of Dispositions and Domestic Violence Recidivism," *Crime and Delinquency* 44 (1998): 388–398; J. David Hirschel, Ira Hutchison, and Charles Dean, "The Failure of Arrest to Deter Spouse Abuse," *Journal of Research in Crime and Delinquency* 29 (1992): 7–33; Franklyn Dunford, David Huizinga, and Delbert Elliott, "The Role of Arrest in Domestic Assault: The Omaha Experiment," *Criminology* 28 (1990): 183–206; Lawrence Sherman, Janell Schmidt, Dennis Rogan, Patrick Gartin, Ellen Cohn, Dean Collins, and Anthony Bacich, "From Initial Deterrence to Long-Term Escalation: Short-Custody Arrest for Domestic Violence," *Criminology* 29 (1991): 821–850; Lawrence Sherman and Richard Berk, "The Specific Deterrent Effects of Arrest for Domestic Assault," *American Sociological Review* 49 (1984): 261–272; Michael Steinman, "Lowering Recidivism among Men Who Batter Women," *Journal of Police Science and Administration* 17 (1990): 124–131; and Susan Miller and Leeann Iovanni, "Determinants of Perceived Risk of Formal Sanction for Courtship Violence," *Justice Quarterly* 11 (1994): 282–312.

---

twice in the same spot," they may reason; no one is that unlucky.[164]

While these results are not encouraging, there are research studies that show that arrest and conviction may under some circumstances lower the frequency of re-offending, a finding that supports specific deterrence.[165]

A few empirical research studies indicate that some offenders who receive harsh punishments will be less likely to recidivate, or if they do commit crimes again, they may do so less frequently. But the consensus is that the association between crime and specific deterrent measures remains uncertain at best.[166] Only the most severe, draconian punishments seem to influence experienced criminals.[167] The

effects of specific deterrence on preventing domestic violence are discussed in the Race, Culture, Gender, and Criminology feature "Deterring Domestic Violence."

⏐⏐⏐⏐⏐⏐ CONNECTIONS ⏐⏐⏐⏐⏐⏐

Theoretically, experiencing punishment should deter future crime. However, punishment stigmatizes people and spoils their identity, a turn of events that may encourage antisocial behavior. The two factors may cancel each other out, helping to explain why punishment does not substantially reduce future criminality. The effects of stigma and negative labels are discussed further in Chapter 7.

Incapacitation

It stands to reason that if more criminals are sent to prison, the crime rate should go down. Because most people age out of crime, the duration of a criminal career is limited. Placing offenders behind bars during their prime crime years should lessen their lifetime opportunity to commit crime. The shorter the span of opportunity, the fewer offenses they can commit during their lives; hence crime is reduced. This theory, known as the **incapacitation effect,** seems logical, but does it work? The past twenty years have witnessed significant growth in the number and percentage of the population held in prison and jails; today more than 2 million Americans are incarcerated. Advocates of incapacitation suggest that this effort has been responsible for the long decline in the crime rate that began in 1993.

This argument is persuasive, but not all criminologists buy into the incapacitation effect. Michael Lynch, for one,

© AP / Wide World Photos

Simply put, if dangerous criminals were incapacitated, they would never have the opportunity to prey upon others. One of the most dramatic examples of the utility of incapacitation is the case of Lawrence Singleton, who in 1978 raped a young California girl, Mary Vincent, and then chopped off her arms with an axe. He served eight years in prison for this vile crime. Upon his release, he moved to Florida, where in 1997 he killed a woman, Roxanne Hayes. Vincent is shown here as she testifies at the penalty phase of Singleton's trial; he was sentenced to death. Should a dangerous predator such as Singleton ever be released from incapacitation? Is rehabilitation even a remote possibility?

shows that as the prison population expanded during another period of time, 1972 to 1993, there was little if any drop in crime rates.[168] Other criminologists believe the association is illusory and that a stable crime rate is actually controlled by factors such as these:

- The size of the teenage population
- The threat of tough new mandatory sentences
- A healthy economy
- Tougher gun laws
- The end of the crack epidemic
- The implementation of tough, aggressive policing strategies in large cities such as New York[169]

CAN INCAPACITATION REDUCE CRIME? Research on the direct benefits of incapacitation has been inconclusive. A number of studies have set out to measure the precise effect of incarceration rates on crime rates, and the results have not supported a strict incarceration policy.[170] If the prison population were cut in half, it has been estimated that the crime rate would most likely go up only 4 percent; if prisons were entirely eliminated, crime might increase 8 percent.[171] Looking at this relationship from another perspective, if the average prison sentence were increased 50 percent, the crime rate might be reduced only 4 percent.[172]

A few criminologists, however, have found an inverse relationship between incarceration rates and crime rates. In a frequently cited study, Reuel Shinnar and Shlomo Shinnar's research on incapacitation in New York led them to conclude that mandatory prison sentences of five years for violent crime and three for property offenses could reduce the reported crime rate by a factor of four or five.[173] In a more recent analysis of incarceration effects, Steven Levitt found that a one-prisoner reduction in the correctional population is associated with an increase of fifteen index crimes per year. Although calculations of the costs of crime are inherently uncertain, Levitt concludes that it appears that the social benefits associated with crime reduction equal or exceed the social costs of incarceration for the marginal prisoner.[174]

| | | | | | | CONNECTIONS | | | | | | |

Chapter 2 discussed the factors that control crime rates. What appears to be an incapacitation effect may actually reflect the effect of some other legal phenomena and not the incarceration of so many criminals. If, for example, the crime rate drops as more people are sent to prison, it would appear that incapacitation works. However, crime rates may really be dropping because potential criminals now fear punishment and are being deterred from crime. What appears to be an incapacitation effect may actually be an effect of general deterrence. Similarly, people may be willing to build new prisons because the economy is robust. If the crime rate drops, it may be because of economic effects and not because of prison construction.

THE LOGIC BEHIND INCARCERATION Incarceration as a crime control strategy should work, considering that the criminals who commit crimes are unable to continue from prison or jail. For example, a recent study of 201 heroin abusers in New York City found that if these abusers were incarcerated for one year, they would not have been able to commit their yearly haul of crimes: 1,000 robberies, 4,000 burglaries, 10,000 shopliftings, and more than 3,000 other property crimes.[175]

Nonetheless, evaluations of incarceration strategies reveal that their impact may be less than expected. For one thing, there is little evidence that incapacitating criminals will deter them from future criminality and even more reason to believe they may be more inclined to commit crimes upon release. In fact, the more prior incarceration experiences inmates have, the more likely they are to recidivate (and return to prison) within 12 months of their release.[176]

By its nature, the prison experience exposes young, first-time offenders to higher-risk, more experienced inmates who can influence their lifestyle and help shape their attitudes. Novice inmates also run an increased risk of becoming infected with AIDS and other health hazards, and that exposure reduces their life chances after release.[177] The short-term crime reduction effect of incapacitating criminals is negated if the prison experience has the long-term effect of escalating frequency of criminal behavior upon release. Furthermore, the economics of crime suggest that if money can be made from criminal activity, there will always be someone to take the place of the incarcerated offender. New criminals will be recruited and trained, offsetting any benefit accrued by incarceration. Imprisoning established offenders may likewise open new opportunities for competitors who were suppressed by more experienced criminals. For example, incarcerating organized crime members may open drug markets to new gangs; the flow of narcotics into the country may increase after organized crime leaders are imprisoned.

Another reason incarceration may not work is that most criminal offenses are committed by teens and very young adult offenders who are unlikely to be sent to prison for a single felony conviction. In addition, incarcerated criminals, aging behind bars, are already past the age when they are likely to commit crime. As a result, a strict incarceration policy may keep people in prison beyond the time they are a threat to society while a new cohort of high-risk adolescents is on the street. It is possible that the most serious criminals are already behind bars and that adding more to the population will have little appreciable effect while adding tremendous costs to the correctional system.[178]

An incapacitation strategy is also terribly expensive. The prison system costs billions of dollars each year. Even if incarceration could reduce the crime rate, the costs would be enormous. Are U.S. taxpayers willing to spend billions more on new prison construction and annual maintenance fees? A strict incarceration policy would result in a growing number of elderly inmates whose maintenance costs, estimated at $69,000 per year, are three times higher than those of younger inmates. Estimates are that in 2005 about 16 percent of the prison population is over age 50.[179]

Finally, relying on incapacitation as a crime control mechanism has resulted in an ever-expanding prison population. Eventually most inmates return to society in a process referred to as re-entry. In most states, prison inmates, especially those convicted of drug crimes, have come from comparatively few urban inner-city areas. Their return may contribute to family disruption, undermine social institutions, and create community disorganization. Rather than act as a crime suppressant, incarceration may have the long-term effect of accelerating crime rates.[180]

SELECTIVE INCAPACITATION A more efficient incapacitation model has been suggested that is based on identifying chronic career criminals. The premise for this model is that if a small number of people account for a relatively large percentage of the nation's crime, then an effort to incapacitate these few troublemakers might have a significant payoff. In an often-cited work, Peter Greenwood of the Rand Corporation suggests that **selective incapacitation** could be an effective crime reduction strategy.[181] In his study of more than 2,000 inmates serving time for theft in California, Michigan, and Texas, he found that selective incapacitation of chronic offenders could reduce the rate of robbery offenses by 15 percent and the inmate population by 5 percent. According to Greenwood's model, chronic offenders can be distinguished on the basis of their offending patterns and lifestyle (for example, their employment record and history of substance abuse). Once identified, high-risk offenders would be eligible for sentencing enhancements that would substantially increase the time they serve in prison.

Another concept receiving widespread attention is the "three strikes and you're out" policy of giving people convicted of three violent offenses a mandatory life term without parole. Many states already employ habitual offender laws that provide long (or life) sentences for repeat offenders. Criminologists retort that although such strategies are politically compelling, they will not work for these reasons:

- Most three-time losers are at the verge of aging out of crime anyway.

- Current sentences for violent crimes are already severe.

- An expanding prison population will drive up already high prison costs.

- There would be racial disparity in sentencing.

- Police would be in danger because two-time offenders would violently resist a third arrest knowing they face a life sentence.[182]

- The prison population probably already contains the highest-frequency criminals.

Those who support a selective incapacitation strategy argue that criminals who are already in prison (high-rate offenders) commit significantly more crimes each year than the average criminal who is on the outside (low-rate offenders). They point to the success of a three strikes policy to bring the crime rate down: Three strikes supporters credit the law for the 46 percent drop in California's crime rate, among the sharpest decline in any state from 1992 to 2002. At least 2 million fewer criminal incidents have occurred, including 6,700 fewer homicides, since the state's three strikes law took effect.[183]

Critics counter that if a broad policy of incarceration were employed—requiring mandatory prison sentences for all those convicted of crimes—more low-rate criminals would be placed behind bars.[184] It would be both costly and nonproductive to incarcerate large groups of people who commit relatively few crimes. It makes more economic sense to focus incarceration efforts on known high-rate offenders by lengthening their sentences. Even in California, where most three strikes sentences originate, citizens are becoming weary of their use. At the time of this writing, three strikes laws are rapidly losing popularity in California for being too harsh and overly punitive, and efforts are underway to curb or limit their application.[185] Concept Summary 4.2 outlines the various methods of crime control and their effects.

 To quiz yourself on this material, go to the Criminology TPT 9e website.

 CONCEPT SUMMARY 4.2

Crime Control Methods

Situational Crime Prevention

- The core concept is that it reduces the payoff of crime.
- Some methods seem to reduce particular crimes.

General Deterrence

- The core concept is that it scares would-be criminals.
- Is it successful? The certainty of punishment is more effective than severity of punishment.

Specific Deterrence

- The core concept is that it scares known criminals.
- Is it successful? It has limited effectiveness underscored by high recidivism rates.

Incapacitation

- The core concept is that it reduces criminal opportunity.
- Is it successful? As prison rates have increased, the crime rate has declined.

PUBLIC POLICY IMPLICATIONS OF CHOICE THEORY

From the origins of classical theory to the development of modern rational choice views, the belief that criminals choose to commit crime has influenced the relationship among law, punishment, and crime. Although research on the core principles of choice theory and deterrence theories produces mixed results, these models have had an important impact on crime prevention strategies.

When police patrol in well-marked cars, it is assumed that their presence will deter would-be criminals. When the harsh realities of prison life are portrayed in movies and TV shows, the lesson is not lost on potential criminals. Nowhere is the idea that the threat of punishment can control crime more evident than in the implementation of tough mandatory criminal sentences to control violent crime and drug trafficking.

Despite its questionable deterrent effect, some advocates argue that the death penalty can effectively restrict criminality; at least it ensures that convicted criminals never again get the opportunity to kill. Many observers are dismayed because people who are convicted of murder sometimes kill again when released on parole. One study of 52,000 incarcerated murderers found that 810 had been previously convicted of murder and had killed 821 people following their previous release from prison.[186] About 9 percent of all inmates on death row have had prior convictions for homicide. Death penalty advocates argue that if these criminals had been executed for their first offenses, hundreds of people would be alive today.[187]

Just Desert

The concept of criminal choice has also prompted the creation of justice policies referred to as **just desert**. The just desert position has been most clearly spelled out by criminologist Andrew Von Hirsch in his book *Doing Justice*.[188] Von Hirsch suggests the concept of desert as a theoretical model to guide justice policy. This utilitarian view purports that punishment is needed to preserve the social equity disturbed by crime. Nonetheless, he claims that the severity of punishment should be commensurate with the seriousness of the crime.[189] Von Hirsch's views can be summarized in these three statements:

1. Those who violate others' rights deserve to be punished.

2. We should not deliberately add to human suffering; punishment makes those punished suffer.

3. However, punishment may prevent more misery than it inflicts; this conclusion re-establishes the need for desert-based punishment.[190]

116. Michael White, James Fyfe, Suzanne Campbell, and John Goldkamp, "The Police Role in Preventing Homicide: Considering the Impact of Problem-Oriented Policing on the Prevalence of Murder," *Journal of Research in Crime and Delinquency* 40 (2003): 194–226.

117. Janice Puckett and Richard Lundman, "Factors Affecting Homicide Clearances: Multivariate Analysis of a More Complete Conceptual Framework," *Journal of Research in Crime and Delinquency* 40 (2003): 171–194.

118. Kenneth Novak, Jennifer Hartman, Alexander Holsinger, and Michael Turner, "The Effects of Aggressive Policing of Disorder on Serious Crime," *Policing* 22 (1999): 171–190.

119. Lawrence Sherman, "Police Crackdowns," *NIJ Reports* (March/April 1990): 2–6, at p. 2.

120. Jacqueline Cohen, Wilpen Gorr, and Piyusha Singh, "Estimating Intervention Effects in Varying Risk Settings: Do Police Raids Reduce Illegal Drug Dealing at Nuisance Bars?" *Criminology* 42 (2003): 257–292.

121. Anthony Braga, David Weisburd, Elin Waring, Lorraine Green Mazerolle, William Spelman, and Francis Gajewski, "Problem-Oriented Policing in Violent Crime Places: A Randomized Controlled Experiment," *Criminology* 37 (1999): 541–580.

122. Fritsch, Caeti, and Taylor, "Gang Suppression through Saturation Patrol, Aggressive Curfew, and Truancy Enforcement."

123. Michael Smith, "Police-Led Crackdowns and Cleanups: An Evaluation of a Crime Control Initiative in Richmond, Virginia," *Crime and Delinquency* 47 (2001): 60–68.

124. Braga, Weisburd, Waring, Mazerolle, Spelman, and Gajewski, "Problem-Oriented Policing in Violent Crime Places."

125. Robert Voas, Scott Tippetts, and James Fell, "Assessing the Effectiveness of Minimum Legal Drinking Age and Zero Tolerance Laws in the United States," *Accident Analysis & Prevention* 35 (2003): 579–588.

126. "Crime and Punishment in America: 1997 Update," National Center for Policy Analysis, Dallas, Texas, 1997.

127. Nagin and Pogarsky, "Integrating Celerity, Impulsivity, and Extralegal Sanction Threats into a Model of General Deterrence," pp. 884–885.

128. Ed Stevens and Brian Payne, "Applying Deterrence Theory in the Context of Corporate Wrongdoing: Limitations on Punitive Damages," *Journal of Criminal Justice* 27 (1999) 195–209; Jeffrey Roth, *Firearms and Violence* (Washington, DC: National Institute of Justice, 1994); and Thomas Marvell and Carlisle Moody, "The Impact of Enhanced Prison Terms for Felonies Committed with Guns," *Criminology* 33 (1995): 247–281.

129. Greg Pogarsky, "Identifying 'Deterrable' Offenders: Implications for Research on Deterrence," *Justice Quarterly* 19 (2002): 431–453.

130. Suzanne Briscoe, "Raising the Bar: Can Increased Statutory Penalties Deter Drunk-Drivers?" *Accident Analysis & Prevention* 36 (2004): 919–929.

131. H. Laurence Ross, "Implications of Drinking-and-Driving Law Studies for Deterrence Research," in *Critique and Explanation, Essays in Honor of Gwynne Nettler,* eds. Timothy Hartnagel and Robert Silverman (New Brunswick, NJ: Transaction Books, 1986), pp. 159–171; H. Laurence Ross, Richard McCleary, and Gary LaFree, "Can Mandatory Jail Laws Deter Drunk Driving? The Arizona Case," *Journal of Criminal Law and Criminology* 81 (1990): 156–167.

132. Wanda Foglia, "Perceptual Deterrence and the Mediating Effect of Internalized Norms among Inner-City Teenagers," *Journal of Research in Crime and Delinquency* 34 (1997): 414–442.

133. Harold Grasmick, Robert Bursik, and Karyl Kinsey, "Shame and Embarrassment as Deterrents to Noncompliance with the Law: The Case of an Anti-Littering Campaign." Paper presented at the annual meeting of the American Society of Criminology, Baltimore, November 1990, p. 3.

134. Charles Tittle, *Sanctions and Social Deviance* (New York: Praeger, 1980).

135. For an opposite view, see Steven Burkett and David Ward, "A Note on Perceptual Deterrence, Religiously Based Moral Condemnation, and Social Control," *Criminology* 31 (1993): 119–134.

136. Ibid.

137. John Snortum, "Drinking–Driving Compliance in Great Britain: The Role of Law as a 'Threat' and as a 'Moral Eye-Opener,'" *Journal of Criminal Justice* 18 (1990): 479–499.

138. Donald Green, "Past Behavior as a Measure of Actual Future Behavior: An Unresolved Issue in Perceptual Deterrence Research," *Journal of Criminal Law and Criminology* 80 (1989): 781–804, at 803; Matthew Silberman, "Toward a Theory of Criminal Deterrence," *American Sociological Review* 41 (1976): 442–461; Linda Anderson, Theodore Chiricos, and Gordon Waldo, "Formal and Informal Sanctions: A Comparison of Deterrent Effects," *Social Problems* 25 (1977): 103–114. See also Maynard Erickson and Jack Gibbs, "Objective and Perceptual Properties of Legal Punishment and Deterrence Doctrine," *Social Problems* 25 (1978): 253–264; and Daniel Nagin and Raymond Paternoster, "Enduring Individual Differences and Rational Choice Theories of Crime," *Law and Society Review* 27 (1993): 467–485.

139. Harold Grasmick and Robert Bursik, "Conscience, Significant Others, and Rational Choices: Extending the Deterrence Model," *Law and Society Review* 24 (1990): 837–861, at 854.

140. Grasmick, Bursik, and Kinsey, "Shame and Embarrassment as Deterrents to Noncompliance with the Law"; Harold Grasmick, Robert Bursik, and Bruce Arneklev, "Reduction in Drunk Driving as a Response to Increased Threats of Shame, Embarrassment, and Legal Sanctions," *Criminology* 31 (1993): 41–69.

141. Harold Grasmick, Brenda Sims Blackwell, and Robert Bursik, "Changes in the Sex Patterning of Perceived Threats of Sanctions," *Law and Society Review* 27 (1993): 679–699.

142. Thomas Peete, Trudie Milner, and Michael Welch, "Levels of Social Integration in Group Contexts and the Effects of Informal Sanction Threat on Deviance," *Criminology* 32 (1994): 85–105.

143. Ernest Van Den Haag, "The Criminal Law as a Threat System," *Journal of Criminal Law and Criminology* 73 (1982): 709–785.

144. David Lykken, "Psychopathy, Sociopathy, and Crime," *Society* 34 (1996): 30–38.

145. George Lowenstein, Daniel Nagin, and Raymond Paternoster, "The Effect of Sexual Arousal on Expectations of Sexual Forcefulness," *Journal of Research in Crime and Delinquency* 34 (1997): 443–473.

146. Ken Auletta, *The Under Class* (New York: Random House, 1982).

147. Foglia, "Perceptual Deterrence and the Mediating Effect of Internalized Norms among Inner-City Teenagers"; Raymond Paternoster, "Decisions to Participate in and Desist from Four Types of Common Delinquency: Deterrence and the Rational Choice Perspective," *Law and Society Review* 23 (1989): 7–29; Raymond Paternoster, "Examining Three-Wave Deterrence Models: A Question of Temporal Order and Specification," *Journal of Criminal Law and Criminology* 79 (1988): 135–163; Raymond Paternoster, Linda Saltzman, Gordon Waldo, and Theodore Chiricos, "Estimating Perceptual Stability and Deterrent Effects: The Role of Perceived Legal Punishment in the Inhibition of Criminal Involvement," *Journal of Criminal Law and Criminology* 74 (1983): 270–297; M. William Minor and Joseph Harry, "Deterrent and Experiential Effects in Perceptual Deterrence Research: A Replication and Extension," *Journal of Research in Crime and Delinquency* 19 (1982): 190–203; Lonn Lanza-Kaduce, "Perceptual Deterrence and Drinking and Driving among College Students," *Criminology* 26 (1988): 321–341.

148. Foglia, "Perceptual Deterrence and the Mediating Effect of Internalized Norms among Inner-City Teenagers," pp. 419–443.

149. Alex Piquero and George Rengert, "Studying Deterrence with Active Residential Burglars," *Justice Quarterly* 16 (1999): 451–462.

150. David Klinger, "Policing Spousal Assault," *Journal of Research in Crime and Delinquency* 32 (1995): 308–324.

151. Paternoster, "Decisions to Participate in and Desist from Four Types of Common Delinquency."

152. James Williams and Daniel Rodeheaver, "Processing of Criminal Homicide Cases in a Large Southern City," *Sociology and Social Research* 75 (1991): 80–88.

153. Wilson, *Thinking about Crime.*

154. James Q. Wilson and Richard Herrnstein, *Crime and Human Nature* (New York: Simon & Schuster, 1985), p. 494.

155. Christina Dejong, "Survival Analysis and Specific Deterrence: Integrating Theoretical and Empirical Models of Recidivism," *Criminology* 35 (1997): 561–576.

156. Paul Tracy and Kimberly Kempf-Leonard, *Continuity and Discontinuity in Criminal Careers* (New York: Plenum Press, 1996).

157. Lawrence Greenfeld, *Examining Recidivism* (Washington, DC: U.S. Government Printing Office, 1985).

158. Allen Beck and Bernard Shipley, *Recidivism of Prisoners Released in 1983* (Washington, DC: Bureau of Justice Statistics, 1989).

159. Dejong, "Survival Analysis and Specific Deterrence," p. 573.

160. David Weisburd, Elin Waring, and Ellen Chayet, "Specific Deterrence in a Sample of Offenders Convicted of White-Collar Crimes," *Criminology* 33 (1995): 587–607.

161. Dejong, "Survival Analysis and Specific Deterrence"; Raymond Paternoster and Alex Piquero, "Reconceptualizing Deterrence: An Empirical Test of Personal and Vicarious Experiences," *Journal of Research in Crime and Delinquency* 32 (1995): 251–258.

162. Dejong, "Survival Analysis and Specific Deterrence"; Paternoster and Piquero, "Reconceptualizing Deterrence."

163. Cassia Spohn and David Holleran, "The Effect of Imprisonment on Recidivism Rates of Felony Offenders: A Focus on Drug Offenders," *Criminology* 40 (2002): 329–359.

164. Greg Pogarsky and Alex R. Piquero "Can Punishment Encourage Offending? Investigating the 'Resetting' Effect," *Journal of Research in Crime and Delinquency* 40(2003): 92–117.

165. Doris Layton MacKenzie and Spencer De Li, "The Impact of Formal and Informal Social Controls on the Criminal Activities of Probationers," *Journal of Research in Crime and Delinquency* 39 (2002): 243–276.

166. Charles Murray and Louis Cox, *Beyond Probation* (Beverly Hills: Sage, 1979); Perry Shapiro and Harold Votey, "Deterrence and Subjective Probabilities of Arrest: Modeling Individual Decisions to Drink and Drive in Sweden," *Law and Society Review* 18 (1984): 111–149; Douglas Smith and Patrick Gartin, "Specifying Specific Deterrence: The Influence of Arrest on Future Criminal Activity," *American Sociological Review* 54 (1989): 94–105.

167. Eleni Apospori and Geoffrey Alpert, "Research Note: The Role of Differential Experience with the Criminal Justice System in Changes in Perceptions of Severity of Legal Sanctions over Time," *Crime and Delinquency* 39 (1993): 184–194.

168. Michael Lynch, "Beating a Dead Horse: Is There Any Basic Empirical Evidence for the Deterrent Effect of Imprisonment?" *Crime, Law and Social Change* 31 (1999): 347–362.

169. Andrew Karmen, "Why Is New York City's Murder Rate Dropping So Sharply?" Unpublished paper, John Jay College, New York City, 1996.

170. Isaac Ehrlich, "Participation in Illegitimate Activities: An Economic Analysis," *Journal of Political Economy* 81 (1973): 521–567; Lee Bowker, "Crime and the Use of Prisons in the United States: A Time Series Analysis," *Crime and Delinquency* 27 (1981): 206–212.

171. David Greenberg, "The Incapacitative Effects of Imprisonment: Some Estimates," *Law and Society Review* 9 (1975): 541–580.

172. Ibid., p. 558.

173. Reuel Shinnar and Shlomo Shinnar, "The Effects of the Criminal Justice System on the Control of Crime: A Quantitative Approach," *Law and Society Review* 9 (1975): 581–611.

174. Steven Levitt, "Why Do Increased Arrest Rates Appear to Reduce Crime: Deterrence, Incapacitation, or Measurement Error?" *Economic Inquiry* 36 (1998):353–372; see also, Thomas Marvell and Carlisle Moody, "The Impact of Prison Growth on Homicide," *Homicide Studies* 1 (1997): 205–233.

175. David Greenberg and Nancy Larkin, "The Incapacitation of Criminal Opiate Users," *Crime and Delinquency* 44 (1998): 205–228.

176. John Wallerstedt, *Returning to Prison, Bureau of Justice Statistics Special Report* (Washington, DC: U.S. Department of Justice, 1984).

177. James Marquart, Victoria Brewer, Janet Mullings, and Ben Crouch, "The Implications of Crime Control Policy on HIV/AIDS-Related Risk among Women Prisoners," *Crime and Delinquency* 45 (1999): 82–98.

178. Jose Canela-Cacho, Alfred Blumstein, and Jacqueline Cohen, "Relationship between the Offending Frequency of Imprisoned and Free Offenders," *Criminology* 35 (1997): 133–171.

179. Kate King and Patricia Bass, "Southern Prisons and Elderly Inmates: Taking a Look Inside," Paper presented at the American Society of Criminology meeting, San Diego, 1997.

180. James Lynch and William Sabol, "Prisoner Reentry in Perspective," Urban Institute: http://www.urban.org/url.cfm?ID=410213. Accessed July 12, 2004.

181. Peter Greenwood, *Selective Incapacitation* (Santa Monica: Rand Corporation, 1982).

182. Marc Mauer, Testimony before the U.S. Congress, House Judiciary Committee, on "Three Strikes and You're Out," 1 March 1994.

183. Bobby Caina Calvan, "Calif. Initiative Seeks to Rewrite Three-Strikes Law," *Boston Globe*, 12 July 2004, p.1.

184. Canela-Cacho, Blumstein, and Cohen, "Relationship between the Offending Frequency of Imprisoned and Free Offenders."

185. Calvan, "Calif. Initiative Seeks to Rewrite Three-Strikes Law."

186. Stephen Markman and Paul Cassell, "Protecting the Innocent: A Response to the Bedeau-Radelet Study," *Stanford Law Review* 41 (1988): 121–170, at 153.

187. James Stephan and Tracy Snell, *Capital Punishment, 1994* (Washington, DC: Bureau of Justice Statistics, 1996), p. 8.

188. Andrew Von Hirsch, *Doing Justice* (New York: Hill and Wang, 1976).

189. Ibid., pp. 15–16.

190. Ibid.

CHAPTER 5

Shasta Kay Groene   Dylan James Groene

© Reuters / Landov

Joseph E. Duncan III, a repeat sex offender, recorded his rambling violent thoughts on his web blog entitled the "Fifth Nail," a reference to a missing nail that was alleged to have pierced the body of Jesus while he was on the cross. He advocated for the the repeal of sex offender laws and discussed his violent fantasies. Duncan is alleged to have broken into the home of two Idaho children—Shasta Groene, age 8, and Dylan Groene, age 9— and killed their mother Brenda, her boyfriend Mark McKenzie, and their older brother Slade. He kidnapped the children and held them hostage for six weeks during which they were repeatedly raped and molested. On July 2, 2005, Shasta Groene was found in Duncan's custody in a Denny's restaurant in Coeur d'Alene, Idaho. A waitress recognized Duncan from a "Wanted" poster and worked with the restaurant manager to delay him until the police arrived.

Is it possible that depraved people such as Joseph Duncan actually "choose" to commit crime as choice theorists would have us believe? Might their crimes be the result of some biological or psychological abnormality, which render them incapable of controlling their urges, impulses, and desires? There is little evidence that Duncan's antisocial behavior was a function of his environment. Are criminals born rather than made?

TRAIT THEORIES

CHAPTER OUTLINE

Foundations of Trait Theory
Impact of Sociobiology
Modern Trait Theories

Biosocial Trait Theories
Biochemical Conditions and Crime

Comparative Criminology:
Diet and Crime: An International Perspective

Neurophysiological Conditions and Crime
Arousal Theory
Genetics and Crime
Evolutionary Theory
Evaluation of the Biosocial Branch of Trait Theory

Psychological Trait Theories
Psychodynamic Theory
Behavioral Theory
Cognitive Theory

The Criminological Enterprise:
The Media and Violence

Psychological Traits and Characteristics
Personality and Crime
Intelligence and Crime

The Criminological Enterprise:
The Antisocial Personality

Public Policy Implications of Trait Theory

CHAPTER OBJECTIVES

1. Be familiar with the concept of sociobiology
2. Know what is meant by the term *equipotentiality*
3. Be able to discuss the relationship between diet and crime
4. Be familiar with the association between hormones and crime
5. Be able to discuss why violent offenders may suffer from neurological problems
6. Know the factors that make up the ADHD syndrome
7. Be able to discuss the role genetics plays in violent behavior
8. Be familiar with the concepts of evolutionary theory
9. Be able to discuss the psychodynamics of criminality
10. Understand the association between media and crime
11. Discuss the role of personality and intelligence in antisocial behaviors.

Beginning with Alfred Hitchcock's film *Psycho*, producers have made millions depicting the ghoulish acts of people who at first seem normal and even friendly but turn out to be demented and dangerous. Lurking out there are crazed baby-sitters (*Hand that Rocks the Cradle*), frenzied airline passengers (*Turbulence*), deranged roommates (*Single, White Female*), psychotic tenants (*Pacific Heights*), demented secretaries (*The Temp*), unhinged police (*Maniac Cop*), mad cab drivers (*The Bone Collector*) irrational fans (*The Fan; Misery*), abnormal girlfriends (*Fatal Attraction*) and boyfriends (*Fear*), unstable husbands (*Enough; Sleeping with the Enemy*) and wives (*Black Widow*), loony fathers (*The Stepfather*), mothers (*Friday the 13th, Part 1*), and grandmothers (*Hush*), unbalanced crime victims (*I Know What You Did Last Summer*), maniacal children (*The Good Son; Children of the Corn*), lunatic high school friends (*Scream*) and college classmates (*Scream II*), possessed dolls (*Child's Play 1–5*) and their mates (*Bride of Chucky*), and nutsy teenaged admirers (*The Crush*). Sometimes they try to kill each other (*Freddy vs. Jason*). No one can ever be safe when the psychologists and psychiatrists who should be treating these disturbed people turn out to be demonic murderers themselves (*Hannibal, Silence of the Lambs, Dressed to Kill,* and *Never Talk to Strangers*). Is it any wonder that we respond to a particularly horrible crime by saying of the perpetrator, "That guy must be crazy" or "She is a monster!"

The view that criminals bear physical and/or mental traits that make them different and abnormal is not restricted to the movie-going public. Since the nineteenth century, some criminologists have suggested that biological and psychological traits may influence behavior. Some people may develop physical or mental traits at birth or soon after that affect their social functioning over the life course and influence their behavior choices. For example, low-birthweight babies have been found to suffer poor educational achievement later in life. Academic deficiency has been linked to delinquency and drug abuse, so it is possible that a condition present at birth (such as low birth weight) will influence antisocial behavior during later adolescence.[1] Possessing these personal differences explains why, when faced with the same life situations, one person commits crime and becomes a chronic offender, whereas another attends school, church, and neighborhood functions and obeys the laws of society. To understand this view of crime causation, we begin with a brief review of the development of trait theories.

FOUNDATIONS OF TRAIT THEORY

As you may recall, Cesare Lombroso's work on the "born criminal" was a direct offshoot of applying the scientific methodology to the study of crime. His identification of primitive, atavistic anomalies was based on what he believed was sound empirical research using established scientific methods.

Lombroso was not alone in the early development of biological theory. A contemporary, Raffaele Garofalo

(1852–1934), shared the belief that certain physical characteristics indicate a criminal nature. For example, Garofalo stated that among criminals "a lower degree of sensibility to physical pain seems to be demonstrated by the readiness with which prisoners submit to the operation of tattooing."[2] Enrico Ferri (1856–1929), another student of Lombroso's, believed that a number of biological, social, and organic factors caused delinquency and crime.[3] Ferri added a social dimension to Lombroso's work and was a pioneer with his view that criminals should not be held personally or morally responsible for their actions because forces outside their control caused criminality.

Advocates of the **inheritance school** traced the activities of several generations of families believed to have an especially large number of criminal members.[4] The body build or **somatotype** school, developed more than fifty years ago by William Sheldon, held that criminals manifest distinct physiques that make them susceptible to particular types of delinquent behavior. *Mesomorphs,* for example, have well-developed muscles and an athletic appearance. They are active, aggressive, sometimes violent, and the most likely to become criminals. *Endomorphs* have heavy builds and are slow moving. They are known for lethargic behavior rendering them unlikely to commit violent crime and more willing to engage in less strenuous criminal activities such as fencing stolen property. *Ectomorphs* are tall, thin, and less social and more intellectual than the other types.[5]

The work of Lombroso and his contemporaries is regarded today as a historical curiosity, not scientific fact. In fact, their research methodology has been discredited because they did not use control groups from the general population to compare results. Many of the traits they assumed to be inherited are not really genetically determined but could be caused by deprivation in surroundings and diet. Even if most criminals shared some biological traits, they might be products not of heredity but of some environmental condition, such as poor nutrition or healthcare. It is equally likely that only criminals who suffer from biological abnormalities are caught and punished by the justice system. In his later writings, even Lombroso admitted that the born criminal was just one of many criminal types. Because of these deficiencies in his theory, the validity of individual-oriented explanations of criminality became questionable and, for a time, was disregarded by the criminological mainstream.

Impact of Sociobiology

What seems no longer tenable at this juncture is any theory of human behavior which ignores biology and relies exclusively on socio-cultural learning. . . . Most social scientists have been wrong in their dogmatic rejection and blissful ignorance of the biological parameters of our behavior.[6]

Biological explanations of crime fell out of favor in the early twentieth century. During this period, criminologists became concerned about the sociological influences on crime, such as the neighborhood, peer group, family life, and social status.

||||||| **CONNECTIONS** |||||||

Biological explanations of criminal behavior first became popular during the middle part of the nineteenth century with the introduction of positivism—the use of the scientific method and empirical analysis to study behavior. Positivism was discussed in Chapter 1 when the history of criminology was described.

The work of biocriminologists was viewed as methodologically unsound and generally invalid by the sociologists who dominated the field and held the view, referred to as **biophobia,** that no serious consideration should be given to biological factors when attempting to understand human nature.[7]

Can sociobiology explain behavior patterns across all animal species and show how it is linked to mating behavior? To find out, read about the mechanism of natural selection in this article: Gerald Holton, "The New Synthesis?" *Society* 35 (January–February 1998): 203.

In the early 1970s, spurred by the publication of *Sociobiology,* by biologist Edmund O. Wilson, the biological basis for crime once again emerged into the limelight.[8] Sociobiology differs from earlier theories of behavior in that it stresses that biological and genetic conditions affect how social behaviors are learned and perceived. These perceptions, in turn, are linked to existing environmental structures. Sociobiologists view the gene as the ultimate unit of life that controls all human destiny. Although they believe environment and experience also have an impact on behavior, their main premise is that most actions are controlled by a person's "biological machine." Most important, people are controlled by the innate need to have their genetic material survive and dominate others. Consequently, they do everything in their power to ensure their own survival and that of others who share their gene pool (relatives, fellow citizens, and so forth). Even when they come to the aid of others, which is called **reciprocal altruism,** people are motivated by the belief that their actions will be reciprocated and that their gene survival capability will be enhanced.

Sociobiologists suggest that when males desire younger females, they are engaging in a procreation strategy that will maximize the chance of producing healthy offspring. Females prefer older males because the survival of their offspring will be enhanced by someone with greater prestige and wealth. To learn more, use "sociobiology" as a subject guide with InfoTrac College Edition.

The study of sociobiology revived interest in finding a biological basis for crime and delinquency. If, as it suggests, biological (genetic) makeup controls human behavior, it follows that it should also be responsible for determining whether a person chooses law-violating or conventional behavior. This view of crime causation is referred to as **trait theory.**

Modern Trait Theories

Trait theorists today do not suggest that a single biological or psychological attribute is thought to adequately explain all criminality. Rather, each offender is considered unique, physically and mentally; consequently, there must be different explanations for each person's behavior. Some may have inherited criminal tendencies, others may be suffering from nervous system (neurological) problems, and still others may have a blood chemistry disorder that heightens their antisocial activity. Criminologists who focus on the individual see many explanations for crime, because, in fact, there are many differences among criminal offenders.

Trait theorists are not overly concerned with legal definitions of crime; they do not try to explain why people violate particular statutory laws such as car theft or burglary. To them, these are artificial legal concepts based on arbitrary boundaries (for example, speeding may be arbitrarily defined as exceeding 65 miles per hour). Instead, trait theorists focus on basic human behavior and drives—aggression, violence, and a tendency to act on impulse—that are linked to antisocial behavior patterns. They also recognize that human traits alone do not produce criminality and that crime-producing interactions involve both personal traits—such as intelligence, personality, and chemical and genetic makeup—and environmental factors, such as family life, educational attainment, economic factors, and neighborhood conditions. Physical or mental traits are, therefore, but one part of a large pool of environmental, social, and personal factors that account for criminality. Some people may have a predisposition toward aggression, but environmental stimuli can either suppress or trigger antisocial acts.

Even the most committed trait theorists recognize that environmental conditions in disadvantaged inner-city areas may have a powerful influence on antisocial behavior. Many people who reside in these areas experience poverty, racism, frustration, and anger, yet relatively few become delinquents and even fewer mature into adult criminals. Because not all humans are born with equal potential to learn and achieve (**equipotentiality**), the combination of physical traits and the environment produces individual behavior patterns. There is a significant link between behavior patterns and physical or chemical changes in the brain, autonomic nervous system, and central nervous system.[9]

To learn how equipotentiality mediates the relationship between economic status and child development, read: Robert Bradley and Robert Corwyn, "Socioeconomic Status and Child Development," *Annual Review of Psychology* (2002): 371–399.

Trait theorists argue that those who do become chronic offenders suffer some biological/psychological condition or trait that renders them incapable of resisting social pressures and problems.[10] As biocriminologists Anthony Walsh and Lee Ellis conclude, "If there is one takeaway lesson from studying biological bases of behavior, it is that the more we study them the more we realize how important the environment is."[11]

Trait theories have gained recent prominence because of what is now known about chronic recidivism and the development of criminal careers. If only a small percentage of all offenders go on to become persistent repeaters, then it is possible that what sets them apart from the criminal population is an abnormal biochemical makeup, brain structure, or genetic constitution.[12] Even if criminals do "choose crime," the fact that some repeatedly make that choice could well be linked to their physical and mental makeup. All people may be aware of and even fear the sanctioning power of the law, but some are unable to control their urges and passions.

Trait theories can be divided into two major subdivisions: one that stresses psychological functioning and another that stresses biological makeup. Although there is often overlap between these views (for example, brain functioning may have a biological basis), each branch has its unique characteristics and will be discussed separately.

 To quiz yourself on this material, go to the Criminology TPT 9e website.

BIOSOCIAL TRAIT THEORIES

Rather than view the criminal as a person whose behavior is controlled by biological conditions determined at birth, biosocial theorists believe physical, environmental, and social conditions work in concert to produce human behavior. Biosocial theory has several core principles.[13] First, it assumes that genetic makeup contributes significantly to human behavior. Further, it contends that not all humans are born with equal potential to learn and achieve (equipotentiality). Biosocial theorists argue that no two people are alike (with rare exceptions, such as identical twins) and that the combination of human genetic traits and the environment produces individual behavior patterns (Figure 5.1). In contrast, social theorists suggest, either explicitly or implicitly, that all people are born equal and that thereafter behavior is controlled by social forces (parents, schools, neighborhoods, and friends).

LEARNING POTENTIAL AND ITS EFFECT ON INDIVIDUAL BEHAVIOR PATTERNS Another critical focus of modern biological theory is the importance of brain functioning, mental processes, and learning. Social behavior, including criminal behavior, is learned, and each individual organism is believed to have a unique potential for learning. The physical and social environments interact to either limit or enhance an organism's capacity for learning. People learn through a process involving the brain and central nervous system. Learning is not controlled by social interactions but by

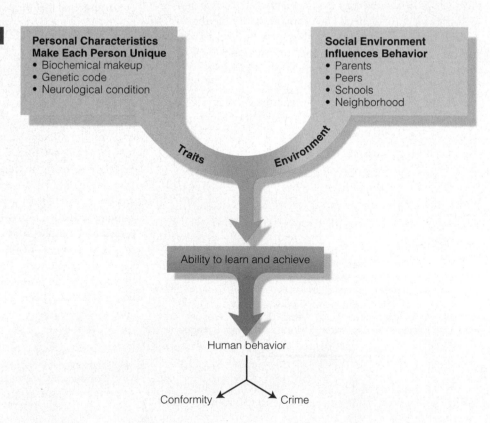

FIGURE 5.1

Biosocial Perspectives on Criminality

Personal Characteristics Make Each Person Unique
• Biochemical makeup
• Genetic code
• Neurological condition

Social Environment Influences Behavior
• Parents
• Peers
• Schools
• Neighborhood

Traits　Environment

Ability to learn and achieve

Human behavior

Conformity　Crime

biochemistry and cellular interaction. Learning can take place only when physical changes occur in the brain. There is a significant link, therefore, between behavior patterns and physical or chemical changes that occur in the brain, autonomic nervous system, and central nervous system.[14]

INSTINCT Some biosocial theorists also believe learning is influenced by instinctual drives. Developed over the course of human history, instincts are inherited, natural, unlearned dispositions that activate specific behavior patterns designed to reach certain goals. For example, people are believed to have a drive to "possess and control" other people and things. Some theft offenses may be motivated by the instinctual need to possess goods and commodities. Rape and other sex crimes may be linked to the primitive instinctual drive males have to "possess and control" females.[15]

The following subsections will examine some of the more important schools of thought within biosocial theory.[16] First, we look at the biochemical factors that are believed to affect how proper behavior patterns are learned. Then the relationship of brain function and crime will be considered. Current ideas about the association between genetic and evolutionary factors and crime will be analyzed. Finally, evolutionary views of crime causation are evaluated.

Biochemical Conditions and Crime

Some trait theorists believe biochemical conditions, including both those that are genetically predetermined and those acquired through diet and environment, control and influence antisocial behavior. Some of the more important biochemical factors that have been linked to criminality are set out in detail here.

CHEMICAL AND MINERAL INFLUENCES Biosocial criminologists maintain that minimum levels of minerals and chemicals are needed for normal brain functioning and growth, especially in the early years of life. Research conducted over the past decade shows that an over- or undersupply of certain chemicals and minerals—including sodium, mercury, potassium, calcium, amino acids, monoamines, and peptides—can lead to depression, mania, cognitive problems, memory loss, and abnormal sexual activity. Even common food additives such as calcium propionate, which is used to preserve bread, have been linked to problem behaviors.[17] In some cases, the relationship is indirect: Chemical and mineral imbalance leads to cognitive and learning deficits and problems, and these factors in turn are associated with antisocial behaviors.[18]

What people eat and take into their bodies may influence their behavior. Some medicines may have detrimental side effects. For example, there has been recent research linking sildenafil, more commonly known as Viagra, with aggressive and violent behavior. While the cause is still unknown, it is possible that sildenafil exerts various biochemical and physiologic effects in the brain and that it affects information processing.[19]

If people with normal needs do not receive the appropriate nutrition, they will suffer from vitamin deficiency. If people have genetic conditions that cause greater than normal needs for certain chemicals and minerals, they are said to suffer from vitamin dependency. People with vitamin deficiency or dependency can manifest many physical, mental, and behavioral problems including lower intelligence test scores.[20] Alcoholics often suffer from thiamine deficiency because of their poor diets and consequently are susceptible to the serious, often fatal **Wernicke-Korsakoff disease**, a deadly neurological disorder.[21]

DIET AND CRIME Another area of biosocial research links diet to crime. In some instances, excessive amounts of harmful substances such as food dyes and artificial colors and /or flavors seem to provoke hostile, impulsive, and otherwise antisocial behaviors.[22]

In other instances the absence in the diet of certain chemicals and minerals—including sodium, potassium, calcium, amino acids, monoamines, and peptides—can lead to

© Tom Boyle/Getty Images

Students purchase soft drinks from vending machines at Jones College Prep High School on April 20, 2004, in Chicago, Illinois. The Chicago Public School system is introducing a new vending policy restricting junk food and a new beverage contract banning carbonated drinks. Under new rules, products in school vending machines must have not more than 30 percent of their calories from fat and no more than 40 percent sugar; candy and chewing gum are banned. New York City has stopped selling soft drinks in schools and replaced them with fruit juices; schools in Los Angeles have also banned soft drinks. A restrictive dietary policy may aid in the control of adolescent obesity. Do you believe that it may also help reduce school crime?

Diet and Crime: An International Perspective

Some recent experimental studies conducted in the United States and abroad have shown that diet and crime may have a significant association.

In Great Britain, Bernard Gesch and his associates studied the behavior of 231 inmates at a maximum security prison. Half of the group received daily capsules containing vitamins, minerals, and essential fatty acids, such as omega-3 and omega-6, while the other half took placebo pills. Antisocial behavior among inmates was recorded before and during distribution of the dietary supplements. Gesch found that the supplement group broke prison rules 25 percent less than those on the placebo. The greatest reduction was for serious offenses—instances of fighting, assaulting guards, or taking hostages dropped 37 percent. There was, however, no significant change in the control group.

In a 2003 Finnish study, 115 depressed outpatients being treated with antidepressants found that those who responded fully to treatment had higher levels of vitamin B12 in their blood at the beginning of treatment and 6 months later. Depression has been linked to antisocial activities. The researchers speculated that vitamin B12 deficiency leads to the accumulation of the amino acid homocysteine, which has been linked to depression.

In the United States, Carlos Iribarren and associates recently (2004) examined the relationship between omega-3 intake and hostility. Using a sample of 3,600 young adults living in urban environments, Iribarren and colleagues controlled for a wide range of factors and found that a higher consumption of the omega-3 fatty acid docosahexaenoic acid (DHA), or of omega-3-rich fish in general, was related to significantly lower levels of hostility.

Stephen Schoenthaler, a well-known biocriminologist, has conducted a number of studies that indicate a significant association between diet and aggressive behavior patterns. In some cases, the relationship is direct; in others, a poor diet may compromise individual functioning, which in turn produces aggressive behavior responses. For example, a poor diet may inhibit school performance, and children who fail at school are at risk for delinquent behavior and criminality.

In one study of 803 New York City public schools, Schoenthaler found that the academic performance of 1.1 million schoolchildren rose 16 percent after their diets were modified. The number of "learning disabled" children fell from 125,000 to 74,000 in one year. No other changes in school programs for the learning disabled were initiated that year. In a similar experiment conducted in a correctional institution, violent and nonviolent antisocial behavior fell an average of 48 percent among 8,047 offenders after dietary changes were implemented. In both these studies, the improvements in behavior and academic performance were attributed to diets containing more vitamins and minerals as compared with the old diets. The greater amounts of these essential nutrients in the new diets were believed to have corrected impaired brain function caused by poor nutrition.

More recently, Schoenthaler conducted three randomized controlled studies in which 66 elementary school children, 62 confined teenage delinquents, and 402 confined adult felons received dietary supplements—the equivalent of a diet providing more fruits, vegetables, and whole grains. In order to remove experimental bias, neither subjects nor researchers knew who received the supplement and who received a placebo. In each study, the subjects receiving the dietary supplement demonstrated significantly less violent and nonviolent antisocial behavior when compared to the control subjects who received placebos. The

---

depression, mania, cognitive problems, memory loss, and abnormal sexual activity.[23] Studies examining the relationship between crime and vitamin deficiency and dependency have identified a close link between antisocial behavior and insufficient quantities of some B vitamins (B3 and B6) and vitamin C. In addition, studies have purported to show that a major proportion of all schizophrenics and children with learning and behavior disorders are dependent on vitamins B3 and B6.[24]

Recent experimental research conducted in the United States and abroad has found that diet and crime may be significantly related. The Comparative Criminology feature reviews some of these findings.

To read more about **diet and crime in England,** go to http://www.thisismidsussex.co.uk/mid_sussex/health/FOOD_FOR_THOUGHT39.html. For an up-to-date list of web links, go to http://cj.wadsworth.com/siegel_crimtpt9e.

SUGAR AND CRIME Another suspected nutritional influence on behavior is a diet especially high in carbohydrates and sugar.[25] For example, some research has found that the way the brain processes glucose is related to scores on tests measuring reasoning power.[26] In addition, sugar intake levels have been associated with attention span deficiencies.[27]

carefully collected data verified that a very good diet, as defined by the World Health Organization, has significant behavioral benefits beyond its health effects.

Schoenthaler and his associates have also evaluated the relationship between nutrition and intelligence. These studies involved 1,753 children and young adults in California, Arizona, Oklahoma, Missouri, England, Wales, Scotland, and Belgium. In each study, subjects who were poorly nourished and who were given dietary supplements showed a greater increase in IQ—an average of 16 points—than did those in the placebo group. (Overall, IQ rose more than 3 points.) The differences in IQ could be attributed to about 20 percent of the children who were presumably inadequately nourished prior to supplementation. The IQ research was expanded to include academic performance in two studies of more than 300 schoolchildren ages 6 to 14 years in Arizona and California. In both studies, children who received daily supplements at school for 3 months achieved significantly higher gains in grade level compared to the matched control group taking placebos. The children taking a supplement improved academically at twice the rate of the children who took placebos.

Schoenthaler concludes that parents with a child who behaves badly, or does poorly in school, may benefit from having the child take a blood test to determine if concentrations of certain nutrients are below the reference norms; if so, a dietary supplement may correct the child's conduct and performance. There is evidence that nineteen nutrients may be critical; low levels appear to adversely affect brain function, academic performance, intelligence, and conduct. When attempting to improve IQ or conduct, it is critical to assess all these nutrients and correct deficiencies as needed. If blood nutrient concentrations are consistently in the normal range, physicians and parents should consider looking elsewhere for the cause of a child's difficulties.

Though more research is needed before the scientific community reaches a consensus on how low is too low, Schoenthaler finds evidence that vitamins, minerals, chemicals, and other nutrients from a diet rich in fruits, vegetables, and whole grains can improve brain function, basic intelligence, and academic performance. These are all variables that have been linked to antisocial behavior.

Critical Thinking

1. If Schoenthaler is correct in his assumptions, should schools be required to provide a proper lunch for all children?

2. How would Schoenthaler explain the aging-out process? Hint: Do people eat better as they mature? What about after they get married?

 InfoTrac College Edition Research

To read more about the relationship between nutrition and behavior, use "nutrition and behavior" as a subject guide with InfoTrac College Edition.

Sources: Jukka Hintikka, Tommi Tolmunen, Antti Tanskanen, and Heimo Viinamäki, "High Vitamin B_{12} Level and Good Treatment Outcome May Be Associated in Major Depressive Disorder," *BMC Psychiatry* 3 (2003): 17–18; C. Iribarren, J. H. Markovitz, D. R. Jacobs, Jr., P. J. Schreiner, M. Daviglus, and J. R. Hibbeln, "Dietary Intake of Omega-3, Omega-6 Fatty Acids and Fish: Relationship with Hostility in Young Adults—The CARDIA Study," *European Journal of Clinical Nutrition* 58 (2004): 24–31; C. Bernard Gesch, Sean M. Hammond, Sarah E. Hampson, Anita Eves, and Martin J. Crowder, "Influence of Supplementary Vitamins, Minerals, and Essential Fatty Acids on the Antisocial Behaviour of Young Adult Prisoners: Randomized, Placebo-Controlled Trial," *British Journal of Psychiatry* 181 (2002): 22–28; Stephen Schoenthaler, "Intelligence, Academic Performance, and Brain Function," California State University, Stanislaus, 2000; see also, S. Schoenthaler and I. Bier, "The Effect of Vitamin–Mineral Supplementation on Juvenile Delinquency among American Schoolchildren: A Randomized Double-Blind Placebo-Controlled Trial," *Journal of Alternative and Complementary Medicine: Research on Paradigm, Practice, and Policy* 6 (2000): 7–18.

Diets high in sugar and carbohydrates also have been linked to violence and aggression. Experiments have been conducted in which children's diets were altered so that sweet drinks were replaced with fruit juices, table sugar with honey, molasses substituted for sugar in cooking, and so on. Results indicate that these changes can reduce aggression levels.[28] Those biocriminologists who believe in a diet–aggression association claim that in every segment of society there are violent, aggressive, and amoral people whose improper food, vitamin, and mineral intake may be responsible for their antisocial behavior. If diet could be improved, they believe the frequency of violent behavior would be reduced.[29]

Although these results are impressive, a number of biologists have questioned this association, and some recent research efforts have failed to find a link between sugar consumption and violence.[30] In one important study, a group of researchers had twenty-five preschool children and twenty-three school-age children described as sensitive to sugar follow a different diet for three consecutive 3-week periods. One diet was high in sucrose, the second substituted Aspartame (Nutrasweet) for a sweetener, and the third relied on saccharin. Careful measurement of the subjects found little evidence of cognitive or behavioral differences that could be linked to diet. If anything, sugar seemed to have a calming effect on the children.[31]

In sum, while some research efforts allege a sugar–violence association, others suggest that many people who maintain diets high in sugar and carbohydrates are not violent or crime prone. In some cases, in fact, sugar intake has been found to possibly reduce or curtail violent tendencies.[32]

GLUCOSE METABOLISM/HYPOGLYCEMIA Research shows that persistent abnormality in the way the brain metabolizes glucose (sugar) can be linked to antisocial behaviors such as substance abuse.[33] **Hypoglycemia** occurs when glucose in the blood falls below levels necessary for normal and efficient brain functioning. The brain is sensitive to the lack of blood sugar because it is the only organ that obtains its energy solely from the combustion of carbohydrates. Thus, when the brain is deprived of blood sugar, it has no alternate food supply to call upon, and brain metabolism slows down, impairing function. Symptoms of hypoglycemia include irritability, anxiety, depression, crying spells, headaches, and confusion.

Research studies have linked hypoglycemia to outbursts of antisocial behavior and violence.[34] Several studies have related assaults and fatal sexual offenses to hypoglycemic reactions.[35] Hypoglycemia has also been connected with a syndrome characterized by aggressive and assaultive behavior, glucose disturbance, and brain dysfunction. Some attempts have been made to measure hypoglycemia using subjects with a known history of criminal activity. Studies of jail and prison inmate populations have found a higher than normal level of hypoglycemia.[36] High levels of reactive hypoglycemia have been found in groups of habitually violent and impulsive offenders.[37]

HORMONAL INFLUENCES Criminologist James Q. Wilson, in his book *The Moral Sense,* concludes that hormones, enzymes, and neurotransmitters may be the key to understanding human behavior. According to Wilson, they help explain gender differences in the crime rate. Males, he writes, are biologically and naturally more aggressive than females, whereas women are more nurturing toward the young and are important for survival of the species.[38] Hormone levels also help explain the aging-out process. Levels of testosterone, the principal male steroid hormone, decline during the life cycle and may explain why violence rates diminish over time.[39]

A number of biosocial theorists are now evaluating the association between violent behavior episodes and hormone levels, and the findings suggest that abnormal levels of male sex hormones (**androgens**) do in fact produce aggressive behavior.[40] Other androgen-related male traits include sensation seeking, impulsivity, dominance, and lesser verbal skills; all of these androgen-related male traits are also related to antisocial behaviors.[41] There is a growing body of evidence suggesting that hormonal changes are also related to mood and behavior and, concomitantly, that adolescents experience more intense mood swings, anxiety, and restlessness than their elders.[42] An association between hormonal activity and antisocial behavior is suggested because rates of both factors peak in adolescence.[43]

One area of concern has been **testosterone,** the most abundant androgen, which controls secondary sex characteristics, such as facial hair and voice timbre.[44] Research conducted on both human and animal subjects has found that prenatal exposure to unnaturally high levels of androgens permanently alters behavior. Girls who were unintentionally exposed to elevated amounts of androgens during their fetal development display an unusually high, long-term tendency toward aggression. Conversely, boys who were prenatally exposed to steroids that decrease androgen levels displayed decreased aggressiveness.[45] In contrast, samples of inmates indicate that testosterone levels were higher in men who committed violent crimes than in the other prisoners.[46] Gender differences in the crime rate then may be explained by the relative difference in androgens between the two sexes. Females may be biologically "protected" from deviant behavior in the same way they are immune from some diseases that strike males.[47]

HOW HORMONES MAY INFLUENCE BEHAVIOR Hormones cause areas of the brain to become less sensitive to environmental stimuli. High androgen levels require people to seek excess stimulation and to be willing to tolerate pain in their quest for thrills. Androgens are linked to brain seizures that, under stressful conditions, can result in emotional volatility. Androgens affect the brain structure itself. They influence the left hemisphere of the **neocortex,** the part of the brain that controls sympathetic feelings toward others.[48] Here are some of the physical reactions produced by hormones that have been linked to violence:

- A lowering of average resting arousal under normal environmental conditions to a point that individuals are motivated to seek unusually high levels of environmental stimulation and are less sensitive to harmful aftereffects resulting from this stimulation

- A lowering of seizure thresholds in and around the limbic system, increasing the likelihood that stressful environmental factors will trigger strong and impulsive emotional responses

- A rightward shift in neocortical functioning, resulting in an increased reliance on the brain hemisphere that is most closely integrated with the limbic system and is least prone to reason in logical-linguistic forms or to respond to linguistic commands.[49]

These effects promote violence and other serious crimes by causing people to seek greater levels of environmental stimulation and to tolerate more punishment, increasing impulsivity, emotional volatility, and antisocial emotions.[50]

Even though some research studies have been unable to demonstrate hormonal differences in samples of violent and nonviolent offenders, drugs that decrease testosterone levels are now being used to treat male sex offenders.[51] The female hormones, estrogen and progesterone, have been administered to sex offenders to decrease their sexual potency.[52]

The long-term side effects of this treatment and the potential danger are still unknown.[53]

Some biologists have claimed that the only difference between men and women is a hormonal system that renders men more aggressive. To research this phemonenon further, use "testosterone" and "violence" as key words with InfoTrac College Edition.

PREMENSTRUAL SYNDROME Hormonal research has not been limited to male offenders. The suspicion has long existed that the onset of the menstrual cycle triggers excessive amounts of the female sex hormones, which affect antisocial, aggressive behavior. This condition is commonly referred to as **premenstrual syndrome,** or **PMS.**[54] The link between PMS and delinquency was first popularized more than twenty-five years ago by Katharina Dalton, whose studies of English women indicated that females are more likely to commit suicide and be aggressive and otherwise antisocial just before or during menstruation.[55]

Dalton's research is often cited as evidence of the link between PMS and crime, but methodological problems make it impossible to accept her findings at face value. There is still significant debate over any link between PMS and aggression. Some doubters argue that the relationship is spurious; it is equally likely that the psychological and physical stress of aggression brings on menstruation and not vice versa.[56]

Diana Fishbein, a noted expert on biosocial theory, concludes that there is in fact an association between elevated levels of female aggression and menstruation. Research efforts, she argues, show (a) that a significant number of incarcerated females committed their crimes during the premenstrual phase and (b) that at least a small percentage of women appear vulnerable to cyclical hormonal changes, which makes them more prone to anxiety and hostility.[57] While the debate is ongoing, it is important to remember that the overwhelming majority of females who do suffer anxiety reactions prior to and during menstruation do not actually engage in violent criminal behavior; so any link between PMS and crime is tenuous at best.[58]

ALLERGIES Allergies are defined as unusual or excessive reactions of the body to foreign substances.[59] For example, hay fever is an allergic reaction caused when pollen cells enter the body and are fought or neutralized by the body's natural defenses. The result of the battle is itching, red eyes, and active sinuses.

Cerebral allergies cause an excessive reaction in the brain, whereas **neuroallergies** affect the nervous system. Neuroallergies and cerebral allergies are believed to cause the allergic person to produce enzymes that attack wholesome foods as if they were dangerous to the body.[60] They may also cause swelling of the brain and produce sensitivity in the central nervous system, conditions linked to mental, emotional, and behavioral problems. Research indicates a connection between allergies and hyperemotionality, depression, aggressiveness, and violent behavior.[61]

Neuroallergy and cerebral allergy problems have also been linked to hyperactivity in children, which may portend antisocial behavior. The foods most commonly involved in producing such allergies are cow's milk, wheat, corn, chocolate, citrus, and eggs; however, about 300 other foods have been identified as allergens. The potential seriousness of the problem has been raised by studies linking the average consumption of one suspected cerebral allergen, corn, to cross-national homicide rates.[62]

ENVIRONMENTAL CONTAMINANTS Recently, the Centers for Disease Control conducted a very extensive evaluation of chemical and mineral contamination in the United States and found that despite some significant improvements there are still many dangerous substances in the environment, including lead, copper, cadmium, mercury, and inorganic gases, such as chlorine and nitrogen dioxide.[63] Prolonged exposure to these substances can cause severe illness or death; at more moderate levels, they have been linked to emotional and behavioral disorders.[64]

Lighting may be another important environmental influence on antisocial behavior. Research projects have suggested that radiation from artificial light sources, such as fluorescent tubes and television sets, may produce antisocial, aggressive behavior.[65]

LEAD LEVELS A number of recent research studies have suggested that lead ingestion is linked to aggressive behaviors on both a macro- and a micro-level.[66] For example, on a macro-level, when criminologists Paul Stretesky and Michael Lynch examined air lead concentrations across counties in the United States, they found that areas with the highest concentrations of lead also reported the highest levels of homicide.[67]

On a micro-level, research finds that delinquents are almost four times more likely to have high bone lead levels than children in the general population.[68] Criminologist Deborah Denno investigated the behavior of more than 900 African American youth and found that lead poisoning was one of the most significant predictors of male delinquency and persistent adult criminality.[69] Herbert Needleman and his associates have conducted a number of studies indicating that youths who had high lead concentrations in their bones were much more likely to report attention problems, delinquency, and aggressiveness than those who were lead free.[70] High lead ingestion is also related to lower IQ scores, a factor also linked to aggressive behavior.[71] There is also evidence linking lead exposure to mental illnesses, such as schizophrenia, which have been linked to antisocial behaviors.[72]

The CDC survey found that among children ages 1 to 5, the average blood lead level was about 2.2 percent, which was down from 4.4 percent a decade ago. While the improvement is welcome, exposure of children to lead in homes containing lead-based paint and lead-contaminated dust remains a serious public health concern.[73]

| | | | | | | CONNECTIONS | | | | | | |

See page 151 in this chapter for more on the link between mental illness and crime.

Neurophysiological Conditions and Crime

Some researchers focus their attention on **neurophysiology,** the study of brain activity.[74] They believe neurological and physical abnormalities are acquired as early as the fetal or prenatal stage or through birth delivery trauma and that they control behavior throughout the life span.[75]

The relationship between neurological dysfunction and crime first received a great deal of attention in 1968 during a tragic incident in Texas. Charles Whitman killed his wife and mother, then barricaded himself in a tower at the University of Texas with a high-powered rifle where he proceeded to kill fourteen people and wound twenty-four others before he was killed by police. An autopsy revealed that Whitman suffered from a malignant infiltrating brain tumor. Whitman had previously experienced uncontrollable urges to kill and had gone to a psychiatrist seeking help for his problems. He kept careful notes documenting his feelings and his inability to control his homicidal urges, and he left instructions for his estate to be given to a mental health foundation so it could study mental problems such as his own.[76]

Since the Whitman case, a great deal of attention has been focused on the association between neurological impairment and crime. Studies conducted in the United States and in other nations have indicated that the relationship is significant between impairment in executive brain functions (for example, abstract reasoning, problem-solving skills, and motor behavior skills) and aggressive behavior.[77] Research indicates that this relationship can be detected quite early and that children who suffer from measurable neurological deficits at birth are more likely to become criminals later in life.[78]

NEUROLOGICAL IMPAIRMENTS AND CRIME   There are numerous ways to measure neurological functioning, including memorization and visual awareness tests, short-term auditory memory tests, and verbal IQ tests. These tests have been found to distinguish criminal offenders from noncriminal control groups.[79]

Traditionally, the most important measure of neurophysiological functioning is the **electroencephalograph (EEG).** An EEG records the electrical impulses given off by the brain.[80] It represents a signal composed of various rhythms and transient electrical discharges, commonly called brain waves, which can be recorded by electrodes placed on the scalp. The frequency is given in cycles per second, measured in hertz (Hz), and usually ranges from 0.5 to 30 Hz. Measurements of the EEG reflect the activity of neurons located in the cerebral cortex. The rhythmic nature of this brain activity is determined by mechanisms that involve subcortical structures, primarily the thalamus portion of the brain.

Studies using the EEG find that violent criminals have far higher levels of abnormal EEG recordings than nonviolent or one-time offenders.[81] Although about 5 percent of the general population has abnormal EEG readings, about 50 to 60 percent of adolescents with known behavior disorders display abnormal recordings.[82] Behaviors highly correlated with abnormal EEG included poor impulse control, inadequate social adaptation, hostility, temper tantrums, and destructiveness.[83] Studies of adults have associated slow and bilateral brain waves with hostile, hypercritical, irritable, nonconforming, and impulsive behavior.[84]

Newer brain scanning techniques, using electronic imaging such as positron emission tomography (PET), brain electrical activity mapping (BEAM), and superconducting interference device (SQUID), have made it possible to assess which areas of the brain are directly linked to antisocial behavior.[85] Violent criminals have been found to have impairment in the prefrontal lobes, thalamus, hypothalamus, medial temporal lobe, superior parietal, and left angular gyrus areas of the brain.[86] For example, some research using PET show that domestic violence offenders have lower metabolism in the right hypothalamus and decreased correlations between cortical and subcortical brain structures than a group of control subjects.[87]

It is possible that antisocial behavior is influenced by what is referred to as prefrontal dysfunction, a condition that occurs when demands on brain activity overload the prefrontal cortex and result in a lack of control over antisocial behaviors. Because the prefrontal lobes have not fully developed in adolescence, they may become overwhelmed at times; it is not surprising that violent behavior peaks in late adolescence before.[88]

A review of existing research by Nathaniel Pallone and James Hennessy finds that chronic violent criminals have far higher levels of brain dysfunction than the general population. Their most striking finding is that the incidence of brain pathology in homicide offenders is thirty-two times greater than in the general population.[89]

MINIMAL BRAIN DYSFUNCTION (MBD)   MBD is related to an abnormality in cerebral structure. It has been defined as an abruptly appearing, maladaptive behavior that interrupts an individual's lifestyle and life flow. In its most serious form, MBD has been linked to serious antisocial acts, an imbalance in the urge-control mechanisms of the brain, and chemical abnormality. Included in the category of minimal brain dysfunction are several abnormal behavior patterns: dyslexia, visual perception problems, hyperactivity, poor attention span, temper tantrums, and aggressiveness. One type of minimal brain dysfunction is manifested through episodic periods of explosive rage. This form of the disorder is considered an important cause of such behavior as spouse beating, child abuse, suicide, aggressiveness, and motiveless homicide. One perplexing feature of this syndrome is that people who are afflicted with it often maintain warm and pleasant personalities between episodes of violence. Some studies measuring the presence of MBD in offender populations

Symptoms of Attention Deficit Hyperactivity Disorder (ADHD)

Lack of Attention

- Frequently fails to finish projects
- Does not seem to pay attention
- Does not sustain interest in play activities
- Cannot sustain concentration on schoolwork or related tasks
- Is easily distracted

Impulsivity

- Frequently acts without thinking
- Often "calls out" in class
- Does not want to wait his or her turn in lines or games
- Shifts from activity to activity
- Cannot organize tasks or work
- Requires constant supervision

Hyperactivity

- Constantly runs around and climbs on things
- Shows excessive motor activity while asleep
- Cannot sit still; is constantly fidgeting
- Does not remain in his or her seat in class
- Is constantly on the go like a "motor"

Source: Adapted from American Psychiatric Association, *Diagnostic and Statistical Manual of Mental Disorders,* 4th ed. (Washington, DC: American Psychiatric Press, 1994).

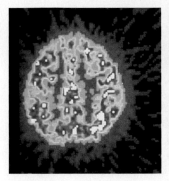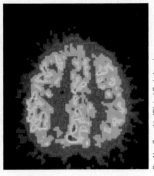

This scan compares a normal brain (left) and an ADHD brain (right). The areas of orange and white demonstrate a higher rate of metabolism; the areas of blue and green represent an abnormally low metabolic rate. Why is ADHD so prevalent in the United States today? Some experts believe our immigrant forebearers were risk-takers who impulsively left their homelands for a life in the new world. They also may have brought with them a genetic predisposition for ADHD.

have found that up to 60 percent exhibit brain dysfunction on psychological tests.[90] Criminals have been characterized as having dysfunction of the dominant hemisphere of the brain.[91] Researchers using brain wave data have predicted with 95 percent accuracy the recidivism of violent criminals.[92] More sophisticated brain scanning techniques, such as PET, have also shown that brain abnormality is linked to violent crime.[93]

ATTENTION DEFICIT HYPERACTIVITY DISORDER (ADHD)

Many parents have noticed that their children do not pay attention to them—they run around and do things in their own way. Sometimes this inattention is a function of age; in other instances, it is a symptom of **attention deficit hyperactivity disorder (ADHD),** in which a child shows a developmentally inappropriate lack of attention, impulsivity, and hyperactivity. The various symptoms of ADHD are described in Exhibit 5.1.

About 3 percent of U.S. children, most often boys, are believed to suffer from this disorder, and it is the most common reason children are referred to mental health clinics. The condition has been associated with poor school performance, grade retention, placement in special needs classes, bullying, stubbornness, and lack of response to discipline.[94] Although the origin of ADHD is still unknown, suspected causes include neurological damage, prenatal stress, and even reactions to food additives and chemical allergies.

Recent research has also suggests a genetic link.[95] There are also ties to family turmoil: Mothers of ADHD children are more likely to be divorced or separated, and ADHD children are much more likely to move to new locales than non-ADHD children.[96] It may be possible then that emotional turmoil either produces symptoms of ADHD or, if they already exist, causes them to intensify.

A series of research studies now link ADHD to the onset and sustenance of a delinquent career.[97] Children with ADHD are more likely to use illicit drugs, alcohol, and cigarettes in adolescence; to be arrested; to be charged with a felony; and to have multiple arrests than non-ADHD youths. There is some evidence that ADHD youths who also exhibit early signs of MBD and conduct disorder (for example, fighting) are the most at risk for persistent antisocial behaviors continuing into adulthood.[98] Many ADHD children also suffer from **conduct disorder (CD)** and continually engage in aggressive and antisocial behavior in early childhood. The disorders are sustained over the life course: Children diagnosed as ADHD are more likely to be suspended from school and engage in criminal behavior as adults. This ADHD–crime association is important because symptoms of ADHD seem stable through adolescence into adulthood.[99] Hyperactive/ADHD children are at greater risk for adolescent antisocial activity and drug use/abuse that persists into adulthood.[100]

The relationship between chronic delinquency and attention disorders may also be mediated by school performance. Kids who are poor readers are the most prone to antisocial behavior; many poor readers also have attention problems.[101] Early school-based intervention programs may be of special benefit to those who suffer ADHD. Early diagnosis and treatment of children suffering ADHD may enhance their life chances. Today, the most typical treatment is doses of stimulants, such as Ritalin, which ironically help control emotional and behavioral outbursts. Other therapies, such as altering diet and food intake, are now being investigated.[102]

TUMORS, LESIONS, INJURY, AND DISEASE The presence of brain tumors and lesions has also been linked to a wide variety of psychological problems, including personality changes, hallucinations, and psychotic episodes.[103] Persistent criminality has been linked to lesions in the frontal and temporal regions of the brain, which play an important role in regulating and inhibiting human behavior, including formulating plans and controlling intentions.[104] Clinical evaluation of depressed and aggressive psychopathic subjects showed a significant number (more than 75 percent) had dysfunction of the temporal and frontal regions of the brain.[105]

There is evidence that people with tumors are prone to depression, irritability, temper outbursts, and even homicidal attacks (for example, the Whitman case). Clinical case studies of patients suffering from brain tumors indicate that previously docile people may undergo behavior changes so great that they attempt to seriously harm their families and friends. When the tumor is removed, their behavior returns to normal.[106] In addition to brain tumors, head injuries caused by accidents, such as falls or auto crashes, have been linked to personality reversals marked by outbursts of antisocial and violent behavior.[107]

A variety of central nervous system diseases have also been linked to personality changes. Some of these conditions include cerebral arteriosclerosis, epilepsy, senile dementia, Wernicke-Korsakoff's syndrome, and Huntington's chorea. Associated symptoms of these diseases are memory deficiency, orientation loss, and affective (emotional) disturbances dominated by rage, anger, and increased irritability.[108]

BRAIN CHEMISTRY Neurotransmitters are chemical compounds that influence or activate brain functions. Those studied in relation to aggression include dopamine, norepinephrine, serotonin, monoamine oxidase, and GABA.[109] Evidence exists that abnormal levels of these chemicals are associated with aggression. For example, several researchers have reported inverse correlations between serotonin concentrates in the blood and impulsive and/or suicidal behavior.[110] Recent studies of habitually violent Finnish criminals show that low serotonin (5-hydroxytryptamine; 5-HT) levels are associated with poor impulse control and hyperactivity. In addition, a relatively low concentration of 5-hydroxyindoleactic acid (5-HIAA) is predictive of increased irritability, sensation seeking, and impaired impulse control.[111]

What is the link between brain chemistry and crime? Prenatal exposure of the brain to high levels of androgens can result in a brain structure that is less sensitive to environmental inputs. Affected individuals seek more intense and varied stimulation and are willing to tolerate more adverse consequences than individuals not so affected.[112] Such exposure also results in a rightward shift in (brain) hemispheric functioning and a concomitant diminution of cognitive and emotional tendencies. One result of this tendency is that left-handers are disproportionately represented in the criminal population since the movement of each hand tends to be controlled by the hemisphere of the brain on the opposite side of the body.

It has also been suggested that individuals with a low supply of the enzyme monoamine oxidase (MAO) engage in behaviors linked with violence and property crime, including defiance of punishment, impulsivity, hyperactivity, poor academic performance, sensation seeking and risk taking, and recreational drug use. Abnormal levels of MAO may explain both individual and group differences in the crime rate. For example, females have higher levels of MAO than males, a condition that may explain gender differences in the crime rate.[113]

The brain and neurological system can produce natural or endogenous opiates that are chemically similar to the narcotics opium and morphine. It has been suggested that the risk and thrills involved in crime cause the neurological system to produce increased amounts of these natural narcotics. The result is an elevated mood state, perceived as an exciting and rewarding experience that acts as a positive reinforcement for crime.[114] The brain then produces its own natural high as a reward for risk-taking behavior. Some people achieve this high by rock climbing and skydiving; others engage in crimes of violence.

Because this linkage has been found, it is not uncommon for violence-prone people to be treated with antipsychotic drugs such as Haldol, Stelazine, Prolixin, and Risperdal, which help control levels of neurotransmitters (such as serotonin/dopamine); these are sometimes referred to as **chemical restraints** or **chemical straitjackets**.

Arousal Theory

It has long been suspected that obtaining thrills is a crime motivator. Adolescents may engage in crimes such as shoplifting and vandalism simply because they offer the attraction of "getting away with it"; from this perspective, delinquency is a thrilling demonstration of personal competence. According to sociologist Jack Katz, there are immediate gratifications from criminality, which he labels the "seductions of crime." These are situational inducements that directly precede the commission of a crime and draw offenders into law violations. For example, someone challenges their authority and they vanquish their opponent with a beating; or they want to do something exciting, so they break into and vandalize a school building.

According to Katz, choosing crime can help satisfy personal needs for thrills and excitement. For some people, shoplifting and vandalism are attractive because getting away with crime is a thrilling demonstration of personal competence; Katz calls this "sneaky thrills." Even murder can have an emotional payoff. Killers behave like the avenging gods of mythology, choosing to have life-or-death control over their victims.[115]

According to **arousal theory,** for a variety of genetic and environmental reasons, some people's brains function differently in response to environmental stimuli. All of us seek to maintain a preferred or optimal level of arousal: Too much stimulation leaves us anxious and stressed out; too little makes us feel bored and weary. There is, however, variation in the way people's brains process sensory input. Some nearly always feel comfortable with little stimulation, whereas others require a high degree of environmental input to feel comfortable. The latter are "sensation seekers," who seek out stimulating activities, which may include aggressive, violent behavior patterns.[116]

The factors that determine a person's level of arousal are not fully determined, but suspected sources include brain chemistry (for example, serotonin levels) and brain structure. Some people have brains with many more nerve cells with receptor sites for neurotransmitters than others. Another view is that people with low heartbeat rates are more likely to commit crime because they seek stimulation to increase their feelings of arousal to normal levels.[117]

Genetics and Crime

Early biological theorists believed that criminality ran in families. Although research on deviant families is not taken seriously today, modern biosocial theorists are still interested in the role of genetics. If some human behaviors are influenced by heredity, would that be the case for antisocial tendencies as well? There is evidence that animals can be bred to have aggressive traits: Pit bulldogs, fighting bulls, and fighting cocks have been selectively mated to produce superior predators. Although no similar data exist with regard to people, a growing body of research is focusing on the genetic factors associated with human behavior.[118] There is evidence, for example, that personality traits including extraversion, openness, agreeableness, and conscientiousness are genetically determined.[119] There are also data suggesting that human traits associated with criminality have a genetic basis.[120] Personality conditions linked to aggression—such as psychopathy, impulsivity, and neuroticism—and psychopathology, such as schizophrenia, may be heritable.[121]

This line of reasoning was cast in the spotlight in the 1970s when genetic testing showed that Richard Speck, the convicted killer of eight nurses in Chicago, allegedly had an abnormal XYY chromosomal structure (XY is normal in males). There was much public concern that all people with XYYs were potential killers and should be closely controlled. Civil libertarians expressed fear that all XYYs could be labeled dangerous and violent regardless of whether they had engaged in violent activities.[122] When it was disclosed that neither Speck nor most violent offenders actually had an extra Y chromosome, interest in the XYY theory dissipated.[123] However, the Speck case drew researchers' attention to looking for a genetic basis of crime.

Researchers have carefully explored the heritability of criminal tendencies by looking at a variety of factors. Some of the most important are described here.

PARENTAL DEVIANCE If criminal tendencies are inherited, then it stands to reason that the children of criminal parents should be more likely to become law violators than the offspring of conventional parents. A number of studies have found that parental criminality and deviance do, in fact, have a powerful influence on delinquent behavior.[124] Some of the most important data on parental deviance were gathered by Donald J. West and David P. Farrington as part of a long-term study of English youth called the Cambridge Study in Delinquent Development (CSDD). Now directed by Dr. Farrington, this research has followed a group of about 1,000 males from the time they were 8 years old until today when many are in their 30s and older. The boys in the study have been repeatedly interviewed and their school and police records evaluated. These cohort data indicate that a significant number of delinquent youths have criminal fathers.[125] While 8.4 percent of the sons of noncriminal fathers eventually became chronic offenders, about 37 percent of youths with criminal fathers were multiple offenders.[126] More recent analysis of the data confirms that delinquent youth grow up to become the parents of antisocial children.[127]

In another important analysis, Farrington found that one type of parental deviance, schoolyard aggression or bullying, may be both inter- and intragenerational. Bullies have children who bully others, and these "second-generation bullies" grow up to become the fathers of children who are also bullies, in a never-ending cycle.[128] Farrington's findings are supported by some recent research data from the Rochester Youth Development Study (RYDS), a longitudinal analysis that has been monitoring the behavior of 1,000 area youths since 1988. Though their data does not allow them to definitively determine whether it is a result of genetics or socialization, the RYDS researchers have also found an intergenerational continuity in antisocial behavior.[129]

The cause of intergenerational deviance is still uncertain. It is possible that environmental, genetic, psychological, or childrearing factors are responsible for the linkage between generations. The link might also have some biological basis. Research on the sons of alcoholic parents shows that these boys suffer many neurological impairments related to chronic delinquency.[130] These results may indicate (a) that prolonged parental alcoholism causes genetic problems related to developmental impairment or (b) that the children of substance-abusing parents are more prone to suffer neurological impairment before, during, or after birth.

The quality of family life may be key in determining children's behavior. Criminal parents should be the ones least likely to have close, intimate relationships with their offspring. Research shows that substance-abusing and/or criminal parents are the ones most likely to use harsh and inconsistent discipline, a factor closely linked to delinquent behavior.[131]

There is no certainty about the nature and causal relationship between parental and child deviance. Data from the CSDD may help shed some light on the association. Recent analysis shows that parental conflict and authoritarian parenting were related to early childhood conduct problems in two successive generations. In addition, males who were poorly supervised by their parents were themselves poor supervisors as fathers. These findings indicate that parenting styles may help explain antisocial behavior in children and that style is passed down from one generation to the next. In addition, CSDD data found that antisocial males tend to partner with antisocial female peers and breed antisocial children. In sum then, the CSDD data indicate that the intergenerational transmission of antisocial behaviors may have both genetic and experiential dimensions.[132] Nonetheless, recent evidence indicates that at least part of the association is genetic in nature.[133] It is also possible that the association is related to the labeling process and family stigma: Social control agents may be quick to fix a delinquent label on the children of known law violators; "the acorn," the reasoning goes, "does not fall far from the tree."[134]

SIBLING SIMILARITIES It stands to reason that if the cause of crime is in part genetic, then the behavior of siblings should be similar because they share genetic material. Research does show that if one sibling engages in antisocial behavior, so does his/her brothers and sisters. The effect is greatest among same sex siblings.[135] Sibling pairs who report warm, mutual relationships and share friends are the most likely to behave in a similar fashion; those who maintain a close relationship also have similar rates of crime and drug abuse.[136]

While the similarity of siblings' behavior seems striking, what appears to be a genetic effect may also be explained by other factors:

- Siblings who live in the same environment are influenced by similar social and economic factors.

- Deviant siblings may grow closer because of shared interests.

- Younger siblings who admire their older siblings may imitate the elder's behavior.

- The deviant sibling forces or threatens the brother or sister into committing criminal acts

- Siblings living in a similar environment may develop similar types of friends; it is peer behavior that is the critical influence on behavior. The influence of peers may negate any observed interdependence of sibling behavior.[137]

TWIN BEHAVIOR As mentioned above, because siblings are usually brought up in the same household and share common life experiences, any similarity in their antisocial behavior might be a function of environmental influences and experiences and not genetics at all. To guard against this, biosocial theorists have compared the behavior of same-sex twins and again found concordance in their behavior patterns.[138]

However, an even more rigorous test of genetic theory involves comparison of the behavior of identical monozygotic

(MZ) twins with fraternal dizygotic (DZ) twins; while the former have an identical genetic makeup, the latter share only about 50 percent of their genetic combinations. Research has shown that MZ twins are significantly closer in their personal characteristics, such as intelligence, than are DZ twins.[139]

The earliest studies conducted on the behavior of twins detected a significant relationship between the criminal activities of MZ twins and a much lower association between those of DZ twins. A review of relevant studies conducted between 1929 and 1961 found that 60 percent of MZ twins shared criminal behavior patterns (if one twin was criminal, so was the other), whereas only 30 percent of DZ twin behavior was similarly related.[140] These findings may be viewed as powerful evidence that a genetic basis for criminality exists.

Other studies have supported these findings. In one well-known work, Danish criminologist Karl Christiansen studied 3,586 male twin pairs and found a 52 percent concordance for MZ pairs and a 22 percent concordance for DZ pairs. This result suggests that the identical MZ twins may share a genetic characteristic that increases the risk of their engaging in criminality.[141] While the behavior of some twin pairs seemed to be influenced by their environment, others displayed behavior disturbances that could only be explained by their genetic similarity.[142]

Since these pioneering studies were conducted, there have been several research efforts confirming the significant correspondence of twin behavior in activities ranging from frequency of sexual activity to crime.[143] For example, David Rowe and D. Wayne Osgood analyzed the factors that influence self-reported delinquency in a sample of twin pairs and concluded that genetic influences actually have significant explanatory power.[144] Genetic effects have been found to be a significant predictor of problem behaviors in children as young as 3 years old.[145] Reviews of twin studies found that in almost all cases, MZ twins have delinquent and antisocial behavior patterns more similar than that of DZ twins.[146] Studies have consistently demonstrated a significantly higher risk for suicidal behavior among monozygotic twin pairs than dizygotic twin pairs.[147] Differences between MZ and DZ twins have been found in tests measuring psychological dysfunctions such as conduct disorders, impulsivity/antisocial behavior, and emotional problems.[148] In one important study, Ginette Dionne and her colleagues found that differences between MZ and DZ twins in such crime relevant measures as level of aggression and verbal skills could be detected as early as 19 months old, a finding suggesting that not only is there a genetic basis of crime but poor verbal ability may be both inherited and a cause of aggressive behavior.[149]

One famous study of twin behavior still underway is the Minnesota Study of Twins Reared Apart. This research compares the behavior of MZ and DZ twin pairs who were raised together with others who were separated at birth and in some cases did not even know of each other's existence. The study shows some striking similarities in behavior and ability for

**Findings from the Minnesota Study
of Twins Reared Apart**

- If you are a DZ twin and your co-twin is divorced, your risk of divorce is 30 percent; If you are an MZ twin and your co-twin is divorced, your risk of divorce is 45 percent, which is 25 percent above the rates for the Minnesota population. Since this was not true for DZ twins, we can conclude that genes do influence the likelihood of divorce.

- MZ twins become *more* similar with respect to abilities such as vocabularies and arithmetic scores as they age. As DZ (fraternal) twins get older, they become less similar with respect to vocabularies and arithmetic scores.

- A P300 is a tiny electrical response (a few millionths of a volt) that occurs in the brain when a person detects something that is unusual or interesting. For example, if a person were shown nine circles and one square, a P300 brain response would appear after seeing the square because it is different. Identical (MZ) twin children have very similar looking P300s. By comparison, children who are fraternal (DZ) twins, do not show as much similarity in their P300s. These results indicate that the way the brain processes information may be greatly influenced by genes.

- An EEG is a measure of brain activity or brain waves that can be used to monitor a person's state of arousal. MZ twins tend to produce strikingly similar EEG spectra; DZ twins show far less similarity.

Source: Minnesota Study of Twins Reared Apart, http://www.psych.umn.edu/psylabs/mtfs/special.htm. Accessed May 5, 2004.

twin pairs raised apart. An MZ twin reared away from a co-twin has about as good a chance of being similar to the co-twin in terms of personality, interests, and attitudes as one who has been reared with his or her co-twin. The conclusion: Similarities between twins are due to genes, not the environment. Because twins reared apart are so similar, the environment, if anything, makes them different (see Exhibit 5.2).[150]

Some experts, including David Rowe, conclude that individuals who share genes are alike in personality regardless of how they are reared; in contrast, environment induces little or no personality resemblance on twin pairs.[151]

EVALUATING GENETIC RESEARCH Twin studies also have their detractors. Some opponents suggest that available evidence provides little conclusive proof that crime is genetically predetermined. Not all research efforts have found that MZ twin pairs are more closely related in their criminal behavior than DZ or ordinary sibling pairs, and some that have found an association note that it is at best "modest."[152] Those who oppose the genes–crime relationship point to the inadequate research designs and weak methodologies of supporting research. The newer, better-designed research studies, critics charge, provide less support than earlier, less methodically sound studies.[153]

Even if the behavior similarities between MZ twins are greater than that between DZ twins, the association may be explained by environmental factors. MZ twins are more likely to look alike and to share physical traits than DZ twins, and they are more likely to be treated similarly. Similarities in their shared behavior patterns may therefore be a function of socialization and/or environment and not heredity.[154]

Twin studies show that some traits, such as bulimia, are environmental, whereas schizophrenia, autism, and bipolar (manic-depressive) disorder seem to be genetic. To learn more about this phenomenon, use Infotrac College Edition to read: Peter McGuffin and Martin Neilson, "Behaviour and Genes," *British Medical Journal* 319 (3 July 1999): 37.

It is also possible that what appears to be a genetic effect picked up by the twin research is actually the effect of sibling influence on criminality referred to as the **contagion effect:** Genetic predispositions and early experiences make some people, including twins, susceptible to deviant behavior, which is transmitted by the presence of antisocial siblings in the household.[155]

The contagion effect may explain in part the higher concordance of deviant behaviors found in identical twins as compared to fraternal twins or mere siblings. The relationship between identical twins may be stronger and more enduring than other sibling pairs so that contagion and not genetics explains their behavioral similarities. According to Marshall Jones and Donald Jones, the contagion effect may also help explain why the behavior of twins is more similar in adulthood than adolescence.[156] Youthful misbehavior is influenced by friends and peer group relationships. As adults, the influence of peers may wane as people marry and find employment. In contrast, twin influence is everlasting; if one twin is antisocial, it legitimizes and supports the criminal behavior in his or her co-twin. This effect may grow even stronger in adulthood because twin relations are more enduring than any other. What seems to be a genetic effect may actually be the result of sibling interaction with a brother or sister who engages in antisocial activity.

ADOPTION STUDIES One way of avoiding the pitfalls of twin studies is to focus attention on the behavior of adoptees. It seems logical that if the behavior of adopted children is more closely aligned to that of their biological parents than to that of their adoptive parents, then the idea of a genetic basis for criminality would be supported. If, on the other hand, adoptees are more closely aligned to the behavior of their adoptive parents than their biological parents, an environmental basis for crime would seem more valid.

Several studies indicate that some relationship exists between biological parents' behavior and the behavior of their children, even when their contact has been nonexistent.[157] In what is considered the most significant study in this area, Barry Hutchings and Sarnoff Mednick analyzed 1,145 male adoptees born in Copenhagen, Denmark, between 1927 and 1941. Of these, 185 had criminal records.[158] After following

143 of the criminal adoptees and matching them with a control group of 143 noncriminal adoptees, Hutchings and Mednick found that the criminality of the biological father was a strong predictor of the child's criminal behavior. When both the biological and the adoptive fathers were criminals, the probability that the youth would engage in criminal behavior greatly increased: 24.5 percent of the boys whose adoptive and biological fathers were criminals had been convicted of a criminal law violation. Only 13.5 percent of those whose biological and adoptive fathers were not criminals had similar conviction records.[159]

A more recent analysis of Swedish adoptees also found that genetic factors are highly significant, accounting for 59 percent of the variation in their petty crime rates. Boys who had criminal parents were significantly more likely to violate the law. Environmental influences and economic status were significantly less important, explaining about 19 percent of the variance in crime. Nonetheless, having a positive environment, such as being adopted into a more affluent home, helped inhibit genetic predisposition.[160]

The genes–crime relationship is controversial because it implies that the propensity to commit crime is present at birth and cannot be altered. It raises moral dilemmas. If in utero genetic testing could detect a gene for violence, and a violence gene was found to be present, what could be done as a precautionary measure?

Evolutionary Theory

Some criminologists believe the human traits that produce violence and aggression are produced through the long process of human evolution.[161] According to this evolutionary view, the competition for scarce resources has influenced and shaped the human species.[162] Over the course of human existence, people whose personal characteristics enable them to accumulate more than others are the most likely to breed and dominate the species. People have been shaped to engage in actions that promote their well-being and ensure the survival and reproduction of their genetic line. Males who are impulsive risk-takers may be able to father more children because they are reckless in their social relationships and have sexual encounters with numerous partners. If, according to evolutionary theories, such behavior patterns are inherited, impulsive behavior becomes intergenerational, passed down from father to son. It is not surprising then that human history has been marked by war, violence, and aggression.

| | | | | | | **CONNECTIONS** | | | | | | |

The relationship between evolutionary factors and crime has just begun to be studied. Criminologists are now exploring how social organizations and institutions interact with biological traits to influence personal decision making, including criminal strategies. See the discussion of latent trait theories in Chapter 9 for more about the integration of biological and environmental factors.

VIOLENCE AND EVOLUTION In their classic book *Homicide,* Martin Daly and Margo Wilson suggest that violent offenses are often driven by evolutionary and reproductive factors. High rates of spouse abuse in modern society may be a function of aggressive men seeking to control and possess "mates." When females are murdered by their spouses, the motivating factor is typically fear of infidelity and the threat of attachment to a new partner. Infidelity challenges male dominance and future reproductive rights. It comes as no surprise that in some cultures, including our own, sexual infidelity discovered in progress by the aggrieved husband is viewed legally as a provocation that justifies retaliatory killing.[163] Men who feel most threatened over the potential of losing mates to rivals are the ones most likely to engage in sexual violence. Research shows that women in common-law marriages, especially those who are much younger than their husbands, are at greater risk than older married women. Abusive males may fear the potential loss of their younger mates, especially if they are not bound by a marriage contract, and may use force for purposes of control and possession.[164] Armed robbery is another crime that may have evolutionary underpinnings. Though most robbers are caught and severely punished, it remains an alluring pursuit for men who both want to show their physical prowess and display resources with which to conquer rivals and attract mates. Violent episodes are far more common among men who are unemployed and unmarried—in other words, those who may want to demonstrate their allure to the opposite sex but who are without the benefit of position or wealth.[165]

GENDER AND EVOLUTION Evolutionary concepts have been linked to gender-based differences in the crime rate. To ensure survival of the gene pool (and the species), it is beneficial for a male of any species to mate with as many suitable females as possible since each can bear his offspring. In contrast, because of the long period of gestation, females require a secure home and a single, stable nurturing partner to ensure their survival. Because of these differences in mating patterns, the most aggressive males mate most often and have the greatest number of offspring. Therefore, over the history of the human species, aggressive males have had the greatest impact on the gene pool. The descendants of these aggressive males now account for the disproportionate amount of male aggression and violence.[166]

Crime rate differences between the genders, then, may be less a matter of socialization than inherent differences in mating patterns that have developed over time.[167] Among young men, reckless, life-threatening "risk proneness" is especially likely to evolve in cultures that force males to find suitable mates to ensure their ability to reproduce. Unless they are aggressive with potential mates and potential rivals for those suitable mates, they are doomed to remain childless.[168]

Other evolutionary factors may have influenced gender differences. With the advent of agriculture and trade in prehistory, feminists have suggested that women were forced into a position of high dependence and limited power. They began to compete among themselves to secure partners who could provide necessary resources. As a result of these early evolutionary developments, inter-gender competition became greatest during periods of resource deprivation—times when women become most dependent on a male for support. These trends can still be observed. For example, during times of high female unemployment, female–female aggression rates increase as women compete with each other for men who can provide them with support. In contrast, as rates of social welfare increase, female–female aggression rates diminish because the state serves as a readily available substitute for a male breadwinner.[169]

THEORIES OF EVOLUTIONARY CRIMINOLOGY There are a number of individual theories of evolutionary criminology, three of which are discussed in detail here.

Rushton's Theory of Race and Evolution One of the most controversial versions of evolutionary theory was formulated by J. Phillippe Rushton and first appeared in his 1995 book, *Race, Evolution and Behavior*.[170] According to Rushton, there is evidence that modern humans evolved in Africa about 200,000 years ago and then began to migrate outward to present-day Europe and Asia. He posits that the further north elements of the populations migrated, the more they encountered harsher climates, which produce the need to gather and store food, gain shelter, make clothes, and raise children successfully during prolonged winters. As these populations evolved into present-day Europeans and Asians, their brain mass increased, and they developed slower rates of maturation and lower levels of sex hormones. This physical change produced reductions in sexual potency and aggression and increases in family stability and longevity. These evolutionary changes are responsible for present-day crime rate differences between the races.

Rushton's work was received harshly by critics, who condemned his definitions of race and crime.[171] Among the many criticisms hurled at Rushton has been his singular focus on street crimes, such as theft, while giving short shrift to white-collar and organized crimes, which are predominantly committed by whites. For example, criminologist Michael Lynch argues that Rushton ignores the fact that men are much more criminal than women even though there is little evidence of significant differences in intelligence or brain size between the genders.

R/K Selection Theory R/K theory holds that all organisms can be located along a continuum based upon their reproductive drives.[172] Those along the "R" end reproduce rapidly whenever they can and invest little in their offspring; those along the "K" end reproduce slowly and cautiously and take care in raising their offspring. Evolutionary theorists believe males today "lean" toward R-selection, because they can reproduce faster without the need for investing in their offspring; females are K-selected, because they have fewer offspring but give more care and devotion to them. K-oriented people are more cooperative and sensitive to others, whereas R-oriented people are more cunning and deceptive.

Males, therefore, tend to partake in more criminal behavior. In general, people who commit violent crimes seem to exhibit R-selection traits, such as a premature birth and early and frequent sexual activity. They are more likely to have been neglected as children and to have a short life expectancy.

Cheater Theory Cheater theory suggests that a subpopulation of men has evolved with genes that incline them toward extremely low parental involvement. They are sexually aggressive and use their cunning to gain sexual conquests with as many females as possible. Because females would not willingly choose them as mates, they use stealth to gain sexual access, including such tactics as mimicking the behavior of more stable males. They use devious and illegal means to acquire resources they need for sexual domination. Their deceptive reproductive tactics spill over into other endeavors, where their talent for irresponsible, opportunistic behavior supports their antisocial activities. Deception in reproductive strategies, then, is linked to a deceitful lifestyle.

Psychologist Byron Roth notes that cheater-type males may be especially attractive to those younger, less intelligent women who begin having children at a very early age.[173] State-sponsored welfare, claims Roth, removes the need for potential mates to have the resources needed to be stable providers and family caretakers. With the state meeting their financial needs, these women are attracted to men who are physically attractive and flamboyant. Their fleeting courtship process produces children with low IQs, aggressive personalities, and little chance of proper socialization in father-absent families. Because the criminal justice system treats them leniently, argues Roth, sexually irresponsible men are free to prey on young girls. Over time, their offspring will supply an ever-expanding supply of cheaters who are both antisocial and sexually aggressive.

For a broad overview of evolutionary psychology, use InfoTrac College Edition to read this article: Linnda R. Caporael, "Evolutionary Psychology: Toward a Unifying Theory and a Hybrid Science," *Annual Review of Psychology* (2001): 607.

Evaluation of the Biosocial Branch of Trait Theory

Biosocial perspectives on crime have raised some challenging questions. Critics find some of these theories to be racist and dysfunctional. If there are biological explanations for street crimes, such as assault, murder, or rape, the argument goes, and if, as the official crime statistics suggest, the poor and minority-group members commit a disproportionate number of such acts, then by implication biological theory says that members of these groups are biologically different, flawed, or inferior.

Biological explanations for the geographic, social, and temporal patterns in the crime rate are also problematic. Is it possible that there are more people genetically predisposed to crime in the South and West than in New England and the Midwest? Furthermore, biological theory seems to divide people into criminals and noncriminals on the basis of their genetic and physical makeup, ignoring self-reports indicating that almost everyone has engaged in some type of illegal activity during his or her lifetime.

Biosocial theorists counter that their views should not be confused with Lombrosian, deterministic biology. Rather than suggest that there are born criminals and noncriminals, they maintain that some people carry the potential to be violent or antisocial and that environmental conditions can sometimes trigger antisocial responses.[174] This would explain why some otherwise law-abiding citizens engage in a single, seemingly unexplainable antisocial act, and conversely, why some people with long criminal careers often engage in conventional behavior. It also explains why there are geographic and temporal patterns in the crime rate: People who are predisposed to crime may simply have more opportunities to commit illegal acts in the summer in Los Angeles and Atlanta than in the winter in Bedford, New Hampshire, and Minot, North Dakota.

The biosocial view is that behavior is a product of interacting biological and environmental events.[175] Physical impairments may make some people "at risk" to crime, but it is when they are linked to social and environmental problems, such as family dysfunction, that they trigger criminal acts.[176] For example, Avshalom Caspi and his associates found that girls who reach physical maturity at an early age are the ones most likely to engage in delinquent acts. This finding might suggest a relationship between biological traits (hormonal activity) and crime. However, the Caspi research found that the association may also have an environmental basis. Physically mature girls are the ones most likely to have prolonged contact with a crime-prone group: older adolescent boys.[177] Here, the combination of biological change, social relationships, and routine opportunities may predict crime rates.

The most significant criticism of biosocial theory has been the lack of adequate empirical testing. In most research efforts, sample sizes are relatively small and nonrepresentative. A great deal of biosocial research is conducted with samples of adjudicated offenders who have been placed in clinical treatment settings. Methodological problems make it impossible to determine whether findings apply only to offenders who have been convicted of crimes and placed in treatment or to the population of criminals as a whole.[178] More research is needed to clarify the relationships proposed by biosocial researchers and to silence critics.

Concept Summary 5.1 summarizes the various biosocial theories of crime.

 To quiz yourself on this material, go to the Criminology TPT 9e website.

CONCEPT SUMMARY 5.1

Biosocial Theories of Crime

Biochemical

- The major premise of the theory is that crime, especially violence, is a function of diet, vitamin intake, hormonal imbalance, or food allergies.

- The strengths of the theory are that it explains irrational violence; it shows how the environment interacts with personal traits to influence behavior.

- The research focuses of the theory are diet, hormones, enzymes, environmental contaminants, and lead intake.

Neurological

- The major premise of the theory is that criminals and delinquents often suffer brain impairment, as measured by the EEG. Attention deficit hyperactivity disorder and minimal brain dysfunction are related to antisocial behavior.

- The strengths of the theory are that it explains irrational violence; it shows how the environment interacts with personal traits to influence behavior.

- The research focuses of the theory are ADD, ADHD, learning disabilities, brain injuries, and brain chemistry.

Genetic

- The major premise of the theory is that criminal traits and predispositions are inherited. The criminality of parents can predict the delinquency of children.

- The strengths of the theory are that it explains why only a small percentage of youth in high-crime areas become chronic offenders.

- The research focuses of the theory are twin behavior, sibling behavior, and parent–child similarities.

Evolutionary

- The major premise of the theory is that as the human race evolved, traits and characteristics have become ingrained. Some of these traits make people aggressive and predisposed to commit crime.

- The strengths of the theory are that it explains high violence rates and aggregate gender differences in the crime rate.

- The research focuses of the theory are gender differences and understanding human aggression.

PSYCHOLOGICAL TRAIT THEORIES

The second branch of trait theories focuses on the psychological aspects of crime, including the association among intelligence, personality, learning, and criminal behavior.

Psychological theories of crime have a long history. In *The English Convict,* Charles Goring (1870–1919) studied the mental characteristics of 3,000 English convicts.[179] He found little difference in the physical characteristics of criminals and noncriminals, but he uncovered a significant relationship between crime and a condition he referred to as **defective intelligence,** which involves such traits as feeblemindedness, epilepsy, insanity, and defective social instinct.[180] Goring believed criminal behavior was inherited and could, therefore, be controlled by regulating the reproduction of families who produced mentally defective children.

Gabriel Tarde (1843–1904) is the forerunner of modern-day learning theorists.[181] Tarde believed people learn from one another through a process of imitation. Tarde's ideas are similar to modern social learning theorists who believe that both interpersonal and observed behavior, such as a movie or television, can influence criminality.

Since the pioneering work of people like Tarde and Goring, psychologists, psychiatrists, and other mental health professionals have long played an active role in formulating criminological theory. In their quest to understand and treat all varieties of abnormal mental conditions, psychologists have encountered clients whose behavior falls within categories society has labeled as criminal, deviant, violent, and antisocial.

This section is organized along the lines of the predominant psychological views most closely associated with the causes of criminal behavior. Some psychologists view antisocial behavior from a **psychoanalytic** or **psychodynamic perspective:** Their focus is on early childhood experience and its effect on personality. In contrast, **behaviorism** stresses social learning and behavior modeling as the keys to criminality. **Cognitive theory** analyzes human perception and how it affects behavior.

Psychodynamic Theory

Psychodynamic (or psychoanalytic) psychology was originated by Viennese psychiatrist Sigmund Freud (1856–1939) and has since remained a prominent segment of psychological theory.[182]

> For a collection of links to libraries, museums, and biographical materials related to **Sigmund Freud and his works**, go to http://users.rcn.com/brill/freudarc.html. For an up-to-date list of web links, go to http://cj.wadsworth.com/siegel_crimtpt9e.

Freud believed that we all carry with us residue of the most significant emotional attachments of our childhood, which then guide future interpersonal relationships. Today the term *psychodynamic* refers to a broad range of theories that focus on the influence of instinctive drives and forces and the importance of developmental processes in shaping personality. Contemporary psychodynamic theory places greater emphasis on conscious experience and its interaction with the unconscious, in addition to the role that social factors play in development. Nonetheless, it still focuses on the influence of early childhood experiences on the development of personality, motivation, and drives.

| | | | | | | **CONNECTIONS** | | | | | | |

Chapter 1 discussed how some of the early founders of psychiatry, including Philippe Pinel and Benjamin Rush, tried to develop an understanding of the "criminal mind." Later theories suggested that mental illness and insanity were inherited and that deviants were inherently mentally damaged by reason of their inferior genetic makeup.

ELEMENTS OF PSYCHODYNAMIC THEORY According to the classic version of the theory, the human personality contains a three-part structure. The **id** is the primitive part of an individual's mental makeup present at birth. It represents unconscious biological drives for sex, food, and other life-sustaining necessities. The id follows the **pleasure principle:** It requires instant gratification without concern for the rights of others.

The **ego** develops early in life, when a child begins to learn that his or her wishes cannot be instantly gratified. The ego is that part of the personality that compensates for the demands of the id by helping the individual guide his or her actions to remain within the boundaries of social convention. The ego is guided by the **reality principle:** It takes into account what is practical and conventional by societal standards.

The **superego** develops as a result of incorporating within the personality the moral standards and values of parents, community, and significant others. It is the moral aspect of an individual's personality; it passes judgments on behavior. The superego is divided into two parts: **conscience** and **ego ideal.** Conscience tells what is right and wrong. It forces the ego to control the id and directs the individual into morally acceptable and responsible behaviors, which may not be pleasurable. Exhibit 5.3 summarizes Freud's personality structure.

PSYCHOSEXUAL STAGES OF HUMAN DEVELOPMENT The most basic human drive present at birth is **eros,** the instinct to preserve and create life. The other is the death instinct (**thanatos**), which is expressed as aggression.

EXHIBIT 5.3		
Freud's Model of the Personality Structure		
Personality Structure	**Guiding Principle**	**Description**
Id	Pleasure principle	Unconscious biological drives; requires instant gratification
Ego	Reality principle	Helps the personality refine the demands of the id; helps person adapt to conventions
Superego	The conscience	The moral aspect of the personality

Eros is expressed sexually. Consequently, very early in their development, humans experience sexuality, which is expressed by seeking pleasure through various parts of the body. During the first year of life, a child attains pleasure by sucking and biting; Freud called this the **oral stage.** During the second and third years of life, the focus of sexual attention is on the elimination of bodily wastes—the **anal stage.** The **phallic stage** occurs during the third year when children focus their attention on their genitals. Males begin to have sexual feelings for their mothers (the **Oedipus complex**) and girls for their fathers (the **Electra complex**). **Latency** begins at age 6. During this period, feelings of sexuality are repressed until the genital stage begins at puberty; this marks the beginning of adult sexuality.

If conflicts are encountered during any of the psychosexual stages of development, a person can become **fixated** at that point. This means, as an adult, the fixated person will exhibit behavior traits characteristic of those encountered during infantile sexual development. For example, an infant who does not receive enough oral gratification during the first year of life is likely as an adult to engage in such oral behavior as smoking, drinking, or drug abuse or to be clinging and dependent in personal relationships. Thus, according to Freud, the roots of adult behavioral problems can be traced to problems developed in the earliest years of life.

THE PSYCHODYNAMICS OF ANTISOCIAL BEHAVIOR Psychologists have long linked criminality to abnormal mental states produced by early childhood trauma. For example, Alfred Adler (1870–1937), the founder of individual psychology, coined the term **inferiority complex** to describe people who have feelings of inferiority and compensate for them with a drive for superiority. Controlling others may help reduce personal inadequacies. Erik Erikson (1902–1984) described the **identity crisis**—a period of serious personal questioning people undertake in an effort to determine their own values and sense of direction. Adolescents undergoing an identity crisis might exhibit out-of-control behavior and experiment with drugs and other forms of deviance.

The psychoanalyst whose work is most closely associated with criminality is August Aichorn.[183] After examining many delinquent youths, Aichorn concluded that societal stress, though damaging, could not alone result in a life of crime unless a predisposition existed that psychologically prepared youths for antisocial acts. This mental state, which he labeled **latent delinquency,** is found in youngsters whose personality requires them to act in these ways:

- Seek immediate gratification (to act impulsively)

- Consider satisfying their personal needs more important than relating to others

- Satisfy instinctive urges without considering right and wrong (that is, they lack guilt)

The psychodynamic model of the criminal offender depicts an aggressive, frustrated person dominated by events that occurred early in childhood. Perhaps because they may have suffered unhappy experiences in childhood or had families that could not provide proper love and care, criminals suffer from weak or damaged egos that make them unable to cope with conventional society. Weak egos are associated with immaturity, poor social skills, and excessive dependence on others. People with weak egos may be easily led into crime by antisocial peers and drug abuse. Some offenders have underdeveloped superegos and consequently lack internalized representations of those behaviors that are punished in conventional society. They commit crimes because they have difficulty understanding the consequences of their actions.[184]

Offenders may suffer from a garden variety of mood and/or behavior disorders. They may be histrionic, depressed, antisocial, or narcissistic.[185] They may suffer from conduct disorders, which include long histories of antisocial behavior, or mood disorders characterized by disturbance in expressed emotions. Among the latter is **bipolar disorder,** in which moods alternate between periods of wild elation and deep depression.[186] Some offenders are driven by an unconscious desire to be punished for prior sins, either real or imaginary. As a result, they may violate the law to gain attention or to punish their parents.

According to this view, crime is a manifestation of feelings of oppression and people's inability to develop the proper psychological defenses and rationales to keep these feelings under control. Criminality enables troubled people to survive by producing positive psychic results: It helps them to feel free and independent, and it gives them the possibility of excitement and the chance to use their skills and imagination. Crime also provides them with the promise of positive gain; it allows them to blame others for their predicament (for example, the police), and it gives them a chance to rationalize their sense of failure ("If I hadn't gotten into trouble, I could have been a success").[187]

MOOD DISORDERS AND CRIME Psychodynamic theorists recognize a variety of mental disorders that may be linked to antisocial behavior. Adolescents who are frequently uncooperative and hostile and who seem to be much more difficult than other children the same age may be suffering from a psychological condition known as *disruptive behavior disorder (DBD)*, which can take on two distinct forms.[188] The first and more mild condition is referred to *oppositional defiant disorder (ODD)*. Children suffering from ODD experience an ongoing pattern of uncooperative, defiant, and hostile behavior toward authority figures that seriously interferes with the youngsters' day-to-day functioning. Symptoms of ODD may include frequent loss of temper and constant arguing with adults; defying adults or refusing adult requests or rules; deliberately annoying others; blaming others for mistakes or misbehavior; being angry and resentful; being spiteful or vindictive; swearing or using obscene language; or having low self-esteem. The person with ODD is moody and easily frustrated and may abuse drugs as a form of self-medication.[189]

The second element of DBD is *conduct disorder (CD)*, which comprises a more serious group of behavioral and emotional problems.[190] Children and adolescents with CD have great difficulty following rules and behaving in socially acceptable ways. They are often viewed by other children, adults, and social agencies as severely antisocial. Research shows that they are frequently involved in such activities as bullying, fighting, committing sexual assaults, and cruelty to animals.

What causes CD? Numerous biosocial and psychological factors are suspected. There is evidence, for example, that interconnections between the frontal lobes and other brain regions may influence CD. There is also research showing that levels of serotonin can influence the onset of CD and that CD has been shown to aggregate in families, suggesting a genetic basis of the disorder.[191]

CRIME AND MENTAL ILLNESS The most serious forms of psychological disturbance will result in mental illness referred to as **psychosis**, which include severe mental **disorders**, such as depression, bipolar disorder (manic depression), and **schizophrenia**—characterized by extreme impairment of a person's ability to think clearly, respond emotionally, communicate effectively, understand reality, and behave appropriately. Schizophrenics may hear nonexistent voices, hallucinate, and make inappropriate behavioral responses. People with severe mental disorders exhibit illogical and incoherent thought processes and a lack of insight into their behavior. For example, they may see themselves as agents of the devil, avenging angels, or the recipients of messages from animals and plants.

David Berkowitz (the "Son of Sam" or the "44-calibre killer"), a noted serial killer who went on a rampage from 1976 to 1977, exhibited these traits when he claimed that his killing spree began when he received messages from a neighbor's dog. **Paranoid schizophrenics,** such as Eugene Weston who went on a shooting rampage in the U.S. capitol building, suffer complex behavior delusions involving wrongdoing or persecution—they think everyone is out to get them.

There are some research efforts that find that offenders who engage in serious, violent crimes suffer from some sort of mental disturbance, such as depression.[192] Female offenders seem to have more serious mental health symptoms, including schizophrenia, paranoia, and obsessive behaviors than male offenders.[193] It is not surprising then that abusive mothers have been found to have mood and personality disorders and a history of psychiatric diagnoses.[194] Juvenile murderers have been described in clinical diagnosis as "overtly hostile," "explosive or volatile," "anxious," and "depressed."[195] Studies of men accused of murder found that 75 percent could be classified as having some mental illness, including schizophrenia.[196] Also, the reported substance abuse among the mentally ill is significantly higher than that of the general population.[197] The diagnosed mentally ill appear in arrest and court statistics at a rate disproportionate to their presence in the population.[198]

Nor is this relationship unique to the United States. Forensic criminologist Henrik Belfrage studied mental patients in Sweden and found that 40 percent of those discharged from institutional care had a criminal record as compared to less than 10 percent of the general public.[199] Australian men diagnosed with schizophrenia are four times more likely than the general population to be convicted for serious violence.[200] And a recent Danish study found a significant positive relationship between mental disorders such as schizophrenia and criminal violence.[201]

A recent (2003) review of the existing literature on the relationship between psychopathology and delinquent behavior concluded that delinquent adolescents have higher rates of clinical mental disorders when compared to adolescents in the general population.[202] In sum, people who suffer paranoid or delusional feelings, for example, and who believe others wish them harm or that their mind is dominated by forces beyond their control, seem to be violence prone.[203]

The **National Mental Health Association (NMHA)** is the country's oldest and largest nonprofit organization addressing all aspects of mental health and mental illness. It is dedicated to improving the mental health of all individuals and achieving victory over mental illnesses. Visit their website at http://www.nmha.org/. For an up-to-date list of web links, go to http://cj.wadsworth.com/siegel_crimtpt9e.

Susan Smith, Darlie Routier, and Andrea Yates all have been convicted of killing their children. Can such behavior be the product of a normal mind, or must their terrible acts be the result of some mental defect or illness?

AP/Wide World Photos

IS THE LINK VALID? Despite this evidence, there are still questions about whether mental illness is a direct cause of crime and violence. The mentally ill may be more likely to withdraw or harm themselves than to act aggressively toward others.[204] Similarly, research shows that upon release prisoners who had prior histories of hospitalization for mental disorders were less likely to be rearrested than those who had never been hospitalized.[205] Mentally disordered inmates who do recidivate upon release appear to do so for the same reasons as the mentally sound—extensive criminal histories, substance abuse, and family dysfunction—rather than as a result of their illness.[206]

It is also possible that the link between mental illness and crime is spurious and an artifact of some intervening factor. For example, the factors that cause mental turmoil also cause antisocial behaviors: People who suffer child abuse are more likely to have mental anguish and commit violent acts; child abuse is the actual cause of both problems.[207]

Mentally ill people may be more likely to lack financial resources than the mentally sound. They are therefore forced to reside in deteriorated high-crime neighborhoods.[208] Living in a stress-filled, urban environment may produce both symptoms of mental illness and crime.[209] A recent Swedish study found that schizophrenic patients are very likely to live in neighborhoods characterized by high levels of disorder, fear of crime, and victimization. The association was circular: The presence of large numbers of mentally ill people helped increase neighborhood fear, leading to neighborhood deterioration, lowered values, and the influx of more diagnosed mentally ill people. Segregating the mentally ill may result in worsening of the illness as well as increasing the deterioration of local areas.[210]

|||||||| CONNECTIONS ||||||||

Chapter 6 will further discuss how fear of crime can result in social disorganization and neighborhood deterioration.

It is also possible that a lack of resources may inhibit the mentally ill from obtaining the proper treatment, which, if made available, would result in reduced criminality. For example, a recent study conducted in North Carolina compared the outcomes for mentally ill patients who received outpatient treatment with an untreated comparison group; treatment significantly reduced arrest probability (12 percent versus 45 percent).[211]

www Here is a site devoted to the relationship between **mental illness and crime:** http://www .karisable.com/crmh.htm. For an up-to-date list of web links, go to http:// cj.wadsworth.com/siegel_crimtpt9e.

Behavioral Theory

Psychological behavior theory maintains that human actions are developed through learning experiences. Rather than focusing on unconscious personality traits or cognitive development patterns produced early in childhood, behavior theorists are concerned with the actual behaviors people engage in during the course of their daily lives. The major premise of behavior theory is that people alter their behavior according to the reactions it receives from others. Behavior is supported by rewards and extinguished by negative reactions or punishments. Behavioral theory is quite complex with many different subareas. With respect to criminal activity, the behaviorist views crimes, especially violent acts, as learned responses to life situations that do not necessarily represent psychologically abnormal responses.

SOCIAL LEARNING THEORY **Social learning** is the branch of behavior theory most relevant to criminology.[212] Social learning theorists, most notably Albert Bandura, argue that people are not actually born with the ability to act violently but that they learn to be aggressive through their life experiences.

www To read about the life and work of **Albert Bandura,** go to http://www.ship.edu/~cgboeree/ bandura.html. For an up-to-date list of web links, go to http://cj.wadsworth.com/siegel_crimtpt9e.

These experiences include personally observing others acting aggressively to achieve some goal or watching people being rewarded for violent acts on television or in movies. People learn to act aggressively when, as children, they model their behavior after the violent acts of adults. Later in life, these violent behavior patterns persist in social relationships. For example, the boy who sees his father repeatedly strike his mother with impunity is the one most likely to grow up to become a battering parent and husband.

Though social learning theorists agree that mental or physical traits may predispose a person toward violence, they believe that activating a person's violent tendencies is achieved by factors in the environment. The specific forms that aggressive behavior takes, the frequency with which it is expressed, the situations in which it is displayed, and the specific targets selected for attack are largely determined by social learning. However, people are self-aware and engage in purposeful learning. Their interpretations of behavior outcomes and situations influence the way they learn from experiences. One adolescent who spends a weekend in jail for drunk driving may find it the most awful experience of her life—one that teaches her to never drink and drive again. Another person, however, may find it an exciting experience about which he can brag to his friends.

SOCIAL LEARNING AND VIOLENCE Social learning theorists view violence as something learned through a process called **behavior modeling.** In modern society, aggressive acts are usually modeled after three principal sources:

1. *Family interaction:* Studies of family life show that aggressive children have parents who use similar tactics when dealing with others. For example, the children of wife batterers are more likely to use aggressive tactics themselves than children in the general population, especially if the victims (their mothers) suffer psychological distress from the abuse.

2. *Environmental experiences:* People who reside in areas in which violence is a daily occurrence are more likely to act violently than those who dwell in low-crime areas whose norms stress conventional behavior.

3. *Mass media:* Films and television shows commonly depict violence graphically. Moreover, violence is often portrayed as an acceptable behavior, especially

Systematic viewing of TV begins at 2½ years of age and continues at a high level during the preschool and early school years. More than 40 percent of U.S. households now have cable TV, which features violent films and shows. The average child views 8,000 TV murders before finishing elementary school. Can the constant bombardment of media violence influence antisocial behavior? If it did, why are violence rates trending downward despite growing access to games, shows, films, and songs with violent themes and content?

In summary, social learning theorists have said that the following four factors may contribute to violent and/or aggressive behavior:

1. *An event that heightens arousal:* such as a person frustrating or provoking another through physical assault or verbal abuse.

2. *Aggressive skills:* learned aggressive responses picked up from observing others, either personally or through the media.

3. *Expected outcomes:* the belief that aggression will somehow be rewarded. Rewards can come in the form of reducing tension or anger, gaining some financial reward, building self-esteem, or gaining the praise of others.

4. *Consistency of behavior with values:* the belief, gained from observing others, that aggression is justified and appropriate, given the circumstances of the current situation.

for heroes who never have to face legal consequences for their actions. For example, David Phillips found the homicide rate increases significantly immediately after a heavyweight championship prize fight.[213]

The Criminological Enterprise feature "The Media and Violence" has more on the effects of the media and violent behavior.

Social learning theorists have tried to determine what triggers violent acts. One position is that a direct, pain-producing physical assault will usually trigger a violent response. Yet the relationship between painful attacks and aggressive responses has been found to be inconsistent. Whether people counterattack in the face of physical attack depends, in part, on their skill in fighting and their perception of the strength of their attackers. Verbal taunts and insults have also been linked to aggressive responses. People who are predisposed to aggression by their learning experiences are likely to view insults from others as a challenge to their social status and to react with violence. Still another violence-triggering mechanism is a perceived reduction in one's life conditions. Prime examples of this phenomenon are riots and demonstrations in poverty-stricken ghetto areas. Studies have shown that discontent also produces aggression in the more successful members of lower-class groups who have been led to believe they can succeed but then have been thwarted in their aspirations. While it is still uncertain how this relationship is constructed, it is apparently complex. No matter how deprived some individuals are they will not resort to violence. It seems evident that people's perceptions of their relative deprivation have different effects on their aggressive responses.

Cognitive Theory

One area of psychology that has received increasing recognition in recent years has been the cognitive school. Psychologists with a cognitive perspective focus on mental processes and how people perceive and mentally represent the world around them and solve problems. The pioneers of this school were Wilhelm Wundt (1832–1920), Edward Titchener (1867–1927), and William James (1842–1920). Today, there are several subdisciplines within the cognitive area. The **moral development** branch is concerned with the way people morally represent and reason about the world. **Humanistic psychology** stresses self-awareness and "getting in touch with feelings." The **information processing** branch focuses on the way people process, store, encode, retrieve, and manipulate information to make decisions and solve problems.

MORAL AND INTELLECTUAL DEVELOPMENT THEORY

The moral and intellectual development branch of cognitive psychology is perhaps the most important for criminological theory. Jean Piaget (1896–1980), the founder of this approach, hypothesized that people's reasoning processes develop in an orderly fashion, beginning at birth and continuing until they are 12 years old and older.[214] At first, children respond to the environment in a simple manner, seeking interesting objects and developing their reflexes. By the fourth and final stage, the formal operations stage, they have developed into mature adults who can use logic and abstract thought.

The Media and Violence

Does the media influence behavior? Does broadcast violence cause aggressive behavior in viewers? This has become a hot topic because of the persistent theme of violence on television and in films. Critics have called for drastic measures, ranging from banning TV violence to putting warning labels on heavy metal albums out of fear that listening to hard-rock lyrics produces delinquency.

If there is in fact a TV–violence link, the problem is indeed alarming. Systematic viewing of TV begins at 2½ years of age and continues at a high level during the preschool and early school years. The Kaiser Foundation study, *Zero to Six: Electronic Media in the Lives of Infants, Toddlers, and Preschoolers,* found that children 6 and under spend an average of 2 hours a day using screen media such as TV and computers, about the same amount of time they spend playing outside and significantly more than the amount they spend reading or being read to (about 39 minutes per day). Nearly half of children 6 and under have used a computer, and just under a third have played video games). Even the youngest children— those under 2—are exposed to electronic media for more than 2 hours per day; more than 40 percent of those under 2 watch TV every day. Marketing research indicates that adolescents ages 11 to 14 rent violent horror movies at a higher rate than any other age group. Children this age use older peers and siblings and apathetic parents to gain access to R-rated films. More than 40 percent of U.S. households now have cable TV, which features violent films and shows. Even children's programming is saturated with violence.

The fact that children watch so much violent TV is not surprising

considering the findings of a well-publicized study conducted by UCLA researchers who found that at least ten network shows made heavy use of violence. Of the 161 television movies monitored (every one that aired that season), twenty-three raised concerns about their use of violence, violent theme, violent title, or inappropriate portrayals of a scene. Of the 118 theatrical films monitored (every one that aired that season), fifty raised concerns about their use of violence.

On-air promotions also reflect a continuing, if not worsening, problem. Some series may contain several scenes of violence, each of which is appropriate within its context. An advertisement for that show, however, will feature those violent scenes only without any of the context. Even some children's television programming had worrisome signs, featuring "sinister combat" as the theme of the show. The characters are usually happy to fight and frequently do so with little provocation. A University of Pennsylvania study also found that children's programming contained an average of thirty-two violent acts per hour, that 56 percent had violent characters, and that 74 percent had characters who became the victims of violence (though "only 3.3 percent had characters who were actually killed"). In all, the average child views 8,000 TV murders before finishing elementary school.

There have been numerous anecdotal cases of violence linked to TV and films. For example, in a famous incident, John Hinckley shot President Ronald Reagan due to his obsession with actress Jodie Foster, which developed after he watched her play a prostitute in the film *Taxi Driver.* Hinckley viewed the film at least fifteen times.

A national survey conducted in the wake of the controversy found that almost 80 percent of the general public

believes violence on TV can cause violence "in real life." Psychologists, however, believe media violence does not in itself *cause* violent behavior, because, if it did, there would be millions of daily incidents in which viewers imitated the aggression they watched on TV or in movies. But most psychologists agree that media violence *contributes* to aggression. There are several explanations for the effects of television and film violence on behavior:

- Media violence can provide aggressive "scripts" that children store in memory. Repeated exposure to these scripts can increase their retention and lead to changes in attitudes.

- Children learn from what they observe. In the same way they learn cognitive and social skills from their parents and friends, children learn to be violent from television.

- Television violence increases the arousal levels of viewers and makes them more prone to act aggressively. Studies measuring the galvanic skin response of subjects—a physical indication of arousal based on the amount of electricity conducted across the palm of the hand—show that viewing violent television shows led to increased arousal levels in young children.

- Watching television violence promotes such negative attitudes as suspiciousness and the expectation that the viewer will become involved in violence. Those who watch television frequently come to view aggression and violence as common and socially acceptable behavior.

- Television violence allows aggressive youths to justify their behavior. It is possible that, instead of causing violence, television helps violent youths rationalize their behavior as a socially acceptable and common activity.

- Television violence may disinhibit aggressive behavior, which is normally controlled by other learning processes. *Disinhibition* takes place when adults are viewed as being rewarded for violence and when violence is seen as socially acceptable. This contradicts previous learning experiences in which violent behavior was viewed as wrong.

A number of experimental approaches have been used to test the link between media and violence. Some of these include:

- Having groups of subjects exposed to violent TV shows in a laboratory setting, then monitoring their behavior afterward compared to control groups who viewed nonviolent programming

- Observing subjects on playgrounds, athletic fields, and residences after they have been exposed to violent television programs

- Requiring subjects to answer attitude surveys after watching violent TV shows

- Using aggregate measures of TV viewing; for example, tracking the number of violent TV shows on the air during a given time period and comparing it to crime rates during the same period

According to a recent analysis of all scientific data since 1975, Brad Bushman and Craig Anderson found that the weight of the evidence is that watching violence on TV is correlated to aggressive behaviors and that the newest, most methodologically sophisticated media show the greatest amount of association. The weight of the experimental results indicates that violent media has an immediate impact on people with a preexisting tendency toward crime and violence.

There is also evidence that kids who watch TV are more likely to persist in aggressive behavior as adults. A recent study conducted by researchers at Columbia University found that kids who watch more than an hour of TV each day show an increase in assaults, fights, robberies, and other acts of aggression later in life. The team, led by Jeffery G. Johnson, studied more than 700 people for seventeen years. Their data indicate that 5.7 percent of 14-year-olds who watched less than an hour of television a day became involved in aggressive acts between the ages of 16 and 22. The rate of aggressive acts skyrocketed to 22.5 percent when kids watched between 1 and 3 hours of TV. For kids who viewed more than 3 hours of TV per day, 28.8 percent were later involved in aggressive acts as adults. This association remained significant after previous aggressive behavior, childhood neglect, family income, neighborhood violence, parental education, and psychiatric disorders were controlled statistically. The Johnson research provides a direct link between TV viewing in adolescence and aggressive behavior in adulthood.

While this research is quite persuasive, not all criminologists accept that watching TV or movies and listening to heavy metal music eventually leads to violent and antisocial behavior. For example, criminologist Simon Singer found that teenage heavy metal fans were no more delinquent than nonlisteners. Candace Kruttschnitt and her associates found that an individual's exposure to violent TV shows is only weakly related to subsequent violent behavior.

There is also little evidence that areas that experience the highest levels of violent TV viewing also have rates of violent crime that are above the norm. Millions of children watch violence every night but do not become violent criminals. In fact, despite the prevalence of violent TV shows, films, and video games, which have become a universal norm, the violence rate among teens has been in a significant decline. If violent TV shows did, indeed, cause interpersonal violence, then there should be few ecological and regional patterns in the crime rate, but there are many. Put another way, how can regional differences in the violence rate be explained considering the fact that people all across the nation watch the same TV shows and films? On the other hand, it is possible that TV viewing may not have an immediate impact on behavior or one that is readily observable. Watching television may create changes in personality and cognition that in the long term may produce behavioral changes. For example, recent research by Dimitri Christakis and his associates found that for every hour of television watched daily between the ages of 1 and 3, the risk of developing attention problems increased by 9 percent over the life course; attention problems have been linked to antisocial behaviors. Further research is needed to clarify this important issue.

Critical Thinking

1. Should the government control the content of TV shows and limit the amount of weekly violence? How could the national news be shown if violence were omitted? What about boxing matches or hockey games?

2. How can we explain the fact that millions of kids watch violent TV shows and remain nonviolent? If there is a TV–violence link, how can we explain the fact that violence rates may have been higher in the Old West than they are today? Do you think violent gang kids stay home and watch TV shows?

(continued)

InfoTrac College Edition Research

For a different take on the effects of TV viewing on violence, check out these articles: David Link, "Facts about Fiction: In Defense of TV Violence," *Reason* 25 (March 1994): 22; Mike Males, "Who Us? Stop Blaming Kids and TV," *The Progressive* 61 (October 1997): 25.

Sources: Victoria Rideout, Elizabeth Vandewater, and Ellen Wartella, *Zero to Six: Electronic Media in the Lives of Infants, Toddler,s and Preschoolers*.(Menlo Park, CA: Kaiser Foundation, 2003); Dimitri Christakis, Frederick Zimmerman, David DiGiuseppe, and Carolyn McCarty, "Early Television Exposure and Subsequent Attentional

Problems in Children," *Pediatrics* 113 (2004): 708–713; Jeffery Johnson, Patricia Cohen, Elizabeth Smailes, Stephanie Kasen, and Judith Brook, "Television Viewing and Aggressive Behavior During Adolescent and Adulthood," *Science* 295 (2002): 2468–2471; Craig Anderson and Brad J. Bushman, "The Effects of Media Violence on Society," *Science* 295 (2002): 2377–2379; Brad Bushman and Craig Anderson, "Media Violence and the American Public," *American Psychologist* 56 (2001): 477–489; UCLA Center for Communication Policy, *Television Violence Monitoring Project* (Los Angeles, 1995); Associated Press, "Hollywood Is Blamed in Token Booth Attack," *Boston Globe,* 28 November 1995, p. 30; Garland White, Janet Katz, and Kathryn Scarborough, "The Impact of Professional Football Games upon Violent Assaults on Women," *Violence and Victims* 7 (1992): 157–171; Simon Singer, "Rethinking Subcultural Theories of Delinquency and the Cultural Resources of Youth." Paper presented at the annual meeting of

the American Society of Criminology, Phoenix, November 1993; Albert Reiss and Jeffrey Roth, eds., *Understanding and Preventing Violence* (Washington, DC: National Academy Press, 1993); Reuters, "Seventy-nine Percent in Survey Link Violence on TV and Crime," *Boston Globe,* 19 December 1993, p. 17; Scott Snyder, "Movies and Juvenile Delinquency: An Overview," *Adolescence* 26 (1991): 121–131; Steven Messner, "Television Violence and Violent Crime: An Aggregate Analysis," *Social Problems* 33 (1986): 218–235; Candace Kruttschnitt, Linda Heath, and David Ward, "Family Violence, Television Viewing Habits, and Other Adolescent Experiences Related to Violent Criminal Behavior," *Criminology* 243 (1986): 235–267; Jonathan Freedman, "Television Violence and Aggression: A Rejoinder," *Psychological Bulletin* 100 (1986): 372–378; Wendy Wood, Frank Wong, and J. Gregory Chachere, "Effects of Media Violence on Viewers' Aggression in Unconstrained Social Interaction," *Psychological Bulletin* 109 (1991): 371–383.

Lawrence Kohlberg first applied the concept of moral development to issues in criminology.[215] He found that people travel through stages of moral development during which their decisions and judgments on issues of right and wrong are made for different reasons. It is possible that serious offenders have a moral orientation that differs from that of law-abiding citizens. Kohlberg's stages of development are listed in Exhibit 5.4.

Kohlberg classified people according to the stage on this continuum at which their moral development ceased to grow. Kohlberg and his associates conducted studies in which criminals were found to be significantly lower in their moral judgment development than noncriminals of the same social background.[216] Since his pioneering efforts, researchers have continued to show that criminal offenders are more likely to be classified in the lowest levels of moral reasoning (Stages 1 and 2), whereas noncriminals have reached a higher stage of moral development (Stages 3 and 4).[217]

Recent research indicates that the decision not to commit crimes may be influenced by one's stage of moral development. People at the lowest levels report that they are deterred from crime because of their fear of sanctions. Those in the middle consider the reactions of family and friends. Those at the highest stages refrain from crime because they believe in duty to others and universal rights.[218]

Moral development theory suggests that people who obey the law simply to avoid punishment or have outlooks mainly characterized by self-interest are more likely to commit crimes than those who view the law as something that benefits all of society. Those at higher stages of moral reasoning tend to sympathize with the rights of others and are

associated with conventional behaviors, such as honesty, generosity, and nonviolence.

EXHIBIT 5.4

Kohlberg's Stages of Development

Stage 1   Right is obedience to power and avoidance of punishment.

Stage 2   Right is taking responsibility for oneself, meeting one's own needs, and leaving to others the responsibility for themselves.

Stage 3   Right is being good in the sense of having good motives, having concern for others, and "putting yourself in the other person's shoes."

Stage 4   Right is maintaining the rules of a society and serving the welfare of the group or society.

Stage 5   Right is based on recognized individual rights within a society with agreed-upon rules—a social contract.

Stage 6   Right is an assumed obligation to principles applying to all humankind—principles of justice, equality, and respect for human life.

Source: Lawrence Kohlberg, *Stages in the Development of Moral Thought and Action* (New York: Holt, Rinehart & Winston, 1969).

|||||||| CONNECTIONS ||||||||

The deterrent effect of informal sanctions and feelings of shame discussed in Chapter 4 may hinge on the level of a person's moral development. The lower one's state of moral development, the less impact informal sanctions may have; increased moral development and informal sanctions may be better able to control crime.

INFORMATION PROCESSING When cognitive theorists who study information processing try to explain antisocial behavior, they do so in terms of mental perception and how people use information to understand their environment. When people make decisions, they engage in a sequence of cognitive thought processes. First, they encode information so that it can be interpreted. Next, they search for a proper response and decide on the most appropriate action. Finally, they act on their decision.[219] Not everyone processes information in the same way, and the differences in interpretation may explain the development of radically different visions of the world.

According to this cognitive approach, people who use information properly, who are better conditioned to make reasoned judgments, and who can make quick and reasoned decisions when facing emotion-laden events are the ones best able to avoid antisocial behavior choices.[220] In contrast, crime-prone people may have cognitive deficits and use information incorrectly when they make decisions.[221] They perceive the world as stacked against them; they believe they have little control over the negative events in their life.[222] Chronic offenders come to believe that crime is an appropriate means to satisfy their immediate personal needs, which take precedence over more distant social needs such as obedience to the law.[223]

SHAPING PERCEPTIONS People whose cognitive processes are skewed or faulty may be relying on mental "scripts" learned in childhood that tell them how to interpret events, what to expect, how they should react, and what the outcome of the interaction should be.[224] Hostile children may have learned improper scripts by observing how others react to events; their own parents' aggressive and inappropriate behavior would have considerable impact. Some may have had early and prolonged exposure to violence (for example, child abuse), which increases their sensitivity to slights and maltreatment. Oversensitivity to rejection by their peers is a continuation of sensitivity to rejection by their parents.[225] Violent behavior responses learned in childhood become a stable behavior because the scripts that emphasize aggressive responses are repeatedly rehearsed as the child matures.[226]

To violence-prone kids, people seem more aggressive than they actually are and intend them ill when there is no reason for alarm. According to information processing theory, as these children mature, they use fewer cues than most people to process information. Some use violence in a calculating fashion as a means of getting what they want; others react in an overly volatile fashion to the slightest provocation. Aggressors are more likely to be vigilant, on edge, or suspicious. When they attack victims, they may believe they are defending themselves, even though they are misreading the situation.[227]

Adolescents who use violence as a coping technique with others are also more likely to exhibit other social problems, such as drug and alcohol abuse.[228] There is also evidence that delinquent boys who engage in theft are more likely to exhibit cognitive deficits than nondelinquent youth.

For example, they have a poor sense of time, leaving them incapable of dealing with or solving social problems in an effective manner.[229] Information processing theory has been used to explain the occurrence of date rape. Sexually violent males believe that when their dates say "No" to sexual advances the women are really "playing games" and actually want to be taken forcefully.[230]

Treatment based on how people process information takes into account that people are more likely to respond aggressively to a provocation because thoughts tend to intensify the insult or otherwise stir feelings of anger. Cognitive therapists, during the course of treatment, attempt to teach explosive people to control aggressive impulses by viewing social provocations as problems demanding a solution rather than retaliation. Programs are aimed at teaching problem-solving skills that may include self-disclosure, role-playing, listening, following instructions, joining in, and using self-control.[231]

Therapeutic interventions designed to make people better problem solvers may involve such measures as (1) enhancing coping and problem-solving skills; (2) enhancing relationships with peers, parents, and other adults; (3) teaching conflict resolution and communication skills and methods for resisting peer pressure related to drug use and violence; (4) teaching consequential thinking and decision-making abilities; (5) modeling prosocial behaviors, including cooperation with others, self-responsibility, respecting others, and public speaking efficacy; and (6) teaching empathy.[232]

Treatment interventions based on learning social skills are relatively new, but there are some indications that this approach can have long-term benefits for reducing criminal behavior.[233]

The various psychological theories of crime are set out in Concept Summary 5.2.

PSYCHOLOGICAL TRAITS AND CHARACTERISTICS

In addition to creating theories of behavior and development, psychologists also study psychological traits and characteristics that define an individual and shape how they function in the world. Certain traits have become associated with psychological problems and the development of antisocial behavior trends. Two of the most critical—personality and intelligence—are discussed in detail in the following sections.

Personality and Crime

Personality can be defined as the reasonably stable patterns of behavior, including thoughts and emotions, that distinguish one person from another.[234] One's personality

Psychological Trait Theories

Psychodynamic

- The major premise of the theory is the development of the unconscious personality early in childhood influences behavior for the rest of the person's life. Criminals have weak egos and damaged personalities.

- The strengths of the theory are that it explains the onset of crime and why crime and drug abuse cut across class lines.

- The research focuses of the theory are on mental disorders, personality development, and unconscious motivations and drives.

Behavioral

- The major premise of the theory is that people commit crime when they model their behavior after others they see being rewarded for similar acts. Behavior is reinforced by rewards and extinguished by punishment.

- The strengths of the theory are that it explains the role of significant others in the crime process; it shows how the media can influence crime and violence.

- The research focuses of the theory are the media and violence, as well as the effects of child abuse.

Cognitive

- The major premise of the theory is that individual reasoning processes influence behavior. Reasoning is influenced by the way people perceive their environment.

- The strengths of the theory are that it shows why criminal behavior patterns change over time as people mature and develop their reasoning powers. It may explain the aging-out process.

- The research focuses of the theory are perception and cognition.

reflects a characteristic way of adapting to life's demands and problems. The way we behave is a function of how our personality enables us to interpret life events and make appropriate behavioral choices. Can the cause of crime be linked to personality? This issue has long caused significant debate.[235] Sheldon Glueck and Eleanor Glueck identified a number of personality traits that they believe characterize antisocial youth:

self-assertiveness	sadism
defiance	lack of concern for others
extroversion	feeling unappreciated
ambivalence	distrust of authority
impulsiveness	poor personal skills
narcissism	mental instability
suspicion	hostility
destructiveness	resentment[236]

||||||| **CONNECTIONS** |||||||

The Glueck research is representative of the view that antisocial people maintain a distinct set of personal traits, which makes them particularly sensitive to environmental stimuli. Once dismissed by mainstream criminologists, the section on life course theories in Chapter 9 shows how the Gluecks' views still influence contemporary criminological theory.

Several other research efforts have attempted to identify criminal personality traits.[237] Suspected traits include impulsivity, hostility, and aggressiveness.[238] For example, Hans Eysenck identified two personality traits that he associated with antisocial behavior: *extroversion-introversion* and *stability-instability.* Extreme introverts are overaroused and avoid sources of stimulation; in contrast, extreme extroverts are unaroused and seek sensation. Introverts are slow to learn and be conditioned; extroverts are impulsive individuals who lack the ability to examine their own motives and behaviors. Those who are unstable, a condition Eysenck calls "neuroticism," are anxious, tense, and emotionally unstable.[239] People who are both neurotic and extroverted lack self-insight and are impulsive and emotionally unstable; they are unlikely to have reasoned judgments of life events. They are the type of offender who will repeat their criminal activity over and over.[240] While extrovert neurotics may act self-destructively (for example, by abusing drugs), more stable people will be able to reason that such behavior is ultimately harmful and life threatening. Eysenck believes that personality is controlled by genetic factors and is heritable.

In a recent study evaluating the most widely used measures of personality, Joshua Miller and Donald Lynam found that variance within two dimensions—agreeableness and conscientious—seem most closely related to antisocial behaviors. *Agreeableness* involves the ability to use appropriate interpersonal strategies when dealing with others; *conscientiousness* involves a person's ability to control impulses, carry out plans and tasks, maintain organizational skills, and follow his or her internal moral code.[241] Miller and Lynam found that personality researchers now link antisocial behaviors to traits such as these: hostile, self-centered, spiteful, jealous, and indifferent to others. Law violators tend to lack ambition and motivation and perseverance, have difficulty controlling their impulses, and hold nonconventional values and beliefs. Miller and Lynam show that these personality traits are linked to crime, but there is still some question about the direction of the linkage. On one hand, it is possible that people who share these personality traits are programmed to commit crimes. On the other hand, it is possible that personality traits interact with environmental factors to alter behavior. For example, kids who are low in conscientiousness will most likely have poor educational and occupational histories, which limit their opportunity for advancement; this blocked opportunity renders them crime prone.[242]

ANTISOCIAL PERSONALITY/PSYCHOPATHY/SOCIOPATHY

As a group, people who share these traits are believed to have a character defect referred to as *antisocial, sociopathic,* or *psychopathic* personality. Though these terms are often used interchangeably, some psychologists distinguish between sociopaths and psychopaths, suggesting that the former are a product of a destructive home environment whereas the latter are a product of a defect or aberration within themselves.[243] This condition is discussed in The Criminological Enterprise feature "The Antisocial Personality."

RESEARCH ON PERSONALITY Since maintaining a deviant personality has been related to crime and delinquency, numerous attempts have been made to devise accurate measures of personality and determine whether they can predict antisocial behavior. One of the most widely used psychological tests is the **Minnesota Multiphasic Personality Inventory,** commonly called the **MMPI.** This test has subscales designed to measure many different personality traits, including psychopathic deviation (Pd scale), schizophrenia (Sc), and hypomania (Ma).[244] Research studies have detected an association between scores on the Pd scale and criminal involvement.[245] Another frequently administered personality test, the **California Personality Inventory (CPI),** has also been used to distinguish deviants from nondeviant groups.[246] The **Multidimensional Personality Questionnaire (MPQ)** allows researchers to assess such personality traits as control, aggression, alienation, and well-being.[247] Evaluations using this scale indicate that adolescent offenders who are "crime prone" maintain "negative emotionality," a tendency to experience aversive affective states, such as anger, anxiety, and irritability. They also are predisposed to weak personal constraints, and they have difficulty controlling impulsive behavior urges. Because they are both impulsive and aggressive, crime-prone people are quick to take action against perceived threats.

Evidence that personality traits predict crime and violence is important because it suggests that the root cause of crime can be found in the forces that influence human development at an early stage of life. If these results are valid, rather than focus on job creation and neighborhood improvement, crime control efforts might be better focused on helping families raise children who are reasoned and reflective and enjoy a safe environment.

Intelligence and Crime

Many early criminologists maintained that many delinquents and criminals have a below-average intelligence quotient and that low IQ is a cause of their criminality. Criminals were believed to have inherently substandard intelligence, and thus, they seemed naturally inclined to commit more crimes than more intelligent persons. Furthermore, it was thought that if authorities could determine which individuals had low IQs, they might identify potential criminals before they committed socially harmful acts.

Social scientists had a captive group of subjects in juvenile training schools and penal institutions, and they began to measure the correlation between IQ and crime by testing adjudicated offenders. Thus, inmates of penal institutions were used as a test group around which numerous theories about intelligence were built, leading ultimately to the nature-versus-nurture controversy that is still going on today. These concepts are discussed in some detail in the following sections.

NATURE THEORY **Nature theory** argues that intelligence is largely determined genetically, that ancestry determines IQ, and that low intelligence, as demonstrated by low IQ, is linked to criminal behavior. When the newly developed IQ tests were administered to inmates of prisons and juvenile training schools in the first decades of the century, the nature position gained support because a very large proportion of the inmates scored low on the tests. During his studies in 1920, Henry Goddard found that many institutionalized persons were what he considered "feebleminded"; he concluded that at least half of all juvenile delinquents were mental defectives.[248] In 1926, William Healy and Augusta Bronner tested groups of delinquent boys in Chicago and Boston and found that 37 percent were subnormal in intelligence. They concluded that delinquents were five to ten times more likely to be mentally deficient than normal boys.[249] These and other early studies were embraced as proof that low IQ scores identified potentially delinquent children and that a correlation existed between innate low intelligence and deviant behavior. IQ tests were believed to measure the inborn genetic makeup of individuals, and many criminologists accepted the idea that individuals with substandard IQs were predisposed toward delinquency and adult criminality.

NURTURE THEORY The rise of culturally sensitive explanations of human behavior in the 1930s led to the nurture school of intelligence. **Nurture theory** states that intelligence must be viewed as partly biological but primarily sociological. Because intelligence is not inherited, low-IQ parents do not necessarily produce low-IQ children.[250] Nurture theorists discredited the notion that people commit crimes because they have low IQs. Instead, they postulated that environmental stimulation from parents, relatives, social contacts, schools, peer groups, and innumerable others create a child's IQ level and that low IQs result from an environment that also encourages delinquent and criminal behavior. Thus, if low IQ scores are recorded among criminals, these scores may reflect criminals' cultural background, not their mental ability.

Studies challenging the assumption that people automatically committed criminal acts because they had below-average IQs began to appear as early as the 1920s. John Slawson studied 1,543 delinquent boys in New York institutions and compared them with a control group of New York

The Criminological Enterprise

The Antisocial Personality

Some violent offenders may have a disturbed character structure commonly and interchangeably referred to as psychopathy, sociopathy, or antisocial personality. Psychopaths exhibit a low level of guilt and anxiety and persistently violate the rights of others. Although they may exhibit superficial charm and above-average intelligence, this often masks a disturbed personality that makes them incapable of forming enduring relationships with others and continually involves them in such deviant behaviors as violence, risk-taking, substance abuse, and impulsivity.

From an early age, many psychopaths have had home lives that were filled with frustrations, bitterness, and quarreling. As a result of this instability and frustration, these individuals developed personalities that became unreliable, unstable, demanding, and egocentric. Most psychopaths are risk-taking, sensation seekers who are constantly involved in a garden variety of antisocial behaviors. They are often described as grandiose, egocentric, manipulative, forceful, and cold-hearted, with shallow emotions and the inability to feel remorse, empathy with others, or anxiety over their misdeeds.

Hervey Cleckley, a leading authority on psychopathy, described them as follows:

> [Psychopaths are] chronically antisocial individuals who are always in trouble, profiting neither from experience nor punishment, and maintaining no real loyalties to any person, group, or code. They are frequently callous and hedonistic, showing marked emotional immaturity, with lack of responsibility, lack of judgment and an ability to rationalize their behavior so that it appears warranted, reasonable and justified.

Considering these personality traits, it is not surprising that research studies show that people evaluated as psychopaths are significantly more prone to criminal and violent behavior when compared to nonpsychopathic control groups. Psychopaths tend to continue their criminal careers long after other offenders burn out or age out of crime. They are continually in trouble with the law and, therefore, are likely to wind up in penal institutions. Criminologists estimate that 10 percent or more of all prison inmates display psychopathic tendencies.

The Cause of Psychopathy

Though psychologists are still not certain of the cause of psychopathy, a number of factors are believed to contribute to its development.

Traumatic Socialization

Some explanations focus on family experiences, suggesting that the influence of an unstable parent, parental rejection, lack of love during childhood, and inconsistent discipline may be related to psychopathy. Children who lack the opportunity to form an attachment to a mother figure in the first three years of life, who suffer sudden separation from the mother figure, or who see changes in the mother figure are most likely to develop psychopathic personalities. According to this view, the path runs from antisocial parenting to psychopathy to criminality. Psychologist David Lykken suggests that psychopaths have an inherited "low fear quotient," which inhibits their fear of punishment. All people have a natural or innate fear of certain stimuli, such as spiders, snakes, fires, or strangers. Psychopaths, as a rule, have few fears. Normal socialization processes depend on punishing antisocial behavior to inhibit future transgressions. Someone who does not fear punishment is simply harder to socialize.

Neurological Disorder

Psychopaths may suffer from lower than normal levels of arousal. Research studies have revealed that psychopaths have lower skin conductance levels and fewer spontaneous responses than "normal" subjects. There may be a link between psychopathy and autonomic nervous system (ANS) dysfunction. The ANS mediates physiological activities associated with emotions and is manifested in such measurements as heartbeat rate, blood pressure, respiration, muscle tension, capillary size, and electrical activity of the skin (called galvanic skin resistance). Psychopaths may be less capable of regulating their activities than other people. While some people may become anxious and afraid when facing the

---

City boys in 1926.[251] Slawson found that although 80 percent of the delinquents achieved lower scores in abstract verbal intelligence, delinquents were about normal in mechanical aptitude and nonverbal intelligence. These results indicated the possibility of cultural bias in portions of the IQ tests. He also found that there was no relationship between the number of arrests, the types of offenses, and IQ.

In 1931, Edwin Sutherland evaluated IQ studies of criminals and delinquents and noted significant variation in the findings, which disproved Goddard's notion that criminals were "feebleminded."[252] Goddard attributed discrepancies to testing and scoring methods rather than to differences in the mental ability of criminals. Sutherland's research all but put an end to the belief that crime was caused by

prospect of committing a criminal act, psychopaths in the same circumstances feel no such fear. James Ogloff and Stephen Wong conclude that their reduced anxiety levels result in behaviors that are more impulsive and inappropriate and in deviant behavior, apprehension, and incarceration.

Brain Abnormality

Another view is that psychopathy is caused by some form of brain abnormality. Some research has linked psychopathy to a dysfunction of the limbic inhibitory system manifested through damage to the frontal and temporal lobes of the brain. Consequently, psychopaths may need greater than average stimulation to bring them up to comfortable levels (similar to arousal theory discussed earlier).

Brain structure has also been linked to psychopathy. For example, Adrian Raine and his associates find that abnormalities in the corpus callosum, a thick band of nerve fibers that connects the two cerebral hemispheres and routes communications between them may be at the heart of the problem: Psychopaths showed an increase in callosal white matter volume, an increase in callosal length, a reduction in callosal thickness, and increased connectivity between brain hemispheres.

Chronic Offending

The antisocial personality concept seems to jibe with what is known about chronic offending. In a recent paper, Lawrence Cohen and Bryan Vila argue that chronic offending should be conceived as a continuum of behavior at whose apex resides the most extremely dangerous and predatory criminals. As many as 80 percent of these high-end chronic offenders exhibit sociopathic behavior patterns. Though comprising about 4 percent of the total male population and less than 1 percent of the total female population, they are responsible for half of all serious felony offenses committed annually. Not all high-rate chronic offenders are sociopaths, but enough are to support a strong link between personality dysfunction and long-term criminal careers.

Critical Thinking

1. Should people diagnosed as psychopaths be separated and treated even if they have not yet committed a crime?

2. Should psychopathic murderers be spared the death penalty because they lack the capacity to control their behavior?

 InfoTrac College Edition Research

To read more about the development of psychopathology check out these articles: John V. Lavigne, Richard Arend, Diane Rosenbaum, Helen J. Binns, Katherine Kaufer Christoffel, Andrew Burns, and Andrew Smith. "Mental Health Service Use among Young Children Receiving Pediatric Primary Care," *Research Journal of the American Academy of Child and Adolescent*

Psychiatry 37 (November 1998): 1175; Shirley Feldman, Jaime Waterman, Hans Steiner, and Elizabeth Cauffman, "Posttraumatic Stress Disorder among Female Juvenile Offenders," *Journal of the American Academy of Child and Adolescent Psychiatry* 37 (November 1998): 1209.

Sources: Kent Kiehl, Andra Smith, Adrianna Mendrek, Bruce Forster, Robert Hare, and Peter F. Liddle, "Temporal Lobe Abnormalities in Semantic Processing by Criminal Psychopaths as Revealed by Functional Magnetic Resonance Imaging," *Psychiatry Research: Neuroimaging* 130 (2004): 27–42; A. Raine, T. Lencz, K. Taylor, J. B. Hellige, S. Bihrle, L. Lacasse, M. Lee, S. Ishikawa, and P. Colletti, "Corpus Callosum Abnormalities in Psychopathic Antisocial Individuals," *Archives of General Psychiatry* 60 (2003): 1134–1142; Grant Harris, Marnie Rice, and Martin Lalumiere, "Criminal Violence: The Roles of Psychopathy, Neurodevelopmental Insults, and Antisocial Parenting," *Criminal Justice and Behavior* 28 (2001): 402–415; David Lykken, "Psychopathy, Sociopathy, and Crime," *Society* 34 (1996): 30–38; Lawrence Cohen and Bryan Vila, "Self-Control and Social Control: An Exposition of the Gottfredson-Hirschi/Sampson-Laub Debate," *Studies on Crime and Crime Prevention* 5 (1996); Donald Lynam, "Early Identification of Chronic Offenders: Who Is the Fledgling Psychopath?" *Psychological Bulletin* 120 (1996): 209–234; James Ogloff and Stephen Wong, "Electrodermal and Cardiovascular Evidence of a Coping Response in Psychopaths," *Criminal Justice and Behavior* 17 (1990): 231–245; Laurie Frost, Terrie Moffitt, and Rob McGee, "Neuro-Psychological Correlates of Psycho-pathology in an Unselected Cohort of Young Adolescents," *Journal of Abnormal Psychology* 98 (1989): 307–313; Hervey Cleckley, "Psychopathic States," in *American Handbook of Psychiatry*, ed. S. Aneti (New York: Basic Books, 1959), pp. 567–569; Spencer Rathus and Jeffrey Nevid, *Abnormal Psychology* (Englewood Cliffs, NJ: Prentice-Hall, 1991), pp. 310–316; Helene Raskin White, Erich Labouvie, and Marsha Bates, "The Relationship between Sensation Seeking and Delinquency: A Longitudinal Analysis," *Journal of Research in Crime and Delinquency* 22 (1985): 197–211.

"feeblemindedness"; the IQ–crime link was all but forgotten in the criminological literature.

REDISCOVERING IQ AND CRIMINALITY The alleged IQ–crime link was dismissed by mainstream criminologists, but it once again became an important area of study when respected criminologists Travis Hirschi and Michael Hindelang published a widely read 1977 paper linking the two variables. After re-examining existing research data, Hirschi and Hindelang concluded that the weight of evidence is that IQ is a more important factor than race and socioeconomic class for predicting criminal and delinquent involvement.[253] Rejecting the notion that IQ tests are race and class biased, they concluded that major differences exist between criminals and noncriminals within similar racial and socioeconomic class categories. They proposed the idea that low IQ increases the likelihood of criminal behavior through its effect on school performance. That is, youths with low IQs do poorly in school, and school failure and academic incompetence are highly related to delinquency and later to adult criminality.

Hirschi and Hindelang's inferences have been supported by research conducted by both U.S. and international scholars.[254] Some studies have found a direct IQ–delinquency link among samples of adolescent boys.[255] When Alex Piquero examined violent behavior among groups of children in Philadelphia, he found that scores on intelligence tests were the best predictors of violent behavior and could be used to distinguish between groups of violent and nonviolent offenders.[256] In contrast, in *Crime and Human Nature,* James Q. Wilson and Richard Herrnstein find that the IQ–crime link is an indirect one: Low intelligence leads to poor school performance, which enhances the chances of criminality.[257] They conclude, "A child who chronically loses standing in the competition of the classroom may feel justified in settling the score outside, by violence, theft, and other forms of defiant illegality."[258]

CROSS-NATIONAL STUDIES The IQ–crime relationship has also been found in cross-national studies. A significant relationship between low IQ and delinquency has been found among samples of youth in Denmark. Researchers found that Danish children with a low IQ tended to engage in delinquent behaviors because their poor verbal ability was a handicap in the school environment.[259] Research by Canadian neural-psychologist Lorne Yeudall and his associates found samples of delinquents possessed IQs about 20 points less than nondelinquent control groups on one of the standard IQ tests, the **Wechsler Adult Intelligence Scale.**[260] An IQ–crime link was also found in a longitudinal study of Swedish youth; low IQ measures taken at age 3 were significant predictors of later criminality over the life course.[261]

IQ AND CRIME RECONSIDERED The Hirschi-Hindelang research increased interest and research on the association between IQ and crime, but the issue is far from settled and is still a matter of significant debate. A number of recent studies find that IQ level has negligible influence on criminal behavior.[262] Also, a recent evaluation of existing knowledge on intelligence conducted by the American Psychological Association concluded that the strength of an IQ–crime link was "very low."[263]

In contrast, *The Bell Curve,* Richard Herrnstein and Charles Murray's influential albeit controversial book on intelligence, comes down firmly for an IQ–crime link. Their extensive review of the available literature shows that people with lower IQs are more likely to commit crime, get caught, and be sent to prison. Conversely, at-risk kids with higher IQs seem to be protected from becoming criminals by their superior ability to succeed in school and in social relationships. Taking the scientific literature as a whole, Herrnstein and Murray conclude that criminal offenders have an average IQ of 92, about 8 points below the mean; chronic

Even if a low IQ is proven to be a "cause" of crime, should criminals with extremely low IQs be punished in the same way as those who are intellectually average or above? Daryl Renard Atkins sits in a York-Poquoson courtroom in York, Virginia. Atkins was convicted and sentenced to death for carjacking and killing an airman in Virginia to get money for beer. One test showed Atkins had an IQ of 59. People who test 70 or below generally are considered mentally retarded or mentally challenged. In Atkins' case, the Supreme Court ruled that the death penalty was not an appropriate punishment for the mentally challenged because their lack of reasoning, judgment, and control of their impulses make them incapable of having the same "moral culpability" or responsibility as people with higher levels of intelligence.

offenders score even lower than the "average" criminal. To those who suggest that the IQ–crime relationship can be explained by the fact that only low IQ criminals get caught, they counter with data showing little difference in IQ scores between self-reported and official criminals.[264] This means that even criminals whose activities go undetected by the authorities have lower IQs than the general public; the IQ–crime relationship cannot be explained away by the fact that slow-witted criminals are the ones most likely to be apprehended by the police.

It is unlikely that the IQ–crime debate will be settled in the near future. Measurement is beset by many methodological problems. The well-documented criticisms suggesting that IQ tests are race and class biased would certainly influence the testing of the criminal population who are besieged with a multitude of social and economic problems. Even if it can be shown that known offenders have lower IQs than the general population, it is difficult to explain many patterns in the crime rate: Why are there more male than female criminals? (Are females three times smarter than males?) Why do crime rates vary by region, time of year, and even weather patterns? Why does aging out occur? IQs do not increase with age, so why should crime rates fall?

FIGURE 5.2

Psychological Perspectives on Criminality

Theory	Cause
PSYCHODYNAMIC (psychoanalytic)	**Intrapsychic processes** • Unconscious conflicts • Mood disorders • Tendencies • Anger • Sexuality
BEHAVIORAL	**Learning processes** • Learning experiences • Stimulus • Rewards and punishments • Direct/indirect observation
COGNITIVE	**Information processing** • Thinking • Planning • Memory • Perception • Ethical values

Characteristic	Cause
PERSONALITY	**Personality processes** • Antisocial personality • Sociopath/psychopath temperament • Abnormal affect, lack of emotional depth
INTELLIGENCE	**Intellectual processes** • Low IQ • Poor school performance • Decision-making ability

The various psychological perspectives, characteristics, and attributes are outlined in Figure 5.2.

To read all about **IQ testing and intelligence**, go to http://www.indiana.edu/~ intell/. For an up-to-date list of web links, go to http://cj.wadsworth.com/siegel _crimtpt9e.

PUBLIC POLICY IMPLICATIONS OF TRAIT THEORY

For most of the twentieth century, biological and psychological views of criminality have influenced crime control and prevention policy. The result has been front-end or **primary** prevention programs that seek to treat personal problems before they manifest themselves as crime. To this end, thousands of family therapy organizations, substance abuse clinics, and mental health associations operate throughout the United States. Teachers, employers, relatives, welfare agencies, and others make referrals to these facilities. These services are based on the premise that if a person's problems can be treated before they become overwhelming, some future crimes will be prevented. **Secondary prevention programs** provide treatment such as psychological counseling to youths and adults who are at risk for law violation. **Tertiary prevention programs** may be a requirement of a probation order, part of a diversionary sentence, or aftercare at the end of a prison sentence.

Biologically oriented therapy is also being used in the criminal justice system. Programs have altered diets, changed lighting, compensated for learning disabilities, treated allergies, and so on.[265] More controversial has been the use of mood-altering chemicals, such as lithium, pemoline, imipramine, phenytoin, and benzodiazepines, to control behavior. Another practice that has elicited concern is the use of psychosurgery (brain surgery) to control antisocial behavior. Surgical procedures have been used to alter the brain structure of convicted sex offenders in an effort to eliminate or control their sex drives. Results are still preliminary, but some critics argue that these procedures are without scientific merit.[266]

Numerous psychologically based treatment methods range from individual counseling to behavior modification. For example, treatment based on how people process information takes into account that people are more likely to respond aggressively to provocation if thoughts intensify the insult or otherwise stir feelings of anger. Cognitive therapists attempt to teach explosive people to control aggressive impulses by viewing social provocations as problems demanding a solution rather than retaliation. Therapeutic interventions designed to make people better problem solvers may involve measures that enhance

- Coping and problem-solving skills
- Relationships with peers, parents, and other adults
- Conflict resolution and communication skills, and methods for resisting peer pressure related to drug use and violence
- Consequential thinking and decision-making abilities
- Prosocial behaviors, including cooperation with others, self-responsibility, respecting others, and public-speaking efficacy
- Empathy[267]

 To quiz yourself on this material, go to the Criminology TPT 9e website.

SUMMARY

- The earliest positivist criminologists were biologists. Led by Cesare Lombroso, these early researchers believed that some people manifested primitive traits that made them born criminals. Today their research is debunked because of poor methodology, testing, and logic.

- Biological views fell out of favor in the early twentieth century. In the 1970s, spurred by the publication of Edmund O. Wilson's *Sociobiology*, several criminologists again turned to study of the biological basis of criminality. For the most part, the effort has focused on the cause of violent crime.

- One area of interest is biochemical factors, such as diet, allergies, hormonal imbalances, and environmental contaminants (such as lead). The conclusion is that crime, especially violence, is a function of diet, vitamin intake, hormonal imbalance, or food allergies.

- Neurophysiological factors, such as brain disorders, ADHD, EEG abnormalities, tumors, and head injuries have been linked to crime. Criminals and delinquents often suffer brain impairment, as measured by the EEG. Attention deficit hyperactivity disorder and minimal brain dysfunction are related to antisocial behavior.

- Some biocriminologists believe that the tendency to commit violent acts is inherited. Research has been conducted with twin pairs and adopted children to determine whether genes are related to behaviors.

- An evolutionary branch holds that changes in the human condition, which have taken millions of years to evolve, may help explain crime rate differences. As the human race evolved, traits and characteristics have become ingrained.

- There are also psychologically based theories of crime. The psychodynamic view, developed by Sigmund Freud, links aggressive behavior to personality conflicts arising from childhood. According to psychodynamic theory, unconscious motivations developed early in childhood propel some people into destructive or illegal behavior. The development of the unconscious personality early in childhood influences behavior for the rest of a person's life. Criminals have weak egos and damaged personalities. According to some psychoanalysts, psychotics are aggressive, unstable people who can easily become involved in crime.

- Behaviorists view aggression as a learned behavior. Children who are exposed to violence and see it rewarded may become violent as adults. People commit crime when they model their behavior after others they see being rewarded for the same acts. Behavior is reinforced by rewards and extinguished by punishment.

- Learning may be either direct and experiential or observational, such as watching TV and movies.

- Cognitive psychology is concerned with human development and how people perceive the world. Cognitive theory stresses knowing and perception. Some people have a warped view of the world.

- Criminality is viewed as a function of improper information processing. Individual reasoning processes influence behavior. Reasoning is influenced by the way people perceive their environment.

- There is evidence that people with abnormal or antisocial personalities are crime prone.

- Psychological traits such as personality and intelligence have been linked to criminality. One important area of study has been the antisocial personality, a person who lacks emotion and concern for others.

- While some criminologists find a link between intelligence and crime, others dispute any linkage between IQ level and law-violating behaviors.

- The controversial issue of the relationship of IQ to criminality has been resurrected once again with the publication of research studies purporting to show that criminals have lower IQs than noncriminals.

Thinking Like a Criminologist

The American Psychiatric Association believes a person should not be held legally responsible for a crime if his or her behavior meets the following standard developed by legal expert Richard Bonnie:

A person charged with a criminal offense should be found not guilty by reason of insanity if it is shown that as a result of mental disease or mental retardation he was unable to appreciate the wrongfulness of his conduct at the time of the offense.

As used in this standard, the terms *mental disease* and *mental retardation* include only those severely abnormal mental conditions that grossly and demonstrably impair a person's perception or understanding of reality and that are not attributable primarily to the voluntary ingestion of alcohol or other psychoactive substances.

As a criminologist with expertise on trait theories of crime, do you agree with this standard? What modifications, if any, might you make to include other categories of offenders who are not excused by this definition?

 ## Doing Research on the Web

Before you give your opinion, you might want to check out the website of the American Psychiatric Association and see what their position is on the insanity defense: http://www.psych.org/public_info/insanity.cfm.

To learn more about the structure of mental illness and how it relates to crime, check out: http://www.mentalhealth.com/book/p40-sc01.html.

Also go to InfoTrac College Edition and use "insanity defense" in a key word search.

BOOK COMPANION WEBSITE

http://cj.wadsworth.com/siegel_crimtpt9e To quiz yourself on the material in this chapter, go to the companion website, where you'll find chapter-by-chapter online tutorial quizzes, a final exam, ABC videos with questions, chapter outlines, chapter review, chapter-by-chapter web links, flash cards, and more!

KEY TERMS

inheritance school (132)
somatotype (132)
biophobia (133)
reciprocal altruism (133)
trait theory (133)
equipotentiality (133)
Wernicke-Korsakoff disease (135)
hypoglycemia (138)
androgens (138)
testosterone (138)
neocortex (138)
premenstrual syndrome (PMS) (139)
cerebral allergies (139)
neuroallergies (139)
neurophysiology (140)
electroencephalograph (EEG) (140)
attention deficit hyperactivity disorder (ADHD) (141)
conduct disorder (CD) (141)
chemical restraints (142)
chemical straitjackets (142)
arousal theory (143)
contagion effect (145)
defective intelligence (149)

psychoanalytic or psychodynamic perspective (149)
behaviorism (149)
cognitive theory (149)
id (149)
pleasure principle (149)
ego (149)
reality principle (149)
superego (149)
conscience (149)
ego ideal (149)
eros (149)
thanatos (149)
oral stage (150)
anal stage (150)
phallic stage (150)
Oedipus complex (150)
Electra complex (150)
latency (150)
fixated (150)
inferiority complex (150)
identity crisis (150)
latent delinquency (150)
bipolar disorder (150)

psychosis (151)
disorders (151)
schizophrenia (151)
paranoid schizophrenic (151)
social learning (152)
behavior modeling (152)
moral development (153)
humanistic psychology (153)
information processing (153)
personality (157)
Minnesota Multiphasic Personality Inventory (MMPI) (159)
California Personality Inventory (CPI) (159)
Multidimensional Personality Questionnaire (MPQ) (159)
nature theory (159)
nurture theory (159)
Wechsler Adult Intelligence Scale (162)
primary prevention programs (163)
secondary prevention programs (163)
tertiary prevention programs (163)

CRITICAL THINKING QUESTIONS

1. What should be done with the young children of violence-prone criminals if in fact research could show that the tendency to commit crime is inherited?

2. After considering the existing research on the subject, would you recommend that young children be forbidden from eating foods with a heavy sugar content?

3. Knowing what you do about trends and patterns in crime, how would you counteract the assertion that people who commit crime are physically or mentally abnormal? For example, how would you explain the fact that crime is more likely to occur in western and urban areas than in eastern or rural areas?

4. Aside from becoming a criminal, what other career paths are open to psychopaths?

5. Research shows that kids who watch a lot of TV in adolescence are more likely to behave aggressively in adulthood. This has led some to conclude that TV watching is responsible for adult violence. Can this relationship be explained in another way?

NOTES

1. Dalton Conley and Neil Bennett, "Is Biology Destiny? Birth Weight and Life Chances," *American Sociological Review* 654 (2000): 458–467.

2. Raffaele Garofalo, *Criminology*, trans. Robert Miller (Boston: Little, Brown, 1914), p. 92.

3. Enrico Ferri, *Criminal Sociology* (New York: D. Appleton, 1909).

4. See Richard Dugdale, *The Jukes* (New York: Putnam, 1910); Arthur Estabrook, *The Jukes in 1915* (Washington, DC: Carnegie Institute of Washington, 1916).

5. William Sheldon, *Varieties of Delinquent Youth* (New York: Harper Bros., 1949).

6. Pierre van den Bergle, "Bringing the Beast Back In: Toward a Biosocial Theory of Aggression," *American Sociological Review* 39 (1974): 779.

7. Lee Ellis, "A Discipline in Peril: Sociology's Future Hinges on Curing Biophobia," *American Sociologist* 27 (1996): 21–41.

8. Edmund O. Wilson, *Sociobiology* (Cambridge, MA: Harvard University Press, 1975).

9. See, generally, Lee Ellis, *Theories of Rape* (New York: Hemisphere Publications, 1989).

10. Anthony Walsh, "Behavior Genetics and Anomie/Strain Theory," *Criminology* 38 (2000): 1,075–1,108.

11. Anthony Walsh and Lee Ellis, "Shoring Up the Big Three: Improving Criminological Theories with Biosocial Concepts." Paper presented at the annual Society of Criminology meeting, San Diego, November 1997, p. 16.

12. Israel Nachshon, "Neurological Bases of Crime, Psychopathy and Aggression," in *Crime in Biological, Social and Moral Contexts,* eds. Lee Ellis and Harry Hoffman (New York: Praeger, 1990), p. 199. Herein cited as *Crime in Biological Contexts.*

13. See, generally, Lee Ellis, "Introduction: The Nature of the Biosocial Perspective," in *Crime in Biological Contexts,* pp. 3–18.

14. See, for example, Tracy Bennett Herbert and Sheldon Cohen, "Depression and Immunity: A Meta-Analytic Review," *Psychological Bulletin* 113 (1993): 472–486.

15. See Ellis, *Theories of Rape.*

16. Leonard Hippchen, "Some Possible Biochemical Aspects of Criminal Behavior," *Journal of Behavioral Ecology* 2 (1981): 1–6; Sarnoff Mednick and Jan Volavka, "Biology and Crime," in *Crime and Justice,* eds. Norval Morris and Michael Tonry (Chicago: University of Chicago Press, 1980), pp. 85–159; Saleem Shah and Loren Roth, "Biological and Psychophysiological Factors in Criminality," in *Handbook of Criminology,* ed. Daniel Glazer (Chicago: Rand McNally, 1974), pp. 125–140.

17. Sue Dengate and Alan Ruben, "Controlled Trial of Cumulative Behavioural Effects of a Common Bread Preservative," *Journal of Pediatrics and Child Health* 38 (2002): 373–376.

18. G. B. Ramirez, O. Pagulayan, H. Akagi, A. Francisco Rivera, L. V. Lee, A. Berroya, M. C. Vince Cruz, and D. Casintahan, "Tagum Study II: Follow-Up Study at Two Years of Age after Prenatal Exposure to Mercury," *Pediatrics* 111 (2003): 289–295.

19. Harold Milman and Suzanne Arnold, "Neurologic, Psychological, and Aggressive Disturbances with Sildenafil," *Annals of Pharmacotherapy* 36 (2002): 1,129–1,134.

20. Ulric Neisser, et al., "Intelligence: Knowns and Unknowns," *American Psychologist* 51 (1996): 77–101, at 88.

21. Leonard Hippchen, ed., *Ecologic-Biochemical Approaches to Treatment of Delinquents and Criminals* (New York: Von Nostram Reinhold, 1978), p. 14.

22. C. Hawley and R. E. Buckley, "Food Dyes and Hyperkinetic Children," *Academy Therapy* 10 (1974): 27–32.

23. Michael Krassner, "Diet and Brain Function," *Nutrition Reviews* 44 (1986): 12–15.

24. Hippchen, *Ecologic-Biochemical Approaches to Treatment of Delinquents and Criminals.*

25. J. Kershner and W. Hawke, "Megavitamins and Learning Disorders: A Controlled Double-Blind Experiment," *Journal of Nutrition* 109 (1979): 819–826.

26. Richard Knox, "Test Shows Smart People's Brains Use Nutrients Better," *Boston Globe,* 16 February 1988, p. 9.

27. Ronald Prinz and David Riddle, "Associations between Nutrition and Behavior in 5-Year-Old Children," *Nutrition Reviews Supplement* 44 (1986): 151–158.

28. Stephen Schoenthaler and Walter Doraz, "Types of Offenses Which Can Be Reduced in an Institutional Setting Using Nutritional Intervention," *International Journal of Biosocial Research* 4 (1983): 74–84; and idem, "Diet and Crime," *International Journal of Biosocial Research* 4 (1983): 74–84. See also, A. G. Schauss, "Differential Outcomes among Probationers Comparing Orthomolecular Approaches to Conventional Casework Counseling." Paper presented at the annual meeting of the American Society of Criminology, Dallas, November 9, 1978; A. Schauss and C. Simonsen, "A Critical

Analysis of the Diets of Chronic Juvenile Offenders, Part I," *Journal of Orthomolecular Psychiatry* 8 (1979): 222–226; A. Hoffer, "Children with Learning and Behavioral Disorders," *Journal of Orthomolecular Psychiatry* 5 (1976): 229.

29. Prinz and Riddle, "Associations between Nutrition and Behavior in 5-Year-Old Children."

30. H. Bruce Ferguson, Clare Stoddart, and Jovan Simeon, "Double-Blind Challenge Studies of Behavioral and Cognitive Effects of Sucrose-Aspartame Ingestion in Normal Children," *Nutrition Reviews Supplement* 44 (1986): 144–158; Gregory Gray, "Diet, Crime and Delinquency: A Critique," *Nutrition Reviews Supplement* 44 (1986): 89–94.

31. Mark Wolraich, Scott Lindgren, Phyllis Stumbo, Lewis Stegink, Mark Appelbaum, and Mary Kiritsy, "Effects of Diets High in Sucrose or Aspartame on the Behavior and Cognitive Performance of Children," *The New England Journal of Medicine* 330 (1994): 303–306.

32. Dian Gans, "Sucrose and Unusual Childhood Behavior," *Nutrition Today* 26 (1991): 8–14.

33. Diana Fishbein, "Neuropsychological Function, Drug Abuse, and Violence, a Conceptual Framework," *Criminal Justice and Behavior* 27 (2000): 139–159.

34. D. Hill and W. Sargent, "A Case of Matricide," *Lancet* 244 (1943): 526–527.

35. E. Podolsky, "The Chemistry of Murder," *Pakistan Medical Journal* 15 (1964): 9–14.

36. J. A. Yaryura-Tobias and F. Neziroglu, "Violent Behavior, Brain Dysrhythmia and Glucose Dysfunction: A New Syndrome," *Journal of Orthopsychiatry* 4 (1975): 182–188.

37. Matti Virkkunen, "Reactive Hypoglycemic Tendency among Habitually Violent Offenders," *Nutrition Reviews Supplement* 44 (1986): 94–103.

38. James Q. Wilson, *The Moral Sense* (New York: Free Press, 1993).

39. Walter Gove, "The Effect of Age and Gender on Deviant Behavior: A Biopsychosocial Perspective," in *Gender and the Life Course,* ed. A. S. Rossi (New York: Aldine, 1985), pp. 115–144.

40. A. Maras, M. Laucht, D. Gerdes, C. Wilhelm, S. Lewicka, D. Haack, L. Malisova, and M. H. Schmidt, "Association of Testosterone and Dihydrotestosterone with Externalizing Behavior in Adolescent Boys and Girls," *Psychoneuroendocrinology* 28 (2003): 932–940; Alan Booth and D. Wayne Osgood, "The Influence of Testosterone on Deviance in Adulthood: Assessing and Explaining the Relationship," *Criminology* 31 (1993): 93–118.

41. Anthony Walsh, "Genetic and Cytogenetic Intersex Anomalies: Can They Help Us to Understand Gender Differences in Deviant Behavior?" *International Journal of Offender Therapy and Comparative Criminology* 39 (1995): 151–166.

42. Christy Miller Buchanan, Jacquelynne Eccles, and Jill Becker, "Are Adolescents the Victims of Raging Hormones? Evidence for Activational Effects of Hormones on Moods and Behavior at Adolescence," *Psychological Bulletin* 111 (1992): 62–107.

43. Alex Piquero and Timothy Brezina, "Testing Moffitt's Account of Adolescent-Limited Delinquency," *Criminology* 39 (2001): 353–370.

44. Booth and Osgood, "The Influence of Testosterone on Deviance in Adulthood."

45. Albert Reiss and Jeffrey Roth, eds. *Understanding and Preventing Violence* (Washington, DC: National Academy Press, 1993), p. 118. Hereafter cited as *Understanding Violence.*

46. L. E. Kreuz and R. M. Rose, "Assessment of Aggressive Behavior and Plasma Testosterone in a Young Criminal Population," *Psychosomatic Medicine* 34 (1972): 321–332.

47. Walsh, "Genetic and Cytogenetic Intersex Anomalies."

48. Lee Ellis, "Evolutionary and Neurochemical Causes of Sex Differences in Victimizing Behavior: Toward a Unified Theory of Criminal Behavior and Social Stratification," *Social Science Information* 28 (1989): 605–636.

49. For a general review, see Lee Ellis and Phyllis Coontz, "Androgens, Brain Functioning, and Criminality: The Neurohormonal Foundations of Antisociality," in *Crime in Biological Contexts,* pp. 162–93.

50. Ibid., p. 181.

51. Robert Rubin, "The Neuroendocrinology and Neuro-Chemistry of Antisocial Behavior," in *The Causes of Crime, New Biological Approaches,* eds. Sarnoff Mednick, Terrie Moffitt, and Susan Stack (Cambridge: Cambridge University Press, 1987), pp. 239–262.

52. J. Money, "Influence of Hormones on Psychosexual Differentiation," *Medical Aspects of Nutrition* 30 (1976): 165.

53. Mednick and Volavka, "Biology and Crime."

54. For a review of this concept, see Anne E. Figert, "The Three Faces of PMS: The Professional, Gendered, and Scientific Structuring of a Psychiatric Disorder," *Social Problems* 42 (1995): 56–72.

55. Katharina Dalton, *The Premenstrual Syndrome* (Springfield, IL: Charles C Thomas, 1971).

56. Julie Horney, "Menstrual Cycles and Criminal Responsibility," *Law and Human Nature* 2 (1978): 25–36.

57. Diana Fishbein, "Selected Studies on the Biology of Antisocial Behavior," in *New Perspectives in Criminology,* ed. John Conklin (Needham Heights, MA: Allyn & Bacon, 1996), pp. 26–38.

58. Ibid.; Karen Paige, "Effects of Oral Contraceptives on Affective Fluctuations Associated with the Menstrual Cycle," *Psychosomatic Medicine* 33 (1971): 515–537.

59. H. E. Amos and J. J. P. Drake, "Problems Posed by Food Additives," *Journal of Human Nutrition* 30 (1976): 165.

60. Ray Wunderlich, "Neuroallergy as a Contributing Factor to Social Misfits: Diagnosis and Treatment," in *Ecologic-Biochemical Approaches to Treatment of Delinquents and Criminals,* ed. Leonard Hippchen (New York: Von Nostram Reinhold, 1978), pp. 229–253.

61. See, for example, Paul Marshall, "Allergy and Depression: A Neurochemical Threshold Model of the Relation between the Illnesses," *Psychological Bulletin* 113 (1993): 23–39.

62. A. R. Mawson and K. J. Jacobs, "Corn Consumption, Tryptophan, and Cross-National Homicide Rates," *Journal of Orthomolecular Psychiatry* 7 (1978): 227–230.

63. Centers for Disease Control. "CDC Releases Most Extensive Assessment Ever of Americans' Exposure to Environmental Chemicals," Centers for Disease Control press release, 31 January 2003.

64. Alexander Schauss, *Diet, Crime, and Delinquency* (Berkeley: Parker House, 1980).

65. John Ott, "The Effects of Light and Radiation on Human Health and Behavior," in *Ecologic-Biochemical Approaches to Treatment of Delinquents and Criminals,* ed. Leonard Hippchen (New York: Von Nostram Reinhold, 1978), pp. 105–83. See also A. Kreuger and S. Sigel, "Ions in the Air," *Human Nature* (July 1978): 46–47; Harry Wohlfarth, "The Effect of Color Psychodynamic Environmental

Modification on Discipline Incidents in Elementary Schools over One School Year: A Controlled Study," *International Journal of Biosocial Research* 6 (1984): 44–53.

66. David C. Bellinger, "Lead," *Pediatrics* 113 (2004): 1,016–1,022.

67. Paul Stretesky and Michael Lynch, "The Relationship between Lead Exposure and Homicide," *Archives of Pediatric Adolescent Medicine* 155 (2001): 579–582.

68. Jeff Evans, "Asymptomatic, High Lead Levels Tied to Delinquency," *Pediatric News* 37 (2003): 13.

69. Deborah Denno, "Considering Lead Poisoning as a Criminal Defense," *Fordham Urban Law Journal* 20 (1993): 377–400.

70. Herbert Needleman, Christine McFarland, Roberta Ness, Stephen Fienberg, and Michael Tobin, "Bone Lead Levels in Adjudicated Delinquents: A Case Control Study," *Neurotoxicology and Teratology* 24 (2002): 711–717; Herbert Needleman, Julie Riess, Michael Tobin, Gretchen Biesecker, and Joel Greenhouse, "Bone Lead Levels and Delinquent Behavior," *Journal of the American Medical Association* 275 (1996): 363–369.

71. Neisser, et al., "Intelligence: Knowns and Unknowns."

72. Mark Opler, Alan Brown, Joseph Graziano, Manisha Desai, Wei Zheng, Catherine Schaefer, Pamela Factor-Litvak, and Ezra S. Susser, "Prenatal Lead Exposure, [Delta]-Aminolevulinic Acid, and Schizophrenia," *Environmental Health Perspectives* 112 (2004): 548–553.

73. Centers for Disease Control. "CDC Releases Most Extensive Assessment Ever of Americans' Exposure to Environmental Chemicals."

74. Terrie Moffitt, "The Neuropsychology of Juvenile Delinquency: A Critical Review," in *Crime and Justice, An Annual Review*, vol. 12, eds. Norval Morris and Michael Tonry (Chicago: University of Chicago Press, 1990), pp. 99–169.

75. Terrie Moffitt, Donald Lynam, and Phil Silva, "Neuropsychological Tests Predicting Persistent Male Delinquency," *Criminology* 32 (1994): 277–300; Elizabeth Kandel and Sarnoff Mednick, "Perinatal Complications Predict Violent Offending," *Criminology* 29 (1991): 519–529; Sarnoff Mednick, Ricardo Machon, Matti Virkkunen, and Douglas Bonett, "Adult Schizophrenia Following Prenatal Exposure to an Influenza Epidemic," *Archives of General Psychiatry* 44 (1987): 35–46; C. A. Fogel, S. A.

Mednick, and N. Michelson, "Hyperactive Behavior and Minor Physical Anomalies," *Acta Psychiatrica Scandinavia* 72 (1985): 551–556.

76. R. Johnson, *Aggression in Man and Animals* (Philadelphia: Saunders, 1972), p. 79.

77. Jean Seguin, Robert Pihl, Philip Harden, Richard Tremblay, and Bernard Boulerice, "Cognitive and Neuropsychological Characteristics of Physically Aggressive Boys," *Journal of Abnormal Psychology* 104 (1995): 614–624; Deborah Denno, "Gender, Crime and the Criminal Law Defenses," *Journal of Criminal Law and Criminology* 85 (1994): 80–180.

78. Adrian Raine, Patricia Brennan, Brigitte Mednick, and Sarnoff Mednick, "High Rates of Violence, Crime, Academic Problems, and Behavioral Problems in Males with Both Early Neuromotor Deficits and Unstable Family Environments," *Archives of General Psychiatry* 53 (1966): 544–549.

79. Deborah Denno, *Biology, Crime and Violence: New Evidence* (Cambridge: Cambridge University Press, 1989).

80. Diana Fishbein and Robert Thatcher, "New Diagnostic Methods in Criminology: Assessing Organic Sources of Behavioral Disorders," *Journal of Research in Crime and Delinquency* 23 (1986): 240–267.

81. See, generally, David Rowe, *Biology and Crime* (Los Angeles: Roxbury Press, 2001).

82. Lorne Yeudall, "A Neuropsychosocial Perspective of Persistent Juvenile Delinquency and Criminal Behavior." Paper presented at the New York Academy of Sciences, September 26, 1979.

83. R. W. Aind and T. Yamamoto, "Behavior Disorders of Childhood," *Electroencephalography and Clinical Neurophysiology* 21 (1966): 148–156.

84. See, generally, Jan Volavka, "Electroencephalogram among Criminals," in *The Causes of Crime, New Biological Approaches,* eds. Sarnoff Mednick, Terrie Moffitt, and Susan Stack (Cambridge: Cambridge University Press, 1987), pp. 137–145; Z. A. Zayed, S. A. Lewis, and R. P. Britain, "An Encephalographic and Psychiatric Study of 32 Insane Murderers," *British Journal of Psychiatry* 115 (1969): 1115–1124.

85. Nathaniel Pallone and James Hennessy, "Brain Dysfunction and Criminal Violence," *Society* 35 (1998): 21–27; P. F. Goyer, P. J. Andreason, and W. E. Semple, "Positronic Emission Tomogra-

phy and Personality Disorders," *Neuropsychopharmacology* 10 (1994): 21–28.

86. Adrian Raine, Monte Buchsbaum, and Lori LaCasse, "Brain Abnormalities in Murderers Indicated by Positron Emission Tomography," *Biological Psychiatry* 42 (1997): 495–508.

87. David George, Robert Rawlings, Wendol Williams, Monte Phillips, Grace Fong, Michael Kerich, Reza Momenan, John Umhau, and Daniel Hommer, "A Select Group of Perpetrators of Domestic Violence: Evidence of Decreased Metabolism in the Right Hypothalamus and Reduced Relationships between Cortical/Subcortical Brain Structures in Positron Emission Tomography," *Psychiatry Research: Neuroimaging* 130 (2004): 11–25.

88. Adrian Raine, "The Role of Prefrontal Deficits, Low Autonomic Arousal, and Early Health Factors in the Development of Antisocial and Aggressive Behavior in Children," *Journal of Child Psychology and Psychiatry* 43 (2002): 417–434.

89. Pallone and Hennessy, "Brain Dysfunction and Criminal Violence," p. 25.

90. D. R. Robin, R. M. Starles, T. J. Kenney, B. J. Reynolds, and F. P. Heald, "Adolescents Who Attempt Suicide," *Journal of Pediatrics* 90 (1977): 636–638.

91. R. R. Monroe, *Brain Dysfunction in Aggressive Criminals* (Lexington, MA: D.C. Heath, 1978).

92. L. T. Yeudall, *Childhood Experiences as Causes of Criminal Behavior* (Senate of Canada, Issue no. 1, Thirteenth Parliament, Ottawa, 1977).

93. Raine, Buchsbaum, and LaCasse, "Brain Abnormalities in Murderers Indicated by Positron Emission Tomography."

94. Leonore Simon, "Does Criminal Offender Treatment Work?" *Applied and Preventive Psychology* (summer 1998); Stephen Faraone, et al., "Intellectual Performance and School Failure in Children with Attention Deficit Hyperactivity Disorder and in Their Siblings," *Journal of Abnormal Psychology* 102 (1993): 616–623.

95. Ibid.

96. Simon, "Does Criminal Offender Treatment Work?"

97. Terrie Moffitt and Phil Silva, "Self-Reported Delinquency, Neuropsychological Deficit, and History of Attention Deficit Disorder," *Journal of Abnormal Child Psychology* 16 (1988): 553–569.

98. Molina Pelham, Jr., "Childhood Predictors of Adolescent Substance Use in a

Longitudinal Study of Children with ADHD," *Journal of Abnormal Psychology* 112 (2003): 497–507; Peter Muris and Cor Meesters, "The Validity of Attention Deficit Hyperactivity and Hyperkinetic Disorder Symptom Domains in Non-clinical Dutch Children," *Journal of Clinical Child and Adolescent Psychology* 32 (2003): 460–466.

99. Elizabeth Hart, et al., "Criterion Validity of Informants in the Diagnosis of Disruptive Behavior Disorders in Children: A Preliminary Study," *Journal of Consulting and Clinical Psychology* 62 (1994): 410–414.

100. Russell Barkley, Mariellen Fischer, Lori Smallish, and Kenneth Fletcher, "Young Adult Follow-Up of Hyperactive Children: Antisocial Activities and Drug Use," *Journal of Child Psychology and Psychiatry* 45 (2004): 195–211.

101. Eugene Maguin, Rolf Loeber, and Paul LeMahieu, "Does the Relationship between Poor Reading and Delinquency Hold for Males of Different Ages and Ethnic Groups?" *Journal of Emotional and Behavioral Disorders* 1 (1993): 88–100.

102. Karen Harding, Richard Judah, and Charles Gant, "Outcome-Based Comparison of Ritalin[R] versus Food-Supplement Treated Children with AD/HD," *Alternative Medicine Review* 8 (2003): 319–330.

103. Rita Shaughnessy, "Psychopharmaco-therapy of Neuropsychiatric Disorders," *Psychiatric Annals* 25 (1995): 634–640.

104. Yeudall, "A Neuropsychosocial Perspective of Persistent Juvenile Delinquency and Criminal Behavior," p. 4; F. A. Elliott, "Neurological Aspects of Antisocial Behavior," in *The Psychopath: A Comprehensive Study of Antisocial Disorders and Behaviors,* ed. W. H. Reid (New York: Brunner/Mazel, 1978), pp. 146–189.

105. Ibid., p. 177.

106. H. K. Kletschka, "Violent Behavior Associated with Brain Tumor," *Minnesota Medicine* 49 (1966): 1,853–1,855.

107. V. E. Krynicki, "Cerebral Dysfunction in Repetitively Assaultive Adolescents," *Journal of Nervous and Mental Disease* 166 (1978): 59–67.

108. C. E. Lyght, ed., *The Merck Manual of Diagnosis and Therapy* (West Point, FL: Merck, 1966).

109. Reiss and Roth, *Understanding Violence,* p. 119.

110. M. Virkkunen, M. J. DeJong, J. Bartko, and M. Linnoila, "Psychobiological Con-

comitants of History of Suicide Attempts among Violent Offenders and Impulsive Fire Starters," *Archives of General Psychiatry* 46 (1989): 604–606.

111. Matti Virkkunen, David Goldman, and Markku Linnoila, "Serotonin in Alcoholic Violent Offenders," *The Ciba Foundation Symposium, Genetics of Criminal and Antisocial Behavior* (Chichester, England: Wiley, 1995).

112. Lee Ellis, "Left- and Mixed-Handedness and Criminality: Explanations for a Probable Relationship," in *Left-Handedness, Behavioral Implications and Anomalies,* ed. S. Coren (Amsterdam: Elsevier, 1990): 485–507.

113. Lee Ellis, "Monoamine Oxidase and Criminality: Identifying an Apparent Biological Marker for Antisocial Behavior," *Journal of Research in Crime and Delinquency* 28 (1991): 227–251.

114. Walter Gove and Charles Wilmoth, "Risk, Crime and Neurophysiologic Highs: A Consideration of Brain Processes that May Reinforce Delinquent and Criminal Behavior," in *Crime in Biological Contexts,* pp. 261–293.

115. Jack Katz, *Seduction of Crime: Moral and Sensual Attractions of Doing Evil* (New York: Basic Books, 1988), pp. 12–15.

116. Lee Ellis, "Arousal Theory and the Religiosity-Criminality Relationship," in *Contemporary Criminological Theory,* eds., Peter Cordella and Larry Siegel (Boston, MA: Northeastern University, 1996), pp. 65–84.

117. Adrian Raine, Peter Venables, and Sarnoff Mednick, "Low Resting Heart Rate at Age 3 Years Predisposes to Aggression at Age 11 Years: Evidence from the Mauritius Child Health Project," *Journal of the American Academy of Adolescent Psychiatry* 36 (1997): 1457–1464.

118. For a general view, see Richard Lerner and Terryl Foch, *Biological-Psychosocial Interactions in Early Adolescence* (Hillsdale, NJ: Erlbaum, 1987).

119. Kerry Jang, W. John Livesley, and Philip Vernon, "Heritability of the Big Five Personality Dimensions and Their Facets: A Twin Study," *Journal of Personality* 64 (1996): 577–589.

120. David Rowe, "As the Twig Is Bent: The Myth of Child-Rearing Influences on Personality Development," *Journal of Counseling and Development* 68 (1990): 606–611; David Rowe, Joseph Rogers, and Sylvia Meseck-Bushey, "Sibling

Delinquency and the Family Environment: Shared and Unshared Influences," *Child Development* 63 (1992): 59–67.

121. Gregory Carey and David DiLalla, "Personality and Psychopathology: Genetic Perspectives," *Journal of Abnormal Psychology* 103 (1994): 32–43.

122. T. R. Sarbin and L. E. Miller, "Demonism Revisited: The XYY Chromosome Anomaly," *Issues in Criminology* 5 (1970): 195–207.

123. Mednick and Volavka, "Biology and Crime," p. 93.

124. For an early review, see Barbara Wooton, *Social Science and Social Pathology* (London: Allen & Unwin, 1959); John Laub and Robert Sampson, "Unraveling Families and Delinquency: A Reanalysis of the Gluecks' Data," *Criminology* 26 (1988): 355–380.

125. D. J. West and D. P. Farrington, eds., "Who Becomes Delinquent?" in *The Delinquent Way of Life* (London: Heinemann, 1977); D. J. West, *Delinquency, Its Roots, Careers, and Prospects* (Cambridge, MA: Harvard University Press, 1982).

126. West, *Delinquency,* p. 114.

127. Carolyn Smith and David Farrington, "Continuities in Antisocial Behavior and Parenting across Three Generations," *Journal of Child Psychology and Psychiatry* 45 (2004): 230–247.

128. David Farrington, "Understanding and Preventing Bullying," in *Crime and Justice,* vol. 17, ed. Michael Tonry (Chicago: University of Chicago Press, 1993), pp. 381–457.

129. Terence Thornberry, Adrienne Freeman-Gallant, Alan Lizotte, Marvin Krohn, and Carolyn Smith. "Linked Lives: The Intergenerational Transmission of Antisocial Behavior," *Journal of Abnormal Child Psychology* 31 (2003): 171–185.

130. Philip Harden and Robert Pihl, "Cognitive Function, Cardiovascular Reactivity, and Behavior in Boys at High Risk for Alcoholism," *Journal of Abnormal Psychology* 104 (1995): 94–103.

131. Laub and Sampson, "Unraveling Families and Delinquency," p. 370.

132. Smith and Farrington, "Continuities in Antisocial Behavior and Parenting across Three Generations."

133. David Rowe and David Farrington, "The Familial Transmission of Criminal Convictions," *Criminology* 35 (1997): 177–201.

134. D. P. Farrington, Gwen Gundry, and D. J. West, "The Familial Transmission of Criminality," in *Crime and the Family*, eds. Alan Lincoln and Murray Straus (Springfield, IL: Charles C Thomas, 1985), pp. 193–206.

135. Abigail Fagan and Jake Najman,"Sibling Influences on Adolescent Delinquent Behaviour: An Australian Longitudinal Study," *Journal of Adolescence* 26 (2003): 547–559.

136. David Rowe and Bill Gulley, "Sibling Effects on Substance Use and Delinquency," *Criminology* 30 (1992): 217–232; see also, David Rowe, Joseph Rogers, and Sylvia Meseck-Bushey, "Sibling Delinquency and the Family Environment: Shared and Unshared Influences," *Child Development* 63 (1992): 59–67.

137. Dana Haynie and Suzanne Mchugh, "Sibling Deviance in the Shadows of Mutual and Unique Friendship Effects?" *Criminology* 41 (2003): 355–393.

138. Louise Arseneault, Terrie Moffitt, Avshalom Caspi, Alan Taylor, Fruhling Rijsdijk, Sara Jaffee, Jennifer Ablow, and Jeffrey Measelle, "Strong Genetic Effects on Cross-Situational Antisocial Behaviour among 5-Year-Old Children According to Mothers, Teachers, Examiner-Observers, and Twins' Self-Reports," *Journal of Child Psychology and Psychiatry* 44 (2003): 832–848.

139. David Rowe, "Sibling Interaction and Self-Reported Delinquent Behavior: A Study of 265 Twin Pairs," *Criminology* 23 (1985): 223–240; Nancy Segal, "Monozygotic and Dizygotic Twins: A Comparative Analysis of Mental Ability Profiles," *Child Development* 56 (1985): 1051–1058.

140. Ibid.

141. See Sarnoff A. Mednick and Karl O. Christiansen, eds., *Biosocial Bases in Criminal Behavior* (New York: Gardner Press, 1977).

142. Michael Lyons, "A Twin Study of Self-Reported Criminal Behavior," and Judy Silberg, Joanne Meyer, Andrew Pickles, Emily Simonoff, Lindon Eaves, John Hewitt, Hermine Maes, and Michael Rutter, "Heterogeneity among Juvenile Antisocial Behaviors: Findings from the Virginia Twin Study of Adolescent Behavioral Development," in *The Ciba Foundation Symposium, Genetics of Criminal and Antisocial Behavior* (Chichester, England: Wiley, 1995).

143. Michael Lyons, Karestan Koenen, Francisco Buchting, Joanne Meyer, Lindon Eaves, Rosemary Toomey, Seth Eisen, Jack Goldberg,Stephen Faraon, Rachel.Ban, Beth Jerskey, and Ming Tsuang, "A Twin Study of Sexual Behavior in Men," *Archives of Sexual Behavior* 33 (2004): 129–136.

144. David Rowe, "Genetic and Environmental Components of Antisocial Behavior: A Study of 265 Twin Pairs," *Criminology* 24 (1986): 513–532; David Rowe and D. Wayne Osgood, "Heredity and Sociological Theories of Delinquency: A Reconsideration," *American Sociological Review* 49 (1984): 526–540.

145. Edwin J. C. G. van den Oord, Frank Verhulst, and Dorret Boomsma, "A Genetic Study of Maternal and Paternal Ratings of Problem Behaviors in 3-Year-Old Twins," *Journal of Abnormal Psychology* 105 (1996): 349–357.

146. Mednick and Volavka, "Biology and Crime," in Norval Morris and Michael Tonry, eds., *Crime and Justice*, vol. 1 (Chicago: University of Chicago Press, 1980), pp. 85–159; Lee Ellis, "Genetics and Criminal Behavior," *Criminology* 10 (1982): 43–66; Karl O. Christiansen, "A Preliminary Study of Criminality among Twins," in S. A. Mednick and Karl O. Christiansen, eds., *The Biosocial Bases of Criminal Behavior* (New York: Gardner Press, 1977).

147. Ping Qin, "The Relationship of Suicide Risk to Family History of Suicide and Psychiatric Disorders," *Psychiatric Times* 20 (2003): http://www.psychiatrictimes.com/p031262.html.

148. Jane Scourfield, Marianne Van den Bree, Neilson Martin, and Peter McGuffin, "Conduct Problems in Children and Adolescents: A Twin Study," *Archives of General Psychiatry*, 61 (2004): 489–496; Jeanette Taylor, Bryan Loney, Leonardo Bobadilla, William Iacono, and Matt McGue, "Genetic and Environmental Influences on Psychopathy Trait Dimensions in a Community Sample of Male Twins," *Journal of Abnormal Child Psychology* 31 (2003): 633–645.

149. Ginette Dionne, Richard Tremblay, Michel Boivin, David Laplante, and Daniel Perusse, "Physical Aggression and Expressive Vocabulary in 19-Month-Old Twins," *Developmental Psychology* 39 (2003): 261–273.

150. Thomas Bouchard, "Genetic and Environmental Influences on Intelligence and Special Mental Abilities," *American Journal of Human Biology* 70 (1998): 253–275; some findings from the Minnesota study can be accessed from their website: http://www.cla.umn.edu/psych/psylabs/mtfs/mtfsspec.htm.

151. David Rowe, *The Limits of Family Influence: Genes, Experiences and Behavior* (New York: Guilford Press, 1995), p. 64.

152. Gregory Carey, "Twin Imitation for Antisocial Behavior: Implications for Genetic and Family Environment Research," *Journal of Abnormal Psychology* 101 (1992): 18–25; David Rowe and Joseph Rodgers, "The Ohio Twin Project and ADSEX Studies: Behavior Genetic Approaches to Understanding Antisocial Behavior." Paper presented at the American Society of Criminology meeting, Montreal, Canada, November 1987.

153. Glenn Walters, "A Meta-Analysis of the Gene–Crime Relationship," *Criminology* 30 (1992): 595–613.

154. Alice Gregory, Thalia. Eley, and Robert Plomin, "Exploring the Association between Anxiety and Conduct Problems in a Large Sample of Twins Aged 2–4," *Journal of Abnormal Child Psychology* 32 (2004): 111–123.

155. Marshall Jones and Donald Jones, "The Contagious Nature of Antisocial Behavior," *Criminology* 38 (2000): 25–46.

156. Jones and Jones, "The Contagious Nature of Antisocial Behavior," p. 31.

157. R. J. Cadoret, C. Cain, and R. R. Crowe, "Evidence for a Gene–Environment Interaction in the Development of Adolescent Antisocial Behavior," *Behavior Genetics* 13 (1983): 301–310.

158. Barry Hutchings and Sarnoff A. Mednick, "Criminality in Adoptees and Their Adoptive and Biological Parents: A Pilot Study," in *Biological Bases in Criminal Behavior*, eds. S. A. Mednick and K. O. Christiansen (New York: Gardner Press, 1977).

159. For similar results, see Sarnoff Mednick, Terrie Moffitt, William Gabrielli, and Barry Hutchings, "Genetic Factors in Criminal Behavior: A Review," in *Development of Antisocial and Prosocial Behavior*, ed. Dan Olweus (New York: Academic Press, 1986), pp. 3–50; Sarnoff Mednick, William Gabrielli, and Barry Hutchings, "Genetic Influences in Criminal Behavior: Evidence from an Adoption Cohort," in *Perspective Studies of Crime and Delinquency*, eds. Katherine Teilmann Van Dusen and Sarnoff Mednick (Boston: Kluver-Nijhoff, 1983), pp. 39–57.

160. Michael Bohman, "Predisposition to Criminality: Swedish Adoption Studies

in Retrospect," in *Genetics of Criminal and Antisocial Behavior,* pp. 99–114.

161. Lawrence Cohen and Richard Machalek, "A General Theory of Expropriative Crime: An Evolutionary Ecological Approach," *American Journal of Sociology* 94 (1988): 465–501.

162. For a general review, see Martin Daly and Margo Wilson, "Crime and Conflict: Homicide in Evolutionary Psychological Theory," in *Crime and Justice, An Annual Edition,* ed. Michael Tonry (Chicago: University of Chicago Press, 1997), pp. 51–100.

163. Martin Daly and Margo Wilson, *Homicide* (New York: Aldine de Gruyter, 1988), p. 194.

164. Margo Wilson, Holly Johnson, and Martin Daly, "Lethal and Nonlethal Violence against Wives," *Canadian Journal of Criminology* 37 (1995): 331–361.

165. Daly and Wilson, *Homicide,* pp. 172–173.

166. Lee Ellis, "The Evolution of Violent Criminal Behavior and Its Nonlegal Equivalent," in *Crime in Biological, Social, and Moral Contexts*, eds. Lee Ellis and Harry Hoffman (New York: Praeger, 1990), pp. 63–65.

167. David Rowe, Alexander Vazsonyi, and Aurelio Jose Figuerdo, "Mating-Effort in Adolescence: A Conditional Alternative Strategy," *Personal Individual Differences* 23 (2002): 105–115.

168. Ibid.

169. Anne Campbell, Steven Muncer, and Daniel Bibel, "Female–Female Criminal Assault: An Evolutionary Perspective," *Journal of Research in Crime and Delinquency* 35 (1998): 413–429.

170. J. Phillipe Rushton, *Race, Evolution and Behavior,* abridged ed. (New Brunswick, NJ: Transaction Books, 1999).

171. Michael Lynch, "J. Phillipe on Crime: An Examination and Critique of the Explanation of Crime and Race," *Social Pathology* 6 (2000): 228–244

172. Lee Ellis, "Sex Differences in Criminality: An Explanation Based on the Concept of R/K Selection," *Mankind Quarterly* 30 (1990): 17–37.

173. Byron Roth, "Crime and Child Rearing," *Society* 34 (1996): 39–45.

174. Deborah Denno, "Sociological and Human Developmental Explanations of Crime: Conflict or Consensus," *Criminology* 23 (1985): 711–741.

175. Israel Nachshon and Deborah Denno, "Violence and Cerebral Function," in *The Causes of Crime, New Biological Approaches,* eds. Sarnoff Mednick, Terrie Moffitt, and Susan Stack (Cambridge: Cambridge University Press, 1987), pp. 185–217.

176. Raine, Brennan, Mednick, and Mednick, "High Rates of Violence, Crime, Academic Problems, and Behavioral Problems in Males with Both Early Neuromotor Deficits and Unstable Family Environments."

177. Avshalom Caspi, Donald Lynam, Terrie Moffitt, and Phil Silva, "Unraveling Girl's Delinquency: Biological, Dispositional, and Contextual Contributions to Adolescent Misbehavior," *Developmental Psychology* 29 (1993): 283–289.

178. Glenn Walters and Thomas White, "Heredity and Crime: Bad Genes or Bad Research," *Criminology* 27 (1989): 455–486, at 478.

179. Charles Goring, *The English Convict: A Statistical Study, 1913* (Montclair, NJ: Patterson Smith, 1972).

180. Edwin Driver, "Charles Buckman Goring," in *Pioneers in Criminology,* ed. Hermann Mannheim (Montclair, NJ: Patterson Smith, 1970), p. 440.

181. Gabriel Tarde, *Penal Philosophy,* trans. R. Howell (Boston: Little, Brown, 1912).

182. See, generally, Donn Byrne and Kathryn Kelly, *An Introduction to Personality* (Englewood Cliffs, NJ: Prentice-Hall, 1981).

183. August Aichorn, *Wayward Youth* (New York: Viking Press, 1935).

184. See, generally, D. A. Andrews and James Bonta, *The Psychology of Criminal Conduct* (Cincinnati, Ohio: Anderson, 1994), pp. 72–75.

185. Paige Crosby Ouimette, "Psychopathology and Sexual Aggression in Nonincarcerated Men," *Violence and Victimization* 12 (1997): 389–397.

186. Robert Krueger, Avshalom Caspi, Phil Silva, and Rob McGee, "Personality Traits Are Differentially Linked to Mental Disorders: A Multitrait-Multidiagnosis Study of an Adolescent Birth Cohort," *Journal of Abnormal Psychology* 105 (1996): 299–312.

187. Seymour Halleck, *Psychiatry and the Dilemmas of Crime* (Berkeley: University of California Press, 1971).

188. Jeffrey Burke, Rolf Loeber, and Boris Birmaher, "Oppositional Defiant Disorder and Conduct Disorder: A Review of the Past 10 Years, Part II," *Journal of the American Academy of Child and Adolescent Psychiatry* 41 (2002): 1275–1294.

189. Ellen Kjelsberg, "Gender and Disorder Specific Criminal Career Profiles in Former Adolescent Psychiatric In-Patients," *Journal of Youth and Adolescence* 33 (2004): 261–270.

190. Richard Rowe, Julie Messer, Robert Goodman, and Howard Meltzer, "Conduct Disorder and Oppositional Defiant Disorder in a National Sample: Developmental Epidemiology," *Journal of Child Psychology and Psychiatry and Allied Disciplines* 45 (2004): 609–621.

191. Paul Rohde, Gregory N. Clarke, David E. Mace, Jenel S. Jorgensen, and John R. Seeley, "An Efficacy/Effectiveness Study of Cognitive-Behavioral Treatment for Adolescents with Comorbid Major Depression and Conduct Disorder," *Journal of the American Academy of Child and Adolescent Psychiatry* 43 (2004): 660–669.

192. Jennifer Beyers and Rolf Loeber, "Untangling Developmental Relations between Depressed Mood and Delinquency in Male Adolescents," *Journal of Abnormal Child Psychology* 31 (2003): 247–267.

193. Dorothy Espelage, Elizabeth Cauffman, Lisa Broidy, Alex Piquero, Paul Mazerolle, and Hans Steiner, "A Cluster-Analytic Investigation of MMPI Profiles of Serious Male and Female Juvenile Offenders," *Journal of the American Academy of Child and Adolescent Psychiatry* 42 (2003): 770–777.

194. Richard Famularo, Robert Kinscherff, and Terence Fenton, "Psychiatric Diagnoses of Abusive Mothers, A Preliminary Report," *Journal of Nervous and Mental Disease* 180 (1992): 658–660.

195. James Sorrells, "Kids Who Kill," *Crime and Delinquency* 23 (1977): 312–320.

196. Richard Rosner, "Adolescents Accused of Murder and Manslaughter: A Five-Year Descriptive Study," *Bulletin of the American Academy of Psychiatry and the Law* 7 (1979): 342–351.

197. Richard Wagner, Dawn Taylor, Joy Wright, Alison Sloat, Gwynneth Springett, Sandy Arnold, and Heather Weinberg, "Substance Abuse among the Mentally Ill," *American Journal of Orthopsychiatry* 64 (1994): 30–38.

198. Bruce Link, Howard Andrews, and Francis Cullen, "The Violent and Illegal Behavior of Mental Patients Reconsidered," *American Sociological Review* 57 (1992): 275–292; Ellen Hochstedler Steury, "Criminal Defendants with Psychiatric Impairment: Prevalence, Probabilities and Rates," *Journal of Criminal Law and Criminology* 84 (1993): 354–374.

199. Henrik Belfrage "A Ten-Year Follow-Up of Criminality in Stockholm Mental Patients: New Evidence for a Relation between Mental Disorder and Crime," *British Journal of Criminology* 38 (1998): 145–155.

200. C. Wallace, P. Mullen, P. Burgess, S. Palmer, D. Ruschena , and C. Browne, "Serious Criminal Offending and Mental Disorder. Case Linkage Study," *British Journal of Psychiatry* 174 (1998): 477–484.

201. Patricia Brennan, Sarnoff Mednick, and Sheilagh Hodgins, "Major Mental Disorders and Criminal Violence in a Danish Birth Cohort," *Archives of General Psychiatry* 57 (2000): 494–500.

202. Robert Vermeiren, "Psychopathology and Delinquency in Adolescents: A Descriptive and Developmental Perspective," *Clinical Psychology Review* 23 (2003): 277–318.

203. John Monahan, *Mental Illness and Violent Crime* (Washington, DC: National Institute of Justice, 1996).

204. Robin Shepard Engel and Eric Silver, "Policing Mentally Disordered Suspects: A Reexamination of the Criminalization Hypothesis," *Criminology* 39 (2001): 225–352; Marc Hillbrand, John Krystal, Kimberly Sharpe, and Hilliard Foster, "Clinical Predictors of Self-Mutilation in Hospitalized Patients," *Journal of Nervous and Mental Disease* 182 (1994): 9–13.

205. Carmen Cirincione, Henry Steadman, Pamela Clark Robbins, and John Monahan, *Mental Illness as a Factor in Criminality: A Study of Prisoners and Mental Patients* (Delmar, N.: Policy Research Associates, 1991). See also, idem, *Schizophrenia as a Contingent Risk Factor for Criminal Violence* (Delmar, NY: Policy Research Associates, 1991).

206. James Bonta, Moira Law, and Karl Hanson, "The Prediction of Criminal and Violent Recidivism among Mentally Disordered Offenders: A Meta-Analysis," *Psychological Bulletin* 123 (1998): 123–142.

207. Eric Silver, "Mental Disorder and Violent Victimization: The Mediating Role of Involvement in Conflicted Social Relationships," *Criminology* 40 (2002): 191–212.

208. Eric Silver, "Extending Social Disorganization Theory: A Multilevel Approach to the Study of Violence among Persons with Mental Illness," *Criminology* 38 (2000): 1043–1074.

209. Stacy DeCoster and Karen Heimer, "The Relationship between Law Violation and Depression: An Interactionist Analysis," *Criminology* 39 (2001): 799–837.

210. B. Lögdberg, L-L. Nilsson, M. T. Levander, and S. Levander, "Schizophrenia, Neighbourhood, and Crime," *Acta Psychiatrica Scandinavica* 110 (2004): 92–97.

211. Jeffrey Wanson, Randy Borum, Marvin Swartz, Virginia Hidaym, H. Ryan Wagner, and Barbara Burns, "Can Involuntary Outpatient Commitment Reduce Arrests among Persons with Severe Mental Illness?" *Criminal Justice and Behavior* 28 (2001): 156–189.

212. This discussion is based on three works by Albert Bandura: *Aggression: A Social Learning Analysis* (Englewood Cliffs, NJ: Prentice-Hall, 1973); *Social Learning Theory* (Englewood Cliffs, NJ: Prentice-Hall, 1977); and "The Social Learning Perspective: Mechanisms of Aggression," in *Psychology of Crime and Criminal Justice,* ed. Hans Toch (New York: Holt, Rinehart & Winston, 1979), pp. 198–236.

213. David Phillips, "The Impact of Mass Media Violence on U.S. Homicides," *American Sociological Review* 48 (1983): 560–568.

214. See, generally, Jean Piaget, *The Moral Judgment of the Child* (London: Kegan Paul, 1932).

215. Lawrence Kohlberg, *Stages in the Development of Moral Thought and Action* (New York: Holt, Rinehart & Winston, 1969).

216. L. Kohlberg, K. Kauffman, P. Scharf, and J. Hickey, *The Just Community Approach in Corrections: A Manual* (Niantic: Connecticut Department of Corrections, 1973).

217. Scott Henggeler, *Delinquency in Adolescence* (Newbury Park, CA: Sage, 1989), p. 26.

218. Carol Veneziano and Louis Veneziano, "The Relationship between Deterrence and Moral Reasoning," *Criminal Justice Review* 17 (1992): 209–216.

219. K. A. Dodge, "A Social Information Processing Model of Social Competence in Children," in *Minnesota Symposium in Child Psychology,* vol. 18, ed. M. Perlmutter (Hillsdale, NJ: Erlbaum, 1986), pp. 77–125.

220. Adrian Raine, Peter Venables, and Mark Williams, "Better Autonomic Conditioning and Faster Electrodermal Half-Recovery Time at Age 15 Years as Possible Protective Factors against Crime at Age 29 Years," *Developmental Psychology* 32 (1996): 624–630.

221. Jean Marie McGloin and Travis Pratt, "Cognitive Ability and Delinquent Behavior among Inner-City Youth: A Life-Course Analysis of Main, Mediating, and Interaction Effects," *International Journal of Offender Therapy and Comparative Criminology* 47 (2003): 253–271.

222. Shadd Maruna, "Desistance from Crime and Explanatory Style: A New Direction in the Psychology of Reform," *Journal of Contemporary Criminal Justice* 20 (2004): 184–200.

223. Tony Ward and Claire Stewart, "The Relationship between Human Needs and Criminogenic Needs," *Psychology, Crime, and Law* 9. (2003): 219–225.

224. L. Huesman and L. Eron, "Individual Differences and the Trait of Aggression," *European Journal of Personality* 3 (1989): 95–106.

225. Rolf Loeber and Dale Hay, "Key Issues in the Development of Aggression and Violence from Childhood to Early Adulthood," *Annual Review of Psychology* 48 (1997): 371–410.

226. Judith Baer and Tina Maschi, "Random Acts of Delinquency: Trauma and Self-Destructiveness in Juvenile Offenders," *Child and Adolescent Social Work Journal* 20 (2003): 85–99.

227. J. E. Lochman, "Self and Peer Perceptions and Attributional Biases of Aggressive and Nonaggressive Boys in Dyadic Interactions," *Journal of Consulting and Clinical Psychology* 55 (1987): 404–410.

228. Kathleen Cirillo, B. E. Pruitt, Brian Colwell, Paul M. Kingery, Robert S. Hurley, and Danny Ballard, "School Violence: Prevalence and Intervention Strategies for At-Risk Adolescents," *Adolescence* 33 (1998): 319–331.

229. Leilani Greening, "Adolescent Stealers' and Nonstealers' Social Problem-Solving Skills," *Adolescence* 32 (1997): 51–56.

230. D. Lipton, E. C. McDonel, and R. McFall, "Heterosocial Perception in Rapists," *Journal of Consulting and Clinical Psychology* 55 (1987): 17–21.

231. *Understanding Violence,* p. 389.

232. Cirillo, Pruitt, Colwell, Kingery, Hurley, and Ballard, "School Violence."

233. See, generally, Walter Mischel, *Introduction to Personality,* 4th ed. (New York: Holt, Rinehart & Winston, 1986).

234. D. A. Andrews and J. Stephen Wormith, "Personality and Crime: Knowledge and Construction in Criminology," *Justice Quarterly* 6 (1989): 289–310; Donald Gibbons, "Comment—Personality and

Crime: Non-Issues, Real Issues, and a Theory and Research Agenda," *Justice Quarterly* (1989): 311–324.

235. Sheldon Glueck and Eleanor Glueck, *Unraveling Juvenile Delinquency* (Cambridge, MA: Harvard University Press, 1950).

236. See, generally, Hans Eysenck, *Personality and Crime* (London: Routledge and Kegan Paul, 1977).

237. Edelyn Verona and Joyce Carbonell, "Female Violence and Personality," *Criminal Justice and Behavior* 27 (2000): 176–195.

238. Hans Eysenck and M. W. Eysenck, *Personality and Individual Differences* (New York: Plenum, 1985).

239. Catrien Bijleveld and Jan Hendriks, "Juvenile Sex Offenders: Differences between Group and Solo Offenders," *Psychology, Crime, and Law* 9 (2003): 237–246.

240. Joshua Miller and Donald Lynam, "Personality and Antisocial Behavior," *Criminology* 39 (2001): 765–799.

241. Ibid., pp. 781–782.

242. David Lykken, "Psychopathy, Sociopathy, and Crime," *Society* 34 (1996): 30–38.

243. See, generally, R. Starke Hathaway and Elio Monachesi, *Analyzing and Predicting Juvenile Delinquency with the MMPI* (Minneapolis: University of Minnesota Press, 1953).

244. R. Starke Hathaway, Elio Monachesi, and Lawrence Young, "Delinquency Rates and Personality," *Journal of Criminal Law, Criminology, and Police Science* 51 (1960): 443–460; Michael Hindelang and Joseph Weis, "Personality and Self-Reported Delinquency: An Application of Cluster Analysis," *Criminology* 10 (1972): 268; Spencer Rathus and Larry Siegel, "Crime and Personality Revisited," *Criminology* 18 (1980): 245–251.

245. See, generally, Edward Megargee, *The California Psychological Inventory Handbook* (San Francisco: Jossey-Bass, 1972).

246. Avshalom Caspi, Terrie Moffitt, Phil Silva, Magda Stouthamer-Loeber, Robert Krueger, and Pamela Schmutte, "Are Some People Crime-Prone? Replications of the Personality–Crime Relationship across Countries, Genders, Races and Methods," *Criminology* 32 (1994): 163–195.

247. Henry Goddard, *Efficiency and Levels of Intelligence* (Princeton, NJ: Princeton University Press, 1920); Edwin Sutherland, "Mental Deficiency and Crime," in *Social*

248. William Healy and Augusta Bronner, *Delinquency and Criminals: Their Making and Unmaking* (New York: Macmillan, 1926).

249. Joseph Lee Rogers, H. Harrington Cleveland, Edwin van den Oord, and David Rowe, "Resolving the Debate over Birth Order, Family Size and Intelligence," *American Psychologist* 55 (2000): 599–612.

250. John Slawson, *The Delinquent Boys* (Boston: Budget Press, 1926).

251. Edwin Sutherland, "Mental Deficiency and Crime," in *Social Attitudes,* ed. Kimball Young (New York: Henry Holt, 1931), chap. 15.

252. Travis Hirschi and Michael Hindelang, "Intelligence and Delinquency: A Revisionist Review," *American Sociological Review* 42 (1977): 471–586.

253. Deborah Denno, "Sociological and Human Developmental Explanations of Crime: Conflict or Consensus," *Criminology* 23 (1985): 711–741; Christine Ward and Richard McFall, "Further Validation of the Problem Inventory for Adolescent Girls: Comparing Caucasian and Black Delinquents and Nondelinquents," *Journal of Consulting and Clinical Psychology* 54 (1986): 732–733; L. Hubble and M. Groff, "Magnitude and Direction of WISC-R Verbal Performance IQ Discrepancies among Adjudicated Male Delinquents," *Journal of Youth and Adolescence* 10 (1981): 179–183; Robert Gordon, "IQ Commensurability of Black–White Differences in Crime and Delinquency." Paper presented at the annual meeting of the American Psychological Association, Washington, DC, August 1986; idem, "Two Illustrations of the IQ-Surrogate Hypothesis: IQ versus Parental Education and Occupational Status in the Race-IQ-Delinquency Model." Paper presented at the annual meeting of the American Society of Criminology, Montreal, Canada, November 1987.

254. Donald Lynam, Terrie Moffitt, and Magda Stouthamer-Loeber, "Explaining the Relation between IQ and Delinquency: Class, Race, Test Motivation, School Failure or Self-Control," *Journal of Abnormal Psychology* 102 (1993): 187–196.

255. Alex Piquero, "Frequency, Specialization, and Violence in Offending Careers," *Journal of Research in Crime and Delinquency* 37 (2000): 392–418.

256. James Q. Wilson and Richard Herrnstein, *Crime and Human Nature* (New York: Simon & Schuster, 1985), p. 148.

257. Ibid., p. 171.

258. Terrie Moffitt, William Gabrielli, Sarnoff Mednick, and Fini Schulsinger, "Socioeconomic Status, IQ, and Delinquency," *Journal of Abnormal Psychology* 90 (1981): 152–156, at 155. For a similar finding, see Hubble and Groff, "Magnitude and Direction of WISC-R Verbal Performance IQ Discrepancies among Adjudicated Male Delinquents."

259. Lorne Yeudall, Delee Fromm-Auch, and Priscilla Davies, "Neuropsychological Impairment of Persistent Delinquency," *Journal of Nervous and Mental Diseases* 170 (1982): 257–265.

260. Hakan Stattin and Ingrid Klackenberg-Larsson, "Early Language and Intelligence Development and Their Relationship to Future Criminal Behavior," *Journal of Abnormal Psychology* 102 (1993): 369–378.

261. H. D. Day, J. M. Franklin, and D. D. Marshall, "Predictors of Aggression in Hospitalized Adolescents," *Journal of Psychology* 132 (1998): 427–435; Scott Menard and Barbara Morse, "A Structuralist Critique of the IQ–Delinquency Hypothesis: Theory and Evidence," *American Journal of Sociology* 89 (1984): 1347–1378; Denno, "Sociological and Human Developmental Explanations of Crime."

262. Neisser, et al., "Intelligence: Knowns and Unknowns," p. 83.

263. Richard Herrnstein and Charles Murray, *The Bell Curve, Intelligence and Class Structure in American Life* (New York: Free Press, 1994).

264. Susan Pease and Craig T. Love, "Optimal Methods and Issues in Nutrition Research in the Correctional Setting," *Nutrition Reviews Supplement* 44 (1986): 122–131.

265. Mark O'Callaghan and Douglas Carroll, "The Role of Psychosurgical Studies in the Control of Antisocial Behavior," in *The Causes of Crime: New Biological Approaches,* ed. Sarnoff Mednick, Terrie Moffitt, and Susan Stack (Cambridge: Cambridge University Press, 1987), pp. 312–328.

266. Reiss and Roth, *Understanding and Preventing Violence,* p. 389.

267. Cirillo, Pruitt, Colwell, Kingery, Hurley, and Ballard, "School Violence."

CHAPTER 6

© Keith Dannemiller / Corbis

Teen gangs have become an ever-present fixture of the American urban experience. The latest national youth gang survey estimates that youth gangs are active in more than 2,300 cities with a population of 2,500 or more and in more than 550 rural/suburban jurisdictions. More than 730,000 kids are active gang members in 21,500 gangs.[1] While gang activity is most prevalent in the largest U.S. cities (population over 100,000)—over 90 percent reported gang activity in each year between 1996 and 2003—more than 70 percent of smaller cities with populations of between 50,000 to 100,000 also experienced gang activity.[2] Gang members are heavily armed, dangerous, and more violent than nonmembers. They are about ten times more likely to carry handguns than non-gang members, and gun-toting gang members commit about ten times more violent crimes than nonmembers; gang homicides seem to be on an upswing. Nowhere is the gang problem more serious than in Los Angeles, where a single gang can have up to 20,000 members.

To criminologists it comes as no surprise that gangs develop in poor, deteriorated urban neighborhoods. Many kids in these areas grow up hopeless and alienated, believing that they have little chance of being part of the American Dream.[3] Joining a gang at least holds the promise of economic rewards and status enhancements that the conventional world simply cannot provide.

SOCIAL STRUCTURE THEORIES

CHAPTER OBJECTIVES

1. Be familiar with the concept of social structure
2. Have knowledge of the socioeconomic structure of American society
3. Be able to discuss the concept of social disorganization
4. Be familiar with the works of Shaw and McKay
5. Know the various elements of ecological theory
6. Be able to discuss the association between collective efficacy and crime
7. Know what is meant by the term *anomie*
8. Be familiar with the concept of strain
9. Understand the concept of cultural deviance

This association between social conditions and crime is not lost on criminologists, many of whom conclude that criminals are indigent and desperate rather than abnormal or evil. Raised in deteriorated parts of town, they lack the social support and economic resources available to more affluent members of society. To understand criminal behavior, we must analyze the influence of these destructive social forces on human behavior. According to this view, it is *social forces*—and not individual traits—that cause crime.

The social environment and its influence on human behavior has been the primary focus of criminology since the early twentieth century, when sociologists Robert Ezra Park (1864–1944), Ernest W. Burgess (1886–1966), Louis Wirth (1897–1952), and their colleagues were teaching and conducting criminological research in the sociology department at the University of Chicago. Their work on the social ecology of the city inspired a generation of scholars to conclude that social forces operating in urban areas create criminal interactions. This perspective came to be known as the Chicago School.

In 1915, Robert Ezra Park called for anthropological methods of description and observation to be applied to urban life.[4] He was concerned with how neighborhood structure developed, how isolated pockets of poverty formed, and what social policies could be used to alleviate urban problems. Later, Park, with Ernest Burgess, studied the social ecology of the city and found that some neighborhoods formed so-called natural areas of wealth and affluence, while others suffered poverty and disintegration.[5] Regardless of their race, religion, or ethnicity, the everyday behavior of people living in these areas was controlled by the social and ecological climate.

Over the next twenty years, Chicago School sociologists carried out an ambitious program of research and scholarship on urban topics, including criminal behavior patterns. Harvey Zorbaugh's *The Gold Coast and the Slum*,[6] Frederick Thrasher's *The Gang*,[7] and Louis Wirth's *The Ghetto*[8] are classic examples of objective, highly descriptive accounts of urban life. Their influence was such that most criminologists have been trained in sociology, and criminology courses are routinely taught in departments of sociology. What is their vision and how do they connect criminality with a person's place in the social structure?

||||||| CONNECTIONS |||||||

Concern about the ecological distribution of crime, the effect of social change, and the interactive nature of crime itself has made sociology the foundation of modern criminology. This chapter reviews sociological theories that emphasize the relationship between social status and criminal behavior. In Chapter 7 the focus shifts to theories that emphasize socialization and its influence on crime and deviance; Chapter 8 covers theories based on the concept of social conflict.

SOCIOECONOMIC STRUCTURE AND CRIME

People in the United States live in a **stratified society.** Social strata are created by the unequal distribution of wealth, power, and prestige. Social classes are segments of the population whose members have a relatively similar portion of desirable things and who share attitudes, values, norms, and an identifiable lifestyle. In U.S. society, it is common to identify people as upper-, middle-, and lower-class citizens, with a broad range of economic variations existing within each group. The upper-upper class is reserved for a small number of exceptionally well-to-do families who maintain enormous financial and social resources. In contrast, the indigent have scant, if any, resources and suffer socially and economically as a result. Today, the poorest fifth (20 percent) of all U.S. households receive only 3.5 percent of the country's aggregate income, the smallest share ever. In contrast, the top fifth (20 percent) of households receive more than 50 percent of all income, a record high; the top 5 percent collect more than 20 percent of all household income, the most in history.[9] Nor is the wealth concentration unique to the United States; it is a worldwide phenomenon. According to the most recent World Wealth Report, there are about 8 million people considered "high net worth" (those with more than $1 million in assets excluding their primary residence) in the world today; collectively, they are worth more than $30.8 trillion, and their numbers are steadily growing.[10]

> To read the **World Wealth Report,** go to http:// www .us.capgemini.com/DownloadLibrary/requestfile .asp?ID=468. For an up-to-date list of web links, go to http: //cj.wadsworth.com/siegel_crimtpt9e.

In contrast, the indigent have scant, if any, resources and suffer socially and economically as a result. The most recent federal data indicates that poverty rose and income levels have been declining; more than 35 million Americans are considered to be living in poverty (Figure 6.1).

Lower-class areas are scenes of inadequate housing and healthcare, disrupted family lives, underemployment, and despair. Members of the lower class also suffer in other ways. They are more prone to depression, less likely to have achievement motivation, and less likely to put off immediate gratification for future gain. For example, they may be less willing to stay in school because the rewards for educational achievement are in the distant future.

Members of the lower class are constantly bombarded by the media with advertisements linking material possessions to self-worth, but they are often unable to attain desired goods and services through conventional means. Though they are members of a society that extols material success above any other, they are unable to satisfactorily compete for such success with members of the upper classes. As a result, they may turn to illegal solutions to their economic plight: They may deal drugs for profit, steal cars and sell them to "chop shops," or commit armed robberies for desperately needed funds. They may become so depressed that they take alcohol and drugs as a form of self-tranquilization, and because of their poverty, they may acquire the drugs and alcohol through illegal channels.

Read the following article for an analysis of poverty research: Howard Glennerster, "United States Poverty Studies and Poverty Measurement: The Past Twenty-Five Years," *Social Service Review* 76 (March 2002): 83–107.

Child Poverty

The timing of poverty also seems to be relevant. Findings suggest that poverty during early childhood may have a more severe impact on behavior than poverty during adolescence and adulthood.[11] This is particularly important today because, as Figure 6.2 shows, children have a higher poverty rate than any other age group.

Children are hit especially hard by poverty. Hundreds of studies have documented the association between family poverty and children's health, achievement, and behavior impairments.[12] Children who grow up in low-income homes are less likely to achieve in school and are less likely to complete their schooling than children with more affluent parents.[13] Poor children are also more likely to suffer from health problems and to receive inadequate healthcare. The number of U.S. children covered by health insurance is declining and will continue to do so for the foreseeable future.[14] Without health benefits or the means to afford medical care, these children are likely to have health problems that impede their long-term development. Children who live in extreme poverty or who remain poor for multiple years appear to suffer the worst outcomes.

Kids Count, a project of the Annie E. Casey Foundation, is a national and state-by-state effort to track the relative status of children in the United States. Go to their website at http://www.aecf.org/kidscount. For an up-to-date list of web links, go to http://cj.wadsworth.com/siegel_crimtpt9e.

Besides their increased chance of physical illness, poor children are much more likely than wealthy children to suffer various social and physical ills, ranging from low birth weight to a limited chance of earning a college degree. Many live in substandard housing—high-rise, multiple-family

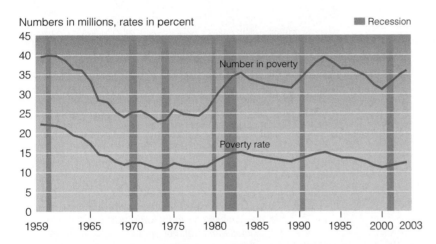

Numbers in millions, rates in percent · Recession

FIGURE 6.1

Number in Poverty and Poverty Rates, 1959–2003

The number of people living in poverty in 2003—35.9 million people—was 1.3 million more than in 2002. This increase led to a poverty rate in 2003 that, at 12.5 percent, is 1.2 percentage points higher than its recent low point of 11.3 percent in 2000.

Note: The data points are placed at the midpoints of the respective years.

Source: U.S. Census Bureau, Current Population Survey (CPS), 2004 Annual Social and Economic Supplement (ASEC). http://www.census.gov/hhes/poverty/poverty03/pov03fig03.pdf.

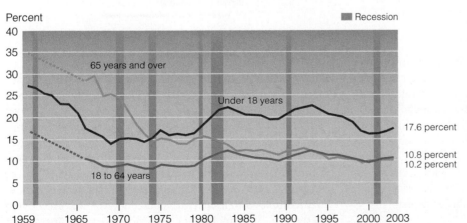

Percent · Recession

FIGURE 6.2

Poverty Rates by Age, 1959–2003

Note: The data points represent the midpoints of the respective years. Data for people 18 to 64 and 65 and older are not available from 1960 to 1965.

Source: U.S. Census Bureau, Current Population Survey (CPS), 2004 Annual Social and Economic Supplement (ASEC). http://www.census.gov/hhes/poverty/poverty03/pov03fig04.pdf

dwellings—which can have a negative influence on their long-term psychological health.[15] Adolescents in the worst neighborhoods share the greatest risk of dropping out of school and becoming teenage parents.

About 25 percent of children under age 6 now live in poverty, a frightening number considering America's self-image as the richest country on earth. There is a distinct racial division in child poverty: Only 6 percent of white children can be described as extremely poor, but about 50 percent of young black children live in extreme poverty.[16] Children who live in extreme poverty or who remain poor for multiple years appear to suffer the worst outcomes. In sum, the general consensus is that poverty during early childhood may have a more significant impact on children than poverty during adolescence or teen years.[17]

Did you know that although income per capita in the United States is among the world's highest, so is its rate of child poverty? To read more about this, use "poverty" and "children" as key words with InfoTrac College Edition.

The Underclass

In 1966, sociologist Oscar Lewis argued that the crushing lifestyle of slum areas produces a **culture of poverty**, which is passed from one generation to the next.[18] Apathy, cynicism, helplessness, and mistrust of social institutions such as schools, government agencies, and the police mark the culture of poverty. This mistrust prevents members of the lower class from taking advantage of the meager opportunities available to them. Lewis's work was the first of a group that described the plight of **at-risk** children and adults. In 1970, Swedish economist Gunnar Myrdal described a worldwide **underclass** that was cut off from society, its members lacking the education and skills needed to be effectively in demand in modern society.[19]

To read about the extent of poverty in the United States and its impact on the nation's poorest citizens, read: John A. Bishop, John P. Formby, and Buhong Zheng, "Extent of Material Hardship and Poverty in the United States: Comment," *Review of Social Economy* 57 (September 1999): 388.

Economic disparity will continually haunt members of the underclass and their children over the course of their life span. Even if they value education and other middle-class norms, their desperate life circumstances (including high unemployment and nontraditional family structures) may prevent them from developing the skills, habits, and lifestyles that lead first to educational success and later to success in the workplace.[20] Their ability to maintain social ties in the neighborhood become attenuated, further weakening a neighborhood's cohesiveness and its ability to regulate the behavior of its citizens.[21]

© William F. Campbell / Time Life Pictures / Getty Images

Members of the underclass are truly disadvantaged. They are socially isolated people who occupy the bottom rung of the social ladder. They are often forced to live in areas in which the basic institutions of society—family, school, housing—have declined. Their life chances are significantly compromised.

To read **conservative social scientists' take on the underclass**, go to http://www.aei.org/docLib/20040311_book268text.pdf. For an up-to-date list of web links, go to http://cj.wadsworth.com/siegel_crimtpt9e.

Minority Group Poverty

The burdens of underclass life are felt most acutely by minority group members. While whites use their economic, social, and political advantages to live in sheltered gated communities protected by security guards and police, minorities are denied similar protections and privileges.[22] Although poverty has actually been declining faster among minorities than among whites, more than 20 percent of African Americans and Latino Americans still live in poverty, compared to less than 10 percent of whites. According to the U.S. Census Bureau, the median family income of

Latino and African Americans is only two-thirds that of whites.[23]

The rates of child poverty in the United States vary significantly by race and ethnicity. Latino and African American children are more than twice as likely to be poor as Asian and white children. A recent study by the UCLA Center for Health Policy Research highlights some of the fallout from these differences in poverty levels. After examining the health, access to healthcare, and well-being of young children in California, the UCLA researchers found that Latino children and those in low-income families are four times less likely to have health insurance as other kids. The study also found large ethnic disparities in the time preschool-age children spend in structured preschool settings. Clearly Latino children in California begin life with significant social and educational deficits.[24]

Minority group problems are exacerbated by ineffective efforts to integrate communities, resulting in neighborhoods that are all black, all white, all Latino, and so on. There is also the perception in minority communities that the police are overzealous in their control of minority neighborhoods.[25] Feelings of injustice are not allayed by the fact that in some neighborhoods a significant portion—up to half—of all minority males are under the control of the criminal justice system. The costs of crime, such as paying for lawyers and court costs, perpetuate poverty by depriving families and children of this money.[26]

According to this view, interracial crime rate differentials can be explained by differences in standard of living. If interracial economic disparity would end, so too might differences in the crime rate.[27] The issue of minority poverty is explored further in the Race, Culture, and Gender and Criminology feature "Bridging the Racial Divide."

www The **Northwestern University/University of Chicago Joint Center for Poverty Research** examines what it means to be poor and live in America: http://www.jcpr.org/. For an up-to-date list of web links, go to http://cj.wadsworth.com/siegel_crimtpt9e.

SOCIAL STRUCTURE THEORIES

The problems caused by poverty and income inequality are not lost on criminologists. They recognize that the various sources of crime data show that crime rates are highest in neighborhoods characterized by poverty and social disorder. Lower-class crime is often the violent, destructive product of youth gangs and marginally and underemployed young adults. Underemployment means that many working adults earn relatively low wages and have few benefits such as health insurance and retirement plans. Their ability to accumulate capital for home ownership is restricted and so, consequently, is their stake in society.

Although members of the middle and upper classes also engage in crime, the crimes of the upper classes are relatively lower in frequency, seriousness, and danger to the general public. The real crime problem is essentially a lower-class phenomenon, which breeds criminal behavior that begins in youth and continues into young adulthood. To explain this phenomenon, criminologists have formulated **social structure theories** that maintain that the social and economic forces operating in deteriorated lower-class areas are the key determinants of criminal behavior patterns.

Most social structure theories focus on children's law-violating behavior. They suggest that the social forces that cause crime begin to affect people while they are relatively young and continue to influence them throughout their lives. Though not all youthful offenders become adult criminals, many begin their training and learn criminal values as members of youth gangs and groups.

Social structure theorists challenge those who suggest that crime is an expression of some personal trait or individual choice. They argue that people living in equivalent social environments tend to behave in a similar, predictable fashion. If the environment did not influence human behavior, then crime rates would be distributed equally across the social structure, which they are not.[28] Because crime rates are higher in lower-class urban centers than in middle-class suburbs, social forces must be operating in urban slums that influence or control behavior.[29]

There are three independent yet overlapping branches within the social structure perspective—social disorganization, strain theory, and cultural deviance theory (outlined in Figure 6.3).

Social disorganization theory focuses on the conditions within the urban environment that affect crime rates. A disorganized area is one in which institutions of social control—such as the family, commercial establishments, and schools—have broken down and can no longer carry out their expected or stated functions. Indicators of social disorganization include high unemployment, school dropout rates, deteriorated housing, low income levels, and large numbers of single-parent households. Residents in these areas experience conflict and despair, and, as a result, antisocial behavior flourishes.

Strain theory holds that crime is a function of the conflict between the goals people have and the means they can use to legally obtain them. Although social and economic goals are common to people in all economic strata, strain theorists argue that the ability to obtain these goals is class dependent. Most people in the United States desire wealth, material possessions, power, prestige, and other life comforts. Members of the lower class are unable to achieve these symbols of success through conventional means. Consequently, they feel anger, frustration, and resentment, which is referred to as **strain**. Lower-class citizens can either accept their condition and live out their days as socially responsible, if unrewarded, citizens, or they can choose an alternative means of achieving success, such as theft, violence, or drug trafficking.

Bridging the Racial Divide

William Julius Wilson, one of the nation's most prominent sociologists, has produced an impressive body of work that details racial problems and racial politics in American society. In 1987, he provided a description of the plight of the lowest levels of the underclass, which he labeled the **truly disadvantaged**. Wilson portrayed members of this group as socially isolated people who dwell in urban inner cities, occupy the bottom rung of the social ladder, and are the victims of discrimination. They live in areas in which the basic institutions of society—family, school, housing—have long since declined. Their decline triggers similar breakdowns in the strengths of inner-city areas, including the loss of community cohesion and the ability of people living in the area to control the flow of drugs and criminal activity. For example, in a more affluent area, neighbors might complain to parents that their children were acting out. In distressed areas, this element of informal social control may be absent because parents are under stress or all too often absent. These effects magnify the isolation of the underclass from mainstream society and promote a ghetto culture and behavior.

Because the truly disadvantaged rarely come into contact with the actual source of their oppression, they direct their anger and aggression at those with whom they are in close and intimate contact, such as neighbors, businesspeople, and landlords. Members of this group, plagued by under- or unemployment, begin to lose self-confidence, a feeling supported by the plight of kin and friendship groups who also experience extreme economic marginality. Self-doubt is a neighborhood norm, overwhelming those forced to live in areas of concentrated poverty.

In his important book *When Work Disappears,* Wilson assesses the effect of joblessness and underemployment on residents in poor neighborhoods on Chicago's south side. He argues that for the first time in the twentieth century, most adults in inner-city ghetto neighborhoods are not working during a typical week. He finds that inner-city life is only marginally affected by the surge in the nation's economy, which has been brought about by new industrial growth connected with technological development. Poverty in these inner-city areas is eternal and unchanging and, if anything, worsening as residents are further shut out of the economic mainstream.

Wilson focuses on the plight of the African American community, which had enjoyed periods of relative prosperity in the 1950s and 1960s. He suggests that as difficult as life was in the 1940s and 1950s for African Americans, they at least had a reasonable hope of steady work. Now, because of the globalization of the economy, those opportunities have evaporated. Though in the past racial segregation had limited opportunity, growth in the manufacturing sector fueled upward mobility and provided the foundation of today's African American middle class. Those opportunities no longer exist as manufacturing plants have moved to inaccessible rural and overseas locations where the cost of doing business is lower. With manufacturing opportunities all but obsolete in the United States, service and retail establishments, which depend on blue-collar spending, have similarly disappeared, leaving behind an economy based on welfare and government supports. In less than twenty years, formerly active African American communities have become crime-infested slums.

The hardships faced by residents in Chicago's south side are not unique to that community. Beyond sustaining inner-city poverty, the absence of employment opportunities has torn at the social fabric of the nation's inner-city neighborhoods. Work helps socialize young people

---

Cultural deviance theory, the third variation of structural theory, combines elements of both strain and social disorganization. According to this view, because of strain and social isolation, a unique lower-class culture develops in disorganized neighborhoods. Each independent **subculture** maintains a unique set of values and beliefs that is in conflict with conventional social norms. Criminal behavior is an expression of conformity to lower-class subcultural values and traditions and not a rebellion from conventional society. Subcultural values are handed down from one generation to the next in a process called **cultural transmission.**

Although each of these theories is distinct in critical aspects, each approach has at its core the view that socially isolated people, living in disorganized neighborhoods, are the ones most likely to experience crime-producing social forces. Each branch of social structure theory will now be discussed in some detail.

▮ SOCIAL DISORGANIZATION THEORIES

Social disorganization theory links crime rates to neighborhood ecological characteristics. Crime rates are elevated in highly transient, mixed-use (where residential and commercial property exist side by side) and/or changing neighborhoods (those

into the wider society, instilling in them such desirable values as hard work, caring, and respect for others. When work becomes scarce, however, the discipline and structure it provides are absent. Community-wide underemployment destroys social cohesion, increasing the presence of neighborhood social problems ranging from drug use to educational failure. Schools in these areas are unable to teach basic skills, and because desirable employment is lacking, there are few adults to serve as role models. In contrast to more affluent suburban households where daily life is organized around job and career demands, children in inner-city areas are not socialized in the workings of the mainstream economy.

In *The Bridge over the Racial Divide: Rising Inequality and Coalition Politics,* Wilson expands on his views of race in contemporary society. He argues that despite economic gains, there is a growing inequality in American society, and ordinary families, of all races and ethnic origins, are suffering. Whites, Latinos, African Americans, Asians, and Native Americans must therefore begin to put aside their differences and concentrate more on what they have in common—their aspirations, problems, and hopes. There needs to be mutual cooperation across racial lines.

One reason for this set of mutual problems is that the government tends to aggravate rather than ease the financial stress being placed on ordinary families. Monetary policy, trade policy, and tax policy are harmful to working-class families. A multiracial citizen's coalition could pressure national public officials to focus on the interests of ordinary people. As long as middle- and working-class groups are fragmented along racial lines, such pressure is impossible.

Wilson finds that racism is becoming more subtle and harder to detect. Whites believe that blacks are responsible for their inferior economic status because of their cultural traits. Because even affluent whites fear corporate downsizing, they are unwilling to vote for governmental assistance to the poor. Whites are continuing to be suburban dwellers, further isolating poor minorities in central cities and making their problems distant and unimportant. He continues to believe that the changing marketplace, with its reliance on sophisticated computer technologies, is continually decreasing demand for low-skilled workers, which impacts African Americans more negatively than other better educated and affluent groups.

Wilson argues for a cross-race, class-based alliance of working- and middle-class Americans to pursue policies that will benefit them rather than the affluent. These include full employment, programs to help families and workers in their private lives, and a reconstructed "affirmative opportunity" program that benefits African Americans without antagonizing whites.

Critical Thinking

1. Is it unrealistic to assume that a government-sponsored public works program can provide needed jobs in this era of budget cutbacks?

2. What are some of the hidden costs of unemployment in a community setting?

3. How would a biocriminologist explain Wilson's findings?

 InfoTrac College Edition Research

For more on Wilson's view of poverty, unemployment, and crime, check out: Gunnar Almgren, Avery Guest, George Immerwahr, and Michael Spittel, "Joblessness, Family Disruption, and Violent Death in Chicago, 1970–90," *Social Forces* 76 (June 1998): 1,465; William Julius Wilson, "Inner-City Dislocations," *Society* 35 (January-February 1998): 270.

Sources: William Julius Wilson, *The Truly Disadvantaged* (Chicago: University of Chicago Press, 1987); *When Work Disappears, The World of the Urban Poor* (New York: Alfred Knopf, 1996); *The Bridge over the Racial Divide: Rising Inequality and Coalition Politics* (Wildavsky Forum Series, 2) (Berkeley: University of California Press, 1999).

---

in which the fabric of social life has become frayed). These localities are unable to provide essential services, such as education, healthcare, and proper housing and, as a result, experience significant levels of unemployment, single-parent families, and families on welfare and Aid to Dependent Children (ADC).

Residents in these crime-ridden neighborhoods want to leave the community at the earliest opportunity. Because they want out, they become uninterested in community matters. The sources of social control common to most neighborhoods—the family, school, business community, social service agencies—become weak and disorganized. Personal relationships are strained because neighbors are constantly moving. Constant resident turnover further weakens communications and blocks any attempt at solving neighborhood problems or establishing common goals.[30]

The problems encountered in such disorganized areas have been described as an "epidemic" that spreads like a contagious disease, destroying the inner workings that enable neighborhoods to survive; they become "hollowed out."[31] As neighborhood quality decreases, the probability that residents will develop problems sharply increases. Crime and violence may also take the form of a "slow epidemic," with periods of onset, peak, and decline. Violence and crime then spread to surrounding areas in a pattern similar to a contagious disease epidemic.[32] The elements of social disorganization theory are shown in Figure 6.4.

FIGURE 6.3

The Three Branches of Social Structure Theory

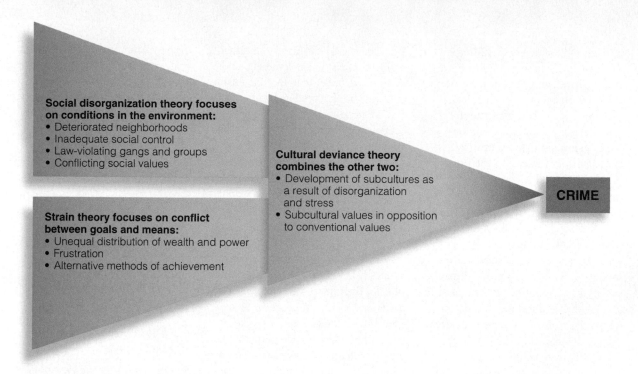

Social disorganization theory focuses on conditions in the environment:
- Deteriorated neighborhoods
- Inadequate social control
- Law-violating gangs and groups
- Conflicting social values

Strain theory focuses on conflict between goals and means:
- Unequal distribution of wealth and power
- Frustration
- Alternative methods of achievement

Cultural deviance theory combines the other two:
- Development of subcultures as a result of disorganization and stress
- Subcultural values in opposition to conventional values

CRIME

Foundations of Social Disorganization Theory

Social disorganization theory was first popularized by the work of two Chicago sociologists, Clifford R. Shaw and Henry D. McKay, who linked life in disorganized, transitional urban areas to neighborhood crime rates. Shaw and McKay began their pioneering work on crime in Chicago during the early 1920s while working as researchers for a state-supported social service agency.[33] They were heavily influenced by Chicago School sociologists Ernest Burgess and Robert Park, who had pioneered the ecological analysis of urban life.

Shaw and McKay began their analysis during a period in the city's history that was fairly typical of the transition that was taking place in many other urban areas. Chicago had experienced a mid-nineteenth-century population expansion, fueled by a dramatic influx of foreign-born immigrants and, later, migrating southern families. Congregating in the central city, the newcomers occupied the oldest housing areas and therefore faced numerous health and environmental hazards.

Sections of the city started to physically deteriorate. This condition prompted the city's wealthy, established citizens to become concerned about the moral fabric of Chicago society. The belief was widespread that immigrants from Europe and the rural South were crime prone and morally dissolute. In fact, local groups were created with the very purpose of "saving" the children of poor families from moral decadence.[34] It was popular to view crime as the property of inferior racial and ethnic groups.

TRANSITIONAL NEIGHBORHOODS Shaw and McKay explained crime and delinquency within the context of the changing urban environment and ecological development of the city. They saw that Chicago had developed into distinct neighborhoods (natural areas), some affluent and others wracked by extreme poverty. These poverty-ridden, **transitional neighborhoods** suffered high rates of population turnover and were incapable of inducing residents to remain and defend the neighborhoods against criminal groups.

Low rents in these areas attracted groups with different racial and ethnic backgrounds. Newly arrived immigrants from Europe and the South congregated in these transitional neighborhoods. Their children were torn between assimilating into a new culture and abiding by the traditional values of their parents. They soon found that informal social control mechanisms that had restrained behavior in the "old country" or rural areas were disrupted. These urban areas were believed to be the spawning grounds of young criminals.

In transitional areas, successive changes in the population composition, disintegration of traditional cultures, diffusion of divergent cultural standards, and gradual industrialization of the area result in dissolution of neighborhood culture and organization. The continuity of conventional neighborhood traditions and institutions is broken, leaving children feeling displaced and without a strong or definitive set of values.

FIGURE 6.4

Social Disorganization Theory

Poverty
- Development of isolated lower-class areas
- Lack of conventional social opportunities
- Racial and ethnic discrimination

∨

Social disorganization
- Breakdown of social institutions and organizations such as school and family
- Lack of informal social control

∨

Breakdown of social control
- Development of gangs, groups
- Peer group replaces family and social institutions

∨

Criminal areas
- Neighborhood becomes crime prone
- Stable pockets of crime develop
- Lack of external support and investment

∨

Cultural transmission
Adults pass norms (focal concerns) to younger generation, creating stable lower-class culture

∨

Criminal careers
Most youths age out of delinquency, marry, and raise families, but some remain in life of crime

---

CONCENTRIC ZONES Shaw and McKay identified the areas in Chicago that had excessive crime rates. Using a model of analysis pioneered by Ernest Burgess, they noted that distinct ecological areas had developed in the city, comprising a series of five concentric circles, or zones, and that there were stable and significant differences in interzone crime rates (Figure 6.5). The areas of heaviest concentration of crime appeared to be the transitional inner-city zones, where large numbers of foreign-born citizens had recently settled.[35] The zones farthest from the city's center had correspondingly lower crime rates.

Analysis of these data indicated a surprisingly stable pattern of criminal activity in the various ecological zones over a 65-year period. Shaw and McKay concluded that, in the transitional neighborhoods, multiple cultures and diverse values, both conventional and deviant, coexist. Children growing up in the street culture often find that adults who have adopted a deviant lifestyle are the most financially successful people in the neighborhood: for example,

the gambler, the pimp, or the drug dealer. Required to choose between conventional and deviant lifestyles, many inner-city kids see the value in opting for the latter. They join other like-minded youths and form law-violating gangs and cliques. The development of teenage law-violating groups is an essential element of youthful misbehavior in slum areas. The values that inner-city youths adopt are often in conflict with existing middle-class norms, which demand strict obedience to the legal code. Consequently, a value conflict occurs that sets the delinquent youth and his or her peer group even further apart from conventional society. The result is a more solid embrace of deviant goals and behavior. To justify their choice of goals, these youths seek support by recruiting new members and passing on the delinquent tradition.

Shaw and McKay's statistical analysis confirmed their theoretical suspicions. Even though crime rates changed, they found that the highest rates were always in Zones I and II (central city and a transitional area). The areas with the highest crime rates retained high rates even when their ethnic composition changed (in the areas Shaw and McKay examined, from German and Irish to Italian and Polish).[36]

THE LEGACY OF SHAW AND MCKAY Social disorganization concepts articulated by Shaw and McKay have remained prominent within criminology for more than seventy-five years. While cultural and social conditions have changed (i.e., we live today in a much more heterogeneous, mobile society than they did), the most important of Shaw and McKay's findings—crime rates correspond to neighborhood structure—still holds up.[37]

Shaw and McKay determined that crime is a function of the destructive social forces operating in lower-class urban neighborhoods. Neighborhood conditions are the cause of crime; criminals are not biologically inferior, intellectually impaired, or psychologically damaged. Their research supported their belief that crime is a constant fixture in areas of poverty regardless of the racial or ethnic identity of its residents. Because the basis of their theory is that neighborhood disintegration and inner-city conditions are the primary causes of criminal behavior, Shaw and McKay paved the way for the many community action and treatment programs developed in the last half-century.

Another important feature of Shaw and McKay's work is that it depicts both adult criminality and delinquent gang membership as normal responses to the adverse social conditions in urban areas. Their findings mirror Émile Durkheim's concept that crime is a "normal" response to societal pressures.

Despite these noteworthy achievements, the validity of Shaw and McKay's findings has been challenged. Some have faulted their assumption that neighborhoods are essentially stable, and others have found their definition of social disorganization confusing.[38] The most important criticism, however, concerns their use of police records to calculate neighborhood crime rates. A zone's high crime rate may be a function of the level of local police surveillance and not

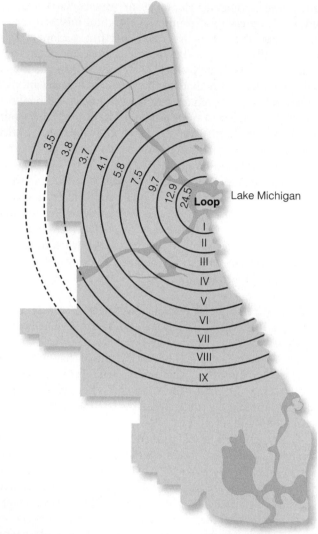

Note: Arabic numerals represent the rate of male delinquency.

interzone crime rate differences. Numerous studies indicate that police use extensive discretion when arresting people and that social status is one factor that influences their decisions.[39] It is possible that people in middle-class neighborhoods commit many criminal acts that never show up in official statistics, whereas people in lower-class areas face a far greater chance of arrest and court adjudication.[40] The relationship between ecology and crime rates, therefore, may reflect police behavior more than criminal behavior.

These criticisms aside, Shaw and McKay's theory provides a valuable contribution to our understanding of the causes of criminal behavior. By introducing a new variable—the ecology of the city—to the study of crime, they paved the way for a whole generation of criminologists to focus on the social influences of criminal and delinquent behavior.

The Social Ecology School

Beginning in the 1980s, a group of criminologists began to study the ecological conditions that support criminality, which changed the direction of social disorganization theory.[41] Contemporary **social ecologists** developed a "purer" form of structural theory that emphasizes the association of community deterioration and economic decline to criminality but places less importance on the value conflict that was a core of Shaw and McKay's vision. In the following sections, some of the more recent social ecological research is discussed in detail.

COMMUNITY DETERIORATION Social ecologists have focused their attention on the association between crime rates and community deterioration: disorder, poverty, alienation, disassociation, and fear of crime.[42] They find that neighborhoods with a high percentage of deserted houses and apartments experience high crime rates; abandoned buildings serve as a "magnet for crime."[43] Areas in which houses are in poor repair, boarded-up and burned out, and whose owners are best described as "slumlords" are also the location of the highest violence rates and gun crime.[44] These are neighborhoods in which retail establishments often go bankrupt, are abandoned, and deteriorate physically.[45]

The concept of **community deterioration and crime** was the subject of a famous *Atlantic Magazine* article titled "Broken Windows": http://www.theatlantic.com/politics/crime. For an up-to-date list of web links, go to http://cj.wadsworth.com/siegel_crimtpt9e.

Poverty becomes consolidated in deteriorated areas as working- and middle-class families flee, and only the most disadvantaged populations remain in inner-city poverty areas.[46] As the working and middle classes move out, they take with them their financial and institutional resources and support. Businesses are disinclined to locate in poverty areas; banks become reluctant to lend money for new housing or businesses.[47] People living in areas of poverty concentration experience significant income and wealth disparities, nonexistent employment opportunities, inferior housing, and unequal access to healthcare; not surprisingly, they also experience high rates of crime.[48]

Minority group members living in these areas are hit particularly hard. They are also exposed to race-based disparity such as income inequality and institutional racism.[49] Black crime rates, more so than white, seem to be influenced by the shift of high-paid manufacturing jobs overseas and their replacement with lower-paid service sector jobs. Both African American men and women seem less able to prosper in a service economy than white men and women, and the resulting economic disadvantage translates into increased levels of violence over time.[50] Some minority group members who suffer chronic financial disadvantage may turn to armed robbery as a means of economic survival. Robberies often go awry, leading to gun play and death. This scenario

One of the areas that current social ecologists study is the deterioration of communities. Neighborhoods with a high percentage of deserted houses and apartments experience high crime rates; abandoned buildings serve as a "magnet for crime." Areas in which houses are in poor repair, boarded-up and burned out, and whose owners are best described as "slumlords" are also the location of the highest violence rates and gun crime. These are neighborhoods in which retail establishments often go bankrupt, are abandoned, and deteriorate physically.

may lead to a rise in interracial violence because robbery victims may be white. However, what appear to be racially motivated crimes may be more a function of economic factors (the shift of jobs overseas) rather than interracial hate or antagonism.[51] The Criminological Enterprise feature "Random Family" focuses on the influence of neighborhood poverty on behavior and lifestyle.

CHRONIC UNEMPLOYMENT As you may recall (Chapter 2), the relationship between unemployment and crime is still unsettled: Aggregate crime rates and aggregate unemployment rates seem weakly related. In other words, crime rates sometimes rise during periods of economic prosperity and fall during periods of economic decline.[52] Yet, as Shaw and McKay claimed, neighborhoods that experience chronic unemployment also encounter social disorganization and crime.[53] Even though short-term economic trends may have

little effect on crime, it is possible that long-term unemployment rates will eventually produce higher levels of antisocial behaviors.[54] Violent crime rates are associated with such variables as the percentage of the neighborhood living below the poverty line, the lack of mortgage investment in a neighborhood, the unemployment rate, and the influx of new immigrants; these factors are usually found in disorganized areas.[55] Though female crime rates may be lower than male rates, women living in deteriorated areas also feel the effects of poverty.[56]

Unemployment destabilizes households, and unstable families are the ones most likely to produce children who put a premium on violence and aggression as a means of dealing with limited opportunity. This lack of opportunity perpetuates higher crime rates, especially when large groups or cohorts of people of the same age compete for relatively scant resources.[57]

Limited employment opportunities also reduce the stabilizing influence of parents and other adults, who may have once been able to counteract the allure of youth gangs. Sociologist Elijah Anderson's analysis of Philadelphia neighborhood life found that "old heads" (respected neighborhood residents) who at one time played an important role in socializing youth have been displaced by younger street hustlers and drug dealers. While the old heads complain that these newcomers may not have "earned" or "worked for" their fortune in the "old-fashioned way," the old heads admire and envy these kids whose gold chains and luxury cars advertise their wealth amid poverty.[58] The old heads may admire the fruits of crime, but they disdain the violent manner in which it is acquired.

COMMUNITY FEAR In neighborhoods where people help one another, residents are less likely to fear crime and be afraid of becoming a crime victim.[59] In contrast, those living in disorganized neighborhoods suffer social and physical **incivilities**—rowdy youth, trash and litter, graffiti, abandoned storefronts, burned-out buildings, littered lots, strangers, drunks, vagabonds, loiterers, prostitutes, noise, congestion, angry words, dirt, and stench. They become afraid when they see neighborhood kids hanging out in community parks and playgrounds or when gangs proliferate in the neighborhood.[60]

Fear is based on experience. Residents who have already been victimized are more fearful of the future than those who have escaped crime.[61] People become afraid when they are approached by someone in the neighborhood selling drugs. They may fear that their children will also be approached and seduced into the drug life.[62] The presence of such incivilities, especially when accompanied by relatively high crime rates, convinces residents that their neighborhood is dangerous; becoming a crime victim seems inevitable.[63]

Fear can become contagious. People tell others when they have been victimized, spreading the word that the neighborhood is getting dangerous and that the chances of future victimization are high.[64] They dread leaving their homes at night and withdraw from community life.

Random Family

In *Random Family,* Adrian Nicole LeBlanc, a talented journalist, tells of the ten years she spent tracing the lives of a Puerto Rican family living in the South Bronx—a journey that she began in the mid-1980s at the height of the crack epidemic and concluded in 2001.

Her book centers around the lives of Latino women who are forced to contend with the vicissitudes and hardships of an urban culture mired in poverty. There are two matriarchs, Foxy and Lourdes, beaten down by their environment, who become grandmothers by the age of 35. Foxy's daughter Coco is in turn tough and big-hearted, ready to defend herself with a hidden razorblade but also willing to wait while the man she loves serves a prison sentence. Coco is smitten with Cesar, Lourdes's macho son who is an aspiring street hood. Cesar hops from jail to jail, never able to control his behavior or to reign in his macho-fueled temper. At last, he is convicted of manslaughter. Lourdes's daughter Jessica is the neighborhood beauty who can get any man she wants. Her downfall begins when she is set up on a blind date with "Boy George," a big-time dope dealer who reads *Yachting* magazine and makes over $100,000 a week dealing heroin by the time he was 21. Jessica loves or at least admires Boy George, even though he beats her; she tattoos his name all over her body.

They live their lives in a neighborhood where going to prison is just like home but in a different place; all your friends are there. Solitary confinement is not so bad; it may be the first time some kids get a sense of peace and quiet. LeBlanc tells how residents view welfare as a scam, but one that can be screwed up by getting caught in a garden variety of misdemeanors and offenses. Kids who cannot pass school and seem illiterate to teachers display fantastic organizational and financial skills when dealing drugs and running cartels. It is not uncommon for 13-year-old girls to have babies in order to keep their government subsidies.

Coco, like so many girls in the neighborhood, hooks up with men who are bad for her; but she has a wild streak herself. She loves Cesar and bears his child, a girl named Mercedes. But when Cesar is locked up, Coco hooks up with an old boyfriend named Kodak and gets pregnant. Though he is enraged by her infidelity, Cesar and Coco get back together when he is released and have yet another daughter, Nautica. When Cesar is sent to jail once again for accidentally killing a friend, Coco again betrays him and has a child by a neighborhood boy named Wishman; true to form, Wishman shows little interest in the baby. Leaving the Bronx behind, Coco moves upstate to Troy with a drug dealer named Frankie and has still another child, a son, LaMonté. By the time she is in her 20s she has five children—one disabled—and spends her time shuttling between housing projects in the Bronx and in Troy. Despite her adversity she is devoted to her children.

By the time she is 19, Jessica has a baby with one boyfriend and a set of twins with the same guy's brother. She has little interest in taking care of her kids who eventually wind up in the care of her friend Milagros after Lourdes refuses to care for the children (even when bribed with cocaine). She works in Boy George's drug business helping to process and move heroin. She is attracted to his fleet of expensive cars, his lavish parties, and the fact that he sends his henchmen to Jessica's apartment to fill her family's refrigerator with food.

He takes her to weekend getaways in the Poconos. When Boy George is busted by drug enforcement agents, Jessica refuses to testify against him and gets a 10-year prison sentence; Boy George gets a life sentence at age 23.

The book paints a bleak picture of inner-city Latino culture. There are few real options for mobility save drug dealing. People consider it a victory if life today is slightly better than it was yesterday: There is food on the table, and you haven't gotten beat up; your kid is a heroin addict but has not taken crack. A girl who has four kids by two boys is considered much better off than a girl who has four by three; a boy who deals drugs and gives the profits to his mother is better than one who spends it on himself. There is little hope and nowhere to go. Even a prison stay does not make Jessica any wiser, just older. There is not much optimism in this place because the demands of the culture overshadow every element of life, leaving little room for individual needs or choices.

Critical Thinking

Does LeBlanc's findings indicate that environmental factors shape behavior? If Coco had been brought up in the suburbs might her life have been any different?

InfoTrac College Edition Research

To read a review of this book, go to Angela Ards, "Welfare family values." (*Random Family: Love, Drugs, Trouble, and Coming of Age in the Bronx; Flat Broke With Children: Women in the Age of Welfare Reform*). *The Women's Review of Books* 21 (2004): p7.

Source: Adrian Nicole LeBlanc, *Random Family: Love, Drugs, Trouble, and Coming of Age in the Bronx* (New York: Scribner's, 2003).

When people live in areas where the death rates are high and life expectancies are short, they may alter their behavior out of fear. They may feel, "Why plan for the future when there is a significant likelihood that I may never see it?" In such areas, young boys and girls may psychologically assimilate by taking risks and discounting the future. Teenage birthrates soar and so do violence rates.[65] For these children, the inevitability of death skews their perspective of how they live their lives.

Fear of repeat victimization may be both instinctual and accurate. Remember that in Chapter 3 we discussed the fact that some people may be "victim prone" and fated to suffer repeated victimization over the life course.

When fear grips a neighborhood, business conditions begin to deteriorate, population mobility increases, and a "criminal element" begins to drift into the area.[66] In essence, fear incites more crime, increasing the chances of victimization, producing even more fear, in a never-ending loop.[67] Fear is often associated with other community-level factors:

1. *Race and fear:* Fear of crime is also bound up in anxiety over racial and ethnic conflicts. Fear becomes most pronounced in areas undergoing rapid and unexpected racial and age-composition changes, especially when they are out of proportion to the rest of the city.[68] Whites become particularly fearful when they sense that they are becoming a racial minority in their neighborhood.[69] The fear experienced by whites may be based on racial stereotypes, but it may also be caused by the sense that they will become less well protected because police do not provide adequate services in predominantly African American neighborhoods.[70]

   Whites are not the only group to experience race-based fear. Minority group members may experience greater levels of fear than whites perhaps because they may have fewer resources to address ongoing social problems.[71] Fear can be found among other racial and ethnic groups, especially when they believe they are in the minority and vulnerable to attack. Ted Chiricos and his associates found that whites feel threatened by Latinos and blacks but only in South Florida where whites are outnumbered by those two groups; in contrast, Latinos are threatened by blacks but only outside of South Florida where Latinos are the minority.[72]

2. *Gangs and fear:* Gangs flourish in deteriorated neighborhoods with high levels of poverty, lack of investment, high unemployment rates, and population turnover.[73] Unlike any other crime, however, gang activity is frequently undertaken out in the open, on the public ways, and in full view of the rest of the community.[74] Brazen criminal activity undermines community solidarity because it signals that the police must be either corrupt or inept. The fact that gangs are willing to openly engage in drug sales and other types of criminal activity shows their confidence that they have silenced or intimidated law-abiding people in their midst. The police and the community alike become hopeless about their ability to restore community stability, producing greater levels of community fear.

3. *Mistrust and fear:* People who report living in neighborhoods with high levels of crime and civil disorder become suspicious and mistrusting.[75] They develop a sense of powerlessness, which amplifies the effect of neighborhood disorder and increases levels of mistrust. Some residents become so suspicious of authority that they develop a **siege mentality** in which the outside world is considered the enemy out to destroy the neighborhood. Elijah Anderson found that residents in the African American neighborhoods he studied believed in the existence of a secret plan to eradicate the population by such strategies as permanent unemployment, police brutality, imprisonment, drug distribution, and AIDS.[76] White officials and political leaders were believed to have hatched this conspiracy, and it was demonstrated by the lax law enforcement efforts in poor areas. Residents felt that police cared little about black-on-black crime because it helped reduce the population. Rumors abounded that federal government agencies, such as the CIA, controlled the drug trade and used profits to fund illegal overseas operations.

This siege mentality results in mistrust of critical social institutions, including business, government, and schools. Government officials seem arrogant and haughty. Residents become self-conscious and are particularly attuned to anyone who disrespects them. Considering this feeling of mistrust, when police ignore crime in poor areas or, conversely, when they are violent and corrupt, anger flares, and people take to the streets and react in violent ways.[77]

COMMUNITY CHANGE In our postmodern society, urban areas undergoing rapid structural changes in racial and economic composition also seem to experience the greatest change in crime rates. In contrast, stable neighborhoods, even those with a high rate of poverty, experience relatively low crime rates and have the strength to restrict substance abuse and criminal activity.[78] Recent studies recognize that change, not stability, is the hallmark of inner-city areas. A neighborhood's residents, wealth, density, and purpose are constantly evolving. Even disorganized neighborhoods acquire new identifying features. Some may become multiracial, while others become racially homogeneous. Some areas become stable and family oriented, while in others, mobile, never-married people predominate.[79]

As areas decline, residents flee to safer, more stable localities. Those who can move to more affluent neighborhoods find that their lifestyles and life chances improve immediately and continue to do so over their lifespan.[80] Those who cannot leave because they cannot afford to live in more affluent communities face an increased risk of victimization. Because of racial differences in economic well-being, those "left behind" are all too often minority citizens.[81] Those who cannot move find themselves surrounded by a constant influx of new residents. High population turnover can have a devastating effect on community culture because it thwarts communication and information flow.[82] In response to this turnover, a culture may develop that dictates standards of dress, language, and behavior to neighborhood youth that are in opposition to those of conventional society. All these factors are likely to produce increased crime rates.

THE CYCLES OF COMMUNITY CHANGE During periods of population turnover, communities may undergo changes that undermine their infrastructure. Urban areas seem to have life cycles, which begin with building residential dwellings and are followed by a period of decline, with marked decreases in socioeconomic status and increases in population density.[83] Later stages in this life cycle include changing racial or ethnic makeup, population thinning, and finally a renewal stage in which obsolete housing is replaced and upgraded (**gentrification**). Areas undergoing such change seem to experience an increase in their crime rates.[84]

 To learn more about the effects of gentrification, use "housing rehabilitation" as a key word with InfoTrac College Edition.

As communities go through cycles, neighborhood deterioration precedes increasing rates of crime and delinquency.[85] Neighborhoods most at risk for crime rate increases contain large numbers of single-parent families and unrelated people living together, have gone from having owner-occupied to renter-occupied units, and have an economic base that has lost semiskilled and unskilled jobs (indicating a growing residue of discouraged workers who are no longer seeking employment).[86] These ecological disruptions strain existing social control mechanisms and inhibit their ability to control crime and delinquency.

Community change may also have racial overtones. A large body of research shows that shifts in the racial makeup of neighborhoods are associated with increased neighborhood crime rates.[87] According to the "racial threat" hypothesis, as the percentage of minority group members in the population increases, so too does the crime rate. Whites may feel threatened as the numbers of minorities in the population increase, and they must compete with minorities for jobs and political power.[88] In changing neighborhoods, adults may actually encourage the law-violating behavior of youths. They may express attitudes that justify violence as a means of protecting their property and way of life by violently resisting newcomers.[89] They may also demand more money be spent on police and other justice agencies. As racial prejudice increases, the call for "law and order" aimed at controlling the minority population grows louder.[90]

COLLECTIVE EFFICACY Cohesive communities, whether urban or rural, with high levels of social control and social integration, where people know one another and develop interpersonal ties, may also develop **collective efficacy**: mutual trust, a willingness to intervene in the supervision of children, and the maintenance of public order.[91] It is the cohesion among neighborhood residents combined with shared expectations for informal social control of public space that promotes collective efficacy.[92] Residents in these areas are able to enjoy a better life because the fruits of cohesiveness can be better education, healthcare, and housing opportunities.[93]

 To read about the internal workings of collective efficacy, go to InfoTrac College Edition and read: Terry E. Duncan, Susan C. Duncan, Hayrettin Okut, Lisa A. Strycker, and Hollie Hix-Small, "A Multilevel Contextual Model of Neighborhood Collective Efficacy," *American Journal of Community Psychology* 32 (2003): 245–253.

In contrast, residents of socially disorganized neighborhoods find that efforts at social control are weak and attenuated. People living in economically disadvantaged areas are significantly more likely to perceive their immediate surroundings in more negative terms (that is, higher levels of incivilities) than those living in areas that maintain collective efficacy.[94] When community social control efforts are blunted, crime rates increase, further weakening neighborhood cohesiveness.[95]

Three forms of social control that shape a neighborhoods' collective efficacy:

1. *Informal social control*: Some elements of collective efficacy operate on the primary or private level and involve peers, families, and relatives. These sources exert informal social control by either awarding or withholding approval, respect, and admiration. Informal control mechanisms include direct criticism, ridicule, ostracism, desertion, or physical punishment.[96]

   The most important wielder of informal social control is the family that may keep at-risk kids in check through such mechanisms as corporal punishment, withholding privileges, or ridiculing lazy or disrespectful behavior. The influence of the family on informal social control takes on greater importance in neighborhoods with few social ties among adults and limited collective efficacy. In these areas parents cannot call upon neighborhood resources to take up the burden of controlling children and face the burden of providing adequate supervision.[97]

   In some areas, neighbors are committed to preserving their immediate environment by confronting destabilizing forces such as teen gangs.[98] By helping neighbors become more resilient and self-confident, adults in these areas provide the external support systems that enable youth to desist from crime. Residents teach one another that they have moral and social obligations to their fellow citizens; children learn to be sensitive to the rights of others and to respect differences.

   Sometimes, neighborhood associations and self-help groups form. The threat of skyrocketing violence rates may draw people to help out one another. While criminologists believe that crime rates are lower in cohesive neighborhoods, it is also possible that an escalating crime rate may bring people closer together to fight a common problem.[99] Some neighbors may get involved in informal social control through surveillance practices, for example, by keeping an "eye out" for intruders when their neighbors go out of town. Informal surveillance has been found to reduce the levels of some crimes such as street robberies; however, if robbery rates remain high, surveillance may be terminated because people become fearful for their safety.[100]

2. *Institutional social control*: Social institutions such as schools and churches cannot work effectively in a climate of alienation and mistrust. Unsupervised peer groups and gangs, which flourish in disorganized areas, disrupt the influence of those neighborhood control agents that do exist.[101]

   People who reside in these neighborhoods find that involvement with conventional social institutions, such as schools and afternoon programs, is often attenuated or blocked.[102] Children are at risk for recruitment into gangs and law-violating groups when there is a lack of effective public services. Gangs become an attractive alternative when adolescents have little to do after school and must rely on out-of-home care rather than more structured school-based programs.[103] As a result, crime may flourish and neighborhood fear increases, conditions that diminish a community's cohesion and thwart the ability of its institutions to exert social control over its residents.[104]

   To combat these influences, communities that have collective efficacy attempt to utilize their local institutions to control crime. Sources of institutional social control include businesses, stores, schools, churches, and social service and volunteer organizations.[105] When their institutions are effective, crime rates decline.[106] Some institutions, such as recreation centers for teens, have been found to lower crime rates because they exert a positive effect; others, such as taverns and bars, can help destabilize neighborhoods and increase the rate of violent crimes such as rape and robbery.[107]

3. *Public social control*: Stable neighborhoods are also able to arrange for external sources of social control. If they can draw on outside help and secure external resources—a process referred to as public social control—they are better able to reduce the effects of disorganization and maintain lower levels of crime and victimization.[108] Racial differences in crime and violence rates may be explained in part by the ability of citizens in affluent, predominantly white neighborhoods to use their economic resources, and the political power it brings, to their own advantage. They demand and receive a level of protection in their communities that is not enjoyed in less affluent minority communities.[109]

   The level of policing, one of the primary sources of public social control, may vary from neighborhood to neighborhood. The police presence is typically greatest when community organizations and local leaders have sufficient political clout to get funding for additional law enforcement personnel. An effective police presence sends a message that the area will not tolerate deviant behavior. Because they can respond vigorously to crime, the police prevent criminal groups from gaining a toehold in the neighborhood.[110] Criminals and drug dealers avoid such areas and relocate to easier and more appealing "targets."[111] In contrast, crime rates are highest in areas where police are mistrusted because they engage in misconduct, such as excessive use of force, or because they are seemingly indifferent to neighborhood problems.[112]

   In more disorganized areas, the absence of political powerbrokers limits access to external funding and protection.[113] Without outside funding, a neighborhood may lack the ability to "get back on its feet."[114] In these areas there are fewer police, and those that do patrol the area are less motivated and their resources are stretched tighter. These communities cannot mount an effective social control effort because as neighborhood disadvantage increases, its level of informal social control decreases.[115]

   The government can also reduce crime by providing economic and social supports through publicly funded social support and welfare programs. Though welfare is often criticized by politicians as being a government handout, there is evidence of a significant negative association between the amount of welfare money people receive and crime rates.[116] Government assistance may help people improve their social status by providing them with the financial resources to clothe, feed, and educate their children while at the same time reducing stress, frustration, and anger. Using government subsidies to reduce crime is controversial, and not all research has found that it actually works as advertised.[117]

   People living in disorganized areas may also be able to draw on resources from their neighbors in more affluent surrounding communities, helping to keep crime rates down.[118] This phenomenon may explain, in part, why violence rates are high in poor African American neighborhoods cut off from outside areas for support.[119]

THE EFFECT OF COLLECTIVE EFFICACY The ramifications of having adequate controls are critical. In areas where collective efficacy remains high, children are less likely to become involved with deviant peers and to engage in problem behaviors.[120] When residents are satisfied that their neighborhoods are good places to live, they feel a sense of obligation to maintain order and are more willing to work hard to encourage informal social control. In areas where social institutions and processes—such as police protection—are working adequately, residents are willing to intervene personally to help control unruly children and uncivil adults.[121]

© San Francisco Chronicle

According to concepts such as social altruism and collective efficacy, neighborhoods where people meet face to face to deal with problems and preserve the immediate environment have been found to experience lower crime rates. Mutual aid can reduce neighborhood disorder. Here, Annette Young Smith (right), who helped start a community garden in a median strip in her San Francisco neighborhood, works with friends in a form of "grass-roots" organizing. Her efforts have helped change the local climate. Her street is now known as a place where neighbors know each other and where things get done.

be countered by the ongoing drain of deep-rooted economic and social deprivation.[124]

www To read an article showing the association between **collective efficacy and crime,** go to http://www.wjh.harvard.edu/soc/faculty/sampson/1997.4.pdf. For an up-to-date list of web links, go to http://cj.wadsworth.com/siegel_crimtpt9e.

According to the social ecology school, then, the quality of community life, including levels of change, fear, incivility, poverty, and deterioration, has a direct influence on an area's crime rate. It is not some individual property or trait that causes people to commit crime but the quality and ambience of the community in which they reside. Conversely, in areas that have high levels of social control and collective efficacy, crime rates have been shown to decrease—no matter what the economic situation. Concept Summary 6.1 sets out the features of social disorganization theory.

In contrast, in disorganized areas, the population is transient, and people want to leave as soon as they can afford to find better housing. Interpersonal relationships remain superficial, and people are less willing to help out neighbors or exert informal controls over their own or neighbors' children. Social institutions like schools and churches cannot work effectively in a climate of alienation and mistrust.[122] Children who live in these neighborhoods find that involvement with conventional social institutions, such as schools and afternoon programs, is blocked; they are instead at risk for recruitment into gangs.[123] These problems are stubborn and difficult to overcome. And even when an attempt is made to revitalize a disorganized neighborhood by creating institutional support programs such as community centers and better schools, the effort may

STRAIN THEORIES

Strain theorists believe that most people share similar values and goals. They want to earn money, have a nice home, drive a great car, and wear stylish clothes. They also want to care for their families and educate their children. Unfortunately, the ability to achieve these personal goals is stratified by socioeconomic class. While the affluent may live out the American Dream, the poor are shut out from achieving their goals. Because they cannot always get what they want, they begin to feel frustrated and angry—a condition referred to as *strain*.

Strain is related to criminal motivation. People who feel economically and socially humiliated may perceive that they have the right to humiliate others in return.[125] Psychologists warn that under these circumstances those who consider

CONCEPT SUMMARY 6.1

Social Disorganization Theories

Theory	Major Premise	Strengths	Research Focus
Shaw and McKay's concentric zones theory	Crime is a product of transitional neighborhoods that manifest social disorganization and value conflict.	Identifies why crime rates are highest in slum areas. Points out the factors that produce crime. Suggests programs to help reduce crime.	Poverty; disorganization, gangs, neighborhood change; community context of crime.
Social ecology theory	The conflicts and problems of urban social life and communities, including fear, unemployment, deterioration, and siege mentality, influence crime rates.	Accounts for urban crime rates and trends. Identifies community level factors that produce high crime rates.	Social control; fear; collective efficacy; unemployment

themselves "losers" begin to fear and envy "winners" who are doing very well at their expense. If they fail to take risky aggressive tactics, they are surely going to lose out in social competition and have little chance of future success.[126] These generalized feelings of **relative deprivation** are precursors to high crime rates.[127]

To read more about this topic, go to InfoTrac College Edition and use "relative deprivation" as a subject guide.

According to strain theorists, sharp divisions between the rich and poor create an atmosphere of envy and mistrust that may lead to violence and aggression.[128] People who feel deprived because of their race or economic class standing eventually develop a sense of injustice and discontent. The less fortunate begin to distrust the society that has nurtured social inequality and obstructed their chances of progressing by legitimate means. The constant frustration that results from these feelings of inadequacy produces pent-up aggression and hostility and, eventually, leads to violence and crime. The effect of inequality may be greatest when the impoverished population believes they are becoming less able to compete in a society where the balance of economic and social power is shifting further toward the already affluent. Under these conditions, the likelihood that the poor will choose illegitimate life-enhancing activities increases.[129] The basic components of strain theory are set out in Figure 6.6.

Strain theories come in two distinct formulations:

- *Structural strain:* Using a sociological lens, structural strain theories suggest that economic and social sources of strain shape collective human behavior.

- *Individual strain:* Using a psychological reference, individual strain theories suggest that individual life experiences cause some people to suffer pain and misery, feelings that are then translated into antisocial behavior.

The Concept of Anomie

The roots of strain theories can be traced to Émile Durkheim's notion of **anomie** (from the Greek *a nomos,* "without norms").

||||||| **CONNECTIONS** |||||||

As you may recall, Durkheim's concept of anomie was discussed in Chapter 1. It remains one of the central concepts in sociology and criminology.

To read more about the work of **Émile Durkheim**, go to http://www.relst.uiuc.edu/durkheim/Biography.html. For an up-to-date list of web links, go to http://cj.wadsworth.com/siegel_crimtpt9e.

According to Durkheim, an anomic society is one in which rules of behavior (values, customs, and norms) have broken down or become inoperative during periods of rapid

FIGURE 6.6

The Basic Components of Strain Theory

Poverty
- Development of isolated lower-class areas
- Lack of conventional social opportunities
- Racial and ethnic discrimination

▽

Maintenance of conventional rules and norms
Residents of lower-class areas remain loyal to conventional values and rules of dominant middle-class culture.

▽

Strain
Lack of opportunity coupled with desire for conventional success produces strain and frustration.

▽

Formation of gangs and groups
Youths form law-violating groups to seek alternative means of achieving success.

▽

Crime and delinquency
Methods of achievement—theft, violence, substance abuse—are defined as illegal by dominant culture.

▽

Criminal careers
Most youthful gang members age out of crime, but some continue as adult criminals.

social change or social crisis such as war or famine. Anomie is most likely to occur in societies that are moving from a **mechanical solidarity** that is characteristic of preindustrial states—held together by traditions, shared values, and unquestioned beliefs—to an **organic solidarity** of postindustrial society, which is highly developed and dependent upon the division of labor. In this modern society, people are connected by their interdependent needs for one another's services and production. The shift in traditions and values creates social turmoil. Established norms begin to erode and lose meaning. If a division occurs between what the population expects and what the economic and productive forces of society can realistically deliver, a crisis situation develops that can manifest itself in normlessness or anomie.

||||||| **CONNECTIONS** |||||||

Can Durkheim's concept of anomie help explain the motivation of terrorists who fear that the Westernization of their culture and the growing influence of globalization directly threaten their traditional religious and social values? The motivation for terrorism is discussed in Chapter 10.

Anomie undermines society's social control function. Every society works to limit people's goals and desires. If a society becomes anomic, it can no longer establish and maintain control over its population's wants and desires. Because people find it difficult to control their appetites, their demands become unlimited. Under these circumstances, obeying legal codes may be strained, and alternative behavior choices, such as crime, may be inevitable.

Anomie theory suggests that American culture prescribes material success as the prime goal while at the same time maintaining social structural arrangements that preclude many from realistic access to legitimate means for achieving that goal. To read more about this concept, use "anomie" as a key word with InfoTrac College Edition.

Merton's Theory of Anomie

Durkheim's ideas were applied to criminology by sociologist Robert Merton in his **theory of anomie**.[130] Merton used a modified version of the concept of anomie to fit social, economic, and cultural conditions found in modern U.S. society.[131] He found that two elements of culture interact to produce potentially anomic conditions: culturally defined goals and socially approved means for obtaining them. Contemporary society stresses the goals of acquiring wealth, success, and power. Socially permissible means include hard work, education, and thrift.

In the United States, Merton argued, legitimate means to acquire wealth are stratified across class and status lines. Those with little formal education and few economic resources soon find that they are denied the ability to legally acquire wealth—the preeminent success symbol. When socially mandated goals are uniform throughout society and access to legitimate means is bound by class and status, the resulting strain produces anomie among those who are locked out of the legitimate opportunity structure. Consequently, they may develop criminal or delinquent solutions to the problem of attaining goals.

SOCIAL ADAPTATIONS Merton argued that each person has his or her own concept of the goals of society and the means at his or her disposal to attain them. Table 6.1 shows Merton's diagram of the hypothetical relationship between social goals, the means for getting them, and the individual actor. Here is a brief description of each of these modes of adaptation.

- *Conformity:* Conformity occurs when individuals both embrace conventional social goals and also have the means at their disposal to attain them. The conformist desires wealth and success and can obtain them through education and a high-paying job. In a balanced, stable society, this is the most common social adaptation. If a majority of its people did not practice conformity, the society would cease to exist.

TABLE 6.1

Typology of Individual Modes of Adaptation

Modes of Adaptation	Cultural Goals	Institutionalized Means
I. Conformity	+	+
I. Innovation	+	−
II. Ritualism	−	+
V. Retreatism	−	−
V. Rebellion	±	±

Source: Robert Merton, "Social Structure and Anomie," in *Social Theory and Social Structure* (Glencoe, Ill.: Free Press, 1957).

- *Innovation:* Innovation occurs when an individual accepts the goals of society but rejects or is incapable of attaining them through legitimate means. Many people desire material goods and luxuries but lack the financial ability to attain them. The resulting conflict forces them to adopt innovative solutions to their dilemma: They steal, sell drugs, or extort money. Of the five adaptations, innovation is most closely associated with criminal behavior.

  If successful, innovation can have serious, long-term social consequences. Criminal success helps convince otherwise law-abiding people that innovative means work better and faster than conventional ones. The prosperous drug dealer's expensive car and flashy clothes give out the message that "crime pays." Merton claims, "The process thus enlarges the extent of anomie within the system, so that others, who did not respond in the form of deviant behavior to the relatively slight anomie which they first obtained, come to do so as anomie is spread and is intensified."[132] This explains why crime is initiated and sustained in certain low-income ecological areas.

- *Ritualism:* Ritualists are less concerned about accumulating wealth and instead gain pleasure from practicing traditional ceremonies regardless of whether they have a real purpose or goal. The strict set of manners and customs in religious orders, feudal societies, clubs, and fraternal orders encourage and appeal to ritualists. Ritualists should have the lowest level of criminal behavior because they have abandoned the success goal, which is at the root of criminal activity.

- *Retreatism:* Retreatists reject both the goals and the means of society. Merton suggests that people who adjust in this fashion are "in the society but not of it." Included in this category are "psychotics, psychoneurotics, chronic autists, pariahs, outcasts, vagrants, vagabonds, tramps, chronic drunkards, and drug addicts." Because such people are morally or otherwise incapable of using both legitimate and illegitimate means, they attempt to escape their lack of success by withdrawing—either mentally or physically.

- *Rebellion:* Rebellion involves substituting an alternative set of goals and means for conventional ones.

Revolutionaries who wish to promote radical change in the existing social structure and who call for alternative lifestyles, goals, and beliefs are engaging in rebellion. Rebellion may be a reaction to a corrupt and hated government or an effort to create alternate opportunities and lifestyles within the existing system.

EVALUATION OF ANOMIE THEORY According to anomie theory, social inequality leads to perceptions of anomie. To resolve the goals—means conflict and relieve their sense of strain, some people innovate by stealing or extorting money, others retreat into drugs and alcohol, others rebel by joining revolutionary groups, and still others get involved in ritualistic behavior by joining a religious cult.

Merton's view of anomie has been one of the most enduring and influential sociological theories of criminality. By linking deviant behavior to the success goals that control social behavior, anomie theory attempts to pinpoint the cause of the conflict that produces personal frustration and consequent criminality. By acknowledging that society unfairly distributes the legitimate means to achieving success, anomie theory helps explain the existence of high-crime areas and the apparent predominance of delinquent and criminal behavior among the lower class. By suggesting that social conditions, not individual personalities, produce crime, Merton greatly influenced the direction taken to reduce and control criminality during the latter half of the twentieth century.

A number of questions are left unanswered by anomie theory.[133] Merton does not explain why people choose to commit certain types of crime. For example, why does one anomic person become a mugger and another deals drugs? Anomie may be used to explain differences in crime rates, but it cannot explain why most young criminals desist from crime as adults. Does this mean that perceptions of anomie dwindle with age? Is anomie short-lived?

Critics have also suggested that people pursue a number of different goals, including educational, athletic, and social success. Juveniles may be more interested in immediate goals, such as having an active social life or being a good athlete, than in long-term "ideal" achievements, such as monetary success. Achieving these goals is not a matter of social class alone; other factors, including athletic ability, intelligence, personality, and family life, can either hinder or assist goal attainment.[134] Anomie theory also assumes that all people share the same goals and values, which is false.[135]

A number of more recent, contemporary versions of strain theory are grounded on Merton's visionary concepts. Some of these are structural theories that hold that the success goal integrated within American society influences the nature and extent of the aggregate crime rate. There are also individual level versions of the theory that focus on how an individual is affected by anomie on a personal or psychological level. Examples of these views are discussed in the sections that follow.

Structural Level Strain: Institutional Anomie Theory

One addition to the strain literature is *Crime and the American Dream* by Steven Messner and Richard Rosenfeld.[136] Their structural version of anomie theory views antisocial behavior as a function of cultural and institutional influences in U.S. society. This is known as the **institutional anomie theory.**

To read research conducted by Messner and Rosenfeld on the utility of institutional anomie theory, use InfoTrac College Edition to access this article: Steven F. Messner and Richard Rosenfeld, "Political Restraint of the Market and Levels of Criminal Homicide: A Cross-National Application of Institutional-Anomie Theory," *Social Forces* 75 (June 1997): 1,393.

Messner and Rosenfeld agree with Merton's view that the success goal is pervasive in American culture. They refer to this as the **American Dream,** a term they employ as both a goal and a process. As a goal, the American Dream involves accumulating material goods and wealth via open individual competition. As a process, it involves both being socialized to pursue material success and believing that prosperity is an achievable goal in American culture. In the United States, the capitalist system encourages innovation in pursuit of monetary rewards. Businesspeople such as Bill Gates, Warren Buffett, and Donald Trump are considered cultural icons and leaders. Anomic conditions occur because the desire to succeed at any cost drives people apart, weakens the collective sense of community, fosters ambition, and restricts desires to achieve anything that is not material wealth. Achieving a "good name" and respect is not sufficient.

What is distinct about American society, according to Messner and Rosenfeld, and what most likely determines the exceedingly high national crime rate, is that anomic conditions have been allowed to "develop to such an extraordinary degree."[137] There do not seem to be any alternatives that would serve the same purpose or strive for the same goal.

IMPACT OF ANOMIE Why does anomie pervade American culture? According to Messner and Rosenfeld, it is because institutions that might otherwise control the exaggerated emphasis on financial success, such as religious or charitable institutions, have been rendered powerless or obsolete.

There are three reasons social institutions have been undermined. First, noneconomic functions and roles have been devalued. Performance in other institutional settings—the family, school, or community—is assigned a lower priority than the goal of financial success. Few students go to college to study the classics; most want to major in a field with good job prospects. Second, when conflicts emerge, noneconomic roles become subordinate to and must accommodate economic roles. The schedules, routines, and demands of the workplace take priority over those of the home, the school, the community, and other aspects of social life. A parent given the opportunity for a promotion thinks nothing of uprooting his family and moving them to another part of the country. And third, economic language, standards, and norms penetrate into noneconomic realms. Economic terms become part of the common vernacular. People want to get to the "bottom line"; spouses view themselves as "partners" who "manage" the household. Retired people say they want to "downsize" their household; we "out source" home repairs instead of doing them ourselves. Corporate leaders run for public office promising to "run the country like a business." People join social clubs to make connections and "network," not to make new friends.

According to Messner and Rosenfeld, the relatively high U.S. crime rates can be explained by the interrelationship between culture and institutions. The dominance of the American Dream mythology ensures that many people will develop wishes and desires for material goods that cannot be satisfied by legitimate means. In their analysis of survey data, Stephen Cernkovich and his associates found that people who valued the American Dream but failed to achieve economic success were crime prone. The effect was more substantial for whites than for African Americans. Cernkovich reasons that whites may have greater expectations of material success than African Americans, whose aspirations have been tempered by a long history of racial and economic deprivation. When whites experience strain, they are more apt to react with anger and antisocial behavior.[138]

At the institutional level, the dominance of economic concerns weakens the informal social control exerted by the family, church, and school. These institutions have lost their ability to regulate behavior and have instead become a conduit for promoting material success. Parents push their kids to succeed at any cost; schools encourage kids to get into the best colleges by any means possible; religious institutions promote their wealth and power.[139] Crime rates may rise even in a healthy economy because national prosperity heightens the attractiveness of monetary rewards, encouraging people to gain financial success by any means possible, including illegal ones. Meanwhile, the importance of social institutions as a means of exerting social control is reduced. In this "culture of competition," self-interest prevails and generates amorality, acceptance of inequality, and disdain for the less fortunate.[140]

The Messner-Rosenfeld version of anomie strain may be a blueprint for crime reduction strategies: If citizens are provided with an economic safety net, they may be able to resist the influence of economic deprivation and commit less crime. Nations that provide such resources—welfare, pension benefits, healthcare—have significantly lower crime rates.[141] In contrast, crime and violence rates are highest in nations with high levels of income inequality.[142]

Individual Level Strain: General Strain Theory

Sociologist Robert Agnew's **General Strain Theory (GST)** helps identify the individual influences of strain. Whereas Merton explains social class differences in the crime rate, Agnew explains why individuals who feel stress and strain are more likely to commit crimes. Agnew also offers a more general explanation of criminal activity among all elements of society rather than restricting his views to lower-class crime.[143]

MULTIPLE SOURCES OF STRESS Agnew suggests that criminality is the direct result of **negative affective states**—the anger, frustration, and adverse emotions that emerge in the wake of negative and destructive social relationships. He finds that negative affective states are produced by a variety of sources of strain (Figure 6.7).

- *Failure to achieve positively valued goals:* This category of strain, similar to what Merton speaks of in his theory of anomie, is a result of the disjunction between aspirations and expectations. This type of strain occurs when a youth aspires for wealth and fame but, lacking financial and educational resources, assumes that such goals are impossible to achieve.

- *Disjunction of expectations and achievements:* Strain can also be produced when there is a disjunction between expectations and achievements. When people compare themselves to peers who seem to be doing a lot better financially or socially (such as making more money or getting better grades), even those doing relatively well feel strain. For example, when a high school senior is accepted at a good college but not a prestige school like some of her friends, she will feel strain. Perhaps she is not being treated fairly because the playing field is tilted against her; "other kids have connections," she may say. Yet perceptions of inequity may result in many adverse reactions, ranging from running away from its source to lowering the benefits of others through physical attacks or vandalizing their property.

- *Removal of positively valued stimuli:* Strain may occur because of the actual or anticipated removal or loss of a

IIIIIII CONNECTIONS IIIIIII

Institutional anomie theory seems in synch with recent scandals involving the looting of some of the nation's most powerful companies including Enron, WorldCom, and Tyco. The desire for wealth seems to have no bounds. Read more about these white-collar crimes in Chapter 12.

IIIIIII CONNECTIONS IIIIIII

The GST is not solely a strain theory because it recognizes non-class-related individual and social psychological sources of strain. In this regard it is similar to the social process theories that are discussed in Chapter 7. However, it is included here because it incorporates the view that social class position can be an important source of strain and because it rests on Merton's theory of anomie, which itself is rooted in structural concepts. Agnew's newest theory, the General Theory of Crime and Delinquency (GTCD) is discussed in Chapter 9. While very different from General Strain Theory, Agnew believes both views have validity.

example, a child who experiences parental divorce early in his life may seek out deviant peers to help fill his emotional needs and in so doing increases his chances of criminality.[146]

■ *Presentation of negative stimuli:* Strain may also be caused by the presence of negative or noxious stimuli. Included within this category are such pain-inducing social interactions as child abuse and neglect, crime victimization, physical punishment, family and peer conflict, school failure, and interaction with stressful life events ranging from verbal threats to air pollution. For example, becoming the target of racism and discrimination may also trigger the anger and aggression predicted by Agnew.[147] Adolescent maltreatment has been linked to delinquency through the rage and anger it generates. Children who are abused at home may take their rage out on younger children at school or become involved in violent delinquency.[148]

According to Robert Agnew, strain may be caused by negative or noxious stimuli, such as stressful life events ranging from extreme poverty to living through a natural disaster. Experiencing strain increases the likelihood that negative emotions, including disappointment, depression, fear, and most important, anger, will develop. Some people may be able to rationalize frustrating circumstances while others try to regain emotional equilibrium through illegal activities. In the aftermath of Hurricane Katrina, insurance company investigators are now looking into fires that may have been set by desperate people who had no flood insurance but want to collect on their homeowners' policies. Could the strain of Katrina have caused them to engage in fraudulent behavior?

positively valued stimulus from the individual.[144] For example, the loss of a girl- or boyfriend can produce strain, as can the death of a loved one, moving to a new neighborhood or school, or the divorce or separation of parents.[145] The loss of positive stimuli may lead to delinquency as the adolescent tries to prevent the loss, retrieve what has been lost, obtain substitutes, or seek revenge against those responsible for the loss. For

According to Agnew, the greater the intensity and frequency of strain experiences, the greater their impact and the more likely they are to cause delinquency.

Each type of strain will increase the likelihood of experiencing such negative emotions as disappointment, depression, fear, and, most important, anger. Anger increases perceptions of being wronged, produces a desire for revenge, energizes individuals to take action, and lowers inhibitions.

FIGURE 6.7

Elements of General Strain Theory (GST)

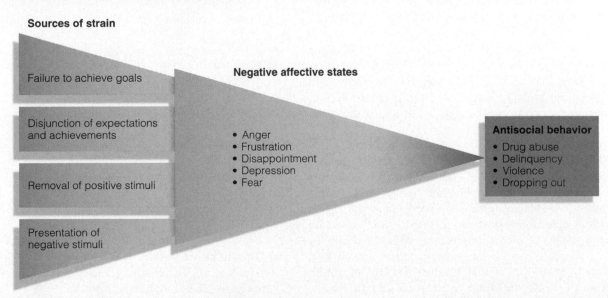

Violence and aggression seem justified if you have been wronged and are righteously angry.

Because it produces these emotions, strain can be considered a predisposing factor for criminality when it is chronic and repetitive and creates a hostile, suspicious, and aggressive attitude. Individual strain episodes may serve as a situational trigger that produces crime, such as when a particularly stressful event ignites a violent reaction.

To read about how strain influences teen suicide, see: Toni Terling Watt and Susan Sharp, "Gender Differences in Strains Associated with Suicidal Behavior among Adolescents," *Journal of Youth and Adolescence* 30 (June 2001): 333–318.

Sources of Strain

There are a variety of sources of strain. Sometimes, it can be a particular individual who is causing problems, such as an abusive parent or a peer group rival. When individuals identify a target to blame for their problems, they are more likely to respond with retaliatory action (for example, "Joe stole my girl away by lying about me, so I beat him up!"). When individuals internalize blame, delinquent behavior is less likely to occur (for example, "I lost my girlfriend because I was unfaithful; it's all my fault"). Sometimes the source of strain is difficult to pinpoint (for example, "I feel depressed because my parents got divorced"); this type of ambiguous strain is unlikely to produce an aggressive response.[149]

SOCIAL SOURCES OF STRAIN People may begin to feel strain because of their membership in a peer or social group. The relationship may be reciprocal. Kids who report feelings of stress and anger are more likely to interact with delinquent peers and engage in criminal behaviors.[150] However, once in a deviant peer group, it is possible that membership conveys pressure to conform to peer expectations, which can produce more strain. Peer groups, deviant or otherwise, convey benefits such as friendship, companionship, and support, but they also force members into behavior patterns (for example, using drugs) that can be the source of unwelcome stress. Feelings of strain and being overwhelmed may become magnified as individuals attempt to comply with peer group demands. Kids may, for example, get involved in an unwanted shoplifting spree to pay for drugs, creating even more stress in their lives.[151]

COMMUNITY SOURCES OF STRAIN GST typically focuses on individual-level sources of strain, yet there are distinct ecological variations in the crime rate. Some regions, cities, and neighborhoods are more crime prone than others. Can ecological differences produce "negative affective states" in large segments of the population, which account for these differences? Agnew suggests that there are, in fact, community-level factors that produce feelings of strain. These strain-producing factors are set out in Exhibit 6.1.

EXHIBIT 6.1

Community-Level Sources of Strain

Sources of Strain

- Certain communities prevent residents from achieving desired levels of positively valued goals such as wealth, respect/status, and justice/fairness.

- These communities also produce feelings of relative deprivation.

- Deprived communities maintain levels of economic deprivation, family disruption, child abuse, overcrowding, and incivility that are much higher than those in surrounding areas. Residents not only experience these traits but witness close friends and family members enduring them; this is "vicarious strain."

- These adverse community traits increase the likelihood of negative emotions, including anger and frustration.

- Residence in these deprived communities increases the likelihood that angry, frustrated individuals will interact with one another, increasing stress levels.

- Some communities will increase the likelihood that angry, frustrated people will commit crime.

Reasons Strain Produces Crime

- Blocked opportunity for advancement or creation of new identities in some areas makes legitimate goals impossible to attain.

- Densely populated communities make it impossible to keep activities and problems private. People may feel pressure to "save face" by acting tough or committing crimes.

- Some communities develop subcultures whose members blame others for their misfortunes. This allows people to blame their aggressive illegal acts on others.

- Residents in deprived areas are less able to develop noncriminal coping strategies for personal problems. They are less able to unite with others to solve their own or community-wide problems.

- Residents in disorganized areas are less able to gain social support from others. They maintain weakened educational, religious, recreational, and other social institutions.

- Deprived areas have weakened agencies of both formal and informal social control.

- Residents of deprived areas are likely to hold values and beliefs conducive to crime.

- The increased presence of criminal groups heightens the chance strain will lead to crime. Such groups serve as models and also reinforce criminal responses.

Source: Robert Agnew, "A Macro-Strain Theory of Community Differences in Crime Rates." Paper presented at the American Society of Criminology meeting, San Diego, 1997.

According to Agnew, communities contribute to strain in several ways:

- They influence the goals people pursue and the ability people have to meet these goals.

- They influence feelings of relative deprivation and exposure to aversive stimuli including family conflict, incivility, and economic deprivation.

- They influence the likelihood that angry, strain-filled individuals will interact with one another.

Consequently, not only does GST predict deviance on an individual level, but it can also account for community-level differences in the crime rate.

Coping with Strain

Not all people who experience strain fall into a life of crime and eventually resort to criminality. Some are able to marshal their emotional, mental, and behavioral resources to cope with the anger and frustration produced by strain. Coping ability may be a function of both individual traits and personal experiences over the life course. Personal temperament, prior learning of delinquent attitudes and behaviors, and association with criminal peers who reinforce anger are among other factors affecting the ability to cope. Juveniles high in negative emotionality and low in constraint will be more likely to react to strain with delinquency and antisocial behaviors.[152]

Although it may be socially disapproved, criminality can provide relief and satisfaction for someone living an otherwise stress-filled life. Using violence for self-protection may increase feelings of self-worth among those who feel inadequate or intellectually insecure. Violent responses may also be used in response to negative stimuli, such as violence. For example, children who report that they hit or strike their parents also report that they had been the target of parental violence (hitting, slapping). In this case, assaulting parents may be viewed as a type of remedy for the strain caused by child abuse.[153]

Some defenses are cognitive; individuals may be able to rationalize frustrating circumstances. Not getting the career they desire is "just not that important"; they may be poor, but the "next guy is worse off"; and if things didn't work out, then they "got what they deserved." Others seek behavioral solutions: They run away from adverse conditions or seek revenge against those who caused the strain. Others will try to regain emotional equilibrium with techniques ranging from physical exercise to drug abuse.

STRAIN AND CRIMINAL CAREERS While some people can effectively cope with strain, how does GST explain both chronic offending and the stability of crime over the life course? GST recognizes that certain people have traits that may make them particularly sensitive to strain. These include an explosive temperament, being overly sensitive or emotional, low tolerance for adversity, and poor problem-solving skills. Kids who suffer from this form of "negative emotionality" are much more likely to engage in antisocial behaviors, especially if they also are lacking in self-control.[154]

Aggressive people who have these traits are likely to have poor interpersonal skills and are more likely to be treated negatively by others; their combative personalities make them feared and disliked. These people are likely to live in families whose caretakers share similar personality traits. They are also more likely to reject conventional peers and join deviant groups. Such individuals are subject to a high degree of strain over the course of their lives.

Crime peaks during late adolescence because this is a period of social stress caused by the weakening of parental supervision and the development of relationships with a diverse peer group. Many kids going through the trauma of family breakup and frequent changes in family structure find themselves feeling a high degree of strain. They may react by becoming involved in precocious sexuality or by turning to substance abuse to mask the strain. For example, research shows that young girls of any social class are more likely to bear out-of-wedlock children if they themselves experienced an unstable family life.[155] Adolescence is also a period during which hormone levels peak, and the behavior moderating aspects of the brain have not fully developed—two factors that make adolescent males susceptible to environmental sources of strain.[156]

As they mature, children's expectations increase; some find that they are unable to meet academic and social demands. Adolescents are very concerned about their standing with peers. Those deficient in these areas may find they are social outcasts, another source of strain. In adulthood, crime rates drop because these sources of strain are reduced, new sources of self-esteem emerge, and adults seem more likely to bring their goals in line with reality.

|||||||| CONNECTIONS ||||||||

Explaining continuity and change in offending rates over the life course has become an important goal of criminologists. Analysis of latent trait and life course theories in Chapter 9 provides some recent thinking on this topic.

Evaluating GST

Agnew's work is important because it both clarifies the concept of strain and directs future research agendas. It also adds to the body of literature describing how social and life history events influence offending patterns. Sources of strain vary over the life course; so too do delinquency rates.

There is also empirical support for GST. Adolescents who score high on self-report test items that measure perceptions of strain (for example, "my classmates don't like me," "adults and friends don't respect my opinions") and negative life events (being a victim of crime, the death of a close friend, serious illness) are also the ones most likely to engage in crime.[157] Some research efforts show that indicators of strain—family breakup, unemployment, moving, feelings of dissatisfaction with friends and school—are positively related to criminality.[158] For example, middle-class youth who drop out of school are more likely to engage in criminal behavior than lower-class dropouts. It is possible that removing this positive stimulus (education) has a greater strain effect on those who are expected to succeed because of their class position than on those who already perceive more limited economic opportunities.[159] There is also

Strain Theories

Theory	Major Premise	Strengths	Research Focus
Anomie theory	People who adopt the goals of society but lack the means to attain them seek alternatives, such as crime.	Points out how competition for success creates conflict and crime. Suggests that social conditions and not personality can account for crime. Explains high lower-class crime rates.	Frustration; anomie; effects of failure to achieve goals
Institutional anomie theory	Material goods pervade all aspects of American life.	Explains why crime rates are so high in American culture.	Frustration; effects of materialism
General strain theory	Strain has a variety of sources. Strain causes crime in the absence of adequate coping mechanisms.	Identifies the complexities of strain in modern society. Expands on anomie theory. Shows the influence of social events on behavior over the life course. Explains middle-class crimes.	Strain; inequality; negative affective states; influence of negative and positive stimuli

evidence that the presence of negative stimulus provokes strain. Agnew himself found evidence that the strain associated with becoming a crime victim and anticipating future victimization may cause people to embrace antisocial behavior.[160]

GENDER ISSUES One of the biggest question marks about GST is its ability to adequately explain gender differences in the crime rate. Females experience as much or more strain, frustration, and anger as males, but their crime rate is much lower. Is it possible that there are gender differences either (a) in the relationship between strain and criminality or (b) in the ability to cope with the effects of strain? Not all sources of strain produce the anger envisioned by Agnew.[161] For example, although females may experience more strain, males may be more deeply affected by interpersonal stress.[162]

There is evidence that stress influences both males and females equally; however, the degree to which it leads to criminal behavior is much higher among males than females.[163] When presented with similar types of strain, males and females respond with a different constellation of negative emotions.[164] Females may be socialized to internalize stress, blaming themselves for their problems; males may take the same type of strain and relieve it by striking out at others and deflecting criticism with aggression.[165] Consequently, males may resort to criminality in the face of stressors of any magnitude, but only extreme levels of strain produce violent reactions from women.[166]

These issues aside, strain theory has proven to be an enduring vision of the cause of criminality. Researchers have continued to show that kids who perceive strain are the ones most likely to engage in delinquent activity.[167] Concept Summary 6.2 sets out the features of strain theory.

CULTURAL DEVIANCE THEORIES

The third branch of social structure theory combines the effects of social disorganization and strain to explain how people living in deteriorated neighborhoods react to social isolation and economic deprivation. Because their lifestyle is draining, frustrating, and dispiriting, members of the lower class create an independent subculture with its own set of rules and values. Middle-class culture stresses hard work, delayed gratification, formal education, and being cautious; the lower-class subculture stresses excitement, toughness, risk taking, fearlessness, immediate gratification, and "street smarts." The lower-class subculture is an attractive alternative because the urban poor find that it is impossible to meet the behavioral demands of middle-class society.

Unfortunately, subcultural norms often clash with conventional values. People who have close personal ties to the neighborhood, especially when they are to deviant networks such as gangs and criminal groups, may find that community norms interfere with their personal desire for neighborhood improvement. So when the police are trying to solve a gang-related killing, neighbors may find that their loyalty to the gang boy and his family outweighs their desire to create a more stable crime-free community by giving information to the police.[168] Figure 6.8 outlines the elements of cultural deviance theory.

Conduct Norms

The concept that the lower class develops a unique culture in response to strain can be traced to Thorsten Sellin's classic 1938 work, *Culture Conflict and Crime,* a theoretical attempt to link cultural adaptation to criminality.[169] Sellin's main premise is that criminal law is an expression of the rules of the dominant culture. The content of the law, therefore, may create a clash between conventional middle-class rules and splinter groups, such as ethnic and racial minorities who are excluded from the social mainstream. These groups maintain their own set of **conduct norms**—rules governing the day-to-day living conditions within these subcultures.[170] Conduct norms can be found in almost any culture and are not the property of any particular group, culture, or political structure.

Complicating matters is the fact that most of us belong to several social groups. In a complex society, the number of

FIGURE 6.8

Elements of Cultural Deviance Theory

Poverty
- Lack of opportunity
- Anomie

Socialization
Lower-class youths are socialized to value middle-class goals and ideas. However, their environment inhibits future success.

Subculture
Blocked opportunities prompt formation of groups with alternative lifestyles and values.

Success goal
Gangs provide alternative methods of gaining success.

Crime and delinquency
New methods of gaining success involve law-violating behaviors such as drug dealing.

Criminal careers
Some gang members can parlay their status into criminal careers; others become drug users or commit violent assault.

groups people belong to—family, peer, occupational, and religious—is quite large. "A conflict of norms is said to exist when more or less divergent rules of conduct govern the specific life situation in which a person may find himself."[171] According to Sellin, **culture conflict** occurs when the rules expressed in the criminal law clash with the demands of group conduct norms. To make his point, Sellin cited the case of a Sicilian father in New Jersey who killed the 16-year-old boy who seduced his daughter and then expressed surprise at being arrested. He claimed that he had "merely defended his family honor in a traditional way."[172]

Focal Concerns

In a classic 1958 paper, Walter Miller identified the unique value system that defines lower-class culture.[173] Conformance to these **focal concerns** dominates life among the lower class. According to Miller, clinging to lower-class focal concerns promotes illegal or violent behavior. Toughness may mean displaying fighting prowess; street smarts may lead to drug deals; excitement may result in drinking, gambling, or drug abuse. Focal concerns do not necessarily represent a rebellion against middle-class values; rather, these values have evolved specifically to fit conditions in lower-class areas. The major lower-class focal concerns are set out in Exhibit 6.2.[174]

It is this adherence to the prevailing cultural demands of lower-class society that causes urban crime. Research, in fact, shows that members of the lower class value toughness and want to show they are courageous in the face of provocation.[175] A reputation for toughness helps them acquire social power while at the same time insulating them from becoming victims. Violence is also seen as a means to acquire the accouterments of wealth (nice clothes, flashy cars, or access to clubs), control or humiliate another person, defy authority, settle drug-related "business" disputes, attain retribution, satisfy the need for thrills or risk taking, and respond to challenges to one's manhood.[176]

To some criminologists, the influence of lower-class focal concerns and culture seem as relevant today as when first identified by Miller fifty years ago. The Race, Culture, Gender, and Criminology feature discusses conflict as a recent version of the concept of cultural deviance.

Theory of Delinquent Subcultures

Albert Cohen first articulated the theory of delinquent subcultures in his classic 1955 book, *Delinquent Boys.*[177] Cohen's central position was that delinquent behavior of lower-class youths is actually a protest against the norms and values of middle-class U.S. culture. Because social conditions make them incapable of achieving success legitimately, lower-class youths experience a form of culture conflict that Cohen labels **status frustration**.[178] As a result, many of them join together in gangs and engage in behavior that is "non-utilitarian, malicious, and negativistic."[179]

Cohen viewed the delinquent gang as a separate subculture, possessing a value system directly opposed to that of the larger society. He describes the subculture as one that "takes its norms from the larger culture, but turns them upside down. The delinquent's conduct is right by the standards of his subculture precisely because it is wrong by the norms of the larger cultures."[180]

According to Cohen, the development of the delinquent subculture is a consequence of socialization practices found in the ghetto or inner-city environment. These children lack the basic skills necessary to achieve social and economic success in the demanding U.S. society. They also lack the proper education and therefore do not have the skills upon which to build a knowledge or socialization foundation. He suggests that lower-class parents are incapable of teaching children the necessary techniques for entering the dominant middle-class culture. The consequences of this deprivation include developmental handicaps, poor speech and communication skills, and inability to delay gratification.

EXHIBIT 6.2

Miller's Lower-Class Focal Concerns

Trouble In lower-class communities, people are evaluated by their actual or potential involvement in making trouble. Getting into trouble includes such behavior as fighting, drinking, and sexual misconduct. Dealing with trouble can confer prestige—for example, when a man establishes a reputation for being able to handle himself well in a fight. Not being able to handle trouble, and having to pay the consequences, can make a person look foolish and incompetent.

Toughness Lower-class males want local recognition of their physical and spiritual toughness. They refuse to be sentimental or soft and instead value physical strength, fighting ability, and athletic skill. Those who cannot meet these standards risk getting a reputation for being weak, inept, and effeminate.

Smartness Members of the lower-class culture want to maintain an image of being streetwise and savvy, using their street smarts, and having the ability to outfox and out-con the opponent. Though formal education is not admired, knowing essential survival techniques, such as gambling, conning, and outsmarting the law, is a requirement.

Excitement Members of the lower class search for fun and excitement to enliven an otherwise drab existence. The search for excitement may lead to gambling, fighting, getting drunk, and sexual adventures. In between, the lower-class citizen may simply "hang out" and "be cool."

Fate Lower-class citizens believe their lives are in the hands of strong spiritual forces that guide their destinies. Getting lucky, finding good fortune, and hitting the jackpot are all slum dwellers' daily dreams.

Autonomy Being independent of authority figures, such as the police, teachers, and parents, is required; losing control is an unacceptable weakness, incompatible with toughness.

Source: Walter Miller, "Lower-Class Culture as a Generating Milieu of Gang Delinquency," *Journal of Social Issues* 14 (1958): 5–19.

MIDDLE-CLASS MEASURING RODS One significant handicap that lower-class children face is the inability to positively impress authority figures, such as teachers, employers, or supervisors. Cohen calls the standards set by these authority figures **middle-class measuring rods.** The conflict and frustration lower-class youths experience when they fail to meet these standards is a primary cause of delinquency. For example, the fact that a lower-class student is deemed by those in power to be substandard or below the average of what is expected can have an important impact on his or her future life chances. A school record may be reviewed by juvenile court authorities and by the military. Because a military record can

influence whether or not someone is qualified for certain jobs, it is quite influential.[181] Negative evaluations become part of a permanent file that follows an individual for the rest of his or her life. When he or she wants to improve, evidence of prior failures is used to discourage advancement.

THE FORMATION OF DEVIANT SUBCULTURES Cohen believes lower-class boys who suffer rejection by middle-class decision makers usually elect to join one of three existing subcultures: the corner boy, the college boy, or the delinquent boy. The **corner boy** role is the most common response to middle-class rejection. The corner boy is not a chronic delinquent but may be a truant who engages in petty or status offenses, such as precocious sex and recreational drug abuse. His main loyalty is to his peer group, on which he depends for support, motivation, and interest. His values, therefore, are those of the group with which he is in close personal contact. The corner boy, well aware of his failure to achieve the standards of the American Dream, retreats into the comforting world of his lower-class peers and eventually becomes a stable member of his neighborhood, holding a menial job, marrying, and remaining in the community.

The **college boy** embraces the cultural and social values of the middle class. Rather than scorning middle-class measuring rods, he actively strives to be successful by those standards. Cohen views this type of youth as one who is embarking on an almost hopeless path, since he is ill-equipped academically, socially, and linguistically to achieve the rewards of middle-class life.

The **delinquent boy** adopts a set of norms and principles in direct opposition to middle-class values. He engages in short-run hedonism, living for today and letting "tomorrow take care of itself."[182] Delinquent boys strive for group autonomy. They resist efforts by family, school, or other sources of authority to control their behavior. They may join a gang because it is perceived as autonomous, independent, and the focus of "attraction, loyalty, and solidarity."[183] Frustrated by their inability to succeed, these boys resort to a process Cohen calls **reaction formation.** Symptoms of reaction formation include overly intense responses that seem disproportionate to the stimuli that trigger them. For the delinquent boy, this takes the form of irrational, malicious, and unaccountable hostility to enemies, which in this case are "the norms of respectable middle-class society."[184] Reaction formation causes delinquent boys to overreact to any perceived threat or slight. They sneer at the college boy's attempts at assimilation and scorn the corner boy's passivity. The delinquent boy is willing to take risks, violate the law, and flout middle-class conventions.

Cohen's work helps explain the factors that promote and sustain a delinquent subculture. By introducing the concepts of status frustration and middle-class measuring rods, Cohen makes it clear that social forces and not individual traits promote and sustain a delinquent career. By introducing the corner boy, college boy, delinquent boy triad, he helps explain why many lower-class youth fail to become chronic offenders: There is more than one social path open

The Code of the Streets

A widely cited view of the interrelationship of culture and behavior is Elijah Anderson's concept of the "code of the streets." He sees that life circumstances are tough for the "ghetto poor"—lack of jobs that pay a living wage, stigma of race, fallout from rampant drug use and drug trafficking, and alienation and lack of hope for the future. Living in such an environment places young people at special risk of crime and deviant behavior.

There are two cultural forces running through the neighborhood that shape their reactions. *Decent values* are taught by families committed to middle-class values and representing mainstream goals and standards of behavior. Though they may be better off financially than some of their street-oriented neighbors, they are generally "working poor." They value hard work and self-reliance and are willing to sacrifice for their children; they harbor hopes that their sons and daughters will achieve a better future. Most go to church and take a strong interest in education. Some see their difficult situation as a test from God and derive great support from their faith and from the church community.

In opposition, *street values*, those of "the streets," are born in the despair of inner-city life and are in opposition to those of mainstream society. The street culture has developed what Anderson calls a *code of the streets*, which are a set of informal rules setting down both proper attitudes and ways to respond if challenged. If the rules are violated, there are penalties and sometimes violent retribution.

At the heart of the code is the issue of respect—loosely defined as being treated "right." The code demands that disrespect be punished or else hard-won respect be lost. With the right amount of respect, a person can avoid "being bothered" in public. If he is bothered, not only may he be in physical danger, but he has been disgraced or "dissed" (disrespected). Some forms of dissing, such as maintaining eye contact for too long, may seem pretty mild. But to street kids who live by the code, these actions become serious indications of the other person's intentions and a warning of imminent physical confrontation.

These two orientations—decent and street—socially organize the community. Their co-existence means that kids who are brought up in "decent" homes must be able to successfully navigate the demands of the "street" culture. Even in decent families, parents recognize that the code must be obeyed or at the very least "negotiated"; it cannot simply be ignored.

The Respect Game

Young men in poor inner-city neighborhoods build their self-image on the foundation of *respect*. Having "juice" (as respect is sometimes called on the street) means that they can take care of themselves even if it means resorting to violence. For street youth, losing respect on the street can be damaging and dangerous. Once they have demonstrated that they can be insulted, beaten up, or stolen from, they become an easy target. Kids from "decent" families may be able to keep their self-respect by getting good grades or a scholarship. Street kids do not have that luxury. With nothing to fall back on, they cannot walk away from an insult. They must retaliate with violence.

One method of preventing attacks is to go on the offensive. Aggressive, violence-prone people are not seen as "easy prey." Robbers do not get robbed, and street fighters are not the favorite targets of bullies. A youth who communicates an image of not being afraid to die and not being afraid to kill has given himself a sense of power on the street.

Anderson's work has been well received by the criminological community. A number of researchers including Timothy Brezina and his colleagues are doing analyses to determine whether Anderson's observations are in fact valid. Using data on violence, their assessment finds a linkage between violent behavior and the social processes uncovered by Anderson.

Critical Thinking

1. Does the code of the street, as described by Anderson, apply in the neighborhood in which you were raised? That is, is it universal?

2. Is there a form of "respect game" being played out on college campuses? If so, what is the substitute for violence?

 InfoTrac College Edition Research

Go to InfoTrac College Edition and use "street culture" in a key word search.

Sources: Elijah Anderson, *Code of the Street: Decency, Violence, and the Moral Life of the Inner City* (New York: Norton, 2000); idem, "Violence and the Inner-City Street Code," in *Violence and Children in the Inner City*, ed. Joan McCord (New York: Cambridge University Press, 1998), pp. 1–30; idem., "The Code of the Streets," *Atlantic Monthly* 273 (May 1994): 80–94; Timothy Brezina, Robert Agnew, Francis T. Cullen, and John Paul Wright, "The Code of the Street: A Quantitative Assessment of Elijah Anderson's Subculture of Violence Thesis and Its Contribution to Youth Violence Research," *Youth Violence and Juvenile Justice* 2 (2004): 303–328.

to indigent youth.[185] His work is a skillful integration of strain and social disorganization theories and has become an enduring element of the criminological literature.

Theory of Differential Opportunity

In their classic work *Delinquency and Opportunity,* written over forty-five years ago, Richard Cloward and Lloyd Ohlin combined strain and social disorganization principles into a portrayal of a gang-sustaining criminal subculture.[186] Cloward and Ohlin agreed with Cohen and found that independent delinquent subcultures exist within society. They consider a delinquent subculture to be one in which certain forms of delinquent activity are essential requirements for performing the dominant roles supported by the subculture.[187]

Youth gangs are an important part of the delinquent subculture. Although not all illegal acts are committed by gang youth, they are the source of the most serious, sustained, and costly criminal behaviors. Delinquent gangs spring up in disorganized areas where youths lack the opportunity to gain success through conventional means. True to strain theory principles, Cloward and Ohlin portray inner-city kids as individuals who want to conform to middle-class values but lack the means to do so.[188]

DIFFERENTIAL OPPORTUNITIES The centerpiece of the Cloward and Ohlin theory is the concept of **differential opportunity,** which states that people in all strata of society share the same success goals but that those in the lower class have limited means of achieving them. People who perceive themselves as failures within conventional society will seek alternative or innovative ways to gain success. People who conclude that there is little hope for advancement by legitimate means may join with like-minded peers to form a gang. Gang members provide the emotional support to handle the shame, fear, or guilt they may develop while engaging in illegal acts. Delinquent subcultures then reward these acts that conventional society would punish. The youth who is considered a failure at school and is only qualified for a menial job at a minimum wage can earn thousands of dollars plus the respect of his or her peers by joining a gang and engaging in drug deals or armed robberies.

Cloward and Ohlin recognize that the opportunity for both successful conventional and criminal careers is limited. In stable areas, adolescents may be recruited by professional criminals, drug traffickers, or organized crime groups. Unstable areas, however, cannot support flourishing criminal opportunities. In these socially disorganized neighborhoods, adult role models are absent, and young criminals have few opportunities to join established gangs or to learn the fine

Kids may join gangs because they are looking for acceptance and respect. The gang may serve as a surrogate family. By providing an alternative, community programs hope to entice kids away from gangs. Some programs have a religious theme. The Venerable Khon Sao, a Buddhist monk, teaches Young Cambodian youths, many of them gang members, how to pray at a Buddhist temple in Lowell, Massachusetts. In conjunction with the police department, the Buddhist temple has begun a program that teaches the fundamentals of Buddhist thought two evenings a week to the teens. In the classes, the youths learn how to pray, meditate, and act peacefully.

© Spencer Platt/Getty Images

points of professional crime. Their most important finding, then, is that all opportunities for success, both illegal and conventional, are closed for the most "truly disadvantaged" youth.

Because of differential opportunity, kids are likely to join one of three types of gangs:

- *Criminal gangs:* Criminal gangs exist in stable lower-class areas in which close connections among adolescent, young adult, and adult offenders create an environment for successful criminal enterprise.[189] Youths are recruited into established criminal gangs that provide a training ground for a successful criminal career. Gang membership provides a learning experience in which the knowledge and skills needed for success in crime are acquired. During this "apprenticeship stage," older, more experienced members of the criminal subculture hold youthful "trainees" on tight reins, limiting activities that might jeopardize the gang's profits (for example, engaging in nonfunctional, irrational violence). Over time, new recruits learn the techniques and attitudes of the criminal world and how to "cooperate successfully with others in criminal enterprises."[190] To become a fully accepted member of the criminal gang, novices must prove themselves reliable and dependable in their contacts with their criminal associates.

To read more about the illegal activities of male and female gang members, use InfoTrac College Edition to access this article: John Hagedorn, Jose Torres, and Greg Giglio, "Cocaine, Kicks, and Strain: Patterns of Substance Use in Milwaukee Gangs," *Contemporary Drug Problems* 25 (spring 1998): 113–145.

Cultural Deviance Theories

Theory	Major Premise	Strengths	Research Focus
Miller's focal concern theory	Citizens who obey the street rules of lower-class life (focal concerns) find themselves in conflict with the dominant culture.	Identifies the core values of lower-class culture and shows their association to crime.	Cultural norms; focal concerns
Cohen's theory of delinquent gangs	Status frustration of lower-class boys, created by their failure to achieve middle-class success, causes them to join gangs.	Shows how the conditions of lower-class life produce crime. Explains violence and destructive acts. Identifies conflict of lower class with middle class.	Gangs; culture conflict; middle-class measuring rods; reaction formation
Cloward and Ohlin's theory of opportunity	Blockage of conventional opportunities causes lower-class youths to join criminal, conflict, or retreatist gangs.	Shows that even illegal opportunities are structured in society. Indicates why people become involved in a particular type of criminal activity. Presents a way of preventing crime.	Gangs; cultural norms; culture conflict; effects of blocked opportunity

- *Conflict gangs:* Conflict gangs develop in communities unable to provide either legitimate or illegitimate opportunities. These highly disorganized areas are marked by transient residents and physical deterioration. Crime in this area is "individualistic, unorganized, petty, poorly paid, and unprotected."[191] There are no successful adult criminal role models from whom youths can learn criminal skills. When such severe limitations on both criminal and conventional opportunity intensify frustrations of the young, violence is used as a means of gaining status. The image of the conflict gang member is the swaggering, tough adolescent who fights with weapons to win respect from rivals and engages in unpredictable and destructive assaults on people and property. Conflict gang members must be ready to fight to protect their own and their gang's integrity and honor. By doing so, they acquire a "rep," which provides them with a means for gaining admiration from their peers and consequently helps them develop their own self-image. Conflict gangs, according to Cloward and Ohlin, "represent a way of securing access to the scarce resources for adolescent pleasure and opportunity in underprivileged areas."[192]

- *Retreatist gangs:* Retreatists are double failures, unable to gain success through legitimate means and unwilling to do so through illegal ones. Some retreatists have tried crime or violence but are either too clumsy, weak, or scared to be accepted in criminal or violent gangs. They then "retreat" into a role on the fringe of society. Members of the retreatist subculture constantly search for ways of getting high—alcohol, pot, heroin, unusual sexual experiences, music. They are always "cool," detached from relationships with the conventional world. To feed their habit, retreatists develop a "hustle"—pimping, conning, selling drugs, and committing petty crimes. Personal status in the retreatist subculture is derived from peer approval. Concept Summary 6.3 sets out the features of cultural deviance theories.

EVALUATING SOCIAL STRUCTURE THEORIES

The social structure approach has significantly influenced both criminological theory and crime prevention strategies. Its core concepts seem to be valid in view of the relatively high crime and delinquency rates and gang activity occurring in the deteriorated inner-city areas of the nation's largest cities.[193] The public's image of the disorganized inner city includes roaming bands of violent teenage gangs, drug users, prostitutes, muggers, and similar frightening examples of criminality. All of these are present today in inner-city areas.

Critics of the approach charge that we cannot be sure that it is lower-class culture itself that promotes crime and not some other force operating in society. Critics of this approach deny that residence in urban areas alone is sufficient to cause people to violate the law.[194] They counter with the charge that lower-class crime rates may be an artifact of bias in the criminal justice system. Lower-class areas seem to have higher crime rates because residents are arrested and prosecuted by agents of the justice system who, as members of the middle class, exhibit class bias.[195] Class bias is often coupled with discrimination against minority group members, who have long suffered at the hands of the justice system.

Even if the higher crime rates recorded in lower-class areas are valid, it is still true that most members of the lower class are not criminals. The discovery of the chronic offender indicates that a significant majority of people living in lower-class environments are not criminals and that a relatively small proportion of the population commits most crimes. If social forces alone could be used to explain crime, how can we account for the vast number of urban poor who remain honest and law abiding? Given these circumstances, law violators must be motivated by some individual mental, physical, or social process or trait.[196]

It is also questionable whether a distinct lower-class culture actually exists. Several researchers have found that gang members and other delinquent youths seem to value middle-class concepts, such as sharing, earning money, and respecting the law, as highly as middle-class youths. Criminologists contend that lower-class youths also value education as highly as middle-class students do.[197] Public opinion polls can also be used as evidence that a majority of lower-class citizens maintain middle-class values. National surveys find that people in the lowest income brackets want tougher drug laws, more police protection, and greater control over criminal offenders.[198] These opinions seem similar to conventional middle-class values rather than representative of an independent, deviant subculture. While this evidence contradicts some of the central ideas of social structure theory, the discovery of stable patterns of lower-class crime, the high crime rates found in disorganized inner-city areas, and the rise of teenage gangs and groups support a close association between crime rates and social class position.

PUBLIC POLICY IMPLICATIONS OF SOCIAL STRUCTURE THEORY

Social structure theory has had a significant influence on public policy. If the cause of criminality is viewed as a schism between lower-class individuals and conventional goals, norms, and rules, it seems logical that alternatives to criminal behavior can be provided by giving inner-city dwellers opportunities to share in the rewards of conventional society.

One approach is to give indigent people direct financial aid through welfare and Aid to Dependent Children (ADC). Although welfare has been curtailed through the Federal Welfare Reform Act of 1996, research shows that crime rates decrease when families receive supplemental income through public assistance payments.[199]

There are also efforts to reduce crime by improving the community structure in high-crime inner-city areas. Crime prevention efforts based on social structure precepts can be traced back to the Chicago Area Project, supervised by Clifford R. Shaw. This program attempted to organize existing community structures to develop social stability in otherwise disorganized slums. The project sponsored recreation programs for children in the neighborhoods, including summer camping. It campaigned for community improvements in such areas as education, sanitation, traffic safety, physical conservation, and law enforcement. Project members also worked with police and court agencies to supervise and treat gang youth and adult offenders. In a 25-year assessment of the project, Solomon Kobrin found that it was successful in demonstrating the feasibility of creating youth welfare organizations in high-delinquency areas.[200] Kobrin also discovered that the project made a distinct contribution to ending the isolation of urban males from the mainstream of society.

Social structure concepts, especially Cloward and Ohlin's views, were a critical ingredient in the Kennedy and Johnson administrations' "War on Poverty," begun in the early 1960s. Rather than organizing existing community structures, as Shaw's Chicago Area Project had done, this later effort called for an all-out attack on the crime-producing structures of inner-city areas. War on Poverty programs included the Job Corps; VISTA (the urban Peace Corps); Head Start and Upward Bound (educational enrichment programs); Neighborhood Legal Services; and the largest community organizing effort, the Community Action Program. War on Poverty programs were sweeping efforts to change the social structure of the inner-city area. They sought to reduce crime by developing a sense of community pride and solidarity in poverty areas and by providing educational and job opportunities for crime-prone youths. Some War on Poverty programs—Head Start, Neighborhood Legal Services, and the Community Action Program—have continued to help people.

Today Operation Weed and Seed is the foremost structural theory-based crime reduction strategy. Its aim is to prevent, control, and reduce violent crime, drug abuse, and gang activity in targeted high-crime neighborhoods across the country. Weed and Seed sites range in size from several neighborhood blocks to 15 square miles.[201] The strategy involves a two-pronged approach. First, law enforcement agencies and prosecutors cooperate in "weeding out" criminals who participate in violent crime and drug abuse and attempt to prevent their return to the targeted area. Then, participating agencies begin "seeding," which brings human services to the area, encompassing prevention, intervention, treatment, and neighborhood revitalization. A community-oriented policing component bridges weeding and seeding strategies. Officers obtain helpful information from area residents for weeding efforts while they aid residents in obtaining information about community revitalization and seeding resources. Operation Weed and Seed is an example of a modern-day crime control approach that relies on changing neighborhood structure to reduce crime rates.

- Sociology has been the main orientation of criminologists because they know that crime rates vary among elements of the social structure, that society goes through changes that affect crime, and that social interaction relates to criminality.

- Social structure theories suggest that people's places in the socioeconomic structure influence their chances of becoming a criminal.

- Poor people are more likely to commit crimes because they are unable to achieve monetary or social success in any other way.

- Social structure theory includes three schools of thought: social disorganization theories, strain theories, and cultural deviance theories.

- Social disorganization theory suggests that the urban poor violate the law because they live in areas in which social control has broken down. The origin of social disorganization theory can be traced to the work of Clifford R. Shaw and Henry D. McKay. Shaw and McKay

- concluded that disorganized areas, marked by divergent values and transitional populations, produce criminality. Modern social ecology theory looks at such issues as community fear, unemployment, and deterioration.

- Strain theories view crime as resulting from the anger people experience over their inability to achieve legitimate social and economic success.

- Strain theories hold that most people share common values and beliefs, but the ability to achieve them is differentiated by the social structure.

- The best-known strain theory is Robert Merton's theory of anomie, which describes what happens when people have inadequate means to satisfy their goals.

- Steven Messner and Richard Rosenfeld show that the core values of American culture produce strain.

- Robert Agnew suggests that strain has multiple sources and is linked to

- anger and frustration that people endure when their goals and aspirations are frustrated or when they lose something they value.

- Cultural deviance theories hold that a unique value system develops in lower-class areas. Lower-class values approve of behaviors such as being tough, never showing fear, and defying authority. People perceiving strain will bond together in their own groups or subcultures for support and recognition.

- Albert Cohen links the formation of subcultures to the failure of lower-class citizens to achieve recognition from middle-class decision makers, such as teachers, employers, and police officers.

- Richard Cloward and Lloyd Ohlin have argued that crime results from lower-class people's perception that their opportunity for success is limited. Consequently, youths in low-income areas may join criminal, conflict, or retreatist gangs.

ThomsonNOW

Thomson NOW! Optimize your study time and master key chapter concepts with **ThomsonNOW™**—the first web-based assessment-centered study tool for Criminology. This powerful resource helps you determine your unique study needs and provides you with a *Personalized Study Plan,* guiding you to interactive media that includes Learning Modules, Topic Reviews, ABC Video Clips with Questions, Animations, an integrated E-book, and more!

Thinking Like a Criminologist

You are a criminologist from a local university who is serving as an advisor to the mayor of Central City, an industrial town with a population of 300,000. The mayor, up for reelection, is disappointed that efforts by the local police force to reduce public disorder and crime rates through a community police program do not seem to be working. He has recently read a report issued by the federal government suggesting that the key to reducing neighborhood crime is to create a sense of "collective efficacy" in city neighborhoods. The report defined collective efficacy as "cohesion among neighborhood residents combined with shared expectations for informal social control of public space." The report, written by criminologists Robert Sampson and Stephen Raudenbush, found that when the rules of comportment are unclear and people mistrust one another, they are unlikely to take action against disorder and crime. When there is cohesion and mutual trust among neighbors, the likelihood is greater that they will share a willingness to intervene for the common good. They found that in neighborhoods where this sense of collective efficacy was strong, rates of violence were low, regardless of neighborhood composition or socioeconomic conditions. Collective efficacy also appeared to deter disorder: Where it was strong, observed levels of physical and social disorder were low.

The mayor wants to apply these concepts to Central City. He asks you to come up with a plan for increasing the collective efficacy of local neighborhoods and determine whether such measures can actually reduce crime. Your problem is twofold: (1) How can collective efficacy be improved? and (2) What test will show whether improvements in collective efficacy levels are responsible for lower violent crime rates?

 ## Doing Research on the Web

You can read the report by Robert J. Sampson and Stephen W. Raudenbush, "Disorder in Urban Neighborhoods: Does It Lead to Crime?" at the National Institute of Justice website: http://www.ncjrs.org/txtfiles1/nij/186049.txt.

To read another report linking collective efficacy to violence, go to http://www.psc.isr.umich.edu/pubs/papers/rr00-451.pdf.

To see how collective efficacy may impact on the behavior and well-being of youth, go to InfoTrac College Edition and read: Rebekah Levine Coley, Jodi Eileen Morris, and Daphne Hernandez, "Out-of-School Care and Problem Behavior Trajectories among Low-Income Adolescents: Individual, Family, and Neighborhood Characteristics as Added Risks," *Child Development* 75 (2004): 948–965.

BOOK COMPANION WEBSITE

http://cj.wadsworth.com/siegel_crimtpt9e To quiz yourself on the material in this chapter, go to the companion website, where you'll find chapter-by-chapter online tutorial quizzes, a final exam, ABC videos with questions, chapter outlines, chapter review, chapter-by-chapter web links, flash cards, and more!

KEY TERMS

stratified society (176)
culture of poverty (178)
at risk (178)
underclass (178)
social structure theory (179)
social disorganization theory (179)
strain theory (179)
strain (179)
truly disadvantaged (180)
cultural deviance theory (180)
subculture (180)
cultural transmission (180)
transitional neighborhoods (182)

social ecologists (184)
incivilities (185)
siege mentality (187)
gentrification (188)
collective efficacy (188)
strain theorists (190)
relative deprivation (191)
anomie (191)
mechanical solidarity (191)
organic solidarity (191)
theory of anomie (192)
institutional anomie theory (193)
American Dream (193)

General Strain Theory (GST) (194)
negative affective states (195)
conduct norms (198)
culture conflict (199)
focal concerns (199)
status frustration (199)
middle-class measuring rods (200)
corner boy (200)
college boy (200)
delinquent boy (200)
reaction formation (200)
differential opportunity (202)

CRITICAL THINKING QUESTIONS

1. Is there a "transitional" area in your town or city? Does the crime rate remain constant in this neighborhood regardless of the racial, ethnic, or cultural composition of its residents?

2. Do you believe a distinct lower-class culture exists? Do you know anyone who has the focal concerns Miller talks about? Did you experience elements of these focal concerns while you were in high school? Will emerging forms of communication such as the Internet reduce cultural differences and create a more homogeneous society, or are subcultures resistant to such influences?

3. Do you agree with Agnew that there is more than one cause of strain? If so, are there other sources of strain that he did not consider?

4. How would a structural theorist explain the presence of middle-class crime?

5. How would biosocial theories explain the high levels of violent crime in lower-class areas?

NOTES

1. Arlen Egley, Jr., *Highlights of the 2002 National Youth Gang Survey* (Washington, DC: Office of Juvenile Justice and Delinquency Prevention, 2003).

2. Arlen Egley, Jr., *Highlights of the 2002–2003 National Youth Gang Surveys* (Washington, DC: Office of Juvenile Justice and Delinquency Prevention, 2005).

3. Steven Messner and Richard Rosenfeld, *Crime and the American Dream* (Belmont, CA: Wadsworth, 1994), p. 11.

4. Robert E. Park, "The City: Suggestions for the Investigation of Behavior in the City Environment," *American Journal of Sociology* 20 (1915): 579–583.

5. Robert Park, Ernest Burgess, and Roderic McKenzie, *The City* (Chicago: University of Chicago Press, 1925).

6. Harvey Zorbaugh, *The Gold Coast and the Slum* (Chicago: University of Chicago Press, 1929).

7. Frederick Thrasher, *The Gang* (Chicago: University of Chicago Press, 1927).

8. Louis Wirth, *The Ghetto* (Chicago: University of Chicago Press, 1928).

9. Sam Roberts, *Who We Are Now: The Changing Face of America in the Twenty-First Century* (New York: Times Books, Henry Holt, 2004).

10. "High Net Worth Wealth Grows Strongly at over 8%, Surpassing $30 Trillion in 2004, According to Merrill Lynch and Capgemini," *World Wealth Report*, June 9, 2005. http://www.us.capgemini.com/worldwealthreport/wwr_pressrelease.asp?ID=48. Accessed August, 17, 2005

11. Jeanne Brooks-Gunn and Greg J. Duncan, "The Effects of Poverty on Children," *Future of Children* 7 (1997): 34–39.

12. Ibid.

13. Greg Duncan, W. Jean Yeung, Jeanne Brooks-Gunn, and Judith Smith, "How Much Does Childhood Poverty Affect the Life Chances of Children?" *American Sociological Review* 63 (1998): 406–423.

14. Ibid., p. 409.

15. Gary Evans, Nancy Wells, and Annie Moch, "Housing and Mental Health: A Review of the Evidence and a Methodological and Conceptual Critique," *Journal of Social Issues* 59 (2003): 475–501.

16. National Center for Children in Poverty, News Release, 11 December 1996.

17. Brooks-Gunn and Duncan, "The Effects of Poverty on Children."

18. Oscar Lewis, "The Culture of Poverty," *Scientific American* 215 (1966): 19–25.

19. Gunnar Myrdal, *The Challenge of World Poverty* (New York: Vintage Books, 1970).

20. James Ainsworth-Darnell and Douglas Downey, "Assessing the Oppositional Culture Explanation for Racial/Ethnic Differences in School Performances," *American Sociological Review* 63 (1998): 536–553.

21. Barbara Warner, "The Role of Attenuated Culture in Social Disorganization Theory," *Criminology* 41 (2003): 73–97.

22. Maria Velez, Lauren Krivo, and Ruth Peterson, "Structural Inequality and Homicide: An Assessment of the Black-White Gap in Killings," *Criminology* 41 (2003): 645–672.

23. U.S. Department of Census Data, *Race and Income* (Washington, DC: Census Bureau, 2003).

24. UCLA Center for Health Policy Research, "The Health of Young Children in California: Findings from the 2001 California Health Interview Survey" (Los Angeles, UCLA Center for Health Policy Research, 2003).

25. John Hagan, Carla Shedd, and Monique Payne, "Race, Ethnicity, and Youth Perceptions of Criminal Injustice," *American Sociological Review* 70 (2005): 381–407.

26. Eric Lotke, "Hobbling a Generation: Young African-American Men in Washington, D.C.'s Criminal Justice System—Five Years Later," *Crime and Delinquency* 44 (1998): 355–366.

27. Thomas McNulty and Paul Bellair, "Explaining Racial and Ethnic Differences in Serious Adolescent Violent Behavior," *Criminology* 41 (2003): 709–748; also Julie A. Phillips, "White, Black, and Latino Homicide Rates: Why the Difference?" *Social Problems* 49 (2002): 349–374.

28. David Brownfield, "Social Class and Violent Behavior," *Criminology* 24 (1986): 421–438.

29. See Charles Tittle and Robert Meier, "Specifying the SES/Delinquency Relationship," *Criminology* 28 (1990): 271–295, at 293.

30. See Ruth Kornhauser, *Social Sources of Delinquency* (Chicago: University of Chicago Press, 1978), p. 75.

31. Jonathan Crane, "The Epidemic Theory of Ghettos and Neighborhood Effects on Dropping Out and Teenage Childbearing," *American Journal of Sociology* 96 (1991): 1,226–1,259; see also Rodrick Wallace, "Expanding Coupled Shock Fronts of Urban Decay and Criminal Behavior: How U.S. Cities Are Becoming 'Hollowed Out,'" *Journal of Quantitative Criminology* 7 (1991): 333–355.

32. Jeffrey Fagan and Garth Davies, "The Natural History of Neighborhood Violence," *Journal of Contemporary Criminal Justice* 20 (2004): 127–147.

33. Clifford R. Shaw and Henry D. McKay, *Juvenile Delinquency and Urban Areas,* rev. ed. (Chicago: University of Chicago Press, 1972).

34. Anthony Platt, *The Child Savers: The Invention of Delinquency* (Chicago: University of Chicago Press, 1968).

35. Shaw and McKay, *Juvenile Delinquency and Urban Areas,* p. 52.

36. Ibid., p. 171.

37. Claire Valier, "Foreigners, Crime and Changing Mobilities," *British Journal of Criminology* 43 (2003): 1–21.

38. For a discussion of these issues, see Robert Bursik, "Social Disorganization and Theories of Crime and Delinquency: Problems and Prospects," *Criminology* 26 (1988): 521–539.

39. Robert Sampson, "Effects of Socioeconomic Context of Official Reaction to Juvenile Delinquency," *American Sociological Review* 51 (1986): 876–885.

40. Jeffrey Fagan, Ellen Slaughter, and Eliot Hartstone, "Blind Justice? The Impact of Race on the Juvenile Justice Process," *Crime and Delinquency* 33 (1987): 224–258; Merry Morash, "Establishment of a Juvenile Police Record," *Criminology* 22 (1984): 97–113.

41. For a general review, see James Byrne and Robert Sampson, eds., *The Social Ecology of Crime* (New York: Springer Verlag, 1985).

42. See, generally, Bursik, "Social Disorganization and Theories of Crime and Delinquency," pp. 519–551.

43. William Spelman, "Abandoned Buildings: Magnets for Crime?" *Journal of Criminal Justice* 21 (1993): 481–493.

44. Keith Harries and Andrea Powell, "Juvenile Gun Crime and Social Stress: Balti-

more, 1980–1990," *Urban Geography* 15 (1994): 45–63.

45. Ellen Kurtz, Barbara Koons, and Ralph Taylor, "Land Use, Physical Deterioration, Resident-Based Control, and Calls for Service on Urban Streetblocks," *Justice Quarterly* 15 (1998): 121–149.

46. Paul Stretesky, Amie Schuck, and Michael Hogan, "Space Matters: An Analysis of Poverty, Poverty Clustering, and Violent Crime," *Justice Quarterly* 21 (2004): 817–841.

47. Jeffrey Morenoff, Robert Sampson, and Stephen Raudenbush, "Neighborhood Inequality, Collective Efficacy, and the Spatial Dynamics of Urban Violence," *Criminology* 39 (2001): 517–560.

48. Gregory Squires and Charis Kubrin, "Privileged Places: Race, Uneven Development, and the Geography of Opportunity in Urban America," *Urban Studies* 42 (2005): 47–68.

49. Karen Parker and Matthew Pruitt, "Poverty, Poverty Concentration, and Homicide," *Social Science Quarterly* 81 (2000): 555–582.

50. Karen Parker, "Industrial Shift, Polarized Labor Markets, and Urban Violence: Modeling the Dynamics between the Economic Transformation and Disaggregated Homicide," *Criminology* 42 (2004): 619–645.

51. Tim Wadsworth and Charis Kubrin, "Structural Factors and Black Interracial Homicide: A New Examination of the Causal Process," *Criminology* 42 (2004): 647–672.

52. Steven Messner, Lawrence Raffalovich, and Richard McMillan, "Economic Deprivation and Changes in Homicide Arrest Rates for White and Black Youths, 1967–1998: A National Time Series Analysis," *Criminology* 39 (2001): 591–614.

53. Steven Messner and Kenneth Tardiff, "Economic Inequality and Levels of Homicide: An Analysis of Urban Neighborhoods," *Criminology* 24 (1986): 297–317.

54. Darrell Steffensmeier and Dana Haynie, "Gender, Structural Disadvantage, and Urban Crime: Do Macrosocial Variables Also Explain Female Offending Rates?" *Criminology* 38 (2000): 403–438; Richard McGahey, "Economic Conditions, Organization, and Urban Crime," in *Communities and Crime,* eds. Albert Reiss and Michael Tonry (Chicago: University of Chicago Press, 1986), pp. 231–270.

55. Adam Dobrin, Daniel Lee, and Jamie Price, "Neighborhood Structure Differences between Homicide Victims and Non-Victims," *Journal of Criminal Justice* 33 (2005): 137–143; G. David Curry and Irving Spergel, "Gang Homicide, Delinquency, and Community," *Criminology* 26 (1988): 381–407.

56. Steffensmeier and Haynie, "Gender, Structural Disadvantage, and Urban Crime."

57. Scott Menard and Delbert Elliott, "Self-Reported Offending, Maturational Reform, and the Easterlin Hypothesis," *Journal of Quantitative Criminology* 6 (1990): 237–268.

58. Elijah Anderson, *Streetwise: Race, Class and Change in an Urban Community* (Chicago: University of Chicago Press, 1990), pp. 243–244.

59. Matthew Lee and Terri Earnest, "Perceived Community Cohesion and Perceived Risk of Victimization: A Cross-National Analysis," *Justice Quarterly* 20 (2003): 131–158.

60. Pamela Wilcox, Neil Quisenberry, and Shayne Jones, "The Built Environment and Community Crime Risk Interpretation," *Journal of Research in Crime and Delinquency* 40 (2003): 322–345.

61. Stephanie Greenberg, "Fear and Its Relationship to Crime, Neighborhood Deterioration, and Informal Social Control," in *The Social Ecology of Crime,* eds. James Byrne and Robert Sampson (New York: Springer Verlag, 1985), pp. 47–62.

62. C. L. Storr, C.-Y. Chen, and J. C. Anthony, "'Unequal Opportunity': Neighborhood Disadvantage and the Chance to Buy Illegal Drugs," *Journal of Epidemiology and Community Health* 58 (2004): 231–238.

63. Pamela Wilcox Rountree and Kenneth Land, "Burglary Victimization, Perceptions of Crime Risk, and Routine Activities: A Multilevel Analysis across Seattle Neighborhoods and Census Tracts," *Journal of Research in Crime and Delinquency* 33 (1996): 147–180.

64. Wesley Skogan, "Fear of Crime and Neighborhood Change," in *Communities and Crime,* eds. Albert Reiss and Michael Tonry (Chicago: University of Chicago Press, 1986), pp. 191–232.

65. Margo Wilson and Martin Daly, "Life Expectancy, Economic Inequality, Homicide, and Reproductive Timing in Chicago Neighborhoods," *British Journal of Medicine* 314 (1997): 1,271–1,274.

66. Skogan, "Fear of Crime and Neighborhood Change."

67. Ibid.

68. Ralph Taylor and Jeanette Covington, "Community Structural Change and Fear of Crime," *Social Problems* 40 (1993): 374–392.

69. Ted Chiricos, Michael Hogan, and Marc Gertz, "Racial Composition of Neighborhood and Fear of Crime," *Criminology* 35 (1997): 107–131.

70. Ibid., p. 125.

71. Jodi Lane and James Meeker, "Social Disorganization Perceptions, Fear of Gang Crime, and Behavioral Precautions among Whites, Latinos, and Vietnamese," *Journal of Criminal Justice,* 32 (2004): 49–62.

72. Ted Chiricos, Ranee Mcentire, and Marc Gertz, "Social Problems, Perceived Racial and Ethnic Composition of Neighborhood and Perceived Risk of Crime," *Social Problems* 48 (2001): 322–341.

73. G. David Curry and Irving Spergel, "Gang Homicide, Delinquency, and Community," *Criminology* 26 (1988): 381–407.

74. Lawrence Rosenthal, "Gang Loitering and Race," *Journal of Criminal Law and Criminology* 91 (2000): 99–160.

75. Catherine E. Ross, John Mirowsky, and Shana Pribesh, "Powerlessness and the Amplification of Threat: Neighborhood Disadvantage, Disorder, and Mistrust," *American Sociological Review* 66 (2001): 568–580.

76. Anderson, *Streetwise: Race, Class, and Change in an Urban Community,* p. 245.

77. William Terrill and Michael Reisig, "Neighborhood Context and Police Use of Force," *Journal of Research in Crime and Delinquency* 40 (2003): 291–321.

78. Bridget Freisthler, Elizabeth Lascala, Paul Gruenewald, and Andrew Treno, "An Examination of Drug Activity: Effects of Neighborhood Social Organization on the Development of Drug Distribution Systems," *Substance Use & Misuse* 40 (2005): 671–686.

79. Finn-Aage Esbensen and David Huizinga, "Community Structure and Drug Use: From a Social Disorganization Perspective," *Justice Quarterly* 7 (1990): 691–709.

80. Micere Keels, Greg Duncan, Stefanie Deluca, Ruby Mendenhall, and James Rosenbaum, "Fifteen Years Later: Can Residential Mobility Programs Provide a Long-Term Escape from Neighborhood Segregation, Crime, and Poverty?" *Demography* 42 (2005): 51–72.

81. Allen Liska and Paul Bellair, "Violent-Crime Rates and Racial Composition: Convergence over Time," *American Journal of Sociology* 101 (1995): 578–610.

82. Wesley Skogan, *Disorder and Decline: Crime and the Spiral of Decay in American Neighborhoods* (New York: Free Press, 1990), pp. 15–35.

83. Robert Bursik and Harold Grasmick, "Decomposing Trends in Community Careers in Crime." Paper presented at the annual meeting of the American Society of Criminology, Baltimore, November 1990.

84. Ralph Taylor and Jeanette Covington, "Neighborhood Changes in Ecology and Violence," *Criminology* 26 (1988): 553–589.

85. Leo Scheurman and Solomon Kobrin, "Community Careers in Crime," in *Communities and Crime*, eds. Albert Reiss and Michael Tonry (Chicago: University of Chicago Press, 1986), pp. 67–100.

86. Ibid.

87. See, generally, Robert Bursik, "Delinquency Rates as Sources of Ecological Change," in *The Social Ecology of Crime*, eds. James Byrne and Robert Sampson (New York: Springer Verlag, 1985), pp. 63–77.

88. Patricia McCall and Karen Parker, "A Dynamic Model of Racial Competition, Racial Inequality, and Interracial Violence," *Sociological Inquiry* 75 (2005): 273–294.

89. Janet Heitgerd and Robert Bursik, "Extracommunity Dynamics and the Ecology of Delinquency," *American Journal of Sociology* 92 (1987): 775–787.

90. Steven Barkan and Steven Cohn, "Why Whites Favor Spending More Money to Fight Crime: The Role of Racial Prejudice," *Social Problems* 52 (2005): 300–314.

91. Jeffrey Michael Cancino, "The Utility of Social Capital and Collective Efficacy: Social Control Policy in Nonmetropolitan Settings," *Criminal Justice Policy Review* 16 (2005): 287–318; Chris Gibson, Jihong Zhao, Nicholas Lovrich, and Michael Gaffney, "Social Integration, Individual Perceptions of Collective Efficacy, and Fear of Crime in Three Cities," *Justice Quarterly* 19 (2002): 537–564.

92. Robert J. Sampson and Stephen W. Raudenbush, *Disorder in Urban Neighborhoods: Does It Lead to Crime?* (Washington, DC: National Institute of Justice, 2001).

93. Andrea Altschuler, Carol Somkin, and Nancy Adler, "Local Services and Amenities, Neighborhood Social Capital, and Health," *Social Science and Medicine* 59 (2004): 1,219–1,230.

94. Michael Reisig and Jeffrey Michael Cancino, "Incivilities in Nonmetropolitan Communities: The Effects of Structural Constraints, Social Conditions, and Crime," *Journal of Criminal Justice* 32 (2004): 15–29.

95. Robert Sampson, Jeffrey Morenoff, and Felton Earls, "Beyond Social Capital: Spatial Dynamics of Collective Efficacy for Children," *American Sociological Review* 64 (1999): 633–660.

96. Donald Black, "Social Control as a Dependent Variable," in *Toward a General Theory of Social Control*, ed. D. Black (Orlando: Academic Press, 1990).

97. Jennifer Beyers, John Bates, Gregory Pettit, and Kenneth Dodge, "Neighborhood Structure, Parenting Processes, and the Development of Youths' Externalizing Behaviors: A Multilevel Analysis," *American Journal of Community Psychology* 31 (2003): 35–53.

98. Ralph Taylor, "Social Order and Disorder of Street Blocks and Neighborhoods: Ecology, Microecology, and the Systemic Model of Social Disorganization," *Journal of Research in Crime and Delinquency* 34 (1997): 113–155.

99. Steven Messner, Eric Baumer, and Richard Rosenfeld, "Dimensions of Social Capital and Rates of Criminal Homicide," *American Sociological Review* 69 (2004): 882–905.

100. Paul Bellair, "Informal Surveillance and Street Crime: A Complex Relationship," *Criminology* 38 (2000): 137–170.

101. Skogan, *Disorder and Decline*.

102. Robert Sampson and W. Byron Groves, "Community Structure and Crime: Testing Social Disorganization Theory," *American Journal of Sociology* 94 (1989): 774–802; Denise Gottfredson, Richard McNeill, and Gary Gottfredson, "Social Area Influences on Delinquency: A Multilevel Analysis," *Journal of Research in Crime and Delinquency* 28 (1991): 197–206.

103. Jodi Eileen Morris, Rebekah Levine Coley, and Daphne Hernandez, "Out-of-School Care and Problem Behavior Trajectories among Low-Income Adolescents: Individual, Family, and Neighborhood," *Child Development* 75 (2004): 948–965.

104. Ruth Triplett, Randy Gainey, and Ivan Sun, "Institutional Strength, Social Control, and Neighborhood Crime Rates," *Theoretical Criminology* 7 (2003): 439–467; Fred Markowitz, Paul Bellair, Allen Liska, and Jianhong Liu, "Extending Social Disorganization Theory: Modeling the Relationships between Cohesion, Disorder, and Fear," *Criminology* 39 (2001): 293–320.

105. Robert Bursik and Harold Grasmick, "The Multiple Layers of Social Disorganization." Paper presented at the annual meeting of the American Society of Criminology, New Orleans, November 1992.

106. George Capowich, "The Conditioning Effects of Neighborhood Ecology on Burglary Victimization," *Criminal Justice and Behavior* 30 (2003): 39–62.

107. Ruth Peterson, Lauren Krivo, and Mark Harris, "Disadvantage and Neighborhood Violent Crime: Do Local Institutions Matter?" *Journal of Research in Crime and Delinquency* 37 (2000): 31–63.

108. Maria Velez, "The Role of Public Social Control in Urban neighborhoods: A Multi-Level Analysis of Victimization Risk," *Criminology* 39 (2001): 837–864.

109. Velez, Krivo, and Peterson, "Structural Inequality and Homicide."

110. David Klinger, "Negotiating Order in Patrol Work: An Ecological Theory of Police Response to Deviance," *Criminology* 35 (1997): 277–306.

111. Rodney Stark, "Deviant Places: A Theory of the Ecology of Crime," *Criminology* 25 (1987): 893–911.

112. Robert Kane, "Compromised Police Legitimacy as a Predictor of Violent Crime in Structurally Disadvantaged Communities," *Criminology* 43 (2005): 469–498.

113. Robert Sampson, "Neighborhood and Community," *New Economy* 11 (2004): 106–113.

114. Robert Bursik and Harold Grasmick, "Economic Deprivation and Neighborhood Crime Rates, 1960–1980," *Law and Society Review* 27 (1993): 263–278.

115. Delbert Elliott, William Julius Wilson, David Huizinga, Robert Sampson, Amanda Elliott, and Bruce Rankin, "The Effects of Neighborhood Disadvantage

on Adolescent Development," *Journal of Research in Crime and Delinquency* 33 (1996): 389–426.

116. James DeFronzo, "Welfare and Homicide," *Journal of Research in Crime and Delinquency* 34 (1997): 395–406.

117. John Worrall, "Reconsidering the Relationship between Welfare Spending and Serious Crime: A Panel Data Analysis with Implications for Social Support Theory," *Justice Quarterly* 22 (2005): 364–391.

118. Sampson, Morenoff, and Earls, "Beyond Social Capital."

119. Thomas McNulty, "Assessing the Race–Violence Relationship at the Macro Level: The Assumption of Racial Invariance and the Problem of Restricted Distribution," *Criminology* 39 (2001): 467–490.

120. Elliott et al., "The Effects of Neighborhood Disadvantage on Adolescent Development," p. 414.

121. Eric Silver and Lisa Miller, "Sources of Informal Social Control in Chicago Neighborhoods," *Criminology* 42 (2004): 551–585.

122. Bursik and Grasmick, "Economic Deprivation and Neighborhood Crime Rates, 1960–1980."

123. Sampson and Groves, "Community Structure and Crime: Testing Social Disorganization Theory"; Gottfredson, McNeill, and Gottfredson, "Social Area Influences on Delinquency: A Multilevel Analysis."

124. Peterson, Krivo, and Harris, "Disadvantage and Neighborhood Violent Crime."

125. John Braithwaite, "Poverty Power, White-Collar Crime, and the Paradoxes of Criminological Theory," *Australian and New Zealand Journal of Criminology* 24 (1991): 40–58.

126. Wilson and Daly, "Life Expectancy, Economic Inequality, Homicide, and Reproductive Timing in Chicago Neighborhoods."

127. Judith Blau and Peter Blau, "The Cost of Inequality: Metropolitan Structure and Violent Crime," *American Sociological Review* 147 (1982): 114–129.

128. P. M. Krueger, Huie S. A. Bond, R. G. Rogers, and R. A. Hummer, "Neighborhoods and Homicide Mortality: An Analysis of Race/Ethnic Differences," *Journal of Epidemiology and Community Health* 58 (2004): 223–230.

129. Gary LaFree and Kriss Drass, "The Effect of Changes in Intraracial Income Inequality and Educational Attainment on Changes in Arrest Rates for African Americans and Whites, 1957 to 1990," *American Sociological Review* 61 (1996): 614–634; Taylor and Covington, "Neighborhood Changes in Ecology and Violence," p. 582; Richard Block, "Community Environment and Violent Crime," *Criminology* 17 (1979): 46–57; Robert Sampson, "Structural Sources of Variation in Race-Age-Specific Rates of Offending across Major U.S. Cities," *Criminology* 23 (1985): 647–673; Richard Rosenfeld, "Urban Crime Rates: Effects of Inequality, Welfare Dependency, Region, and Race," in *The Social Ecology of Crime,* eds. James Byrne and Robert Sampson (New York: Springer Verlag, 1985), pp. 116–130.

130. Robert Merton, *Social Theory and Social Structure,* enlarged ed. (New York: Free Press, 1968).

131. For an analysis, see Richard Hilbert, "Durkheim and Merton on Anomie: An Unexplored Contrast in Its Derivatives," *Social Problems* 36 (1989): 242–256.

132. Ibid., p. 243.

133. Albert Cohen, "The Sociology of the Deviant Act: Anomie Theory and Beyond," *American Sociological Review* 30 (1965): 5–14.

134. Robert Agnew, "The Contribution of Social Psychological Strain Theory to the Explanation of Crime and Delinquency," in *Advances in Criminological Theory,* vol. 6, *The Legacy of Anomie,* eds. Freda Adler and William Laufer (New Brunswick, NJ: Transaction Press, 1995), pp. 111–122.

135. These criticisms are articulated in Messner and Rosenfeld, *Crime and the American Dream,* p. 60.

136. Messner and Rosenfeld, *Crime and the American Dream.*

137. Steven Messner and Richard Rosenfeld, "An Institutional-Anomie Theory of the Social Distribution of Crime." Paper presented at the annual meeting of the American Society of Criminology, Phoenix, November 1993.

138. Stephen Cernkovich, Peggy Giordano, and Jennifer Rudolph, "Race, Crime, and the American Dream," *Journal of Research in Crime and Delinquency* 37 (2000): 131–170.

139. Jon Gunnar Bernburg, "Anomie, Social Change, and Crime: A Theoretical Examination of Institutional-Anomie

Theory," *British Journal of Criminology* 42 (2002): 729–743.

140. John Hagan, Gerd Hefler, Gabriele Classen, Klaus Boehnke, and Hans Merkens, "Subterranean Sources of Subcultural Delinquency beyond the American Dream," *Criminology* 36 (1998): 309–340.

141. Jukka Savolainen, "Inequality, Welfare State, and Homicide: Further Support for the Institutional Anomie Theory," *Criminology* 38 (2000): 1,021–1,042.

142. Kate Pickett, Jessica Mokherjee, and Richard Wilkinson, "Adolescent Birth Rates, Total Homicides, and Income Inequality in Rich Countries," *American Journal of Public Health* 95 (2005): 1,181–1,183.

143. Robert Agnew, "Foundation for a General Strain Theory of Crime and Delinquency," *Criminology* 30 (1992): 47–87.

144. Ibid., p. 57.

145. Tami Videon, "The Effects of Parent–Adolescent Relationships and Parental Separation on Adolescent Well-Being," *Journal of Marriage and the Family* 64 (2002): 489–504.

146. Cesar Rebellon, "Reconsidering the Broken Homes/Delinquency Relationship and Exploring Its Mediating Mechanism(s)," *Criminology* 40 (2002): 103–135.

147. Ronald Simons, Yi Fu Chen, and Eric Stewart, "Incidents of Discrimination and Risk for Delinquency: A Longitudinal Test of Strain Theory with an African American Sample," *Justice Quarterly* 20 (2003): 827–854.

148. Timothy Brezina, "Adolescent Maltreatment and Delinquency: The Question of Intervening Processes," *Journal of Research in Crime and Delinquency* 35 (1998): 71–99.

149. Paul Mazerolle and Alex Piquero, "Linking General Strain with Anger: Investigating the Instrumental, Escapist, and Violent Adaptations to Strain." Paper presented at the American Society of Criminology meeting, Boston, November 1995.

150. Paul Mazerolle, Velmer Burton, Francis Cullen, T. David Evans, and Gary Payne, "Strain, Anger, and Delinquent Adaptations Specifying General Strain Theory," *Journal of Criminal Justice* 28 (2000): 89–101; Paul Mazerolle and Alex Piquero, "Violent Responses to Strain: An Examination of Conditioning Influences," *Violence and Victimization* 12 (1997): 323–345.

151. George E. Capowich, Paul Mazerolle, and Alex Piquero, "General Strain Theory, Situational Anger, and Social Networks: An Assessment of Conditioning Influences," *Journal of Criminal Justice* 29 (2001): 445–461.

152. Robert Agnew, Timothy Brezina, John Paul Wright, and Francis T. Cullen, "Strain, Personality Traits, and Delinquency: Extending General Strain Theory," *Criminology* 40 (2002): 43–71.

153. Timothy Brezina, "The Functions of Aggression: Violent Adaptations to Interpersonal Violence." Paper presented at the American Society of Criminology Meeting, San Diego, 1997.

154. Agnew, Brezina, Wright, and Cullen, "Strain, Personality Traits, and Delinquency"; Robert Agnew, "Stability and Change in Crime over the Life Course: A Strain Theory Explanation," in *Advances in Criminological Theory*, vol. 7, *Developmental Theories of Crime and Delinquency*, ed. Terence Thornberry (New Brunswick, NJ: Transaction Books, 1995), pp. 113–137.

155. Lawrence Wu, "Effects of Family Instability, Income, and Income Instability on the Risk of Premarital Birth," *American Sociological Review* 61 (1996): 386–406.

156. Anthony Walsh, "Behavior Genetics and Anomie/Strain Theory," *Criminology* 38 (2000): 1,075–1,108.

157. Robert Agnew and Helene Raskin White, "An Empirical Test of General Strain Theory," *Criminology* 30 (1992): 475–499.

158. John Hoffman and Alan Miller, "A Latent Variable Analysis of General Strain Theory," *Journal of Quantitative Criminology* 13 (1997): 111–113; Raymond Paternoster and Paul Mazerolle, "General Strain Theory and Delinquency: A Replication and Extension," *Journal of Research in Crime and Delinquency* 31 (1994): 235–263.

159. G. Roger Jarjoura, "The Conditional Effect of Social Class on the Dropout–Delinquency Relationship," *Journal of Research in Crime and Delinquency* 33 (1996): 232–255.

160. Robert Agnew, "Experienced, Vicarious, and Anticipated Strain: An Exploratory Study on Physical Victimization and Delinquency," *Justice Quarterly* 19 (2002): 603–633.

161. Lisa Broidy, "A Test of General Strain Theory," *Criminology* 39 (2001): 9–36.

162. Robert Agnew and Timothy Brezina, "Relational Problems with Peers, Gender, and Delinquency," *Youth and Society* 29 (1997): 84–111.

163. John Hoffmann and S. Susan Su, "The Conditional Effects of Stress on Delinquency and Drug Use: A Strain Theory in Assessment of Sex Differences," *Journal of Research in Crime and Delinquency* 34 (1997): 46–78.

164. Lisa Broidy, "The Role of Gender in General Strain Theory." Paper presented at the meeting of the American Society of Criminology, Boston, November 1995.

165. Lisa Broidy and Robert Agnew, "Gender and Crime: A General Strain Theory Perspective," *Journal of Research in Crime and Delinquency* 34 (1997): 275–306.

166. Robbin Ogle, Daniel Maier-Katkin, and Thomas Bernard, "A Theory of Homicidal Behavior among Women," *Criminology* 33 (1995): 173–193.

167. Teresa LaGrange and Robert Silverman, "Investigating the Interdependence of Strain and Self-Control," *Canadian Journal of Criminology and Criminal Justice* 45 (2003): 431–464.

168. Christopher Browning, Seth Feinberg, and Robert D. Dietz, "The Paradox of Social Organization: Networks, Collective Efficacy, and Violent Crime in Urban Neighborhoods," *Social Forces* 83 (2004): 503–534.

169. Thorsten Sellin, *Culture Conflict and Crime*, Bulletin No. 41 (New York: Social Science Research Council, 1938).

170. Ibid., p. 22.

171. Ibid., p. 29.

172. Ibid., p. 68.

173. Walter Miller, "Lower-Class Culture as a Generating Milieu of Gang Delinquency," *Journal of Social Issues* 14 (1958): 5–19.

174. Ibid., pp. 14–17.

175. Fred Markowitz and Richard Felson, "Social-Demographic Attitudes and Violence," *Criminology* 36 (1998): 117–138.

176. Jeffrey Fagan, *Adolescent Violence: A View from the Street*, NIJ Research Preview (Washington, DC: National Institute of Justice, 1998).

177. Albert Cohen, *Delinquent Boys* (New York: Free Press, 1955).

178. Ibid., p. 25.

179. Ibid., p. 28.

180. Ibid.

181. Clarence Schrag, *Crime and Justice American Style* (Washington, DC: U.S. Government Printing Office, 1971), p. 74.

182. Cohen, *Delinquent Boys*, p. 30.

183. Ibid., p. 31.

184. Ibid., p. 133.

185. J. Johnstone, "Social Class, Social Areas, and Delinquency," *Sociology and Social Research* 63 (1978): 49–72; Joseph Harry, "Social Class and Delinquency: One More Time," *Sociological Quarterly* 15 (1974): 294–301.

186. Richard Cloward and Lloyd Ohlin, *Delinquency and Opportunity* (New York: Free Press, 1960).

187. Ibid., p. 7.

188. Ibid., p. 85.

189. Ibid., p. 171.

190. Ibid., p. 23.

191. Ibid., p. 73.

192. Ibid., p. 24.

193. Finn-Aage Esbensen and David Huizinga, "Gangs, Drugs and Delinquency in a Survey of Urban Youth," *Criminology* 31 (1993): 565–587.

194. For a general criticism, see Kornhauser, *Social Sources of Delinquency*.

195. Charles Tittle, "Social Class and Criminal Behavior: A Critique of the Theoretical Foundations," *Social Forces* 62 (1983): 334–358.

196. James Q. Wilson and Richard Herrnstein, *Crime and Human Nature* (New York: Simon & Schuster, 1985).

197. Kenneth Polk and F. Lynn Richmond, "Those Who Fail," in *Schools and Delinquency*, eds. Kenneth Polk and Walter Schafer (Englewood Cliffs, NJ: Prentice-Hall, 1974), p. 67.

198. Kathleen Maguire and Ann Pastore, *Sourcebook of Criminal Justice Statistics, 1996* (Washington, DC: U.S. Government Printing Office, 1996), pp. 150–166.

199. James DeFronzo, "Welfare and Burglary," *Crime and Delinquency* 42 (1996): 223–230.

200. Solomon Kobrin, "The Chicago Area Project—25-Year Assessment," *Annals of the American Academy of Political and Social Science* 322 (1959): 20–29.

201. Community Capacity Development Office website: http://www.ojp.usdoj.gov/eows/nutshell.htm#Strategy. Accessed August 1, 2004.

CHAPTER 7

© AP Photo / Corpus Christi Caller-Times, David Pellerin / Wide World Photos

Under the Alaska Sex Offender Registration Act, an incarcerated sex offender or child kidnapper must register with the Department of Corrections before release from prison. The law requires that the offender's name, aliases, address, photograph, and physical description be published on the Internet. Both the act's registration and notification requirements were made retroactive to previously convicted offenders.

In a recent case, the Supreme Court upheld the Alaska Sex Offender Registration Act's requirement that offenders who had been incarcerated prior to its passage be made to conform to its provisions.[1] Reasoning that the law was nonpunitive, the Court ruled that the Alaska legislature's intent was to protect the public from sex offenders.

While some lawmakers may view sex offender registration as an effective method of alerting citizens to the presence of dangerous predators in their community, such methods may also have their downside. Sex registration stigmatizes people who have already paid their debt to society and labels them as a continuing threat even though correctional authorities have ordered their release. Is it possible that such drastic measures, which turn former offenders into social outcasts, might actually encourage rather than deter deviant behaviors?

SOCIAL PROCESS THEORIES

CHAPTER OBJECTIVES

1. Be familiar with the concept of socialization
2. Discuss the effect of schools, family, and friends on crime
3. Be able to discuss the differences of learning, control, and reaction
4. Be familiar with the concept of differential association
5. Be able to discuss what is meant by a definition toward criminality
6. Understand the concept of neutralization
7. Be able to discuss the relationship between self-concept and crime
8. Know the elements of the social bond
9. Describe the labeling process and how it leads to criminal careers
10. Be familiar with the concepts of primary and secondary deviance
11. Show how the process of labeling leads to criminal careers

To some criminologists, an individual's relationship with critical elements of the social process is the key to understanding the onset and continuation of criminal behaviors. They believe that criminality is a function of individual socialization and the interactions people have with various organizations, institutions, and processes of society. Most people are influenced by their family relationships, peer group associations, educational experiences, and interactions with authority figures, including teachers, employers, and agents of the justice system. If these relationships are positive and supportive, people can succeed within the rules of society; if these relationships are dysfunctional and destructive, conventional success may be impossible, and criminal solutions may become a feasible alternative. Taken together, this view of crime is referred to as **social process theory.**

|||||||| CONNECTIONS ||||||||

Chapter 2's analysis of the class–crime relationship showed why this association is still a hotly debated topic. Although serious criminals may be found disproportionately in lower-class areas, self-report studies show that criminality cuts across class lines. The discussion of drug use in Chapter 13, which shows that members of the middle class use and abuse recreational substances, suggests that law violators are not necessarily economically motivated.

Many criminologists question whether a person's place in the social structure alone can control or predict the onset of criminality. After all, the majority of people residing in the nation's most deteriorated urban areas are law-abiding citizens who hold conventional values and compensate for their lack of social standing and financial problems with hard work, frugal living, and keeping an eye to the future. Conversely, self-report studies tell us that many members of the privileged classes engage in theft, drug use, and other crimes.

Today, more than 30 million Americans live below the poverty line. Even were we to assume that all criminals come from the lower class—which they do not—it is evident that the great majority of the most indigent Americans do not commit criminal acts even though they may have a great economic incentive to do so. As discussed in Chapter 6, neighborhood deterioration and disorganization alone cannot explain why one individual embarks on a criminal career while another, living in the same environment, obeys the law, gets an education, and seeks legitimate employment.[2]

Relatively few delinquent offenders living in the most deteriorated areas remain persistent, chronic offenders; most desist despite the continuing pressure of social decay. Some other social forces, then, must be at work to explain why the majority of at-risk individuals do not become persistent criminal offenders.

SOCIALIZATION AND CRIME

To explain these contradictory findings, attention has been focused on social-psychological processes and interactions common to people at all segments of the social structure. Social process theories share one basic concept: all people, regardless of their race, class, or gender, have the potential to become delinquents or criminals. Although members of the lower class may have the added burdens of poverty, racism, poor schools, and disrupted family lives, these social forces may be counteracted by positive peer relations, a supportive family, and educational success. In contrast, even the most affluent members of society may turn to antisocial behavior if their life experiences are intolerable or destructive.

The influence of social process theories has endured because the relationship between social class and crime is still uncertain. Most residents of inner-city areas refrain from criminal activity, and few of those who do commit crimes remain persistent chronic offenders into their adulthood. If poverty were the sole cause of crime, then indigent adults would be as criminal as indigent teenagers. The association between economic status and crime has been called problematic because class position alone cannot explain crime rates.[3]

Criminologists have long studied the critical elements of socialization to determine how they contribute to a burgeoning criminal career. Prominent among these elements are the family, the peer group, and the school.

Family Relations

For some time, family relationships have been considered a major determinant of behavior.[4] In fact, there is abundant evidence that parenting factors, such as the ability to communicate and to provide proper discipline, may play a critical role in determining whether people misbehave as children and even later as adults. This is one of the most replicated findings in the criminological literature.[5]

|||||||| CONNECTIONS ||||||||

Chapter 3 noted that victims of abuse may suffer significant social problems and emotional stress related to criminal activity. Process theories recognize the role of family relations in escalating criminal activity.

Youth who grow up in households characterized by conflict and tension, where parents are absent or separated, or where there is a lack of familial love and support are susceptible to the crime-promoting forces in the environment. Even those children living in so-called high-crime areas will be better able to resist the temptations of the streets if they receive fair discipline, care, and support from parents who provide them with strong, positive role models.[6] Nonetheless, living in a disadvantaged neighborhood places terrific strain on family functioning, especially in single-parent

According to social process theory, youths who grow up in a household characterized by conflict and tension, where parents are absent or separated, or where there is a lack of familial love and support, are susceptible to the crime-promoting forces in the environment. In contrast, children will be able to resist crime if they receive fair discipline, care, and support from parents and other family members who provide them with strong, positive role models.

criminal behaviors. The lack of supervision in the aftermath of divorce may expose some kids to the negative effects of antisocial peers.[11] There is evidence that children who live with single parents receive less encouragement and less help with schoolwork. Poor school achievement and limited educational aspirations have been associated with delinquent behavior. Also, because they are receiving less attention as a result of having just one parent, these children may be more prone to rebellious acts, such as running away and truancy.[12] Children in two-parent households, on the other hand, are more likely to want to go on to college than kids in single-parent homes.[13]

Because their incomes may decrease substantially in the aftermath of marital breakup, some divorced mothers are forced to move to residences in deteriorated neighborhoods. Some of these disorganized neighborhoods may place children at risk of crime and drug abuse.[14] In poor neighborhoods single parents cannot call upon neighborhood resources to take up the burden of controlling children, and, as a result, a greater burden is placed on families to provide adequate supervision.[15]

When a mother remarries, it does not seem to mitigate the effects of divorce on youth. Children living with a stepparent exhibit as many problems as youth in single-parent families and considerably more problems than those who are living with both biological parents.[16]

families that experience social isolation from relatives, friends, and neighbors. Children who are raised within such distressed families are at risk for delinquency.[7]

 Use "parental deprivation" as a subject guide in InfoTrac College Edition to find out the effects of parental absence on children.

The relationship between family structure and crime is critical when the high rates of divorce and single parents are considered. The U.S. Census Bureau estimates that the percentage of children living in homes headed by married couples is on the decline and should be further reduced from about 35 percent today to about 29 percent in 2010.[8] This trend is important when we consider the fact that since 1960 the number of single-parent households in the population has been significantly related to arrest rates.[9]

At one time, growing up in a so-called broken home was considered a primary cause of criminal behavior. However, many criminologists today discount the association between family structure and the onset of criminality, claiming that family conflict and discord are more important determinants of behavior than family structure.[10] Not all experts discount the effects of family structure on crime, however. Even if single mothers (or fathers) can make up for the loss of a second parent, the argument goes, it is simply more difficult to do so, and the chances of failure increase. Single parents may find it difficult to provide adequate supervision. Kids whose parents are divorced are more likely to engage in delinquency, especially if they hang out with peers who engage in

 Does remarriage help the educational achievement of kids who live in single-parent households? To find out, read this article in InfoTrac College Edition: William Jeynes, "Effects of Remarriage following Divorce on the Academic Achievement of Children," *Journal of Youth and Adolescence* 28 (June 1999): 385.

Other family factors with predictive value include inconsistent discipline, poor supervision, and the lack of a warm, loving, supportive parent–child relationship.[17] Parents who are supportive and effectively control their children in a noncoercive fashion (*parental efficacy*) are more likely to raise children who refrain from delinquency.[18] Delinquency will be reduced if parents provide the type of structure that integrates children into families while giving them the ability to assert their individuality and regulate their own behavior.[19] Kids who report having troubled home lives also exhibit lower levels of self-esteem and are more prone to antisocial behaviors.[20] In contrast, children who have warm and affectionate ties to their parents report greater levels of self-esteem beginning in adolescence and extending into their adulthood; high self-esteem is inversely related to criminal behavior.[21]

Children growing up in homes where a parent suffers from mental impairment are also at risk for delinquency.[22] Even children as young as 2 years old who are the children of drug abusers exhibit personality defects such as excessive anger and negativity.[23] These children, and those who are older, are more likely to become persistent substance abusers than the children of nonabusers.[24] John Laub and Robert Sampson find that parents who engage in criminality and substance abuse are more likely to raise children who engage in law-violating behavior than the offspring of conventional law-abiding parents.[25]

| | | | | | | CONNECTIONS | | | | | | |

Sampson and Laub's research will be discussed more fully in Chapter 9. Although deviant parents may encourage offending, Sampson and Laub believe that life experiences can either encourage crime-prone people to offend or conversely aid them in their return to a conventional lifestyle.

CHILD ABUSE AND CRIME There is also a suspected link between child abuse, neglect, sexual abuse, and crime.[26] Mental health and delinquency experts have found that abused kids experience mental and social problems across their life span, ranging from substance abuse to possession of a damaged personality.[27] A number of studies show that there is a significant association between child maltreatment and serious self-reported and official delinquency, even when taking into account gender, race, and class.[28] Children who are subject to even minimum amounts of physical punishment may be more likely to use violence themselves in personal interactions. The effect seems greatest among white children and less among African American and Latino children.[29] In nonviolent societies, parents rarely punish their children physically; in more violent societies, there is a link between corporal punishment, delinquency, anger, spousal abuse, depression, and adult crime.[30]

The effect of abuse on delinquency has also been observed in other cultures. Research conducted in ten European countries shows that the degree to which parents and teachers approve of corporal punishment is related to the overall homicide rate as well as the infant homicide rate.[31] Studies of Chinese families show that those who provide firm support inhibit delinquency, whereas families that have one or both parents who are deviant are more likely to have children who are involved in deviant activities.[32]

Educational Experience

The educational process and adolescent achievement in school have been linked to criminality. Studies show that children who do poorly in school, lack educational motivation, and feel alienated are the most likely to engage in criminal acts.[33] Children who fail in school have been found to offend more frequently than those who are successful in school. These children commit more serious and violent offenses and persist in their offending into adulthood.[34]

Schools contribute to criminality when they label problem youths and set them apart from conventional society. One way in which schools perpetuate this stigmatization is the "track system," which identifies some students as college bound and others as academic underachievers or potential dropouts.[35] Those children placed in tracks labeled advanced placement, college prep, or honors will develop positive self-images and achievement motivation, whereas those assigned to lower level or general courses of study may believe academic achievement is closed to someone of their limited skills.

Another significant educational problem is that many students leave high school without gaining a diploma. Though national dropout rates are in decline, more than 10 percent of Americans ages 16 to 24 have left school permanently without a diploma; of these more than 1 million withdrew before completing 10th grade. According to a recent report by the nonprofit Urban Institute, the national graduation rate is 68 percent, with nearly one-third of all public high school students failing to graduate. These researchers found tremendous racial gaps in graduation rates. Students from historically disadvantaged minority groups (American Indian, Latino, black) have little more than a fifty-fifty chance of finishing high school with a diploma; by comparison, graduation rates for whites and Asians are 75 and 77 percent nationally.[36] These results are disturbing because research indicates that many school dropouts, especially those who have been expelled, face a significant chance of entering a criminal career.[37] In contrast, doing well in school and developing attachments to teachers have been linked to crime resistance.[38] Efforts to keep children in school are discussed in the Policy and Practice in Criminology feature highlighting a program called Communities In Schools.

Schools can also be the scene of crime and violence. For example, bullying is a sad but common occurrence in the U.S. educational system that occurs in almost every school system.[39] Research by Tonja Nansel found that more than 16 percent of U.S. schoolchildren say they have been bullied by other students during the current school term, and approximately 30 percent of 6th- through 10th-grade students reported being involved in some aspect of moderate to frequent bullying, either as a bully, the target of bullying, or both.[40]

The latest national survey on school crime (2003) estimates that about 1.5 million violent incidents occur in public elementary and secondary schools each year.[41] Few schools are immune: More than 70 percent of public schools experienced one or more violent incidents, and 36 percent of schools reported one or more such incidents to the police. Twenty percent of schools experienced one or more serious violent incidents including rape, possession of a weapon, and threat of and actual armed robbery; almost half of all public schools experienced one or more thefts. These translate into an estimated 61,000 serious violent incidents and 218,000 thefts at public schools each year. About 15 percent of public schools report one or more serious violent incidents to the police, and 28 percent report one or more thefts to the police.

To learn what is being done to improve school security, read: Teresa Anderson, "School Security," *Security Management* 45 (2001): 96–98.

School level and size have a significant impact on the likelihood of experiencing theft and violence. Secondary schools are more likely to have a violent incident than elementary, middle, or combined schools. Likewise, larger schools are more likely to have a violent incident and report one or more violent incidents to the police than smaller schools: About 90 percent of all schools with 1,000 students or more had a violent incident, compared with 60 percent of schools with less than 300 students. School location also seems to have a significant influence on school crime. Urban schools are more likely than suburban and rural schools to experience or report crime to the police.

To access the **school crime survey,** go to http://nces.ed.gov/pubsearch/ pubsinfo.asp?pubid = 2004004. For an up-to-date list of web links, go to http://cj.wadsworth .com/siegel_crimtpt9e.

The presence of weapons and violence is not lost on the average student. Data from a recent (2004) survey of high school students found that almost half report having seen other students carry knives at school, roughly one in ten report having seen other students carry guns at school, and more than one in five reported being fearful of weapon-associated victimization at school.[42]

Peer Relations

Psychologists have long recognized that the peer group has a powerful effect on human conduct and can have a dramatic influence on decision making and behavior choices.[43] Peer influence on behavior has been recorded in different cultures and may be a universal norm.[44]

Early in children's lives, parents are the primary source of influence and attention. Between the ages of 8 and 14, children begin to seek out a stable peer group. If all goes as it should, both the number and variety of friendships increase as children go through adolescence. Soon, friends begin having a greater influence over decision making than parents.[45]

By their early teens, children report that their friends give them emotional support when they are feeling badly and that they can confide intimate feelings to peers without worrying about their confidences being betrayed. As children begin to talk to their friends about deviant behavior— such as getting together to use drugs—their level of participation in antisocial behavior increases as well.[46] In later adolescence, peer approval has a major impact on socialization. As they go through adolescence, children form cliques, small groups of friends who share activities and confidences. They also belong to crowds, loosely organized groups of

© Lawrence Manning/Corbis

As kids mature, peers replace parents as the primary source of influence and attention. Kids seek out a stable peer group and both the number and variety of friendships increase as children go through adolescence. By their early teens, friends give emotional support; they can be told intimate feelings. Close connections with peers who are antisocial may encourage young people to engage in antisocial behavior themselves.

Keeping Kids in School: The Communities In Schools Program

Millions of Americans have not completed high school; they are dropouts. Research indicates that they will earn less over their lifetimes and be at risk for criminality. Four in ten dropouts said they left high school because they were failing or they did not like school; an equal number of males and females reported they were leaving school because of personality conflicts with teachers. More males than females dropped out because of school suspension or expulsion.

A popular program designed to reduce the number of students who drop out of school is the Communities In Schools (CIS) network (formerly known as Cities In Schools). This program includes a web of local, state, and national partnerships working together to bring at-risk youth four basic necessities to help motivate them to stay in school:

- A personal one-on-one relationship with a caring adult

- A safe place to learn and grow

- A marketable skill to use upon graduation

- A chance to give back to peers and community

A student's decision to drop out of school may result from a variety of social and emotional problems, such as family dissention, drug and alcohol abuse, illiteracy, or teenage pregnancy. Therefore, the entire community, not just the schools, must take responsibility for preventing youth from dropping out. CIS brings together businesses and public and private agencies in communities—welfare and health professionals, employment counselors, social workers and recreation leaders, the clergy, and members of community groups—to help the schools. CIS caters to the student and his or her family, bringing together in one place a support system of caring adults. They ensure that the student has access to the resources that can help him or her build self-worth and the skills needed to embark on a productive and constructive life.

Most CIS programs take place inside traditional schools, but another method of service delivery is the CIS academy, an easily identifiable free-standing facility or wing of an existing school, sponsored largely by an individual corporation or organization.

In general, CIS projects are grouped into three broad categories:

- Traditional school site projects that pattern themselves as closely as possible after the normal classroom routine

- Projects in which repositioned health and human services staff assume the primary role

- Projects that function as alternative schools

The first two categories apply to the classroom model; the third applies to the academy model.

The CIS *classroom model* enables students to sign up for the program as an elective class. Instruction focuses on life-skills education, such as employment, remedial education, and tutoring. CIS classrooms often involve community volunteers who mentor and tutor students. The classroom model also can provide in-school activities such as conflict resolution, violence abatement, and community service. The classroom structure is patterned closely after a normal routine. Teachers assigned by the school district to the CIS program lead these activities. In certain situations, repositioned health and human services staff assume the primary leadership role.

The *academy model* has all the basic elements of the CIS classroom model but is organized as an alternative school. These academies can be "schools within schools," located in a separate wing or section of the school where the CIS students attend classes together or can occupy a completely

---

children who share interests and activities. While clique members share intimate knowledge, crowds are brought together by mutually shared activities, such as sports, religion, or hobbies. Though bonds in this wider circle of friends may not be intimate, adolescents learn a lot about themselves and their world while navigating through these relationships.[47] Some adolescents who are considered popular may be members of a variety of cliques and crowds. The most popular youths, in general, tend to do well in school and are socially astute. In contrast, children who are rejected by their peers are more likely to display aggressive behavior and disrupt group activities through bickering, bullying, or other

antisocial behavior.[48] Peer relations, then, are a vital aspect of maturation.

Because of the powerful influence adolescents feel from their peers, they feel a persistent pressure to conform to group values. When peer pressure is exerted from positive relationships, peers guide one another and help their friends learn to share and cooperate, cope with aggressive impulses, and discuss feelings they would not dare bring up at home. In these relationships, youths can compare their own experiences and learn that others have similar concerns and problems. Through these friendships, they realize they are not alone. When the peer group is not among friends

separate building. A student who meets CIS program eligibility criteria and has parental permission is assigned a case manager who assesses the student's needs. The case manager then contacts the proper agencies to provide the specific services needed. Through the CIS program, the young person can receive counseling either individually or as part of a group. If the CIS program cannot provide a needed service directly, the student, and sometimes parents and family members, are referred to an appropriate service agency.

CIS programs serve a target population of at-risk youth and youth who have already crossed the line into risky behaviors and consequences. If not for the CIS program, most of these students would be expected to leave school before graduation.

CIS has been quite popular. As of 2004:

■ There are 194 operational CIS programs in 28 states, serving nearly 3,000 education sites.

■ Nearly 2 million students have access to services through CIS.

■ Approximately 985,000 students receive direct services through CIS.

■ More than 180,000 parents, families and guardians of students also receive services.

Evaluations of the program show the following results:

■ The overall dropout rate for CIS-tracked students was 1 percent.

■ Eighty-seven percent of eligible CIS seniors graduated from high school.

■ CIS students who had had serious to moderately severe problems in attendance and academic performance improved their performance in these areas. About 70 percent of students with high absenteeism prior to participation in CIS improved their attendance, and 60 percent with low initial grades improved.

Of those students with the lowest grades (GPA below 1.0), 79 percent raised their GPA, with an average increase of a full grade point. The majority of the students believed they had benefited from CIS and expressed high levels of satisfaction with the program.

Schools that have the program show overall improvement:

■ Eighty-seven percent of schools that were assigned a grade for annual overall school performance improved or maintained a satisfactory school grade.

■ Ninety-two percent of schools assessed for overall school safety improved or maintained their safety assessment.

■ Almost 89 percent improved or maintained satisfactory overall student academic achievement.

Critical Thinking

1. Why does the CIS program seem to be making a difference for at-risk youth?

2. What is it about the way the program is structured that allows students the opportunity to succeed?

3. What other alternatives may be available to help motivate kids to stay in school? What other special programs may be helpful?

InfoTrac College Edition Research

To learn more, read these articles: Adel Wassef, Gayle Mason, Melissa Lassiter Collins, Michael O'Boyle, and Denise Ingham, "Student Assessment of School-Based Support Groups," *Adolescence* 31 (spring 1996): 1; Clyde A. Winters, "Learning Disabilities, Crime, Delinquency, and Special Education Placement," *Adolescence* 32 (summer 1997): 451–458.

Sources: *Communities In Schools,* http://www.cisnet.org/. Accessed on August 1, 2004; Susan Siegel, *Communities In Schools Network Report 2002–2003, Improving Schools, Changing Lives, Choosing Success* (Alexandria, VA: Communities In Schools, 2004); Sharon Cantelon and Donni LeBoeuf, *Keeping Young People in School: Community Programs that Work* (Washington, DC: National Institute of Justice, 1997).

who are positive influences on one another, however, adolescent criminal activity can begin to be initiated as a group process.[49]

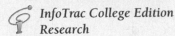 There are many studies examining the relationship of peer influence on crime. Read one on InfoTrac College Edition: David Fergusson, Nicola Swain-Campbell, and L. John Horwood, "Deviant Peer Affiliations, Crime, and Substance Use: A Fixed Effects Regression Analysis," *Journal of Abnormal Child Psychology* 34 (2002): 419–430.

PEER REJECTION/PEER ACCEPTANCE Kids who are considered unpopular, out of control, or unruly may be abandoned or snubbed by their peers. Peer rejection helps lock these already aggressive kids into a cycle of persistent violence that is likely to continue into early adulthood.[50]

Peer rejection may help increase and sustain antisocial behaviors because outcast kids become suspicious of other people's motives, see them as hostile, and become more likely to respond in an antisocial manner. Because the most popular kids reject them, these troubled youth have fewer positive social options and may be drawn to lower-status and deviant peer groups. Hoping to belong and to be accepted in at least one peer group, no matter its damaged reputation, they feel compelled to engage in more antisocial activity in an effort to gain standing and approval.

If peer rejection promotes criminality, can peer acceptance reverse its tide? Having prosocial friends who are committed to conventional success may help shield kids from crime-producing inducements in their environment. Recently, using data from a national survey of youth, John Paul Wright and Francis Cullen found that associating with prosocial friends and coworkers helped lure adolescents away from delinquent peer networks. Peer acceptance helped reduce adolescent criminal behavior and drug use; the effect continued on to their adulthood. [51]

PEERS AND CRIMINALITY Though experts have long debated the exact relationship between peer group interaction and delinquency, research shows that adolescents who report inadequate or strained peer relations, and who say they are not popular with the "opposite sex," are the ones most likely to become delinquent.[52] The association between peers and the onset and continuation of criminality may take one of a number of different paths:

- Delinquent friends cause law-abiding youth to "get in trouble." Kids who fall in with a "bad crowd" are at risk for delinquency. Youths who maintain friendships with antisocial peers are more likely to become delinquent regardless of their own personality or the type of supervision they receive at home.[53] Even previously law-abiding youths are more likely to get involved in delinquency if they become associated with friends who initiate them into delinquent careers.[54]

- Antisocial youths seek out and join up with like-minded friends; deviant peers sustain and amplify delinquent careers.[55] Those who choose aggressive or violent friends are more likely to begin engaging in antisocial behavior themselves and suffer psychological deficits.[56]

- As children move through the life course, antisocial friends help youths maintain delinquent careers and obstruct the aging-out process.[57] In contrast, nondelinquent friends moderate delinquency.[58] If adulthood brings close and sustaining ties to conventional friends, marriage, and family, the level of deviant behavior will decline.[59]

- Troubled kids choose delinquent peers out of necessity rather than desire. The social baggage they cart around prevents them from developing associations with conventional peers. Because they are impulsive, they may hook up with friends who are dangerous and get them into trouble.[60] Deviant peers do not cause straight kids to go bad, but they amplify the likelihood of a troubled kid getting further involved in antisocial behaviors.[61]

Regardless of how they are chosen, criminal peers may exert tremendous influence on behavior, attitudes, and be-

liefs.[62] In every level of the social structure, youths who fall in with a "bad crowd" become more susceptible to criminal behavior patterns.[63] These deviant peers provide friendship networks that support delinquency and drug use.[64] Activities such as riding around, staying out late, and partying with deviant peers provide these groups with the opportunity to commit deviant acts.[65] Because delinquent friends tend to be, as criminologist Mark Warr puts it, "sticky" (once acquired, they are not easily lost), peer influence may continue throughout the life span.[66]

Some children join more than one deviant group, playing a leadership role in one and being a follower in another. Even when some of these groups are short lived, being exposed to so many deviant influences in multiple groups may help explain why deviant group membership is highly correlated with personal offending rates.[67] The more antisocial the peer group, the more likely its members will engage in delinquency; nondelinquent friends will help moderate delinquency.[68]

As children grow and move forward, friends will influence their behavior, and their behavior will influence their friends.[69] Antisocial friends guide delinquent careers so they withstand the aging-out process.[70] People who maintain close relations with antisocial peers will sustain their own criminal behavior into their adulthood.

Institutional Involvement and Belief

It follows that people who hold high moral values and beliefs, who have learned to distinguish "right from wrong," and who regularly attend religious services should also eschew crime and other antisocial behaviors. Religion binds people together and forces them to confront the consequences of their behavior. Committing crimes would violate the principles of all organized religions.

Sociologists Travis Hirschi and Rodney Stark found in a classic study that, contrary to expectations, the association between religious attendance and belief and delinquent behavior patterns is negligible and insignificant.[71] However, some research efforts have reached an opposite conclusion, finding that attending religious services significantly helps reduce crime.[72] Kids living in disorganized high-crime areas who attend religious services are better able to resist illegal drug use.[73] Interestingly, participation seems to be a more significant inhibitor of crime than merely having religious beliefs and values.[74] Cross-national research shows that countries with high rates of church membership and attendance have lower crime rates than less "devout" nations.[75]

|||||||| CONNECTIONS ||||||||

Arousal theory would predict that church attendance is inversely correlated with crime rates because criminals are people who need large amounts of stimulation and would not be able to sit through religious services. See Chapter 5 for more on arousal theory.

The Effects of Socialization on Crime

To many criminologists, the elements of socialization described up to this point are the chief determinants of criminal behavior. According to this view, people living in even the most deteriorated urban areas can successfully resist inducements to crime if they have a positive self-image, learn moral values, and have the support of their parents, peers, teachers, and neighbors. The girl with a positive self-image who is chosen for a college scholarship has the warm, loving support of her parents and is viewed as someone "going places" by friends and neighbors. She is less likely to adopt a criminal way of life than another adolescent who is abused at home, lives with criminal parents, and whose bond to her school and peer group is shattered because she is labeled a troublemaker.[76] The boy who has learned criminal behavior from his parents and siblings and then joins a neighborhood gang is much more likely to become an adult criminal than his next-door neighbor who idolizes his hard-working, deeply religious parents. It is socialization, not the social structure, which determines life chances. The more social problems encountered during the socialization process, the greater the likelihood that youths will encounter difficulties and obstacles as they mature, such as being unemployed or becoming a teenage mother.

Theorists who believe that an individual's socialization determines the likelihood of criminality adopt the social process approach to human behavior. The social process approach has several independent branches (Figure 7.1).

The first branch, **social learning theory**, suggests that people learn the techniques and attitudes of crime from close and intimate relationships with criminal peers; crime is a learned behavior. The second, **social control theory**, maintains that everyone has the potential to become a criminal but that most people are controlled by their bonds to society. Crime occurs when the forces that bind people to society are weakened or broken. The third branch, **social reaction theory (labeling theory),** says people become criminals when significant members of society label them as such, and they accept those labels as a personal identity.

Put another way, social learning theory assumes people are born good and learn to be bad; social control theory assumes people are born bad and must be controlled in order to be good; social reaction theory assumes that, whether good or bad, people are controlled by the reactions of others. Each of these independent branches will be discussed separately.

 To quiz yourself on this material, go to the Criminology TPT 9e website.

SOCIAL LEARNING THEORY

Social learning theorists believe crime is a product of learning the norms, values, and behaviors associated with criminal activity. Social learning can involve the actual techniques

FIGURE 7.1

The Social Processes that Control Human Behavior

Social learning theory
Criminal behavior is learned through human interaction.

Social control theory
Human behavior is controlled through close associations with institutions and individuals.

SOCIAL PROCESS APPROACH

Social reaction theory (labeling theory)
Some people are labeled "criminal" by police and court authorities; labeled people are known as troublemakers, criminals, and so on and are shunned by conventional society.

of crime—how to hot-wire a car or roll a joint—as well as the psychological aspects of criminality—how to deal with the guilt or shame associated with illegal activities. This section briefly reviews the three most prominent forms of social learning theory: differential association theory, differential reinforcement theory, and neutralization theory.

Not only can learning theories be applied to a wide assortment of criminal activity, they are also used to explain noncriminal activities. To find out more, go to InfoTrac College Edition and use "learning theory" as a key word.

Differential Association Theory

One of the most prominent social learning theories is Edwin H. Sutherland's **differential association theory.** Often considered the preeminent U.S. criminologist, Sutherland first put forth his theory in his 1939 text, *Principles of Criminology.*[77] The final version of the theory appeared in 1947. When Sutherland died in 1950, Donald Cressey, his long-time associate, continued his work. Cressey was so successful in explaining and popularizing his mentor's efforts that differential association remains one of the most enduring explanations of criminal behavior.

Sutherland's research on white-collar crime, professional theft, and intelligence led him to dispute the notion that crime was a function of the inadequacy of people in the lower classes.[78] To Sutherland, criminality stemmed neither from individual traits nor from socioeconomic position; instead, he believed it to be a function of a learning process that could affect any individual in any culture. Acquiring a behavior is a social learning process, not a political or legal process. Skills and motives conducive to crime are learned as a result of contacts with pro-crime values, attitudes, and definitions and other patterns of criminal behavior.

Edwin H. Sutherland served as the twenty-ninth president of the American Sociological Society. His presidential address, "White-Collar Criminality," was delivered at the organization's annual meeting in Philadelphia in December 1939. To read Sutherland's groundbreaking talk on white-collar crime, go to http://www.asanet.org/governance/PresidentialAddress1939.pdf. For an up-to-date list of web links, go to http://cj.wadsworth.com/siegel_crimtpt9e.

PRINCIPLES OF DIFFERENTIAL ASSOCIATION The basic principles of differential association are explained as follows:[79]

- *Criminal behavior is learned:* This statement differentiates Sutherland's theory from prior attempts to classify criminal behavior as an inherent characteristic of criminals. By suggesting that delinquent and criminal behavior is learned, Sutherland implied that it can be classified in the same manner as any other learned behavior, such as writing, painting, or reading.

- *Learning is a by-product of interaction:* Criminal behavior is learned as a by-product of interacting with others. Sutherland believed individuals do not start violating the law simply by living in a crimogenic environment or by manifesting personal characteristics, such as low IQ or family problems, associated with criminality. People actively participate in the learning process as they interact with other individuals. Thus, criminality cannot occur without the aid of others; it is a function of socialization.

- *Learning occurs within intimate groups:* Learning criminal behavior occurs within intimate personal groups. People's contacts with their most intimate social companions—family, friends, peers—have the greatest influence on their deviant behavior and attitude development. Relationships with these influential individuals color and control the way individuals interpret everyday events. For example, research shows that children who grow up in homes where parents abuse alcohol are more likely to view drinking as being socially and physically beneficial.[80] The intimacy of these associations far outweighs the importance of any other form of communication—for example, movies or television. Even on those rare occasions when violent motion pictures seem to provoke mass criminal episodes, these outbreaks can be more readily explained as a reaction to peer group pressure than as a reaction to the films themselves.

- *Criminal techniques are learned:* Learning criminal behavior involves learning the techniques of committing the crime, which are sometimes very complicated and sometimes very simple. This requires learning the specific direction of motives, drives, rationalizations, and attitudes. Young delinquents learn from their associates the proper way to pick a lock, shoplift, and obtain and use narcotics. In addition, novice criminals learn to use the proper terminology for their acts and then acquire "proper" reactions to law violations. For example, getting high on marijuana and learning the proper way to smoke a joint are behavior patterns usually acquired from more experienced companions. Moreover, criminals must learn how to react properly to their illegal acts, such as when to defend them, rationalize them, or show remorse for them.

- *Perceptions of legal code influence motives and drives:* The specific direction of motives and drives is learned from perceptions of various aspects of the legal code as being favorable or unfavorable. The reaction to social rules and laws is not uniform across society, and people constantly come into contact with others who maintain different views on the utility of obeying the legal code. Some people they admire may openly disdain or flout the law or ignore its substance. People experience what Sutherland calls *culture conflict* when they are exposed to different and opposing attitudes toward what is right and wrong, moral and immoral. The conflict of social attitudes and cultural norms is the basis for the concept of differential association.

■ *Differential associations may vary in frequency, duration, priority, and intensity:* Whether a person learns to obey the law or to disregard it is influenced by the quality of social interactions. Those of lasting *duration* have greater influence than those that are brief. Similarly, *frequent* contacts have greater effect than rare and haphazard contacts. Sutherland did not specify what he meant by *priority,* but Cressey and others have interpreted the term to mean the age of children when they first encounter definitions of criminality. Contacts made early in life probably have a greater and more far-reaching influence than those developed later on. Finally, *intensity* is generally interpreted to mean the importance and prestige attributed to the individual or groups from whom the definitions are learned. For example, the influence of a father, mother, or trusted friend far outweighs the effect of more socially distant figures.

■ *The process of learning criminal behavior by association with criminal and anticriminal patterns involves all of the mechanisms involved in any other learning process:* This suggests that learning criminal behavior patterns is similar to learning nearly all other patterns and is not a matter of mere imitation.

■ *Criminal behavior is an expression of general needs and values, but it is not excused by those general needs and values because noncriminal behavior is also an expression of those same needs and values:* This principle suggests that the motives for criminal behavior cannot logically be the same as those for conventional behavior. Sutherland rules out such motives as desire to accumulate money or social status, personal frustration, or low self-concept as causes of crime because they are just as likely to produce noncriminal behavior, such as getting a better education or working harder on a job. It is only the learning of deviant norms through contact with an excess of definitions favorable toward criminality that produces illegal behavior.

FIGURE 7.2

Differential Associations

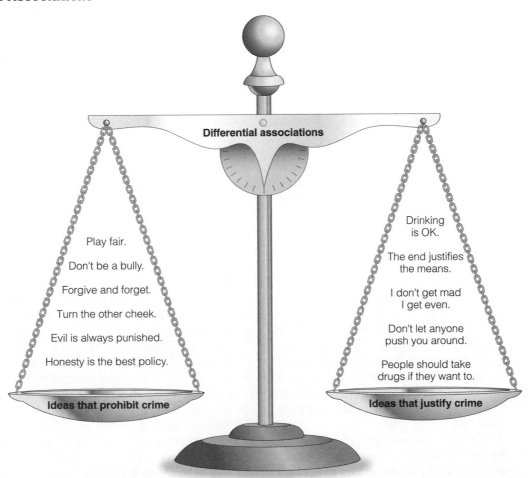

A person becomes a criminal when he or she perceives more favorable than unfavorable consequences to violating the law (Figure 7.2). According to Sutherland's theory, individuals become law violators when they are in contact with people, groups, or events that produce an excess of definitions favorable toward criminality and are isolated from counteracting forces. A definition favorable toward criminality occurs, for example, when a person is exposed to friends sneaking into a theater to avoid paying for a ticket or talking about the virtues of getting high on drugs. A definition unfavorable toward crime occurs when friends or parents demonstrate their disapproval of crime. Neutral behavior, such as reading a book, is neither positive nor negative with respect to law violation. Cressey argues that neutral behavior is important; for example, when a child is occupied doing something neutral, it prevents him or her from being in contact with those involved in criminal behaviors.[81]

In sum, differential association theory holds that people learn criminal attitudes and behavior while in their adolescence from close and trusted friends and/or relatives. A criminal career develops if learned antisocial values and behaviors are not at least matched or exceeded by conventional attitudes and behaviors. Criminal behavior, then, is learned in a process that is similar to learning any other human behavior.

TESTING DIFFERENTIAL ASSOCIATION THEORY Despite the importance of differential association theory, research devoted to testing its assumptions has been relatively sparse. It has proven difficult to conceptualize the principles of the theory so that they can be empirically tested. For example, social scientists find it difficult to evaluate such vague concepts as "definition toward criminality." It is also difficult to follow people over time, establish precisely when definitions toward criminality begin to outweigh prosocial definitions, and determine if this imbalance produces criminal behavior.

Despite these limitations, several notable research efforts have supported the core principles of this theory. These generally show a correlation between (a) having deviant friends, (b) holding deviant attitudes, and (c) committing deviant acts.[82] People who report having attitudes that support deviant behavior are also likely to engage in deviant behavior.[83] In a classic work, criminologist James Short surveyed institutionalized youths and found that they had, in fact, maintained close associations with delinquent youths prior to their law-violating acts.[84] Association with deviant peers has been found to sustain the deviant attitudes that support crime both in group settings and in solo ventures.[85] Mark Warr found that antisocial children who maintain delinquent friends over a long duration are much more likely to persist in their delinquent behavior than those without such peer support.[86] Scales measuring differential association have been significantly correlated with criminal behaviors among samples taken in other nations and cultures.[87]

Differential association also seems especially relevant in trying to explain the onset of substance abuse and a career in the drug trade. This requires learning proper techniques and attitudes from an experienced user or dealer.[88] In his interview study of low-level drug dealers, Kenneth Tunnell found that many novices were tutored by a more experienced criminal dealer who helped them make connections with buyers and sellers. One told him:

> I had a friend of mine who was an older guy, and he introduced me to selling marijuana to make a few dollars. I started selling a little and made a few dollars. For a young guy to be making a hundred dollars or so, it was a lot of money. So I got kind of tied up in that aspect of selling drugs.[89]

Tunnell found that making connections is an important part of the dealer's world. Adolescent drug users are likely to have intimate relationships with a peer friendship network that supports their substance abuse and teaches them how to deal within the drug world.[90]

Differential association may also be used to explain the gender difference in the crime rate. Males are more likely to socialize with deviant peers than females and, when they do, are more deeply influenced by peer relations.[91] Females are shielded by their unique moral sense, which makes caring about people and avoiding social harm a top priority. Males, in contrast, have a more cavalier attitude toward others and are more interested in their own self-interests. They are therefore more susceptible to the influence of deviant peers.

ANALYSIS OF DIFFERENTIAL ASSOCIATION THEORY There have been a number of important critiques of the theory. According to the *cultural deviance critique,* differential association is invalid because it suggests that criminals are people "properly" socialized into a deviant subculture; that is, they are taught criminal norms by significant others. Supporters counter that differential association also recognizes that individuals can embrace criminality because they have been improperly socialized into the normative culture.[92]

Differential association theory also fails to explain why one youth who is exposed to delinquent definitions eventually succumbs to them, while another, living under the same conditions, is able to avoid criminal entanglements. It fails to account for the origin of delinquent definitions. How did the first "teacher" learn delinquent attitudes and definitions in order to pass them on? Another apparently valid criticism of differential association is that it assumes criminal and delinquent acts to be rational and systematic. This ignores spontaneous and wanton acts of violence and damage that appear to have little utility or purpose, such as the isolated psychopathic killing or serial rapist.

Another critique concerns the relationship between deviant peers and criminality. It is possible that youths learn about crime and then commit criminal acts, but it is also possible that experienced delinquents and criminals seek out like-minded peers after they engage in antisocial acts and that the internalization of deviant attitudes follows, rather than precedes, criminality ("birds of a feather flock together").[93]

Despite these criticisms, differential association theory maintains an important place in the study of criminal behavior. For one thing, it provides a consistent explanation of all types of delinquent and criminal behavior. Unlike social structure theories, it is not limited to the explanation of a single facet of antisocial activity, such as lower-class gang activity. The theory can also account for the extensive delinquent behavior found even in middle- and upper-class areas, where youths may be exposed to a variety of pro-delinquent definitions from such sources as overly opportunistic parents and friends.

Differential Reinforcement Theory

Differential reinforcement theory is another attempt to explain crime as a type of learned behavior. First proposed by Ronald Akers in collaboration with Robert Burgess in 1966, it is a version of the social learning view that employs both differential association concepts along with elements of psychological learning theory.

| | | | | | | | **CONNECTIONS** | | | | | | |

Psychological learning theories were first discussed in Chapter 5. These trait theories maintain that human actions are developed through learning experiences. Behavior is supported by rewards and extinguished by negative reactions or punishments. Behavior is constantly being shaped by life experiences.

According to Akers, the same process is involved in learning both deviant and conventional behavior. People learn to be neither "all deviant" nor "all conforming" but rather strike a balance between the two opposing poles of behavior. This balance is usually stable, but it can undergo revision over time.[94]

A number of learning processes shape behavior. **Direct conditioning**, also called **differential reinforcement**, occurs when behavior is reinforced by being either rewarded or punished while interacting with others. When behavior is punished, this is referred to as **negative reinforcement.** This type of reinforcement can be distributed by using either negative stimuli (punishment) or loss of a positive reward. Whether deviant or criminal behavior has been initiated or persists depends on the degree to which it has been rewarded or punished and the rewards or punishments attached to its alternatives.

According to Akers, people learn to evaluate their own behavior through their interactions with significant others and groups in their lives. These groups control sources and patterns of reinforcement, define behavior as right or wrong, and provide behaviors that can be modeled through observational learning. The more individuals learn to define their behavior as good or at least as justified, rather than as undesirable, the more likely they are to engage in it. For example, adolescents who hook up with a drug-abusing peer group whose members value drugs and alcohol, encourage their use, and provide opportunities to observe people abusing substances will be encouraged, through this social learning experience, to use drugs themselves.

Akers's theory posits that the principal influence on behavior comes from "those groups which control individuals' major sources of reinforcement and punishment and expose them to behavioral models and normative definitions."[95] The important groups are the ones with which a person is in differential association—peer and friendship groups, schools, churches, and similar institutions. Within the context of these critical groups, according to Akers, "deviant behavior can be expected to the extent that it has been differentially reinforced over alternative behavior . . . and is defined as desirable or justified."[96] Once people are indoctrinated into crime, their behavior can be reinforced by being exposed to deviant behavior models, associating with deviant peers, and lacking negative sanctions from parents or peers. The deviant behavior, originally executed by imitating someone else's behavior, is sustained by social support. It is possible that differential reinforcements help establish criminal careers and are a key factor in explaining persistent criminality.

TESTING DIFFERENTIAL REINFORCEMENT The principles of differential reinforcement have been subject to empirical review by Akers and other criminologists.[97] In an important test of his theory, Akers and his associates surveyed 3,065 male and female adolescents on drug- and alcohol-related activities and their perception of variables related to social learning and differential reinforcement. Items in the scale included the respondents' perceptions of esteemed peers' attitudes toward drug and alcohol abuse, the number of people they admired who actually used controlled substances, and whether people they admired would reward or punish them for substance abuse. Akers found a strong association between drug and alcohol abuse and social learning variables: Those who believed they would be rewarded for deviance by those they respect were the ones most likely to engage in deviant behavior.[98]

Akers also found that the learning–deviant behavior link is not static. The learning experience continues within a deviant group as behavior is both influenced by, and exerts influence over, group processes. For example, adolescents may learn to smoke because their friends are smoking and, therefore, approve of this behavior. Over time, smoking influences friendships and peer group memberships as smokers seek out one another for companionship and support.[99]

Differential reinforcement theory is an important perspective that endeavors to determine the cause of criminal activity. It considers how the content of socialization conditions crime. Because not all socialization is positive, it accounts for the fact that negative social reinforcements and experiences can produce criminal results. This concurs with research that demonstrates that parental deviance is related to adolescent antisocial behavior.[100] Parents may reinforce their children's deviant behavior by supplying negative social reinforcements. Akers's work also fits well with rational choice theory because they both suggest that people learn the techniques and attitudes necessary to commit crime. Criminal knowledge is gained through experience. After considering the outcome of their past experiences, potential offenders decide which criminal acts will be profitable and which are dangerous and should be avoided.[101] Integrating these perspectives, people make rational choices about crime because they have learned to balance risks against the potential for criminal gain.

Neutralization Theory

Neutralization theory is identified with the writings of David Matza and his associate Gresham Sykes.[102] They view the process of becoming a criminal as a learning experience in which potential delinquents and criminals master techniques that enable them to counterbalance or neutralize conventional values and drift back and forth between illegitimate and conventional behavior. One reason this is possible is the subterranean value structure of American society. **Subterranean values** are morally tinged influences that have become entrenched in the culture but are publicly condemned. They exist side by side with conventional values and while condemned in public may be admired or practiced in private. Examples include viewing pornographic films, drinking alcohol to excess, and gambling on sporting events. In American culture, it is common to hold both subterranean and conventional values; few people are "all good" or "all bad."

Matza argues that even the most committed criminals and delinquents are not involved in criminality all the time; they also attend schools, family functions, and religious services. Their behavior can be conceived as falling along a continuum between total freedom and total restraint. This process, which he calls **drift,** refers to the movement from one extreme of behavior to another, resulting in behavior that is sometimes unconventional, free, or deviant and at other times constrained and sober.[103] Learning techniques of neutralization enables a person to temporarily "drift away" from conventional behavior and get involved in more subterranean values and behaviors including crime and drug abuse.[104]

Sykes and Matza base their theoretical model on these observations:[105]

- *Criminals sometimes voice a sense of guilt over their illegal acts:* If a stable criminal value system existed in opposition to generally held values and rules, it would be unlikely that criminals would exhibit any remorse for their acts, other than regret at being apprehended.

- *Offenders frequently respect and admire honest, law-abiding people:* Really honest people are often revered; and if for some reason such people are accused of misbehavior, the criminal is quick to defend their integrity. Those admired may include sports figures, priests and other clergy, parents, teachers, and neighbors.

- *Criminals draw a line between those whom they can victimize and those whom they cannot:* Members of

similar ethnic groups, churches, or neighborhoods are often off limits. This practice implies that criminals are aware of the wrongfulness of their acts.

- *Criminals are not immune to the demands of conformity:* Most criminals frequently participate in many of the same social functions as law-abiding people—for example, in school, church, and family activities.

Because of these factors, Sykes and Matza conclude that criminality is the result of the neutralization of accepted social values through the learning of a standard set of techniques that allow people to counteract the moral dilemmas posed by illegal behavior.[106]

TECHNIQUES OF NEUTRALIZATION Sykes and Matza suggest that people develop a distinct set of justifications for their law-violating behavior. These neutralization techniques enable them to temporarily drift away from the rules of the normative society and participate in subterranean behaviors. These techniques of neutralization include the following patterns:

- *Deny responsibility:* Young offenders sometimes claim their unlawful acts were simply not their fault. Criminals' acts resulted from forces beyond their control or were accidents.

- *Deny injury:* By denying the wrongfulness of an act, criminals are able to neutralize illegal behavior. For example, stealing is viewed as borrowing; vandalism is considered mischief that has gotten out of hand. Delinquents may find that their parents and friends support their denial of injury. In fact, they may claim that the behavior was merely a prank, helping affirm the offender's perception that crime can be socially acceptable.

- *Deny victim:* Criminals sometimes neutralize wrongdoing by maintaining that the victim of crime "had it coming." Vandalism may be directed against a disliked teacher or neighbor; or homosexuals may be beaten up by a gang because their behavior is considered offensive. Denying the victim may also take the form of ignoring the rights of an absent or unknown victim: for example, stealing from the unseen owner of a department store. It becomes morally acceptable for the criminal to commit such crimes as vandalism when the victims, because of their absence, cannot be sympathized with or respected.

- *Condemn condemners:* An offender views the world as a corrupt place with a dog-eat-dog code. Because police and judges are on the take, teachers show favoritism, and parents take out their frustrations on their kids, it is ironic and unfair for these authorities to condemn his or her misconduct. By shifting the blame to others, criminals are able to repress the feeling that their own acts are wrong.

FIGURE 7.3
Techniques of Neutralization

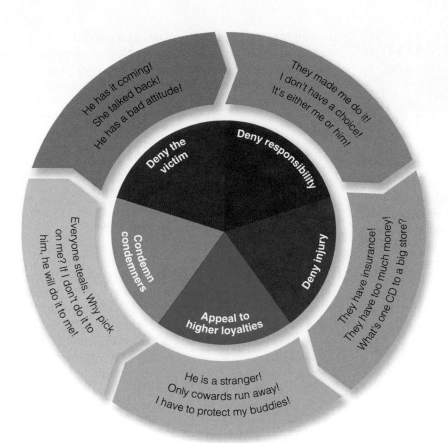

- *Appeal to higher loyalties:* Novice criminals often argue that they are caught in the dilemma of being loyal to their own peer group while at the same time attempting to abide by the rules of the larger society. The needs of the group take precedence over the rules of society because the demands of the former are immediate and localized (Figure 7.3).

||||||| CONNECTIONS |||||||

Denial of the victim may help explain the hate crime phenomenon in which people are victimized simply because they belong to the wrong race, religion, ethnic group, or because of their sexual orientation. Hate crimes are discussed in Chapter 10.

In sum, the theory of neutralization presupposes a condition that allows people to neutralize unconventional norms and values by using such slogans as "I didn't mean to do it," "I didn't really hurt anybody," "They had it coming to them," "Everybody's picking on me," and "I didn't do it for myself." These excuses allow people to drift into criminal modes of behavior.

TESTING NEUTRALIZATION THEORY Attempts have been made to verify the assumptions of neutralization theory empirically, but the results have been inconclusive.[107] One area of research has been directed at determining whether there really is a need for law violators to neutralize moral constraints. The thinking behind this research is this: If criminals hold values *in opposition* to accepted social norms, then there is really no need to neutralize. So far, the evidence is mixed. Some studies show that law violators approve of criminal behavior, such as theft and violence, and still others find evidence that even though they may be active participants themselves criminals voice disapproval of illegal behavior.[108] Some studies indicate that law violators approve of social values such as honesty and fairness; others come to the opposite conclusion.[109]

Although the existing research findings may be ambiguous, the weight of the evidence is that (a) most adolescents generally *disapprove* of deviant behaviors such as violence and that (b) neutralizations do in fact enable youths to engage in socially disproved of behavior.[110] Equally important is some recent evidence showing that, as Matza predicted, people drift in and out of antisocial behavior. Jeffery Fagan's interviews with 150 young men who had experiences with violent crimes while living in some of New York City's toughest neighborhoods found that many alternated their demeanor between "decent" and "street" codes of behavior, language, and dress. Both orientations lived side by side within the same individuals. The street code's rules for getting and maintaining respect through aggressive behavior forced many "decent" youths to situationally adopt a tough demeanor and perhaps behave violently in order to survive an otherwise hostile and possibly dangerous environment.[111]

| | | | | | | CONNECTIONS | | | | | | |

The concept of "decent" and "street" codes of behavior is discussed in the Race, Culture, Gender, and Criminology feature "The Code of the Streets" in Chapter 6.

The theory of neutralization, then, is a major contribution to the literature of crime and delinquency. It can account for the aging-out process: Youths can forgo criminal behavior as adults because they never really rejected the morality of normative society. It helps explain the behavior of the occasional or nonchronic delinquent, who is able to successfully age out of crime. Because teens are not committed to criminality, as they mature they simply drift back into conventional behavior patterns. While they are young, justifications and excuses neutralize guilt and enable individuals to continue to feel good about themselves.[112] In contrast, people who remain criminals as adults may be using newly learned techniques to neutralize the wrongfulness of their actions and avoid guilt. For example, psychotherapists accused of sexually exploiting their clients blame the victim for "seducing them"; some claim there was little injury caused by the sexual encounter; others seek scapegoats to blame for their actions.[113]

Are Learning Theories Valid?

Learning theories make a significant contribution to our understanding of the onset of criminal behavior. Nonetheless, the general learning model has been subject to some criticism. One complaint is that learning theorists fail to account for the origin of criminal definitions. How did the first "teacher" learn criminal techniques and definitions? Who came up with the original neutralization technique?

Learning theories also imply that people systematically learn techniques that enable them to be active and successful criminals, but they fail to adequately explain spontaneous and wanton acts of violence and damage and other expressive crimes that appear to have little utility or purpose. Principles of differential association can easily explain shoplifting, but is it possible that a random shooting is caused by excessive deviant definitions? It is estimated that about 70 percent of all arrestees were under the influence of drugs and alcohol when they committed their crime: Do "crack heads" pause to neutralize their moral inhibitions before mugging a victim? Do drug-involved kids stop to consider what they have "learned" about moral values?[114]

Little evidence exists substantiating that people learn the techniques that enable them to become criminals before they actually commit criminal acts. It is equally plausible that people who are already deviant seek out others with similar lifestyles. Early onset of deviant behavior is now considered a key determinant of criminal careers. It is difficult to see how extremely young adolescents had the opportunity to learn criminal behavior and attitudes within a peer group setting.

Despite these criticisms, learning theories maintain an important place in the study of delinquent and criminal behavior. Unlike social structure theories, these theories are not limited to the explanation of a single facet of antisocial activity—for example, lower-class gang activity; they may be used to explain criminality across all class structures. Even corporate executives may be exposed to a variety of pro-criminal definitions and learn to neutralize moral constraints.

 To quiz yourself on this material, go to the Criminology TPT 9e website.

SOCIAL CONTROL THEORY

Social control theories maintain that all people have the potential to violate the law and that modern society presents many opportunities for illegal activity. Criminal activities, such as drug abuse and car theft, are often exciting pastimes that hold the promise of immediate reward and gratification.

Considering the attractions of crime, the question control theorists pose is, Why do people obey the rules of society? A choice theorist would respond that it is the fear of punishment; structural theorists would say that obedience is a function of having access to legitimate opportunities; learning theorists would explain that obedience is acquired through contact with law-abiding parents and peers. In contrast, social control theorists argue that people obey the law because behavior and passions are being controlled by internal and external forces. Some individuals have **self-control,** manifested through a strong moral sense, which renders them incapable of hurting others and violating social norms. Other people develop a **commitment to conformity,** which is adhered to because there is a real, present, and logical reason to obey the rules of society.[115] Individuals may believe that getting caught at criminal activity will hurt a dearly loved parent or jeopardize their chance at a college scholarship, or perhaps they feel that their job will be forfeited if they get in trouble with the law. In other words, people's behavior, including criminal activity, is controlled by their attachment and commitment to conventional institutions, individuals, and processes. If that commitment is absent, they are free to violate the law and engage in deviant behavior. Those who are "uncommitted" are not deterred by the threat of legal punishments.[116]

Self-Concept and Crime

Early versions of control theory speculated that low self-control was a product of weak self-concept and poor self-esteem. Youths who felt good about themselves and maintained a positive attitude were able to resist the temptations of the streets. As early as 1951, sociologist Albert Reiss described how delinquents had weak egos and lacked the self-control to produce conforming behavior.[117] Scott Briar and Irving Piliavin noted that youths who believe criminal activity will damage their self-image and their relationships with others will be most likely to conform to social rules; they have a commitment to conformity. In contrast, those less concerned about their social standing are free to violate the law.[118] In his **containment theory,** pioneering control theorist Walter Reckless argued that a strong self-image insulates a youth from the pressures and pulls of crimogenic influences in the environment.[119] In a series of studies conducted within the school setting, Reckless and his colleagues found that nondelinquent youths are able to maintain a positive self-image in the face of environmental pressures toward delinquency.[120]

How does self-concept influence delinquent and criminal behavior? To find out, read this article in InfoTrac College Edition: Kenneth St.C. Levy, "The Contribution of Self-Concept in the Etiology of Adolescent Delinquents," *Adolescence* 32 (1997): 671–686.

Sociologist Howard Kaplan believes youths with poor self-concepts are the ones most likely to engage in delinquent behavior; successful participation in criminality actually helps raise their self-esteem.[121] Kaplan's self-enhancement theory suggests that adolescents structure their behavior to enhance their self-image and to minimize negative self-attitudes.

According to Kaplan, youth conform to social rules of society, seek membership in **normative groups** (for example, the high school "in-crowd"), and perform conventional tasks as long as their efforts pay off in positive, esteem-enhancing feedback. If they feel threatened, rebuked, or belittled, they may experience "self-rejection" (for example, "I feel I do not have much to be proud of"; "I feel useless at times"). Because of this rejection, they may then turn to deviant groups made up of youths who have been similarly rejected to meet their need for self-esteem. While conventional society may reject them, their new criminal friends give them positive feedback and support. To further enhance their new identity, they may engage in deviant behaviors.[122] Youths who maintain both the lowest self-image and the greatest need for approval are the ones most likely to seek self-enhancement by engaging in criminal activities. There is also evidence that perceptions of relative deprivation may produce the negative self-feelings imagined by Kaplan: Kids who perceive economic deprivation relative to their friends, neighbors, and the general population also develop negative self-feelings, which motivate antisocial behaviors.[123]

I I I I I I CONNECTIONS I I I I I I		

Kaplan's views help explain the deviance-producing effect of relative deprivation discussed in Chapter 6. Tying relative deprivation to self-concept helps to explain why some people, but not all, in disadvantaged areas are crime prone. It also suggests means to reduce crime rates: for example, by providing self-concept enhancing opportunities for relatively disadvantaged youth.

Hirschi's Social Bond Theory

Social bond theory (also called *social control theory*), articulated by Travis Hirschi in his 1969 book *Causes of Delinquency,* is now the dominant version of control theory.[124] Hirschi links the onset of criminality to the weakening of the ties that bind people to society. Hirschi assumes that all individuals are potential law violators, but they are kept under control because they fear that illegal behavior will damage their relationships with friends, parents, neighbors, teachers, and employers. Without these social ties or bonds, and in the absence of sensitivity to and interest in others, a person is free to commit criminal acts. Hirschi does not view society as containing competing subcultures with unique value systems. Most people are aware of the prevailing moral and legal code. He suggests, however, that in all elements of society people vary in how they respond to conventional social rules and values. Among all ethnic, religious, racial, and social groups, people whose bond to society is weak may fall prey to crimogenic behavior patterns.

In the three *American Pie* films, high school buddies Jim Levinstein (Jason Biggs), Chris "Oz" Ostreicher (Chris Klein), Kevin Myers (Thomas Ian Nicholas), Paul Finch (Eddie Kaye Thomas), and Steve Stiffler (Seann William Scott) scheme their way through various indescribable plots and escapades. Their friendship extends to the marriage of Jim and his high school girlfriend, Michelle Flaherty (Alyson Hannigan). While the boys may have had their share of adolescent escapades, Hirschi would argue that their attachment to one another and their commitment to the future were factors that helped them escape involvement in serious antisocial behaviors.

Universal / The Kobal Collection / Zink, Vivian

I I I I I I I CONNECTIONS I I I I I I I

Though his work has achieved a prominent place in criminological literature, Hirschi, along with Michael Gottfredson, has restructured his concept of control by integrating
biosocial, psychological, and rational choice theory ideas
into a "general theory of crime." This theory is essentially
developmental and integrated, and it will be discussed
more fully in Chapter 9.

ELEMENTS OF THE SOCIAL BOND Hirschi argues that the
social bond a person maintains with society is divided into
four main elements: attachment, commitment, involvement,
and belief (Figure 7.4).

■ *Attachment:* Attachment refers to a person's sensitivity
to and interest in others.[125] Without a sense of attachment, psychologists believe a person becomes a psychopath and loses the ability to relate coherently to the
world. The acceptance of social norms and the development of a social conscience depend on attachment
to and caring for other human beings.

Hirschi views parents, peers, and schools as the
important social institutions with which a person
should maintain ties. Attachment to parents is the most
important. Even if a family is shattered by divorce or
separation, a child must retain a strong attachment to
one or both parents. Without this attachment, it is unlikely that feelings of respect for others in authority
will develop.

■ *Commitment:* Commitment involves the time, energy,
and effort expended in conventional lines of action,
such as getting an education and saving money for
the future. If people build a strong commitment to
conventional society, they will be less likely to engage
in acts that will jeopardize their hard-won position.
Conversely, the lack of commitment to conventional
values may foreshadow a condition in which risk-
taking behavior, such as crime, becomes a reasonable
behavior alternative.

■ *Involvement:* Heavy involvement in conventional activities leaves little time for illegal behavior. When people
become involved in school, recreation, and family,
Hirschi believes it insulates them from the potential
lure of criminal behavior, whereas idleness enhances it.

■ *Belief:* People who live in the same social setting often
share common moral beliefs; they may adhere to such
values as sharing, sensitivity to the rights of others,
and admiration for the legal code. If these beliefs are
absent or weakened, individuals are more likely to
participate in antisocial or illegal acts.

Hirschi further suggests that the interrelationship
of social bond elements controls subsequent behavior.
For example, people who feel kinship and sensitivity to
parents and friends should be more likely to adopt and
work toward legitimate goals. A person who rejects
such social relationships is more likely to lack commitment to conventional goals. Similarly, people who are
highly committed to conventional acts and beliefs are
more likely to be involved in conventional activities.

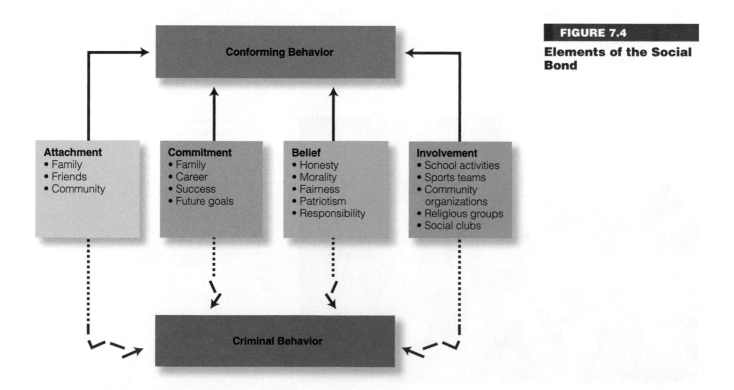

FIGURE 7.4

Elements of the Social Bond

TESTING SOCIAL BOND THEORY One of Hirschi's most significant contributions was his attempt to test the principal hypotheses of social bond theory. He administered a detailed self-report survey to a sample of more than 4,000 junior and senior high school students in Contra Costa County, California.[126] In a detailed analysis of the data, Hirschi found considerable evidence to support the control theory model. Among Hirschi's more important findings are the following:

- Youths who were strongly attached to their parents were less likely to commit criminal acts.

- Commitment to conventional values, such as striving to get a good education and refusing to drink alcohol and "cruise around," was indicative of conventional behavior.

- Youths involved in conventional activity, such as homework, were less likely to engage in criminal behavior.

- Youths involved in unconventional behavior, such as smoking and drinking, were more delinquency prone.

- Youths who maintained weak and distant relationships with people tended toward delinquency.

- Those who shunned unconventional acts were attached to their peers.

- Delinquents and nondelinquents shared similar beliefs about society.

SUPPORTING RESEARCH Hirschi's data lent important support to the validity of control theory. Even when the statistical significance of his findings was less than he expected, the direction of his research data was notably consistent. Only in very rare instances did his findings contradict the theory's most critical assumptions.

Hirschi's version of social control theory has been corroborated by numerous research studies showing that delinquent youth often feel detached from society.[127] Their relationships within the family, peer group, and school often appear strained, indicative of a weakened social bond.[128] Associations among indicators of lack of attachment, belief, commitment, and involvement with measures of delinquency have tended to be positive and significant.[129] In contrast, strong positive attachments help control delinquency.[130]

- *Attachment:* Research indicates that, as Hirschi predicts, kids who are attached to their families, friends, and school are less likely to get involved in a deviant peer group and consequently less likely to engage in criminal activities.[131] Teens who are attached to their parents are also able to develop the social skills that equip them both to maintain harmonious social ties and to escape life stresses such as school failure.[132] In contrast, family detachment—including intrafamily conflict, abuse of children, and lack of affection,

supervision, and family pride—are predictive of delinquent conduct.[133]

Attachment to education is equally important. Youths who are detached from the educational experience are at risk to criminality; those who are committed to school are less likely to engage in delinquent acts.[134] Youths who fail at school and are detached from the educational experience are at risk of criminality; those who seem attached to school are less likely to engage in delinquent acts.[135] In a recent study of adolescent motherhood, Trina Hope, Esther Wilder, and Toni-Terling Watt found important support for social control theory. They discovered that adolescent mothers did not have delinquency levels higher than those of their never-pregnant peers. They found that in contrast to adolescent females who end their pregnancies with an abortion, those who keep their babies reduce deviant activities such as smoking and marijuana use. The birth of a child serves as a mechanism of social control and reduces the likelihood of delinquent behavior. Attachment to a child, even during difficult circumstances, may produce the behavior change predicted by Hirschi.[136]

- *Belief:* Other research efforts have shown that holding positive beliefs are inversely related to criminality. Children who are involved in religious activities and hold conventional religious beliefs are less likely to become involved in substance abuse.[137] Kids who live in areas marked by strong religious values and who hold strong religious beliefs themselves are less likely to engage in delinquent activities than adolescents who do not hold such beliefs or who live in less devout communities.[138]

- *Commitment:* As predicted by Hirschi, kids who are committed to school and educational achievement are less likely to become involved in delinquent behaviors than those who lack such commitment.[139]

- *Involvement:* Research shows that youths who are involved in conventional leisure activities, such as supervised social activities and noncompetitive sports, are less likely to engage in delinquency than those who are involved in unconventional leisure activities and unsupervised, peer-oriented social pursuits.[140] One study found that students who engage in a significant amount of extracurricular activities from 8th grade through 12th grade are more likely to experience high academic achievement and prosocial behaviors extending into young adulthood.[141]

Cross-national surveys have also supported the general findings of Hirschi's control theory.[142] For example, one study of Canadian youth found that perceptions of parental attachment were the strongest predictor of delinquent or law-abiding behavior. Teens who are attached to their parents may develop the social skills that equip them both to maintain harmonious social ties and to escape life stresses such as school failure.[143]

OPPOSING VIEWS More than seventy published attempts have been made to corroborate social control theory by replicating Hirschi's original survey techniques.[144] There has been significant empirical support for Hirschi's work, but there are also those who question some or all of its elements. Here are some elements that have come under criticism and need further study.

■ *Friendship:* One significant criticism concerns Hirschi's contention that delinquents are detached loners whose bond to their family and friends has been broken. Some critics have questioned whether delinquents (1) do have strained relations with family and peers and (2) whether they may be influenced by close relationships with deviant peers and family members. A number of research efforts do show that delinquents maintain relationships with deviant peers and are influenced by members of their deviant peer group.[145] Delinquents, however, may not be "lone wolves" whose only personal relationships are exploitive; their friendship patterns seem quite close to those of conventional youth.[146] In fact, some types of offenders, such as drug abusers, may maintain even more intimate relations with their peers than nonabusers.[147]

■ *Not all elements of the bond are equal:* Hirschi makes little distinction between the importance of each element of the social bond, yet research evidence suggests that there may be differences. Some adolescents who report high levels of "involvement," which Hirschi suggests should reduce delinquency, are involved in criminal behavior. As kids get involved in behaviors outside the home, it is possible that parental control weakens, and youths have greater opportunity to commit crime.[148] When asked, children report that concepts such as "involvement" and "belief" have relatively little influence over behavior patterns.[149]

■ *Deviant peers and parents:* Hirschi's conclusion that any form of social attachment is beneficial, even to deviant peers and parents, has also been disputed. Rather than deter delinquency attachment to deviant peers, it may support and nurture antisocial behavior. Though his classic study supported the basic principles of control theory, criminologist Michael Hindelang found that attachment to delinquent peers escalated rather than restricted criminality.[150] In a similar fashion, a number of research efforts have found that youths attached to drug-abusing parents are more likely to become drug users themselves.[151] Attachment to deviant family members, peers, and associates may help motivate youths to commit crime and facilitate their antisocial acts.[152]

■ *Restricted in scope:* There is some question as to whether the theory can explain all modes of criminality (as Hirschi maintains) or is restricted to particular groups or forms of criminality. For example, control variables seem better able to explain minor delinquency (such as alcohol and marijuana abuse) than more serious criminal acts.[153] Research efforts have found control variables are more predictive of female than male behavior.[154] Perhaps girls are more deeply influenced by the quality of their bond to society.

■ *Changing bonds:* Social bonds seem to change over time, a phenomenon ignored by Hirschi.[155] It is possible then that at one age level weak bonds (to parents) lead to delinquency, while at another strong bonds (to peers) lead to delinquency.

■ *Crime and social bonds:* The most severe criticism of control theory has been leveled by sociologist Robert Agnew, who claims that Hirschi miscalculated the direction of the relationship between criminality and a weakened social bond.[156] Hirschi's theory projects that a weakened bond leads to delinquency, but Agnew suggests that the chain of events may flow in the opposite direction. In other words, perhaps kids who break the law find that their bond to parents, schools, and society eventually becomes weak and attenuated. Other studies have also found that criminal behavior weakens social bonds and not vice versa.[157]

Although these criticisms need to be addressed with further research, the weight of existing empirical evidence supports control theory, and it has emerged as one of the preeminent theories in criminology.[158] For many criminologists, it is perhaps the most important way of understanding the onset of youthful misbehavior.

 To quiz yourself on this material, go to the Criminology TPT 9e website.

 To read more about **Hirschi's work,** go to http://home.comcast.net/~ ddemelo/crime /hirschi.html. For an up-to-date list of web links, go to http://cj.wadsworth.com/siegel_crimtpt9e.

SOCIAL REACTION THEORY

Social reaction theory, commonly called labeling theory (the two terms are used interchangeably here), explains how criminal careers form based on destructive social interactions and encounters. Its roots are found in the **symbolic interaction theory** of sociologists Charles Horton Cooley and George Herbert Mead, and later, Herbert Blumer.[159] Symbolic interaction theory holds that people communicate via symbols—gestures, signs, words, or images—that stand for or represent something else.

People interpret symbolic gestures from others and incorporate them in their self-image. Symbols are used by others to let people know how well they are doing and whether they are liked or appreciated. How people view reality then depends on the content of the messages and situations they encounter, the subjective interpretation of these interactions, and how they shape future behavior. There is no objective reality. People interpret the reactions of others, and this interpretation assigns meaning. Because interpretation changes over time, so do the meanings of concepts and symbols.

Social reaction theory picks up on these concepts of *interaction* and *interpretation*.[160] Throughout their lives, people are given a variety of symbolic labels and ways to interact with others. These labels represent behavior and attitude characteristics; labels help define not just one trait but the whole person. For example, people labeled insane are also assumed to be dangerous, dishonest, unstable, violent, strange, and otherwise unsound. Valued labels, including smart, honest, and hard-working, suggest overall competence. These labels can improve self-image and social standing. Research shows that people who are labeled with one positive trait, such as being physically attractive, are assumed to maintain other traits, such as being intelligent and competent.[161] In contrast, negative labels—including troublemaker, mentally ill, and stupid—help stigmatize the recipients of these labels and reduce their self-image. Those who have accepted these labels are more prone to engage in delinquent behaviors than those whose self-image has not been so tarnished.[162]

Both positive and negative labels involve subjective interpretation of behavior: A troublemaker is merely someone who people label as troublesome. There need not be any objective proof or measure indicating that the person is actually a troublemaker. Though a label may be a function of rumor, innuendo, or unfounded suspicion, its adverse impact can be immense.

If a devalued status is conferred by a significant other—teacher, police officer, elder, parent, or valued peer—the negative label may cause permanent harm. The degree to which a person is perceived as a social deviant may affect his or her treatment at home, at work, at school, and in other social situations. Children may find that their parents consider them a bad influence on younger brothers and sisters. School officials may limit them to classes reserved for people with behavioral problems. Likewise, when adults are labeled as criminal, ex-con, or drug addict, they may find their eligibility for employment severely restricted. Furthermore, if the label is bestowed as the result of conviction for a criminal offense, the labeled person may be subjected to official sanctions ranging from a mild reprimand to incarceration.

Beyond these immediate results, labeling advocates maintain that, depending on the visibility of the label and the manner and severity with which it is applied, a person will have an increasing commitment to a deviant career. As one

FIGURE 7.5

The Labeling Process

Initial criminal act
People commit crimes for a number of reasons.

Detection by the justice system
Arrest is influenced by racial, economic, and power relations.

Decision to label
Some are labeled "official" criminals by police and court authorities.

Creation of a new identity
Those labeled are known as troublemakers, criminals, and so on, and are shunned by conventional society.

Acceptance of labels
Labeled people begin to see themselves as outsiders (secondary deviance, self-labeling).

Deviance amplification
Stigmatized offenders are now locked into criminal careers.

national commission put it: "Thereafter he may be watched; he may be suspect . . . he may be excluded more and more from legitimate opportunities."[163] Labeled people may find themselves turning to others similarly stigmatized for support and companionship. Isolated from conventional society, they may identify themselves as members of an outcast group and become locked into a deviant career. Figure 7.5 illustrates this process.

Because the process of acquiring stigma is essentially interactive, labeling theorists blame criminal career formation on the social agencies originally designed for its control. Often mistrustful of institutions—such as police, courts, and correctional agencies—labeling advocates find it logical that these institutions produce the stigma that is so harmful to the very people they are trying to help, treat, or correct. Rather than reduce deviant behavior, for which they were designed, such label-bestowing institutions actually help to maintain and amplify criminal behavior.

> To check out **stigma impacts on the mentally ill,** go to http://www.mentalhealthworks.ca/facts/sheets/stigma.asp. For an up-to-date list of web links, go to http://cj.wadsworth.com/siegel_crimtpt9e.

Crime and Labeling Theory

Labeling theorists use an interactionist definition of crime. In a defining statement, sociologist Kai Erickson argues, "Deviance is not a property inherent in certain forms of behavior, it is a property conferred upon those forms by the audience which directly or indirectly witnesses them."[164] Crime and deviance, therefore, are defined by the social audience's reaction to people and their behavior and the subsequent effects of that reaction; they are not defined by the moral content of the illegal act itself.[165]

In a famous statement, Becker sums up the importance of the audience's reaction:

> Social groups create deviance by making rules whose infractions constitute deviance, and by applying those rules to particular people and labeling them as outsiders. From this point of view, deviance is not a quality of the act a person commits, but rather a consequence of the application by others of rules and sanctions to an "offender." The deviant is one to whom the label has successfully been applied; deviant behavior is behavior that people so label.[166]

In its purest form, social reaction theory argues that such crimes as murder, rape, and assault are only bad or evil because people label them as such. After all, the difference between an excusable act and a criminal one is often a matter of legal definition, which changes from place to place and from year to year. For example, acts such as abortion, marijuana use, possession of a handgun, and gambling have been legal at some points and places in history and illegal at others.

Howard Becker refers to people who create rules as *moral entrepreneurs.* An example of a moral entrepreneur today might be members of an ultra orthodox religious group who target the gay lifestyle and mount a campaign to prevent gays from adopting children or conducting same-sex marriages.[167]

A social reaction theorist views crime as a subjective concept whose definition is totally dependent on the viewing audience. An act that is considered illegal and/or criminal to one person may be perfectly acceptable behavior to another. Because crime is defined by those in power, the shape of the criminal law is defined by the values of those who rule and not by an objective standard of moral conduct.

Differential Enforcement

An important principle of social reaction theory is that the law is differentially applied, benefiting those who hold economic and social power and penalizing the powerless. The probability of being brought under the control of legal authority is a function of a person's race, wealth, gender, and social standing. A core concept of social reaction theory is that police officers are more likely to formally arrest males, minority group members, and those in the lower class and to use their discretionary powers to give beneficial treatment to more favored groups.[168] Minorities and the poor are more likely to be prosecuted for criminal offenses and to receive harsher punishments when convicted.[169] Judges may sympathize with white defendants and help them avoid criminal labels, especially if they seem to come from "good families," whereas minority youth are not afforded that luxury.[170]

This evidence is used to support the labeling concept that personal characteristics and social interactions are more important variables in developing criminal careers than merely violating the law. Social reaction theorists also argue that the content of the law reflects power relationships in society. They point to the evidence that white-collar crimes—economic crimes usually committed by members of the upper class—are most often punished by a relatively small fine and rarely result in a prison sentence. This treatment contrasts with long prison sentences given to those convicted of "street crimes," such as burglary or car theft, which are the province of the lower, powerless classes.[171]

In sum, a major premise of social reaction theory is that the law is differentially constructed and applied, depending on the offenders. It favors the powerful members of society who direct its content and penalizes people whose actions represent a threat to those in control, such as minority group members and the poor who demand equal rights.[172]

Becoming Labeled

Social reaction theory is not especially concerned with why people originally engage in acts that result in their being labeled.[173] Crime may be a result of greed, personality, social structure, learning, or control. Regardless of why they commit crime, the less personal power and resources a person has, the greater the chance he or she will become labeled. Race, class, and ethnic differences between those in power and those who are not influence the likelihood of labeling. For example, the poor or minority group teenager may run a greater chance of being officially processed for criminal acts by police, courts, and correctional agencies than the wealthy white youth. This helps to explain why there are significant racial and economic differences in the crime rate.

Not all labeled people have chosen to engage in label-producing activities, such as crime. Some negative labels are bestowed on people for behaviors over which they have little control. Negative labels of this sort include mentally ill and mentally deficient. In these categories, the probability of being labeled may depend on how visible that person is in the

The Scary Guy (his legal name) is covered from head to toe in tattoos. What do you think he is like? What are his personality traits? Would you want him to meet your family? Are you labeling him?

community, the tolerance of the community for unusual behavior, and the person's own power to combat labels.

Consequences of Labeling

Social reaction theorists are most concerned with two effects of labeling: the creation of **stigma** and the effect on self-image. Labels are believed to produce stigma. The labeled deviant becomes a social outcast who may be prevented from enjoying a higher education, well-paying jobs, and other social benefits. Such alienation leads to a low self-image.

Labeling theorists consider public condemnation an important part of the label-producing process. It may be accomplished in such ceremonies as a hearing, in which a person is found to be mentally ill, or a trial, in which an individual is convicted of a crime. A public record of the deviant acts, such as an arrest or conviction record, causes the denounced person to be ritually separated from the legitimate order and placed outside the world occupied by citizens of good standing. Harold Garfinkle has called transactions that produce irreversible, permanent labels "successful degradation ceremonies."[174]

IIIIIII **CONNECTIONS** IIIIIII

Fear of stigma has prompted efforts to reduce the impact of criminal labels through such programs as pretrial diversion and community treatment programs. In addition, some criminologists have called for noncoercive "peacemaking" solutions to interpersonal conflict. This peacemaking, or restorative justice movement, is reviewed in Chapter 8.

DIFFERENTIAL SOCIAL CONTROL According to the concept of **differential social control,** the process of labeling may produce a re-evaluation of the self, which reflects actual or perceived appraisals made by others. Kids who view themselves as delinquents after being labeled as such are giving an inner voice to their perceptions of how parents, teachers, peers, and neighbors view them. When they believe that others view them as antisocial or troublemakers, they take on attitudes and roles that reflect this assumption; they expect to become suspects and then to be rejected.[175] This process has been linked to delinquent behavior and other social problems including depression.[176]

Tempering or enhancing the effect of this **reflective role taking** are informal and institutional social control processes. Families, schools, peers, and the social system can either help control children and dissuade them from crime or encourage and sustain deviance. When these groups are dysfunctional, such as when parents use drugs, they encourage, rather than control, antisocial behavior.[177]

JOINING DEVIANT CLIQUES When children are labeled as deviant, they may join up with similarly outcast delinquent peers who facilitate their behavior. Eventually, antisocial behavior becomes habitual and automatic.[178] The desire to join deviant cliques and groups may stem from a self-rejecting attitude ("At times, I think I am no good at all"), which eventually results in a weakened commitment to conventional values and behaviors. In turn, these children may acquire motives to deviate from social norms. Facilitating this attitude and value transformation is the bond social outcasts form with similarly labeled peers in the form of a deviant subculture.[179]

Membership in a deviant subculture often involves conforming to group norms that conflict with those of conventional society. Deviant behaviors that defy conventional values can serve a number of different purposes. Some acts are defiant, designed to show contempt for the source of the negative labels. Other acts are planned to distance the transgressor from further contact with the source of criticism (for example, an adolescent runs away from critical parents).[180]

RETROSPECTIVE READING Beyond any immediate results, labels tend to redefine the whole person. For example, the label ex-con may create in people's imaginations a whole series of behavior descriptions—tough, mean, dangerous, aggressive, dishonest, sneaky—that a person who has been in prison may or may not possess. People begin to react to the label description and what it signifies instead of reacting to the actual behavior of the person who bears it. This is referred to as **retrospective reading,** a process in which the past of the labeled person is reviewed and re-evaluated to fit his or her current status. For example, boyhood friends of an assassin are interviewed by the media and report that the suspect was withdrawn, suspicious, and negativistic as a youth. By a retrospective reading, we can now understand what prompted his current behavior; therefore, the label must be accurate.[181]

DRAMATIZATION OF EVIL Labels become the basis of personal identity. As the negative feedback of law enforcement agencies, parents, friends, teachers, and other figures amplifies the force of the original label, stigmatized offenders may begin to re-evaluate their own identities. If they are not really evil or bad, they may ask themselves, why is everyone making such a fuss? Frank Tannenbaum, a social reaction theory pioneer, referred to this process as the **dramatization of evil.** With respect to the consequences of labeling delinquent behavior, Tannenbaum stated:

> The process of making the criminal, therefore, is a process of tagging, defining, identifying, making conscious and self-conscious; it becomes a way of stimulating, suggesting and evoking the very traits that are complained of. If the theory of relation of response to stimulus has any meaning, the entire process of dealing with the young delinquent is mischievous insofar as it identifies him to himself or to the environment as a delinquent person. The person becomes the thing he is described as being.[182]

Primary and Secondary Deviance

One of the best-known views of the labeling process is Edwin Lemert's concept of primary deviance and secondary deviance.[183] According to Lemert, **primary deviance** involves norm violations or crimes that have very little influence on the actor and can be quickly forgotten. For example, a college student takes a "five-finger discount" at the campus bookstore. He successfully steals a textbook, uses it to get an A in a course, goes on to graduate, is admitted into law school, and later becomes a famous judge. Because his shoplifting goes unnoticed, it is a relatively unimportant event that has little bearing on his future life.

In contrast, **secondary deviance** occurs when a deviant event comes to the attention of significant others or social control agents who apply a negative label. The newly labeled offender then reorganizes his or her behavior and personality around the consequences of the deviant act. The shoplifting student is caught by a security guard and expelled from college. With his law school dreams dashed and his future cloudy, his options are limited; people who know him say he "lacks character," and he begins to share their opinion. He eventually becomes a drug dealer and winds up in prison (Figure 7.6).

Secondary deviance involves resocialization into a deviant role. The labeled person is transformed into one who, according to Lemert, "employs his behavior or a role based upon it as a means of defense, attack, or adjustment to the overt and covert problems created by the consequent social reaction to him."[184] Secondary deviance produces a deviance amplification effect. Offenders feel isolated from the mainstream of society and become firmly locked within their deviant role. They may seek out others similarly labeled to form deviant subcultures or groups. Ever more firmly enmeshed in their deviant role, they are locked into an escalating cycle of deviance, apprehension, more powerful labels, and identity transformation. Lemert's concept of secondary deviance

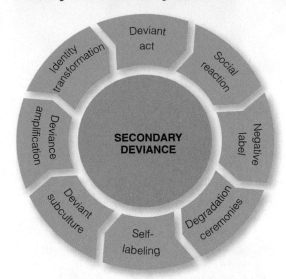

FIGURE 7.6
Primary and Secondary Deviance

expresses the core of social reaction theory: deviance is a process in which one's identity is transformed. Efforts to control the offenders, whether by treatment or punishment, simply help lock them in their deviant role.

Research on Social Reaction Theory

Research on social reaction theory can be classified into two distinct categories. The first focuses on the characteristics of offenders who are chosen for labels. The theory maintains that these offenders should be relatively powerless people who are unable to defend themselves against the negative labeling. The second type of research attempts to discover the effects of being labeled. Labeling theorists predict that people who are negatively labeled should view themselves as deviant and commit increasing amounts of criminal behavior.

WHO GETS LABELED? The poor and powerless people are victimized by the law and justice system; labels are not equally distributed across class and racial lines. Critics charge that although substantive and procedural laws govern almost every aspect of the American criminal justice system, discretionary decision making controls its operation at every level. From the police officer's decision on whom to arrest, to the prosecutor's decisions on whom to charge and for how many and what kind of charges, to the court's decision on whom to release or on whom to permit bail, to the grand jury's decision on indictment, to the judge's decision on the length of the sentence, discretion works to the detriment of minorities, including African Americans, Latinos, Asian Americans, and Native Americans.[185] Reviews indicate that race bias adversely influences decision making in many critical areas of the justice system.[186] There is also evidence that those in power try to streamline the labeling process by discounting or ignoring the "protestations of innocence" made by suspects accused of socially undesirable acts such as rape, sex crimes, and child abuse.[187]

Although these arguments are persuasive, little definitive evidence exists that the justice system is inherently unfair and biased. Procedures such as arrest, prosecution, and sentencing seem to be more often based on legal factors, such as prior record and severity of the crime, than on personal characteristics, such as class and race.[188] However, it is possible that discriminatory practices in the labeling process are subtle and hidden. For example, in a thorough review of sentencing disparity, Samuel Walker, Cassia Spohn, and Miriam DeLone identify what they call **contextual discrimination.** This term refers to judges' practices in some jurisdictions of imposing harsher sentences on African Americans only in some instances, such as when they victimize whites and not other African Americans.[189] They may also be more likely to impose prison sentences on racial minorities in "borderline" cases for which whites get probation. According to their view, racism is very subtle and hard to detect, but it still exerts an influence in the distribution of criminal sanctions.

THE EFFECTS OF LABELING There is empirical evidence that negative labels actually have a dramatic influence on self-image and subsequent behavior. Considerable empirical evidence indicates that social sanctions lead to self-labeling and deviance amplification.[190]

Family interaction can influence the labeling process. Children negatively labeled by their parents routinely suffer a variety of problems, including antisocial behavior and school failure.[191] This process is important because once they are labeled troublemakers, adolescents begin to reassess their self-image. Parents who label their kids as troublemakers promote deviance amplification: Labeling causes parents to become alienated from their child; negative labels reduce a child's self-image and increase delinquency.[192]

To read more about the process of reflected appraisals and how it reflects gender differences, read: Dawn Jeglum Bartusch and Ross L. Matsueda, "Gender, Reflected Appraisals, and Labeling: A Cross-Group Test of an Interactionist Theory of Delinquency," *Social Forces* 75 (1996): 145–176.

As they mature, children are in danger of receiving repeat and intensive official labeling, which has been shown to produce self-labeling and damaged identities.[193] Kids labeled troublemakers in school are the ones most likely to drop out; dropping out has been linked to delinquent behavior.[194] Even as adults, the labeling process can take its toll. Male drug users labeled as addicts by social control agencies eventually become self-labeled and increase their drug use.[195] People arrested in domestic violence cases, especially those with a low "stake in conformity" (for example, jobless and unmarried), increase offending after being given official labels.[196] And once in prison, inmates labeled high risk are more likely to have disciplinary problems than those who are spared such negative labels.[197]

LABELING AND CRIMINAL CAREERS Until recently, scant attention had been paid to the fact that stigma and negative labels may be critical factors in a criminal career.[198] In fact, the very definition of a chronic offender is a person who has been arrested and therefore labeled multiple times over the course of his or her offending career.

Empirical evidence supports the fact that labeling plays an important role in persistent offending.[199] Maintaining a damaged identity after official labeling may, along with other negative social reactions from society, produce a "cumulative disadvantage," which provokes some adolescents into repeating their antisocial behaviors.[200] Using longitudinal data obtained from youths ages 13 to 22, Jön Gunnar Bernburg and Marvin Krohn found evidence that, rather than deterring future offending, the "cumulative disadvantage" created by official intervention actually increases the probability that a labeled person will get involved in subsequent involvement in antisocial behavior. A label triggers exclusionary processes that limit conventional opportunities, such as educational attainment and employment. Kids who were labeled in adolescence were much more likely to engage in crime in early adulthood unless they were able to overcome labels and do well in school and obtain meaningful employment opportunities.[201]

In sum, there is considerable evidence that people who are negatively labeled by parents, schools, and the criminal justice system are likely to partake in criminal behaviors. However, it is still unclear whether this outcome is actually a labeling effect or the product of some other personal and social factors that also caused the labeling to occur.

Is Labeling Theory Valid?

Labeling theory has been the subject of academic debate in criminological circles. Those who criticize it point to its inability to specify the conditions that must exist before an act or individual is labeled deviant; that is, why some people are labeled and others remain "secret deviants."[202] Critics also charge that social reaction theory fails to explain differences in crime rates; if crime is a function of stigma and labels, why are crime rates higher in some parts of the country at particular times of the year?[203] Labeling also ignores the onset of deviant behavior (that is, it fails to ask why people commit the initial deviant act) and does not deal with the reasons delinquents and criminals decide to forgo a deviant career.[204]

In an in-depth analysis of research on the crime-producing effects of labels, criminologist Charles Tittle found little evidence that stigma produces crime.[205] Tittle claims that many criminal careers occur without labeling; that labeling often comes after, rather than before, chronic offending; and that criminal careers may not follow even when labeling takes place. There is growing evidence that the onset of criminal careers occurs early in life and that those who go on to a "life of crime" are burdened with so many social, physical, and psychological problems that negative labeling may be a relatively insignificant event.[206]

LABELING REEXAMINED Criticisms of social reaction theory have reduced the importance of labeling in the criminological literature, but its use to explain crime and deviance should not be dismissed. Criminologists Raymond Paternoster and Leeann Iovanni have identified some other features of the labeling perspective that are important contributions to the study of criminality:[207]

- The labeling perspective identifies the role played by social control agents in the process of crime causation. Criminal behavior cannot be fully understood if the agencies and individuals empowered to control and treat it are neglected.

- Labeling theory recognizes that criminality is not a disease or pathological behavior. It focuses attention on the social interactions and reactions that shape individuals and their behavior.

- Labeling theory distinguishes between criminal acts (primary deviance) and criminal careers (secondary deviance) and shows that these concepts must be interpreted and treated differently.

Labeling theory is also important because of its focus on interaction as well as the situations surrounding the crime. Rather than view the criminal as a robotlike creature whose actions are predetermined, it recognizes that crime is often the result of complex interactions and processes. The decision to commit crime involves actions of a variety of people including peers, the victim, the police, and other key characters. Labels may expedite crime because they guide the actions of all parties involved in these criminal interactions. Actions deemed innocent when performed by one person are considered provocative when someone who has been labeled as deviant engages in them. Similarly, labeled people may be quick to judge, take offense, or misinterpret behavior of others because of past experience.

Labeling theory is also supported by research showing that convicted criminals who are placed in treatment programs aimed at reconfiguring their self-image may be able to develop revamped identities and desist from crime. Some are able to go through "redemption rituals" in which they are able to cast off their damaged identities and develop new ones. As a result, they develop an improved "looking-glass self-concept," which reflects the positive reinforcement they receive while in treatment.[208] Finally, international data seems to support the impact of stigma on crime, a finding that suggests that the labeling process is universal.[209]

 To quiz yourself on this material, go to the Criminology TPT 9e website.

EVALUATING SOCIAL PROCESS THEORIES

The branches of social process theory—social learning, social control, and social reaction—are compatible because they suggest that criminal behavior is part of the socialization process. Criminals are people whose interactions with critically important social institutions and processes—the family, schools, justice system, peer groups, employers, and neighbors—are troubled and disturbed. Though there is some disagreement about the relative importance of those influences and the form they take, there seems to be little question that social interactions shape the behavior, beliefs, values, and self-image of the offender. People who have learned deviant social values, find themselves detached from conventional social relationships, or are the subject of stigma and labels from significant others will be the most likely to fall prey to criminal behavior. These negative influences can affect people in all walks of life, beginning in their youth and continuing through their majority. The major strength of the social process view is the vast body of empirical data showing that delinquents and criminals are people who grew up in dysfunctional families, who had troubled childhoods, and who failed at school, at work, and in marriage. Prison data show that these characteristics are typical of inmates.

Although persuasive, these theories do not always account for the patterns and fluctuations in the crime rate. If social process theories are valid, for example, people in the West and South must be socialized differently from those in the Midwest and New England because these latter regions have much lower crime rates. How can the fact that crime rates are lqwer in October than in July be explained if crime is a function of learning or control? How can social processes explain why criminals escalate their activity or why they desist from crime as they age? Once a social bond is broken, how can it be "reattached"? Once crime is "learned," how can it be "unlearned"?

Concept Summary 7.1 sets out the premises, strengths, and research focus of social process theories.

 To quiz yourself on this material, go to the Criminology TPT 9e website.

PUBLIC POLICY IMPLICATIONS OF SOCIAL PROCESS THEORY

Social process theories have had a major influence on policy-making since the 1950s. Learning theories have greatly influenced the way criminal offenders are dealt with and treated. The effect of these theories has mainly been felt by young offenders, who are viewed as being more salvageable than "hardened" criminals. If people become criminal by learning definitions and attitudes toward criminality, advocates of the social learning approach argue that they can "unlearn" them by being exposed to definitions toward conventional behavior. It is common today for residential and nonresidential programs to offer treatment programs that teach offenders about the harmfulness of drugs, to forgo delinquent behavior, and to stay in school. If learning did not affect behavior, such exercises would be futile.

Social Process Theories

Theory	Major Premise	Strengths	Research Focus
Social Learning Theories			
Differential association theory	People learn to commit crime from exposure to antisocial definitions.	Explains onset of criminality. Explains the presence of crime in all elements of social structure. Explains why some people in high-crime areas refrain from criminality. Can apply to adults and juveniles.	Measuring definitions toward crime; influence of deviant peers and parents
Differential reinforcement theory	Criminal behavior depends on the person's experiences with rewards for conventional behaviors and punishment for deviant ones. Being rewarded for deviance leads to crime.	Adds psychological learning theory principles to differential associational. Links sociological and psychological principles.	Differential reinforcement theory studies the cause of criminal activity. It considers how the content of socialization conditions crime.
Neutralization theory	Youths learn ways of neutralizing moral restraints and periodically drift in and out of criminal behavior patterns.	Explains why many delinquents do not become adult criminals. Explains why youthful law violators can participate in conventional behavior.	Do people who use neutralizations commit more crimes? Beliefs, values, and crime
Social Control Theory			
Hirschi's control theory	A person's bond to society prevents him or her from violating social rules. If the bond weakens, the person is free to commit crime.	Explains the onset of crime; can apply to both middle- and lower-class crime. Explains its theoretical constructs adequately so they can be measured. Has been empirically tested.	The association between commitment, attachment, involvement, belief, and crime
Social Reaction Theory			
Labeling theory	People enter into law-violating careers when they are labeled for their acts and organize their personalities around the labels.	Explains the role of society in creating deviance. Explains why some juvenile offenders do not become adult criminals. Develops concepts of criminal careers.	Self-concept and crime; differential application of labels; effect of stigma

© Mario Villafuerte/Getty Images

Head Start has been a highly successful program for many years. Here, children play outside of the Brown E. Moore Head Start Center in Shreveport, Louisiana. During the summer the Moore Head Start Center has a student body of 220 pre-school students. There may be some changes in the administration of Head Start. Louisiana is among eight states that could be involved in a proposed federal program that shifts the funding for Head Start to state control.

Head Start

Head Start is probably the best-known effort to help lower-class youths achieve proper socialization and, in so doing, reduce their potential for future criminality. Head Start programs were instituted in the 1960s as part of President Johnson's War on Poverty. In the beginning, Head Start was a 2-month summer program for children who were about to enter school that was aimed at embracing the "whole child." In embracing the whole child, the school offered comprehensive programming that helped improve physical health, enhance mental processes, and improve social and emotional development, self-image, and interpersonal relationships. Preschoolers were provided with an enriched educational environment to develop their learning and cognitive skills. They were given the opportunity to use pegs and pegboards, puzzles, toy animals, dolls, letters and numbers, and other materials that middle-class children take for granted. These opportunities provided the children a leg up in the educational process. The program is divided into four segments:

- *Education:* Head Start's educational program is designed to meet the needs of each child, the community served, and its ethnic and cultural characteristics. Every child receives a variety of learning experiences to foster intellectual, social, and emotional growth.

- *Health:* Head Start emphasizes the importance of the early identification of health problems. Every child is involved in a comprehensive health program, which includes immunizations; medical, dental, and mental health; and nutritional services.

- *Parent involvement:* An essential part of Head Start is the involvement of parents in parent education, program planning, and operating activities.

- *Social services:* Specific services are geared to each family including community outreach; referrals; family need assessments; recruitment and enrollment of children; and emergency assistance and/or crisis intervention.

Today, with annual funding of more than $6.5 billion, the Head Start program is administered by the Head Start Bureau; the Administration on Children, Youth, and Families (ACFY); the Administration for Children and Families (ACF); and the Department of Health and Human Services (DHHS). Head Start teachers strive to provide a variety of learning experiences appropriate to the child's age and development. These experiences encourage the child to read books, to understand cultural diversity, to express feelings, and to play with and relate to peers in an appropriate fashion. Students are guided in developing gross and fine motor skills and self-confidence.

Healthcare is also an issue, and most children enrolled in the program receive comprehensive health screening, physical and dental examinations, and appropriate followup. Many programs provide meals, and in so doing help children receive proper nourishment.

Head Start programs now serve parents in addition to their preschoolers. Some programs allow parents to enroll in classes, which cover parenting, literacy, nutrition/weight loss, domestic violence prevention, and other social issues; social services, health, nutrition, and educational services are also available.

Considerable controversy has surrounded the success of the Head Start program. In 1970, the Westinghouse Learning Corporation issued an evaluation of the Head Start effort and concluded that there was no evidence of lasting cognitive gains on the part of the participating children. While disappointing, this evaluation focused on IQ levels and gave short shrift to improvement in social competence and other survival skills. More recent research has produced dramatically different results. One report found that, by age 5, children who experienced the enriched daycare offered by Head Start averaged more than 10 points higher on their IQ scores than their peers who did not participate in the program. Other research that carefully compared Head Start children to similar youngsters who did not attend

Control theories have also influenced criminal justice and other public policy. Programs have been developed to increase people's commitment to conventional lines of action. Some work at creating and strengthening bonds early in life before the onset of criminality. The educational system has been the scene of numerous programs designed to improve basic skills and create an atmosphere in which youths will develop a bond to their schools. The most famous of these efforts, the Head Start Program, is profiled in the Policy and Practice in Criminology feature.

Control theories have focused on the family and have played a key role in putting into operation programs designed to strengthen the bond between parent and child. Others attempt to repair bonds that have been broken and frayed. Examples of this approach are the career, work furlough, and educational opportunity programs being developed in the nation's prisons. These programs are designed to help inmates maintain a stake in society so they will be less willing to resort to criminal activity on their release.

the program found that the former made significant intellectual gains. Head Start children were less likely to have been retained in a grade or placed in classes for slow learners; they outperformed peers on achievement tests; and they were more likely to graduate from high school.

Head Start kids also made strides in nonacademic areas: They appear to have better health, immunization rates, nutrition, and enhanced emotional characteristics after leaving the program. Research also shows that the Head Start program can have important psychological benefits for the mothers of participants, such as decreasing depression and anxiety and increasing feelings of life satisfaction. The best available evidence suggests that:

■ Head Start is associated with short-term gains in cognitive skills as well as longer-term gains in school completion, and even greater gains are possible if children receive good follow-up in the early grades.

■ Head Start may be focused too heavily on social supports at the expense of language and literacy training.

■ Although Head Start centers vary in quality, on average they are better than privately run childcare centers, have achieved short-term benefits, and would pay for themselves if they produced even a fraction of

the long-term benefits associated with model programs. For this reason, they merit some expansion and greater attention paid to their quality.

If, as many experts believe, there is a close link between school performance, family life, and crime, programs such as Head Start can help some potentially criminal youths avoid problems with the law. By implication, their success indicates that programs that help socialize youngsters can be used to combat urban criminality. While some problems have been identified in individual centers, the government has shown its faith in Head Start as a socialization agent. Head Start's mission is to help low-income children start school ready to learn by providing early childhood education, child development, comprehensive health, and social services.

Since 1965, local Head Start programs across the country have served more than 21 million children and built strong partnerships with parents and families. Table 7-A illustrates the size of this vast program:

TABLE 7-A

Head Start, 2003

Number of grantees	1,670
Number of classrooms	47,000
Number of centers	19,200
Average cost per child	$7,092
Paid staff	206,000
Volunteers	1,372,000

Critical Thinking

1. If crime were a matter of human traits, as some criminologists suggest, would a program such as Head Start help kids avoid criminal careers?

2. Are there any other types of programs that would help parents or children avoid involvement in drugs and/or crime?

3. Were you in Head Start? If so, did it help you attain your current academic success?

 InfoTrac College Edition Research

To learn more about the Head Start program and its current status, use "Head Start" as a subject guide in InfoTrac College Edition.

Sources: Head Start statistics can be accessed at the Head Start bureau website: http://www.acf.hhs.gov/programs/hsb/research/2004.htm. Accessed August 1, 2004; Janet Currie, *A Fresh Start for Head Start?* (Washington, DC: Brookings Institute, March 2001); Statement by Wade F. Horn, Assistant Secretary for Children and Families, "Head Start and Child Care in the Context of Early Learning," before the House Committee on Appropriations, Subcommittee on Labor, Health, and Human Services, and Education, April 17, 2002; Edward Zigler and Sally Styfco, "Head Start, Criticisms in a Constructive Context," *American Psychologist* 49 (1994): 127–132; Nancy Kassebaum, "Head Start, Only the Best for America's Children," *American Psychologist* 49 (1994):123–126; Faith Lamb Parker, Chaya Piorkowski, and Lenore Peay, "Head Start as Social Support for Mothers: The Psychological Benefits of Involvement," *American Journal of Orthopsychiatry* 57 (1987): 220–233.

Labeling theorists caution against too much intervention. Rather than ask social agencies to attempt to rehabilitate people having problems with the law, they argue, "less is better." Put another way, the more institutions try to "help" people, the more these people will be stigmatized and labeled. For example, a special education program designed to help problem readers may cause them to label themselves and others as slow or stupid. Similarly, a mental health rehabilitation program created with the best intentions may cause clients to be labeled as crazy or dangerous.

The influence of labeling theory can be viewed in the development of diversion and restitution programs. **Diversion programs** are designed to remove both juvenile and adult offenders from the normal channels of the criminal justice process by placing them in programs designed for rehabilitation. For example, a college student whose drunken driving causes injury to a pedestrian may, before a trial occurs, be placed for 6 months in an alcohol treatment program. If he successfully completes the program, charges against him will be dismissed. Thus, he avoids the stigma of a criminal label. Such programs are common throughout the nation. Often, they offer counseling; vocational, educational, and family services; and medical advice.

Another label-avoiding innovation that has gained popularity is restitution. Rather than face the stigma of a formal trial, an offender is asked to either pay back the victim of the crime for any loss incurred or do some useful work in the community in lieu of receiving a court-ordered sentence.

Despite their good intentions, stigma-reducing programs have not met with great success. Critics charge that they substitute one kind of stigma for another—for instance, attending a mental health program in place of a criminal trial. In addition, diversion and restitution programs usually screen out violent offenders and repeat offenders. Finally, there is little hard evidence that the recidivism rate of people placed in alternative programs is less than that of people sent to traditional programs.

 To quiz yourself on this material, go to the Criminology TPT 9e website.

SUMMARY

- Social process theories view criminality as a function of people's interaction with various organizations, institutions, and processes in society.

- People in all walks of life have the potential to become criminals if they maintain destructive social relationships. Improper socialization is a key component of crime.

- Social process theories say that the way people are socialized controls their behavior choices, and there is strong evidence that social relations influence behavior.

- Children growing up with conflict, abuse, and neglect are at risk for crime and delinquency. As well, educational failure has been linked to criminality.

- Adolescents who associate with deviant peers are more likely to engage in crime than those who maintain conventional peer group relations. Kids who are socialized to have proper values and beliefs are less likely to get involved in crime than those without normative belief systems.

- Social process theory has three main branches: Social learning theory stresses that people learn how to commit crimes. Social control theory analyzes the failure of society to control criminal tendencies. Labeling theory maintains that negative labels produce criminal careers.

- Social learning theory suggests that people learn criminal behaviors much as they learn conventional behavior.

- Differential association theory, formulated by Sutherland, holds that criminality is a result of a person perceiving an excess of definitions in favor of crime over definitions that uphold conventional values.

- Differential reinforcement theory recasts differential association in terms of operant conditioning. It stresses reward and punishment.

- Sykes and Matza's theory of neutralization stresses that youths learn behavior rationalizations that enable them to overcome societal values and norms and break the law.

- Social control theories maintain that behavior is a function of the attachment that people feel toward society. People who have a weak commitment to conformity are free to commit crime. Control theory maintains that all people have the potential to become criminals, but their bonds to conventional society prevent them from violating the law. This view suggests that a person's self-concept aids his or her commitment to conventional action. A strong self-image may insulate people from crime.

- Hirschi's social control theory describes the social bond as containing elements of attachment, commitment, involvement, and belief. Weakened bonds allow youths to behave antisocially.

- Social reaction or labeling theory holds that criminality is promoted by becoming negatively labeled by significant others. Such labels as criminal, ex-con, and junkie isolate people from society and lock them into lives of crime.

- Labels create expectations that the labeled person will act in a certain way; labeled people are always watched and suspected. Eventually these people begin to accept their labels as personal identities, locking them further into lives of crime and deviance.

- Lemert suggests that people who accept labels are involved in secondary deviance while primary deviants are able to maintain an undamaged identity.

- Some critics have charged that labeling theory lacks credibility as a description of crime causation. However, supporters reply that it helps explain the continuity of crime and the maintenance of a criminal career.

- Social process theories have greatly influenced social policy. They have controlled treatment orientations as well as community action policies.

Thomson NOW! Optimize your study time and master key chapter concepts with **ThomsonNOW™**—the first web-based assessment-centered study tool for Criminology. This powerful resource helps you determine your unique study needs and provides you with a *Personalized Study Plan,* guiding you to interactive media that includes that Learning Modules, Topic Reviews, ABC Video Clips with Questions, Animations, an integrated E-book, and more!

Thinking Like a Criminologist

As a criminologist, you have been asked by the governor to help her deal with the state's emerging gang problem. The head of the state police views the gang problem as part of a criminal conspiracy designed to provide profits for highly motivated young criminals. Kids turn to gangs, he argues, as a method of obtaining desired goods and services, either directly through theft and extortion or indirectly through the profits generated by drug dealing and weapons sales. He argues that the best method to control this rational choice is to increase police gang control units and pass legislation heavily penalizing gang activity.

As a social process theorist, you believe the gang is a refuge for young men and women who have learned criminal attitudes and behaviors at home. Many have weak ties to their parents and families. Many do poorly in school. You are aware of research that shows that significant numbers of gang members have been sexually abused at home and that their homes are very likely to include drug users and people arrested for crimes.

Considering these data, you believe joining a gang can be an assertion of independence not only from the family but also from cultural and class constraints; the gang is a substitute institution that can provide meaning and identity.

If gang control is the objective, what programs would you suggest the governor implement? Do you believe a "get tough" program could actually work, or may it backfire? How would you convince the governor that your ideas are valid and worthwhile?

Doing Research on the Web

Before you tackle the question above, go to InfoTrac College Edition and read the following two articles in order to gain insight on gang life and culture: L. Thomas Winfree, Jr., Frances Bernat, and Finn-Aage Esbensen, "Hispanic and Anglo Gang Membership in Two Southwest-ern Cities," *Social Science Journal* 38 (2001): 105–118; John M. Hagedorn, Jose Torres, and Greg Giglio, "Cocaine, Kicks, and Strain: Patterns of Substance Use in Milwaukee Gangs," *Contemporary Drug Problems* 25 (spring 1998): 113–145.

For a general overview of gangs in America, see http://www.ncjrs.org/pdffiles/167249.pdf and the National Youth Gang Center, www.iir.com/nygc/faq.htm#.

http://cj.wadsworth.com/siegel_crimtpt9e To quiz yourself on the material in this chapter, go to the companion website, where you'll find chapter-by-chapter online tutorial quizzes, a final exam, ABC videos with questions, chapter outlines, chapter review, chapter-by-chapter web links, flash cards, and more!

social process theory (214)
social learning theory (221)
social control theory (221)
social reaction theory (221)
labeling theory (221)
differential association theory (222)
differential reinforcement theory (225)
direct conditioning (225)
differential reinforcement (225)
negative reinforcement (225)

neutralization theory (226)
subterranean values (226)
drift (226)
self-control (228)
commitment to conformity (228)
containment theory (229)
normative groups (229)
social bond (230)
symbolic interaction theory (232)

stigma (235)
differential social control (235)
reflective role taking (235)
retrospective reading (235)
dramatization of evil (236)
primary deviance (236)
secondary deviance (236)
contextual discrimination (237)
diversion programs (241)

CRITICAL THINKING QUESTIONS

1. Do negative labels cause crime? Or do people who commit crime become negatively labeled? That is, are labels a cause of crime or a result?

2. Once weakened, can a person's bonds to society become reattached? What social processes might help reattachment?

3. Can you devise a test of Sutherland's differential association theory? How would you go about measuring an excess of definitions toward criminality?

4. Can you think of ways you may have supported your peers' or siblings' antisocial behavior by helping them learn criminal techniques or attitudes?

5. Do you recall neutralizing any guilt you might have felt for committing a criminal or illegal act? Did your neutralizations come before or after you committed the act in question?

NOTES

1. *Smith et al. v. Doe et al.* No. 01—729. Decided March 5, 2003.

2. Alan Lizotte, Terence Thornberry, Marvin Krohn, Deborah Chard-Wierschem, and David McDowall, "Neighborhood Context and Delinquency: A Longitudinal Analysis," in *Cross-National Longitudinal Research on Human Development and Criminal Behavior,* eds. E. M. Weitekamp and H. J. Kerner (Netherlands: Kluwer, 1994), pp. 217–227.

3. Charles Tittle and Robert Meier, "Specifying the SES/Delinquency Relationship," *Criminology* 28 (1990): 271–299, at 274.

4. Sheldon Glueck and Eleanor Glueck, *Unraveling Juvenile Delinquency* (Cambridge, MA: Harvard University Press, 1950); Ashley Weeks, "Predicting Juvenile Delinquency," *American Sociological Review* 8 (1943): 40–46.

5. Denise Kandel, "The Parental and Peer Contexts of Adolescent Deviance: An Algebra of Interpersonal Influences," *Journal of Drug Issues* 26 (1996): 289–315; Ann Goetting, "The Parenting Crime Connection," *Journal of Primary Prevention* 14 (1994): 167–184.

6. Joseph Weis, Katherine Worsley, and Carol Zeiss, "The Family and Delinquency: Organizing the Conceptual Chaos." Monograph. (Seattle: Center for Law and Justice, University of Washington, 1982).

7. Susan Stern and Carolyn Smith, "Family Processes and Delinquency in an Ecological Context," *Social Service Review* 37 (1995): 707–731.

8. *Families with Children under 18 by Type: 1995 to 2010,* Series 1, 2, and 3 (Washington, DC: U.S. Bureau of the Census, 1996).

9. Jukka Savolainen, "Relative Cohort Size and Age-Specific Arrest Rates: A Conditional Interpretation of the Easterlin Effect," *Criminology* 38 (2000): 117–136.

10. Lawrence Rosen and Kathleen Neilson, "Broken Homes," in *Contemporary Criminology,* eds. Leonard Savitz and Norman Johnston (New York: Wiley, 1982), pp. 126–132.

11. Cesar Rebellon, "Reconsidering the Broken Homes/Delinquency Relationship and Exploring Its Mediating Factors," *Criminology* 40 (2002): 103–136.

12. L. Edward Wells and Joseph Rankin, "Families and Delinquency: A Meta-Analysis of the Impact of Broken Homes," *Social Problems* 38 (1991): 71–90.

13. Nan Marie Astone and Sara McLanahan, "Family Structure, Parental Practices, and High School Completion," *American Sociological Review* 56 (1991): 309–320.

14. Mary Pat Traxler, "The Influence of the Father and Alternative Male Role Models on African-American Boys' Involvement in Antisocial Behavior." Paper presented at the annual meeting of the American Society of Criminology, New Orleans, November 1992.

15. Jennifer Beyers, John Bates, Gregory Pettit, and Kenneth Dodge, "Neighborhood Structure, Parenting Processes, and the Development of Youths' Externalizing Behaviors: A Multilevel Analysis," *American Journal of Community Psychology* 31 (2003): 35–53.

16. Paul Amato and Bruce Keith, "Parental Divorce and the Well-Being of Children: A Meta-Analysis," *Psychological Bulletin* 110 (1991): 26–46.

17. Joseph Rankin and L. Edward Wells, "The Effect of Parental Attachments and Direct Controls on Delinquency," *Journal of Research in Crime and Delinquency* 27 (1990): 140–165.

18. John Paul Wright and Francis Cullen, "Parental Efficacy and Delinquent Behavior: Do Control and Support Matter?" *Criminology* 39 (2001): 677–706.

19. Carter Hay, "Parenting, Self-Control, and Delinquency: A Test of Self-Control Theory," *Criminology* 39 (2001): 707–736.

20. Robert Vermeiren, Jef Bogaerts, Vladislav Ruchkin, Dirk Deboutte, and Mary Schwab-Stone, "Subtypes of Self-Esteem and Self-Concept in Adolescent Violent and Property Offenders," *Journal of Child Psychology and Psychiatry* 45 (2004): 405–411.

21. Robert Roberts and Vern Bengston, "Affective Ties to Parents in Early Adulthood and Self-Esteem across 20 Years," *Social Psychology Quarterly* 59 (1996): 96–106.

22. Robert Johnson, S. Susan Su, Dean Gerstein, Hee-Choon Shin, and John Hoffman, "Parental Influences on Deviant Behavior in Early Adolescence: A Logistic Response Analysis of Age- and Gender-Differentiated Effects," *Journal of Quantitative Criminology* 11 (1995): 167–192.

23. Judith Brook and Li-Jng Tseng, "Influences of Parental Drug Use, Personality, and Child Rearing on the Toddler's Anger and Negativity," *Genetic, Social and General Psychology Monographs* 122 (1996): 107–128.

24. Thomas Ashby Wills, Donato Vaccaro, Grace McNamara, and A. Elizabeth Hirky, "Escalated Substance Use: A Longitudinal Grouping Analysis from Early to Middle Adolescence," *Journal of Abnormal Psychology* 105 (1996): 166–180.

25. John Laub and Robert Sampson, "Unraveling Families and Delinquency: A Reanalysis of the Gluecks' Data," *Criminology* 26 (1988): 355–380.

26. Richard Famularo, Karen Stone, Richard Barnum, and Robert Wharton, "Alcoholism and Severe Child Maltreatment," *American Journal of Orthopsychiatry* 56 (1987): 481–485; Richard Gelles, "Child Abuse and Violence in Single-Parent Families: Parent Absence and Economic Deprivation," *American Journal of Orthopsychiatry* 59 (1989): 492–501; Cecil Willis and Richard Wells, "The Police and Child Abuse: An Analysis of Police Decisions to Report Illegal Behavior," *Criminology* 26 (1988): 695–716; Carolyn Webster-Stratton, "Comparison of Abusive and Nonabusive Families with Conduct-Disordered Children," *American Journal of Orthopsychiatry* 55 (1985): 59–69.

27. Fred Rogosch and Dante Cicchetti, "Child Maltreatment and Emergent Personality Organization: Perspectives from the Five-Factor Model," *Journal of Abnormal Child Psychology* 32 (2004): 123–145.

28. Carolyn Smith and Terence Thornberry, "The Relationship between Childhood Maltreatment and Adolescent Involvement in Delinquency," *Criminology* 33 (1995): 451–479.

29. Eric Slade and Lawrence Wissow, "Spanking in Early Childhood and Later Behavior Problems: A Prospective Study of Infants and Young Toddlers," *Pediatrics* 113 (2004): 1,321–1,330.

30. Murray A. Straus, "Spanking and the Making of a Violent Society: The Short- and Long-Term Consequences of Corporal Punishment," *Pediatrics* 98 (1996): 837–843.

31. Ibid.

32. Lening Zhang and Steven Messner, "Family Deviance and Delinquency in China," *Criminology* 33 (1995): 359–387.

33. *The Forgotten Half: Pathways to Success for America's Youth and Young Families* (Washington, DC: William T. Grant Foundation, 1988); Lee Jussim, "Teacher Expectations: Self-Fulfilling Prophecies, Perceptual Biases, and Accuracy," *Journal of Personality and Social Psychology* 57 (1989): 469–480.

34. Eugene Maguin and Rolf Loeber, "Academic Performance and Delinquency," in *Crime and Justice: A Review of Research*, vol. 20, ed. Michael Tonry (Chicago: University of Chicago Press, 1996), pp. 145–264.

35. Jeannie Oakes, *Keeping Track, How Schools Structure Inequality* (New Haven, CT: Yale University Press, 1985).

36. Christopher B. Swanson, *Who Graduates? Who Doesn't? A Statistical Portrait of Public High School Graduation, Class of 2001* (Washington, DC: Urban Institute, 2004).

37. G. Roger Jarjoura, "Does Dropping Out of School Enhance Delinquent Involvement? Results from a Large-Scale National Probability Sample," *Criminology* 31 (1993): 149–172; Terence Thornberry, Melaine Moore, and R. L. Christenson, "The Effect of Dropping Out of High School on Subsequent Criminal Behavior," *Criminology* 23 (1985): 3–18.

38. Carolyn Smith, Alan Lizotte, Terence Thornberry, and Marvin Krohn, *Resilient Youth: Identifying Factors that Prevent High-Risk Youth from Engaging in Delinquency and Drug Use* (Albany, NY: Rochester Youth Development Study, 1994), pp. 19–21.

39. Catherine Dulmus, Matthew Theriot, Karen Sowers, and James Blackburn, "Student Reports of Peer Bullying Victimization in a Rural School," *Stress, Trauma & Crisis: An International Journal* 7 (2004): 1–15;

40. Tonja Nansel, Mary Overpeck, and Ramani Pilla, "Bullying Behaviors among U.S. Youth: Prevalence and Association with Psychosocial Adjustment," *Journal of the American Medical Association* 285 (2001): 2,094–3,100.

41. Jill DeVoe, Katharin Peter, Sally Ruddy, Amanda Miller, Mike Planty, Thomas Snyder, and Michael Rand, *Indicators of School Crime and Safety, 2003* (Washington, DC: U.S. Department of Education and Bureau of Justice Statistics, 2004).

42. Ben Brown and William Reed Benedict, "Bullets, Blades, and Being Afraid in Hispanic High Schools: An Exploratory Study of the Presence of Weapons and Fear of Weapon-Associated Victimization among High School Students in a Border Town," *Crime and Delinquency* 50 (2004): 372–395.

43. Irving Janis, *Groupthink: Psychological Studies of Policy Decisions and Fiascoes* (Boston: Houghton Mifflin, 1982).

44. Zhang and Messner, "Family Deviance and Delinquency in China."

45. Thomas Berndt, "The Features and Effects of Friendships in Early Adolescence," *Child Development* 53 (1982): 1,447–1,469; Thomas Berndt and T. B. Perry, "Children's Perceptions of Friendships as Supportive Relationships," *Developmental Psychology* 22 (1986): 640–648; Spencer Rathus, *Understanding Child Development* (New York: Holt, Rinehart & Winston, 1988), p. 462.

46. Isabela Granic and Thomas Dishion, "Deviant Talk in Adolescent Friendships: A Step toward Measuring a Pathogenic Attractor Process," *Social Development* 12 (2003): 314–334.

47. Peggy Giordano, "The Wider Circle of Friends in Adolescence," *American Journal of Sociology* 101 (1995): 661–697.

48. Delbert Elliott, David Huizinga, and Suzanne Ageton, *Explaining Delinquency and Drug Use* (Beverly Hills: Sage, 1985); Helene Raskin White, Robert Padina, and Randy LaGrange, "Longitudinal Predictors of Serious Substance Use and Delinquency," *Criminology* 6 (1987): 715–740.

49. See, generally, John Hagedorn, *People and Folks: Gangs, Crime and the Underclass in a Rustbelt City* (Chicago: Lakeview Press, 1988).

50. This section is adapted from Gail Wasserman, Kate Keenan, Richard Tremblay, John Coie, Todd Herrenkohl, Rolf Loeber, and David Petechuk, "Risk and Protective Factors of Child Delinquency," *Child Delinquency Bulletin Series* (Washington, DC: Office of Juvenile Justice and Delinquency Prevention, 2003).

51. John Paul Wright and Francis Cullen, "Employment, Peers, and Life-Course Transitions," *Justice Quarterly* 21 (2004): 183–205.

52. Robert Agnew and Timothy Brezina, "Relational Problems with Peers, Gender, and Delinquency," *Youth and Society* 29 (1997): 84–111.

53. Kate Keenan, Rolf Loeber, Quanwu Zhang, Magda Stouthamer-Loeber, and Welmoet Van Kammen, "The Influence of Deviant Peers on the Development of Boys' Disruptive and Delinquent Behavior: A Temporal Analysis," *Development and Psychopathology* 7 (1995):715–726.

54. John Cole, Robert Terry, Shari-Miller Johnson, and John Lochman, "Longitudinal Effects of Deviant Peer Groups on Criminal Offending in Late Adolescence." Paper presented at the American Society of Criminology meeting, Boston, November 1995.

55. Terence Thornberry and Marvin Krohn, "Peers, Drug Use, and Delinquency," in *Handbook of Antisocial Behavior,* eds. David Stoff, James Breiling, and Jack Maser (New York: Wiley, 1997), pp. 218–233; Thomas Dishion, Deborah Capaldi, Kathleen Spracklen, and Fuzhong Li, "Peer Ecology of Male Adolescent Drug Use," *Development and Psychopathology* 7 (1995): 803–824.

56. Sylvie Mrug, Betsy Hoza, and William Bukowski, "Choosing or Being Chosen by Aggressive-Disruptive Peers: Do They Contribute to Children's Externalizing and Internalizing Problems?" *Journal of Abnormal Child Psychology* 32 (2004): 53–66.

57. Mark Warr, "Age, Peers, and Delinquency," *Criminology* 31 (1993): 17–40.

58. Sara Battin, Karl Hill, Robert Abbott, Richard Catalano, and J. David Hawkins, "The Contribution of Gang Membership to Delinquency beyond Delinquent Friends," *Criminology* 36 (1998): 93–116.

59. Mark Warr, "Life-Course Transitions and Desistance from Crime," *Criminology* 36 (1998): 502–536.

60. Stephen W. Baron, "Self-Control, Social Consequences, and Criminal Behavior: Street Youth and the General Theory of Crime," *Journal of Research in Crime and Delinquency* 40 (2003): 403–425.

61. Daneen Deptula and Robert Cohen, "Aggressive, Rejected, and Delinquent Children and Adolescents: A Comparison of Their Friendships," *Aggression and Violent Behavior* 9 (2004): 75–104.

62. Scott Menard, "Demographic and Theoretical Variables in the Age-Period Cohort Analysis of Illegal Behavior," *Journal of Research in Crime and Delinquency* 29 (1992): 178–199.

63. Patrick Jackson, "Theories and Findings about Youth Gangs," *Criminal Justice Abstracts* (June 1989): 313–327.

64. Marvin Krohn and Terence Thornberry, "Network Theory: A Model for Understanding Drug Abuse among African-American and Hispanic Youth," in *Drug Abuse among Minority Youth: Advances in Research and Methodology,* eds. Mario De La Rosa and Juan-Luis Recio Adrados (Washington, DC: U.S. Department of Health and Human Services, 1993).

65. D. Wayne Osgood, Janet Wilson, Patrick O'Malley, Jerald Bachman, and Lloyd Johnston, "Routine Activities and Individual Deviant Behavior," *American Sociological Review* 61 (1996): 635–655.

66. Mark Warr, "Age, Peers, and Delinquency," *Criminology* 31 (1993): 17–40.

67. Mark Warr, "Organization and Instigation in Delinquent Groups," *Criminology* 34 (1996): 11–35.

68. Sara Battin, Karl Hill, Robert Abbott, Richard Catalano, and J. David Hawkins, "The Contribution of Gang Membership to Delinquency beyond Delinquent Friends," *Criminology* 36 (1998): 93–116.

69. Terence Thornberry, Alan Lizotte, Marvin Krohn, Margaret Farnworth, and Sung Joon Jang, "Delinquent Peers, Beliefs, and Delinquent Behavior: A Longitudinal Test of Interactional Theory." Working paper no. 6, rev. (Albany, NY: Rochester Youth Development Study, Hindelang Criminal Justice Research Center, 1992), pp. 8–30.

70. Warr, "Age, Peers and Delinquency."

71. Travis Hirschi and Rodney Stark, "Hellfire and Delinquency," *Social Problems* 17 (1969): 202–213.

72. Colin Baier and Bradley Wright, "If You Love Me, Keep My Commandments: A Meta-Analysis of the Effect of Religion on Crime," *Journal of Research in Crime and Delinquency* 38 (2001): 3–21; Byron Johnson, Sung Joon Jang, David Larson, and Spencer De Li, "Does Adolescent Religious Commitment Matter? A Reexamination of the Effects of Religiosity on Delinquency," *Journal of Research in Crime and Delinquency* 38 (2001): 22–44.

73. Sung Joon Jang and Byron Johnson, "Neighborhood Disorder, Individual Religiosity, and Adolescent Use of Illicit Drugs: A Test of Multilevel Hypothesis," *Criminology* 39 (2001): 109–144.

74. T. David Evans, Francis Cullen, R. Gregory Dunaway, and Velmer Burton, Jr., "Religion and Crime Reexamined: The Impact of Religion, Secular Controls, and Social Ecology on Adult Criminality," *Criminology* 33 (1995): 195–224.

75. Lee Ellis and James Patterson, "Crime and Religion: An International Comparison among Thirteen Industrial Nations," *Personal Individual Differences* 20 (1996): 761–768.

76. Walter Miller, *Violence by Youth Gangs and Youth Groups as a Crime Problem in Major American Cities* (Washington, DC: U.S. Government Printing Office, 1975).

77. Edwin H. Sutherland, *Principles of Criminology* (Philadelphia: Lippincott, 1939).

78. See, for example, Edwin Sutherland, "White-Collar Criminality," *American Sociological Review* 5 (1940): 2–10.

79. See Edwin Sutherland and Donald Cressey, *Criminology,* 8th ed. (Philadelphia: Lippincott, 1970), pp. 77–79.

80. Sandra Brown, Vicki Creamer, and Barbara Stetson, "Adolescent Alcohol Expectancies in Relation to Personal and Parental Drinking Patterns," *Journal of Abnormal Psychology* 96 (1987): 117–121.

81. Ibid.

82. Matthew Ploeger, "Youth Employment and Delinquency: Reconsidering A Problematic Relationship," *Criminology* 35 (1997): 659–675.

83. Paul Vowell and Jieming Chen, "Predicting Academic Misconduct: A Comparative Test of Four Sociological Explanations," *Sociological Inquiry* 74 (2004): 226–249.

84. James Short, "Differential Association as a Hypothesis: Problems of Empirical Testing," *Social Problems* 8 (1960): 14–25.

85. Andy Hochstetler, Heith Copes, and Matt DeLisi, "Differential Association in Group and Solo Offending," *Journal of Criminal Justice* 30 (2002): 559–566.

86. Warr, "Age, Peers, and Delinquency."

87. Clayton Hartjen and S. Priyadarsini, "Gender, Peers, and Delinquency," *Youth and Society* 34 (2003): 387–414.

88. Denise Kandel and Mark Davies, "Friendship Networks, Intimacy, and Illicit Drug Use in Young Adulthood: A Comparison of Two Competing Theories," *Criminology* 29 (1991): 441–467.

89. Kenneth Tunnell, "Inside the Drug Trade: Trafficking from the Dealer's Perspective," *Qualitative Sociology* 16 (1993): 361–381, at 367.

90. Krohn and Thornberry, "Network Theory," pp. 123–124.

91. Daniel Mears, Matthew Ploeger, and Mark Warr, "Explaining the Gender Gap in Delinquency: Peer Influence and Moral Evaluations of Behavior," *Journal of Research in Crime and Delinquency* 35 (1998): 251–266.

92. Ronald Akers, "Is Differential Association/Social Learning Cultural Deviance Theory," *Criminology* 34 (1996): 229–247; for an opposing view, see Travis Hirschi, "Theory without Ideas: Reply to Akers," *Criminology* 34 (1996): 249–256.

93. Robert Burgess and Ronald Akers, "A Differential Association–Reinforcement Theory of Criminal Behavior," *Social Problems* 14 (1966): 128–147.

94. Ronald Akers, *Deviant Behavior: A Social Learning Approach,* 2nd ed. (Belmont, CA: Wadsworth, 1977).

95. Ronald Akers, Marvin Krohn, Lonn Lanza-Kaduce, and Marcia Radosevich, "Social Learning and Deviant Behavior: A Specific Test of a General Theory," *American Sociological Review* 44 (1979): 638.

96. Ibid.

97. Marvin Krohn, William Skinner, James Massey, and Ronald Akers, "Social Learning Theory and Adolescent Cigarette Smoking: A Longitudinal Study," *Social Problems* 32 (1985): 455–471.

98. L. Thomas Winfree, Christine Sellers, and Dennis L. Clason, "Social Learning and Adolescent Deviance Abstention: Toward Understanding the Reasons for Initiating, Quitting, and Avoiding Drugs," *Journal of Quantitative Criminology* 9 (1993): 101–125.

99. Ronald Akers and Gang Lee, "A Longitudinal Test of Social Learning Theory: Adolescent Smoking," *Journal of Drug Issues* 26 1996): 317–343.

100. Gary Jensen and David Brownfield, "Parents and Drugs," *Criminology* 21 (1983): 543–554.

101. Ronald Akers, "Rational Choice, Deterrence and Social Learning Theory in Criminology: The Path Not Taken," *Journal of Criminal Law and Criminology* 81 (1990): 653–676.

102. Gresham Sykes and David Matza, "Techniques of Neutralization: A Theory of Delinquency," *American Sociological Review* 22 (1957): 664–670; David Matza, *Delinquency and Drift* (New York: Wiley, 1964).

103. Matza, *Delinquency and Drift,* p. 51.

104. Sykes and Matza, "Techniques of Neutralization," pp. 664–670; see also David Matza, "Subterranean Traditions of Youths," *Annals of the American Academy of Political and Social Science* 378 (1961): 116.

105. Sykes and Matza, "Techniques of Neutralization," pp. 664–670.

106. Ibid.

107. Ian Shields and George Whitehall, "Neutralization and Delinquency among Teenagers," *Criminal Justice and Behavior* 21 (1994): 223–235; Robert A. Ball, "An Empirical Exploration of Neutralization Theory," *Criminologica* 4 (1966): 22–32. See also M. William Minor, "The Neutralization of Criminal Offense," *Criminology* 18 (1980): 103–120; Robert Gordon, James Short, Desmond Cartwright, and Fred Strodtbeck, "Values and Gang Delinquency: A Study of Street Corner Groups," *American Journal of Sociology* 69 (1963): 109–128.

108. Michael Hindelang, "The Commitment of Delinquents to Their Misdeeds: Do Delinquents Drift?" *Social Problems* 17 (1970): 500–509; Robert Regoli and Eric Poole, "The Commitment of Delinquents to Their Misdeeds: A Reexamination," *Journal of Criminal Justice* 6 (1978): 261–269.

109. Larry Siegel, Spencer Rathus, and Carol Ruppert, "Values and Delinquent Youth: An Empirical Reexamination of Theories of Delinquency," *British Journal of Criminology* 13 (1973): 237–244.

110. Robert Agnew, "The Techniques of Neutralization and Violence," *Criminology* 32 (1994): 555–580.

111. Jeffrey Fagan, "Adolescent Violence: A View from the Street," *NIJ Research Preview* (Washington, DC: National Institute of Justice, 1998).

112. John Hamlin, "Misplaced Role of Rational Choice in Neutralization Theory," *Criminology* 26 (1988): 425–438.

113. Mark Pogrebin, Eric Poole, and Amos Martinez, "Accounts of Professional Misdeeds: The Sexual Exploitation of Clients by Psychotherapists," *Deviant Behavior* 13 (1992): 229–252.

114. Eric Wish, *Drug Use Forecasting 1990* (Washington, DC: National Institute of Justice, 1991).

115. Scott Briar and Irving Piliavin, "Delinquency: Situational Inducements and Commitment to Conformity," *Social Problems* 13 (1965–1966): 35–45.

116. Lawrence Sherman and Douglas Smith, with Janell Schmidt and Dennis Rogan, "Crime, Punishment, and Stake in Conformity: Legal and Informal Control of Domestic Violence," *American Sociological Review* 57 (1992): 680–690.

117. Albert Reiss, "Delinquency as the Failure of Personal and Social Controls," *American Sociological Review* 16 (1951): 196–207.

118. Briar and Piliavin, "Delinquency: Situational Inducements and Commitment to Conformity."

119. Walter Reckless, *The Crime Problem* (New York: Appleton-Century-Crofts, 1967), pp. 469–483.

120. Among the many research reports by Reckless and his colleagues are Frank Scarpitti, Ellen Murray, Simon Dinitz, and Walter Reckless, "The Good Boy in a High Delinquency Area: Four Years Later," *American Sociological Review* 23 (1960): 555–558; Walter Reckless, Simon Dinitz, and Ellen Murray, "The Good Boy in a High Delinquency Area," *Journal of Criminal Law, Criminology, and Police Science* 48 (1957): 12–26; idem, "Self-Concept as an Insulator against Delinquency," *American Sociological Review* 21 (1956): 744–746; Walter Reckless and Simon Dinitz, "Pioneering with Self-Concept as a Vulnerability Factor in Delinquency," *Journal of Criminal Law, Criminology, and Police Science* 58 (1967): 515–523; Walter Reckless, Simon Dinitz, and Barbara Kay, "The Self-Component in Potential Delinquency and Potential Non-Delinquency," *American Sociological Review* 22 (1957): 566–570.

121. Howard Kaplan, *Deviant Behavior in Defense of Self* (New York: Academic Press, 1980); idem, "Self-Attitudes and Deviant Response," *Social Forces* 54 (1978): 788–801.

122. Kaplan, *Deviant Behavior in Defense of Self,* pp. 30–50.

123. Beverly Stiles, Xiaoru Liu, and Howard Kaplan, "Relative Deprivation and Deviant Adaptations: The Mediating Effects of Negative Self-Feelings," *Journal of Research in Crime and Delinquency* 37 (2000): 64–90.

124. Travis Hirschi, *Causes of Delinquency* (Berkeley: University of California Press, 1969).

125. Ibid., p. 231.

126. Ibid., pp. 66–74.

127. Michael Wiatrowski, David Griswold, and Mary K. Roberts, "Social Control Theory and Delinquency," *American Sociological Review* 46 (1981): 525–541.

128. Patricia Van Voorhis, Francis Cullen, Richard Mathers, and Connie Chenoweth Garner, "The Impact of Family Structure and Quality on Delinquency: A Comparative Assessment of Structural and Functional Factors," *Criminology* 26 (1988): 235–261.

129. Marc LeBlanc, "Family Dynamics, Adolescent Delinquency, and Adult Criminality." Paper presented at the Society for Life History Research conference, Keystone, Colorado, October 1990, p. 6.

130. Bobbi Jo Anderson, Malcolm Holmes, and Erik Ostresh, "Male and Female Delinquent's Attachments and Effects

of Attachments on Severity of Self-Reported Delinquency," *Criminal Justice and Behavior* 26 (1999): 435–452.

131. Helen Garnier and Judith Stein, "An 18-Year Model of Family and Peer Effects on Adolescent Drug Use and Delinquency," *Journal of Youth and Adolescence* 31 (2002): 45–56.

132. Teresa LaGrange and Robert Silverman, "Perceived Strain and Delinquency Motivation: An Empirical Evaluation of General Strain Theory." Paper presented at the American Society of Criminology meeting, Boston, November 1995.

133. Voorhis, Cullen, Mathers, and Garner, "The Impact of Family Structure and Quality on Delinquency."

134. Thomas Vander Ven, Francis Cullen, Mark Carrozza, and John Paul Wright, "Home Alone: The Impact of Maternal Employment on Delinquency," *Social Problems* 48 (2001): 236–257; Patricia Jenkins, "School Delinquency and the School Social Bond," *Journal of Research in Crime and Delinquency* 34 (1997): 337–367.

135. Patricia Jenkins, "School Delinquency and the School Social Bond," *Journal of Research in Crime and Delinquency* 34 (1997): 337–367.

136. Trina Hope, Esther Wilder, and Toni-Terling Watt, "The Relationships among Adolescent Pregnancy, Pregnancy Resolution, and Juvenile Delinquency," *Sociological Quarterly* 44 (2003): 555–576.

137. John Cochran and Ronald Akers, "An Exploration of the Variable Effects of Religiosity on Adolescent Marijuana and Alcohol Use," *Journal of Research in Crime and Delinquency* 26 (1989): 198–225.

138. Mark Regnerus and Glen Elder, "Religion and Vulnerability among Low-Risk Adolescents," *Social Science Research* 32 (2003): 633–658; Mark Regnerus, "Moral Communities and Adolescent Delinquency: Religious Contexts and Community Social Control," *Sociological Quarterly* 44 (2003): 523–554.

139. Michael Cretacci, "Religion and Social Control: An Application of a Modified Social Bond of Violence," *Criminal Justice Review* 28 (2003): 254–277.

140. Robert Agnew and David Peterson, "Leisure and Delinquency," *Social Problems* 36 (1989): 332–348.

141. Jonathan Zaff, Kristin Moore, Angela Romano Papillo, and Stephanie Williams, "Implications of Extracurricular Activity Participation during Adolescence on Positive Outcomes," *Journal of Adolescent Research* 18 (2003): 599–631.

142. Marianne Junger and Ineke Haen Marshall, "The Interethnic Generalizability of Social Control Theory: An Empirical Test," *Journal of Research in Crime and Delinquency* 34 (1997): 79–112; Josine Junger-Tas, "An Empirical Test of Social Control Theory," *Journal of Quantitative Criminology* 8 (1992): 18–29.

143. LaGrange and Silverman, "Perceived Strain and Delinquency Motivation."

144. Kimberly Kempf, "The Empirical Status of Hirschi's Control Theory," in *Advances in Criminological Theory,* eds. Bill Laufer and Freda Adler (New Brunswick, NJ: Transaction Books, 1992).

145. Vander Ven, Cullen, Carrozza, and Wright, "Home Alone: The Impact of Maternal Employment on Delinquency," p. 253.

146. Peggy Giordano, Stephen Cernkovich, and M.D. Pugh, "Friendships and Delinquency," *American Journal of Sociology* 91 (1986): 1170–1202.

147. Denise Kandel and Mark Davies, "Friendship Networks, Intimacy, and Illicit Drug Use in Young Adulthood: A Comparison of Two Competing Theories," *Criminology* 29 (1991): 441–467.

148. Velmer Burton, Francis Cullen, T. David Evans, R. Gregory Dunaway, Sesha Kethineni, and Gary Payne, "The Impact of Parental Controls on Delinquency," *Journal of Criminal Justice* 23 (1995): 111–126.

149. Kimberly Kempf Leonard and Scott Decker, "The Theory of Social Control: Does It Apply to the Very Young," *Journal of Criminal Justice* 22 (1994): 89–105.

150. Michael Hindelang, "Causes of Delinquency: A Partial Replication and Extension," *Social Problems* 21 (1973): 471–487.

151. Gary Jensen and David Brownfield, "Parents and Drugs," *Criminology* 21 (1983): 543–554. See also M. Wiatrowski, D. Griswold, and M. Roberts, "Social Control Theory and Delinquency," *American Sociological Review* 46 (1981): 525–541.

152. Leslie Samuelson, Timothy Hartnagel, and Harvey Krahn, "Crime and Social Control among High School Dropouts," *Journal of Crime and Justice* 18 (1990): 129–161.

153. Marvin Krohn and James Massey, "Social Control and Delinquent Behavior: An Examination of the Elements of the Social Bond," *Sociological Quarterly* 21 (1980): 529–543.

154. Jill Leslie Rosenbaum and James Lasley, "School, Community Context, and Delinquency: Rethinking the Gender Gap," *Justice Quarterly* 7 (1990): 493–513.

155. Randy LaGrange and Helene Raskin White, "Age Differences in Delinquency: A Test of Theory," *Criminology* 23 (1985): 19–45.

156. Robert Agnew, "Social Control Theory and Delinquency: A Longitudinal Test," *Criminology* 23 (1985): 47–61.

157. Alan E. Liska and M. D. Reed, "Ties to Conventional Institutions and Delinquency: Estimating Reciprocal Effects," *American Sociological Review* 50 (1985): 547–560.

158. Michael Wiatrowski, David Griswold, and Mary K. Roberts, "Social Control Theory and Delinquency," *American Sociological Review* 46 (1981): 525–541.

159. George Herbert Mead, *Mind, Self and Society* (Chicago: University of Chicago Press, 1934); idem, *The Philosophy of the Act* (Chicago: University of Chicago Press, 1938); Charles Horton Cooley, *Human Nature and the Social Order* (New York: Schocken, 1964), originally published in 1902; Herbert Blumer, *Symbolic Interactionism: Perspective and Method* (Englewood Cliffs, NJ: Prentice-Hall, 1969).

160. Bruce Link, Elmer Streuning, Francis Cullen, Patrick Shrout, and Bruce Dohrenwend, "A Modified Labeling Theory Approach to Mental Disorders: An Empirical Assessment," *American Sociological Review* 54 (1989): 400–423.

161. Linda Jackson, John Hunter, and Carole Hodge, "Physical Attractiveness and Intellectual Competence: A Meta-Analytic Review," *Social Psychology Quarterly* 58 (1995): 108–122.

162. Mike Adams, Craig Robertson, Phyllis Gray-Ray, and Melvin Ray, "Labeling and Delinquency," *Adolescence* (2003): 171–186.

163. *President's Commission on Law Enforcement and the Administration of Youth Crime, Task Force Report: Juvenile Delinquency and Youth* (Washington, DC: U.S. Government Printing Office, 1967), p. 43.

164. Kai Erickson, "Notes on the Sociology of Deviance," *Social Problems* 9 (1962): 397–414.

165. Edwin Schur, *Labeling Deviant Behavior* (New York: Harper & Row, 1972), p. 21.

166. Howard Becker, *Outsiders, Studies in the Sociology of Deviance* (New York: Macmillan, 1963), p. 9.

167. Laurie Goodstein, "The Architect of the 'Gay Conversion' Campaign," *New York Times,* 13 August 1998, p. A10.

168. Christy Visher, "Gender, Police Arrest Decision, and Notions of Chivalry," *Criminology* 21 (1983): 5–28.

169. Marjorie Zatz, "Race, Ethnicity and Determinate Sentencing," *Criminology* 22 (1984): 147–171.

170. Christina DeJong and Kenneth Jackson, "Putting Race into Context: Race, Juvenile Justice Processing, and Urbanization," *Justice Quarterly* 15 (1998): 487–504.

171. Roland Chilton and Jim Galvin, "Race, Crime and Criminal Justice," *Crime and Delinquency* 31 (1985): 3–14.

172. Joan Petersilia, "Racial Disparities in the Criminal Justice System: A Summary," *Crime and Delinquency* 31 (1985): 15–34.

173. Walter Gove, *The Labeling of Deviance: Evaluating a Perspective* (New York: Wiley, 1975), p. 5.

174. Harold Garfinkle, "Conditions of Successful Degradation Ceremonies," *American Journal of Sociology* 61 (1956): 420–424.

175. Karen Heimer and Ross Matsueda, "Role-Taking, Role-Commitment, and Delinquency: A Theory of Differential Social Control," *American Sociological Review* 59 (1994): 400–437.

176. Stacy DeCoster and Karen Heimer, "The Relationship between Law Violation and Depression: An Interactionist Analysis," *Criminology* 39 (2001): 799–837.

177. Karen Heimer, "Gender, Race, and the Pathways to Delinquency: An Interactionist Explanation," in *Crime and Inequality*, eds. John Hagan and Ruth Peterson (Stanford, CA: Stanford University Press, 1995), pp. 32–57.

178. Heimer and Matsueda, "Role-Taking, Role-Commitment, and Delinquency."

179. See, for example, Howard Kaplan and Hiroshi Fukurai, "Negative Social Sanctions, Self-Rejection, and Drug Use," *Youth and Society* 23 (1992): 275–298; Howard Kaplan and Robert Johnson, "Negative Social Sanctions and Juvenile Delinquency: Effects of Labeling in a Model of Deviant Behavior," *Social Science Quarterly* 72 (1991): 98–122; Howard Kaplan, Robert Johnson, and Carol Bailey, "Deviant Peers and Deviant Behavior: Further Elaboration of a Model," *Social Psychology Quarterly* 30 (1987): 277–284.

180. Howard Kaplan, *Toward a General Theory of Deviance: Contributions from Perspectives on Deviance and Criminality* (College Station: Texas A&M University, n.d.).

181. John Lofland, *Deviance and Identity* (Englewood Cliffs, NJ: Prentice-Hall, 1969).

182. Frank Tannenbaum, *Crime and the Community* (New York: Columbia University Press, 1938), pp. 19–20.

183. Edwin Lemert, *Social Pathology* (New York: McGraw-Hill, 1951).

184. Ibid., p. 75.

185. National Minority Advisory Council on Criminal Justice, *The Inequality of Justice* (Washington, DC: author, 1981), p. 200.

186. Carl Pope and William Feyerherm, "Minority Status and Juvenile Justice Processing," *Criminal Justice Abstracts* 22 (1990): 327–236; see also Carl Pope, "Race and Crime Revisited," *Crime and Delinquency* 25 (1979): 347–357.

187. Leslie Margolin, "Deviance on Record: Techniques for Labeling Child Abusers in Official Documents," *Social Problems* 39 (1992): 58–68.

188. Charles Corley, Stephen Cernkovich, and Peggy Giordano, "Sex and the Likelihood of Sanction," *Journal of Criminal Law and Criminology* 80 (1989): 540–553.

189. Samuel Walker, Cassia Spohn, and Miriam DeLone, *The Color of Justice, Race, Ethnicity, and Crime in America* (Belmont, CA: Wadsworth, 1996), pp. 145–146.

190. Kaplan and Johnson, "Negative Social Sanctions and Juvenile Delinquency."

191. Ruth Triplett, "The Conflict Perspective, Symbolic Interactionism, and the Status Characteristics Hypothesis," *Justice Quarterly* 10 (1993): 540–558.

192. Ross Matsueda, "Reflected Appraisals: Parental Labeling, and Delinquency: Specifying a Symbolic Interactionist Theory," *American Journal of Sociology* 97 (1992): 1577–1611.

193. Suzanne Ageton and Delbert Elliott, *The Effect of Legal Processing on Self-Concept* (Boulder, CO: Institute of Behavioral Science, 1973).

194. Christine Bowditch, "Getting Rid of Troublemakers: High School Disciplinary Procedures and the Production of Dropouts," *Social Problems* 40 (1993): 493–507.

195. Melvin Ray and William Downs, "An Empirical Test of Labeling Theory Using Longitudinal Data," *Journal of Research in Crime and Delinquency* 23 (1986): 169–194.

196. Sherman and Smith, with Schmidt and Rogan, "Crime, Punishment, and Stake in Conformity."

197. Lawrence Bench and Terry Allen, "Investigating the Stigma of Prison Classification: An Experimental Design," *Prison Journal* 83 (2003): 367–382.

198. Charles Tittle, "Two Empirical Regularities (Maybe) in Search of an Explanation: Commentary on the Age/Crime Debate," *Criminology* 26 (1988): 75–85.

199. Ibid.

200. Robert Sampson and John Laub, "A Life-Course Theory of Cumulative Disadvantage and the Stability of Delinquency," in *Developmental Theories of Crime and Delinquency*, ed. Terence Thornberry (New Brunswick, NJ: Transaction Books, 1997), pp. 133–161.

201. Jön Gunnar Bernburg and Marvin Krohn, "Labeling, Life Chances, and Adult Crime: The Direct and Indirect Effects of Official Intervention in Adolescence on Crime in Early Adulthood," *Criminology* 41 (2003): 1287–1319.

202. Jack Gibbs, "Conceptions of Deviant Behavior: The Old and the New," *Pacific Sociological Review* 9 (1966): 11–13.

203. Schur, *Labeling Deviant Behavior*, p. 14.

204. Ronald Akers, "Problems in the Sociology of Deviance," *Social Problems* 46 (1968): 463.

205. Charles Tittle, "Labeling and Crime: An Empirical Evaluation," in *The Labeling of Deviance: Evaluating a Perspective*, ed. Walter Gove (New York: Wiley, 1975), pp. 157–179.

206. David Farrington, "Early Predictors of Adolescent Aggression and Adult Violence," *Violence and Victims* 4 (1989): 79–100.

207. Raymond Paternoster and Leeann Iovanni, "The Labeling Perspective and Delinquency: An Elaboration of the Theory and an Assessment of the Evidence," *Justice Quarterly* 6 (1989): 358–394.

208. Shadd Maruna, Thomas Lebel, Nick Mitchell, and Michelle Maples, "Pygmalion in the Reintergration Process: Desistance from Crime through the Looking Glass," *Psychology, Crime, and Law* 10 (2004): 271–281.

209. Lening Zhang, "Official Offense Status and Self-Esteem among Chinese Youths," *Journal of Criminal Justice* 31(2003): 99–105.

CHAPTER 8

© Getty Images

In the past few years, between 6 and 10 million people in up to 60 countries are thought to have marched in protest against the U.S. involvement in Iraq. These are the largest antiwar demonstrations since the Vietnam War. In London, organizers claimed that more than 2 million people protested (police estimates were a more modest 750,000), while in Barcelona, Spanish police estimated that up to 1.3 million people marched. Europeans were not alone in venting their anger against U.S. military operations; there were also widespread demonstrations on American soil, including a large protest in New York City with around 100,000 people marching, filling 20 city blocks.

Although these protests drew worldwide attention, it was the presence of Cindy Sheehan, an American woman whose son had been killed in the war, at President George W. Bush's Crawford, Texas ranch that vaulted the antiwar movement into national consciousness. What began as a solitary campaign by Sheehan in August 2005 to force a meeting with President Bush by setting up camp along the road to his ranch quickly turned into a national media event.

SOCIAL CONFLICT THEORIES: CRITICAL CRIMINOLOGY AND RESTORATIVE JUSTICE

CHAPTER OUTLINE

CHAPTER OBJECTIVES

1. Be familiar with the concept of social conflict and how it shapes behavior
2. Be able to discuss elements of conflict in the justice system
3. Be familiar with the idea of critical criminology
4. Be able to discuss the difference between structural and instrumental Marxism
5. Know the various techniques of critical research
6. Be able to discuss the term *left realism*
7. Understand the concept of patriarchy
8. Know what is meant by feminist criminology
9. Be able to discuss peacemaking
10. Understand the concept of restorative justice

It would be unusual to pick up the morning paper and not see headlines loudly proclaiming renewed strife between the United States and its overseas adversaries, between union negotiators and management attorneys, between citizens and police authorities, or between feminists and reactionary males protecting their turf. The world is filled with conflict. Conflict can be destructive when it leads to war, violence, and death; it can be functional when it results in positive social change.

Criminologists who view crime as a function of social conflict and economic rivalry are called social conflict theorists. Some conflict theorists stress the role that the capitalist economic system has on crime rates. These scholars are sometimes called **Marxist criminologists** or **radical criminologists,** but here we will refer to them generically as *critical criminologists* and their field of study as **critical criminology.** Among their affiliated sub-branches are peacemaking, left realism, radical feminism, and postmodernism (also called deconstructionism).

Social conflict/critical criminologists explain crime within economic and social contexts and to express the connection among social conflict, crime, and social control.[1] They are concerned with issues such as

- The role that government plays in creating a crimogenic environment

---

FIGURE 8.1

The Branches of Social Conflict Theory

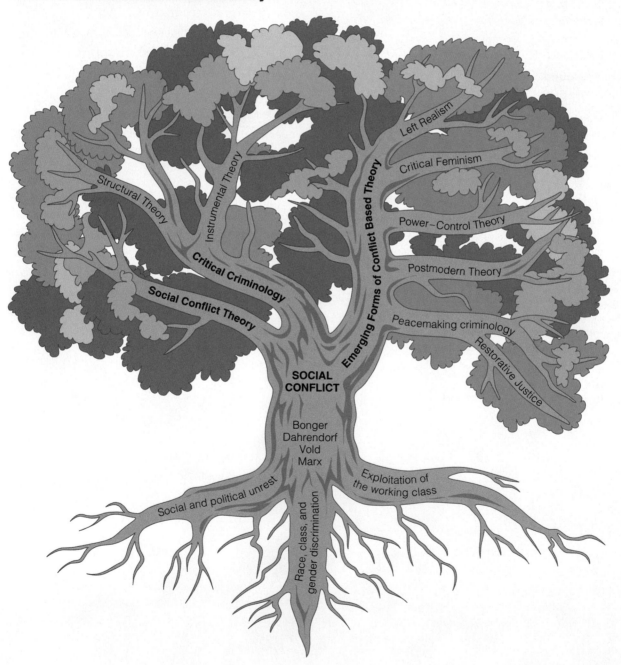

- The relationship between personal or group power and the shaping of criminal law

- The prevalence of bias in justice system operations

- The relationship between a capitalist, free enterprise economy and crime rates

Conflict promotes crime by creating a social atmosphere in which the law is a mechanism for controlling dissatisfied, have-not members of society while the wealthy maintain their power. This is why crimes that are the province of the wealthy, such as illegal corporate activities, are sanctioned much more leniently than those, such as burglary, that are considered lower-class activities.

This chapter reviews criminological theories that allege that criminal behavior is a function of conflict, a reaction to the unfair distribution of wealth and power in society. It looks at the development of critical criminology and important critical concepts. It also discusses emerging forms of **social conflict theory** including left realism, feminist, peacemaking, and postmodern thought. Figure 8.1 illustrates these and other independent branches of social conflict theory. Finally, the chapter will review how critical concepts have been meshed into a new way of looking at the use and misuse of criminal punishment, which is referred to as restorative justice.

MARXIST THOUGHT

As you may recall (Chapter 1), Karl Marx identified the economic structures in society that control all human relations. Those criminologists who gain their inspiration from Marx reject the notion that criminals are malevolent people who wish to trample the rights of others and the criminal law is designed to control them and maintain a tranquil, fair society. If it were, then acts of racism, sexism, imperialism, unsafe working conditions, inadequate childcare, substandard housing, pollution of the environment, and warmaking as a tool of foreign policy would be the "true crimes." The crimes of the helpless—burglary, robbery, and assault—are more expressions of rage over unjust conditions than actual crimes.[2]

Marx's view of society was shaped by the economic trends and structures of that period. He lived in an era of unrestrained capitalist expansion.[3] The tools of the Industrial Revolution had become regular features of society by 1850. Mechanized factories, the use of coal to drive steam engines, and modern transportation all inspired economic development. Production had shifted from cottage industries to large factories. Industrialists could hire workers on their own terms; as a result, conditions in factories were atrocious. Owners and government agents, who were the agents of capitalists, ruthlessly suppressed trade unions that promised workers salvation from these atrocities.

Marx's early career as a journalist was interrupted by government suppression of the newspaper where he worked because of the paper's liberal editorial policy. He then moved to Paris, where he met Friedrich Engels (1820–1895), who would become his friend and economic patron. By 1847, Marx and Engels had joined with a group of primarily German socialist revolutionaries known as the Communist League.

Productive Forces and Productive Relations

In 1848, Marx issued his famous **communist manifesto.** In this document, Marx focused his attention on the economic conditions perpetuated by the capitalist system. He stated that its development had turned workers into a dehumanized mass who lived an existence that was at the mercy of their capitalist employers. He wrote of the injustice of young children being sent to work in mines and factories from dawn to dusk. He focused on the people who were being beaten down by a system that demanded obedience and cooperation and offered little in return. These oppressive conditions led Marx to conclude that the character of every civilization is determined by its mode of production—the way its people develop and produce material goods (materialism).

Did you know that at one time Karl Marx was a reporter for the *New York Tribune*? To read more about Marx's life, use his name as a subject guide in Info-Trac College Edition and check out the encyclopedia reference. Then read some of the many periodical selections devoted to his thought and philosophy.

Marx identified the economic structures in society that control all human relations. Production has two components: (1) **productive forces,** which include such things as technology, energy sources, and material resources; and (2) **productive relations,** which are the relationships that exist among the people producing goods and services. The most important relationship in industrial culture is between the owners of the means of production, the **capitalist bourgeoisie,** and the people who do the actual labor, the proletariat.

Throughout history, society has been organized this way—master–slave, lord–serf, and now capitalist–proletariat. According to Marx, capitalist society is subject to the development of a rigid class structure with the capitalist bourgeoisie at the top, followed by the working proletariat, who actually produce goods and services, and at the bottom, the fringe, nonproductive members who produce nothing and live, parasitically, off the work of others—the **lumpen proletariat** (Figure 8.2).

In Marxist theory, the term *class* does not refer to an attribute or characteristic of a person or a group; rather, it denotes position in relation to others. Thus, it is not necessary to have a particular amount of wealth or prestige to be a member of the capitalist class; it is more important to have the power to exploit others economically, legally, and socially. The political and economic philosophy of the dominant class influences all aspects of life. Consciously or unconsciously, artists, writers, and teachers bend their work to the whims of the capitalist system. Thus, the economic system controls all facets of human life. Consequently, people's lives revolve around the means of production.

As Marx said:

> In all forms of society, there is one specific kind of production which predominates over the rest, whose relations thus assign rank and influence to the others. It is a general illumination which bathes all the other colours and modifies their particularity. It is a particular ether which determines the specific gravity of every being which has materialized within it.[4]

Marx believed societies and their structures were not stable and, therefore, could change through slow evolution or sudden violence. Historically, such change occurs because

FIGURE 8.2
The Marxist View of Class

The owners of production
Capitalist bourgeoisie

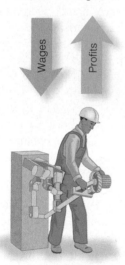

The worker
Proletariat

The nonproductive
Lumpen proletariat

of contradictions present in a society. These contradictions are antagonism or conflicts between elements in the existing social arrangement, which in the long run are incompatible with one another. If these social conflicts are not resolved, they tend to destabilize society, leading to social change.

To read about **Marx and his vision,** go to http://www.philosophypages.com/ph/marx.htm. For an up-to-date list of web links, go to http://cj.wadsworth.com/siegel_crimtpt9e.

Surplus Value

How could social change occur in capitalist society? Marx held that the laboring class produces goods that exceed wages in value (the theory of **surplus value**). The excess value goes into the hands of the capitalists as profit; they then use most of it to acquire an ever-expanding capitalist base that relies on

In capitalist societies, workers commonly protest unfair pay and conditions. According to the theory of surplus value, excess profits go into the hands of the capitalists who then use most of it to acquire advanced technology so that they can produce goods more efficiently and cheaply. Ways capitalists can stay competitive are to pay workers the lowest possible wages, replace them with labor-saving machinery, or ship jobs overseas.

advanced technology for efficiency. Capitalists are in constant competition with one another, so they must find ways of producing goods more efficiently and cheaply. One way is to pay workers the lowest possible wages or to replace them with labor-saving machinery (Figure 8.3). Soon the supply of efficiently made goods outstrips the ability of the laboring classes to purchase them, a condition that precipitates an economic crisis. During this period of crisis, weaker enterprises go under and are consequently incorporated into ever-expanding, monopolistic mega-corporations strong enough to further exploit the workers. For example, between the 1980s and today, many giant corporations have merged to form even larger enterprises: Disney and ABC; AOL and Time Warner; Exxon and Mobil, and Mercedes Benz and Chrysler. This allowed management to control costs, cut excess labor, and reduce the power of workers to demand benefits or wage increases. Also, in an era of globalization, mergers enable companies to have a worldwide reach and to exploit labor in developing nations.

Marx believed the ebb and flow of the capitalist business cycle contained the seeds of its own destruction. He predicted that from its ashes would grow a socialist state in which the workers themselves would own the means of production. In his analysis, Marx used the **dialectic method,** based on the analysis developed by the philosopher Georg Hegel (1770–1831). Hegel argued that for every idea, or **thesis,** there exists an opposing argument, or **antithesis.** Since neither position can ever be truly accepted, the result is a merger of the two ideas, a **synthesis.** Marx adapted this analytic method for his study of class struggle. History, argued Marx, is replete with examples of two opposing forces whose conflict promotes social change. When conditions are bad enough, the oppressed will rise up to fight the owners and eventually replace them. Thus, in the end, the capitalist system will destroy itself.

 The theory of **surplus value** can be quite complex. Read more about it at http://www.marxists.org/archive/marx/works/1863/theories-surplus-value/. For an up-to-date list of web links, go to http:// cj.wadsworth .com/siegel_crimtpt9e.

Marx on Crime

Marx did not write a great deal on the subject of crime, but he mentioned it in a variety of passages scattered throughout his writing. He viewed crime as the product of law enforcement policies akin to a labeling process theory.[5] He also saw a connection between criminality and the inequities found in the capitalist system. He reasoned: "There must be something rotten in the very core of a social system which increases in wealth without diminishing its misery, and increases in crime even more rapidly than in numbers."[6]

His collaborator, Friedrich Engels, however, did spend some time on the subject in his work, *The Condition of the Working Class in England in 1844.*[7] Engels portrayed crime as a function of social demoralization—a collapse of people's humanity reflecting a decline in society. Workers, demoralized by capitalist society, are caught up in a process that leads to crime and violence. According to Engels, workers are social outcasts, ignored by the structure of capitalist society and treated as brutes.[8] Left to their own devices, working people committed crime because their choice is a slow death of starvation or a speedy one at the hands of the law. The brutality of the capitalist system, he believed, turns workers into animal-like creatures without a will of their own.

To quiz yourself on this material, go to the Criminology TPT 9e website.

FIGURE 8.3

Surplus Value

Worker produces goods that exceed wages in value → Profit → Capitalist keeps profits → Uses profits to buy machines and replace workers → Workers make less and buy less → **Economic crisis**

DEVELOPING A CONFLICT-BASED THEORY OF CRIME

The writings of Karl Marx greatly influenced the development of the view of crime that rested on the concept of social conflict. Even though Marx himself did not write much on the topic of crime, his views on the relationship between the economic structure and social behavior deeply influenced other thinkers.

The concept of social conflict was first applied to criminology by three distinguished scholars: Willem Bonger, Ralf Dahrendorf, and George Vold. In some instances, their works share the Marxist view that industrial society is wracked by conflict between the proletariat and the bourgeoisie; in other instances, their writings diverge from Marxist dogma. The writing of each of these pioneers is briefly discussed next.

The Contribution of Willem Bonger

Willem Bonger was born in 1876 in Holland and committed suicide in 1940 rather than submit to Nazi rule. He is famous for his Marxist socialist concepts of crime causation, which were first published in 1916.[9]

Bonger believed crime is of social and not biological origin, and that with the exception of a few special cases, crime lies within the boundaries of normal human behavior. According to Bonger, no act is naturally immoral or criminal. He viewed crimes as antisocial acts that reflect current morality. Because the social structure changes continually, ideas of what is moral and what is not also are in constant flux.

Bonger believed society is divided into haves and have-not groups, not on the basis of people's innate ability, but because of the system of production that is in force. In every society that is divided into a ruling class and an inferior class, penal law serves the will of the ruling class. Even though criminal laws may appear to protect members of both classes, hardly any act is punished that does not injure the interests of the dominant ruling class. Crimes, then, are considered to be antisocial acts because they are harmful to those who have the power at their command to control society.

Bonger argued that attempts to control law violations through force are a sign of a weak society. He viewed the capitalist system, characterized by extreme competition, as being held together by force rather than consensus, thus making it a weak system. As a consequence of this force, he claimed, the social order is maintained for the benefit of the capitalists at the expense of the population as a whole. Everyone may desire wealth, but it is only the most privileged people, with the most capital, who can enjoy luxuries and advantages. Within this society, people care only for their own lives and pleasures and ignore the plight of the disadvantaged. Because of this dramatic inequity between the haves and have-nots, Bonger claimed, people have become very egotistical and more capable of crime than if the system had developed under a socialist philosophy.

Although the capitalist system makes both the proletariat and the bourgeoisie crime prone, only the former are likely to become officially recognized criminals. The reason for this is twofold. First, the legal system discriminates against the poor by defending the actions of the wealthy, and second, it is the proletariat who are deprived of the materials that are monopolized by the bourgeoisie.

Upper-class individuals will commit crime if (1) they sense a good opportunity to make a financial gain, and (2) their lack of moral sense enables them to violate social rules. It is the drive toward success at any price that pushes wealthier individuals toward criminality.

Recognized, official crimes are a function of poverty. The relationship can be direct, as when a person steals to survive, or indirect, as when poverty kills the social sentiments in each person and between people.

It is not the absolute amount of wealth that affects crime, but its distribution, posits Bonger. If wealth is distributed unequally throughout the social structure and people are taught to equate economic advantage with superiority, then those who are poor and therefore inferior will be crime prone. The economic system will intensify any personal disadvantage people have—for example, psychological problems—and increase their propensity to commit crime.

Bonger concluded that almost all crime will disappear if society progresses from competitive capitalism, to monopoly capitalism (in which a relatively few enterprises control the means of production), to having the means of production held in common, to the ultimate state of society. In other words, Bonger believed that redistribution of property according to the maxim "each according to his needs" would be the demise of crime. If this stage of society cannot be reached, a residue of crime will always remain. If socialism can be achieved, however, then remaining crimes will be of the irrational psychopathic type caused by individual mental problems. Bonger's writing continues to be one of the most often-cited sources of Marxist thought.

The Contribution of Ralf Dahrendorf

In formulating their views, today's conflict theorists also rely heavily on the writings of pioneering social thinker Ralf Dahrendorf, who argues that modern society is organized into what he called **imperatively coordinated associations**.[10] These associations comprise two groups: those who possess authority and use it for social domination and those who lack authority and are dominated. Because the domination of one segment of society (for example, industry) does not mean dominating another (such as government), society is a plurality of competing interest groups.

In his classic work *Class and Class Conflict in Industrial Society,* Dahrendorf attempted to show how society has changed since Marx formulated his concepts of class, state, and conflict. Dahrendorf argued that Marx did not foresee the changes that have occurred in the laboring classes. "The working class of today," Dahrendorf stated, "far from being a homogeneous group of equally unskilled and impoverished people, is in fact a stratum differentiated by numerous subtle and not so subtle distinctions."[11] Workers are divided into the unskilled, semiskilled, and skilled; the interests of one group may not match the needs of the others. Accordingly, Marx's concept of a cohesive proletarian class has proved inaccurate. As a result of his differing perspectives, Dahrendorf embraced a non-Marxist conflict orientation. Dahrendorf proposed a unified conflict theory of human behavior, which can be summarized as follows:

- Every society is at every point subject to processes of change; social change is everywhere.

- Every society displays at every point dissent and conflict; social conflict is everywhere.

- Every element in a society renders a contribution to its disintegration and change.

- Every society is based on the coercion of some of its members by others.

Dahrendorf did not speak directly to the issue of crime, but his model of conflict serves as a pillar of modern conflict criminology.

 To review an in-depth interview with **Ralf Dahrendorf,** go to http://globetrotter.berkeley.edu/Elberg/Dahrendorf/dahrendorf0.html. For an up-to-date list of web links, go to http://cj.wadsworth.com/siegel_crimtpt9e.

The Contribution of George Vold

Although Dahrendorf contributed its theoretical underpinnings, conflict theory was actually adapted to criminology by George Vold.[12] Vold argued that crime can also be explained by social conflict. Laws are created by politically oriented groups, who seek the government's assistance to help them defend their rights and protect their interests. If a group can marshal enough support, a law will be created to hamper and curb the interests of some opposition group. Every stage of the process—from passing the law, to prosecuting the case, to developing relationships between inmate and guard, parole agent and parolee—is marked by conflict. Vold found that criminal acts are a consequence of direct contact between forces struggling to control society. Although their criminal content may mask their political meaning, closer examination of even the most basic violent acts often reveals political undertones.

Vold's model cannot be used to explain all types of crime. It is limited to situations in which rival group loyalties collide. It cannot explain impulsive, irrational acts unrelated to any group's interest. Despite this limitation, Vold found that a great deal of criminal activity results from intergroup clashes.

 To quiz yourself on this material, go to the Criminology TPT 9e website.

SOCIAL CONFLICT THEORY

The association between social conflict and crime began to be a focus of criminological scholarship during the 1960s, when self-report studies began to yield data suggesting that the class–crime correlation found in official crime data was spurious. The self-reports showed that crime and delinquency were distributed much more evenly through the social structure than indicated by official statistics, which reported more crime in lower-class environments.[13] If these self-reports were accurate, middle-class participation in crime was going unrecorded while the lower class was subjected to discriminatory law enforcement practices.[14]

The theme that dominated much of this scholarship was the contention that criminal legislation was determined by the relative power of groups determined to use criminal law to advance their own special interests or to impose their own moral preferences on others.[15] This movement was aided by the widespread social and political upheaval of the late 1960s and early 1970s. These social forces included anti–Vietnam War demonstrations, counterculture movements, and various forms of political protest. Conflict theory flourished within this framework because it provided a systematic basis for challenging the legitimacy of the government's creation and application of law. The federal government's crackdown on political dissidents and prosecution of draft resisters seemed designed to maintain control in the hands of political power brokers.

As social conflict theory began to influence criminological study, several influential scholars embraced its ideas. William Chambliss and Robert Seidman wrote the well-respected treatise *Law, Order, and Power,* which documented how the justice system protects the rich and powerful.[16] Some common objectives of conflict criminology that appear in Chambliss and Seidman's writing include

- Describing how control of the political and economic system affects the way criminal justice is administered

- Showing how definitions of crime favor those who control the justice system

- Analyzing the role of conflict in contemporary society

In another influential work, Richard Quinney spelled out what he terms the **social reality of crime.**[17] According to Quinney, criminal definitions (law) represent the interests of those who hold power in society. Where there is conflict between social groups—for example, the wealthy and the poor—those who hold power will be the ones to create the laws that benefit themselves and hold rivals in check. Law is not an abstract body of rules that represents an absolute moral code; rather, law is an integral part of society, a force that represents a way of life and a method of doing things. Crime is a function of power relations and an inevitable result of social conflict. Criminals are not simply social misfits, but people who have come up short in the struggle for success and are seeking alternative means of achieving wealth, status, or even survival.

This scholarship showed that the justice system in the United States was tilted toward the wealthy and powerful. Crime is defined by those in power. The term **power,** as used here, refers to the ability of persons and groups to determine and control the behavior of others and to shape public opinion to meet their personal interests. Because those in power shape the content of the law, it comes as no surprise that their behavior is often exempt from legal sanctions. Those who deserve the most severe sanctions (wealthy white-collar criminals whose crimes cost society millions of dollars) usually receive lenient punishments while those whose relatively minor crimes are committed out of economic necessity (petty thieves and drug dealers) receive stricter penalties especially if they are minority group members who lack social and economic power.[18]

> ||||||| **CONNECTIONS** |||||||
>
> The enforcement of laws against illegal business activities such as price fixing, restraint of trade, environmental crimes, and false advertising is discussed in Chapter 12. Although some people are sent to prison for these white-collar offenses, many offenders are still punished with a fine or economic sanction.

Social Conflict Research

Criminologists have used a variety of methods to determine whether indicators of social conflict are highly correlated with rates and trends in crime. One method is to compare the crime rates of members of powerless groups with those of members of the elite classes. Because of social and economic inequality, members of the lower class are forced to commit larceny and burglary, engage in robberies, and sell drugs as a means of social and economic survival. In some instances, the disenfranchised will engage in rape, assault,

and senseless homicides as a means of expressing their rage, frustration, and anger. There is a considerable body of research supporting this view. Criminologists routinely have found evidence that measures of social inequality—such as income level, deteriorated living conditions, and relative economic deprivation—are highly associated with crime rates.[19] For example, recent research by Travis Pratt and Christopher Lowenkamp found a significant relationship between economic conditions and homicide rates; the effect was strongest for felony murders that typically accompany robberies and burglaries.[20] Their conclusion is that with economic **marginalization,** people turn to violent crime for survival, producing an inevitable upswing in the murder rate.

> ||||||| **CONNECTIONS** |||||||
>
> For more on the different categories of murder, go to Chapter 11. A felony murder is one committed in connection with some other crime, such as a burglary, and is typically punished severely. All those involved in the felony can be charged even if they did not take part in the murder.

Criminologists have also examined the justice system to uncover whether it hands out fair and even-handed justice or is rife with bias and discrimination, factors related to social conflict. For example, research shows that a suspect's race is an important factor in shaping police discretion and decision making. Using data from a nationally drawn survey of citizen attitudes and behavior, Ronald Weitzer and Steven Tuch found that about 40 percent of African American respondents claimed they were stopped by police because of their race as compared to just 5 percent of whites; almost three-quarters of young African American men, ages 18 to 34, said they were the victim of profiling.[21] Recent research by Albert Meehan and Michael Ponder found that police are more likely to use racial profiling to stop black motorists as they travel farther into the boundaries of predominantly

Research on social conflict may look at efforts of hate groups to control or intimidate minorities and the poor. Here, police keep protesters away from Richard Barrett, the head of the Mississippi-based Nationalist Movement, as Barrett spoke in support of racial profiling July 4, 2001, in Morristown. Critical criminologists view racial profiling as a function of social conflict.

© Nancy Wegard/Getty Images

white neighborhoods: A black motorist discovered driving in an all-white neighborhood sends up a "red flag" because they are "out of place."[22] Research also shows that police brutality complaints are highest in minority neighborhoods, especially those that experience relative deprivation (African American residents earn significantly less money than the white majority).[23]

Criminal courts are also more likely to dole out harsh punishments to members of powerless, disenfranchised groups.[24] Both white and black offenders have been found to receive stricter sentences if their personal characteristics (single, young, urban, male) show them to be members of the "dangerous classes."[25] Unemployed racial minorities may be perceived as "social dynamite" who present a real threat to society and must be controlled and incapacitated.[26] Race also plays a role in prosecution and punishment. African American defendants are more likely to be prosecuted under habitual offender statutes if they commit crimes where there is a greater likelihood of a white victim—for example, larceny and burglary—than if they commit violent crimes that are largely intraracial; where there is a perceived "racial threat" punishment is enhanced.[27]

Considering these examples of how conflict controls the justice process, it is not surprising when analysis of national population trends and imprisonment rates shows that as the percentage of minority group members increases in a population, the imprisonment rate does likewise.[28] Similarly, states with a substantial minority population have a much higher imprisonment rate than those with predominantly white populations.[29]

 To quiz yourself on this material, go to the Criminology TPT 9e website.

CRITICAL CRIMINOLOGY

In the 1960s, theories that focused on the relationship between crime and conflict in any society began to be supplanted by more radical critical theories that examined the specific role of capitalism in law and criminality. In 1968, a group of British sociologists formed the National Deviancy Conference (NDC). With about 300 members, this organization sponsored several national symposiums and dialogues. Members came from all walks of life, but at its core was a group of academics who were critical of the positivist criminology being taught in British and American universities. More specifically, they rejected the conservative stance of criminologists and their close financial relationship with government funding agencies.

The NDC was not conceived as a Marxist-oriented group; rather, it investigated the concept of deviance from a labeling perspective. It called attention to ways in which social control might actually cause deviance rather than just respond to antisocial behavior. Many conference members became concerned about the political nature of social

control. In time, a schism developed within the NDC, with one group clinging to the interactionist/labeling perspective while the second embraced Marxist thought.

In 1973, critical theory was given a powerful academic boost when British scholars Ian Taylor, Paul Walton, and Jock Young published *The New Criminology*.[30] This brilliant, thorough, and well-constructed critique of existing concepts in criminology called for the development of new methods of criminological analysis and critique. *The New Criminology* became the standard resource for scholars critical of both the field of criminology and the existing legal process.

To learn more about the early development of critical criminology, read: Ian Taylor, "Crime and Social Criticism," *Social Justice* 26 (1999): 150–161; and Gregory Shank, "Looking Back: Radical Criminology and Social Movements," *Social Justice* 26 (1999): 114–127.

During the same period, a small group of scholars in the United States also began to follow a new critical approach to criminology. The locus of the critical school was the criminology program at the University of California at Berkeley. The most noted Marxist scholars at that institution were Anthony Platt, Paul Takagi, Herman Schwendinger, and Julia Schwendinger. At other U.S. academic institutions, some scholars who had earlier embraced social conflict theory—including Richard Quinney, William Chambliss, Steven Spitzer, and Barry Krisberg—became more critical in their approach.

In the United States, critical criminologists were influenced by the widespread social ferment during the late 1960s and early 1970s. The war in Vietnam, prison struggles, and the civil rights and feminist movements produced a climate in which criticism of the ruling class seemed a natural by-product. Mainstream, positivist criminology was criticized as being overtly conservative, pro-government, and antihuman. Critical criminologists scoffed when their fellow scholars used statistical analysis of computerized data to describe criminal and delinquent behavior.

In the early 1980s, the left realism school was started by scholars affiliated with Middlesex Polytechnic and the University of Edinburgh in Great Britain. In the United States, scholars influenced in part by the pioneering work of Dennis Sullivan and Larry Tifft laid the foundation for what eventually became known as the peacemaking movement, which calls for a humanist vision of justice.[31] At the same time, feminist scholars began to critically analyze the relationship between gender, power, and criminality.

Since the 1980s critical criminologists have been deeply concerned with the conservative trend in American politics and the creation of what they consider to be an American empire. The conservative agenda, initiated by Ronald Reagan, called for the lowering of labor costs through union busting, welfare limitations, tax cuts that favor the wealthy, ending affirmative action, and reducing environmental control and regulation. While spending was cut on social programs, spending on the military expanded. The rapid buildup of the prison system and passage of draconian criminal laws that threatened civil rights and liberties—for example, three strikes laws and the Patriot Act—are other elements of the conservative agenda. Critical criminologists believe that they are responsible for informing the public about the dangers of these developments.[32]

Critical criminologists have turned their attention to the threat competitive capitalism presents to the working class. In addition to perpetuating male supremacy and racialism, they believe that modern global capitalism helps destroy the lives of workers in less developed countries. For example, capitalists hailed China's entry into the World Trade Organization in 2001 as a significant economic event. However, critical thinkers point out that the economic boom has significant costs: The average manufacturing wage in China is 20 to 25 cents per hour; during the first half of 2001, 47,000 workers were killed, and 35.2 million Chinese workers were permanently or temporarily disabled at work.[33]

Fundamentals of Critical Criminology

Critical criminologists view crime as a function of the capitalist mode of production and not the social conflict which might occur in any society regardless of its economic system. According to **critical criminology**, capitalism produces haves and have-nots, each engaging in a particular branch of criminality.[34] The mode of production shapes social life. Because economic competitiveness is the essence of capitalism, conflict increases and eventually destabilizes social institutions and the individuals within them.[35]

In a capitalist society, those with economic and political power control the definition of crime and the manner in which the criminal justice system enforces the law.[36] Consequently, the only crimes available to the poor, or proletariat, are the severely sanctioned "street crimes": rape, murder, theft, and mugging. Members of the middle class, or *petite bourgeoisie,* cheat on their taxes and engage in petty corporate crime (employee theft), acts that generate social disapproval but are rarely punished severely. The wealthy bourgeoisie are involved in acts that should be described as crimes but are not, such as racism, sexism, and profiteering. Although regulatory laws control illegal business activities, these are rarely enforced, and violations are lightly punished. One reason is that an essential feature of capitalism is the need to expand business and create new markets. This goal often comes in conflict with laws designed to protect the environment and creates clashes with those who seek their enforcement. In advanced capitalist society the need for expansion usually triumphs. For example, corporate spokespeople and their political allies will brand environmentalists as "tree huggers" who stand in the way of jobs and prosperity.[37]

The rich are insulated from street crimes because they live in areas far removed from crime. Those in power use the fear of crime as a tool to maintain their control over society. The poor are controlled through incarceration, and the middle class is diverted from caring about the crimes of the powerful by their fear of the crimes of the powerless.[38] Ironically, they may have more to lose from the economic crimes committed by the rich than the street crimes of the poor. Stock market swindles and savings and loan scams cost the public billions of dollars but are typically settled with fines and probationary sentences.

Because private ownership of property is the true measure of success in capitalism (as opposed to being, say, a worthy person), the state becomes an ally of the wealthy in protecting their property interests. As a result, theft-related crimes are often punished more severely than are acts of violence because while the former may be interclass, the latter are typically intraclass.

GLOBALIZATION Critical criminologists believe that the nature of a society controls the direction of its criminality; criminals are not social misfits, but products of the society and its economic system. Capitalism as a mode of production has always produced a relatively high level of crime and violence.[39] Critical thinkers are wary of how capitalism is becoming the predominant economic system in the world, replacing the socialist regimes in the former Soviet Union and eastern Europe. China is now a center for free market enterprise. This new global capitalist economy is a particular vexing development for critical theorists and impacts the concept of surplus value; globalization of industry has shifted the focus of critical inquiry to a world perspective.

Globalization is hard to define. It usually refers to the process of creating transnational markets, politics, and legal systems—that is, creating a global economy. Globalization began when large companies decided to establish themselves in foreign markets by adapting their products or services to the local culture. The process took off with the fall of the Soviet Union, which opened new European markets. The development of China into a super-industrial power encouraged foreign investors to take advantage of China's huge supply of workers. As the Internet and communication revolution unfolded, companies were able to establish instant communications with their far-flung corporate empires, a technological breakthrough that further aided trade and foreign investments. A series of transnational corporate mergers (for example, Daimler Chrysler) and takeovers (Ford and Volvo) produced ever-larger transnational corporations.

While some experts believe that globalization can improve the standard of living in Third World nations by providing jobs and training, critical thinkers question the altruism of multinational corporations.[40] Their motives, critical thinkers charge, are the exploitation of natural resources, avoiding regulation, and taking advantage of desperate workers. When these giant corporations set up a factory in a developing nation it is not to help the local population but to get around environmental laws and take advantage of needy workers who may be forced to labor in substandard conditions. Globalization has replaced imperialism and colonization as a new form of economic domination and oppression. Conflict thinkers David Friedrichs and Jessica Friedrichs warn that globalization presents the following four-pronged threat to the world economy:

1. The growing global dominance and reach of the free-market capitalist system that disproportionately benefits wealthy and powerful organizations and individuals

2. The increasing vulnerability of indigenous people with a traditional way of life to the forces of globalized capitalism

3. The growing influence and impact of international financial institutions (such as the World Bank) and the related relative decline of power of local or state-based institutions

4. The nondemocratic operation of international financial institutions[41]

While many critical criminologists blame globalization for the recent upswing in international crime rates, legal scholar Jean-Germain Gros argues that it alone cannot increase crime unless it occurs in so-called failed or collapsed states.[42] Globalization may produce crime in places such as the Congo, Liberia, Somalia, Sierra Leone, and Chechnya where there is widespread looting and banditry, where criminal warlords have more power than the government, and where arms traffickers can ply their trade unimpeded by government regulation.[43]

Instrumental versus Structural Theory

Although these themes can be found throughout critical criminology, there are actually two different schools of thought on the relationship between capitalism and crime. These are the instrumental and structural models set out below.

THE INSTRUMENTAL VIEW According to **instrumental critical theory**, criminal law and the criminal justice system act solely as instruments for controlling the poor, have-not members of society. The state and its agencies of control—police, courts, and correctional system—are solely the tool of capitalists.

According to the instrumental view, capitalist justice serves the powerful and rich and enables them to impose their morality and standards of behavior on the entire society. Under capitalism, those who wield economic power are able to extend their self-serving definition of illegal or criminal behavior to encompass those who might threaten the status quo or interfere with their quest for ever-increasing profits.[44] For example, the concentration of economic assets in the nation's largest industrial firms translates into the political power needed to control tax laws to limit the firms' tax liabilities.[45] Some have the economic clout to hire top attorneys to defend themselves against antitrust actions, making them almost immune to regulation. For example, in 2004 Congress was presented with legislation to change the tax

structure for professional sports teams that would allow their owners benefits of such magnitude that they would significantly increase the value of the franchise. If the legislation is signed into law, the value of the teams, currently estimated to be about $41 billion, would increase 5 percent or $2 billion.[46]

The poor, according to this branch of critical theory, may or may not commit more crimes than the rich, but they certainly are arrested and punished more often. Under the capitalist system, the poor are driven to crime because a natural frustration exists in a society in which affluence is well publicized but unattainable. When class conflict becomes unbearable, frustration can spill out in riots, such as the one that occurred in Los Angeles on April 29, 1992, which was described as a "class rebellion of the underprivileged against the privileged."[47] Because of class conflict, a deep-rooted hostility is generated among members of the lower class toward a social order they are not allowed to shape and whose benefits are unobtainable.[48]

An important goal of instrumental theorists is to **demystify** law and justice—that is, to unmask its true purpose. Criminological theories that focus on family structure, intelligence, peer relations, and school performance keep the lower classes servile by showing why they are more criminal, less intelligent, and more prone to school failure and family problems than the middle class. Demystification involves identifying the destructive intent of capitalist inspired and funded criminology.[49]

THE STRUCTURAL VIEW According to **structural critical theory**, the relationship between law and capitalism is unidirectional, not always working for the rich and against the poor.[50] Law is not the exclusive domain of the rich but rather is used to maintain the long-term interests of the capitalist system and control members of any class who threaten its existence. If law and justice were purely instruments of the capitalist class, why would laws controlling corporate crimes, such as price fixing, false advertising, and illegal restraint of trade, have been created and enforced?

To a structuralist, the law is designed to keep the capitalist system operating efficiently, and anyone, capitalist or proletarian, who rocks the boat is targeted for sanction. For example, antitrust legislation is designed to prevent any single capitalist from dominating the system. If the capitalist system is to function, no single person can become too powerful at the expense of the economic system as a whole. Structuralists would regard the efforts of the U.S. government to break up large corporations such as AT&T and Microsoft as examples of capitalists controlling capitalists to keep the system on an even keel. The long prison sentences given to corporate executives who engage in insider trading is a warning to capitalists that they must play by the rules. Though some may view the conviction of Martha Stewart as unfair, a structuralist sees Stewart as a sacrificial lamb, thrown to the wolves in order to prove the system works for everyone. Meanwhile, wealthy capitalists enjoy tax breaks and protection from prosecutions.

On September 15, 2004, in New York City, Martha Stewart made a statement to the media that she had decided to surrender for prison as soon as possible, citing the need to get on with her life. Stewart, the millionaire businesswoman, was sentenced in July of 2004 to five months in prison and five months of house arrest after she was convicted of lying about a stock sale. Some critical thinkers who use the structural view might see Stewart's punishment as indicating that the system requires even the wealthiest people to play by the rules of the capitalist economy.

Research on Critical Criminology

Critical criminologists rarely use standard social science methodologies to test their views because many believe the traditional approach of measuring research subjects is anti-human and insensitive.[51] They believe that the research conducted by mainstream liberal and positivist criminologists is designed to unmask weak and powerless members of society so they can be better dealt with by the legal system. They are particularly offended by purely empirical studies, such as those designed to show that minority group members have

lower IQs than whites or that the inner city is the site of the most serious crime whereas middle-class areas are relatively crime-free.

Empirical research, however, is not considered totally incompatible with critical criminology, and there have been some important efforts to test its fundamental assumptions quantitatively.[52] For example, research has shown that the property crime rate reflects a change in the level of surplus value; the capitalist system's emphasis on excessive profits accounts for the need of the working class to commit property crime.[53] Nonetheless, critical research tends to be historical and analytical, not quantitative and empirical. Social trends are interpreted with regard to how capitalism has affected human interaction. Critical criminologists investigate both macro-level issues, such as how the accumulation of wealth affects crime rates, and micro-level issues, such as the effect of criminal interactions on the lives of individuals living in a capitalist society. Of particular importance to critical thinkers is analyzing the historical development of capitalist social control institutions, such as criminal law, police agencies, courts, and prison systems.

CRIME, THE INDIVIDUAL, AND THE STATE Critical criminologists devote considerable attention to the relationships among crime, victims, the criminal, and the state. Two common themes emerge: (1) Crime and its control are a function of capitalism; (2) the justice system is biased against the working class and favors upper-class interests.

Critical analysis of the criminal justice system is designed to identify the often-hidden processes that control people's lives. It takes into account how conditions, processes, and structures evolved into what they are today. One issue considered is the process by which deviant behavior is defined as criminal or delinquent in U.S. society.[54] Another issue is the degree to which class affects the justice system's decision-making process.[55] Also subject to analysis is how power relationships help undermine any benefit the lower class receives from sentencing reforms.[56]

In general, critical research efforts have yielded evidence linking operations of the justice system to class bias.[57] In addition, some researchers have attempted to show how capitalism intervenes across the entire spectrum of crime-related phenomena. In addition to conducting studies showing the relationship between crime and the state, some critical researchers have attempted to show how capitalism influences the distribution of punishment. Robert Weiss found that the expansion of the prison population is linked to the need for capitalists to acquire a captive and low-paid labor force in order to compete with overseas laborers and domestic immigrant labor. Employing immigrants has its political downside because it displaces "American" workers and antagonizes their legal representatives. In contrast, using prison labor can be viewed as a humanitarian gesture. Weiss also observes that an ever-increasing prison population is politically attractive because it masks unemployment rates. Many inmates were chronically unemployed before their imprisonment;

incarcerating the chronically unemployed allows politicians to claim they have lowered unemployment. When the millions of people who are on probation and parole and who must maintain jobs are added to the mix, the correctional system is now playing an ever-more important role in suppressing wages and maintaining the profitability of capitalism.[58]

> Research shows that African Americans are sent to prison on drug charges at up to fifty times the rate of whites. To read more about the effects of racial discrimination, use "race discrimination" as a subject guide in InfoTrac College Edition.

This type of research does not set out to prove statistically that capitalism causes crime but rather to show that it creates an environment in which crime is inevitable. Critical research is humanistic, situational, descriptive, and analytical rather than statistical, rigid, and methodological. Critical theorists argue that there must be a thorough rethinking of the role and purpose of the criminal justice system, giving the powerless a greater voice to express their needs and concerns, if these inequities are to be addressed.[59]

HISTORICAL ANALYSIS Another type of critical research focuses on the historical background of commonly held institutional beliefs and practices. One goal is to show how changes in criminal law correspond to the development of the capitalist economy. The second goal is to investigate the development of modern police agencies.

To examine the changes in criminal law, historian Michael Rustigan analyzed historical records to show that law reform in nineteenth-century England was largely a response to pressure from the business community to increase punishment for property law violations in order to protect their rapidly increasing wealth.[60] Other research has focused on topics such as how the relationship between convict work and capitalism evolved during the nineteenth century. During this period, prisons became a profitable method of centralized state control over lower-class criminals, whose labor was exploited by commercial concerns. These criminals were forced to labor in order to pay off wardens and correctional administrators.[61]

Critique of Critical Criminology

Critical criminology has been sharply criticized by some members of the criminological mainstream, who charge that its contribution has been "hot air, heat, but no real light."[62] In turn, critical criminologists have accused mainstream criminologists of being culprits in developing state control over individual lives and selling out their ideals for the chance to receive government funding.

Mainstream criminologists have also attacked the substance of critical thought. Some argue that critical theory simply rehashes the old tradition of helping the underdog, in which the poor steal from the rich to survive.[63] In reality,

most theft is for luxury, not survival. While the wealthy do commit their share of illegal acts, these are nonviolent and leave no permanent injuries.[64] People do not live in fear of corrupt businessmen and stock traders; they fear muggers and rapists.

Other critics suggest that critical criminologists unfairly neglect the capitalist system's efforts to regulate itself—for example, by instituting antitrust regulations and putting violators in jail. Similarly, they ignore efforts to institute social reforms aimed at helping the poor.[65] There seems to be no logic in condemning a system that helps the poor and empowers them to take on corporate interests in a court of law. Even inherently conservative institutions such as police departments have made attempts at self-regulation when they become aware of class- and race-based inequality such as the use of racial profiling in making traffic stops.[66]

Some argue that critical criminologists refuse to address the problems and conflicts that exist in socialist countries, such as the gulags and purges of the Soviet Union under Stalin. Similarly, they fail to explain why some highly capitalist countries, such as Japan, have extremely low crime rates. Critical criminologists are too quick to blame capitalism for every human vice without adequate explanation or regard for other social and environmental factors.[67] In so doing, they ignore objective reality and refuse to acknowledge that members of the lower classes tend to victimize one another. Critical criminologists ignore the plight of the lower classes, who must live in crime-ridden neighborhoods, while condemning the capitalist system from the security of the ivory tower.

Critical scholars claim their detractors rely on "traditional" variables, such as class and poverty, in their analysis of radical thought. Although important, these factors do not reflect the key issues in the structural and economic process. In fact, like crime, they too may be the outcome of the capitalist system.[68] Critical criminologists also point out that although other capitalist nations may have lower crime rates, this does not mean they are crime-free. Even Japan has significant problems with teen prostitution and organized crime.

 To quiz yourself on this material, go to the Criminology TPT 9e website.

CONTEMPORARY FORMS OF CRITICAL THEORY

We have noted that contemporary critical theory can be subdivided into the structural and instrumental branches. In addition, there are a number of new branches of thought and scholarship which have sprung from the same roots: the appreciation of social conflict and the economic determinism of Marxist thought. Some of the more important of these are discussed below.

Left Realism

Some critical scholars are now addressing the need for the left wing to respond to the increasing power of right-wing conservatives. They are troubled by the emergence of a strict "law and order" philosophy, which has as its centerpiece a policy of severe and strict punishment. At the same time, they find the focus of most left-wing scholarship—the abuse of power by the ruling elite—too narrow. It is wrong, they argue, to ignore inner-city gang crime and violence, which often target indigent people.[69] The approach of scholars who share these concerns is referred to as **left realism**.[70]

Left realism is most often connected to the writings of British scholars John Lea and Jock Young. In their well-respected 1984 work, *What Is to Be Done About Law and Order?* they reject the utopian views of "idealistic" critical criminologists who portray street criminals as revolutionaries.[71] They take the more "realistic" approach that street criminals prey on the poor and disenfranchised, thus making the poor doubly abused, first by the capitalist system and then by members of their own class.

Lea and Young's view of crime causation borrows from conventional sociological theory and closely resembles the relative deprivation approach, which posits that experiencing poverty in the midst of plenty creates discontent and breeds crime. As they put it, "The equation is simple: relative deprivation equals discontent; discontent plus lack of political solution equals crime."[72]

In a more recent book, *Crime in Context: A Critical Criminology of Market Societies,* Ian Taylor recognizes that critical criminologists who expect an instant socialist revolution to take place are simply engaging in wishful thinking.[73] He uses data from both Europe and North America to show that the world is currently in the midst of multiple crises that are shaping all human interaction, including criminality. These crises include those involving job creation, social inequality, social fear, political incompetence and failure, gender conflict, and family and parenting. They have led to a society in which the government seems incapable of creating positive social change, where people have become more fearful and isolated from one another and some are excluded from the mainstream because of racism and discrimination, and where manufacturing jobs have been exported overseas to nations that pay extremely low wages and in which fiscal constraints inhibit the possibility of reform. These problems often fall squarely on the shoulders of young black men who not only suffer from exclusion and poverty but who have also suffered from economic dislocation caused by the erosion of manufacturing jobs due to globalization of the economy. In response, they engage in a hyper-form of masculinity that helps increase their crime rates.[74]

CRIME PROTECTION Left realists argue that crime victims in all classes need and deserve protection; crime control reflects community needs. They do not view police and the courts as inherently evil tools of capitalism whose tough tactics alienate the lower classes. In fact, they recognize that these institutions offer life-saving public services. The left realists wish, however, that police would reduce their use of force and increase their sensitivity to the public.[75]

Preemptive deterrence is an approach in which community organization efforts eliminate or reduce crime before police involvement becomes necessary. The reasoning behind this approach is that if the number of marginalized youths (those who feel they are not part of society and have nothing to lose by committing crime) could be reduced, then delinquency rates would decline.[76]

Although implementing a socialist economy might help eliminate the crime problem, left realists recognize that something must be done to control crime under the existing capitalist system. To develop crime control policies, left realists not only welcome radical ideas but also build on the work of strain theorists, social ecologists, and other mainstream views. Community-based efforts seem to hold the greatest promise of crime control.

Left realism has been criticized by radical thinkers as legitimizing the existing power structure: By supporting existing definitions of law and justice, it suggests that the "deviant" and not the capitalist system causes society's problems. Critics question whether left realists advocate the very institutions that "currently imprison us and our patterns of thought and action."[77] In rebuttal, left realists would say that it is unrealistic to speak of a socialist state lacking a police force or a system of laws and justice. They believe that the criminal code does, in fact, represent public opinion.

Critical Feminist Theory

Most of the efforts of critical theorists have been devoted to explaining male criminality.[78] To remedy this theoretical lapse, a number of critical scholars have attempted to explain the cause of crime, gender differences in crime rates, and the exploitation of female victims from a **critical feminist** perspective. Critical feminists view gender inequality as stemming from the unequal power of men and women in a capitalist society, which leads to the exploitation of women by fathers and husbands. Under this system, women are considered a commodity worth possessing, like land or money.[79]

The origin of gender differences can be traced to the development of private property and male domination of the laws of inheritance, which led to male control over property and power.[80] A patriarchal system developed in which men's work was valued and women's work was devalued. As capitalism prevailed, the division of labor by gender made women responsible for the unpaid maintenance and reproduction of the current and future labor force, which was derisively called "domestic work." Although this unpaid work done by women is crucial and profitable for capitalists, who reap these free benefits, such labor is exploitative and oppressive for women.[81] Even when women gained the right to work for pay, they were exploited as cheap labor. The dual exploitation of women within the household and in the labor market means that women produce far greater surplus value for capitalists than men.

Critical feminists view gender inequality as a function of female exploitation by men. Women have become a "commodity" worth possessing, like land or money. The origin of gender differences can be traced to the development of private property and male domination over the laws of inheritance, which led to their control over property and power. Are these teen prostitutes—shown here waiting to be booked at the Maricopa, Arizona, jail—a by-product of this view of women as commodities, which was engendered by the capitalist system?

Capitalism lends itself to male supremacy and capitalist societies are built around **patriarchy,** a system in which men dominate public, social, economic, and political affairs. This system sustains female oppression at home and in the workplace.[82] Although the number of traditional patriarchal families is in steep decline, in those that still exist, a wife's economic dependence ties men more securely to wage-earning jobs, further serving the interests of capitalists by undermining potential rebellion against the system.

PATRIARCHY AND CRIME Critical feminists link criminal behavior patterns to the gender conflict created by the economic and social struggles common in postindustrial societies. In his book *Capitalism, Patriarchy, and Crime,* James Messerschmidt argues that capitalist society is marked by both patriarchy and class conflict. Capitalists control the labor of workers, while men control women both economically and biologically.[83] This "double marginality" explains why females in a capitalist society commit fewer crimes than males. Because they are isolated in the family, they have fewer opportunities to engage in elite deviance (white-collar and economic crimes). Although powerful females as well as males will commit white-collar crimes, the female crime rate is restricted because of the patriarchal nature of the capitalist system.[84] Women are also denied access to male-dominated street crimes. Because capitalism renders lower-class women powerless, they are forced to commit less serious, nonviolent, self-destructive crimes, such as abusing drugs.

Powerlessness also increases the likelihood that women will become targets of violent acts.[85] When lower-class males are shut out of the economic opportunity structure, they try to build their self-image through acts of machismo; such acts may involve violent abuse of women. This type of reaction accounts for a significant percentage of female victims who are attacked by a spouse or intimate partner.

In *Masculinities and Crime,* Messerschmidt expands on these themes.[86] He suggests that in every culture, males try to emulate "ideal" masculine behaviors. In Western culture, this means being authoritative, in charge, combative, and controlling. Failure to adopt these roles leaves men feeling effeminate and unmanly. Their struggle to dominate women in order to prove their manliness is called "doing gender." Crime is a vehicle for men to "do gender" because it separates them from the weak and allows them to demonstrate physical bravery. Violence directed toward women is an especially economical way to demonstrate manhood. Would a weak, effeminate male ever attack a woman?

Feminist writers have supported this view by maintaining that in contemporary society men achieve masculinity at the expense of women. In the best case scenario they must convince others that in no way are they feminine or have female qualities—for example, they are sloppy and do no cooking or housework because these are "female" activities. More ominously, they may work at excluding, hurting, denigrating, exploiting, or otherwise abusing actual women. Even in all-male groups men often prove their manhood by treating the weakest member of the group as "woman-like" and abusing them accordingly. Men's need to defend themselves at all costs from being contaminated with femininity, and these efforts begin in children's playgroups and continue into adulthood and marriage.[87]

According to this view, female victimization should decline as women's place in society is elevated, and they are able to obtain more power at home, in the workplace, and in government. A recent (2004) cross-national study of educational and occupational status of women supports this hypothesis. In nations where the status of women is generally high, sexual violence rates are significantly lower than in nations where women do not enjoy similar educational and occupational opportunities.[88]

EXPLOITATION AND CRIMINALITY Critical feminists also focus on the social forces that shape women's lives and experiences to explain female criminality.[89] For example, they attempt to show how the sexual victimization of females is a function of male socialization because so many young males learn to be aggressive and to exploit females. Males seek out same-sex peer groups for social support; these groups encourage members to exploit and sexually abuse females. On college campuses, peers encourage sexual violence against women who are considered "teasers," "bar pickups," or "loose women." These derogatory labels allow the males to justify their actions; a code of secrecy then protects the aggressors from retribution.[90]

According to the critical feminist view, exploitation triggers the onset of female delinquent and deviant behavior. When female victims run away and abuse substances, they may be reacting to abuse they have suffered at home or at school. Their attempts at survival are labeled as deviant or delinquent behavior.[91] In a sense, the female criminal is herself a victim.

Research shows that a significant number of girls who are sent to hospital emergency rooms to be treated for sexual abuse later report engaging in physical fighting as teens or as adults. Many of these abused girls later form romantic attachments with abusive partners. Clearly many girls involved in delinquency, crime, and violence have themselves been the victims of violence in their youth and later as adults.[92]

Critical feminist opinions differ on certain issues. For example, some feminist scholars charge that the movement focuses on the problems and viewpoints of white, middle-class, heterosexual women without taking into account the special interests of lesbians and women of color.[93] The Race, Culture, Gender, and Criminology feature traces the history of patriarchy.

HOW THE JUSTICE SYSTEM PENALIZES WOMEN Radical feminists have indicted the justice system and its patriarchal hierarchy as contributing to the onset of female delinquency. Some have studied the early history of the justice system and uncovered an enduring pattern of discrimination. From its inception, the juvenile justice system has viewed most female delinquents as sexually precocious girls who have to be brought under control. Writing about the "girl problem," Ruth Alexander has described how working-class young women desiring autonomy and freedom in the 1920s were considered delinquents and placed in reformatories. Lacking the ability to protect themselves from the authorities, these young girls were considered outlaws in a male-dominated society because they flouted the very narrow rules of appropriate behavior that were applied to females. Girls who rebelled against parental authority or who engaged in sexual behavior deemed inappropriate were incarcerated in order to protect them from a career in prostitution.[94]

Mary Odem and Steven Schlossman researched the lives of young women who entered the Los Angeles Juvenile Court in 1920 and found that the majority were petitioned for either suspected sexual activity or behavior that placed them at risk of sexual relations. Despite the limited seriousness of these charges, most of the girls were detained before their trials, and while in juvenile hall, all were given a compulsory pelvic exam. Girls adjudged sexually delinquent on the basis of the exam were segregated from the merely incorrigible girls to prevent moral corruption. Those testing positive for venereal disease were usually confined in the juvenile hall hospital for 1 to 3 months. More than 29 percent of these female adolescents were eventually committed to custodial institutions.[95]

A well-known feminist writer, Meda Chesney-Lind, has written extensively about the victimization of female delinquents by agents of the juvenile justice system.[96] She suggests that because female adolescents have a much narrower range of acceptable behavior than male adolescents, any sign of misbehavior in girls is seen as a substantial challenge to authority and to the viability of the double standard of sexual inequality. Female delinquency is viewed as relatively more serious than male delinquency and therefore is more likely to be severely sanctioned.

Power–Control Theory

John Hagan and his associates have created a radical feminist model that uses gender differences to explain the onset of criminality.[97] Hagan's view is that crime and delinquency rates are a function of two factors: (1) class position (power) and (2) family functions (control).[98] The link between these two variables is that, within the family, parents reproduce the power relationships they hold in the workplace; a position of dominance at work is equated with control in the household. As a result, parents' work experiences and class position influence the criminality of children.[99]

In **paternalistic families,** fathers assume the traditional role of breadwinners, while mothers tend to have menial jobs or remain at home to supervise domestic matters. Within the paternalistic home, mothers are expected to control the behavior of their daughters while granting greater freedom to sons. In such a home, the parent–daughter relationship can be viewed as a preparation for the "cult of domesticity," which makes girls' involvement in delinquency unlikely, whereas boys are freer to deviate because they are not subject to maternal control. Girls growing up in patriarchal families are socialized to fear legal sanctions more than are males; consequently, boys in these families exhibit more delinquent behavior than their sisters. The result is that boys not only engage in more antisocial behaviors but have greater access to legitimate adult-type behaviors, such as working at part time jobs and/or possessing transportation. In contrast, without these legitimate behavioral outlets, girls who are unhappy or dissatisfied with their status are forced to seek out risky **role exit behaviors,** including such desperate measures as running away and contemplating suicide.

In **egalitarian families**—those in which the husband and wife share similar positions of power at home and in the

Race, Culture, Gender, and Criminology

Capitalism and Patriarchy

Feminist scholar Nancy Jurik has described the historical association between patriarchy and capitalism and how both worked to subjugate women. Patriarchy first emerged in precapitalist agricultural societies in which a male head presided over his family, controlling work and the marriages of its members. In these early societies, the household was the center of production. With the development of industrialization and the emergence of labor, capitalism interacted with patriarchy to change family life. With the advent of mass production, the factory and not the home became the center of production.

At the onset of industrialization, all family members, including children, went out to work. Gradually, however, social reformers and even some capitalists arranged for the removal of women and children from the harsh conditions of factory life. Male-controlled unions fought for job protection by forcing legislation, which prohibited women from competing for factory jobs. Capitalists eventually agreed to pay a "family wage" that would be large enough to support wives and children. Capitalism then rendered men as the sole "breadwinners" while at the same time satisfying the owners' need for a stable and healthy workforce. Despite the ideology that all men should earn enough

to keep their wives at home, men of color, nonunion whites, and immigrants rarely earned a family wage.

Women began to be exploited because they provided free reproductive labor in their homes. Their labor, though unappreciated, allowed men to work. Women produced and cared for the next generation of laborers (their children). Women's reproductive labor limited their ability to engage in paid work or to participate in the political process. They were denied control over their sexuality and reproduction.

Men's domination was both a function of their control of social institutions and their constant threat of physical violence. Lack of opportunity relegated women to seek men's protection in monogamous nuclear families. The law even denied a woman's right to control her own sexuality by limiting access to birth control and abortions.

For those women who did hold jobs outside the home, their role in the workplace defined the way they were viewed. In the event a woman was forced to seek work, she was reduced to "help" and "support" work, which was viewed as less skilled than the work men did and was therefore lower paid. Keeping women's wages low also helped capitalists dominate male workers by threatening to replace them with lower-paid women. This fear allowed them to deny raises and to limit benefits. This further alienated and enraged men, convincing them of the urgency of preventing women from

joining unions and from gaining employment in traditional male occupations.

Patriarchy may have preceded capitalism, but beginning with the Industrial Age both capitalism and patriarchy have been intertwined in an effort to sustain the subordination of women.

Critical Thinking

1. How would you respond to someone who claims that the social roles of men and women have converged, and, if anything, women actually have more power today?

2. Can you think of institutions and practices that show gender discrimination to be a continuing and contemporary problem?

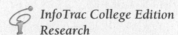

InfoTrac College Edition Research

For more on the concept of patriarchy and how it influences women, see: Heidi Gottfried, "Beyond Patriarchy? Theorising Gender and Class," *Sociology* 32 (August 1998): 451; Stanley Rothman and Amy E. Black, "Who Rules Now? American Elites in the 1990s," *Society* 35 (September–October 1998): 17.

Source: Nancy Jurik, "Socialist Feminism, Criminology, and Criminal Justice," in *Social Justice/Criminal Justice,* ed. Bruce Arrigo (Belmont, CA: West/Wadsworth, 1999), pp. 31–51.

---

workplace—daughters gain a kind of freedom that reflects reduced parental control. These families produce daughters whose law-violating behavior mirrors their brothers' behavior. In an egalitarian family, girls may have greater opportunity to engage in legitimate adult-status behaviors and have less need to enact deviant role exits.[100]

Ironically, these relationships also occur in female-headed households with absent fathers. Hagan and his associates found that when fathers and mothers hold equally

valued managerial positions, the similarity between the rates of their daughters' and sons' delinquency is greatest. By implication, middle-class girls are the most likely to violate the law because they are less closely controlled than their lower-class counterparts. In homes in which both parents hold positions of power, girls are more likely to have the same expectations of career success as their brothers. Consequently, siblings of both sexes will be socialized to take risks and engage in other behavior related to delinquency.

EVALUATING POWER–CONTROL This **power–control theory** has received a great deal of attention in the criminological community because it encourages a new approach to the study of criminality, one that includes gender differences, class position, and the structure of the family. Empirical analysis of its premises has generally been supportive. For example, Brenda Sims Blackwell's research supports a key element of power–control theory: Females in paternalistic households have learned to fear legal sanctions more than have their brothers.[101]

Not all research is as supportive.[102] Some critics have questioned its core assumption that power and control variables can explain crime.[103] More specifically, critics fail to replicate the finding that upper-class kids are more likely to deviate than their lower-class peers or that class and power interact to produce delinquency.[104] Some researchers have found few gender-based supervision and behavior differences in worker-, manager-, or owner-dominated households.[105] It is possible that the concept of class employed by Hagan may have to be reconsidered. Moreover, power–control theory must now consider the multitude of power and control relationships that are emerging in postmodern society: for example, blended families, and families where mothers hold managerial positions and fathers are blue-collar workers, and so forth.[106]

Postmodern Theory

A number of radical thinkers, referred to as **postmodernists** or **deconstructionists**, have embraced semiotics as a method of understanding all human relations, including criminal behavior. **Semiotics** refers to the use of language elements as signs or symbols beyond their literal meaning. Thus, deconstructionists critically analyze communication and language in legal codes to determine whether they contain language and content that institutionalize racism or sexism.[107]

Postmodernists rely on semiotics to conduct their research efforts. For example, the term *special needs children* is designed to describe these youngsters' learning needs, but it may also characterize the children themselves as mentally challenged, dangerous, or uncontrollable. Postmodernists believe that value-laden language can promote inequities. *Truth, identity, justice, and power* are all concepts whose meaning is derived from the language dictated by those in power.[108] Laws, legal skill, and justice are commodities that can be bought and sold like any other service or product.[109] For example, the OJ Simpson case is vivid proof that the affluent can purchase a different brand of justice than the indigent.[110]

Postmodernists assert that there are different languages and ways of knowing. Those in power can use their own language to define crime and law while excluding or dismissing those who oppose their control, such as prisoners and the poor. By dismissing these oppositional languages, certain versions of how to think, feel, or act are devalued and excluded. This exclusion is seen as the source of conflict in society.[111]

Peacemaking Theory

One of the newer movements in radical theory is **peacemaking** criminology. To members of the peacemaking movement, the main purpose of criminology is to promote a peaceful, just society. Rather than standing on empirical analysis of data, peacemaking draws its inspiration from religious and philosophical teachings ranging from Quakerism to Zen.[112]

Peacemakers view the efforts of the state to punish and control as crime-encouraging rather than crime-discouraging. These views were first articulated in a series of books with an anarchist theme written by criminologists Larry Tifft and Dennis Sullivan in 1980.[113] Tifft argues, "The violent punishing acts of the state and its controlling professions are of the same genre as the violent acts of individuals. In each instance these acts reflect an attempt to monopolize human interaction."[114]

Sullivan stresses the futility of correcting and punishing criminals in the context of our conflict-ridden society: "The reality we must grasp is that we live in a culture of severed relationships, where every available institution provides a form of banishment but no place or means for people to become connected, to be responsible to and for each other."[115] Sullivan suggests that mutual aid rather than coercive punishment is the key to a harmonious society. In *Restorative Justice* (2001), Sullivan and Tifft reaffirm their belief that

Peacemakers believe in restoration and not revenge, even for the most heinous crimes. They are firmly against the death penalty. Here, Scott Langley, Chris Banner, and Virginia Hodges sing together for death row inmates at the U.S. Federal Penitentiary in Terre Haute, Indiana. The three participated in an 80-mile march from Indianapolis to Terre Haute in protest of the death penalty.

Social Conflict/Critical Criminology Theories

Social Conflict Theory

- The major premise is that crime is a function of class conflict. Law is defined by people who hold social and political power.

- The strengths of the theory are that it accounts for class differentials in the crime rate and shows how class conflict influences behavior.

Critical Criminology

- The major premise of the theory is that the capitalist means of production creates class conflict. Crime is a rebellion of the lower class. The criminal justice system is an agent of class warfare.

- The strength of the theory is that it accounts for the associations between economic structure and crime rates.

Instrumental Critical Theory

- The major premise of the theory is that criminals are revolutionaries. The real crimes are sexism, racism, and profiteering.

- The strengths of the theory are that it broadens the definition of crime and demystifies or explains the historical development of the law.

Structural Critical Theory

- The major premise of the theory is that the law is designed to sustain the capitalist economic system.

- The major strength of the theory is that it explains the existence of white-collar crime and business control laws.

Left Realism

- The major premise of the theory is that class conflicts create crime.

- The strength of the theory is that it provides a fair and humane prescription for crime control in an unjust society.

Critical Feminist Theory

- The major premise of the theory is that gender conflict in male-dominated patriarchal societies create crime.

- The strength of the theory is that it explains how gender differences in the crime rate are a function of capitalist competition and the exploitation of women.

Power–Control Theory

- The major premise of the theory is that gender differences in crime are a function of economic power (class position, one- versus two-earner families) and parental control (paternalistic versus egalitarian families).

- The major strength of the theory is that it encourages a new approach to the study of criminality, one that includes gender differences, class position, and the structure of the family.

Postmodern Theory

- The major premise of the theory is that language and understanding are related to definitions of antisocial behavior.

- The strength of the theory is that it provides a framework for the study of modern society and its control over human behavior.

Peacemaking Theory

- The major premise of the theory is that peace and humanism can reduce crime; conflict resolution strategies can work.

- The strength of the theory is that it offers a new approach to crime control through mediation.

---

society must seek humanitarian forms of justice without resorting to brutal punishments:

> By allowing feelings of vengeance or retribution to narrow our focus on the harmful event and the person responsible for it—as others might focus solely on a sin committed and the "sinner"—we tell ourselves we are taking steps to free ourselves from the effects of the harm or the sin in question. But, in fact, we are putting ourselves in a servile position with respect to life, human growth, and the further enjoyment of relationships with others.[116]

Today, advocates of the peacemaking movement, such as Harold Pepinsky and Richard Quinney (who has shifted his theoretical orientation from conflict theory to Marxism and now to peacemaking), try to find humanist solutions to crime and other social problems.[117] Rather than punishment and prison, they advocate such policies as mediation and conflict resolution.[118]

Concept Summary 8.1 sets out the major sub-branches of social conflict theory and critical criminology.

PUBLIC POLICY IMPLICATIONS OF SOCIAL CONFLICT THEORY: RESTORATIVE JUSTICE

At the core of all the varying branches of critical criminology is the fact that conflict causes crime. If conflict and competition in society could somehow be reduced, it is possible that crime rates would fall. Some critical theorists believe this goal can only be accomplished by thoroughly reordering society so that capitalism is destroyed and a socialist state is created. Others call for a more practical application of critical principles. Nowhere has this been more successful than in the **restorative justice** movement.

Influenced by the peacemaking movement, restorative justice advocates have made an ongoing effort to reduce the conflict created by the criminal justice system when it hands out harsh punishments to offenders, many of whom are powerless social outcasts. Based on the principle of reducing social harm, restorative justice advocates argue that the old methods of punishment are a failure and that upwards of two-thirds of all prison inmates recidivate soon after their release. They scoff at claims that the crime rate has dropped because the number of people in prison is at an all-time high, countering these claims with studies that show that imprisonment rates are not at all related to crime rates; there is no consistent finding that locking people up helps reduce crimes.[119]

> ||||||| **CONNECTIONS** |||||||
>
> Contrast this approach with the crime-control deterrence policies advocated by rational choice theorists in Chapter 4.

Encompassing both academic thinkers and justice system personnel, the restorative approach relies on nonpunitive strategies for crime prevention and control.[120] The next sections discuss the foundation and principles of restorative justice.

Reintegrative Shaming

One of the key foundations of the restoration movement is contained in John Braithwaite's influential book *Crime, Shame, and Reintegration*.[121] Braithwaite notes that countries such as Japan, in which conviction for crimes brings an inordinate amount of shame, have extremely low crime rates. In Japan, criminal prosecution proceeds only when the normal process of public apology, compensation, and the victim's forgiveness breaks down.

Shame is a powerful tool of informal social control. Citizens in cultures in which crime is not shameful, such as the United States, do not internalize an abhorrence for crime because when they are punished, they view themselves as mere victims of the justice system. Their punishment comes at the hands of neutral strangers, like police and judges, who are being paid to act. In contrast, reintegrative shaming relies on the victim's participation.[122]

Braithwaite divides the concept of shame into two distinct types. The most common form of shaming typically involves stigmatization. This form of shaming involves an ongoing process of degradation in which the offender is branded as an evil person and cast out of society. Shaming can occur at a school disciplinary hearing or a criminal court trial. Bestowing stigma and degradation may have a general deterrent effect: It makes people afraid of social rejection and public humiliation. As a specific deterrent, stigma is doomed to failure: people who suffer humiliation at the hands of the justice system are just as likely to "reject their rejectors" by joining a deviant subculture of like-minded people who collectively resist social control. Despite these dangers, there has been an ongoing effort to brand offenders and make their shame both public and permanent. Most states have passed sex offender registry and notification laws that make public the names of those convicted of sex offenses and warn neighbors of their presence in the community.[123]

Braithwaite argues that crime control can be better achieved through a policy of **reintegrative shaming**. Here disapproval is extended to the offenders' evil deeds, while at the same time they are cast as respected people who can be reaccepted by society. A critical element of reintegrative shaming occurs when the offenders begin to understand and recognize their wrongdoing and shame themselves. To be reintegrative, shaming must be brief and controlled and then followed by ceremonies of forgiveness, apology, and repentance.

To prevent crime, Braithwaite charges, society must encourage reintegrative shaming. For example, the women's movement can reduce domestic violence by mounting a crusade to shame spouse abusers.[124] Similarly, parents who use reintegrative shaming techniques in their childrearing practices may improve parent–child relationships and ultimately reduce the delinquent involvement of their children.[125] Because informal social controls may have a greater impact than legal or formal ones, it may not be surprising that the fear of personal shame can have a greater deterrent effect than the fear of legal sanctions. It may also be applied to produce specific deterrence. Offenders can meet with victims so that the offenders can experience shame. Family members and peers can be present to help the offender reintegrate.[126] Such efforts can humanize a system of justice that today relies on repression rather than forgiveness as the basis of specific deterrence.

> ||||||| **CONNECTIONS** |||||||
>
> The use of reintegrative shaming has been advocated by criminologists who consider harsh punishment counterproductive. If shame can convince people to refrain from crime, then it follows that they are following a logical process in choosing criminal over conventional solutions to their problems. This jibes with the choice theory model discussed in Chapter 4.

The Concept of Restorative Justice

According to Howard Zehr, a leader of the restorative justice movement, the term *restorative justice* is often hard to define because it encompasses a variety of programs and practices. Zehr observes that, "Restorative justice requires, at minimum, that we address victims' harms and needs, hold offenders accountable to put right those harms, and involve victims, offenders, and communities in this process." Its core value can be put into one word: respect. He states: "Respect for all, even those who are different from us, even those who seem to be our enemies. Respect reminds us of our interconnectedness but also of our differences. Respect insists that we balance concern for all parties." At its core it is "a set of principles, a philosophy, an alternate set of guiding questions" that provide an alternative framework for thinking about "wrongdoing."[127]

The traditional justice system has done little to involve the community in the process of dealing with this "wrongdoing." What has developed is a system of coercive punishments, administered by bureaucrats, that are inherently harmful to offenders and that reduce the likelihood they will ever become productive members of society. This system relies on punishment, stigma, and disgrace. In his controversial book *The Executed God: The Way of the Cross in Lockdown America,* theology professor Mark Lewis Taylor discusses the similarities between this contemporary, coercive justice system and that which existed in imperial Rome, when Jesus and many of his followers were executed because they were considered a threat who served as an inspiration to the poor and slave populations. Jesus created a popular movement that threatened the power structure and had to be put down if the system of imperial privilege was to remain intact. So too is our modern justice system designed to keep the downtrodden in place. Taylor suggests that there should be a movement to reduce coercive elements of justice such as police brutality and the death penalty before our "lockdown society" becomes the model around the globe.[128]

Advocates of restorative justice argue that rather than today's lockdown mentality, what is needed instead is a justice policy that repairs the harm caused by crime and that includes all parties who have suffered from that harm, including the victim, the community, and the offender. The principles of this approach are set out in Exhibit 8.1.

An important aspect of achieving these goals is for offenders to accept accountability for their actions and accept the responsibility for the harm their actions caused. Only then can they be restored as productive members of their community. Restoration involves turning the justice system into a healing process rather than being a distributor of retribution and revenge.

Most people involved in offender–victim relationships actually know each other or were related in some way before the criminal incident took place. Instead of treating one of the involved parties as a victim deserving of sympathy and the other as a criminal deserving of punishment, it is more productive to address the issues that produced conflict between these people. Rather than take sides and choose whom to isolate and punish, society should try to reconcile the parties involved in conflict.[129] The effectiveness of justice ultimately depends on the stake a person has in the community (or a particular social group). If people do not value their membership in the group, they will be unlikely to accept responsibility, show remorse, or repair the injuries caused by their actions. In contrast, people who have a stake in the community and its principal institutions—such as work, home, and school—find that their involvement enhances their personal and familial well-being.[130] If offenders can truly understand the problems and hurt they cause and are remorseful for their acts, they are less likely to re-offend.[131]

> The **Center for Restorative Justice and Peacemaking** provides links and information on the ideals of restoration and programs based on its principles: http://2ssw.che.umn.edu/rjp/. For an up-to-date list of web links, go to http://cj.wadsworth.com/siegel_crimtpt9e.

The Process of Restoration

The restoration process begins by redefining crime in terms of a conflict among the offender, the victim, and the affected constituencies (families, schools, workplaces, and so on). Therefore, it is vitally important that the resolution take place within the context in which the conflict originally occurred rather than be transferred to a specialized institution that has no social connection to the community or group from which the conflict originated. In other words, most conflicts are better settled in the community than in a court. By maintaining "ownership" or jurisdiction over the conflict, the community is able to express its shared outrage about the offense. Shared community outrage is directly communicated to the offender. The victim is also given a chance to voice his or her story, and the offender can directly communicate his or her need for social reintegration and treatment.

DEVELOPING RESTORATION Restoration programs typically involve the parties caught in the complex web of a criminal act—the victim, the offender, families, witnesses, neighbors, and the community—in a mutual healing process. Although programs may differ in structure and style, they generally include:

1. An element in which the offender is asked to recognize that he or she caused injury to personal and social relations and a determination and acceptance of responsibility (ideally accompanied by a statement of remorse)

2. A commitment to both material restitution (for instance, monetary) and symbolic reparation (for instance, an apology)

3. A determination of community support and assistance for both victim and offender

The intended result of the process is to repair injuries suffered by the victim and the community while assuring reintegration of the offender.

Kay Pranis, a trainer and consultant on restorative philosophy and peacemaking practices, has conducted trainings on the use of peacemaking circles in schools, universities, social services, the workplace, juvenile residential facilities, prisons, neighborhoods and families.

RESTORATION PROGRAMS Negotiation, mediation, consensus building, and peacemaking have been part of the dispute resolution process in European and Asian communities for centuries.[132] North American native peoples have long used the type of community participation in the adjudication process (for example, sentencing circles, sentencing panels, elders panels) that restorative justice advocates are now embracing.[133] The adaptation of these programs holds the promise of bringing a more humanistic approach to the treatment of people enmeshed in the justice system.[134]

To read more about **sentencing circles,** go to http://www.ojp.usdoj.gov/nij/rest-just/CH5/3_sntcir .htm. For an up-to-date list of web links, go to http:// cj.wadsworth.com/siegel_crimtpt9e.

In some Native American communities, people accused of breaking the law will meet with community members, victims (if any), village elders, and agents of the justice system in a **sentencing circle.** Members of the circle express their feelings about the act that was committed and raise questions or concerns. The accused can express regret about his or her actions and a desire to change the harmful behavior. People may suggest ways the offender can make things up to the community and those he or she harmed. A treatment program, such as Alcoholics Anonymous, can be suggested, if appropriate.

Restorative justice is now being embraced on many levels within the society and the justice system.

- *Community:* Communities that isolate people and have few mechanisms for interpersonal interaction encourage and sustain crime. Those that implement forms of community dialogue to identify problems and plan tactics for their elimination, guided by restorative justice practices and principles, may create a climate in which violent crime is less likely to occur.[135]

- *Schools:* Some schools have embraced restorative justice practices in order to deal with students who are involved in drug and alcohol abuse without having to resort to more punitive measures such as expulsion. Schools in Minnesota, Colorado, and elsewhere are now trying to involve students in "relational rehabilitation" programs, which strive to improve the person's relationships with key figures in the community who may have been harmed by the student's actions.[136]

- *Police:* Restorative justice has also been implemented when crime is first encountered by police. Community policing, which views police officers as mediators and community counselors, is an attempt to bring restorative concepts into law enforcement. Restorative justice relies on the fact that criminal justice policymakers need to listen and respond to the needs of those who are to be affected by their actions, and community policing relies on policies established with input and exchanges between officers and citizens.[137] Restorative justice program are not unique to American policing and have been tried abroad. For example, New Zealand employs police officers called youth aid officers whose duties include restoring community balance that may have been upset by the actions of juvenile offenders.[138]

- *Courts:* In the court system, restorative programs typically involve diverting the formal court process; these programs instead encourage meeting and reconciling the conflicts between offenders and victims via victim advocacy, mediation programs, and sentencing circles, in which crime victims and their families are brought together with offenders and their families in an effort to formulate a sanction that addresses the needs of each party. Victims are given a chance to voice their stories, and offenders can help compensate them financially or provide some service (such as fixing damaged property).[139] The goal is to enable offenders to appreciate the damage they have caused, to make amends, and to be reintegrated back into society.

BALANCED AND RESTORATIVE JUSTICE (BARJ) According to a number of restorative justice experts (Gordon Bazemore and his associates), restorative justice should be centered on the principle of balance.[140] According to this approach, the justice system should give equal weight to:

1. Holding offenders accountable to victims. *Offender accountability* refers specifically to the requirement that offenders "make amends" for the harm resulting from their crimes by repaying or restoring losses to victims and the community.

2. Providing competency development for offenders in the system so they can pursue legitimate endeavors after release. *Competency development*, the rehabilitative goal for intervention, requires that people who enter the justice system should exit the system more capable of being productive and responsible in the community.

3. Ensuring community safety. The *community protection* goal explicitly acknowledges and endorses a long-term public expectation: a safe and secure community.

The balanced approach means that justice policies and priorities should seek to address each of the three goals in each case and that system balance should be pursued. The goal of achieving balance suggests that no one objective take precedence over any other (avoiding creating a system that is "out of balance") and implies that efforts to achieve one goal should not hinder efforts to achieve other goals.

BARJ is founded on the belief that justice is best served when the victim, community, and offender are viewed as equal clients of the justice system who will receive fair and balanced attention, be actively involved in the justice process, and gain tangible benefits from their interactions with the justice system. Most BARJ programs are located today within the juvenile justice system. (See the Comparative Criminology feature "Practicing Restorative Justice Abroad.")

The Challenge of Restorative Justice

While restorative justice holds great promise, there are also some concerns. John Braithwaite warns that even though restorative justice recognizes that individual differences between offenders must be taken into account when dispensing justice, restorative programs must create standards so that clients are treated more or less equally. Fairness cannot be sacrificed for the sake of restoration.[141]

As well, restorative justice programs must be wary of the cultural and social differences that can be found throughout our heterogeneous society. What may be considered "restorative" in one subculture may be considered insulting and damaging in another.[142] Similarly, there are so many diverse programs that call themselves "restorative" that it is difficult to assess their effectiveness as each may have a unique objective. In other words, there is still no single definition of what constitutes restorative justice.[143]

Possibly the greatest challenge to restorative justice is the difficult task of balancing the needs of offenders with those of their victims. If programs focus solely on reconciling victims' needs, they may risk ignoring the offender's needs and increasing the likelihood of re-offending. This one-sided view,

argues critic Declan Roche, a lecturer in law at the London School of Economics in *Accountability in Restorative Justice,* may blind admirers to the benefits of traditional methods and prevent them from understanding or appreciating the pitfalls of restoration. Is there danger inherent in restorative justice's reliance on informal process, without lawyers, and with little or no oversight on the outcome? He warns of giving participants in the justice process unchecked power; procedural safeguards should be installed in restoration programs.[144]

Sharon Levrant and her colleagues suggest that restorative justice programs that feature short-term interactions with victims fail to help offenders learn prosocial ways of behaving. Restorative justice advocates may falsely assume that relatively brief interludes of public shaming will change deeply rooted criminal predispositions.[145] In contrast, programs that focus on the offender may turn off victims and their advocates. Some victim advocacy groups have voiced concerns about the focus of restorative justice programs (Exhibit 8.2).

EXHIBIT 8.2

Victim Concerns about Restorative Justice

- Restorative justice processes can cast victims as little more than props in a psychodrama focused on the offender, to restore him and thereby render him less likely to offend again.

- A victim, supported by family and intimates while engaged in restorative conferencing, and feeling genuinely free to speak directly to the offender, may press a blaming rather than restorative shaming agenda.

- The victim's movement has focused for years on a perceived imbalance of "rights." Criminal defendants enjoy the presumption of innocence, the right to proof beyond a reasonable doubt, the right not to have to testify, and lenient treatment when found guilty of crime. Victims were extended no rights at all in the legal process. Is restorative justice another legal giveaway to criminals?

- Victim's rights are threatened by some features of the restorative justice process, such as respectful listening to the offender's story and consensual dispositions. These features seem to be affronts to a victim's claim of the right to be seen as a victim, to insist on the offender being branded a criminal, to blame the offender, and not to be "victimized all over again by the process."

- Many victims do want an apology, if it is heartfelt and easy to get, but some want, even more, to put the traumatic incident behind them; to retrieve stolen property being held for use at trial; to be assured that the offender will receive treatment he is thought to need if he is not to victimize someone else. For victims such as these, restorative justice processes can seem unnecessary at best.

- Restorative processes depend, case by case, on victims' active participation in a role more emotionally demanding than that of complaining witness in a conventional criminal prosecution—which is itself a role avoided by many, perhaps most, victims.

Source: Michael E. Smith, *What Future for "Public Safety" and "Restorative Justice" in Community Corrections* (Washington, DC: National Institute of Justice, 2001).

Practicing Restorative Justice Abroad

While the restorative justice philosophy is catching on in the United States, it is widely practiced abroad. Below are just a few of the many programs found around the world.

South Africa

After fifty years of oppressive white rule in South Africa, the race-dividing apartheid policy was abolished in the early 1990s, and in 1994 Nelson Mandela, leader of the African National Congress (ANC), was elected president. Some black leaders wanted revenge for the political murders carried out during the apartheid era, but Mandela established the Truth and Reconciliation Commission. Rather than seeking vengeance for the crimes, this government agency investigated the atrocities with the mandate of granting amnesty to those individuals who confessed their roles in the violence and could prove that their actions served some political motive rather than being based on personal factors such as greed or jealousy. Supporters of the commission believe that this approach would help heal the nation's wounds and prevent years of racial and ethnic strife. Mandela, who had been unjustly jailed for twenty-seven years by the regime, had reason to desire vengeance. Yet, he wanted to move the country forward after the truth of what happened in the past had been established. Though many South Africans, including some ANC members, believe that the commission is too lenient, Mandela's attempts at reconciliation have prevailed. The commission is a model of restoration over revenge.

Australia

The justice system in Australia makes use of the conferencing process to divert offenders from the justice system. This offers offenders the opportunity to attend a conference to discuss and resolve their offense instead of being charged and appearing in court. (Those who deny guilt are not offered conferencing.) The conference, normally lasting 1 to 2 hours, is attended by the victims and their supporters, the defendant and his or her supporters, and other concerned parties. The conference coordinator focuses the discussion on condemning the act without condemning the character of the actor. Offenders are asked to tell their side of the story, what happened, how they have felt about the crime, and what they think should be done. The victims and others are asked to describe the physical, financial, and emotional consequences of the crime. This discussion may lead the offenders, their families, and their friends to experience the shame of the act, prompting an apology to the victim. A plan of action is developed and signed by key participants. The plan may include the offender paying compensation to the victim, doing work for the victim or the community, or similar solutions. It is the responsibility of the conference participants to determine the outcomes that are most appropriate for these particular victims and these particular offenders.

All eight states and territories in Australia have used the conference model, but there are five in which conferencing is active. Of these five jurisdictions, all but one (the Australian Capital Territory or ACT) has legislatively established conferencing. South Australia began to use conferences routinely in 1994, Western Australia and the ACT in 1995, and New South Wales in 1998. While Queensland is an active jurisdiction, it is experimenting with several formats of organizational placement and delivery, and conferencing is not available on a statewide basis. Tasmania passed legislation in 1997, which gave statutory authority to establish conferences, but a conferencing program has not yet started. The State of Victoria, like the ACT, is without a statutory scheme, but a community organization,

---

These are a few of the obstacles that restorative justice programs must overcome in order for it to be successful and productive. Yet, because the method holds so much promise, criminologists are now conducting numerous demonstration projects to find the most effective means of returning the ownership of justice to the people and the community.

 To quiz yourself on this material, go to the Criminology TPT 9e website.

 The **Justice Studies Association (JSA)** is a non-for-profit group established in 1998 to foster progressive writing, research, and practice in all areas of criminal, social, and restorative justice. Visit their website at http://www.justicestudies.org/. For an up-to-date list of web links, go to http://cj.wadsworth.com/siegel_crimtpt9e.

working in partnership with state agencies, uses the conference model in selected cases as a presentencing option.

Ireland

The Nenagh Community Reparation Project is managed by a local committee representing different community interests in partnership with the Probation and Welfare Service. It began on the initiative of Judge Michael Reilly, who with the cooperation of the community and various agencies has sought to use reparation in his court. In cases where an offender has admitted guilt, the judge can, at his or her discretion, offer the offender the choice of either the normal course of jail or participation in the community reparation project. At this point the court adjourns for approximately 30 minutes while the probation officer explains the project to the offender. If the offender decides to participate in the project, a meeting will be called in the near future.

This meeting is always attended by the offender, two panel members representing the community, the police officers who have been involved in the case, and the probation officer. If the crime involves victims, they are also invited to attend the meeting, although their participation is not mandatory.

At the meeting, offenders are asked to explain the circumstances of the offense, why it happened, how they felt about it then, and how they feel about their actions now. Together, the group decides how the offender might make reparation to the victim and/or the community for the damage caused by the offense.

Once agreement is reached about the form of the reparation, a contract is drawn up that sets out treatment courses (for example, treatment for alcoholism, substance abuse, anger management, and so on as appropriate) the offender will be expected to take. Reparation may include letters of apology to the victim, monetary restitution, and other proportionate and appropriate activities. Contracts generally cover a period of approximately 6 months and are monitored by the probation officer. If the terms of the contract are successfully completed, the record of the offense will be dropped. If the terms are not met, the case will go back to court and proceed in the normal manner.

Critical Thinking

Restorative justice may be the model that best serves alternative sanctions. How can this essentially humanistic approach be sold to the general public that now supports more punitive sanctions? For example, would it be

reasonable to expect that using restorative justice with nonviolent offenders frees up resources for the relatively few dangerous people in the criminal population? Explain.

 InfoTrac College Edition Research

To learn more about the restorative justice approach, see: Gordon Bazemore, "Restorative Justice and Earned Redemption: Communities, Victims, and Offender Reintegration," *American Behavioral Scientist* 41 (1998): 768; Tag Evers, "A Healing Approach to Crime," *The Progressive* 62 (1998): 30; Carol La Prairie, "The Impact of Aboriginal Justice Research on Policy: A Marginal Past and an Even More Uncertain Future," *Canadian Journal of Criminology* 41 (1999): 249.

Sources: Leena Kurki, *Incorporating Restorative and Community Justice into American Sentencing and Corrections* (Washington, DC: National Institute of Justice, 1999); Australian Government, Australian Institute of Criminology, "Restorative Justice: An Australian Perspective," http://www.aic.gov.au/rjustice/australia.html. Accessed August 4, 2004; Restorative Justice in Ireland, Nenagh Community Reparation Project, Co. Tipperary: http://www.extern.org/restorative/. Accessed August 4, 2004; John W. De Gruchy, *Reconciliation: Restoring Justice.* (Minneapolis: Fortress, 2002).

SUMMARY

- Social conflict theorists view crime as a function of the conflict that exists in society.

- Social conflict has its theoretical basis in the works of Karl Marx, as interpreted by Bonger, Dahrendorf, and Vold.

- Conflict theorists suggest that crime in any society is caused by class

conflict. Laws are created by those in power to protect their rights and interests.

- Social conflict theory is aimed at identifying "real" crimes in U.S. society, such as profiteering, sexism, and racism. It seeks to evaluate how criminal law is used as a mechanism of social control, and it describes

how power relations create inequities in U.S. society. Racism and classism pervade the U.S. justice system and shape crime rates.

- All criminal acts have political undertones. Quinney has called this concept "the social reality of crime."

- Research efforts to validate the conflict approach have not produced significant findings. One of conflict theory's most important premises is that the justice system is biased and designed to protect the wealthy. Research has not been unanimous in supporting this point.

- Critical criminology views the competitive nature of the capitalist system as a major cause of crime. The poor commit crimes because of their frustration, anger, and need. The wealthy engage in illegal acts because they are used to competition and because they must do so to keep their positions in society. In this view, the state serves the interests of the ruling capitalist class.

- Criminal law is an instrument of economic oppression. Capitalism demands that the subordinate classes remain oppressed.

- Critical scholars have attempted to show that the law is designed to protect the wealthy and powerful and to control the poor, have-not members of society.

- There are two main branches of critical theory referred to as instrumental and structural theory. Instrumental theorists believe that the legal system supports the owners at the expense of the workers. Structural theorists believe that the law also ensures that no capitalist becomes too powerful. The law is used to maintain the long-term interests of the capitalist system.

- Research on critical theory focuses on how the system of justice is designed to protect the interests of the upper classes. Critical research uses historical analysis to show how the capitalist classes have exerted their control over the police, courts, and correctional agencies. Critical criminology has been heavily criticized by conservatives who believe that it contains fundamental errors in the concept of ownership and class interest.

- Left realists take a centrist position on crime by showing its rational and destructive nature.

- Critical feminist writers draw attention to the influence of patriarchal society on crime and how abusive relationships lead to female criminality.

- Power–control theory considers that that gender differences in crime are a function of economic power (class position, one- versus two-earner families) and parental control (paternalistic versus egalitarian families).

- Postmodernism and deconstructionism look at the symbolic meaning of law and culture.

- Peacemaking theory brings a call for humanism to criminology.

- According to restorative justice, rather than punishing, shaming, and excluding those who violate the law, efforts should be made to use humanistic techniques that reintegrate people into society. Restorative programs rely on victims, relatives, neighbors, and community institutions rather than courts and prisons.

Thinking Like a Criminologist

An interim evaluation of Restoration House's New Hope for Families program, a community-based residential treatment program for women with dependent children, shows that 70 percent of women who complete follow-up interviews 6 months after treatment have maintained abstinence or reduced their drug use. The other 30 percent, however, lapse back into their old habits.

The program relies on restorative justice techniques in which community people meet with the women to discuss the harm drug use can cause and how it can damage both them and their children. The community members show their support and help the women find a niche in the community.

Women who complete the Restoration House program improve their employment, reduce parenting stress, retain custody of their children, and restore their physical, mental, and emotional health. The program focuses not only on reducing drug and alcohol use but also on increasing health, safety, self-sufficiency, and positive attitudes.

As a criminologist, would you consider this program a success? What questions would have to be answered before it gets your approval? How do you think the program should handle women who do not succeed in the program? Are there any other approaches you would try with these women? If so, explain.

Doing Research on the Web

Go to Restorative Justice Online, a nonpartisan source of information on restorative justice, to begin researching your answer: http://www.restorative justice.org/.

The Centre for Restorative Justice, at Simon Frazer University in British Columbia, Canada, in partnership with individuals, the community, and justice agencies, exists to support and promote the principles and practices of restorative justice by providing education, training, evaluation, and research. Visit their website at http://www.sfu.ca/crj/.

You might also want to use "restorative justice" in a key word search in InfoTrac College Edition.

| | | | | | | | | | | | | | | | | | | | | | | | | | | | | | | | | | | | | | | | | | | |

BOOK COMPANION WEBSITE

 http://cj.wadsworth.com/siegel_crimtpt9e To quiz yourself on the material in this chapter, go to the companion website, where you'll find chapter-by-chapter online tutorial quizzes, a final exam, ABC videos with questions, chapter outlines, chapter review, chapter-by-chapter web links, flash cards, and more!

KEY TERMS

Marxist criminologists (252)
radical criminologists (252)
social conflict theory (253)
communist manifesto (253)
productive forces (253)
productive relations (253)
capitalist bourgeoisie (253)
lumpen proletariat (253)
surplus value (254)
dialectic method (255)
thesis (255)
antithesis (255)
synthesis (255)

imperatively coordinated
   associations (256)
social reality of crime (257)
power (258)
marginalization (258)
critical criminologists (260)
critical criminology (260)
globalization (260)
instrumental critical theory (261)
demystify (261)
structural critical theory (261)
left realism (264)
preemptive deterrence (264)

critical feminist (264)
patriarchy (265)
paternalistic families (266)
role exit behaviors (266)
egalitarian families (266)
power–control theory (268)
postmodernists (268)
deconstructionists (268)
semiotics (268)
peacemaking (268)
restorative justice (269)
reintegrative shaming (270)
sentencing circle (272)

CRITICAL THINKING QUESTIONS

1. How would a conservative reply to a call for more restorative justice? How would a restorative justice advocate respond to a conservative call for more prisons?

2. Considering recent changes in American culture, how would a power–control theorist explain recent drops in the U.S. crime rate?

3. Is conflict inevitable in all cultures? If not, what can be done to reduce the level of conflict in our own society?

4. If Marx were alive today, what would he think about the prosperity enjoyed by the working class in industrial societies? Might he alter his vision of the capitalist system?

NOTES

1. Michael Lynch, "Rediscovering Criminology: Lessons from the Marxist Tradition," in *Marxist Sociology: Surveys of Contemporary Theory and Research,* eds. Donald McQuarie and Patrick McGuire (New York: General Hall Press, 1994).

2. Michael Lynch and W. Byron Groves, *A Primer in Radical Criminology,* 2nd ed.

(Albany, NY: Harrow & Heston, 1989), pp. 32–33.

3. See, generally, Karl Marx and Friedrich Engels, *Capital: A Critique of Political Economy,* trans. E. Aveling (Chicago: Charles Kern, 1906); Karl Marx, *Selected Writings in Sociology and Social Philosophy,* trans. P. B. Bottomore (New York: McGraw-Hill,

1956). For a general discussion of Marxist thought, see Lynch and Groves, *A Primer in Radical Criminology,* pp. 6–26.

4. Karl Marx, *Grundrisse: Introduction to the Critique of Political Economy,* trans. Martin Nicolaus (New York: Vintage, 1973), pp. 106–107.

5. Lynch, "Rediscovering Criminology."

6. Karl Marx, "Population, Crime and Pauperism," in *Karl Marx and Friedrich Engels, Ireland and the Irish Question* (Moscow: Progress, 1859, reprinted 1971), p. 92.

7. Friedrich Engels, *The Condition of the Working Class in England in 1844* (London: Allen & Unwin, 1950).

8. Lynch, "Rediscovering Criminology," p. 5.

9. Willem Bonger, *Criminality and Economic Conditions,* abridged ed. (Bloomington: Indiana University Press, 1969). [Originally published 1916]

10. Ralf Dahrendorf, *Class and Class Conflict in Industrial Society* (Palo Alto, CA: Stanford University Press, 1959).

11. Ibid., p. 48.

12. George Vold, *Theoretical Criminology* (New York: Oxford University Press, 1958).

13. James Short and F. Ivan Nye, "Extent of Undetected Delinquency: Tentative Conclusions," *Journal of Criminal Law, Criminology, and Police Science* 49 (1958): 296–302.

14. See, generally, Robert Meier, "The New Criminology: Continuity in Criminological Theory," *Journal of Criminal Law and Criminology* 67 (1977): 461–469.

15. David Greenberg, ed., *Crime and Capitalism* (Palo Alto, CA: Mayfield, 1981), p. 3.

16. William Chambliss and Robert Seidman, *Law, Order, and Power* (Reading, MA: Addison-Wesley, 1971), p. 503.

17. Richard Quinney, *The Social Reality of Crime* (Boston: Little, Brown, 1970).

18. John Braithwaite, "Retributivism, Punishment, and Privilege," in *Punishment and Privilege,* eds. W. Byron Groves and Graeme Newman (Albany, NY: Harrow & Heston, 1986), pp. 55–66.

19. Judith Blau and Peter Blau, "The Cost of Inequality: Metropolitan Structure and Violent Crime," *American Sociological Review* 147 (1982): 114–129; Richard Block, "Community Environment and Violent Crime," *Criminology* 17 (1979): 46–57; Robert Sampson, "Structural Sources of Variation in Race-Age-Specific Rates of Offending across Major U.S. Cities," *Criminology* 23 (1985): 647–673.

20. Travis Pratt and Christopher Lowenkamp, "Conflict Theory, Economic Conditions, and Homicide: A Time-Series Analysis," *Homicide Studies* 6 (2002): 61–84.

21. Ronald Weitzer and Steven Tuch, "Perceptions of Racial Profiling: Race, Class, and Personal Experience," *Criminology* 40 (2002): 435–456.

22. Albert Meehan and Michael Ponder, "Race and Place: The Ecology of Racial Profiling African American Motorists," *Justice Quarterly* 29 (2002): 399–431.

23. Malcolm Homes, "Minority Threat and Police Brutality: Determinants of Civil Rights Criminal Complaints in U.S. Municipalities," *Criminology* 38 (2000): 343–368.

24. Darrell Steffensmeier and Stephen Demuth, "Ethnicity and Judges' Sentencing Decisions: Hispanic-Black-White Comparisons," *Criminology* 39 (2001): 145–178; Alan Lizotte, "Extra-Legal Factors in Chicago's Criminal Courts: Testing the Conflict Model of Criminal Justice," *Social Problems* 25 (1978): 564–580.

25. Terance Miethe and Charles Moore, "Racial Differences in Criminal Processing: The Consequences of Model Selection on Conclusions about Differential Treatment," *Sociological Quarterly* 27 (1987): 217–237.

26. Tracy Nobiling, Cassia Spohn, and Miriam DeLone, "A Tale of Two Counties: Unemployment and Sentence Severity," *Justice Quarterly* 15 (1998): 459–485.

27. Charles Crawford, Ted Chiricos, and Gary Kleck, "Race, Racial Threat, and Sentencing of Habitual Offenders," *Criminology* 36 (1998): 481–511.

28. Thomas Arvanites, "Increasing Imprisonment: A Function of Crime or Socioeconomic Factors?" *American Journal of Criminal Justice* 17 (1992): 19–38.

29. David Greenberg and Valerie West, "State Prison Populations and their Growth, 1971–1991," *Criminology* 39 (2001): 615–654.

30. Ian Taylor, Paul Walton, and Jock Young, *The New Criminology: For a Social Theory of Deviance* (London: Routledge and Kegan Paul, 1973).

31. See, for example, Larry Tifft and Dennis Sullivan, *The Struggle to Be Human: Crime, Criminology, and Anarchism* (Over-the-Water-Sanday, Scotland: Cienfuegos Press, 1979); Dennis Sullivan, *The Mask of Love* (Port Washington, NY: Kennikat Press, 1980).

32. Tony Platt and Cecilia O'Leary, "Patriot Acts," *Social Justice* 30 (2003): 5–21.

33. Garrett Brown, "The Global Threats to Workers' Health and Safety on the Job," *Social Justice* 29 (2002): 12–25.

34. This section borrows heavily from Richard Sparks, "A Critique of Marxist Criminology," in *Crime and Justice,* vol. 2, eds. Norval Morris and Michael Tonry (Chicago: University of Chicago Press, 1980), pp. 159–208.

35. Barbara Sims, "Crime, Punishment, and the American Dream: Toward a Marxist Integration," *Journal of Research in Crime and Delinquency* 34 (1997): 5–24.

36. Jeffery Reiman, *The Rich Get Richer and the Poor Get Prison* (New York: Wiley, 1984), pp. 43–44.

37. Rob White, "Environmental Harm and the Political Economy of Consumption," *Social Justice* 29 (2002): 82–102.

38. Sims, "Crime, Punishment, and the American Dream."

39. Ibid., p. 4.

40. Bill Dixon, "In Search of Interactive Globalisation: Critical Criminology in South Africa's Transition," *Crime, Law, and Social Change* 41 (2004): 359–384.

41. David Friedrichs and Jessica Friedrichs, "The World Bank and Crimes of Globalization: A Case Study," *Social Justice* 29 (2002): 13–36.

42. Jean-Germain Gros, "Trouble in Paradise: Crime and Collapsed States in the Age of Globalization," *British Journal of Criminology* 43 (2003): 63–80.

43. Robert Rotberg, *State Failure and State Weakness in a Time of Terror* (Washington, DC: World Peace Foundation, 2003).

44. Gresham Sykes, "The Rise of Critical Criminology," *Journal of Criminal Law and Criminology* 65 (1974): 211–229.

45. David Jacobs, "Corporate Economic Power and the State: A Longitudinal Assessment of Two Explanations," *American Journal of Sociology* 93 (1988): 852–881.

46. Associated Press, "Bill Could Raise Values of Sports Teams," *New York Times,* 2 August 2004, p. A1.

47. Deanna Alexander, "Victims of the L.A. Riots: A Theoretical Consideration." Paper presented at the annual meeting of the American Society of Criminology, Phoenix, November 1993.

48. Richard Quinney, "Crime Control in Capitalist Society," in *Critical Criminol-*

ogy, eds. Ian Taylor, Paul Walton, and Jock Young (London: Routledge and Kegan Paul, 1975), p. 199.

49. Ibid.

50. John Hagan, *Structural Criminology* (New Brunswick, NJ: Rutgers University Press, 1989), pp. 110–119.

51. Roy Bhaskar, "Empiricism," in *A Dictionary of Marxist Thought,* ed. T. Bottomore (Cambridge, MA: Harvard University Press, 1983), pp. 149–150.

52. Byron Groves, "Marxism and Positivism," *Crime and Social Justice* 23 (1985): 129–150; Michael Lynch, "Quantitative Analysis and Marxist Criminology: Some Old Answers to a Dilemma in Marxist Criminology," *Crime and Social Justice* 29 (1987): 110–117.

53. Alan Lizotte, James Mercy, and Eric Monkkonen, "Crime and Police Strength in an Urban Setting: Chicago, 1947–1970," in *Quantitative Criminology,* ed. John Hagan (Beverly Hills: Sage, 1982), pp. 129–148.

54. William Chambliss, "The State, the Law, and the Definition of Behavior as Criminal or Delinquent," in *Handbook of Criminology,* ed. D. Glazer (Chicago: Rand McNally, 1974), pp. 7–44.

55. Timothy Carter and Donald Clelland, "A Neo-Marxian Critique, Formulation, and Test of Juvenile Dispositions as a Function of Social Class," *Social Problems* 27 (1979): 96–108.

56. David Greenberg, "Socio-Economic Status and Criminal Sentences: Is There an Association?" *American Sociological Review* 42 (1977): 174–175; David Greenberg and Drew Humphries, "The Co-Optation of Fixed Sentencing Reform," *Crime and Delinquency* 26 (1980): 206–225.

57. Steven Box, *Power, Crime and Mystification* (London: Tavistock, 1984); Gregg Barak, *In Defense of Whom? A Critique of Criminal Justice Reform* (Cincinnati: Anderson, 1980). For an opposing view, see Franklin Williams, "Conflict Theory and Differential Processing: An Analysis of the Research Literature," in *Radical Criminology: The Coming Crisis,* ed. J. Inciardi (Beverly Hills: Sage, 1980), pp. 213–231.

58. Robert Weiss, "Repatriating Low-Wage Work: The Political Economy of Prison Labor Reprivatization in the Postindustrial United States," *Criminology* 39 (2001): 253–292.

59. Dragan Milovanovic, "Postmodern Criminology: Mapping the Terrain," *Justice Quarterly* 13 (1996): 567–610.

60. Michael Rustigan, "A Reinterpretation of Criminal Law Reform in Nineteenth-Century England," in *Crime and Capitalism,* ed. D. Greenberg (Palo Alto, CA: Mayfield, 1981), pp. 255–278.

61. Rosalind Petchesky, "At Hard Labor: Penal Confinement and Production in Nineteenth-Century America," in *Crime and Capitalism,* ed. D. Greenberg (Palo Alto, CA: Mayfield, 1981), pp. 341–357; Paul Takagi, "The Walnut Street Jail: A Penal Reform to Centralize the Powers of the State," *Federal Probation* 49 (1975): 18–26.

62. Jack Gibbs, "An Incorrigible Positivist," *Criminologist* 12 (1987): 2–3.

63. Jackson Toby, "The New Criminology Is the Old Sentimentality," *Criminology* 16 (1979): 513–526.

64. Sparks, "A Critique of Marxist Criminology."

65. Carl Klockars, "The Contemporary Crises of Marxist Criminology," in *Radical Criminology: The Coming Crisis,* ed. J. Inciardi (Beverly Hills: Sage, 1980), pp. 92–123.

66. Matthew Petrocelli, Alex Piquero, and Michael Smith, "Conflict Theory and Racial Profiling: An Empirical Analysis of Police Traffic Stop Data," *Journal of Criminal Justice* 31 (2003): 1–10.

67. Ibid.

68. Michael Lynch, W. Byron Groves, and Alan Lizotte, "The Rate of Surplus Value and Crime: A Theoretical and Empirical Examination of Marxian Economic Theory and Criminology," *Crime, Law, and Social Change* 18 (1994): 1–11.

69. Anthony Platt, "Criminology in the 1980s: Progressive Alternatives to 'Law and Order,'" *Crime and Social Justice* 21–22 (1985): 191–199.

70. See, generally, Roger Matthews and Jock Young, eds., *Confronting Crime* (London: Sage, 1986); for a thorough review of left realism, see Martin Schwartz and Walter DeKeseredy, "Left Realist Criminology: Strengths, Weaknesses, and the Feminist Critique," *Crime, Law, and Social Change* 15 (1991): 51–72.

71. John Lea and Jock Young, *What Is to Be Done About Law and Order?* (Harmondsworth, England: Penguin, 1984).

72. Ibid., p. 88.

73. Ian Taylor, *Crime in Context: A Critical Criminology of Market Societies* (Boulder, CO: Westview Press, 1999).

74. Ibid., pp. 30–31.

75. Richard Kinsey, John Lea, and Jock Young, *Losing the Fight against Crime* (London: Blackwell, 1986).

76. Martin Schwartz and Walter DeKeseredy, *Contemporary Criminology* (Belmont, CA: Wadsworth, 1993), p. 249.

77. Schwartz and DeKeseredy, "Left Realist Criminology."

78. For a general review of this issue, see Kathleen Daly and Meda Chesney-Lind, "Feminism and Criminology," *Justice Quarterly* 5 (1988): 497–538; Douglas Smith and Raymond Paternoster, "The Gender Gap in Theories of Deviance: Issues and Evidence," *Journal of Research in Crime and Delinquency* 24 (1987): 140–172; and Pat Carlen, "Women, Crime, Feminism, and Realism," *Social Justice* 17 (1990): 106–123.

79. Herman Schwendinger and Julia Schwendinger, *Rape and Inequality* (Newbury Park, CA: Sage, 1983).

80. Daly and Chesney-Lind, "Feminism and Criminology."

81. Janet Saltzman Chafetz, "Feminist Theory and Sociology: Underutilized Contributions for Mainstream Theory," *Annual Review of Sociology* 23 (1997): 97–121.

82. Ibid.

83. James Messerschmidt, *Capitalism, Patriarchy, and Crime* (Totowa, NJ: Rowman and Littlefield, 1986); for a critique of this work, see Herman Schwendinger and Julia Schwendinger, "The World According to James Messerschmidt," *Social Justice* 15 (1988): 123–145.

84. Kathleen Daly, "Gender and Varieties of White-Collar Crime," *Criminology* 27 (1989): 769–793.

85. Jane Roberts Chapman, "Violence against Women as a Violation of Human Rights," *Social Justice* 17 (1990): 54–71.

86. James Messerschmidt, *Masculinities and Crime: Critique and Reconceptualization of Theory* (Lanham, MD: Rowman and Littlefield, 1993).

87. Angela P. Harris, "Gender, Violence, Race, and Criminal Justice," *Stanford Law Review* 52 (2000): 777–810

88. Carrie Yodanis, "Gender Inequality, Violence against Women, and Fear," *Journal of Interpersonal Violence* 19 (2004): 655–675.

89. Suzie Dod Thomas and Nancy Stein, "Criminality, Imprisonment, and Women's Rights in the 1990s," *Social Justice* 17 (1990): 1–5.

90. Walter DeKeseredy and Martin Schwartz, "Male Peer Support and Woman Abuse: An Expansion of DeKeseredy's Model," *Sociological Spectrum* 13 (1993): 393–413.

91. Daly and Chesney-Lind, "Feminism and Criminology." See also Drew Humphries and Susan Caringella-MacDonald, "Murdered Mothers, Missing Wives: Reconsidering Female Victimization," *Social Justice* 17 (1990): 71–78.

92. Jane Siegel and Linda Meyer Williams, "Aggressive Behavior among Women Sexually Abused as Children." Paper presented at the annual meeting of the American Society of Criminology, Phoenix, 1993, revised version.

93. Susan Ehrlich Martin and Nancy Jurik, *Doing Justice, Doing Gender* (Thousand Oaks, CA: Sage, 1996), p. 27.

94. Ruth Alexander, *The "Girl Problem": Female Sexual Delinquency in New York, 1900–1930* (Ithaca, NY: Cornell University Press, 1995).

95. Mary Odem and Steven Schlossman, "Guardians of Virtue: The Juvenile Court and Female Delinquency in Early 20th-Century Los Angeles," *Crime and Delinquency* 37 (1991): 186–203.

96. Meda Chesney-Lind, "Judicial Enforcement of the Female Sex Role: The Family Court and the Female Delinquent," *Issues in Criminology* 8 (1973): 51–69. See also Meda Chesney-Lind, "Women and Crime: The Female Offender," *Signs: Journal of Women in Culture and Society* 12 (1986): 78–96; "Female Offenders: Paternalism Reexamined," in *Women, the Courts, and Equality,* eds. Laura L. Crites and Winifred L. Hepperle (Newbury Park, CA: Sage, 1987): 114–139; "Girls' Crime and a Woman's Place: Toward a Feminist Model of Female Delinquency." Paper presented at the annual meeting of the American Society of Criminology, Montreal, 1987.

97. Hagan, *Structural Criminology.*

98. John Hagan, A. R. Gillis, and John Simpson, "The Class Structure and Delinquency: Toward a Power-Control Theory of Common Delinquent Behavior," *American Journal of Sociology* 90 (1985): 1151–1178; John Hagan, John Simpson, and A. R. Gillis, "Class in the Household: A Power-Control Theory of Gender and Delinquency," *American Journal of Sociology* 92 (1987): 788–816.

99. John Hagan, Bill McCarthy, and Holly Foster, "A Gendered Theory of Delinquency and Despair in the Life Course," *Acta Sociologica* 45 (2002): 37–47.

100. Brenda Sims Blackwell, Christine Sellers, and Sheila Schlaupitz, "A Power-Control Theory of Vulnerability to Crime and Adolescent Role Exits—Revisited," *Canadian Review of Sociology and Anthropology* 39 (2002): 199–219.

101. Brenda Sims Blackwell, "Perceived Sanction Threats, Gender, and Crime: A Test and Elaboration of Power-Control Theory," *Criminology* 38 (2000): 439–488.

102. Christopher Uggen, "Class, Gender, and Arrest: An Intergenerational Analysis of Workplace Power and Control," *Criminology* 38 (2001): 835–862.

103. Gary Jensen, "Power-Control versus Social-Control Theory: Identifying Crucial Differences for Future Research." Paper presented at the annual meeting of the American Society of Criminology, Baltimore, November 1990.

104. Gary Jensen and Kevin Thompson, "What's Class Got to Do with It? A Further Examination of Power-Control Theory," *American Journal of Sociology* 95 (1990): 1009–1023. For some critical research, see Simon Singer and Murray Levine, "Power Control Theory, Gender, and Delinquency: A Partial Replication with Additional Evidence on the Effects of Peers," *Criminology* 26 (1988): 627–648.

105. Kevin Thompson, "Gender and Adolescent Drinking Problems: The Effects of Occupational Structure," *Social Problems* 36 (1989): 30–38.

106. See, generally, Uggen, "Class, Gender, and Arrest."

107. See, generally, Lynch, "Rediscovering Criminology," pp. 27–28.

108. See, generally, Stuart Henry and Dragan Milovanovic, *Constitutive Criminology: Beyond Postmodernism* (London: Sage, 1996).

109. Dragan Milovanovic, *A Primer in the Sociology of Law* (Albany, NY: Harrow & Heston, 1988), pp. 127–128.

110. See, generally, Henry and Milovanovic, *Constitutive Criminology.*

111. Bruce Arrigo and Thomas Bernard, "Postmodern Criminology in Relation to Radical and Conflict Criminology," *Critical Criminology* 8 (1997): 39–60.

112. Liz Walz, "One Blood," *Contemporary Justice Review* 6 (2003): 25–36.

113. See, for example, Tifft and Sullivan, *The Struggle to Be Human*; Sullivan, *The Mask of Love.*

114. Larry Tifft, "Foreword," in Sullivan, *The Mask of Love,* p. 6.

115. Sullivan, *The Mask of Love,* p. 141.

116. Dennis Sullivan and Larry Tifft, *Restorative Justice* (Monsey, NY: Willow Tree Press, 2001).

117. Richard Quinney, "The Way of Peace: On Crime, Suffering, and Service," in *Criminology as Peacemaking,* eds. Harold Pepinsky and Richard Quinney (Bloomington: Indiana University Press, 1991), pp. 8–9.

118. For a review of Quinney's ideas, see Kevin B. Anderson, "Richard Quinney's Journey: The Marxist Dimension," *Crime and Delinquency* 48 (2002): 232–242.

119. Robert DeFina and Thomas Arvanites, "The Weak Effect of Imprisonment on Crime: 1971–1998," *Social Science Quarterly* 83 (2002): 635–654.

120. Kathleen Daly and Russ Immarigeon, "The Past, Present, and Future of Restorative Justice: Some Critical Reflections," *Contemporary Justice Review* 1 (1998): 21–45.

121. John Braithwaite, *Crime, Shame, and Reintegration* (Melbourne, Australia: Cambridge University Press, 1989).

122. Ibid., p. 81.

123. Anthony Petrosino and Carolyn Petrosino, "The Public Safety Potential of Megan's Law in Massachusetts: An Assessment from a Sample of Criminal Sexual Psychopaths," *Crime and Delinquency* 45 (1999): 140–158.

124. For more on this approach, see Jane Mugford and Stephen Mugford, "Shame and Reintegration in the Punishment and Deterrence of Spouse Assault." Paper presented at the annual meeting of the American Society of Criminology, San Francisco, 1991.

125. Carter Hay, "An Exploratory Test of Braithwaite's Reintegrative Shaming Theory," *Journal of Research in Crime and Delinquency* 38 (2001): 132–153.

126. Mugford and Mugford, "Shame and Reintegration in the Punishment and Deterrence of Spouse Assault."

127. Howard Zehr, *The Little Book of Restorative Justice* (Intercourse, PA: Good Books, 2002), pp. 1-10.

128. Mark Lewis Taylor, *The Executed God: The Way of the Cross in Lockdown America* (Minneapolis: Fortress Press, 2001).

129. Gene Stephens, "The Future of Policing: From a War Model to a Peace Model," in *The Past, Present, and Future of American Criminal Justice,* eds. Brendan Maguire and Polly Radosh (Dix Hills, NY: General Hall, 1996), pp. 77–93.

130. Rick Shifley, "The Organization of Work as a Factor in Social Well-Being," *Contemporary Justice Review* 6 (2003): 105–126.

131. Hennessey Hayes and Kathleen Daly, "Youth Justice Conferencing and Reoffending," *Justice Quarterly* 20 (2003): 725–764.

132. Kay Pranis, "Peacemaking Circles: Restorative Justice in Practice Allows Victims and Offenders to Begin Repairing the Harm," *Corrections Today* 59 (1007): 74; see also, Kay Pranis, Stuart Barry, and Mark Wedge, *Peacemaking Circles: From Crime to Community* (St. Paul, MN: Living Justice Press, 2003).

133. Carol LaPrairie, "The 'New' Justice: Some Implications for Aboriginal Communities," *Canadian Journal of Criminology* 40 (1998): 61–79.

134. Edward Gumz, "American Social Work, Corrections, and Restorative Justice: An Appraisal," *International Journal of Offender Therapy & Comparative Criminology* 48 (2004): 449–460.

135. Diane Schaefer, "A Disembodied Community Collaborates in a Homicide: Can Empathy Transform a Failing Justice System?" *Contemporary Justice Review* 6 (2003): 133–143.

136. David R. Karp and Beau Breslin, "Restorative Justice in School Communities," *Youth and Society* 33 (2001): 249–272.

137. Paul Jesilow and Deborah Parsons, "Community Policing as Peacemaking," *Policing and Society* 10 (2000): 163–183.

138. L. Thomas Winfree, Jr., "New Zealand Police and Restorative Justice Philosophy," *Crime and Delinquency* 50 (2004): 189–213.

139. Gordon Bazemore and Curt Taylor Griffiths, "Conferences, Circles, Boards, and Mediations: The 'New Wave' of Community Justice Decision Making," *Federal Probation* 61 (1997): 25–37.

140. This section is based on Gordon Bazemore and Mara Schiff, "Paradigm Muddle or Paradigm Paralysis? The Wide and Narrow Roads to Restorative Justice Reform (or, a Little Confusion May Be a Good Thing)," *Contemporary Justice Review* 7 (2004): 37–57.

141. John Braithwaite, "Setting Standard for Restorative Justice," *British Journal of Criminology* 42 (2002): 563–577.

142. David Altschuler, "Community Justice Initiatives: Issues and Challenges in the U.S. Context," *Federal Probation* 65 (2001): 28–33.

143. Lois Presser and Patricia Van Voorhis, "Values and Evaluation: Assessing Processes and Outcomes of Restorative Justice Programs," *Crime and Delinquency* 48 (2002): 162–189.

144. Declan Roche, *Accountability in Restorative Justice* (Clarendon Studies in Criminology) (London: Oxford University Press, 2004).

145. Sharon Levrant, Francis Cullen, Betsy Fulton, and John Wozniak, "Reconsidering Restorative Justice: The Corruption of Benevolence Revisited?" *Crime and Delinquency* 45 (1999): 3–28.

CHAPTER 9

© AP Photo/Doug Dreyer/Wide World Photos

William Janklow was a major force in South Dakota politics, serving terms as attorney general, governor, and then congressman. On August 16, 2003, he killed Randy Scott, who was on a motorcycle when Janklow ran a stop sign and hit him. Despite his political prominence, Janklow, 64, was charged with manslaughter, reckless driving, running a stop sign, and speeding. At his trial the defense argued that Janklow, a diabetic, was suffering the effects of low blood sugar at the time of the crash but did not know it because the symptoms were masked by heart medication. Witnesses rebuked that defense and testified that Janklow was driving in a reckless fashion, plowing through a stop sign at more than 70 miles per hour.

Though the prosecution wanted to enter evidence of Janklow's long history of irresponsible behavior, the trial judge prohibited prosecutors from mentioning his 12 prior speeding tickets and three accidents. Yet, most South Dakotans knew that Janklow loved roaring down the South Dakota roads, flaunting the speed limits. He bragged about his uncontrolled driving in speeches, and, as the state's attorney general and governor, he had his car equipped with a siren and flashing red light. On December 18, 2003, he was found guilty of all four charges. After serving 100 days, he walked out of the Minnehaha County Jail on May 17, 2004.

DEVELOPMENTAL THEORIES: LIFE COURSE AND LATENT TRAIT

CHAPTER OBJECTIVES

1. Be familiar with the concept of developmental theory
2. Know the factors that influence the life course
3. Recognize that there are different pathways to crime
4. Know what is meant by problem behavior syndrome
5. Differentiate between adolescent-limited and life course persistent offenders
6. Be familiar with the turning points in crime
7. Be able to discuss the influence of social capital on crime
8. Know what is meant by a latent trait
9. Be familiar with the concepts of impulsivity and self-control
10. Be able to discuss Gottfredson and Hirschi's General Theory of Crime

How can the chronic, risk-taking behavior of a Bill Janklow be explained? Certainly his antisocial acts were not the product of economic needs, a deprived background, or a troubled childhood. What could explain such reckless and impulsive risk taking?

Some experts believe antisocial behavior is a function of some personal trait, such as a low IQ or impulsive personality, which is present at birth or soon afterward. Yet, if the onset of crime is explained by abnormally low intelligence or a defective personality, why is it that most people **desist** or age out of crime as they mature? It seems unlikely that intelligence increases as young offenders mature or that personality flaws disappear. And why is it that most antisocial people start their criminal career with relatively minor crimes, such as shoplifting or smoking marijuana, and then commit progressively more serious crimes, such as burglary and rape? Even if the onset of criminality can be explained by a single biological or personal trait, some other factor must explain its change, development, and continuance or termination.

||||||| **CONNECTIONS** |||||||

Chapter 2 addressed the issues of both chronic offending and aging out. These two issues are the cornerstones of contemporary criminological theories.

Concern over these critical issues has prompted some criminologists to identify, describe, and understand the developmental factors that explain the onset and continuation of a criminal career. Rather than look at a single factor, such as poverty or low intelligence, and suggest that people who maintain this trait are predisposed to crime, **developmental theories** attempt to provide a more global vision of a criminal career, encompassing its onset, continuation, and termination.

FOUNDATIONS OF DEVELOPMENTAL THEORY

The foundation of developmental theory can be traced to the pioneering work of Sheldon and Eleanor Glueck. While at Harvard University in the 1930s, the Gluecks popularized research on the life cycle of delinquent careers. In a series of longitudinal research studies, they followed the careers of known delinquents to determine the factors that predicted persistent offending.[1] The Gluecks made extensive use of interviews and records in their elaborate comparisons of delinquents and nondelinquents.[2]

The Gluecks' research focused on early onset of delinquency as a harbinger of a criminal career: "[T]he deeper the roots of childhood maladjustment, the smaller the chance of adult adjustment."[3] They also noted the stability of offending careers: Children who are antisocial early in life are the most likely to continue their offending careers into adulthood.

The Gluecks identified a number of personal and social factors related to persistent offending, the most important of which was family relations. This factor was considered in terms of quality of discipline and emotional ties with parents. The adolescent raised in a large, single-parent family of limited economic means and educational achievement was the most vulnerable to delinquency.

||||||| **CONNECTIONS** |||||||

Social process theories lay the foundation for assuming that peer, family, educational, and other interactions, which vary over the life course, influence behaviors. See the first few sections of Chapter 7 for a review of these issues. As you may recall from Chapter 2, a great deal of research has been conducted on the relationship of age and crime and the activities of chronic offenders. This scholarship has prompted interest in the life cycle of crime.

The Gluecks did not restrict their analysis to social variables. When they measured such biological and psychological traits as body type, intelligence, and personality, they found that physical and mental factors also played a role in determining behavior. Children with low intelligence, who had a background of mental disease, and who had a powerful (mesomorph) physique were the most likely to become persistent offenders.

The Gluecks' research was virtually ignored for nearly thirty years as the study of crime and delinquency shifted almost exclusively to social and social-psychological factors (such as poverty, neighborhood deterioration, and socialization) that formed the nucleus of structural and process theories. The Gluecks' methodology and their integration of biological, psychological, and social factors were heavily criticized, and for many years their work was ignored in criminology texts and overlooked in the academic curriculum.

Do scientists still believe that body build and physique can shape behavior? To find out, read: Alan Dixson, Gayle Halliwell, Rebecca East, Praveen Wignarajah, and Matthew Anderson, "Masculine Somatotype and Hirsuteness as Determinants of Sexual Attractiveness to Women, " *Archives of Sexual Behavior* 32 (2003): 29–40.

During the 1990s, the Glueck legacy was rediscovered in a series of papers by criminologists Robert Sampson and John Laub who used modern statistical techniques to reanalyze the Gluecks' carefully drawn empirical measurements. Their findings, published in a series of books and articles, fueled the popularity of the developmental approach.[4]

||||||| **CONNECTIONS** |||||||

Laub and Sampson's findings, drawn from the Glueck data, are covered later in this chapter.

The critical Philadelphia cohort research by Marvin Wolfgang and his associates was another milestone prompting interest in explaining criminal career development.[5]

As you may recall, Wolfgang found that while many offenders commit a single criminal act and desist from crime, a small group of chronic offenders engage in frequent and repeated criminal activity and continue to do so across their life span. Wolfgang's research focused attention on criminal careers. Criminologists were now asking this fundamental question: What prompts one person to engage in persistent criminal activity while another, who on the surface suffers the same life circumstances, finds a way to steer clear of crime and travel along a more conventional path?

A 1990 review paper by Rolf Loeber and Marc LeBlanc was another important event that generated interest in developmental theory. In this landmark work, Loeber and LeBlanc proposed that criminologists should devote time and effort to understanding some basic questions about the evolution of criminal careers: Why do people begin committing antisocial acts? Why do some stop while others continue? Why do some escalate the severity of their criminality (that is, go from shoplifting to drug dealing to armed robbery) while others deescalate and commit less serious crimes as they mature? If some terminate their criminal activity, what, if anything, causes them to begin again? Why do some criminals specialize in certain types of crime, whereas others are generalists engaging in a variety of antisocial behavior? According to Loeber and LeBlanc's developmental view, criminologists must pay attention to how a criminal career unfolds, how it begins, why it is sustained, and how it comes to an end.[6]

To read a paper cowritten by Rolf Loeber, go to: Jennifer M. Beyers and Rolf Loeber, "Untangling Developmental Relations between Depressed Mood and Delinquency in Male Adolescents," *Journal of Abnormal Child Psychology* 31 (2003): 247–266.

These scholarly advances created enormous excitement among criminologists and focused their attention on criminal career research. As research on criminal careers has evolved, two distinct viewpoints have taken shape: the life course view and the latent trait view. **Life course theories** view criminality as a dynamic process, influenced by a multitude of individual characteristics, traits, and social experiences. As people travel through the life course, they are constantly bombarded by changing perceptions and experiences, and as a result their behavior will change directions, sometimes for the better and sometimes for the worse (Figure 9.1).

In contrast, **latent trait theories** hold that human development is controlled by a "master trait," present at birth or soon after. Some latent trait theorists maintain that this master trait is inflexible, stable, and unchanging throughout a person's lifetime, while others recognize that under some circumstances a latent trait can be altered or influenced by experiences and interactions (Concept Summary 9.1). In either event, this trait is always there in people's lives, directing their behavior and shaping their life course. Because this master trait is enduring, the ebb and flow of criminal behavior is directed by the impact of external forces such as interpersonal interactions and criminal opportunity; although people do not change, their opportunities and experiences do. Each of these positions is discussed in detail in the following sections.

CONCEPT SUMMARY 9.1

Two Types of Latent Traits

Constant Latent Trait	Evolving Latent Trait
Inflexible	Flexible
Unchanging	Varying
Influenced by psychological/biological traits and conditions	Influenced by human interaction: relationships, contacts, and associations

FIGURE 9.1

Life Course and Latent Trait Theories

Latent Trait Theory

Master trait guides behavior
• Impulsivity
• Control-Balance
• Oppression

Life Course Theory

The propensity for crime changes over the life course.
Multiple pathways to crime.
Multiple classes of criminals.
Crime and its causes are interactional: They affect each other.

Criminal careers are a passage; Personal, social, and/or environmental factors influence the decision to commit crime; Crime not a constant but may increase or decrease in severity, frequency, and variety; Developmental factors produce not only crime but other antisocial, risky behaviors.

LIFE COURSE FUNDAMENTALS

According to the life course view, even as toddlers people begin relationships and behaviors that will determine their adult life course. At first they must learn to conform to social rules and function effectively in society. Later they are expected to begin to think about careers, leave their parental homes, find permanent relationships, and eventually marry and begin their own families.[7] These transitions are expected to take place in order—beginning with finishing school, then entering the workforce, getting married, and having children.

Some individuals, however, are incapable of maturing in a reasonable and timely fashion because of family, environmental, or personal problems. In some cases, transitions can occur too early—an adolescent girl who engages in precocious sex, gets pregnant, and is forced to drop out of high school. In other cases, transitions may occur too late—a teenage male falls in with the wrong crowd, goes to prison, and finds it difficult to break into the job market; he puts off getting married because of his diminished economic circumstances. Sometimes interruption of one trajectory can harm another—a teenager who has family problems may find that her educational and career development is upset.

Republished with permission of Globe Newspaper Company, Inc.

This is Richard Marinick, who started out as a bouncer in local bars, earned a black belt in Karate and became a State Police officer in Massachusetts. Developing a drug habit, he quit the police, joined a gang and got involved in enforcement beatings, truck-hijacking, bank robberies, and armored car holdups. After being caught and sentenced to prison, he decided to change his life. In prison, he got religion, earned two college degrees, and went into counseling. Released after serving 10 years, he got married, found work, and became an author. Is Marinick unique? Do most people have the power to alter the direction of their life course?

Because the transition from one stage of life to another can be a bumpy ride, the propensity to commit crimes is neither stable nor constant: It is a developmental process. A positive life experience may help some criminals desist from crime for a while, whereas a negative one may cause them to resume their activities. Criminal careers are said to be developmental because people are influenced by the behavior of those around them, and they, in turn, influence others' behavior. A youth's antisocial behavior may turn his more conventional friends against him; their rejection solidifies and escalates his antisocial behavior.[8]

Disruptions in life's major transitions can be destructive and ultimately can promote criminality. Those who are already at risk because of socioeconomic problems or family dysfunction are the most susceptible to these awkward transitions. Criminality, according to this view, cannot be attributed to a single cause, nor does it represent a single underlying tendency.[9] People are influenced by different factors as they mature. Consequently, a factor that may have an important influence at one stage of life (such as delinquent peers) may have little influence later on.[10]

These negative life events can become cumulative: As people acquire more personal deficits, the chances of acquiring additional ones increases.[11] The cumulative impact of these disruptions sustains criminality from childhood into adulthood.[12]

| | | | | | | | CONNECTIONS | | | | | | | |

In Chapter 8 the "cumulative disadvantage" created by official intervention and labels was discussed. Labeling may obstruct the developmental process by increasing the likelihood of antisocial behavior.

Life course theories also recognize that as people mature, the factors that influence their behavior change.[13] As people make important life transitions—from child to adolescent, from adolescent to adult, from unwed to married—the nature of social interactions changes.[14]

At first, family relations may be most influential. It comes as no shock to life course theorists when research shows that criminality runs in families and that having criminal relatives is a significant predictor of future misbehaviors.[15] In later adolescence, school and peer relations predominate; in adulthood, vocational achievement and marital relations may be the most critical influences. Some antisocial children who are in trouble throughout their adolescence may manage to find stable work and maintain intact marriages as adults; these life events help them desist from crime. In contrast, less fortunate adolescents who develop arrest records and get involved with the wrong crowd may find themselves limited to menial jobs and at risk for criminal careers.

A view of crime has emerged that incorporates personal change and growth. The factors that produce crime and delinquency at one point in the life cycle may not be relevant at another; as people mature, the social, physical, and environmental influences on their behavior are transformed.

People may show a propensity to offend early in their lives, but the nature and frequency of their activities are often affected by forces beyond their control, which elevate and sustain their criminal activity.[16]

The next sections review some of the more important concepts associated with the developmental perspective and discuss some prominent life course theories.

Problem Behavior Syndrome

Most criminological theories portray crime as the outcome of social problems. Learning theorists view a troubled home life and deviant friends as precursors of criminality; structural theorists maintain that acquiring deviant cultural values leads to criminality. In contrast, the developmental view is that criminality may best be understood as one of many social problems faced by at-risk youth, a view called **problem behavior syndrome (PBS).** According to this view, crime is one among a group of interrelated antisocial behaviors that cluster together and typically involve family dysfunction, sexual and physical abuse, substance abuse, smoking, precocious sexuality and early pregnancy, educational underachievement, suicide attempts, sensation seeking, and unemployment.[17] People who suffer from one of these conditions typically exhibit many symptoms of the rest.[18] All varieties of criminal behavior, including violence, theft, and drug offenses, may be part of a generalized PBS, indicating that all forms of antisocial behavior have similar developmental patterns (Exhibit 9.1).[19]

Many examples support the existence of PBS:[20]

- Adolescents with a history of gang involvement are more likely to have been expelled from school, be a binge drinker, test positively for marijuana, have been in three or more fights in the past 6 months, have a nonmonogamous partner, and test positive for sexually transmitted diseases.[21]

- Kids who gamble and take risks at an early age also take drugs and commit crimes.[22]

- People who exhibit one of these conditions typically exhibit many of the others.[23]

Those who suffer PBS are prone to more difficulties than the general population.[24] They find themselves with a range of personal dilemmas ranging from drug abuse to being accident prone, to requiring more healthcare and hospitalization, to becoming teenage parents, to having mental health problems.[25] PBS has been linked to individual-level personality problems (such as impulsiveness, rebelliousness, and low ego), family problems (such as intrafamily conflict and parental mental disorder), substance abuse, and educational failure.[26] Research shows that social problems such as drug abuse, low income, aggression, single parenthood, residence in isolated urban areas, lack of family support or resources, racism, and prolonged exposure to poverty are all interrelated.[27] According to this view, crime is a type of social problem rather than the product of other social problems.[28]

EXHIBIT 9.1
Problem Behaviors

Social
- Family dysfunction
- Unemployment
- Educational underachievement
- School misconduct

Personal
- Substance abuse
- Suicide attempts
- Early sexuality
- Sensation seeking
- Early parenthood
- Accident prone
- Medical problems
- Mental disease
- Anxiety
- Eating disorders (bulimia, anorexia)

Environmental
- High-crime area
- Disorganized area
- Racism
- Exposure to poverty

Pathways to Crime

Some life course theorists recognize that career criminals may travel more than a single road: Some may specialize in violence and extortion; some may be involved in theft and fraud; others may engage in a variety of criminal acts. Some offenders may begin their careers early in life, whereas others are late bloomers who begin committing crime when most people desist. Some are frequent offenders while others travel a more moderate path.[29]

Some of the most important research on delinquent paths or trajectories has been conducted by Rolf Loeber and his associates. Using data from a longitudinal study of Pittsburgh youth, Loeber has identified three distinct paths to a criminal career (Figure 9.2).[30]

1. The **authority conflict pathway** begins at an early age with stubborn behavior. This leads to defiance (doing things one's own way, disobedience) and then to authority avoidance (staying out late, truancy, running away).

2. The **covert pathway** begins with minor, underhanded behavior (lying, shoplifting) that leads to property damage (setting nuisance fires, damaging property). This behavior eventually escalates to more serious forms of criminality, ranging from joyriding, pocket picking, larceny, and fencing to passing bad checks,

FIGURE 9.2

Loeber's Pathways to Crime

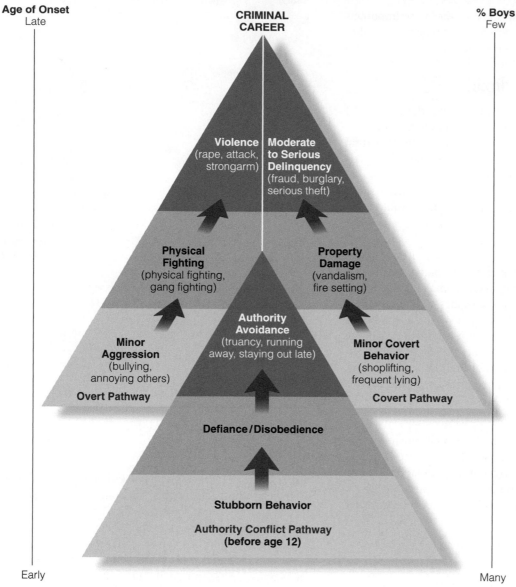

Age of Onset
Late

% Boys
Few

Early

Many

Source: "Serious and Violent Juvenile Offenders," *Juvenile Justice Bulletin,* May 1998.

using stolen credit cards, stealing cars, dealing drugs, and breaking and entering.

3. The **overt pathway** escalates to aggressive acts beginning with aggression (annoying others, bullying), leading to physical (and gang) fighting, and then to violence (attacking someone, forced theft).

The Loeber research indicates that each of these paths may lead to a sustained deviant career. Some people enter two and even three paths simultaneously: They are stubborn, lie to teachers and parents, are bullies, and commit petty thefts. These adolescents are the most likely to become persistent offenders as they mature.

Although some persistent offenders may specialize in one type of behavior, others engage in varied criminal acts and antisocial behaviors as they mature. As adolescents they cheat on tests, bully kids in the schoolyard, take drugs, commit burglary, steal a car, and then shoplift from a store. As adults, some specialize in a particular criminal activity, such as drug trafficking, while others are involved in an assortment of deviant acts—selling drugs, committing robberies and break-ins—when the situation arises and the opportunities are present.[31] There may be a multitude of criminal career subgroupings (for example, prostitutes, drug dealers) that each have their own distinctive career paths.

Age of Onset/Continuity of Crime

Most life course theories assume that the seeds of a criminal career are planted early in life and that early onset of deviance strongly predicts later and more serious criminality.[32] Research supports this by showing that children who will later become the most serious delinquents begin their deviant careers at a very early (preschool) age and that the earlier the onset of criminality the more frequent, varied, and sustained the criminal career.[33] Early-onset criminals are involved in such behaviors as truancy, cruelty to animals, lying, and theft and also appear to be more violent than their less precocious peers.[34] In contrast, late starters are more likely to be involved in nonviolent crimes such as theft.[35] Because symptoms appear early in life, it is not surprising that teacher evaluations of children during their public school years have been found to be a significant predictor of troublesome and aggressive behavior in adulthood.[36]

The earlier the onset of crime, the longer its duration.[37] As they emerge into adulthood, persisters report less emotional support, lower job satisfaction, distant peer relationships, and more psychiatric problems than those who desist.[38]

CONTINUITY AND DESISTANCE What causes some kids to begin offending at an early age? Research shows that poor parental discipline and monitoring seem to be a key to the early onset of criminality and that these influences may follow kids into their adulthood. The psychic scars of childhood are hard to erase.[39]

Children who are improperly socialized by unskilled parents are the most likely to rebel by wandering the streets with deviant peers.[40] Parental influences may be replaced: In middle childhood, social rejection by conventional peers and academic failure sustains antisocial behavior; in later adolescence, commitment to a deviant peer group creates a training ground for crime. While the youngest and most serious offenders may persist in their criminal activity into late adolescence and even adulthood, others are able to age out of crime or desist. Why and how some people are able to turn their lives around is the subject of The Criminological Enterprise feature "Desisting from Crime."

GENDER AND DESISTANCE As they mature, both males and females who have early experiences with antisocial behavior are the ones most likely to persist with this behavior throughout their life course. Like boys, early-onset girls continue to experience difficulties—increased drug and alcohol use, poor school adjustment, mental health problems, poor sexual health, psychiatric problems, higher rates of mortality, criminal behavior, insufficient parenting skills, relationship dysfunction, lower performance in academic and occupational environments, involvement with social service assistance, and adjustment problems—as they enter young adulthood and beyond.[41]

There are also some distinct gender differences. For males, the path runs from early onset in childhood to later problems at work and involvement with substance abuse. For females, the path seems somewhat different: Early antisocial behavior leads to relationship problems, depression, suicidal tendencies, and poor health in adulthood.[42] Males seem to be more deeply influenced by an early history of childhood aggression: Males who exhibited chronic physical aggression during the elementary school years exhibit

According to the concept of early onset, the most serious offenders begin their offending career at a very young age and then persist in their criminality. Twelve-year-old Alex King (upper left inset) and his brother, 13-year-old Derek King, were indicted by a Grand Jury as adults on first-degree murder and arson charges December 11, 2001, for the bludgeoning death of their father Terry King, whose body was found in his burning home. Both boys were later found guilty of second-degree murder but the judge overturned the conviction. They pled to a lesser charge and are currently serving 7- and 8-year sentences in a juvenile facility in Florida.

© Getty Images

The Criminological Enterprise

||||||||||||||||||||||||||||||||||||||

Desisting from Crime

Why do people desist from crime? Understanding desistance has become an important target for criminological research. In one important work, *Making Good: How Ex-Convicts Reform and Rebuild Their Lives*, criminologist Shadd Maruna interviewed a group of serious criminals in order to understand how they could be reformed. These men, who had been in trouble for most of their lives, were able to turn their lives around although their background suggests otherwise.

Maruna found that desistance was a process, not an instantaneous event. Desisters undergo a long-term cognitive change in which they begin to see themselves as a "new person" or have a new outlook on life. They begin to try to understand their past and develop insights into why they behaved the way they did and understand why and how things went wrong. Desisters begin to feel a sense of fulfillment in engaging in productive behaviors and, in so doing, become agents of their own change. They start feeling in control of their future and have a newfound purpose in life. Importantly, rather than run from their past, they view their prior history as a learning experience, finding a silver lining in an otherwise awful situation.

Sociologists Peggy Giordano, Stephen Cernkovich, and Jennifer Rudolph also link desistance to a process of cognitive change. They believe that under some circumstances changes in their environment help some people to construct a kind of psychic "scaffolding" that makes it possible for them to create significant life change. These behavior changes can include desisting from crime.

To be eligible for desistance, individuals must discard their old bad habits and begin the process of crafting a different way of life. Because at first the new lifestyle is usually only a distant dream or faint possibility, people who want to change must find it within themselves to resonate with, move toward, or select the various environmental catalysts for change.

Cognitive Transformations

Giordano and her associates believe there are certain "hooks for change" within the environment. These hooks are positive life experiences that help people turn their lives around; people have to latch onto these opportunities when and if they become available. If they can manage to seize the right opportunity, the former offender may undergo a *cognitive transformation*—a process in which the person reshapes

his or her thought and behavior patterns into a more conventional and rewarding lifestyle. Giordano and her associates have identified four critical cognitive transformations that are the key to the healing process:

1. *A shift in the actor's basic openness to change.* In order to change a person must be ready and willing to change.

2. *Exposure to a particular hook or set of hooks for change.* While a general openness to change is necessary, by itself it is often insufficient to produce meaningful results. There must also be some environmental catalyst available to "hook on to." The potential desister must not only regard the new environmental situation as a positive development (for example, experience high attachment to a spouse), but must define the new state of affairs as fundamentally incompatible with continued deviation.

3. To desist, the person must be able to envision and begin to fashion an appealing and conventional *replacement self* that he or she can substitute for the older, damaged identity. People can begin to escape their deviant lifestyle only when they begin to believe in their new persona

---

the risk of continued physical violence and delinquency during adolescence; there is less evidence of a link between childhood physical aggression and adult aggression among females.[43]

Adolescent-Limiteds and Life Course Persisters

But not all persistent offenders begin at an early age. Some are precocious, beginning their criminal careers early and persisting into adulthood.[44] Others stay out of trouble in adolescence and do not violate the law until their teenage years. Some offenders may peak at an early age, whereas

others persist into adulthood. Some youth maximize their offending rates at a relatively early age and then reduce their criminal activity; others persist into their 20s. Some are high-rate offenders, whereas others offend at relatively low rates.[45]

Some kids who do not begin their deviant behavior at an early age may "catch up" later in their adolescence. According to psychologist Terrie Moffitt, most young offenders follow one of two paths. **Adolescent-limited offenders** may be considered "typical teenagers" who get into minor scrapes and engage in what might be considered rebellious teenage behavior with their friends.[46] As they reach their mid-teens, adolescent-limited delinquents begin to mimic the antisocial

and think, "It is inappropriate for someone like me to do something like that." The new identity must serve as a basis for decision making as the person moves into new and novel situations: "I may have smoked pot as a kid, but now that I am a husband the new me would never take the risk." The concept of a replacement self is critical when the actor faces stressful life circumstances (such as divorce and unemployment), and the person is forced to make decisions that differ from the ones he or she made in the past (and which turned out to be destructive).

4. *A transformation in the way the actor views the deviant behavior or lifestyle itself.* The desistance process can be seen as complete when the actor no longer sees the past life and behaviors as positive, viable, or even personally relevant. What the person did in the past was foolish and destructive: "It is no longer cool to get high, but selfish and destructive."

Using these cognitive shifts, the desistance process proceeds from an overall "readiness" to change, to encountering one or more environmental hooks for change, to a shift in iden-

tity, and to the maintenance of a positive identity that gradually decreases the desirability of the former deviant behavior.

Giordano and associates tested their views by using data collected from incarcerated delinquent youth who were first interviewed in 1982 and re-interviewed in 1995. They found that kids who desisted from crime as adults did in fact experience cognitive transformations. However, the hooks that got them to change were varied. For males, going to prison was a life-transforming event. For many females, having a religious conversion served as a catalyst for change. Females also believed that having children was the hook that helped them reform. Some desisters told Giordano that having a romantic relationship was a key factor in their personal turnaround because supportive partners helped them raise their self-esteem: "He said I didn't belong where I was at." By seeking out conventional partners, desisters are demonstrating a cognitive shift ("I am the type of person who wants to associate with this respectable man/woman"). The potential desister, tired of being dishonest, is helped when he or she is able to connect to someone who demonstrates what it means to be honest on a daily basis.

The Giordano, Cernkovich, and Rudolph research helps us better understand the life-transforming processes that help some people desist from crime.

Critical Thinking

Many of the women told the researchers that they had crafted highly traditional replacement selves (such as child of God, the good wife, involved mother) and that these new identities helped them with their successful exits from criminal activities. Giordano fears that latching on to these identities might be helpful in the short term but may be highly repressive and cut into women's becoming economically self-sustaining and independent in the long term. Do you agree?

 InfoTrac College Edition Research

You can obtain the original Giordano research in InfoTrac College Edition. Use "cognitive transformation" as a key word to access the article.

Sources: Shadd Maruna, *Making Good: How Ex-Convicts Reform and Rebuild Their Lives* (Washington, DC: American Psychological Association, 2000); Peggy Giordano, Stephen Cernkovich, and Jennifer Rudolph, "Gender, Crime, and Desistance: Toward a Theory of Cognitive Transformation," *American Journal of Sociology* 107 (2002): 990–1,065.

---

behavior of more troubled teens, only to reduce the frequency of their offending as they mature to around age 18.[47]

The second path is the one taken by a small group of **life course persisters** who begin their offending career at a very early age and continue to offend well into adulthood.[48] Moffitt finds that life course persisters combine family dysfunction with severe neurological problems that predispose them to antisocial behavior patterns. These afflictions can be the result of maternal drug abuse, poor nutrition, or exposure to toxic agents such as lead. It is not surprising then that life course persisters display social and personal dysfunctions including lower than average verbal ability, reasoning skills, learning ability, and school achievement.

Terrie Moffitt has written on a number of topics involving psychological issues and criminal involvement. Use her name as a subject guide in InfoTrac College Edition and read some of her research papers.

Research shows that the persistence patterns predicted by Moffitt are valid and accurate.[49] Life course persisters offend more frequently and engage in a greater variety of antisocial acts than other offenders; they also manifest significantly more mental health problems, including psychiatric pathologies, than adolescent-limited offenders.[50]

EXHIBIT 9.2

Some Important Life Course Theories

Name

Social Development Model (SDM)

Principal Theorists

J. David Hawkins and Richard Catalano

Major Premise

In the social development model (SDM), community-level risk factors make some people susceptible to antisocial behaviors. Preexisting risk factors are either reinforced or neutralized by socialization. To control the risk of antisocial behavior, a child must maintain prosocial bonds. Over the life course involvement in prosocial or antisocial behavior determines the quality of attachments. Commitment and attachment to conventional institutions, activities, and beliefs insulate youths from the crimogenic influences in their environment. The prosocial path inhibits deviance by strengthening bonds to prosocial others and activities. Without the proper level of bonding, adolescents can succumb to the influence of deviant others.

Name

Interactional Theory

Principal Theorists

Terence Thornberry, Marvin Krohn, Alan Lizotte, and Margaret Farnworth

Major Premise

According to interactional theory, the onset of crime can be traced to a deterioration of the social bond during adolescence, marked by weakened attachment to parents, less commitment to school, and lack of belief in conventional values. The cause of crime and delinquency is bidirectional: Weak bonds lead kids to develop friendships with deviant peers and get involved in delinquency. Frequent delinquency involvement further weakens bonds and makes it difficult to reestablish conventional ones. Delinquency-promoting factors tend to reinforce one another and sustain a chronic criminal career. Kids who go through stressful life events, such as a family financial crisis, are more likely to later get involved in antisocial behaviors and vice versa. Criminality is a developmental process that takes on different meaning and form as a person matures. During early adolescence, attachment to the family is critical; by mid-adolescence, the influence of the family is replaced by friends, school, and youth culture; by adulthood, a person's behavioral choices are shaped by his or her place in conventional society and his or her own nuclear family. Although crime is influenced by these social forces, it also influences these processes and associations. Therefore, crime and social processes are interactional.

There is also evidence, as predicted by Moffitt, that the cause of early-onset/life course persistent delinquency can be found at the individual level. Life course persisters are more likely to manifest traits such as low verbal ability and hyperactivity, they display a negative or impulsive personality, and they seem particularly impaired on spatial and memory functions.[51] Individual traits rather than environmental ones seem to have the greatest influence on life course persistence.[52]

Some recent research shows that there may be more than one subset of life course persisters based on the presence of attention deficit hyperactive disorder. Some begin acting out during the preschool years; these youth show signs of ADHD and do not outgrow the levels of disobedience typical of the preschool years. The second group shows few symptoms of ADHD but, from an early age, is aggressive, underhanded, and in constant opposition to authority.[53]

||||||| CONNECTIONS |||||||

Moffitt views adolescent-limited kids as following the social learning perspective discussed in Chapter 7. Kids learn that violating the norms of society is an act of independence; some such actions, like smoking and drinking, may be efforts at gaining a pseudo-maturity. These acts are neither serious nor violent.

THEORIES OF THE CRIMINAL LIFE COURSE

A number of systematic theories have been formulated that account for onset, continuance, and desistance from crime. It is not uncommon for life course theories to interconnect *personal*

Name	Principal Theorist
General Theory of Crime and Delinquency (GTCD)	Robert Agnew

Major Premise

Crime and social relations are reciprocal. Family relationships, work experiences, school performance, and peer relations influence crime. In turn, antisocial acts have a significant impact on family relationships, work experiences, school performance, and peer relations. Engaging in crime leads to a weakened bond with significant others and a strengthening of the association with criminal peers. Close ties to criminal peers weakens bonds to conventional society. Crime is most likely to occur when the constraints against crime (fear of punishment, stake in conformity, self-control) are low, and the motivations for crime (beliefs favorable to crime, exposure to criminals, criminal learning experiences) are high. The way an individual reacts to constraints and motivations are shaped by five key elements of human development called life domains:

1. *self*—irritability and/or low self-control;

2. *family*—poor parenting and no marriage or a bad marriage;

3. *school*—negative school experiences and limited education;

4. *peers*—delinquent friends; and

5. *work*—unemployment or having a bad job.

The structure and impact of each of the life domains are continuously evolving; each has an influence over the other; they are mutually interdependent.

Sources: Robert Agnew, *Why Do Criminals Offend? A General Theory of Crime and Delinquency* (Los Angeles: Roxbury Publishing, 2005); Terence Thornberry, "Toward an Interactional Theory of Delinquency," *Criminology* 25 (1987): 863–891; Richard Catalano and J. David Hawkins, " The Social Development Model: A Theory of Antisocial Behavior, " in *Delinquency & Crime: Current Theories*, ed. J. David Hawkins (New York: Cambridge University Press, 1996, pp. 149–197).

factors such as personality and intelligence, *social factors* such as income and neighborhood, *socialization factors* such as marriage and military service, *cognitive factors* such as information processing and attention/perception, and *situational factors* such as criminal opportunity, effective guardianship, and apprehension risk into complex multifactor explanations of human behavior. In this sense they are **integrated theories** because they incorporate social, personal, and developmental factors into complex explanations of human behavior. They do not focus on the relatively simple question: Why do people commit crime? but on more complex issues: Why do some offenders persist in criminal careers while others desist from or alter their criminal activity as they mature?[54] Why do some people continually escalate their criminal involvement while others slow down and turn their lives around? Are all criminals similar in their offending patterns, or are there different types of offenders and paths to offending?

Life course theorists want to know not only why people enter a criminal way of life but why, once they do, they are able to alter the trajectory of their criminal involvement. Below one of the more important life course theories, Sampson and Laub's Age-Graded Theory, is set out in some detail. Exhibit 9.2 sets out the principles of some other life course theories.

Sampson and Laub: Age-Graded Theory

If there are various pathways to crime and delinquency, are there trails back to conformity? In an important 1993 work, *Crime in the Making,* Robert Sampson and John Laub identify the **turning points** in a criminal career.[55] As devotees of the life course perspective, Sampson and Laub find that the stability of delinquent behavior can be affected by events that occur later in life, even after a chronic delinquent career has been undertaken. They agree with other criminologists that formal and informal social controls restrict criminality and that crime begins early in life and continues over the life course; they disagree that once this course is set, nothing can impede its progress.

Laub and Sampson reanalyzed the data originally collected by the Gluecks more than forty years ago. Using modern statistical analysis, Laub and Sampson found evidence supporting the developmental view. They state that children who enter delinquent careers are those who have trouble at home and at school and maintain deviant friends; these findings are similar to those from earlier research on delinquent careers.

TURNING POINTS Laub and Sampson's most important contribution is identifying the life events that enable adult offenders to desist from crime (Figure 9.3). Two critical turning points are marriage and career. For example, adoles-

cents who are at risk for crime can live conventional lives if they can find good jobs or achieve successful careers. Their success may hinge on a lucky break. Even those who have been in trouble with the law may turn from crime if employers are willing to give them a chance despite their records.

When they achieve adulthood, adolescents who had significant problems with the law are able to desist from crime if they become attached to a spouse who supports and sustains them even when the spouse knows they had gotten in trouble when they were young. Happy marriages are life sustaining, and marital quality improves over time (as people work less and have fewer parental responsibilities).[56] Spending time in marital and family activities also reduces exposure to deviant peers, which in turn reduces the opportunity to become involved in delinquent activities.[57] People who cannot sustain secure marital relations are less likely to desist from crime.

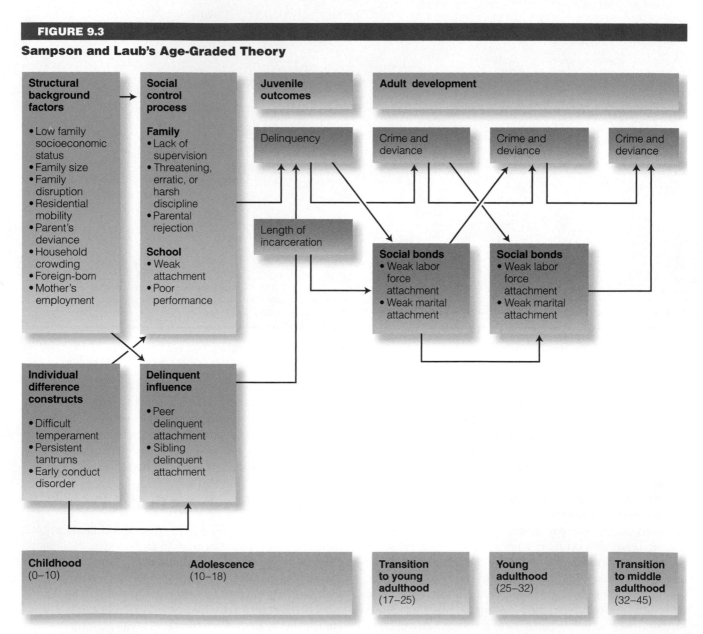

FIGURE 9.3

Sampson and Laub's Age-Graded Theory

Source: Robert Sampson and John Laub, *Crime in the Making: Pathways and Turning Points through Life* (Cambridge, MA: Harvard University Press, 1993), pp. 244–245.

SOCIAL CAPITAL Laub and Sampson recognize that people build **social capital**—positive relations with individuals and institutions that are life sustaining. In the same manner that building financial capital improves the chances for personal success, building social capital supports conventional behavior and inhibits deviant behavior. For example, a successful marriage creates social capital when it improves a person's stature, creates feelings of self-worth, and encourages people to trust the individual. A successful career inhibits crime by creating a stake in conformity; why commit crime when you are doing well at your job? The relationship is reciprocal. If people are chosen to be employees, they return the favor by doing the best job possible; if they are chosen as spouses, they blossom into devoted partners. In contrast, people who fail to accumulate social capital are more prone to commit criminal acts.[58]

The fact that social capital influences the trajectory of a criminal career underscores the life course view that events that occur in later adolescence and adulthood do in fact influence behavior choices. Life events that occur in adulthood can help either terminate or sustain deviant careers.

TESTING AGE-GRADED THEORY Empirical research now shows that, as forecast by Sampson and Laub, people change over the life course and that the factors that predict delinquency in adolescence, such as a weak social bond, may have less of an impact on adult crime.[59] Criminality appears to be dynamic and is affected by behaviors occurring over the life course, such as accumulating deviant peers: The more deviant friends one accumulates over time, the more likely the person is to get involved in crime.[60] Of critical importance is early labeling by the justice system: Adolescents who are convicted of crime at an early age are more likely to develop antisocial attitudes later in life. They later develop low educational achievement, declining occupational status, and unstable employment records.[61] People who get involved with the justice system as adolescents may find that their career paths are blocked well into adulthood.[62] The relationship is reciprocal:

Men who are unemployed or underemployed report higher criminal participation rates than employed men.[63]

Evidence is also available that confirms Sampson and Laub's suspicion that criminal career trajectories can be reversed if life conditions improve.[64] For example, youth who have a positive high school experience, facilitated by occupationally oriented course work, small class size, and positive peer climates, are less likely to become incarcerated as adults than those who do not enjoy these social benefits.[65] In contract, kids who have long-term exposure to poverty will find that their involvement in crime escalates. Their involvement in crime will diminish if life circumstances improve because parents are able to escape poverty and move to more attractive environments. Recent research by Ross Macmillan and his colleagues shows that children whose mothers were initially poor but escaped from poverty were no more likely to develop behavior problems than children whose mothers were never poor. Gaining social capital then may help erase some of the damage caused by its absence.[66]

A number of research efforts have supported Sampson and Laub's position that accumulating social capital reduces crime rates. For example, youths who accumulate social capital in childhood (by doing well in school or having a tightly knit family) are also the most likely to maintain steady work as adults; employment may help insulate them from crime.[67] Delinquents who enter the military, serve overseas, and receive veterans' benefits enhance their occupational status (social capital) while reducing criminal involvement.[68] Similarly, high-risk adults who are fortunate enough to obtain high-quality jobs are likely to reduce their criminal activities even if they have a prior history of offending.[69]

THE MARRIAGE FACTOR People who maintain a successful marriage and become parents are the most likely to mature out of crime.[70] Marriage stabilizes people and helps them build social capital; it also may discourage crime by reducing contact with criminal peers. As Mark Warr states:

Research supports Sampson and Laub's views on the constructive influence marriage has on behavior. People who maintain a successful marriage and become parents are the most likely to mature out of crime. Marriage stabilizes people and helps them build social capital; it also may discourage crime by reducing contact with criminal peers.

© Amy Etra/PhotoEdit Inc.

For many individuals, it seems, marriage marks a transition from heavy peer involvement to a preoccupation with one's spouse. That transition is likely to reduce interaction with former friends and accomplices and thereby reduce the opportunities as well as the motivation to engage in crime.[71]

Even people who have histories of criminal activity and have been convicted of serious offenses reduce the frequency of their offending if they live with spouses and maintain employment when they are in the community.[72] The marriage benefit may also be intergenerational: Children who grow up in two-parent families are more likely to later have happier marriages themselves than children who are the product of divorced or never-married parents.[73] If people with marital problems are more crime prone, their children will also suffer a greater long-term risk of marital failure and antisocial activity.

One important new research study further confirms the benefits of marriage as a crime-reducing social event. Researchers Alex Piquero, John MacDonald, and Karen Parker tracked each of 524 men in their late teens and early 20s for a 7-year period after they were paroled from the California Youth Authority during the 1970s and 1980s. The sample of men, who had been incarcerated for lengthy periods of time, was 48.5 percent white, 33 percent black, 16.6 percent Latino, and 1.9 percent other races.[74] The research team found former offenders were far less likely to return to crime if they settled down into the routines of a solid marriage. Common-law marriages or living with a partner did not have the same crime-reducing effect as did traditional marriages in which the knot is tied, the union is registered at the courthouse, and there is a general expectation to lead a steady life. Among non-Caucasians, parolees cohabiting without the benefit of marriage actually increased their recidivism rates. Piquero explains his findings by suggesting that

> People who are married often have schedules where they work 9-to-5 jobs, come home for dinner, take care of children if they have them, watch television, go to bed and repeat that cycle over and over again; people who are not married have a lot of free rein to do a lot of what they want, especially if they are not employed. There's something about crossing the line of getting married that helps these men stay away from crime. If they don't cross that line, they can continue their lifestyles, which are pretty erratic.[75]

While the Piquero research is persuasive, some important questions still need to be answered: Why do some people enter strong marriages while others fail? Does the influence of marriage have an equal effect on men and women? Research by Ronald Simons and his associates found that while marriage significantly improves a woman's life chances, it has less impact on men.[76] However, for both males and females, having an antisocial romantic partner as a young adult increased the likelihood of later criminal behavior, a finding that supports Laub and Sampson.

FUTURE RESEARCH DIRECTIONS Although age-graded theory has received enormous attention, there are still many research questions left unanswered. For example, what is it about a military career that helps reduce future criminality? Does the connection between military service and desistance suggest universal military service as a crime prevention alternative? Why are some troubled youth able to conform to the requirements of a job or career while others cannot? If acquiring social capital—family, friends, education, marriage, and employment—aids in the successful recovery from crime, does the effect produce an actual change in the propensity to commit crime or merely the reduction of criminal opportunity?[77] To answer some of these questions, Laub and Sampson contacted the surviving members of the Glueck cohort, and some of their findings are discussed in The Criminological Enterprise feature "Shared Beginnings, Divergent Lives."

LATENT TRAIT FUNDAMENTALS

On August 7, 2005, police in Concord, New Hampshire, arrested Thaddeus Duprey, aged 19, and three of his friends for driving around town and shooting at pedestrians with a BB gun.[78] The crime was rather unremarkable, and no one was seriously injured. But the incident made headlines in local newspapers because Duprey, a graduate of pricey Derryfield School (a local private academy that caters to affluent students) was formerly a member of Derryfield's crew team and at the time of the incident was a student at the prestigious University of Pennsylvania. The police said the motive for the shootings appeared to have been boredom.

What would motivate a privileged youth such as Thad Duprey to shoot at people he had never met? Certainly, his behavior was not a result of economic hardship or feelings of strain. Could some underlying trait, unknown and unseen to people who knew him well, be the catalyst for this inexplicable outburst of violence? Was this a singular incident or one in an ongoing pattern of antisocial activity? Had Duprey been involved in prior incidents of antisocial activity from early in his childhood that had heretofore gone undetected?

In a critical 1990 article, David Rowe, D. Wayne Osgood, and W. Alan Nicewander proposed the concept of latent traits to explain the flow of crime over the life cycle. Their model assumes that a number of people in the population have a personal attribute or characteristic that controls their inclination or propensity to commit crimes.[79] This disposition, or **latent trait,** may be either present at birth or established early in life, and it can remain stable over time. Suspected latent traits include defective intelligence, damaged or impulsive personality, genetic abnormalities, the physical-chemical functioning of the brain, and environmental influences on brain function such as drugs, chemicals, and injuries.[80]

Regardless of gender or environment, those who maintain one of these suspect traits may be at risk to crime and in danger of becoming career criminals; those who lack the traits have a much lower risk.[81]

Because latent traits are stable, people who are antisocial during adolescence are the most likely to persist in crime.

The positive association between past and future criminality detected in the cohort studies of career criminals reflects the presence of this underlying crimogenic trait. That is, if low IQ contributes to delinquency in childhood, it should also cause the same people to offend as adults because intelligence is usually stable over the life span.

Whereas the propensity to commit crime is stable, the opportunity to commit crime fluctuates over time. People age out of crime: As they mature and develop, there are simply fewer opportunities to commit crimes and greater inducements to remain "straight." They may marry, have children, and obtain jobs. The former delinquents' newfound adult responsibilities leave them little time to hang with their friends, abuse substances, and get into scrapes with the law.

To understand this concept better, assume that intelligence as measured by IQ tests is a stable latent trait associated with crime. Intelligence remains stable and unchanging over the life course, but crime rates decline with age. How can latent trait theory explain this phenomenon? Teenagers have more opportunity to commit crime than adults, so at every level of intelligence, adolescent crime rates will be higher. As they mature, however, teens with both high and low IQs will commit less crime because their adult responsibilities provide them with fewer criminal opportunities. They may get married and raise a family, get a job, and buy a home. And like most people, as they age they lose strength and vigor, qualities necessary to commit crime. Though their IQ remains stable and their propensity to commit crime is unchanged, their living environment and biological condition have undergone radical change. Even had they wanted to engage in antisocial activities, the former delinquents may lack the opportunity and the energy to engage in criminal activities.

Crime and Human Nature

Latent trait theorists were encouraged when two prominent social scientists, James Q. Wilson and Richard Herrnstein, published *Crime and Human Nature* in 1985 and suggested that personal traits—such as genetic makeup, intelligence, and body build—may outweigh the importance of social variables as predictors of criminal activity.[82]

According to Wilson and Herrnstein's **human nature theory**, all human behavior, including criminality, is determined by its perceived consequences. A criminal incident occurs when an individual chooses criminal over conventional behavior (referred to as *non-crime*) after weighing the potential gains and losses of each: "The larger the ratio of net rewards of crime to the net rewards of non-crime, the greater the tendency to commit the crime."[83]

Wilson and Herrnstein's model assumes that both biological and psychological traits influence the crime–non-crime choice. They see a close link between a person's decision to choose crime and such biosocial factors as low intelligence, mesomorphic body type, genetic influences (parental criminality), and possessing an autonomic nervous system that responds too quickly to stimuli. Psychological traits, such as an impulsive or extroverted personality or generalized hostility, also determine the potential to commit crime.

In their focus on the association between these constitutional and psychological factors and crime, Wilson and Herrnstein seem to be suggesting the existence of an elusive latent trait that predisposes people to commit crime.[84] Their vision helped inspire other criminologists to identify the elusive latent trait that causes criminal behavior. The most prominent latent trait theory is Michael Gottfredson and Travis Hirschi's General Theory of Crime. Exhibit 9.3 on pages 300–301 discusses some other important contributions to the latent trait model.

General Theory of Crime

In their important work, *A General Theory of Crime,* Michael Gottfredson and Travis Hirschi modified and redefined some of the principles articulated in Hirschi's social control theory by integrating the concepts of control with those of biosocial, psychological, routine activities, and rational choice theories.[85]

| | | | | | | | **CONNECTIONS** | | | | | | |

In his original version of control theory, discussed in Chapter 7, Hirschi focused on the social controls that attach people to conventional society and insulate them from criminality. In this newer work, he concentrates on self-control as a stabilizing force. The two views are connected, however, because both social control (or social bonds) and self-control are acquired through early experiences with effective parenting.

THE ACT AND THE OFFENDER In their **General Theory of Crime (GTC)**, Gottfredson and Hirschi consider the criminal offender and the criminal act as separate concepts (Figure 9.4 on page 301). On one hand, criminal acts, such as robberies or burglaries, are illegal events or deeds that offenders engage in when they perceive them to be advantageous. For example, burglaries are typically committed by young males looking for cash, liquor, and entertainment; the crime provides "easy, short-term gratification."[86] This aspect of the theory relies on concepts developed first as classical theory and later as rational choice and routine activities theories: Crime is rational and predictable; people commit crime when it promises rewards with minimal threat of pain; the threat of punishment can deter crime. If targets are well guarded, crime rates diminish. Only the truly irrational offender would dare to strike under those circumstances.

While criminal offenders are people predisposed to commit crimes, they are not robots who commit crime without restraint; their days are also filled with conventional behaviors, such as going to school, parties, concerts, and church. But given the same set of criminal opportunities, such as having a lot of free time for mischief and living in a neighborhood with unguarded homes containing valuable merchandise, crime-prone people have a much higher probability of violating the law than do noncriminals. The

| | | | | | | | | | | | | | | | | | | | | | | | | | | | | | |

Shared Beginnings, Divergent Lives

Why are some delinquents destined to become persistent criminals as adults? John Laub and Robert Sampson are now conducting a follow-up to their reanalysis of Sheldon and Eleanor Glueck's study that matched 500 delinquent boys with 500 nondelinquents. The individuals in the original sample were re-interviewed by the Gluecks at ages 25 and 32. Now Sampson and Laub have located the survivors of the delinquent sample, the oldest 70 years old and the youngest 62, and have re-interviewed this cohort.

Persistence and Desistance

Laub and Sampson find that delinquency and other forms of antisocial conduct in childhood are strongly related to adult delinquency and drug and alcohol abuse. Former delinquents also suffer consequences in other areas of social life, such as school, work, and family life. For example, delinquents are far less likely to finish high school than are nondelinquents and subsequently are more likely to be unemployed, receive welfare, and experience separation or divorce as adults.

In their latest research, Laub and Sampson address one of the key questions posed by life course theories: Is it possible for former delinquents to turn their lives around as adults? They find that most antisocial children do not remain antisocial as adults. For example, of men in the study cohort who survived to age 50, 24 percent had no arrests for delinquent acts of violence and property after age 17 (6 percent had no arrests for total delinquency); 48 percent had no arrests for these predatory delinquency after age 25 (19 percent for total delinquency); 60 percent had no arrests for predatory delinquency after age 31 (33 percent for total delinquency); and 79 percent had no arrests for predatory delinquency after age 40 (57 percent for total delinquency). They conclude that desistance from delinquency is the norm and that most, if not all, serious delinquents desist from delinquency.

Why Do Delinquents Desist?

Laub and Sampson's earlier research indicated that building social capital through marriage and jobs were key components of desistance from delinquency. However, in this new round of research, Laub and Sampson were able to find out more about long-term desistance by interviewing fifty-two men as they approached age 70. The follow-up showed a dramatic drop in criminal activity as the men aged: Between the ages of 17 and 24, 84 percent of the subjects had committed violent crimes; in their 30s and 40s, that number dropped to 14 percent; it fell to just 3 percent as the men reached their 60s and 70s. Property crimes and alcohol- and drug-related crimes showed significant decreases. They found that men who desisted from crime were rooted in structural routines and had strong social ties to family and community. Drawing on the men's own words, they found that one important element for "going straight" is the "knifing off" of individuals from their immediate environment and offering the men a new script for the future. Joining the military can provide this knifing-off effect, as does marriage or changing one's residence. One former delinquent (age 69) told them:

> I'd say the turning point was, number one, the Army. You get into an outfit, you had a sense of belonging, you made your friends. I think I became a pretty good judge of character. In the Army, you met some good ones, you met some foul balls. Then I met the wife. I'd say probably that would be the turning point. Got married, then naturally, kids come. So now you got to get a better job, you got to make more money. And that's how I got to the Navy Yard and tried to improve myself.

Former delinquents who "went straight" were able to put structure into their lives. Structure often led the men to disassociate from delinquent peers, reducing the opportunity to get into trouble. Getting married, for example, may limit the number of nights men can

---

propensity to commit crimes remains stable throughout a person's life. Change in the frequency of criminal activity is purely a function of change in criminal opportunity.

By recognizing that there are stable differences in people's propensity to commit crime, the GTC adds a biosocial element to the concept of social control. Individual differences are stable over the life course, and so is the propensity to commit crime; only opportunity changes. The factors that make people impulsive and thereafter crime prone may have physical or social roots, or perhaps both.

Recent research shows that children who suffer anoxia (oxygen starvation) during the birthing process are the ones most likely to lack self-control later in life, suggesting that impulsivity may have a biological basis.[87] There is also evidence that low self-control may develop through incompetent or absent parenting. If a child is not properly socialized, his or her neural pathways are physically affected. Once experiences are ingrained, the brain establishes a pattern of electrochemical activation that remains for life.[88]

"hang with the guys." As one wife of a former delinquent said, "It is not how many beers you have, it's who you drink with." Even multiple offenders who did time in prison were able to desist with the help of a stabilizing marriage.

Former delinquents who can turn their life around, who have acquired a degree of maturity by taking on family and work responsibilities, and who have forged new commitments are the ones most likely to make a fresh start and find new direction and meaning in life. It seems that men who desisted changed their identity as well, and this, in turn, affected their outlook and sense of maturity and responsibility. The ability to change did not reflect delinquency "specialty": Violent offenders followed the same path as property offenders.

While many former delinquents desisted from delinquency, they still faced the risk of an early and untimely death. Thirteen percent (N = 62) of the delinquent as compared to only 6 percent (N = 28) of the nondelinquent subjects died unnatural deaths such as violence, cirrhosis of the liver caused by alcoholism, poor self-care, suicide, and so on. By age 65, 29 percent (N = 139) of the delinquent and 21 percent (N = 95) of the nondelinquent subjects had died from natural causes. Frequent delinquent involvement in adolescence and alcohol abuse were the strongest predictors of an early and

unnatural death. So while many troubled youth are able to reform, their early excesses may haunt them across their life span.

Policy Implications

Laub and Sampson find that youth problems—delinquency, substance abuse, violence, dropping out, teen pregnancy—often share common risk characteristics. Intervention strategies, therefore, should consider a broad array of antisocial, criminal, and deviant behaviors and not limit the focus to just one subgroup or delinquency type. Because criminality and other social problems are linked, early prevention efforts that reduce delinquency will probably also reduce alcohol abuse, drunk driving, drug abuse, sexual promiscuity, and family violence. The best way to achieve these goals is through four significant life-changing events: marriage, joining the military, getting a job, and changing one's environment or neighborhood. What appears to be important about these processes is that they all involve, to varying degrees, the following items: a knifing off of the past from the present; new situations that provide both supervision and monitoring as well as new opportunities of social support and growth; and new situations that provide the opportunity for transforming identity. Prevention of delinquency must be a policy at all times and at all stages of life.

Critical Thinking

1. Do you believe that the factors that influenced the men in the original Glueck sample are still relevant for change, for example a military career?

2. Would it be possible for men such as these to join the military today?

3. Do you believe that some sort of universal service program might be beneficial and help people turn their lives around?

 InfoTracCollege Edition Research

Read a review of Laub and Sampson's *Crime in the Making* at: Roland Chilton, "Crime in the Making: Pathways and Turning Points through Life," *Social Forces* 74 (September 1995): 357.

To learn more about the concept of "social capital," use it as a key word term in InfoTrac College Edition.

Sources: John Laub and Robert Sampson, *Shared Beginnings, Divergent Lives: Delinquent Boys to Age 70* (Cambridge, MA: Harvard University Press, 2003); John Laub and Robert Sampson, "Understanding Desistance from Delinquency," in *Delinquency and Justice: An Annual Review of Research*, vol. 28, ed. Michael Tonry, (Chicago: University of Chicago Press, 2001), pp. 1–71; John Laub and George Vaillant, "Delinquency and Mortality: A 50-Year Follow-Up Study of 1,000 Delinquent and Nondelinquent Boys," *American Journal of Psychiatry* 157 (2000): 96–102.

IMPULSIVITY AND CRIME? What, then, causes people to become excessively crime prone? Gottfredson and Hirschi attribute the tendency to commit crimes to a person's level of self-control. People with limited self-control tend to be impulsive; they are insensitive to other people's feelings, physical (rather than mental), risk-takers, shortsighted, and nonverbal.[89] They have a here-and-now orientation and refuse to work for distant goals; they lack diligence, tenacity, and persistence.

People lacking self-control tend to be adventuresome, active, physical, and self-centered. As they mature, they often have unstable marriages, jobs, and friendships.[90] They are less likely to feel shame if they engage in deviant acts and are more likely to find them pleasurable.[91] They are also more likely to engage in dangerous behaviors such as drinking, smoking, and reckless driving; all of these behaviors are associated with criminality.[92]

Because those with low self-control enjoy risky, exciting, or thrilling behaviors with immediate gratification, they are more likely to enjoy criminal acts, which require stealth, agility, speed, and power, than conventional acts, which demand

Some Important Latent Trait Theories

Name	Principal Theorist	Latent Trait
Integrated Cognitive Antisocial Potential (ICAP) Theory	David Farrington	Antisocial potential

Major Premise

People maintain a range of *antisocial potential (AP),* the potential to commit antisocial acts. AP can be viewed as both a long- and short-term phenomenon. Those with high levels of long-term AP are at risk for offending over the life course; those with low AP levels live more conventional lives. Though AP levels are fairly consistent over time, they peak in the teenage years because of the effects of maturational factors—such as increase in peer influence and decrease in family influence—that directly influence crime rates. Long-term AP can be reduced of decreased by changing life events such as marriage.

There is also short-term AP when immediate life events may increase a personal antisocial potential so that, in the immediate moment, people may increase their location on the AP continuum. For example, a person with a relatively low long-term AP may suffer a temporary amplification if he is bored, angry, drunk, or frustrated. According to the ICAP theory, the commission of offenses and other types of antisocial acts depend on the interaction between the individual (with his immediate level of AP) and the social environment (especially criminal opportunities and victims).

Name	Principal Theorist	Latent Trait
Differential Coercion Theory	Mark Colvin	Perceptions of coercion

Major Premise

Perceptions of *coercion* begin early in life when children experience punitive forms of discipline including both physical attacks and psychological coercion including negative commands, critical remarks, teasing, humiliation, whining, yelling, and threats. Through these destructive family interchanges, coercion becomes ingrained and guides reactions to adverse situations that arise in both family and nonfamily settings.

There are two sources of coercion: interpersonal and impersonal. *Interpersonal coercion* is direct, involving the use or threat of force and intimidation from parents, peers, and significant others. *Impersonal coercion* involves pressures beyond individual control, such as economic and

long-term study and cognitive and verbal skills. As Gottfredson and Hirschi put it, they derive satisfaction from "money without work, sex without courtship, revenge without court delays."[93] Many of these individuals who have a propensity for committing crime also engage in other behaviors such as smoking, drinking, gambling, and illicit sexuality.[94] Although these acts are not illegal, they too provide immediate, short-term gratification. Exhibit 9.4 lists the elements of self-control.

Gottfredson and Hirschi trace the root cause of poor self-control to inadequate childrearing practices. Parents who refuse or who are unable to monitor a child's behavior, who do not recognize deviant behavior when it occurs, and who do not punish that behavior will produce children who lack self-control. Children who are not attached to their parents, who are poorly supervised, and whose parents are criminal or deviant themselves are the most likely to develop poor self-control. In a sense, lack of self-control occurs naturally when steps are not taken to stop its development.[95]

Low self-control develops early in life and remains stable into and through adulthood.[96] Considering the continuity of criminal motivation, Hirschi and Gottfredson have questioned the utility of the juvenile justice system and of giving more lenient treatment to young delinquent offenders. Why separate youthful and adult offenders legally when the source

social pressure caused by unemployment, poverty, or competition among businesses or other groups. High levels of coercion produce criminality especially when the coercion is inconsistent and random because it teaches people that they cannot control their lives: Chronic offenders grew up in homes where parents used erratic control and applied it in an inconsistent fashion.

Name	Principal Theorist	Latent Trait
Control Balance Theory	Charles Tittle	Control/balance

Major Premise

According to Control Balance Theory, the concept of control has two distinct elements: the amount of control one is subject to by others and the amount of control one can exercise over others. Conformity results when these two elements are in balance; control imbalances produce deviant and criminal behaviors.

Those people who sense a deficit of control turn to three types of behavior to restore balance: (1) *Predation* involves direct forms of physical violence, such as robbery, sexual assault, or other forms of physical violence; (2) *defiance* challenges control mechanisms but stops short of physical harm—for example, vandalism, curfew violations, and unconventional sex; (3) *submission* involves passive obedience to the demands of others, such as submitting to physical or sexual abuse without response.

An excess of control can result in crimes of (1) *exploitation,* which involves using others to commit crimes such as contract killers or drug runners; (2) *plunder,* which involves using power without regard for others, such as committing a hate crime or polluting the environment; or (3) *decadence,* which involves spur of the moment, irrational acts such as child molesting.

Sources: David P. Farrington, "Developmental and Life-Course Criminology: Key Theoretical and Empirical Issues." Sutherland Award Address at the American Society of Criminology meeting in Chicago, November 2002, revised March 2003; Charles Tittle, *Control Balance: Toward a General Theory of Deviance* (Boulder, CO: Westview Press, 1995); Mark Colvin, *Crime and Coercion: An Integrated Theory of Chronic Criminality* (New York: Palgrave Press, 2000).

FIGURE 9.4

Gottfredson and Hirschi's General Theory of Crime

Criminal Offender

Impulsive personality
- Physical
- Insensitive
- Risk-taking
- Short-sighted
- Nonverbal

Low self-control
- Poor parenting
- Deviant parents
- Lack of supervision
- Active
- Self-centered

Weakening of social bonds
- Attachment
- Involvement
- Commitment
- Belief

+

Criminal Opportunity
- Presence of gangs
- Lack of supervision
- Lack of guardianship
- Suitable targets

=

Criminal Act
- Delinquency
- Smoking
- Drinking
- Underage sex
- Substance abuse

EXHIBIT 9.4

The Elements of Impulsivity: Signs that a Person Has Low Self-Control

Insensitive
Physical
Shortsighted
Nonverbal
Here-and-now orientation
Unstable social relations
Enjoys deviant behaviors
Risk-taker
Refuses to work for distant goals
Lacks diligence
Lacks tenacity
Adventuresome
Self-centered
Shameless
Imprudent
Lacks cognitive and verbal skills
Enjoys danger and excitement

of their criminality (for example, impulsivity) is essentially the same?[97]

SELF-CONTROL AND CRIME Gottfredson and Hirschi claim that the principles of **self-control theory** can explain all varieties of criminal behavior and all the social and behavioral correlates of crime. That is, such widely disparate crimes as burglary, robbery, embezzlement, drug dealing, murder, rape, and insider trading all stem from a deficiency of self-control. Likewise, gender, racial, and ecological differences in crime rates can be explained by discrepancies in self-control. Put another way, the male crime rate is higher than the female crime rate because males have lower levels of self-control.

Unlike other theoretical models that explain only narrow segments of criminal behavior (such as theories of teenage gang formation), Gottfredson and Hirschi argue that self-control applies equally to all crimes, ranging from murder to corporate theft. For example, Gottfredson and Hirschi maintain that white-collar crime rates remain low because people who lack self-control rarely attain the positions necessary to commit those crimes. However, relatively few white-collar criminals lack self-control to the same degree and in the same manner as criminals such as rapists and burglars. Although the criminal activity of individuals with low self-control also declines as those individuals mature, they maintain an offense rate that remains consistently higher than those with strong self-control.

SUPPORT FOR GTC Since the publication of *A General Theory of Crime,* numerous researchers have attempted to test the validity of Gottfredson and Hirschi's theoretical views. One approach involved identifying indicators of impulsiveness and self-control to determine whether scales measuring these factors correlate with measures of criminal activity. A number of studies conducted both in the United States and abroad have successfully showed this type of association.[98] Some of the most important findings are included in Exhibit 9.5. When Alexander Vazsonyi and his associates analyzed self-control and deviant behavior with samples drawn from a number of different countries (Hungary, Switzerland, the Netherlands, the United States, and Japan), they found that low-self control is significantly related to antisocial behavior and that the association can be seen regardless of culture or national settings.[99]

ANALYZING THE GENERAL THEORY OF CRIME By integrating the concepts of socialization and criminality, Gottfredson and Hirschi help explain why some people who lack self-control can escape criminality, and, conversely, why some people who have self-control might not escape criminality. People who are at risk because they have impulsive personalities may forgo criminal careers because there are no criminal opportunities that satisfy their impulsive needs; instead, they may find other outlets for their impulsive personalities. In contrast, if the opportunity is strong enough, even people with relatively strong self-control may be tempted to violate the law; the incentives to commit crime may overwhelm self-control.

Integrating criminal propensity and criminal opportunity can explain why some children enter into chronic offending while others living in similar environments are able to resist criminal activity. It can also help us understand why the corporate executive with a spotless record gets caught up in business fraud. Even a successful executive may find self-control inadequate if the potential for illegal gain is large. The driven executive, accustomed to both academic and financial success, may find that the fear of failure can overwhelm self-control. During tough economic times, the impulsive manager who fears dismissal may be tempted to circumvent the law to improve the bottom line.[100]

Although the General Theory seems persuasive, several questions and criticisms remain unanswered. Among the most important are the following:

■ *Tautological:* Some critics argue that the theory is tautological or involves circular reasoning: How do we know when people are impulsive? When they commit crimes! Are all criminals impulsive? Of course, or else they would not have broken the law![101]

Gottfredson and Hirschi counter by saying that impulsivity is not itself a propensity to commit crime but a condition that inhibits people from appreciating the long-term consequences of their behavior. Consequently, if given the opportunity, they are more likely to indulge in criminal acts than their nonimpulsive counterparts.[102] According to Gottfredson and Hirschi, impulsivity and criminality are neither identical nor equivalent. Some impulsive people may channel their reckless energies into noncriminal activity, such as trading on the commodities markets or real estate speculation, and make a legitimate fortune for their efforts.

EXHIBIT 9.5

Empirical Evidence Supporting the General Theory of Crime

1. Novice offenders, lacking in self-control, commit a garden variety of criminal acts.

2. More mature and experienced criminals become more specialized in their choice of crime (for example, robbers, burglars, drug dealers).

3. Male and female drunk drivers are impulsive individuals who manifest low self-control.

4. Repeat violent offenders are more impulsive than their less violent peers.

5. Incarcerated youth enjoy risk-taking behavior and hold values and attitudes that suggest impulsivity.

6. Kids who take drugs and commit crime are impulsive and enjoy engaging in risky behaviors.

7. Measures of self-control can predict deviant and antisocial behavior across age groups ranging from teens to adults age 50.

8. People who commit white-collar and workplace crime have lower levels of self-control than nonoffenders.

9. Gang members have lower levels of self-control than the general population; gang members report lower levels of parental management, a factor associated with lower self-control.

10. Low self-control shapes perceptions of criminal opportunity and consequently conditions the decision to commit crimes.

11. People who lack self-control expect to commit crime in the future.

12. Kids whose problems develop early in life are the most resistant to change in treatment and rehabilitation programs.

13. Gender differences in self-control are responsible for crime rate differences. Females who lack self-control are as crime prone as males with similar personalities.

14. Parents who manage their children's behavior increase their self-control, which helps reduce their delinquent activities.

15. Having parents (or guardians) available to control behavior may reduce the opportunity to commit crime.

16. Victims have lower self-control than nonvictims. Impulsivity predicts both the likelihood that a person will engage in criminal behavior and the likelihood that the person will become a victim of crime.

17. People with poor impulse control are the most likely to engage in serious violent crime.

Notes: 1. Xiaogang Deng and Lening Zhang, "Correlates of Self-Control: An Empirical Test of Self-Control Theory," *Journal of Crime and Justice* 21 (1998): 89–103; 2. Alex Piquero, Raymond Paternoster, Paul Mazeroole, Robert Brame, and Charles Dean, "Onset Age and Offense Specialization," *Journal of Research in Crime and Delinquency* 36 (1999): 275–299; 3. Carl Keene. Paul Maxim, and James Teevan, "Drinking and Driving, Self-Control, and Gender: Testing a General Theory of Crime," *Journal of Research in Crime and Delinquency* 30 (1993): 30–46; 4. Judith DeJong, Matti Virkkunen, and Marku Linnoila, "Factors Associated with Recidivism in a Criminal Population," *Journal of Nervous and Mental Disease* 180 (1992): 543–550; 5. David Cantor," Drug Involvement and Offending among Incarcerated Juveniles." Paper presented at the annual meeting of the American Society of Criminology, Boston, November 1995; 6. David Brownfield and Ann Marie Sorenson, "Self-Control and Juvenile Delinquency: Theoretical Issues and an Empirical Assessment of Selected Elements of a General Theory of Crime," *Deviant Behavior* 14 (1993): 243–264; John Cochran, Peter Wood, and Bruce Arneklev, "Is the Religiosity-Delinquency Relationship Spurious? A Test of Arousal and Social Control Theories," *Journal of Research in Crime and Delinquency* 31 (1994): 92–123; 7. Velmer Burton, T. David Evans, Francis Cullen, Kathleen Olivares, and R. Gregory Dunaway, "Age, Self-Control, and Adults' Offending Behaviors: A Research Note Assessing a General Theory of Crime," *Journal of Criminal Justice* 27 (1999): 45–54; John Gibbs and Dennis Giever, "Self-Control and Its Manifestations among University Students: An Empirical Test of Gottfredson and Hirschi's General Theory," *Justice Quarterly* 12 (1995): 231–255; 8. Carey Herbert, "The Implications of Self-Control Theory for Workplace Offending." Paper presented at the annual meeting of the American Society of Criminology, San Diego, 1997; 9. Dennis Giever, Dana Lynskey, and Danette Monnet, "Gottfredson and Hirschi's General Theory of Crime and Youth Gangs: An Empirical Test on a Sample of Middle School Youth." Paper presented at the annual meeting of the American Society of Criminology, San Diego, 1997; 10. Douglas Longshore, Susan Turner, and Judith Stein, "Self-Control in a Criminal Sample: An Examination of Construct Validity," *Criminology* 34 (1996): 209–228; 11. Deng and Zhang, "Correlates of Self-Control: An Empirical Test of Self-Control Theory"; 12. Linda Pagani, Richard Tremblay, Frank Vitaro, and Sophie Parent, "Does Preschool Help Prevent Delinquency in Boys with a History of Perinatal Complications?" *Criminology* 36 (1998): 245–268; 13. Velmer Burton, Francis Cullen, T. David Evans, Leanne Fiftal Alarid, and R. Gregory Dunaway, "Gender, Self-Control, and Crime," *Journal of Research in Crime and Delinquency* 35 (1998): 123–147; 14. John Gibbs, Dennis Giever, and Jamie Martin, "Parental Management and Self-Control: An Empirical Test of Gottfredson and Hirschi's General Theory," *Journal of Research in Crime and Delinquency* 35 (1998): 40–70; 15. Vic Bumphus and James Anderson, "Family Structure and Race in a Sample of Offenders," *Journal of Criminal Justice* 27 (1999): 309–320; 16. Christopher Schreck, "Criminal Victimization and Low Self-Control: An Extension and Test of a General Theory of Crime," *Justice Quarterly* 16 (1999): 633–654; 17. Daniel Nagin and Greg Pogarsky, "Time and Punishment: Delayed Consequences and Criminal Behavior," *Journal of Quantitative Criminology* 20 (2004): 295–317.

- *Different classes of criminals:* As you may recall, Moffitt has identified two classes of criminals—adolescent-limited and life course persistent.[103] Other researchers have found that there may be different criminal paths or trajectories. People offend at a different pace, commit different kinds of crimes, and are influenced by different external forces.[104] For example, most criminals tend to be "generalists" who engage in a garden variety of criminal acts. However, people who commit violent crimes may be different from nonviolent offenders who

have maintained a unique set of personality traits and problem behaviors.[105] This would contradict the GTC vision that a single factor causes crime and that there is a single class of offender.

- *Ecological differences:* The GTC also fails to address individual and ecological patterns in the crime rate. For example, if crime rates are higher in Los Angeles than in Albany, New York, can it be assumed that residents of Los Angeles are more impulsive than residents of

Albany? There is little evidence of regional differences in impulsivity or self-control. Can these differences be explained solely by variation in criminal opportunity? Few researchers have tried to account for the influence of culture, ecology, economy, and so on.

Gottfredson and Hirschi might counter that crime rate differences may reflect criminal opportunity: One area may have more effective law enforcement, more draconian laws, and higher levels of guardianship. In their view, opportunity is controlled by economy and culture.

■ *Racial and gender differences:* Although distinct gender differences in the crime rate exist, there is little evidence that males are more impulsive than females (although females and males differ in many other personality traits).[106] Some research efforts have found gender differences in the association between self-control and crime; the theory predicts no such difference should occur.[107]

Looking at this relationship from another perspective, males who persist in crime exhibit characteristics that are different than female persisters. Women seem to be influenced by their place of residence, childhood and recent abuses, living with a criminal partner, selling drugs, stress, depression, fearfulness, their romantic relationships, their children, and whether they have suicidal thoughts. In contrast, men are more likely to persist because of their criminal peer associations, carrying weapons, alcohol abuse, and aggressive feelings. Impulsivity alone may not be able to explain why males and females persist or desist.[108]

Similarly, Gottfredson and Hirschi explain racial differences in the crime rate as a failure of childrearing practices in the African American community.[109] In so doing, they overlook issues of institutional racism, poverty, and relative deprivation, which have been shown to have a significant impact on crime rate differentials.

■ *Moral beliefs:* The General Theory also ignores the moral concept of right and wrong, or "belief," which Hirschi considered a cornerstone in his earlier writings on the social bond.[110] Does this mean that learning and assimilating moral values have little effect on criminality? Belief may be the weakest of the bonds associated with crime, and the General Theory reflects this relationship.[111]

■ *Peer influence:* A number of research efforts show that the quality of peer relations either enhance or control criminal behavior and that these influences vary over time.[112] As children mature, peer influence continues to grow.[113] Research shows that kids who lack self-control also have trouble maintaining relationships with law-abiding peers. They may either choose (or be forced) to seek out friends who are similarly limited in their ability to maintain self-control. Similarly, as they

mature they may seek out romantic relationships with law-violating boyfriends and/or girlfriends, and these entanglements enhance the likelihood that they will get further involved in crime (girls seem to be more deeply influenced by their delinquent boyfriends than boys by their delinquent girlfriends).[114]

This finding contradicts the GTC, which suggests the influence of friends should be stable and unchanging and that a relationship established later in life (for example, making friends) should not influence criminal propensity. Gottfredson and Hirschi might counter that it should come as no surprise that impulsive kids, lacking in self-control, seek out peers with similar personality characteristics.

■ *People change:* One of the most important questions raised about the GTC concerns its assumption that criminal propensity does not change. Is it possible that human personality and behavior patterns remain unaltered over the life course? Research shows that changing life circumstances, such as starting and leaving school, abusing substances and then "getting straight," and starting or ending personal relationships, all influence the frequency of offending.[115] As people mature, they may be better able to control their impulsive behavior and reduce their criminal activities.[116]

Ronald Simons has found that boys who were involved in deviant and oppositional behavior during childhood were able to turn their lives around if they

Rebecca Fallon, shown here, was committed to prison for life at 15 for the murder of a taxi driver. Gottfredson and Hirschi might argue that the impulsive personality that caused her to commit crime is unlikely to change and that a long prison sentence is justified because her lack of self-control is unlikely to improve behind bars. Do you agree? Can someone like Rebecca Fallon change?

later experienced improved parenting, increased school commitment, and/or reduced involvement with deviant peers. So while early childhood antisocial behavior may increase the chances of later criminality, even the most difficult children are at no greater risk for delinquency than are their conventional counterparts if they later experience positive changes in their daily lives and increased ties with significant others and institutions.[117]

While the Simons research seems to contradict the GTC, Gottfredson and Hirschi acknowledge that external factors such as parenting and school involvement may indeed reduce crime because they limit the opportunity to commit illegal acts. The child's criminal propensity remains the same, and if these external supports were once again weakened or removed, they would still be at risk for criminality.

■ *Modest relationship:* Some research results support the proposition that self-control is a causal factor in criminal and other forms of deviant behavior but that the association is at best quite modest.[118] This would indicate that other forces influence criminal behavior and that low self-control alone cannot predict the onset of a criminal or deviant career. Perhaps antisocial behavior is best explained by a condition that either develops subsequent to the development of self-control or is independent of a person's level of impulsivity.[119] This alternative quality, which may be the real stable latent trait, is still unknown.

■ *Cross-cultural differences:* There is some evidence that criminals in other countries do not lack self-control, indicating that the GTC may be culturally limited. For example, Otwin Marenin and Michael Resig actually found equal or higher levels of self-control in Nigerian criminals than in noncriminals.[120] Behavior that may be considered imprudent in one culture may be socially acceptable in another and therefore cannot be viewed as "lack of self-control."[121] There is, however, emerging evidence that the GTC may have validity in predicting criminality abroad.[122]

■ *Misreads human nature:* According to Francis Cullen, John Paul Wright, and Mitchell Chamlin, the GTC makes flawed assumptions about human character.[123] It assumes that people are essentially selfish, self-serving, and hedonistic and must therefore be controlled lest they gratify themselves at the expense of others. A more plausible view is that humans are inherently generous and kind; selfish hedonists may be a rare exception.

■ *One of many causes:* Research shows that even if lack of self-control is a prerequisite to crime, so are other social, neuropsychological, and physiological factors.[124] Social cultural factors have been found to make an independent contribution to criminal offending patterns.[125] Among the many psychological characteristics

that set criminals apart from the general population is their lack of self-direction; their behavior has a here and now orientation rather than being aimed at providing long-term benefits.[126] Law violators exhibit lower resting heart rate and perform poorly on tasks that trigger cognitive functions.[127]

■ *More than one kind of impulsivity:* Gottfredson and Hirschi assume that impulsivity is a singular construct—that is, one is either impulsive or not. However, there may be more than one kind of impulsive personality. For example, some people may be impulsive because they are sensation seekers who are constantly looking for novel experiences, while others lack deliberation and rarely think through problems. Some may give up easily while others act without thinking when they get upset.[128]

To read a critique of the GTC, use InfoTrac College Edition to access this article: Charles R. Tittle and Harold G. Grasmick, "Criminal Behavior and Age: A Test of Three Provocative Hypotheses," *Journal of Criminal Law and Criminology* 88 (fall 1997): 309–342.

Although questions like these remain, the strength of GTC lies in its scope and breadth: It attempts to explain all forms of crime and deviance, from lower-class gang delinquency to sexual harassment in the business community.[129] By integrating concepts of criminal choice, criminal opportunity, socialization, and personality, Gottfredson and Hirschi make a plausible argument that all deviant behaviors may originate at the same source. Continued efforts are needed to test the GTC and establish the validity of its core concepts. It remains one of the key developments of modern criminological theory.

A number of other theories suggesting that a master trait controls human development and the propensity to commit crime have been formulated. Concept Summary 9.2 summarizes the most prominent developmental theories.

EVALUATING DEVELOPMENTAL THEORIES

Although the differences between the views presented in this chapter may seem irreconcilable, they in fact share some common ground. They indicate that a criminal career must be understood as a passage along which people travel, that it has a beginning and an end, and that events and life circumstances influence the journey. The factors that affect a criminal career may include structural factors, such as income and status; socialization factors, such as family and peer relations; biological factors, such as size and strength; psychological factors, including intelligence and personality; and opportunity factors, such as free time, inadequate police protection, and a supply of easily stolen merchandise.

Developmental Theories

Theory	Major Premise	Strengths	Research Focus
Life Course Theories	As people go through the life course, social and personal traits undergo change and influence behavior.	Explains why some at-risk children desist from crime.	Identify critical moments in a person's life course that produce crime.
Integrated Cognitive Antisocial Potential (ICAP) Theory	People with antisocial potential (AP) are at risk to commit antisocial acts. AP can be viewed as both a long- and short-term phenomenon.	Identifies different types of criminal propensity and shows how they may influence behavior in both the short and long term.	Identify the components of long- and short-term AP.
Interactional Theory	Criminals go through lifestyle changes during their offending career.	Combines sociological and psychological theories.	Identify crime-producing interpersonal interactions and their reciprocal effects.
General Theory of Crime and Delinquency (GTCD)	Five critical life domains shape criminal behavior and are shaped by criminal behavior.	Shows that crime and other aspects of social life are interactive and developmental.	Measure the relationship between life domains and crime.
Age-Graded Theory	As people mature, the factors that influence their propensity to commit crime change. In childhood, family factors are critical; in adulthood, marital and job factors are key.	Shows how crime is a developmental process that shifts in direction over the life course.	Identify critical points in the life course that produce crime. Analyze the association between social capital and crime.
Latent Trait Theories	A master trait controls human development.	Explains the continuity of crime and chronic offending.	Identify master trait that produces crime.
General Theory of Crime	Crime and criminality are separate concepts. People choose to commit crime when they lack self-control. People lacking self-control will seize criminal opportunities.	Integrates choice and social control concepts. Identifies the difference between crime and criminality.	Measure association among impulsivity, low self-control, and criminal behaviors.
Differential Coercion Theory	Individuals exposed to coercive environments develop social-psychological deficits that enhance their probability of engaging in criminal behavior.	Explains why feeling of coercion is a master trait that determines behavior.	Measuring the sources of coercion.
Control Balance Theory	A person's "control ratio" influences his or her behavior.	Explains how the ability to control one's environment is a master trait.	Measuring control balance and imbalance.

Life course theories emphasize the influence of changing interpersonal and structural factors (that is, people change along with the world they live in). Latent trait theories place more emphasis on the fact that behavior is linked less to personal change and more to changes in the surrounding world.

These perspectives differ in their view of human development. Do people constantly change, as life course theories suggest, or are they stable, constant, and changeless, as the latent trait view indicates? Are the factors that produce criminality different at each stage of life, as the life course view suggests, or does a master trait, for example, control balance, self-control, or coercion, steer the course of human behavior?

It is also possible that these two positions are not mutually exclusive, and each may make a notable contribution to understanding the onset and continuity of a criminal career.

For example, research by Bradley Entner Wright and his associates found evidence supporting both latent trait and life course theories.[130] Their research, conducted with subjects in New Zealand, indicates that low self-control in childhood predicts disrupted social bonds and criminal offending later in life, a finding that supports latent trait theory. They also found that maintaining positive social bonds helps reduce criminality and that maintaining prosocial bonds could even counteract the effect of low self-control. Latent traits are an important influence on crime, but their findings indicate that social relationships that form later in life appear to influence criminal behavior "above and beyond" individuals' preexisting characteristics.[131] This finding may reflect the fact that there are two classes of criminals: a less serious group who are influenced by life events, and a more chronic group whose latent traits insulate them from any positive prosocial relationships.[132]

The Fast Track Project

Fast Track is designed to prevent serious antisocial behavior and related adolescent problems in high-risk children entering first grade. The intervention is guided by a developmental approach that suggests that antisocial behavior is the product of the interaction of multiple social and psychological influences:

1. Residence in low-income, high-crime communities places stressors and influences on children and families that increase their risk levels. In these areas, families characterized by marital conflict and instability make consistent and effective parenting difficult to achieve, particularly with children who are impulsive and of difficult temperament.

2. Children of high-risk families usually enter the education process poorly prepared for its social, emotional, and cognitive demands. Their parents often are unprepared to relate effectively with school staff, and a poor home–school bond often aggravates the child's adjustment problems. They may be grouped with other children who are similarly unprepared. This peer group may be negatively influenced by disruptive classroom contexts and punitive teachers.

3. Over time, aggressive and disruptive children are rejected by families and peers and tend to receive less support from teachers. All of these processes increase the risk of antisocial behaviors, in a process that begins in elementary school and lasts throughout adolescence. During this period, peer influences, academic difficulties, and dysfunctional personal identity development can contribute to serious conduct problems and related risky behaviors.

What Does Fast Track Do?

The Fast Track provides intervention based on the assumption that improving child competencies, parenting effectiveness, school context, and school–home communications will, over time, contribute to preventing antisocial behavior across the period from early childhood through adolescence. To carry out this mission, in four sites across the United States, Fast Track coordinators identified (by their conduct problems at home and at school) a sample of 445 high-risk children in kindergarten; a matched control group of 446 youth was also identified. Treatment was provided in a number of phases stretching from 1st to 10th grade:

Elementary School Phase of the Intervention (Grades 1–5)

- Teacher-led classroom curricula (called PATHS) as a universal intervention directed toward the development of emotional concepts, social understanding, and self-control (including weekly teacher consultation about classroom management); and the following five programs administered to high-risk intervention subjects:

(continued)

PUBLIC POLICY IMPLICATIONS OF DEVELOPMENTAL THEORY

There have been a number of policy-based initiatives based on premises of developmental theory. These typically feature multi-systemic treatment efforts designed to provide at-risk kids with personal, social, educational, and family services. For example, one program found that an intervention that promotes academic success, social competence, and educational enhancement during the elementary grades can reduce risky sexual practices and their accompanying health consequences in early adulthood.[133]

Other programs are now employing multidimensional strategies and are aimed at targeting children in preschool through the early elementary grades in order to alter the direction of their life course. Many of the most successful programs are aimed at strengthening children's social-emotional competence and positive coping skills and suppressing the development of antisocial, aggressive behavior.[134] Research evaluations indicate that the most promising multicomponent crime and substance abuse prevention programs for youths, especially those at high risk, are aimed at improving their developmental skills. They may include a school component, an after-school component, and a parent-involvement component. All of these components have the common goal of increasing protective factors and decreasing risk factors in the areas of the family, the community, the school, and the individual.[135] For example, the Boys and Girls Clubs and School Collaborations' Substance Abuse Prevention Program includes a school component called SMART (skills mastery and resistance training) Teachers, an after-school component called SMART Kids, and a parent-involvement component called SMART Parents. Each component is designed to reduce specific risk factors in the children's school, family, community, and personal environments.[136] The Policy and Practice in Criminology feature "The Fast Track Project" describes a developmentally based program designed to impact youth early in their life course.

- Parent training groups designed to promote the development of positive family–school relationships and to teach parents behavior management skills, particularly in the use of praise, time-out, and self-restraint.

- Home visits for the purpose of fostering parents' problem-solving skills, self-efficacy, and life management.

- Child social skill training groups (called Friendship Groups).

- Child tutoring in reading; and child friendship enhancement in the classroom (called Peer Pairing).

Adolescent Phase of the Intervention (Grades 6–10)

- Standard and individualized activities for high-risk youth and families. Group-based interventions were de-emphasized in order to avoid promoting engagement with deviant peers.

- Curriculum-based parent and youth group meetings were included in the intervention, to support children in their transition into middle school (grades 5–7).

- Individualized services, designed to strengthen protective factors and reduce risk factors in areas of particular need for each youth, which included academic tutoring, mentoring, support for positive peer-group involvement, home visiting and family problem solving, and liaisons with school and community agencies.

Evaluation of the Fast Track Program

The efficacy of the Fast Track prevention program is tested periodically by comparing the group of children receiving intervention services to children in the control group, with regard to a wide range of problem-behavior outcomes and their development over time. Significant progress was made toward the goal of improving competencies of the children receiving intervention services and their parents. Compared to the control group, the intervention children improved their social-cognitive and academic skills, and their parents reduced their use of harsh discipline. These group differences also were reflected in behavioral improvements during the elementary school years and beyond. Compared with children in the control group, children in the intervention group displayed significantly less aggressive behavior at home, in the classroom, and on the playground. By the end of 3rd grade, 37 percent of the intervention group had become free of conduct problems, in contrast with 27 percent of the control group. By the end of elementary school, 33 percent of the intervention group had a developmental trajectory of decreasing conduct problems, as compared with 27 percent of the control group. Furthermore, placement in special education by the end of elementary school was about one-fourth lower in the intervention group than in the control group.

Group differences continued through adolescence. Court records indicate that by 8th grade, 38 percent of the intervention group boys had been arrested, in contrast with 42 percent of the control group. Finally, psychiatric interviews after 9th grade indicate that the Fast Track intervention has reduced serious conduct disorder by over a third, from 27 percent to 17 percent. These effects generalized across gender and ethnic groups and across the wide range of child and family characteristics measured by Fast Track.

Critical Thinking

1. The success of the Fast Track program has led to its implementation in several school systems across the country, as well as in several schools in Great Britain, Australia, and Canada. Would you want such a program implemented in your local school system?

2. Should the government devote significant resources to helping at-risk kids or might the funds be better off spent on programs that provide advanced training to the academically gifted?

InfoTrac College Edition Research

The Fast Track program is certainly not unique. To read an analysis of the effects of other complex developmental treatment programs on criminal behavior, go to InfoTrac College Edition and read: David Farrington and Brandon Welsh, "Family-Based Prevention of Offending: A Meta-Analysis," *Australian and New Zealand Journal of Criminology* 36 (2003): 127–151.

Source: Project overview, Fast Track Data Center: http://www.fasttrackproject.org/datacenter.htm and http://www.fasttrackproject.org/fasttrack-overview.htm. Accessed September1, 2005.

- Life course theories argue that events that take place over the life course influence criminal choices.

- The cause of crime constantly changes as people mature. At first, the nuclear family influences behavior; during adolescence, the peer group dominates; in adulthood, marriage and career are critical.

- There are a variety of pathways to crime: some kids are sneaky, others hostile, and still others defiant.

- Crime may be part of a variety of social problems, including health, physical, and interpersonal troubles.

- Maruna's research shows that going straight is a long process that begins when offenders feel a sense of fulfillment in engaging in productive behaviors; they start feeling in control of their future and have a newfound purpose in life.

- Sampson and Laub's age-graded theory holds that the social sources of behavior change over the life course.

- People who develop social capital are best able to avoid antisocial entanglements.

- There are important life events or turning points that enable adult offenders to desist from crime.

- Among the most important are getting married and serving in the military.

- Laub and Sampson have found that while many criminals desist from crime, they still face other risks such as an untimely death.

- Latent trait theories hold that some underlying condition present at birth or soon after controls behavior.

- Suspect traits include low IQ, impulsivity, and personality structure. This underlying trait explains the

- continuity of offending because, once present, it remains with a person throughout his or her life.

- Opportunity to commit crime varies; latent traits remain stable.

- The General Theory of Crime, developed by Gottfredson and Hirschi, integrates choice theory concepts. People with latent traits choose crime over non-crime; the opportunity for crime mediates their choice.

- Impulsive people have low self-control and a weak bond to society; they often cannot resist criminal opportunities.

- Programs that are based on developmental theory are typically multidimensional and multifaceted.

ThomsonNOW

Thomson NOW! Optimize your study time and master key chapter concepts with **ThomsonNOW™**—the first web-based assessment-centered study tool for Criminology. This powerful resource helps you determine your unique study needs and provides you with a *Personalized Study Plan,* guiding you to interactive media that includes Learning Modules, Topic Reviews, ABC Video Clips with Questions, Animations, an integrated E-book, and more!

Thinking Like a Criminologist

Gary L. Sampson, 41, addicted to alcohol and cocaine, was a deadbeat dad, a two-bit thief, and a bank robber with a long history of violence. On August 1, 2001, he turned himself in to the Vermont State Police after fleeing from a string of three murders he committed in Massachusetts and New Hampshire.

Those who knew Sampson speculated that his murders were a desperate finale to a troubled life. During his early life in New England, he once bound, gagged, and beat three elderly women in a candy store, hijacked cars at knife-

point, and had been medically diagnosed as schizophrenic. In 1977, he married a 17-year-old girl he had impregnated; 2 months later he was arrested and charged with rape for having "unnatural intercourse with a child under 16." Although he was acquitted of that charge, his wife noticed that Sampson had started developing a hair-trigger temper and had become increasingly violent; their marriage soon ended. As the years passed, Sampson had at least four failed marriages, was an absentee father to two children, and became an alcoholic and a

drug user; he spent nearly half of his adult life behind bars.

Jumping bail after being arrested for theft from an antique store, he headed south to North Carolina and took on a new identity: Gary Johnson, a construction worker. He took up with Ricki Carter, a transvestite, but their relationship was anything but stable. Sampson once put a gun to Carter's head, broke his ribs, and threatened to kill his family. After his breakup with Carter, Sampson moved in with a new girlfriend, Karen Anderson, and began pulling bank jobs.

When the police closed in, Sampson fled north. Needing transportation, he pulled three carjackings and killed the drivers, one a 19-year-old college freshman who had stopped to give Sampson a hand. In December 2003, Sampson received a sentence of death from a jury who was not swayed by his claim that he was mentally unfit.

The governor is unsettled by the verdict. She wants to grant clemency in the case and reduce Sampson's sentence to life in prison. She asks you to help her make the judgment: Were Sampson's crimes a product of his impaired development? Should he be spared death?

Doing Research on the Web

Before you answer, you might want to think about the victims of predatory criminals. Go to InfoTrac College Edition and read: Dean G. Kilpatrick, "Interpersonal Violence and Public Policy: What about the Victims?" *Journal of Law, Medicine & Ethics* 32 (2004): 73–81.

Should we use harsh punishments to bring down the crime rate? Would they work with chronic offenders? Go to InfoTrac College Edition and read: Matthew Yglesias, "The Research Wars: Hard-Liners Gave Long Prison Sentences Credit for the Drop in Crime. They Were Mostly Wrong," *The American Prospect* 14 (2003): 39–41.

Go to the National Center for Policy Analysis for a conservative take on this issue: http://www.ncpa.org/pi/crime/crime33b.html#D.

| | | | | | | | | | | | | | | | | | | | | | | | | | | | | | | | | | | | | | | | | | | | | |

BOOK COMPANION WEBSITE

http://cj.wadsworth.com/siegel_crimtpt9e To quiz yourself on the material in this chapter, go to the companion website, where you'll find chapter-by-chapter online tutorial quizzes, a final exam, ABC videos with questions, chapter outlines, chapter review, chapter-by-chapter web links, flash cards, and more!

KEY TERMS

desist (284)
developmental theories (284)
life course theories (285)
latent trait theories (285)
problem behavior syndrome (PBS) (287)

authority conflict pathway (287)
covert pathway (287)
overt pathway (288)
adolescent-limited offenders (290)
life course persisters (291)
integrated theories (293)

turning points (293)
social capital (295)
latent trait (296)
human nature theory (297)
General Theory of Crime (GTC) (297)
self-control theory (302)

CRITICAL THINKING QUESTIONS

1. Do you consider yourself to have social capital? If so, what form does it take?

2. Someone you know gets a perfect score on the SAT. What personal, family, and social characteristics do you think this individual has? Another person becomes a serial killer. Without knowing this person, what personal, family, and social charac-

teristics do you think this individual has? If "bad behavior" is explained by multiple problems, is "good behavior" explained by multiple strengths?

3. Do you believe it is a latent trait that makes a person crime prone, or is crime a function of environment and socialization?

4. Do you agree with Loeber's multiple pathways model? Do you know people who have traveled down those paths?

5. Do people really change, or do they stay the same but appear to be different because their life circumstances have changed?

1. See, generally, Sheldon Glueck and Eleanor Glueck, *500 Criminal Careers* (New York: Knopf, 1930); Sheldon Glueck and Eleanor Glueck, *One Thousand Juvenile Delinquents* (Cambridge, MA: Harvard University Press, 1934); Sheldon Glueck and Eleanor Glueck, *Predicting Delinquency and Crime* (Cambridge, MA: Harvard University Press, 1967), pp. 82–83.

2. Sheldon Glueck and Eleanor Glueck, *Unraveling Juvenile Delinquency* (Cambridge, MA: Harvard University Press, 1950).

3. Ibid., p. 48.

4. See, generally, John Laub and Robert Sampson, "The Sutherland–Glueck Debate: On the Sociology of Criminological Knowledge," *American Journal of Sociology* 96 (1991): 1,402–1,440; John Laub and Robert Sampson, "Unraveling Families and Delinquency: A Reanalysis of the Gluecks' Data," *Criminology* 26 (1988): 355–380.

5. Marvin Wolfgang, Robert Figlio, and Thorsten Sellin, *Delinquency in a Birth Cohort* (Chicago: University of Chicago Press, 1972).

6. Rolf Loeber and Marc LeBlanc, "Toward a Developmental Criminology," in *Crime and Justice*, vol. 12, eds. Norval Morris and Michael Tonry (Chicago: University of Chicago Press, 1990), pp. 375–473; Rolf Loeber and Marc LeBlanc, "Developmental Criminology Updated," in *Crime and Justice*, vol. 23, ed. Michael Tonry (Chicago: University of Chicago Press, 1998), pp. 115–198.

7. Marvin Krohn, Alan Lizotte, and Cynthia Perez, "The Interrelationship between Substance Use and Precocious Transitions to Adult Sexuality," *Journal of Health and Social Behavior* 38 (1997): 87–103, at 88.

8. Bradley Entner Wright, Avashalom Caspi, Terrie Moffitt, and Phil Silva, "The Effects of Social Ties on Crime Vary by Criminal Propensity: A Life-Course Model of Interdependence," *Criminology* 39 (2001): 321–352.

9. Joan McCord, "Family Relationships, Juvenile Delinquency, and Adult Criminality," *Criminology* 29 (1991): 397–417.

10. Paul Mazerolle, "Delinquent Definitions and Participation Age: Assessing the Invariance Hypothesis," *Studies on Crime and Crime Prevention* 6 (1997): 151–168.

11. Peggy Giordano, Stephen Cernkovich, and Jennifer Rudolph, "Gender, Delinquency, and Desistance: Toward a Theory of Cognitive Transformation?" *American Journal of Sociology* 107(2002): 990–1,064.

12. John Hagan and Holly Foster, "S/He's a Rebel: Toward a Sequential Stress Theory of Delinquency and Gendered Pathways to Disadvantage in Emerging Adulthood," *Social Forces* 82 (2003): 53–86.

13. G. R. Patterson, Barbara DeBaryshe, and Elizabeth Ramsey, "A Developmental Perspective on Antisocial Behavior," *American Psychologist* 44 (1989): 329–335.

14. Robert Sampson and John Laub, "Crime and Deviance in the Life Course," *American Review of Sociology* 18 (1992): 63–84.

15. David Farrington, Darrick Jolliffe, Rolf Loeber, Madga Stouthamer-Loeber, and Larry Kalb, "The Concentration of Offenders in Families, and Family Criminality in the Prediction of Boys' Delinquency," *Journal of Adolescence* 24 (2001): 579–596.

16. Raymond Paternoster, Charles Dean, Alex Piquero, Paul Mazerolle, and Robert Brame, "Generality, Continuity, and Change in Offending," *Journal of Quantitative Criminology* 13 (1997): 231–266.

17. Magda Stouthamer-Loeber and Evelyn Wei, "The Precursors of Young Fatherhood and Its Effect on Delinquency of Teenage Males," *Journal of Adolescent Health* 22 (1998): 56–65; Richard Jessor, John Donovan, and Francis Costa, *Beyond Adolescence: Problem Behavior and Young Adult Development* (New York: Cambridge University Press, 1991); Xavier Coll, Fergus Law, Aurelio Tobias, Keith Hawton, and Joseph Tomas, "Abuse and Deliberate Self-Poisoning in Women: A Matched Case-Control Study," *Child Abuse and Neglect* 25 (2001): 1,291–1,293.

18. Richard Miech, Avshalom Caspi, Terrie Moffitt, Bradley Entner Wright, and Phil Silva, "Low Socioeconomic Status and Mental Disorders: A Longitudinal Study of Selection and Causation during Young Adulthood," *American Journal of Sociology* 104 (1999): 1,096–1,131; Krohn, Lizotte, and Perez, "The Interrelationship between Substance Use and Precocious Transitions to Adult Sexuality," p. 88; Richard Jessor, "Risk Behavior in Adolescence: A Psychosocial Framework for Understanding and Action," in *Adolescents at Risk: Medical and Social Perspectives*, eds. D. E. Rogers and E. Ginzburg (Boulder, CO: Westview Press, 1992).

19. Deborah Capaldi and Gerald Patterson, "Can Violent Offenders Be Distinguished from Frequent Offenders: Prediction from Childhood to Adolescence," *Journal of Research in Crime and Delinquency* 33 (1996): 206–231; D. Wayne Osgood, "The Covariation among Adolescent Problem Behaviors." Paper presented at the annual meeting of the American Society of Criminology, Baltimore, November 1990.

20. For an analysis of more than thirty studies, see Mark Lipsey and James Derzon, "Predictors of Violent or Serious Delinquency in Adolescence and Early Adulthood: A Synthesis of Longitudinal Research," in *Serious and Violent Juvenile Offenders: Risk Factors and Successful Interventions*, eds. Rolf Loeber and David Farrington (Thousand Oaks, CA: Sage, 1998).

21. Gina Wingood, Ralph DiClemente, Rick Crosby, Kathy Harrington, Susan Davies, and Edward Hook, III, "Gang Involvement and the Health of African American Female Adolescents," *Pediatrics* 110 (2002): 57.

22. David Husted, Nathan Shapira, and Martin Lazoritz, "Adolescent Gambling, Substance Use, and Other Delinquent Behavior," *Psychiatric Times* 20 (2003): 52–55;

23. Krohn, Lizotte, and Perez, "The Interrelationship between Substance Use and Precocious Transitions to Adult Sexuality," p. 88; Richard Jessor, "Risk Behavior in Adolescence: A Psychosocial Framework for Understanding and Action," in *Adolescents at Risk: Medical and Social Perspectives*, ed. D. E. Rogers and E. Ginzburg (Boulder, CO: Westview Press, 1992).

24. Terence Thornberry, Carolyn Smith, and Gregory Howard, "Risk Factors for Teenage Fatherhood," *Journal of Marriage and the Family* 59 (1997): 505–522; Todd Miller, Timothy Smith, Charles Turner,

Margarita Guijarro, and Amanda Hallet, "A Meta-Analytic Review of Research on Hostility and Physical Health," *Psychological Bulletin* 119 (1996): 322–348; Marianne Junger, "Accidents and Crime," in *The Generality of Deviance*, eds. T. Hirschi and M. Gottfredson (New Brunswick, NJ: Transaction Books, 1993).

25. James Marquart, Victoria Brewer, Patricia Simon, and Edward Morse, "Lifestyle Factors among Female Prisoners with Histories of Psychiatric Treatment," *Journal of Criminal Justice* 29 (2001): 319–328; Rolf Loeber, David Farrington, Magda Stouthamer-Loeber, Terrie Moffitt, Avshalom Caspi, and Don Lynam, "Male Mental Health Problems, Psychopathy, and Personality Traits: Key Findings from the First 14 Years of the Pittsburgh Youth Study," *Clinical Child and Family Psychology Review* 4 (2002): 273–297.

26. Robert Johnson, S. Susan Su, Dean Gerstein, Hee-Choon Shin, and John Hoffman, "Parental Influences on Deviant Behavior in Early Adolescence: A Logistic Response Analysis of Age and Gender-Differentiated Effects," *Journal of Quantitative Criminology* 11 (1995): 167–192; Judith Brooks, Martin Whiteman, and Patricia Cohen, "Stage of Drug Use, Aggression, and Theft / Vandalism," in *Drugs, Crime and Other Deviant Adaptations: Longitudinal Studies*, ed. Howard Kaplan (New York: Plenum Press, 1995), pp. 83–96.

27. Helene Raskin White, Peter Tice, Rolf Loeber, and Magda Stouthamer-Loeber, "Illegal Acts Committed by Adolescents under the Influence of Alcohol and Drugs," *Journal of Research in Crime and Delinquency* 39 (2002): 131–153. Candace Kruttschnitt, Jane McLeod, and Maude Dornfeld, "The Economic Environment of Child Abuse," *Social Problems* 41 (1994): 299–312.

28. David Fergusson, L. John Horwood, Elizabeth Ridder, "Show Me the Child at Seven II: Childhood Intelligence and Later Outcomes in Adolescence and Young Adulthood,"*Journal of Child Psychology & Psychiatry & Allied Disciplines* 46 (2005): 850–859.

29. Margit Wiesner and Ranier Silbereisen,"Trajectories of Delinquent Behaviour in Adolescence and Their Co-variates: Relations with Initial and Time-Averaged Factors," *Journal of Adolescence* 26 (2003): 753–771.

30. Rolf Loeber, Phen Wung, Kate Keenan, Bruce Giroux, Magda Stouthamer-

Loeber, Wemoet Van Kammen, and Barbara Maughan, "Developmental Pathways in Disruptive Behavior," *Development and Psychopathology* (1993): 12–48.

31. Sheila Royo Maxwell and Christopher Maxwell, "Examining the 'Criminal Careers' of Prostitutes within the Nexus of Drug Use, Drug Selling, and Other Illicit Activities," *Criminology* 38 (2000): 787–809.

32. Alex R. Piquero and He Len Chung, "On the Relationships between Gender, Early Onset, and the Seriousness of Offending," *Journal of Criminal Justice* 29 (2001): 189–206.

33. David Nurco, Timothy Kinlock, and Mitchell Balter, "The Severity of Preaddiction Criminal Behavior among Urban, Male Narcotic Addicts and Two Nonaddicted Control Groups," *Journal of Research in Crime and Delinquency* 30 (1993): 293–316.

34. W. Alex Mason, Rick Kosterman, J. David Hawkins, Todd Herrenkohi, Liliana Lengua, and Elizabeth McCauley, "Predicting Depression, Social Phobia, and Violence in Early Adulthood from Childhood Behavior Problems," *Journal of the American Academy of Child and Adolescent Psychiatry* 43 (2004): 307–315; Rolf Loeber and David Farrington, "Young Children Who Commit Crime: Epidemiology, Developmental Origins, Risk Factors, Early Interventions, and Policy Implications," *Development and Psychopathology* 12 (2000): 737–762; Patrick Lussier, Jean Proulx, and Marc LeBlanc, Criminal Propensity, Deviant Sexual Interests and Criminal Activity of Sexual Aggressors against Women: A Comparison of Explanatory Models," *Criminology* 43 (2005): 249–281.

35. Dawn Jeglum Bartusch, Donald Lynam, Terrie Moffitt, and Phil Silva, "Is Age Important? Testing a General versus a Developmental Theory of Antisocial Behavior," *Criminology* 35 (1997): 13–48.

36. Hanno Petras, Nicholas Ialongo, Sharon Lambert, Sandra Barrueco, Cindy Schaeffer, Howard Chilcoat, and Sheppard Kellam, "The Utility of Elementary School TOCA-R Scores in Identifying Later Criminal Court Violence among Adolescent Females,". *Journal of the American Academy of Child and Adolescent Psychiatry* 44 (2005): 790–797; Hanno Petras, Howard Chilcoat, Philip Leaf, Nicholas Ialongo, and Sheppard Kellam, "Utility of TOCA-R Scores during the Elementary School Years in Identifying Later Violence

among Adolescent Males," *Journal of the American Academy of Child and Adolescent Psychiatry* 43 (2004): 88–96.

37. W. Alex Mason, Rick Kosterman, J. David Hawkins, Todd Herrenkohl, Liliana Lengua, and Elizabeth McCauley, "Predicting Depression, Social Phobia, and Violence in Early Adulthood from Childhood Behavior Problems," *Journal of the American Academy of Child and Adolescent Psychiatry* 43 (2004): 307–315; Ronald Prinz and Suzanne Kerns, "Early Substance Use by Juvenile Offenders," *Child Psychiatry and Human Development* 33(2003): 263–268.

38. Glenn Clingempeel and Scott Henggeler, "Aggressive Juvenile Offenders Transitioning into Emerging Adulthood: Factors Discriminating Persistors and Desistors," *American Journal of Orthopsychiatry* 73 (2003): 310–323.

39. David Gadd and Stephen Farrall, "Criminal Careers, Desistance, and Subjectivity: Interpreting Men's Narratives of Change," *Theoretical Criminology* 8 (2004): 123–156.

40. G. R. Patterson, L. Crosby, and S. Vuchinich, "Predicting Risk for Early Police Arrest," *Journal of Quantitative Criminology* 8 (1992): 335–355.

41. Holly Hartwig and Jane Myers, "A Different Approach: Applying a Wellness Paradigm to Adolescent Female Delinquents and Offenders," *Journal of Mental Health Counseling* 25 (2003): 57–76.

42. Terrie Moffitt, Avshalom Caspi, Michael Rutter, and Phil Silva, *Sex Differences in Antisocial Behavior: Conduct Disorder, Delinquency, and Violence in the Dunedin Longitudinal Study* (London: Cambridge University Press, 2001).

43. Lisa Broidy, Richard Tremblay, Bobby Brame, David Fergusson, John Horwood, Robert Laird, Terrie Moffitt, Daniel Nagin, John Bates, Kenneth Dodge, Rolf Loeber, Donald Lynam, Gregory Pettit, and Frank Vitaro, "Developmental Trajectories of Childhood Disruptive Behaviors and Adolescent Delinquency: A Six-Site, Cross-National Study," *Developmental Psychology* 39 (2003): 222–245.

44. Ick-Joong Chung, Karl G Hill, J. David Hawkins, Lewayne Gilchrist, and Daniel Nagin, "Childhood Predictors of Offense Trajectories," *Journal of Research in Crime and Delinquency* 39 (2002): 60–91.

45. Amy D'Unger, Kenneth Land, Patricia McCall, and Daniel Nagin, "How Many Latent Classes of Delinquent/Criminal Careers? Results from Mixed Poisson Regression Analyses," *American Journal of Sociology* 103 (1998): 1,593–1,630.

46. Alex Piquero and Timothy Brezina, "Testing Moffitt's Account of Adolescent-Limited Delinquency," *Criminology* 39 (2001): 353–370.

47. Terrie Moffitt, "Adolescence-Limited and Life-Course Persistent Antisocial Behavior: A Developmental Taxonomy," *Psychological Review* 100 (1993): 674–701.

48. Terrie Moffitt, "Natural Histories of Delinquency," in *Cross-National Longitudinal Research on Human Development and Criminal Behavior,* eds. Elmar Weitekamp and Hans-Jurgen Kerner (Dordrecht, Netherlands: Kluwer, 1994), pp. 3–65.

49. Andrea Donker, Wilma Smeenk, Peter van der Laan, and Frank Verhulst, "Individual Stability of Antisocial Behavior from Childhood to Adulthood: Testing the Stability Postulate of Moffitt's Developmental Theory," *Criminology* 41 (2003): 593–609.

50. Robert Vermeiren, "Psychopathology and Delinquency in Adolescents: A Descriptive and Developmental Perspective," *Clinical Psychology Review* 23 (2003): 277–318; Paul Mazerolle, Robert Brame, Ray Paternoster, Alex Piquero, and Charles Dean, "Onset Age, Persistence, and Offending Versatility: Comparisons across Sex," *Criminology* 38 (2000): 1,143–1,172.

51. Adrian Raine, Rolf Loeber, Magda Stouthamer-Loeber, Terrie Moffitt, Avshalom Caspi, and Don.Lynam, "Neurocognitive Impairments in Boys on the Life-Course Persistent Antisocial Path," *Journal of Abnormal Psychology* 114 (2005): 38–49.

52. Per-Olof Wikstrom and Rolf Loeber, "Do Disadvantaged Neighborhoods Cause Well-Adjusted Children to Become Adolescent Delinquents? A Study of Male Juvenile Serious Offending, Individual Risk and Protective Factors, and Neighborhood Context," *Criminology* 38 (2000): 1,109–1,142.

53. Rolf Loeber and Magda Stouthamer-Loeber, "Development of Juvenile Aggression and Violence," *American Psychologist* 53 (1998): 242–259.

54. Stephen Farrall and Benjamin Bowling, "Structuration, Human Development, and Desistance from Crime," *British Journal of Criminology* 39 (1999): 253–268.

55. Robert Sampson and John Laub, *Crime in the Making: Pathways and Turning Points through Life* (Cambridge, MA: Harvard University Press, 1993); John Laub and Robert Sampson, "Turning Points in the Life Course: Why Change Matters to the Study of Crime." Paper presented at the annual meeting of the American Society of Criminology, New Orleans, November 1992.

56. Terri Orbuch, James House, Richard Mero, and Pamela Webster, "Marital Quality over the Life Course," *Social Psychology Quarterly* 59 (1996): 162–171; Lee Lillard and Linda Waite, "'Til Death Do Us Part: Marital Disruption and Mortality," *American Journal of Sociology* 100 (1995): 1,131–1,156.

57. Mark Warr, "Life-Course Transitions and Desistance from Crime," *Criminology* 36 (1998): 183–216.

58. Daniel Nagin and Raymond Paternoster, "Personal Capital and Social Control: The Deterrence Implications of a Theory of Criminal Offending," *Criminology* 32 (1994): 581–606.

59. Leonore M. J. Simon, "Social Bond and Criminal Record History of Acquaintance and Stranger Violent Offenders," *Journal of Crime and Justice* 22 (1999): 131–146.

60. Raymond Paternoster and Robert Brame, "Multiple Routes to Delinquency? A Test of Developmental and General Theories of Crime," *Criminology* 35 (1997): 49–84.

61. Spencer De Li, "Legal Sanctions and Youths' Status Achievement: A Longitudinal Study," *Justice Quarterly* 16 (1999): 377–401.

62. Shawn Bushway, "The Impact of an Arrest on the Job Stability of Young White American Men," *Journal of Research on Crime and Delinquency* 35 (1999): 454–479.

63. Candace Kruttschnitt, Christopher Uggen, and Kelly Shelton, "Individual Variability in Sex Offending and Its Relationship to Informal and Formal Social Controls." Paper presented at the American Society of Criminology meeting, San Diego, 1997; Mark Collins and Don Weatherburn, "Unemployment and the Dynamics of Offender Populations," *Journal of Quantitative Criminology* 11 (1995): 231–245.

64. Robert Hoge, D. A. Andrews, and Alan Leschied, "An Investigation of Risk and Protective Factors in a Sample of Youthful Offenders," *Journal of Child Psychology and Psychiatry* 37 (1996): 419–424.

65. Richard Arum and Irenee Beattie, "High School Experience and the Risk of Adult Incarceration," *Criminology* 37 (1999): 515–540.

66. Ross Macmillan, Barbara J. McMorris, and Candace Kruttschnitt, "Linked Lives: Stability and Change in Maternal Circumstances and Trajectories of Antisocial Behavior in Children," *Child Development* 75 (2004): 205–220.

67. Avshalom Caspi, Terrie Moffitt, Bradley Entner Wright, and Phil Silva, "Early Failure in the Labor Market: Childhood and Adolescent Predictors of Unemployment in the Transition to Adulthood," *American Sociological Review* 63 (1998): 424–451.

68. Robert Sampson and John Laub, "Socioeconomic Achievement in the Life Course of Disadvantaged Men: Military Service as a Turning Point, circa 1940–1965," *American Sociological Review* 61 (1996): 347–367.

69. Christopher Uggen, "Ex-Offenders and the Conformist Alternative: A Job Quality Model of Work and Crime," *Social Problems* 46 (1999): 127–151.

70. Erich Labouvie, "Maturing Out of Substance Use: Selection and Self-Correction," *Journal of Drug Issues* 26 (1996): 457–474.

71. Mark Warr, "Life-Course Transitions and Desistance from Crime," *Criminology* 36 (1998): 502–535.

72. Doris Layton MacKenzie and Spencer De Li, "The Impact of Formal and Informal Social Controls on the Criminal Activities of Probationers," *Journal of Research in Crime and Delinquency* 39 (2002): 243–278.

73. Pamela Webster, Terri Orbuch, and James House, "Effects of Childhood Family Background on Adult Marital Quality and Perceived Stability," *American Journal of Sociology* 101 (1995): 404–432.

74. Alex Piquero, John MacDonald, and Karen Parker, "Race, Local Life Circumstances, and Criminal Activity over the Life-Course," *Social Science Quarterly* 83 (2002): 654–671.

75. Personal Communication with Alex Piquero, September 24, 2002.

76. Ronald Simons, Eric Stewart, Leslie Gordon, Rand Conger, and Glen Elder, Jr., "Test of Life-Course Explanations for Stability and Change in Antisocial Behavior from Adolescence to Young Adulthood," *Criminology* 40 (2002): 401–435.

77. Dunlop and Johnson, "Family and Human Resources in the Development of a Female Crack-Seller Career."

78. Allison Steele, "Four Teenagers Arrested in BB Gun Shootings" *Concord Monitor,* 9 August 2005, p. 1.

79. David Rowe, D. Wayne Osgood, and W. Alan Nicewander, "A Latent Trait Approach to Unifying Criminal Careers," *Criminology* 28 (1990): 237–270.

80. Lee Ellis, "Neurohormonal Bases of Varying Tendencies to Learn Delinquent and Criminal Behavior," in *Behavioral Approaches to Crime and Delinquency,* eds. E. Morris and C. Braukmann (New York: Plenum, 1988), pp. 499–518.

81. David Rowe, Alexander Vazsonyi, and Daniel Flannery, "Sex Differences in Crime: Do Means and Within-Sex Variation Have Similar Causes?" *Journal of Research in Crime and Delinquency* 32 (1995): 84–100.

82. James Q. Wilson and Richard Herrnstein, *Crime and Human Nature* (New York: Simon & Schuster, 1985).

83. Ibid., p. 44.

84. Ibid., p. 171.

85. Michael Gottfredson and Travis Hirschi, *A General Theory of Crime* (Stanford, CA: Stanford University Press, 1990).

86. Ibid., p. 27.

87. Kevin Beaver and John Paul Wright, "Evaluating the Effects of Birth Complications on Low Self-Control in a Sample of Twins," *International Journal of Offender Therapy & Comparative Criminology* 49 (2005): 450–472.

88. Anthony Walsh and Lee Ellis, "Shoring up the Big Three: Improving Criminological Theories with Biosocial Concepts." Paper presented at the annual Society of Criminology meeting, San Diego, November 1997, p. 15.

89. Gottfredson and Hirschi, *A General Theory of Crime,* p. 90.

90. Ibid., p. 89.

91. Alex Piquero and Stephen Tibbetts, "Specifying the Direct and Indirect Effects of Low Self-Control and Situational Factors in Offenders' Decision Making: Toward a More Complete Model of Rational Offending," *Justice Quarterly* 13 (1996): 481–508.

92. David Forde and Leslie Kennedy, "Risky Lifestyles, Routine Activities, and the General Theory of Crime," *Justice Quarterly* 14 (1997): 265–294.

93. Gottfredson and Hirschi, *A General Theory of Crime,* p. 112.

94. Ibid.

95. Dennis Giever, "An Empirical Assessment of the Core Elements of Gottfredson and Hirschi's General Theory of Crime." Paper presented at the American Society of Criminology meeting, Boston, November 1995.

96. Robert Agnew, "The Contribution of Social-Psychological Strain Theory to the Explanation of Crime and Delinquency," *Anomie Theory: Advances in Criminological Theory,* vol. 6, eds. Freda Adler and William Laufer (New Brunswick, NJ: Transaction Books, 1995), pp. 81–96.

97. Travis Hirschi and Michael Gottfredson, "Rethinking the Juvenile Justice System," *Crime and Delinquency* 39 (1993): 262–271.

98. David Brownfield and Ann Marie Sorenson, "Self-Control and Juvenile Delinquency: Theoretical Issues and an Empirical Assessment of Selected Elements of a General Theory of Crime," *Deviant Behavior* 14 (1993): 243–264; Harold Grasmick, Charles Tittle, Robert Bursik, and Bruce Arneklev, "Testing the Core Empirical Implications of Gottfredson and Hirschi's General Theory of Crime," *Journal of Research in Crime and Delinquency* 30 (1993): 5–29; John Cochran, Peter Wood, and Bruce Arneklev, "Is the Religiosity–Delinquency Relationship Spurious? A Test of Arousal and Social Control Theories," *Journal of Research in Crime and Delinquency* 31 (1994): 92–123; Marc LeBlanc, Marc Ouimet, and Richard Tremblay, "An Integrative Control Theory of Delinquent Behavior: A Validation 1976–1985," *Psychiatry* 51 (1988): 164–176.

99. Alexander Vazsonyi, Janice Clifford Wittekind, Lara Belliston, andTimothy Van Loh, "Extending the General Theory of Crime to "The East:" Low Self-Control in Japanese Late Adolescents," *Journal of Quantitative Criminology* 20 (2004): 189–216; Alexander Vazsonyi, Lloyd Pickering, Marianne Junger, and Dick Hessing, "An Empirical Test of a General Theory of Crime: A Four-Nation Comparative Study of Self-Control and the Prediction of Deviance," *Journal of Research in Crime and Delinquency* 38 (2001): 91–131.

100. Michael Benson and Elizabeth Moore, "Are White-Collar and Common Offenders the Same? An Empirical and Theoretical Critique of a Recently Proposed General Theory of Crime," *Journal of Research in Crime and Delinquency* 29 (1992): 251–272.

101. Ronald Akers, "Self-Control as a General Theory of Crime," *Journal of Quantitative Criminology* 7 (1991): 201–211.

102. Gottfredson and Hirschi, *A General Theory of Crime,* p. 88.

103. Moffitt, "Adolescence-Limited and Life-Course Persistent Antisocial Behaviors."

104. Alex Piquero, Robert Brame, Paul Mazerolle, and Rudy Haapanen, "Crime in Emerging Adulthood," *Criminology* 40 (2002): 137–170.

105. Donald Lynam, Alex Piquero, and Terrie Moffitt, "Specialization and the Propensity to Violence: Support from Self-Reports but Not Official Records," *Journal of Contemporary Criminal Justice* 20 (2004): 215–228.

106. Alan Feingold, "Gender Differences in Personality: A Meta Analysis," *Psychological Bulletin* 116 (1994): 429–456.

107. Charles Tittle, David Ward, and Harold Grasmick, "Gender, Age, and Crime/Deviance: A Challenge to Self-Control Theory," *Journal of Research in Crime and Delinquency* 40 (2003): 426–453.

108. Brent Benda, "Gender Differences in Life-Course Theory of Recidivism: A Survival Analysis," *International Journal of Offender Therapy & Comparative Criminology* 49 (2005): 325–342.

109. Gottfredson and Hirschi, *A General Theory of Crime,* p. 153.

110. Ann Marie Sorenson and David Brownfield, "Normative Concepts in Social Control." Paper presented at the annual meeting of the American Society of Criminology, Phoenix, November 1993.

111. Brent Benda, "An Examination of Reciprocal Relationship between Religiosity and Different Forms of Delinquency within a Theoretical Model," *Journal of Research in Crime and Delinquency* 34 (1997): 163–186.

112. Delbert Elliott and Scott Menard, "Delinquent Friends and Delinquent Behavior: Temporal and Developmental

Patterns," in *Crime and Delinquency: Current Theories*, ed. J. David Hawkins (Cambridge: Cambridge University Press, 1996).

113. Graham Ousey and David Aday, "The Interaction Hypothesis: A Test Using Social Control Theory and Social Learning Theory." Paper presented at the American Society of Criminology Meeting, Boston, 1995.

114. Dana Haynie, Peggy Giordano, Wendy Manning, and Monica Longmore, "Adolescent Romantic Relationships and Delinquency Involvement," *Criminology* 43 (2005): 177–210.

115. Julie Horney, D. Wayne Osgood, and Ineke Haen Marshall, "Criminal Careers in the Short-Term: Intra-Individual Variability in Crime and Its Relations to Local Life Circumstances," *American Sociological Review* 60 (1995): 655–673; Martin Daly and Margo Wilson, "Killing the Competition," *Human Nature* 1 (1990): 83–109.

116. Charles R. Tittle and Harold G. Grasmick, "Criminal Behavior and Age: A Test of Three Provocative Hypotheses," *Journal of Criminal Law and Criminology* 88 (1997): 309–342.

117. Ronald Simons, Christine Johnson, Rand Conger, and Glen Elder, "A Test of Latent Trait versus Life-Course Perspectives on the Stability of Adolescent Antisocial Behavior," *Criminology* 36 (1998): 217–244.

118. Carter Hay, "Parenting, Self-Control, and Delinquency: A Test of Self- Control Theory," *Criminology* 39 (2001): 707–736; Douglas Longshore, "Self-Control and Criminal Opportunity: A Prospective Test of the General Theory of Crime," *Social Problems* 45 (1998): 102–114; Finn-Aage Esbensen and Elizabeth Piper Deschenes, "A Multisite Examination of Youth Gang Membership: Does Gender Matter?" *Criminology* 36 (1998): 799–828.

119. Raymond Paternoster and Robert Brame, "The Structural Similarity of Processes Generating Criminal and Analogous Behaviors," *Criminology* 36 (1998): 633–670.

120. Otwin Marenin and Michael Resig, "A General Theory of Crime and Patterns of Crime in Nigeria: An Exploration of Methodological Assumptions," *Journal of Criminal Justice* 23 (1995): 501–518.

121. Bruce Arneklev, Harold Grasmick, Charles Tittle, and Robert Bursik, "Low Self-Control and Imprudent Behavior," *Journal of Quantitative Criminology* 9 (1993): 225–246.

122. Peter Muris and Cor Meesters, "The Validity of Attention Deficit Hyperactivity and Hyperkinetic Disorder Symptom Domains in Nonclinical Dutch Children," *Journal of Clinical Child and Adolescent Psychology* 32 (2003): 460–466.

123. Francis Cullen, John Paul Wright, and Mitchell Chamlin, "Social Support and Social Reform: A Progressive Crime Control Agenda," *Crime and Delinquency* 45 (1999): 188–207.

124. Alex Piquero, John MacDonald, Adam Dobrin, Leah Daigle, and Francis Cullen, "Self-Control, Violent Offending, and Homicide Victimization: Assessing the General Theory of Crime," *Journal of Quantitative Criminology* 21 (2005): 55–71.

125. Ibid.

126. Richard Wiebe, "Reconciling Psychopathy and Low Self-Control," *Justice Quarterly* 20 (2003): 297–336.

127. Elizabeth Cauffman, Laurence Steinberg, and Alex Piquero, "Psychological, Neuropsychological, and Physiological Correlates of Serious Antisocial Behavior in Adolescence: The Role of Self-Control," *Criminology* 43 (2005): 133–176.

128. Donald Lynam and Joshua Miller, "Personality Pathways to Impulsive Behavior and Their Relations to Deviance: Results from Three Samples," *Journal of Quantitative Criminology* 20 (2004): 319–341.

129. Kevin Thompson, "Sexual Harassment and Low Self-Control: An Application of Gottfredson and Hirschi's General The-

ory of Crime." Paper presented at the annual meeting of the American Society of Criminology, Phoenix, November 1993.

130. Bradley Entner Wright, Avashalom Caspi, Terrie Moffitt, and Phil Silva, "Low Self-Control, Social Bonds, and Crime: Social Causation, Social Selection, or Both?" *Criminology* 37 (1999): 479–514.

131. Ibid., p. 504.

132. Stephen Cernkovich and Peggy Giordano, "Stability and Change in Antisocial Behavior: The Transition from Adolescence to Early Adulthood," *Criminology* 39 (2001): 371–410.

133. Heather Lonczk, Robert Abbott, J. David Hawkins, Rick Kosterman, and Richard Catalano, "Effects of the Seattle Social Development Project on Sexual Behavior, Pregnancy, Birth, and Sexually Transmitted Disease Outcomes by Age 21 Years," *Archive of Pediatrics and Adolescent Medicine* 156 (2002): 438–447.

134. Kathleen Bodisch Lynch, Susan Rose Geller, and Melinda G. Schmidt, "Multi-Year Evaluation of the Effectiveness of a Resilience-Based Prevention Program for Young Children," *Journal of Primary Prevention* 24 (2004): 335–353.

135. This section leans on Thomas Tatchell, Phillip Waite, Renny Tatchell, Lynne Durrant, and Dale Bond, "Substance Abuse Prevention in Sixth Grade: The Effect of a Prevention Program on Adolescents' Risk and Protective Factors," *American Journal of Health Studies* 19 (2004): 54–61.

136. Nancy Tobler and Howard Stratton, "Effectiveness of School Based Drug Prevention Programs: A Meta-Analysis of the Research," *Journal of Primary Prevention* 18 (1997): 71–128.

PART Three

CRIME TYPOLOGIES

||||||||||||||||||||||||||||

Criminologists group criminal offenders and/or criminal behaviors into categories or typologies so they may be more easily studied and understood. Are there common traits or characteristics that link offenders together and that make them distinct from nonoffenders? Are there common areas between seemingly different acts such as murder and rape?

In this section, we focus on crime typologies, clustered into five groups: violent crime (Chapter 10); economic crimes involving common theft offenses (Chapter 11); enterprise crimes involving white-collar criminals and criminal organizations (Chapter 12); public order crimes, such as prostitution and drug abuse (Chapter 13); and cyber crimes (Chapter 14). This format groups criminal behaviors by their focus and consequence: bringing physical harm to others; misappropriating other people's property; violating laws designed to protect public morals; and using technology to commit crime.

Typologies can be useful in classifying large numbers of criminal offenses or offenders into easily understood categories. This text has grouped offenses and offenders on the basis of their legal definitions and their collective goals, objectives, and consequences.

CHAPTER 10

© Nelson "Speedy" Andrad/EPA/Landov

Natalee Holloway, 18, from the Birmingham, Alabama, suburb of Mountain Brook, celebrated her high school graduation by going on a holiday to the Caribbean island of Aruba with about 100 classmates and several parent chaperones. On the night of May 30, 2005, she went to a local bar and was later seen leaving with three men—two brothers from Surinam and a local boy, the son of a high-ranking Dutch judicial official. Natalee never returned to her hotel.

The three young men told the police that they took Natalee to Arashi Beach, on Aruba's northern tip, and at 2 A.M. dropped her off at her hotel, where they saw her being approached by a security guard as they drove off. The young men, prime suspects in the case, were arrested, released, arrested again, and released again. Despite a massive hunt and investigation, at the time of this writing the fate of the young woman who wanted to become a doctor remains unknown.[1]

VIOLENT CRIME

CHAPTER OBJECTIVES

1. Be familiar with the various causes of violent crime
2. Know the concept of the brutalization process
3. Be able to discuss the history of rape and know the different types of rape
4. Be able to discuss the legal issues in rape prosecution
5. Recognize that there are different types of murder
6. Be able to discuss the differences among serial killing, mass murder, and spree killing
7. Be familiar with the nature of assault in the home
8. Understand the careers of armed robbers
9. Be able to discuss newly emerging forms of violence such as stalking, hate crimes, and workplace violence
10. Understand the different types of terrorism and what is being done to combat terrorist activities

The Holloway case grabbed national attention. Rumors of her fate abounded: Had the three young men raped and murdered Natalee? Was there a cover-up because one of the suspects was the son of a public official? Did they dispose of Natalee's body in a panic after she died from a drug or alcohol overdose? Had she been abducted and forced to become a member of the international sex trade?

|||||||| **CONNECTIONS** ||||||||

Chapter 13 has more on the significant illegal sex trade that forces thousands of young boys and girls into prostitution each year.

Whatever her fate, Natalee's case proved to the American public that violent crime could be encountered anywhere, even on a tranquil Caribbean island known for its beautiful beaches. No matter where they go, people may encounter violent acts. Some are **expressive violence**—acts that vent rage, anger, or frustration—and some are **instrumental violence**—acts designed to improve the financial or social position of the criminal, for example, through an armed robbery or murder for hire.

This chapter explores the concept of violence in some depth. First, it reviews the suggested causes of violent crime. Then it focuses on specific types of interpersonal violence—rape, homicide, assault, robbery, and newly recognized types of interpersonal violence such as stalking and workplace violence. Finally, it briefly examines political violence and terrorism.

THE CAUSES OF VIOLENCE

What sets off a violent person? Criminologists have a variety of views on this subject. Some believe that violence is a function of human traits and makeup. Others point to improper socialization and upbringing. Violent behavior may be culturally determined and relate to dysfunctional social values.[2] The various sources of violence are set out in Figure 10.1.

Psychological Abnormality

On March 13, 1995, an ex–Boy Scout leader named Thomas Hamilton took four high-powered rifles into the primary school of the peaceful Scottish town of Dunblane and slaughtered sixteen kindergarten children and their teacher. This horrific crime shocked the British Isles into implementing strict controls on all guns.[3] Bizarre outbursts such as Hamilton's support a link between violence and psychological abnormality.

> To read more about the **Dunblane massacre,** go to http://www.guardiancentury.co.uk/1990-1999/Story/ 0,6051,112749,00.html. For an up-to-date list of web links, go to http://cj.wadsworth.com/siegel_crimtpt9e.

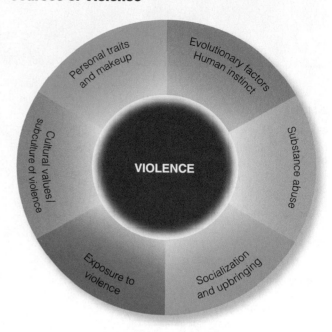

FIGURE 10.1
Sources of Violence

Research has shown that a significant number of people who are involved in violent episodes may be suffering from severe mental abnormalities.[4] Research conducted by psychologist Dorothy Otnow Lewis and her associates has shown that kids who kill may be suffering from multiple symptoms of psychological abnormality: neurological impairment (such as abnormal EEGs, multiple psychomotor impairments, and severe seizures), low intelligence, and psychotic symptoms (such as paranoia, illogical thinking, and hallucinations).[5] In her book *Guilty by Reason of Insanity*, Lewis finds that death row inmates have a history of mental impairment and intellectual dysfunction.[6]

Lewis's research is not unique. Abnormal personality structures—including such traits as depression, impulsivity, aggression, dishonesty, pathological lying, lack of remorse, borderline personality syndrome, and psychopathology—have all been associated with various forms of violence.[7] It comes as no surprise to psychologists that many murderers kill themselves shortly after committing their crime.[8]

|||||||| **CONNECTIONS** ||||||||

As you may recall from Chapter 5, biosocial theorists link violence to a number of biological irregularities, including but not limited to genetic influences and inheritance, the action of hormones, the functioning of neurotransmitters, brain structure, and diet. Psychologists link violent behavior to observational learning from violent TV shows, traumatic childhood experiences, low intelligence, mental illness, impaired cognitive processes, and abnormal (psychopathic) personality structure.

To read an interview with Dorothy Otnow Lewis in which she discusses how the problems in an aggressive boy's life should be evaluated and how appropriate treatment should be provided, go to: Rena Large, "New Path for Aggressive Boys," *NEA Today* 17 (October 1998): 29.

Evolutionary Factors/Human Instinct

Sigmund Freud believed that human behavior is shaped by two instinctual drives: *eros,* the life instinct, which drives people toward self-fulfillment and enjoyment; and *thanatos,* the death instinct, which produces self-destruction. Thanatos can be expressed externally (as violence and sadism) or internally (as suicide, alcoholism, or other self-destructive habits).[9]

To learn more about Freud's views, go to InfoTrac College Edition and use his name as a key word.

In his celebrated book, *On Aggression,* anthropologist Konrad Lorenz argued that aggressive energy is produced by inbred instincts that are independent of environmental forces.[10] In the animal kingdom, aggression usually serves a productive purpose—for example, it leads members of grazing species such as zebras and antelopes to spread out over available territory to ensure an ample food supply and the survival of the fittest. Lorenz found that humans possess some of the same aggressive instincts as animals. But among lower species, aggression is rarely fatal; when a conflict occurs, the winner is determined through a test of skill or endurance. This inhibition against killing members of their own species protects animals from self-extinction. Humans, lacking this inhibition against fatal violence, are capable of killing their own kind in war or as a result of interpersonal conflicts. Lorenz feared that as technology develops and more lethal weapons are produced, the extinction of the human species becomes a significant possibility.

To read the **autobiography of Konrad Lorenz,** who won the Nobel Prize in medicine in 1973, go to http://www.nobel.se/medicine/laureates/1973/lorenz-autobio.html. For an up-to-date list of web links, go to http://cj.wadsworth.com/siegel_crimtpt9e.

Substance Abuse

Substance abuse has been associated with violence on both the individual and social levels: Substance abusers have higher rates of violence than nonabusers; and neighborhoods with high levels of substance abuse have higher violence rates when compared to areas with low use rates.[11] A direct association has been found between community levels of crack cocaine and heroin use and the incidence of street robberies.[12]

High-use areas may also face social disorganization, poverty, and unemployment, factors that further escalate violence rates.[13]

The link between substance abuse and violence appears in three different formats:[14]

1. *Psychopharmacological relationship:* Violence may be the direct consequence of ingesting mood-altering substances. Experimental evidence shows that high doses of drugs such as PCP and amphetamines produce violent, aggressive behavior.[15] For example, binge drinking has been closely associated with violent crime rates.[16] Heavy drinking reduces cognitive ability, information processing skills, and the ability to process and react to verbal and nonverbal behavior. As a result, miscommunication becomes more likely, and the capacity for rational dialogue is compromised.[17] It is not surprising that males involved in sexual assaults often claim that they were they were drinking and misunderstood their victims' intentions.[18]

2. *Economic compulsive behavior:* Drug users/ resort to violence to obtain the financial resources to support their habit. Studies conducted in the United States and Europe show that addicts commit hundreds of crimes each year.[19]

3. *Systemic link:* Violence escalates when drug-dealing gangs flex their muscle to dominate territory and drive out rivals. Studies of gangs that sell drugs show that their violent activities may result in a significant proportion of all urban homicides.[20]

Socialization and Upbringing

Another view is that improper socialization and upbringing is responsible for the onset of violent acts. Absent or deviant parents, inconsistent discipline, physical abuse, and lack of supervision have all been linked to persistent violent offending.[21]

Although infants demonstrate individual temperaments, who they become may have a lot to do with how they are treated during their early years. Some children are harder to soothe than others; in some cases, difficult infant temperament has been associated with later aggression and behavioral problems.[22] Parents who fail to set adequate limits or to use proper, consistent discipline reinforce a child's coercive behavior.[23] The effects of inadequate parenting and early rejection may affect violent behavior throughout life.[24] There is evidence that children who are maltreated and neglected in early childhood are the ones most likely to be initiated into criminality and thereafter continue or persist in a criminal career.[25]

There are also indications that children who are subject to even minimal amounts of physical punishment may be more likely one day to use violence themselves.[26] Sociologist Murray Straus reviewed the concept of discipline in a series of surveys and found a powerful relationship between exposure to physical punishment and later aggression.[27] The effect of physical punishment may be mediated or neutralized

Socialization and upbringing have been linked to the onset of violent acts. Kids who are raised by deviant parents and subject to inconsistent discipline, physical abuse, and lack of supervision are more likely to engage in violent offending. Considering the link between socialization and crime, do you believe that parents who introduce their children to guns at an early age are leading them down the path toward violence?

© Les Stone/Corbis Sygma

to some extent if parents also provide support, warmth, and care. When kids experience physical punishment in the absence of parental involvement, they feel angry and unjustly treated and are more willing to defy their parents and engage in antisocial behavior.[28]

ABUSED CHILDREN A number of research studies have found that children who are clinically diagnosed as abused later engage in delinquent behaviors, including violence, at a rate significantly greater than that of children who were not abused.[29] Samples of convicted murderers reveal a high percentage of seriously abused youth.[30] The abuse–violence association has been established in many cases in which parents have been killed by their children; sexual abuse is also a constant factor in father (patricide) and mother (matricide) killings.[31] Dorothy Otnow Lewis found that juvenile death row inmates all have long histories of intense child abuse.[32]

Abuse may have the greatest effect if it is persistent and extends from childhood to adolescence.[33] Children who are physically punished by their parents are likely to physically abuse a sibling and later engage in spouse abuse and other forms of criminal violence.[34] They may become spousal abusers in their adulthood: There is evidence that batterers received significantly less love and more punishment from their mothers than did men in a general population comparison group. Abusive childhood experiences may be a key factor in the later development of relationship aggression.[35]

THE BRUTALIZATION PROCESS Lonnie Athens is one well-known criminologist who links violence to early experiences with child abuse. Athens finds that people can be classified into three groups based on their aggressive tendencies: nonviolent, violent (those who attack others physically with the intention of harming them), and incipiently violent (those

who are willing and ready to attack but limit themselves to violent ultimatums and/or intimidating physical gestures). Athens also finds that there are actually four distinct types of violent acts: physically defensive (in which the perpetrator sees his violent act as one of self-defense), frustrative (in which the offender acts out of anger due to frustration when he cannot get his way), malefic (in which the victim is considered to be extremely evil or malicious), and frustrative-malefic (a combined type). Antisocial careers are often created in a series of stages that begin with brutal episodes during early adolescence.

- The first stage involves the *brutalization process,* during which a young victim begins the process of developing a belligerent, angry demeanor. The brutalization can come at the hands of abusive parents or caretakers. But the brutalization process is broader than parental physical or sexual abuse. It may also result from violent coaching by peers, neighbors, and schoolmates. Although most brutalization occurs early in life, some people can be brutalized as they mature.

- Brutalized youth may become belligerent and angry. When confronted at home, school, or on the street, these belligerent youth respond with *violent performances* of angry, hostile behavior. The success of their violent confrontations provides them with a sense of power and achievement.

- In the *virulency stage*, emerging criminals develop a violent identity that makes them feared; they enjoy intimidating others. To Athens, this process takes violent youths full circle from being the victims of aggression to its initiators; they are now the same person they grew up despising, ready to begin the process with their own children.[36]

Athens recognizes that brutalization alone is not a sufficient condition to cause someone to become a dangerous violent criminal. One must complete the full cycle of the "violentization process"—belligerence, violent performances, and virulency—to become socialized into violence. Many brutalized children do not go on to become violent criminals, and some later reject the fact that they were abused as youths and redefine their early years as normative.

 To learn more about the nature and extent of child abuse, use "child abuse" in a subject guide search in InfoTrac College Edition.

Exposure to Violence

People who are constantly exposed to violence in the environment may adopt violent methods themselves. Children living in areas marked by extreme violence may become desensitized to the persistent brutality, succumbing to violent behaviors as well.[37] Much of the difference in rates of violent crime between whites and racial minorities can be explained by the fact that the latter are often forced to live in high-crime neighborhoods that increase their risk of exposure to violence.[38]

Social scientist Felton Earls and his associates are now conducting the Project on Human Development in Chicago Neighborhoods—a government-funded longitudinal study of pathways to violence among 7,000 Chicago area people in eighty different, randomly selected neighborhoods.[39] Interviews with youths aged 9 to 15 show that large numbers of these children have been victims of or witnesses to violence and that many carry weapons.

To read more about the **Project on Human Development in Chicago Neighborhoods,** go to their website at http://www.hms.harvard.edu/chase/projects/chicago. For an up-to-date list of web links, go to http://cj.wadsworth.com/siegel_crimtpt9e.

Between 30 and 40 percent of the children who reported exposure to violence displayed significant violent behavior themselves. A 2005 report by Earls and his associates finds that young teens who witness gun violence are more than twice as likely as non-witnesses to commit violent crime themselves in the following years.[40] Even a single exposure to firearm violence doubles the chance that a young person will later engage in violent behavior.

||||||| **CONNECTIONS** |||||||

The Project on Human Development in Chicago Neighborhoods has served as a source of data showing that collective efficacy and concentrated poverty are key determinants of neighborhood crime rates. These concepts were discussed more fully in Chapter 6.

Children living in these conditions become **"crusted over"**: They do not let people inside, nor do they express their feelings. They exploit others and in turn are exploited by those older and stronger; as a result, they develop a sense of hopelessness. They find that parents and teachers focus on their failures and problems, not their achievements. Consequently, they are vulnerable to the lure of delinquent gangs and groups.[41]

Cultural Values/Subculture of Violence

Violence may be the product of cultural beliefs, values, and behaviors that develop in poor and disorganized neighborhoods.[42] To explain this phenomenon, criminologists Marvin Wolfgang and Franco Ferracuti formulated the famous concept that some areas contain an independent **subculture of violence.**[43]

||||||| **CONNECTIONS** |||||||

Delinquent subcultures were discussed in some detail in Chapter 6. Recall that subculture theorists portray delinquents not as rebels from the normative culture but rather as people who are in accord with the informal rules and values of their immediate culture. By adhering to cultural norms, they violate the law.

The norms of the subculture of violence are separate from society's central, dominant value system. In this subculture, a potent theme of violence influences lifestyles, the socialization process, and interpersonal relationships. Even though the subculture's members share some of the dominant culture's values, they expect that violence will be used to solve social conflicts and dilemmas. In some cultural subgroups, then, violence has become legitimized by customs and norms. It is considered appropriate behavior within culturally defined conflict situations in which an individual who has been offended by a negative outcome in a dispute seeks reparations through violent means; a concept referred to as **disputatiousness.**[44]

There is evidence that a subculture of violence may be found in areas that experience concentrated poverty and social disorganization.[45] Though most people abhor violence, income inequality and racial disparity may help instill a sense of hopelessness that nourishes pro-violence norms and values.[46] In these areas people are more likely to carry weapons and use them in assaults and robberies. Victims are aware of these tactics and are less likely to fight back forcibly when attacked.[47] However, when pressed to the limit, even passive victims may eventually fight back. When Charis Kubrin and Ronald Weitzer studied homicide in St. Louis, Missouri, they discovered that a certain type of killing referred to as *cultural retaliatory homicide* is common in neighborhoods that suffer economic disadvantage. In these areas, residents resolve interpersonal conflicts informally—without calling the police—even if it means killing their opponent; neighbors understand and support their violent methods.[48] Because police and other agencies of formal social control are devalued as weak, understaffed, and possibly corrupt, people are willing to take matters into their own hands, and violence rates increase accordingly.[49]

PEER GROUP INFLUENCES Empirical evidence shows that violence rates are highest in urban areas where subcultural values support teenage gangs whose members typically embrace the use of violence.[50] Gang boys are more likely to own guns and other weapons than non–gang members. They are also more likely to have peers who are gun owners and are more likely to carry guns outside the home.[51] Ominously, major metropolitan areas such as Los Angeles and Chicago are now reporting a significant increase in the number of street gang-related killings.[52]

The association between gang membership and violence has a number of roots. It can result from drug-trafficking activities and turf protection but also stems from personal vendettas and a perceived need for self-protection.[53] Gang boys are much more likely to own guns and to associate with violent peers than nonmembers.[54] Those who choose aggressive or violent friends are more likely to begin engaging in antisocial behavior themselves and suffer psychological deficits.[55] The risky gang lifestyle increases the likelihood a boy will himself become a victim of violent crime. Experiencing victimization brings on retaliation, creating a cycle of violence begetting even more violence.[56] Criminologist Scott Decker found that gang violence may be initiated for a variety of reasons:

- It enables new members to show toughness during initiation ceremonies.

- It can be used to retaliate against rivals for actual or perceived grievances.

- It protects ownership, such as when violence erupts when graffiti is defaced by rivals.

- It protects turf from incursions by outsiders.[57]

- While many boys are predisposed toward violence before joining a gang, research shows that once in gangs their violent behavior quickly escalates; after they leave, it significantly declines.[58]

REGIONAL VALUES Criminologists have suggested that regional values promote violence.[59] Historian Eric Monkkonen analyzed nearly two centuries of Los Angeles homicide data and found that regional cultural differences contributed to relatively high rates of homicide.[60] From its western days, Los Angelinos accepted street justice, and the city has always had high rates of "justifiable homicides." A considerable number of "executions," says Monkkonen, were left to the discretion of individuals who "happened to be armed at the moment of need."[61]

In a famous study, sociologist Raymond Gastil found a significant relationship between murder rates and southern culture that values personal honor and firearm ownership.[62] Southerners seem more willing to defend family and home against any perceived threat.[63] Some criminologists dispute Gastil's southern subculture of violence concept and argue that southern homicide rates are high because of economic and social factors, not any "southern culture of lethal violence."[64]

NATIONAL VALUES Some nations—including the United States, Sri Lanka, Angola, Uganda, and the Philippines—have relatively high violence rates; others are much more peaceful. According to research by sociologist Jerome Neapolitan, a number of national characteristics are predictive of violence: a high level of social disorganization, economic stress, high child abuse rates, approval of violence by the government, political corruption, and an inefficient justice system.[65] Children in high-violence nations are likely to be economically deprived and socially isolated, exposed to constant violence, and lacking in hope and respect for the law. Guns are common in these nations because, lacking an efficient justice system, people arm themselves or hire private security forces for protection.[66] In contrast, nations such as Japan have relatively low violence rates because of cultural and economic strengths. Japan boasts a system of exceptionally effective informal social controls that help reduce crime. It also has had a robust economy that may alleviate the stresses that produce violence.[67]

Does the United States maintain values that promote violence? Did these originate in the early development of the nation? The Criminological Enterprise feature "Violent Land" explores these questions.

Each of these factors is believed to influence violent crime, including traditional common-law crimes, such as rape, murder, assault, and robbery, and newly recognized problems, such as workplace violence, hate crimes, and terrorism and political violence. Each of these forms of violent behavior is discussed in some detail in this chapter.

FORCIBLE RAPE

Rape (from the Latin *rapere,* to take by force) is defined in common law as "the carnal knowledge of a female forcibly and against her will."[68] It is one of the most loathed, misunderstood, and frightening crimes. Under traditional common-law definitions, rape involves nonconsensual sexual intercourse that a male performs against a female he is neither married to nor cohabitating with.[69] There are of course other forms of sexual assault, including male on male, female on female, and female on male sexual assaults, but these were not contained within the traditional definition of rape.[70] However, recognizing these other forms of sexual assault, all but three states have now revised their statutes to make them gender neutral.[71] In *Michael M. v. Superior Court of Sonoma City,* the Supreme Court of the United States upheld a California statute that defines statutory rape as "an act of sexual intercourse accomplished with a female not the wife of the perpetrator, where the female is under the age of 18 years." The Court allowed the gendered

The Criminological Enterprise

||||||||||||||||||||||||||||||||||

Violent Land

David Courtwright, an authority on the sociocultural roots of violence, describes a nineteenth-century American society much more violent than today. According to Courtwright, societies with the highest rates of violent crime have been populations with an overabundance of young males who are "awash with testosterone" and unrestrained by social controls such as marriage and family.

Until the mid-twentieth century, the U.S. population was disproportionately young and male. The male-to-female gender ratio of those who settled here involuntarily—indentured servants and slaves—was more than 2 to 1. Poor laborers who paid for their passage by signing labor contracts were almost all male; the gender ratio among Chinese laborers was an astounding 27 to 1. Aside from Ireland, which furnished slightly more female than male immigrants, Europeans who arrived voluntarily were also predominantly male. Because these young men outnumbered women, not all men were able to marry, and those who did not remained unrestrained by the calming influences of family life and parental responsibility.

Cultural factors worsened these population trends. Frontier culture was characterized by racism and preoccupation with personal honor. Some ethnic groups drank heavily and frequented saloons and gambling halls, where petty arguments could become lethal because most patrons carried guns and knives. Violent acts often went unpunished, however, because law enforcement agencies were unable or unwilling to take action. Nowhere were these cultural and population effects felt more acutely than on the western frontier. Here the population was mostly young bachelors who were sensitive about

honor, hostile racists, heavy drinkers, morally indifferent, heavily armed, and unchecked by adequate law enforcement. It is not surprising, considering this explosive mix, that 20 percent of the 89,000 miners who arrived in California during the 1849 gold rush were dead within 6 months. Many died from disease, but others succumbed to drink and violence. Smoking, gambling, and heavy drinking became a cultural imperative, and those who were disinclined to indulge were considered social outcasts.

Over time, gender ratios equalized as more men brought families to the frontier, and children of both sexes were born. Many men died, returned home, or drifted elsewhere. By the mid-twentieth century, America's overall male surplus was disappearing, and a balanced population helped bring down the crime rate.

According to Courtwright, rising violence rates in the 1960s and 1970s can be attributed to the fact that men were avoiding, delaying, or terminating marriage. In 1960 Americans spent an average of 62 percent of their lives with spouses and children, an all-time high; in 1980 they spent 43 percent with families, an all-time low. Both the illegitimacy and divorce rates began to spiral upward, guaranteeing that the number of poorly socialized and supervised children would increase dramatically. The inner-city urban ghetto became the frontier community of today. Gangs such as the Crips and Bloods in Los Angeles and the Mara Salvatrucha, or MS-13, which is located in more than 30 states and has upwards of 20,000 members, are the modern descendants of the Old West gangs of Jesse James and Butch Cassidy and the Sundance Kid's Hole in the Wall Gang. And although the male-to-female ratio is more balanced than on the western frontier, the presence of

unsupervised, poorly socialized males, who have easy access to guns, drugs, and vice, has produced a crime rate of similar proportions. Violence rates have stabilized lately, but they may rise again as the decline in the family remains unchecked.

Courtwright's analysis shows that violence is not a recent development and that demographic and cultural forces determine violent crime rates. It disputes the contention that some artifact of modern life, like violent films and TV, is causing American violence. The factors that predispose societies to violence can be found in demographic and cultural factors that are unique neither to our society nor to our times.

Critical Thinking

1. According to Courtwright, crime rates were exceedingly high in the nineteenth century before TV, movies, and rap videos had been created. What, if anything, does this say about the effect of media on crime?

2. Is it possible that America's frontier values influence contemporary culture? Do we still admire legendary heroes such as Wild Bill Hickok and Wyatt Earp and their use of gunplay to settle disagreements? Do you think that these factors still cause violence today?

InfoTrac College Edition Research

If you are interested in reading more about the early history of violence in the West, look up: Margaret Walsh, "New Horizons for the American West," *History Today* 44 (March 1994): 44.

Sources: David Courtwright, "Violence in America," *American Heritage* 47 (1996): 36–52, quote at 36; David Courtwright, *Violent Land: Single Men and Social Disorder from the Frontier to the Inner City* (Cambridge, MA: Harvard University Press, 1996).

language because the intent of the law was to prevent "teenage pregnancies," a goal with "significant social, medical, and economic consequences for both the mother and her child, and the State."[72]

 Use "rape" as a subject guide to search for more information in InfoTrac College Edition.

History of Rape

Rape has been a recognized crime throughout history. It has been the subject of art, literature, film, and theater. Paintings such as the *Rape of the Sabine Women* by Nicolas Poussin, novels such as *Clarissa* by Samuel Richardson, poems such as *The Rape of Lucrece* by William Shakespeare, and films such as *The Accused* have sexual violence as their central theme.

In early civilization rape was common. Men staked a claim of ownership on women by forcibly abducting and raping them. This practice led to males' solidification of power and their historical domination of women.[73] Under Babylonian and Hebraic law, the rape of a virgin was a crime punishable by death. However, if the victim was married, then both she and her attacker were considered equally to blame, and unless her husband intervened, both were put to death.

During the Middle Ages, it was common for ambitious men to abduct and rape wealthy women in an effort to force them into marriage. The practice of "heiress stealing" illustrates how feudal law gave little thought or protection to women and equated them with property.[74] Only in the late fifteenth century, after a monetary economy developed, was forcible sex outlawed. Thereafter, the violation of a virgin caused an economic hardship on her family, who expected a significant dowry for her hand in marriage. However, the law only applied to the wealthy; peasant women and married women were not considered rape victims until well into the sixteenth century. During this period, prevailing moral values condemned casual sex and portrayed women as evil, having lust in their hearts, and redeemable only by motherhood. A woman who was raped was almost automatically suspected of contributing to her attack.

Rape and the Military

Although rape has long been associated with military conquest, the nation was still stunned when in 1996 the national media revealed the presence of a "rape ring" at the Aberdeen Proving Grounds in Maryland. Nearly twenty noncommissioned officers were accused of raping and sexually harassing nineteen female trainees. The investigation prompted more than 5,000 female soldiers to call military hot lines to report similar behavior at Army bases around the country. The Army scandal was especially disturbing because it involved drill instructors, who are given almost total control over the lives of young female recruits who in turn depended on the instructors for support, training, and nurturing.[75]

The link between the military and rape is inescapable. Throughout recorded history, rape has been associated with armies and warfare. Soldiers of conquering armies have considered sexual possession of their enemies' women one of the spoils of war. Among the ancient Greeks, rape was socially acceptable within the rules of warfare. During the Crusades, even knights and pilgrims, ostensibly bound by vows of chivalry and Christian piety, took time to rape as they marched toward Constantinople.

The belief that women are part of the spoils of war has continued. During World War II the Japanese army forced as many as 200,000 Korean women into frontline brothels, where they were repeatedly raped. In a 1998 Japanese ruling, the surviving Korean women were awarded the equivalent of $2,300 each in compensation.[76] The systematic rape of Bosnian and Kosovar women by Serbian army officers during the civil war in the former Yugoslavia horrified the world during the 1990s. These crimes seemed particularly atrocious because they appeared to be part of an official policy of genocide: Rape was deliberately used to impregnate Bosnian women with Serbian children.

||||||| CONNECTIONS |||||||

State-sponsored terrorism, often directed at minority groups who share some personal characteristic such as religion or ethnic background, will be discussed later in this chapter in the sections on political terrorism.

On March 9, 1998, Dragoljub Kunarac, 37, a former Bosnian Serb paramilitary commander, admitted before an international tribunal in the Netherlands that he had raped Muslim women during the Bosnian war in 1992. His confession made him the first person to plead guilty to rape as a war crime.[77] Human rights groups have estimated that more than 30,000 women and young girls were sexually abused in the Balkan fighting.

Though shocking, the war crimes discovered in Bosnia have not deterred conquering armies from using rape as a weapon. In 2004 pro-government militias in the Darfur region of Sudan were accused of using rape and other forms of sexual violence "as a weapon of war" to humiliate African women and girls as well as the rebels fighting the Sudanese government in Khartoum.[78]

Incidence of Rape

According to the most recent UCR data, about 92,000 rapes or attempted rapes were reported to U.S. police in 2004, a rate of about 32 per 100,000 inhabitants or more relevantly, 62 per 100,000 females.[79] Like other violent crimes, the rape rate has been in a decade-long decline, and the 2004 totals are significantly below 1992 levels when 84 women per 100,000 were rape victims.

Population density influences the rape rate. Metropolitan areas today have rape rates significantly higher than rural areas; nonetheless, urban areas have experienced a much greater drop in rape reports than rural areas. The police make arrests in slightly more than half of all reported rape offenses. Of the offenders arrested, typically about half are under 25 years of age, and about two-thirds are white. The racial and age pattern of rape arrests has been fairly consistent for some time. Finally, rape is a warm-weather crime—most incidents occur during July and August, with the lowest rates occurring during December, January, and February.

These data must be interpreted with caution because rape is a traditionally underreported crime. As many as 10 percent of all adult women may have been raped during their lifetime.[80] According to the National Crime Victimization Survey (NCVS), in 2004 almost 210,000 rapes and attempted rapes took place, suggesting that slightly less than half of all rape incidents are not reported to police.[81] Many people fail to report rapes because they are embarrassed, believe nothing can be done, or blame themselves. Some victims of sexual assaults may even question whether they have really been "raped"; research indicates that when the assault involved a boyfriend, if the woman was severely impaired by alcohol or drugs, or if the act involved oral or digital sex, the women were unlikely to label their situations as being a "real" rape.[82]

Types of Rape and Rapists

Some rapes are planned, others are spontaneous; some focus on a particular victim, whereas others occur almost as an afterthought during the commission of another crime, such as a burglary. Some rapists commit a single crime, whereas others are multiple offenders; some attack alone, and others engage in group or gang rapes.[83] Because there is no single type of rape or rapist, criminologists have attempted to define and categorize the vast variety of rape situations.

Criminologists now recognize that there are numerous motivations for rape and as a result various types of rapists. One of the best-known attempts to classify the personalities of rapists was made by psychologist A. Nicholas Groth, an expert on classifying and treating sex offenders. According to Groth, every rape encounter contains at least one of these three elements: anger, power, and sadism.[84] Consequently, rapists can be classified according to one of the three dimensions described in Exhibit 10.1. In treating rape offenders, Groth found that about 55 percent were of the power type; about 40 percent, the anger type; and about 5 percent, the sadistic type.[85]

GANG RAPE Some research estimates that as many as 25 percent or more of rapes involve multiple offenders.[86] There is generally little difference in the demographic characteristics of single- or multiple-victim rapes. However, women who are attacked by multiple offenders are subject to more violence, such as beatings and the use of weapons, and the rapes are more likely to be completed than individual rapes. Gang rape victims are more likely to resist and face injury than those attacked by single offenders. Gang rape victims are more likely to call police, to seek therapy, and to contemplate suicide.

EXHIBIT 10.1

Varieties of Forcible Rape

- *Anger rape:* This rape occurs when sexuality becomes a means of expressing and discharging pent-up anger and rage. The rapist uses far more brutality than would have been necessary if his real objective had been simply to have sex with his victim. His aim is to hurt his victim as much as possible; the sexual aspect of rape may be an afterthought. Often the anger rapist acts on the spur of the moment after an upsetting incident has caused him conflict, irritation, or aggravation. Surprisingly, anger rapes are less psychologically traumatic for the victim than might be expected. Because a woman is usually physically beaten during an anger rape, she is more likely to receive sympathy from her peers, relatives, and the justice system and consequently be immune from any suggestion that she complied with the attack.

- *Power rape:* This type of rape involves an attacker who does not want to harm his victim as much as he wants to possess her sexually. His goal is sexual conquest, and he uses only the amount of force necessary to achieve his objective. The power rapist wants to be in control, to be able to dominate women and have them at his mercy. Yet it is not sexual gratification that drives the power rapist; in fact, he often has a consenting relationship with his wife or girlfriend. Rape is instead a way of putting personal insecurities to rest, asserting heterosexuality, and preserving a sense of manhood. The power rapist's victim usually is a woman equal in age to or younger than the rapist. The lack of physical violence may reduce the support given the victim by family and friends. Therefore, the victim's personal guilt over her rape experience is increased—perhaps, she thinks, she could have done something to get away.

- *Sadistic rape:* This type of rape involves both sexuality and aggression. The sadistic rapist is bound up in ritual— he may torment his victim, bind her, or torture her. Victims are usually related, in the rapist's view, to a personal characteristic that he wants to harm or destroy. The rape experience is intensely exciting to the sadist; he gets satisfaction from abusing, degrading, or humiliating his captive. Sadistic rape is particularly traumatic for the victim. Victims of such crimes need psychiatric care long after their physical wounds have healed.

Source: A. Nicholas Groth and Jean Birnbaum, *Men Who Rape* (New York: Plenum Press, 1979).

Gang rapes then, as might be expected, are more severe in violence and outcome.

SERIAL RAPE Some rapists are one-time offenders, but others engage in multiple or **serial rapes.** Some serial rapists constantly increase their use of force; others do not. Research by Janet Warren and her associates determined that increasers (about 25 percent of serial rapists) tend to be white males who attack multiple victims who are typically older than the norm. During these attacks, the rapist uses excessive profanity and takes more time than during typical rapes. Increasers have a limited criminal history for other crimes,

Some rapists are one-time offenders, but others engage in multiple or serial rapes over a long period of time. Research shows that serial rapists tend to be white males who are typically older than the norm. A Miami police poster shows information relating to a suspect accused of at least seven rapes as well as four attempted rapes between September 2002 and September 2003 (when he was captured). The victims ranged in age from 11 to 79. The suspect is currently awaiting trail.

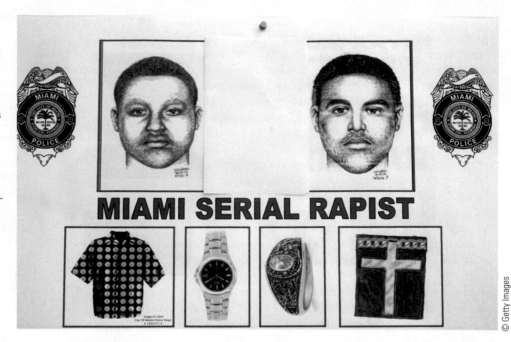

© Getty Images

a fact suggesting that their behavior is focused almost solely on sexual violence.[87]

Some serial rapists commit "blitz rapes," in which they attack their victims without warning, whereas others try to "capture" their victims by striking up a conversation or offering them a ride. Others use personal or professional relationships to gain access to their targets.[88]

ACQUAINTANCE RAPE **Acquaintance rape** involves someone known to the victim, including family members and friends. Included within acquaintance rapes are the subcategories of *date rape,* which involves a sexual attack during a courting relationship; **statutory rape,** in which the victim is underage; and **marital rape,** which is forcible sex between people who are legally married to each other.

It is difficult to estimate the ratio between rapes involving strangers and those in which victim and assailant are in some way acquainted because women may be more reluctant to report acts involving acquaintances. By some estimates, about 50 percent of rapes involve acquaintances.[89] Stranger rapes are typically more violent than acquaintance rapes; attackers are more likely to carry a weapon, threaten the victim, and harm her physically. However, stranger rapes may be less likely to be prosecuted than acquaintance rapes because victims may be more reluctant to recount their ordeal at trial if the attack involved a stranger than if their attacker was someone they knew or had been involved with in an earlier relationship.[90]

DATE RAPE One disturbing trend of rape involves people who are in some form of courting relationship. There is no single form of date rape. Some occur on first dates, others after a relationship has been developing, and still others occur after the couple has been involved for some time. In long-term

or close relationships, the male partner may feel he has invested so much time and money in his partner that he is owed sexual relations or that sexual intimacy is an expression that the involvement is progressing. He may make comparisons to other couples who have dated as long and are sexually active.[91] Some use a variety of strategies to coerce sex, including getting their dates drunk, threatening them with termination of the relationship, threatening to disclose negative information, making them feel guilty, or uttering false promises (like "we'll get engaged") to obtain sex.[92]

Date rape is believed to be frequent on college campuses. It has been estimated that 15 percent to 20 percent of all college women are victims of rape or attempted rape. One self-report survey conducted on a midwestern campus found that 100 percent of all rapists knew their victims beforehand.[93]

The actual incidence of date rape may be even higher than surveys indicate, because many victims blame themselves and do not recognize the incident as a rape, saying, for example, "I should have fought back harder" or "I shouldn't have gotten drunk."[94] Victims tend to have histories of excessive drinking and prior sexuality, conditions that may convince them that their intemperate and/or immoderate behavior contributed to their own victimization.[95] Some victims do not report rapes because they do not view their experience as a "real rape," which, they believe, involves a strange man "jumping out of the bushes." Other victims are embarrassed and frightened. Many tell their friends about their rape while refusing to let authorities know what happened; reporting is most common in the most serious cases, for example, when a weapon is used; it is less common when drugs and alcohol are involved.[96]

In sum, coercive sexual encounters have become disturbingly common in our culture. As criminologist Martin Schwartz has stated:

The conclusion is inescapable that a very substantial minority of women on American college campuses have experienced an event which would fit most states' definitions of felony rape or sexual assault.[97]

Does watching films that degrade women influence the commission of date rape? To find out, read: Michael Milburn, Roxanne Mather, and Sheree D. Conrad, "The Effects of Viewing R-Rated Movie Scenes that Objectify Women on Perceptions of Date Rape," *Sex Roles: A Journal of Research* (November 2000): 645.

MARITAL RAPE In 1978 Greta Rideout filed rape charges against her husband John. This Oregon case grabbed headlines because it was the first in which a husband was prosecuted for raping his wife while sharing a residence with her. John was acquitted, and the couple briefly reconciled; later, continued violent episodes culminated in divorce and a jail term for John.[98]

Traditionally, a legally married husband could not be charged with raping his wife; this was referred to as the **marital exemption.** The origin of this legal doctrine can be traced to the sixteenth-century pronouncement of Matthew Hale, England's chief justice, who wrote

> But the husband cannot be guilty of rape committed by himself upon his lawful wife, for by their mutual matrimonial consent and contract the wife hath given up herself in this kind unto the husband which she cannot retract.[99]

However, research indicates that many women are raped each year by their husbands as part of an overall pattern of spousal abuse, and they deserve the protection of the law. Although popular myth, illustrated by Rhett Butler overcoming the objections of his reluctant bride Scarlett O'Hara in the classic film *Gone with the Wind,* says that marital rapes are the result of "healthy male sexuality," the reality is quite the opposite. Many spousal rapes are accompanied by brutal, sadistic beatings and have little to do with normal sexual interests.[100] Not surprisingly, the marital exemption has undergone significant revision. In 1980, only three states had laws against marital rape; today almost every state recognizes marital rape as a crime.[101] Piercing the marital exemption is not unique to U.S. courts; it has also been abolished in Canada, Israel, Scotland, and New Zealand.[102] However, although marital rape is now recognized, most states do not give wives the same legal protection as they would nonmarried couples, and when courts do recognize marital rape, the perpetrators are sanctioned less harshly than are those accused of nonmarital sexual assaults. For example, some will only prosecute when women suffer severe physical harm.[103]

STATUTORY RAPE The term *statutory rape* refers to sexual relations between an underage minor and an adult. Although the sex is not forced or coerced, the law says that young people are incapable of giving informed consent, so the act is legally considered nonconsensual. Typically a state's law will define an age of consent above which there can be no criminal prosecution for sexual relations.

Although each state is different, most evaluate the age differences between the parties to determine whether an offense has taken place. For example, Indiana law mandates prosecution of men aged 21 or older who have consensual sex with girls younger than 14. In some states, defendants can claim they mistakenly assumed their victims were above the age of consent, whereas in others, "mistake-of-age" defenses are ignored. An American Bar Association (ABA) survey found that prosecution is often difficult in statutory rape cases because the young victims are reluctant to testify. Often parents have given their blessing to the relationships, and juries are reluctant to convict men involved in consensual sex even with young teenaged girls. The ABA report calls for stricter enforcement of these cases, noting that many states are already toughening their laws by raising the age of consent to protect minors from the psychological scars of precocious sexuality with an older predatory partner.[104]

To read a report on a **victim-oriented approach to dealing with statutory rape,** go to http://www.ojp.usdoj.gov/ovc/publications/infores/statutoryrape/trainguide/welcome.html. For an up-to-date list of web links, go to http://cj.wadsworth.com/siegel_crimtpt9e.

The Causes of Rape

What factors predispose some men to commit rape? Criminologists' responses to this question are almost as varied as the crime itself. However, most explanations can be grouped into a few consistent categories.

EVOLUTIONARY, BIOLOGICAL FACTORS One explanation for rape focuses on the evolutionary, biological aspects of the male sexual drive. This perspective suggests that rape may be instinctual, developed over the ages as a means of perpetuating the species. In more primitive times, forcible sexual contact may have helped spread genes and maximize offspring. Some believe that these prehistoric drives remain: Males still have a natural sexual drive that encourages them to have intimate relations with as many women as possible.[105] The evolutionary view is that the sexual urge corresponds to the unconscious need to preserve the species by spreading one's genes as widely as possible. Men who are sexually aggressive will have a reproductive edge over their more passive peers. In contrast, women are more cautious and want stable partners who seem willing to make a long-term commitment to childrearing. This difference produces sexual tension that causes men to employ forceful copulatory tactics, especially when the chance of punishment is low.[106] Rape is bound up with sexuality as well as violence because, according to biosocial theorist Lee Ellis, the act involves the "drive to possess and control others to whom one is sexually attracted."[107]

MALE SOCIALIZATION In contrast to the evolutionary biological view, some researchers argue that rape is a function of modern male socialization. Some men have been socialized to be aggressive with women and believe that the use of violence or force is legitimate if their sexual advances are rebuffed—that is, "women like to play hard to get and expect to be forced to have sex." Those men who have been socialized to believe that "no means yes" are more likely to be sexually aggressive.[108] The use of sexual violence is aggravated if pro-force socialization is reinforced by peer group members who share similar values.[109] The Criminological Enterprise feature, "Masculinity and Sexual Violence among the Urban Poor," explores this topic further.

Diana Russell, a leading expert on sexual violence, suggests that rape is actually not a deviant act but one that conforms to the qualities regarded as masculine in U.S. society.[110] Russell maintains that from an early age boys are taught to be aggressive, forceful, tough, and dominating. Men are taught to dominate at the same time that they are led to believe that women want to be dominated. Russell describes the **virility mystique**—the belief that males must separate their sexual feelings from needs for love, respect, and affection. She believes men are socialized to be the aggressors and expect to be sexually active with many women; consequently, male virginity and sexual inexperience are shameful. Similarly, sexually aggressive women frighten some men and cause them to doubt their own masculinity. Sexual insecurity may lead some men to commit rape to bolster their self-image and masculine identity.[111]

Feminists suggest that as the nation moves toward gender equality there may be an immediate increase in rape rates because of increased threats to male virility and dominance. However, in the long term, gender equality will reduce rape rates because there will be an improved social climate toward women.[112]

> **||||||| CONNECTIONS |||||||**
> Recall that Chapter 8 described how the need to prove masculinity helps men justify their abuse of women. Sexually violent men, the argument goes, are viewed as virile and masculine by their peers.

PSYCHOLOGICAL ABNORMALITY Another view is that rapists suffer from some type of personality disorder or mental illness. Research shows that a significant percentage of incarcerated rapists exhibit psychotic tendencies, and many others have hostile, sadistic feelings toward women.[113] A high proportion of serial rapists and repeat sexual offenders exhibit psychopathic personality structures.[114] There is evidence linking rape proclivity with **narcissistic personality disorder,** a pattern of traits and behaviors that indicate infatuation and fixation with one's self to the exclusion of all others and the egotistic and ruthless pursuit of one's gratification, dominance, and ambition.[115]

SOCIAL LEARNING This perspective submits that men learn to commit rapes much as they learn any other behavior. For example, sexual aggression may be learned through interaction with peers who articulate attitudes supportive of sexual violence.[116]

Nicholas Groth found that 40 percent of the rapists he studied were sexually victimized as adolescents.[117] A growing body of literature links personal sexual trauma with the desire to inflict sexual trauma on others.[118] Watching violent or pornographic films featuring women who are beaten, raped, or tortured has been linked to sexually aggressive behavior in men.[119] In one startling case, a 12-year-old Providence, Rhode Island, boy sexually assaulted a 10-year-old girl on a pool table after watching television trial coverage of a case in which a woman was similarly raped (the incident was made into a film, *The Accused,* starring Jodie Foster).[120]

> **||||||| CONNECTIONS |||||||**
> This view is explored further in Chapter 13 when the issue of pornography and violence is analyzed in greater detail. Most research does not show that watching pornography is directly linked to sexual violence, but there may be a link between sexual aggression and viewing movies with sexual violence as their theme.

SEXUAL MOTIVATION Most criminologists believe rape is a violent act that is not sexually motivated. Yet it might be premature to dismiss the sexual motive from all rapes.[121] NCVS data reveal that rape victims tend to be young and that rapists prefer younger, presumably more attractive, victims. Data show an association between the ages of rapists and their victims, indicating that men choose rape targets of approximately the same age as consensual sex partners. And, although younger criminals are usually the most violent, older rapists tend to harm their victims more than younger rapists. This pattern indicates that older criminals may rape for motives of power and control, whereas younger offenders may be seeking sexual gratification and may therefore be less likely to harm their victims.

Rape and the Law

Of all violent crimes, none has created such conflict in the legal system as rape. Even if women choose to report sexual assaults to police, they are often initially reluctant because of the sexist fashion in which rape victims are treated by police, prosecutors, and court personnel and the legal technicalities that authorize invasion of women's privacy when a rape case is tried in court.[122] Police officers may be hesitant to make arrests and testify in court when the alleged assaults do not yield obvious signs of violence or struggle (presumably showing the victim strenuously resisted the attack). However, police and courts are now becoming more sensitive to the plight of rape victims and are just as likely to investigate acquaintance rapes as they are **aggravated rapes** involving multiple offenders, weapons, and victim injuries. In some

The Criminological Enterprise

ΙΙΙΙΙΙΙΙΙΙΙΙΙΙΙΙΙΙΙΙΙΙΙΙΙΙΙΙΙΙΙ

Masculinity and Sexual Violence among the Urban Poor

In an important work, Walter DeKeseredy, Shahid Alvi, Martin Schwartz, and E. Andreas Tomaszewski studied the lives of people whose economic circumstances force them to live in urban housing projects. DeKeseredy and his associates found that as the economy of North America shifts from manufacturing to service based, a greater percentage of working-class men and women end up in urban public housing. Unable to care for their families and live up to their culturally defined role as breadwinner, socially and economically excluded men experience high levels of stress because their normal paths for personal power and prestige are blocked. Stress prompts them to seek support from male peers with similar problems. Peer group support may be helpful, but it has consequences. Socially and economically excluded males in and around public housing complexes view wife beating, rape, and other forms of male-to-female victimization as legitimate and effective means of repairing their damaged masculinity. Keeping women under control helps shore up their fragile self-identity.

Compounding the problem, many male public housing residents are not emotionally attached to women and have little interest in marriage and family. These single, unemployed inner-city men become heavily integrated into peer groups that pressure them to be sexually active, brag about their sexual encounters, and reward them for breaching the sexual defenses of women. Young males in this culture are expected to have high or exaggerated levels of sexual involvement, which for most men, regardless of their social class position, is almost impossible to achieve. If their peers see them as failures with women, they will face group ridicule and experience sexual frustration. Sexual violence and rape may be an outcome of peer pressure to constantly prove one's manhood.

DeKeseredy and his colleagues note that poor urban women are not simply passive victims of this patriarchal domination and control. A growing number of them are creating autonomy for themselves and their "sisters." When they make the financial decisions for the household and put the lease for the car in their own name, their actions are perceived by their mates as an assault on their masculinity. Some men deal with their partner's economic autonomy by leaving them, while others use violence as a means of sabotaging women's attempts to gain economic independence. For example, women who have obtained better economic resources through welfare reform are at greater risk of being abused because the male partner fears that the woman will be able to leave him or meet a more attractive, financially secure man in the workplace.

Social service providers are now hearing many reports of women who are stalked or assaulted in their workplaces by their economically disenfranchised partner as a means of making them lose their job and economic independence. Male violence deters women from participating in the paid labor market. Many abused female public housing residents, like other poor battered women, are forced to return to their violent partner out of economic necessity.

Critical Thinking

1. Discuss the following statement: Some men assault and/or rape women in a misguided attempt to deflect accusations that they are weak and passive around women.

2. Is sexual assault used as a means of keeping women in their place so that they will not challenge male economic superiority?

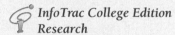 **InfoTrac College Edition Research**

Use "rape" and "sexual assault" in a key word search in InfoTrac College Edition.

Sources: Walter S. DeKeseredy, Shahid Alvi, Martin D. Schwartz, and E. Andreas Tomaszewski. *Under Siege: Poverty and Crime in a Public Housing Community* (Lexington Books, 2003); Walter S. DeKeseredy and Martin D. Schwartz, "Theorizing Public Housing Women Abuse as a Function of Economic Exclusion and Male Peer Support," *Women's Health & Urban Life: An International and Interdisciplinary Journal* 1 (2002): 26–45.

---

jurisdictions, the justice system takes all rape cases seriously and does not ignore those in which victim and attacker have had a prior relationship or those that did not involve serious injury.[123]

PROVING RAPE Proving guilt in a rape case is extremely challenging for prosecutors. Although the law does not recognize it, jurors are sometimes swayed by the insinuation that the rape was victim precipitated; thus the blame is shifted from rapist to victim. To get a conviction, prosecutors must establish that the act was forced and violent and that no question of voluntary compliance exists. They may be reluctant to prosecute cases where they have questions about the victim's moral character or if they believe that the victim's demeanor and attitude will turn off the jury and undermine the chance of conviction.[124] For example, prosecutors may be more willing to bring charges in interracial rape cases because they know that juries are more likely to believe victims and convict defendants in cases involving interracial rape than in intraracial rape.[125]

As well, there is always the concern that a frightened and traumatized victim may identify the wrong man, which happened in the case of Dennis Maher, a Massachusetts man freed in 2003 after spending more than nineteen years in prison for rapes he did not commit. Though three victims provided eyewitness identification at trial, DNA testing proved that Maher could not have been the rapist.[126]

CONSENT Rape represents a major legal challenge to the criminal justice system for a number of reasons.[127] One issue involves the concept of **consent.** It is essential to prove that the attack was forced and that the victim did not give voluntary consent to her attacker. In a sense, the burden of proof is on the victim to show that her character is beyond question and that she in no way encouraged, enticed, or misled the accused rapist.

Proving victim dissent is not a requirement in any other violent crime. For example, robbery victims do not have to prove they did not entice their attackers by flaunting expensive jewelry; yet the defense counsel in a rape case can create reasonable doubt about the woman's credibility. A common defense tactic is to introduce suspicion in the minds of the jury that the woman may have consented to the sexual act and later regretted her decision. Conversely, it is difficult for a prosecuting attorney to establish that a woman's character is so impeccable that the absence of consent is a certainty. Such distinctions are important in rape cases because male jurors may be sympathetic to the accused if the victim is portrayed as unchaste. Referring to the woman as "sexually liberated" or "promiscuous" may be enough to result in exoneration of the accused, even if violence and brutality were used in the attack.[128]

When Cassia Spohn and David Holleran studied prosecutors' decisions in rape cases, they found that perception of the victim's character was still a critical factor in their decision to file charges. In cases involving acquaintance rape, prosecutors were reluctant to file charges when the victim's character was questioned—for example, when police reports described the victim as sexually active or engaged in sexually oriented occupations such as "stripper." In stranger cases, prosecutors were more likely to take action if a gun or knife were used. Spohn and Holleran conclude that prosecutors are still influenced by perceptions of what constitutes "real rape" and who are "real victims."[129] And, even if prosecuted and found guilty in a sexual assault case, punishment is significantly reduced if the victim is believed to have negative personal characteristics such as being a transient, hitchhiker, alone in a bar, or a drug and alcohol abuser.[130]

REFORM Because of the difficulty rape victims have in obtaining justice, rape laws have been changing around the country. Efforts for reform include changing the language of statutes, dropping the condition of victim resistance, and changing the requirement of use of force to include the threat of force or injury.[131] A number of states and the federal government have replaced rape laws with the more gender-neutral term "crimes of sexual assault."[132] Sexual assault laws outlaw any type of forcible sex, including homosexual rape.[133]

Most states and the federal government have developed **shield laws,** which protect women from being questioned about their sexual history unless it directly bears on the case. In some instances these laws are quite restrictive, whereas in others they grant the trial judge considerable discretion to admit prior sexual conduct in evidence if it is deemed relevant for the defense. In an important 1991 case, *Michigan v. Lucas,* the U.S. Supreme Court upheld the validity of shield laws and ruled that excluding evidence of a prior sexual relationship between the parties did not violate the defendant's right to a fair trial.[134]

In addition to requiring evidence that consent was not given, the common law of rape required corroboration that the crime of rape actually took place. This involved the need for independent evidence from police officers, physicians, and witnesses that the accused was actually the person who committed the crime, that sexual penetration took place, and that force was present and consent absent. This requirement shielded rapists from prosecution in cases where the victim delayed reporting the crime or in which physical evidence had been compromised or lost. Corroboration is no longer required except under extraordinary circumstances, such as when the victim is too young to understand the crime, has had a previous sexual relationship with the defendant, or gives a version of events that is improbable and self-contradictory.[135]

The federal government may have given rape victims another source of redress when it passed the Violence Against Women Act in 1994. This statute allows rape victims to sue in federal court on the grounds that sexual violence violates their civil rights; the provisions of the act have so far been upheld by appellate courts.[136]

MURDER AND HOMICIDE

Murder is defined in common law as "the unlawful killing of a human being with malice aforethought."[137] It is the most serious of all common-law crimes and the only one that can still be punished by death. Western society's abhorrence of murderers is illustrated by the fact that there is no statute of limitations in murder cases. Whereas state laws limit prosecution of other crimes to a fixed period, usually 7 to 10 years, accused killers can be brought to justice at any time after their crimes were committed.

To legally prove that a murder has taken place, most state jurisdictions require prosecutors to show that the accused maliciously intended to kill the victim. "Express or actual malice" is the state of mind assumed to exist when someone kills another person in the absence of any apparent provocation. "Implied or constructive malice" is considered to exist when a death results from negligent or unthinking behavior. In these cases, even though the perpetrator did not wish to kill the victim, the killing resulted from an inherently dangerous act and therefore is considered murder. An unusual example of this concept is the attempted murder conviction of Ignacio Perea, an AIDS-infected Miami man who kidnapped and raped an

11-year-old boy. Perea was sentenced to up to 25 years in prison when the jury agreed with the prosecutor's contention that the AIDS virus is a deadly weapon.[138]

Degrees of Murder

There are different levels or degrees of homicide.[139] **First-degree murder** occurs when a person kills another after premeditation and deliberation. **Premeditation** means that the killing was considered beforehand and suggests that it was motivated by more than a simple desire to engage in an act of violence. **Deliberation** means the killing was planned after careful thought rather than carried out on impulse: "To constitute a deliberate and premeditated killing, the slayer must weigh and consider the question of killing and the reasons for and against such a choice; having in mind the consequences, he decides to and does kill."[140] The planning implied by this definition need not be a long process; it may be an almost instantaneous decision to take another's life. Also, a killing accompanying a felony, such as robbery or rape, usually constitutes first-degree murder (**felony murder**).

Second-degree murder requires the killer to have malice aforethought but not premeditation or deliberation. A second-degree murder occurs when a person's wanton disregard for the victim's life and his or her desire to inflict serious bodily harm on the victim result in the victim's death.

Homicide without malice is called **manslaughter** and is usually punished by anywhere from 1 to 15 years in prison. Voluntary or **nonnegligent manslaughter** refers to a killing committed in the heat of passion or during a sudden quarrel that provoked violence. Although intent may be present, malice is not. **Involuntary** or **negligent manslaughter** refers to a killing that occurs when a person's acts are negligent and without regard for the harm they may cause others. Most involuntary manslaughter cases involve motor vehicle deaths—for example, when a drunk driver kills a pedestrian. However, one can be held criminally liable for the death of another in any instance where disregard of safety kills.

One of the most famous cases illustrating the difference between murder and manslaughter occurred on January 26, 2001, when Diane Whipple, a San Francisco woman, died after two large bull mastiff dogs attacked her in the hallway of her apartment building. The dogs' owners—Marjorie Knoller and her husband Robert Noel—were charged with second-degree murder and involuntary manslaughter, respectively. Knoller faced the more severe charge of second-degree murder because she was present during the attack. After the couple's conviction on March 21, 2002, Judge James Warren overturned the murder conviction of Diane Knoller and instituted one of manslaughter. He stated that Knoller could not have known that her two dogs would fatally attack Whipple, and therefore the facts did not support the charge of second-degree murder.[141] Nonetheless, the case involved manslaughter because the couple knew the dogs were dangerous and did not exercise the proper precautions to ensure they would not attack people.

"BORN AND ALIVE" One issue that has received national attention is whether a murder victim can be a fetus that has not yet been delivered; this is referred to as **feticide.** In some instances, fetal harm involves a mother whose behavior endangers an unborn child; in other cases, feticide results from the harmful action of a third party.

Some states have prosecuted women for endangering or killing their unborn fetuses by their drug or alcohol abuse. Some of these convictions have been overturned because the law applies only to a "human being who has been born and is alive."[142] At least 200 women in thirty states have been arrested and charged in connection with harming (though not necessarily killing) a fetus; appellate courts have almost universally overturned such convictions on the basis that they were without legal merit or were unconstitutional.[143] However, in *Whitner v. State,* the Supreme Court of South Carolina ruled that a woman could be held liable for actions during pregnancy that could affect her viable fetus.[144] In holding that a fetus is a "viable person," the court opened the door for a potential homicide prosecution if a mother's action resulted in fetal death.

State laws more commonly allow prosecutions for murder when a third party's actions kill a fetus. Four states (Illinois, Missouri, South Dakota, and West Virginia) extend wrongful death action to the death of any fetus, whereas the remaining states require that the fetus be viable. A viable fetus is able to live outside the mother's body; therefore, the law extends the definition of murder to a fetus that is born alive but dies afterward due to injuries sustained in utero.[145] In a Texas case, a man was convicted of manslaughter in the death of a baby who was delivered prematurely after he caused an auto accident while intoxicated. It was one of the first cases to hold that a person can be held criminally liable for harming an unborn child.[146]

The Nature and Extent of Murder

It is possible to track U.S. murder rate trends from 1900 to the present with the aid of coroners' reports and UCR data. The murder rate peaked in 1933, a time of high unemployment and lawlessness, and then fell until 1958. The homicide rate doubled from the mid-1960s to the late 1970s and then peaked at 10.2 per 100,000 population in 1980. After a brief decline, the murder rate rose again in the late 1980s and early 1990s to a peak of 9.8 per 100,000 in 1991. The murder rate has since been in a decline. In 2004, about 16,000 murders were reported to police, a rate of about 5.5 per 100,000 population, half the 1980 level.

|||||||| **CONNECTIONS** ||||||||

Is it possible that the recent decline in the murder rate is linked to a relatively mundane factor such as improved healthcare? Read about Anthony Harris's study on the effects of improved healthcare on the murder rate in the feature "Explaining Crime Trends" in Chapter 2.

What else do official crime statistics tell us about murder today? Murder tends to be an urban crime. More than half of the homicides occur in cities with a population of 100,000 or more.[147] Almost one-quarter of homicides occur in cities with a population of more than 1 million. Not surprisingly, murder in urban areas is more commonly crime and gang related than in less populated areas. Large cities are much more commonly the site of drug-related killings, gang-related murders, and relatively less likely the location of family-related homicides, including murders of intimates.

Some murders involve very young children, a crime referred to as **infanticide** (killing older children is called **filicide**), and others involve senior citizens, referred to as **eldercide**.[148] The younger the child, the greater the risk of infanticide. At the opposite end of the age spectrum, less than 5 percent of all homicides involve people age 65 or older.

People arrested on murder charges tend to be males (about 90 percent); males are also much more likely to be murder victims. Approximately one-third of murder victims and almost half the offenders are under the age of 25. For both victims and offenders, the rate per 100,000 peaks in the 18- to 24-year-old age group.

Slightly less than half of all victims are African Americans and slightly less than half are white. African Americans are disproportionately represented as both homicide victims and offenders. They are six times more likely to be victimized and eight times more likely to commit homicide than are whites. Murder, like rape, tends to be an intraracial crime; about 90 percent of victims are slain by members of their own race. Similarly, people arrested for murder are generally young (under 35) and male (about 90 percent), and ex-offenders; a significant portion of murderers had prior criminal records.[149]

Murderers typically have a long involvement in crime; few people begin a criminal career by killing someone. When Philip Cook, Jens Ludwig, and Anthony Braga examined all arrests and felony convictions in Illinois between 1990 and 2001, they found that people arrested for homicide were significantly more likely to have been in trouble with the law than the average citizen (that is, the rest of the Illinois population): 42 percent of the murderers had at least one prior felony conviction compared with 4 percent of the general population; 71 percent had experienced an arrest compared with 18 percent of average citizens.[150]

Today few would deny that some relationship exists between social and ecological factors and murder. The following section explores some of the more important issues related to these factors.

Murderous Relations

One factor that has received a great deal of attention from criminologists is the relationship between the murderer and the victim.[151] Some murders are expressive, motivated by rage or anger; others are instrumental, the outcome of a botched robbery or drug deal. Murderous relations are also shaped by gender: Males more likely to kill others of similar social standing in more public contexts; women kill family members and intimate partners in private locations.[152]

||||||| CONNECTIONS |||||||		

Recall from Chapter 3 the discussion of victim precipitation. The argument made by some criminologists is that murder victims help create the "transactions" that lead to their death.

SPOUSAL RELATIONS The rate of homicide among cohabitating couples has declined significantly during the past two decades, a finding that can be attributed to the shift away from marriage in modern society. There are, however, significant gender differences in homicide trends among unmarried people. The number of unmarried men killed by their partners has declined (mirroring the overall trend in the murder rate), but the number of women killed by the men they live with has increased dramatically.

It is possible that men kill their spouses or partners because they fear losing control and power. Because unmarried people who live together have a legally and socially more open relationship, males in such relationships may be more likely to feel loss of control and exert their power with violence.[153]

Research indicates that most females who kill their mates do so after suffering repeated violent attacks.[154] Perhaps the number of males killed by their partners has declined because alternatives to abusive relationships, such as battered women's shelters, are becoming more prevalent around the United States. Regions that provide greater social support for battered women and that have passed legislation to protect abuse victims also have lower rates of female-perpetrated homicide.[155]

Some people kill their mates because they find themselves involved in a love triangle.[156] Interestingly, women who kill out of jealousy aim their aggression at their partners; in contrast, men are more likely to kill their mates' suitors. Love triangles tend to become lethal when the offenders believe they have been lied to or betrayed. Lethal violence is more common when (1) the rival initiated the affair, (2) the killer knew the spouse was already in a steady relationship outside the marriage, and (3) the killer was repeatedly lied to or betrayed.[157]

||||||| CONNECTIONS |||||||

It is possible that men who perceive loss of face aim their aggression at rivals who are competing with them for a suitable partner. Biosocial theory (Chapter 5) suggests that this behavior is motivated by the male's instinctual need to replenish the species and protect his place in the gene pool. Killing a rival would help a spouse maintain control over a potential mother for his children.

PERSONAL RELATIONS Most murders occur among people who are acquainted. Although on the surface the killing might have seemed senseless, it often is the result of a long-simmering dispute motivated by revenge, dispute resolution,

FIGURE 10.2

Murder Transactions

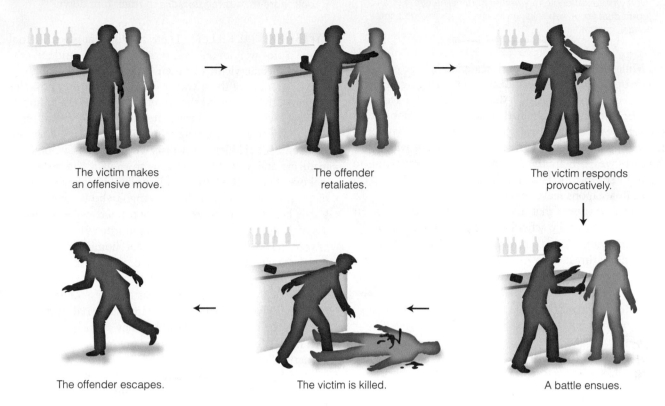

The victim makes an offensive move.

The offender retaliates.

The victim responds provocatively.

The offender escapes.

The victim is killed.

A battle ensues.

jealousy, drug deals, racial bias, or threats to identity or status.[158] For example, a prior act of violence, motivated by profit or greed, may generate revenge killing, such as when a buyer robs his dealer during a drug transaction.

How do these murderous relations develop between two people who may have had little prior conflict? In a classic study, David Luckenbill studied murder transactions to determine whether particular patterns of behavior are common between the killer and the victim.[159] He found that many homicides follow a sequential pattern. First, the victim makes what the offender considers an offensive move. The offender typically retaliates verbally or physically. An agreement to end things violently is forged with the victim's provocative response. The battle ensues, leaving the victim dead or dying. The offender's escape is shaped by his or her relationship to the victim or the reaction of the audience, if any (Figure 10.2).

STRANGER RELATIONS While in the past people seemed to kill someone they knew or were related to, over the past decade, the number of stranger homicides has increased. Today more than half of murderers are strangers to their victims, a significant increase from years past. Stranger homicides occur most often as felony murders during rapes, robberies, and burglaries. Others are random acts of urban violence that fuel public fear. For example, a homeowner tells a motorist to move his car because it is blocking the driveway, an argument ensues, and the owner gets a pistol and kills the motorist; or consider a young boy who kills a store manager because, he says, "something came into my head to hurt the lady."[160]

Why do stranger killings now make up a greater percentage of all murders than in years past? It is possible that tough new sentencing laws such as the three strikes laws used in California and other habitual criminal statutes are responsible. These laws mandate that a "three-time loser" be given a life sentence if convicted of multiple felonies. It is possible, as Tomislav Kovandzic and his associates found, that these laws encourage criminals to kill while committing burglaries and robberies. Why hesitate to kill now because if they are caught they will receive a life sentence anyway?[161]

STUDENT RELATIONS Sadly, violence in schools has become commonplace. About 90 percent of all schools with 1,000 or more students experience a violent incident each year.[162] Violence and bullying have become routine; surveys indicate that more than 16 percent of U.S. schoolchildren have been bullied by other students during the current school term, and approximately 30 percent of 6th- through 10th-grade students reported being involved in some aspect of moderate to frequent bullying, either as a bully, the target of bullying, or both.[163] Sometimes violence and bullying can escalate into a school shooting, such as the Columbine High School massacre, which resulted in the deaths of fifteen people.

To read about some of the more publicized **school shootings**, go to http://www.washingtonpost.com/ wpsrv/national/longterm/juvmurders/timeline.htm. For an up-to-date list of web links, go to http://cj.wadsworth.com/ siegel_crimtpt9e.

While relatively rare, these incidents may be expected because up to 10 percent of students report bringing weapons to school on a regular basis.[164] Many of these kids have a history of being abused and bullied; many perceive a lack of support from peers, parents, and teachers.[165] Kids who have been the victims of crime themselves and who hang with peers who carry weapons are the ones most likely to bring guns to school.[166] Troubled kids with little social support but carrying deadly weapons make for an explosive situation.

Research shows that most shooting incidents occur around the start of the school day, the lunch period, or the end of the school day.[167] In most of the shootings (55 percent), a note, threat, or other action indicating risk for violence occurred prior to the event. Shooters were also likely to have expressed some form of suicidal behavior and to have been bullied by their peers.[168]

In some shooting incidents, the perpetrators claim to have been picked on and bullied by the school's star athletes. Did you know that in sports a team reflects the personality of the coach? If the coach is very aggressive, players may follow this example. To research the effects of coaching on team violence, use "sports violence" as a key word in InfoTrac College Edition. You may want to read this article as well: Edgar Shields, "Intimidation and Violence by Males in High School Athletics," *Adolescence* 34 (fall 1999): 503.

Serial Murder

For 31 years, the notorious serial killer in Wichita, Kansas— known as BTK for Bind, Torture, Kill—eluded the police. During his murder spree, the BTK killer sent taunting letters and packages to the police and the media. After committing some gruesome killings in the 1970s, he went underground and disappeared from view. After 25 years of silence, he suddenly renewed his communications with a local news station. His last communication contained a computer disk that was traced to 59-year-old Dennis Rader after an FBI analysis of deleted data on the disk. Rader later confessed to ten murders in an effort to escape the death penalty.

Criminologists consider a **serial killer**, such as Rader, to be a person who kills three or more persons in three or more separate events. In between the murders, the serial killer reverts to his normal lifestyle. Rader worked as a supervisor of the Compliance Department at Park City, Kansas, which put him in charge of animal control, housing problems, zoning, general permit enforcement, and a variety of nuisance cases. A married father of two, he served as a county commissioner, a Cub Scout leader, and a member of Christ Lutheran Church where he had been elected president of the

Congregation Council. Rader's biography and personal life give few clues to his murderous path, which is perhaps why it took more than three decades to track him down.[169]

TYPES OF SERIAL KILLERS There are different types of serial killers. Some wander the countryside killing at random; others lure specific victims to their death.[170] Theodore Bundy, convicted killer of three young women and suspected killer of many others, roamed the country in the 1970s, killing as he went. Wayne Gacy, during the same period, killed more than thirty boys and young men without leaving Chicago.

Some serial killers are sadists who gain satisfaction from torturing and killing.[171] Sadists wish to gain complete control over their victims through humiliation, shame, enslavement, and terror. Dr. Michael Swango, who is suspected of killing between thirty-five and sixty patients, wrote in his diary of the pleasure he obtained from murder. He wrote of the "sweet, husky, close smell of indoor homicide" and how murders were "the only way I have of reminding myself that I'm still alive."[172]

While Swango obtained pleasure from killing, other healthcare workers who have committed serial murder rationalize their behavior by thinking they are helping patients end their suffering when they put them to death. Harold Frederick Shipman, Britain's most notorious serial killer, was a general practitioner convicted of fifteen murders, most involving elderly patients. After he committed suicide in 2004, further investigation found that he had actually killed at least 218 patients and perhaps even more.[173]

Another type of serial killer, the psychopathic killer, is motivated by a character disorder that causes an inability to experience shame, guilt, sorrow, or other normal human emotions; these murderers are concerned solely with their own needs and passions.

Serial murder experts James Alan Fox and Jack Levin have developed the following typology of serial killer motivations:

- *Thrill killers* strive for either sexual sadism or dominance. This is the most common form of serial murderer.

- *Mission killers* want to reform the world or have a vision that drives them to kill.

- *Expedience killers* are out for profit or want to protect themselves from a perceived threat.[174]

FEMALE SERIAL KILLERS An estimated 10 to 15 percent of serial killers are women. A study by criminologists Belea Keeney and Kathleen Heide investigated the characteristics of a sample of fourteen female serial killers and found some striking differences between the way male and female killers carried out their crimes.[175] Males were much more likely than females to use extreme violence and torture. Whereas males used a "hands-on" approach, including beating, bludgeoning, and strangling their victims, females were more likely to poison or smother their victims. Men tracked or stalked their victims, but women were more likely to lure victims to their death. There were also gender-based personality and behavior characteristics. Female killers, somewhat older than their male counterparts, abused both alcohol and drugs; males were not likely to be substance abusers. Women were diagnosed as having histrionic, manic-depressive, borderline, dissociative, and antisocial personality disorders; men were more often diagnosed as having antisocial personalities. Aileen Wuornos, executed for killing seven men, was diagnosed with a severe psychopathic personality, a product most likely of her horrific childhood marred by beatings, alcoholism, rape, incest, and prostitution.[176]

The profile of the female serial killer that emerges is a person who smothers or poisons someone she knows. During childhood she suffered from an abusive relationship in a disrupted family. Female killers' education levels are below average, and if they hold jobs, they are in low-status positions.

WHY DO SERIAL KILLERS KILL? The cause of serial murder eludes criminologists. Such disparate factors as mental illness, sexual frustration, neurological damage, child abuse and neglect, smothering relationships with mothers (David Berkowitz, the notorious Son of Sam, slept in his parents' bed until he was 10), and childhood anxiety are suspected. Most experts view serial killers as sociopaths who from early childhood demonstrate bizarre behavior, such as torturing animals. This behavior extends to the pleasure that they reap from killing, their ability to ignore or enjoy their victims' suffering, and their propensity for basking in the media limelight when apprehended for their crimes. Killing provides a way to fill their emotional hunger and reduce their anxiety levels.[177] Wayne Henley, Jr., who along with Dean Corill killed twenty-seven boys in Houston, offered to help prosecutors find the bodies of additional victims so he could break Chicago killer Wayne Gacy's record of thirty-three murders.[178]

According to experts Fox and Levin, serial killers enjoy the thrill, the sexual gratification, and the dominance they achieve over the lives of their victims. The serial killer rarely uses a gun because this method is too quick and would deprive him of his greatest pleasure: exalting in his victim's suffering. Levin and Fox dispute the notion that serial killers have some form of biological or psychological problem, such as genetic anomalies or schizophrenia. Even the most sadistic serial murderers are not mentally ill or driven by delusions or hallucinations. Instead, they typically exhibit a sociopathic personality that deprives them of pangs of conscience or guilt to guide their behavior. Serial killers are not insane, they claim, but "more cruel than crazy."[179]

CONTROLLING SERIAL KILLERS Serial killers come from diverse backgrounds. To date, law enforcement officials have been at a loss to control random killers who leave few clues, constantly move, and have little connection to their victims. Catching serial killers is often a matter of luck. To help local law enforcement officials, the FBI has developed a profiling system to identify potential suspects. Because serial killers often use the same patterns in each attack, they leave a signature that might help in their capture.[180]

In addition, the Justice Department's Violent Criminal Apprehension Program (VICAP), a computerized information service, gathers information and matches offense characteristics on violent crimes around the country.[181] This program links crimes to determine if they are the product of a single culprit.

Mass Murder

In contrast to serial killings, **mass murder** involves the killing of four or more victims by one or a few assailants within a single event.[182] The murderous incident can last but a few minutes or as long as several hours. In order to qualify as a mass murder, the incident must be carried out by one or a few offenders. Highly organized or institutionalized killings (such as war crimes and large-scale acts of political terrorism, as well as certain acts of highly organized crime rings), while atrocious, are not considered mass murder and are motivated by a totally different set of factors. The 2004 brutal and senseless X-Box murders, which involved the killing of six people in Florida by a gang of four men out to revenge the theft of clothes and video games, is a mass murder; the genocide of Hitler's Third Reich or the terrorist attack of 9/11 is not.

Mass murderers engage in a single, uncontrollable outburst called "simultaneous killing." Examples include Charles Whitman, who killed fourteen people and wounded thirty others from atop the 307-foot tower on the University of Texas campus on August 1, 1966; James Huberty, who killed twenty-one people in a McDonald's restaurant in San Ysidro, California, on July 18, 1984; and George Hennard, a deranged Texan who, on October 16, 1991, smashed his truck through a plate glass window in a cafeteria in Killeen, Texas, got out, and systematically killed twenty-two people before committing suicide as police closed in.

Fox and Levin define four types of mass murderers:

1. *Revenge killers* seek to get even with individuals or society at large. Their typical target is an estranged wife and "her" children or an employer and "his" employees.

2. *Love killers* are motivated by a warped sense of devotion. They are often despondent people who commit suicide and take others, such as a wife and children, with them.

3. *Profit killers* are usually trying to cover up a crime, eliminate witnesses, and carry out a criminal conspiracy.

4. *Terrorist killers* are trying to send a message. Gang killings tell rivals to watch out; cult killers may actually leave a message behind to warn society about impending doom.[183]

While it often appears that today's society has spawned incidents of mass murder, a recent study by Grant Duwe shows that more than 900 mass killings took place between 1900 and 1999 and that mass killings were nearly as common during the 1920s and 1930s as they are today. More of the earlier incidents involved **familicide** (killing of one's family), and killers were more likely to be older and more suicidal than they are today.

The most significant differences between contemporary mass murders and those in the past are that more killers use guns today and more incidents involve drug trafficking.[184]

SPREE KILLERS Spree killers engage in a rampage of violence taking place over a period of days or weeks. Unlike mass murderers, their killing is not confined to a single outburst, and they do not return to their "normal" identities in between killings. The most notorious spree killing to date occurred in October 2002, in the Washington, DC, area.[185] John Lee Malvo, 17, a Jamaican citizen, and his traveling companion John Allen Muhammad, 41, an Army veteran with an expert's rating in marksmanship, went on a rampage that left more than ten people dead.

Some spree killers target a specific group or class. Joseph Paul Franklin targeted mixed-race couples, African Americans and Jews, committing over twenty murders in twelve states in an effort to instigate a race war. Franklin also shot and paralyzed *Hustler* publisher Larry Flynt because he published pictures of interracial sex.[186] Others, like the DC snipers Malvo and Muhammad, kill randomly and do not seek out a specific class of victim; their targets include the young and old, African Americans and whites, men and women.[187]

ASSAULT AND BATTERY

Although many people mistakenly believe the term *assault and battery* refers to a single act, they are actually two separate crimes. *Battery* requires offensive touching, such as slapping, hitting, or punching a victim. *Assault* requires no actual touching but involves either attempted battery or intentionally frightening the victim by word or deed. Although common law originally intended these twin crimes to be misdemeanors, most jurisdictions now upgrade them to felonies either when a weapon is used or when they occur during the commission of a felony (for example, when a person is assaulted during a robbery). In the UCR, the FBI defines serious assault, or aggravated assault, as "an unlawful attack by one person upon another for the purpose of inflicting severe or aggravated bodily injury"; this definition is similar to the one used in most state jurisdictions.[188]

Under common law, battery required bodily injury, such as broken limbs or wounds. However, under modern law, an assault and battery occurs if the victim suffers a temporarily painful blow, even if no injury results. Battery can also involve offensive touching, such as if a man kisses a woman against her will or puts his hands on her body.

The Nature and Extent of Assault

The pattern of criminal assault is similar to that of homicide; one could say that the only difference between the two is that the victim survives.[189] Assaults may be common in our society simply because of common life stresses. Motorists who assault each other have become such a familiar occurrence that the

According to their legal definitions, battery requires offensive touching, such as slapping, hitting, or punching a victim, while an assault involves intentionally frightening a victim by word or deed. Even the rich and famous sometimes let their emotions get carried away, leading them to commit assault and battery. Here actor Russell Crowe arrives at a New York City criminal court on November 18, 2005, to settle his assault case for which he pleaded guilty to throwing a phone at a hotel concierge.

term **road rage** has been coined. There have even been frequent incidents of violent assault among frustrated passengers who lose control while traveling.

Every citizen is bound by the law of assault, even police officers. Excessive use of force can result in criminal charges being filed even if it occurs while police officers are arresting a dangerous felony suspect. Only the minimum amount of force needed to subdue the suspect is allowed by law, and if police use more aggressive tactics than required, they may find themselves the target of criminal charges and civil lawsuits that can run into the millions of dollars.[190]

In 2004, the FBI recorded about 850,000 assaults, a rate of about 294 per 100,000 inhabitants. Like other violent crimes, the number of assaults has been in decline, down about 25 percent in the past decade. People arrested for assault and those identified by victims are usually young, male (about 80 percent), and white, although the number of African Americans arrested for assault (33 percent) is disproportionate to their representation in the population. Assault victims tend to be male, but females also face a significant danger. Assault rates are highest in urban areas, during summer, and in southern and western regions. The most common weapons used in assaults are blunt instruments and hands and feet.

The NCVS indicates that only about half of all serious assaults are reported to the police. Victims reported about 1.1 million aggravated assaults in 2003 and 3.5 million simple or weaponless assaults. Like other violent crimes, the NCVS indicates that the number of assaults has been in steep decline, dropping more than 50 percent during the past decade, a decline that far exceeds the one reported in the UCR.

Assault in the Home

Violent attacks in the home are one of the most frightening types of assault. Criminologists recognize that intrafamily violence is an enduring social problem in the United States and abroad.

The UN's World Health Organization (WHO) found that around the world, women often face the greatest risk for violence in their own homes and in familiar settings. Almost half the women who die due to homicide are killed by their current or former husbands or boyfriends; in some countries about 70 percent of all female deaths are domestic homicides. It is possible that nearly one in four women will experience sexual violence by an intimate partner in their lifetime, and most of these are subjected to multiple acts of violence over extended periods of time. In addition to physical abuse, a third to over half of these cases are accompanied by sexual violence; in some countries, up to one-third of adolescent girls report forced sexual initiation.[191] The WHO report found that the percentage of women assaulted by a spouse or intimate partner varied considerably around the world: less than 3 percent in the United States, Canada, and Australia and up to 38 percent of the married women in the Republic of Korea and 52 percent of Palestinian women on the West Bank and Gaza Strip.[192] In many places assaults and even murders occur because men believe that their partners have been defiled sexually, either through rape or sex outside of marriage. In some societies the only way to cleanse the family honor is by killing the offending female. In Alexandria, Egypt, 47 percent of the women who were killed by a relative were murdered after they had been raped.[193]

CHILD ABUSE One area of intrafamily violence that has received a great deal of media attention is **child abuse.** This term describes any physical or emotional trauma to a child for which no reasonable explanation, such as an accident or ordinary disciplinary practices, can be found.[194]

Child abuse can result from actual physical beatings administered to a child by hands, feet, weapons, belts, sticks, burning, and so on. Another form of abuse results from **neglect**—not providing children with the care and shelter to which they are entitled.

Yearly national surveys conducted by the Department of Health and Human Services show that the problem is huge: Child protective services (CPS) agencies throughout the United States receive nearly 2 million reports of suspected child abuse or neglect per year. Of these about two-thirds are considered unfounded, which leaves an estimated 900,000 children across the country who are victims of abuse or neglect, or about 12.3 out of every 1,000 children.[195] The National Child Abuse and Neglect Data System (NCANDS) reported an estimated 1,400 child fatalities in 2002 or 1.98 children per 100,000 children in the general population.[196] However, as Figure 10.3 shows, maltreatment rates are lower today than they were a decade ago.

More than half (59 percent) of victims experienced neglect, meaning a caretaker failed to provide for the child's basic needs. Fewer victims were found to have been physically abused (19 percent) or sexually abused (10 percent), and 7 percent were found to be victims of emotional abuse, which includes criticizing, rejecting, or refusing to nurture a child.[197]

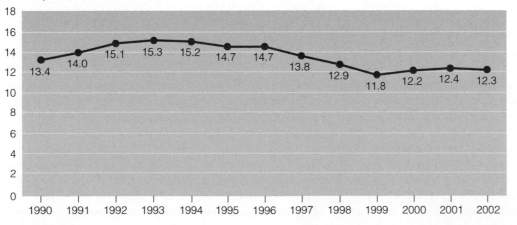

FIGURE 10.3

Child Maltreatment Rates, 1990–2002

Victims per 1,000 children

13.4, 14.0, 15.1, 15.3, 15.2, 14.7, 14.7, 13.8, 12.9, 11.8, 12.2, 12.4, 12.3

Source: National Child Abuse and Neglect Data System (NCANDS), 2004. http://nccanch.acf.hhs.gov/pubs/factsheets/fatality.cfm

Why do parents physically assault their children? Such maltreatment is a highly complex problem with neither a single cause nor a readily available solution. It cuts across ethnic, religious, and socioeconomic lines. Abusive parents cannot be categorized by sex, age, or educational level; they come from all walks of life.[198]

A number of factors have been commonly linked to abuse and neglect:

- Family violence seems to be perpetuated from one generation to another within families.

- The behavior of abusive parents can often be traced to negative experiences in their own childhood— physical abuse, lack of love, emotional neglect, incest, and so on.

- Blended families, which include children living with an unrelated adult such as a stepparent or another unre- lated co-resident, have also been linked to abuse. For example, children who live with a mother's boyfriend are at much greater risk for abuse than children living with two genetic parents. Some stepparents do not have strong emotional ties to their nongenetic children, nor do they reap emotional benefits from the parent–child relationship.[199]

Parents may also become abusive if they are isolated from friends, neighbors, or relatives who can help in times of crisis. Potentially abusive parents are often alienated from society; they have carried the concept of the shrinking nuclear family to its most extreme form and are cut off from ties of kinship and contact with other people in the neighborhood.[200]

SEXUAL ABUSE Another aspect of the abuse syndrome is **sexual abuse**—the exploitation of children through rape, incest, and molestation by parents or other adults. It is diffi- cult to estimate the incidence of sexual abuse, but a number of attempts have been made to gauge the extent of the prob- lem. In a classic study, Diana Russell's survey of women in the San Francisco area found that 38 percent had experi- enced intra- or extrafamilial sexual abuse by the time they reached age 18.[201] Others have estimated that at least 20 per- cent of females suffer some form of sexual violence; that is, at least one in five girls suffer sexual abuse.[202]

Although sexual abuse is still prevalent, the number of reported cases has been in a significant decline.[203] However, this trend must be interpreted with caution. While it is possible that the actual number of cases is truly in decline be- cause of the effectiveness of prevention programs, increased prosecution, and public awareness campaigns, declines might be the result of more cases being overlooked because of (1) increased evidentiary requirements to substantiate cases, (2) increased caseworker caution due to new legal rights for caregivers, and (3) increasing limitations on the types of cases that agencies accept for investigation.[204]

Sexual abuse is of particular concern because children who have been abused experience a long list of symp- toms, including fear, posttraumatic stress disorder, behavior problems, sexualized behavior, and poor self-esteem.[205] Women who were abused as children are also at greater risk to be re-abused as adults than those who escaped childhood victimization.[206] The amount of force used during the abuse, its duration, and its frequency are all related to the extent of the long-term effects and the length of time needed for recovery.

PARENTAL ABUSE Parents are sometimes the target of abuse from their own children. Research conducted by Arina Ulman and Murray Straus found:

1. The younger the child, the higher the rate of child-to- parent violence (CPV).

2. At all ages, more children were violent to mothers than to fathers.

3. Both boys and girls hit mothers more than fathers.

4. At all ages, slightly more boys than girls hit parents.

Ulman and Straus found that child-to-parent violence or CPV was associated with some form of violence by parents, which could either be husband-to-wife, wife-to-husband, corporal punishment of children, or physical abuse. They suggest that if the use of physical punishment could be elim- inated or curtailed, then child-to-parent violence would sim- ilarly decline.[207]

SPOUSAL ABUSE Spousal abuse has occurred throughout recorded history. Roman men had the legal right to beat their wives for minor acts such as attending public games without permission, drinking wine, or walking outdoors with their faces uncovered.[208] More serious transgressions, such as adultery, were punishable by death. During the later stages of the Roman Empire, the practice of wife beating abated; and by the fourth century, excessive violence on the part of husband or wife was grounds for divorce.[209] During the early Middle Ages, there was a separation of love and marriage.[210] The ideal woman was protected, cherished, and loved from afar. In contrast, the wife, with whom marriage had been ar- ranged by family ties, was guarded jealously and could be punished severely for violating her duties. A husband was expected to beat his wife for "misbehaviors" and might him- self be punished by neighbors if he failed to do so.[211]

Through the later Middle Ages and into modern times (from 1400 to 1900), there was little community objection to a man using force against his wife as long as the assault did not exceed certain limits, usually construed as death or dis- figurement. By the mid-nineteenth century, severe wife beat- ing fell into disfavor, and accused wife beaters were subject to public ridicule. Nonetheless, limited chastisement was still the rule. By the close of the nineteenth century, England and the United States outlawed wife beating. Yet the long his- tory of husbands' domination of their wives made physical coercion hard to control. Until recent times, the subordinate position of women in the family was believed to give hus- bands the legal and moral obligation to manage their wives' behavior. Even after World War II, English courts found domestic assault a reasonable punishment for a wife who had disobeyed her husband.[212] These ideas form the foundation of men's traditional physical control of women and have led to severe cases of spousal assault.

THE NATURE AND EXTENT OF SPOUSAL ABUSE It is difficult to estimate how widespread spousal abuse is today; however, some statistics indicate the extent of the problem. In their classic study of family violence, Richard Gelles and Murray Straus found that 16 percent of surveyed families had experienced husband–wife assaults.[213] In police departments around the country, 60 to 70 percent of evening calls involve domestic disputes.

Nor is violence restricted to marriage: National surveys indicate that between 20 and 40 percent of females experience violence while dating.[214] According to a survey conducted by researchers from the Harvard School of Public Health, one in five high school girls suffered sexual or physical abuse from a boyfriend. The study found that teen girls who had been abused by their boyfriends also were much more likely to use drugs or alcohol, to have unsafe sex, and to acquire eating disorders among other social problems.[215] Some of the personal attributes and characteristics of spouse abusers and abusive situations are listed in Exhibit 10.2.

To read this study, go to the **Harvard School of Public Health** website: http://www.hsph.harvard .edu/press/releases/press7312001.html. For an up-to-date list of web links, go to http://cj.wadsworth.com/ siegel_crimtpt9e.

ROBBERY

The common-law definition of *robbery* (and the one used by the FBI) is "the taking or attempting to take anything of value from the care, custody or control of a person or persons by force or threat of force or violence and/or by putting the victim in fear."[216] A robbery is considered a violent crime because it involves the use of force to obtain money or goods. Robbery is punished severely because the victim's life is put in jeopardy. In fact, the severity of punishment is based on the amount of force used during the crime, not the value of the items taken.

In 2004 the FBI recorded about 400,000 robberies, a rate of about 140 per 100,000 population. As with most other violent crimes, there has been a significant reduction in the robbery rate during the past decade; the robbery rate is down more than 40 percent since 1994. The ecological pattern for robbery is similar to that of other violent crimes, with one significant exception: Northeastern states by far have the highest robbery rate.

According to the NCVS, about 500,000 robberies were committed or attempted in 2004, a decrease of about 90,000 from the prior year. The recent downturn in robbery victim-

ization continues a decade-long drop in the robbery rate, from 6 per 1,000 population in 1993 to about 2 today, a decline of 63 percent! Whether this dramatic decline in robberies will continue into the future remains to be seen.

- *Robbery of people who, as part of their employment, are in charge of money or goods:* This category includes robberies in jewelry stores, banks, offices, and other places in which money changes hands.

- *Robbery in an open area:* These robberies include street muggings, purse snatchings, and other attacks. Street robberies are the most common type, especially in urban areas where this type of robbery constitutes about 60 percent of reported totals. Street robbery is most closely associated with mugging or yoking, which refers to grabbing victims from behind and threatening them with a weapon. Street muggers often target unsavory characters such as drug dealers or pimps who carry large amounts of cash because these victims would find it awkward to report the crime to the police. Most commit their robberies within a short distance from their homes.

- *Commercial robbery:* This type of robbery occurs in businesses ranging from banks to liquor stores. Banks are among the most difficult targets to rob, usually because they have more personnel and a higher level of security.

- *Robbery on private premises:* This type of robbery involves breaking into people's homes. FBI records indicate that this type of robbery accounts for about 10 percent of all offenses.

- *Robbery after a short, preliminary association:* This type of robbery comes after a chance meeting—in a bar, at a party, or after a sexual encounter.

- *Robbery after a longer association between victim and offender:* An example of this type of robbery would be an intimate acquaintance robbing his paramour and then fleeing the jurisdiction.

- *Carjacking:* This is a completed or attempted theft of a motor vehicle by force or threat of force.

Sources: Patsy Klaus, *Carjackings in the United States, 1992–96* (Washington, DC: Bureau of Justice Statistics, 1999); Peter J. van Koppen and Robert Jansen, "The Road to the Robbery: Travel Patterns in Commercial Robberies," *British Journal of Criminology* 38 (1998): 230–247; F. H. McClintock and Evelyn Gibson, *Robbery in London* (London: Macmillan, 1961), p. 15.

- *Professional robbers:* These robbers have a long-term commitment to crime as a source of livelihood. This type of robber plans and organizes crimes prior to committing them and seeks money to support a hedonistic lifestyle. Some professionals are exclusively robbers, whereas others engage in additional types of crimes. Professionals are committed to robbing because it is direct, fast, and profitable. They hold no other steady job and plan three or four "big scores" a year to support themselves. Planning and skill are the trademarks of the professional robber, who usually operates in groups with assigned roles. Professionals usually steal large amounts from commercial establishments. After a score, they may stop for a few weeks until "things cool off."

- *Opportunist robbers:* These robbers steal to obtain small amounts of money when an accessible target presents itself. They are not committed to robbery but will steal from cab drivers, drunks, the elderly, and other vulnerable persons if they need some extra spending money. Opportunists are usually young minority group members who do not plan their crimes. Although they operate within the milieu of the juvenile gang, they are seldom organized and spend little time discussing weapon use, getaway plans, or other strategies.

- *Addict robbers:* These people steal to support their drug habits. They have a low commitment to robbery because of its danger but a high commitment to theft because it supplies needed funds. The addict is less likely to plan crime or use weapons than the professional robber but is more cautious than the opportunist. Addicts choose targets that present minimal risk; however, when desperate for funds, they are sometimes careless in selecting the victim and executing the crime. They rarely think in terms of the big score; they just want enough money to get their next fix.

- *Alcoholic robbers:* These people steal for reasons related to their excessive consumption of alcohol. Alcoholic robbers steal (1) when, in a disoriented state, they attempt to get some money to buy liquor or (2) when their condition makes them unemployable and they need funds. Alcoholic robbers have no real commitment to robbery as a way of life. They plan their crimes randomly and give little thought to their victim, circumstance, or escape. For that reason, they are the most likely to be caught.

Source: John Conklin, *Robbery and the Criminal Justice System* (New York: Lippincott, 1972), pp. 1–80.

Attempts have been made to classify and explain the nature and dynamics of robbery. One approach is to characterize robberies by type (Exhibit 10.3), and another is to characterize types of robbers based on their specialties (Exhibit 10.4).

As these typologies indicate, the typical armed robber is unlikely to be a professional who carefully studies targets while planning a crime. People walking along the street, convenience stores, and gas stations are much more likely robbery targets than banks or other highly secure environments. Robbers, therefore, seem to be diverted by modest defensive measures, such as having more than one clerk in a store or locating stores in strip malls; they are more likely to try an isolated store.[217]

Acquaintance Robbery

As Exhibit 10.4 suggests, one type of robber may focus on people they know, a phenomenon referred to as **acquaintance robbery.** This seems puzzling because victims can easily identify their attackers and report them to the police. However, despite this threat, acquaintance robbery may be attractive for a number of rational reasons:[218]

- Victims may be reluctant to report these crimes because they do not want to get involved with the police: They may be involved in crime themselves (drug dealers, for example), or they may fear retaliation if they report the crime. Some victims may be reluctant to gain the label of "rat" or "fink" if they go to the police.

- Some robberies are motivated by street justice. The robber has a grievance against the victim and settles the dispute by stealing the victim's property. In this instance, robbery may be considered a substitute for an assault: The robber wants retribution and revenge rather than remuneration.[219]

- Because the robber knows the victim personally, the robber has inside information that there will be a "good take." Offenders may target people they know to be carrying a large amount of cash or who just purchased expensive jewelry.

- When a person in desperate need for immediate cash runs out of money, the individual may target people in close proximity simply because they are convenient targets.

When Richard Felson and his associates studied acquaintance robbery, they found that victims were more likely to be injured in acquaintance robberies than in stranger robberies, indicating that revenge rather than reward was the primary motive.[220] Similarly, robberies of family members were more likely to have a bigger payoff than stranger robberies, an indication that the offender was aware that the target had a large amount of cash on hand.

Rational Robbery

Most robbers may be opportunistic rather than professional, but the patterns of robbery suggest that it is not merely a random act committed by an alcoholic or drug abuser. Though most crime rates are higher in the summer, robberies seem to peak during the winter months. One reason may be that the cold weather allows for greater disguise; another reason is that robbers may be attracted to the high amounts of cash people and merchants carry during the Christmas shopping season.[221] Robbers may also be attracted to the winter because days are shorter, affording them greater concealment in the dark.

Robbers also choose vulnerable victims. According to research by criminologist Jody Miller, female armed robbers are likely to choose female targets, reasoning that they will be more vulnerable and offer less resistance.[222] When robbing males, women "set them up" in order to catch them off guard; some feign sexual interest or prostitution to gain the upper hand.[223] In an important book, Scott Decker and Richard Wright interviewed active robbers in St. Louis, Missouri.[224] Their findings, presented in The Criminological Enterprise feature "Armed Robbers in Action," also suggest that robbers are rational decision makers.

||||||| **CONNECTIONS** |||||||

Chapter 4 discussed the rationality of robbers. Even when robbers are stealing to support a drug habit, their acts do not seem haphazard or irrational. Only the most inebriated might fail to take precautions. The fact that robbery is gender specific is also evidence that robbers are rational decision makers.

EMERGING FORMS OF INTERPERSONAL VIOLENCE

Assault, rape, robbery, and murder are traditional forms of interpersonal violence. As more data become available, criminologists have recognized relatively new subcategories within these crime types, such as serial murder and date rape. Additional new categories of interpersonal violence are now receiving attention in criminological literature; the next sections describe three of these forms of violent crime.

Hate Crimes

In the fall of 1998 Matthew Shepard, a gay college student, was kidnapped and severely beaten. He died 5 days after he was found unconscious on a Wyoming ranch, where he had been left tied to a fence for 18 hours in near freezing temperatures.[225] His two killers, Aaron J. McKinney and Russell A. Henderson, both 22, were sentenced to life in prison after the Shepard family granted them mercy. At McKinney's sentencing, Matthew's father, Dennis Shepard, addressed the young man:

> I would like nothing better than to see you die, McKinney. However, this is the time to begin the healing process, to show mercy to someone who refused to show any mercy.

AP/Wide World Photos

An image of a murdered Indian immigrant, Balbir Singh Sodhi, is shown at a memorial service in Phoenix, Arizona. Sodhi was killed in a hate crime after the September 11 attack in the mistaken belief that he was of Middle Eastern descent. Should hate crimes be punished more severely than crimes motivated by revenge or greed?

Armed Robbers in Action

Criminologists Richard Wright and Scott Decker have identified and interviewed a sample of eighty-six active armed robbers in St. Louis, Missouri. Their sample, primarily young African American men, helped provide an in-depth view of armed robbery that had been missing from the criminological literature.

Wright and Decker found that most armed robberies are motivated by a pressing need for cash. Many robbers careen from one financial crisis to the next, prompted by their endless quest for stimulation and thrills. Interviewees told of how they partied, gambled, drank, and abused substances until they were broke. Their partying not only provided excitement, but it helped generate a street reputation as a "hip" guy who can "make things happen." Robbers had a "here and now" mentality, which required a constant supply of cash to fuel their appetites. Those interviewed showed little long-range planning or commitment to the future. Because of their street hustler mentality, few if any of the robbers were able to obtain or keep legitimate employment, even if it was available.

Armed robbery also provided a psychic thrill. It was a chance to hurt or humiliate victims, or to get even with someone who may have wronged them in the past. As one robber explained, "This might sound stupid, but I [also] like to see a person get scared, be scared of the pistol. . . . You got power. I come in here with a big old pistol and I ain't playing."

Robbers show evidence of being highly rational offenders. Many choose victims who themselves are involved in illegal behavior, most often drug dealers. Ripping off a dealer kills three birds with one stone, providing both money and drugs while at the same time targeting victims who are quite unlikely to call the police. Another ideal target is a married man who is looking for illicit sexual adventures. He also is disinclined to call the police and bring attention to himself. One told them why he chose to be a robber:

I feel more safer doing a robbery because doing a burglary, I got a fear of breaking into somebody's house not knowing who might be up in there. . . . On robbery I can select my victims, I can select my place of business. I can watch and see who all work in there or I can rob a person and pull them around in the alley or push them up in a doorway and rob them. (p. 52)

Others target noncriminal victims. They like to stay in their own neighborhood, relying on their intimate knowledge of streets and alleys to avoid detection. Although some range far afield seeking affluent victims, others believe that residents in the city's poorest areas are more likely to carry cash (wealthy people carry checks and credit cards). Because they realize that the risk of detection and punishment is the same whether the victim is carrying a load of cash or is penniless, experienced robbers use discretion in selecting targets. People whose clothing, jewelry, and demeanor mark them as carrying substantial amounts of cash make suitable targets; people who look

---

Mr. McKinney, I am going to grant you life, as hard as it is for me to do so, because of Matthew. Every time you celebrate Christmas, a birthday or the Fourth of July, remember that Matthew isn't. Every time you wake up in that prison cell, remember that you had the opportunity and the ability to stop your actions that night. You robbed me of something very precious, and I will never forgive you for that. May you live a long life and may you thank Matthew every day for it.[226]

Hate crimes or **bias crimes** are violent acts directed toward a particular person or members of a group merely because the targets share a discernible racial, ethnic, religious, or gender characteristic.[227] Hate crimes can include the desecration of a house of worship or cemetery, harassment of a minority group family that has moved into a previously all-white neighborhood, or a racially motivated murder. For example, on August 23, 1989, Yusuf Hawkins, a black youth, was killed in the Bensonhurst section of Brooklyn, New York, because he had wandered into a racially charged white neighborhood.[228]

Hate crimes usually involve convenient, vulnerable targets who are incapable of fighting back. There have been numerous reported incidents of teenagers attacking vagrants and the homeless in an effort to rid their town or neighborhood of people they consider undesirable.[229] Another group targeted for hate crimes is gay men and women: Gay bashing has become common in U.S. cities.

Racial and ethnic minorities have also been the targets of attack. In California, Mexican laborers have been attacked and killed; in New Jersey, Indian immigrants have been the targets of racial hatred.[230] Although hate crimes are often mindless attacks directed toward "traditional" minority victims, political and economic trends may cause this form of violence to be redirected. Asians have been attacked by groups who resent the growing economic power of Japan and Korea as well as the commercial success of Asian Americans.[231] The factors that precipitate hate crimes are listed in Exhibit 10.5.

like they can fight back are avoided. Some station themselves at cash machines to spot targets who are flashing rolls of money.

Robbers have racial, gender, and age preferences in their selection of targets. Some African American robbers prefer white targets because they believe they are too afraid to fight back. Others concentrate on African American victims, who are more likely to carry cash than credit cards. As one interviewee revealed, "White guys can be so paranoid [that] they just want to get away. . . . They're not . . . gonna argue with you." Likewise, intoxicated victims in no condition to fight back were favored targets. Some robbers tend to target women because they feel they are easy subjects; however, others avoid them because they believe they will get emotionally upset and bring unwanted attention. Most agree that the elderly are less likely to put up a fuss than younger, stronger targets.

Some robbers choose commercial targets, such as convenience stores or markets that are cash businesses open late at night. Gas stations are a favorite victim. Security is of little consequence to experienced robbers, who may bring an accomplice to subdue guards.

Once they choose their targets, robbers carefully orchestrate the criminal incidents. They immediately impose their will on their chosen victims, leaving little room for the victims to maneuver and making sure the victims feel threatened enough to offer no resistance. Some approach from behind so they cannot be identified, and others approach victims head-on, showing that they are tough and bold. By convincing the victims of their impending death, the robber takes control.

Critical Thinking

1. It is unlikely that the threat of punishment can deter robbery (most robbers refuse to think about apprehension and punishment), but Wright and Decker suggest that eliminating cash and relying on debit and credit cards may be the most productive method to reduce the incidence of robbery. Although this seems far-fetched, our society is becoming progressively more cashless; it is now possible to buy both gas and groceries with credit cards. Would a cashless society end the threat of robbery, or would innovative robbers find new targets?

2. Based on what you know about how robbers target victims, how can you better protect yourself from robbery?

InfoTrac College Edition Research

To learn more about robbery, see: Peter J. van Koppen and Robert W. J. Jansen, "The Road to the Robbery: Travel Patterns in Commercial Robberies," *British Journal of Criminology* 38 (spring 1998): 230; D. J. Pyle and D. F. Deadman, "Crime and the Business Cycle in Post-War Britain," *British Journal of Criminology* 34 (summer 1994): 339–357.

Source: Richard Wright and Scott Decker, *Armed Robbers in Action, Stickups and Street Culture* (Boston: Northeastern University Press, 1997).

THE ROOTS OF HATE Why do people commit bias crimes? In their book *Hate Crimes,* Jack McDevitt and Jack Levin identify three motivations for hate crimes:

- **Thrill-seeking hate crimes:** In the same way some kids like to get together to shoot hoops, hatemongers join forces to have fun by bashing minorities or destroying property. Inflicting pain on others gives them a sadistic thrill.

- **Reactive (defensive) hate crimes:** Perpetrators of these crimes rationalize their behavior as a defensive stand taken against outsiders whom they believe threaten their community or way of life. A gang of teens that attacks a new family in the neighborhood because they are the "wrong" race is committing a reactive hate crime.

- **Mission hate crimes:** Some disturbed individuals see it as their duty to rid the world of evil. Those on a "mission," like Skinheads, the Ku Klux Klan (KKK), and white supremacist groups, may seek to eliminate people who threaten their religious beliefs because they are members of a different faith or threaten "racial purity" because they are of a different race.[232]

More recent research (2002) by McDevitt and Levin with Susan Bennett used data from the Community Disorders Unit (CDU) of the Boston Police Department to uncover a new category of hate crime: **retaliatory hate crimes.** These offenses are committed in response to a hate crime, whether real or perceived; whether the original incident actually occurred is irrelevant. Their more recent research indicates that most hate crimes can be classified as thrill motivated (66 percent) followed by defensive (25 percent) and retaliative (8 percent). Few cases were mission-oriented offenses.[233]

In his 2002 book *The Violence of Hate,* Levin notes that in addition to the traditional hatemongers, hate crimes can be committed by "dabblers"—people who are not committed to hate but drift in and out of active bigotry. They may be young people who get drunk on Saturday night and assault a gay couple or attack an African American man who happens by; they then go back to work or school on Monday. Some are thrill seekers while others may be reacting to the presence of members of a disliked group in their neighborhood. Levin also notes that some people are "sympathizers": They may not attack African Americans but think nothing of telling jokes with racial themes or agreeing with people who despise gays. Finally, there are "spectators" who may not actively participate in bigotry but who do nothing to stop its course. They may even vote for politicians who are openly bigoted because they agree with their tax policies or some other positions, neglecting to process the fact that their vote empowers prejudice and leads to hate.[234]

THE NATURE AND EXTENT OF HATE CRIME
According to the FBI, during 2004 opposition toward a particular race, religion, sexual orientation, ethnicity/national origin, or physical or mental disability prompted hate crimes against 9,528 victims. There were about 7,649 bias-motivated incidents, which include 9,035 separate offenses.[235]

What form do hate crimes take, and whom do they target? The latest FBI data shows that more than half of all incidents are motivated by racial bigotry, about 20 percent are caused by religious intolerance, about 16 percent are the result of a sexual-orientation bias, and almost 13 percent are triggered by an ethnicity/national origin bias; the remainder involves a bias against a disability.[236] An analysis of 3,000 hate crime cases reported to the police found that about 60 percent involved a violent act, most commonly intimidation or simple assault, and 40 percent of the incidents involved property crimes, most commonly damage, destruction, or vandalism of property.[237] While intimidation was the most common form of hate crime, in 2004 the FBI recorded five bias-motivated murders.

In crimes where victims could actually identify the culprits, most victims reported that they were acquainted with

their attackers or that their attackers were actually friends, coworkers, neighbors, or relatives.[238] Younger victims were more likely to be victimized by people known to them. Hate crimes can occur in many settings, but most are perpetrated in public settings.

> **www** To examine the **FBI's hate crime data** go to http://www.fbi.gov/ucr/cius_01/01crime2.pdf. For an up-to-date list of web links, go to http://cj.wadsworth.com/siegel_crimtpt9e.

CONTROLLING HATE CRIMES
Because of the extent and seriousness of the problem, a number of legal jurisdictions have made a special effort to control the spread of hate crimes. Boston maintains the Community Disorders Unit, and the New York City Police Department formed the Bias Incident Investigating Unit in 1980. When a crime anywhere in the city is suspected of being motivated by bias, the unit initiates an investigation. The unit also assists victims and works with concerned organizations such as the Commission on Human Rights and the Gay and Lesbian Task Force. These agencies deal with noncriminal bias incidents through mediation, education, and other forms of prevention.[239]

> **www** To read more about the **Boston Community Disorder Unit,** go to http://www.usmayors.org/uscm/us_mayor_newspaper/documents/08_16_99/usm_0816199921.HTM. For an up-to-date list of web links, go to http://cj.wadsworth.com/siegel_crimtpt9e.

There are also specific hate crime laws that actually originated after the Civil War and that were designed to protect the rights of freed slaves.[240] Today, almost every state jurisdiction has enacted some form of legislation designed to combat hate crimes: Thirty-nine states have enacted laws against bias-motivated violence and intimidation; nineteen states have statutes that specifically mandate the collection of hate crime data.

Some critics argue that it is unfair to punish criminals motivated by hate any more severely than those who commit similar crimes whose motivation is revenge, greed, or anger. There is also the danger that what appears to be a hate crime, because the target is a minority group member, may actually be motivated by some other factor such as vengeance or monetary gain. In November 2004, Aaron McKinney, who is serving a life sentence for killing Matthew Shepard, told ABC News correspondent Elizabeth Vargas that he was high on methamphetamine when he killed Mr. Shepard and that his intent was robbery and not hate. His partner, Russell Henderson, who is appealing his sentence, also claims that the killing was simply a robbery gone bad: "It was not because me and Aaron had anything against gays."[241]

However, in his important book *Punishing Hate: Bias Crimes under American Law,* Frederick Lawrence argues that criminals motivated by bias deserve to be punished more severely than those who commit identical crimes for other motives.[242] He suggests that a society dedicated to the equality of all its people must treat bias crimes differently from other crimes and in so doing enhance the punishment of these crimes.[243]

Some criminals choose their victims randomly; others select specific victims, for example, as in crimes of revenge. Bias crimes are different. They are crimes in which (a) distinct identifying characteristics of the victim are critical to the perpetrator's choice of victim, and (b) the individual identity of the victim is irrelevant.[244] Lawrence views a bias crime as one that would not have been committed but for the victim's membership in a particular group.[245] Bias crimes should be punished more severely because the harm caused will exceed that caused by crimes with other motivations:[246]

- Bias crimes are more likely to be violent and involve serious physical injury to the victim.

- Bias crimes will have significant emotional and psychological impact on the victim; they result in a "heightened sense of vulnerability," which causes depression, anxiety, and feelings of helplessness.

- Bias crimes harm not only the victim but also the "target community."

- Bias crimes violate the shared value of equality among citizens and racial and religious harmony in a heterogeneous society.

Recent research by McDevitt and his associates that made use of bias crime records collected by the Boston police supports Lawrence's position. McDevitt found that the victims of bias crime experience more severe post-crime psychological trauma, for a longer period of time, than do victims of similar crimes that are not motivated by hate or bias. Hate crime victims are more likely to suffer intrusive thoughts, feelings of danger, nervousness, and depression at a higher level than non-bias crime victims.[247] Considering the damage caused by bias crimes, it seems appropriate that they be punished more severely than typical common-law crimes.

LEGAL CONTROLS Should symbolic acts of hate such as drawing a swastika or burning a cross be banned or are they protected by the free speech clause of the First Amendment? The U.S. Supreme Court helped answer this question in the case of *Virginia v. Black* (2003) when it upheld a Virginia statute that makes it a felony "for any person . . . , with the intent of intimidating any person or group . . . , to burn . . . a cross on the property of another, a highway or other public place," and specifies that "[a]ny such burning . . . shall be prima facie evidence of an intent to intimidate a person or group." In its decision, the Court upheld Virginia's law that criminalized cross burning. The Court ruled that cross burning was intertwined with the Ku Klux Klan and its reign of terror throughout the South. The Court has long held that statements in which the speaker intends to communicate intent to commit an act of unlawful violence to a particular

individual or group of individuals is not protected free speech and can be criminalized; the speaker need not actually intend to carry out the threat.[248]

Workplace Violence

Paul Calden, a former insurance company employee, walked into a Tampa cafeteria and opened fire on a table at which his former supervisors were dining. Calden shouted, "This is what you all get for firing me!" and began shooting. When he finished, three were dead and two others were wounded.[249] It has become commonplace to read of irate employees or former employees attacking coworkers or sabotaging machinery and production lines. **Workplace violence** is now considered one of the leading causes of occupational injury or death.[250]

Who engages in workplace violence? The typical offender is a middle-aged white male who faces termination in a worsening economy. The fear of economic ruin is especially strong in agencies such as the U.S. Postal Service, where long-term employees fear job loss because of automation and reorganization. In contrast, younger workers usually kill while committing a robbery or another felony.

CREATING WORKPLACE VIOLENCE A number of factors precipitate workplace violence. One suspected cause is a management style that appears cold and insensitive to workers. As corporations cut their staffs because of some economic downturn or workers are summarily replaced with cost-effective technology, long-term employees may become irate and irrational; their unexpected layoff can lead to a violent reactions.[251] The effect is most pronounced when managers are unsympathetic and nonsupportive; their callous attitude may help trigger workplace violence. Not all workplace violence is triggered by management-induced injustice. In some incidents coworkers have been killed because they refused romantic relationships with the assailants or reported them for sexual harassment. Others have been killed because they got a job the assailant coveted.

Irate clients and customers have also killed because of poor service or perceived slights. Although a hospital is designed to help people deal with their problems, patients whose demands are not met may attack those people who are there to be caregivers: Healthcare and social services workers have the highest rate of nonfatal assault injuries. Nurses are three times more likely to experience workplace violence than any other professional group.[252] In one Los Angeles incident, a former patient shot and critically wounded three doctors because his demand for painkillers had gone unheeded.[253]

There are a variety of responses to workplace provocations. Some people take out their anger and aggression by attacking their supervisors in an effort to punish the company that dismissed them; this is a form of murder by proxy.[254] Disgruntled employees may also attack family members or friends, misdirecting the rage and frustration caused by their work situation. Others are content with sabotaging company equipment; computer databases are particularly vulnerable to tampering. The aggrieved party may do nothing to rectify the situation; this inaction is referred to as **sufferance.** Over time, the unresolved conflict may be compounded by other events that cause an eventual eruption.

THE EXTENT OF WORKPLACE VIOLENCE According to security experts Michael Mantell and Steve Albrecht, the cost of workplace violence for American businesses runs more than $4 billion annually, including lost work time, employee medical benefits, legal expenses, replacing lost employees and retraining new ones, decreased productivity, higher insurance premiums, raised security costs, bad publicity, lost business, and expensive litigation.[255]

These huge costs can be explained by the fact that on average violence in the workplace accounts for about 18 percent of all violent crime or, at last count, 1.7 million violent criminal acts, including: 1.3 million simple assaults; 325,000 aggravated assaults; 36,500 rapes and sexual assaults; 70,000 robberies; and 900 homicides.[256] Which occupation is most dangerous? Not surprisingly, police officers are at the greatest risk to be victims of workplace violence. Other occupations at risk are correctional officers, taxicab drivers, private security workers, and bartenders. As mentioned above, an occupation that is unexpectedly high risk is hospital workers. They average 8.3 assaults per 10,000 employees, which is significantly higher than the rate of nonfatal assaults for all public sector industries—2 per 10,000.[257]

||||||| **CONNECTIONS** |||||||

Does the fact that occupations such as police officer, taxicab driver, and correctional worker have the highest risk of injury support routine activities theory? People in high-risk jobs who are out late at night and, in the case of taxicab drivers, do business in cash seem to have the greatest risk of injury on the job. See Chapter 3 for more on routine activities and crime.

CAN WORKPLACE VIOLENCE BE CONTROLLED? One approach is to use third parties to mediate disputes. The restorative justice movement (discussed in Chapter 8) advocates the use of mediation to resolve interpersonal disputes. Restorative justice techniques may work particularly well in the workplace, where disputants know one another, and tensions may be simmering over a long period. This may help control the rising tide of workplace violence. Another idea is a human resources approach, with aggressive job retraining and continued medical coverage after layoffs; it is also important to use objective, fair hearings to thwart unfair or biased terminations. Perhaps rigorous screening tests can help identify violence-prone workers so that they can be given anger management training. Most importantly, employers may want to establish policies restricting weapons in the workplace: Recent research shows that workplaces where guns were specifically permitted were five to seven times more likely to be the site of a worker homicide than those where all weapons were prohibited.[258]

Stalking

In Wes Craven's popular *Scream* movies, the heroine Sydney (played by Neve Campbell) is stalked by a mysterious adversary who scares her half to death while killing off most of her peer group. Although obviously extreme even by Hollywood standards, the *Scream* movies focus on a newly recognized form of long-term and repeat victimization: stalking.[259]

While it is a complex phenomenon, **stalking** can be defined as a course of conduct directed at a specific person that involves repeated physical or visual proximity, nonconsensual communication, or verbal, written, or implied threats sufficient to cause fear in a reasonable person.[260] According to a leading government survey, it is a problem that affects an estimated 1.4 million victims annually.[261] Recent research by Bonnie Fisher and her associates suggest that even that substantial figure may undercount the actual problem. They found that about 13 percent of the women in a nationally drawn sample of more than 4,000 college women were the victims of stalking. Considering that there are more than 6.5 million women attending college in the United States, about 700,000 women are being stalked each year on college campuses alone.[262] Though students most likely have a lifestyle that increases the risk of stalking compared to women in the general population, this data make it clear that stalking is a very widespread phenomenon.

||||||| **CONNECTIONS** |||||||

The Fisher research found that the likelihood of becoming stalked may be related to the victim's lifestyle and routine activities. Female students who are the victims of stalking tend to date more, go out at night to bars and parties, and live alone. Their lifestyle both brings them into contact with potential stalkers and makes them vulnerable to stalking. For more on routine activities and stalking, go to Chapter 3.

Most victims know their stalker. Women are most likely to be stalked by an intimate partner—a current spouse, a former spouse, someone they lived with, or even a date. In contrast, men typically are stalked by a stranger or an acquaintance. The typical female victim is stalked because her assailant wants to control her, scare her, or keep her in a relationship. Victims of both genders find that there is a clear relationship between stalking and other emotionally controlling and physically abusive behavior.

Stalkers behave in ways that induce fear, but they do not always make overt threats against their victims. Many follow or spy upon their victims, some threaten to kill pets, and others vandalize property. However, as criminologist Mary Brewster found, stalkers who make verbal threats are the ones most likely to later attack their victims.[263]

Though stalking is a serious problem, research indicates that many cases are dropped by the courts even though the stalkers often have extensive criminal histories and are frequently the subject of protective orders. A lenient response may be misplaced considering that there is evidence that stalkers repeat their criminal activity within a short time of the lodging of a stalking charge with police authorities.[264] Victims experience its social and psychological consequences long afterward. About one-third seek psychological treatment, and about one-fifth lose time from work; some never return to work.

Why does stalking stop? Most often because the victim moved away or the police got involved or, in some cases, when the stalker met another love interest.

TERRORISM

As we all watched on September 11, 2001, two hijacked airliners crashed into the World Trade Center in New York City. Thousands were killed when the towers collapsed more than an hour after the impacts. A third hijacked airliner crashed into the Pentagon. A fourth jet, possibly bound for another target in Washington, DC, crashed in Somerset County, Pennsylvania, after passengers were able to overpower the hijackers. The events of September 11 were quickly traced to followers of Osama bin Laden and his al-Qaeda terrorist organization based in Afghanistan. Acting swiftly, the United States began military operations in Afghanistan to root out bin Laden and topple the Taliban government that had sheltered his activities. At the time of this writing, the fight against the Taliban continues.

Since 9/11, terrorism has been the number one concern of the U.S. government. In this section we will define terrorism, briefly discuss its history, mention the various forms it takes, try to understand why someone would want to become a terrorist, and finally review some of the post–9/11 actions taken to curb its occurrence.

What Is Terrorism?

Despite its long history, it is often difficult to precisely define terrorism and to separate terrorist acts from interpersonal crimes of violence. For example, if a group robs a bank to obtain funds for its revolutionary struggles, should the act be treated as terrorism or as a common bank robbery? In this instance, defining a crime as terrorism depends on the kind of legal response the act evokes from those in power. To be considered **terrorism,** which is a political crime, an act must carry with it the intent to disrupt and change the government and must not be merely a common-law crime committed for greed or egotism.

Because of its complexity, an all-encompassing definition of terrorism is difficult to formulate, although most experts agree that it generally involves the illegal use of force against innocent people to achieve a political objective. According to the U.S. State Department, the term *terrorism* means premeditated, politically motivated violence perpetrated against

noncombatant targets by subnational groups or clandestine agents, usually intended to influence an audience. The term **international terrorism** means terrorism involving citizens or the territory of more than one country. A **terrorist group** is any group practicing, or that has significant subgroups that practice, international terrorism.[265]

Terrorism usually involves a type of political crime that emphasizes violence as a mechanism to promote change. Whereas some political criminals may demonstrate, counterfeit, sell secrets, spy, and the like, terrorists systematically murder and destroy or threaten such violence to frighten individuals, groups, communities, or governments into conceding to the terrorists' political demands.[266] However, it may be erroneous to equate terrorism with political goals, because not all terrorist actions are aimed at political change. Some terrorists may try to bring about what they consider to be economic or social reform—for example, by attacking women wearing fur coats or sabotaging property during a labor dispute. Terrorism must also be distinguished from conventional warfare, because it requires secrecy and clandestine operations to exert social control over large populations.[267]

TERRORIST AND GUERILLA The word *terrorist* is often used interchangeably with the term **guerilla;** however the terms are quite different. *Guerilla* comes from the Spanish term meaning "little war," which developed out of the Spanish rebellion against French troops after Napoleon's 1808 invasion of the Iberian Peninsula.[268] Terrorists have an urban focus. Operating in small bands, or cadres, of three to five members, they target the property or persons of their enemy, such as members of the ruling class.[269] Guerillas, on the other hand, are located in rural areas and attack the military, the police, and government officials. Their organizations can grow quite large and eventually take the form of a conventional military force. However, guerillas can infiltrate urban areas in small bands, and terrorists can make forays into the countryside; consequently, the terms are used interchangeably.[270]

A Brief History of Terrorism

Acts of terrorism have been known throughout history. The assassination of Julius Caesar on March 15, 44 BCE, is considered an act of terrorism. Terrorism became widespread at the end of the Middle Ages, when political leaders were subject to assassination by their enemies. The word *assassin* was derived from an Arabic term meaning "hashish eater"; it originally referred to members of a drug-using Muslim terrorist organization that carried out plots against prominent Christians and other religious enemies.[271] The literal translation of *assassin* refers to the acts of ritual intoxication undertaken by the warriors before their missions. In the first century CE, a Jewish sect known as the Zealots took up arms against the Roman occupation, using daggers to slit the throats of Romans and of Jews who collaborated.

When rulers had absolute power, terrorist acts were viewed as one of the only means of gaining political rights. At times European states encouraged terrorist acts against their enemies. For example, Queen Elizabeth I empowered her naval leaders, including famed captains John Hawkins and Francis Drake, to attack the Spanish fleet. These privateers would have been considered pirates had they not operated with government approval. American privateers attacked the British during the Revolutionary War and the War of 1812 and were considered heroes for their actions against the English Navy.

The term *terrorist* first became popular during the French Revolution. From the fall of the Bastille on July 14, 1789, until July 1794, thousands suspected of counterrevolutionary activity were killed on the guillotine. Here again, the relative nature of political crime is documented: whereas most victims of the French Reign of Terror were revolutionaries who had been denounced by rival factions, thousands of the hated nobility lived in relative tranquility. The end of the terror was signaled by the death of its prime mover, Maximilien Robespierre, on July 28, 1794, as the result of a successful plot to end his rule. He was executed on the same guillotine to which he had sent almost 20,000 people.

In the hundred years after the French Revolution, terrorism continued around the world. The Hur Brotherhood in India was made up of religious fanatics who carried out terrorist acts against the ruling class. In Eastern Europe the Internal Macedonian Revolutionary Organization campaigned against the Turkish government, which controlled its homeland (Macedonia became part of the former Yugoslavia). Similarly, the protest of the Union of Death Society, or Black Hand, against the Austro-Hungarian Empire's control of Serbia led to the group's assassination of Archduke Franz Ferdinand, which started World War I. The Irish Republican Army, established around 1916, steadily battled British forces from 1919 to 1923, culminating in the Republic of Ireland gaining independence. Between the world wars, right-wing terrorism existed in Germany, Spain, and Italy. Conversely, Russia was the scene of left-wing revolutionary activity, which killed the czar in 1917 and gave birth to the Marxist state.

During World War II, resistance to the occupying German troops was common throughout Europe. The Germans considered the resistors to be terrorists, but the rest of the world considers them heroes. Meanwhile, in Palestine, Jewish terrorist groups—the Haganah, Irgun, and Stern Gang, whose leaders included Menachem Begin, who later became Israel's prime minister—waged war against the British to force them to allow Jewish survivors of the Holocaust to settle in their traditional homeland. Today, of course, many of these alleged terrorists are considered freedom fighters who laid down their lives for a just cause.

Contemporary Forms of Terrorism

Today the term *terrorism* encompasses many different behaviors and goals. Some of the more common forms are briefly described here.

REVOLUTIONARY TERRORISTS Revolutionary terrorists use violence to frighten those in power and their supporters in order to replace the existing government with a regime that

Belgian Muriel Degauque became Europe's first female suicide bomber when her life came to an end on November 9, 2005, in Baquba, north of Baghdad, where she blew herself up in an attack on an Iraqi police patrol. Five policemen were killed outright and a sixth officer and four civilians were seriously injured. Muriel had converted to Islam when she married a man of north African origin who is alleged to have influenced her radical Islamist beliefs.

holds acceptable political or religious views. Terrorist actions such as kidnapping, assassination, and bombing are designed to draw repressive responses from governments trying to defend themselves. These responses help revolutionaries to expose, through the skilled use of media coverage, the government's inhumane nature. The original reason for the government's harsh response may be lost as the effect of counterterrorist activities is felt by uninvolved people. For example, On October 12, 2002, a powerful bomb exploded in a nightclub on the Indonesian island of Bali, killing more than 180 foreign tourists. In the aftermath of the attack, the Indonesian government declared that the attack was the work of a fundamentalist Islamic group, Jemaah Islamiyah, a secretive terrorist organization aligned with al-Qaeda. Jemaah Islamiyah is believed to be intent on driving away foreign tourists and ruining the nation's economy so that they can usurp the government and set up a pan-Islamic nation in Indonesia and neighboring Malaysia.[272]

Some revolutionary terrorisits direct their attacks at people or groups who oppose the terrorists' political ideology or whom the terrorists define as "outsiders" who must be destroyed. Though classified as revolutionaries, these political terrorists may not want to replace the existing government but to replace its leaders with those who are sympathetic with their views.

In the U.S. political/revolutionary terrorists tend to be heavily armed groups organized around such themes as white supremacy, militant tax resistance, and religious revisionism. Identified groups have included the Aryan Republican Army, the Aryan Nation, the Posse Comitatus, and the Ku Klux Klan. Although unlikely to topple the government, these individualistic acts of terror are difficult to predict or control. On April 19, 1995, 168 people were killed during the Oklahoma City bombing. This is the most severe example of political terrorism in the United States.

NATIONALIST TERRORISM Nationalist terrorism promotes the interests of a minority ethnic or religious group that believes it has been persecuted under majority rule and wishes to carve out its own independent homeland.

In the Middle East, terrorist activities have been linked to the Palestinians' desire to wrest their former homeland from Israel. The leading group, the Palestinian Liberation Organization (PLO), had directed terrorist activities against Israel. Although the PLO now has political control over the West Bank and the Gaza Strip, splinter groups have broken from the PLO. These groups, Hamas and the Iranian-backed Hezbollah, are perpetuating the conflict that Israel and the PLO sought to resolve and are behind a spate of suicide bombings and terrorist attacks designed to elicit a sharp response from Israel and set back any chance for peace in the region. Hundreds on both sides of the conflict have been killed during terrorist attacks and reprisals.

The Middle East is not the only source of nationalistic terrorism. The Chinese government has been trying to suppress separatist groups fighting for an independent state in the northwestern province of Xinjiang. The rebels are drawn from the region's Uyghur, most of whom practice Sufi Islam, speak a Turkic language, and wish to set up a Muslim state called Eastern Turkistan. During the past decade the Uyghur separatists have organized demonstrations, bombings, and political assassinations. The province has witnessed more than 200 attacks since 1990, causing more than 150 deaths.[273] In Russia, Chechen terrorists have been intent on creating a free Chechen homeland and have been battling the Russian government to achieve their goal. And in Spain the ETA (Euskadi Ta Askatasuna, which means "Basque Fatherland and Liberty") uses terror tactics including bombings and assassinations in hopes of forming an independent Basque state in parts of northern Spain and southwestern France.

CAUSE-BASED TERRORISM Some terrorists espouse a particular social or religious cause and use violence to attract followers to their standard. They do not wish to set up their own homeland or topple a government but rather want to attack and intimidate groups that oppose their social and religious views. Anti-abortion groups have demonstrated at abortion clinics, and some members have attacked clients, bombed offices, and killed doctors who perform abortions. On October 23, 1998, Dr. Barnett Slepian was shot by a sniper and killed in his Buffalo, New York, home; he was one of a growing number of abortion providers believed to be the victims of terrorists who ironically claim to be "pro-life." The Comparative Criminology feature further explores this relatively new form of terrorist activity.

ENVIRONMENTAL TERRORISM On August 22, 2003, members of the extremist environmental group Earth Liberation Front (ELF) claimed responsibility for fires that destroyed about a dozen sport utility vehicles at a Chevrolet dealership in West Covina, California.[274] This was neither the first nor the most costly of their attacks. On October 19, 1998, several suspicious fires were set atop Vail Mountain, a luxurious ski resort in Colorado. Soon after, the Earth Liberation Front claimed that it set the fires to stop a ski operator from expanding into animal habitats (especially that of the mountain lynx). The fires, which caused an estimated $12 million in damages, are the most costly of the more than 1,500 terrorist acts committed by environmental terrorists during the past two decades; these groups commit terrorism in an effort to slow down developers who they believe are threatening the environment or harming animals. Fires have also been set in government labs where animal research is conducted. Spikes are driven into trees to prevent logging in fragile areas. Members of such groups as the Animal Liberation Front (ALF) and Earth First! take responsibility for these attacks; they have also raided turkey farms before Thanksgiving and rabbit farms before Easter. Their activities have had significant impact on the commercial aspects of scientific testing, driving up the price of products, such as drugs, which rely on animal experimentation.[275]

> The **Animal Liberation Front** maintains a website at http://www.animalliberation.net. For an up-to-date list of web links, go to http://cj.wadsworth.com/siegel_crimtpt9e.

The Earth Liberation Front has been active for several years in the United States and abroad. In addition to its raid on Vail developers and car dealerships in California and Oregon, members have conducted arson attacks on property ranging from a Nike shop in a mall north of Minneapolis to new homes on Long Island, New York. Their latest attack on February 7, 2004, targeted construction equipment at a 30-acre development site in Charlottesville, Virginia. The FBI has determined that ELF merits investigating as a terrorist network.[276]

STATE-SPONSORED TERRORISM State-sponsored terrorism occurs when a repressive government regime forces its citizens into obedience, oppresses minorities, and stifles political dissent. **Death squads** and the use of government troops to destroy political opposition parties are often associated with Latin American political terrorism. Much of what we know about state-sponsored terrorism comes from the efforts of human rights groups. London-based Amnesty International

Transnational Terrorism in the New Millennium

The traditional image of the armed professional terrorist group with a clear-cut goal such as nationalism or independence is giving way to a new breed of terrorists with diverse motives and sponsors. Rather than a unified central command, they are organized in far-flung nets. Not located in any particular nation or area, they have no identifiable address. They are capable of attacking anyone at anytime with great destructive force. They may employ an arsenal of weapons of mass destruction—chemical, biological, nuclear—without fear of contaminating their own homelands because in reality they may not actually have one.

Nor do contemporary transnational terrorists rely solely on violence to achieve their goals. They may use technology to attack their targets' economic infrastructure—such as through computers and the Internet—and actually profit from the resulting economic chaos by buying or selling securities in advance of their own attack. And they may use terror attacks to influence the economy of their target. Research by Sanjeev Gupta and his associates shows that terror attacks are associated with lower economic growth and higher inflation and also has adverse effects on government tax revenues and investment. It results in higher government spending on defense, which can slow growth in other areas of the economy. These outcomes can weaken the terrorists' targets and undermine their resolve to continue to resist.

The "postmodern terrorist" is becoming more lethal, and as a result, terrorism fatalities have steadily increased throughout the decade. Terrorism expert Bruce Hoffman believes this may be attributed to the rise of religiously motivated terrorist groups such as al-Qaeda, which grew sixfold from 1980 to 1992 and has continued to increase steadily ever since. He suggests that religiously inspired terrorist attacks are more likely to result in higher casualties because they are motivated not by efforts to obtain political freedom or a national homeland but because of culture conflict. Maintaining a differing value system allows the perpetrators to justify in their minds the deaths of large numbers of people: "for the religious terrorist, violence is a divine duty . . . executed in direct response to some theological demand . . . and justified by scripture" (p. 20).

Osama bin Laden and al-Qaeda are the paradigm of the new value-oriented terrorist organization. His masterminding of the 9/11 attack was not designed to restore his homeland or bring about a new political state but to have his personal value structure adopted by Muslim nations. His attack may have been designed to create a military invasion of Afghanistan, which he hoped to exploit for his particular brand of revolution. According to Michael Scott Doran, bin Laden believed his acts would reach the audience that concerned him the most: the *umma,* or universal Islamic community. The media would show Americans killing innocent civilians in Afghanistan, and the *umma* would find it shocking how Americans nonchalantly caused Muslims to suffer and die. The ensuing outrage would open a chasm between the Muslim population of the Middle East and the ruling governments in states such as Saudi Arabia, which were

---

maintains that tens of thousands of people continue to become victims of security operations that result in disappearances and executions. Political prisoners are now being tortured in about 100 countries; people have disappeared or are being held in secret detention in about twenty countries; and government-sponsored death squads have been operating in more than thirty-five countries. Countries known for encouraging violent control of dissidents include Brazil, Colombia, Guatemala, Honduras, Peru, Iraq, and the Sudan.

CRIMINAL TERRORISM In December 2001 six men were arrested by Russian security forces as they were making a deal for weapons-grade uranium. Some of the men were members of the Balashikha criminal gang, and they were in possession of 2 pounds of top-grade radioactive material, which can be used to build weapons. They were asking $30,000 for the deadly merchandise.[277] Since 1990 there have been a half-dozen cases involving theft and transportation of nuclear material and other cases involving people who offered to sell agents material not yet in their possession. These are the known cases; it is impossible to know if client states have already purchased enriched uranium or plutonium.

Sometimes terrorist groups become involved in common-law crimes such as drug dealing and kidnapping, even selling nuclear materials. According to terrorism expert Chris Dishman, these illegal activities may on occasion become so profitable that they replace the group's original focus. Burmese insurgents continue to actively cultivate, refine, and traffic opium and heroin out of the Golden Triangle (the border between Myanmar (Burma), Thailand, and Laos), and some have even moved into the methamphetamine market.

In some cases there has been close cooperation between organized criminal groups and guerillas. In other instances the relationship is more superficial. The Revolutionary Armed Forces of Colombia (FARC) imposes a tax on Colom-

allied with the West. On October 7, 2001, bin Laden made a broadcast in which he said that the Americans and the British "have divided the entire world into two regions—one of faith, where there is no hypocrisy, and another of infidelity, from which we hope God will protect us."

According to Doran, bin Laden's true aim was to cause an Islamic revolution within the Muslim world itself, in Saudi Arabia especially, and not to win a war with the United States. Bin Laden viewed the leaders of the Arab and Islamic worlds as hypocrites and idol worshippers propped up by American military might. His attack was designed to force those governments to choose: You are either with the idol-worshipping enemies of God, or you are with the true believers. The attack on the United States was merely an instrument designed to help his brand of extremist Islam survive and flourish among the believers who could bring down these corrupt governments. Americans, in short, were drawn into somebody else's civil war.

This new generation of terrorists is especially frightening because they have no need to live to enjoy the fruits of victory. They do not hope to regain a homeland or a political voice; hence, they are willing to engage in suicide missions to achieve their goals. The devoted members of al-Qaeda are willing to martyr themselves because they believe they are locked in a life-or-death struggle with the forces of nonbelievers. They consider themselves true believers surrounded by blasphemers and conclude that the future of religion itself, and therefore the world, depends on them and their battle against idol worship. They believe that victory and salvation can be achieved in a martyr's death.

Critical Thinking

1. Are there parallels between an inner-city youth joining a gang in Los Angeles and a disaffected youth who joins an international terrorist group? Do they have the same goals? The same psychological needs?

2. Would you be willing to give up some of your civil rights, such as personal privacy, if it meant that the government could mount a more effective campaign against terrorist groups? For example, should government agents be allowed to search the homes of suspected terrorists without a warrant?

 InfoTrac College Edition Research

What can be done to prevent terrorism in the new millennium? Can technology hold the key? Find out by reading: Richard K. Betts, "Fixing Intelligence," *Foreign Affairs* 81 (January–February 2002): 43.

Sources: Sanjeev Gupta, Benedict Clements, Rina Bhattacharya, and Shamit.Chakravarti, "Fiscal Consequences of Armed Conflict and *Terrorism* in Low- and Middle-Income Countries," *European Journal of Political Economy* 20 (2004): 403–421; Andrew Chen and Thomas Siems, "Effects of Terrorism on Global Capital Markets," *European Journal of Political Economy* 20 (2004): 349–356; Michael Scott Doran, "Somebody Else's Civil War," *Foreign Affairs* 81 (January–February 2002): 22–25; Bruce Hoffman, "Change and Continuity in Terrorism," *Studies in Conflict and Terrorism* 24 (2001); Harvey Kushner, *Terrorism in America, A Structured Approach to Understanding the Terrorist Threat* (Springfield, IL: Charles C Thomas, 1998); Ian Lesser, Bruce Hoffman, John Arquilla, David Ronfeldt, and Michele Zanini, *Countering the New Terrorism* (Washington, DC: Rand, 1999); Jessica Stern, *The Ultimate Terrorists* (Cambridge, MA: Harvard University Press, 1999).

bian drug producers, but evidence indicates that the group cooperates with Colombia's top drug barons in running the trade. In some instances, the line between being a terrorist organization with political support and vast resources and being an organized criminal group engaging in illicit activities for profit becomes blurred. What appears to be a politically motivated action, such as the kidnapping of a government official for ransom, may turn out to be merely a for profit crime.[278]

What Motivates Terrorists?

In the aftermath of September 11, many Americans asked themselves the same simple question: Why? What could motivate someone like Osama bin Laden to order the deaths of thousands of innocent people? How could someone who had never been to the United States or suffered personally at its hands develop such lethal hatred?

Some experts believed the attacks had a political basis, claiming that bin Laden's anger was an outgrowth of America's Middle East policies. Others saw a religious motivation and claimed that the terrorists were radical Muslims at war with the liberal religions of the West. Another view was that bin Laden's rage was fueled by deep-rooted psychological problems.

Bin Laden's motivations will probably never be fully understood, but it is possible that his violent urges stemmed from the same web of emotions that fuel the thousands of predatory criminals who prowl society looking for unwary victims. If so, his actions, although extreme, are certainly not unique.

Terrorists engage in criminal activities, such as bombings, shootings, and kidnappings. What motivates these individuals to risk their lives and those of innocent people? One view is that terrorists are emotionally disturbed individuals who act out their psychosis within the confines of violent groups. According to this view, terrorist violence is not so much a political instrument as an end in itself; it is the result of compulsion or psychopathology. Terrorists do what they do because of garden-variety emotional problems, including but not limited to self-destructive urges, disturbed emotions combined with problems with authority, and inconsistent and troubled parenting.[279] As terrorism expert Jerrold M. Post puts it, "political terrorists are driven to commit acts of violence as a consequence of psychological forces, and . . . their special psychology is constructed to rationalize acts they are psychologically compelled to commit."[280]

Another view is that terrorists hold extreme ideological beliefs that prompt their behavior. At first they have heightened perceptions of oppressive conditions, believing that they are being victimized by some group or government. Once these potential terrorists recognize that these conditions can be changed by an active governmental reform effort that has not happened, they conclude that they must resort to violence to encourage change. The violence need not be aimed at a specific goal. Rather, terror tactics must help set in motion a series of events that enlists others in the cause and leads to long-term change. "Successful" terrorists believe that their "self-sacrifice" outweighs the guilt created by harming innocent people. Terrorism, therefore, requires violence without guilt; the cause justifies the violence.

Ironically, many terrorists appear to be educated members of the upper class. Osama bin Laden was a multimillionaire, and at least some of his followers were highly educated and trained. The acts of the modern terrorist—using the Internet; logistically complex and expensive assaults; and writing and disseminating formal critiques, manifestos, and theories—require the training and education of the social elite, not the poor and oppressed.

Use "terrorism" in a key word search in InfoTrac College Edition.

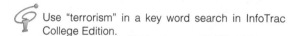

Responses to Terrorism

In the aftermath of 9/11, a great deal of criticism was directed at the U.S antiterrorism and information-gathering agencies: How could they have let this happen? Critics may have failed to comprehend the difficulty in gathering intelligence about these closed, highly secretive groups.

In *Nuclear Terrorism* (2004), Graham Allison, an expert on nuclear weapons and national security, describes the almost superhuman effort it would take to seal the nation's borders from nuclear attack. Every day, 30,000 trucks, 6,500 rail cars, and 140 ships deliver more than 50,000 cargo containers into the United States. And while fewer than 5 percent ever get screened, those that do are given nonphysical inspections that may not detect nuclear weapons or fissile material.[281]

LEGAL RESPONSES Antiterrorist legislation provides jurisdiction over terrorist acts committed abroad against U.S. citizens and gives the United States the right to punish people

Can the fear of terrorism go too far and lead to harassment and even violence? Calling herself a "Legal Observer," Kristen Dillon uses the roof of her group's van as a perch to monitor the activity of Minuteman Project volunteers along the U.S./Mexico border west of Douglass, Arizona. Minuteman volunteers were manning observation posts around the clock for the month of April 2005 along the border in the eastern part of Arizona to bring attention to the number of illegal immigrants coming north from Mexico. The Legal Observers, who are affiliated with the American Civil Liberties Union, were concerned that Minuteman Project volunteers, some of whom are armed, could harm illegal immigrants.

for killing foreign officials and politically protected persons. The 1994 Violent Crime Control Act authorized the death penalty for international terrorists who kill U.S. citizens abroad.[282] The World Trade Center attack forever changed U.S. policy on terrorism. What have been some of the major efforts to combat terrorist groups?

Soon after the attack, Congress moved quickly to pass legislation giving the law enforcement agencies a freer hand to investigate and apprehend suspected terrorists. Congress quickly enacted the **USA Patriot Act (USAPA)**.[283] The bill, over 342 pages, created new laws and made changes to over 15 different existing statutes. Its aims were to give sweeping new powers to domestic law enforcement and international intelligence agencies in an effort to fight terrorism, to expand the definition of terrorist activities, and to alter sanctions for violent terrorism.

© Fred Greaves/Reuters/Landov

While it is impossible to discuss here every provision of this sweeping legislation, a few of its more important elements will be examined below. Among its provisions, USAPA expands all four traditional tools of surveillance—wiretaps, search warrants, "pen/trap" orders (installing devices that record phone calls), and subpoenas. The Foreign Intelligence Surveillance Act (FISA), which allows domestic operations by intelligence agencies, was also expanded. USAPA gave greater power to the FBI to check and monitor phone, Internet, and computer records without first needing to demonstrate that they were being used by a suspect or target of a court order.

The government may now serve a single wiretap or pen/trap order on any person regardless of whether that person or entity is named in a court order. Prior to the Patriot Act, telephone companies could be ordered to install pen/trap devices on their networks that would monitor calls coming to a surveillance target and to whom the surveillance target made calls. The USAPA extends this monitoring to the Internet. Law enforcement agencies may now obtain the e-mail addresses and websites visited by a target and e-mails of those people with whom they communicate. It is possible to require that an Internet service provider (ISP) install a device that records e-mail and other electronic communications on an ISP's servers, looking for communications initiated or received by the target of an investigation. Under USAPA, the government does not need to show a court that the information or communication is relevant to a criminal investigation, nor does it have to report where the order was served or what information was received.

The Patriot Act also allows enforcement agencies to monitor cable operators and obtain access to cable operators' records and systems. Prior to the legislation, the cable company had to give prior notice to the customer, even if that person was a target of an investigation. Information can be obtained about people with whom the cable subscriber communicates, the content of their communications, and their subscription records; prior notice is still required if law enforcement agencies want to learn what television programming a subscriber purchases.

The Patriot Act also expands the definition of terrorism and enables the government to monitor more closely those people suspected of "harboring" and giving "material support" to terrorists (§§ 803, 805). It further increases the authority of the attorney general to detain and deport noncitizens with little or no judicial review. The attorney general may certify that he or she has "reasonable grounds to believe" that a noncitizen endangers national security and therefore is eligible for deportation. The attorney general and secretary of state are also given the authority to designate domestic groups as terrorist organizations and may deport any noncitizens who are its members.

While law enforcement agencies may applaud these new laws, civil libertarians are troubled because they view the Patriot Act as eroding civil rights. They are troubled by provisions that permit the government to share information from grand jury proceedings and from criminal wiretaps with intelligence agencies. The First Amendment activities of American citizens—such as watching TV—may be violated. The new and sweeping authority of the act is not limited to true terrorism investigations but covers a much broader range of activity involving reasonable political action.[284] At the time of this writing, the main provisions of the USAPA remain the law of the land though concern about using it to spy on U.S. citizens has been the subject of national debate.

JUSTICE RESPONSES To respond to terrorism, the United States government has revamped the mission of existing agencies and created new ones designed to coordinate counterterrorism activity.

The FBI is currently expanding its force and concentrating on hiring agents with scientific and technological skills as well as foreign language proficiency in priority areas, such as Arabic, Farsi, Pashtu, Urdu, all dialects of Chinese, Japanese, Korean, Russian, Spanish, and Vietnamese; the FBI is also looking for those with backgrounds in foreign counterintelligence, counterterrorism, and military intelligence. These new agents, as well as helping in counterterrorism activities, will help staff the Cyber Division, which coordinates, oversees, and facilitates FBI investigations in which the Internet, online services, and computer systems and networks are the principal instruments or targets of terrorists.

The National Strategy for Homeland Security and the Homeland Security Act of 2002 established the Department of Homeland Security (DHS) whose mission is to unify the loosely defined and structured organizations involved in national security. Today the department employs more than 180,000 people who are charged with

- Preventing terrorist attacks within the United States

- Reducing America's vulnerability to terrorism

- Minimizing the damage and recovery from attacks that do occur

The DHS now has five independent branches:

1. *Border and Transportation Security (BTS):* BTS is responsible for maintaining the security of our nation's borders and transportation systems.

2. *Emergency Preparedness and Response (EPR):* This branch ensures that our nation is prepared for, and able to recover from, terrorist attacks and natural disasters.

3. *Science and Technology (S&T):* Coordinates the department's efforts in research and development, including preparing for and responding to the full range of terrorist threats involving weapons of mass destruction.

4. *Information Analysis and Infrastructure Protection (IAIP):* IAIP merges the capability to identify and assess intelligence information concerning threats to the homeland under one roof, issue timely warnings, and take appropriate preventive and protective action.

5. *Management:* This branch is responsible for budget, management, and personnel issues in DHS.

In addition, the U.S. government has created two new agencies to combat terrorism. The National Counterterrorism Center (NCTC) —staffed by terrorism experts from the CIA, FBI, and the Pentagon; the Privacy and Civil Liberties Board; and the National Counterproliferation Center— serves as the primary organization in the U.S. government for analyzing and integrating all intelligence possessed or acquired pertaining to terrorism and counterterrorism, excepting purely domestic counterterrorism information.

As well, the office of Director of National Intelligence (DNI) has been created. The DNI is charged with coordinating data from the nation's primary intelligence-gathering agencies and serves as the principal intelligence advisor to the president and the statutory intelligence advisor to the National Security Council. The first person to hold the post of director of national intelligence is John Negroponte, former ambassador to Iraq, who was confirmed on April 21, 2005.

SUMMARY

- Violence has become an all too common aspect of modern life. Among the various explanations of sources of violent crime are exposure to violence, personal traits and makeup, evolutionary factors and human instincts, cultural values and a subculture of violence, substance abuse, and socialization and upbringing.

- Rape, the carnal knowledge of a female forcibly and against her will, has been known throughout history, but the view of rape has evolved. At present, more than 90,000 rapes are reported to U.S. police each year; the actual number of rapes is probably much higher. However, like other violent crimes, the rape rate is in decline.

- There are numerous forms of rape including statutory, acquaintance, and date rape. Rape is an extremely difficult charge to prove in court. The victim's lack of consent must be proven; therefore, it almost seems that the victim is on trial. Rape shield laws have been developed to protect victims from having their personal life placed on trial.

- Murder is defined as killing a human being with malice aforethought. There are different degrees of murder, and punishments vary accordingly. Like rape the murder rate and number of annual murders is in decline.

- Murder can involve a single victim or multiple killings as in serial murder, mass murder, or spree killing.

- One important characteristic of murder is that the victim and criminal often know each other. Murder often involves an interpersonal transaction in which a hostile action by the victim precipitates a murderous relationship.

- Assault involves physically harming another. Assaults often occur in the home, including child abuse and spouse abuse. There also appears to be a trend toward violence between dating couples.

- Robbery involves theft by force, usually in a public place. Robbery is considered a violent crime because it can and often does involve violence. Robbery that involves people

who know each other is acquaintance robbery.

- There are newly emerging forms of violent crime including hate crimes, stalking, and workplace violence.

- Terrorism is a significant form of violence. Many terrorist groups exist at both the national and international levels.

- There are a variety of terrorist goals including political, nationalist, cause based, criminal, state sponsored, and environmental protection.

- Terrorists may be motivated by criminal gain, psychosis, grievance against the state, or ideology.

- The FBI and the Department of Homeland Security have been assigned the task of protecting the nation from terrorist attacks. The USA Patriot Act was passed to provide these agencies with greater powers.

- The National Counterterrorism Center and the Director of National Intelligence are two agencies created to coordinate counterterrorism activities.

ThomsonNOW

Thomson NOW! Optimize your study time and master key chapter concepts with **ThomsonNOW™**—the first web-based assessment-centered study tool for Criminology. This powerful resource helps you determine your unique study needs and provides you with a *Personalized Study Plan,* guiding you to interactive media that includes Learning Modules, Topic Reviews, ABC Video Clips with Questions, Animations, an integrated E-book, and more!

Thinking Like a Criminologist

You have been hired as a terror expert by the director of national intelligence. He tells you that the United States and its coalition allies have vowed to eliminate the network of al-Qaeda cells thought to have been established throughout the western world. Already, numerous al-Qaeda and Taliban suspects captured in Afghanistan and elsewhere have been imprisoned on U.S. military bases including Guantanamo Bay in Cuba. There have been hundreds of arrests made in more than fifty countries, and a number of allies have actually changed their laws to make it easier to apprehend alleged activists. Yet, despite these efforts the threat of terror goes on unabated. The director would like you to make three recommendations, to be implemented immediately, which will help reduce the terrorist threat. How would you respond?

Doing Research on the Web

Use "antiterror" in a key word search in InfoTrac College Edition.

You may want to read about antiterror activities in the United Kingdom as well. Go to http:// www.commonwealthtuc.org/ CHRI%20Report.doc.

The entire 9/11 Commission report can be accessed at http://www. 9-11commission.gov.

Here is the site for the FBI's 2004 to 2009 reorganization plan: http://www.fbi .gov/publications/strategicplan/ strategicplanfull.pdf.

KEY TERMS

expressive violence (320)
instrumental violence (320)
crusted over (323)
subculture of violence (323)
disputatiousness (323)
rape (324)
gang rape (327)
serial rape (327)
acquaintance rape (328)
statutory rape (328)
marital rape (328)
marital exemption (329)
virility mystique (330)
narcissistic personality disorder (330)
aggravated rape (330)
consent (332)
shield laws (332)
murder (332)

first-degree murder (333)
premeditation (333)
deliberation (333)
felony murder (333)
second-degree murder (333)
manslaughter (333)
nonnegligent manslaughter (333)
involuntary manslaughter (333)
negligent manslaughter (333)
feticide (333)
infanticide (334)
filicide (334)
eldercide (334)
serial killer (336)
mass murder (337)
familicide (337)
road rage (338)
child abuse (339)

neglect (339)
sexual abuse (340)
acquaintance robbery (342)
hate crimes (344)
bias crimes (344)
thrill-seeking hate crimes (345)
reactive (defensive) hate crimes (345)
mission hate crimes (345)
retaliatory hate crimes (346)
workplace violence (347)
sufferance (348)
stalking (348)
terrorism (349)
international terrorism (349)
terrorist group (349)
guerilla (349)
death squads (351)
USA Patriot Act (USAPA) (354)

1. Should different types of rape receive different legal sanctions? For example, should someone who rapes a stranger be punished more severely than someone who is convicted of marital rape or date rape? If your answer is yes, do you also think that someone who kills a stranger should be more severely punished than someone who kills his wife or girlfriend?

2. Is there a subculture of violence in your home city or town? If so, how would you describe its environment and values?

3. There have been significant changes in rape laws regarding issues such as corroboration and shield laws. What other measures would you take to protect the victims of rape when they are forced to testify in court? Should the names of rape victims be published in the press? Do they deserve more protection than those accused of rape?

4. Should hate crimes be punished more severely than crimes motivated by greed, anger, or revenge? Why should crimes be distinguished by the motivations of the perpetrator?

Is hate a more heinous motivation than revenge?

5. In light of the 9/11 attack, should acts of terrorism be treated differently from other common-law violent crimes? For example, should terrorists be executed for their acts even if no one is killed during their attack?

NOTES

1. CNN. "Missing Teen's Mother Leaves Aruba." http://www.cnn.com/2005/LAW/07/31/aruba.missing. Accessed September 2, 2005.

2. Robert Nash Parker and Catherine Colony, "Relationships, Homicides, and Weapons: A Detailed Analysis." Paper presented at the annual meeting of the American Society of Criminology, Montreal, November 1987.

3. Stryker McGuire, "The Dunblane Effect," Newsweek, 28 October 1996, p. 46.

4. Rokeya Farrooque, Ronnie Stout, and Frederick Ernst, "Heterosexual Intimate Partner Homicide: Review of Ten Years of Clinical Experience," Journal of Forensic Sciences 50 (2005): 648–651; Miltos Livaditis, Gkaro Esagian, Christos Kakoulidis, Maria Samakouri, and Nikos Tzavaras, "Matricide by Person with Bipolar Disorder and Dependent Overcompliant Personality," Journal of Forensic Sciences 50 (2005): 658–661.

5. Dorothy Otnow Lewis, Ernest Moy, Lori Jackson, Robert Aaronson, Nicholas Restifo, Susan Serra, and Alexander Simos, "Biopsychosocial Characteristics of Children Who Later Murder," American Journal of Psychiatry 142 (1985): 1,161–1,167.

6. Dorothy Otnow Lewis, Guilty by Reason of Insanity (New York: Fawcett Columbine, 1998).

7. Richard Rogers, Randall Salekin, Kenneth Sewell, and Keith Cruise, "Prototypical Analysis of Antisocial Personality Disorder," Criminal Justice and Behavior 27 (2000): 234–255; Amy Holtzworth-Munroe and Gregory Stuart, "Typologies of Male Batterers: Three Subtypes and the Differences among Them," Psychological Bulletin 116 (1994): 476–497.

8. Katherine Van Wormer and Chuk Odiah, "The Psychology of Suicide-Murder and the Death Penalty," Journal of Criminal Justice 27 (1999): 361–370.

9. Sigmund Freud, Beyond the Pleasure Principle (London: Inter-Psychoanalytic Press, 1922).

10. Konrad Lorenz, On Aggression (New York: Harcourt Brace Jovanovich, 1966).

11. Arnie Nielsen, Ramiro Martinez, and Matthew Lee, "Alcohol, Ethnicity, and Violence: The Role of Alcohol Availability for Latino and Black Aggravated Assaults and Robberies," Sociological Quarterly 46 (2005): 479–502.

12. Chris Allen, "The Links between Heroin, Crack Cocaine, and Crime: Where Does Street Crime Fit In?" British Journal of Criminology, 45 (2005): 355–372.

13. Steven Messner, Glenn Deane, Luc Anselin, and Benjamin Pearson-Nelson, "Locating the Vanguard in Rising and Falling Homicide Rates across Cities," Criminology 43 (2005): 661–696.

14. Paul Goldstein, Henry Brownstein, and Patrick Ryan, "Drug-Related Homicide in New York: 1984–1988," Crime and Delinquency 38 (1992): 459–476.

15. Albert Reiss and Jeffrey Roth, Understanding and Preventing Violence (Washington, DC: National Academy Press, 1993), pp. 193–194.

16. Robert Brewer and Monica Swahn, "Binge Drinking and Violence,". Journal of the American Medical Association 294 (2005): 16–20.

17. Tomika Stevens, Kenneth Ruggiero, Dean Kilpatrick, Heidi Resnick, and Benjamin Saunders, "Variables Differentiating Singly and Multiply Victimized Youth: Results from the National Survey of Adolescents and Implications for Secondary Prevention," Child Maltreatment 10 (2005): 211–223; James Collins and Pamela Messerschmidt, "Epidemiology of Alcohol-Related Violence," Alcohol Health and Research World 17 (1993): 93–100.

18. Antonia Abbey, Tina Zawacki, Philip Buck, Monique Clinton, and Pam McAuslan, "Sexual Assault and Alcohol Consumption: What Do We Know about Their Relationship and What Types of Research Are Still Needed?" Aggression and Violent Behavior 9 (2004): 271–303.

19. Martin Grann and Seena Fazel, "Substance Misuse and Violent Crime: Swedish Population Study," British Medical Journal 328 (2004): 1,233–1,234; Susanne Rogne Gjeruldsen, Bjørn Myrvang, and Stein Opjordsmoen, "Criminality in Drug Addicts: A Follow-Up Study over 25 Years," European Addiction Research 10 (2004): 49–56.

20. Paul Goldstein, Patricia Bellucci, Barry Spunt, and Thomas Miller, "Volume of Cocaine Use and Violence: A Comparison between Men and Women," *Journal of Drug Issues* 21 (1991): 345–367.

21. Todd Herrenkohl, Bu Huang, Emiko Tajima, and Stephen Whitney, "Examining the Link between Child Abuse and Youth Violence," *Journal of Interpersonal Violence* 18 (2003): 1,189–1,208; Pamela Lattimore, Christy Visher, and Richard Linster, "Predicting Rearrest for Violence among Serious Youthful Offenders," *Journal of Research in Crime and Delinquency* 32 (1995): 54–83.

22. Rolf Loeber and Dale Hay, "Key Issues in the Development of Aggression and Violence from Childhood to Early Adulthood," *Annual Review of Psychology* 48 (1997): 371–410.

23. Deborah Capaldi and Gerald Patterson, "Can Violent Offenders Be Distinguished from Frequent Offenders: Prediction from Childhood to Adolescence," *Journal of Research in Crime and Delinquency* 33 (1996): 206–231.

24. Adrian Raine, Patricia Brennan, and Sarnoff Mednick, "Interaction between Birth Complications and Early Maternal Rejection in Predisposing Individuals to Adult Violence: Specificity to Serious, Early-Onset Violence," *American Journal of Psychiatry* 154 (1997): 1,265–1,271.

25. John Lemmon, "How Child Maltreatment Affects Dimensions of Juvenile Delinquency in a Cohort of Low-Income Urban Youths," *Justice Quarterly* 16 (1999): 357–376.

26. Eric Slade and Lawrence Wissow, "Spanking in Early Childhood and Later Behavior Problems: A Prospective Study of Infants and Young Toddlers," *Pediatrics* 113 (2004): 1,321–1,330.

27. Murray Straus, "Discipline and Deviance: Physical Punishment of Children and Violence and Other Crime in Adulthood," *Social Problems* 38 (1991): 101–123.

28. Ronald Simons, Chyi-In Wu, Kuei-Hsiu Lin, Leslie Gordon, and Rand Conger, "A Cross-Cultural Examination of the Link between Corporal Punishment and Adolescent Antisocial Behavior," *Criminology* 38 (2000): 47–79.

29. Robert Scudder, William Blount, Kathleen Heide, and Ira Silverman, "Important Links between Child Abuse, Neglect, and Delinquency," *International Journal of Offender Therapy* 37 (1993): 315–323.

30. Dorothy Lewis, et al., "Neuropsychiatric, Psychoeducational, and Family Characteristics of 14 Juveniles Condemned to Death in the United States," *American Journal of Psychiatry* 145 (1988): 584–588.

31. Charles Patrick Ewing, *When Children Kill* (Lexington, MA: Lexington Books, 1990), p. 22.

32. Lewis, *Guilty by Reason of Insanity,* pp. 11–35.

33. Timothy Ireland, Carolyn Smith, and Terence Thornberry, "Developmental Issues in the Impact of Child Maltreatment on Later Delinquency and Drug Use," *Criminology* 40 (2002): 359–401.

34. Straus, "Discipline and Deviance."

35. Alan Rosenbaum and Penny Leisring, "Beyond Power and Control: Towards an Understanding of Partner Abusive Men," *Journal of Comparative Family Studies* 34 (2003): 7–26.

36. Lonnie Athens, *The Creation of Dangerous Violent Criminals* (Urbana: University of Illinois Press, 1992), pp. 27–80.

37. Eric Stewart, Ronald Simons, and Rand Conger, "Assessing Neighborhood and Social Psychological Influences on Childhood Violence in an African-American Sample," *Criminology* 40 (2002): 801–830.

38. Joanne Kaufman, "Explaining the Race/Ethnicity–Violence Relationship: Neighborhood Context and Social Psychological Processes," *Justice Quarterly* 22 (2005): 224–251; David Farrington, Rolf Loeber, and Madga Stouthamer-Loeber, "How Can the Relationship between Race and Violence be Explained?" in *Violent Crimes: Assessing Race and Ethnic Differences,* ed. D. F. Hawkins (New York: Cambridge University Press, 2003), pp. 213–237.

39. Felton Earls, *Linking Community Factors and Individual Development* (Washington, DC: National Institute of Justice, 1998).

40. Jeffrey B. Bingenheimer, Robert T. Brennan, and Felton J. Earls, "Firearm Violence Exposure and Serious Violent Behavior," *Science* 308 (2005): 1,323–1,326; "Witnessing Gun Violence Significantly Increases Likelihood that a Child Will Also Commit Violent Crime; Violence May Be Viewed as Infectious Disease," *AScribe Health News Service,* 26 May 2005.

41. Michael Greene, "Chronic Exposure to Violence and Poverty: Interventions That Work for Youth," *Crime and Delinquency* 39 (1993): 106–124.

42. Robert Baller, Luc Anselin, Steven Messner, Glenn Deane, and Darnell Hawkins, "Structural Covariates of U.S. County Homicide Rates Incorporating Spatial Effects," *Criminology* 39 (2001): 561–590.

43. Marvin Wolfgang and Franco Ferracuti, *The Subculture of Violence* (London: Tavistock, 1967).

44. David Luckenbill and Daniel Doyle, "Structural Position and Violence: Developing a Cultural Explanation," *Criminology* 27 (1989): 419–436.

45. Robert Sampson and William Julius Wilson, "Toward a Theory of Race, Crime, and Urban Inequality," in *Crime and Inequality,* eds. John Hagan and Ruth Peterson (Stanford, CA: Stanford University Press, 1995), p. 51.

46. Liqun Cao, Anthony Adams, and Vickie Jensen, "A Test of the Black Subculture of Violence Thesis," *Criminology* 35 (1997): 367–379.

47. Eric Baumer, Julie Horney, Richard Felson, and Janet Lauritsen, "Neighborhood Disadvantage and the Nature of Violence," *Criminology* 41 (2003): 39–71.

48. Charis Kubrin and Ronald Weitzer, "Retaliatory Homicide: Concentrated Disadvantage and Neighborhood Culture," *Social Problems* 50 (2003): 157–180.

49. Robert J. Kane, "Compromised Police Legitimacy as a Predictor of Violent Crime in Structurally Disadvantaged Communities," *Criminology* 43 (2005): 469–499.

50. Steven Messner, "Regional and Racial Effects on the Urban Homicide Rate: The Subculture of Violence Revisited," *American Journal of Sociology* 88 (1983): 997–1,007; Steven Messner and Kenneth Tardiff, "Economic Inequality and Levels of Homicide: An Analysis of Urban Neighborhoods," *Criminology* 24 (1986): 297–317.

51. Beth Bjerregaard and Alan Lizotte, "Gun Ownership and Gang Membership," *Journal of Criminal Law and Criminology* 86 (1995): 37–58.

52. Fox Butterfield, "Rise in Killings Spurs New Steps to Fight Gangs," *New York Times,* 17 January 2004, p. A1.

53. James Howell, "Youth Gang Homicides: A Literature Review," *Crime and Delinquency* 45 (1999): 208–241.

54. Alan Lizotte and David Sheppard, *Gun Use by Male Juveniles* (Washington, DC: Office of Juvenile Justice and Delinquency Prevention, 2001); Daneen Deptula and Robert Cohen, "Aggressive, Rejected, and Delinquent Children and Adolescents: A Comparison of Their Friendships," *Aggression and Violent Behavior* 9 (2004): 75–104.

55. Sylvie Mrug, Betsy Hoza, and William Bukowski, "Choosing or Being Chosen by Aggressive-Disruptive Peers: Do They Contribute to Children's Externalizing and Internalizing Problems?" *Journal of Abnormal Child Psychology* 32 (2004): 53–66.

56. Daniel Neller, Robert Denney, Christina Pietz, and R. Paul Thomlinson, "Testing the Trauma Model of Violence," *Journal of Family Violence* 20 (2005): 151–159.

57. Scott Decker, "Gangs and Violence: The Expressive Character of Collective Involvement." Unpublished manuscript, University of Missouri–St. Louis: 1994, p. 11.

58. Rachel Gordon, Benjamin Lahey, Eriko Kawai, Rolf Loeber, Magda Stouthamer-Loeber, and David Farrington, "Antisocial Behavior and Youth Gang Membership," *Criminology* 42 (2004): 55–88.

59. See, generally, Kirk Williams and Robert Flewelling, "The Social Production of Criminal Homicide: A Comparative Study of Disaggregated Rates in American Cities," *American Sociological Review* 53 (1988): 421–431.

60. Eric Monkkonen, "Homicide in Los Angeles, 1827–2002,"*Journal of Interdisciplinary History*, 36 (2005): 167–183.

61. Ibid., 177–178.

62. Raymond Gastil, "Homicide and the Regional Culture of Violence," *American Sociological Review* 36 (1971): 12–27; see also, Keith Harries, *Serious Violence: Patterns of Homicide and Assault in America* (Springfield, IL: Charles C Thomas, 1990).

63. Edem Avakame, "How Different Is Violence in the Home: An Examination of Some Correlates of Stranger and Intimate Homicide," *Criminology* 36 (1998): 601–632.

64. Howard Erlanger, "Is There a Subculture of Violence in the South?" *Journal of Criminal Law and Criminology* 66 (1976): 483–490; Colin Loftin and Robert Hill, "Regional Subculture of Violence: An Examination of the Gastil-Hackney Thesis," *American Sociological Review* 39 (1974): 714–724.

65. Jerome Neapolitan, "A Comparative Analysis of Nations with Low and High Levels of Violent Crime," *Journal of Criminal Justice* 27 (1999): 259–274.

66. Ibid., p. 271.

67. Aki Roberts and Gary Lafree, "Explaining Japan's Postwar Violent Crime Trends," *Criminology* 42 (2004): 179–210.

68. William Green, *Rape* (Lexington, MA: Lexington Books, 1988), p. 5.

69. Susan Randall and Vicki McNickle Rose, "Forcible Rape," in *Major Forms of Crime,* ed. Robert Meyer (Beverly Hills: Sage, 1984), p. 47.

70. Barbara Krah, Renate Scheinberger-Olwig, and Steffen Bieneck, "Men's Reports of Nonconsensual Sexual Interactions with Women: Prevalence and Impact," *Archives of Sexual Behavior* 32 (2003): 165–176.

71. Siegmund Fred Fuchs, "Male Sexual Assault: Issues of Arousal and Consent," *Cleveland State Law Review* 51 (2004): 93–108.

72. *Michael M. v. Superior Court of Sonoma City* 450 U.S. 464 (1981).

73. Susan Brownmiller, *Against Our Will: Men, Women, and Rape* (New York: Simon & Schuster, 1975).

74. Green, *Rape,* p. 6.

75. Gregory Vistica, "Rape in the Ranks," *Newsweek,* 25 November 1996, pp. 29–31.

76. Yuri Kageyama, "Court Orders Japan to Pay Sex Slaves," *Boston Globe*, 28 April 1998, p. A2.

77. Marlise Simons, "Bosnian Serb Pleads Guilty to Rape Charge before War Crimes Tribunal," *New York Times,* 10 March 1998, p. 8.

78. Marc Lacey, "Amnesty Says Sudan Militias Use Rape as Weapon," *New York Times,* 19 July 2004, p. A9.

79. FBI, *Crime in the United States, 2004*, pp. 27. Crime data in this chapter comes from this source.

80. Maria Testa, Jennifer Livingston, Carol Vanzile-Tamsen, and Michael Frone, "The Role of Women's Substance Use in Vulnerability to Forcible and Incapacitated Rape," *Journal of Studies on Alcohol* 64 (2003): 756–766.

81. Shannan Catalano, *Criminal Victimization 2004* (Washington, DC: Bureau of Justice Statistics, 2005), p. 2.

82. Carol Vanzile-Tamsen, Maria Testa, and Jennifer Livingston, "The Impact of Sexual Assault History and Relationship Context on Appraisal of and Responses to Acquaintance Sexual Assault Risk," *Journal of Interpersonal Violence* 20 (2005): 813–822; Arnold Kahn, Jennifer Jackson, Christine Kully, Kelly Badger, and Jessica Halvorsen, "Calling It Rape: Differences in Experiences of Women Who Do or Do Not Label Their Sexual Assault as Rape," *Psychology of Women Quarterly* 27 (2003): 233–242.

83. Mark Warr, "Rape, Burglary, and Opportunity," *Journal of Quantitative Criminology* 4 (1988): 275–288.

84. A. Nicholas Groth and Jean Birnbaum, *Men Who Rape* (New York: Plenum Press, 1979).

85. For another typology, see Raymond Knight, "Validation of a Typology of Rapists," in *Sex Offender Research and Treatment: State-of-the-Art in North America and Europe,* eds. W. L. Marshall and J. Frenken (Beverly Hills: Sage, 1997), pp. 58–75.

86. Sarah Ullman, "A Comparison of Gang and Individual Rape Incidents," *Violence and Victimization* 14 (1999): 123–134.

87. Janet Warren, Roland Reboussin, Robert Hazlewood, Natalie Gibbs, Susan Trumbetta, and Andrea Cummings, "Crime Scene Analysis and the Escalation of Violence in Serial Rape," *Forensic Science International* (1998): 56–62.

88. James LeBeau, "Patterns of Stranger and Serial Rape Offending Factors Distinguishing Apprehended and At-Large Offenders," *Journal of Criminal Law and Delinquency* 78 (1987): 309–326.

89. Julie Allison and Lawrence Wrightsman, *Rape: The Misunderstood Crime* (Newbury Park, CA: Sage, 1993), p. 51.

90. Cassia Spohn, Dawn Beichner, and Erika Davis-Frenzel, "Prosecutorial Justifications for Sexual Assault Case Rejection: Guarding the 'Gateway to Justice,'" *Social Problems* 48 (2001): 206–235.

91. R. Lance Shotland, "A Model of the Causes of Date Rape in Developing and Close Relationships," in *Close Relationships,* ed. C. Hendrick (Newbury Park, CA: Sage, 1989), pp. 247–270.

92. Kimberly Tyler, Danny Hoyt, and Les Whitbeck, "Coercive Sexual Strategies," *Violence and Victims* 13 (1998): 47–63.

93. Thomas Meyer, "Date Rape: A Serious Campus Problem that Few Talk About," *Chronicle of Higher Education* 29 (5 December 1984): 15.

94. Allison and Wrightsman, *Rape: The Misunderstood Crime,* p. 64.

95. Amy Buddie and Maria Testa, "Rates and Predictors of Sexual Aggression among Students and Nonstudents," *Journal of Interpersonal Violence* 20 (2005): 713–725.

96. Bonnie Fisher, Leah Daigle, Francis Cullen, and Michael Turner, "Reporting Sexual Victimization to the Police and Others: Results from a National-Level Study of College Women," *Criminal Justice and Behavior* 30 (2003): 6–39.

97. Martin Schwartz, "Humanist Sociology and Date Rape on the College Campus," *Humanity and Society* 15 (1991): 304–316.

98. Allison and Wrightsman, *Rape: The Misunderstood Crime,* pp. 85–87.

99. Cited in Diana Russell, "Wife Rape," in *Acquaintance Rape: The Hidden Crime,* eds. A. Parrot and L. Bechhofer (New York: Wiley, 1991), pp. 129–139, at 129.

100. David Finkelhor and K. Yllo, *License to Rape: Sexual Abuse of Wives* (New York: Holt, Rinehart & Winston, 1985).

101. Allison and Wrightsman, *Rape: The Misunderstood Crime,* p. 89.

102. Associated Press, "British Court Rejects Precedent, Finds a Man Guilty of Raping Wife," *Boston Globe,* 15 March 1991, p. 68.

103. Jill Elaine Hasday, "Contest and Consent: A Legal History of Marital Rape," *California Law Review* 88 (2000): 1,373–1,433.

104. Sharon Elstein and Roy Davis, *Sexual Relationships between Adult Males and Young Teen Girls: Exploring the Legal and Social Responses* (Chicago: American Bar Association, 1997).

105. Donald Symons, *The Evolution of Human Sexuality* (Oxford: Oxford University Press, 1979).

106. Lee Ellis and Anthony Walsh, "Gene-Based Evolutionary Theories in Criminology," *Criminology* 35 (1997): 229–276.

107. Lee Ellis, "A Synthesized (Biosocial) Theory of Rape," *Journal of Consulting and Clinical Psychology* 39 (1991): 631–642.

108. Suzanne Osman, "Predicting Men's Rape Perceptions Based on the Belief that 'No' Really Means 'Yes,'" *Journal of Applied Social Psychology* 33 (2003): 683–692.

109. Martin Schwartz, Walter DeKeseredy, David Tait, and Shahid Alvi, "Male Peer Support and a Feminist Routine Activities Theory: Understanding Sexual Assault on the College Campus," *Justice Quarterly* 18 (2001): 623–650.

110. Diana Russell, *The Politics of Rape* (New York: Stein and Day, 1975).

111. Diana Russell and Rebecca M. Bolen, *The Epidemic of Rape and Child Sexual Abuse in the United States* (Thousand Oaks, CA: Sage, 2000).

112. Rachel Bridges Whaley, "The Paradoxical Relationship between Gender Inequality and Rape: Toward a Refined Theory," *Gender and Society* 15 (2001): 531–555.

113. Paul Gebhard, John Gagnon, Wardell Pomeroy, and Cornelia Christenson, *Sex Offenders: An Analysis of Types* (New York: Harper & Row, 1965), pp. 198–205; Richard Rada, ed., *Clinical Aspects of the Rapist* (New York: Grune & Stratton, 1978), pp. 122–130.

114. Stephen Porter, David Fairweather, Jeff Drugge, Huues Herve, Angela Birt, and Douglas Boer, "Profiles of Psychopathy in Incarcerated Sexual Offenders," *Criminal Justice and Behavior* 27 (2000): 216–233.

115. Brad Bushman, Angelica Bonacci, Mirjam van Dijk, and Roy Baumeister, "Narcissism, Sexual Refusal, and Aggression: Testing a Narcissistic Reactance Model of Sexual Coercion," *Journal of Personality and Social Psychology,* 84 (2003): 1,027–1,040.

116. Schwartz, DeKeseredy, Tait, and Alvi, "Male Peer Support and a Feminist Routine Activities Theory."

117. Groth and Birnbaum, *Men Who Rape,* p. 101.

118. See, generally, Edward Donnerstein, Daniel Linz, and Steven Penrod, *The Question of Pornography* (New York: Free Press, 1987); Diana Russell, *Sexual Exploitation* (Beverly Hills: Sage, 1985), pp. 115–116.

119. Neil Malamuth and John Briere, "Sexual Violence in the Media: Indirect Effects on Aggression against Women," *Journal of Social Issues* 42 (1986): 75–92.

120. Associated Press, "Trial on TV May Have Influenced Boy Facing Sexual-Assault Count," *Omaha World Herald,* 18 April 1984, p. 50.

121. Richard Felson and Marvin Krohn, "Motives for Rape," *Journal of Research in Crime and Delinquency* 27 (1990): 222–242.

122. Laura Monroe, Linda Kinney, Mark Weist, Denise Spriggs Dafeamekpor, Joyce Dantzler, and Matthew Reynolds, "The Experience of Sexual Assault: Findings from a Statewide Victim Needs Assessment," *Journal of Interpersonal Violence* 20 (2005): 767–776.

123. Julie Horney and Cassia Spohn, "The Influence of Blame and Believability Factors on the Processing of Simple versus Aggravated Rape Cases," *Criminology* 34 (1996): 135–163.

124. Spohn, Beichner, and Davis-Frenzel, "Prosecutorial Justifications for Sexual Assault Case Rejection."

125. Patricia Landwehr, Robert Bothwell, Matthew Jeanmard, Luis Luque, Roy Brown III, and Marie-Anne Breaux, "Racism in Rape Trials," *Journal of Social Psychology* 142 (2002): 667–670.

126. "Man Wrongly Convicted of Rape Released 19 Years Later," *The Forensic Examiner* (May–June 2003): 44.

127. Gerald Robin, "Forcible Rape: Institutionalized Sexism in the Criminal Justice System," *Crime and Delinquency* 23 (1977): 136–153.

128. Associated Press, "Jury Stirs Furor by Citing Dress in Rape Acquittal," *Boston Globe,* 6 October 1989, p. 12.

129. Cassia Spohn and David Holleran, "Prosecuting Sexual Assault: A Comparison of Charging Decisions in Sexual Assault Cases Involving Strangers, Acquaintances, and Intimate Partners," *Justice Quarterly* 18 (2001): 651–688.

130. Rodney Kingsworth, Randall MacIntosh, and Jennifer Wentworth, "Sexual Assault: The Role of Prior Relationship and Victim Characteristics in Case Processing," *Justice Quarterly* 16 (1999): 276–302.

131. Susan Estrich, *Real Rape* (Cambridge, MA: Harvard University Press, 1987), pp. 58–59.

132. See, for example, Mich. Comp. Laws Ann. 750.5200-(1); Florida Statutes Annotated, Sec. 794.011; see, generally, Gary LaFree, "Official Reactions to Rape," *American Sociological Review* 45 (1980): 842–854.

133. Martin Schwartz and Todd Clear, "Toward a New Law on Rape," *Crime and Delinquency* 26 (1980): 129–151.

134. *Michigan v. Lucas* 90-149 (1991); Comment, "The Rape Shield Paradox: Complainant Protection amidst Oscillating Trends of State Judicial Interpretation," *Journal of Criminal Law and Criminology* 78 (1987): 644–698.

135. Andrew Karmen, *Crime Victims* (Pacific Grove, CA: Brooks/Cole, 1990), p. 252.

136. "Court Upholds Civil Rights Portion of Violence Against Women Act," *Criminal Justice Newsletter* 28 (1 December 1997): 3.

137. Donald Lunde, *Murder and Madness* (San Francisco: San Francisco Book, 1977), p. 3.

138. Lisa Baertlein, "HIV Ruled Deadly Weapon in Rape Case," *Boston Globe,* 2 March 1994, p. 3.

139. The legal principles here come from Wayne LaFave and Austin Scott, *Criminal Law* (St. Paul: West, 1986; updated 1993). The definitions and discussion of legal principles used in this chapter lean heavily on this work.

140. LaFave and Scott, *Criminal Law.*

141. Evelyn Nieves, "Woman Gets 4-Year Term in Fatal Dog Attack," *New York Times,* 16 July 2002, p.1.

142. Pauline Arrillaga, "Jurors Give Drunk Driver 16 Years in Fetus's Death," *Manchester Union Leader,* 22 October 1996, p. B20.

143. Center for Reproductive Law and Policy, *Punishing Women for Their Behavior during Pregnancy* (New York: author, 1996), pp. 1–2.

144. *Whitner v. State of South Carolina,* Supreme Court of South Carolina, Opinion Number 24468, July 15, 1996.

145. Janet Kreps, *Feticide and Wrongful Death Laws* (New York: Center for Reproductive Law and Policy, 1996), pp. 1–2.

146. Arrillaga, "Jurors Give Drunk Driver 16 Years in Fetus's Death."

147. James Alan Fox and Marianne Zawitz, *Homicide Trends in the United States* (Washington, DC: Bureau of Justice Statistics, 2001).

148. Todd Shackelford, Viviana Weekes-Shackelford, and Shanna Beasley, "An Exploratory Analysis of the Contexts and Circumstances of Filicide-Suicide in Chicago, 1965–1994," *Aggressive Behavior* 31 (2005):399–406.

149. FBI, *Crime in the United States, 2004.* http://www.fbi.gov/ucr/cius_04/offenses_reported/violent_crime/murder.html.

150. Philip Cook, Jens Ludwig, and Anthony Braga, "Criminal Records of Homicide Offenders," *Journal of the American Medical Association* 294 (2005): 598–601.

151. See, generally, Marc Reidel and Margaret Zahn, *The Nature and Pattern of American Homicide* (Washington, DC: U.S. Government Printing Office, 1985).

152. Terance Miethe and Wendy Regoeczi, with Kriss Drass, *Rethinking Homicide: Exploring the Structure and Process Underlying Deadly Situations* (Cambridge, MA: Cambridge University Press, 2004).

153. Angela Browne and Kirk Williams, "Gender, Intimacy, and Lethal Violence: Trends from 1976 through 1987," *Gender and Society* 7 (1993): 78–98.

154. Linda Saltzman and James Mercy, "Assaults between Intimates: The Range of Relationships Involved," in *Homicide: The Victim/Offender Connection,* ed. Anna Victoria Wilson (Cincinnati: Anderson Publishing, 1993), pp. 65–74.

155. Angela Browne and Kirk Williams, "Exploring the Effect of Resource Availability and the Likelihood of Female-Perpetrated Homicides," *Law and Society Review* 23 (1989): 75–94.

156. Richard Felson, "Anger, Aggression, and Violence in Love Triangles," *Violence and Victimization* 12 (1997): 345–363.

157. Ibid., p. 361.

158. Scott Decker, "Deviant Homicide: A New Look at the Role of Motives and Victim–Offender Relationships," *Journal of Research in Crime and Delinquency* 33 (1996): 427–449.

159. David Luckenbill, "Criminal Homicide as a Situational Transaction," *Social Problems* 25 (1977): 176–186.

160. Margaret Zahn and Philip Sagi, "Stranger Homicides in Nine American Cities," *Journal of Criminal Law and Criminology* 78 (1987): 377–397.

161. Tomislav Kovandzic, John Sloan, and Lynne Vieraitis, "Unintended Consequences of Politically Popular Sentencing Policy: The Homicide Promoting Effects of 'Three Strikes' in U.S. Cities (1980–1999)," *Criminology and Public Policy* 3 (2002): 399–424.

162. Jill DeVoe, Katharin Peter, Sally Ruddy, Amanda Miller, Mike Planty, Thomas Snyder, and Michael Rand, *Indicators of School Crime and Safety, 2003* (Washington, DC: U.S. Department of Education and Bureau of Justice Statistics, 2004).

163. Tonja Nansel, Mary Overpeck, and Ramani Pilla, "Bullying Behaviors among US Youth: Prevalence and Association with Psychosocial Adjustment," *Journal of the American Medical Association* 285 (2001): 2,094–3,100.

164. Christine Kerres Malecki and Michelle Kilpatrick Demaray, "Carrying a Weapon to School and Perceptions of Social Support in an Urban Middle School," *Journal of Emotional and Behavioral Disorders* 11 (2003): 169–178.

165. Ibid.

166. Pamela Wilcox and Richard Clayton, "A Multilevel Analysis of School-Based Weapon Possession," *Justice Quarterly* 18 (2001): 509–542.

167. Mark Anderson, Joanne Kaufman, Thomas Simon, Lisa Barrios, Len Paulozzi, George Ryan, Rodney Hammond, William Modzeleski, Thomas Feucht, Lloyd Potter, and the School-Associated Violent Deaths Study Group, "School-Associated Violent Deaths in the United States, 1994–1999," *Journal of the American Medical Association* 286 (2001): 2,695–2,702.

168. Bryan Vossekuil, Marisa Reddy, Robert Fein, Randy Borum, and William Modzeleski, *Safe School Initiative, An Interim Report on the Prevention of Targeted Violence in Schools* (Washington, DC: United States Secret Service, 2000).

169. "BTK Killer Blames 'Demon' for Murders," July 7, 2005. http://www.usatoday.com/news/nation/2005-07-07-btk-killings_x.htm. Accessed September 2, 2005.

170. Alasdair Goodwill and Laurence Alison, "Sequential Angulation, Spatial Dispersion, and Consistency of Distance Attack Patterns from Home in Serial Murder, Rape, and Burglary," *Journal of Psychology, Crime & Law* 11 (2005): 161–176.

171. Ronald Holmes and Stephen Holmes, *Murder in America* (Thousand Oaks, CA: Sage, 1994), pp. 13–14.

172. http://www.crimelibrary.com/serial_killers/weird/swango/pleasure_8.html. Accessed September 3, 2005.

173. Aneez Esmail, "Physician as Serial Killer—The Shipman Case," *New England Journal of Medicine* 352 (2005): 1,483–1,844.

174. James Alan Fox and Jack Levin, *Overkill: Mass Murder and Serial Killing Exposed*

(New York: Plenum, 1994); James Alan Fox, Jack Levin, and Kenna Quinet, *The Will to Kill: Making Sense of Senseless Murder,* 2nd ed. (Boston: Allyn & Bacon, 2004).

175. Belea Keeney and Kathleen Heide, "Gender Differences in Serial Murderers: A Preliminary Analysis," *Journal of Interpersonal Violence* 9 (1994): 37–56.

176. Wade Myers, Erik Gooch, and Reid Meloy, "The Role of Psychopathy and Sexuality in a Female Serial Killer," *Journal of Forensic Sciences* 50 (2005): 652–658.

177. Terry Whitman and Donald Akutagawa, "Riddles in Serial Murder: A Synthesis," *Aggression and Violent Behavior* 9 (2004): 693–703.

178. Holmes and Holmes, *Murder in America,* p. 106.

179. James Alan Fox and Jack Levin, *Overkill: Mass Murder and Serial Killing Exposed* (New York: Plenum, 1994).

180. Gabrielle Salfati and Alicia Bateman, "Serial Homicide: An Investigation of Behavioural Consistency," *Journal of Investigative Psychology & Offender Profiling* 2 (2005): 121–144.

181. Jennifer Browdy, "VI-CAP System to Be Operational This Summer," *Law Enforcement News,* 21 May 1984, p. 1.

182. James Alan Fox and Jack Levin, "Multiple Homicide: Patterns of Serial and Mass Murder," in *Crime and Justice: An Annual Edition,* vol. 23, ed. Michael Tonry (Chicago: University of Chicago Press, 1998), pp. 407–455; Fox and Levin, *Overkill: Mass Murder and Serial Killing Exposed*; James Alan Fox, Jack Levin, and Kenna Quinet, *The Will to Kill: Making Sense of Senseless Murder,* 2nd ed. (Boston: Allyn & Bacon, 2004); James Allan Fox and Jack Levin, "A Psycho-Social Analysis of Mass Murder," in *Serial and Mass Murder: Theory, Policy, and Research,* eds. Thomas O'Reilly-Fleming and Steven Egger (Toronto: University of Toronto Press, 1993).

183. James Alan Fox and Jack Levin, "Mass Murder: An Analysis of Extreme Violence," *Journal of Applied Psychoanalytic Studies* 5 (2003): 47–64.

184. Grant Duwe, "The Patterns and Prevalence of Mass Murder in Twentieth-Century America," *Justice Quarterly,* 21 (2004): 729–761.

185. Elissa Gootman, "The Hunt for a Sniper: The Victim; 10th Victim Is Recalled as Motivator on Mission," *New York Times,*

14 October 2002, p. A15; Sarah Kershaw, "The Hunt for a Sniper: The Investigation; Endless Frustration but Little Evidence in Search for Sniper," *New York Times,* 14 October 2002, p. A1.

186. *Mugshots, Court TV's Criminal Biography Series, Profiles Racist Serial Killer Joseph Paul Franklin.* http://www.courttv.com/archive/press/Franklin.html. Accessed September 3, 2005.

187. Francis X. Clines with Christopher Drew, "Prosecutors to Discuss Charges as Rifle Is Tied to Sniper Killings," *New York Times,* 25 October 2002, p. A1.

188. Federal Bureau of Investigation, *Crime in the United States, 2000* (Washington, DC: U.S. Government Printing Office, 2001), p. 34.

189. Keith Harries, "Homicide and Assault: A Comparative Analysis of Attributes in Dallas Neighborhoods, 1981–1985," *Professional Geographer* 41 (1989): 29–38.

190. Kevin Flynn, "Record Payouts in Settlements of Lawsuits against the New York City Police Are Set for Year," *New York Times,* 1 October 1999, p. 12.

191. Etienne Krug, Linda Dahlberg, James Mercy, Anthony Zwi, and Rafael Lozano, *World Report on Violence and Health* (Geneva: World Health Organization, 2002).

192. Ibid., p. 89.

193. Ibid., p. 93.

194. See, generally, Ruth S. Kempe and C. Henry Kempe, *Child Abuse* (Cambridge, MA: Harvard University Press, 1978).

195. U.S. Department of Health and Human Services, Administration for Children and Families, Children's Bureau, *Child Maltreatment, 2002* (Washington, DC: U.S. Department of Health and Human Services, 2004).

196. National Clearinghouse on Child Abuse and Neglect, *Child Abuse and Neglect Fatalities: Statistics and Interventions, 2004.* http://nccanch.acf.hhs.gov/pubs/factsheets/fatality.cfm. Accessed August 8, 2004.

197. U.S. Department of Health and Human Services, Administration for Children and Families, Children's Bureau, *Child Maltreatment, 2001* (Washington, DC: U.S. Government Printing Office, 2003).

198. Glenn Wolfner and Richard Gelles, "A Profile of Violence toward Children: A National Study," *Child Abuse and Neglect* 17 (1993): 197–212.

199. Martin Daly and Margo Wilson, "Violence against Step Children," *Current Directions in Psychological Science* 5 (1996): 77–81.

200. Ruth Inglis, *Sins of the Fathers: A Study of the Physical and Emotional Abuse of Children* (New York: St. Martin's, 1978), p. 53.

201. Diana Russell, "The Incidence and Prevalence of Intrafamilial and Extrafamilial Sexual Abuse of Female Children," *Child Abuse and Neglect* 7 (1983): 133–146; see also David Finkelhor, *Sexually Victimized Children* (New York: Free Press, 1979), p. 88.

202. Jeanne Hernandez, "Eating Disorders and Sexual Abuse in Adolescents." Paper presented at the annual meeting of the American Psychosomatic Society, Charleston, South Carolina, March 1993; Wolfner and Gelles, "A Profile of Violence toward Children."

203. Lisa Jones and David Finkelhor, *The Decline in Child Sexual Abuse Cases* (Washington, DC: Office of Juvenile Justice and Delinquency Prevention, 2001).

204. Lisa Jones, David Finkelhor, and Kathy Kopie, "Why Is Sexual Abuse Declining? A Survey of State Child Protection Administrators," *Child Abuse and Neglect* 25 (2001): 1,139–1,141.

205. Eva Jonzon, and Frank Lindblad, "Adult Female Victims of Child Sexual Abuse," *Journal of Interpersonal Violence* 20 (2005): 651–666.

206. Jane Siegel and Linda Williams, "Risk Factors for Sexual Victimization of Women," *Violence Against Women* 9 (2003): 902–930.

207. Arina Ulman and Murray Straus, "Violence by Children against Mothers in Relation to Violence between Parents and Corporal Punishment by Parents," *Journal of Comparative Family Studies* 34 (2003): 41–63.

208. R. Emerson Dobash and Russell Dobash, *Violence against Wives* (New York: Free Press, 1979).

209. Julia O'Faolain and Laura Martines, eds., *Not in God's Image: Women in History* (Glasgow: Fontana/Collins, 1974).

210. Laurence Stone, "The Rise of the Nuclear Family in Modern England: The Patriarchal Stage," in *The Family in History,* ed. Charles Rosenberg (Philadelphia: University of Pennsylvania Press, 1975), p. 53.

211. Dobash and Dobash, *Violence against Wives,* p. 46.

212. John Braithwaite, "Inequality and Republican Criminology." Paper

presented at the annual meeting of the American Society of Criminology, San Francisco, November 1991, p. 20.

213. Richard Gelles and Murray Straus, "Violence in the American Family," *Journal of Social Issues* 35 (1979): 15–39.

214. Miguel Schwartz, Susan O'Leary, and Kimberly Kendziora, "Dating Aggression among High School Students," *Violence and Victimization* 12 (1997): 295–307; James Makepeace, "Social Factor and Victim–Offender Differences in Courtship Violence," *Family Relations* 33 (1987): 87–91.

215. Jay Silverman, Anita Raj, Lorelei Mucci, and Jeanne Hathaway, "Dating Violence against Adolescent Girls and Associated Substance Abuse, Unhealthy Weight Control, Sexual Risk Behavior, Preg- nancy, and Suicidality," *Journal of the American Medical Association* 286 (2001): 572–579.

216. FBI, *Crime in the United States*, 2000, p. 29.

217. James Calder and John Bauer, "Conve- nience Store Robberies: Security Mea- sures and Store Robbery Incidents," *Journal of Criminal Justice* 20 (1992): 553–566.

218. Richard Felson, Eric Baumer, and Steven Messner, "Acquaintance Robbery," *Jour- nal of Research in Crime and Delinquency* 37 (2000): 284–305.

219. Ibid., p. 287.

220. Ibid.

221. Peter Van Koppen and Robert Jansen, "The Time to Rob: Variations in Time of Number of Commercial Robberies," *Journal of Research in Crime and Delinquency* 36 (1999): 7–29.

222. Jody Miller, "Up It Up: Gender and the Accomplishment of Street Robbery," *Criminology* 36 (1998): 37–67.

223. Ibid., pp. 54–55.

224. Richard Wright and Scott Decker, *Armed Robbers in Action, Stickups and Street Culture* (Boston: Northeastern University Press, 1997).

225. James Brooke, "Gay Student Who Was Kidnapped and Beaten Dies," *New York Times,* 13 October 1998, A1.

226. Michael Janofsky, "Wyoming Man Gets Life Term in Gay's Death," *New York Times,* 5 November 1999, p. 1.

227. James Garofalo, "Bias and Non-Bias Crimes in New York City: Preliminary Findings." Paper presented at the annual

meeting of the American Society of Criminology, Baltimore, November 1990.

228. Ronald Powers, "Bensonhurst Man Guilty," *Boston Globe,* 18 May 1990, p. 3.

229. "Boy Gets 18 Years in Fatal Park Beating of Transient," *Los Angeles Times,* 24 December 1987, p. 9B.

230. Ewing, *When Children Kill*, pp. 65–66.

231. Mike McPhee, "In Denver, Attacks Stir Fears of Racism," *Boston Globe,* 10 December 1990, p. 3.

232. Jack Levin and Jack McDevitt, *Hate Crimes: The Rising Tide of Bigotry and Bloodshed* (New York: Plenum Press, 1993).

233. Jack McDevitt, Jack Levin, and Susan Bennett, "Hate Crime Offenders: An Expanded Typology," *Journal of Social Issues* 58 (2002): 303–318.

234. Jack Levin, *The Violence of Hate, Con- fronting Racism, Anti-Semitism, and other Forms of Bigotry* (Boston: Allyn & Bacon, 2002), pp. 29–56.

235. FBI, *Hate Crime Statistics, 2004* (Washington, DC: FBI, 2005).

236. Ibid. at http://www.fbi.gov/ucr/cius_04/ offenses_reported/hate_crime/index .html#table_32.

237. Kevin J. Strom, *Hate Crimes Reported in NIBRS, 1997–99* (Washington, DC: Bureau of Justice Statistics, 2001).

238. Gregory Herek, Jeanine Cogan, and Roy Gillis, "Victim Experiences in Hate Crimes Based on Sexual Orientation," *Journal of Social Issues* 58 (2002): 319–340.

239. Garofalo, "Bias and Non-Bias Crimes in New York City," p. 3.

240. Brian Levin, "From Slavery to Hate Crime Laws: The Emergence of Race and Status-Based Protection in American Criminal Law" *Journal of Social Issues* 58 (2002): 227–246.

241. Felicia Lee, "Gays Angry over TV Report on a Murder," *New York Times,* 16 No- vember 2004, p. A3.

242. Frederick M. Lawrence, *Punishing Hate: Bias Crimes under American Law* (Cambridge, MA: Harvard University Press, 1999).

243. Ibid., p. 3.

244. Ibid., p. 9.

245. Ibid., p. 11.

246. Ibid., pp. 39–42.

247. Jack McDevitt, Jennifer, Balboni, Luis Garcia, and Joann Gu, "Consequences for Victims: A Comparison of Bias- and Non-Bias-Motivated Assaults," *American Behavioral Scientist* 45 (2001): 697–714.

248. *Virginia v. Black et al.* No. 01—1107. 2003.

249. Carl Weiser, "This Is What You Get for Firing Me," *USA Today,* 28 January 1993, p. 3A.

250. James Alan Fox and Jack Levin, "Firing Back: The Growing Threat of Workplace Homicide," *Annals* 536 (1994): 16–30.

251. John King, "Workplace Violence: A Conceptual Framework." Paper presented at the annual meeting of the American Society of Criminology, Phoenix, November 1993.

252. Janet R. Copper, "Response to 'Workplace Violence in Health Care: Recognized but not Regulated' by Kathleen M. McPhaul and Jane A. Lipscomb (September 30, 2004)," *Online Journal of Issues in Nursing* 10 (2005): 53–55.

253. Associated Press, "Gunman Wounds 3 Doctors in L.A. Hospital," *Cleveland Plain Dealer,* 9 February 1993, p. 1B.

254. Fox and Levin, "Firing Back," p. 5.

255. Michael Mantell and Steve Albrecht, *Ticking Bombs: Defusing Violence in the Workplace* (New York: Irwin, 1994).

256. Detis Duhart, *Workplace Violence, 1993–99* (Washington, DC: Bureau of Justice Statistics, 2001).

257. Centers for Disease Control, National In- stitute for Occupational Safety and Health, *Violence, Occupational Hazards in Hospitals* (Atlanta: National Institutes of Health, 2002).

258. Dana Loomis, Stephen Marshall, and Myduc Ta, "Employer Policies toward Guns and the Risk of Homicide in the Workplace," *American Journal of Public Health,* 95 (2005): 830–832.

259. The following sections rely heavily on Patricia Tjaden, *The Crime of Stalking: How Big Is the Problem?* (Washington, DC: National Institute of Justice, 1997); see also, Robert M. Emerson, Kerry O. Ferris, and Carol Brooks Gardner, "On Being Stalked," *Social Problems* 45 (1998): 289–298.

260. Patrick Kinkade, Ronald Burns, and Angel Ilarraza Fuentes, "Criminalizing Attractions: Perceptions of Stalking and

the Stalker," *Crime and Delinquency* 51 (2005): 3–25.

261. Patricia Tjaden, *The Crime of Stalking*.

262. Bonnie Fisher, Francis Cullen, and Michael Turner, "Being Pursued: Stalking Victimization in a National Study of College Women," *Criminology and Public Policy* 1 (2002): 257–309.

263. Mary Brewster, "Stalking by Former Intimates: Verbal Threats and Other Predictors of Physical Violence," *Violence and Victims* 15 (2000): 41–51.

264. Carol Jordan, T. K. Logan, and Robert Walker, "Stalking: An Examination of the Criminal Justice Response," *Journal of Interpersonal Violence* 18 (2003): 148–165.

265. Title 22 of the United States Code section 2656f (d) (1999).

266. Paul Wilkinson, *Terrorism and the Liberal State* (New York: Wiley, 1977), p. 49.

267. Jack Gibbs, "Conceptualization of Terrorism," *American Sociological Review* 54 (1989): 329–340, at 330.

268. Robert Friedlander, *Terrorism* (Dobbs Ferry, NY: Oceana Publishers, 1979), p. 14.

269. Daniel Georges-Abeyie, "Political Crime and Terrorism," in *Crime and Deviance: A Comparative Perspective,* ed. Graeme Newman (Beverly Hills: Sage, 1980), pp. 313–333.

270. Georges-Abeyie, "Political Crime and Terrorism," p. 319.

271. This section relies heavily on Friedlander, *Terrorism,* pp. 8–20.

272. Associated Press, "Malaysia Arrests Five Militants," *New York Times,* 15 October 2002, p. A2.

273. Chung Chien-Peng, "China's War on Terror," *Foreign Affairs* 81 (July–August 2002): 8–13.

274. Jocelyn Parker, "Vehicles Burn at Dealership: SUV Attacks Turn Violent," *Detroit Free Press,* 23 August 2003, p. 1.

275. Fiona Proffitt, "Costs of Animal Rights Terror," *Science* 304 (18 June 2004): 1,731–1,739.

276. "Brutal Elves in the Woods," *The Economist* 359 (14 April 2001): 28–30.

277. Jeffrey Kluger, "The Nuke Pipeline: The Trade in Nuclear Contraband Is Approaching Critical Mass. Can We Turn Off the Spigot?" *Time,* 17 December 2001, p. 40.

278. Chris Dishman, "Terrorism, Crime, and Transformation," *Studies in Conflict & Terrorism* 24 (2001): 43–56.

279. Mark Jurgensmeyer, *Terror in the Mind of God* (Berkeley and Los Angeles: University of California Press, 2000).

280. Jerrold M. Post, "Terrorist Psycho-Logic: Terrorist Behavior as a Product of Psychological Forces," in *Origins of Terrorism: Psychologies, Ideologies Theologies, States of Mind,* ed. Walter Reich (Cambridge: Cambridge University Press, 1990), p. 12.

281. Graham Allison, *Nuclear Terrorism: The Ultimate Preventable Catastrophe* (New York: Times Books, 2004).

282. 18 U.S.C.A 2332 (a) (1) (West Supp., 1997).

283. "Hunting Terrorists Using Confidential Informant Reward Programs," *FBI Law Enforcement Bulletin* 71(2002): 26–28; Sara Sun Beale and James Felman, "The Consequences of Enlisting Federal Grand Juries in the War on Terrorism: Assessing the USA Patriot Act's Changes to Grand Jury Secrecy," *Harvard Journal of Law and Public Policy* 25 (2002): 699–721.

284. Morton Halperin, "Less Secure, Less Free: Striking Terror at Civil Liberty," *The American Prospect* 12 (19 November 2001): 10–13.

Hey Kids!
This is the Deal
On the Scavenger Hunt

2,000 Kids Seated in Two Rows at 460 Decorated Tables

The Entire Coconut Grove Convention Center is Decorated
And is Full of Christmas Trees From Around the World

2,000 Christmas Presents Are Underneath the Trees

Everybody Gets a Clipboard with 250 Questions

250 Answers Were Hidden Around the Exhibit

You Get 10 Raffle Tickets to Start!
You Get One Ticket for Every 10 Answers You Find!

Over 35 Chances for You to Win
There Is a Gift Given Away Every 2 Minutes

When A Ticket Wins!
A Bingo Machine Pops Up A Number; The Winner Can
Choose Anything Under The Tree Matching That Number.
On Stage there is a Continuous Christmas Music Show

The Cost is $20.00 Per Person a Night!
There are 2 Evening Shows a Day
Wed. thru Fri: 4:00pm to 8:30pm / 8:30pm to 10:30pm
The Morning Matinee Is Sold Out and Not Open to the Public

Call David Lee at 305-970-1707 for Tickets

In 2003, David Lee Ellisor, who had a long track record in staging events, promoted an elaborate Christmas pageant for Miami schoolchildren and their families. Ellisor sent out slick brochures proclaiming a three-day "Christmas from Around the World" spectacular, with pageantry, presents, and even live reindeer. Ellisor arranged meetings with local school officials, dazzling them with promises of a stage filled with Christmas trees and lights, an elaborate holiday show, and a lunchtime feast with a Harry Potter look-alike.

To back up his claims, Ellisor named prominent businesses and local police and fire departments as event sponsors. To show his stature in the community, he printed promotional materials on stolen University of Miami letterhead. And to convince school officials of his good track record in staging similar special events, he showed them a letter of thanks he had received eight years earlier from the Miami FBI field office for staging a career-day event.

However, Ellisor was no longer a legitimate businessman but a con artist staging an elaborate fraud. Who were his victims? More than 2,700 students from 22 Miami-area schools who handed over $10 each for tickets. Some schools even held bake sales to raise money for children whose families could not afford to pay the fee. Ellisor collected more than $38,000 in a bank account he set up for the "event." But when busloads of teachers, parents, and students arrived for the spectacular in December 2003, clutching their $20 tickets, they found an empty, shuttered convention center and no sign of Ellisor. On the morning the holiday spectacular was to begin, Ellisor had cleaned out the bank account while parents and teachers tried to console thousands of devastated children in the convention center parking lot. Later that day, federal warrants charging Ellisor with mail fraud were issued. Meanwhile, Ellisor quickly used $3,800 of the take to make the final payment on a luxury Jaguar automobile and fled.

Ellisor had never intended to hold the pageant and had spent the children's money on lobster dinners, lavish hotel suites, movie rentals, wine, luxury rental cars, special-order clothing, and a $5,000 watch. In 2005, Ellisor was convicted of eight counts of mail fraud, sentenced to more than 7 years in prison, and ordered to pay more than $38,500 in restitution to the children and their families.

PROPERTY CRIME

CHAPTER OBJECTIVES

1. Be familiar with the history of theft offenses
2. Recognize the differences between professional and amateur thieves
3. Know the similarities and differences between the various types of larceny
4. Understand the different forms of shoplifting
5. Be able to discuss the concept of fraud
6. Know what is meant by a confidence game
7. Understand what it means to burgle a home
8. Know what it takes to be a good burglar
9. Understand the concept of arson

Though average citizens may be puzzled and enraged by violent crimes, believing them to be both senseless and cruel, they often view economic crimes with a great deal more ambivalence. Society generally disapproves of crimes involving theft and corruption, but the public seems quite tolerant of the "gentleman bandit," even to the point of admiring such figures. They pop up as characters in popular myths and legends—the famed English outlaw Robin Hood, western bank robber Jesse James, 1930s outlaws Bonnie Parker and Clyde Barrow (the subjects of the 1967 award-winning film *Bonnie and Clyde* starring Warren Beatty and Faye Dunaway). There are the semi-heroic subjects of books and films such as *48 Hours* (1982), in which Eddie Murphy plays a thief who helps a police officer (Nick Nolte) catch even more dangerous criminals; *Heat* (1995), in which Robert DeNiro plays a master thief and Al Pacino the detective who tracks him down; *Heist* (2001), in which Gene Hackman plays a clever thief who steals gold bullion by the ton; and *Ocean's 11* (2001) and *Ocean's 12* (2004) in which a suave George Clooney leads a band of rogues who loot hundreds of millions of dollars from casinos, galleries, and so on.

To see thieves glorified as heroes, go to the **Ocean's 12** website at http://oceans12.warnerbros .com/. For an up-to-date list of web links, go to http:// cj.wadsworth.com/siegel_crimtpt9e.

How can such ambivalence toward criminality be explained? For one thing, if self-report surveys are accurate, national tolerance toward economic criminals may be prompted by the fact that almost every U.S. citizen has at some time been involved in economic crime. Even those among us who would never consider ourselves lawbreakers may have at one time engaged in petty theft, cheated on our income tax, stolen a textbook from a college bookstore, or pilfered from our place of employment. Consequently, it may be difficult for society to condemn economic criminals without feeling hypocritical.

People may also be somewhat more tolerant of economic crimes because they never seem to seriously hurt anyone— banks are insured, large businesses pass along losses to consumers, stolen cars can be easily replaced and, in most cases, are insured. The true pain of economic crime often goes unappreciated. Convicted offenders, especially businesspeople who commit white-collar crimes involving millions of dollars, often are punished rather lightly.

This chapter is the first of two that reviews the nature and extent of economic crime in the United States. It is divided into two principal sections. The first deals with the concept of professional crime and focuses on different types of professional criminals, including the **fence,** a buyer and seller of stolen merchandise. The chapter then turns to a discussion of common theft-related offenses or **street crime.** Included within these general offense categories are such common crimes as auto theft, shoplifting, and credit card fraud. Next, the chapter discusses a more serious form of theft, burglary, which involves forcible entry into a person's home or place of work for the purpose of theft. Finally, the crime of arson is discussed briefly. In Chapter 12 attention will be given to white-collar crimes and economic crimes that involve organizations devoted to criminal enterprise.

■ A BRIEF HISTORY OF THEFT

As a group, **economic crime** can be defined as acts in violation of the criminal law designed to bring financial reward to an offender. In U.S. society, the range and scope of criminal activity motivated by financial gain is tremendous: Self-report studies show that property crime among the young in every social class is widespread. National surveys of criminal behavior indicate that millions of personal and household thefts occur annually, including auto thefts, shoplifting incidents, embezzlements, burglaries, and larcenies. Between 10 and 15 percent of the U.S. population are victims of theft offenses each year.

Property crimes are not new to this century. This painting illustrates fourteenth-century thieves plundering a home in Paris.

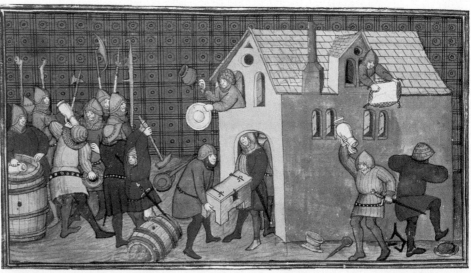

Theft, however, is not a phenomenon unique to modern times; the theft of personal property has been known throughout recorded history. The Crusades of the eleventh century inspired peasants and downtrodden noblemen to leave the shelter of their estates to prey on passing pilgrims.[2] Crusaders felt it within their rights to appropriate the possessions of any infidels—Greeks, Jews, or Muslims—they happened to encounter during their travels.

The Crusades actually lasted for centuries. Read about them and why they ended: Nigel Saul, "The Vanishing Vision: Late Medieval Crusading," *History Today* 47 (June 1997): 23.

By the thirteenth century, returning pilgrims, not content to live as serfs on feudal estates, gathered in the forests of England and the Continent to poach on game that was the rightful property of their lord or king and, when possible, to steal from passing strangers. By the fourteenth century, many such highwaymen and poachers were fulltime livestock thieves, stealing great numbers of cattle and sheep.[3] The fifteenth and sixteenth centuries brought hostilities between England and France in what has come to be known as the Hundred Years' War. Foreign mercenary troops fighting for both sides roamed the countryside; loot and pillage were viewed as a rightful part of their pay. As cities developed and a permanent class of propertyless urban poor was established,[4] theft became more professional. By the eighteenth century, three separate groups of property criminals were active: skilled thieves, smugglers, and poachers.

- **Skilled thieves** typically worked in the larger cities, such as London and Paris. This group included pickpockets, forgers, and counterfeiters, who operated freely. They congregated in **flash houses**—public meeting places, often taverns, that served as headquarters for gangs. Here, deals were made, crimes were plotted, and the sale of stolen goods was negotiated.[5]

- **Smugglers** were the second group of thieves. They moved freely in sparsely populated areas and transported goods, such as spirits, gems, gold, and spices, without bothering to pay tax or duty.

- **Poachers,** the third type of thief, typically lived in the country and supplemented their diet and income with game that belonged to a landlord.

Is poaching still a crime? To find out, use "poaching" as a subject guide in InfoTrac College Edition.

By the eighteenth century, professional thieves in the larger cities had banded together into gangs to protect themselves, increase the scope of their activities, and help dispose of stolen goods. Jack Wild, perhaps London's most famous thief, perfected the process of buying and selling stolen goods and gave himself the title of Thief-Taker General of Great Britain and Ireland. Before he was hanged, Wild controlled

numerous gangs and dealt harshly with any thief who violated his strict code of conduct.[6] During this period, individual theft-related crimes began to be defined by the common law. The most important of these categories are still used today.

 To read more about **Jack Wild** and his times, go to the website of the Old Bailey Court in England: http://www.oldbaileyonline.org/history/crime/policing .html. For an up-to-date list of web links, go to http://cj .wadsworth.com/siegel_crimtpt9e.

To quiz yourself on this material, go to the Criminology TPT 9e website.

MODERN THIEVES

Of the millions of property and theft-related crimes that occur each year, most are committed by **occasional criminals** who do not define themselves by a criminal role or view themselves as committed career criminals; other theft-offenders are in fact skilled **professional criminals.** The following sections review these two orientations toward property crime.

To read about the lives of three professional criminals, use InfoTrac College Edition to access this article: Dick Hobbs, "Professional Crime: Change, Continuity, and the Enduring Myth of the Underworld," *Sociology* 31 (February 1997): 57.

Occasional Criminals

Though criminologists are not certain, they suspect that the great majority of economic crimes are the work of amateur criminals whose decision to steal is spontaneous and whose acts are unskilled, impulsive, and haphazard. Millions of theft-related crimes occur each year, and most are not reported to police agencies. Many of these theft offenses are committed by school-age youths who are unlikely to enter into a criminal career and whose behavior has been described as drifting between conventional and criminal behavior. Added to the pool of amateur thieves are the millions of adults whose behavior may occasionally violate the criminal law—shoplifters, pilferers, tax cheats—but whose main source of income comes from conventional means and whose self-identity is not criminal. Added together, their behaviors form the bulk of theft crimes.

Occasional property crime occurs when there is an opportunity or **situational inducement** to commit crime.[7] Opportunities are available to members of all classes, but members of the upper class have the opportunity to engage in the more lucrative business-related crimes of price fixing, bribery, embezzlement, and so on, which are closed to the lower classes. Hence, lower-class individuals are overrepresented in street crime.

Occasional criminals are amateurs whose decision to steal is spontaneous and whose acts are unskilled, impulsive, and haphazard. They might even take advantage of an opportunity created by Mother Nature. With his shotgun sitting on a chair beside him, Terry Frye sits in front of his home, which was devastated by Hurricane Charley, in Port Charlotte, Florida, early August 14, 2004. Frye scrawled a note on the wall behind him to protect his home and scare off looters. Is Frye being overly cautious or should he worry about occasional criminals?

Situational inducements are short-term influences on a person's behavior that increase risk taking. These include psychological factors, such as financial problems, and social factors, such as peer pressure. Opportunity and situational inducements are not the cause of crime; rather, they are the occasion for crime, hence, the term *occasional criminal.*

The opportunity to commit crime and the short-run inducements to do so are not randomly situated; some people, typically poor young males, have an ample supply of both. Consequently, the frequency of occasional property crime varies according to age, class, sex, and so on. Occasional offenders are not professional criminals, nor do they make crime their occupation. They do not rely on skills or knowledge to commit their crimes, they do not organize their daily activities around crime, and they are not committed to crime as a way of life.

Occasional criminals have little group support for their acts. Unlike professionals, they do not receive informal peer group support for their crimes. In fact, they will deny any connection to a criminal lifestyle and instead view their transgressions as being "out of character." They may see their crimes as being motivated by necessity. For example, they were only borrowing the car the police caught them with; they were going to pay for the merchandise that they stole from the store—eventually. Because of their lack of commitment to a criminal lifestyle, occasional offenders may be the most likely to respond to the general deterrent effect of the law.

Professional Criminals

In contrast to occasional criminals, professional criminals make a significant portion of their income from crime. Professionals do not delude themselves with the belief that their acts are impulsive, one-time efforts, nor do they employ elaborate rationalizations to excuse the harmfulness of their action ("shoplifting doesn't really hurt anyone"). Consequently, professionals pursue their craft with vigor, attempting to learn from older, experienced criminals the techniques that will earn them the most money with the least risk. Though their numbers are relatively few, professionals engage in crimes that produce the greater losses to society and perhaps cause the more significant social harm.

Professional theft traditionally refers to nonviolent forms of criminal behavior that are undertaken with a high degree of skill for monetary gain and that exploit interests tending to maximize financial opportunities and minimize the possibilities of apprehension. The most typical forms include pocket-picking, burglary, shoplifting, forgery and counterfeiting, extortion, sneak theft, and confidence swindling.[8]

Relatively little is known about the career patterns of professional thieves and criminals. From the literature on crime and delinquency, three patterns emerge:

- Youth come under the influence of older, experienced criminals who teach them the trade.

- Juvenile gang members continue their illegal activities at a time when most of their peers have "dropped out" to marry, raise families, and take conventional jobs.

- Youth sent to prison for minor offenses learn the techniques of crime from more experienced thieves.

Harry King, a professional thief, relates this story about his entry into crime after being placed in a shelter-care home by his recently divorced mother:

> It was while I was at this parental school that I learned that some of the kids had been committed there by the court for stealing bikes. They taught me how to steal and

where to steal them and where to sell them. Incidentally, some of the "nicer people" were the ones who bought bikes from the kids. They would dismantle the bike and use the parts: the wheels, chains, handlebars, and so forth.[9]

Here we can see how would-be criminals may be encouraged in their illegal activities by so-called honest people who are willing to buy stolen merchandise and gain from criminal enterprise.

There is some debate in the criminological literature over who may be defined as a professional criminal. In his classic works, Edwin Sutherland used the term to refer only to thieves who do not use force or physical violence in their crimes and who live solely by their wits and skill.[10] However, some criminologists use the term to refer to any criminal who identifies with a criminal subculture, who makes the bulk of his or her living from crime, and who possesses a degree of skill in his or her chosen trade.[11] Thus, one can become a professional safecracker, burglar, car thief, or fence. Some criminologists would not consider drug addicts who steal to support their habit as professionals; they lack skill and therefore are amateur opportunists rather than professional technicians. However, professional criminals who take drugs might still be considered under the general pattern of professional crime. If the sole criterion for being judged a professional criminal were using crime as one's primary source of income, then many drug users would have to be placed in the professional category.

Sutherland's Professional Criminal

What we know about the lives of professional criminals has come to us through their journals, diaries, autobiographies, and the first-person accounts they have given to criminologists. The best-known account of professional theft is the life of a professional thief or con man, Chic Conwell, in Sutherland's classic book, *The Professional Thief*.[12] Conwell and Sutherland's concept of professional theft has two critical dimensions.

First, professional thieves engage in limited types of crime, which are described in Exhibit 11.1.[13] Professionals depend solely on their wit and skill. Thieves who use force or commit crimes that require little expertise are not considered worthy of the title "professional." Their areas of activity include "heavy rackets," such as bank robbery, car theft, burglary, and safecracking. You can see that Conwell and Sutherland's criteria for professionalism are weighted heavily toward con games and trickery and give little attention to common street crimes.

The second requirement of professional theft is the exclusive use of wits, front (a believable demeanor), and talking ability. Manual dexterity and physical force are of little importance. Professional thieves must acquire status in their profession. Status is based on their technical skill, financial standing, connections, power, dress, manners, and wide knowledge base. In their world, "thief" is a title worn with pride. Conwell and Sutherland also argue that professional

EXHIBIT 11.1

Sutherland's Typology of Professional Thieves

- Pickpocket (cannon)
- Thief in rackets related to confidence games
- Forger
- Extortionist from those engaging in illegal acts (shakedown artist)
- Confidence game artist (con artist)
- Thief who steals from hotel rooms (hotel prowl)
- Jewel thief who substitutes fake gems for real ones (pennyweighter)
- Shoplifter (booster)
- Sneak thief from stores, banks, and offices (heel)

Source: Edwin Sutherland and Chic Conwell, *The Professional Thief* (Chicago: University of Chicago Press, 1937).

thieves share feelings, sentiments, and behaviors. Of these, none is more important than the code of honor of the underworld; even under the threat of the most severe punishment, a professional thief must never inform (squeal) on his or her fellows. Sutherland and Conwell view professional theft as an occupation with much the same internal organization as that characterizing such legitimate professions as advertising, teaching, or police work. They conclude:

> A person can be a professional thief only if he is recognized and received as such by other professional thieves. Professional theft is a group way of life. One can get into the group and remain in it only by the consent of those previously in the group. Recognition as a professional thief by other professional thieves is the absolutely necessary, universal and definitive characteristic of the professional thief.[14]

Professional thieves have changed their behavior over time in response to crime control technology. The Criminological Enterprise feature "Transforming Theft" shows how these technology-inspired shifts in criminality began as early as the nineteenth century.

The Professional Fence

Some experts have argued that Sutherland's view of the professional thief may be outdated because modern thieves often work alone, are not part of a criminal subculture, and were not tutored early in their careers by other criminals.[15] However, some important research efforts show that the principles set down by Sutherland still have value for understanding the behavior of one contemporary criminal type— the **professional fence,** who earns his or her living solely by buying and reselling stolen merchandise. The fence's critical role in criminal transactions has been recognized since the eighteenth century.[16] They act as middlemen who purchase stolen merchandise—ranging from diamonds to auto

The Criminological Enterprise

Transforming Theft: Train Robbers and Safecrackers

According to Neal Shover, the activities of professional thieves began to be influenced by technology before the twentieth century. For example, train robbery flourished toward the end of the nineteenth century because professional robbers considered them easy pickings. Law enforcement was decentralized, and robbers could escape over the border to a neighboring state to avoid detection. Security arrangements were minimal, and robbers could stop, board, and loot trains with little fear of capture. As the threat to trains increased, technological improvements were initiated in an effort to deter would-be robbers:

- Plainclothes officers were placed on trains and rode unobtrusively among the passengers.

- Baggage cars were equipped with ramps and stalls containing fleet horses that could be used to immediately pursue bandits.

- Cars were made with finer precision and strength to make them impregnable.

- Forensic science made it easier to identify robbers, and improved communication made it easier to capture them.

- Federal involvement in train protection extended the ability of law enforcement beyond the county or state in which the robbery occurred.

As a result of these innovations, the number of train robberies decreased from twenty-nine in 1900 to seven in 1905; by 1920, train robbers had all but disappeared.

Safecracking also underwent a dramatic change due to technological changes in the design of safes. In the early 1900s, safes were made of manganese steel because it was resistant to drilling and was fireproof. With the invention and distribution of acetylene torches in the latter part of the nineteenth century, safes constructed of manganese became vulnerable and encouraged safecrackers to commit bold crimes. Safe manufacturers fought back by constructing safes with alternative sheets of copper and steel. The copper diffused heat and made the safe resistant to being torched. In response, safecrackers shifted their approach to attacking safes' locks and locking mechanisms. They developed mechanical devices that either dismantled or destroyed locks. Some burglars developed methods of peeling the laminated layers of the safe apart.

After World War II, safecrackers began using carbide and then diamond drill bits, which tore through metal. Safe manufacturers responded by lining safes with new metals designed to chip or break drill bits. They also developed sophisticated security systems featuring light beams, which would trip an alarm if the beam was interrupted by an intruder. When thieves learned how to neutralize these alarms, they were supplanted by motion detectors and ultrasonic systems, which fill space with sound waves and set off alarms when they are disturbed. Though these systems can be defeated, it requires expensive electronic gear, which most criminals can neither afford nor operate. As a result, the number of safecrackers has declined, and the crime of safecracking is relatively rare.

Critical Thinking

1. Technology changes the nature and extent of theft crimes. Although train robbing and safecracking may be rare today, using bogus credit cards and stealing from ATM machines has increased in both number of crimes and value. What are some other crime patterns that have been created by technological innovation?

2. What types of crime involving technological innovations have been prevented or deterred?

 InfoTrac College Edition Research

To read about the life of an actual train robber, check out this article: Stephen Fox, "Chris Evans Could Always Be Relied on to Pull a Fast One," *Smithsonian* 26 (May 1995): 84.

Source: Neal Shover, *Great Pretenders, Pursuits, and Careers of Persistent Thieves* (Boulder, CO: Westview Press, 1996), pp. 50–51.

---

hubcaps—and resell them to merchants who market them to legitimate customers.[17]

Carl Klockars examined the life and times of one successful fence who used the alias Vincent Swaggi. Through 400 hours of listening to and observing Swaggi, Klockars found that this highly professional criminal had developed techniques that made him almost immune to prosecution. During the course of a long and profitable career in crime, Swaggi spent only 4 months in prison. He stayed in business, in part, because of his sophisticated knowledge of the law of stolen property. To convict someone of receiving stolen goods, the prosecution must prove that the accused was in possession of the goods and knew that they had been stolen. Swaggi had the skills to make sure that these elements could never be proved. Also helping Swaggi stay out of the law's grasp were the close working associations he maintained with society's upper classes, including influential members of the justice system. Swaggi helped them purchase stolen items at below-cost, bargain prices. He also helped authorities recover stolen goods and therefore remained in their good graces. Klockars's work strongly suggests that fences customarily cheat their thief-clients and at the same time cooperate with the law.

Sam Goodman, a fence interviewed by sociologist Darrell Steffensmeier, lived in a world similar to Vincent Swaggi's. He also purchased stolen goods from a wide variety of thieves and suppliers, including burglars, drug addicts, shoplifters, dockworkers, and truck drivers. According to Goodman, to be successful, a fence must meet the following conditions:

- *Upfront cash:* All deals are cash transactions, so an adequate supply of ready cash must always be on hand.

- *Knowledge of dealing—learning the ropes:* The fence must be schooled in the knowledge of the trade, including developing a "larceny sense"; learning to "buy right" at acceptable prices; being able to "cover one's back" and not get caught; finding out how to make the right contacts; and knowing how to "wheel and deal" and how to create opportunities for profit.

- *Connections with suppliers of stolen goods:* The successful fence must be able to engage in long-term relationships with suppliers of high-value stolen goods who are relatively free of police interference. The warehouse worker who pilfers is a better supplier than the narcotics addict, who is more likely to be apprehended and talk to the police.

- *Connections with buyers:* The successful fence must have continuing access to buyers of stolen merchandise who are inaccessible to the common thief. For example, they must make contacts with local pawn shops and other distributors of secondhand goods and be able to move their material without drawing attention from the authorities.[18]

- *Complicity with law enforcers:* The fence must work out a relationship with law enforcement officials who invariably find out about the fence's operations. Steffensmeier found that to stay in business the fence must either bribe officials with good deals on merchandise and cash payments or act as an informer who helps police recover particularly important merchandise and arrest thieves.

Fences handle a tremendous number of products—televisions, cigarettes, stereo equipment, watches, autos, and cameras.[19] In dealing their merchandise, they operate through many legitimate fronts, including art dealers, antique stores, furniture and appliance retailers, remodeling companies, salvage companies, trucking companies, and jewelry stores. When deciding what to pay the thief for goods, the fence uses a complex pricing policy: Professional thieves who steal high-priced items are usually given the highest amounts—about 30 to 50 percent of the wholesale price. For example, furs valued at $5,000 may be bought for $1,500.

However, the amateur thief or drug addict who is not in a good bargaining position may receive only 10 cents on the dollar.

Fencing seems to contain many of the elements of professional theft as described by Sutherland: Fences live by their wits, never engage in violence, depend on their skill in negotiating, maintain community standing based on connections and power, and share the sentiments and behaviors of their fellows. The only divergence between Sutherland's thief and the fence is the code of honor; it seems likely that the fence is much more willing to cooperate with authorities than most other professional criminals.

The Nonprofessional Fence

Professional fences have attracted the attention of criminologists, but like other forms of theft, fencing is not dominated solely by professional criminals. A significant portion of all fencing is performed by amateur or occasional criminals. For example, novice burglars, such as juveniles and drug addicts, often find it so difficult to establish relationships with professional fences that they turn instead to nonprofessionals to unload the stolen goods.[20]

One type of occasional fence is the part-timer who, unlike professional fences, has other sources of income. Part-timers are often "legitimate" businesspeople who integrate the stolen merchandise into their regular stock. For example, the manager of a local video store who buys stolen DVD players and DVDs and rents them along with his legitimate merchandise is a part-time fence. An added benefit of the illegitimate part of his work is the profit he makes on these stolen items, which are not reported for tax purposes.

Some merchants become actively involved in theft either by specifying the merchandise they want the burglars to steal or by "fingering" victims. Some businesspeople sell merchandise and then describe the customers' homes and vacation plans to known burglars so that they can steal it back!

Associational fences are amateur fences who barter stolen goods for services. These amateurs typically have legitimate professional dealings with known criminals including bail bonds agents, police officers, and attorneys. A lawyer may demand an expensive watch from a client in exchange for legal services. Bartering for stolen merchandise avoids taxes and becomes a transaction in the underground economy.

Neighborhood hustlers buy and sell stolen property as one of the many ways they make a living. They keep some of the booty for themselves and sell the rest in the neighborhood. These dealmakers are familiar figures to neighborhood burglars looking to get some quick cash by selling them stolen merchandise.

Amateur receivers can be complete strangers approached in a public place by someone offering a great deal on valuable commodities. It is unlikely that anyone buying a $2,000 stereo for $200 cash would not suspect that it may have been stolen. Some amateur receivers make a habit of buying suspect merchandise at reasonable prices from a "trusted friend," establishing an ongoing relationship. This practice encourages crime because the criminals know that there will always be someone to buy their merchandise. In addition to the professional fence, the nonprofessional fence may account for a great deal of criminal receiving. Both professional and amateur thieves have a niche in the crime universe.

Criminologists and legal scholars recognize that common theft offenses fall into several categories linked together because they involve the intentional misappropriation of property for personal gain. In fencing, goods are bought from another who is in illegal possession of those goods. In the case of embezzlement, burglary, and larceny, the property is taken through stealth. In other kinds of theft, such as bad checks, fraud, and false pretenses, goods are obtained through deception. Some of the major categories of common theft offenses are discussed in the next sections in some detail.

 To quiz yourself on this material, go to the Criminology TPT 9e website.

LARCENY/THEFT

Larceny/theft was one of the earliest common-law crimes created by English judges to define acts in which one person took for his or her own use the property of another.[21] According to common law, larceny was defined as "the trespassory taking and carrying away of the personal property of another with intent to steal."[22] Most state jurisdictions have incorporated the common-law crime of larceny in their legal codes. Today, definitions of larceny often include such familiar acts as shoplifting, passing bad checks, and other theft offenses that do not involve using force or threats on the victim (robbery) or forcibly breaking into a person's home or place of work (burglary).

When it was originally construed, larceny involved taking property that was in the possession of the rightful owners. For example, it would have been considered larceny for someone to go secretly into a farmer's field and steal a cow. Thus, the original common-law definition required a "trespass in the taking"; this meant that for an act to be considered larceny, goods must have been taken from the physical possession of the rightful owner. In creating this definition of larceny, English judges were more concerned with people disturbing the peace than they were with thefts. If someone tried to steal property from another's possession, they reasoned that the act could eventually lead to a physical confrontation and possibly the death of one party or the other, thereby disturbing the peace! Consequently, the original definition of larceny did not include crimes in which the thief had come into the possession of the stolen property by trickery or deceit. For example, if someone entrusted with another person's property decided to keep it, it was not considered larceny.

The growth of manufacturing and the development of the free enterprise system required greater protection for private property. The pursuit of commercial enterprise often required that one person's legal property be entrusted to a second party; therefore, larceny evolved to include the theft of goods that had come into the thief's possession through legitimate means.

To get around the element of "trespass in the taking," English judges created the concept of **constructive possession.** This legal fiction applied to situations in which persons voluntarily and temporarily gave up custody of their property but still believed the property was legally theirs. For example, if a person gave a jeweler her watch for repair, she would still believe she owned the watch even though she had handed it over to the jeweler. Similarly, when a person misplaces his wallet and someone else finds it and keeps it— although identification of the owner can be plainly seen— the concept of constructive possession makes the person who has kept the wallet guilty of larceny.

Larceny Today

Most state jurisdictions have, as mentioned, incorporated larceny in their criminal codes. Larceny is usually separated by state statute into **petit (petty) larceny** and **grand larceny.** The former involves small amounts of money or property; it is punished as a misdemeanor. Grand larceny, involving merchandise of greater value, is considered a felony and is punished by a sentence in the state prison. Each state sets its own boundary between grand larceny and petty larceny. So, for example, in Massachusetts if the goods or services stolen were worth over $250, it is considered a felony offense, under $250 the crime is a misdemeanor.[23] This distinction often presents a serious problem for the justice system. Car thefts and other larcenies involving high-priced merchandise are easily classified, but it is often difficult to decide whether a particular theft should be considered petty or grand larceny. For example, if a 10-year-old watch that originally cost $500 is stolen, should its value be based on its original cost, on its current worth ($50), or on its replacement cost ($1,000)? As most statutes are worded, the current market value of the property governs its worth. Thus, the theft of the watch would be considered petty larceny because its worth today is only $50. However, if a painting originally bought for $25 has a current market value of $500, its theft would be considered grand larceny. The distinction between petit and grand larceny can be especially significant in states such as California, which employ three strikes laws mandating that someone convicted of a third felony be given a life sentence. The difference may not be lost on potential criminals: Research by John Worrall shows that larceny rates in California have been significantly lowered since passage of the three strikes law.[24]

Larceny/theft is probably the most common criminal offense. The FBI recorded a little more than 7 million acts of larceny in 2003 essentially unchanged from the year before; the larceny rate is about 2,400 per 100,000 people. Larceny rates declined about 20 percent between 1994 and 2003. Preliminary data show larceny declined 2 percent between 2003 and 2004.[25]

There are many different varieties of larceny. Some involve small items of little value. Many of these go unreported, however, especially if the victims were business owners who do not want to take the time to get involved with police. They simply write off the losses as part of doing business. For example, hotel owners estimate that guests filch $100 million a year in towels, bathrobes, ashtrays, bedspreads, shower heads, flatware, and even television sets and wall paintings.[26] Another favorite is stolen car parts that can be taken from stolen autos (see below) or simply ripped off on the street. Among the most attractive targets:

- *Head lights:* Blue-white, high-intensity discharge headlights. New ones go for $500 and up per light, sometimes $3,000 per car.

- *Air bags:* About 10 percent of all theft claims involve an air bag. The driver's side bag, mounted in the steering wheel, is the easiest to remove and costs $500 to $1,000 to replace.

- *Wheels:* Custom rims are attractive to thieves, especially the "spinners" that keep revolving when the car is stopped. They go from $100 each up to $15,000 for a set of super-luxe models.[27]

Other larcenies involve complex criminal conspiracies, and no one, not even the U.S. government, is immune. Thieves steal millions of dollars worth of government equipment and supplies each year. For example, the Department of Energy reported more than $20 million in property missing from its site in Rocky Flats, Colorado. Missing items included semi-trailers, forklifts, cameras, desks, radios, and more than 1,800 pieces of computer equipment.[28]

Shoplifting

Shoplifting is a common form of theft involving taking goods from retail stores. Usually shoplifters try to snatch items— jewelry, clothes, records, or appliances—when store personnel are otherwise occupied, and they then hide the goods on their person. The five-finger discount is an extremely common form of crime, and retailers lose an estimated $30 billion to inventory shrinkage; on average, stores small and large lose at least 2 percent of total sales to thieves.[29] Shoplifting is certainly not unique to the United States. In England, about 5 percent of the population is convicted of shoplifting by age 40. Surveys of retailers in the United Kingdom suggest that there are more than 4 million known shoplifting incidents, 1.3 million apprehended shoplifters, and 800,000 shoplifters reported to the police each year. One reason for the popularity of shoplifting may be lax treatment. Although about one in seven apprehended offenders is eventually convicted in court, less than one in twenty shoplifting attempts result in apprehension.[30]

Retail security measures add to the already high cost of this crime, all of which is passed on to the consumer. Some studies estimate that about one in every nine shoppers steals from department stores. Moreover, the increasingly popular discount stores, such as Costco, Wal-Mart, and Target, have a minimum of sales help and depend on highly visible merchandise displays to attract purchasers, all of which makes them particularly vulnerable to shoplifters.

> To learn more about shoplifting control, use InfoTrac College Edition, and read: Ann Longmore-Etheridge, "Bagging Profits Instead of Thieves," *Security Management* 45 (October 2001): 70.

PROFILE OF A SHOPLIFTER In the early 1960s, Mary Owen Cameron conducted a classic study of shoplifting.[31] In her pioneering effort, Cameron found that about 10 percent of all shoplifters were professionals who derived the majority of their income from shoplifting. Sometimes called **boosters** or **heels,** she found that professional shoplifters steal with the intention of reselling stolen merchandise to pawnshops or fences, usually at half the original price.[32]

Cameron found that the majority of shoplifters are amateur pilferers, called **snitches** in thieves' argot. Snitches are usually respectable people who do not conceive of themselves as thieves but are systematic shoplifters who steal merchandise for their own use. They are not simply overcome by an uncontrollable urge to take something that attracts them; they come equipped to steal. Snitches who are arrested usually have never been apprehended before. For the most part, they are people who lack the kind of criminal experience that suggests extensive association with a criminal subculture.

Criminologists view shoplifters as people who are likely to reform if apprehended. Because snitches are not part of a criminal subculture and do not think of themselves as criminals, Cameron reasoned that they are deterred by an initial contact with the law. Getting arrested has a traumatic effect on them, and they will not risk a second offense.[33] This argument seems plausible, but some criminologists argue that apprehension may have a labeling effect that inhibits deterrence and results in repeated offending.[34]

CONTROLLING SHOPLIFTING One major problem associated with combating shoplifting is that many customers who observe pilferage are reluctant to report it to security agents. Store employees themselves are often loathe to get involved in apprehending a shoplifter. In fact, less than 10 percent of shoplifting incidents are detected by store employees; customers who notice boosters are unwilling to report even serious cases to managers.[35] It is also likely that a store owner's decision to prosecute shoplifters will be based on the value of the goods stolen, the nature of the goods stolen, and the manner in which the theft was realized. For example, shoplifters who planned their crime by using a concealed apparatus, such as a bag pinned to the inside of their clothing, were more apt to be prosecuted than those who had impulsively put merchandise into their pockets.[36] The concealment indicated that the crime was premeditated and not a spur of the moment loss of control.

To encourage the arrest of shoplifters, a number of states have passed *merchant privilege laws* designed to protect retailers and their employers from litigation stemming from improper or false arrests of suspected shoplifters.[37] These laws protect but do not immunize merchants from lawsuits. They require that arrests be made on reasonable grounds or probable cause, detention be of short duration, and store employees or security guards conduct themselves in a reasonable fashion.

PREVENTION STRATEGIES Retail stores are now initiating a number of strategies designed to reduce or eliminate shoplifting. **Target removal strategies** involve putting dummy or disabled goods on display while the real merchandise is kept under lock and key. For example, audio equipment with missing parts is displayed, and only after items are purchased are the necessary components installed. Some stores sell from a catalogue while keeping merchandise in stockrooms.

Target hardening strategies involve locking goods in place or having them monitored by electronic systems. Clothing stores may use racks designed to prevent large quantities of garments from being slipped off easily. Store owners may rely on electronic article surveillance (EAS) systems, featuring tags with small electronic sensors that trip sound and light alarms if not removed by employees before the item leaves the store. Security systems now feature source

tagging, a process by which manufacturers embed the tag in the packaging or in the product itself. Thieves are hard-pressed to remove or defeat such tags, and retailers save on the time and labor needed to attach the tags at their stores.[38]

Situational measures place the most valuable goods in the least vulnerable places, use warning signs to deter potential thieves, and use closed-circuit cameras. Goods may be tagged with devices that activate an alarm if they are taken out of the shop. Exhibit 11.2 illustrates some additional measures that stores can take to deter shoplifters.

Another approach to shoplifting prevention is to create specialized programs that use methods such as doing community service, paying monetary restitution, writing essays, watching anti-shoplifting videos, writing apology letters, and being placed in individual and/or family counseling. Evaluations indicate that such programs can be successful in reducing recidivism of young shoplifters.[39]

Bad Checks

Another form of larceny is cashing bad bank checks, knowingly and intentionally drawn on a nonexistent or underfunded bank account, to obtain money or property. In general, for a person to be guilty of passing a bad check, the bank the check is drawn on must refuse payment, and the check casher must fail to make the check good within 10 days after finding out the check was not honored.

Edwin Lemert conducted the best-known study of check forgers more than forty years ago.[40] Lemert found that the majority of check forgers—he calls them **naive check forgers**—are amateurs who do not believe their actions will hurt anyone. Most naive check forgers come from middle-class backgrounds and have little identification with a criminal subculture. They cash bad checks because of a financial crisis that demands an immediate resolution—perhaps they have lost money at the horse track and have some pressing bills to pay. Lemert refers to this condition as **closure.** Naive check forgers are often socially isolated people who have been unsuccessful in their personal relationships. They are risk prone when faced with a situation that is unusually stressful for them. The willingness of stores and other commercial establishments to cash checks with a minimum of fuss to promote business encourages the check forger to risk committing a criminal act. Some of the different techniques used in check fraud schemes, which may cost retail establishment upwards of $1 billion annually, are set out in Exhibit 11.3.

Not all check forgers are amateurs. Lemert found that a few professionals—whom he calls **systematic forgers**—make a substantial living by passing bad checks. However, professionals constitute a relatively small segment of the total population of check forgers. It is difficult to estimate the number of such forgeries committed each year or the amounts involved. Stores and banks may choose not to press charges because the effort to collect the money due them is often not worth their while. It is also difficult to separate the true check forger from the neglectful shopper.

Credit Card Theft

The use of stolen credit cards has become a major problem in U.S. society. It has been estimated that fraud has been responsible for a billion-dollar loss in the credit card industry. Most credit card abuse is the work of amateurs who acquire stolen cards through theft or mugging and then use them for two or three days. However, professional credit card rings may be getting into the act. They collect or buy from employees the names and credit card numbers of customers in retail establishments; then they buy plain plastic cards and have the numbers of the customers embossed on them. They create fictitious wholesale companies and apply for and received authorization to accept credit cards from the customers. They then use the phony cards to charge nonexistent purchases on the accounts of the people whose names and card numbers they had collected.

To combat losses from credit card theft, Congress passed a law in 1971 limiting a person's liability to $50 per stolen card. Similarly, some states, such as California, have passed specific statutes making it a misdemeanor to obtain property

or services by means of cards that have been stolen, forged, canceled, or revoked, or whose use is for any reason unauthorized.[41] However, while the public is protected, merchants may have to foot the bill. For example, Website Billing.com, a Hollywood, Florida-based web company that processes payments for merchants, was required to pay the Visa credit card company $15 for each fraudulent transaction that it processed. But because fraudulent purchases exceeded 5 percent of all its international transactions, Visa assessed an additional $100 penalty for each fraudulent transaction; in a single year, Website paid Visa more than $1 million in fees. Merchants argue that these fees—which generate an estimated $500 million in revenue for the card industry each year—eliminate much of the card companies' incentive to pursue credit card fraud.[42]

| | | | | | | CONNECTIONS | | | | | | |

Similar frauds are conducted over the Internet. These will be discussed in Chapter 14.

Want to avoid **credit card theft**? The Federal Trade Commission has some important tips: http://www.ftc.gov/bcp /conline/pubs/credit/ cards.htm. For an up-to-date list of web links, go to http://cj.wadsworth.com/ siegel_crimtpt9e.

The problem of credit card misuse is being compounded by thieves who set up bogus Internet sites strictly to trick people into giving them their credit card numbers, which they then use for their own gain. The problem is growing so rapidly that a number of new technologies are being prepared, aimed at combating credit card number theft over the Internet. One method is to incorporate digital signatures into computer operating systems, which can be accessed with a digital key that comes with each computer. Owners of new systems can present three forms of identification to a notary public and trade a notarized copy of their key for a program that will sign files. The basis of the digital signature is a digital certificate, a small block of data that contains a person's "public key." This certificate is signed, in turn, by a certificate authority. This digital certificate will act like a credit card with a hologram and a photograph and identify the user to the distant website and vice versa.[43] The Criminological Enterprise feature discusses one such Internet credit card scheme.

Auto Theft

Motor vehicle theft is another common larceny offense. Yet because of its frequency and seriousness, it is treated as a separate category in the UCR. The FBI recorded about 1.2 million auto thefts in 2003, accounting for a total loss of more than $8 billion. Like other crimes, motor vehicle theft has declined during the past decade, down 18 percent from

Credit Card Fraud

Philip Arcand and his wife, Roberta Galway, lived a life of luxury. They owned two homes, one in British Columbia and one in Las Vegas. They had a Mercedes, Corvette, and Ferrari in their driveways. They took frequent trips around the world. All this without having a job. How did they do it? Through credit card fraud!

Arcand wrote high-pressure scripts to lure victims, arranged for telemarketing companies to make the pitch, and set up front businesses to process the illegal monies. The telemarketers claimed to be from a credit card company. They told victims how easy it is to steal a credit card number, especially over the Internet. They offered to sell protection policies that would insure that the buyer would not have to pay if thieves ran up a huge tab on their account. The telemarketers told the victims that if they did not get this protection, they would have to foot the bill for any unauthorized charges made if their credit cards were stolen. After making their pitch, the victims were asked: "May we have your credit card number, please?" Later, a charge of between $199 and $389 appeared on their account, even if they did not sign up for the service.

The scheme was bogus, illegal, and entirely unnecessary because most major credit card companies protect you from fraudulent charges. Still, thousands of Americans were victimized by this scam—the overwhelming majority elderly victims who lived across the country, from Massachusetts and West Virginia to California and Hawaii. In all, they were defrauded of more than $12 million.

Arcand and Galway were ultimately caught when some of the victims reported their suspicions and complaints to authorities. Because they were Canadian citizens, a joint partnership of Canadian and U.S. law enforcement agencies—including the Royal Canadian Mounted Police (RCMP), the FBI's Los Angeles field office, and the Federal Trade Commission (FTC)—pursued the case, which was called Project Emptor. In August 2002, the couple was arrested by FBI agents while living in Las Vegas, and on November 17, 2003, Arcand was sentenced to 10 years in federal prison; his wife Roberta Galway pled guilty and was sentenced to 6 months in jail. The couple also paid a $100,000 civil judgment in a case initiated by the FTC. Other charges are still outstanding.

Critical Thinking

1. Should a person such as Arcand be sentenced to 10 years in prison for credit card fraud? Is this too severe a punishment for someone whose victims actually lost relatively little money on an individual basis?

2. Should it be a crime to sell people services they are unaware of but are already eligible to receive? Is this fraud or merely taking advantage of the uninformed?

 InfoTrac College Edition Research

To learn more, use "credit card fraud" in a key word search in InfoTrac College Edition.

Source: Federal Bureau of Investigation, "Credit Card Con: Canadian Man Gets 10 Years for $12 Million Telemarketing Scam." http://www.fbi.gov/page2/nov03/credit112803 .htm. Accessed August 11, 2004.

1994. UCR projections on auto theft are actually similar to the projections of the National Crime Victimization Survey (about 1 million thefts in 2003). The similarity of data between these sources occurs because almost every state jurisdiction requires owners to insure their vehicles. Auto theft is the most highly reported of all major crimes (80 percent of all auto thefts are reported to police).

A number of attempts have been made to categorize the various forms of auto theft. Distinctions typically are made between theft for temporary personal use, for resale, and for chopping or stripping cars for parts. One of the most detailed typologies was developed by Charles McCaghy and his associates after examining data from police and court files in several state jurisdictions.[44] The researchers uncovered five categories of auto theft transactions:

- *Joyriding:* Many car thefts are motivated by teenagers' desire to acquire the power, prestige, sexual potency, and recognition associated with an automobile. Joyriders do not steal cars for profit or gain but to experience, even briefly, the benefits associated with owning an automobile.

- *Short-term transportation:* Auto theft for short-term transportation is most similar to joyriding. It involves the theft of a car simply to go from one place to another. In more serious cases, the thief may drive to another city or state and then steal another car to continue the journey.

- *Long-term transportation:* Thieves who steal cars for long-term transportation intend to keep the cars for their personal use. Usually older than joyriders and from a lower-class background, these auto thieves may repaint and otherwise disguise cars to avoid detection.

A tow truck pulls Nicolas Cage's 1989 Porsche Sportster from the Lake of the Ozarks, Missouri. The $100,000 collectors' item was in transport from California to Pennsylvania when it was stolen Christmas Day 2001 from a parking lot in Arnold, south of St. Louis. About one million cars are stolen each year, most often Toyota Camrys and Honda Accords.

© Getty Images

■ *Profit:* Auto theft for profit is motivated by hope for monetary gain. At one extreme are highly organized professionals who resell expensive cars after altering their identification numbers and falsifying their registration papers. At the other end of the scale are amateur auto strippers who steal batteries, tires, and wheel covers to sell them or reequip their own cars.

■ *Commission of another crime:* A small portion of auto thieves steal cars to use in other crimes, such as robberies and thefts. This type of auto thief desires both mobility and anonymity.

At one time, joyriding was the predominant motive for auto theft, and most cars were taken by relatively affluent, white, middle-class teenagers looking for excitement.[45] There appears to be a change in this pattern: Fewer cars are being taken today while, concomitantly, fewer stolen cars are being recovered. Part of the reason is that there has been an increase in professional car thieves who are linked to chop shops, export rings, or both. Export of stolen vehicles has become a global problem, and the emergence of capitalism in eastern Europe has increased the demand for U.S.-made cars.[46] Heath Copes has found that persistent auto theft may be more popular now because street hustlers view auto theft as a valuable tool to enlarge their bankroll and improve their street image. While few experienced thieves want to drive around in a stolen vehicle, they are more than willing to use their profit from selling a stolen car to buy a suitable ride. Even those without a connection to a chop shop or theft ring can profit handsomely from stealing cars.[47]

WHICH CARS ARE TAKEN MOST? Car thieves show signs of rational choice when they make their target selections.

Today, luxury cars and utility vehicles are in greatest demand. According to the National Insurance Crime Bureau (NICB), the following ten cars are the most popular with auto thieves:

1. Toyota Camry

2. Honda Accord

3. Honda Civic

4. Chevrolet full-size C/K pickup

5. Ford full-size pickup (150/250/350)

6. Jeep Cherokee/Grand Cherokee

7. Oldsmobile Cutlass/Supreme/Ciera

8. Dodge Caravan/Grand Caravan

9. Ford Taurus

10. Toyota Corolla [48]

According to the NICB, thieves typically choose these vehicles because of the high profit potential when the cars are stripped of their component parts, which are then sold on the black market. These vehicles are popular overseas, and once taken, organized theft rings will illegally export them to foreign destinations. Many of the highly desired cars are never recovered because they are immediately shipped abroad where they command prices three times higher than their U.S. sticker price.[49]

Car models that have been in production for a few years without many design changes stand the greatest risk of theft. These vehicles are popular because their parts are most valued in the secondary market. Luxury cars, on the other hand, typically experience a sharp decline in their theft rate soon after a design change. Enduring models are also in demand because older cars are more likely to be uninsured, and demand for stolen used parts is higher for these vehicles.

||||||| **CONNECTIONS** |||||||

Chapter 4 discusses the rational choice view of car theft. As you may recall, cars with expensive radios and parts are more often the target of rational thieves.

CARJACKING You may have read about gunmen approaching a car and forcing the owner to give up the keys; in some cases, people have been killed when they reacted too slowly. This type of auto theft has become so common that it has its own name, **carjacking**.[50] Carjacking is legally considered a type of robbery because it involves force to steal. According to NCVS data, about 38,000 carjacking victimizations occur annually. During the past decade, that meant that there was an average of 1.7 victimizations per 10,000 persons annually; about 15 people are killed in auto-related crimes each year.[51]

Both victims and offenders in carjackings tend to be young black men. Urban residents are more likely to experience carjacking than suburban or rural residents. About half of all carjackings are typically committed by gangs or groups. These crimes are most likely to occur in the evening, in the central city, in an open area, or in a parking garage. This pattern may reflect the fact that carjacking seems to be a crime of opportunity; it is the culmination of the carjacker's personal needs and desires coinciding with the immediate opportunity for gain. This decision is also shaped by the carjacker's participation in urban street culture.[52]

Weapons, most often guns, were used in about three-quarters of all carjacking victimizations.[53] Despite the presence of weapons, victims resisted the offender in two-thirds of carjackings, and, not surprisingly, about 32 percent of victims of completed carjackings and about 17 percent of victims of attempted carjackings were injured. Serious injuries, such as gunshot or knife wounds, broken bones, or internal injuries, occurred in about 9 percent of carjackings. More minor injuries, such as bruises and chipped teeth, occurred in about 15 percent of cases.

COMBATING AUTO THEFT Auto theft is a significant target of situational crime prevention efforts. One approach to theft deterrence has been to increase the risks of apprehension. Hot lines offer rewards for information leading to the arrest of car thieves. A Michigan-based program, Operation HEAT (Help Eliminate Auto Theft), is credited with recovering more than 900 vehicles, worth $11 million, and resulting in the arrest of 647 people. Another approach has been to place fluorescent decals on windows that indicate that the car is never used between 1 A.M. and 5 A.M.; if police spot a car with the decal being operated during this period, they know it is stolen.[54]

The Lojack system involves installing a hidden tracking device in cars that gives off a signal, enabling the police to pinpoint its location. Research evaluating the effectiveness of this device finds that it has a significant crime reduction capability.[55] Because car thieves cannot tell that Lojack has been installed, it does not reduce the likelihood that a protected car will be stolen. However, cars installed with Lojack have a much higher recovery rate. There may also be a general deterrent effect: Areas with high rates of Lojack use experience significant reductions in their auto theft rates. Ironically, Lojack owners actually accrue a smaller than anticipated reward for their foresight than the general public because they have to pay for installation and maintenance of the device. Those without it actually gain more because they benefit from a lower auto theft rate without paying any additional cost.

Other prevention efforts involve making it more difficult to steal cars. Publicity campaigns have been directed at encouraging people to lock their cars. Parking lots have been equipped with theft-deterring closed-circuit TV cameras and barriers. Manufacturers have installed more sophisticated steering column locking devices and other security systems that make theft more difficult.

A study by the Highway Loss Data Institute (HLDI) found that most car theft prevention methods, especially alarms, have little effect on theft rates. The most effective methods appear to be devices that immobilize a vehicle by cutting off the electrical power needed to start the engine when a theft is detected.[56]

 Want to learn how to **prevent auto theft**? Go to http://www.prevent-crime.com/auto-theft.html. For an up-to-date list of web links, go to http://cj.wadsworth .com/siegel_crimtpt9e.

To learn more, use "Lojack" in a key word search in InfoTrac College Edition.

False Pretenses or Fraud

The crime of **false pretenses**, or **fraud**, involves misrepresenting a fact in a way that causes a victim to willingly give his or her property to the wrongdoer, who then keeps it.[57] In 1757, the English Parliament defined false pretenses to cover an area of law left untouched by larceny statutes. The first false pretenses law punished people who "knowingly and designedly by false pretense or pretenses, [obtained] from any person or persons, money, goods, wares or merchandise with intent to cheat or defraud any person or persons of the same."[58]

False pretense differs from traditional larceny because the victims willingly give their possessions to the offender, and the crime does not, as does larceny, involve a "trespass in the taking." An example of false pretenses would be an unscrupulous merchant selling someone a chair by claiming it was an antique, but knowing all the while that it was a cheap copy. Another example would be a phony healer selling a victim a bottle of colored sugar water as an elixir that would cure a disease.

Fraud may also occur when people conspire to cheat a third party or institution—for example, by selling fake IDs, tickets, vouchers, tokens, or licenses, which can be used to fraudulently gain services or illegal access. One example of an innovative cheating scheme was instituted by a man named Po Chieng Ma, who conspired to sell answers to the Graduate Management Administration Test (GMAT), the Graduate Record Examinations (GRE), and the Test of English as a Foreign Language (TOEFL) to an estimated 788 customers, each of whom had paid him $2,000 to $9,000. In the scheme, people were paid to take the multiple-choice tests in Manhattan and then call California, where the same tests were to be given, with the answers. The answers were passed on to Ma, who, taking advantage of the 3-hour time difference, carved the answers in code on the sides of pencils, which were then given to his customers. Ma pled guilty to conspiracy and obstruction of justice and received a 4-year prison term for his efforts. In this case, there were many victims, including the testing service, universities, and the students who lost places in school because those who inflated their scores through the scheme were admitted instead.[59]

Confidence Games

Confidence games are run by swindlers who aspire to separate a victim (or "sucker") from his or her hard-earned money. These con games usually involve getting a **mark,** the target of a con man or woman, interested in some get-rich-quick scheme, which may have illegal overtones. The criminal's hope is that when victims lose their money they will either be too embarrassed or too afraid to call the police. There are hundreds of varieties of con games. The most common is called the **pigeon drop.**[60] Here, a package or wallet containing money is "found" by a con man or woman. A passing victim is stopped and asked for advice about what to do, since no identification can be found. Another "stranger," who is part of the con, approaches and enters the discussion. The three decide to split the money; but first, to make sure everything is legal, one of the swindlers goes off to consult a lawyer. Upon returning, he or she says that the lawyer claims the money can be split up; first, however, each party must prove he or she has the means to reimburse the original owner, should one show up. The victim then is asked to give some good-faith money for the lawyer to hold. When the victim goes to the lawyer's office to pick up a share of the loot, he or she finds the address bogus and the money gone.

In the new millennium, the pigeon drop has been appropriated by corrupt telemarketers, who contact people over the phone, typically elderly victims, to bilk them out of their savings. The FBI estimates that illicit telephone pitches cost Americans some $40 billion a year.[61] In one scam, a salesman tried to get $500 out of a 78-year-old woman by telling her the money was needed as a deposit to make sure she would get $50,000 in cash she had supposedly won in a contest. In another scheme, a Las Vegas–based telephone con game used the name Feed America Inc. to defraud people out of more than $1.3 million by soliciting donations for various causes, including families of those killed in the Oklahoma City bombing. With the growth of direct-mail marketing and "900" telephone numbers that charge callers more than $2.50 per minute for conversations with what are promised to be beautiful, willing sex partners, a flood of new confidence games may be about to descend on the U.S. public. Some common confidence games include:

- Con artists read the obituary column and then send a surviving spouse bills supposedly owed by the person deceased. Or they deliver an item—like a Bible—that they say the deceased relative ordered just before he died.

- A swindler, posing as a bank employee, stops a customer as he or she is about to enter the bank. The swindler claims to be an investigator who is trying to catch a dishonest teller. He asks the customer to withdraw cash to see if he or she got the right amount. After the cash is withdrawn, the swindler asks that it be turned over to them so he can check the serial numbers.

- Pyramid schemes involve the selling of phony franchises. The investor buys a franchise to sell golf clubs or some other commodity paying thousands of dollars. He is asked to recruit some friends to buy more franchises and promised a percentage of the sales of every new franchisee he recruits. Eventually there are hundreds of distributors, few customers, and the merchandise is typically unavailable. Those at the top make lots of money before the pyramid collapses, leaving the individual investors without their cash.

- Shady contractors offer an unusually low price for an expensive job such as driveway repair and then use old motor oil rather than asphalt to make the repairs. The first rain brings disaster. Some offer a low rate but conduct a "free" inspection that turns up several expensive repairs that are actually bogus.

- A business office receives a mailing that looks like an invoice with a self-addressed envelope that makes it look like it comes from the phone company (walking fingers on a yellow background). It appears to be a contract for an ad in the Yellow Pages. On the back, in small print, will be written, "By returning this confirmation, you're signing a contract to be an advertiser in the upcoming, and all subsequent, issues." If the invoice is returned, the business soon finds that it has agreed to a long-term contract to advertise in some private publication that is not widely distributed.

In all, about 300,000 people were arrested for fraud in 2003, most likely a very small percentage of all swindlers, scam artists, and defrauders.

> To learn how con artists operate, go to: "How Not to Buy a Bridge; Con Artists Prey on the Unwary, as This Entrepreneur Discovered. A Few Simple Precautions Could Have Made All the Difference," *Business Week Online,* 11 April 2002. In InfoTrac College Edition, use "confidence games" as a subject guide to learn more.

Embezzlement

Embezzlement was mentioned in early Greek culture when, in his writings, Aristotle alluded to theft by road commissioners and other government officials.[62] It was first codified in law by the English Parliament during the sixteenth century to fill a gap in the larceny law.[63] Until then, to be guilty of theft, a person had to take goods from the physical possession of another (trespass in the taking). However, as explained earlier, this definition did not cover instances in which one person trusted another and willfully gave that person temporary custody of his or her property. For example, in everyday commerce, store clerks, bank tellers, brokers, and merchants gain lawful possession but not legal ownership of other people's money. Embezzlement occurs when someone who is so trusted with property fraudulently converts it—that is, keeps it for his or her own use or the use of others. It can be distinguished from fraud on the basis of when the criminal intent was formed. Most U.S. courts require that a serious breach of trust must have occurred before a person can be convicted of embezzlement. The mere act of moving property without the owner's consent, or damaging it or using it, is not considered embezzlement. However, using it up, selling it, pledging it, giving it away, or holding it against the owner's will is considered to be embezzlement.[64]

Although it is impossible to know how many embezzlement incidents occur annually, the FBI found that only 18,000 people were arrested for embezzlement in 2003—probably an extremely small percentage of all embezzlers. However, the number of people arrested for embezzlement has increased more than 40 percent since 1991, indicating that (1) more employees are willing to steal from their employers, (2) more employers are willing to report instances of embezzlement, or (3) law enforcement officials are more willing to prosecute embezzlers. There has also been a rash of embezzlement-type crimes around the world, especially in Third World countries where poverty is all too common and the economy is poor and supported by foreign aid and loans. Government officials and businessmen who have their hands on this money are tempted to convert it for their own use—a scenario that is sure to increase the likelihood of embezzlement.[65]

 To quiz yourself on this material, go to the Criminology TPT 9e website.

BURGLARY

In common law, the crime of burglary is defined as "the breaking and entering of a dwelling house of another in the nighttime with the intent to commit a felony within."[66] Burglary is considered a much more serious crime than larceny/theft because it often involves entering another's home, a situation in which the threat of harm to occupants is great. Even though the home may be unoccupied at the time of the burglary, the potential for harm to the occupants is so significant that most state jurisdictions punish burglary as a felony.

The legal definition of burglary has undergone considerable change since its common-law origins. When first created by English judges during the late Middle Ages, laws against burglary were designed to protect people whose homes might be set upon by wandering criminals. Including the phrase "breaking and entering" in the definition protected people from unwarranted intrusions; if an invited guest stole something, it would not be considered a burglary. Similarly, the requirement that the crime be committed at nighttime was added because evening was considered the time when honest people might fall prey to criminals.[67]

In more recent times, state jurisdictions have changed the legal requirements of burglary, and most have discarded the necessity of forced entry. Many now protect all structures, not just dwelling houses. A majority of states have removed the nighttime element from burglary definitions as well. It is common for states to enact laws creating different degrees of burglary. In this instance, the more serious and heavily punished crimes involve a nighttime forced entry into the home; the least serious involve a daytime entry into a nonresidential structure by an unarmed offender. Several gradations of the offense may be found between these extremes.

The Nature and Extent of Burglary

The FBI's definition of burglary is not restricted to burglary from a person's home; it includes any unlawful entry of a structure to commit theft or felony. Burglary is further categorized into three subclasses: forcible entry, unlawful entry where no force is used, and attempted forcible entry. According to the UCR, about 2.1 million burglaries occurred in 2003. The burglary rate has dropped by almost 30 percent since 1994; both residential and commercial burglaries underwent steep declines during this period. Preliminary data indicates a decline of 2 percent between 2003 and 2004. Overall, the average loss for a burglary was about $1,600 per victim, for a total of about $3.5 billion.

The NCVS reports that about 3.3 million residential burglaries were either attempted or completed in 2003. Despite this significant number, the NCVS indicates that the number of burglaries has declined significantly during the past decade; burglary rates are down 49 percent since 1993. According to the NCVS, those most likely to be burglarized are relatively poor Latino and African American families (annual income under $7,500). Owner-occupied and single-family residences had lower burglary rates than renter-occupied and multiple-family dwellings.

Residential Burglary

Some burglars are crude thieves who will smash a window and enter a vacant home or structure with minimal preparation; others plan out a strategy. For example, experienced burglars learn to avoid areas of the city in which most residents are renters and not homeowners, reasoning that renters are less likely to be suitable targets than are more affluent homeowners.[68] Because it involves planning, risk, and skill, burglary has been a crime long associated with professional thieves who carefully learn their craft. For example, Francis Hoheimer, an experienced professional burglar, has described how he learned the "craft of burglary" from a fellow inmate, Oklahoma Smith, when the two were serving time in the Illinois State Penitentiary. Among Smith's recommendations are these:

> Never wear deodorant or shaving lotion; the strange scent might wake someone up. The more people there are in a house, the safer you are. If someone hears you moving around, they will think it's someone else. . . . If they call, answer in a muffled sleepy voice. . . . Never be afraid of dogs, they can sense fear. Most dogs are friendly, snap your finger, they come right to you.[69]

Despite his elaborate preparations, Hoheimer spent many years in confinement.

Burglars must "master" the skills of their "trade," learning to spot environmental cues "nonprofessionals" fail to notice.[70] For example, they must learn which targets contain valuables worth stealing and which are most likely to prove to be a dry hole. Research shows that burglary rates for student-occupied apartments is actually much lower than the rate for other residences in the same neighborhoods; burglars appear to have learned which apartments to avoid.[71] Experienced burglars are more willing to travel to find rich targets. They have access to transportation that enables them to select a wider variety of targets than younger, more inexperienced thieves.[72]

In an important book titled *Burglars on the Job,* Richard Wright and Scott Decker describe the working conditions of active burglars.[73] Most are motivated by the need for cash in order to get high; they want to enjoy the good life, "keeping the party going" without having to work. As Exhibit 11.4 shows, they approach their "job" in a rational workmanlike fashion, but their lives are controlled by their culture and environment. Unskilled and uneducated, urban burglars make the choices they do because there are few conventional opportunities for success.

Research also shows that gender plays an important role in shaping the lives and motivations of burglars. This is the topic of the Race, Culture, Gender, and Criminology feature.

EXHIBIT 11.4

Burglars on the Job

According to active burglars:

- Most avoid occupied residences, considering them high-risk targets.
- Most are not deterred by alarms and elaborate locks; in fact, these devices tell them there is something inside worth stealing.
- Some call occupants from a pay phone, and if the phone is still ringing when they arrive, they know no one is home.
- Once entering a residence, anxiety turns to calm as they first turn to the master bedroom for money and drugs. They also search kitchens believing that some people keep money in the mayonnaise jar!
- Most work in groups, one serving as a lookout while the other(s) ransacks the place.
- Some dispose of goods through a professional fence; others try to pawn the goods. Some exchange goods for drugs; some sell them to friends and relatives; and a few keep the stolen items for themselves, especially guns and jewelry.
- Many approach a target masquerading as workmen such as carpenters or house painters.
- Some stake out residences to learn occupants' routine.
- Tipsters help them select attractive targets.
- Drug dealers are favored targets because they tend to have a lot of cash and drugs, and victims are not going to call police!
- Targets are often acquaintances.

Source: Richard Wright and Scott Decker, *Burglars on the Job: Streetlife and Residential Break-Ins* (Boston: Northeastern University Press, 1994).

Commercial Burglary

Some burglars prefer to victimize commercial property rather than private homes. Of all business establishments, retail stores are burglars' favorite targets. They display merchandise so that burglars know exactly what to look for, where it can be found, and—because the prices are displayed—how much they can hope to gain in resale to a fence. Burglars can legitimately enter a retail store during business hours and gain knowledge about what the store contains and where it is stored; they can also check for security alarms and devices. Commercial burglars perceive retail establishments as quick sources of merchandise that can be easily sold.

Other commercial establishments such as service centers, warehouses, and factories are less attractive targets because it is more difficult to gain legitimate access to plan the theft. The burglar must use a great deal of guile to scope out these places, perhaps posing as a delivery person. In addition, the merchandise is more likely to be used, and it may be more difficult to fence at a premium price.

If burglars choose to attack factories, warehouses, or service centers, the most vulnerable properties are those

Are There Gender Differences in Burglary?

Does gender play a role in shaping burglary careers? Are there differences in the way professional male and female burglars approach their craft? Do gender roles influence the burglar lifestyle? To find out, Christopher Mullins and Richard Wright used interviews with eighteen active female burglars and thirty-six males, matched approximately for age. Their findings indicate that significant gender-based differences exist in the way males and females begin and end their offending careers and how they carry out their criminal tasks.

There were similarities in the way most offenders, male or female, were initiated into residential burglary. Both became involved via interaction in intimate groups, such as older friends, family members, or street associates. One told them:

> [M]e and my brother, we wanted, you know, he came and got me and say he know where a house at to break into. And, uhm, we go there and uh, we just do it . . . me and my brother, he and some more friends.

But there was one key difference between the male and female offenders: The men typically became involved in burglary with male peers; women more often were introduced to crime by their boyfriends. Males are more likely to bring their male peers and family members into their offending networks and resist working with women except their girlfriend or female relative. And when they do include women, they put them in a subservient role, such as a lookout.

Why do they get involved in a burglary career in the first place? Both males and females generally said they got involved in break-ins to finance a party lifestyle centered on drug use and to buy bling bling like designer clothing and jewelry. There were some differences: Males reportededly wanted money to pursue sexual conquests; female burglars were far more likely to say that they needed money to buy necessities for their children.

When asked what they were looking for in a prospective residential burglary target, the male and female offenders expressed similar preferences; both wanted to find a dwelling that was (a) unoccupied and (b) contained something of value. Both the men and the women wanted to know something about the people who lived in the residence, be familiar with their day-to-day routine, and to have an idea of the target's valuables. Male offenders used their legitimate jobs as home remodelers, cable television installers, or gardeners to scout potential burglary targets. Female burglars who lacked legitimate entry had to rely on information generated by the men in their immediate criminal social network. Some used sexual attraction to gain the victim's confidence and gather information.

Mullins and Wright also found that men preferred to commit residential burglaries by themselves, while women most often worked with others. Males seemed unwilling to trust accomplices and were also unwilling to share the proceeds. Females, on the other hand, reported that they lacked the knowledge or skills needed to break into a dwelling on their own and were therefore more willing to work with a team.

Finally, when asked what it would take to make them stop committing crime, both male and female offenders claimed that a good job that paid well and involved little or no disciplined subordination to authority would be required to get them to give up their careers in crime. Men also claimed they would probably give up burglary once they settled down and started a family. Because they were dependent on male help, female burglars needed to sever their relationships with criminally involved males in order to reduce their offending. Female burglars were also more sensitive than the males to shaming and ostracism at the hands of their relatives and might quit under family pressure.

Mullins and Wright found that residential burglary is a significantly gender-stratified offense; the processes of initiation, commission, and potential desistance are heavily structured by gender. Women have to negotiate the male-dominated world of burglary to accomplish their crimes. Gender, they find, plays a significant role in shaping opportunity (such as initiation) and the events leading up to residential burglaries (for example, information gathering), while playing a lesser but still important role in molding actual offense commission.

Critical Thinking

1. Do the gender differences in burglary reflect the gender differences found in other segments of society?

2. Do you think gender discrimination helps reduce the female crime rate? If gender equality were achieved, would differences in the crime rate narrow?

 InfoTrac College Edition Research

Use "burglary" and "burglars" in key word searches in InfoTrac College Edition.

Source: Christopher Mullins and Richard Wright, "Gender, Social Networks, and Residential Burglary," *Criminology* 41 (2003): 813–839.

located far from major thoroughfares and away from pedestrian traffic. Establishments located within three blocks of heavily traveled thoroughfares have been found to be less vulnerable to burglary than those located farther away; commercial establishments in wealthier communities have a higher probability of burglary.[74]

Though alarms have been found to be an effective deterrent to burglary, they are less effective in isolated areas because it takes police longer to respond than on more heavily patrolled thoroughfares, and an alarm is less likely to be heard by a pedestrian who would be able to call for help. Even in the most remote areas, however, burglars are wary of alarms and try to choose targets without elaborate or effective security systems. One study found that the probability of burglary of non-alarmed properties is 4.57 times higher than that of similar property with alarms.[75]

Careers in Burglary

Some criminals make burglary their career and continually develop new and specialized skills to aid their profession. Neal Shover has studied the careers of professional burglars and has uncovered the existence of a particularly successful type—the **good burglar**.[76] Professional burglars use this title to characterize colleagues who have distinguished themselves as burglars. Characteristics of the good burglar include:

- Technical competence
- Maintenance of personal integrity
- Specialization in burglary
- Financial success
- The ability to avoid prison sentences

To receive recognition as good burglars, Shover found that novices must develop four key requirements of the trade.

First, they must learn the many skills needed to commit lucrative burglaries. This process may include learning techniques such as how to gain entry into homes and apartment houses; how to select targets with high potential payoffs; how to choose items with a high resale value; how to open safes properly, without damaging their contents; and how to use the proper equipment, including cutting torches, electric saws, explosives, and metal bars.

Second, the good burglar must be able to team up to form a criminal gang. Choosing trustworthy companions is essential if the obstacles to completing a successful job—police, alarms, and secure safes—are to be overcome.

Third, the good burglar must have inside information. Without knowledge of what awaits them inside, burglars can spend a tremendous amount of time and effort on empty safes and jewelry boxes.

Finally, the good burglar must cultivate fences or buyers for stolen wares. Once the burglar gains access to people who buy and sell stolen goods, he or she must also learn how to successfully sell these goods for a reasonable profit. Evidence of these skills was discovered in a study of more than 200 career burglars in Australia. Burglars reported that they had developed a number of relatively safe methods for disposing of their loot. Some traded stolen goods directly for drugs; others used fences, legitimate businesses, pawnbrokers, and secondhand dealers as trading partners. Surprisingly, many sold their illegal gains to family or friends. Burglars report that disposing of stolen goods was actually low risk and more efficient than expected. One reason was that in many cases fences and shady businesspeople put in a request for particular items, and the readymade market allowed the stolen merchandise to be disposed of quickly, often in less than 1 hour. Though the typical markdown was 67 to 75 percent of the price of the goods, most reported that they could still earn a good living, averaging AUS$2,000 per week (about $1,000 in U.S. dollars). Those who benefited most from these transactions were the receivers of stolen property, who make considerable profits and are unlikely to be caught.[77]

According to Shover, a person becomes a good burglar by learning the techniques of the trade from older, more experienced burglars. During this process, the older burglar teaches the novice how to handle such requirements as dealing with defense attorneys, bail bond agents, and other agents of the justice system. Apprentices must be known to have the appropriate character before they are taken under the wing of the old pro. Usually, the opportunity to learn burglary comes as a reward for being a highly respected juvenile gang member; from knowing someone in the neighborhood who has made a living at burglary; or, more often, from having built a reputation for being solid while serving time in prison. Consequently, the opportunity to become a good burglar is not open to everyone.

I I I I I I I CONNECTIONS I I I I I I I

Shover finds that the process of becoming a professional burglar is similar to the process described in Sutherland's theory of Differential Association. You can read more about this theory in Chapter 7.

THE BURGLARY "CAREER LADDER" Paul Cromwell, James Olson, and D'Aunn Wester Avary interviewed thirty active burglars in Texas and found that burglars go through stages of career development. They begin as young *novices* who learn the trade from older more experienced burglars, frequently siblings or relatives. Novices will continue to get this tutoring as long as they can develop their own markets (fences) for stolen goods. After their education is over, novices enter the *journeyman* stage, characterized by forays in search of lucrative targets and careful planning. At this point, they develop reputations as experienced reliable criminals. Finally, they become *professional* burglars when they have developed advanced skills and organizational abilities that give them the highest esteem among their peers.

The Texas burglars also displayed evidence of rational decision making. Most seemed to carefully evaluate potential costs and benefits before deciding to commit crime. There is evidence that burglars follow this pattern in their choice of burglary sites. Burglars show a preference for corner houses because they are easily observed and offer the maximum number of escape routes.[78] They look for houses that show evidence of long-term care and wealth. Though people may erect fences and other barriers to deter burglars, these devices may actually attract crime because they are viewed as protecting something worth stealing: If there is nothing valuable inside, why go through so much trouble to secure the premises?[79]

Cromwell, Olson, and Avary also found that many burglars had serious drug habits and that their criminal activity was, in part, aimed at supporting their substance abuse.

REPEAT BURGLARY To what extent do burglars strike the same victim more than once? Research suggests that burglars may in fact return to the scene of the crime to repeat their offenses. One reason is that many burgled items are indispensable (for example, televisions and VCRs); therefore, it is safe to assume that they will quickly be replaced.[80] Research shows that some burglars repeat their acts to steal these replacement goods.[81] Graham Farrell, Coretta Phillips, and Ken Pease have articulated why burglars would most likely try to hit the same target more than once:

- It takes less effort to burgle a home or apartment known to be a suitable target than an unknown or unsuitable one.

- The burglar is already aware of the target's layout.

- The ease of entry of the target has probably not changed, and escape routes are known.

- The lack of protective measures and the absence of nosy and intrusive neighbors that made the first burglary a success have probably not changed.

- Goods have been observed that could not be taken out the first time.[82]

The repeat burglary phenomenon should mean that homes in close proximity to a burgled dwelling have an increased burglary risk, especially if they are similar in structure to the initial target. When this hypothesis was recently tested by Michael Townsley and his colleagues in Brisbane, Australia, they found that the lack of diversity in the physical construction and general appearance of dwellings in a neighborhood, helped reduce repeat victimization. Townsley reasons that housing diversity allows offenders a choice of targets, and favored targets will be "revisited" by burglars. If houses are identical, there is no motive for an offender to favor one property over another, and therefore the risk of repeat victimization is limited.[83]

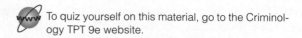

To quiz yourself on this material, go to the Criminology TPT 9e website.

|||||||| CONNECTIONS ||||||||

In Chapter 3, repeat victimization was discussed. As you may recall, it is common for particular people and places to be the targets of numerous predatory crimes.

ARSON

Arson is the willful and malicious burning of a home, public building, vehicle, or commercial building. About 71,000 known arsons were recorded in 2003. Many of these fires are set by adolescents, causing at least 300 deaths, 2,000 injuries, and more than $300 million in damage; juveniles comprise about 40 percent of all people arrested for arson annually.[84] Arson arrests declined 7 percent between 2003 and 2004.

Use "arson" as a key word in InfoTrac College Edition to learn more about the nature and extent of fire setting.

Arson is not just an American phenomenon. According to the Arson Prevention Bureau, a British group that coordinates a national campaign to reduce arson, every week in England:

- There are 2,100 arson attacks.

- One or two people die in arson attacks.

- Fifty-five people are injured.

- Four churches or places of worship are damaged or destroyed.

- Twenty schools are damaged or destroyed by arson.

- Sixty million dollars of damage and costs result from arson.[85]

There are several motives for arson. Adult arsonists may be motivated by severe emotional turmoil. Some psychologists view fire starting as a function of a disturbed personality. Arson, therefore, should be viewed as a mental health problem and not a criminal act.[86] It is alleged that arsonists often experience sexual pleasure from starting fires and then observing their destructive effects. Although some arsonists may be aroused sexually by their activities, there is little evidence that most arsonists are psychosexually motivated.[87] It is equally likely that fires are started by angry people looking for revenge against property owners or by teenagers out to vandalize property. Research on the background characteristics

© Getty Images

There are numerous motivations for arson. Some fires are set by terrorist groups in an effort to undermine their opponents. The Earth Liberation Front (ELF) set four fires at different new home construction sites around the Carmel Valley section of San Diego, California, in September 2003. They also took responsibility for a $50 million fire on August 3, 2003 that destroyed an apartment complex under construction in University City in the San Diego area. The activities of environmental terrorist groups like the ELF were also discussed in Chapter 10.

of juvenile fire setters shows that their acts are often associated with antisocial behavior and psychopathology.[88] These findings support the claim that arson should be viewed as a mental health problem, not a criminal act, and that it should be treated with counseling and other therapeutic measures rather than severe punishments.[89]

Juveniles, the most prolific fire starters, may get involved in arson for a variety of reasons as they mature. Juvenile fire setting has long been associated with conduct problems, such as disobedience and aggressiveness, anger, hostility, and resentment over parental rejection. The Criminological Enterprise feature discusses the topic of juvenile fire setting.

During the past decade, hundreds of jurisdictions across the nation have established programs to address the growing problem of juvenile fire setting. Housed primarily within the fire service, these programs are designed to identify, evaluate, and treat juvenile fire setters to prevent the recurrence of fire-setting behaviors. A promising approach is the FireSafe Families effort in Rhode Island, which combines a training curriculum for fire-safety educators, a training program for community professionals to identify potential behavior that may lead to arson and a cognitive-behavioral therapy (CBT) program to treat children and their families who are at risk to becoming juvenile fire starters.[90]

Other arsons are set by professional arsonists who engage in **arson for profit.** People looking to collect insurance money, but who are afraid or unable to set the fire themselves, hire professional arsonists. These professionals have acquired the skills to set fires yet make the cause seem accidental (for example, like an electrical short). Another form is **arson fraud,** which involves a business owner burning his or her property, or hiring someone to do it, to escape financial problems.[91] Over the years, investigators have found that businesspeople are willing to become involved in arson to

collect fire insurance or for various other reasons, including but not limited to these:

- Obtaining money during a period of financial crisis

- Getting rid of outdated or slow-moving inventory

- Destroying outmoded machines and technology

- Paying off legal and illegal debt

- Relocating or remodeling a business; for example, when a theme restaurant has not been accepted by customers

- Taking advantage of government funds available for redevelopment

- Applying for government building money, pocketing it without making repairs, and then claiming that fire destroyed the "rehabilitated" building

- Planning bankruptcies to eliminate debts, after the merchandise supposedly destroyed was secretly sold before the fire

- Eliminating business competition by burning out rivals

- Employing extortion schemes that demand that victims pay up or the rest of their holdings will be burned

- Solving labor–management problems; arson may be committed by a disgruntled employee

- Concealing another crime, such as embezzlement

Some recent technological advances may help prove that many alleged arsons were actually accidental fires. There is now evidence of a fire effect called **flashover.** During the course of an ordinary fire, heat and gas at the ceiling of a room can reach 2,000 degrees. This causes clothes and

The Criminological Enterprise

IIIIIIIIIIIIIIIIIIIIIIIIIIIIIIIIIIIIIII

What Motivates Juvenile Fire Setters?

What motivates young people to commit arson? According to research by sociologist Wayne Wooden, juvenile arsonists can be classified in one of four categories:

■ The "playing with matches" fire setter: This is the youngest fire starter, usually between the ages of 4 and 9, who sets fires because parents are careless with matches and lighters. Proper instruction on fire safety can help prevent fires set by these young children.

■ The "crying for help" fire setter: This type of fire setter is a 7- to 13-year-old who turns to fire to reduce stress. The source of the stress is family conflict, divorce, death, or abuse. These youngsters have difficulty expressing their feelings of sorrow, rage, or anger and turn to fire as a means of relieving stress or getting back at their antagonists.

■ The "delinquent" fire setter: Some youth set fires to school property or surrounding areas to retaliate for some slight experienced at school. These kids may break into the school to vandalize property with friends and later set a fire to cover up their activities.

■ The "severely disturbed" fire setter: This youngster is obsessed with

	Group 1 Under 7 Years	Group 2 8–12 Years	Group 3 13–18 Years
Reason(s) for fire-setting behavior	Accident or curiosity	Curiosity or psychological conflict	History of fire-starting behavior, or psychological conflict, or intentional criminal behavior

TABLE 11-A
Fire-Setting Groups

fires and often dreams about them in "vibrant colors." This is the most disturbed type of juvenile fire setter and the one most likely to set numerous fires with the potential for death and damage.

Another research effort, by Eileen M. Garry, concluded that juvenile fire setters fall into three general groups. The first is made up of children under 7 years of age. Generally, fires started by these children are the result of accidents or curiosity. In the second group of fire setters are children ranging in age from 8 to 12. Although the fire setting of some of these children is motivated by curiosity or experimentation, a greater proportion of their fire setting represents underlying psychosocial conflicts. The third group comprises adolescents between the ages of 13 and 18. These youth tend to have a long history of undetected fire play and fire-starting behavior. Their current fire-setting episodes are usually either the result of psychosocial conflict and turmoil or intentional criminal behavior. This behavior is summarized in Table 11-A.

Critical Thinking

1. Have you ever been fascinated with fire? Did this result in experimenting with matches? If not, what stopped you from acting on your impulses?

2. If you knew of someone who frequently tampered with matches to the point of concern, how would you handle this situation?

 InfoTrac College Edition Research

To read more on the subject of arson, check out this article: Herschel Prins, "Arson: A Review of the Psychiatric Literature," *British Journal of Criminology* 36 (winter 1996): 162–163.

Sources: Wayne Wooden, "Juvenile Firesetters in Cross-Cultural Perspective: How Should Society Respond?" in *Official Responses to Problem Juveniles: Some International Reflections,* ed. James Hackler (Onati, Spain: Onati Publications, 1991), pp. 339–348; Eileen M. Garry, *Juvenile Firesetting and Arson* (Washington, DC: Office of Juvenile Justice and Delinquency Prevention, 1997).

---

furniture to burst into flame, duplicating the effects of arsonists' gasoline or explosives. It is possible that many suspected arsons are actually the result of flashover.[92]

 To quiz yourself on this material, go to the Criminology TPT 9e website.

The **Bureau of Alcohol, Tobacco, and Firearms** is the federal agency that has jurisdiction over violations of the federal law involving arson. You may go to their home page at http://www.atf.treas.gov/. For an up-to-date list of web links, go to http://cj.wadsworth.com/siegel _crimtpt9e.

SUMMARY

- Theft offenses are common throughout recorded history. During the Middle Ages, poachers stole game, smugglers avoided taxes, and thieves worked as pickpockets and forgers.

- Economic crimes are designed to financially reward the offender. Opportunistic amateurs commit the majority of economic crimes. Amateurs steal because of situational inducements.

- Economic crime has also attracted professional criminals. Professionals earn most of their income from crime, view themselves as criminals, and possess skills that aid them in their law-breaking behavior. A good example of the professional criminal is the fence who buys and sells stolen merchandise.

- Common theft offenses include larceny, fraud, and embezzlement. These are common-law crimes, originally defined by English judges.

- Larceny involves taking the legal possessions of another. Petty larceny is typically theft of amounts under $100; grand larceny usually refers to amounts over $100. Larceny is the most common theft crime and involves such activities as shoplifting, passing bad checks, and stealing or illegally using credit cards.

- Some shoplifters are amateurs who steal on the spur of the moment, while others are professionals who use sophisticated techniques to help them avoid detection.

- The crime of false pretenses, or fraud, is similar to larceny in that it involves the theft of goods or money; it differs in that the criminal tricks victims into voluntarily giving up their possessions.

- Embezzlement involves people taking something that was temporarily entrusted to them, such as bank tellers taking money out of the cash drawer and keeping it for themselves.

- Auto theft usually involves amateur joyriders who borrow cars for short-term transportation and professional auto thieves who steal cars often to sell off their parts, which are highly valuable.

- Burglary, a more serious theft offense, was defined in common law as the "breaking and entering of a dwelling house of another in the nighttime with the intent to commit a felony within." This definition has also evolved over time. Today most states have modified their definitions of burglary to include theft from any structure at any time of day.

- Because burglary involves planning and risk, it attracts professional thieves. The most competent have technical ability and personal integrity, specialize in burglary, are financially successful, and avoid prison sentences.

- Professional burglars are able to size up the value of a particular crime and balance it out with the perceived risks. Many have undergone training in the company of older, more experienced burglars. They have learned the techniques to make them good burglars.

- Arson is another serious property crime. Although most arsonists are teenage vandals, there are professional arsonists who specialize in burning commercial buildings for profit.

Thinking Like a Criminologist

You are approached by the local police chief who is quite concerned about high burglary rates in some areas of the city. She is a former student of yours and well aware of recent developments in criminological theory. The chief is a strong advocate of rational choice theory and has already instituted a number of programs based on a deterrence/situational crime prevention model of control. The existing police initiatives include these programs:

- The police offer target hardening measures to repeat victims. They install high-tech security equipment in their homes so that the homes can be monitored on a 24-hour basis. The police plan an advertising campaign to alert would-be offenders that they are on watch at prior target residences.

- A new police initiative identifies repeat burglars in the area and provides intervention designed to supply them with legitimate economic opportunities to reduce their criminal motivation.

■ A new school-based program designed to reduce criminal motivation seeks to raise young people's awareness of the dangers of burglary and how it can result in a long prison sentence.

■ The police have developed a series of environmental improvements in the target area with a view to minimizing burglary opportunities. These include improved visibility, better access control, and lighting in areas that have relatively high burglary rates. They have also instituted high-visibility police patrols in these areas to deter criminals from committing crimes here.

■ A Burglary Control Model House, fitted with low-cost methods of security, such as strengthened door/window frames, bolts, locks, and so on, has been built and will be advertised to encourage residents to help themselves.

The chief has asked you to look over these initiatives and comment on their anticipated effectiveness. She wants to know whether there are any pitfalls and whether you can suggest other policy initiatives that might prove effective in reducing the opportunity to commit burglary and deter potential burglars.

Doing Research on the Web

Before you answer the questions above, you may want to see what the Metropolitan Police Service, by far the largest of the police services that operate in greater London, suggest. Go to http://www .met.police.uk/crimeprevention/ burglary.htm.

Likewise, the Burglary Prevention Council offers advice at http://www .burglaryprevention.org/10tips.htm.

To get some advice on changing the environment to prevent burglary, go to http://www.longbeach.gov/civica/ filebank/blobdload.asp?BlobID=4467.

KEY TERMS

fence (368)
street crime (368)
economic crime (368)
skilled thieves (369)
flash houses (369)
smugglers (369)
poachers (369)
occasional criminals (369)
professional criminals (369)
situational inducement (369)
professional fence (371)
constructive possession (374)

petit (petty) larceny (374)
grand larceny (374)
shoplifting (375)
boosters (375)
heels (375)
snitches (375)
target removal strategies (376)
target hardening strategies (376)
naive check forgers (376)
closure (376)
systematic forgers (376)
carjacking (380)

false pretenses (380)
fraud (380)
confidence games (381)
mark (381)
pigeon drop (381)
embezzlement (382)
good burglar (385)
arson for profit (387)
arson fraud (387)
flashover (387)

CRITICAL THINKING QUESTIONS

1. Differentiate between an occasional and a professional criminal. Which one would be more likely to resort to violence? Which one would be more easily deterred?

2. What crime occurs when a person who owns an antique store sells a client an "original" Tiffany lamp that the person knows is a fake? Would it still be a crime if the person selling the lamp was not aware that it was a fake? As an antique dealer, should the seller have a duty to determine the authenticity of the products he or she sells?

3. What are the characteristics of good burglars? Can you compare their career path to any other professionals, such as doctors or lawyers? Which theory of criminal behavior best predicts the development of the good burglar?

4. You have been the victim of repeat burglaries. What could you do to reduce the chances of future victimization? (Hint: buying a gun is not an option!)

NOTES

1. Federal Bureau of Investigation, Press Release, "The Crook Who Stole Christmas: Florida Man Sentenced for Scamming Children with Holiday Pageant Scheme." December 5, 2005. http://www.fbi.gov/page2/dec05/holidayscam120505.htm.

2. Andrew McCall, *The Medieval Underworld* (London: Hamish Hamilton, 1979), p. 86.

3. Ibid., p. 104.

4. J. J. Tobias, *Crime and Police in England, 1700–1900* (London: Gill and Macmillan, 1979).

5. Ibid., p. 9.

6. Marilyn Walsh, *The Fence* (Westport, CT: Greenwood Press, 1977), pp. 18–25.

7. John Hepburn, "Occasional Criminals," in *Major Forms of Crime,* ed. Robert Meier (Beverly Hills: Sage, 1984), pp. 73–94.

8. James Inciardi, "Professional Crime," in *Major Forms of Crime,* p. 223.

9. Harry King and William Chambliss, *Box Man: A Professional Thief's Journal* (New York: Harper & Row, 1972), p. 24.

10. Edwin Sutherland, "White-Collar Criminality," *American Sociological Review* 5 (1940): 2–10.

11. Gilbert Geis, "Avocational Crime," in *Handbook of Criminology,* ed. D. Glazer (Chicago: Rand McNally, 1974), p. 284.

12. Edwin Sutherland and Chic Conwell, *The Professional Thief* (Chicago: University of Chicago Press, 1937).

13. Ibid., pp. 197–198.

14. Ibid., p. 212.

15. See, for example, Edwin Lemert, "The Behavior of the Systematic Check Forger," *Social Problems* 6 (1958): 141–148.

16. Cited in Walsh, *The Fence,* p. 1.

17. Carl Klockars, *The Professional Fence* (New York: Free Press, 1976); Darrell Steffensmeier, *The Fence: In the Shadow of Two Worlds* (Totowa, NJ: Rowman and Littlefield, 1986); Walsh, *The Fence,* pp. 25–28.

18. Simon Fass and Janice Francis, "Where Have All the Hot Goods Gone? The Role of Pawnshops," *Journal of Research in Crime and Delinquency* 41 (2004): 156–179.

19. Walsh, *The Fence,* p. 34.

20. Paul Cromwell, James Olson, and D'Aunn Avary, "Who Buys Stolen Property? A New Look at Criminal Receiving," *Journal of Crime and Justice* 16 (1993): 75–95.

21. This section depends heavily on a classic book, Wayne La Fave and Austin Scott, *Handbook on Criminal Law* (St. Paul, MN: West Publishing, 1972).

22. Ibid., p. 622.

23. General Laws of Massachusetts, Part IV, Crimes, Punishments, and Proceedings in Criminal Cases, Title I, Crimes and Punishments, Chapter 266. Crimes against Property, Chapter 266: Section 30 Larceny; General Provisions and Penalties: http://www.mass.gov/legis/laws/mgl/266-30.htm.

24. John Worrall, "The Effect of Three-Strikes Legislation on Serious Crime in California," *Journal of Criminal Justice* 32 (2004): 283–296.

25. FBI, *Crime in the United States, 2003* (Washington, DC: U.S. Government Printing Office, 2004). All official crime data used in this chapter comes from this source

26. Margaret Loftus, "Gone: One TV," *U.S. News & World Report,* 14 July 1997, p. 61.

27. "Hot Cars: Parts Crooks Love Best," *Business Week* (15 September 2003): 104.

28. Timothy W. Maier, "Uncle Sam Gets Rolled," *Insight on the News,* 10 March 1997, p. 13.

29. Jill Jordan Siedfer, "To Catch a Thief, Try This: Peddling High-Tech Solutions to Shoplifting," *U.S. News & World Report* (23 September 1996): 71.

30. David Farrington, "Measuring, Explaining and Preventing Shoplifting: A Review of British Research," *Security Journal* 12 (1999): 9–27.

31. Mary Owen Cameron, *The Booster and the Snitch* (New York: Free Press, 1964).

32. Ibid., p. 57.

33. Lawrence Cohen and Rodney Stark, "Discriminatory Labeling and the Five–Finger Discount: An Empirical Analysis of Differential Shoplifting Dispositions," *Journal of Research on Crime and Delinquency* 11 (1974): 25–35.

34. Lloyd Klemke, "Does Apprehension for Shoplifting Amplify or Terminate Shoplifting Activity?" *Law and Society Review* 12 (1978): 390–403.

35. Erhard Blankenburg, "The Selectivity of Legal Sanctions: An Empirical Investigation of Shoplifting," *Law and Society Review* 11 (1976): 109–129.

36. Michael Hindelang, "Decisions of Shoplifting Victims to Invoke the Criminal Justice Process," *Social Problems* 21 (1974): 580–595.

37. George Keckeisen, *Retail Security versus the Shoplifter* (Springfield, IL: Charles C Thomas, 1993), pp. 31–32.

38. Siedfer, "To Catch a Thief, Try This," p. 71.

39. Thomas Kelley, Daniel Kennedy, and Robert Homant, "Evaluation of an Individualized Treatment Program for Adolescent Shoplifters," *Adolescence* 38 (2003): 725–733.

40. Edwin Lemert, "An Isolation and Closure Theory of Naive Check Forgery," *Journal of Criminal Law, Criminology and Police Science* 44 (1953): 297–298.

41. La Fave and Scott, *Handbook on Criminal Law*, p. 672.

42. Paul Beckett and Jathon Sapsford, "As Credit-Card Theft Grows, a Tussle over Paying to Stop It," *Wall Street Journal*, 1 May 2003, p. A1.

43. Peter Wayner, "Bogus Web Sites Troll for Credit Card Numbers," *New York Times*, 12 February 1997, p. A18.

44. Charles McCaghy, Peggy Giordano, and Trudy Knicely Henson, "Auto Theft," *Criminology* 15 (1977): 367–381.

45. Donald Gibbons, *Society, Crime and Criminal Careers* (Englewood Cliffs, NJ: Prentice-Hall, 1977), p. 310.

46. Kim Hazelbaker, "Insurance Industry Analyses and the Prevention of Motor Vehicle Theft," in *Business and Crime Prevention*, eds. Marcus Felson and Ronald Clarke (Monsey, NY: Criminal Justice Press, 1997), pp. 283–293.

47. Heith Copes, "Streetlife and the Rewards of Auto Theft," *Deviant Behavior* 24 (2003): 309–333.

48. National Insurance Crime Bureau, "2002 Top 25 Make and Model Thefts." http://www.nicb.org/public/newsroom/whereismycar/top25makemodel.cfm. Accessed August 11, 2004.

49. Hazelbaker, "Insurance Industry Analyses and the Prevention of Motor Vehicle Theft," p. 287.

50. Michael Rand, *Carjacking* (Washington, DC: Bureau of Justice Statistics, 1994), p. 1.

51. Patsy Klaus, *Carjacking, 1993–2002* (Washington, DC: Bureau of Justice Statistics, 2004).

52. Bruce Jacobs, Volkan Topalli, and Richard Wright, "Carjacking, Streetlife, and Offender Motivation," *British Journal of Criminology* 43 (2003): 673–688.

53. Klaus, *Carjacking, 1993–2002*.

54. Ronald Clarke and Patricia Harris, "Auto Theft and Its Prevention," in *Crime and Justice: An Annual Review*, eds. N. Morris and M. Tonry (Chicago: Chicago University Press, 1992).

55. Ian Ayres and Steven D. Levitt, "Measuring Positive Externalities from Unobservable Victim Precaution: An Empirical Analysis of Lojack," *Quarterly Journal of Economics* 113 (1998): 43–78.

56. Hazelbaker, "Insurance Industry Analyses and the Prevention of Motor Vehicle Theft," p. 289.

57. La Fave and Scott, *Handbook on Criminal Law*, p. 655.

58. 30 Geo. III, C. 24 (1975).

59. Benjamin Weiser, "4-Year Sentence for Mastermind of Scheme to Cheat on Graduate School Tests," *New York Times*, 3 October 1998, p. 8.

60. As described in Charles McCaghy, *Deviant Behavior* (New York: Macmillan, 1976), pp. 230–231.

61. Susan Gembrowski and Tim Dahlberg, "Over 100 Here Indicted after Telemarketing Fraud Probe around the U.S.," *San Diego Daily Transcript* [Online], 8 December 1995. http://www.sddt.com/files/library/95headlines/DN95_12_08/DN95_12_08_02.html.

62. Jerome Hall, *Theft, Law and Society* (Indianapolis: Bobbs-Merrill, 1952), p. 36.

63. La Fave and Scott, *Handbook on Criminal Law*, p. 644.

64. Ibid., p. 649.

65. Dawit Kiros Fantaye, "Fighting Corruption and Embezzlement in Third World Countries," *Journal of Criminal Law* 68 (April 2004): 170–177.

66. La Fave and Scott, *Handbook on Criminal Law*, p. 708.

67. E. Blackstone, *Commentaries on the Laws of England* (London: 1769), p. 224.

68. Elizabeth Groff and Nancy La Vigne, "Mapping an Opportunity Surface of Residential Burglary," *Journal of Research in Crime and Delinquency* 38 (2001): 257–278.

69. Frank Hoheimer, *The Home Invaders: Confessions of a Cat Burglar* (Chicago: Chicago Review, 1975).

70. Richard Wright, Robert Logie, and Scott Decker, "Criminal Expertise and Offender Decision Making: An Experimental Study of the Target Selection Process in Residential Burglary," *Journal of Research in Crime and Delinquency* 32 (1995): 39–53.

71. Matthew Robinson, "Accessible Targets, but Not Advisable Ones: The Role of 'Accessibility' in Student Apartment Burglary," *Journal of Security Administration* 21 (1998): 28–44.

72. Brent Snook, "Individual Differences in Distance Travelled by Serial Burglars,". *Journal of Investigative Psychology & Offender Profiling* 1 (2004): 53–66.

73. Richard Wright and Scott Decker, *Burglars on the Job: Streetlife and Residential Break-Ins* (Boston: Northeastern University Press, 1994).

74. Simon Hakim and Yochanan Shachmurove, "Spatial and Temporal Patterns of Commercial Burglaries," *American Journal of Economics and Sociology* 55 (1996): 443–457.

75. Ibid., pp. 443–456.

76. See, generally, Neal Shover, "Structures and Careers in Burglary," *Journal of Criminal Law, Criminology and Police Science* 63 (1972): 540–549.

77. Richard Stevenson, Lubica Forsythe, and Don Weatherburn, "The Stolen Goods Market in New South Wales, Australia: An Analysis of Disposal Avenues and Tactics," *British Journal of Criminology* 41 (winter 2001): 101–118.

78. Paul Cromwell, James Olson, and D'Aunn Wester Avary, *Breaking and Entering: An Ethnographic Analysis of Burglary* (Newbury Park, CA: Sage, 1991), pp. 48–51.

79. See, M. Taylor and C. Nee, "The Role of Cues in Simulated Residential Burglary: A Preliminary Investigation," *British Journal of Criminology* 28 (1988): 398–401; Julia MacDonald and Robert Gifford, "Territorial Cues and Defensible Space Theory: The Burglar's Point of

View," *Journal of Environmental Psychology* 9 (1989): 193–205.

80. Roger Litton, "Crime Prevention and the Insurance Industry," in *Business and Crime Prevention,* p. 162.

81. "Explaining Repeat Residential Burglaries: An Analysis of Property Stolen," Ronald Clarke, Elizabeth Perkins, and Donald Smith, in *Repeat Victimization,* Crime Prevention Studies, vol. 12, eds. Graham Farrell and Ken Pease (Monsey, NY: Criminal Justice Press, 2001): 119–132.

82. Graham Farrell, Coretta Phillips, and Ken Pease, "Like Taking Candy, Why Does Repeat Victimization Occur?" *British Journal of Criminology* 35 (1995): 384–399, at 391.

83. Michael Townsley, Ross Homel, and Janet Chaseling, "Infectious Burglaries," *British Journal of Criminology* 43 (2003): 615–634.

84. Jeffrey Zaslow, "Dangerous Games— Medical Mystery: Why Some Children Keep Setting Fires—Without Consensus on Cure, Groups Try Safety Lessons, Therapy and Scare Tactics—Sleeping Mom's Singed Hair," *Wall Street Journal,* 27 June 2003, p. A1.

85. Arson Prevention Bureau of Justice, key facts. http://www.arsonprevention-bureau.org.uk/News/. Accessed October 15, 2003.

86. Nancy Webb, George Sakheim, Luz Towns-Miranda, and Charles Wagner, "Collaborative Treatment of Juvenile Firestarters: Assessment and Outreach," *American Journal of Orthopsychiatry* 60 (1990): 305–310.

87. Vernon Quinsey, Terry Chaplin, and Douglas Unfold, "Arsonists and Sexual Arousal to Fire Setting: Correlations Unsupported," *Journal of Behavior Therapy and Experimental Psychiatry* 20 (1989): 203–209.

88. Pekka Santtila, Helina Haikkanen, Laurence Alison, Laurence Whyte, and Carrie Whyte, "Juvenile Firesetters: Crime Scene Actions and Offender Characteristics," *Legal and Criminological Psychology* 8 (2003): 1–20.

89. John Taylor, Ian Thorne, Alison Robertson, and Ginny Avery, "Evaluation of a Group Intervention for Convicted Arsonists with Mild and Borderline Intellectual Disabilities." *Criminal Behaviour and Mental Health* 12 (2002): 282–294.

90. Scott Turner, "Funding Sparks Effort to Cut Juvenile Arson Rate," *George Street Journal* 27 (31 January 2003): 1. http://www.brown.edu/Administration/George_Street_Journal/vol27/27GSJ16f.html.

91. Leigh Edward Somers, *Economic Crimes* (New York: Clark Boardman, 1984), pp. 158–168.

92. Michael Rogers, "The Fire Next Time," *Newsweek* (26 November 1990): 63.

CHAPTER 12

Chip East / Reuters / Landov

On October 15, 2002, Dr. Samuel Waksal, the founder of the biotech company ImClone Systems, pled guilty to charges of securities fraud, perjury, and obstruction of justice. The charges were a result of an investigation into the dumping of ImClone stock by Waksal and his friends and family shortly before the company announced that its application for approval of a cancer drug had been rejected by the Food and Drug Administration. The fraud charge involved, among other acts, the sale of nearly 40,000 ImClone shares by Waksal's daughter Aliza, whom he called the day before the failure was made public and told to sell all her stock so that she would have cash to buy an apartment. "I have made terrible mistakes," Waksal, 55, told reporters after his courtroom appearance. "I deeply regret what has happened. I was wrong."[1] Ironically, in June 2003, clinical trials of ImClone drug Erbitux proved positive, and the stock boomed at about the same time Waksal was sentenced to 7 years in prison.

Another player in the ImClone case was domestic guru Martha Stewart, who dumped her shares just prior to the negative announcement. Stewart's suspicious stock sales quickly made her the target of a government probe. She was never actually accused of insider trading—the more serious charge of selling the ImClone stock based on privileged knowledge not available to the general public. Instead, Stewart was convicted of lying to the government when she claimed that she had a prior agreement with her stockbroker to sell ImClone stock at a certain price. Stewart was also convicted of altering a telephone log about a call from the broker before changing it back. People wondered how someone as wealthy and savvy as Stewart could get herself sent to prison for involvement in a legally questionable scheme. On March 4, 2005, Stewart was released from a federal women's prison in Alderson, West Virginia, after serving 5 months; she returned to her estate in Katonah, New York, where she finished out the rest of her sentence—5 months under house arrest.

ENTERPRISE CRIME: WHITE-COLLAR AND ORGANIZED CRIME

CHAPTER OBJECTIVES

1. Understand the concept of enterprise crime
2. Be familiar with the various types of white-collar crime
3. Be familiar with the various types of corporate crime
4. Recognize the extent and various causes of white-collar crime
5. Be able to discuss the different approaches to combating white-collar crime
6. List the different types of illegal behavior engaged in by organized crime figures
7. Describe the evolution of organized crime
8. Explain how the government is fighting organized crime

ENTERPRISE CRIME

It has become routine in our free enterprise, global economy for people such as Waksal and Stewart to use illegal tactics to make profit. We refer here to these crimes of the marketplace as **enterprise crime**.

In this chapter we divide these crimes of illicit entrepreneurship into two distinct categories: white-collar crime and organized crime. **White-collar crime** involves illegal activities of people and institutions whose acknowledged purpose is profit through legitimate business transactions. **Organized crime** involves illegal activities of people and organizations whose acknowledged purpose is profit through illegitimate business enterprise.

Crimes of Business Enterprise

White-collar crime and organized crime are linked here because in each category offenders twist the legal rules of commercial enterprise for criminal purposes. These crimes often overlap. Organized criminals may engage in ongoing fraud schemes and then seek legitimate enterprises to launder money, diversify their sources of income, increase their power and influence, and gain and enhance respectability.[2] Otherwise legitimate businesspeople may turn to organized criminals to help them with economic problems (such as breaking up a strike or dumping hazardous waste products), stifle or threaten competition, and increase their influence.[3] Whereas some corporate executives cheat to improve their company's position in the business world, others are motivated purely for personal gain, acting more like organized criminals than indiscreet businesspeople.[4]

These organizational crimes taint and corrupt the free market system. They mix and match illegal and legal methods and legal and illegal products in all phases of commercial activity. Organized criminals often use illegal marketing techniques (threat, extortion, and smuggling) to distribute otherwise legal products and services (lending money, union activities, selling securities); they also engage in the distribution of products and services (drugs, sex, gambling, and prostitution) that have been outlawed. White-collar criminals use illegal business practices (embezzlement, price fixing, bribery, and so on) to merchandise what are normally legitimate commercial products (securities, medical care, online auctions).[5]

Surprisingly, enterprise crime can involve violence. Although the use of force and coercion by organized crime members has been popularized in the media and therefore comes as no shock, that white-collar criminals may inflict pain and suffering seems more astonishing. Yet experts claim that more than 200,000 occupational deaths occur each year and that "corporate violence" annually kills and injures more people than all street crimes combined.[6]

WHITE-COLLAR CRIME

In the late 1930s, the distinguished criminologist Edwin Sutherland first used the phrase "white-collar crime" to describe the criminal activities of the rich and powerful. He defined white-collar crime as "a crime committed by a person of respectability and high social status in the course of his occupation."[7] As Sutherland saw it, white-collar crime involved conspiracies by members of the wealthy classes to use their position in commerce and industry for personal gain without regard to the law. Often these actions were handled by civil courts because injured parties were more concerned with recovering their losses than with seeing the offenders punished criminally. Consequently, Sutherland believed that the great majority of white-collar criminals did not become the subject of criminological study. Yet the cost of white-collar crime is probably several times greater than all the crimes customarily regarded as the crime problem. And, in contrast to street crimes, white-collar offenses breed distrust in economic and social institutions, lower public morale, and undermine faith in business and government.[8]

Redefining White-Collar Crime

Although Sutherland's work is considered a milestone in criminological history, his focus was on corporate criminality, including the crimes of the rich and powerful. Contemporary definitions of white-collar crime are typically much broader and include both middle-income Americans and corporate titans who use the marketplace for their criminal activity.[9] Included within recent views of white-collar crime are such acts as income tax evasion, credit card fraud, and bankruptcy fraud. Other white-collar criminals use their positions of trust in business or government to commit crimes. Their activities might include pilfering, soliciting bribes or kickbacks, and embezzlement. Some white-collar criminals set up business for the sole purpose of victimizing the general public. They engage in land swindles (for example, representing swamps as choice building sites), securities theft, medical fraud, and so on.

In addition to acting as individuals, some white-collar criminals become involved in criminal conspiracies designed to improve the market share or profitability of their corporations. This type of white-collar crime, which includes antitrust violations, price fixing, and false advertising, is known as **corporate crime**.[10]

It is difficult to estimate the extent and influence of white-collar crime on victims because all too often those who suffer the consequences of white-collar crime are ignored by victimologists.[11] Some experts place its total monetary value in the hundreds of billions of dollars, far outstripping the expense of any other type of crime. Nor is it likely that the full extent of white-collar crime will ever be fully known because victims are often reluctant to report their crime to police, believing that nothing can be done and that getting further involved is pointless.[12]

Beyond the monetary cost, white-collar crime often damages property and kills people. Violations of safety standards, pollution of the environment, and industrial accidents due to negligence can be classified as corporate violence. White-collar crime also destroys confidence, saps the integrity of commercial life, and has the potential for devastating destruction. Think of the possible results if nuclear regulatory rules are flouted or if toxic wastes are dumped into a community's drinking water supply.[13]

COMPONENTS OF WHITE-COLLAR CRIME

White-collar crime today represents a range of behaviors involving individuals acting alone and within the context of a business structure. The victims of white-collar crime can be the general public, the organization that employs the offender, or a competing organization. Numerous attempts have been made to create subcategories or typologies of white-collar criminality.[14] This text adapts a typology created by criminologist Mark Moore to organize the analysis of white-collar crime.[15] Moore's typology contains seven elements, ranging from an individual using a business enterprise to commit theft-related crimes, to an individual using his or her place within a business enterprise for illegal gain, to business enterprises collectively engaging in illegitimate activity.

Stings and Swindles

For more than a decade, the Gold Club in Atlanta was the hottest spot in town, the destination for conventioneers and businessmen looking for a rowdy night filled with good cigars, strong drinks, and nude dancers.[16] It became the home away from home for well-known professional athletes who stopped by to receive sexual favors from the girls who worked at the club. The federal government filed charges, claiming that the Gold Club manager, Steven Kaplan, was in cahoots with the Gambino organized crime family of New York to overcharge or double bill credit cards of unsuspecting customers. The club owners were also charged with ordering women in their employ to provide sexual services to professional athletes and celebrities to encourage their presence at the club. The government won its case when Kaplan pled guilty and received a 3- to 5-year prison sentence and a $5 million fine. Ironically, as part of the deal, the federal government took over the Gold Club, making it the manager of one of the largest strip clubs in the nation!

Kaplan and his co-conspirators were found guilty of engaging in an **sting or swindle,** a white-collar crime in which people use their institutional or business position to

trick others out of their money. Offenses in this category range from fraud involving the door-to-door sale of faulty merchandise to passing millions of dollars in counterfeit stock certificates to an established brokerage firm. Swindlers have little shame when defrauding people people out of their money; they often target the elderly, sick, and infirm. In the aftermath of the devastating Hurricane Katrina, the FBI felt it necessary to issue warnings about swindlers who use the tragedy to solicit relief funds from charitable and well-meaning victims.[17] If caught, white-collar swindlers are usually charged with common-law crimes such as embezzlement or fraud.

||||||| **CONNECTIONS** |||||||

In Chapter 11 fraud was described as a common theft offense. While these crimes are similar, common fraud involves a crime in which one person uses illegal methods to bilk another out of money, while white-collar fraud involves a person using his or her institutional or business position to reach the same goal. Common-law fraud is typically a short-term transaction whereas white-collar fraud involves a long-term criminal conspiracy. Although the ends are similar, the means are somewhat different.

The collapse of the Bank of Credit and Commerce International (BCCI) in 1991 was one of the most notorious swindles in recent history and cost depositors billions of dollars. BCCI was the world's seventh largest private bank, with assets of about $23 billion. Investigators believe bank officials made billions of dollars in loans to confederates who had no intention of repaying them; BCCI officers also used false accounting methods to defraud depositors. Its officers helped clients—such as Colombian drug cartel leaders and dictators Saddam Hussein and Ferdinand Marcos—launder money, finance terrorist organizations, and smuggle illegal arms. BCCI officers aided drug dealers and helped launder drug money so that it could be shifted to legitimate banks.[18] After the bank was closed, in addition to the billions of lost deposits, hundreds of millions were spent to pay auditors to liquidate the bank's holdings.[19] Despite the notoriety of the BCCI case, investors continue to bite at bogus investment schemes promising quick riches.

To read more about the infamous case of the **Bank of Credit and Commerce International,** go to http://www.apfn.org/apfn/BCCI.htm. For an up-to-date list of web links, go to http://cj.wadsworth.com/siegel_crimtpt9e.

RELIGIOUS SWINDLES When oil prices skyrocketed in 2003 and 2004, one enterprising swindler, Linda Stetler of Albany, Kentucky-based Vision Oil Company, lured investors into risky schemes by claiming that God (and not geologists) guided her company's oil exploration: "God gave me a vision of three oil wells," she said in a letter sent to potential investors. State regulators found that Stetler and her company engaged in illegal practices, including inadequate disclosures of risks and selling to unsuitable investors; Vision Oil and its agents were fined by the state and ordered to pay restitution to investors.[20]

It is estimated that fake religious organizations bilk thousands of people out of $100 million every year.[21] Swindlers take in worshippers of all persuasions: Jews, Baptists, Lutherans, Catholics, Mormons, and Greek Orthodox have all fallen prey to religious swindles. How do religious swindlers operate? Some create fraudulent chartiable organizations and convince devout people to contribute to their seemingly worthwhile cause. Some use religious television and radio shows to sell their products. Others place verses from the Scriptures on their promotional literature to comfort hesitant investors.

Chiseling

Chiseling, the second category of white-collar crime, involves regularly cheating an organization, its consumers, or both. Chiselers may be individuals looking to make quick profits in their own businesses or employees of large organizations who decide to cheat on obligations to their own company or its clients by doing something contrary to either the law or company policy. Chiseling can involve charging for bogus auto repairs, cheating customers on home repairs, or short-weighting (intentionally tampering with the accuracy of scales used to weigh products) in supermarkets or dairies. In one scheme, some New York City cab drivers routinely tapped the dashboards of their cabs with pens loaded with powerful magnets to zap their meters and jack up the fares.[22]

In some cases, workers use their position in an organization to conduct illegal schemes or help others benefit illegally. For example, racetrack tellers at Belmont, Aqueduct, and Saratoga in New York were arrested when it was discovered that they used the flow of cash through betting windows to launder money for drug dealers. The tellers exchanged more than $300,000 in small bills for large ones.[23] In 2005 the federal government announced the success of Operation Bullpen aimed at stopping chiseling in the sports memorabilia industry. Convicted in the investigation was the largest seller in the world of signed celebrity photos: Truly Unique Collectibles, who through its website, sold millions of dollars in forged and fraudulent posters, photos, and other items. Its celebrity-signed pictures and posters were obtained by "runners," people who happen to catch a celebrity at an event and obtain a signed picture there. Though runners may have obtained one or two signatures from famous athletes, they simply forged many more, claiming all were genuine. The investigation found that the overwhelming number of celebrity-signed

photographs and posters being sold throughout the world are sold under this pretense; they are almost all forgeries.[24]

Chiseling may even involve illegal use of information about company policies that have not been disclosed to the public. The secret information can be sold to speculators or used to make money in the stock market. Use of the information violates the obligation to keep company policy secret.

PROFESSIONAL CHISELING It is not uncommon for professionals to use their positions to chisel clients. Pharmacists have been known to alter prescriptions or substitute - low-cost generic drugs for more expensive name brands.[25] In one case that made national headlines in 2001, Kansas City pharmacist Robert R. Courtney was charged with fraud when it was discovered that he had been selling diluted mixtures of the cancer medications Taxol, Gemzar, Paraplatin, and Platinol, which are used to treat a variety of illnesses including pancreatic and lung cancer, advanced ovarian and breast cancer, and AIDS-related Kaposi's sarcoma. In one instance, Courtney provided a doctor with only 450 milligrams of Gemzar for a prescription that called for 1,900 mg, a transaction that netted him a profit of $779.[26] After he pled guilty, Courtney told authorities that his drug dilution activities were not limited to the conduct he admitted to at the time of his guilty plea. His criminal activities had actually begun in 1992 or even earlier, affected the patients of 400 doctors, involved 98,000 prescriptions, and harmed approximately 4,200 patients.[27] There is no telling how many people died or

Kansas City pharmacist Robert R. Courtney was charged with fraud after it was discovered that he had been selling diluted mixtures of the cancer medications Taxol, Gemzar, Paraplatin, and Platinol. These drugs are used to treat a variety of illnesses including pancreatic and lung cancer, advanced ovarian and breast cancer, and AIDS-related Kaposi's sarcoma. A plea bargain helped Courtney avoid a life sentence, but he will spend about 30 years in prison.

suffered serious medical complications because of Courtney's criminal conduct.

SECURITIES FRAUD A great deal of chiseling takes place on the commodities and stock markets, where individuals engage in deceptive practices that are prohibited by federal law.[28] Some investment counselors and insurance agents use their positions to cheat individual clients by misleading them on the quality of their investments; financial organizations cheat their clients by promoting risky investments as being iron-clad safe. For example, in 2005, Richard Banville and Harold Howell from Orange County, California, were indicted on fraud charges stemming from their operation of a scheme that defrauded elderly and retired victims out of nearly $1.7 million. According to the indictment, Banville and Howell operated a company called Trading West, Inc. (TWI), which solicited investments for foreign currency exchange trading. Promising huge returns on investments, they told potential investors that they were really in luck because a world-renowned trader—David Zachary of La Jolla, California—would be doing the trades. Though they promised returns of 10 percent to 40 percent per month, they failed to mention that David Zachary did not really exist and that most of the money had been diverted to Banville and Howell for personal gain. When victims asked to withdraw their funds, Banville and Howell explained that an "early withdrawal penalty" of up to 75 percent of the principal would be assessed in order to disguise the fact that the scheme diverted victims' monies for the personal benefit of Banville and Howell.[29]

Stockbrokers violate accepted practices when they engage in **churning** the client's account by repeated, excessive, and unnecessary buying and selling of stock.[30] Other broker fraud includes **front running,** in which brokers place personal orders ahead of a large customer's order to profit from the market effects of the trade, and **bucketing,** which is skimming customer trading profits by falsifying trade information.[31]

As discussed in the ImClone case, securities chiseling can also involve using one's position of trust to profit from inside business information, referred to as **insider trading.** The information can then be used to buy and sell securities, giving the trader an unfair advantage over the general public, which lacks this inside information.

Insider trading violations can occur in a variety of situations. As originally conceived, it was illegal for corporate employees with direct knowledge of market-sensitive information to use that information for their own benefit—for example, by buying stock in a company that they learn will be taken over by the larger concern for which they work. In recent years, the definition of insider trading has been expanded by federal courts to include employees of financial institutions, such as law or banking firms, who misappropriate confidential information on pending corporate actions to purchase stock or give the information to a third party so that party may buy shares in the company. Courts have ruled that such actions are deceptive and violate security trading codes.[32]

When the stock market collapsed in 2000, securities fraud became a major national issue. Leading market analysts have been accused of providing false and misleading information in order to pump up the price of stocks to secure business for their firms. On April 28, 2003, the Securities and Exchange Commission announced a settlement in which leading Wall Street brokerage firms—including Salomon Smith Barney, CSFB (Credit Suisse First Boston), Morgan Stanley, Goldman Sachs, Bear Stearns, J.P. Morgan, Lehman Brothers, UBS Warburg, and U.S. Bancorp Piper Jaffray—paid a $1.4 billion fine.[33] Some leading analysts were fined millions of dollars and barred from the security industry for life.

Individual Exploitation of an Institutional Position

Another type of white-collar crime involves individuals' exploiting their power or position in organizations to take advantage of other individuals who have an interest in how that power is used. For example, a fire inspector who demands that the owner of a restaurant pay him to be granted an operating license is abusing his institutional position. In most cases, this type of offense occurs when the victim has a clear right to expect a service, and the offender threatens to withhold the service unless an additional payment or bribe is forthcoming.

On the local and state levels, scandals commonly emerge in which liquor license board members, food inspectors, and fire inspectors are named as exploiters. A striking example of exploitation made national headlines on October 6, 1998, when San Francisco 49ers co-owner Eddie DeBartolo, Jr., pled guilty to concealing an extortion plot by the former governor of Louisiana, Edwin Edwards. According to the authorities, Edwards demanded payments of $400,000 or he would use his influence to prevent DeBartolo from obtaining a license for a riverboat gambling casino.[34] Here a former politician is alleged to have used his still-considerable political clout to demand payment from a businessman desiring to engage in a legitimate business enterprise.

Exploitation can also occur in private industry. Purchasing agents in large companies often demand a piece of the action for awarding contracts to suppliers and distributors. Managing agents in some of New York City's most luxurious buildings have been convicted on charges that they routinely extorted millions of dollars from maintenance contractors and building suppliers. Building managers have been charged with steering repair and maintenance work to particular contractors in exchange for kickbacks totaling millions of dollars.[35] In 1998, the FBI arrested executives of Bayship Management Inc. (BSM), one of the largest private ship management companies in the United States. In a sting operation, FBI agents created a bogus undercover marine contracting business, which did business with BSM on government contracts. BSM employees directed the undercover agents to fraudulently inflate the dollar amounts of contracts to cover the cost of bribes! Fraudulent contracts were issued for work that was never performed in order to entertain the BSM employees at dinners, golf outings, and trips and for cash payoffs. BSM was "charging" its subcontractors for the right to work on government jobs.[36]

In some foreign countries, soliciting bribes to do business is a common, even expected, practice. Not surprisingly, U.S. businesses have complained that stiff penalties for bribery give foreign competitors an edge over them. In European countries, such as Italy and France, giving bribes to secure contracts is perfectly legal; and in West Germany, corporate bribes are actually tax deductible.[37] Some government officials solicit bribes to allow American firms to do business in their countries.[38]

Influence Peddling and Bribery

Sometimes individuals holding important institutional positions sell power, influence, and information to outsiders who have an interest in influencing or predicting the activities of the institution. Offenses within this category include government employees' taking kickbacks from contractors in return for awarding them contracts they could not have won on merit, or outsiders' bribing government officials, such as those in the Securities and Exchange Commission, who might sell information about future government activities. Political leaders have been convicted of accepting bribes to rig elections that enable their party to control state politics.[39]

Charges of influence peddling sometimes reach to the highest levels of governments. Here, U.S. House of Representatives Majority Leader Tom DeLay (R-TX) makes a brief statement to the news media after he announced on September 28, 2005, at the Capitol in Washington, D.C., that he was stepping down from his leadership position. DeLay was indicted on charges of criminal conspiracy and money laundering in his home state of Texas.

One major difference distinguishes **influence peddling** from the previously discussed exploitation, which involves forcing victims to pay for services to which they have a clear right. In contrast, influence peddlers and bribe takers use their institutional positions to grant favors and sell information to which their co-conspirators are not entitled. In sum, in crimes of institutional exploitation, the victim is threatened and forced to pay, whereas the victim of influence peddling is the organization compromised by its employees for their own interests.

INFLUENCE PEDDLING IN GOVERNMENT In 2005 business consultant Nate Gray was convicted of bribing corrupt public officials with cash, Super Bowl tickets, massages, and limousines. Part of the scheme involved bribing East Cleveland Mayor Emmanuel Onunwor as payment for his awarding a no-bid, $3.9 million contract to one of Gray's clients.[40] In a major 2006 case, powerful lobbyist Jack Abramoff plead guilty to charges of conspiracy, fraud, and tax evasion, after he used campaign contributions, lavish trips, meals and other perks to influence lawmakers and their aides.

Agents of the criminal justice system have also gotten caught up in official corruption, a circumstance that is particularly disturbing because society expects a higher standard of moral integrity from people empowered to uphold the law and judge their fellow citizens. Police officers have been particularly vulnerable to charges of corruption. Thirty years ago, the Knapp Commission found that police corruption in New York City was pervasive and widespread, ranging from patrol officers' accepting small gratuities from local businesspeople to senior officers receiving payoffs in the thousands of dollars from gamblers and narcotics violators.[41] Despite years of effort to eradicate police corruption, instances still abound. For example, in 1998 more than twenty officers were alleged to have been patrons of prostitutes working at 335 West 39th Street and a nearby massage parlor; some officers were filmed demanding sex.[42]

INFLUENCE PEDDLING IN BUSINESS Politicians and government officials are not the only ones accused of bribery; business has had its share of scandals. The 1970s witnessed revelations that multinational corporations regularly made payoffs to foreign officials and businesspeople to secure business contracts. Gulf Oil executives admitted paying $4 million to the South Korean ruling party; Burroughs Corporation admitted paying $1.5 million to foreign officials; and Lockheed Aircraft admitted paying $202 million.

McDonnell-Douglas Aircraft Corporation was indicted for paying $1 million in bribes to officials of Pakistani International Airlines to secure orders.[43]

In response to these revelations, in 1977 Congress passed the Foreign Corrupt Practices Act (FCPA), which makes it a criminal offense to bribe foreign officials or to make other questionable overseas payments. Violations of the FCPA draw strict penalties for both the defendant company and its officers.[44] Moreover, all fines imposed on corporate officers are paid by them, not absorbed by the company. For example, for violating the antibribery provisions of the FCPA, a domestic corporation can be fined up to $1 million. Company officers, employees, or stockholders who are convicted of bribery may have to serve a prison sentence of up to 5 years and pay a $10,000 fine.

Congressional dissatisfaction with the harshness and ambiguity of the bill has caused numerous revisions to be proposed. Despite the penalties imposed by the FCPA, corporations that deal in foreign trade have continued to give bribes to secure favorable trade agreements.[45] On June 16, 2004, Schering-Plough Corporation agreed to pay a civil penalty of $500,000 for violating provisions of the FCPA. An employee of Schering-Plough's Polish subsidiary made a payment to a charitable foundation headed by a Polish government official. The government charged that these "charitable" payments were designed to influence the official to purchase Schering-Plough's pharmaceutical products for his region's health fund.[46] In 2005 the U.S. Department of Justice announced it was investigating the bribing of government officials in Africa and Latin America by the Daimler Chrysler auto company after it was discovered that the firm maintained forty offshore bank accounts used to fund the payment of bribes. And in another 2005 case, an investigation was launched into the dealings in Equatorial Guinea of Amerada Hess, Marathon Oil Corp., and ChevronTexaco. There is suspicion that money given to charity in that poor nation goes directly into the hands of the ruling family in exchange for privileges.[47]

To find out more about the **FCPA** and read its provisions, go to its website: http://www.usdoj.gov/ criminal/fraud/fcpa/dojdocb.htm. For an up-to-date list of web links, go to http://cj.wadsworth.com/siegel_crimtpt9e.

Embezzlement and Employee Fraud

Another type of white-collar crime involves individuals' use of their positions to embezzle company funds or appropriate company property for themselves. Here the company or organization that employs the criminal, rather than an outsider, is the victim of white-collar crime.

BLUE-COLLAR FRAUD In 2002, three employees and a friend allegedly stole moon rocks from a NASA laboratory in Houston. FBI agents arrested them after they tried to sell the contraband to an undercover agent in Orlando, Florida. The would-be seller reportedly asked $2,000 per gram for the rocks initially but later bumped the price to $8,000 per gram.[48] While the theft of moon rocks does not happen very often, systematic theft of company property by employees, or **pilferage**, is common.[49]

Employee theft is most accurately explained by factors relevant to the work setting, such as job dissatisfaction and the workers' belief that they are being exploited by employers or supervisors; economic problems play a relatively small role in the decision to pilfer. So, although employers attribute employee fraud to economic conditions and declining personal values, workers themselves say they steal because of strain and conflict.

Though it is difficult to determine the value of goods taken by employees, some recent surveys indicate it is substantial and not confined to the United States. Shrinkage costs the European economy $29 billion—more than the losses due to car theft and/or domestic burglary.[50] Shrinkage may be on the rise because employees are influenced by economic conditions. A study co-sponsored by the National Food Service Security Council found the average restaurant worker now steals $204 in cash or merchandise per year, up from $96 in 1998 when the economy was in better shape.[51] However, these figures may underestimate the problem because they rely on employee self-reporting; experts believe that, on average, each worker takes $1,500 each year![52] This evidence indicates that the scope of employee theft is truly staggering, amounting to almost $35 billion per year.[53]

Where do you go to report cases of employee fraud? The **National Whistleblower Center** is a nonprofit educational advocacy organization that works for the enforcement of environmental laws, nuclear safety, civil rights, and government and industry accountability through the support and representation of employee whistleblowers: http://www.whistleblowers.org. For an up-to-date list of web links, go to http://cj.wadsworth.com/siegel_crimtpt9e.

MANAGEMENT FRAUD Blue-collar workers are not the only employees who commit corporate theft. Management-level fraud is also quite common. Such acts include converting company assets for personal benefit; fraudulently receiving increases in compensation (such as raises or bonuses); fraudulently increasing personal holdings of company stock; retaining one's present position within the company by manipulating accounts; and concealing unacceptable performance from stockholders.[54]

Management fraud has involved some of the nation's largest companies and richest people. The Criminological Enterprise feature focuses on three of the most prominent cases of recent years.

The Criminological Enterprise

‖‖‖‖‖‖‖‖‖‖‖‖‖‖‖‖‖‖‖‖‖‖‖‖‖‖‖‖‖‖‖‖‖

Tyco, Enron, and WorldCom: Enterprise Crime at the Highest Levels

The Tyco Case

Tyco International Ltd. is a gigantic corporate entity that today operates in all fifty U.S. states and over 100 countries and employs more than 250,000 people. Despite its great success, the U.S. government indicted Tyco's Chief Executive Officer L. Dennis Kozlowski and Chief Financial Officer Marc Swartz on a variety of fraud and larceny charges including misappropriating $170 million in company funds by hiding unauthorized bonuses and secretly forgiving loans to themselves. Kozlowski and Swartz were also accused of making more than $430 million by lying about Tyco's financial condition in order to inflate the value of their stock.

Kozlowski has been tried twice. During the first trial in 2004, the government tried to establish a motive by showing jurors elements of his extravagant lifestyle. Kozlowski spent more than $2 million on a party for his wife on the Italian island of Sardinia that featured a performance by singer Jimmy Buffett; young men and women—dressed as Roman soldiers and maidens—danced and served the guests. He also spent $15 million to furnish an $18 million Tyco-owned apartment on Fifth Avenue in New York City; his expenses included a $15,000 umbrella holder, a $2,200 gilt metal trash basket, and a $6,000 shower curtain.

The defense claimed that Kozlowski and Swartz were merely highly paid executives and that everything they received was approved by Tyco's board of directors and their accounting firm, PricewaterhouseCoopers.

Because there was no stealth, there could be no embezzlement. However, on April 2, 2004, before the jury could decide on the matter, the judge was forced to declare a mistrial after a juror revealed that she had been the subject of threats.

During the second trial, Kozlowski testified on his own behalf, stating that his pay package was "confusing" and "almost embarrassingly big," but that he never committed a crime as the company's top executive. However, Kozlowski was convicted on June 17, 2005, for misappropriation of Tyco's corporate funds, among other charges. The prosecution won a total of twenty-two counts of grand larceny for $150 million in unauthorized bonuses. Kozlowski was convicted of fraud against the company shareholders for an amount of more than $400 million. On September 19, 2005, he was sentenced to between 8 and 25 years in prison.

The Enron Case

Enron Corporation, an oil and gas trading firm, was one of the largest companies in the United States before it collapsed and cost thousands of employees their life savings and millions of investors their hard-earned money.

Enron was an aggressive energy company that sought to transform itself into the world's biggest energy trader. Enron's share price collapsed when word got out that the company had been setting up shell companies and limited partnerships to conceal debts so they did not show up in the company's accounts.

In one incident, six Enron executives negotiated complex deals in which they made at least $42 million on personal investments totaling $161,000, all the while knowing that

the limited partnerships they sold to retirement plans and private foundations were collapsing in value. It is also suspected that Enron engaged in sham transactions in late 2000 that drove up electricity prices in California and helped worsen the energy crisis that plagued the West for more than a year.

Enron's auditors—Arthur Andersen, a prestigious accounting firm—actually shredded key documents to keep them out of the hands of the government. One man involved in the incident, David Duncan, a former Andersen partner who was head of the team that audited Enron, agreed to serve as a government witness after pleading guilty to obstruction of justice. Duncan admitted in court that he "knowingly, intentionally, and corruptly persuaded and attempted to persuade" Andersen employees to withhold records, documents, and other objects from an investigation by the Securities and Exchange Commission (SEC). In 2005, the U.S. Supreme Court overturned an obstruction of justice conviction against Arthur Andersen though it came too late to save the company from bankruptcy.

In the aftermath of the Enron collapse, Chairman Kenneth L. Lay was charged with conspiracy, securities fraud, wire fraud, bank fraud, and making false statements. Enron CEO Jeffrey K. Skilling and former Enron Chief Accounting Officer Richard Causey were also charged with money laundering and conspiracy. The government claimed that Lay, Skilling, Causey, and others oversaw a massive conspiracy to delude investors into believing that Enron was a growing company when, in fact, it was undergoing business setbacks.

The government charges indicate that between 1999 and 2001, these executives used their position of trust to engage in a wide-ranging scheme to deceive the public and the SEC about the true performance of Enron's businesses. Their fraud helped inflate Enron's stock price from $30 per share in early 1998 to over $80 per share in January 2001. The three allegedly orchestrated a series of accounting frauds designed to make up the shortfall between what the company actually earned and what was expected by Wall Street analysts. The government contends that, after Lay participated in management committee meetings at which reports showed that Enron was losing billions, Lay stated on an online forum (on September 26, 2001) with thousands of Enron employees, many of whom were investors in Enron stock, that Enron was doing great and was going to "hit [its] numbers."

What would motivate the head of one of the nation's largest companies to commit fraud? The government believes it was greed: Between 1998 and 2001, Lay received approximately $300 million from the sale of Enron stock options and restricted stock and made over $217 million in profit; he was also paid more than $19 million in salary and bonuses. If convicted of all the charges in the indictment, Lay faces a maximum sentence of 175 years in prison and millions of dollars in fines.

At the time of this writing, a number of Enron executives have already pled guilty to securities fraud. Andrew S. Fastow, the former chief financial officer (CFO) of Enron Corporation, pled guilty to two counts of conspiracy to commit securities and wire fraud and is cooperating with an ongoing criminal investigation into Enron's collapse. On August 25, 2004, Mark Koenig, former director of investor relations and executive vice president at Enron, also pled guilty to security charges and admitted that he was aware that Enron's publicly reported financial results and filings with the SEC did not truthfully present Enron's financial position.

Lay, Skilling, and Causey are set to be tried in January 2006. A few other executives have been found not guilty recently, calling into question the government's chances for conviction.

The WorldCom Case

On March 15, 2005, WorldCom CEO Bernie Ebbers was found guilty and received a 25-year sentence for falsifying the company's financial statements by more than $9 billion; WorldCom was forced to file for the largest bankruptcy in U.S. history. One of the most important elements of the case was the more than $400 million that WorldCom loaned or guaranteed to loan Ebbers at an interest rate of 2.15 percent.

Ebbers began his career by creating the LDDS (Long Distance Discount Services), which gained many of America's largest corporations as customers for its voice and data network. He then bought IDB Company and renamed it WorldCom. Through a series of acquisitions, WorldCom became one of the largest Internet hookup and networking companies in the United States; its stock value increased 7,000 percent during the 1990s.

When the market collapsed in 2000, WorldCom was heavily in debt and hemorrhaging money. While people were being laid off, the company made its loans to Ebbers so he could hold onto his company stock, for which he had taken out loans to purchase. Then on June 25, 2002, WorldCom announced that it had illegally treated $3.8 billion in ordinary costs as capital expenditures. The bottom dropped out of the stock, creditors began to sue, and Ebbers was in no position to pay back the loans. The company admitted to overstating profits by a whopping $74.4 billion between 2000 and 2001, including at least $10.6 billion that the firm attributed to accounting "errors" as well as "improper" and "inappropriate" accounting.

Critical Thinking

1. Considering the various theories of criminal behavior we have discussed, how would you explain the alleged behavior of millionaire businesspeople such as Dennis Kozlowski, Bernie Ebbers, and Kenneth Lay? Are they impulsive? Do they lack "self-control"? Is there a personality deficit that can explain their behavior?

2. Should white-collar criminals be punished with a prison sentence or would society be better served if all their ill-gotten gains were confiscated?

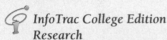 InfoTrac College Edition Research

Look up the Tyco, Enron, and World-Com, and cases in InfoTrac College Edition.

Sources: Lynne W. Jeter, *Disconnected: Deceit and Betrayal at WorldCom* (New York: Wiley, 2003); Bethany McLean and Peter Elkind, *Smartest Guys in the Room: The Amazing Rise and Scandalous Fall of Enron* (New York: Penguin, 2003); Kurt Eichenwald, "Ex-Andersen Partner Pleads Guilty in Record-Shredding," *New York Times,* 12 April 2002, p. C1; John A. Byrne, "At Enron, the Environment Was Ripe for Abuse," *Business Week* (25 February 2002):12; Peter Behr and Carrie Johnson, "Govt. Expands Charges against Enron Execs," *Washington Post,* 1 May 2003, p.1; Associated Press, "Ex-Tyco CEO Dennis Kozlowski Found Guilty," MSNBC, 17 June 2005. http://www.msnbc.msn.com/id/8258729. Accessed November 4, 2005.

Client Fraud

Another component of white-collar crime is theft by an economic client from an organization that advances credit to its clients or reimburses them for services rendered. These offenses are linked because they involve cheating an organization (such as a government agency or insurance company) with many individual clients that the organization supports financially (such as welfare clients), reimburses for services provided (such as healthcare providers), covers losses of (such as insurance policyholders), or extends credit to (such as bank clients or taxpayers). Included in this category are insurance fraud, credit card fraud, fraud related to welfare and Medicare programs, and tax evasion. For example, some critics suggest that welfare recipients cheat the federal government out of billions each year. As eligibility for public assistance becomes more limited, recipients are resorting to a number of schemes to maintain their status. Some women collect government checks while working on the side or living illegally with boyfriends or husbands. Some young mothers tell children to answer exam questions incorrectly to be classified as disabled and receive government assistance.[55]

HEALTHCARE FRAUD It is also common for doctors to violate their ethical vows and engage in fraud in obtaining patients and administering their treatment.

Another target of medical fraud is the federal Medicaid program. Under Medicaid, recipients under age 21 are entitled to dental checkups and cleanings twice a year and a limited number of other treatments. In 2001, prosecutors in Miami filed charges against two former dentists, Joel Berger and Charles Kravitz, for allegedly setting up a Medicaid fraud scheme that cost the state millions in bogus fees. Berger was charged with hiring recruiters to pick up children, some as young as 2, from street corners, school buses, and daycare centers and take them to dental facilities for unneeded procedures that included cleanings, X-rays, and even extractions. Recruiters received $25 for every child they placed in a dental chair; the kids got $5 for participating. The procedures were frequently administered by untrained dental employees. The scheme involved a dozen dentists and nearly ninety recruiters and dental workers and may have cost taxpayers up to $20 million in illegal Medicaid payments. Similar, albeit smaller-scale, frauds have been uncovered in Texas, Kansas, and other states.[56] However, statewide Medicaid systems have also been the target of enterprise criminals: New York State officials estimate that 10 percent of the entire program, billions of dollars, has been lost due to fraudulent practices.[57]

Abusive and deceptive healthcare practices include such techniques as "ping-ponging" (referring patients to other physicians in the same office), "gang visits" (billing for multiple services), and "steering" (directing patients to particular pharmacies). Doctors who abuse their Medicaid or Medicare patients in this way are liable to civil suits and even criminal penalties.

In addition to individual physicians, some large healthcare providers have been accused of routinely violating the law to obtain millions in illegal payments. In 1998 the federal government filed suit against two of the nation's largest hospital chains, Columbia/HCA Healthcare Corporation (320 hospitals) and Quorum Health Group (250 hospitals), alleging that they routinely overstated expenses to bilk Medicare.[58] It has been estimated that $100 billion spent annually on federal healthcare is lost to fraudulent practices.[59] Despite the magnitude of this abuse, state and federal governments have been reluctant to prosecute Medicaid fraud.[60]

The government has attempted to tighten control over the industry in order to restrict the opportunity for physicians to commit fraud. Healthcare companies providing services to federal healthcare programs are also regulated by federal laws that prohibit kickbacks and self-referrals. For example, it is a crime, punishable by up to 5 years in prison, to provide anything of value, money or otherwise, directly or indirectly, with the intent to induce a referral of a patient or a healthcare service. Liability attaches to both parties in the transaction—the entity or individual providing the kickbacks and the individual receiving payment of the referral.

Federal law also prohibits so-called physicians and other healthcare providers from referring beneficiaries in federal healthcare programs to clinics or other facilities in which the physician or healthcare provider has a financial interest. For example, it would be illegal for a doctor to refer her patients to a blood-testing lab in which she has an ownership share. These practices—kickbacks and self-referrals—are prohibited under federal law because they would compromise a medical professional's independent judgment. Federal law prohibits arrangements that tend to corrupt medical judgment and put the provider's bottom line ahead of the patient's well-being.[61]

BANK FRAUD Bank fraud can encompass such diverse schemes as **check kiting** (Exhibit 12.1), check forgery, false statements on loan applications, sale of stolen checks, bank credit card fraud, unauthorized use of automatic teller machines (ATMs), auto title fraud, and illegal transactions with offshore banks.[62] To be found guilty of bank fraud, one must knowingly execute or attempt to execute a scheme to fraudulently obtain money or property from a financial institution. For example, a car dealer would commit bank fraud by securing loans on titles to cars it no longer owned. A real estate owner would be guilty of bank fraud if he or she obtained a false appraisal on a piece of property with the intention of obtaining a bank loan in excess of the property's real worth. Penalties for bank fraud include a maximum fine of $1 million and up to 30 years in prison.

TAX EVASION Another important aspect of client fraud is tax evasion. Here the victim is the government that is cheated by one of its clients, the errant taxpayer to whom it extended credit by allowing the taxpayer to delay paying taxes on money he or she had already earned. Tax fraud is a particularly challenging area for criminological study because so many U.S. citizens regularly underreport their income, and it is often difficult to separate honest error from deliberate tax evasion.

The basic law on tax evasion is contained in the U.S. Internal Revenue Code, section 7201, which states:

> Any person who willfully attempts in any manner to evade or defeat any tax imposed by this title or the payment thereof shall, in addition to other penalties provided by law, be guilty of a felony and, upon conviction thereof, shall be fined not more than $100,000 or imprisoned not more than five years, or both, together with the costs of prosecution.

To prove tax fraud, the government must find that the taxpayer either underreported his or her income or did not report taxable income. No minimum dollar amount is stated before fraud exists, but the government can take legal action when there is a "substantial underpayment of tax." A second element of tax fraud is "willfulness" on the part of the tax evader. In the major case on this issue, willfulness was defined as a "voluntary, intentional violation of a known legal duty and not the careless disregard for the truth."[63] Finally, to prove tax fraud, the government must show that the taxpayer has purposely attempted to evade or defeat a tax payment. If the offender is guilty of passive neglect, the offense is a misdemeanor. Passive neglect means simply not paying taxes, not reporting income, or not paying taxes when due. On the other hand, affirmative tax evasion, such as keeping double books, making false entries, destroying books or records, concealing assets, or covering up sources of income, constitutes a felony.

Although tax cheating is a serious crime, the great majority of major tax cheats (in some categories, four of five cheaters) are not prosecuted because the IRS lacks the money to enforce the law.[64] Today, the IRS has a budget that amounts to only 41 cents per tax return; this is 10 percent less, after adjusting for inflation, than in 1997. In addition, because most IRS resources are devoted to processing tax returns, there is less money for audits, investigations, and collections than there was a decade ago.

The problem of tax fraud is significant, and honest taxpayers are forced to bear the costs that may run into the hundreds of billions. For example, the IRS must process each year more than 13 million cases in which financial documents from business partnerships do not match up with reports on individual tax returns. But the agency has the resources to pursue only a fifth of these cases. The losses from the failure to report income from partnerships alone could be as high as $64 billion per year. Another loophole in the tax law is the use of offshore accounts to evade taxes. Interest earned in these accounts may not be reported as income on U.S. tax returns, costing the federal government an estimated $70 billion annually. And though the IRS has identified more than 80,000 people currently using this type of scheme to defraud the government, budget restraints mean that it can only investigate about 20 percent of the cases.

Corporate Crime

Yet another component of white-collar crime involves situations in which powerful institutions or their representatives willfully violate the laws that restrain these institutions from doing social harm or require them to do social good. This is also known as corporate or **organizational crime.**

Interest in corporate crime first emerged in the early 1900s, when a group of writers, known as the muckrakers, targeted the monopolistic business practices of John D. Rockefeller, and other corporate business leaders. In a 1907 article, sociologist E. A. Ross described the "criminaloid": a business leader who while enjoying immunity from the law victimized an unsuspecting public.[65] Edwin Sutherland focused theoretical attention on corporate crime when he began his research on the subject in the 1940s; corporate crime was probably what he had in mind when he coined the phrase "white-collar crime."[66]

Corporate crimes are socially injurious acts committed by people who control companies to further their business interests. The target of their crimes can be the general public, the environment, or even company workers. What makes these crimes unique is that the perpetrator is a legal fiction—a corporation—and not an individual. In reality, it is company employees or owners who commit corporate crimes and who ultimately benefit through career advancement or greater profits. For a corporation to be held criminally liable, the employee committing the crime must be acting within the scope of his employment and must have actual or apparent

A 24-foot long representation of a screw is hoisted into position outside Federal Hall in New York's financial district on June 11, 2003, at a protest against a possible $500 million settlement between WorldCom Inc., the bankrupt long-distance telephone company, and securities regulators. WorldCom was the target of one of the biggest accounting fraud investigations in U.S. history.

authority to engage in the particular act in question. **Actual authority** occurs when a corporation knowingly gives authority to an employee; **apparent authority** is satisfied if a third party, like a customer, reasonably believes the agent has the authority to perform the act in question. Courts have ruled that actual authority may occur even when the illegal behavior is not condoned by the corporation but is nonetheless within the scope of the employee's authority.[67]

Some of the acts included within corporate crime are price fixing and illegal restraint of trade, false advertising, and the use of company practices that violate environmental protection statutes. The variety of crimes contained within this category is great, and they cause vast damage. The following subsections examine some of the most important offenses.

ILLEGAL RESTRAINT OF TRADE AND PRICE FIXING

A restraint of trade involves a contract or conspiracy designed to stifle competition, create a monopoly, artificially maintain prices, or otherwise interfere with free market competition.[68] The control of restraint of trade violations has its legal basis in the **Sherman Antitrust Act,** which subjects to criminal or civil sanctions any person "who shall make any contract or engage in any combination or conspiracy" in restraint of interstate commerce.[69] For violations of its provisions, this federal law created criminal penalties of up to 3 years imprisonment and $100,000 in fines for individuals and $10 million in fines for corporations.[70] The act outlaws conspiracies between corporations designed to control the marketplace.

In most instances, the act lets the presiding court judge whether corporations have conspired to "unreasonably restrain competition." However, four types of market conditions are considered so inherently anticompetitive that federal courts, through the Sherman Antitrust Act, have defined them as illegal per se, without regard to the facts or circumstances of the case:

- **Division of markets:** Firms divide a region into territories, and each firm agrees not to compete in the others' territories.

- **Tying arrangement:** A corporation requires customers of one of its services to use other services it offers. For example, it would be an illegal restraint of trade if a railroad required that companies doing business with it or supplying it with materials ship all goods they produce on trains owned by the rail line.[71]

- **Group boycott**: An organization or company boycotts retail stores that do not comply with its rules or desires.

- **Price fixing:** A conspiracy to set and control the price of a necessary commodity is considered an absolute violation of the act.

DECEPTIVE PRICING

Even the largest U.S. corporations commonly use deceptive pricing schemes when they respond to contract solicitations. Deceptive pricing occurs when contractors provide the government or other corporations with incomplete or misleading information on how much it will actually cost to fulfill the contracts on which they are bidding or use mischarges once the contracts are signed.[72] For example, defense contractors have been prosecuted for charging the government for costs incurred on work they are doing for private firms or shifting the costs on fixed-price contracts to ones in which the government

©Reuters/Corbis

reimburses the contractor for all expenses ("cost-plus" contracts). One well-known example of deceptive pricing occurred when the Lockheed Corporation withheld information that its labor costs would be lower than expected on the C-5 cargo plane. The resulting overcharges were an estimated $150 million. Although the government was able to negotiate a cheaper price for future C-5 orders, it did not demand repayment on the earlier contract. The government prosecutes approximately 100 cases of deceptive pricing in defense work each year, involving 59 percent of the nation's largest contractors.[73]

FALSE CLAIMS ADVERTISING Executives in even the largest corporations sometimes face stockholders' expectations of ever-increasing company profits that seem to demand that sales be increased at any cost. At times executives respond to this challenge by making claims about their products that cannot be justified by actual performance. However, the line between clever, aggressive sales techniques and fraudulent claims is fine. It is traditional to show a product in its best light, even if that involves resorting to fantasy. It is not fraudulent to show a delivery service vehicle taking off into outer space or to imply that taking one sip of beer will make people feel they have just jumped into a freezer. However, it is illegal to knowingly and purposely advertise a product as possessing qualities that the manufacturer realizes it does not have, such as the ability to cure the common cold, grow hair, or turn senior citizens into rock stars (though some rock stars are senior citizens these days).

In 2003 the U.S. Supreme Court, in the case of *Illinois Ex Rel. Madigan v. Telemarketing Associates,* helped define the line separating illegal claims from those that are artistic hyperbole protected by free speech.[74] Telemarketing Associates, a for-profit fundraising corporation, was retained by a charity to solicit donations to aid Vietnam veterans in the state of Illinois. Though donors were told that a significant portion of the money would go to the vets, the telemarketers actually retained 85 percent of all the money collected. The Illinois attorney general filed a complaint in state court, alleging that such representations were knowingly deceptive and materially false. The telemarketers said they were exercising their First Amendment free speech rights when they made their pitch for money.

The Supreme Court disagreed and found that states may charge fraud when fundraisers make false or misleading representations designed to deceive donors about how their donations will be used. The Court held that it is false and misleading for a solicitor to fool potential donors into believing that a substantial portion of their contributions would fund specific programs or services, knowing full well that was not the case.

WORKER SAFETY/ENVIRONMENTAL CRIMES Much attention has been paid to intentional or negligent environmental pollution caused by many large corporations. The numerous allegations in this area involve almost every aspect of U.S. business. There are many different types of environmental crimes. Some corporations have endangered the lives of their own workers by maintaining unsafe conditions in their plants and mines. It has been estimated that more than 20 million workers have been exposed to hazardous materials while on the job. Some industries have been hit particularly hard by complaints and allegations. The control of workers' safety has been the province of the Occupational Safety and Health Administration (OSHA). OSHA sets industry standards for the proper use of such chemicals as benzene, arsenic, lead, and coke. Intentional violation of OSHA standards can result in criminal penalties.

The major enforcement arm against environmental crimes is the Environmental Protection Agency, which was given full law enforcement authority in 1988. The EPA has successfully prosecuted significant violations across all major environmental statutes, including data fraud cases (for instance, private laboratories submitting false environmental data to state and federal environmental agencies); indiscriminate hazardous waste dumping that resulted in serious injuries and death; industry-wide ocean dumping by cruise ships; oil spills that caused significant damage to waterways, wetlands, and beaches; international smuggling of CFC refrigerants that damage the ozone layer and increase skin cancer risk; and illegal handling of hazardous substances such as pesticides and asbestos that exposed children, the poor, and other especially vulnerable groups to potentially serious illness.[75] Its Criminal Investigation Division (EPA CID) investigates allegations of criminal wrongdoing prohibited by various environmental statutes. Such investigations involve, but are not limited to:

- The illegal disposal of hazardous waste

- The export of hazardous waste without the permission of the receiving country

- The illegal discharge of pollutants to a water of the United States; the removal and disposal of regulated asbestos containing materials in a manner inconsistent with the law and regulations

- The illegal importation of certain restricted or regulated chemicals into the United States

- Tampering with a drinking water supply

- Mail fraud

- Wire fraud

- Conspiracy and money laundering relating to environmental criminal activities

Most environmental crime statutes contain overlapping civil, criminal, and administrative penalty provisions that give the government latitude in enforcement. Over time, Congress has elevated some violations from misdemeanors to felonies and has increased potential jail sentences and fines for those convicted.[76]

CAUSES OF WHITE-COLLAR CRIME

Ivan Boesky was a famous Wall Street trader who had amassed a fortune of about $200 million by betting on corporate takeovers, a practice called *arbitrage*. In 1986, he was investigated by the Securities and Exchange Commission for insider trading. To escape serious punishment, he informed on several associates. In exchange for cooperation, Boesky received a sentence of 3½ years in prison and a $100 million fine. Released after serving 2 years, Boesky was barred from working in the securities business for the remainder of his life.

Caught in the web was billionaire junk bond trader Michael Milken. Indicted by a federal grand jury, Milken pled guilty to five securities and reporting violations and was sentenced to 10 years in prison; he served 22 months. He also paid a $200 million fine and another $400 to $800 million in settlements relating primarily to civil lawsuits.

How can people with so much disposable wealth get involved in risky schemes to produce even more? There are probably as many explanations for white-collar crime as there are white-collar crimes.

Many offenders feel free to engage in business crime because they can easily rationalize its effects. Some convince themselves that their actions are not really crimes because the acts involved do not resemble street crimes. A banker who uses his position of trust to lend his institution's assets to a company he secretly controls may see himself as a shrewd businessman, not as a criminal. Or a pharmacist who chisels customers on prescription drugs may rationalize her behavior by telling herself that it does not really hurt anyone. Further, some businesspeople feel justified in committing white-collar crimes because they believe government regulators do not really understand the business world or the problems of competing in the free enterprise system.

Even when caught, many white-collar criminals cannot see the error of their ways. For example, one offender who was convicted in an electrical industry price fixing conspiracy categorically denied the illegality of his actions. "We did not fix prices," he said; "I am telling you that all we did was recover costs."[77] Some white-collar criminals believe that everyone violates business laws, so it is not so bad if they do so themselves. Rationalizing greed is a common trait of white-collar criminals.

Greedy or Needy?

When a Kansas City pharmacist was asked after his arrest why he substituted improper doses of drugs instead of what doctors had prescribed, Courtney told investigators he cut the drugs' strength "out of greed."[78]

Greed is not the only motivation for white-collar crime; need also plays an important role. Executives may tamper with company books because they feel the need to keep or improve their jobs, satisfy their egos, or support their children. Blue-collar workers may pilfer because they need to

keep pace with inflation or buy a new car. Kathleen Daly's analysis of convictions in seven federal district courts indicates that many white-collar crimes involve relatively trivial amounts. Women convicted of white-collar crime typically work in lower-echelon positions, and their acts seem motivated more by economic survival than by greed and power.[79]

Even people in the upper echelons of the financial world, such as Boesky, may carry scars from an earlier needy period in their lives that can be healed only by accumulating ever-greater amounts of money. As one of Boesky's associates put it:

> I don't know what his devils were. Maybe he's greedy beyond the wildest imaginings of mere mortals like you and me. And maybe part of what drives the guy is an inherent insecurity that was operative here even after he had arrived. Maybe he never arrived.[80]

A well-known study of embezzlers by Donald Cressey illustrates the important role need plays in white-collar crime. According to Cressey, embezzlement is caused by what he calls a "nonshareable financial problem." This condition may be the result of offenders' living beyond their means, perhaps piling up gambling debts; offenders feel they cannot let anyone know about such financial problems without ruining their reputations.

THEORIES OF WHITE-COLLAR CRIME

Why do they do it? Why do otherwise respectable people decide to break the law? As we have noted, most criminal offenders begin their offending careers when they are quite young. Yet by its very nature white-collar crime requires people to attain a certain position in the workplace before they can commit crime. Can the theories that predict common-law crime also be applied to white-collar crime? There are a number of theories of white-collar crime. The next sections describe three of the most prominent.

Rationalization/Neutralization View

In his research on fraud, Donald Cressey found that the door to solving personal financial problems through criminal means is opened by the rationalizations people develop for white-collar crime: "Some of our most respectable citizens got their start in life by using other people's money temporarily"; "in the real estate business, there is nothing wrong about using deposits before the deal is closed"; "all people steal when they get in a tight spot."[81] Offenders use these and other rationalizations to resolve the conflict they experience over engaging in illegal behavior. Rationalizations allow offenders' financial needs to be met without compromising their values.

In a recent study of Medicare/Medicaid fraud by speech, occupational, and physical therapists working in hospitals, nursing homes, and with home health agencies, researchers found the healthcare workers frequently engaged in two fraudulent practices: cutting sessions short while charging for

Comparative Criminology

Snakes and Ladders: Confronting White-Collar Crime in Britain

How do otherwise law-abiding people cope with the emotional turmoil created when they are cast as white-collar criminals? This issue was explored by Sara Willott, Christine Griffin, and Mark Torrance through a series of interviews they conducted with groups of working-class and professional men in Great Britain who had been convicted of white-collar offenses.

Willott and her colleagues found that members of both groups used linguistic devices to justify their behavior. The working-class men argued that they were the breadwinners of their families and were forced by dire economic circumstances to commit crime. Their crimes were not for personal gain but simply to feed their families. They also viewed themselves as modern-day Robin Hoods who were taking from the rich to help the poor, who in this case were their own families. Rather than accept blame, they positioned themselves as decent men who were forced to commit crimes: It was not their fault but the government's for failing to provide them with a safety net during a time of financial crisis. And, having been forced into crime by an unfair system, the men claimed they were revictimized and humiliated when sent to prison. They viewed themselves as the bottom of life's barrel, as pawns similar to the ones used in the children's game Snakes and Ladders (called Chutes and Ladders in the United States). They were being kept in place by powerful forces beyond their control.

The professional men used some similar linguistic tools to justify their behavior. They also saw themselves as breadwinners who used other people's money to help their families. But, unlike the blue-collar workers, they saw their professional responsibilities as adding to their burden. As businesspeople, they saw themselves as protectors of a wider circle of dependents, including their employees and their families. They did not steal but were "digging into funds" when the need arose. They were careful to point out that they did not use the funds to support an extravagant lifestyle but to shoulder the responsibility they had been socialized to carry.

The professionals were also aware of the high social standing demanded by their profession and lifestyle. Along with power come the obligations and trappings of power, and they were forced to violate the law to meet these obligations.

Some of the professional men viewed themselves as victims of bureaucrats who relentlessly pursued them to enhance their careers in government. They viewed law enforcers, many of whom had lower-class backgrounds, as ruthlessly ambitious people who used the prosecutions as stepping stones to success. Class envy, then, was responsible in part for their current dilemma.

The businesspeople believed the conditions that produced their descent were not of their doing and were beyond their control. Economic decline and recession had pushed them down the slippery slope. And, once in the "system," their entire world was rocked to its very foundations. They were aliens in a strange land of courts and correctional facilities: Although working-class criminals might feel at home in their current surroundings, they complained that as professionals "we have fallen out of the structures of our lives" (p. 457). And, even though they viewed themselves as competent professionals in the business world, their amateurism as criminals helped get them into their current predicament. They sought to distinguish themselves as being morally superior to both working-class criminals and the justice officials who led them to their disgrace.

Critical Thinking

1. Willott and her colleagues found that both working-class and professional-class white-collar offenders created elaborate justifications for their behavior. They were pawns in an economic and social system beyond their control. Do their findings seem similar to Cressey's earlier research, which indicates that white-collar criminals are more likely to view themselves as victims than predators?

2. Would you put violators in prison? Or should white-collar criminals be given economic sanctions alone?

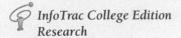

InfoTrac College Edition Research

Use "white-collar crime" as a key word in InfoTrac College Edition and access the articles in the *American Criminal Law Review*, annual edition, which reviews all the recent case law on business-related crimes.

Source: Sara Willott, Christine Griffin, and Mark Torrance, "Snakes and Ladders: Upper-Middle-Class Male Offenders Talk about Economic Crime," *Criminology* 39 (2001): 441–466.

---

the entire session and charging individual session rates for group therapy sessions.[82] When interviewed, the workers described using three techniques of neutralization that enabled them to defuse guilt over what they recognized as deviant practices: (1) everyone else does it, (2) its not my fault or responsibility, and (3) no one is hurt except wealthy insurance companies. The Comparative Criminology feature discusses this view in greater detail.

Corporate Culture View

The corporate culture view is that some business organizations promote white-collar criminality in the same way that lower-class culture encourages the development of juvenile gangs and street crime. According to the corporate culture view, some business enterprises cause crime by placing excessive demands on employees while at the same time maintaining a business climate tolerant of employee deviance. New employees learn the attitudes and techniques needed to commit white-collar crime from their business peers.

The corporate culture theory can be used to explain the collapse of Enron. A new CEO had been brought in to revitalize the company, and he wanted to become part of the "new economy" based on the Internet. Layers of management were wiped out, and hundreds of outsiders were recruited. Huge cash bonuses and stock options were granted to top performers. Young managers were given authority to make $5 million decisions without higher approval. It became common for executives to change jobs two or three times in an effort to maximize bonuses and pay. Seminars were conducted showing executives how to hide profits and avoid taxes.[83]

|||||||| CONNECTIONS ||||||||

The view that white-collar crime is a learning process is reminiscent of Edwin Sutherland's description of how gang boys learn the techniques of drug dealing and burglary from older youths through differential association. See Chapter 7 for a description of this process.

Those holding the corporate culture view would point to the Enron scandal as a prime example of what happens when people work in organizations in which the cultural values stress profit over fair play, government scrutiny is limited and regulators are viewed as the enemy, and senior members encourage newcomers to believe that "greed is good."

Self-Control View

Not all criminologists agree with corporate culture theory. Travis Hirschi and Michael Gottfredson take exception to the hypothesis that white-collar crime is a product of corporate culture.[84] If that were true, there would be much more white-collar crime than actually exists, and white-collar criminals would not be embarrassed by their misdeeds, as most seem to be. Instead, Hirschi and Gottfredson maintain that the motives that produce white-collar crimes—quick benefits with minimal effort—are the same as those that produce any other criminal behaviors.

|||||||| CONNECTIONS ||||||||

As you may recall from Chapter 9, Gottfredson and Hirschi's General Theory of Crime holds that criminals lack self-control. Because Gottfredson and Hirschi believe all crime has a similar basis, the motivation and pressure to commit white-collar crime is the same as for any other form of crime.

White-collar criminals have low self-control and are inclined to follow momentary impulses without considering the long-term costs of such behavior.[85] White-collar crime is relatively rare because, as a matter of course, business executives tend to hire people with self-control, thereby limiting the number of potential white-collar criminals. Hirschi and Gottfredson have collected data showing that the demographic distribution of white-collar crime is similar to other crimes. For example, gender, race, and age ratios are the same for crimes such as embezzlement and fraud as they are for street crimes such as burglary and robbery.

WHITE-COLLAR LAW ENFORCEMENT SYSTEMS

On the federal level, detection of white-collar crime is primarily in the hands of administrative departments and agencies.[86] The decision to pursue criminal rather than civil violations usually is based on the seriousness of the case and the perpetrator's intent, actions to conceal the violation, and prior record. Any evidence of criminal activity is then sent to the Department of Justice or the FBI for investigation. Some other federal agencies, such as the Securities and Exchange Commission and the U.S. Postal Service, have their own investigative arms. Enforcement generally is reactive (generated by complaints) rather than proactive (involving ongoing investigations or the monitoring of activities). Investigations are carried out by the various federal agencies and the FBI. If criminal prosecution is called for, the case will be handled by attorneys from the criminal, tax, antitrust, and civil rights divisions of the Justice Department. If insufficient evidence is available to warrant a criminal prosecution, the case will be handled civilly or administratively by some other federal agency. For example, the Federal Trade Commission can issue a cease and desist order in antitrust or merchandising fraud cases.

The number of state-funded technical assistance offices to help local prosecutors has increased significantly; more than forty states offer such services. On the state and local levels, law enforcement officials have made progress in a number of areas, such as controlling consumer fraud. For example, the Environmental Crimes Strike Force in Los Angeles County, California, is considered a model for the control of illegal dumping and pollution.[87] Some of the more common environmental offenses investigated and prosecuted by the task force include:

- The illegal transportation, treatment, storage or disposal of hazardous waste

- Oil spills

- Fraudulent certification of automobile smog tests [88]

Nonetheless, while local agencies recognize the seriousness of enterprise-type crimes, they rarely have the funds necessary for effective enforcement.[89]

Since 1999, **Florida's Department of Environmental Protection** has fielded a multi-agency Strike Force—led by the Department's Division of Law Enforcement—to investigate pollutant discharges and the release of hazardous material statewide: http://www.savefl.org/strike/backgrd.htm. For an up-to-date list of web links, go to http://cj.wadsworth.com/siegel_crimtpt9e.

Local prosecutors pursue white-collar criminals more vigorously if they are part of a team effort involving a network of law enforcement agencies.[90] National surveys of local prosecutors find that many do not consider white-collar crimes particularly serious problems. They are more willing to prosecute cases if the offense causes substantial harm and if other agencies fail to act. Relatively few prosecutors participate in interagency task forces designed to investigate white-collar criminal activity.[91]

Controlling White-Collar Crime

The prevailing wisdom is that, unlike lower-class street criminals, white-collar criminals are rarely prosecuted and, when convicted, receive relatively light sentences. There have also been charges that efforts to control white-collar crime are biased against specific classes and races: Authorities seem to be less diligent when victims are poor or minority group members or the crimes take place in minority areas. For example, Michael Lynch and his associates studied whether petroleum refineries violating environmental laws in black, Latino, and low-income communities receive smaller fines than those refineries in white and affluent communities; they found that violations of the Clean Air Act, the Clean Water Act, and/or the Resource Conservation and Recovery Act in minority areas received much smaller fines than the same types of violations occuring in white areas ($108,563 versus $341,590).[92]

In years past, it was rare for a corporate or white-collar criminal to receive a serious criminal penalty.[93] White-collar criminals are often considered nondangerous offenders because they usually are respectable older citizens who have families to support. These "pillars of the community" are not seen in the same light as a teenager who breaks into a drugstore to steal a few dollars. Their public humiliation at being caught is usually deemed punishment enough; a prison sentence seems unnecessarily cruel.

The prevailing wisdom, then, is that many white-collar criminals avoid prosecution, and those that are prosecuted receive lenient punishment. What efforts have been made to bring violators of the public trust to justice? White-collar criminal enforcement typically involves two strategies designed to control organizational deviance: compliance and deterrence.[94]

COMPLIANCE STRATEGIES Compliance strategies aim for law conformity without the necessity of detecting, processing, or penalizing individual violators. At a minimum, they ask for cooperation and self-policing among the business community. Compliance systems attempt to create conformity by giving companies economic incentives to obey the law. They rely on administrative efforts to prevent unwanted conditions before they occur. Compliance systems depend on the threat of economic sanctions or civil penalties to control corporate violators.

One method of compliance is to set up administrative agencies to oversee business activity. For example, the Securities and Exchange Commission regulates Wall Street activities, and the Food and Drug Administration regulates drugs, cosmetics, medical devices, meats, and other foods. The legislation creating these agencies usually spells out the penalties for violating regulatory standards. This approach has been used to control environmental crimes, for example, by levying heavy fines based on the quantity and quality of pollution released into the environment.[95] It is easier and less costly to be in compliance, the theory goes, than to pay costly fines and risk criminal prosecution for repeat violations. Moreover, the federal government bars people and businesses from receiving government contracts if they have engaged in repeated business law violations.

Another approach is to force corporate boards to police themselves and take more oversight responsibility. In the wake of the Enron and WorldCom debacles, the federal government enacted the Sarbanes–Oxley (SOX) legislation in 2002 to combat fraud and abuse in publicly traded companies.[96] This law limits the nonaudit services auditing firms can perform for publicly traded companies in order to make sure accounting firms do not fraudulently collude with corporate officers; as well, it places greater responsibilities on boards to preserve an organization's integrity and reputation, primarily for U.S. publicly traded companies. It also penalizes any attempts to alter or falsify company records in order to delude shareholders:

> Sec. 802(a) Whoever knowingly alters, destroys, mutilates, conceals, covers up, falsifies, or makes a false entry in any record, document, or tangible object with the intent to impede, obstruct, or influence the investigation or proper administration of any matter within the jurisdiction of any department or agency of the United States or any case filed under title 11, or in relation to or contemplation of any such matter or case, shall be fined under this title, imprisoned not more than 20 years, or both.

It seems that enforcing compliance with civil penalties is on the upswing. For example, the antitrust division of the U.S. Department of Justice reports that between 1997 and 2003, over $2 billion in criminal fines was levied on business violators, an amount equal to more than all the money collected for violations of the Sherman Antitrust Act between 1890 and 1997! In the ten years prior to 1997, the Anti-Trust Division obtained, on average, $29 million in criminal fines annually; by 2001, fines amounted to over $280 million. Among the biggest settlements:

- $500 million against F. Hoffmann-La Roche (vitamin cartel–May 1999), largest fine ever imposed in a criminal prosecution of any kind

- $225 million against BASF AG (vitamin cartel–May 1999)

- $135 million against SGL Carbon AG (graphite electrodes cartel–May 1999)

- $134 million against Mitsubishi Corp. (graphite electrodes cartel–May 2001)

- $110 million against UCAR International (graphite electrodes cartel–April 1998)

- $100 million against Archer Daniels Midland Company (lysine and citric acid cartels–October 1996)[97]

In sum, compliance strategies attempt to create a marketplace incentive to obey the law; for example, the more a company pollutes, the more costly and unprofitable that pollution becomes. Compliance strategies also avoid stigmatizing and shaming businesspeople by focusing on the act, rather than the actor, in white-collar crime.[98]

DETERRENCE STRATEGIES Some criminologists say that the punishment of white-collar crimes should include a retributive component similar to that used in common-law crimes. White-collar crimes, after all, are immoral activities that have harmed social values and deserve commensurate punishment.[99] Even the largest fines and penalties are no more than a slap on the wrist to multibillion-dollar companies. Corporations can get around economic sanctions by moving their rule-violating activities overseas, where legal controls over injurious corporate activities are lax or nonexistent.[100] They argue that the only way to limit white-collar crime is to deter potential offenders through fear of punishment.

Deterrence strategies involve detecting criminal violations, determining who is responsible, and penalizing the offenders to deter future violations.[101] Deterrence systems are oriented toward apprehending violators and punishing them rather than creating conditions that induce conformity to the law.

Deterrence strategies should work—and they have—because white-collar crime by its nature is a rational act whose perpetrators are extremely sensitive to the threat of criminal sanctions. Perceptions of detection and punishment for white-collar crimes appear to be powerful deterrents to future law violations. Although deterrence strategies may prove effective, federal agencies have traditionally been reluctant to throw corporate executives in jail. For example, the courts have not hesitated to enforce the Sherman Antitrust Act in civil actions, but they have limited application of the criminal sanctions. Similarly, the government seeks criminal indictments in corporate violations only in "instances of outrageous conduct of undoubted illegality," such as price fixing.[102] The government has also been lenient with companies and individuals that cooperate voluntarily after an investigation has begun; leniency is not given as part of a confession or plea arrangement. Those who comply with the leniency policy are charged criminally for the activity reported.[103]

Some federal courts are likely to send convicted white-collar criminals to prison, whereas others seem reluctant to use incarceration. For a news report on this phenomenon, go to InfoTrac College Edition and read this article: "Wide Disparity in White-Collar Sentences," USA Today 128 (April 2000): 11.

Is the Tide Turning?

Despite years of neglect, there is growing evidence that white-collar crime deterrence strategies have become normative. For example, Adelphia cable operator John Rigas was sentenced to 15 years in prison for bank and securities fraud, and his son Timothy Rigas was sentenced to 20 years after their conviction on charges that they used company funds to support their profligate lifestyle. John Rigas took advantage of a shared line of credit with Adelphia, using the company's money—stockholder's money—for personal extravagances.[104]

This get-tough deterrence approach appears to be affecting all classes of white-collar criminals. Although many people believe affluent corporate executives usually avoid serious punishment, public displeasure with such highly publicized white-collar crimes may be producing a backlash that is resulting in more frequent use of prison sentences.[105] With the Enron scandal depriving so many people of their life savings, the general public has become educated as to the damage caused by white-collar criminals and may now consider white-collar crimes as more serious offenses than common-law theft offenses.[106]

As a result, the government has stepped up investigations against senior executives and financial reporting personnel. From July 2002 through May 2004, federal prosecutors obtained 500 convictions or guilty pleas on corporate fraud charges against 900 defendants, 60 of whom were corporate presidents or CEOs.[107]

Some commentators now argue that the government may actually be going overboard in its efforts to punish white-collar criminals, especially for crimes that are the result of negligent business practices rather than intentional criminal conspiracy.[108] Nonetheless, the government has continued to pass legislation increasing penalties for business-related crimes. For example, the Antitrust Criminal Penalty Enhancement and Reform Act of 2004 imposes significantly higher criminal antitrust penalties for individuals and businesses committing violations under Sections 1 or 3 of the Sherman Antitrust Act or a violation of any similar state law. These penalties include:

- The maximum corporate fine is raised to $100 million from $10 million.

- The maximum individual fine is raised to $1 million from $350,000.

- The maximum prison sentence is increased to 10 years from 3 years.

When the act was passed, R. Hewitt Pate, Assistant Attorney General for Antitrust, issued a statement that said in part:

The enhanced enforcement measures provided for by the Act will aid in the continued successful detection, prosecution, punishment, and deterrence of hard core cartel activity, further protecting free and open competition.[109]

Such measures show that in the wake of the Enron and WorldCom scandals, white-collar crime has become a signficant focus of government interest.

ORGANIZED CRIME

A second branch of enterprise crime involves organized crime—ongoing criminal enterprise groups whose ultimate purpose is personal economic gain through illegitimate means. Here a structured enterprise system is set up to continually supply consumers with merchandise and services banned by criminal law but for which a ready market exists: prostitution, pornography, gambling, and narcotics. The system may resemble a legitimate business run by an ambitious chief executive officer, his or her assistants, staff attorneys, and accountants, with thorough, efficient accounts receivable and complaint departments.[110]

Because of its secrecy, power, and fabulous wealth, a great mystique has grown up about organized crime. Its legendary leaders—Al Capone, Meyer Lansky, Lucky Luciano—have been the subjects of books and films. The famous *Godfather* films popularized and humanized organized crime figures; the media often glamorize organized crime figures.[111] Watching the exploits of Tony Soprano and his family life has become a national craze.

> Want to learn more about the **Sopranos?** There are a number of websites devoted to Tony and his clan. Go to http://www.the-sopranos.com. Want to learn Tony's "business secrets"? Go to http://www.businessknowhow.com/growth/soprano.htm. For an up-to-date list of web links, go to http://cj.wadsworth.com/siegel_crimtpt9e.

Most citizens believe organized criminals are capable of taking over legitimate business enterprises if given the opportunity. Almost everyone is familiar with such terms as mob, underworld, Mafia, wise guys, syndicate, or La Cosa Nostra, which refer to organized crime. Although most of us have neither met nor seen members of organized crime families, we feel sure that they exist, and we fear them. This section briefly defines organized crime, reviews its history, and discusses its economic effect and control.

Characteristics of Organized Crime

A precise description of the characteristics of organized crime is difficult to formulate, but here are some of its general traits:[112]

- Organized crime is a conspiratorial activity, involving the coordination of numerous people in the planning and execution of illegal acts or in the pursuit of a legitimate objective by unlawful means (for example, threatening a legitimate business to get a stake in it). Organized crime involves continuous commitment by primary members, although individuals with specialized skills may be brought in as needed. Organized crime is usually structured along hierarchical lines—a chieftain supported by close advisers, lower subordinates, and so on.

- Organized crime has economic gain as its primary goal, although power and status may also be motivating factors. Economic gain is achieved through maintenance of a near-monopoly on illegal goods and services, including drugs, gambling, pornography, and prostitution.

- Organized crime activities are not limited to providing illicit services. They include such sophisticated activities as laundering illegal money through legitimate businesses, land fraud, and computer crime.

- Organized crime employs predatory tactics, such as intimidation, violence, and corruption. It appeals to greed to accomplish its objectives and preserve its gains.

- By experience, custom, and practice, organized crime's conspiratorial groups are usually very quick and effective in controlling and disciplining their members, associates, and victims. The individuals involved know that any deviation from the rules of the organization will evoke a prompt response from the other participants. This response may range from a reduction in rank and responsibility to a death sentence.

- Organized crime is not synonymous with the Mafia, which is really a common stereotype of organized crime. Although several families in the organization called the Mafia are important components of organized crime activities, they do not hold a monopoly on underworld activities.

- Organized crime does not include terrorists dedicated to political change. Although violent acts are a major tactic of organized crime, the use of violence does not mean that a group is part of a confederacy of organized criminals.

Activities of Organized Crime

What are the main activities of organized crime? The traditional sources of income are derived from providing illicit materials and using force to enter into and maximize profits in legitimate businesses.[113] Most organized crime income comes from narcotics distribution, loan sharking (lending money at illegal rates), and prostitution. However, additional billions come from gambling, theft rings, pornography, and other illegal enterprises. Organized criminals have infiltrated labor unions and taken control of

© Desmond Boylan / Reuters / Landov

Young girls from the close-knit tribe known as the Dhimal, who live in eastern India near Nepal, have become the newest target of international organized crime figures who traffic in the international sex trade. Trafficking in people for forced labor is one of the most lucrative and fastest-growing criminal enterprises in the world, with an estimated 600,000–800,000 men, women, and children forced into slavery each year. There is evidence that criminal syndicates are switching from drugs to human trafficking, finding it easier to transport people than cocaine or heroin. Moreover, while drugs can only be sold once, people can be resold again and again.

their pension funds and dues.[114] Hijacking of shipments and cargo theft are other sources of income. Underworld figures fence high-value items and maintain international sales territories. In recent years they have branched into computer crime and other white-collar activities. Organized crime figures have also kept up with the information age by using computers and the Internet to sell illegal material such as pornography.

Organized crime figures are also involved in stock market manipulation. The FBI notes that organized crime groups target "small cap" or "micro cap" stocks, over-the-counter stocks, and other types of thinly traded stocks that can be easily manipulated and sold to elderly or inexperienced investors. The conspirators use offshore bank accounts to conceal their participation in the fraud scheme and to launder the illegal proceeds in order to avoid paying income tax.[115]

The Concept of Organized Crime

The term *organized crime* conjures up images of strong men in dark suits, machine gun–toting bodyguards, rituals of allegiance to secret organizations, professional "gangland" killings, and meetings of "family" leaders who chart the course of crime much as the board members at General Motors decide on the country's transportation needs. These images have become part of what criminologists refer to as the **alien conspiracy theory** concept of organized crime. This is the belief, adhered to by the federal government and many respected criminologists, that organized crime is a direct offshoot of a criminal society—the **Mafia**—that first originated in Italy and Sicily and now controls racketeering in major U.S. cities. A major premise of the alien conspiracy theory is that the Mafia is centrally coordinated by a national committee that settles disputes, dictates policy, and assigns territory.[116]

Not all criminologists believe in this narrow concept of organized crime, and many view the alien conspiracy theory as a figment of the media's imagination.[117] Their view depicts organized crime as a group of ethnically diverse gangs or groups who compete for profit in the sale of illegal goods and services or who use force and violence to extort money from legitimate enterprises. These groups are not bound by a central national organization but act independently on their own turf. We will now examine these perspectives in some detail.

Alien Conspiracy Theory

According to the alien conspiracy theory, organized crime is made up of a national syndicate of twenty-five or so Italian-dominated crime families that call themselves **La Cosa Nostra**. The major families have a total membership of about 1,700 "made men," who have been inducted into organized crime families, and another 17,000 "associates," who are criminally involved with syndicate members. The families control crime in distinct geographic areas. New York City, the most important organized crime area, alone contains five families—the Gambino, Columbo (formerly Profaci), Lucchese, Bonnano, and Genovese families—named after their founding "godfathers"; in contrast, Chicago contains a single mob organization called the "outfit," which also influences racketeering in such cities as Milwaukee, Kansas City, and Phoenix.[118] The families are believed to be ruled by a "commission" made up of the heads of the five New York families and bosses from Detroit, Buffalo, Chicago, and Philadelphia, which settles personal problems and jurisdictional conflicts and enforces rules that allow members to gain huge profits through the manufacture and sale of illegal goods and services.

In sum, the alien conspiracy theory sees organized crime as being run by an ordered group of ethnocentric (primarily of Italian origin) criminal syndicates, maintaining unified leadership and shared values. These syndicates communicate closely with other groups and obey the decisions of a national commission charged with settling disputes and creating crime policy.

Contemporary Organized Crime Groups

Even such devoted alien conspiracy advocates as the U.S. Justice Department now view organized crime as a loose confederation of ethnic and regional crime groups, bound together by a commonality of economic and political objectives.[119] Some of these groups are located in fixed geographical areas. Chicano crime families are found in areas with significant Latino populations, such as California and Arizona. White-ethnic crime organizations are found across the nation. Some Italian and Cuban groups operate internationally. Some have preserved their past identity, whereas others are constantly changing organizations.

One important contemporary change in organized crime is the interweaving of ethnic groups into the traditional structure. African American, Latino, and Asian racketeers now compete with the more traditional groups, overseeing the distribution of drugs, prostitution, and gambling in a symbiotic relationship with old-line racketeers.

EASTERN EUROPEAN CRIME GROUPS Eastern Europe has been the scene of a massive buildup in organized crime since the fall of the Soviet Union. Trading in illegal arms, narcotics, pornography, and prostitution, they operate a multibillion-dollar transnational crime cartel. For example, organized groups prey upon women in the poorest areas of Europe—Romania, Ukraine, Bosnia—and sell them into virtual sexual slavery. Many of these women are transported as prostitutes around the world, some finding themselves in the United States.

In September 2002, an intensive European enforcement operation conducted with American assistance to eliminate some of the major players in the international sex trade resulted in the arrest of 293 traffickers. However, this is the tip of the iceberg: It is estimated that 700,000 women are transported, mostly involuntarily, over international borders each year for the sex trade. One reason for the difficulty in creating effective enforcement is the complicity of local authorities with criminal organizations. For example, during the 2002 raids, the United Nations Mission in Sarajevo dismissed eleven Bosnian police officers, including members of the antitrafficking squad, after they were apprehended visiting brothels and abusing prostitutes.[120]

Since 1970, Russian and other eastern European groups have been operating on U.S. soil. Some groups are formed by immigrants from former satellites of the Soviet Union. For example, in 1998 the FBI established the Yugoslavian/Albanian/Croatian/Serbian (YACS) Crime Group initiative as a response to the increasing threat of criminal activity by people originating from these areas. YACS gangs focus on highly organized and specialized thefts from ATM machines in the New York City area.[121]

Some experts believe Russian crime families, thanks to their control of gasoline terminals and distributorships in the New York metropolitan area, evade as much as $5 billion a year in state and federal taxes. Some of that money then goes to pay off their allies, the Italian Mafia. To find out more, use "Russian organized crime" as a subject guide in InfoTrac College Edition. Also, read this article: Sherry Ricchiardi, "The Best Investigative Reporter You've Never Heard of," American Journalism Review 22 (January 2000): 44.

In addition, as many as 2,500 Russian immigrants are believed to be involved in criminal activity, primarily in Russian enclaves in New York City. Beyond extortion from immigrants, Russian organized crime groups have cooperated with Mafia families in narcotics trafficking, fencing stolen property, money laundering, and other traditional organized crime schemes.[122]

Some of these gangs have engaged in wide-ranging multinational conspiracies. In 1999, after a 2-year criminal investigation in Italy, investigators turned up evidence that alleged Russian organized crime operators had funneled millions of dollars through the Bank of New York in a massive money-laundering scheme.[123] Italian prosecutors found that the Russian criminal gangs were raising money in Italy through a mixture of legitimate business activities as well as extortion and tax fraud. Their targets were the Russian businessmen and immigrants who had flooded into Italy with the collapse of communism. The illegal funds were then routed to Moscow and New York, where they were transferred to accounts belonging to suspected organized crime operators. Between 1996 and 1999, the Russian mob is believed to have moved at least $7.5 billion from Russia into the Bank of New York. For more on the Russian mob, see the Comparative Criminology feature.

The Evolution of Organized Crime

Have these newly emerging groups achieved the same level of control as traditional crime families? Some experts argue that minority gangs will have a tough time developing the network of organized corruption, which involves working with government officials and unions, that traditional crime families enjoyed.[124] As law enforcement pressure has been put on traditional organized crime figures, other groups have filled the vacuum. For example, the Hell's Angels motorcycle club is now believed to be one of the leading distributors of narcotics in the United States. Similarly, Chinese criminal gangs have taken over the dominant role in New York City's heroin market from the traditional Italian-run syndicates.

In sum, most experts now agree that it is simplistic to view organized crime in the United States as a national syndicate that controls all illegitimate rackets in an orderly

Russian Organized Crime

In the decade since the collapse of the Soviet Union, criminal organizations in Russia and other former Soviet republics such as the Ukraine have engaged in a variety of crimes: drugs and arms trafficking, stolen automobiles, trafficking in women and children, and money laundering, No area of the world seems immune to this menace, especially not the United States. America is the land of opportunity for unloading criminal goods and laundering dirty money.

Unlike Colombian, Italian, Mexican, or other well-known forms of organized crime, Russian organized crime is not primarily based on ethnic or family structures. Instead, Russian organized crime is based on economic necessity that was nurtured by the oppressive Soviet regime. Here, a professional criminal class developed in Soviet prisons during the Stalinist period that began in 1924—the era of the gulag. These criminals adopted behaviors, rules, values, and sanctions that bound them together in what was called the thieves' world, led by the elite *vory v zakone*, criminals who lived according to the "thieves' law." This thieves' world, and particularly the *vory,* created and maintained the bonds and climate of trust necessary for carrying out organized crime.

The following are some specific characteristics of Russian organized crime in the post-Soviet era:

■ Russian criminals make extensive use of the state governmental apparatus to protect and promote their criminal activities. For example, most businesses in Russia—legal, quasi-legal, and illegal—must operate with the protection of a *krysha* (roof). The protection is often provided by police or security officials employed outside their "official" capacities for this purpose. In other cases, officials are "silent partners" in criminal enterprises that they, in turn, protect.

■ The criminalization of the privatization process has resulted in the massive use of state funds for criminal gain. Valuable properties are purchased through insider deals for much less than their true value and then resold for lucrative profits.

■ Criminals have been able to directly influence the state's domestic and foreign policy to promote the interests of organized crime, either by attaining public office themselves or by buying public officials.

Beyond these particular features, organized crime in Russia shares other characteristics that are common to organized crime elsewhere in the world:

■ Systematic use of violence, including both the threat and the use of force

■ Hierarchical structure

■ Limited or exclusive membership

■ Specialization in types of crime and a division of labor

■ Military-style discipline, with strict rules and regulations for the organization as a whole

---

fashion. This view ignores the variety of gangs and groups, their membership, and their relationship to the outside world.[125] Mafia-type groups may play a major role in organized crime, but they are by no means the only ones that can be considered organized criminals.[126]

For a site devoted to **organized crime** and links to other similar sites, go to http://organizedcrime. about.com. For an up-to-date list of web links, go to http:// cj.wadsworth.com/siegel_crimtpt9e.

Controlling Organized Crime

George Vold has argued that the development of organized crime parallels early capitalist enterprises. Organized crime employs ruthless monopolistic tactics to maximize profits; it is also secretive, protective of its operations, and defensive against any outside intrusion.[127] Consequently, controlling its activities is extremely difficult.

Federal and state governments actually did little to combat organized crime until fairly recently. One of the first measures aimed directly at organized crime was the Interstate and Foreign Travel or Transportation in Aid of Racketeering Enterprises Act (Travel Act).[128] The Travel Act prohibits travel in interstate commerce or use of interstate facilities with the intent to promote, manage, establish, carry on, or facilitate an unlawful activity; it also prohibits the actual or attempted engagement in these activities. In 1970 Congress passed the Organized Crime Control Act. Title IX of the act, probably its most effective measure, has been called the **Racketeer Influenced and Corrupt Organization (RICO) Act.**[129]

RICO did not create new categories of crimes but rather new categories of offenses in racketeering activity, which it defined as involvement in two or more acts prohibited by twenty-four existing federal and eight state statutes. The offenses listed in RICO include state-defined crimes, such as murder, kidnapping, gambling, arson, robbery, bribery, extortion, and narcotic violations; and federally defined crimes,

- Possession of high-tech equipment, including military weapons; threats, blackmail, and violence are used to penetrate business management and assume control of commercial enterprises or, in some instances, to found their own enterprises with money from their criminal activities.

As a result of these activities:

- Russia has high rates of homicide that are now more than twenty times those in western Europe and approximately three times the rates recorded in the United States. The rates more closely resemble those of a country in civil war or in conflict than those of a country ten years into a transition.

- Corruption and organized crime are globalized. Russian organized crime is active in Europe, Africa, Asia, and North and South America.

- Massive money laundering is now common. It allows Russian and foreign organized crime to flourish. In some cases, it is tied to terrorist funding.

The organized crime threat to Russia's national security is now becoming a global threat. Russian organized crime operates both on its own and in cooperation with foreign groups. The latter cooperation often comes in the form of joint money laundering ventures. Russian criminals have become involved in killings for hire in central and western Europe, Israel, Canada, and the United States.

However, in the United States, with the exception of extortion and money laundering, Russians have had little or no involvement in some of the more traditional types of organized crime, such as drug trafficking, gambling, and loan sharking. Instead, these criminal groups are extensively engaged in a broad array of frauds and scams, including healthcare fraud, insurance scams, stock frauds, antiquities swindles, forgery, and fuel tax evasion schemes. Recently, for example, Russians have become the main purveyors of credit card fraud in the United States. Legitimate businesses, such as the movie business and textile industry,

have become targets of criminals from the former Soviet Union, and they are often used for money laundering.

Critical Thinking

The influence of new immigrant groups in organized crime seems to suggest that illegal enterprise is a common practice among "new" Americans. Do you believe that there is some aspect of American culture that causes immigrants to choose a criminal lifestyle? Or does our open culture encourage criminal activities that may have been incubating in people's native lands?

InfoTrac College Edition Research

To read more about Russian organized crime, go to InfoTrac College Edition and access: Scott O'Neal, "Russian Organized Crime," *FBI Law Enforcement Bulletin* 69 (May 2000): 1.

Sources: Louise I. Shelley, "Crime and Corruption: Enduring Problems of Post-Soviet Development," *Demokratizatsiya* 11 (2003): 110–114; James O. Finckenauer and Yuri A. Voronin, *The Threat of Russian Organized Crime* (Washington, DC: National Institute of Justice, 2001).

---

such as bribery, counterfeiting, transmission of gambling information, prostitution, and mail fraud. RICO is designed to limit patterns of organized criminal activity by prohibiting involvement in acts intended to

- Derive income from racketeering or the unlawful collection of debts and use or invest such income

- Acquire through racketeering an interest in or control over any enterprise engaged in interstate or foreign commerce

- Conduct business through a pattern of racketeering

- Conspire to use racketeering as a means of making income, collecting loans, or conducting business

An individual convicted under RICO is subject to 20 years in prison and a $25,000 fine. Additionally, the accused must forfeit to the U.S. government any interest in a business in violation of RICO. These penalties are much more potent than simple conviction and imprisonment.

RICO's success has shaped the way the FBI attacks organized crime groups. They now use the **enterprise theory of investigation (ETI)** model as their standard investigative tool. Rather than investigate crimes after they are committed, under the ETI model the focus is on criminal enterprise and investigation attacks on the structure of the criminal enterprise rather than on criminal acts viewed as isolated incidents.[130] For example, a drug trafficking organization must get involved in such processes as transportation and distribution of narcotics, finance such as money laundering, and communication with clients and dealers. The ETI identifies and then targets each of these areas simultaneously, focusing on the subsystems that are considered the most vulnerable.

The Future of Organized Crime

Indications are that the traditional organized crime syndicates are in decline. Law enforcement officials in Philadelphia, New Jersey, New England, New Orleans, Kansas City, Detroit, and Milwaukee all report that years of federal and state interventions have severely eroded the Mafia organizations in their areas.

What has caused this alleged erosion of Mafia power? First, a number of the reigning family heads are quite old, in their 80s and older, prompting some law enforcement officials to dub them "the Geritol gang."[131] A younger generation of mob leaders is stepping in to take control of the families, and they seem to lack the skill and leadership of the older bosses. In addition, active government enforcement policies have halved what the estimated mob membership was twenty-five years ago, and a number of the highest-ranking leaders have been imprisoned.

Additional pressure comes from newly emerging ethnic gangs that want to muscle in on traditional syndicate activities, such as drug sales and gambling. For example, Chinese Triad gangs in New York and California have been active in the drug trade, loan sharking, and labor racketeering. Other ethnic crime groups include black and Colombian drug cartels and the Sicilian Mafia, which operates independently of U.S. groups.

The Mafia has also been hurt by changing values in U.S. society. White, ethnic, inner-city neighborhoods, which were the locus of Mafia power, have been shrinking as families move to the suburbs. (It comes as no surprise that fictional character Tony Soprano lives in suburban New Jersey and his daughter goes to Columbia.) Organized crime groups have consequently lost their political and social base of operations. In addition, the code of silence that protected Mafia leaders is now broken regularly by younger members who turn informer rather than face prison terms. It is also possible that their success has hurt organized crime families: Younger members are better educated than their forebears and are equipped to seek their fortunes through legitimate enterprise.[132]

If traditional organized gangs are in decline, that does not mean the end of organized crime. Russian, Caribbean, and Asian gangs seem to be thriving, and there are always new opportunities for illegal practices. Law enforcement officials believe that Internet gambling sites are a tempting target for enterprise criminals. It is not surprising then that Illinois, Louisiana, Nevada, Oregon, and South Dakota have recently passed laws specifically banning Internet gambling.[133] It is unlikely, considering the demand for illegal goods and services and the emergence of newly constituted crime families, that organized criminal behavior will ever be eradicated.

SUMMARY

- Enterprise crime involves illicit entrepreneurship and commerce.

- White-collar and organized crimes are linked because they involve entrepreneurship. Losses from enterprise crime may far outstrip any other type of crime.

- Enterprise crime involves criminal acts that twist the legal rules of commercial enterprise for criminal purposes.

- There are various types of white-collar crime: Stings and swindles involve long-term efforts to cheat people out of their money; chiseling involves regular cheating of an organization or its customers; exploitation involves coercing victims (clients) into paying for services for which they are entitled by threatening consequences if they refuse; influence peddling and bribery involve demanding payment for a service for which the payer is clearly not entitled (the victim here is the organization).

- Embezzlement and employee fraud occur when a person uses a position of trust to steal from an organization.

- Client fraud involves theft from an organization that advances credit, covers losses, or reimburses for services.

- Corporate crime involves various illegal business practices such as price fixing, restraint of trade, and false advertising.

- There are numerous explanations for white-collar crime: Some offenders are motivated by greed; others offend due to personal problems.

- The rationalization/neutralization view suggests that offenders use rationalizations to resolve the conflict they experience over engaging in illegal behavior. Rationalizations allow offenders' financial needs to be met without compromising their values.

- Corporate culture theory suggests that some businesses actually encourage employees to cheat or cut corners.

- The self-control view is that white-collar criminals are like any other law violators: impulsive people who lack self-control.

- Little has been done in the past to combat white-collar crime. Most offenders do not view themselves as criminals and therefore do not seem to be deterred by criminal statutes. Although thousands of white-collar criminals are prosecuted each year, their numbers are insignificant compared with the magnitude of the problem.

- The government has used various law enforcement strategies to combat white-collar crime. Some involve deterrence, which uses punishment to frighten potential abusers. Others involve economic or compliance strategies, which create economic incentives to obey the law.

- Organized crime supplies alcohol, gambling, drugs, prostitutes, and pornography to the public. It is immune from prosecution because of public apathy and because of its own strong political connections.

- Organized criminals used to be white ethnics—Jews, Italians, and Irish—but today African Americans, Latinos, and other groups have become involved in organized crime

activities. The old-line "families" are now more likely to use their criminal wealth and power to buy into legitimate businesses.

- There is debate over the control of organized crime. Some experts believe a national crime cartel controls all activities. Others view organized crime as a group of disorganized,

competing gangs dedicated to extortion or to providing illegal goods and services. Efforts to control organized crime have been stepped up. The federal government has used antiracketeering statutes to arrest syndicate leaders. But as long as huge profits can be made, illegal enterprises will continue to flourish.

ThomsonNOW

Thomson NOW! Optimize your study time and master key chapter concepts with **ThomsonNOW™**—the first web-based assessment-centered study tool for Criminology. This powerful resource helps you determine your unique study needs and provides you with a *Personalized Study Plan,* guiding you to interactive media that includes Learning Modules, Topic Reviews, ABC Video Clips with Questions, Animations, an integrated E-book, and more!

Thinking Like a Criminologist

As a criminologist you have been asked by a federal judge to help her make a sentencing decision in the case of Frank and Miriam Martin of Richmond, Virginia. The Martins have just pled guilty to conspiracy to commit identification document fraud for their involvement in issuing and selling genuine Virginia driver's licenses. The judge tells you the following facts of the case:

Until his arrest in July 2005, Frank Martin, age 57, was the manager of the Virginia Department of Motor Vehicles (DMV) customer service center at the Springfield Mall in Springfield, Virginia, and had been a DMV employee since 1990. Miriam Martin, age 57, worked as a clerk at the DMV in Tyson's Corner, Virginia, from 1996 to 1998 and then again briefly in 2003.

The defendants, as former DMV employees, were intimately familiar with the procedures and policies of the DMV with regard to eligibility for obtaining driver's licenses. For approximately 4 years, Frank and Miriam Martin were the critical players in a conspiracy to produce and sell authentic

Virginia driver's licenses to immigrants unlawfully in the United States and other unqualified applicants in exchange for fees of up to $3,500. Frank Martin abused his position from within DMV to produce driver's licenses for immigrants located and sent to the DMV customer service center by his wife Miriam and another conspirator. He falsified DMV records to make it appear that the immigrants who received the licenses were residents who had recently moved to Virginia from another state. Specifically, he would falsify records to show that the immigrant applicant had surrendered a valid driver's license from another state, knowing that the applicant surrendered no license at all and never lived in that state.

Miriam Martin served as the critical link between her husband and the unqualified applicants. She would obtain the names and other personal information that the unqualified applicants wanted their licenses to bear to pass along to her husband. She would also provide instructions to the unqualified applicants and collect fees from them. In return for a genuine Virginia driver's

license, each immigrant was charged a fee of up to $3,500. In most cases the immigrants buying the licenses were not qualified to obtain a valid Virginia driver's license because they were unlawfully present in the United States or because their driving privileges had been suspended.

As a result of their joint actions, Frank and Miriam Martin allowed numerous illegal immigrants to conceal their true identities and obtain valid identification documents that they then could and did use for commercial and other reasons. Their joint bank account indicates that they made over $350,000 from the illegal scheme.

Neither Frank nor Miriam has been in trouble with the law before. They have three children and own their own home. Their neighbors describe them as polite, cordial, and friendly. They pose no threat to society now that their scheme has been uncovered. The judge asks you to analyze the case and make a sentence recommendation. The choices are probation with a fine or a period of incarceration of up to 5 years. Which would you choose and why?

Doing Research on the Web

Are we really getting tough on white-collar crime? Check out the testimony of Department of Homeland Security Secretary Michael Chertoff, then Assistant Attorney General, before the U.S. Senate Committee on the Judiciary, "Penalties for White-Collar Crime: Are We Really Getting Tough on Crime?" July 10, 2002: http://judiciary.senate.gov/print_testimony.cfm?id=310&wit_id=66.

For an opposing view, go to: Clifton Leaf, "White-Collar Criminals: Enough Is Enough," *Fortune* (18 March 2002), which can be found at: http://www.doublestandards.org/leaf1.html.

BOOK COMPANION WEBSITE

 http://cj.wadsworth.com/siegel_crimtpt9e To quiz yourself on the material in this chapter, go to the companion website, where you'll find chapter-by-chapter online tutorial quizzes, a final exam, ABC videos with questions, chapter outlines, chapter review, chapter-by-chapter web links, flash cards, and more!

KEY TERMS

enterprise crime (396)
white-collar crime (396)
organized crime (396)
corporate crime (396)
sting or swindle (397)
chiseling (398)
churning (399)
front running (399)
bucketing (399)
insider trading (399)

exploitation (399)
influence peddling (400)
pilferage (401)
check kiting (404)
organizational crime (405)
actual authority (406)
apparent authority (406)
Sherman Antitrust Act (406)
division of markets (406)
tying arrangement (406)

group boycott (406)
price fixing (406)
alien conspiracy theory (414)
Mafia (414)
La Cosa Nostra (414)
Racketeer Influenced and Corrupt Organization (RICO) Act (416)
enterprise theory of investigation (ETI) (417)

CRITICAL THINKING QUESTIONS

1. How would you punish a corporate executive whose product killed people if the executive had no knowledge that the product was potentially lethal? What if the executive did know?

2. Is organized crime inevitable as long as immigrant groups seek to become part of the American Dream?

3. Does the media glamorize organized crime? Does it paint an inaccurate picture of noble crime lords fighting to protect their families?

4. Apply traditional theories of criminal behavior to white-collar and organized crime. Which one seems to best predict why someone would engage in these behaviors?

NOTES

1. Constance Hays, "ImClone Founder Pleads Guilty to 6 Charges," *New York Times*, 16 October 2002, p. A1.

2. Nikos Passas and David Nelken, "The Thin Line between Legitimate and Criminal Enterprises: Subsidy Frauds in the European Community," *Crime, Law, and Social Change* 19 (1993): 223–243.

3. For a thorough review, see David Friedrichs, *Trusted Criminals* (Belmont, CA: Wadsworth, 1996).

4. Kitty Calavita and Henry Pontell, "Savings and Loan Fraud as Organized Crime: Toward a Conceptual Typology of Corporate Illegality," *Criminology* 31 (1993): 519–548.

5. Mark Haller, "Illegal Enterprise: A Theoretical and Historical Interpretation," *Criminology* 28 (1990): 207–235.

6. Nancy Frank and Michael Lynch, *Corporate Crime, Corporate Violence* (Albany, NY: Harrow & Heston, 1992), p. 7.

7. Edwin Sutherland, *White-Collar Crime: The Uncut Version* (New Haven, CT: Yale University Press, 1983).

8. Edwin Sutherland, "White-Collar Criminality," *American Sociological Review* 5 (1940): 2–10.

9. David Weisburd and Kip Schlegel, "Returning to the Mainstream," in *White-Collar Crime Reconsidered*, eds. Kip Schlegel and David Weisburd (Boston: Northeastern University Press, 1992), pp. 352–365.

10. Ronald Kramer and Raymond Michalowski, "State-Corporate Crime." Paper presented at the annual meeting of the American Society of Criminology, Baltimore, November 1990.

11. Elizabeth Moore and Michael Mills, "The Neglected Victims and Unexamined Costs of White-Collar Crime," *Crime and Delinquency* 36 (1990): 408–418.

12. Natalie Taylor, "Under-Reporting of Crime against Small Business: Attitudes towards Police and Reporting Practices," *Policing and Society* 13 (2003): 79–90.

13. Gilbert Geis, "White-Collar and Corporate Crime," in *Major Forms of Crime,* ed. Robert Meier (Beverly Hills: Sage, 1984), p. 145.

14. Marshall Clinard and Richard Quinney, *Criminal Behavior Systems: A Typology* (New York: Holt, Rinehart & Winston, 1973), p. 117.

15. Mark Moore, "Notes toward a National Strategy to Deal with White-Collar Crime," in *A National Strategy for Containing White-Collar Crime,* eds. Herbert Edelhertz and Charles Rogovin (Lexington, MA: Lexington Books, 1980), pp. 32–44.

16. David Firestone, "In Racketeering Trial, Well-Dressed Strip Club Takes the Stage," *New York Times,* 5 May 2001, p. 3.

17. Internet Crime Complaint Center, "Fraudulent Sites Capitalizing on Relief Efforts of Hurricane Katrina." http://www.ifccfbi.gov/strategy/katrina_warning.pdf. Accessed September 6, 2005.

18. Nikos Passas, "Structural Sources of International Crime: Policy Lessons from the BCCI Affair," *Crime, Law and Social Change* 19 (1994): 223–231.

19. Nikos Passas, "Accounting for Fraud: Auditors' Ethical Dilemmas in the BCCI Affair," in *The Ethics of Accounting and Finance,* eds. W. Michael Hoffman, Judith Brown Kamm, Robert Frederick, and Edward Petry (Westport, CT: Quorum Books, 1996), pp. 85–99.

20. North American Securities Administrators Association (NASAA), "Beware of Oil and Gas Schemes, State Securities Regulators Warn Investors, Con Artists May Seek to Exploit Fears over Mideast, Oil Supply." http://www.nasaa.org/nasaa/abtnasaa/display_top_story.asp?stid=348. Accessed August 25, 2004.

21. Earl Gottschalk, "Churchgoers Are the Prey as Scams Rise," *Wall Street Journal,* 7 August 1989, p. C1.

22. Associated Press, "NYC Cab Scam Warning Given," *Boston Globe,* 19 September 1997, p. 13.

23. Richard Pérez-Peña, "Indictments Charge 4 Racetrack Tellers with Laundering Money at Betting Windows," *New York Times,* 20 July 2001, p. A4.

24. Federal Bureau of Investigation, Operation Bullpen, http://www.fbi.gov/hq/cid/fc/ec/sm/smoverview.htm. Accessed September 6, 2005.

25. Richard Quinney, "Occupational Structure and Criminal Behavior: Prescription Violation of Retail Pharmacists," *Social Problems* 11 (1963): 179–185; see also John Braithwaite, *Corporate Crime in the Pharmaceutical Industry* (London: Routledge and Kegan Paul, 1984).

26. Pam Belluck, "Prosecutors Say Greed Drove Pharmacist to Dilute Drugs" *New York Times,* 18 August 2001, p. 3.

27. Press Release, April 22, 2002, Kansas City Division, Federal Bureau of Investigation.

28. Anish Vashista, David Johnson, and Muhtashem Choudhury. "Securities Fraud," *American Criminal Law Review* 42 (2005): 877–942.

29. U.S. Department of Justice, "Two Men Arraigned in Fraud Scheme that Cost Victims Nearly $1.7 Million," September 6, 2005. http://www.usdoj.gov/usao/cac/pr2005/126.html. Accessed September 7, 2005.

30. James Armstrong, et al., "Securities Fraud," *American Criminal Law Review* 33 (1995): 973–1,016.

31. Scott McMurray, "Futures Pit Trader Goes to Trial," *Wall Street Journal,* 8 May 1990, p. C1; Scott McMurray, "Chicago Pits' Dazzling Growth Permitted a Free-for-All Mecca," *Wall Street Journal,* 3 August 1989, p. A4.

32. *Carpenter v. United States* 484 U.S. 19 (1987); also see John Boland, "The SEC Trims the First Amendment," *Wall Street Journal,* 4 December 1986, p. 28.

33. Securities and Exchange Commission Press Release, "Ten of Nation's Top Investment Firms Settle Enforcement Actions Involving Conflicts of Interest between Research and Investment Banking. Historic Settlement Requires Payments of Penalties of $487.5 Million, Disgorgement of $387.5 Million, Payments of $432.5 Million to Fund Independent Research, and Payments of $80 Million to Fund Investor Education and Mandates Sweeping Structural Reforms." Monday, April 28, 2003.

34. Kevin Sack, "49ers Owner Pleads Guilty in Louisiana Casino Case," *New York Times,* 7 October 1998, p. 1.

35. Charles V. Bagli, "Kickback Investigation Extends to Middle-Class Buildings in New York," *New York Times,* 14 October 1998, p. A19.

36. Press Release, FBI National Press Office, August 19, 1999.

37. Marshall Clinard and Peter Yeager, *Corporate Crime* (New York: Free Press, 1980), p. 67.

38. Ibid.

39. United Press International, "Minority Leader in N.Y. Senate Is Charged," *Boston Globe,* 17 September 1987, p. 20.

40. U.S. Department of Justice News Release, 2 September 2005. http://www.usdoj.gov/usao/ohn/news/02September2005_2.htm. Accessed September 6, 2005.

41. *The Knapp Commission Report on Police Corruption* (New York: George Braziller, 1973), pp. 1–3, 170–182.

42. David Kocieniewski and David M. Halbfinger, "New York's Most Respected Officers Led Precinct Where Sex Scandal Festered," *New York Times,* 20 July 1998, p. 1.

43. Cited in Hugh Barlow, *Introduction to Criminology,* 2nd ed. (Boston: Little, Brown, 1984).

44. PL No. 95-213, 101-104, 91 Stat. 1494.

45. Thomas Burton, "The More Baxter Hides Its Israeli Boycott Role, the More Flak It Gets," *Wall Street Journal,* 25 April 1991, p. 1.

46. Foreign Corrupt Practices Act Update, "Schering-Plough Settles FCPA Case with SEC for Payments to Charity Headed by Government Official." http://wilmer.admin.hubbardone.com/files/tbl_s29Publications%5CFileUpload5665%5C4421%5CFCPA%2006-30-04.pdf. Accessed June 30, 2004.

47. Terence O'Hara, "Chrysler Probe Reflects Trend, U.S. More Vigilant against Domestic, Foreign Bribery," *Washington Post,* 6 August 2005, p. D-1.

48. Adrian Cho, "Hey Buddy. . . Wanna Buy a Moon Rock?" *Science Now,* 7 July 2002, p. 1.

49. Charles McCaghy, *Deviant Behavior* (New York: Macmillan, 1976), p. 178.

50. "While Stocks Last," *The Economist* 364 (21 September 2002): 64–67.

51. The National Food Service Council, 2002. The council's website can be accessed at http://www.nfssc.com.

52. Joshua Kurlantzick, "Those Sticky Fingers," *U.S. News & World Report* 130 (4 June 2001): 44.

53. National Food Service Council. http://www.nfssconline.org/Newsletters/NLv5i3.pdf. Accessed August 26, 2004.

54. J. Sorenson, H. Grove, and T. Sorenson, "Detecting Management Fraud: The Role of the Independent Auditor," in *White-Collar Crime, Theory and Research,* eds. G. Geis and E. Stotland (Beverly Hills: Sage, 1980), pp. 221–251.

55. Joe Sexton, "In Brooklyn Neighborhood, Welfare Fraud Is Nothing New," *New York Times,* 19 March 1997, p. A1.

56. Dana Canedy, "Children Are Prey in a Medicaid Dental Scheme," *New York Times,* 17 August 2001, p. 1.

57. Michael Luo and Clifford J. Levy, "As Medicaid Balloons, Watchdog Force Shrinks," *New York Times*, 19 July 2005, p. A1.

58. Kurt Eichenwald, "Hospital Chain Cheated U.S. on Expenses, Documents Show," *New York Times,* 18 December 1997, p. B1.

59. Laura Johannes and Wendy Bounds, "Corning Agrees to Pay $6.8 Million to Settle Medicare Billing Charges," *Wall Street Journal,* 22 February 1996, p. B2.

60. Ibid.

61. 42 U.S.C. 1320a-7b(b); 42 U.S.C. 1320a-7b(b)(3); 42 C.F.R. 1001.952 (regulatory safe harbors). 42 U.S.C. 1395nn (codifying "Stark I" and "Stark II" statutes).

62. 18 U.S.C. section 1344 (1994).

63. *United States v. Bishop,* 412 U.S. 346 (1973).

64. David Cay Johnston, "Departing Chief Says I.R.S. Is Losing War on Tax Cheats," *New York Times,* 5 November 2002, p. 1.

65. Cited in Frank and Lynch, *Corporate Crime, Corporate Violence,* pp. 12–13.

66. Sutherland, "White-Collar Criminality," pp. 2–10.

67. Joseph S. Hall, "Corporate Criminal Liability," *American Criminal Law Review* 35 (1998): 549–560.

68. Kylie Cooper and Adrienne Dedjinou, "Antitrust Violations," *American Criminal Law Review* 42 (2005): 179–221.

69. 15 U.S.C. section 1 (1994).

70. 15 U.S.C. 1–7 (1976).

71. *Northern Pacific Railways v. United States,* 356 U.S. 1 (1958).

72. Tim Carrington, "Federal Probes of Contractors Rise for Year," *Wall Street Journal,* 23 February 1987, p. 50.

73. Ibid.

74. *Illinois Ex Rel. Madigan v. Telemarketing Associates, Inc., et al.* Number 01-1806 (2003).

75. Environmental Protection Agency, Criminal Investigation Division. http://www.epa.gov/compliance/criminal/index.html.

76. Andrew Oliveira, Christopher Schenck, Christopher Cole, and Nicole Janes. "Environmental Crimes. (Annual Survey of White Collar Crime)," *American Criminal Law Review* 42 (2005): 347–380.

77. Herbert Edelhertz and Charles Rogovin, eds., *A National Strategy for Containing White-Collar Crime* (Lexington, MA: Lexington Books, 1980), Appendix A, pp. 122–123.

78. Belluck, "Prosecutors Say Greed Drove Pharmacist to Dilute Drugs," p. 3.

79. Kathleen Daly, "Gender and Varieties of White-Collar Crime," *Criminology* 27 (1989): 769–793.

80. Quoted in Tim Metz and Michael Miller, "Boesky's Rise and Fall Illustrate a Compulsion to Profit by Getting Inside Track on Market," *Wall Street Journal,* 17 November 1986, p. 28.

81. Donald Cressey, *Other People's Money: A Study of the Social Psychology of Embezzlement* (Glencoe, IL: Free Press, 1973), p. 96.

82. Rhonda Evans and Dianne Porche, "The Nature and Frequency of Medicare/Medicaid Fraud and Neutralization Techniques among Speech, Occupational, and Physical Therapists," *Deviant Behavior* 26 (2005): 253–271.

83. John A. Byrne, "At Enron, the Environment Was Ripe for Abuse," *Business Week,* 25 February 2002, p. 14.

84. Travis Hirschi and Michael Gottfredson, "Causes of White-Collar Crime," *Criminology* 25 (1987): 949–974.

85. Michael Gottfredson and Travis Hirschi, *A General Theory of Crime* (Stanford, CA: Stanford University Press, 1990), p. 191.

86. This section relies heavily on Daniel Skoler, "White-Collar Crime and the Criminal Justice System: Problems and Challenges," in *A National Strategy for Containing White-Collar Crime,* eds. Herbert Edelhertz and Charles Rogovin (Lexington, MA: Lexington Books, 1980), pp. 57–76.

87. Theodore Hammett and Joel Epstein, *Prosecuting Environmental Crime: Los Angeles County* (Washington, DC: National Institute of Justice, 1993).

88. Information provided by Los Angeles County District Attorney's Office, April 2003.

89. Ronald Burns, Keith Whitworth, Carol Thompson, "Assessing Law Enforcement Preparedness to Address Internet Fraud," *Journal of Criminal Justice* 32 (2004): 477–493.

90. Michael Benson, Francis Cullen, and William Maakestad, "Local Prosecutors and Corporate Crime," *Crime and Delinquency* 36 (1990): 356–372.

91. Ibid., pp. 369–370.

92. Michael Lynch, Paul Stretesky, and Ronald Burns, "Slippery Business," *Journal of Black Studies* 34 (2004): 421–440.

93. David Simon and D. Stanley Eitzen, *Elite Deviance* (Boston: Allyn & Bacon, 1982), p. 28.

94. This section relies heavily on Albert Reiss, Jr., "Selecting Strategies of Social Control over Organizational Life," in *Enforcing Regulation,* eds. Keith Hawkins and John M. Thomas (Boston: Klowver Publications, 1984), pp. 25–37.

95. John Braithwaite, "The Limits of Economism in Controlling Harmful Corporate Conduct," *Law and Society Review* 16 (1981–1982): 481–504.

96. Sarbanes–Oxley Act, H.R. 3763-2 (2002).

97. Status Report: Criminal Fines: Criminal Enforcement Division, Anti-Trust Division, U.S. Department of Justice, June 1, 2002.

98. Michael Benson, "Emotions and Adjudication: Status Degradation among White-Collar Criminals," *Justice Quarterly* 7 (1990): 515–528; John Braithwaite, *Crime, Shame, and Reintegration* (Sydney: Cambridge University Press, 1989).

99. Kip Schlegel, "Desert, Retribution and Corporate Criminality," *Justice Quarterly* 5 (1988): 615–634.

100. Raymond Michalowski and Ronald Kramer, "The Space between Laws: The Problem of Corporate Crime in a Transnational Context," *Social Problems* 34 (1987): 34–53.

101. Ibid.

102. Christopher M. Brown and Nikhil S. Singhvi, "Antitrust Violations," *American Criminal Law Review* 35 (1998): 467–501.

103. Howard Adler, "Current Trends in Criminal Antitrust Enforcement," *Business Crimes Bulletin* 4 (1996): 1.

104. CNNMoney, "John Rigas Guilty of Conspiracy: Adelphia Founder, Son, Found Guilty on Some Charges that They Looted Cable Company," July 8, 2004. http://money.cnn.com/2004/07/08/news/midcaps/adelphia_verdict. Accessed November 8, 2005.

105. David Weisburd, Elin Waring, and Stanton Wheeler, "Class, Status, and the Punishment of White-Collar Criminals," *Law and Social Inquiry* 15 (1990): 223–243.

106. Sean Rosenmerkel, "Wrongfulness and Harmfulness as Components of Seriousness of White-Collar Offenses," *Journal of Contemporary Criminal Justice* 17 (2001): 308–328.

107. Joseph Savage and Christine Sgarlata Chung, "Trends in Corporate Fraud Enforcement: A Calm During the Storm?" *Business Crimes Bulletin* 13 (2005): 1–3.

108. Mark Cohen, "Environmental Crime and Punishment: Legal/Economic Theory and Empirical Evidence on Enforcement of Federal Environmental Statutes," *Journal of Criminal Law and Criminology* 82 (1992): 1,054–1,109.

109. U.S. Department of Justice, "Assistant Attorney General for Antitrust, R. Hewitt Pate, Issues Statement on Enactment of Antitrust Criminal Penalty Enhancement and Reform Act of 2004," June 23, 2004. http://www.usdoj.gov/opa/pr/2004/June/04_at_432.htm. Accessed November 8, 2005.

110. See, generally, President's Commission on Organized Crime, *Report to the President and the Attorney General, The Impact: Organized Crime Today* (Washington, DC: U.S. Government Printing Office, 1986). Herein cited as *Organized Crime Today.*

111. Frederick Martens and Michele Cunningham-Niederer, "Media Magic, Mafia Mania," *Federal Probation* 49 (1985): 60–68.

112. *Organized Crime Today,* pp. 7–8.

113. Alan Block and William Chambliss, *Organizing Crime* (New York: Elsevier, 1981).

114. Alan Block, *East Side/West Side* (New Brunswick, NJ: Transaction Books, 1983), pp. vii, 10–11.

115. Statement for the record of Thomas V. Fuentes, Chief Organized Crime Section, Criminal Investigative Division, Federal Bureau of Investigation, "Organized Crime before the House Subcommittee on Finance and Hazardous Materials." September 13, 2000.

116. Donald Cressey, *Theft of the Nation* (New York: Harper & Row, 1969).

117. Dwight Smith, *The Mafia Mystique* (New York: Basic Books, 1975).

118. Stanley Einstein, and Menachem Amir, *Organized Crime: Uncertainties and Dilemmas* (Chicago: University of Illinois at Chicago, Office of International Criminal Justice, 1999); William Kleinknecht, *The New Ethnic Mobs: The Changing Face of Organized Crime in America* (New York: Free Press, 1996); Don Liddick, *An Empirical, Theoretical, and Historical Overview of Organized Crime* (Lewiston, NY: Edwin Mellen Press, 1999); Maria Minniti, "Membership Has Its Privileges: Old and New Mafia Organizations," *Comparative Economic Studies* 37 (1995): 31–47.

119. *Organized Crime Today,* p. 11.

120. David Binder, "In Europe, Sex Slavery Is Thriving Despite Raids," *New York Times,* 19 October 2002, p. A3.

121. Richard A. Ballezza, "YACS Crime Groups: An FBI Major Crime Initiative," *FBI Law Enforcement Bulletin* 67 (1998): 7–13.

122. Omar Bartos, "Growth of Russian Organized Crime Poses Serious Threat," *CJ International* 11 (1995): 8–9.

123. John Tagliabue, "Russian Racket Linked to New York Bank," *New York Times,* 28 September 1999, p. 1.

124. Robert Kelly and Rufus Schatzberg, "Types of Minority Organized Crime: Some Considerations." Paper presented at the annual meeting of the American Society of Criminology, Montreal, November 1987.

125. Phillip Jenkins and Gary Potter, "The Politics and Mythology of Organized Crime: A Philadelphia Case Study," *Journal of Criminal Justice* 15 (1987): 473–484.

126. William Chambliss, *On the Take* (Bloomington: Indiana University Press, 1978).

127. George Vold, *Theoretical Criminology,* 2nd ed., rev. Thomas Bernard (New York: Oxford University Press, 1979).

128. 18 U.S.C. 1952 (1976).

129. PL 91-452, Title IX, 84 Stat. 922 (1970) (codified at 18 U.S.C. 1961–68, 1976).

130. Richard McFeely, "Enterprise Theory of Investigation," *FBI Law Enforcement Bulletin* 70 (2001): 19–26.

131. Selwyn Raab, "A Battered and Ailing Mafia Is Losing Its Grip on America," *New York Times,* 22 October 1990, p. 1.

132. Raab, "A Battered and Ailing Mafia Is Losing Its Grip on America," p. B7.

133. Rebecca Porter, "Prosecutors, Plaintiffs Aim to Curb Internet Gambling," *Trial* 40 (August 2004): 14.

CHAPTER 13

© AP Photo/Bill Krostroun/Wide World Photos

When star baseball player Rafael Palmeiro testified before the House Committee on Government Reform, he pointed his finger at the committee and emphatically denied any use of steroids to enhance his performance on the field. "I was just speaking from the heart, man," he said. "I just wanted to make sure I got my point across and that I was sincere about it." Five months later, the Baltimore Orioles slugger became baseball's highest-profile player to be suspended 10 days for using steroids. The 40-year-old Palmeiro became the seventh player to fail a test under Major League Baseball's new drug-testing policy that took effect in March 2005.

Another star, Yankee first baseman Jason Giambi, was subpoenaed in a federal grand jury probe of BALCO, a nutritional supplement firm suspected of concocting a type of steroid that could not be detected by routine drug testing. While the investigation was ongoing, the San Francisco Chronicle released the fact that Giambi, a former American League MVP, had told the grand jury investigating BALCO that he used steroids obtained from Greg Anderson, the personal trainer for San Francisco Giants star Barry Bonds. While he never actually admitted using tetrahydrogestrinone, Giambi publicly apologized to fans and his teammates for his behavior.[1]

The steroid scandal rocked baseball and tainted the reputation of some of its greatest stars. But is it wrong to take substances such as steroids as long as no one else is hurt?

PUBLIC ORDER CRIME

To read more about this controversial topic, use "gay marriage" in a key word search in InfoTrac College Edition.

To read more about **Dworkin** and her life, go to http://www.washingtonpost.com/wp-dyn/articles/A45447-2005Apr11.html. For an up-to-date list of web links, go to http://cj.wadsworth.com/siegel_crimtpt9e.

Crimes involving sexuality and morality are often referred to as **public order crimes** or **victimless crimes**, although this latter term can be misleading.[2] Public order crimes involve acts that interfere with the operations of society and the ability of people to function efficiently.

Put another way, common-law crimes such as rape or robbery are considered inherently wrong and damaging, but other behaviors are outlawed (public order crimes) because they conflict with social policy, prevailing moral rules, and current public opinion. Statutes designed to uphold public order usually prohibit the manufacture and distribution of morally questionable goods and services such as erotic material, commercial sex, and mood-altering drugs. Statutes like these are controversial in part because millions of otherwise law-abiding citizens often engage in these outlawed activities and consequently become criminals. These statutes are also controversial because they selectively prohibit desired goods, services, and behaviors; in other words, they outlaw sin and vice.

This chapter covers these public order crimes; it first briefly discusses the relationship between law and morality. Next the chapter addresses public order crimes of a sexual nature: homosexuality, paraphilias, prostitution, and pornography. The chapter concludes by focusing on the abuse of drugs and alcohol.

LAW AND MORALITY

Legislation of moral issues has continually frustrated lawmakers. There is little debate that the purpose of criminal law is to protect society and reduce social harm. When a store is robbed or a child assaulted, it is relatively easy to see and condemn the harm done the victim. It is, however, more difficult to sympathize with or even identify the victims of immoral acts, such as pornography or prostitution, where the parties involved may be willing participants. If there is no victim, can there be a crime?

To answer this question, we might first consider whether there is actually a victim in so-called victimless crimes. Some participants may have been coerced into their acts; they are therefore its victims. Opponents of pornography, such as Andrea Dworkin, charge that women involved in adult films, far from being highly paid stars, are "dehumanized—turned into objects and commodities."[3]

Research on prostitution shows that many young runaways and abandoned children are coerced into a life on the streets, where they are cruelly treated and held as virtual captives.[4]

Even if public order crimes do not actually harm their participants, perhaps society as a whole should be considered the victim of these crimes. Is the community harmed when an adult bookstore opens or a brothel is established? Does this signal that a neighborhood is in decline? Does it teach children that deviance is to be tolerated and profited from?

Debating Morality

Some scholars argue that acts like pornography, prostitution, and drug use erode the moral fabric of society and therefore should be prohibited and punished. They are crimes, according to the great legal scholar Morris Cohen, because "it is one of the functions of the criminal law to give expression to the collective feeling of revulsion toward certain acts, even when they are not very dangerous."[5] In his classic statement on the function of morality in the law, legal scholar Sir Patrick Devlin states,

> Without shared ideas on politics, morals, and ethics no society can exist. . . . If men and women try to create a society in which there is no fundamental agreement about good and evil, they will fail; if having based it on common agreement, the agreement goes, the society will disintegrate. For society is not something that is kept together physically; it is held by the invisible bonds of common thought. If the bonds were too far relaxed, the members would drift apart. A common morality is part of the bondage. The bondage is part of the price of society; and mankind, which needs society, must pay its price.[6]

According to this view, so-called victimless crimes are prohibited because one of the functions of criminal law is to express a shared sense of public morality.[7]

Some influential legal scholars have questioned the propriety of legislating morals. H. L. A. Hart states,

> It is fatally easy to confuse the democratic principle that power should be in the hands of the majority with the utterly different claim that the majority, with power in their hands, need respect no limits. Certainly there is a special risk in a democracy that the majority may dictate how all should live.[8]

Hart may be motivated by the fact that defining morality may be an impossible task: Who defines morality? Are we not punishing differences rather than social harm? As U.S. Supreme Court Justice William O. Douglas once so succinctly put it, "What may be trash to me may be prized by others."[9] After all, many of the great works of Western art depict nude males and females, some quite young. Are the paintings of Rubens or the sculpture of Michelangelo obscene?

© Alinari /Art Resources, New York

Michelangelo's statue of David is one of the most important and beloved pieces of Western art. Is it possible that some might consider the unclothed David obscene or prurient? If so, should children be prevented from viewing the statue? Should it be covered up? If David's nudity is not offensive or sexually suggestive, then what does it take to make a statue or photo "pornographic"?

Joseph Gusfield argues that the purpose of outlawing immoral acts is to show the moral superiority of those who condemn the acts over those who partake of them. The legislation of morality "enhances the social status of groups carrying the affirmed culture and degrades groups carrying that which is condemned as deviant."[10] Research indicates

that people who define themselves as liberals are also the most tolerant of sexually explicit material. Demographic attributes such as age, educational attainment, and occupational status may also influence views of pornography: The young and better educated tend to be more tolerant than older, less-educated people.[11] Whose views should prevail?

And, if a majority of the population chooses to engage in what might objectively be considered immoral or deviant behavior, would it be to prohibit or control such behavior or render it criminal? According to Hitwise, an Internet monitoring corporation, online porn sites get about three times more visits than the top three web search engines, including Google, Yahoo! Search and MSN Search: Adult websites accounted for about 18.8 percent of all Internet visits by U.S. users for the week ending May 29, 2004, compared to 5.5 percent for these three widely used search engines, combined. Should pornography be criminalized or sanctioned if so many people are active users and wish to enjoy its content?[12] And if the law tried to define or limit objectionable material, might it not eventually inhibit free speech and political dissent? Not so, according to social commentator Irving Kristol:

> If we start censoring pornography and obscenity, shall we not inevitably end up censoring political opinion? A lot of people seem to think this would be the case—which only shows the power of doctrinaire thinking over reality. We had censorship of pornography and obscenity for 150 years, until almost yesterday, and I am not aware that freedom of opinion in this country was in any way diminished as a consequence of this fact.[13]

Cultural clashes may ensue when behavior that is considered normative in one society is deplored by those living in another. For example, by 2004, Amnesty International estimates that 135 million of the world's females will have undergone genital mutilation.[14] Custom and tradition are by far the most frequently cited reasons for mutilation, and it is often carried out in a ritual during which the young woman is initiated into adulthood.[15] The surgery is done to ensure virginity, remove sexual sensation, and render the females suitable for marriage; a girl in these societies cannot be considered an adult unless she has undergone genital mutilation.

Critics of this practice, led by American author Alice Walker (*The Color Purple*), consider the procedure mutilation and torture; others argue that this ancient custom should be left to the discretion of the indigenous people who consider it part of their culture. "Torture," counters Walker, "is not culture." Can an outsider define the morality of another culture?[16] Amnesty International and the United Nations have worked to end the practice. Because of outside pressure, several African nations south of the Sahara have now instituted bans that are enforced with fines and jail terms. The procedure is now forbidden in Senegal, Egypt, Burkina Faso, the Central African Republic, Djibouti, Ghana, Guinea, and Togo. Other countries, among them Uganda, discourage it. In North Africa, the Egyptian Supreme Court upheld a ban on the practice and also ruled it had no place in Islam.[17] Despite these efforts, approximately 6,000 girls are still subject to female circumcision every day in Africa and the Middle East and in Muslim areas all over the world.

> While almost universally condemned in the West, female circumcision is still common in Africa and the Middle East. To find out why, read this article in InfoTrac College Edition: Richard A. Shweder, "What about 'Female Genital Mutilation'? and Why Understanding Culture Matters in the First Place," *Daedalus* 129 (2000): 209.

Social Harm

Stuart J. Roll built a thriving business selling mustard, ketchup, jelly, and jam that did $10 million in sales each year and made him a multimillionaire. Then he decided to branch out into prostitution. Roll solicited women through ads in local newspapers seeking a "companion/housekeeper." When women applied, he proposed that they become prostitutes.

He employed at least three women and charged customers $150 for half an hour or $250 for an hour, which he split fifty-fifty with the women. He got customers through classified ads in New York magazines that promised "pvt. relaxation for the refined gentleman. Elegant European beauty. Private res. Upscale/Expensive."

After his arrest, Roll, 68, told the media that he set up the new business using the same kind of principles— catering to his customers' needs and paying meticulous attention to detail—that he had used to start his food business. "What we are performing here is more of a community service than breaking the law," Roll said of his new enterprise. "People need love so badly. Here a man can come in and have his sanctuary, his peace of mind and his fantasy all wrapped in a million-dollar home ready to serve him. . . . It is a victimless crime. . . . I want to take sex out of the street and put it in the home, where it belongs," he claimed.[18]

Were Roll's activities really harmful, or do you agree with his viewpoint that his prostitution ring was providing a desirable community service? Unfortunately for him, most societies have long banned or limited behaviors that are believed to run contrary to social norms, customs, and values. However, many acts that most of us deem highly immoral and objectionable are not in fact criminal. There is no law against lust, gluttony, avarice, sloth, envy, pride, or anger, although they are considered the seven deadly sins. Nor is it a crime in most jurisdictions to ignore the pleas of a drowning person, even though such callous behavior is quite immoral. How then do we distinguish between acts that are criminal and outlawed and those that are merely objectionable but tolerated and legal?

In our society, immoral acts can be distinguished from crimes on the basis of the **social harm** they cause. Acts that are believed to be extremely harmful to the general public

are usually outlawed; those that may only harm the actor are more likely to be tolerated. Yet even this perspective does not always hold sway. Some acts that cause enormous amounts of social harm are perfectly legal. It is well documented that the consumption of tobacco and alcohol is extremely harmful, but these products remain legal to produce and sell; manufacturers continue to sell sports cars and motorcycles that can accelerate to more than 100 mph, but the legal speed limit is usually 65 mph. More people die each year from alcohol-, tobacco-, and auto-related deaths than from all illegal drugs combined. Should drugs be legalized and fast cars outlawed?

Moral Crusaders

In the early West, vigilance committees were set up in San Francisco and other boom towns to pursue cattle rustlers and stage coach robbers and to dissuade undesirables from moving in. These **vigilantes** held a strict standard of morality that, when they caught their prey, resulted in sure and swift justice.

The avenging vigilante has remained part of popular culture. Fictional do-gooders who take it on themselves to enforce the law, battle evil, and personally deal with those whom they consider immoral have become enmeshed in the public psyche. From the Lone Ranger to Spiderman, the righteous vigilante is expected to go on moral crusades without any authorization from legal authorities. The assumption that it is okay to take matters into your own hands if the cause is right and the target is immoral is not lost on the younger generation. Gang boys sometimes take on the street identity of Batman or Superman so they can battle their rivals with impunity.

Fictional characters are not the only ones who take it upon themselves to fight for moral decency; members of special interest groups are also ready to do battle. Popular targets of moral crusaders are abortion clinics, pornographers, gun dealers, and logging companies. For example, after the 9/11 attacks, minister Jerry Falwell, pastor of the 22,000-member Thomas Road Baptist Church, claimed on a broadcast of the Christian television program *The 700 Club*,

> I really believe that the pagans, and the abortionists, and the feminists, and the gays and the lesbians who are actively trying to make that an alternative lifestyle, the ACLU, People For the American Way, all of them who have tried to secularize America. I point the finger in their face and say "you helped this happen."

He viewed the attacks as God's judgment on America for "throwing God out of the public square, out of the schools. The abortionists have got to bear some burden for this because God will not be mocked." Falwell, under pressure from gay and lesbian groups, later apologized for his stormy rhetoric.[19]

Moral crusaders (also known as *moral entrepreneurs*) are rule creators who engage in activities to rid the world of behavior they consider wrong and depraved; "the crusader is fervent and righteous, often self-righteous."[20] Today moral crusaders take on a number of far-ranging issues, from teaching evolution to controlling Internet pornography.

While many moral crusaders campaign within the confines of the law, others become fanatical and engage in immoral and/or illegal conduct to achieve their goals: Some abortion foes have resorted to violence to rid the nation of pro-choice healthcare providers; animal rights activists have attacked biology labs; antiwar protestors have defaced government websites.

Some moral crusaders justify their actions by claiming that the very structure of our institutions and beliefs are in danger because of immorality. For example, Andrea Friedman's analysis of anti-obscenity campaigns during the Cold War era (post–World War II) found that the politics of the times led to images of aggressive, even violent, males that were used in comic books and pornography. Moral crusaders argued that this depiction was threatening to family values, which led them to advocate a ban on violent comics and porn magazines.[21]

Moral crusades are directed against acts that some people believe threaten the moral fabric of society and are a danger to the public order. Those public order crimes discussed in this chapter are divided into two broad areas. The first relates to what conventional society considers deviant sexual practices: homosexual acts, paraphilias, prostitution, and pornography. The second area concerns the use of substances that have been outlawed or controlled because of the alleged harm they cause: drugs and alcohol.

Moral crusaders come in many different forms. Read about how some early feminists tried to shape the sexual cultural during Victorian times: Jesse F. Battan, "You Cannot Fix the Scarlet Letter on My Breast!": Women Reading, Writing, and Reshaping the Sexual Culture of Victorian America," *Journal of Social History* 37 (2004): 601–624.

HOMOSEXUALITY

It may be surprising that a section on homosexuality is still included in a criminology text, but today homosexual men and women not only face archaic legal restrictions that criminalize their behavior but are targeted for so many violent hate crimes that a specific term, **gay bashing**, has been coined to describe violent acts directed at people because of their sexual orientation.

Homosexuality (the word derives from the Greek *homos,* meaning "same") refers to erotic interest in members of one's own sex. However, engaging in homosexual behavior does not necessarily mean one is a homosexual. People may engage in homosexuality because heterosexual partners are unavailable. Some may have sex forced on them by aggressive homosexuals, a condition common in prisons. Some adolescents may experiment with partners of the same sex although their sexual affiliation is heterosexual.[22] Finally, it is possible to be a homosexual but not to engage in sexual conduct with members of the same sex. To avoid this confusion, it might be helpful to adopt the definition of a homosexual as one "who is motivated in adult life by a definite preferential erotic attraction to members of the same sex and who usually (but not necessarily) engages in overt sexual relations with them."[23]

Homosexual behavior has existed in most societies. Records of it can be found in prehistoric art and hieroglyphics.[24] Even when homosexuality was banned or sanctioned, it persisted.[25] The U.S. Census Bureau now measures the number of unmarried, same-sex partner households in the United States; today there are more than 600,000 gay partnerships (more than 1.2 million people), a 314 percent increase over the 145,130 same-sex, unmarried partner households tallied in the 1990 census. More than 99 percent of all counties in the United States have same-sex households; only twenty-two counties in the entire country reported no same-sex households.[26]

Attitudes toward Homosexuality

Throughout much of Western history, homosexuals have been subject to discrimination, sanction, and violence. The Bible implies that God destroyed the ancient cities of Sodom and Gomorrah because of their residents' deviant behavior, presumably homosexuality; Sodom is the source of the term **sodomy** (deviant intercourse). The Bible expressly forbids homosexuality—in Leviticus in the Old Testament; Paul's Epistles, Romans, and Corinthians in the New Testament—and this prohibition has been the basis for repressing homosexual behavior.[27]

Intolerance continues today. In 2002 three men in Saudi Arabia were beheaded after they "committed acts of sodomy, married each other, seduced young men, and attacked those who rebuked them."[28] Gay bashing still remains a common occurrence around the world.[29]

The cause of antigay feelings or **homophobia** is uncertain. Some religious leaders argue that the Bible condemns same-sex relations and that this behavior is therefore a sin. Some people are ignorant about the lifestyle of gays and fear that homosexuality is a contagious disease or that homosexuals will seduce their children.[30] Other people develop a deep-rooted hatred of gays because they are insecure about their own sexual identity. Research shows that males who express homophobic attitudes are also likely to become aroused by erotic images of homosexual behavior. Homophobia, then, may be associated with homosexual arousal that the homophobe is either unaware of or denies.[31]

||||||| **CONNECTIONS** |||||||
As you may recall from Chapter 10, gay men and women are still subject to thousands of incidents of violence and other hate crimes each year.

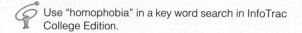Use "homophobia" in a key word search in InfoTrac College Edition.

Homosexuality and the Law

Homosexuality, considered a legal and moral crime throughout most of Western history, is no longer a crime in the United States. In the case of *Robinson v. California,* the U.S. Supreme Court determined that people could not be criminally prosecuted because of their status (such as drug addict or homosexual).[32] Despite this protection, most states and the federal government criminalize the lifestyle and activities of homosexuals. For example, no state or locality save Massachusetts allows same-sex marriage, and homosexuals cannot obtain a marriage license to legitimize their relationship. The Defense of Marriage Act, which President Clinton signed in 1996, declared that states are not obligated to recognize single-sex marriages performed in other states.[33]

The military still bans openly gay people from serving but has compromised with a "don't ask, don't tell" policy: The military does not ask about sexual orientation; gay people can serve as long as their sexuality remains secret. In 1996, the U.S. Supreme Court tacitly approved this policy by declining to hear a case brought by Navy Lieutenant Paul Thomasson, who was discharged in 1994 for openly declaring himself homosexual.[34] In January 1998, a federal judge barred the U.S. Navy from dismissing Chief Petty Officer Timothy McVeigh, who had posted sexually oriented material on the Internet. The judge ruled that the Navy had violated McVeigh's privacy when it asked America Online to divulge his identity; in so doing, the Navy violated the spirit of the "don't ask, don't tell" policy.[35] Gays have also lost custody of their children because of their sexual orientation, although more courts are now refusing to consider a gay lifestyle alone as evidence of parental unfitness.[36] And in an important 2000 case, *Boy Scouts of America v. Dale,* the Supreme Court ruled that the Boy Scouts are entitled to exclude openly gay scouts and scout leaders.[37] In their decision, the Court recognized that employing an openly gay scout leader would significantly burden the organization's right to oppose or disfavor homosexual conduct.

Is the Tide Turning?

Although there are still negative attitudes toward gays and they still face legal burdens, there seems to be a long overdue increase in social tolerance. Surveys show that a significant majority of Americans now support gays in the military and equality in employment, housing, inheritance rights, and Social Security benefits for same-sex couples.[38]

While some believe that recent Supreme Court decisions have heralded a new era of legal and civil rights for gay men and women, some states still punish gay people more harshly than heterosexuals. For example, Kansas law punishes someone having sex with a minor of the same sex much more harshly than it does someone having sexual relations with an opposite-sex minor. In the case of *State v. Limon,* a 19-year-old boy was sentenced to more than 17 years in prison for having sex with a 14-year-old boy; had Limon engaged in sex with an underage girl, he could have been sentenced to no more than 1 year and 3 months in prison.[39]

■ PARAPHILIAS

Between 2002 and 2004, the archdiocese of Boston was rocked by allegations that a significant number of priests had engaged in sexual relations with minor children. The archdiocese eventually turned over the names of nearly 100 priests to prosecutors. As the scandal spread, clergy elsewhere in the United States and abroad resigned amid allegations that they had abused children or failed to stop abuse of which they had knowledge. In Ireland the Most Rev. Brendan Comiskey, the Bishop of Ferns, offered his resignation to the pope, and an archbishop in Wales was forced to resign because he had ignored complaints about two priests later convicted of sexually abusing children. Responding to the crisis, Pope John Paul II called a special meeting of American Catholic leaders in April 2002 to create new policies on sex abuse. The pope issued a statement in which he said that there is "no place in the priesthood . . . for those who would harm the young." He added that sexual abuse by the clergy was not only an "appalling sin" but a crime, and he noted that "many are offended at the way in which church leaders are perceived to have acted in this matter."[40]

Nowhere did the scandal take on greater proportion than in the Boston area where Cardinal Bernard Law was forced to step down as leader of the diocese. Numerous churches were closed or sold to help raise money for legal fees and victim compensation. Among the most notorious offenders was Father James Porter, accused of molesting at least 125 children of both sexes over a 30- year period reaching back to the early 1960s. Porter was eventually sentenced to an 18- to 20-year prison term.

To read more about the **clergy scandal,** go to http://www.boston.com/globe/spotlight/abuse. For an up-to-date list of web links, go to http://cj.wadsworth .com/siegel_crimtpt9e.

Paraphilias have been recorded for thousands of years. From the Greek *para,* "to the side of," and *philos,* "loving," **paraphilias** are bizarre or abnormal sexual practices involving recurrent sexual urges focused on (1) nonhuman objects (such as underwear, shoes, or leather), (2) humiliation or the experience of receiving or giving pain (such as in sadomasochism or bondage), or (3) children or others who cannot grant consent. More than 2000-year-old Buddhist texts contain references to sexually deviant behaviors among monastic communities including sexual activity with animals and sexual interest in corpses. Richard von Krafft-Ebing's *Psychopathia Sexualis,* first published in 1887, was the first text to discuss such paraphilias as sadism, bestiality, and incest.[41]

Some paraphilias, such as wearing clothes normally worn by the opposite sex (transvestite fetishism), can be engaged in by adults in the privacy of their homes and do not involve a third party; these are usually out of the law's reach. Others, however, risk social harm and are subject to criminal penalties. Included in this group of outlawed sexual behaviors are these practices:

- *Asphyxiophilia (autoerotic asphyxia):* By means of a noose, ligature, plastic bag, mask, volatile chemicals, or chest compression, attempting partial asphyxia and oxygen deprivation to the brain to enhance sexual gratification. Almost all cases of hypoxyphilia involve males.

- *Frotteurism:* Rubbing against or touching a nonconsenting person in a crowd, elevator, or other public area.

- *Voyeurism:* Obtaining sexual pleasure from spying on a stranger while he or she disrobes or engages in sexual behavior with another.

- *Exhibitionism:* Deriving sexual pleasure from exposing the genitals to surprise or shock a stranger.

- *Sadomasochism:* Deriving pleasure from receiving pain or inflicting pain on another.

- *Pedophilia:* Attaining sexual pleasure through sexual activity with prepubescent children. Research indicates that more than 20 percent of males report sexual attraction to at least one child, although the rate of sexual fantasies and the potential for sexual contacts are much lower.[42]

Paraphilias that involve unwilling or underage victims are illegal. Most state criminal codes also ban indecent exposure and voyeurism. Others prosecute paraphilias under common-law assault and battery or sodomy statutes. In their extreme, paraphilias can lead to sexual assaults in which the victims suffer severe harm.

PROSTITUTION

Prostitution has been known for thousands of years. The term derives from the Latin *prostituere,* which means "to cause to stand in front of." The prostitute is viewed as publicly offering his or her body for sale. The earliest record of prostitution appears in ancient Mesopotamia, where priests engaged in sex to promote fertility in the community. All women were required to do temple duty, and passing strangers were expected to make donations to the temple after enjoying its services.[43]

Modern commercial sex appears to have its roots in ancient Greece, where Solon established licensed **brothels** in 500 BCE. The earnings of Greek prostitutes helped pay for the temple of Aphrodite. Famous men openly went to prostitutes to enjoy intellectual, aesthetic, and sexual stimulation; prostitutes, however, were prevented from marrying.[44]

Although some early Christian religious leaders, such as St. Augustine and St. Thomas Aquinas, tolerated prostitution as a necessary evil, this tolerance disappeared after the reformation. Martin Luther advocated abolishing prostitution on moral grounds, and Lutheran doctrine depicted prostitutes as emissaries of the devil who were sent to destroy the faith.[45]

During the early nineteenth century, prostitution was tied to the rise of English breweries: Saloons controlled by the companies employed prostitutes to attract patrons and encourage them to drink. This relationship was repeated in major U.S. cities, such as Chicago, until breweries were forbidden to own the outlets that distributed their product.

Today there are many variations, but in general, **prostitution** can be defined as granting nonmarital sexual access, established by mutual agreement of the prostitutes, their clients, and their employers, for remuneration. This definition is sexually neutral because prostitutes can be straight or gay and male or female.

Prostitutes are referred to by sociologists as "street-level sex workers" whose activities are similar to any other service industry. These conditions are usually present in a commercial sexual transaction:

- *Activity that has sexual significance for the customer:* This includes the entire range of sexual behavior, from sexual intercourse to exhibitionism, sadomasochism, oral sex, and so on.

- *Economic transaction:* Something of economic value, not necessarily money, is exchanged for the activity.

- *Emotional indifference:* The sexual exchange is simply for economic consideration. Although the participants may know each other, their interaction has nothing to do with affection.[46] Men believe that the lack of involvement makes hiring a prostitute less of a hassle and less trouble than becoming involved in a romantic relationship.[47]

Sociologist Monica Prasad observed these conditions when she interviewed both men and women about their motivation to employ a prostitute. Although their choice was shaped by sexuality, she found that their decision was also influenced by pressure from friends to try something different and exciting, the wish for a sexual exchange free from obligations, and curiosity about the world of prostitution. Prasad found that most customers who became "regulars" began to view prostitution merely as a "service occupation."[48]

The Natasha Trade: International Trafficking in Prostitution

Trafficking in women and girls for the purpose of sexual exploitation is market valued at $7 billion annually, in U.S. dollars. Trafficking may be the result of force, coercion, manipulation, deception, abuse of authority, initial consent, family pressure, past and present family and community violence, economic deprivation, or other conditions of inequality for women and children. Women are trafficked to, from, and through every region in the world.

Exact numbers are unknown, but international agencies and governmental bodies estimate that each year over 1 million women and girls are trafficked for sexual exploitation in sex industries. The U.S. State Department estimates that 50,000 to 100,000 women and children are trafficked into the United States each year for labor or sexual exploitation. The money-makers are transnational networks

of traffickers and pimps who prey on women seeking employment and opportunities. These illegal activities and related crimes not only harm the women involved; they also undermine the social, political, and economic fabric of the nations where they occur.

Countries with large sex industries create the demand for women; countries where traffickers easily recruit women provide the supply. For decades, the primary sending countries were in Asia. But the collapse of the Soviet Union opened up a pool of millions of women from which traffickers can recruit. Former Soviet republics such as Belarus, Latvia, Moldova, Russia, and the Ukraine have become major suppliers of women to sex industries all over the world. These young women are the "Natashas" who fuel the international sex trade.

In the sex industry today, the most popular and valuable women are from Russia and the Ukraine. Authorities in the Ukraine estimate that more than 100,000 women were trafficked

during the previous decade. Popular destination countries include Canada, the Czech Republic, Germany, Greece, Hungary, the Netherlands, Turkey, the United Arab Emirates, the United States, and Yugoslavia. Large numbers of Ukrainian women are trafficked into Korea to be used as prostitutes near military bases.

Migration from the former Soviet Republics has aided trafficking. Members of organized crime rings establish contacts with collaborators in overseas communities and work within migrating populations to build criminal networks. Increased migration also serves as a cover for traffickers transporting women. Computer technologies also have enabled the increased volume and complexity of international financial transactions, increasing opportunities for transnational crime and decreasing the probability of detection.

Recruiting Women

Recruiters, traffickers, and pimps have developed common operating methods. One strategy is advertisements

Incidence of Prostitution

It is difficult to assess the number of prostitutes operating in the United States. Fifty years ago, about two-thirds of non–college-educated men and one-quarter of college-educated men had visited a prostitute.[49] It is likely that the number of men who hire prostitutes has declined sharply; the number of arrests for prostitution has remained stable for the past two decades while the population has increased.[50]

How can these changes be accounted for? The sexual revolution has liberalized sexuality so that men are less likely to use prostitutes because legitimate alternatives for sexuality are now available. In addition, the prevalence of sexually transmitted diseases has caused many men to avoid visiting prostitutes for fear of irreversible health hazards.

Despite such changes, the Uniform Crime Report (UCR) indicates that about 80,000 prostitution arrests are made annually, with the gender ratio about 2 to 1 female to male.[51]

More alarming is the fact that about 1,000 arrests involved minors under the age of 18, including almost 150 kids aged 15 and under. Arguments that criminal law should not interfere with sexual transactions because no one is harmed are undermined by these disturbing statistics.

International Sex Trade

There is also a troubling overseas trade in prostitution in which men from wealthy countries frequent semi-regulated sex areas in needy nations such as Thailand in order to procure young girls forced or sold into prostitution—a phenomenon known as *sex tourism*. In addition to sex tours, there has also been a soaring demand for pornography, strip clubs, lap dancing, escorts, and telephone sex in developing countries.[52]

In addition, every year, hundreds of thousands of women and children—primarily from Southeast Asia and eastern Europe—are lured by the promise of good jobs and then end up forced into brothels or as circuit travelers in

in newspapers offering lucrative job opportunities in foreign countries for low-skilled jobs, such as waitresses and nannies. Another method of recruitment is through "marriage agencies," sometimes called mail-order bride agencies or international introduction services.

But the most common way for women to be recruited is through a friend or acquaintance who gains the woman's confidence. "Second wave" recruiting occurs when a trafficked woman returns home to draft other women. Once a woman has been trafficked and trapped in the sex industry, she has few options. One of the few means of escaping the brutality of being forced to have sex with multiple men each day is to move from victim to perpetrator. Once they reach the destination country, travel documents are confiscated, the women are subjected to violence, and threats are made to harm their family members. They are told they owe thousands in travel costs and must pay them off through prostitution. The women get to keep little, if any, of the money.

The women must repay their purchase price and travel and other expenses before they are allowed to leave. They can expect little help from law enforcement authorities who are either ambivalent or working with the traffickers.

Combating Trafficking

Recently, the United States made stopping the trafficking of women a top priority. In 1998, the "Memorandum on Steps to Combat Violence Against Women and the Trafficking of Women and Girls" was issued that directed the secretary of state, the attorney general, and the president's Interagency Council on Women to expand their work against violence against women to include work against the trafficking of women.

In the former Soviet Union, prevention education projects are aimed at potential victims of trafficking, and nongovernmental organizations have established hotlines for victims or women seeking information about the risks of accepting job offers abroad.

Critical Thinking

1. If put in charge, what would you do to slow or end the international sex trade? Before you answer, remember the saying that prostitution is the oldest profession, which implies that curbing it may prove quite difficult.

2. Should men who hire prostitutes be punished very severely in order to deter them from getting involved in the exploitation of these vulnerable young women?

 InfoTrac College Edition Research

For more on the international sex trade, go to: Brenda Platt, "Commercial Sexual Exploitation of Children: A Global Problem Requiring Global Action," *Sexual Health Exchange* (2002): 10–12.

Source: Donna Hughes, "The 'Natasha' Trade: Transnational Sex Trafficking," *National Institute of Justice Journal* (January 2001). http://ncjrs.org/pdffiles1/jr000246c.pdf. Accessed November 15, 2004.

---

labor camps. It is believed that traffickers import up to 50,000 women and children every year into the United States despite legal prohibitions (in addition to prostitution, some are brought in to work in sweat shops).[53] The international trade in prostitution is the subject of the Comparative Criminology feature titled "The Natasha Trade."

To read Amnesty International's report on the exploitation of women in Kosovo and Bosnia and their forced entry in the **international sex trade,** go to http://web.amnesty.org/library/Index/ENGEUR700102004. For an up-to-date list of web links, go to http://cj.wadsworth.com/siegel_crimtpt9e.

Types of Prostitutes

Several different types of prostitutes operate in the United States. As you will see, each group operates in a particular venue.

STREETWALKERS Prostitutes who work the streets in plain sight of police, citizens, and customers are referred to as *hustlers, hookers,* or *streetwalkers.* Although glamorized by the Julia Roberts character in the film *Pretty Woman* (who winds up with the multimillionaire character played by Richard Gere), streetwalkers are considered the least attractive, lowest paid, most vulnerable men and women in the profession. They are most likely to be impoverished members of ethnic or racial minorities. Many are young runaways who gravitate to major cities to find a new, exciting life and escape from sexual and physical abuse at home.[54] In the United States and abroad, street workers tend to be younger than other prostitutes, start working at a younger age, and have less education. More use money from sex work for drugs and use drugs at work; they are more likely than other prostitutes to be the targets of extreme forms of violence.[55]

Streetwalkers wear bright clothing, makeup, and jewelry to attract customers; they take their customers to hotels. The term *hooker,* however, is not derived from the ability of streetwalkers to hook clients on their charms. It actually stems from the popular name given women who followed Union General "Fighting Joe" Hooker's army during the Civil War.[56] Because streetwalkers must openly display their occupation, they are likely to be involved with the police.

The street life is very dangerous. Recent interviews conducted with 325 sex workers in Miami by Hilary Surratt and her colleagues found that over 40 percent experienced violence from clients in the prior year: 24.9 percent were beaten, 12.9 percent were raped, and 13.8 percent were threatened with weapons.[57] If they survive and gain experience, street workers learn to adopt sex practices that promote their chances of survival, such as refusing to trade sex for drugs and refusing to service clients they consider too dangerous or distasteful for sex.[58]

BAR GIRLS B-girls, as they are also called, spend their time in bars, drinking and waiting to be picked up by customers. Although alcoholism may be a problem, B-girls usually work out an arrangement with the bartender so they are served diluted drinks or water colored with dye or tea, for which the customer is charged an exorbitant price. In some bars, the B-girl is given a credit for each drink she gets the customer to buy. It is common to find B-girls in towns with military bases and large transient populations.[59]

BROTHEL PROSTITUTES Also called bordellos, cathouses, sporting houses, and houses of ill repute, brothels flourished in the nineteenth and early twentieth centuries. They were large establishments, usually run by madams that housed several prostitutes. A **madam** is a woman who employs prostitutes, supervises their behavior, and receives a fee for her services; her cut is usually 40 to 60 percent of the prostitute's earnings. The madam's role may include recruiting women into prostitution and socializing them in the trade.[60]

Brothels declined in importance following World War II. The closing of the last brothel in Texas is chronicled in the play and movie *The Best Little Whorehouse in Texas.* Today the most well-known brothels exist in Nevada, where prostitution is legal outside large population centers (one, the Mustang Ranch, has an official website that sells souvenirs!). Despite their decline, some madams and their brothels have achieved national prominence. In 1984 socialite Sydney Biddle Barrows was arrested by New York police for operating a $1 million per year prostitution ring out of a bordello on West 74th Street.[61] Descended from a socially prominent family who traced their lineage to the Mayflower, Barrows ranked her twenty women on looks and personality from A ($125 per hour) to C ($400 per hour) and kept 60 percent of their take. Her book of clients was described by police as a mini "Who's Who" of celebrities.

Read more about the life of **Sydney Biddle Barrows** at http://www.annonline.com/interviews/970211/biography.html. For an up-to-date list of web links, go to http://cj.wadsworth.com/siegel_crimtpt9e.

CALL GIRLS The aristocrats of prostitution are **call girls.** Some charge customers thousands per night and net more than $100,000 per year. Some gain clients through employment in escort services, and others develop independent customer lists. Many call girls come from middle-class backgrounds and service upper-class customers. Attempting to dispel the notion that their service is simply sex for money, they concentrate on making their clients feel important and attractive. Working exclusively via telephone "dates," call girls get their clients by word of mouth or by making arrangements with bellhops, cab drivers, and so on. They either entertain clients in their own apartments or visit clients' hotels and apartments. Upon retiring, a call girl can sell her "date book" listing client names and sexual preferences for thousands of dollars. Despite the lucrative nature of their business, call girls suffer considerable risk by being alone and unprotected with strangers. They often request the business cards of their clients to make sure they are dealing with "upstanding citizens."

ESCORT SERVICES/CALL HOUSES Some escort services are fronts for prostitution rings. Both male and female sex workers can be sent out after the client calls an ad in the yellow pages. In 2003, Las Vegas had 561 listings for adult services in the yellow pages; New York City had 135.

A relatively new phenomenon, call houses, combines elements of the brothel and call girl rings: A madam receives a call from a prospective customer, and if she finds the client acceptable, she arranges a meeting between the caller and a prostitute in her service. The madam maintains a list of prostitutes who are on call rather than living together in a house.

The call house insulates the madam from arrest because she never meets the client or receives direct payment.[62]

CIRCUIT TRAVELERS Prostitutes known as circuit travelers move around in groups of two or three to lumber, labor, and agricultural camps. They ask the foremen for permission to ply their trade, service the whole crew in an evening, and then move on. Some circuit travelers seek clients at truck stops and rest areas.

Sometimes young girls are forced to become circuit travelers by unscrupulous pimps. In 1998, sixteen people were charged with enslaving at least twenty women from Mexico, some as young as 14, and forcing them to work for months as prostitutes in agricultural migrant camps in Florida and South Carolina. Their captors, known as *ticketeros,* forced them to work 6 days a week under the threat of violence and for little pay; the women were paid $3 for each sexual act, but the *ticketeros* charged $20.[63]

SKEEZERS Surveys conducted in New York and Chicago have found that a significant portion of female prostitutes have substance abuse problems, and more than half claim that prostitution is how they support their drug habits; on the street, women who barter drugs for sex are called **skeezers.** Not all drug-addicted prostitutes barter sex for drugs, but those that do report more frequent drug abuse and sexual activity than other prostitutes.[64]

MASSAGE PARLORS/PHOTO STUDIOS Some "working girls" are based in massage parlors and photo studios. Although it is unusual for a masseuse to offer all the services of prostitution, oral sex and manual stimulation are common. Most localities have attempted to limit commercial sex in massage parlors by passing ordinances specifying that the masseuse keep certain parts of her body covered and limiting the areas of the body that can be massaged. Some photo studios allow customers to put body paint on models before the photo sessions start.

CYBER PROSTITUTE In 2004, nearly seventy men were arrested in Odessa, Texas, after a year-long prostitution sting that focused on a massage parlor run by a woman named Misty Lane. Lane had her own website, was known as Hot Fort Worth Girl, and contacted her clients via e-mail.[65] As Lane seemed to know, the technological revolution has altered the world of prostitution. Cyber prostitutes set up personal websites or put listings on web boards such as Adult Friendfinder that carry personals. They may use loaded phrases such as "looking for generous older man" in their self-descriptions. When contacted, they ask to exchange e-mails, chat online, or make voice calls with perspective clients. They may even exchange pictures. This allows them to select who they want to be with and avoid clients who may be threatening or dangerous. Some cyber prostitution rings offer customers the opportunity to choose women from their Internet page and then have them flown in from around the country.

Becoming a Prostitute

Why does someone turn to prostitution? In the United States, both male and female street-level sex workers often come from troubled homes marked by extreme conflict and hostility and from poor urban areas or rural communities. Divorce, separation, or death splits the family; most prostitutes grew up in homes with absent fathers. One recent survey of street-level sex workers in Phoenix found that women engaging in prostitution have limited educational backgrounds; most did not complete high school. They had experienced high rates of physical and sexual abuse in childhood, as well as parental substance abuse.[66]

Lower-class girls who get into "the life" report conflict with school authorities, poor grades, and an overly regimented school experience; a significant portion have long histories of drug abuse.[67] Young girls who frequently use drugs and begin using at an early age are most at risk for prostitution to support their habits.[68]

Once they get into the life, personal danger begins to escalate. Their continuous exposure to violence, both as victims and as witnesses, leaves street workers suffering from emotional trauma that, in the absence of adequate support services, may cause them to increase their drug intake in an attempt to cope with the harsh realities of their daily lives. Life on the street increases women's risk for physical, emotional, and sexual abuse as well as their risk for HIV/AIDS. Prostitutes then find themselves in a vicious cycle of violence, substance abuse, and AIDS risk.[69]

Studies conducted abroad, especially in Third World countries, are more likely to find that prostitution is linked to economic necessity. Prostitutes in Dakar, Senegal, report that they are in the life because sexual relations with men are an important means to achieving social and economic status and, for some, a necessary means for survival.[70]

Another recent survey of female sex workers in Tijuana, Mexico, found that many of the women were single mothers (40 percent) who entered the trade because of its flexible work hours and good income. While sex work has risks such as physical assault, diseases, and unwanted pregnancies, the women believed that sex work did have some upside: It provided women with an easy and simple way to get off the streets and avoid homelessness.[71] However, despite its economic benefits there are significant downsides to entering sex work. The Dakar prostitutes reported a significant chance of contracting HIV.

CHILD SEXUAL ABUSE AND PROSTITUTION Child prostitution is not a recent development. For example, it was routine for poor young girls to serve as prostitutes in nineteenth-century England.[72] In contemporary society, child prostitution has been linked to sexual trauma experienced at an early age.[73] Many prostitutes were initiated into sex by family members at ages as young as 10 to 12 years; they have long histories of sexual exploitation and abuse.[74] The early experiences with sex help teach them that their bodies have value and that sexual encounters can be used to obtain affection, power, or money. In a detailed study of child sexual exploitation in North America, Richard J. Estes and Neil Alan Weiner found that the problem of child sexual abuse is much more widespread than has been previously believed or documented.[75] Their research indicated that each year in the United States, 25,000 children are subjected to some form of sexual exploitation, which often begins with sexual assaults by relatives and acquaintances, such as a teacher, coach, or a neighbor. Abusers are nearly always men, and about a quarter of them are married with children.

Once they fled an abusive situation at home, kids were vulnerable to life on the streets. Some get hooked up in the sex trade, starting as strippers and lap dancers and drifting into prostitution and pornography. They remain in the trade because they have lost hope and are resigned to their fate.[76] Some meet pimps who quickly turn them to a life of prostitution and beat them if they do not make their daily financial quotas. Others who fled to the streets exchange sex for money, food, and shelter. Some have been traded between prostitution rings, and others are shipped from city to city and even sent overseas as prostitutes. About 20 percent of sexually exploited children were involved in prostitution rings that worked across state lines.

Controlling Prostitution

In the late nineteenth and early twentieth century, efforts were made to regulate prostitution in the United States through medical supervision and the licensing and zoning of brothels in districts outside residential neighborhoods.[77] After World War I, prostitution became associated with disease, and the desire to protect young servicemen from harm helped to end almost all experiments with legalization in the United States.[78] Some reformers attempted to paint pimps and procurers as immigrants who used their foreign ways to snare unsuspecting American girls into prostitution. Such fears prompted passage of the federal Mann Act (1925), which prohibited bringing women into the country or transporting them across state lines for the purposes of prostitution. Often called the "white slave act," it carried a $5,000 fine, 5 years in prison, or both.[79]

Today, prostitution is considered a misdemeanor, punishable by a fine or a short jail sentence. In practice, most law enforcement is uneven and aims at confining illegal activities to particular areas in the city.[80] Prostitution is illegal in all states except Nevada (in the counties in which Las Vegas and Reno are located), where it is a highly regulated business enterprise. Some local police agencies concerned about prostitution have used high-visibility patrols to discourage prostitutes and their customers, undercover work to arrest prostitutes and drug dealers, and collaboration with hotel and motel owners to identify and arrest pimps and drug dealers.[81]

There has also been an effort to reduce prostitution and protect children forced into the life by punishing sex tourism (see the section above on international sex trade). The Violent Crime Control and Law Enforcement Act of 1994 included a provision, referred to as the Child Sexual Abuse Prevention Act, which made it a criminal offense to travel abroad for the purpose of engaging in sexual activity with a minor.[82] Some loopholes in the law were closed when President George W. Bush signed the Protect Act into law in 2003.[83] Despite these efforts, prosecuting sex tourists is often tricky due to the difficulty of gathering evidence of crimes that were committed in other countries and that involve minor children.[84]

Legalize Prostitution?

Feminists have staked out conflicting views of prostitution. One position is that women must become emancipated from male oppression and reach sexual equality. The *sexual equality view* considers the prostitute a victim of male dominance. In patriarchal societies, male power is predicated on female subjugation, and prostitution is a clear example of this gender exploitation.[85] In contrast, for some feminists, the fight for equality depends on controlling all attempts by men or women to impose their will on women. The *free choice view* is that prostitution, if freely chosen, expresses women's equality and is not a symptom of subjugation.

Advocates of both positions argue that the penalties for prostitution should be reduced (decriminalized); neither side advocates outright legalization. Decriminalization would relieve already desperate women of the additional burden of severe legal punishment. In contrast, legalization might be coupled with regulation by male-dominated justice agencies. For example, required medical examinations would mean increased male control over women's bodies.

Both positions have had significant influence around the world. In Sweden, feminists have succeeded in getting legislation passed that severely restricts prostitution and criminalizes any effort to buy sexual activities.[86] In contrast, Holland legalized brothels in 2001 but ordered that they be

A female police officer poses as a prostitute on Holt Boulevard in Pomona (known to sex workers throughout southern California as "the track") during a major prostitution sting operation on November 12, 2004. Approximately 60 to 80 men are arrested each night during the sting operations. Cars driven by the arrested men are seized and become city property until a $1000 fine is paid. Each vehicle is then labeled with a large window sticker stating that the car was seized for solicitation of prostitution and the photos of the men appear in a full-page ad in the local newspaper. Do you think such aggressive police tactics can successfully reduce or eliminate prostitution?

© Getty Images

run under a strict set of guidelines.[87] The English government is considering licensing brothels and creating managed areas or "toleration zones" to combat street prostitution.[88] Should prostitution be legalized in the United States? In her book *Brothel,* Alexa Albert, a Harvard-trained physician who interviewed young women working at a legal brothel in Nevada, makes a compelling case for legalization. She found that the women remained HIV-free and felt safer working in a secure environment than alone on city streets. Despite long hours and rules that gave too much profit to the owners, the women actually took pride in their work. In addition to the added security, most earned between $300 and $1,500 per day.[89]

IIIIIII CONNECTIONS IIIIIII

Research that highlights the survival skills of streetwalkers seems to support the rational choice approach discussed in Chapter 4. Such rules of behavior would not be learned and adopted if prostitutes were compulsive or irrational.

▌ PORNOGRAPHY

The term **pornography** derives from the Greek *porne,* meaning "prostitute," and *graphein,* meaning "to write." In the heart of many major cities are stores that display and sell books, magazines, and films depicting every imaginable explicit sex act. Suburban video stores also rent and sell sexually explicit tapes, which make up 15 to 30 percent of the home rental market. The Internet contains at least 200,000 websites offering pornographic material and adult sex films.

The purpose of this material is to provide sexual titillation and excitement for paying customers. Although material depicting nudity and sex is typically legal, protected by the First Amendment's provision limiting governmental control of speech, most criminal codes prohibit the production, display, and sale of obscene material.

Obscenity, derived from the Latin *caenum,* for "filth," is defined by Webster's dictionary as "deeply offensive to morality or decency . . . designed to incite to lust or depravity."[90] The problem of controlling pornography centers on this definition of obscenity. Police and law enforcement officials can legally seize only material that is judged obscene. But who, critics ask, is to judge what is obscene? At one time, such novels as *Tropic of Cancer* by Henry Miller, *Ulysses* by James Joyce, and *Lady Chatterley's Lover* by D. H. Lawrence were prohibited because they were considered obscene; today they are considered works of great literary value. Thus, what is obscene today may be considered socially acceptable at a future time. After all, *Playboy* and other adult magazines, sold openly on most college campuses, display nude models in all kinds of sexually explicit poses.

Allowing individual judgments on what is obscene makes the Constitution's guarantee of free speech unworkable. Could not anti-obscenity statutes also be used to control political and social dissent? The uncertainty surrounding this issue is illustrated by Supreme Court Justice Potter Stewart's famous 1964 statement on how he defined obscenity: "I know it when I see it." Because of this legal and moral ambiguity, a global pornography industry is becoming increasingly mainstream, currently generating up to $60 billion per year in revenue. In fact, some Internet pornography companies are now listed on the NASDAQ stock exchange.[91]

Prior to the nineteenth century, pornography essentially involved the written word. During the 1880s and 1890s, the photographic image began to replace older forms of pornography. The content stayed remarkably similar: Visual pornography continued to focus on women as the objects of sexual desire. To read more about the history of pornography, go to InfoTrac College Edition and read: Lisa Z. Sigel, "Filth in the Wrong People's Hands: Postcards and the Expansion of Pornography in Britain and the Atlantic World, 1880–1914," *Journal of Social History* 33 (summer 2000): 859.

Child Pornography

The use of children in pornography is the most controversial and reprehensible aspect of the business. Each year more than a million children are believed to be used in pornography or prostitution, many of them runaways whose plight is exploited by adults.[92] Sexual exploitation by child pornography rings can devastate victims, causing them physical problems ranging from headaches and loss of appetite to genital soreness, vomiting, and urinary tract infections and psychological problems including mood swings, withdrawal, edginess, and nervousness. In cases of extreme, prolonged victimization, children may lock onto the sex group's behavior and become prone to further victimization or even become victimizers themselves.

Child pornography has become widespread on the Internet. In his book, *Beyond Tolerance: Child Pornography on the Internet,* sociologist Philip Jenkins argues that activists are focused on stamping out Internet pornography but that they have not focused on its most dangerous form, kiddie porn, which sometimes involves pictures of 4- and 5-year-old girls in sexual encounters.

When an effort is made to target pedophilic websites, investigators often go in the wrong direction, failing to recognize that most sites are short-lived entities whose addresses are passed around to users. Jenkins suggests that kiddie porn is best combated by more effective law enforcement: Instead of focusing on users, efforts should be directed against suppliers. He also suggests that newsgroups and bulletin boards that advertise and discuss kiddie porn be criminalized.[93]

Does Pornography Cause Violence?

An issue critical to the debate over pornography is whether viewing it produces sexual violence or assaultive behavior. This debate was given added attention when serial killer Ted Bundy claimed his murderous rampage was fueled by reading pornography.

The evidence is mixed. Some studies indicate that viewing sexually explicit material actually has little effect on sexual violence. For example, when Neil Malamuth, Tamara Addison, and Mary Koss surveyed 2,972 male college students, they discovered that frequent use of pornography was not related to sexual aggression. There were only relatively minor differences in sexual aggression between men who report using pornography very frequently when compared to those who said they rarely used it at all. However, men who were both at high risk for sexual aggression and who were very frequent users of pornography were much more likely to engage in sexual aggression than their counterparts who consume pornography less frequently. Put simply, if a person has relatively aggressive sexual inclinations resulting from various personal and cultural factors, exposure to pornography may activate and reinforce associated coercive tendencies and behaviors. But even high levels of exposure to pornography do not turn nonaggressive men into sexual predators.[94]

How might we account for this surprisingly modest association?[95] It is possible that viewing erotic material may act as a safety valve for those whose impulses might otherwise lead them to violence. Convicted rapists and sex offenders report less exposure to pornography than a control group of nonoffenders.[96] Viewing prurient material may have the unintended side effect of satisfying erotic impulses that otherwise might result in more sexually aggressive behavior.

While the pornography–violence link seems modest, there is more evidence that people exposed to material that portrays violence, sadism, and women enjoying being raped and degraded are also likely to be sexually aggressive toward female victims.[97] Laboratory experiments conducted by a number of leading authorities have found that men exposed to violent pornography are more likely to act aggressively and hold aggressive attitudes toward women.[98] James Fox and Jack Levin find it common for serial killers to collect and watch violent pornography. Some make their own "snuff" films starring their victims.[99] On a macro-level, cross-national research indicates that nations that consume the highest levels of pornography also have extremely high rape rates.[100] However, it is still not certain if such material drives people to sexual violence or whether people predisposed to sexual violence are drawn to pornography with a violent theme.

| | | | | | | CONNECTIONS | | | | | | |

Chapter 5 discusses the effects of media on violence. As you may recall, while there is some evidence that people exposed to violent media will become violent themselves, the association is still being debated.

Pornography and the Law

All states and the federal government prohibit the sale and production of pornographic material. Child pornography is usually a separate legal category that involves either (1) the creation or reproduction of materials depicting minors engaged in actual or simulated sexual activity ("sexual exploitation of minors") or (2) the publication or distribution of obscene, indecent, or harmful materials to minors.[101] Under existing federal law, trafficking in obscenity (18 U.S.C. Sec. 1462, 1464, 1466), child pornography (18 U.S.C. Sec. 2252), harassment (18 U.S.C. Sec. 875(c)), illegal solicitation or luring of minors (18 U.S.C. Sec. 2423(b)), and threatening to injure someone (18 U.S.C. Sec. 875(c)) are all felonies punished by long prison sentences.

While these laws are designed to control obscene material, the First Amendment of the U.S. Constitution protects free speech and prohibits police agencies from limiting the public's right of free expression. This legal protection has sent the government along a torturous road in the attempt to define when material is criminally obscene and eligible for legal control. For example, the Supreme Court held in the twin cases of *Roth v. United States* and *Alberts v. California* that the First Amendment protects all "ideas with even the slightest redeeming social importance—unorthodox ideas, controversial ideas, even ideas hateful to the prevailing climate of opinion, but implicit in the history of the First Amendment is the rejection of obscenity as utterly without redeeming social importance."[102] In the 1966 case of *Memoirs v. Massachusetts,* the Supreme Court again required that for a work to be considered obscene it must be shown to be "utterly without redeeming social value."[103] These decisions left unclear how obscenity is defined. If a highly erotic movie tells a "moral tale," must it be judged legal even if 95 percent of its content is objectionable? A spate of movies made after the *Roth* decision alleged that they were educational so they could not be said to lack redeeming social importance. Many state obscenity cases were appealed to federal courts so judges could decide whether the films totally lacked redeeming social importance. To rectify the situation, the Supreme Court redefined its concept of obscenity in the case of *Miller v. California:*

> The basic guidelines for the trier of fact must be (a) whether the average person applying contemporary community standards would find that the work taken as a whole appeals to the prurient interest; (b) whether the work depicts or describes, in a patently offensive way, sexual conduct specifically defined by the applicable state law, and (c) whether the work, taken as a whole, lacks serious literary, artistic, political or scientific value.[104]

To convict a person of obscenity under the *Miller* doctrine, the state or local jurisdiction must specifically define obscene conduct in its statute, and the pornographer must engage in that behavior. The Court gave some examples of what is considered obscene: "patently offensive representations or descriptions of masturbation, excretory functions and lewd exhibition of the genitals." In subsequent cases the Court overruled convictions for "offensive" or "immoral" behavior; these are not considered obscene. The *Miller* doctrine has been criticized for not spelling out how community standards are to be determined. Obviously, a plebiscite cannot be held to determine the community's attitude for every trial concerning the sale of pornography. Works that are considered obscene in Omaha might be considered routine in New York, but how can we be sure? To resolve this dilemma, the Supreme Court articulated in *Pope v. Illinois* a reasonableness doctrine: A work is not obscene if a reasonable person applying objective standards would find that the material in question has at least some social value:[105]

> The ideas that a work represents need not obtain majority approval to merit protection, and the value of that work does not vary from community to community based on the degree of local acceptance it has won. The proper inquiry is not whether an ordinary member of any given community would find serious value in the allegedly obscene material, but whether a reasonable person would find such value in the material, taken as a whole.[106]

To read **Pope v. Illinois,** go to http://caselaw.lp.findlaw.com/scripts/getcase.pl?court5US&vol5. For an up-to-date list of web links, go to http://cj.wadsworth.com/siegel_crimtpt9e.

Controlling Pornography

Sex for profit predates Western civilization. Considering its longevity, there seems to be little evidence that it can be controlled or eliminated by legal means alone. In 1986, the Attorney General's Commission on Pornography advocated a strict law enforcement policy to control obscenity, directing that "the prosecution of obscene materials that portray sexual violence be treated as a matter of special urgency."[107] Since then, there has been a concerted effort by the federal government to prosecute adult movie distributors. Law enforcement has been so fervent that industry members have filed suit claiming they are the victims of a "moral crusade" by right-wing zealots.[108]

Although politically appealing, controlling sex for profit is difficult because of the public's desire to purchase sexually related material and services. Law enforcement crusades may not necessarily obtain the desired effect. A get-tough policy could make sex-related goods and services scarce, driving up prices and making their sale even more desirable and profitable. Going after national distributors may help decentralize the adult movie and photo business and encourage local rings to expand their activities, for example, by making and marketing videos as well as still photos or distributing them through computer networks.

An alternative approach has been to restrict the sale of pornography within acceptable boundaries. Some municipal governments have tolerated or even established adult entertainment zones in which obscene material can be openly sold. In the case of *Young v. American Mini Theaters,* the Supreme Court permitted a zoning ordinance that restricted theaters showing erotic movies to one area of the city, even though it did not find that any of the movies shown were obscene.[109] The state, therefore, has the right to regulate adult films as long as the public has the right to view them. Some jurisdictions have responded by limiting the sale of sexually explicit material in residential areas and restricting the number of adult stores that can operate in a particular area. For example, New York City has enacted zoning that seeks to break up the concentration of peep shows, topless bars, and X-rated businesses in several neighborhoods, particularly in Times Square.[110] The law forbids sex-oriented businesses within 500 feet of residential zones, schools, churches, or daycare centers. Sex shops cannot be located within 500 feet of each other, so concentrated "red light" districts must be dispersed. Rather than close their doors, sex shops got around the law by adding products like luggage, cameras, T-shirts, and classic films. The courts have upheld the law, ruling that stores can stay in business if no more than 40 percent of their floor space and inventory are dedicated to adult entertainment.[111]

Technological Change

Technological change will provide the greatest challenge to those seeking to control the sex-for-profit industry. Adult movie theaters are closing as people are able to buy or rent tapes in their local video stores and play them in the privacy of their homes.[112] Adult CD-ROMs are now a staple of the computer industry. Internet sex services include live, interactive stripping and sexual activities.[113] The government has moved to control the broadcast of obscene films via satellite and other technological innovations. On February 15, 1991, Home Dish Only Satellite Networks was fined $150,000 for broadcasting pornographic movies to its 30,000 clients throughout the United States; it was the first prosecution of the illegal use of satellites to broadcast obscene films.[114]

Despite these cases, the First Amendment right to free speech makes legal control of pornography, even kiddie porn, quite difficult. For example, to control the spread of Internet pornography, Congress passed the Communications Decency Act (CDA), which made all Internet service providers, commercial online services, bulletin board systems, and electronic mail providers criminally liable whenever their services were used to transmit material considered "obscene, lewd, lascivious, filthy, or indecent" (S 314, 1996). However, In *Reno v. ACLU* (1997), the Supreme Court ruled that the CDA unconstitutionally restricted free speech, once again illustrating the difficulty enforcement have when trying to balance the need to control obscenity with the First Amendment.[115]

In 1996 Congress again attempted to control the growth of Internet porn when it passed the Child Pornography Prevention Act (CPPA). CPPA expanded the federal prohibition on child pornography to include not only pornographic images made using actual children but also

The technological revolution represented by the Internet poses a major obstacle for people who want to control or limit sex-related entertainment. Here, Ashley West, one of the roommates on the VoyeurDorm.com website, poses in front of a new recreational vehicle owned by the site while Faith Gardner demonstrates the real-time video being shot inside. Clients pay a monthly fee to watch the girls 24 hours a day. Should such activities be criminalized? Or are they legitimate and harmless business transactions between consenting adults?

© AP/Wide World Photos

any visual depiction that is or appears to be of a minor engaging in sexually explicit conduct. The careful language of the act was used to ban "virtual child pornography" that appears to depict minors, whether or not minors are actually used.[116] However, in 2002, the U.S. Supreme Court struck down some sections of CPPA as being unconstitutionally deficient, especially those that ban "virtual porn":

> Finally, the First Amendment is turned upside down by the argument that, because it is difficult to distinguish between images made using real children and those produced by computer imaging, both kinds of images must be prohibited. The overbreadth doctrine prohibits the Government from banning unprotected speech if a substantial amount of protected speech is prohibited or chilled in the process.[117]

Since the Court's ruling, the act has not been enforced. The legal difficulties encountered by the CPPA illustrate the difficulty society has controlling the distribution of sexually related materials. Recent reports indicate that the sex business is currently booming and now amounts to $10 billion per year.[118]

SUBSTANCE ABUSE

The problem of substance abuse stretches across the United States. Large urban areas are beset by drug-dealing gangs, drug users who engage in crime to support their habits, and alcohol-related violence. Rural areas are important staging centers for the shipment of drugs across the country and are often the production sites for synthetic drugs and marijuana farming.[119] Nor is the United States alone in experiencing a problem with substance abuse. In Australia 19 percent of

youths in detention centers and 40 percent of adult prisoners report having used heroin at least once; in Canada, cocaine and crack are considered serious urban problems; South Africa reports increased cocaine and heroin abuse; Thailand has a serious heroin and methamphetamine problem; and British police have found a major increase in heroin abuse.[120]

For a list of the most **commonly used drugs and an explanation of their effects,** go to http://www.nida.nih.gov/DrugPages/DrugsofAbuse.html. For an up-to-date list of web links, go to http://cj.wadsworth.com/siegel_crimtpt9e.

Another indication of the concern about drugs has been the increasing number of drug-related arrests: from less than half a million in 1977 to more than 1.5 million today.[121] Similarly, the proportion of prison inmates incarcerated for drug offenses has increased by 300 percent since 1986.[122] Clearly the justice system views drug abuse as a major problem and is taking what decision makers regard as decisive measures for its control.

Despite the scope of the drug problem, some still view it as another type of victimless public order crime. There is great debate over the legalization of drugs and the control of alcohol. Some consider drug use a private matter and drug control another example of government intrusion into people's private lives. Furthermore, legalization could reduce the profit of selling illegal substances and drive suppliers out of the market.[123] Others see these substances as dangerous, believing that the criminal activity of users makes the term *victimless* nonsensical. Still another position is that the possession and use of all drugs and alcohol should be legalized but that the sale and distribution of drugs should be heavily penalized. This would punish those profiting from drugs and would enable users to be helped without fear of criminal punishment.

When Did Drug Use Begin?

The use of chemical substances to change reality and to provide stimulation, relief, or relaxation has gone on for thousands of years. Mesopotamian writings indicate that opium was used 4,000 years ago—it was known as the "plant of joy."[124] The ancient Greeks knew and understood the problem of drug use. At the time of the Crusades, the Arabs were using marijuana. In the Western hemisphere, natives of Mexico and South America chewed coca leaves and used "magic mushrooms" in their religious ceremonies.[125] Drug use was also accepted in Europe well into the twentieth century. Recently uncovered pharmacy records circa 1900 to 1920 showed sales of cocaine and heroin solutions to members of the British royal family; records from 1912 show that Winston Churchill, then a member of Parliament, was sold a cocaine solution while staying in Scotland.[126]

In the early years of the United States, opium and its derivatives were easily obtained. Opium-based drugs were used in various patent medicine cure-alls. Morphine was used extensively to relieve the pain of wounded soldiers in the Civil War. By the turn of the century, an estimated 1 million U.S. citizens were opiate users.[127]

Several factors precipitated the current stringent U.S. drug laws. The rural religious creeds of the nineteenth century—especially those of the Methodists, Presbyterians, and Baptists—emphasized individual human toil and self-sufficiency while designating the use of intoxicating substances as an unwholesome surrender to the evils of urban morality. Religious leaders were thoroughly opposed to the use and sale of narcotics. The medical literature of the late 1800s began to designate the use of morphine and opium as a vice, a habit, an appetite, and a disease. Nineteenth- and early twentieth-century police literature described drug users as habitual criminals. Moral crusaders in the nineteenth century defined drug use as evil and directed that local and national entities should outlaw the sale and possession of drugs. Some well-publicized research efforts categorized drug use as highly dangerous.[128] Drug use was also associated with the foreign immigrants recruited to work in factories and mines; they brought with them their national drug habits. Early antidrug legislation appears to be tied to prejudice against immigrating ethnic minorities.[129]

After the Spanish-American War of 1898, the United States inherited Spain's opium monopoly in the Philippines. Concern over this international situation, along with the domestic issues just outlined, led the U.S. government to participate in the First International Drug Conference, held in Shanghai in 1908, and a second one at The Hague in 1912. Participants in these two conferences were asked to strongly oppose free trade in drugs. The international pressure, coupled with a growing national concern, led to the passage of the antidrug laws discussed here.

Alcohol and Its Prohibition

The history of alcohol and the law in the United States has also been controversial and dramatic. At the turn of the century, a drive was mustered to prohibit the sale of alcohol. This **temperance movement** was fueled by the belief that the purity of the U.S. agrarian culture was being destroyed by the growth of the city. Urbanism was viewed as a threat to the lifestyle of the majority of the nation's population, then living on farms and in villages. The forces behind the temperance movement were such lobbying groups as the Anti-Saloon League led by Carrie Nation, the Women's Temperance Union, and the Protestant clergy of the Baptist, Methodist, and Congregationalist faiths.[130] They viewed the growing city, filled with newly arriving Irish, Italian, and eastern European immigrants, as centers of degradation and wickedness. The propensity of these ethnic people to drink heavily was viewed as the main force behind their degenerate lifestyle. The eventual prohibition of the sale of alcoholic beverages brought about by ratification of the Eighteenth Amendment in 1919 was viewed as a triumph of the morality of middle- and upper-class Americans over the threat posed to their culture by the "new Americans."[131]

Prohibition failed. It was enforced by the Volstead Act, which defined intoxicating beverages as those containing one-half of 1 percent, or more, alcohol.[132] What doomed Prohibition? One factor was the use of organized crime to supply illicit liquor. Also, the law made it illegal only to sell alcohol, not to purchase it; this cut into the law's deterrent capability. Finally, despite the work of Elliot Ness and his "Untouchables," law enforcement agencies were inadequate, and officials were likely to be corrupted by wealthy bootleggers.[133] Eventually, in 1933, the Twenty-First Amendment to the Constitution repealed Prohibition, signaling the end of the "noble experiment."

The Extent of Substance Abuse

Despite continuing efforts at control, the use of mood-altering substances persists in the United States. Some of the most commonly abused drugs are described in Exhibit 13.1. What is the extent of the substance abuse problem today? A number of national surveys attempt to chart trends in drug abuse in the general population. Results from two of the most important sources are described in the next sections.

MONITORING THE FUTURE (MTF) One important source of information on drug use is the annual self-report survey of drug abuse among high school students conducted by the Institute of Social Research (ISR) at the University of Michigan.[134] This survey is based on the self-report responses of nearly 50,000 high school students in the 8th, 10th, and 12th grades in almost 400 schools across the United States (8th and 10th graders were added to the survey in 1991).

EXHIBIT 13.1

Commonly Used Drugs

Anesthetics
Anesthetics, such as PCP or "angel dust," are drugs used as nervous system depressants. They act on the brain to produce a generalized loss of sensation, stupor, or unconsciousness (called narcosis).

Volatile liquids
Volatile liquids are liquids that are easily vaporized. Some substance abusers inhale vapors from lighter fluid, paint thinner, cleaning fluid, and model airplane glue to reach a drowsy, dizzy state sometimes accompanied by hallucinations. The psychological effect produced by inhaling these substances is a short-term sense of excitement and euphoria followed by a period of disorientation, slurred speech, and drowsiness.

Barbiturates
These hypnotic, sedative drugs depress the central nervous system into a sleeplike condition. On the illegal market, barbiturates are called "goofballs" or "downers" or are known by the color of the capsules—"reds" (Seconal), "blue dragons" (Amytal), and "rainbows" (Tuinal).

Tranquilizers
Tranquilizers relieve uncomfortable emotional feelings by reducing levels of anxiety; they ease tension and promote a state of relaxation. The major tranquilizers are used to control the behavior of the mentally ill who are suffering from psychoses, aggressiveness, and agitation. They are known by their brand names—Ampazine, Thorazine, Pacatal, Largactil, and Sparine. Improper dosages can lead to addiction, and withdrawal can be painful and hazardous.

Amphetamines
Amphetamines (Dexedrine, "dex"), Dexamyl, Bephetamine ("whites"), and Methedrine ("meth," "speed," "crystal meth," "ice") are synthetic drugs that stimulate action in the central nervous system. They produce an intense physical reaction: mood elevation and increased blood pressure, breathing rate, and bodily activity. Amphetamines also produce psychological effects, such as increased confidence, euphoria, fearlessness, talkativeness, impulsive behavior, and loss of appetite. Methedrine is probably the most widely used and most dangerous amphetamine. Long-term heavy use can result in exhaustion, anxiety, prolonged depression, and hallucinations.

Cannabis (marijuana)
Commonly called "pot," "grass," "ganja," "maryjane," "dope," and a variety of other names, marijuana is produced from the leaves of Cannabis sativa, a plant grown throughout the world. Hashish (hash) is a concentrated form of cannabis made from unadulterated resin from the female plant. Smoking large amounts of pot or hash can cause drastic distortion in auditory and visual perception, even producing hallucinatory effects.

Hallucinogens
Hallucinogens are drugs, either natural or synthetic, that produce vivid distortions of the senses without greatly disturbing the viewer's consciousness. Some produce hallucinations, and others cause psychotic behavior in otherwise normal people. D-lysergic acid diethylamide-25, commonly called LSD, is a powerful substance that stimulates cerebral sensory centers to produce visual hallucinations in all ranges of colors, to intensify hearing, and to increase sensitivity.

Cocaine
Cocaine is an alkaloid derivative of the coca leaf first isolated in 1860 by Albert Niemann of Göttingen, Germany. When originally discovered, it was considered a medicinal breakthrough that could relieve fatigue,

---

||||||| CONNECTIONS |||||||

The MTF is a prime example of the use of self-report surveys. Go to Chapter 2 for a review of this data collection technique. Can this survey be valid considering the problem of absenteeism, dropping out, and so on?

As Figure 13.1 shows, drug use declined from a high point around 1980 until 1990, when it began once again to increase until 1996; since then teenage drug use has either stabilized or declined.[135] Marijuana, the most widely used of the illicit drugs, accounted for most of the increase in overall illicit drug use during the 1990s, but use is now in decline and more kids view it as dangerous. Even though marijuana use has now stabilized, more than one-third of all seniors said they smoked pot at least once during the prior 12 months. The MTF survey shows that the popularity of Ecstasy increased dramatically in the period from 1998 to 2001 until about 12 percent of seniors reported having ever used the drug. Its usage is now in decline as kids have begun to realize the danger it presents. Though alcohol use has stabilized since 1990, 12 percent of 8th graders, 22 percent of 10th graders, and more than

27 percent of 12th graders report having five drinks in a row (binge drinking) in the past 2 weeks.

NATIONAL SURVEY ON DRUG USE AND HEALTH Each year the Substance Abuse and Mental Health Services Administration (SAMHSA), a division of the Department of Health and Human Services, conducts the National Survey on Drug Use and Health (NSDUH) (the survey was called the National Household Survey on Drug Abuse—NHSDA— prior to 2002). The NSDUH collects information from all U.S. residents of households, noninstitutional group quarters (such as shelters, rooming houses, dormitories), and civilians living on military bases (it excludes homeless people who do not use shelters, military personnel on active duty, and residents of institutional group quarters, such as jails and hospitals).

According to the last available data (2003), an estimated 19.5 million Americans aged 12 or older (about 8 percent of the population) were current illicit drug users, meaning they had used an illicit drug during the month prior to the survey interview. There was no change in the overall rate of illicit drug use between 2002 and 2003. Marijuana is the most commonly used illicit drug, with a rate of 6.2 percent. Of the

depression, and various other symptoms. Cocaine, or coke, is the most powerful natural stimulant. Its use produces euphoria, laughter, restlessness, and excitement. Overdoses can cause delirium, increased reflexes, violent manic behavior, and possible respiratory failure.

Freebase

Freebase is a chemical produced from street cocaine by treating it with a liquid to remove the hydrochloric acid with which pure cocaine is bonded during manufacture. The free cocaine, or cocaine base (hence the term "freebase") is then dissolved in a solvent, usually ether, that crystallizes the purified cocaine. The resulting crystals are crushed and smoked in a special glass pipe; the high produced is more immediate and powerful than snorting street-strength coke.

Crack

Crack is processed street cocaine. Its manufacture involves using ammonia or baking soda to remove the hydrochlorides and create a crystalline form of cocaine base that can then be smoked. Crack is not a pure form of cocaine and contains both remnants of hydrochloride and additional residue from the baking soda (sodium bicarbonate); it gets its name from the fact that the sodium bicarbonate often emits a crackling sound when the substance is smoked. It is relatively cheap and provides a powerful high; users rapidly become psychologically addicted to crack.

Narcotics/ Heroin

Narcotic drugs produce insensibility to pain (analgesia) and free the mind of anxiety and emotion (sedation). Users experience a rush of euphoria, relief from fear and apprehension, release of tension, and elevation of spirits. After experiencing this uplifting mood for a short period, users become apathetic and drowsy and nod off. Heroin, the most commonly used narcotic, was first produced in 1875 and used as a painkiller (the drug's name derives from the fact it was considered a "hero" because of its painkilling ability when it was first isolated). It is also possible to create synthetic narcotics in the laboratory. Synthetics include Demerol, Methadone, Nalline, and Darvon.

Steroids

Anabolic steroids are used to gain muscle bulk and strength for athletics and bodybuilding. Although not physically addicting, steroid use can be an obsession among people who desire athletic success. Steroids are dangerous because of the significant health problems associated with long-term use: liver ailments, tumors, hepatitis, kidney problems, sexual dysfunction, hypertension, and mental problems such as depression.

Alcohol

Although the purchase and sale of alcohol are legal today in most U.S. jurisdictions, excessive alcohol consumption is considered a major substance abuse problem. Drinkers report that alcohol reduces tension, diverts worries, enhances pleasure, improves social skills, and transforms experiences for the better. Long-term use has been linked with depression and numerous physical ailments ranging from heart disease to cirrhosis of the liver (although some research links moderate drinking to a reduction in the probability of heart attack).

Club drugs

Club drugs are primarily synthetic substances that are commonly used at nightclubs, bars, and raves. Within this category are MDMA (Ecstasy), GHB (gamma hydroxybutyrate), Rohypnol, DMT and 2c-B or "Nexus," Ketamine, and methamphetamine. MDMA (Ecstasy) combines an amphetaminelike rush with hallucinogenic experiences. Rohypnol is a central nervous system depressant that has been connected with sexual assault, rape, and robbery. OxyContin (also known by its generic name oxycodone) is widely used as a painkiller. Though it should be released slowly into the system, abusers grind tablets into powder and snort or inject the drug to produce feelings of euphoria.

Percent who used drugs in the last 12 months

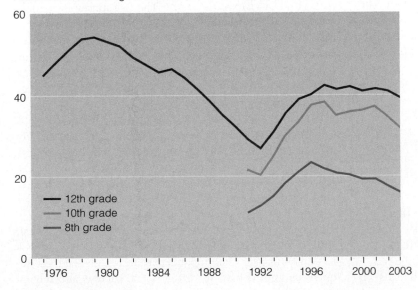

FIGURE 13.1

Trends in Annual Prevalence of Teenage Illicit Drug Use

Source: Monitoring the Future, 2003.

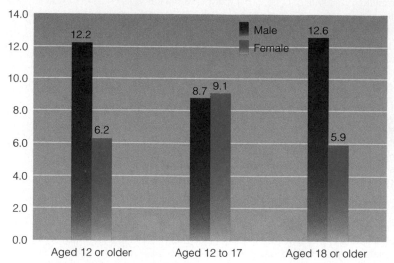

Percent dependent or abusing in past year

FIGURE 13.2

Past Year Illicit Drug or Alcohol Dependence or Abuse, by Age and Gender: 2003

Source: National Survey on Drug Abuse and Health, 2003 (Washington, DC: U.S. Department of Health and Human Services, 2003). http://www.oas.samhsa.gov/nhsda/2k3nsduh/2k3Overview.htm#ch3.

14.6 million Americans who claim to have used marijuana in the past month, about one-third, or 4.8 million people, used it on 20 or more days.[136]

Agreeing with the MTF survey, the NSDUH indicates that drug use trends have been in decline since 1996. However, as Figure 13.2 shows, both male and female Americans still use a significant amount of illegal drugs, and they continue to do so from childhood into young adulthood and beyond.

NATIONAL CENTER ON ADDICTION AND SUBSTANCE ABUSE (CASA) SURVEY

Surveys conducted by the National Center on Addiction and Substance Abuse show that alcohol abuse begins at an early age and remains an extremely serious problem over the life course. According to CASA research conducted at Columbia University, children under the age of 21 drink about 19 percent of the alcohol consumed in the United States. More than 5 million high school students (31.5 percent) admit to binge drinking at least once a month. The age at which children begin drinking is dropping: Since 1975, the proportion of children who begin drinking in the 8th grade or earlier has jumped by almost a third, from 27 to 36 percent.[137] In addition, there appears to be a significant association between teen drinking and precocious sexuality:

- Compared to teens with no sexually active friends, teens who report half or more of their friends are sexually active are more than six and one-half times likelier to drink; 31 times likelier to get drunk; 22.5 times likelier to have tried marijuana; and more than five and one-half times likelier to smoke.

- Teens who spend 25 or more hours a week with a boyfriend/girlfriend are two and one-half times likelier to drink; five times likelier to get drunk; 4.5 times likelier to have tried marijuana; and more than 2.5 times likelier to smoke than teens who spend less than 10 hours a week with a boyfriend/girlfriend.

- Girls with boyfriends 2 or more years older are more than twice as likely to drink; almost six times likelier to get drunk; six times likelier to have tried marijuana; and four and one-half times likelier to smoke than girls whose boyfriends are less than two years older or who do not have a boyfriend.[138]

The **National Center on Addiction and Substance Abuse** is devoted to informing Americans about the economic and social costs of substance abuse and its impact on their lives: http://www.casacolumbia.org. For an up-to-date list of web links, go to http://cj.wadsworth.com/siegel_crimtpt9e.

The various drug use surveys are set out in Concept Summary 13.1.

ARE THE SURVEYS ACCURATE? The ISR survey is methodologically sophisticated, but it relies on self-report evidence that is subject to error. Drug users may boastfully exaggerate the extent of their substance abuse, underreport out of fear, or simply be unaware or forgetful. About 20 percent of the ISR survey respondents say they would not provide or are not sure if they provide honest answers.

Another problem is that these national surveys overlook important segments of the drug-using population. For example, the NSDUH survey misses people who are homeless, in prison, in drug rehabilitation or AIDS clinics, and those (about 20 percent of the people contacted) who refuse to participate in the interview. The ISR survey omits kids who are institutionalized, who are absent on the day the survey is administered, who refuse to answer target questions such as their racial background, and who have dropped out of school. Research indicates that dropouts may, in fact, be the most frequent users of dangerous drugs.[139] The surveys also rely on accurate self-reporting by drug users, a group whose recall and

Drug Use Surveys

	GENERAL INFORMATION		COVERAGE		DATES
Title	Agency	Description	Population	Geographic Area	Frequency
National Survey on Drug Use and Health (NSDUH) (formerly National Household Survey on Drug Abuse)	SAMHSA	The primary source of information on the prevalence, patterns, and consequences of drug and alcohol use and abuse	General U.S. civilian non institutionalized population, aged 12 and older	National, regional, state	Annually; started 1976; most recent 2002
Monitoring the Future (MTF)	NIDA	An ongoing study of the drug-related behaviors, attitudes, and values of American secondary school students, college students, and young adults	8th, 10th, 12th graders, college students, and young adults	National	Annually; started 1972; most recent 2003
National Center on Addiction and Substance Abuse (CASA)	Columbia University	An ongoing survey of teen attitudes and the factors that produce drug usage	1,000 teens; 500 parents	National	Annually; started 1996; most recent 2004
Arrestee Drug Abuse Monitoring Program (ADAM)	NIJ	Traces trends in the prevalence and types of drug use among booked arrestees in urban areas (formerly Drug Use Forecasting—DUF)	Adult arrestees and juvenile detainees	Local, multi-jurisdictional	Annually; started 1997; most recent 2003 (DUF 1986 to 1996)

dependability may be questionable. A number of studies indicate that serious abusers underreport drug use in surveys.[140] There is evidence that reporting may be affected by social and personal traits: Girls are more willing than boys to admit taking drugs; kids from two-parent homes are less willing to admit taking drugs than kids growing up in single-parent homes.[141]

These surveys also use statistical estimating methods to project national use trends from relatively small samples.[142] Although these weaknesses are troubling, the surveys are administered yearly, in a consistent fashion, so that the effects of over- and underreporting and missing subjects should have a consistent effect in every survey year. The surveys have attempted to improve their methodologies to increase validity. For example, the ISR survey now includes 8th and 10th graders in an attempt to survey youths before they drop out of school.

AIDS and Drug Use

Intravenous (IV) drug use is closely tied to the threat of AIDS.[143] Since monitoring the spread of AIDS began in 1981, about one-fourth of all adult AIDS cases reported to the Centers for Disease Control in Atlanta have occurred among IV drug users. It is now estimated that as many as one-third of all IV drug users are AIDS carriers.[144]

One reason for the AIDS–drug use relationship is the widespread habit of needle sharing among IV users. For example, a recent study of Los Angeles drug "shooting galleries" conducted by researcher Douglas Longshore found that about one-quarter of users shoot drugs in these abandoned buildings, private apartments, or other sites, where for a small entry fee injection equipment can be borrowed or rented.[145] Most users (72 percent) shared needles, and although some tried to use bleach as a disinfectant, the majority ignored this safety precaution. Asking for or bringing bleach ruined the moment because it reminded the addicts of the risk of AIDS; others were too high to be bothered. As one user told Longshore,

> After I started shooting coke, all hell broke loose, no holds barred, couldn't be bothered to get bleach. That was out of the question. Literally picking needles up that I had no idea who had used. . . . I was just out of my mind insane. [HIV] wasn't a consideration. It was more like, I hope this is going to be okay. You just aren't in your right mind anymore.[146]

Needle sharing has been encouraged by efforts to control drugs by outlawing the over-the-counter sale of hypodermic needles. Consequently, some jurisdictions have developed outreach programs to help these drug users; others have made an effort to teach users how to clean their needles and syringes; a few states have gone so far as to give addicts sterile needles.[147]

The threat of AIDS may be changing the behavior of recreational and middle-class users, but drug use may still be increasing among the poor, high school dropouts, and other disadvantaged groups. If that pattern is correct, then the recently observed decline in substance abuse may be restricted to one segment of the at-risk population while another is continuing to use drugs at ever-increasing rates.

What Causes Substance Abuse?

What causes people to abuse substances? Although there are many different views on the causes of drug use, most can be characterized as seeing the onset of an addictive career as being either an environmental or a personal matter.

SUBCULTURAL VIEW Those who view drug abuse as having an environmental basis concentrate on lower-class addiction. Because a disproportionate number of drug abusers are poor, the onset of drug use can be tied to such factors as racial prejudice, devalued identities, low self-esteem, poor socioeconomic status, and the high level of mistrust, negativism, and defiance found in impoverished areas. Residents feel trapped in a cycle of violence, drug abuse, and despair.[148] Youths in these disorganized areas may join peers to learn the techniques of drug use and receive social support for their habit. Research shows that peer influence is a significant predictor of drug careers that actually grow stronger as people mature.[149] Drug use splits some communities into distinct groups of relatively affluent abstainers and desperately poor abusers.[150]

PSYCHOLOGICAL VIEW Not all drug abusers reside in lower-class slum areas; the problem of middle-class substance abuse is very real. Consequently, some experts have linked substance abuse to psychological deficits such as impaired cognitive functioning, personality disturbance, and emotional problems that can strike people in any economic class.[151]

Drugs may help people deal with unconscious needs and impulses and relieve dependence and depression. People may turn to drug abuse as a form of self-medication in order to reduce the emotional turmoil of adolescence, deal with troubling impulses, or cope with traumatic life experiences.[152] For example, survivors of sexual assault and physical abuse may turn to drug and alcohol abuse as a coping mechanism.[153] Depressed people may use drugs as an alternative to more radical solutions to their pain such as suicide.[154]

Research on the psychological characteristics of drug abusers does in fact reveal the presence of a significant degree of personal pathology. Studies have found that addicts suffer personality disorders characterized by a weak ego, low frustration tolerance, anxiety, and fantasies of omnipotence. Many addicts exhibit psychopathic or sociopathic behavior characteristics, forming what is called an addiction-prone personality.[155] One study of abusers conducted in five large U.S. cities found a significant association between mental illness and drug abuse: About 53 percent of drug abusers and 37 percent of alcohol abusers have at least one serious mental illness. Conversely, 29 percent of the diagnosed mentally ill people in the survey have substance abuse problems.[156]

GENETIC FACTORS Research shows that substance abuse may have a genetic basis.[157] For example, a number of studies comparing alcoholism among identical twins and fraternal twins have found that the degree of concordance (both siblings behaving identically) is twice as high among the identical twin groups.[158]

Taken as a group, studies of the genetic basis of substance abuse suggest that people whose parents were alcoholic or drug dependent have a greater chance of developing a problem than the children of nonabusers, and this relationship occurs regardless of parenting style or the quality of the parent–child relationship.[159] However, not all children of abusing parents become drug dependent themselves, suggesting that even if drug abuse is heritable, environment and socialization must play some role in the onset of abuse.[160]

SOCIAL LEARNING Social psychologists suggest that drug abuse may also result from observing parental drug use. Parental drug abuse begins to have a damaging effect on children as young as 2 years old, especially when parents manifest drug-related personality problems such as depression or poor impulse control.[161] Children whose parents abuse drugs are more likely to have persistent abuse problems than the children of non-abusers.[162]

People who learn that drugs provide pleasurable sensations may be the most likely to experiment with illegal substances; a habit may develop if the user experiences lower anxiety, fear, and tension levels.[163] Having a history of family drug and alcohol abuse has been found to be a characteristic of violent teenage sexual abusers.[164] Heroin abusers report an unhappy childhood that included harsh physical punishment and parental neglect and rejection.[165]

PROBLEM BEHAVIOR SYNDROME (PBS) For many people, substance abuse is just one of many problem behaviors. Longitudinal studies show that drug abusers are maladjusted, alienated, and emotionally distressed and that drug use is only one among many social problems.[166] Having a deviant lifestyle begins early in life and is punctuated with criminal relationships, family history of substance abuse, educational failure, and alienation. Crack cocaine use has been linked to sexual abuse as children and social isolation as adults.[167] There is robust support for the interconnection of problem drinking and drug abuse, delinquency, precocious sexual behavior, school failure, running away, homelessness, family conflict, and other similar social problems.[168]

RATIONAL CHOICE Not all people who abuse drugs do so because of personal pathology. Some may use drugs and alcohol because they want to enjoy their effects: get high, relax, improve creativity, escape reality, and increase sexual responsiveness. Research indicates that adolescent alcohol abusers believe that getting high will make them powerful, increase their sexual performance, and facilitate their social behavior; they care little about negative future consequences.[169] Claire Sterk-Elifson's research on middle-class drug-abusing women shows that most were introduced by friends in the context of "just having some fun."[170]

Substance abuse, then, may be a function of the rational but mistaken belief that drugs can benefit the user. The decision to use drugs involves evaluations of personal consequences (such as addiction, disease, and legal punishment) and the expected benefits of drug use (such as peer approval, positive affective states, heightened awareness, and relaxation). Adolescents may begin using drugs because they believe their peers expect them to do so.[171]

Is There a Drug Gateway?

Some experts believe that, regardless of its cause, most people fall into drug abuse slowly, beginning with alcohol and then following with marijuana and more serious drugs as the need for a more powerful high intensifies. A number of research efforts have confirmed this **gateway model.** For example, James Inciardi, Ruth Horowitz, and Anne Pottieger found a clear pattern of adult involvement in adolescent drug abuse. Kids on crack started their careers with early experimentation with alcohol at age 7, began getting drunk at age 8, had alcohol with an adult present by age 9, and became regular drinkers by the time they were 11 years old.[172] Drinking with an adult present, presumably a parent, was a significant precursor of future substance abuse and delinquency. "Adults who gave children alcohol," they argue, "were also giving them a head start in a delinquent career."[173] Other research efforts support this view when they find that the most serious drug users have a history of alcohol abuse.[174] Kids who begin using alcohol in adolescence become involved in increasing levels of deviant behavior as they mature.[175]

The drug gateway vision is popular, but not all research efforts find that users progress to ever-more potent drugs, and some show that, surprisingly, many hard-core drug abusers never actually smoked pot or used alcohol.[176] And although many American youths have tried marijuana, few actually progress to crack or heroin abuse.[177]

In sum, there may be no single cause of substance abuse. People may try and continue to use illegal substances for a variety of reasons. As Inciardi points out,

> There are as many reasons people use drugs as there are individuals who use drugs. For some, it may be a function of family disorganization, or cultural learning, or maladjusted personality, or an "addiction-prone" personality. . . . For others, heroin use may be no more than a normal response to the world in which they live.[178]

Types of Drug Users

The general public often groups all drug users together without recognizing that there are many varieties, ranging from adolescent recreational drug users to adults who run large smuggling operations.[179]

■ *Adolescents who distribute small amounts of drugs:* Many adolescents begin their involvement in the drug trade by using and distributing small amounts of drugs; they do not commit any other serious criminal acts. Kenneth Tunnell found in his interviews with low-level drug dealers that many started out as "stash dealers" who sold drugs to maintain a consistent access to drugs for their own consumption; their customers are almost always personal acquaintances, including friends and relatives.[180] They are insulated from the legal system because their activities rarely result in apprehension and sanction.

■ *Adolescents who frequently sell drugs:* A small number of adolescents, most often multiple-drug users or heroin or cocaine users, are high-rate dealers who bridge the gap between adult drug distributors and the adolescent user. Frequent dealers often have adults who "front" for them—that is, loan them drugs to sell without up-front cash. The teenagers then distribute the drugs to friends and acquaintances, returning most of the proceeds to the supplier while keeping a commission for themselves. Frequent dealers are more likely to sell drugs in public and can be seen in known drug user hangouts in parks, schools, or other public places. Deals are irregular, so the chances of apprehension are slight.

■ *Teenage drug dealers who commit other delinquent acts:* A more serious type of drug-involved youth comprises those who use and distribute multiple substances and also commit both property and violent crimes; many are gang members.[181] Although these youngsters make up about 2 percent of the teenage population, they commit 40 percent of the robberies and assaults and about 60 percent of all teenage felony thefts and drug sales.

These youths are frequently hired by older dealers to act as street-level drug runners. Each member of a crew of three to twelve boys will handle small quantities of drugs, perhaps three bags of heroin, which are received on consignment and sold on the street; the supplier receives 50 to 70 percent of the drug's street value. The crew members also act as lookouts, recruiters, and guards. Between drug sales, the young dealers commit robberies, burglaries, and other thefts.[182]

■ *Adolescents who cycle in and out of the justice system:* Some drug-involved youths are failures at both dealing and crime. They do not have the savvy to join gangs or groups and instead begin committing unplanned, opportunistic crimes that increase their chances of arrest. They are heavy drug users, which both increases apprehension risk and decreases their value

Some drug users are "winners." They commit hundreds of crimes each year but are rarely arrested. On the streets, they are known for their calculated violence. Their crimes are carefully planned and coordinated. However, on occasion their activities are cut short by dedicated police action. An illustration put together by the Providence, Rhode Island, police department details the players in "Operation Royal Flush," a 10-month-long drug investigation that ended on November 10, 2004. Officials said 21 members of the Latin Kings street gang or their associates have been either arrested or indicted by a federal grand jury for their involvement in a drug trafficking ring. Authorities said they are still looking for five other people involved.

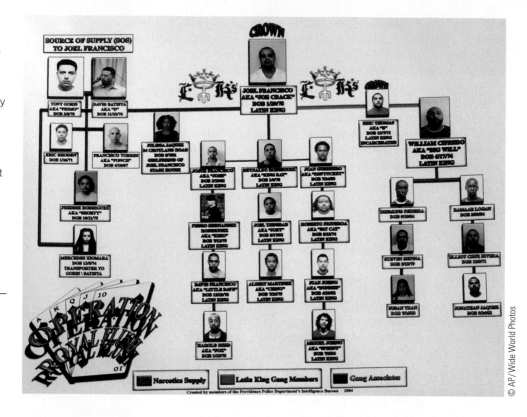

© AP/Wide World Photos

for organized drug distribution networks. Drug-involved "losers" can earn a living steering customers to a seller in a "copping" area, "touting" drug availability for a dealer, or acting as a lookout. However, they are not considered trustworthy or deft enough to handle drugs or money. They may bungle other criminal acts, which solidifies their reputation as undesirable.

■ *Drug-involved youth who continue to commit crimes as adults:* Although about two-thirds of substance-abusing youths continue to use drugs after they reach adulthood, about half desist from other criminal activities. Those who persist in both substance abuse and crime as adults exhibit a garden variety of social and developmental problems. Some evidence also exists that these drug-using persisters have low nonverbal IQs and poor physical coordination.

■ *Outwardly respectable adults who are top-level dealers:* A few outwardly respectable adult dealers sell large quantities of drugs to support themselves in high-class lifestyles. Outwardly respectable dealers often seem indistinguishable from other young professionals. Upscale dealers seem to drift into dealing from many different walks of life. Some begin as campus dealers whose lifestyle and outward appearance are indistinguishable from other students (though they are more frequently involved in illegal behavior outside of drug dealing).[183] Frequently they are drawn from professions and occupations that are unstable, have irregular working hours, and accept drug abuse. Former graduate students, musicians, performing

artists, and bar-keepers are among those who are likely to fit the pro- file of the adult who begins dealing drugs in his or her 20s. Some use their business skills and drug profits to get into legitimate enterprises or illegal scams. Others drop out of the drug trade because they are the victims of violent crime committed by competitors or disgruntled customers; a few wind up in jail or prison.

■ *Smugglers:* Smugglers import drugs into the United States. They are generally men, middle-aged or older, who have strong organizational skills, established connections, capital to invest, and a willingness to take large business risks. Smugglers are a loosely organized, competitive group of individual entrepreneurs. There is a constant flow in and out of the business as some sources become the target of law enforcement activities, new drug sources become available, older smugglers become dealers, and former dealers become smugglers.

■ *Adult predatory drug users who are frequently arrested:* Many users who begin abusing substances in early adolescence continue in drugs and crime in their adulthood. Getting arrested, doing time, using multiple drugs, and committing predatory crimes are a way of life for them. They have few skills, did poorly in school, and have long criminal records. The threat of conviction and punishment has little effect on their criminal activities. These "losers" have friends and relatives involved in drugs and crime. They specialize in robberies, burglaries, thefts, and drug sales. They filter in and out of the justice system and begin committing crimes as soon as they are released. In some populations, at least one-third of adult males are involved in drug trafficking and other criminal acts well into their adulthood.[184]

If they make a "big score," perhaps through a successful drug deal, they may significantly increase their drug use. Their increased narcotics consumption then destabilizes their lifestyle, destroying family and career ties. When their finances dry up, they may become *street junkies,* people whose traditional lifestyle has been destroyed, who turn to petty crime to maintain an adequate supply of drugs. Cut off from a stable source of quality heroin, not knowing from where their next fixes or the money to pay for them will come, looking for any opportunity to make a buck, getting sick or "jonesing," being pathetically unkempt and unable to maintain even the most primitive routines of health or hygiene, street junkies live a very difficult existence. Because they are unreliable and likely to become police informants, street junkies pay the highest prices for the poorest quality heroin; lack of availability increases their need to commit habit-supporting crimes.[185]

■ *Adult predatory drug users who are rarely arrested:* Some drug users are "winners." They commit hundreds of crimes each year but are rarely arrested. On the streets, they are known for their calculated violence. Their crimes are carefully planned and coordinated. They often work with partners and use lookouts to carry out the parts of their crimes that have the highest risk of apprehension. These "winners" are more likely to use recreational drugs, such as coke and pot, than the more addicting heroin or opiates. Some become high-frequency users and risk apprehension and punishment. But for the lucky few, their criminal careers can stretch for up to 15 years without interruption by the justice system.

These users are sometimes referred to as *stabilized junkies* who have learned the skills needed to purchase and process larger amounts of heroin. Their addiction enables them to maintain normal lifestyles, although they may turn to drug dealing to create contacts with drug suppliers. They are employable, but earning legitimate income does little to reduce their drug use or dealing activities.[186]

■ *Less predatory drug-involved adult offenders:* Most adult drug users are petty criminals who avoid violent crime. These occasional users are people just beginning their addiction, who use small amounts of narcotics, and whose habit can be supported by income from conventional jobs; narcotics have relatively little influence on their lifestyles.[187] They are typically high school graduates and have regular employment that supports their drug use. They usually commit petty thefts or pass bad checks. They stay on the periphery of the drug trade by engaging in such acts as helping addicts shoot up, bagging drugs for dealers, operating shooting galleries, renting needles and syringes, and selling small amounts of drugs. These petty criminal drug users do not have the stomach for a life of hard crime and drug dealing. They violate the law in proportion to the amount and cost of the drugs they are using. Pot smokers have a significantly lower frequency of theft violations than daily heroin users, whose habit is considerably more costly.

■ *Women who are drug-involved offenders:* Women who are drug-involved offenders constitute a separate type of substance abuser. Although women are far less likely than men to use addictive drugs, female offenders are just as likely to be involved in drugs as male offenders. Though infrequently violent criminals, they are often involved in prostitution and low-level drug dealing; a few become top-level dealers. Many are pregnant or are already mothers, and because they share needles, they are at high risk of contracting AIDS and passing the HIV virus to their newborn children. They maintain a high risk of victimization. One study of 171 women using crack cocaine found that since initiating crack use, 62 percent of the women reported suffering a physical attack and 32 percent suffered rape; more than half were forced to seek medical care for their injuries.[188]

Drugs and Crime

One of the main reasons for the criminalization of particular substances is the assumed association between drug abuse and crime. Research suggests that many criminal offenders have extensive experience with drug use and that drug users commit an enormous amount of crime; alcohol abuse has also been linked to criminality.[189] Research shows that almost four in ten violent crimes and fatal motor vehicle accidents involve alcohol.[190] This pattern is not unique to the United States. Research conducted in England found that about 61 percent of arrestees tested positively for at least one drug, a finding comparable to arrestees in the United States.[191]

Although the drug–crime connection is powerful, the true relationship between them is still uncertain because many users have had a history of criminal activity before the onset of their substance abuse.[192] It is possible that:

■ Chronic criminal offenders begin to abuse drugs and alcohol after they have engaged in crime; that is, crime causes drug abuse.

■ Substance abusers turn to a life of crime to support their habits; that is, drug abuse causes crime.

■ Drug use and crime co-occur in individuals; that is, both crime and drug abuse are caused by some other common factor. For example, people with a fondness for risk-taking activities may take drugs and also commit crime.[193]

■ Drug users begin to engage in activities such as heavy drinking, which leads them to commit crime.[194]

Considering these possible scenarios, it is impossible to make a definitive statement such as "drugs cause crime." However, while it is not certain whether drug use turns otherwise law-abiding citizens into criminals, it certainly amplifies the extent of their criminal activities.[195] And, as addiction levels increase, so does the frequency and seriousness of criminality.[196] Two approaches have been used to study the relationship between drugs and crime. One has been to survey known addicts to assess the extent of their law violations; the other has been to survey known criminals to see if they were or are drug users. These are discussed separately next.

USER SURVEYS Numerous studies have examined the criminal activity of drug users. As a group, they show that people who take drugs have extensive involvement in crime.[197] Youths who abuse alcohol are also the most likely to engage in violence during their life course; violent adolescents report histories of alcohol abuse; adults with long histories of drinking are also more likely to report violent offending patterns.[198]

One often-cited study of this type was conducted by sociologist James Inciardi. After interviewing 356 addicts in Miami, Inciardi found that they reported 118,134 criminal offenses during a 12-month period; of these, 27,464 were index crimes.[199] If this behavior is typical, the country's estimated 300,000 to 700,000 heroin users could be responsible for a significant amount of all criminal behavior. An English study using a sample of 100 known abusers found that more than half of the subjects reported involvement in crime in the month prior. The most common offenses were shoplifting, receiving stolen goods, and theft; violence was used relatively rarely (11 percent).[200]

SURVEYS OF KNOWN CRIMINALS The second method used to link drugs and crime involves testing known criminals to determine the extent of their substance abuse. For example, the NSDUH survey found that youths who self-reported delinquent behavior during the past year were also more likely to use illicit drugs in the past month than other youths. Those who reported getting into a serious fight at school or work (20.7 versus 9.3 percent); carrying a handgun (34.6 versus 10.8 percent); selling illegal drugs (68.8 versus 9.0 percent); and stealing or trying to steal something worth $50 or more (43.8 versus 9.9 percent) were significantly more likely to use drugs than those who did not engage in such antisocial behaviors.[201]

Surveys of prison inmates disclose that many (80 percent) are lifelong substance abusers. More than one-third claim to have been under the influence of drugs when they committed their last offense.[202] These data support the view that a strong association exists between substance abuse and serious crime.

Another important source of data on the drug abuse–crime connection is the federally sponsored Arrestee Drug Abuse Monitoring Program (ADAM), which interviews and tests thousands of arrestees for drug abuse each year. Its most recent surveys indicate that approximately two-thirds of both female and male arrestees tested positive for at least one of the following drugs: cocaine, opiates, marijuana, methamphetamine, and PCP. Marijuana was the drug most commonly used by male arrestees, followed by cocaine, opiates, methamphetamine, and PCP. Cocaine was the drug most commonly used by female arrestees, followed by marijuana, methamphetamine, opiates, and PCP.[203]

THE DRUG–CRIME CONNECTION It is of course possible that most criminals are not actually drug users but that police are more likely to apprehend muddle-headed substance abusers than clear-thinking abstainers. A second, and probably more plausible, interpretation is that most criminals are in fact substance abusers. While the drug–crime link is still uncertain, drug use interferes with maturation and socialization. Drug abusers are more likely to drop out of school, be underemployed, engage in premarital sex, and become unmarried parents. These factors have been linked to a weakening of the social bond that may lead to antisocial behaviors.[204]

In sum, research testing both the criminality of known narcotics users and the narcotics use of known criminals produces a very strong association between drug use and crime. Even if the crime rate of drug users were actually half that reported in the research literature, users would be responsible for a significant portion of the total criminal activity in the United States.

Drugs and the Law

The federal government first initiated legal action to curtail the use of some drugs early in the twentieth century.[205] In 1906 the Pure Food and Drug Act required manufacturers to list the amounts of habit-forming drugs in products on the labels but did not restrict their use. However, the act prohibited the importation and sale of opiates except for medicinal purposes. In 1914 the Harrison Narcotics Act restricted importation, manufacture, sale, and dispensing of narcotics.

It defined *narcotic* as any drug that produces sleep and relieves pain, such as heroin, morphine, and opium. The act was revised in 1922 to allow importation of opium and coca (cocaine) leaves for qualified medical practitioners. The Marijuana Tax Act of 1937 required registration and payment of a tax by all who imported, sold, or manufactured marijuana. Because marijuana was classified as a narcotic, those registering would also be subject to criminal penalty.

In later years, other federal laws were passed to clarify existing drug statutes and revise penalties. For example, the Boggs Act of 1951 provided mandatory sentences for violating federal drug laws. The Durham-Humphrey Act of 1951 made it illegal to dispense barbiturates and amphetamines without a prescription. The Narcotic Control Act of 1956 increased penalties for drug offenders. In 1965 the Drug Abuse Control Act set up stringent guidelines for the legal use and sale of mood-modifying drugs, such as barbiturates, amphetamines, LSD, and any other "dangerous drugs," except narcotics prescribed by doctors and pharmacists. Illegal possession was punished as a misdemeanor and manufacture or sale as a felony. And in 1970 the Comprehensive Drug Abuse Prevention and Control Act set up unified categories of illegal drugs and associated penalties with their sale, manufacture, or possession. The law gave the U.S. attorney general discretion to decide in which category to place any new drug.

Since then, various federal laws have attempted to increase penalties imposed on drug smugglers and limit the manufacture and sale of newly developed substances. For example, the 1984 Controlled Substances Act set new, stringent penalties for drug dealers and created five categories of narcotic and non-narcotic substances subject to federal laws.[206] The Anti-Drug Abuse Act of 1986 again set new standards for minimum and maximum sentences for drug offenders, increased penalties for most offenses, and created a new drug penalty classification for large-scale offenses (such as trafficking in more than 1 kilogram of heroin), for which the penalty for a first offense was 10 years to life in prison.[207] With then-President George Bush's endorsement, Congress passed the Anti-Drug Abuse Act of 1988, which created a coordinated national drug policy under a "drug czar," set treatment and prevention priorities, and, symbolizing the government's hard-line stance against drug dealing, imposed the death penalty for drug-related killings.[208]

For the most part, state laws mirror federal statutes. Some states now apply extremely heavy penalties for selling or distributing dangerous drugs, involving long prison sentences of up to 25 years.

Drug Control Strategies

Substance abuse remains a major social problem in the United States. Politicians looking for a safe campaign issue can take advantage of the public's fear of drug addiction by calling for a war on drugs. These wars have been declared even when drug usage is stable or in decline.[209] Can these efforts pay off? Can illegal drug use be eliminated or controlled?

A number of different drug control strategies have been tried with varying degrees of success. Some aim to deter drug use by stopping the flow of drugs into the country,

apprehending and punishing dealers, and cracking down on street-level drug deals. Others focus on preventing drug use by educating potential users to the dangers of substance abuse (convincing them to "say no to drugs") and by organizing community groups to work with the at-risk population in their area. Still another approach is to treat known users so they can control their addictions. Some of these efforts are discussed here.

SOURCE CONTROL One approach to drug control is to deter the sale and importation of drugs through the systematic apprehension of large-volume drug dealers, coupled with the enforcement of strict drug laws that carry heavy penalties. This approach is designed to capture and punish known international drug dealers and deter those who are considering entering the drug trade. A major effort has been made to cut off supplies of drugs by destroying overseas crops and arresting members of drug cartels in Central and South America, Asia, and the Middle East, where many drugs are grown and manufactured. The federal government has been in the vanguard of encouraging exporting nations to step up efforts to destroy drug crops and prosecute dealers. However, translating words into deeds is a formidable task. Drug lords are willing and able to fight back through intimidation, violence, and corruption when necessary.

The amount of narcotics grown each year is so vast that even if three-quarters of the opium crop were destroyed, the U.S. market would still require only 10 percent of the remainder to sustain the drug trade. Radically reducing the amount of illegal drugs produced each year might have little effect on U.S. consumption. Drug users in the United States are more able and willing to pay for drugs than anyone else in the world. Even if the supply were reduced, whatever drugs there were would find their way to the United States.

Adding to control problems is the fact that the drug trade is an important source of foreign revenue, and destroying the drug trade undermines the economies of Third World nations. Even if the government of one nation were willing to cooperate in vigorous drug suppression efforts, suppliers in other nations, eager to cash in on the sellers' market, would be encouraged to turn more acreage over to coca or poppy production. For example, between 1994 and 1999, enforcement efforts in Peru and Bolivia were so successful that they altered cocaine cultivation patterns. Colombia became the premier coca cultivating country, growing or refining 80 percent of the world's cocaine supply. Rather than rely on shaky foreign sources, the drug cartels are encouraging local growers to cultivate coca plants. When the Colombian government mounted an effective eradication campaign in the traditional growing areas, the cartel linked up with rebel groups in remote parts of the country for their drug supply.[210] There are also indications that the drug syndicates may be planting a higher yield variety of coca and improving refining techniques to replace crops lost to government crackdowns.

Adding to the problem of source control is the fact that the United States has little influence in some key drug-producing areas such as Vietnam, Cambodia, and Myanmar (formerly Burma).[211] War and terrorism also may make source control strategies problematic. After the United States destroyed Afghanistan's Taliban government, local warlords seized power and resumed the drug trade; Afghanistan now supplies 75 percent of the world's opium.[212] And while the Colombian guerillas may not be interested in joining or colluding with crime cartels, they finance their war against the government by aiding drug traffickers and "taxing" crops and sales.[213]

INTERDICTION STRATEGIES Law enforcement efforts have also been directed at intercepting drug supplies as they enter the country. Border patrols and military personnel using sophisticated hardware have been involved in massive interdiction efforts; many impressive multimillion-dollar seizures have been made. Yet the U.S. borders are so vast and unprotected that meaningful interdiction is impossible. And even if all importation were shut down, homegrown marijuana and laboratory-made drugs, such as "ice," LSD, and PCP, could become the drugs of choice. Even now, their easy availability and relatively low cost are increasing their popularity among the at-risk population.

LAW ENFORCEMENT STRATEGIES Local, state, and federal law enforcement agencies have been actively fighting against drugs. One approach is to direct efforts at large-scale drug rings. The long-term consequence has been to decentralize drug dealing and encourage young independent dealers to become major suppliers. Ironically, it has proven easier for federal agents to infiltrate and prosecute traditional organized crime groups than to take on drug-dealing gangs. Consequently, some nontraditional groups have broken into the drug trade. For example, the Hell's Angels motorcycle club has become one of the primary distributors of cocaine and amphetamines in the United States.

Police can also target, intimidate, and arrest street-level dealers and users in an effort to make drug use so much of a hassle that consumption is cut back and the crime rate reduced. Approaches that have been tried are reverse stings, in which undercover agents pose as dealers to arrest users who approach them for a buy. One approach is to direct efforts at large-scale drug rings. However, this effort has merely served to decentralize drug dealing. Asian, Latin American, and Jamaican groups, motorcycle clubs, and local gangs, such as the Crips and Bloods, are all involved in large-scale dealing. Colombian syndicates have established cocaine distribution centers on every continent, and Mexican organizations are responsible for large methamphetamine

shipments to U.S., Russian, Turkish, Italian, Nigerian, Chinese, Lebanese, and Pakistani heroin trafficking syndicates, which are now competing for dominance.

In terms of weight and availability, there is still no commodity more lucrative than illegal drugs. They cost relatively little to produce and provide large profit margins to dealers and traffickers. At an average street price of $100 per gram in the United States (the current price according to the Office of National Drug Control Policy), a metric ton of pure cocaine is worth $100 million; cutting it and reducing purity can double or triple the value.[214] It is difficult for law enforcement agencies to counteract the inducement of drug profits. When large-scale drug busts are made, supplies become scarce and market values increase, encouraging more people to enter the drug trade. There are also suspicions that a displacement effect occurs: Stepped-up efforts to curb drug dealing in one area or city simply encourage dealers to seek out friendlier territory.[215]

PUNISHMENT STRATEGIES Even if law enforcement efforts cannot produce a general deterrent effect, the courts may achieve the required result by severely punishing known drug dealers and traffickers. A number of initiatives have made the prosecution and punishment of drug offenders a top priority. State prosecutors have expanded their investigations into drug importation and distribution and created special prosecutors to focus on drug dealers. Once convicted, drug dealers can get very long sentences.

However, these efforts often have their downside. Defense attorneys consider delay tactics to be sound legal maneuvering in drug-related cases. Courts are so backlogged that prosecutors are anxious to plea bargain. The consequence of this legal maneuvering is that about 25 percent of people convicted on federal drug charges are granted probation or some other form of community release. Even so, prisons have become jammed with inmates, many of whom were involved in drug-related cases. Many drug offenders sent to prison do not serve their entire sentences because they are released in an effort to relieve prison overcrowding. The mean sentence for a drug crime is 47 months, but the actual time served is 23 months or about half of the original sentence.[216]

It is unlikely that the public would approve of a drug control strategy that locks up large numbers of traffickers; research indicates that the public already believes drug trafficking penalties are too harsh (while supporting the level of punishment for other crimes).[217] And some critics are disturbed because punishment strategies seem to have a disproportionate effect on minority group members and the impoverished. Some have gone as far as suggesting that government agencies are either ignoring or covering up the toll harsh drug penalties have on society's disadvantaged because it is politically expedient to be a tough defender of the nation's moral climate.[218]

COMMUNITY STRATEGIES Another type of drug-control effort relies on the involvement of local community groups to lead the fight against drugs. Representatives of various local government agencies, churches, civic organizations, and similar institutions are being brought together to create drug prevention and awareness programs.

Citizen-sponsored programs attempt to restore a sense of community in drug-infested areas, reduce fear, and promote conventional norms and values.[219] These efforts can be classified into one of four distinct categories.[220] The first involves law enforcement-type efforts, which may include block watches, cooperative police–community efforts, and citizen patrols. Some of these citizen groups are nonconfrontational: They simply observe or photograph dealers, write down their license plate numbers, and then notify police. On occasion, telephone hot lines have been set up to take anonymous tips on drug activity. Other groups engage in confrontational tactics that may even include citizens' arrests. Area residents have gone as far as contracting with private security firms to conduct neighborhood patrols.

Another tactic is to use the civil justice system to harass offenders. Landlords have been sued for owning properties that house drug dealers; neighborhood groups have scrutinized drug houses for building code violations. Information acquired from these various sources is turned over to local authorities, such as police and housing agencies, for more formal action.

There are also community-based treatment efforts in which citizen volunteers participate in self-help support programs, such as Narcotics Anonymous or Cocaine Anonymous, which have more than 1,000 chapters nationally. Other programs provide youths with martial arts training, dancing, and social events as an alternative to the drug life.

The fourth drug prevention effort is designed to enhance the quality of life, improve interpersonal relationships, and upgrade the neighborhood's physical environment. Activities might include the creation of drug-free school zones (which encourage police to keep drug dealers away from the vicinity of schools). Consciousness-raising efforts include demonstrations and marches to publicize the drug problem and build solidarity among participants. Politicians have been lobbied to get better police protection or tougher laws passed; New York City residents even sent bags filled with crack collected from street corners to the mayor and police commissioner to protest drug dealing. Residents have cleaned up streets, fixed broken streetlights, and planted gardens in empty lots to broadcast the message that they have local pride and do not want drug dealers in their neighborhoods.

Community crime prevention efforts seem appealing, but there is little conclusive evidence that they are an effective drug control strategy. Some surveys indicate that most residents do not participate in programs. There is also evidence that community programs work better in stable, middle-income areas than in those that are crime ridden and disorganized.[221] Although these findings are discouraging, some studies do find that on occasion deteriorated areas can sustain successful antidrug programs.[222] Future evaluations of community control efforts should determine whether they can work in the most economically depressed areas. The most common community-based program is Drug Abuse Resistance Education (DARE), which is discussed more fully in the Policy and Practice in Criminology feature.

DRUG-TESTING PROGRAMS Drug testing of private employees, government workers, and criminal offenders is believed to deter substance abuse. In the workplace, employees are tested to enhance on-the-job safety and productivity. In some industries, such as mining and transportation, drug testing is considered essential because abuse can pose a threat to the public.[223] Business leaders have been enlisted in the fight against drugs. Mandatory drug-testing programs in government and industry are common: More than 40 percent of the country's largest companies, including IBM and AT&T, have drug-testing programs. The federal government requires employee testing in regulated industries such as nuclear energy and defense contracting. About 4 million transportation workers are subject to testing.

Drug testing is also common in government and criminal justice agencies. About 30 percent of local police departments test applicants, and 16 percent routinely test field officers. However, larger jurisdictions serving populations over 250,000 are much more likely to test applicants (84 percent) and field officers (75 percent). Drug testing is also part of the federal government's Drug-Free Workplace Program, which has the goal of improving productivity and safety. Employees most likely to be tested include presidential appointees, law enforcement officers, and people in positions of national security.

Criminal defendants are now routinely tested at all stages of the justice system, from arrest to parole. The goal is to reduce criminal behavior by detecting current users and curbing their abuse. Can such programs reduce criminal activity? Two evaluations of pretrial drug-testing programs found little evidence that monitoring defendants' drug use influenced their behavior.[224]

TREATMENT STRATEGIES A number of approaches are taken to treat known users, getting them clean of drugs and alcohol, and thereby reducing the at-risk population. One approach rests on the assumption that users have low self-esteem and treatment efforts must focus on building a sense of self. For example, users have been placed in worthwhile programs of outdoor activities and wilderness training to create self-reliance and a sense of accomplishment.[225] More intensive efforts use group therapy approaches relying on group leaders who have been substance abusers; through such sessions users get the skills and support to help them reject social pressure to use drugs. These programs are based on the Alcoholics

Drug Abuse Resistance Education

The most widely known drug education program, Drug Abuse Resistance Education (DARE), is an elementary school course designed to give students the skills for resisting peer pressure to experiment with tobacco, drugs, and alcohol. It is unique because it employs uniformed police officers to carry the antidrug message to the students before they enter junior high school. The program focuses on five major areas:

1. Providing accurate information about tobacco, alcohol, and drugs

2. Teaching students techniques to resist peer pressure

3. Teaching students respect for the law and law enforcers

4. Giving students ideas for alternatives to drug use

5. Building the self-esteem of students

DARE is based on the concept that the young students need specific analytical and social skills to resist peer pressure and say no to drugs. Instructors work with children to raise their self-esteem, provide them with decision-making tools, and help them identify positive alternatives to substance abuse. Millions of students have already taken the DARE program. More than 40 percent of all school districts incorporate assistance from local law enforcement agencies in their drug prevention programming. New community policing strategies commonly incorporate the DARE program in their efforts to provide services to local neighborhoods at the grassroots level.

Does DARE Work?

DARE is popular with both schools and police agencies, but a highly sophisticated evaluation of the program by Dennis Rosenbaum and his associates found that it had only a marginal impact on student drug use and attitudes. A longitudinal study by psychologist Donald Lynam and his colleagues found that DARE had no effect on students' drug use at any time through 10th grade, and a 10-year followup failed to find any hidden or delayed "sleeper" effects. At age 20, there were no differences in drug use between those who received DARE and those who did not; the only difference was that those who received DARE reported slightly lower levels of self-esteem at age 20, an effect that proponents were not aiming for.

Changing the DARE Curriculum

Although national evaluations have questioned the validity of DARE and a few communities have discontinued its use, it is still widely employed in school districts around the United States. To meet criticism head on, DARE began testing a new curriculum in 2001. The new program is aimed at older students and relies more on having them question their assumptions about drug use than on listening to lectures on the subject. Among other changes, the new program will work largely on changing social norms, teaching students to question whether they really have to use drugs to fit in with their peers. Police officers will now serve more as coaches than as lecturers, encouraging students to challenge the social norm of drug use in discussion groups. Students also do role playing in an effort to learn decision-making skills. There is also an emphasis on the role of media and advertising in shaping behavior.

Critical Thinking

1. If DARE does not work as expected, what policy might be the best strategy to reduce teenage drug use? Source control? Reliance on treatment? Community-level enforcement?

2. Should all teens who are receiving a free education from the state be tested for drugs and alcohol in order to remain in school?

3. Do you think that the DARE program would be more successful if taught by people other than police officers? What about ex-addicts?

 InfoTrac College Edition Research

Use "Drug Abuse Resistance Education" as a subject guide in InfoTrac College Edition. To learn more about the Lynam research, read this article: "DARE: Doubtful after 10 Years," *Harvard Mental Health Letter* 17 (August 2000).

Sources: Kate Zernike, "Antidrug Program Says It Will Adopt a New Strategy," *New York Times*, 15 February 2001, p.1; Donald R. Lynam, Rich Milich, Rick Zimmerman, Scott Novak, T. K. Logan, Catherine Martin, Carl Leukefeld, and Richard Clayton, "Project D.A.R.E.: No Effects at 10-Year Follow-Up," *Journal of Consulting and Clinical Psychology* 67 (1999): 590–593; Dennis Rosenbaum, Robert Flewelling, Susan Bailey, Chris Ringwalt, and Deanna Wilkinson, "Cops in the Classroom: A Longitudinal Evaluation of Drug Abuse Resistance Education (D.A.R.E.)," *Journal of Research in Crime and Delinquency* 31 (1994): 3–31; David Carter, *Community Policing and D.A.R.E.: A Practitioner's Perspective* (Washington, DC: Bureau of Justice Assistance, 1995).

Anonymous approach, which holds that users must find within themselves the strength to stay clean and that peer support from those who understand their experiences can help them achieve a drug-free life.

There are also residential programs for the more heavily involved, and a large network of drug treatment centers has been developed. Some detoxification units use medical procedures to wean patients from the more addicting drugs

Walden House residents Dennis, left, and his mentor, Jamal, talk during the group's morning walk to Alamo Square in San Francisco. New clients are assigned a senior member of the program who is responsible for teaching them the rules and systems of the house. California has embarked on an ambitious experiment to divert thousands of nonviolent drug offenders out of the prison system and into community treatment programs like this one in the tough Mission District.

© AP/Wide World Photos

to others, such as methadone, that can be more easily regulated. Methadone is a drug similar to heroin, and addicts can be treated at clinics where they receive methadone under controlled conditions. However, methadone programs have been undermined because some users sell their methadone on the black market, and others supplement their dosages with illegally obtained heroin. Other programs utilize drugs such as Naxalone, which counter the effects of narcotics and ease the trauma of withdrawal, but results have not been conclusive.[226]

Cocaine Anonymous is a fellowship of men and women who share their experience, strength, and hope with one another so that they may solve their common problem and help others to recover from their addiction: http://www.ca.org. For an up-to-date list of web links, go to http://cj.wadsworth.com/siegel_crimtpt9e.

Other therapeutic programs attempt to deal with the psychological causes of drug use. Hypnosis, aversion therapy (getting users to associate drugs with unpleasant sensations, such as nausea), counseling, biofeedback, and other techniques are often used.

The long-term effects of treatment on drug abuse are still uncertain. Critics charge that a stay in a residential program can help stigmatize people as addicts even if they never used hard drugs; and in treatment they may be introduced to hard-core users with whom they will associate after release. Users do not often enter these programs voluntarily and have little motivation to change.[227] And even those who could be helped soon learn that there are simply more users who need treatment than there are beds in treatment facilities. Many facilities are restricted to users whose health insurance will pay for short-term residential

care; when their insurance coverage ends, patients are often released, even though their treatment is incomplete.

Narcotics Anonymous can be reached at http://www.na.org/. For an up-to-date list of web links, go to http://cj.wadsworth.com/siegel_crimtpt9e.

Supporters of treatment argue that many addicts are helped by intensive in- and out-patient treatment. As one District of Columbia program shows, clients who complete treatment programs are less likely to use drugs than those who drop out.[228] Although such data support treatment strategies, it is also possible that completers are motivated individuals who would have stopped using drugs even if they had not been treated.

Although these and similar results are encouraging, treatment strategies have been thwarted because relatively few drug-dependent people actually receive the rehabilitation efforts they so desperately need. Unfortunately, those requiring treatment may not often receive the proper care. More than 4.1 million people may now be drug dependent, but less than 1 million are receiving treatment. The treatment gap is most pronounced for adolescents: The number of people aged 12 to 25 dependent on illicit drugs is nearly six times greater than the number receiving treatment.

EMPLOYMENT PROGRAMS Research indicates that drug abusers who obtain and keep employment will end or reduce the incidence of their substance abuse.[229] Not surprisingly, then, there have been a number of efforts to provide vocational rehabilitation for drug abusers. One approach is the supported work program, which typically involves jobsite training, ongoing assessment, and job-site intervention. Rather than teach work skills in a classroom, support programs rely on helping drug abusers deal with real work settings. Other programs that have merit provide training to overcome the barriers to employment and improve work skills, including help with motivation, education, experience, the job market, job-seeking skills, and personal issues.[230]

Drug Legalization

Considering these problems, some commentators have called for the legalization or decriminalization of restricted drugs. The so-called war on drugs is expensive, costing more than $500 billion over the past twenty years—money that could have been spent on education and economic development. Drug enforcement and treatment now costs federal, state, and local governments about $100 billion per year. The National Center on Addiction and Substance Abuse at Columbia University claims that a conservative estimate of what the states have spent on substance abuse and addiction is $81.3 billion,13.1 percent of the $620 billion of total state spending.[231] The federal government plans to spend close to $12 billion more on drug control, up from $7 billion in 1995; this figure does not reflect treatment costs.[232]

Despite the massive effort to control drugs through prevention, deterrence, education, and treatment strategies, the fight against substance abuse has not proved successful. It is difficult to get people out of the drug culture because of the enormous profits involved in the drug trade. It has also proven difficult to control drugs by convincing known users to quit; few treatment efforts have been successful. Legalization is warranted, according to drug expert Ethan Nadelmann, because the use of mood-altering substances is customary in almost all human societies; people have always wanted, and will find ways of obtaining, psychoactive drugs.[233] Banning drugs creates networks of manufacturers and distributors, many of whom use violence as part of their standard operating procedures. Although some believe that drug use is immoral, Nadelmann questions whether it is any worse than the unrestricted use of alcohol and cigarettes, both of which are addicting and unhealthful. Far more people die each year because they abuse these legal substances than are killed in drug wars or from abusing illegal substances.

Nadelmann also states that just as Prohibition failed to stop the flow of alcohol in the 1920s while it increased the power of organized crime, the policy of prohibiting drugs is similarly doomed to failure. When drugs were legal and freely available in the early twentieth century, the proportion of Americans using drugs was not much greater than today. Most users led normal lives, probably because of the legal status of their drug use.

If drugs were legalized, the argument goes, price and distribution could be controlled by the government. This would reduce addicts' cash requirements, so crime rates would drop because users would no longer need the same cash flow to support their habits. Drug-related deaths would decline because government control would reduce needle sharing and the spread of AIDS. Legalization would also destroy the drug-importing cartels and gangs. Because drugs would be bought and sold openly, the government would reap a tax windfall both from taxes on the sale of drugs and from income taxes paid by drug dealers on profits that have been part of the hidden economy. Of course, drug distribution would be regulated, like alcohol, keeping drugs away from adolescents, public servants such as police and airline pilots, and known felons. Those who favor legalization point to the Netherlands as a country that has legalized drugs and remains relatively crime free.[234]

THE CONSEQUENCES OF LEGALIZATION Critics claim the legalization approach might have the short-term effect of reducing the association between drug use and crime, but it might also have grave social consequences. Legalization might increase the nation's rate of drug usage, creating an even larger group of nonproductive, drug-dependent people who must be cared for by the rest of society.[235] If drugs were legalized and freely available, drug users might significantly increase their daily intake. In countries like Iran and Thailand, where drugs are cheap and readily available, the rate of narcotics use is quite high. Historically, the availability of cheap narcotics has preceded drug-use epidemics, as was the case when British and American merchants sold opium in nineteenth-century China.

Furthermore, if the government tried to raise money by taxing legal drugs, as it now does with liquor and cigarettes, that might encourage drug smuggling to avoid tax payments; these "illegal" drugs might then fall into the hands of adolescents.

THE LESSON OF ALCOHOL The problems of alcoholism should serve as a warning of what can happen when controlled substances are made readily available. Because women may more easily become dependent on crack than men, the number of drug-dependent babies could begin to match or exceed the number delivered with fetal alcohol syndrome.[236] Drunk-driving fatalities, which today number about 25,000 per year, might be matched by deaths due to driving under the influence of pot or crack. And although distribution would be regulated, it is likely that adolescents would have the same opportunity to obtain potent drugs as they now have to obtain alcoholic beverages.

Decriminalization or legalization of controlled substances is unlikely in the near term, but further study is warranted. What effect would a policy of partial decriminalization (for example, legalizing small amounts of marijuana) have on drug use rates? Would a get-tough policy help to "widen the net" of the justice system and actually deepen some youths' involvement in substance abuse? Can society provide alternatives to drugs that will reduce teenage drug dependency?[237] The answers to these questions have proven elusive.

- Public order crimes are acts considered illegal because they conflict with social policy, accepted moral rules, and public opinion. There is usually great debate over public order crimes. Some charge that public order crimes are not crimes at all and that it is foolish to legislate morality. Others view such morally tinged acts as prostitution, gambling, and drug abuse as harmful and therefore subject to public control.

- Many public order crimes are sex related.

- Although homosexuality is not a crime, homosexual acts are subject to legal control. Gay people are still not allowed to married and are barred from the military and other groups such as the Boy Scouts. In 2003 the Supreme Court ruled that sexual relations between gay people cannot be criminalized.

- Prostitution is another sex-related public order crime. Although prostitution has been practiced for thousands of years and is legal in some areas, most states outlaw commercial sex.

- The international sex trade is a multibillion-dollar business; it involves tricking young girls from primarily eastern Europe and Asia into becoming prostitutes.

- There are a variety of prostitutes, including streetwalkers, B-girls, and call girls. A new type of prostitution is cyber prostitution, which is Internet based.

- Studies indicate that prostitutes came from poor, troubled families and have abusive parents. However, there is little evidence that prostitutes are emotionally disturbed, addicted to drugs, or sexually abnormal.

- Although prostitution is illegal, some cities have set up adult entertainment areas where commercial sex is tolerated by law enforcement agents.

- Pornography involves the sale of sexually explicit material intended to sexually excite paying customers. The depiction of sex and nudity is not illegal, but it does violate the law when it is judged obscene. *Obscenity* is a legal term that today is defined as material offensive to community standards. Thus, each local jurisdiction must decide what pornographic material is obscene. A growing problem is the exploitation of children in obscene materials (kiddie porn), which has been expanded through the Internet.

- The Supreme Court has ruled that local communities can pass statutes outlawing any sexually explicit material. There is no hard evidence that pornography is related to crime or aggression, but data suggest that sexual material with a violent theme is related to sexual violence by those who view it.

- Substance abuse is another type of public order crime. Most states and the federal government outlaw a wide variety of drugs they consider harmful, including narcotics, amphetamines, barbiturates, cocaine, hallucinogens, and marijuana.

- One of the main reasons for the continued ban on drugs is their relationship to crime. Numerous studies have found that drug addicts commit enormous amounts of property and violent crime.

- Alcohol is another commonly abused substance. Although alcohol is legal to possess, it too has been linked to crime. Drunk driving and deaths caused by drunk drivers are growing national problems.

- There are many different strategies to control substance abuse, ranging from source control to treatment. So far, no single method seems effective. Although hotly debated, because so many people already take drugs and because there is an association of drug abuse with crime, legalization is unlikely in the near term.

ThomsonNOW

Thomson NOW! Optimize your study time and master key chapter concepts with **ThomsonNOW™**—the first web-based assessment-centered study tool for Criminology. This powerful resource helps you determine your unique study needs and provides you with a *Personalized Study Plan,* guiding you to interactive media that includes Learning Modules, Topic Reviews, ABC Video Clips with Questions, Animations, an integrated E-book, and more!

Thinking Like a Criminologist

You have been called upon by the director of the Department of Health and Human Services to give your opinion on a recent national survey finding that serious mental illness is highly correlated with illicit drug use. Among adults who used an illicit drug in the past year, 17.1 percent had serious mental illness in that year, while the rate of serious mental illness was 6.9 percent among adults who did not use an illicit drug. Among adults with serious mental

Percent using

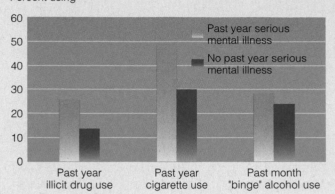

FIGURE 13-A

Rates of Serious Mental Illness Correlated with Illicit Drug, Alcohol, and Cigarette Use among Adults Aged 18 or Older, 2002

Source: National Household Survey on Drug Abuse, 2002 (Washington, DC: U.S. Department of Health and Human Services, 2003).

illness, 28.9 percent used an illicit drug in the past year, while the rate of illicit drug use was 12.7 percent among those without serious mental illness. The relationship is illustrated in 13-A.

Among adults with serious mental illness, 23.2 percent (4 million) were dependent on or abused alcohol or illicit drugs, while the rate among adults without serious mental illness was only 8.2 percent. Adults with serious mental illness were more likely than those without serious mental illness to be dependent on or abuse illicit drugs (9.6 versus 2.1 percent) and more likely to be dependent on or abuse alcohol (18.0 versus 7.0 percent). Among adults with substance dependence or abuse, 20.4 percent had serious mental illness. The rate of serious mental illness was 7.0 percent among adults who did not have substance abuse or dependence.

The director realizes that one possible explanation of this data is that drugs cause people to become mentally ill. He asks you to comment on other possible explanations. What do you tell him?

Doing Research on the Web

To learn more about the association between mental illness and drug abuse, check out the website of the National Alliance for Mental Illness: http://web. nami.org/ helpline/dualdiagnosis.htm.

You may also want to check out research at a Substance Abuse and Mental Health Service Administration website: http://www.gainsctr.com/ pdfs /fact _sheets/gainsjailprev.pdf.

For more on drugs and mental illness, go to http://www.nlm.nih.gov/medlineplus /drugabuse.html.

BOOK COMPANION WEBSITE

http://cj.wadsworth.com /siegel_crimtpt9e To quiz yourself on the material in this chapter, go to the companion website, where you'll find chapter-by-chapter online tutorial quizzes, a final exam, ABC videos with questions, chapter outlines, chapter review, chapter-by-chapter web links, flash cards, and more!

KEY TERMS

public order crimes (426)
victimless crimes (426)
social harm (428)
vigilantes (428)
moral crusaders (428)
gay bashing (429)
homosexuality (429)

sodomy (429)
homophobia (429)
paraphilias (430)
brothels (431)
prostitution (431)
madam (434)
call girls (434)

skeezers (434)
pornography (437)
obscenity (437)
temperance
    movement (441)
gateway model (447)

CRITICAL THINKING QUESTIONS

1. Under what circumstances, if any, might the legalization or decriminalization of drugs be beneficial to society?

2. Do you consider alcohol a drug? Should greater control be placed on the sale of alcohol?

3. Do TV shows and films glorify drug usage and encourage youths to enter the drug trade? Should all images on TV of drugs and alcohol be banned?

4. Is prostitution really a crime? Should a man or woman have the right to sell sexual favors if they so choose?

5. Do you believe there should be greater controls placed on the distribution of sexually explicit material on the Internet? Would you approve of the online sale of sexually explicit photos of children if they were artificial images created by computer animation?

6. Which statement is more accurate: (a) Sexually aggressive men are drawn to pornography because it reinforces their preexisting hostile orientation to sexuality; or (b) Reading or watching pornography can make men become sexually aggressive.

7. Are there objective standards of morality? Does the existing criminal code reflect contemporary national moral standards? Or are laws banning sexual behaviors and substance abuse the product of a relatively few "moral entrepreneurs" who seek to control other people's behaviors?

NOTES

1. Associated Press, "Palmeiro Very Happy He Appeared," March 18, 2005. http://sports.espn.go.com/mlb/news/story?id=2016305; ESPN.Com News Services, "Admissions before BALCO Grand Jury Detailed," December 2, 2005. http://sports.espn.go.com/espn/news/story?id=1936592. Accessed December 5, 2005.

2. Edwin Schur, *Crimes without Victims* (Englewood Cliffs, NJ: Prentice-Hall, 1965).

3. Andrea Dworkin, quoted in "Where Do We Stand on Pornography," *Ms* (January–February 1994): 34.

4. Jennifer Williard, *Juvenile Prostitution* (Washington, DC: National Victim Resource Center, 1991).

5. Morris Cohen, "Moral Aspects of the Criminal Law," *Yale Law Journal* 49 (1940): 1017.

6. Sir Patrick Devlin, *The Enforcement of Morals* (New York: Oxford University Press, 1959), p. 20.

7. See Joel Feinberg, *Social Philosophy* (Englewood Cliffs, NJ: Prentice-Hall, 1973), chap. 2, 3.

8. H. L. A. Hart, "Immorality and Treason," *Listener* 62 (1959): 163.

9. *United States v. 12 200-ft Reels of Super 8mm Film,* 413 U.S. 123 (1973) at 137.

10. Joseph Gusfield, "On Legislating Morals: The Symbolic Process of Designating Deviancy," *California Law Review* 56 (1968): 58–59.

11. John Franks, "The Evaluation of Community Standards," *Journal of Social Psychology,* 139 (1999): 253–255.

12. Information provided by Hitwise, Inc. June 4, 2004; http://www.hitwise.com.

13. Irving Kristol, "Liberal Censorship and the Common Culture," *Society* 36 (September 1999): 5.

14. Amnesty International, http://www.amnesty.org/ailib /intcam /femgen/ fgm1.htm. Accessed September 8, 2004.

15. Barbara Crossette, "Senegal Bans Cutting of Genitals of Girls," *New York Times,* 18 January 1999, p. A11.

16. David Kaplan, "Is It Torture or Tradition?" *Newsweek* (20 December 1993): 124.

17. Crossette, "Senegal Bans Cutting of Genitals of Girls."

18. Al Baker, "L. I. Millionaire's Newest Venture Was Oldest Profession, Police Say," *New York Times,* 21 July 2001.

19. CNN News Service, "Falwell Apologizes to Gays, Feminists, Lesbians," 14 September 2001. http://www.cnn.com/2001/US/09/14/Falwell.apology/.

20. Howard Becker, *Outsiders* (New York: Macmillan, 1963), pp. 13–14.

21. Andrea Friedman, "Sadists and Sissies: Anti-Pornography Campaigns in Cold War America," *Gender and History* 15 (2003): 201–228.

22. Albert Reiss, "The Social Integration of Queers and Peers," *Social Problems* 9 (1961): 102–120.

23. Judd Marmor, "The Multiple Roots of Homosexual Behavior," in *Homosexual Behavior,* ed. J. Marmor (New York: Basic Books, 1980), p. 5.

24. J. Money, "Sin, Sickness, or Status? Homosexual Gender Identity and Psychoneuroendocrinology," *American Psychologist* 42 (1987): 384 –399.

25. C. S. Ford and F. A. Beach, *Patterns of Sexual Behavior* (New York: Harper, 1951).

26. U.S. Census Bureau, *Current Population Survey,* March 2000.

27. J. McNeil, *The Church and the Homosexual* (Kansas City, MO: Sheed, Andrews, and McNeel, 1976).

28. "Executing Injustice," *The Advocate* (5 February 2002): 16.

29. Sue Headley, "Anti-Homosexual Homicides Most Often Perpetrated by Young Males," *Youth Studies Australia* 22 (2003): 55.

30. Ibid., p. 19.

31. Henry Adams, Lester Wright, and Bethany Lohr, "Is Homophobia Associated with Homosexual Arousal?" *Journal*

of Abnormal Psychology 105 (1996): 440–445.

32. 376 U.S. 660; 82 S.Ct. 1417; 8 L.Ed.2d 758 (1962).

33. Elsa Arnett, "Efforts Grow to Cap Gay-Rights Gains," *Boston Globe,* 12 April 1998, p. A10.

34. John Biskupic, "Justice Let Stand 'Don't Ask, Don't Tell' Policy," *Boston Globe,* 22 October 1996, p. A6.

35. Michael Joseph Gross, "A Problem with Privacy, and with Openness," *Boston Globe,* 15 February 1998, p. C3.

36. Associated Press, "Court Gives Sons Back to Gay Father," *Boston Globe,* 16 October 1996, p. A5.

37. *Boy Scouts of America v. Dale* 530 U.S. 640 (2000).

38. National Gay and Lesbian Task Force, press release, "Eye on Equality: Pride and Public Opinion," July 5, 1998.

39. *State v. Limon,* Court of Appeals of the State of Kansas, 2004. No. 85, 898.

40. Charles M. Sennott, "Pope Calls Sex Abuse Crime, Pontiff Says Cases Mishandled, Voices Solidarity with Victims," *Boston Globe,* 24 April 2002, p. A1; Kevin Cullen, "Irish Bishop Quits over Priest Case, Prelate Admits He Failed to Stop Abuse of Children," *Boston Globe,* 2 April 2002, p. A6.

41. W. P. de Silva, "Sexual Variations," *British Medical Journal* 318 (1999): 654–655.

42. Kathy Smiljanich and John Briere, "Self-Reported Sexual Interest in Children: Sex Differences and Psychosocial Correlates in a University Sample," *Violence and Victims* 11 (1996): 39–50.

43. See, generally, V. Bullogh, *Sexual Variance in Society and History* (Chicago: University of Chicago Press, 1958), pp. 143–144.

44. Spencer Rathus, *Human Sexuality* (New York: Holt, Rinehart & Winston, 1983), p. 463.

45. Annette Jolin, "On the Backs of Working Prostitutes: Feminist Theory and Prostitution Policy," *Crime and Delinquency* 40 (1994): 60–83.

46. Charles McCaghy, *Deviant Behavior* (New York: Macmillan, 1976), pp. 348–349.

47. Marian Pitts, Anthony Smith, Jeffrey Grierson, Mary O'Brien, and Sebastian Misson, "Who Pays for Sex and Why? An Analysis of Social and Motivational Factors Associated with Male Clients of Sex Workers," *Archives of Sexual Behavior* 33 (2004): 353–358.

48. Monica Prasad, "The Morality of Market Exchange: Love, Money, and Contractual Justice," *Sociological Perspectives* 42 (1999): 181–187.

49. Cited in McCaghy, *Deviant Behavior.*

50. FBI, *Crime in the United States, 1999* (Washington, DC: U.S. Government Printing Office, 2000), p. 217; updated with data from FBI, *Crime in the United States, 2000* (Washington, DC: U.S. Government Printing Office, 2001), p. 217.

51. FBI, *Crime in the United States, 2003,* p. 270.

52. Elizabeth Bernstein, 'The Meaning of the Purchase: Desire, Demand, and the Commerce of Sex," *Ethnography* 2 (2001): 389–420.

53. David Enrich, "Trafficking in People," *U.S. News & World Report* 131 (23 July 2001): 34.

54. Mark-David Janus, Barbara Scanlon, and Virginia Price, "Youth Prostitution," in *Child Pornography and Sex Rings,* ed. Ann Wolbert Burgess (Lexington, MA: Lexington Books, 1989), pp. 127–146.

55. Libby Plumridge and Gillian Abel, "A 'Segmented' Sex Industry in New Zealand: Sexual and Personal Safety of Female Sex Workers," *Australian and New Zealand Journal of Public Health* 25 (2000): 78–83.

56. Charles Winick and Paul Kinsie, *The Lively Commerce* (Chicago: Quadrangle Books, 1971), p. 58.

57. Hilary Surratt, James Inciardi, Steven Kurtz, and Marion Kiley, "Sex Work and Drug Use in a Subculture of Violence," *Crime and Delinquency* 50 (2004): 43–60.

58. Lisa Maher, "Hidden in the Light: Occupational Norms among Crack-Using Street-Level Sex Workers," *Journal of Drug Issues* 26 (1996): 143–173.

59. Winick and Kinsie, *The Lively Commerce,* pp. 172–173.

60. Paul Goldstein, "Occupational Mobility in the World of Prostitution: Becoming a Madam," *Deviant Behavior* 4 (1983): 267–279.

61. Alessandra Stanley, "Case of the Classy Madam," *Time* (29 October 1984): 39.

62. Goldstein, "Occupational Mobility in the World of Prostitution," pp. 267–270.

63. Mireya Navarro, "Group Forced Illegal Aliens into Prostitution, U.S. Says," *New York Times,* 24 April 1998, p. A10.

64. Paul Goldstein, Lawrence Ouellet, and Michael Fendrich, "From Bag Brides to Skeezers: A Historical Perspective on Sex-for-Drugs Behavior," *Journal of Psychoactive Drugs* 24 (1992): 349–361.

65. Sarah Bahari, "Online Prostitution a Problem on the Web," Knight Ridder/Tribune News Service, 24 August 2004, p. K7343.

66. Lisa Kramer and Ellen Berg, "A Survival Analysis of Timing of Entry into Prostitution: The Differential Impact of Race, Educational Level, and Childhood/Adolescent Risk Factors," *Sociological Inquiry* 73 (2003): 511–529.

67. John Potterat, Richard Rothenberg, Stephen Muth, William Darrow, and Lynanne Phillips-Plummer, "Pathways to Prostitution: The Chronology of Sexual and Drug Abuse Milestones," *Journal of Sex Research* 35 (1998): 333–342.

68. Sheila Royo Maxwell and Christopher Maxwell, "Examining the 'Criminal Careers' of Prostitutes within the Nexus of Drug Use, Drug Selling, and Other Illicit Activities," *Criminology* 38 (2000): 787–809.

69. Nancy Romero-Daza, Margaret Weeks, and Merrill Singer, " 'Nobody Gives a Damn If I Live or Die' ": Violence, Drugs, and Street-Level Prostitution in Inner-City Hartford, Connecticut," *Medical Anthropology* 22 (2003): 233–259.

70. Maria Eugênia Do Espirito Santo and Gina Etheredge, " 'And Then I Became a Prostitute' " . . . Some Aspects of Prostitution and Brothel Prostitutes in Dakar, Senegal," *Social Science Journal* 41 (2004): 137–146.

71. Jesus Bucardo, Shirley Semple, Miguel Fraga-Vallejo, Wendy Davila, and Thomas Patterson, "A Qualitative Exploration of Female Sex Work in Tijuana, Mexico," *Archives of Sexual Behavior* 33 (2004): 343–352.

72. Alyson Brown and David Barrett, *Knowledge of Evil: Child Prostitution and Child Sexual Abuse in Twentieth Century England* (Devon, England: Willan, 2002).

73. Jocelyn Brown, Patricia Cohen, Henian Chen, Elizabeth Smailes, and Jeffrey Johnson, "Sexual Trajectories of Abused

and Neglected Youths," *Journal of Developmental and Behavioral Pediatrics* 25 (2004): 77–83.

74. Gerald Hotaling and David Finkelhor, *The Sexual Exploitation of Missing Children* (Washington, DC: U.S. Department of Justice, 1988).

75. Richard Estes and Neil Alan Weiner, *The Commercial Sexual Exploitation of Children in the U.S., Canada, and Mexico* (Philadelphia: University of Pennsylvania Press, 2001).

76. Shu-ling Hwang and Olwen Bedford, "Juveniles' Motivations for Remaining in Prostitution," *Psychology of Women Quarterly* 28 (2004):136–137.

77. Barbara G. Brents and Kathryn Hausbeck, "State-Sanctioned Sex: Negotiating Formal and Informal Regulatory Practices in Nevada Brothels," *Sociological Perspectives* 44 (2001): 307–335.

78. Ibid.

79. Mara Keire, "The Vice Trust: A Reinterpretation of the White Slavery Scare in the United States, 1907–1917," *Journal of Social History* 35 (2001): 5–42.

80. Ronald Weitzer, "The Politics of Prostitution in America," in *Sex for Sale,* ed. Ronald Weitzer (New York: Routledge, 2000): 159–180.

81. Sherry Plaster Carter, Stanley Carter, and Andrew Dannenberg, "Zoning Out Crime and Improving Community Health in Sarasota, Florida: Crime Prevention through Environmental Design," *American Journal of Public Health* 93 (2003): 1442–1445.

82. 18 U.S.C. [section] 2423(b) (2000).

83. The Protect Act, Public Law 108-21. April 30, 2003.

84. Sara K. Andrews, "U.S. Domestic Prosecution of the American International Sex Tourist: Efforts to Protect Children from Sexual Exploitation," *Journal of Criminal Law and Criminology* 94 (2004): 415–453.

85. Andrea Dworkin, *Pornography* (New York: Dutton, 1989).

86. Arthur Gould, "The Criminalisation of Buying Sex: The Politics of Prostitution in Sweden," *Journal of Social Policy* 30 (2001): 437–438.

87. Suzanne Daley, "New Rights for Dutch Prostitutes, but No Gain," *New York Times,* 12 August 2001, p. A4.

88. James Morton, "Legalising Brothels," *Journal of Criminal Law* 68 (2004): 87–90.

89. Alexa Albert, *Brothel: Mustang Ranch and Its Women* (New York: Random House, 2001).

90. *Merriam-Webster Dictionary* (New York: Pocket Books, 1974), p. 484.

91. Neil Malamuth, Tamara Addison, and Mary Koss, "Pornography and Sexual Aggression: Are There Reliable Effects and Can We Understand Them?" *Annual Review of Sex Research* 11 (2000): 26–94.

92. Albert Belanger, et al., "Typology of Sex Rings Exploiting Children," in *Child Pornography and Sex Rings,* ed. Ann Wolbert Burgess (Lexington, MA: Lexington Books, 1984), pp. 51–81.

93. Philip Jenkins, *Beyond Tolerance: Child Pornography Online* (New York: New York University Press, 2001).

94. Neil Malamuth, Tamara Addison, and Mary Koss, "Pornography and Sexual Aggression: Are There Reliable Effects and Can We Understand Them?" *Annual Review of Sex Research* 11 (2000): 26–94.

95. Berl Kutchinsky, "The Effect of Easy Availability of Pornography on the Incidence of Sex Crimes," *Journal of Social Issues* 29 (1973): 95–112.

96. Michael Goldstein, "Exposure to Erotic Stimuli and Sexual Deviance," *Journal of Social Issues* 29 (1973): 197–219.

97. See Edward Donnerstein, Daniel Linz, and Steven Penrod, *The Question of Pornography* (New York: Free Press, 1987).

98. Edward Donnerstein, "Pornography and Violence against Women," *Annals of the New York Academy of Science* 347 (1980): 277–288; E. Donnerstein and J. Hallam, "Facilitating Effects of Erotica on Aggression against Women," *Journal of Personality and Social Psychology* 36 (1977): 1270–1277.

99. James Alan Fox and Jack Levin, "Multiple Homicide: Patterns of Serial and Mass Murder," in *Crime and Justice: An Annual Edition,* vol. 23, ed. Michael Tonry (Chicago: University of Chicago Press, 1998): 418–419.

100. John Court, "Sex and Violence: A Ripple Effect," *Pornography and Aggression,* eds.

Neil Malamuth and Edward Donnerstein (Orlando: Academic Press, 1984).

101. State Laws on Obscenity, Child Pornography, and Harassment. http://www.itaa .org/porn1.htm.

102. *Roth v. United States,* 354 U.S. 476 (1957).

103. *A Book Named "John Cleland's Memoirs of a Woman of Pleasure" v. Attorney General of Massachusetts* 383 U.S. 413 (1966).

104. *Miller v. California,* 413 U.S. 15 (1973).

105. *Pope v. Illinois,* 481 U.S. 497 (1987).

106. Ibid.

107. *Pornography Commission,* pp. 376–377.

108. Bob Cohn, "The Trials of Adam and Eve," *Newsweek* (7 January 1991): 48.

109. 427 U.S. 50 (1976).

110. Thomas J. Lueck, "At Sex Shops, Fear that Ruling Means the End Is Near," *New York Times,* 25 February 1998, p.1.

111. David Rohde, "In Giuliani's Crackdown on Porn Shops, Court Ruling Is a Setback," *New York Times,* 29 August 1998, p. A11.

112. Joseph Scott, "Violence and Erotic Material—The Relationship between Adult Entertainment and Rape." Paper presented at the annual meeting of the American Association for the Advancement of Science, Los Angeles, 1985.

113. Anthony Flint, "Skin Trade Spreading across U.S.," *Boston Globe,* 1 December 1996, pp. 1, 36–37.

114. Associated Press, "N.Y. Firm Fined for Broadcasting Pornographic Films by Satellite," *Boston Globe,* 16 February 1991, p. 12.

115. *ACLU, Reno v. ACLU,* No. 96–511.

116. ACLU, news release, "ACLU v. Reno, Round 2: Broad Coalition Files Challenge to New Federal Net Censorship Law." October 22, 1998.

117. *Ashcroft, Attorney General, et al. v. Free Speech Coalition, et al.* 00–795. April 16, 2002.

118. Flint, "Skin Trade Spreading Across U.S."

119. Ralph Weisheit, "Studying Drugs in Rural Areas: Notes from the Field," *Journal of Research in Crime and Delinquency* 30 (1993): 213–232.

120. "British Officials Report Skyrocketing Heroin Use," *Alcoholism & Drug Abuse Weekly* 10 (August 17, 1998): 7;

National Institute on Drug Abuse, Community Epidemiology Work Group, *Epidemiological Trends in Drug Abuse, Advance Report* (Washington, DC: National Institute on Drug Abuse, 1997).

121. FBI, *Uniform Crime Report,* 2002, p. 234.

122. Allen Beck and Paige Harrison, *Prisoners in 2000* (Washington, DC: Bureau of Justice Statistics, 2002), p. 2.

123. Arnold Trebach, *The Heroin Solution* (New Haven, CN: Yale University Press, 1982).

124. James Inciardi, *The War on Drugs* (Palo Alto, CA: Mayfield, 1986), p. 2.

125. See, generally, David Pittman, "Drug Addiction and Crime," in *Handbook of Criminology,* ed. D. Glazer (Chicago: Rand McNally, 1974), pp. 209–232; Board of Directors, National Council on Crime and Delinquency, "Drug Addiction: A Medical, Not a Law Enforcement, Problem," *Crime and Delinquency* 20 (1974): 4–9.

126. Associated Press, "Records Detail Royals' Turn-of-Century Drug Use," *Boston Globe,* 29 August 1993, p. 13.

127. See Edward Brecher, *Licit and Illicit Drugs* (Boston: Little, Brown, 1972).

128. James Inciardi, *Reflections on Crime* (New York: Holt, Rinehart & Winston, 1978), p. 15.

129. William Bates and Betty Crowther, "Drug Abuse," in *Deviants: Voluntary Actors in a Hostile World,* eds. E. Sagarin and F. Montanino (New York: Foresman and Co., 1977), p. 269.

130. Inciardi, *Reflections on Crime,* pp. 8–10. See also, A. Greeley, William Mc-Cready, and Gary Theisen, *Ethnic Drinking Subcultures* (New York: Praeger, 1980).

131. Joseph Gusfield, *Symbolic Crusade* (Urbana: University of Illinois Press, 1963), chap. 3.

132. McCaghy, *Deviant Behavior,* p. 280.

133. Ibid.

134. The annual survey is conducted by Lloyd Johnston, Jerald Bachman, and Patrick O'Malley of the Institute of Social Research, University of Michigan, Ann Arbor.

135. Lloyd Johnston, Patrick O'Malley, Gerald Bachman, and John Schulenberg, *Ecstasy Use Falls for Second Year in a Row, Overall Teen Drug Use Drops* (Ann Arbor: University of Michigan News and Information Services, 19 December

2003). www.monitoringthefuture.org. Accessed September 8, 2004.

136. Substance Abuse and Mental Health Services Administration, *Overview of Findings from the 2003 National Survey on Drug Use and Health,* NSDUH Series H–24, DHHS Publication No. SMA 04–3963 (Rockville, MD: Office of Applied Studies, 2004).

137. National Center on Addiction and Substance Abuse, *Teen Tipplers: America's Underage Drinking Epidemic,* rev. ed. (New York: National Center on Addiction and Substance Abuse, 2003). http://www.casacolumbia.org/usr_doc/Teen_Tipplers_February_2003R.pdf. Accessed October 25, 2003.

138. National Center on Addiction and Substance Abuse, *National Survey of American Attitudes on Substance Abuse IX: Teen Dating Practices and Sexual Activity* (New York City: author, 2004).

139. Eric Wish, *Drug Use Forecasting Program, Annual Report 1990* (Washington, DC: National Institute of Justice, 1990).

140. Thomas Gray and Eric Wish, *Maryland Youth at Risk: A Study of Drug Use in Juvenile Detainees* (College Park, MD: Center for Substance Abuse Research, 1993); Eric Wish and Christina Polsenberg, "Arrestee Urine Tests and Self-Reports of Drug Use: Which Is More Related to Rearrest?" Paper presented at the annual meeting of the American Society of Criminology, Phoenix, November 1993.

141. Julia Yun Soo Kim, Michael Fendrich, and Joseph Wislar, "The Validity of Juvenile Arrestees' Drug Use Reporting: A Gender Comparison," *Journal of Research in Crime and Delinquency* 37 (2000): 419–432.

142. Thomas Mieczkowski, "The Prevalence of Drug Use in the United States," in *Crime and Justice, A Review of Research,* vol. 20, ed. Michael Tonry (Chicago: University of Chicago Press, 1996), pp. 349–414, at 376.

143. See, generally, Mark Blumberg, ed., *AIDS: The Impact on the Criminal Justice System* (Columbus, OH: Merrill Publishing, 1990).

144. Scott Decker and Richard Rosenfeld, "Intravenous Drug Use and the AIDS Epidemic: Findings for a Twenty-City Sample of Arrestees." Paper presented at the annual meeting of the American Society of Criminology, Baltimore, November 1990.

145. Douglas Longshore, "Prevalence and Circumstances of Drug Injection at Los Angeles Shooting Galleries," *Crime and Delinquency* 42 (1996): 21–35.

146. Ibid., p. 30.

147. Mark Blumberg, "AIDS and the Criminal Justice System: An Overview," in *AIDS: The Impact on the Criminal Justice System,* p. 11.

148. Susan James, Janice Johnson, and Chitra Raghavan, "I Couldn't Go Anywhere," *Violence Against Women* 10 (2004): 991–1,015.

149. Marvin Krohn, Alan Lizotte, Terence Thornberry, Carolyn Smith, and David McDowall, "Reciprocal Causal Relationships among Drug Use, Peers, and Beliefs: A Five-Wave Panel Model," *Journal of Drug Issues* 26 (1996): 205–428.

150. Kellie Barr, Michael Farrell, Grace Barnes, and John Welte, "Race, Class, and Gender Differences in Substance Abuse: Evidence of Middle-Class / Underclass Polarization among Black Males," *Social Problems* 40 (1993): 314–326.

151. Peter Giancola, "Constructive Thinking, Antisocial Behavior, and Drug Use in Adolescent Boys with and without a Family History of a Substance Use Disorder," *Personality and Individual Differences* 35 (2003): 1,315–1,331.

152. Spencer Rathus, *Psychology,* 4th ed. (New York: Holt, Rinehart & Winston, 1990), p. 158.

153. Daniel Smith, Joanne Davis, and Adrienne Fricker-Elhai, "How Does Trauma Beget Trauma? Cognitions about Risk in Women with Abuse Histories," *Child Maltreatment* 9 (2004): 292–302.

154. Sean Kidd, "The Walls Were Closing in, and We Were Trapped," *Youth and Society* 36 (2004): 30–55.

155. Jerome J. Platt, *Heroin Addiction and Theory, Research and Treatment: The Addict, the Treatment Process and Social Control* (Melbourne, Fl.: Krieser Publishing, 1995), p. 127.

156. Alison Bass, "Mental Ills, Drug Abuse Linked," *Boston Globe,* 21 November 1990, p. 3.

157. Tracy Hampton, "Genes Harbor Clues to Addiction, Recovery," *Journal of the American Medical Association* 292 (2004): 321–323.

158. D. W. Goodwin, "Alcoholism and Genetics," *Archives of General Psychiatry* 42 (1985): 171–174.

159. Martha Vungkhanching, Kenneth Sher, Kristina Jackson, and Gilbert Parra, "Relation of Attachment Style to Family History of Alcoholism and Alcohol Use Disorders in Early Adulthood," *Drug and Alcohol Dependence* 75 (2004): 47–54.

160. For a thorough review of this issue, see John Petraitis, Brian Flay, and Todd Miller, "Reviewing Theories of Adolescent Substance Use: Organizing Pieces in the Puzzle," *Psychological Bulletin* 117 (1995): 67–86.

161. Judith Brooks and Li-Jung Tseng, "Influences of Parental Drug Use, Personality, and Child Rearing on the Toddler's Anger and Negativity," *Genetic, Social and General Psychology Monographs* 122 (1996): 107–128.

162. Thomas Ashby Wills, Donato Vaccaro, Grace McNamara, and A. Elizabeth Hirky, "Escalated Substance Use: A Longitudinal Grouping Analysis from Early to Middle Adolescence," *Journal of Abnormal Psychology* 105 (1996): 166–180.

163. Denise Kandel and Mark Davies, "Friendship Networks, Intimacy, and Illicit Drug Use in Young Adulthood: A Comparison of Two Competing Theories," *Criminology* 29 (1991): 441–471.

164. J. S. Mio, G. Nanjundappa, D. E. Verlur, and M. D. DeRios, "Drug Abuse and the Adolescent Sex Offender: A Preliminary Analysis," *Journal of Psychoactive Drugs* 18 (1986): 65–72.

165. D. Baer and J. Corrado, "Heroin Addict Relationships with Parents During Childhood and Early Adolescent Years," *Journal of Genetic Psychology* 124 (1974): 99–103.

166. John Wallace and Jerald Bachman, "Explaining Racial / Ethnic Differences in Adolescent Drug Use: The Impact of Background and Lifestyle," *Social Problems* 38 (1991): 333–357.

167. Amy Young, Carol Boyd, and Amy Hubbell, "Social Isolation and Sexual Abuse among Women Who Smoke Crack," *Journal of Psychosocial Nursing* 39 (2001): 16–19.

168. Xiaojin Chen, Kimberly Tyler, Les Whitbeck, and Dan Hoyt, "Early Sexual Abuse, Street Adversity, and Drug Use among Female Homeless and Runaway Adolescents in the Midwest," *Journal of Drug Issues,* 34 (2004): 1–20; John Donovan, "Problem-Behavior Theory and the Explanation of Adolescent Marijuana Use," *Journal of Drug Issues* 26 (1996): 379–404.

169. A. Christiansen, G. T. Smith, P. V. Roehling, and M. S. Goldman, "Using Alcohol Expectancies to Predict Adolescent Drinking Behavior after One Year," *Journal of Counseling and Clinical Psychology* 57 (1989): 93–99.

170. Claire Sterk-Elifson, "Just for Fun?: Cocaine Use Among Middle-Class Women," *Journal of Drug Issues* 26 (1996): 63–76, at 69.

171. Icek Ajzen, *Attitudes, Personality and Behavior* (Homewood, IL: Dorsey Press, 1988).

172. James Inciardi, Ruth Horowitz, and Anne Pottieger, *Street Kids, Street Drugs, Street Crime: An Examination of Drug Use and Serious Delinquency in Miami* (Belmont, CA: Wadsworth, 1993), p. 43.

173. Ibid.

174. Mary Ellen Mackesy-Amiti, Michael Fendrich, and Paul Goldstein, "Sequence of Drug Use among Serious Drug Users: Typical vs. Atypical Progression," *Drug and Alcohol Dependence* 45 (1997): 185–196.

175. Bu Huang, Helene White, Rick Kosterman, Richard Catalano, and J. David Hawkins, "Developmental Associations between Alcohol and Interpersonal Aggression during Adolescence," *Journal of Research in Crime and Delinquency* 38 (2001): 64–83.

176. Andrew Golub and Bruce Johnson, "The Multiple Paths Through Alcohol, Tobacco and Marijuana to Hard Drug Use among Arrestees." Paper presented at the annual Society of Criminology meeting, San Diego, November 1997.

177. Andrew Golub and Bruce D. Johnson, *The Rise of Marijuana as the Drug of Choice among Youthful Adult Arrestees* (Washington, DC: National Institute of Justice, 2001).

178. Inciardi, *The War on Drugs,* p. 60.

179. These lifestyles are described in Marcia Chaiken and Bruce Johnson, *Characteristics of Different Types of Drug-Involved Offenders* (Washington, DC: National Institute of Justice, 1988).

180. Kenneth Tunnell, "Inside the Drug Trade: Trafficking from the Dealer's Perspective," *Qualitative Sociology* 16 (1993): 361–381.

181. Lening Zhang, John Welte, and William Wieczorek, "Youth Gangs, Drug Use and Delinquency," *Journal of Criminal Justice* 27 (1999): 101–109.

182. Carolyn Rebecca Block, Antigone Christakos, Ayad Jacob, and Roger Przybylski, *Street Gangs and Crime* (Chicago: Illinois Criminal Justice Information Authority, 1996).

183. Richard Tewksbury and Elizabeth Ehrhardt Mustaine, "Lifestyle of the Wheelers and Dealers: Drug Dealing among American College Students," *Journal of Crime and Justice* 21 (1998): 37.

184. Hilary Saner, Robert MacCoun, and Peter Reuter, "On the Ubiquity of Drug Selling among Youthful Offenders in Washington, D.C., 1985–1991: Age, Period, or Cohort Effect?" *Journal of Quantitative Criminology* 11 (1995): 362–373.

185. Charles Faupel and Carl Klockars, "Drugs–Crime Connections: Elaborations from the Life Histories of Hard-Core Heroin Addicts," *Social Problems* 34 (1987): 54–68.

186. Charles Faupel, "Heroin Use, Crime and Unemployment Status," *Journal of Drug Issues* 18 (1988): 467–479.

187. Faupel and Klockars, "Drugs–Crime Connections."

188. Russel Falck, Jichuan Wang, and Robert Carlson, "The Epidemiology of Physical Attack and Rape among Crack-Using Women," *Violence and Victims* 16 (2001): 79–89.

189. Marvin Dawkins, "Drug Use and Violent Crime among Adolescents," *Adolescence* 32 (1997): 395–406.

190. U.S. Department of Justice, press release, "Four in Ten Criminal Offenders Report Alcohol as a Factor in Violence." 5 April 1998.

191. Arrestee Drug Abuse Monitoring Program, *1997 Drug Use Forecasting, Annual Report on Adult and Juvenile Arrestees* (Washington, DC: National Institute of Justice, 1998); *Center for Substance Abuse Research Report,* 7 September 1998.

192. George Speckart and M. Douglas Anglin, "Narcotics Use and Crime: An Overview

of Recent Research Advances," *Contemporary Drug Problems* 13 (1986): 741–769; Faupel and Klockars, "Drugs–Crime Connections."

193. Evelyn Wei, Rolf Loeber, and Helene White, "Teasing Apart the Developmental Associations Between Alcohol and Marijuana Use and Violence," *Journal of Contemporary Criminal Justice* 20 (2004): 166–183.

194. Susan Martin, Christopher Maxwell, Helene White, and Yan Zhang, "Trends in Alcohol Use, Cocaine Use, and Crime," *Journal of Drug Issues* 34 (2004): 333–360.

195. M. Douglas Anglin, Elizabeth Piper Deschenes, and George Speckart, "The Effect of Legal Supervision on Narcotic Addiction and Criminal Behavior." Paper presented at the annual meeting of the American Society of Criminology, Montreal, November 1987, p. 2.

196. Speckart and Anglin, "Narcotics Use and Crime: An Overview of Recent Research Advances," p. 752.

197. Ibid.

198. Bu Huang, Helene White, Rick Kosterman, Richard Catalano, and J. David Hawkins, "Developmental Associations between Alcohol and Interpersonal Aggression during Adolescence," *Journal of Research in Crime and Delinquency* 38 (2001): 64–83; Helene Raskin White and Stephen Hansell, "The Moderating Effects of Gender and Hostility on the Alcohol–Aggression Relationship," *Journal of Research in Crime and Delinquency* 33 (1996): 450–470.

199. James Inciardi, "Heroin Use and Street Crime," *Crime and Delinquency* 25 (1979): 335–346; see also, W. McGlothlin, M. Anglin, and B. Wilson, "Narcotic Addiction and Crime," *Criminology* 16 (1978): 293–311.

200. David Best, Clare Sidwell, Michael Gossop, et al., "Crime and Expenditure amongst Polydrug Misusers Seeking Treatment: The Connection between Prescribed Methadone and Crack Use, and Criminal Involvement," *British Journal of Criminology* 41 (2001): 119–126.

201. Overview of findings from the 2002 National Survey on Drug Use and Health. http://www.oas.samhsa.gov/nhsda/ 2k2nsduh/Overview/ 2k2Overview .htm#chap5. Accessed September 8, 2004.

202. Allen Beck, Darrell Gilliard, Lawrence Greenfeld, Caroline Harlow, Thomas Hester, Lewis Jankowski, Tracy Snell, James Stephen, and Danielle Morton, *Survey of State Prison Inmates, 1991* (Washington, DC: Bureau of Justice Statistics, 1993). The survey of prison inmates is conducted by the Bureau of Justice Statistics every 5 to 7 years.

203. National Institute of Justice, *2000 Arrestee Drug Abuse Monitoring* (Washington, DC: National Institute of Justice, 2003). http://www.ncjrs.org/ txtfiles1/nij/193013.txt. Accessed September 8, 2004.

204. Paul Goldstein, "The Drugs–Violence Nexus: A Tripartite Conceptual Framework," *Journal of Drug Issues* 15 (1985): 493–506; Marvin Krohn, Alan Lizotte, and Cynthia Perez, "The Interrelationship between Substance Use and Precocious Transitions to Adult Sexuality," *Journal of Health and Social Behavior* 38 (1997): 87–103, at 88; Richard Jessor, "Risk Behavior in Adolescence: A Psychosocial Framework for Understanding and Action," in *Adolescents at Risk: Medical and Social Perspectives,* eds. D. E. Rogers and E. Ginzburg (Boulder, CO: Westview Press, 1992).

205. See Kenneth Jones, Louis Shainberg, and Carter Byer, *Drugs and Alcohol* (New York: Harper & Row, 1979), pp. 137–146.

206. Controlled Substance Act, 21 U.S.C. 848 (1984).

207. Anti-Drug Abuse Act of 1986, PL 99-570, U.S.C. 841 (1986).

208. Anti-Drug Abuse Act of 1988, PL 100-690; 21 U.S.C. 1501; Subtitle A—Death Penalty, Sec. 7001, Amending the Controlled Substances Abuse Act, 21 U.S.C. 848.

209. Eric Jensen, Jurg Gerber, and Ginna Babcock, "The New War on Drugs: Grass Roots Movement or Political Construction?" *Journal of Drug Issues* 21 (1991): 651–667.

210. U.S. Department of State, *1998 International Narcotics Control Strategy Report,* February 1999.

211. George Rengert, *The Geography of Illegal Drugs* (Boulder, CO: Westview Press, 1996), p. 2.

212. Fareed Zakaria, "Warlords, Drugs, and Votes; Drugs Have Become the Dominating Feature of Afghanistan's Economy, and Corruption Has Infected Every Aspect of Afghan Political Life," *Newsweek* (9 August 2004): 39.

213. Francisco Gutierrez, "Institutionalizing Global Wars: state Transformations in Colombia, 1978–2002: Colombian Policy Directed at Its Wars, Paradoxically, Narrows the Government's Margin of Maneuver Even as It Tries to Expand It," *Journal of International Affairs* 57 (2003): 135–152.

214. Office of National Drug Control Policy, Cocaine. http://www.whitehousedrugpolicy.gov/drugfact /cocaine/index.html. Accessed September 11, 2004.

215. Mark Moore, *Drug Trafficking* (Washington, DC: National Institute of Justice, 1988).

216. Matthew Durose and Patrick Langan, *Felony Sentences in State Courts, 2000* (Washington, DC: Bureau of Justice Statistics, 2003).

217. Peter Rossi, Richard Berk, and Alec Campbell, "Just Punishments: Guideline Sentences and Normative Consensus," *Journal of Quantitative Criminology* 13 (1997): 267–283.

218. Michael Welch, Russell Wolff, and Nicole Bryan, "Recontextualizing the War on Drugs: A Content Analysis of NIJ Publications and Their Neglect of Race and Class," *Justice Quarterly* 15 (1998): 719–742.

219. Robert Davis, Arthur Lurigio, and Dennis Rosenbaum, eds., *Drugs and the Community* (Springfield, IL: Charles C Thomas, 1993), pp. xii–xv.

220. Saul Weingart, "A Typology of Community Responses to Drugs," in Davis, Lurigio, and Rosenbaum, *Drugs and the Community,* pp. 85–105.

221. Davis, Lurigio, and Rosenbaum, *Drugs and the Community,* pp. xii–xiii.

222. Marianne Zawitz, *Drugs, Crime and the Justice System* (Washington, DC: Bureau of Justice Statistics, 1992), pp. 109–112.

223. Ibid., pp. 115–122.

224. John Goldkamp and Peter Jones, "Pretrial Drug-Testing Experiments in Milwaukee and Prince George's County: The Context of Implementation," *Journal of Research in Crime and Delinquency* 29 (1992): 430–465; Chester Britt,

Michael Gottfredson, and John Goldkamp, "Drug Testing and Pretrial Misconduct: An Experiment on the Specific Deterrent Effects of Drug Monitoring Defendants on Pretrial Release," *Journal of Research in Crime and Delinquency* 29 (1992): 62–78.

225. See, generally, Peter Greenwood and Franklin Zimring, *One More Chance* (Santa Monica, CA: Rand, 1985).

226. Tracy Beswick, David David, Jenny Bearn, Michael Gossop, Sian Rees, and John Strang, "The Effectiveness of Combined Naloxone/Lofexidine in Opiate Detoxification: Results from a Double-Blind Randomized and Placebo-Controlled Trial," *American Journal on Addictions* 12 (2003): 295–306.

227. Eli Ginzberg, Howard Berliner, and Miriam Ostrow, *Young People at Risk: Is Prevention Possible?* (Boulder, CO: Westview Press, 1988), p. 99.

228. National Evaluation Data and Technical Assistance Center, *The District of Columbia's Drug Treatment Initiative (DCI)* (Washington, DC: author, February 1998).

229. The following section is based on material found in Jerome Platt, "Vocational Rehabilitation of Drug Abusers," *Psychological Bulletin* 117 (1995): 416–433.

230. Celia Lo, "Sociodemographic Factors, Drug Abuse, and Other Crimes: How They Vary among Male and Female Arrestees," *Journal of Criminal Justice* 32 (2004): 399–409.

231. The National Center on Addiction and Substance Abuse, *Shoveling Up: The Impact of Substance Abuse on State Budgets* (New York: author, 2001).

232. Office of National Drug Control Policy, *National Drug Control Strategy: FY 2004 Budget Summary* (Washington, DC: author, February 2003).

233. Ethan Nadelmann, "The U.S. Is Addicted to War on Drugs," *Globe and Mail,* 20 May 2003, p.1; Ethan Nadelmann, "America's Drug Problem," *Bulletin of the American Academy of Arts and Sciences* 65 (1991): 24–40.

234. See, generally, Ralph Weisheit, *Drugs, Crime, and the Criminal Justice System* (Cincinnati: Anderson, 1990).

235. David Courtwright, "Should We Legalize Drugs? History Answers No," *American Heritage* (February–March 1993): 43–56.

236. James Inciardi and Duane McBride, "Legalizing Drugs: A Gormless, Naive Idea," *Criminologist* 15 (1990): 1–4.

237. Kathryn Ann Farr, "Revitalizing the Drug Decriminalization Debate," *Crime and Delinquency* 36 (1990): 223–237.

CHAPTER 14

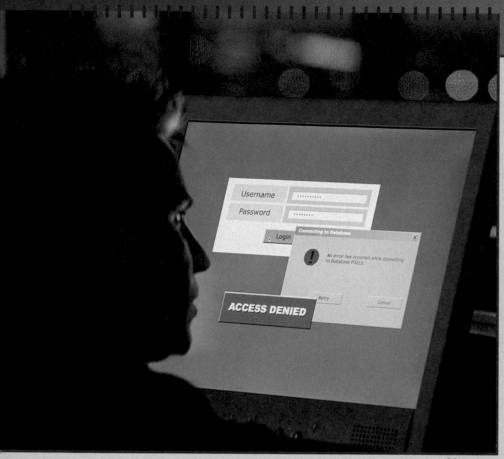

©Digital Vision

Jason Salah Arabo, 18, of Southfield, Michigan, represents a new breed of criminal.[1] He was arrested in 2005 on charges that he "did knowingly and intentionally conspire and agree with others to cause the transmission of a program, information, code, and command, and as a result of such conduct, intentionally cause damage without authorization, to a protected computer, namely, a computer that was used in interstate and foreign commerce and communication." What prompted his arrest? Arabo ran two web-based companies— www.customleader.com and www.jerseydomain.com—that sold sports apparel, including historic sports uniform reproductions, popularly known as "retro" or "throwback" jerseys. To thwart the competition, Arabo hired a New Jersey juvenile to engage in a highly destructive computer attack on his competitors. The attack not only damaged his competitors' online sportswear business but caused major disruption of the Internet service providers that carried their websites. The attack also disrupted the service of the providers' other clients, affecting businesses as far away as Europe.

How did the attacks take place? Arabo's juvenile co-conspirator is alleged to have secretly infected thousands of computers with copies of a program known as a "bot" (short for "robot"), which is used to gain unauthorized access to and control over computers that it infects. The bot causes the infected computers to attack other computers. For a payment of some shoes and sports gear, the New Jersey juvenile remotely ordered hundreds of the implanted bots to attack computer servers that supported Arabo's competitors' websites. The bots caused the infected computers to access the targeted website all at once, overloading the website's hosting computer server and causing it to crash.

CYBER CRIME AND TECHNOLOGY

CHAPTER OBJECTIVES

1. Understand the concept of cyber crime and why it is becoming so important

2. Distinguish among cyber theft, cyber vandalism, and cyber terrorism

3. Know the various types of computer crimes such as computer frauds, illegal copyright infringement, and Internet securities fraud

4. Be familiar with the terms *identity theft* and *phishing*

5. Know the differences among worms, viruses, Trojan horses, logic bombs, and spam

6. Discuss how the Internet can be used for spying

7. Be able to debate the issue of cyber terrorism

8. Be familiar with the various methods being used to control cyber crime

9. Discuss the role technology now plays in the criminal justice system

10. Understand both sides of the debate over the use of technology and civil liberties

The criminal enterprise of Jason Salah Arabo could not have existed 20 years ago. Innovation brings change and with it new opportunities to commit crime. The technological revolution has provided new tools to misappropriate funds, damage property, and sell illicit material. It has created **cyber crime**, a new breed of offenses that can be singular or ongoing but typically involve the theft and/or destruction of information, resources, or funds utilizing computers, computer networks, and the Internet.

> **||||||| CONNECTIONS |||||||**
>
> Chapter 12 reviews the concept of criminal enterprise and its motivations. Cyber crime can be viewed as a type of enterprise crime employing sophisticated technology to achieve illegal profits.

Cyber crime presents a compelling challenge for the justice system for a number of reasons: (1) It is rapidly evolving with new schemes being created daily; (2) it is difficult to detect through traditional law enforcement channels; and (3) its control demands that agents of the justice system develop technical skills that match those of the perpetrators.[2]

Why has cyber crime become so important? The widespread use of both computers and the Internet have ushered in the age of **information technology (IT)** and made it an intricate part of daily life in most industrialized societies. IT can involve computer networking, the Internet, and/or advanced communications. It is the key to the economic system and will become more important as major industries shift their manufacturing plants to other areas of the world where production is much cheaper. IT is responsible for the **globalization** phenomenon or the process of creating transnational markets, politics, and legal systems; in other words, IT is responsible for creating a global economy. The Internet, coupled with ever-more powerful computers, is now the chosen medium to provide a wide range of global services, ranging from entertainment and communication to research and education.

The cyber age has also generated an enormous amount of revenue. Spending on IT and telecommunications is growing by more than 6 percent each year and will soon reach about $2 trillion.[3] Today more than 1 billion people are e-mail users, and 240 million are mobile Internet users. Magnifying the importance of the Internet is the fact that many critical infrastructure functions are now being conducted online, ranging from banking to control of shipping on the Mississippi River.[4]

This vast network has now become a target for illegal activities and enterprise. As a group, these actions are referred to as *cyber crime*—any criminal act that involves communication, computer, and Internet networks. Some cyber crimes use modern technology to accumulate goods and services. **Cyber theft** schemes range from illegal copying of copyrighted material to using technology to commit traditional theft-based offenses such as larceny and fraud.

Another type of cyber criminal is motivated less by profit and more by the urge to commit **cyber vandalism** or technological destruction. These offenders aim their malicious attacks at disrupting, defacing, and destroying technology that they find offensive. A third type of cyber crime is **cyber terrorism**, acts that are aimed at undermining the social, economic, and political system of an enemy by destroying its electronic infrastructure and disrupting its economy.

In sum, some cyber criminals are high-tech thieves while others are high-tech vandals; the property they destroy is electronic rather then physical. And some may combine theft and vandalism in cyber terror attacks.

This chapter reviews the various forms of cyber crime. It also looks at how law enforcement agencies are beginning to fight back against cyber criminals by learning to apply some of the emerging technology to deal with traditional crime problems.

CYBER THEFT: CYBER CRIMES FOR PROFIT

Since the industrial revolution, every technological breakthrough (for example, the telephone and the automobile) has not only dramatically improved society but created new opportunities for criminal wrongdoing: Criminals used the telephone to place bets and threaten victims, and cars were stolen and sold for big profits.[5] The same pattern is now occurring with the IT revolution: The computer and Internet provide fantastic opportunities for socially beneficial endeavors—such as education, research, commerce, and entertainment—while at the same time serving as tools to facilitate illegal activity.

Computer-based technology allows criminals to operate more efficiently and effectively. Cyber thieves now have the luxury of remaining anonymous, living in any part of the planet, conducting their business during the day or in the evening, working alone or in a group, while at the same time reaching a much wider number of potential victims than ever before. No longer are con artists or criminal entrepreneurs limited to fleecing victims in a particular geographic locale; the whole world can be their target. And the technology revolution has opened novel methods for cyber theft—ranging from the unlawful distribution of computer software to Internet securities fraud—that previously were nonexistent. Cyber thieves conspire to use cyber space to either distribute illegal goods and services or to defraud people for quick profits. Some of the most common methods are set out in the following.

Computer Fraud

In 2004 Jessica Sabathia, 31, a California woman pled guilty to counts of computer fraud for using her computer to embezzle more than $875,000 from North Bay Health Care Group. Sabathia, an accounts payable clerk for North Bay, used her computer to access North Bay's accounting software without the authority of her employer and issued approximately 127 checks payable to herself and others. To conceal the fraud, she then altered the electronic check register to make it appear that the checks had been payable to North Bay's vendors. Jessica cashed several of the checks, deposited many in her bank account and the accounts of others, and used some money for personal expenses.[6]

Sabathia's crime falls under the general category of computer fraud. Computer fraud is not a unique offense but rather a common-law crime committed using contemporary technology. Consequently, many computer crimes are prosecuted under such traditional criminal statutes as larceny or fraud. However, not all computer crimes fall under common-law statutes because the property stolen may be intangible, that is, electronic and/or magnetic impulse. Some of these crimes are listed in Exhibit 14.1.

||||||| CONNECTIONS |||||||

As computer frauds have proliferated, new laws specifically designed for their control have been implemented. These are discussed later in the chapter under the heading, "Controlling Cyber Crime."

There are a number of recent trends in computer frauds. Internal attacks are now outgrowing external attacks at the world's largest financial institutions. According to a recent global security survey (2005), 35 percent of financial institutions encountered attacks from inside their organization within the last twelve months (up from 14 percent in 2004) compared to 26 percent from external sources (up from 23 percent in 2004).[7] The shift from external to internal attacks may be explained by improved security technologies that make it more difficult for people unfamiliar with the system to misuse it for personal gain. It has now become easier for disgruntled employees to attack the company's computers than for outsiders to breach their defenses.

There has also been a growing trend to commit fraud using devices that rely on IT for their operations. For example, **automatic teller machines (ATMs)** are now attracting the attention of cyber criminals looking for easy profits.[8] One criminal approach is to use a thin, transparent-plastic overlay on an ATM keypad that captures a user's identification code as it is entered. Though the plastic covering looks like some sort of cover to protect the keys, in fact it contains microchips to record every keystroke. Another transparent device inside the card slot captures card data. While the client completes the transaction, a computer attached to the overlay records all the data necessary to clone the card. Here we can readily compare the significant differences between common-law crime and cyber crime: Rather than rob an ATM user at gunpoint, the cyber criminal relies on stealth and technological skill to commit the crime.

Distributing Illegal Sexual Material

The IT revolution has revitalized the porn industry. The Internet is an ideal venue for selling and distributing obscene material, and the computer is an ideal device for storing and viewing it. Because of their vast number, it is difficult to estimate how many websites feature sexual content, including nude photos, videos, live sex acts, and web-cam strip sessions, among other forms of "adult entertainment."[9] N2H2, a Seattle-based web-filtering company, estimates that the number of pornography web pages has soared during the past six years, and there are now over 1.3 million sites containing about 260 million pages of erotic content—all aimed at cashing in on the billions in revenue spent on Internet porn annually.[10] The number of visits to pornographic sites surpasses those made to Internet search engines; some individual sites report as many as 50 million hits per year.

How do adult sites operate today?[11]

- A large firm sells annual subscriptions in exchange for unlimited access to content.

- Password services charge an annual fee to deliver access to hundreds of small sites, which share the subscription revenues.

- Large firms provide free content to smaller "affiliate" sites. The affiliates post the free content and then try to channel visitors to the large sites, which give the smaller sites a percentage of the fees paid by those who sign up.

- Webmasters forward traffic to another porn site in return for a small per-consumer fee. In many cases,

The distribution of Internet pornography has become a billion-dollar business and has revitalized the "adult entertainment" industry. Al Goldstein, former editor of the racy *Screw Magazine* went from multimillionaire to pauper after his adult publishing empire collapsed. Now he is making a comeback at the age of 69 serving as the national marketing director for XonDemand, an Internet on-demand video porn website.

site for access to these pornographic images of minors and was the only gateway to these child pornography websites.[13] The sites, off limits to U.S. control because they were located in Russia and Indonesia, had a fee-sharing arrangement with Landslide's owners, Thomas and Janice Reedy. The Reedys pocketed millions, drove a Mercedes, and lived in a luxury home. Reedy was sentenced to life in prison for his crimes.

Despite this successful prosecution, it has been difficult to control Internet pornography. The various federal legislative efforts including the Communications Decency Act (1996), the Child Online Protection Act (1998), and the Children's Internet Protection Act (2000) have been successfully challenged in the courts under the First Amendment. Filtering devices used extensively in schools and libraries fail to block out a lot of obscene material, giving youngsters the opportunity to use computers away from home to surf the Internet for adult content. It is unlikely that any law enforcement efforts will put a dent in the Internet porn industry.

the consumer is sent to the other sites involuntarily, which is known in the industry as "mousetrapping." Web surfers who try to close out a window after visiting an adult site are sent to another web page automatically. This can repeat dozens of times, causing users to panic and restart their computers in order to escape.

- Adult sites cater to niche audiences looking for specific kinds of adult content.

While some sites cater to adult tastes, others cross the legal border by peddling access to either obscene material or kiddie porn. In one well-known case, Landslide Productions of Fort Worth, Texas, operated as a highly profitable Internet-based pornography ring, taking in as much as $1.4 million in 1 month.[12] Having at least 250,000 subscribers worldwide, it offered access to websites that advertised themselves with such phrases as "Child Rape" or "Cyber Lolita." Landslide provided a credit card verification service that acted as an electronic gateway to the pictures and movies of minors engaging in sexually explicit conduct. Internet customers were required to provide a credit card number as well as a charge authorization in order to gain access, by a user name and password provided by Landslide, to the pornographic productions on the websites. Landslide charged each customer approximately $29.95 per month per

| | | | | | | **CONNECTIONS** | | | | | | |

Pornography is discussed more fully in Chapter 13. The ability to access pornographic material over the Internet has helped expand the sale of sexually related material. People wishing to purchase sexually related material no longer face the risk of public exposure in adult bookstores or movie theaters. Sellers of adult films and photos can now reach a much wider international audience.

Denial of Service Attack

A **denial of service attack** is characterized as an attempt to extort money from legitimate users of an Internet service by threatening to prevent the users from having access to the service.[14] Examples include:

- Attempts to "flood" a computer network, thereby preventing legitimate network traffic

- Attempts to disrupt connections within a computer network, thereby preventing access to a service

- Attempts to prevent a particular individual from accessing a service

- Attempts to disrupt service to a specific system or person

Established in 1988, the **CERT Coordination Center (CERT/CC)** is a hub of Internet security expertise, located at the Software Engineering Institute, a federally funded research and development center operated by Carnegie Mellon University: http://www.cert.org/nav/index_main.html. For an up-to-date list of web links, go to http://cj.wadsworth.com/siegel_crimtpt9e.

A denial of service attack may involve threatening or actually flooding an Internet site with millions of bogus messages or orders so that the services will be tied up and unable to perform as promised. Unless the site operator pays extortion, the attackers threaten to keep up the interference until real consumers become frustrated and abandon the site. Even so-called respectable businesspeople have been accused of launching denial of service attacks against rival business interests. In 2004 Jay R. Echouafni of Orbit Communication Corporation left the country rather than face charges that he had hired hackers to set up online attacks that interfered with rivals' websites.[15] As in the case described at the beginning of the chapter with Jason Arabo, the juvenile accomplice flooded competitors' websites to destroy their ability to do business.

Online gambling casinos—a $7 billion a year industry—have proven particularly vulnerable to attack. Hundreds of attacks have been launched against online casinos located in Costa Rica, the Caribbean, and Great Britain. If the attack coincides with a big sporting event such as the Super Bowl, the casinos may give in and make payments rather than lose revenue and fray customer relations.[16]

Illegal Copyright Infringement

For the past decade, groups of individuals have been working together to illegally obtain software and then "crack" or "rip" its copyright protections, before posting it on the Internet for other members of the group to use; this is called **warez**.

Frequently, these new pirated copies reach the Internet days or weeks before the legitimate product is commercially available. The government has actively pursued members of the warez community, and some have been charged and convicted under the Computer Fraud and Abuse Act (CFAA), which criminalizes accessing computer systems without authorization to obtain information[17] and the Digital Millennium Copyright Act (DMCA), which makes it a crime to circumvent antipiracy measures built into most commercial software and also outlaws the manufacture, sale, or distribution of code-cracking devices used to illegally copy software.[18]

FILE SHARING Another form of illegal copyright infringement involves file-sharing programs that allow Internet users to download music and other copyrighted material without paying the artists and record producers their rightful royalties. Theft through the illegal reproduction and distribution of movies, software, games, and music is estimated to cost U.S. industries $19 billion worldwide each year. Although some students routinely share files and download music, criminal copyright infringement represents a serious economic threat. The U.S. Criminal Code provides penalties for a first-time offender of 5 years' incarceration and a fine of $250,000.[19] Other provisions provide for the forfeiture and destruction of infringing copies and all equipment used to make the copies.[20]

In August 2004, the FBI announced it had carried out Operation Digital Gridlock, the first criminal enforcement action against peer-to-peer copyright piracy. Operation Digital Gridlock targeted illegal file sharing of copyrighted materials over five direct connect peer-to-peer networks that belonged to a group known as the Underground Network. Members were required to share a minimum of 1 to 100 gigabytes of

Michael Petricone of the Consumer Electronic Association (center) and Rick Carnes, a songwriter and president of the Songwriters Guild of America (right), confront each other during a protest outside the U.S. Supreme Court on March 29, 2005. During the demonstrations, justices were hearing the case of *MGM v. Grokster* on the issues of Internet file sharing and copyright protection. On June 27, 2005, the Court ruled that the providers of software designed to enable "file-sharing" of copyrighted works may be held liable for the copyright infringement that takes place using that software.

© Dennis Brack / Bloomberg News / Landov

computer files with other users on the network so that each user could download shared files from the hard drives of all other members on the network.[21]

On June 27 copyright protection of music and other types of entertainment distributed via the internet was upheld by the Supreme Court in the case of MGM Studios, Inc. v. Grokster 125 S. Ct. 2764. The Court ruled unanimously that software distributors such as Grokster could be sued for inducing copyright infringement if they market file sharing software that might induce people to illegally copy protected material even if that software could also be used for legitimate purposes. Justice Souter wrote:

"[O]ne who distributes a device with the object of promoting its use to infringe copyright, as shown by clear expression or other affirmative steps taken to foster infringement, is liable for the resulting acts of infringement by third parties . . . [but] mere knowledge of infringing potential or of actual infringing uses would not be enough here to subject a distributor to liability. Nor would ordinary acts incident to product distribution, such as offering customers technical support or product updates, support liability in themselves. The inducement rule, instead, premises liability on *purposeful, culpable expression and conduct* . . . ."

As a result of the opinion, on November 7, 2005 Grokster announced that it would suspend its file sharing service; it was also forced to pay $50 million to the music and recording industries. While a triumph for the music industry, the Grokster case raises many issues: How can an innovator know if their new device can be used for illegal purposes. For example, is an iPod illegal because it can record copyrighted music even though its inventors did not intend it for copyright infringement?

MEDIA PIRACY As you may recall, movie pirates such as Johnny Ray Gasca (Chapter 4) who use the Internet to sell illegally copied films have become such a serious problem that the federal government was forced to create the Family Entertainment and Copyright Act of 2005. One part of that statute, known as the ART Act (Artists' Rights and Theft Prevention Act of 2005), criminalizes the use of recording equipment to make copies of films while in movie theaters. The statute also makes it illegal to copy a work in production and put it on the Internet so it will be accessible to the public when the individual making the copy knew or should have known the work was intended for commercial distribution.[22]

Internet Securities Fraud

Jonathan Lebed, 15, was charged with securities fraud by the SEC after he repeatedly bought low-cost, thinly traded stocks and then spread hundreds of false and misleading messages concerning them—generally baseless price predictions. After their values were artificially inflated, Lebed sold the securities at an exaggerated price. His smallest one-day gain was $12,000, and on one particular day he made $74,000. Lebed agreed to findings of fraud but later questioned whether he had done anything wrong; on Sept. 20, 2000, he was forced to hand over his illicit gains, plus interest, which came to $285,000.[23]

Though he might not agree, young Lebed's actions are considered Internet fraud because they involve using the Internet to intentionally manipulate the securities marketplace for profit. There are actually three major types of Internet securities fraud today:

■ *Market manipulation:* Stock market manipulation occurs when an individual tries to control the price of stock by interfering with the natural forces of supply and demand. There are two principal forms of this crime: the "pump and dump" and the "cyber smear." In a pump and dump scheme, erroneous and deceptive information is posted online to get unsuspecting investors to become interested in a stock while those spreading the information sell previously purchased stock at an inflated price. The cyber smear is a reverse pump and dump: Negative information is spread online about a stock, driving down its price and enabling people to buy it at an artificially low price before rebuttals by the company's officers reinflate the price.[24]

■ *Fraudulent offerings of securities:* Some cyber criminals create websites specifically designed to fraudulently sell securities. To make the offerings look more attractive than they are, assets may be inflated, expected returns overstated, and risks understated. In these schemes, investors are promised abnormally high profits on their investments. No investment is actually made. Early investors are paid returns with the investment money received from the later investors. The system usually collapses, and the later investors do not receive dividends and lose their initial investment.

An example of fraudulent security offerings occurred when the Tri-West Investment Company solicited investments in "prime bank notes" from 1999 to 2001.[25] Visitors to their website were promised an annualized rate of return of 120 percent plus return of their principal at the end of a year, as well as substantial referral fees of 15 percent of all referred investments. The website, which contained alleged testimonials describing instant wealth from early investors, also told visitors that their investments were "guaranteed." Investors contributed $60 million in funds to Tri-West, and some "dividends" were paid. However, no money was actually invested, the dividends were paid from new investments, and most of the cash was siphoned off by the schemers.

■ *Illegal touting:* This crime occurs when individuals make securities recommendations and fail to disclose that they are being paid to disseminate their favorable opinions. Section 17(b) of the Securities Act of 1933 requires that paid touters disclose the nature, source, and amount of their compensation. If those who tout stocks fail to disclose their relationship with the company, information misleads investors into believing that the speaker is objective and credible rather than bought and paid for.

Identity Theft

Identity theft occurs when a person uses the Internet to steal someone's identity and/or impersonate the victim to open a new credit card account or conduct some other financial transaction. It is a type of cyber crime that has grown at surprising rates over the past few years.[26]

Identity theft can destroy people's lives by manipulating credit records or stealing from their bank accounts. Identity thieves use a variety of techniques to steal information. They may fill out change of address cards at the post office and obtain people's credit card bills and bank statements. They may then call the credit card issuer and, pretending to be the victim, ask for a change in address on the account. They can then charge numerous items over the Internet and have the merchandise sent to the new address. It may take months for the victim to realize the fraud because the victim is not getting bills from the credit card company.

Some identity theft schemes are extremely elaborate. For example, in 2004 nineteen people were indicted on charges that they had created an organization called Shadowcrew to provide stolen credit card numbers and identity documents through an online marketplace. The stolen account numbers were contributed by approved "vendors" who had been granted permission to sell on the Shadowcrew site after being vetted through a complex review process. Shadowcrew members allegedly trafficked in at least 1.7 million stolen credit card numbers and caused total losses in excess of $4 million dollars.[27]

PHISHING Some identity thieves create false e-mails and/or websites that look legitimate but are designed to gain illegal access to a victim's personal information; this is known as **phishing** (or **carding and spoofing**).

Some phishers send out e-mails that look like they come from a credit card company or online store telling the victim that there was a problem with their account credit or balance. To fix the problem and update their account, they are asked to submit their name, address, phone numbers, personal information, credit card account numbers, and Social Security number (SSN). Or the e-mail may direct them to a phony website that purports to be a legitimate company or business enterprise. Once a victim accesses the website, he or she is asked to provide personal information or financial account information to the website so that the problem can be fixed.

Once phishers have a victim's personal information, they can do three things with it: (1) They can gain access to preexisting accounts—banking and credit cards—and buy things with those accounts; (2) phishers can use the information to open new bank and credit card accounts without the victim's knowledge; (3) phishers can implant viruses into their software that forwards the phishing e-mail to other recipients once one person responds to the original e-mail,

---

EXHIBIT 14.2

Common Phisher Scams

- *Account verification scams:* Individuals purchase domain names that are similar to those of legitimate companies. It may be in a form such as Amazon.Accounts.net. The real company is Amazon, but it does not have an "accounts" in its domain. These con artists then send out millions of e-mails asking consumers to verify account information and requesting Social Security numbers.

- *Sign-in rosters:* There are some companies and governmental agencies (such as colleges and state-sponsored programs) that ask you to put your name and Social Security number on a sign-in roster. Identity thieves may sign up toward the end of a page so that they can copy and collect personal identifying information.

- *"Help move money from my country" or the Nigerian 419 scam:* A bogus e-mail is sent from an alleged representative of a foreign government asking the victim to help move money from one account to another. Some forms include requests to help a dying woman or free a political prisoner. Some claim that the victim has been the recipient of a legacy or a winning lottery ticket. Nigerian money offers now account for about 12 percent of the scams.

- *Canadian/Netherlands lottery:* Originating from the Netherlands and other foreign countries, these lottery scams usually ask for money to hold the prize until the victim can collect in person.

- *Free credit report:* Almost all "free credit report" e-mails are scams. Either the person is trying to find out the victim's Social Security number, or the victim is billed for services later on.

- *"You have won a free gift":* Victims receive an e-mail about a free gift or prize. They just have to send their credit card information to take care of shipping and handling. Responding may result in hundreds of spams or telemarketing calls.

- *E-mail chain letters/pyramid schemes:* Victims are sent an official-looking e-mail requesting cooperation by sending a report to five friends or relatives. Those who respond are then contacted for money in order to keep the chain going.

- *"Find out everything on anyone":* This e-mail is trying to solicit money in order to buy a CD or program that you can use to find out personal information on someone. What are being sold are always public records, and the seller may be someone who just wants access to credit account numbers.

- *Job advertisement scams:* Fraudulent internet job websites contact a victim promising a high-paying job. They solicit information including Social Security numbers.

- *VISA/MasterCard scam:* A VISA or MasterCard "employee" sends an e-mail asking to confirm unusual spending activity and asks the victim for the security code on the back of the credit card.

Source: Identity Theft Resource Center (ITRC), Scams and Consumer Alerts. http://www.idtheftcenter.org/alerts.shtml#current.

---

thereby luring more potential victims in the net. Some common phisher scams are listed in Exhibit 14.2.

Phishing e-mails and websites have become even more of a problem now that cyber criminals can easily copy brand names, corporate letterheads with personnel and their titles, and company logos directly into the e-mail. The look may be so authentic that victims do not doubt that the e-mail comes from the advertised company. Most phishers send out spam e-mails to a large number of recipients knowing that some of those recipients will have accounts with the company that they are impersonating.

To meet the increasing threat of phishing and identity theft, Congress passed the Identity Theft and Assumption Deterrence Act of 1998 (Identity Theft Act) to make it a federal crime when anyone:

> knowingly transfers or uses, without lawful authority, a means of identification of another person with the intent to commit, or to aid or abet, any unlawful activity that constitutes a violation of Federal law, or that constitutes a felony under any applicable State or local law.[28]

Violations of the act are investigated by federal investigative agencies such as the U.S. Secret Service, the FBI, and the U.S. Postal Inspection Service. In 2004 the Identity Theft Penalty Enhancement Act was signed into law; the act increases existing penalties for the crime of identity theft, establishes aggravated identity theft as a criminal offense, and establishes mandatory penalties for aggravated identity theft. According to the new law, anyone who knowingly "transfers, possesses, or uses, without lawful authority" someone else's identification will be sentenced to an extra prison term of 2 years with no possibility of probation. Committing identity fraud while engaged in crimes associated with terrorism—such as aircraft destruction, arson, airport violence, or kidnapping top government officials—will receive a mandatory sentence enhancement of 5 years.[29]

E-Tailing Fraud

New fraud schemes are evolving to reflect the fact that billions of dollars of goods are sold on the Internet each year. **E-tailing fraud** involves using the Internet for both illegally buying and selling merchandise.

Some e-tailing scams involve failure to deliver on promised purchases or services while others involve the substitution of cheaper or used material for higher quality purchases. So, for example, a woman buys expensive jewelry on an Internet site and receives a somewhat less valuable piece than she expected. EBay, the online auction site, is fertile ground for such fraud. In one case a California man named Jie Dong built a record of satisfied customers on eBay by selling $150,000 worth of merchandise at low prices; however, before he fled the country, Dong sold $800,000 worth of goods, like DVD players and digital cameras, to 5,000 people and never delivered the products.[30]

Not only do e-tail frauds involve selling merchandise, but they can also involve buyer fraud. One scam involves purchasing top-of-the-line electronic equipment over the Internet and then purchasing a second, similar-looking but cheaper model of the same brand. The cheaper item is then returned to the e-tailer after switching bar codes and boxes

with the more expensive unit. Because e-tail return processing centers do not always check returned goods closely, they may send a refund for the value of the higher priced model.

Another tactic is called "shoplisting"; a thief pays maybe $10 for an unexpired receipt covering $500 of legitimately bought electronics or clothing, shoplifts the listed items, and returns them for a refund or gift card. The cards are then sold over the Internet. Not surprisingly, the underground market for receipts has been growing, as stores have liberalized return policies.[31] One of the more ingenious online auction scams is described in Exhibit 14.3.

CYBER VANDALISM: CYBER CRIME WITH MALICIOUS INTENT

On September 8, 2005, an unnamed Massachusetts juvenile pled guilty in federal court and was sentenced to 11 months' detention in a juvenile facility, to be followed by 2 years of supervised release. During his periods of detention and supervised release, the juvenile was barred from possessing or using any computer, cell phone, or other electronic equipment capable of accessing the Internet.

The basis for the charges was a course of criminal conduct that took place over a 15-month period beginning in March

2004 when the juvenile sent an e-mail to a Florida school with the caption, "this is URGENT!!!" The text of the e-mail read:

"your all going to perish and flourish . . . you will all die

Tuesday, 12:00 p.m.

we're going to have a "blast"

hahahahahaha wonder where I'll be? youll all be destroyed. im sick of your [expletive deleted] school and piece of [expletive deleted] staff, your all gonna [expletive deleted] die you pieces of crap!!!!

DIE MOTHER [expletive deleted] IM GONA BLOW ALL YOU UP AND MYSELF

ALL YOU NAZI LOVING MEXICAN FAGGOT BITCHES ARE DEAD"

As a result of this bomb threat, the school was closed for 2 days, while a bomb squad, a canine team, the fire department, and Emergency Medical Services were called in.

The juvenile engaged in numerous other acts. In January 2005, he gained access to the internal computer system of a major telephone service provider that allowed him to look up account information of the telephone service provider's customers. He used this computer system to discover key information about an individual who had an account with the telephone service. He then accessed the information stored on this individual's mobile telephone and posted the information on the Internet.[32]

Some cyber criminals, such as the boy in Massachusetts, may not be motivated by greed or profit but by the desire for revenge, destruction, and to achieve a malicious intent. Cyber vandalism ranges from sending destructive viruses and worms to terrorist attacks designed to destroy important computer networks. Cyber vandals are motivated more by malice than by greed:

- Some cyber vandals target computers and networks seeking revenge for some perceived wrong.

- Some desire to exhibit their technical prowess and superiority.

- Some wish to highlight the vulnerability of computer security systems (see Exhibit 14.4).

- Some desire to spy on other people's private financial and personal information ("computer voyeurism").

- Some want to destroy computer security because they believe in a philosophy of open access to all systems and programs.[33]

What forms does cyber vandalism take?

Worms, Viruses, Trojan Horses, Logic Bombs, and Spam

The most typical use of cyber space for destructive intent involves sending or implanting disruptive programs— viruses, worms, Trojan horses, logic bombs, and spam.

VIRUSES AND WORMS A **computer virus** is one type of malicious software program (also called **malware**) that disrupts or destroys existing programs and networks, causing them to perform the task for which the virus was designed.[34] The virus is then spread from one computer to another when a user sends out an infected file through e-mail, a network, or a disk. **Computer worms** are similar to viruses but use computer networks or the Internet to self-replicate and "send themselves" to other users, generally via e-mail without the aid of the operator.

The damage caused by viruses and worms can be considerable. On March 26, 1999, the Melissa virus disrupted e-mail service around the world when it was posted to an Internet newsgroup, causing more than $80 million in damage. Its creator, David Smith, pled guilty to state and federal charges and was later sentenced to 20 months in prison (leniency was granted because he cooperated with authorities in thwarting other hackers).[35] Another damaging malware was the MS Blaster worm—also known as W32.Blaster and W32/Lovsan—which took advantage of a vulnerability in a widely used feature of Microsoft Windows and infected more than 120,000 computers worldwide.[36]

TROJAN HORSES Some hackers may introduce a **Trojan horse** program in a computer system. The Trojan horse looks like a benign application, but it contains illicit codes that can damage the system operations. Sometimes hackers with a sense of irony will install a Trojan horse and claim that it is an antivirus program. When it is opened, it spreads viruses in the computer system. While Trojan horses do not replicate themselves like viruses, they can be just as destructive.

LOGIC BOMBS A fourth type of destructive attack that can be launched on a computer system is the **logic bomb,** a program that is secretly attached to a computer system, monitors the network's output, and waits for a particular signal such as a date to appear. Also called a *slag code,* it is a type of delayed-action virus that is also set off when a program user unwittingly inputs a specific command or makes an inputting error. A logic bomb may cause a variety of problems ranging from displaying or printing a spurious message to deleting or corrupting data.

In a 2005 incident, William Shea was convicted of placing malicious computer code on the network of Bay Area Credit Services of San Jose, California, causing the deletion and modification of financial records and disruption of the proper functioning of the company's computer network.[37] Shea's bomb affected more than 50,000 debtor accounts and caused the company more than $100,000 in damages. Shea, a disgruntled former employee, still had administrative-level access to and familiarity with the company's computer systems, including the database server. Company officials did not know that at the time Shea left the company he had placed malicious code on the computer network that was set to delete and modify data at the end of the month.

SPAM An unsolicited advertisement or promotional material, **spam** typically comes in the form of an unwanted e-mail message; spammers use electronic communications to send unsolicited messages in bulk. While e-mail is the most common form of spam, it can also be sent via instant messaging, usenet newsgroup, and mobile phone messaging, among other mediums.

Spam can simply be in the form of an unwanted and unwelcome advertisement. For example, spam may advertise sexually explicit websites and find its way to minors. A more dangerous and malicious form of spam contains a Trojan horse disguised as an e-mail attachment, advertising some commodity such as free software or an electronic game. If the recipient downloads or opens the attachment, a virus may be launched that corrupts the victim's computer; the Trojan horse may also be designed to capture important data from the victim's hard drive and send it back to the hacker's e-mail address.

Sending spam can become a crime and even lead to a prison sentence when it causes serious harm to a computer or network. In 2005 Allan Eric Carlson was convicted of 79 counts of computer fraud and identity fraud and received a 4-year prison term for spamming. Carlson was a dissatisfied Philadelphia Phillies fan. To express his frustration over his team's failures, he hacked into computers and launched hundreds of thousands of spam e-mails complaining about the Phillies. He faked the e-mail addresses of writers at the *Philadelphia Daily News* and the *Philadelphia Inquirer* and of employees of the Philadelphia Phillies, among others. Because many of the e-mail addresses that Carlson sent his messages to were no longer valid, tens of thousands of e-mails were "returned" to the e-mail boxes of the persons whose addresses were spoofed. By flooding the victims' systems, the businesses they support were severely affected and they lost business. Sometimes fan loyalty goes too far.[38]

Web Defacement

Cyber vandals may also aim their attention at the websites of their victims. **Web defacement** is a type of cyber vandalism that occurs when a computer hacker intrudes on another person's website by inserting or substituting codes that expose site visitors to misleading or provocative information. Defacement can range from installing humorous graffiti to sabotaging or corrupting the site. In some instances, defacement efforts are not easily apparent or noticeable, for example, when they are designed to give misinformation by substituting or replacing authorized text on a company's web page. The false information may mislead customers and frustrate their efforts to utilize the site or make it difficult for people using search engines to find the site as they surf the net.

Almost all defacement attacks are designed to vandalize web pages rather than to bring profits or gain to the intruders (although some defacers may eventually extort money from their targets). Some defacers are simply trying to impress the hacking community with their skills. Others may target a corporation when they oppose its business practices and policies—for example, oil companies, tobacco companies, defense contractors, and so on. Some defacement has political goals such as disrupting the web page of a rival political party or fund-raising group. In the aftermath of the war in Iraq, there were approximately 20,000 website defacements, both pro and antiwar, with most taking place within the first few days of the outset of the conflict. Five British government sites were compromised by a hacking group protesting the war with Iraq; graffiti slamming U.S. President George W. Bush, British Prime Minister Tony Blair, and Israeli Prime Minister Ariel Sharon were posted. In response, the English language Al Jazeera website, which posted disturbing images of civilian victims, was attacked by hackers.[39]

Content analysis of web page defacements indicates that about 70 percent are pranks instituted by hackers while the rest have a political motive. Defacers are typically members of an extensive social network who are eager to demonstrate their reasons for hacking and often leave calling cards, greetings, and taunts on web pages.[40]

Web defacement is a significant and major threat to online businesses and government agencies. It can harm the credibility and reputation of the organization and demonstrate that its security measures are inadequate. As a result, clients lose trust and may be reluctant to share personal information such as credit card numbers and identification data. An e-tailer may lose business if potential clients believe the site is not secure. Financial institutions, such as web-based banks and brokerage houses, are particularly vulnerable because they rely on e-security and credibility to protect their clients' accounts.[41]

Cyber Stalking

For two years, Georges Debeir contacted adolescent girls he met in Internet chat rooms and promised gifts and money in exchange for sex. In April 1998, Debeir initiated a conversation in a "teensex" chat room with a 14-year-old Baltimore girl named Kathy. After weeks of trading explicit e-mail messages, Debeir eventually asked Kathy to meet him in person for sex, all the while stressing the importance of keeping their relationship confidential. Unfortunately for Debeir, Kathy

Cyber stalking is becoming a more common occurrence. Here William Lepeska, stalker of tennis star Anna Kournikova, is shown in custody. After finding her address on the Internet, Lepeska, a 40-year-old homeless man, swam nude across Biscayne Bay in Miami searching for Kournikova's mansion, but instead landed at a house three doors down. Lepeska, who has Kournikova's first name tattooed on his right arm, was arrested while screaming "Anna! Save me!"

was actually an undercover FBI agent working for Innocent Images, a computer crimes unit targeting sexual predators and child pornographers on the Internet. Debeir was arrested at a Baltimore shopping mall where he had arranged to meet Kathy. He pled guilty to one count of traveling interstate with the intent to have sex with a minor, a federal charge that carries a maximum sentence of 10 years in prison.[42]

Cyber stalking refers to the use of the Internet, e-mail, or other electronic communication devices to stalk another person.[43] Traditional stalking involves repeated harassing or threatening behavior, such as following a person, appearing at a person's home or place of business, making harassing phone calls, leaving written messages or objects, or vandalizing a person's property. Some stalkers, such as Debeir, pursue minors through online chat rooms, establish a relationship with the child, and later make contact for the purpose of engaging in criminal sexual activities. Others harass their victims electronically. They may send repeated, threatening, or harassing messages via e-mail and use programs to send messages at regular or random intervals without being physically present at a computer terminal. A cyber stalker may trick others into harassing or threatening a victim by impersonating the victim on Internet bulletin boards and/or chat rooms and posting messages that are provocative, such as, "I want to have sex." The stalker than posts the victim's name, phone number, or e-mail address hoping that other chat participants will stalk or hassle the victim without the stalker's personal involvement.

Cyber Spying

On July 21, 2005, Carlos Enrique Perez-Melara, the creator and marketer of a spyware program called "Loverspy," was indicted by a federal grand jury and charged with such crimes as manufacturing a surreptitious interception device, sending a surreptitious interception device, and advertising a surreptitious interception device.[44]

Loverspy was a computer program designed and marketed by Perez for people to use to spy on others. Prospective purchasers, after paying $89 through a website in Texas, were electronically redirected to Perez's computers in San Diego. Purchasers would then select from a menu an electronic greeting card to send to up to five different victims or e-mail addresses. Unbeknownst to the victims, once the e-mail greeting cards were opened, Loverspy secretly installed itself on their computers and recorded all their activities including e-mails sent and received, websites visited, and passwords entered. Loverspy also gave the purchaser the ability to remotely control the victim's computer, including accessing, changing, and deleting files, and turning on web-enabled cameras connected to the victim computers. Over 1,000 purchasers from the United States and the rest of the world purchased Loverspy and used it against more than 2,000 victims.[45]

Perez was indicted for engaging in **cyber spying**, illegally using the Internet to gather information that is considered private and confidential. Cyber spies have a variety of motivations. Some people are involved in marital disputes and may want to seize the e-mails of their estranged spouse.

Business rivals might hire a disgruntled employee, consultants, and outside contractors to steal information from their competitors. These commercial cyber spies target upcoming bids, customer lists, product designs, software source code, voice-mail messages, and confidential e-mail messages.[46] Some commercial spying is conducted by foreign competitors who seek to appropriate trade secrets in order to gain a business advantage.[47]

CYBER ESPIONAGE Cyber spying has taken on greater importance because intelligence agencies around the world are now employing hackers to penetrate secure computer networks at the country's most sensitive military bases, defense contractors, and aerospace companies in order to steal important data. Chinese agents have been able to penetrate secure computers, enter hidden sections of a hard drive, zip up as many files as possible, and transmit the data to way stations in South Korea, Hong Kong, or Taiwan before sending them to mainland China. The spy ring, known as Titan Rain, is thought to rank among the most pervasive cyber espionage threats ever faced by computer networks in the United States. It is believed that the agents have compromised secure networks ranging from the Redstone Arsenal military base to NASA to the World Bank; the U.S. army's flight-planning software has been electronically stolen. Hundreds of Defense Department computer systems have been penetrated, and similar attacks have been launched against secure systems in Britain, Canada, Australia, and New Zealand.[48]

CYBER TERRORISM: CYBER CRIME WITH POLITICAL MOTIVES

The justice system must now also be on guard against attacks that integrate terrorist goals with cyber capabilities: cyber terrorism. While the term may be difficult to define, *cyber terrorism* can be viewed as an effort by covert forces to disrupt the intersection between the virtual electronic reality of computers and the physical world.[49] It has been defined as "the premeditated, politically motivated attack against information, computer systems, computer programs, and data which result in violence against noncombatant targets by sub-national groups or clandestine agents."[50] Cyber terrorism may involve use of computer network tools to shut down critical national infrastructures or to coerce or intimidate a government or civilian population.[51]

Terrorist organizations are now beginning to understand the power that cyber crime can inflict on their enemies, even though, ironically, they come from a region where computer databases and the Internet are not widely used. Terrorist organizations are now adapting IT into their arsenal, and agencies of the justice system have to be ready for a sustained attack on the nation's electronic infrastructure.

Common examples of infrastructure at risk for attacks would be water treatment plants, electric plants, dams, oil refineries, and nuclear power plants. These industries all provide vital services to society by allowing people to go about their daily lives. Terrorist computer hackers could make a dam overflow or cause real property damage to oil refineries or nuclear plants by shutting down safeguards in the system that prevent catastrophic meltdowns.

Why Terrorism in Cyber Space?

Cyberspace is a handy battlefield for terrorists because an attack can strike directly at a target that bombs will not affect: the economy of their sworn enemy. Terror attacks designed to cripple the enemy nation may be aimed at destroying or reducing its economic growth, creating an inflationary economy, and at the same time reducing tax revenues. Battered by cyber terrorist attacks, the enemy's staggered economy will not be able to fund existing social programs while at the same time devoting adequate sums to the military and security to keeps the terrorists at bay. These outcomes can weaken the terrorist's target and undermine its resolve to continue to resist.[52]

Cyber terrorism also seems more efficient and less dangerous than the more traditional forms of terrorist activity. There is no loss of life and no need to infiltrate "enemy" territory. Cyber terrorists can commit crimes from anyplace in the world, and the costs are minimal. Nor do terror organizations lack for skilled labor to mount cyber attacks. There are a growing number of highly educated experts who are available at reasonable costs in developing countries in the Middle East and former Soviet Union.

Cyber Attacks

Has the United States already been the target of cyber attacks? While it may be difficult to separate the damage caused by hackers from deliberate attacks by terrorists, the Center for Strategic and International Studies claims to have uncovered attacks on the National Security Agency, the Pentagon, and a nuclear weapons laboratory; security breaches disrupted operations in each of these sites.[53] The financial service sector is a prime target and has been victimized by information warfare. Between January 1 and June 30, 2002, financial service firms received an average of 1,018 attacks per company, and 46 percent of these firms had at least one server attack during the period.[54]

What form may cyber attacks take today and perhaps in the future? Here are some possible scenarios:

- Logic bombs are implanted in an enemy's computer. They can go undetected for years until they are instructed through the Internet to overwhelm a computer system.

- Programs are used to allow terrorists to enter "secure" systems and disrupt or destroy the network.

Some cyber criminals attack government installations. Gary McKinnon of North London enters the Bow Street Magistrates Court on July 27, 2005, in London, England. McKinnon, 39, was wanted by the U.S. government for illegally accessing and making unauthorized modifications to 53 computers belonging to NASA, the Pentagon, the U.S. Army, Navy, and Air Force, and the Department of Defense, causing $1 million in damage. Is this a form of cyber terrorism or just cyber vandalism?

© Getty Images

- Using conventional weapons, terrorists overload a network's electrical system thereby threatening computer security.[55]

- Computers allow terrorist groups to remain connected and communicate covertly with agents around the world. Networks are a cost-effective tool for planning and striking.[56]

- The computer system of a corporation whose welfare is vital to national security—such as Boeing or Raytheon—is breached and disrupted.

- Internet-based systems used to manage basic infrastructure needs, such as an oil pipeline's flow or water levels in dams, are attacked and disrupted, posing a danger of loss of life and interruption of services.

- Cyber terrorists may directly attack the financial system. In ever-increasing numbers, people are spending and investing their money electronically, using online banking, credit card payment, and online brokerage services. The banking/financial system transacts billions of dollars each day through a complex network of institutions and systems. Efficient and secure electronic functioning is required if people are willing to conduct credit and debit card purchases, money transfers, and stock trading. A cyber attack can disrupt these transactions and interfere with the nation's economic well-being.[57]

- Terrorists can use the Internet to recruit new members and disseminate information. For example, Islamic militant organizations use the Internet to broadcast anti-Western slogans and information. An organization's charter and political philosophy can be displayed on its website, which can also be used to solicit funds.

Is Cyber Terrorism a Real Threat?

Some experts question the existence of cyber terrorism, going so far as to claim that not a single case of cyber terrorism has yet been recorded, that cyber vandals and hackers are regularly mistaken for terrorists, and that cyber defenses are more robust than is commonly supposed. James Lewis of the Center for Strategic and International Studies points out that fears of cyber terrorism may be exaggerated or misplaced for a number of important reasons:[58]

- The infrastructure that would be the target of cyber attacks is not easy to hack into and might defeat most terrorists who have not had advanced programming training.

- Even if they could enter the system, a failure of such locations would not cause a widespread panic. There are hundreds of different sites throughout the country that provide infrastructure services. For example, water treatment plants are not all connected; neither are the nation's electric plants. As a result, these plants do not share a common computer network so it would require a large number of hackers, working toward a common goal, to gain access to a number of plants to cause a systemwide problem.

- Power outages or problems with water treatment plants are not uncommon across the United States. Cities and states have experienced problems with these industries, and none of the past problems have resulted in mass panic or physical damage to property or life.

- The most likely use of these types of attacks would be in conjunction with a more traditional physical attack. Most of the attention in recent years has been focused on terrorist organizations, like al-Qaeda. However, it does not appear that al-Qaeda would want to use cyber attacks to gain their goals.

As noted by Lewis, terrorists seek to complete their political goals by inflicting psychological and physical damage. It does not appear that al-Qaeda would spend extra time trying to orchestrate cyber attacks that would cause neither death nor widespread destruction. There is a greater fear that terrorist organizations would attempt to hack into economic or military sites in the attempt to steal money for their attacks or to gain intelligence information. The weaknesses of computer systems, including systems that control the nation's national security, are prime targets for terrorist organizations that need to collect information on targets. These organizations need to be as hidden as possible in the attempt to gather as much intelligence as possible.

So far there have been no reports of major widespread cyber terrorism attacks in the United States. Even so, the potential threat is still there, likely to increase, and steps must be taken to address the dangers ahead.[59]

THE EXTENT AND COSTS OF CYBER CRIME

How common is cyber crime and how costly is it to American businesses and the general public? The Internet has become a vast engine for illegal profits. Criminal entrepreneurs view this vast pool as a prime target for cyber crime, and though an accurate accounting of cyber crime will probably never be made because so many offenses go unreported, there is little doubt that its incidence is growing rapidly.

Though thousands of breaches occur each year, most are not reported to local, state, or federal authorities. Some cyber crime goes unreported because it involves low-visibility acts, such as copying computer software in violation of copyright law, that simply never get detected.[60] Some businesses choose not to report cyber crime because they fear revealing the weaknesses in their network security systems. However, the information that is available indicates that the profit in cyber crime is vast and continually growing.[61] Losses are now in the billions and rising with the continuing growth of e-commerce. A number of watchdog groups have attempted to decipher estimated costs due to theft, loss of work product, damage to computer networks, and so on.

- *Illegal copying:* The Business Software Alliance (BSA), a professional watchdog group, found in a recent survey that 36 percent of the software installed on computers worldwide (including operating systems, consumer software, and local market software) was pirated, representing a loss of nearly $29 billion. The study found that while $80 billion in software was installed on computers, only $51 billion was legally purchased.[62]

- *Payment fraud:* Credit card fraud on the Internet has increased from $1.6 billion in 2000 to more than $15.5 billion today.[63]

- *Computer security breaches:* When the Computer Security Institute (CSI), an independent security watchdog group, contacted 700 computer security practitioners in U.S. corporations, government agencies, financial institutions, medical institutions and universities in 2005, it found that the average loss from computer security breaches was $204,000 (though this cost has been trending downward).[64] The 2005 survey showed that such crimes as unauthorized access of computer systems and theft of information have undergone a dramatic increase in recent years. Ironically, the percentage of organizations reporting computer intrusions to law enforcement has been in decline. The key reason cited for not reporting intrusions to law enforcement is the concern for negative publicity.

- *Phishing and identity theft:* The cost of phishing and identity theft now runs in the billions in the United States. Fifty-seven million U.S. adults think they have received a phishing e-mail. Nearly 1 million users have suffered from identity theft fraud, costing banks and card issuers billions in direct losses in the past year.[65] In June 2005, the Anti-Phishing Working Group reported over 15,000 phishing attempts that used different legitimate brand names. A recent survey by the Identity Theft Center indicates that businesses victimized by identity thieves averaged almost $50,000 in losses in 2004 compared to $41,717 in 2003. Individual victims reported lost wages ranging from $1,820 to $14,340 with the median loss of about $4,000 in 2004. Victims also reported expenses ranging from $851 to $1,378 for such items as phone calls, copies, affidavits, travel, notary fees, court documents, attorney fees, and certified mail to deal with the aftermath of the incident.[66] The U.S is not alone in experiencing losses due to identity theft. In Britain, identity (ID) fraud is one of the fastest-growing criminal trends and costs the British economy around £1.3 billion per year (more than $2 billion); it takes victims up to 300 hours of effort to regain their former status with banks and credit reference agencies.[67]

- *Employee abuse:* The Computer Security Institute found that 78 percent of employers had detected employee abuse of Internet access privileges (for example, downloading pirated software or inappropriate use of e-mail systems), and 38 percent suffered unauthorized access or misuse on their web.[68] About 25 percent of those reported attacks involved from two to five incidents; 39 percent reported ten or more incidents.[69]

- *Cyber vandalism:* Symantec Corp. conducts an annual Internet security threat report. The latest effort, which makes use of data from over 24,000 security devices deployed in over 180 countries, shows that online attackers are increasingly using stealthy attacks on personal computers in the pursuit of profit rather than simply to vandalize computer networks. Hackers and malicious software writers unleashed huge numbers of low-grade attacks designed to advance identity theft, spamming, extortion, and other schemes. There has been a significant increase in attack programs using malicious codes with the aim that at least some will get past defenses. Attackers are also targeting their assaults more carefully and using less familiar methods, such as lacing websites with attacks. Personal computers are increasingly the target of attacks because they are considered the weak links in corporate network security and at the same time contain valuable consumer data, such as financial account numbers, passwords, and identifying information. During the first 6 months of 2005, Symantec documented 10,866 new viruses and worms for computers running the Microsoft Windows operating system, by far the largest target, up 48 percent from 7,360 in the second half of 2004. Virus writers now routinely tweak old programs to create new variants in an effort to evade antivirus software. Also, attackers have been launching "bots," or programs that provide remote control of victims' computers, as described in the chapter opening, at a record pace; more than 10,000 are now being launched daily.[70]

CONTROLLING CYBER CRIME

The proliferation of cyber crime and its cost to the economy has created the need for new laws and enforcement processes specifically aimed at controlling its emerging formulations. Because technology evolves so rapidly, the enforcement challenges are particularly vexing. There have been numerous organizations set up to provide training and support for law enforcement agents. In addition, new federal and state laws have been aimed at particular areas of high-tech crimes.

Congress has treated computer-related crime as a distinct federal offense since the passage of the Counterfeit Access Device and Computer Fraud and Abuse Law in 1984.[71] The 1984 act protected classified U.S. defense and foreign relations information, financial institution and consumer reporting agency files, and access to computers operated for the government. The act was supplemented in 1996 by the National Information Infrastructure Protection Act (NIIPA), which significantly broadens the scope of the law. The key provisions of this act are set out in Exhibit 14.5.

Because cyber crime is relatively new, existing laws sometimes are inadequate to address the problem. Therefore new legislation has been drafted to protect the public from this new breed of cyber criminal. For example, before October 30, 1998, when the Identity Theft and Assumption Act of 1998 became law, there was no federal statute that made identity theft a crime. Today, federal prosecutors are making substantial use of the statute and are actively prosecuting cases of identity theft.[72] Since then all states except

---

EXHIBIT 14.5

Key Provisions of the National Information Infrastructure Protection Act (NIIPA)

- NIIPA makes it a crime to access computer files without authorization, or in excess of authorization, and subsequently to transmit classified government information.

- The act criminalizes gaining information without access, or in excess of authorized access, from financial institutions, the U.S. government, or private sector computers used in interstate commerce.

- The act proscribes intentionally accessing a U.S. department or agency nonpublic computer without authorization. If the government or a government agency does not use the computer exclusively, the illegal access must affect the government's use.

- The act prohibits accessing a protected computer, without or beyond authorization, with the intent to defraud and obtain something of value. There is an exception if the defendant only obtained computer time with a value less than $5,000 per year.

- The act extends the protection against computer hacking by including interstate, government, and financial institution computers as "protected" computers. It prohibits unauthorized access that causes damage regardless of whether or not the damage was "recklessly caused."

- The act criminalizes knowingly causing the transmission of a program, code, or command, and as a result, intentionally causing damage to a protected computer (without regard as to authorization to access the computer). Company employees and other authorized users can be culpable for intentional damage to a protected computer. The act makes unauthorized users, such as hackers, who cause the transmission of viruses responsible even if the transmission was not intentional because it was only reckless or negligent.

- The act prohibits one with intent to defraud from trafficking in passwords, which either would permit unauthorized access to a government computer or affect interstate or foreign commerce.

- The act makes it illegal to transmit in interstate or foreign commerce any threat to cause damage to a protected computer with intent to extort something of value. For example, hackers threatening to crash a system if not given system privileges or encrypting a company's data and demanding money for the key would be held criminally liable.

Source: Public Law 104-294, Title II, [sections] 201, 110 Stat. 3488, 3491-94 (1996).

Vermont and the District of Columbia have passed laws related to identity theft.

In the wake of the 9/11 attacks, NIIPA has been amended by sections of the USA Patriot Act to make it easier to enforce crimes by terrorists and other organized enemies against the nation's computer systems. Subsection 1030(a)(5)(A)(i) of the act criminalizes knowingly causing the transmission of a program, code, or command, and as a result, intentionally causing damage to a protected computer. This section applies regardless of whether the user had authorization to access the protected computer; company insiders and authorized users can be culpable for intentional damage to a protected computer. The act also prohibits intentional access without authorization that results in damage but does not require intent to damage; the attacker can merely be negligent or reckless.

In addition to these main acts, computer-related crimes can also be charged under at least forty different federal statutes. In additon to some of the statutes discussed earlier in the chapter, these include the Copyright Act and Digital Millennium Copyright Act, the National Stolen Property Act, the mail and wire fraud statutes, the Electronic Communications Privacy Act, the Communications Decency Act of 1996, the Child Online Protection Act, the Child Pornography Prevention Act of 1996, and the Internet False Identification Prevention Act of 2000.[73]

Cyber Crime Enforcement Agencies

To enforce these laws, the federal government is now operating a number of organizations to control cyber crime. One approach is to create working groups that coordinate the activities of numerous agencies involved in investigating cyber crime. The Interagency Telemarketing and Internet Fraud Working Group brings together representatives of numerous U.S. attorneys' offices, the FBI, the Secret Service, the Postal Inspection Service, the Federal Trade Commission, the Securities and Exchange Commission, and other law enforcement and regulatory agencies to share information about trends and patterns in Internet fraud schemes.[74]

Specialized enforcement agencies have been created. The Internet Fraud Complaint Center, based in Fairmont, West Virginia, is run by the FBI and the National White-Collar Crime Center. It brings together about 1,000 state and local law enforcement officials and regulators. Its goal is to analyze fraud-related complaints in order to find distinct patterns, develop information on particular cases, and send investigative packages to law enforcement authorities in the jurisdiction that appears likely to have the greatest investigative interest in the matter. In 2004 the center received almost 200,000 complaints, an increase of more than 60 percent in a single year.[75] Law enforcement has made remarkable strides in dealing with identity theft as a crime problem over the last several years.

One of the most successful federal efforts is the New York Electronic Crimes Task Force (NYECTF), a partnership between the U.S. Secret Service and a host of other public safety agencies and private corporations. Today, the task force consists of over 250 individual members representing federal, state, and local law enforcement, the private sector, and computer science specialists from 18 different universities. Since 1995, the New York task force has charged over 1,000 individuals with electronic crime losses exceeding $1 billion. It has trained over 60,000 law enforcement personnel, prosecutors, and private industry representatives in cyber crime prevention. Its success has prompted similar task forces to be set up in Boston, Miami, Charlotte, Chicago, Las Vegas, San Francisco, Los Angeles, and Washington, DC.[76]

Local Enforcement Efforts

Local police departments are now creating special units to crack down on cyber criminals. In Toronto, Canada, the police department's child exploitation section concentrates on cracking high-profile and difficult cases of Internet child pornography by using inventive and aggressive investigative methods. They estimate that there are perhaps 100,000 children depicted in as many as 1 million pictures that circulate via the Internet. The efforts of the 4-year-old Toronto police unit have led to 300 arrests so far, and only half have been made in the Toronto area. The unit looks for even the smallest clues to lead them to perpetrators. In one well-known case, investigators honed in on a computer keyboard where the character ñ—unique to Spanish—was visible. In the same series of pictures, they noticed a train ticket that appeared to be European in a child's hand. Sharing the information with Interpol, the international police consortium led to the breakup of a sadistic child porn ring operating south of Madrid led by a man who had been using his position as a baby-sitter to gain access to small children.[77]

CONTROLLING CRIME USING INFORMATION TECHNOLOGY

Criminal justice agencies are turning the tables on criminals and scam artists by using modern technology to increase their own effectiveness. Information technology (IT) now plays a significant role in law enforcement. This effort was given a jumpstart in 1998 when the federal government, recognizing the vital role information, identification, and communication technologies could and must play in the criminal justice system, enacted the Crime Identification Technology Act of 1998 (CITA); this act provided more than a billion dollars in grants to the states to upgrade their IT capabilities in areas such as criminal history record and identification systems and to promote the compatibility and integration of national, state, and local computer systems. The areas that CITA aided are set out in Exhibit 14.6.

CITA helped initiate the use of information technology in the criminal justice system. How have the various elements of criminal justice—police, courts, and corrections—adopted IT in their daily activities?

Law Enforcement Technology

IT has become a necessity in contemporary law enforcement because, as criminality has entered the cyber age, budget realities demand that police leaders make the most effective use of their forces, and technology is an important method of increasing productivity at a relatively low cost. The introduction of technology has already been explosive. In 1964, for example, only one city, St. Louis, had a police computer

Areas for Criminal Justice Improvement Designated by the Crime Identification Technology Act (CITA)

- Improving adult and juvenile criminal history record information systems.

- Creating automated fingerprint identification systems that are compatible with standards established by the Commerce Department's National Institute of Standards and Technology (NIST) and are interoperable with the Federal Bureau of Investigation (FBI) Integrated Automated Fingerprint System.

- Establishing finger imaging, live scan, and other automated systems to digitize and communicate fingerprints consistent with NIST standards and ensure interoperability with print systems operated by the states and the FBI.

- Augmenting state and local participation in the Interstate Identification Index of the National Crime Information System.

- Improving systems to allow any compact relating to the Interstate Identification Index to participate fully in the National Crime Information System.

- Enhancing systems to enhance state and local participation in the FBI's National Instant Check System (NICS), which was authorized with the creation of the Brady Handgun Violence Prevention Act.

- Creating an integrated criminal justice system, so that law enforcement agencies, courts, prosecutors, and corrections agencies have access to the same information.

- Improving criminal history record information to determine eligibility to purchase firearms under NICS.

- Developing court-based criminal justice information systems that integrate with other criminal justice information systems and promote the reporting of dispositions to central state repositories and to the FBI.

- Accessing ballistics identification programs and technology that are compatible with the Bureau of Alcohol, Tobacco, and Firearms' National Integrated Ballistics Network

- Enhancing the capabilities of forensic science laboratories and medical examiner programs.

- Improving sex offender identification, tracking, and registration systems.

- Creating systems to track and share information about domestic violence offenders.

- Supporting fingerprint-supported background checks for noncriminal justice purposes.

- Developing criminal justice information systems that provide research and statistical analysis.

- Establishing multi-agency, multijurisdictional communications systems among the states to share information among federal, state, and local law enforcement agencies.

- Enhancing the capability of the criminal justice system to deliver timely, accurate, and complete criminal record information to child welfare agencies, organizations, and programs that are engaged in the assessment of risk and other activities related to the protection of children, including protection against child sexual abuse, and placement of children in foster care.

Source: Office of Justice Programs Crime Identification Technology Act. http://it.ojp.gov/fund/files/cita.html#17%20Purposes. Accessed September 15, 2005.

system; by 1968, ten states and fifty cities had state-level criminal justice information systems; today, almost every city of more than 50,000 people has some sort of computer-support services.[78]

Law enforcement effectiveness is now being enhanced by the application of sophisticated electronic gadgetry: computers, cellular phones, and digital communication devices. What are some of the applications that are in use or in development?

IDENTIFYING CRIMES AND CRIMINALS Some criminal activities are so subtle that they have gone undetected. But IT now allows investigations using a wide variety of tools. Recently, for example, Texas recouped $437 in taxes when the Audit Division of the Texas Comptroller of Public Accounts created a database that consolidated information from internal sources, such as tax returns and taxpayer records, and external sources, such as wage records from the Texas Workers Compensation Commission and results from prior audits. The agency then used analytics software from SPSS Inc. to create an in-depth scoring system that helps target tax audits. The system analyzes more than 750,000 business tax accounts and returns a score that indicates the statistical probability of noncompliance with the tax laws. This allows auditors to hone in on those businesses with the most potential to yield a claim.

DATA MINING Law enforcement agencies have begun to use sophisticated computer software to conduct analysis of behavior patterns, a process called **data mining,** in an effort to identify crime patterns and link them to suspects.[79] By discovering patterns in burglaries, especially those involving multiple offenders, computer programs can be programmed to recognize a particular way of working at crime and thereby identify suspects most likely to fit the working profile. Advanced computer software has also helped in the investigations of Internet crime. For example, in one recent case in England, police used forensic software to show in court that a defendant had used a particular Internet search engine to find web pages that contained information about child pornography and then followed links to sites that he used to obtain and view kiddie porn. The Internet evidence was used to obtain his conviction.[80]

CRIMINAL IDENTIFICATION One of the most important computer-aided tasks is the identification of criminal suspects. Computers now link neighboring agencies so that they can share information on cases, suspects, and warrants. On a broader jurisdictional level, the FBI implemented the National Crime Information Center in 1967. This system provides rapid collection and retrieval of data about persons wanted for crimes anywhere in the fifty states.

Law enforcement agents are using computerized imaging systems to replace mug books. Photos or sketches are stored in computer memory and easily retrieved for viewing. Several software companies have developed identification programs that help witnesses create a composite picture of

Computer images are now being used to reconstruct facial features in order to identify suspects. Biometric crime-solving methods will become more important in the future.

© Digital Art./Corbis

the perpetrator. A vast library of photographed or drawn facial features can be stored in computer files and accessed on a terminal screen. Witnesses can scan through thousands of noses, eyes, and lips until they find those that match the suspect's. Eyeglasses, mustaches, and beards can be added; skin tones can be altered. When the composite is created, an attached camera makes a hard copy for distribution.

Computer systems now used in the booking process can also help in the suspect identification process. During booking, a visual image of the suspect is stored in a computer's memory, along with other relevant information. By calling up color photos on the computer monitor, police can then easily create a "photo lineup" of all suspects having a particular characteristic described by a witness.

New techniques are constantly being developed. Soon, through the use of genetic algorithms (mathematical models), a computerized composite image of a suspect's face will be constructed from relatively little information. Digitization of photographs will enable the reconstruction of blurred images. Videotapes of bank robbers or blurred photos of license plates, even bite marks, can be digitized using highly advanced mathematical models.

New computer software is being created that allows two-dimensional mug shots to be re-created on a three-dimensional basis. This technology has the human face divided into sixty-four features. For each feature, such as nose, mouth, and chin, there are 256 different types to choose from within the program. The result is that virtually anyone's face can be re-created according to a witness or victim's description. Once re-created, the image can be compared with over 1 million mug shots in less than a second to search for

a match. Rather than relying on an artist's sketch based on a victim's description of a suspect, investigators can work with a victim on a computer to come up with a matching description. Once detectives have mug shots, they can take the three-dimensional facial images contained in the software and create a match with the mug shot. Once this is done for all sixty-four features, a two-dimensional mug shot can be enhanced to make a three-dimensional head. Effects on the three-dimensional image such as lighting and angles can also be changed to make a better re-creation of an environment in which a crime has taken place.[81]

AUTOMATED FINGERPRINT IDENTIFICATION SYSTEMS

The use of computerized **automated fingerprint identification systems (AFIS)** is a widely used criminal identification process in the United States. Using mathematical models, AFIS can classify fingerprints and identify up to 250 characteristics (minutiae) of the print. These automated systems use high-speed silicon chips to plot each point of minutiae and count the number of ridge lines between that point and its four nearest neighbors, which substantially improves its speed and accuracy over earlier systems. Some police departments report that computerized fingerprint systems are allowing them to make over 100 identifications a month from fingerprints taken at a crime scene.

AFIS files have been regionalized. For example, the Western Identification Network (WIN) consists of eight central site members (Alaska, Idaho, Montana, Nevada, Oregon, Utah, Wyoming, and Portland Police Bureau), two interface members (California and Washington), multiple local members, and six federal members (Drug Enforcement Administration, Federal

Bureau of Investigation, Immigration and Naturalization Service, Internal Revenue Service, Postal Inspection Service, and Secret Service).[82] When it first began, the system had a centralized automated database of 900,000 fingerprint records; today, with the addition of new jurisdictions (Alaska, California, and Washington), the system's number of searchable fingerprint records has increased to more than 14 million.

To learn more about automated fingerprint identification systems, go to the **Western Identification Network** website at http://www.winid.org/history.htm. For an up-to-date list of web links, go to http://cj.wadsworth.com/siegel_crimtpt9e.

If these computerized fingerprint files become standardized and a national database is formed, it will be possible to check records in all fifty states to determine whether the suspect's fingerprints match those taken at the crime scene of previously unsolved cases. A national fingerprint identification system will become an even more effective tool because laser technology will vastly improve fingerprint analysis. Investigators will soon be able to recover prints that in the past were too damaged to be used as evidence. New breeds of fingerprint analysis will soon be available. The FBI plans to create an integrated AFIS that will allow local departments to scan fingerprints, send them electronically to a national depository, and receive back identification and criminal history of suspects.

Police are also using modern technology to preserve and analyze crime scenes, a topic that is explored more fully in the Policy and Practice feature, "Crime Scene Investigation Goes High Tech."

CRIME ANALYSIS Rather than employ their forces randomly along preordained routes, police departments are now using computer mapping programs that can translate addresses into map coordinates that allow departments to identify problem areas for particular crimes, such as drug dealing. Computer maps enable police to identify the location, time of day, and link among criminal events and to concentrate their forces accordingly.[83]

|||||||| CONNECTIONS ||||||||

Both crime mapping and data mining are discussed in Chapter 2. They have become entrenched as indispensable tools for both criminological researchers and law enforcement investigators who are searching for patterns in large amounts of crime data.

Crime maps offer police administrators graphic representations of where crimes are occurring in their jurisdiction. Computerized crime mapping gives the police the power to analyze and correlate a wide array of data to create immediate, detailed visuals of crime patterns. The simplest maps display crime locations or concentrations and are used to help direct patrols to places they are most needed. More complex maps can be used to chart trends in criminal activity and have been proved valuable in solving individual criminal cases. For example, a serial rapist may be caught by observing and understanding the patterns of his crimes so that detectives may predict where he will strike next and stake out the area with police decoys.

Computerized crime mappings let the police detect patterns of crimes and pathologies of related problems. It enables them to work with multiple layers of information and scenarios, thus to identify far more successfully emerging hot spots of criminal activity and target resources accordingly. A survey conducted by the National Institute of Justice found that 36 percent of agencies with 100 or more sworn officers are now using some form of computerized crime mapping.[84]

ALTERNATIVE MAPPING INITIATIVES Mapping may soon serve other purposes than resource allocation. Law enforcement officials in the state of Washington are now developing a new Internet-based mapping system that will provide critical information about public infrastructures to help them handle terrorist or emergency situations. The new initiative, known as Critical Incident Planning and Mapping System, is expected to provide access to tactical response plans, satellite imagery, photos, floor plans, and hazardous chemical locations.[85] In West Virginia, local and state government entities are working with private firms to develop an emergency 911 system that can pinpoint the location of callers even if they are unable to speak English, they are unconscious, or they hang up. The West Virginia Statewide Addressing and Mapping Board is using geospatial information technology to produce maps that show a callers exact locations by a given number and street name. The project is designed to improve emergency response times and disaster recovery planning, floodplain mapping, security, evacuation routing, counterterrorism efforts, crime analysis, and more.[86]

BIOMETRICS Biometrics is defined as automated methods of recognizing a person based on a physiological or behavioral characteristic.[87] Some biometric measures, such as fingerprint identification, have been used for years by law enforcement to identify criminals. However, recent improvements in computer technology have expanded the different types of measures that can be used for identification. Biometrics are now used to identify individuals based voice, retina, facial features, and handwriting analysis, just to name a few.

The field of biometrics can be used by all levels of government, including the military and law enforcement, and is also helpful in private businesses. Financial institutions, retail shopping, and other health and social fields can all utilize biometrics as a way to limit access to financial information or to secure Internet sites or physical locations. As opposed to current identification methods, such as personal identification numbers (PINs) used for bank machines and Internet transactions, biometric authenticators are unique to the user and as a result cannot be stolen and used without that individual's knowledge.

Crime Scene Investigation Goes High Tech

Crime scene investigation (CSI) techniques have caught the public interest now that *CSI*-type programs are routine TV fare. But, in truth, CSI technology is undergoing considerable change as cyber capabilities are being added to the investigators' bag of tricks.

Traditionally, to investigate and evaluate a crime scene, detectives relied on photographic evidence and two-dimensional drawings. However, it can be difficult to visualize the positional relationships of evidence with two-dimensional tools. Now, through a combination of laser and computer technology, high-definition surveying (HDS) creates a virtual crime scene that allows investigators to maneuver every piece of evidence.

High-definition surveying gives law enforcement a complete picture of a crime scene. HDS reflects a laser light off of objects in the crime scene and back to a digital sensor, creating three-dimensional spatial coordinates that are calculated and stored using algebraic equations. An HDS device projects light in the form of a laser in a 360-degree horizontal circumference, measuring millions of points, creating a "point cloud." The data points are bounced back to the receiver, collected, converted, and used to create a virtual image of any location. A personal computer can now take the data file and project that site onto any screen.

Not only does HDS technology allow the crime scene to be preserved exactly, but the perspective can be manipulated to provide additional clues. For instance, if the crime scene were the front room of an apartment, the three-dimensional image allows the investigator to move around and examine different points of view. Or, if a victim was found seated, an investigator could see and show a jury what the victim might have seen just before the crime occurred. If witnesses outside said they looked in a living room window, an investigator could zoom around and view what the witnesses could or could not have seen through that window.

HDS technology can also limit the crime scene contamination. Investigators may inadvertently touch an object at a crime scene leaving their fingerprints, or move or take evidence from the scene, perhaps by picking up fibers on their shoes. Evidence is compromised if moved or disturbed from its resting place, which may contaminate the scene and undermine the case. HDS technology is a "stand off" device, allowing investigators to approach the scene in stages by scanning from the outer perimeter and moving inward, reducing the chances of contamination.

The investigative and prosecutorial value of virtual crime scenes is evident. If an HDS device is used at the scene, detectives, prosecutors, and juries can return to a crime scene in its preserved state. Showing a jury exactly what a witness could or could not have seen can be very valuable. In addition to crime scenes, HDS technology plays an important role in other criminal functions, including investigations, civil liability, training, and emergency preparedness. For example, HDS scans can be made of critical structures such as schools, hospitals, and airports and kept on record. In a hostage situation, the HDS could produce a virtual school and, combined with real-time information, could give tactical teams an edge over the hostage takers.

Critical Thinking

1. How would you explain the fact that despite the addition of innovative technology, the percentage of crimes solved by police hovers at around 20 percent and has not improved in more than 40 years?

2. Would you approve of a program that inserted monitoring chips under the skin of all convicted felons? If not, why?

InfoTrac College Edition Research

To learn more about the impact of IT on criminal investigations, go to InfoTrac College Edition and read: Carole Longendyke, "Data Forensics Investigations," *New Jersey Law Journal* (28 February 2005): na; Alan Dove, "Molecular Cops: Forensic Genomics Harnessed for the Law," *Genomics and Proteomics* 4–5 (2004): 23.

Source: Raymond E. Foster, "Crime Scene Investigation," *Government Technology* (March 2005). http://www.govtech.net/magazine/story.php?id=93225&issue=3:2005. Accessed September 17, 2005.

The process of recording biometric data occurs in four steps. First, the raw biometric data is captured or recorded by a videocamera or a fingerprint reading device. Second, the distinguishing characteristics of the raw data are used to create a biometric template. Third, the template is changed into a mathematical representation of the biometric sample and is stored in a database. Finally, a verification process will occur when an individual attempts to gain access to a restricted site. The individual will have to present his or her fingerprint or retina to be read and then matched to the biometric sample on record. Once verification is made, the individual will have access to restricted areas.

Currently, a number of programs are in effect. The Immigration and Naturalization Service (INS, now ICE for

Immigration and Customs Enforcement) has been using hand geometry systems at major U.S. airports to check frequent international travelers. Law enforcement agencies now have access to automated fingerprint identification systems or AFIS, which can match a sample fingerprint with a national database of fingerprints with no human interaction. Casinos around the country have started to implement facial recognition software into their security systems to notify them when a known cheater has entered their premises.

The field of biometrics is growing every day in response to breaches in security in major industries and in government. Biometrics is discussed further in the Policy and Practice in Criminology feature, "Biometric Technology."

COMMUNICATIONS IT is also being applied to communications and information dissemination. Many larger departments have equipped officers with portable computers, which significantly cuts down on the time needed to write and duplicate reports. Police can now use terminals to draw accident diagrams, communicate with city traffic engineers, and merge their incident reports into other databases. Pen computing, in which officers write directly on a computer screen, eliminates paperwork and increases the accuracy of reports.[88] To make this material more accessible to the officer on patrol, head-up display (HUD) units now project information onto screens located on patrol car windshields; police officers can now access computer readouts without taking their eyes off the road.[89]

Some departments are linking advanced communications systems with computers, making use of electronic bulletin boards that link officers in an active online system, enabling them to communicate faster and more easily. The U.S. government is encouraging communications by funding the development of interoperable communications networks that enable emergency service personnel to communicate directly during crises. When an incident occurs, interoperable communications will enable first responders to communicate with other agencies in the area in order to coordinate all available resources and share information in real time.[90]

COMBATING TERRORISM WITH COMMUNICATIONS Communication technology has become even more important now that police agencies are involved in a war on terrorism. Keeping surveillance on suspected terrorist groups is not an easy task. However, when Congress passed the Communications Assistance for Law Enforcement Act (CALEA) in 1994, it aided law enforcement's ability to monitor suspects. The act required that communication equipment manufacturers and carriers design equipment, facilities, and services that are compatible with electronic surveillance needs.[91] Under the law, telecommunications carriers must ensure that equipment has the capability to facilitate the isolation and interception of communications content and call-identifying information and make it easy to deliver this data to law enforcement agencies.[92] CALEA allows that upon issue of a court order or other lawful authorization, communication carriers must be able to:

1. Expeditiously isolate all wire and electronic communications of a target transmitted by the carrier within its service area

2. Expeditiously isolate call-identifying information of a target

3. Provide intercepted communications and call-identifying information to law enforcement

4. Carry out intercepts unobtrusively, so targets are not made aware of the electronic surveillance, and in a manner that does not compromise the privacy and security of other communications

Under CALEA the government reimburses telecommunications carriers for the costs of developing software to intercept communications.

SURVEILLANCE Closed-circuit cameras have long been the mainstay of British police departments. Britain has 4 million videocameras monitoring streets, parks, and government buildings, more than any other country. London alone has 500,000 cameras watching for signs of illicit activity.

| | | | | | | CONNECTIONS | | | | | | |

The deadly London bombings that occurred in the summer of 2005 are discussed later in this chapter. While surveillance cameras did not prevent the bombings, they were instrumental in identifying the bombers and arresting accomplices.

Although not as popular in the United States, that is going to change as the country goes on high alert for terror activity. The Department of Homeland Security is now giving $800 million to fifty cities to help set up surveillance systems, and not just to stop terrorists:

■ In Los Angeles, eight cameras installed last year in crime-ridden MacArthur Park helped police make more than 600 arrests.

■ In Chicago, 250 cameras are being added in high-crime areas and linked to 2,000 cameras that monitor highways and public buildings. The cameras have helped drive crime rates to 40-year lows.[93]

Because of problem-oriented approaches (combined with advanced technology), it is no longer as easy for thieves to steal cars in many jurisdictions. In order to reduce the high number of car thefts occurring each year, some police departments have invested in "bait cars," which are parked in high-theft areas and are equipped with technology that alarms law enforcement personnel when someone has stolen the car. A signal goes off when either a door is opened or the engine begins. Then, equipped with global positioning satellite (GPS) technology, police officers are able to watch the movement of the car. Some cars are also equipped with microscopic videos and audio recorders that allow officers to

Biometric Technology

Since the terrorist attacks on September 11, 2001, added security measurements have been installed to help protect U.S. citizens. Biometrics, the science of using digital technology to identify individuals, has been implemented in many facets of the country's security system. Biometric technology has been installed in both airports and immigration centers to ensure that people are not using fake identities for illegal behavior.

Airports

Airports have started to implement the use of biometrics into their systems to prevent nonemployees from entering secured locations; in addition, biometric technology allows for control of passengers onto airplanes. For example, the most popular type of biometrics being used in airports is iris scanning. While looking into a camera, a computer scans your eye, records information regarding your iris, and stores the information into a database. Once your eye has been scanned, you are then permitted onto the plane. In order to depart from the plane at your destination, your iris scan must match the one in the database to ensure that you are the person who is supposed to be departing the plane. For those who travel frequently, this procedure has proved effective, because it does not require the individual to continuously stop at checkpoints and have identification checked; the person simply looks into a camera and within seconds is permitted to pass through all the checkpoints.

In addition, airport managers and security personnel have used the system to keep unwanted individuals from entering secure facilities. Previously, with the use of swipe cards and/or codes, people were allowed to walk in behind personnel to gain entry into secured areas; however, this is no longer a problem with the use of biometrics. Employees of the Charlotte, NC airport have their irises scanned, and the information gained remains in a database. In order to access the secured areas, personnel must look into a tube and have their match confirmed to be allowed entrance. Although fingerprints have also been used for this purpose, an iris scan can match over 400 different points of identification compared to only 60 to 70 points of a fingerprint.

Other airports have incorporated another type of biometric technology within their security system: facial recognition. Facial recognition systems measure facial features, noting the distance of one feature to another, along with sizes of features, and so forth. An airport in Florida uses a facial recognition system that contains the images of the FBI's top ten most wanted, along with other sought after individuals. Passengers are required to look into cameras to verify that they do not match any of the images in the system. If no matches are found, passengers are permitted to pass through and board their airplane. There is hope that with the continued success of this system, facial recognition systems will help locate fugitives, terrorists, and abducted children who are passing through transportation terminals.

Immigration

The Department of Homeland Security has implemented the U.S. Visitor and Immigrant Status Indicator Technology or US-Visit. US-Visit was developed to provide more security to the nation's airports while keeping transportation into and out of the country open. This is accomplished by using

---

see and hear the suspect(s) within the car and remote engine and door locks that can trap the thief inside.

The technology has been used in conjunction with an advertising campaign to warn potential car thieves about the program. The system has been instituted in Vancouver, Canada, and Minneapolis, Minnesota, with impressive results: Motor vehicle theft dropped over 40 percent in Minneapolis over a 3-year period in which bait cars were used and 30 percent in Vancouver within 6 months of being instituted. In addition to cutting down on auto theft, the system, which costs roughly $3,500 per car, seems to decrease the incidence of dangerous high-speed pursuits because police officers know they will be able to identify and locate the suspects.[94]

INFORMATION PROCESSING Not only can law enforcement agencies use IT to solve crimes and communicate with one another, they are now using the growing electronic net to gather and disseminate information. Several websites offer police agencies advice, e-mail, publications, and information on policies, conferences, ordinances, programs, and innovations in the law enforcement community.[95] Justice Technology Information Network (JUSTNET, http://www.justnet.org) and the International Association of Chiefs of Police (IACPNet, http://services.login-inc.com/iacpnet) are examples of the sort. Each offers information to the criminal justice community, collects and disseminates information, and features advances in criminal justice technology, such as the results of testing and evaluation of products such as body armor and handcuffs.

Most large police departments now have their own websites designed to improve public relations by enhancing communication. Websites give both police and community

biometric scans to determine the identity of all travelers from foreign countries that attempt to enter the United States.

Almost all foreign citizens, regardless of country of origin, who wish to travel in the United States must comply with US-Visit requirements. The process of registering for travel in the United States under the new US-Visit starts far from U.S. soil. An individual who wishes to travel to the United States must first visit a U.S. consulate office in his or her country and apply for a visa to travel to the United States. When the individual applies for the visa, he or she will have biometrics collected in two separate ways. First, photographs will be taken of every applicant, and those photographs will be entered into the US-Visit database along with digital finger scans. The digital finger scans will be taken of both the right and left index fingers of the applicant. This information will be loaded into a database and then checked to see if it matches any criminals or suspected terrorists already in the system.

Once an applicant passes the database check, the individual can be issued a visa to travel to the United States. Upon arrival at a U.S. port of entry, the traveler will be required to scan the left and right index fingers to determine if the individual at the point of entry is the same as the person who applied for the visa.

Entry procedures were started in 115 airports at the beginning of 2004, and by the end of 2005, all airports that receive international flights had US-Visit capabilities. Currently, there are twelve airports within the U.S. that are taking part in the US-Visit exit procedures. Also there are two separate seaports that are testing the exit procedures for US-Visit. The exit procedure requires each traveler to scan his or her fingers to determine the identity of the individual leaving the country.

The Department of Homeland Security believes that implementing these new security features will result in fewer criminals or terrorists entering the country; at the same time, the procedures will reduce the amount of identity theft and fraud that may occur upon entry or exit of the country. However, there are critics who say that the information available to U.S. Customs and Immigration is much too personal. Despite privacy concerns, the Department of Homeland Security is set on using the US-Visit program in conjunction with other government programs to increase the security of the United States.

Critical Thinking

1. Are you afraid that futuristic security methods such as biometric technology will lead to the loss of personal privacy and the erosion of civil liberties?

2. Would you want your personal medical information to be posted on a computer website where it potentially could be accessed by future employers and others?

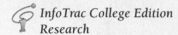

InfoTrac College Edition Research

To learn more about the subject, use "biometric technology" as a key word on InfoTrac College Edition.

Sources: U.S. Visitor and Immigrant Status Indicator Technology, Electronic Privacy Information Center. http://www.epic.org/privacy/us-visit. Accessed September 1, 2005; US-Visit, Travel and Transportation, U.S. Department of Homeland Security. http://www.dhs.gov/dhspublic/interapp/content_multi_image/content_multi_image_0006.xml. Accessed September 1, 2005; William Scott, "Israeli Screening System Exploits Biometric ID," *Aviation Week & Space Technology* 156 (2002): 50.

members an opportunity to share crime information. Police websites now allow the public to file complaints, offer employment qualifications and opportunities, distribute crime alerts, and serve as a link to many other civil and social services. Some provide a link to sexual offender registries, allowing the user to submit a name or address to see the status of an offender and his current location.

Each department site has its own special features. The police website in Tempe, Arizona, has interactive capability for the public to use and also distributes information for analysts, community managers, and department personnel.[96] The Los Angeles police website has a section devoted to stolen art and objects and shows bulletins with suspects' pictures, as well as images of recovered and stolen items with a small description of each object and incident.[97]

Court Technology

IT is also being applied in the courts in such areas as videotaped testimonies, new court-reporting devices, information systems, and data processing systems to handle such functions as court docketing and jury management.[98] In 1968, only ten states had state-level automated information systems; today, all states employ such systems for a mix of tasks and duties. A survey of Georgia courts found that 84 percent used computers for three or more court administration applications. What are some other developing areas of court technology?

COMMUNICATIONS Court jurisdictions are cooperating with police departments in the installation of communications gear that allows defendants to be arraigned via closed-circuit

The virtual courtroom will employ a variety of information technologies that will help make the justice process more effective and efficient. From witness statements to the presentation of evidence, the Internet will continue to play an ever-increasing role in the trial process.

television while they are in police custody. Closed-circuit television has been used for judicial conferences and scheduling meetings. Courts are using voice-activated cameras to record all testimony during trials; these are the sole means of keeping trial records.

VIDEOCONFERENCING About 400 courts across the country have videoconferencing capability. It is now being employed for juvenile detention hearings, expert witness testimony at trial, oral arguments on appeal, and parole hearings. More than 150 courts are using two-way live, televised remote linkups for first appearance and arraignment. In the usual arrangement, the defendant appears from a special location in the jail where he or she is able to see and hear and be seen and heard by the presiding magistrate. Such appearances are now being authorized by state statute, for example, Virginia Code § 19.2-3. 1. Televised appearances minimize delays in prisoner transfer, effect large cost savings through the elimination of transportation and security costs, and reduce escape and assault risks.

EVIDENCE PRESENTATION Many high-tech courtrooms are now equipped for real-time transcription and translation, audio-video preservation of the court record, remote witness participation, computer graphics displays, television monitors for jurors, and computers for counsel and judge. The Harris County Criminal Justice Center in Texas now has the largest evidence display and courtroom video distribution project in the history of the U.S. court system.[99] The facility-wide, hub-based videoconferencing system supports a total of 105 rooms, with conferencing ability among multiple parties from various locations throughout the building. This system was designed to allow witnesses to testify without having contact with criminal defendants. The technology includes:

- Digital evidence presentation system

- Simultaneous evidence viewing via high-resolution 52-inch monitors

- Annotation capabilities

- Flat panel display for judges' viewing

- Seamless technical integration via Court-Wide

- Under-carpet cable installation

- Remote participation via videoconferencing

CASE MANAGEMENT In the 1970s, municipal courts installed tracking systems, which used databases to manage court data. These older systems were limited and could not process the complex interrelationships of information pertaining to persons, cases, time, and financial matters that occur in court cases.

Contemporary relational databases now provide the flexibility to handle complex case management. To help programmers define the multiplicity of relationships that occur in a court setting, the National Center for State Courts in Williamsburg, Virginia, has developed a methodology for structuring a case management system that tracks a person to the case or cases in which he is a defendant, the scheduling of the cases to avoid any conflicts, and, of increasing importance, the fines that have been levied and the accounts to which the money goes. One of the more advanced current approaches to statewide court system automation has been undertaken by Wisconsin, which has developed and implemented an information system called the Circuit Court Automation Program (CCAP), used to improve day-to-day operations of courts, such as case records management and court calendaring, as well as jury selection and financial management.[100]

INTERNET RECORDS The Internet has become increasingly involved in the court system. For example, in the federal system, J-Net is the judiciary's website. It makes it easier for judges and court personnel to receive important information in a timely fashion.[101] The federal court's administrative office has begun sending official correspondence by electronic mail, a method that provides instantaneous communication of important information. In 1999, an automated library management system was developed, which meant that judges could access a web-based virtual law library. An electronic network providing the public with access to court records and other information via the Internet was also implemented. In 2002, eleven federal courts announced that they would allow Internet access to criminal case files. This was the first time the public could gain access to criminal case files.

The U.S. Supreme Court's Public Access to Court Electronic Records (PACER) offers an inexpensive, fast, and comprehensive case information service to any individual with a personal computer and Internet access. The PACER system permits people to request information about a particular individual or case. The data is displayed instantly and is simple enough that little user training or documentation is required.[102]

Corrections Technology

IT has also had its influence in the correctional field.[103] The correctional establishment—the managers of the jail, prison, probation, and parole systems—and their sponsors in elected office are seeking more cost-effective ways to increase public safety as the number of people under correctional supervision continues to grow. A correctional establishment that takes advantage of all the potential offered by new technologies to reduce the costs of supervising criminal offenders and minimize the risks they pose to society will define the field of **technocorrections**. How is information technology being used within the correctional system?

LOCATING AND MONITORING INMATES Some jails at the city and town level as well as state and federal prisons are now using Internet-based inmate locators. The Federal Bureau of Prisons maintains a database that includes all federal inmates from 1982 to the present; a query will return either the location of the offender (which prison, halfway house, and so on) or when the inmate was released. States have also used IT to locate inmates. The Arkansas system allows for searches by identification number of offender, first and last name, race, age, sex, county, or facility; alternately, a user can search for all of the people committing one particular crime. This function allows for a mini-database to be downloaded. The Florida Department of Corrections has similar search capability, including an Inmate Escape Information Search and Supervised Population Information Search.

Correctional departments are now using the Internet to monitor offenders in the community. Some use kiosks, similar to the size and workings of an ATM machine, that allow for probationers/parolees/pretrial defendants to report to their case manager. Identification is matched via a bar-coded card/login and a biometric sample (fingerprint/palm print). The offender is then guided through a series of questions and e-mail notices from the case manager; the individual can also submit employment records at the kiosk. The case manager then can access the client's new input via middleware software on the Internet. Some cities such as New York and Los Angeles, whose caseworkers tend to have larger caseloads,

are using these kiosks for low-risk/nonviolent offenders. The obvious benefits are efficient use of time on behalf of the case manager, reduced data entry time, increased accuracy, and real-time access to monitoring data.

IT FOR PRISON SECURITY Technological innovation is also common within secure institutions to maintain prison security. What are some of these new technologies?

- *Ground penetrating radar:* The Special Technologies Laboratories has developed a technology called ground penetrating radar (GPR), which is able to locate tunnels inmates use to escape. GPR works almost like an old-fashioned Geiger counters, held in the hand and swept across the ground by an operator. Instead of detecting metal, the GPR system detects changes in ground composition, such as buried contraband in the recreation yard, or voids, such as those created by a tunnel.

- *Heartbeat monitoring:* The weakest security link in any prison has always been the sally port, where trucks unload their supplies and where trash and laundry is taken out of the facility. Over the years, inmates have hidden in loads of trash, old produce, laundry—any possible container that might be exiting the facility. Now it is possible to prevent escapes by monitoring inmates' heartbeats! The Advanced Vehicle Interrogation and Notification System (AVIAN)—being marketed by Geo Vox Security—works by identifying the shock wave generated by the beating heart, which couples to any surface the body touches. The system takes all the frequencies of movement, such as the expansion and contraction of the engine and rain hitting the roof, and determines if there is a pattern similar to a human heartbeat.

- *Satellite monitoring:* Pro Tech Monitoring Inc. of Palm Harbor, Florida, has developed a system to monitor offenders by using cellular technology combined with the federal government's global positioning system of satellites. While in the community, each offender wears an ankle bracelet and carries a 3-pound portable tracking device (smart box), programmed with information on his or her geographic restrictions. For instance, a sex offender may be forbidden to come within 5 miles of his victim's home or workplace, or a pedophile may be barred from getting close to a school. A satellite monitors the geographic movements of the offender, either in real time or by transmitting the information to the smart box for later retrieval. The smart box and the ankle bracelet sound an alarm when boundaries are breached, alerting potential victims.

- *Sticky Shocker:* This is a less-than-lethal projectile that uses stun gun technology to temporarily incapacitate a person at stand-off range. The Sticky Shocker is a low-impact wireless projectile fired from compressed gas or powder launchers and is accurate to within 10 meters.

- *Back-scatter imaging system for concealed weapons:* This system utilizes a back-scatter imager to detect weapons and contraband. The major advantage of this device over current walk-through portals is that it can detect nonmetallic as well as metallic weapons. It uses low-power X-rays equal to about 5 minutes of exposure to the sun at sea level. While these X-rays penetrate clothing, they do not penetrate the body.

- *Body scanning screening system:* This is a stationary screening system to detect nonmetallic weapons and contraband in the lower body cavities. It uses simplified magnetic resonance imaging (MRI) as a noninvasive alternative to X-ray and physical body cavity searches. The stationary screening system makes use of first-generation medical MRI.

- *Transmitter wristbands:* Developed by Technology Systems International, these broadcast a unique serial number via radio frequency every 2 seconds so that antennas throughout the prison can pick up the signals and pass the data via a local area network to a central monitoring station computer. The bands can sound an alert when a prisoner gets dangerously close to the perimeter fence or when an inmate does not return from a furlough on time; they can even tag gang members and notify guards when rivals get into contact with one another.

- *Personal health status monitor:* To monitor inmates who may be a threat to commit suicide, correctional authorities are developing a personal health status monitor that, in its initial form, will use acoustics to track the heartbeat and respiration of a person in a cell. The monitor does not actually need to be located on the person of the inmate; it is the size of two packs of cigarettes and can be placed on the ceiling or just outside a cell. The device is similar to those installed inside infant cribs in hospitals. More advanced monitors are now being developed that can track five or more vital signs at once, and based on the combination of findings, produce an assessment of an inmate's state of health. While this more advanced monitor may take another decade to develop, the current version will be able to help prevent suicides in the very near future.

- *All-in-one drug detection spray:* For the past several years, Mistral Security of Bethesda, Maryland, has marketed drug detection sprays for marijuana, methamphetamines, heroin, and cocaine. A specially made paper is wiped on a surface; when sprayed with one of the aerosol sprays, it changes color within 15 seconds if as little as 4 to 20 micrograms of drugs are present. A new detection device uses a single spray that will test for all drugs at once. The test paper will turn different colors depending on which drugs the spray contacts, and several positive results will be possible with a single use of the spray.

- *Radar vital signs monitor/radar flashlight:* Researchers at Georgia Tech have developed a hand-held radar flashlight that can detect the respiration of a human in a cell from behind a 20-centimeter hollow-core concrete wall or an 8-inch cinder block wall. It instantly gives the user a bar graph readout that is viewed on the apparatus itself. Other miniature radar detectors give users heartbeat and respiration readings. The equipment is expected to be a useful tool to find hidden people, since the only thing that successfully blocks its functioning is a metal wall or conductive material in the direction it is pointed. The radars can also be used in telemedicine and for individuals to whom electrodes would be difficult to apply.

- *Personal alarm location system:* It is now possible for prison employees to carry a tiny transmitter linking them with a computer in a central control room. In an emergency, they can hit an alarm button and transmit to a computer that automatically records whose distress button has been pushed. An architectural map of the facility instantly appears on-screen that shows the exact location of the unfortunate staff member.

INORMATION TECHNOLOGY, CRIME, AND CIVIL LIBERTIES

Though the new IT provides increased effectiveness and efficiency within criminal justice agencies, it comes with a price. Some critics believe that IT can compromise the privacy and liberty of U.S citizens who have not engaged in any form of illegal activity. Wary of Big Brother, the American Civil Liberties Union (ACLU) warns that we are turning into a surveillance society, constantly watched by a plethora of computers, cameras, sensors, wireless communication, GPS, biometrics, and other technologies. And, they warn, there are new technologies on the horizon, ranging from biometrics to implantable microchips that threaten privacy.[104]

Privacy concerns often focus on the new surveillance techniques, ranging from closed-circuit surveillance cameras to biometrics. Critics believe that an identification system based on face recognition technology poses several threats to civil liberties, the most telling being false positives where a person is falsely identified and then investigated, a process that unfairly impinges on the privacy of innocent people. Biometrics can also be used to locate and physically track people, prying into their movements that may have little to do with any crime or terrorist activity.[105] As a result, people wary of being watched and recorded by the government will alter their activities and actions and, in so doing, lose the right to self-determination of their own behavior.[106]

There are also concerns about the linkage of surveillance information to fast and inexpensive data processing and storage systems. The result is a permanent record that is easily accessed. Every move an individual makes over the course of a day—from using an E-ZPass at a particular exit on the throughway to the items the person bought at the drugstore—can be tied across various databases to create a detailed dossier on daily activities.[107] Who should have access to this information and for what purpose are critical questions.

Although these intrusions are troubling, people also want to be protected from harmful criminal activity, ranging from identity theft to terrorism. Protection of civil liberties is important, but so is protection from civil dangers. The level of intrusion and surveillance people will tolerate may depend in large part on their assessment of the risks they face and their willingness to sacrifice civil liberties to reduce these risks.[108] As the threat of terrorism and cyber crime grows, so too may tolerance for invasions of privacy. A number of factors may tip the balance of public opinion to either support the use of IT in law enforcement or attempt to restrict its use:

- *Not much to fear:* Is the government really intent on keeping the public under surveillance? Some commentators view concerns about using IT in criminal justice as misplaced. When they gather data or use IT in surveillance, police agencies may simply be trying to do their job more effectively, not attempting to create a Big Brother society. While the media and some civil liberties advocates warn about the loss of privacy, average citizens have much more to worry about from terrorist cells and identity thieves whose phishing expeditions compromise their financial and personal well-being and security than from the police.[109]

- *It really does work:* Modern IT may not be foolproof, but it does increase safety. Intrusions into personal space may be warranted if lives are saved. Security cameras, for example, have proliferated in England and are now a vital tool in the government's war on terrorism. While they did not prevent the bombing of the London subway system that killed fifty-six Londoners in 2005, the images they produced encouraged thousands of tips and led to the arrest of other terrorists in the group, including one who had fled to Italy. While civil liberties groups fear that the success of the surveillance may lead to expanded coverage, that risk is offset by the fact that the bombers will not be able to strike again.[110]

- *What's the big deal?:* While IT makes surveillance and data storage more efficient, it does not gather information that human investigators did not collect in the past. It just does it more efficiently. The new technology is not invading homes but gathering information from public spaces, albeit in the real or electronic world. It is illogical to say that IT should not be used to collect data that any police officer or private citizen is free to observe and record.

- *IT in criminal justice can be controlled:* There is no question that abuses may occur if national security and law enforcement agents are given free reign to use IT for surveillance and control. However, strict national standards on the use of IT can keep it within acceptable boundaries. A number of national groups, including the American Bar Association (ABA), have already created model rules for IT. The ABA suggests that electronic surveillance must consider the following in order that it not invade people's privacy:

  a. The nature of the place, activity, condition, or location to be surveilled
  b. The care that has been taken to enhance the privacy of such place, activity, condition, or location
  c. The lawfulness of the vantage point, including whether either the surveillance or installation of surveillance equipment requires a physical intrusion
  d. The availability and sophistication of the surveillance technology
  e. The extent to which the surveillance technology enhances the law enforcement officer's natural senses
  f. The extent to which the surveillance of subjects is minimized in time and space
  g. The extent to which the surveillance of nonsubjects is likewise minimized
  h. Whether the surveillance is covert or overt

  And, if surveillance is required, it should be governed by the following considerations:

  a. The subjects of the surveillance should not be selected in an arbitrary or discriminatory manner.
  b. The scope of the surveillance should be limited to its authorized objectives and be terminated when those objectives are achieved.
  c. When a particular surveillance device makes use of more than one regulated technology and the technologies are governed by differing rules, the more restrictive rules should apply.
  d. The particular surveillance technique should be capable of doing what it purports to do and be used solely for that purpose by officers trained in its use.
  e. Notice of the surveillance should be given when appropriate.[111]

As the use of IT in criminal justice proliferates, whether it is to track and apprehend terrorists, cyber criminals, or common-law felons, its intrusion into the life of the average citizen will also continue to grow. While civil libertarians warn of its expansion, the dangers present in contemporary society may override considerations of liberty and privacy.

- Cyber crime is a new breed of offenses that involves the theft and/or destruction of information, resources, or funds utilizing computers, computer networks, and the Internet. Cyber crime presents a challenge for the justice system because it is rapidly evolving, it is difficult to detect through traditional law enforcement channels, and its control demands that agents of the justice system develop technical skills that match those of the perpetrators.

- Cyber crime has grown because information technology (IT) has become part of daily life in most industrialized societies. Some of the many types of cyber crime are cyber theft, cyber vandalism, cyber terrorism, and identity theft.

- The Internet has become an important source for selling and distributing obscene material. Some sites cater to adult tastes, while others illegally peddle access to obscene material or kiddie porn. It is unlikely that any law enforcement efforts will put a dent in the Internet porn industry.

- A denial-of-service attack is characterized as an attempt to extort money from legitimate users of an Internet service by threatening to block the user's access to the service.

- Warez refers to groups of individuals who work together to illegally obtain software and then "crack" or "rip" its copyright protections before posting it on the Internet for other members of the group to use.

- File sharing is another type of illegal copyright infringement that allows Internet users to download music and other copyrighted material without paying the artists and record producers royalties.

- Internet security fraud involves using the Internet to intentionally manipulate the securities marketplace for profit.

- Identity theft occurs when a person uses the Internet to steal someone's identity and/or impersonate the victim to open credit card accounts or conduct other financial transactions. Identity theft can destroy a person's life by manipulating financial information.

- Phishing involves the creation of false e-mails and/or websites to gain access to a victim's personal information.

- E-tailing scams involve either the failure to deliver on promised purchases or services or the substitution of cheaper or used material for higher quality purchases.

- Some cyber criminals may be motivated by the desire for revenge, destruction, and to achieve a malicious intent. Cyber vandalism involves malicious attacks aimed at disrupting, defacing, and destroying technology that the vandals find offensive. It can range from sending destructive viruses and worms to hacker attacks designed to destroy important computer networks, and may involve computer viruses, worms, Trojan horses, logic bombs, and spam. Web defacement is another type of cyber vandalism.

- Cyber stalking refers to the use of the Internet, e-mail, or other electronic communications devices to stalk another person. Some cyber stalkers pursue minors through online chat rooms while others harass their victims electronically.

- Cyber spying involves illegally using the Internet to gather information that is considered private and confidential.

- Cyber terrorism can be viewed as an effort by covert forces to disrupt the intersection where the virtual electronic reality of computers meets with the physical world. Some experts question the existence of cyber terrorism, claiming that not a single case of cyber terrorism has yet been recorded, that cyber vandals and hackers are regularly mistaken for terrorists, and that cyber defenses are more robust than is commonly supposed.

- As the Internet has become a vast engine for illegal profits, a need for new laws and enforcement processes specifically aimed at controlling cyber crime has developed. Since 1984, Congress has treated computer-related crime as a distinct federal offense, and new legislation has been drafted to protect the public from cyber crime. As well, new enforcement techniques through numerous agencies have been implemented.

- Criminal justice agencies are using IT to increase their own effectiveness with such methods as data mining, crime mapping, and computer-aided identification of criminal suspects.

- Biometrics, automated methods of recognizing a person based on a physiological or behavioral characteristic, is also being used for identification and security in law enforcement.

- IT is also being applied in the courts in such areas as videotaped testimonies, new court-reporting devices, information systems, and data processing systems to handle such functions as court docketing and jury management.

- IT has also influenced the corrections field. States have used IT to locate inmates, and correctional departments are now using the Internet to monitor offenders in the community. Prisons are also making use of IT to maintain security.

- Though IT techniques provide the opportunity to increase the effectiveness and efficiency within criminal agencies, critics believe they can compromise the privacy and liberty of U.S citizens who have not engaged in any form of illegal activity. A number of factors may tip the balance of public opinion to either support the use of IT in law enforcement or attempt to restrict its use.

||||||||||||||||||||||||||||||||||||||||||||||||

Thinking Like a Criminologist

The president's national security advisor approaches you with a problem. A tracking device has been developed that can be implanted under the skin that will allow people to be constantly monitored. Implanted at birth, the data surveillance device could potentially cover *everyone*, with a record of every transaction and activity entered into powerful computers where search engines keep them under constant surveillance. The surveillance device would enable the government to keep tabs on people's whereabouts as well as monitoring their biological activities such as brain waves, heart rate, and so on.

The benefits are immense. Once a person becomes a suspect in a crime or is believed to be part of a terrorist cell, he or she can be easily monitored from a distance without danger to any government agent. The person cannot hide or escape detection. Physical readings could be made to determine if the suspect is under stress, using banned substances, and so on.

The advisor wants your opinion on this device. Is it worthwhile, considering the threats faced by America from terrorists and criminals, or does it violate personal privacy and freedom?

Doing Research on the Web

Before answering this question, you should go to the American Civil Liberties Union website: http://www.aclu.org/Privacy/PrivacyMain.cfm. The ACLU states:

> The United States is at risk of turning into a full-fledged surveillance society. The tremendous explosion in surveillance-enabling technologies, combined with the ongoing weakening in legal restraints that protect our privacy, mean that we are drifting toward a surveillance society. The good news is that it can be stopped. Unfortunately, right now the big picture is grim.

You may also want to look at the website of the Center for Democracy and Technology (CDT), a nonprofit public policy organization dedicated to promoting the democratic potential of today's open, decentralized global Internet. Their mission is to conceptualize, develop, and implement public policies to preserve and enhance free expression, privacy, open access, and other democratic values in the new and increasingly integrated communications medium: http://www.cdt.org.

||||||||||||||||||||||||||||||||||||||||||||||||

KEY TERMS

cyber crime (468)
information technology (IT) (468)
globalization (468)
cyber theft (468)
cyber vandalism (468)
cyber terrorism (468)
automatic teller machines (ATMs) (469)
denial of service attack (470)

warez (471)
identity theft (473)
phishing (carding or spoofing) (473)
e-tailing fraud (474)
computer virus (475)
malware (475)
computer worm (475)
Trojan horse (476)
logic bomb (476)

spam (476)
web defacement (476)
cyber stalking (477)
cyber spying (477)
data mining (483)
automated fingerprint identification systems (AFIS) (484)
biometrics (485)
technocorrections (491)

1. Which theories of criminal behavior best explain the actions of cyber criminals, and which ones do you believe fail to explain cyber crime?

2. How would you punish a web page defacer who placed an antiwar message on a government site? Prison? Fine?

3. What guidelines would you recommend for the use of IT in law enforcment?

4. Are we creating a Big Brother society, and and is the loss of personal privacy worth the price of safety?

NOTES

1. U.S. Department of Justice, "Michigan Man Arrested for Using New Jersey Juvenile to Launch Destructive 'DDOS for Hire' Computer Attacks on Competitors." http://www.usdoj.gov/usao/nj/publicaffairs/NJ_Press/files/arab0318_r.htm. Accessed November 8, 2005.

2. Statement of Michael A. Vatis, director of the FBI's National Infrastructure Protection Center, on cyber crime before the Senate Judiciary Committee, Criminal Justice Oversight Subcommittee, and House Judiciary Committee, Crime Subcommittee, Washington, DC, 29 February 2000. www.cybercrime.gov/vatis. htm. Accessed July 12, 2005.

3. Ed Frauenheim, "IDC: Cyberterror and Other Prophecies," CNET News.com, 12 December 2002. Accessed August 14, 2005.

4. Giles Trendle, "An E-Jihad against Government?" EGOV Monitor, September 2002.

5. "A Report of the President's Working Group on Unlawful Conduct on the Internet: The Electronic Frontier" (Washington, DC: 2000). http://www.usdoj .gov/criminal/cybercrime/unlawful.htm#EXECSUM.

6. Department of States Attorney, Eastern District of California, Press Release, "Vallejo Woman Admits to Embezzling More than $875,035: Not-for-Profit Organization Victim of Computer Fraud." http://www.cybercrime .gov/sabathiaPlea.htm. Accessed September 14, 2005.

7. Deloitte & Touche, 2005 Global Security Survey. http://www.deloitte.com/dtt/cda/doc/content/Deloitte+2005+Global+Security+Survey.pdf. Accessed November 11, 2005.

8. Chris Richard, "Guard Your Card: ATM Fraud Grows More Sophisticated," Christian Science Monitor 95 (July 21, 2003):15.

9. Andreas Philaretou, "Sexuality and the Internet," Journal of Sex Research 42 (2005): 180–181.

10. N2H2 communication. http://www.n2h2.com/index.php.

11. Jeordan Legon, "Sex Sells, Especially to Web Surfers: Internet Porn a Booming, Billion-Dollar Industry," CNNThursday, 11 December 2003. http://www.cnn.com/2003/TECH/internet/12/10/porn.business. Accessed September 12, 2005.

12. Christopher Marquis, "U.S. Says It Broke Pornography Ring Featuring Youths," New York Times, 9 August 2001, p. 6.

13. U.S. Department of Justice, Press Release, "Thomas Reedy Sentenced to Life Imprisonment in Child Porn Case," August 6, 2001. http://www.usdoj.gov/usao/txn/PressRel01/reedy_sent_pr.htm. Accessed August 25, 2004.

14. This section relies heavily on CERT® Coordination Center Denial of Service Attacks: http://www.cert.org/tech_tips/denial_of_service.html. Accessed September 8, 2005.

15. Saul Hansell, "U.S. Tally in Online-Crime Sweep: 150 Charged," New York Times, 27 August 2004, p. C1.

16. Stephen Baker and Brian Grow, "Gambling Sites, This Is a Holdup," Business Week 3895 (9 August 2004): 60–62.

17. The Computer Fraud and Abuse Act (CFAA). 18 U.S.C. §1030 (1998).

18. The Digital Millennium Copyright Act, Public Law 105-304 (1998).

19. Title 18, U.S. Code, Section 2319.

20. Title 17, U.S. Code, Section 506.

21. U.S. Department of Justice, Press Release, "Attorney General Ashcroft Announces First Criminal Enforcement Action against Peer-to-Peer Copyright Piracy," August 25, 2004.

http://www.usdoj.gov/opa/pr/2004/August/04_ag_578.htm.

22. Family Entertainment and Copyright Act of 2005, Title 18, U.S. Code Section 2319B.

23. This section is based on Richard Walker and David M. Levine, " 'You've Got Jail': Current Trends in Civil and Criminal Enforcement of Internet Securities Fraud," American Criminal Law Review 38 (2001): 405–430.

24. Jim Wolf, "Internet Scams Targeted in Sweep: A 10-Day Crackdown Leads to 62 Arrests and 88 Indictments," Boston Globe, 22 May 2001, p. A2.

25. U.S. Department of Justice, Press Release, "Alleged Leaders of $60 Million Internet Scam Indicted on Fraud and Money Laundering Charges Massive Internet Investment Fraud Case Involves 15,000 Investors from 60 Countries." January 3, 2003.

26. These sections rely on "Phishing Activity Trends Report, June 2005," Anti-Phishing Working Group. http://www.ncjrs.org/spotlight/identity_theft/publications.html#phishing. Accessed August 30, 2005; U.S. Department of Justice, Criminal Division, "Special Report of 'Phishing' (2004)." http://www.ncjrs.org/spotlight/identity_theft/publications.html#phishing. Accessed August 30, 2005.

27. U.S. Department of Justice, Press Release, "Nineteen Individuals Indicted in Internet 'Carding' Conspiracy," October 28, 2004.

28. Identity Theft and Assumption Deterrence Act, as amended by Public Law 105-318, 112 Stat. 3007 (October 30, 1998).

29. Public Law 108-275 (2004).

30. Hansell, "U.S. Tally in Online-Crime Sweep: 150 Charged."

31. Elizabeth Woyke and Dan Beucke, "Many Not-So-Happy Returns," *Business Week* (9 August 2005): 10.

32. U.S. Department of Justice, District of Massachusetts, Press Release, "Massachusetts Teen Convicted for Hacking into Internet and Telephone Service Providers and Making Bomb Threats to High Schools in Massachusetts and Florida," September 8, 2005. http://www.cybercrime.gov/juvenileSentboston.htm. Accessed September 25, 2005.

33. Anne Branscomb, "Rogue Computer Programs and Computer Rogues: Tailoring Punishment to Fit the Crime," *Rutgers Computer and Technology Law Journal* 16 (1990): 24–26.

34. Heather Jacobson and Rebecca Green, "Computer Crimes," *American Criminal Law Review* 39 (2002): 272–326.

35. U.S. Department of Justice, "Creator of 'Melissa' Computer Virus Pleads Guilty to State and Federal Charges." December 9, 1999. http://www.cybercrime.gov/melissa.htm. Accessed October 21, 2002. See Jacobson and Green, "Computer Crimes," 273–275.

36. Robert Lemos, "'MSBlast' Worm Widespread but Slowing," CNET News.com, 12 August 2003. http://news.com.com/2100-1002-5062655.html?tag=nl. Accessed September 25, 2005.

37. Department of Justice, Northern District of California, Press Release, "Federal Jury Convicts Former Technology Manager of Computer Hacking Offense: Defendant Found Guilty of Placing Computer 'Time Bomb' on Employer's Network Following Employment Dispute," September 8, 2005.

38. Department of Justice, Eastern District, Pennsylvania, Press Release, "Disgruntled Phillies Fan/Spammer Sent to Prison for Four Years," July, 14 2005. http://www.cybercrime.gov/carlson-Sent.htm. Accessed September14, 2004.

39. "Cyber Threat!" *Middle East* 335 (2003): 38–41.

40. Hyung-jin Woo, Yeora Kim, and Joseph, Dominick, "Hackers: Militants or Merry Pranksters? A Content Analysis of Defaced Web Pages," *Media Psychology* 6 (2004): 63–82.

41. Yona Hollander, "Prevent Web Page Defacement," *Internet Security Advisor* 2(2000): 1–4.

42. Debra Baker, "When Cyber Stalkers Walk," *American Bar Association Journal* 85 (1999): 50–54.

43. U.S. Department of Justice, "Cyberstalking: A New Challenge for Law Enforcement and Industry," A Report from the Attorney General to the Vice President, Washington, DC, 1999. http://www.usdoj.gov/criminal/cybercrime/cyberstalking.htm. Accessed September 12, 2005.

44. Manufacturing a Surreptitious Interception Device 3 Title 18, U.S. Code, Section 2512(1)(b); Manufacturing a Surreptitious Interception Device Title 18, U.S. Code, Section 2512(1)(b); Advertising a Surreptitious Interception Device Title 18, U.S. Code, Section 2512(1)(c)(i).

45. U.S. Department of Justice, Southern District of California, News Release, "Creator and Four Users of Loverspy Spyware Program Indicted," August 26, 2005. http://www.cybercrime.gov/perezIndict.htm. Accessed September 12, 2005.

46. Tom Yager, "Cyberspying: No Longer a Crime for Geeks Only," *InfoWorld* 22 (2000): 62.

47. Nathan Vardi, "Chinese Take Out," *Forbes* 176 (25 July 2005).

48. Nathan Thornburgh, Matthew Forney, Brian Bennett, Timothy Burger, and Elaine Shannon, "The Invasion of the Chinese Cyberspies (and the Man Who Tried to Stop Them)," *Time* 166 (5 September 2005): 10.

49. Barry C. Collin, "The Future of Cyber-Terrorism: Where the Physical and Virtual Worlds Converge," 2004. http://afgen.com/terrorism1.html. Accessed August 14, 2005.

50. Mark Pollitt, "Cyberterrorism—Fact or Fancy?" FBI Laboratory. http://www.cs.georgetown.edu/~denning/infosec/pollitt.html. Accessed August 17, 2005.

51. James Lewis, "Assessing the Risks of Cyber Terrorism, Cyber War, and Other Cyber Threats," Center for Strategic and International Studies, Washington DC, 2002.

52. Sanjeev Gupta et al., "Fiscal Consequences of Armed Conflict and Terrorism in Low- and Middle-Income Countries," *European Journal of Political Economy* 20(2004): 403–421.

53. Daniel Benjamin, *America and the World in the Age of Terrorism* (Washington, DC: CSIS Press, 2005), pp. 1–216.

54. General Accounting Office, "Critical Infrastructure Protection: Efforts of the Financial Services Sector to Address Cyber Threats Reports to the Technology Committee" (Washington, DC: January 2003).

55. Yael Shahar, "Information Warfare: The Perfect Terrorist Weapon," Institute for Counter-Terrorism,1997. http://www.ict.org.il/articles/infowar.htm. Accessed August 17, 2005.

56. Michael Whine, "Cyberspace—A New Medium for Communication, Command, and Control by Extremists," Institute for Counter-Terrorism, 1999. www.ict.org.il/articles/articledet.cfm?articleid=76, Accessed August 14, 2005.

57. General Accounting Office, "Critical Infrastructure Protection: Efforts of the Financial Services Sector to Address Cyber Threats."

58. Lewis, "Assessing the Risks of Cyber Terrorism, Cyber War, and Other Cyber Threats."

59. Gabriel Weimann, "Cyberterrorism: The Sum of All Fears?" *Studies in Conflict and Terrorism* 28 (2005): 129–150.

60. Clyde Wilson, "Software Piracy: Uncovering Mutiny on the Cyberseas," *Trial* 32 (1996): 24–31.

61. Deloitte, "2005 Global Security Survey." http://www.deloitte.com/dtt/cda/doc/content/dtt_financialservices_2005GlobalSecuritySurvey_2005-07-21.pdf. Accessed September 14, 2005.

62. Business Software Alliance, "BSA Seventh Annual Global Software Piracy Study," 2003. http://www.bsa.org/globalstudy/loader.cfm?url=/commonspot/security/getfile.cfm&pageid=16947&hitbox-done=yes. Accessed August 25, 2004.

63. Jeanne Capachin and Dave Potterton, "Online Card Payments, Fraud Solutions Bid to Win," *Meridien Research Report,* 18 January 2001.

64. Computer Security Institute, "CSI/FBI Computer Crime and Security Survey, 2005." http://www.gocsi.com. Accessed September 12, 2005.

65. Avivah Litan, "Phishing Victims Likely Will Suffer Identity Theft Fraud," May 14, 2004 (Gartner Group). http://www.gartner.com/Init.

66. Henry Pontell and Anastasia Tosouni, "Identity Theft: The Aftermath 2004, with Comparisons to the Aftermath 2003," Survey Identity Theft Resource Center, 2005.

67. David Porter, "Identity Fraud: The Stealth Threat to UK PLC," *Computer Fraud & Security* (2004): 4–7.

68. Computer Security Institute, Press Release, "Cybercrime Bleeds U.S. Corporations, Survey Shows; Financial Losses from Attacks Climb for Third Year in a Row," April 7, 2002.

69. Ibid.

70. Dean Turner, "Symantec Internet Security Threat Report," April 21, 2005.

71. Public Law 98-473, Title H, Chapter XXI, [sections] 2102(a), 98 Stat. 1837, 2190 (1984).

72. Jacobson and Green, "Computer Crime"; Identity Theft and Assumption Act of 1998 (18 U.S.C. S 1028(a)(7)).

73. Comprehensive Crime Control Act of 1984, PL 98–473, 2101–03, 98 Stat. 1837, 2190 (1984), adding 18 U.S.C. 1030 (1984); Counterfeit Active Device and Computer Fraud and Abuse Act Amended by PL 99–474, 100 Stat. 1213 (1986) codified at 18 U.S.C. 1030 (Supp. V 1987); Computer Abuse Amendments Act 18 U.S.C. section 1030 (1994); Copyright Infringement Act 17 U.S.C. section 506(a) 1994; Electronic Communications Privacy Act of 198618 U.S.C. 2510–2520 (1988 and Supp. II 1990).

74. Bruce Swartz, Deputy Assistant General, Criminal Division, Justice Department, "Internet Fraud Testimony before the House Energy and Commerce Committee," May 23, 2001.

75. IC3 Annual Internet Fraud Report, January 1, 2004–December 31, 2004. http://www.ifccfbi.gov/strategy/2004_IC 3Report.pdf.

76. Statement of Bob Weaver, Deputy Special Agent in Charge, New York Field Office, U.S. Secret Service, before the House Financial Services Committee, Subcommittee on Financial Institutions and Consumer Credit, and the Subcommittee on Oversight and Investigations, U.S. House of Representatives, April 3, 2003.

77. Steven Frank, "Toronto's Child Porn Sleuths: A Canadian Team Leads the Way in Tracking Down Global Perpetrators of Grisly Internet Child Pornography," *Time Canada* 166 (2005): 30.

78. Lois Pliant, "Information Management," Police Chief 61 (1994): 31–35.

79. Bill Goodwin, "Burglars Captured by Police Data Mining Kit," *Computer Weekly* (8 August 2002): 3.

80. "Forensic Computing Expert Warns Interpol about Computer Crime," *Information Systems Auditor* (August 2002): 2.

81. "Spotlight on Computer Imaging," *Police Chief* 66 (1999): 6–8.

82. Laura Moriarty and David Carter, *Criminal Justice Technology in the 21st Century* (Springfield, IL: Charles C Thomas Publishers, 1998).

83. William W. Bratton and Peter Knobler, *Turnaround: How America's Top Cop Reversed the Crime Epidemic* (New York: Random House, 1998), p. 289.

84. Kent.Reichert, "Use of Information Technology by Law Enforcement," University of Pennsylvania Jerry Lee Center of Criminology, Forum on Crime and Justice (December 2001).

85. U.S. Department of Justice, Office of Justice Programs, Information Technology Initiatives, "Washington State Develops Mapping System." http://it.ojp.gov/index.jsp. Accessed September 18, 2005.

86. U.S. Department of Justice, Office of Justice Programs, Information Technology Initiatives, "Where's the Emergency?" http://it.ojp.gov/index.jsp. Accessed September 18, 2005.

87. "Introduction to Biometrics," 2005. http://www.biometrics.org. Accessed August 25, 2005; Fernando L. Podio, "Biometrics—Technologies for Highly Secure Personal Authentication," *ITL Bulletin,* National Institute of Standards and Technology, 2001.

88. "Pen Computing: The Natural 'Next Step' for Field Personnel," *Law and Order* 43 (1995): 37.

89. Miller McMillan, "High Tech Enters the Field of View," *Police Chief* 62 (1994): 29.

90. Office of Community Oriented Policing Service, Press Release, "COPS Office Awards $92.7M to Help First Responders Communicate," September 9, 2005. http://www.cops.usdoj.gov/Default.asp?Item=1600. Accessed September 17, 2005.

91. Communications Assistance for Law Enforcement Act of 1994. Public L. No. 103-414, 108 Stat. 4279.

92. Michael P. Clifford, "Communications Assistance for Law Enforcement Act (CALEA)," *FBI Law Enforcement Bulletin* 71 (2002): 11–14.

93. "Today's Debate: Privacy in an Era of Terror (Part I)," *USA Today*, 2 August 2005.

94. C. Jewett, "Police Use Bait Cars to Reduce Theft," Knight Ridder/*Tribune Business News* (3 March 2003); Licensing Road Safety Autoplan Insurance, "Vancouver Police Bait Car Program," North Vancouver, Canada. December 3, 2003.

95. This and the following section rely heavily on Roberta Griffith,

96. www.tempe.gov.

97. http://www.lapdonline.org/portal/getinvolved.php?page=/get_involved/stolen_art/art_theft_main.htm. Accessed September 22, 2005.

98. This section relies heavily on Fredric I. Lederer, "The Road to the Virtual Courtroom? Consideration of Today's—and Tomorrow's—High Technology Courtrooms," *South Carolina Law Review* 799 (1999); "Criminal Court Records Go Online," *The Quill* 90 (2002): 39; Donald C. Dilworth, "New Court Technology Will Affect How Attorneys Present Trials," *Trial* 33 (1997): 100–114.

99. Doar Inc. http://www.doar.com/court_tech/evidence/index.asp. Accessed September 22, 2005.

100. http://wcca.wicourts.gov.Accessed September 30, 2005.

101. http://www.uscourts.gov/library/dirrpt00/part4.pdf. Accessed September 28, 2005.

102. http://pacer.psc.uscourts.gov. Accessed September 25, 2005.

103. The following section relies heavily on Ann H. Crowe, "Electronic Supervision: From Decision-Making to Implementation," *Corrections Today* 64 (August 2002):130: Mark Robert, "Big Brother Goes Behind Bars," *Fortune* 146 (30 September 2002): 44; Tony Fabelo, *"Technocorrections": The Promises, the Uncertain Threats Series: Sentencing & Corrections: Issues for the 21st Century* (Washington, DC: National Institute of Justice, 2000); Irwin Soonachan, "The Future of Corrections: Technological Developments Are Turning Science Fiction Into Science Fact," *Corrections Today* 62 (2000): 64–66;. Steve Morrison, "How Technology Can Make Your Job Safer," *Corrections Today* 62 (2000): 58–60.

104. Jay Stanley and Barry Steinhardt, *Bigger Monster, Weaker Chains: The Growth of an American Surveillance Society* (New York: American Civil Liberties Union, 2003).

105. Margaret Johnson and Neville Holmes, "Biometrics and the Threat to Civil Liberties," *Computer* 37 (2004): 92–94.

106. Benjamin Hale, "Identity Crisis: Face Recognition Technology and Freedom of the Will," *Ethics, Place & Environment* 8 (2005): 141–158.

107. Catherine Yang, Kerry Capell, and Otis Port, "The State of Surveillance," *Business Week* 3946 (8 August 2005): 52–59.

108. W. Kip Viscusi and Richard J. Zeckhauser, "Sacrificing Civil Liberties to Reduce Terrorism Risks," Harvard University, Olin Center for Law, Economics, and Business, 2003. http://www.law.harvard.edu/programs/olin_center.

109. Craig Arndt, "The Loss of Privacy and Identity," *Biometric Technology Today* 13 (2005): 6–7.

110. "Today's Debate: Privacy in an Era of Terror (Part I)," *USA Today* (8 February 2005).

111. American Bar Association, "Technologically-Assisted Physical Surveillance," Standard 2-9.1, General Principles. http://www.abanet.org/crimjust/standards/taps_toc.html. Accessed September 22, 2005.

acquaintance rape Forcible sex in which offender and victim are acquainted with each other.

acquaintance robbery Robbers who focus their thefts on people they know.

active precipitation The view that the source of many criminal incidents is the aggressive or provocative behavior of victims.

actual authority The authority a corporation knowingly gives to an employee.

actus reus An illegal act. The *actus reus* can be an affirmative act, such as taking money or shooting someone, or a failure to act, such as failing to take proper precautions while driving a car.

adolescent-limited offender Offender who follows the most common criminal trajectory, in which antisocial behavior peaks in adolescence and then diminishes.

aggravated rape Rape involving multiple offenders, weapons, and victim injuries.

aging out The process by which individuals reduce the frequency of their offending behavior as they age. It is also known as spontaneous remission, because people are believed to spontaneously reduce the rate of their criminal behavior as they mature. Aging out is thought to occur among all groups of offenders.

alien conspiracy theory The view that organized crime was imported to the United States by Europeans and that crime cartels have a policy of restricting their membership to people of their own ethnic background.

American Dream The goal of accumulating material goods and wealth through individual competition; the process of being socialized to pursue material success and to believe it is achievable.

anal stage In Freud's schema, the second and third years of life, when the focus of sexual attention is on the elimination of bodily wastes.

androgens Male sex hormones.

anomie A condition produced by normlessness. Because of rapidly shifting moral values, the individual has few guides to what is socially acceptable. According to Merton, anomie is a condition that occurs when personal goals cannot be achieved by available means. In Agnew's revision, anomie can occur when positive or valued stimuli are removed or negative or painful ones applied.

antithesis An opposing argument.

apparent authority Authority that a third party, like a customer, reasonably believes the agent has to perform the act in question.

arousal theory A view of crime suggesting that people who have a high arousal level seek powerful stimuli in their environment to maintain an optimal level of arousal. These stimuli are often associated with violence and aggression. Sociopaths may need greater than average stimulation to bring them up to comfortable levels of living; this need explains their criminal tendencies.

arson The intentional or negligent burning of a home, structure, or vehicle for criminal purposes such as profit, revenge, fraud, or crime concealment.

arson for profit People looking to collect insurance money, but who are afraid or unable to set the fire themselves, hire professional arsonists. These professionals have acquired the skills to set fires yet make the cause seem accidental.

arson fraud A business owner burns his or her property, or hires someone to do it, to escape financial problems.

assault An attack that may not involve physical contact; includes attempted battery or intentionally frightening the victim by word or deed.

atavistic anomalies According to Lombroso, the physical characteristics that distinguish born criminals from the general population and are throwbacks to animals or primitive people.

at risk Children and adults who lack the education and skills needed to be effectively in demand in modern society.

attention deficit hyperactivity disorder (ADHD) A psychological disorder in which a child shows developmentally inappropriate impulsivity, hyperactivity, and lack of attention.

authority conflict pathway The path to a criminal career that begins with early stubborn behavior and defiance of parents.

automated fingerprint identification systems (AFIS) A criminal identification process that uses mathematical models to classify fingerprints and identify up to 250 characteristics (minutiae) of the print.

automatic teller machines (ATMs) An unattended electronic machine in a public place connected to a data system and related equipment and used by bank customers to obtain cash withdrawals and other banking services.

battery A physical attack that includes hitting, punching, slapping, or other offensive touching of a victim.

behavior modeling Process of learning behavior (notably aggression) by observing others. Aggressive models may be parents, criminals in the neighborhood, or characters on television or in video games and movies.

behaviorism The branch of psychology concerned with the study of observable behavior rather than unconscious motives. It focuses on the relationship between particular stimuli and people's responses to them.

bias crimes Violent acts directed toward a particular person or members of a group merely because the targets share a discernible racial, ethnic, religious, or gender characteristic; also called hate crimes.

biological determinism A belief that crimogenic traits can be acquired through indirect heredity from a degenerate family whose members suffered from such ills as insanity, syphilis, and alcoholism, or through direct heredity—being related to a family of criminals.

biometrics Automated methods of recognizing a person based on a physiological or behavioral characteristic.

biophobia Sociologists who held the view that no serious consideration should be given to biological factors when attempting to understand human nature.

biosocial theory An approach to criminology that focuses on the interaction between biological and social factors as they relate to crime.

bipolar disorder An emotional disturbance in which moods alternate between periods of wild elation and deep depression.

boosters Professional shoplifters who steal with the intention of reselling stolen merchandise.

bourgeoisie In Marxist theory, the owners of the means of production; the capitalist ruling class.

brothel A house of prostitution, typically run by a madam who sets prices and handles "business" arrangements.

brutalization effect The belief that capital punishment creates an atmosphere of brutality that enhances rather than deters the level of violence in society. The death penalty reinforces the view that violence is an appropriate response to provocation.

bucketing A form of stockbroker chiseling in which brokers skim customer trading profits by falsifying trade information.

burglary Breaking into and entering a home or structure for the purposes of committing a felony.

California Personality Inventory (CPI) A frequently administered personality test used to distinguish deviants from nondeviant groups.

call girls Prostitutes who make dates via the phone and then service customers in hotel rooms or apartments. Call girls typically have a steady clientele who are repeat customers.

capable guardians Effective deterrents to crime, such as police or watchful neighbors.

capitalist bourgeoisie The owners of the means of production.

career criminals Persons who repeatedly violate the law and organize their lifestyle around criminality.

carjacking Theft of a car by force or threat of force.

cartographic school of criminology An approach developed in Europe in the early nineteenth century making use of social statistics to provide important demographic information on the population, including density, gender, religious affiliations, and wealth. Many of the relationships between crime and social phenomena identified then still serve as a basis for criminology today.

cerebral allergies A physical condition that causes brain malfunction due to exposure to some environmental or biochemical irritant.

check kiting Fraud that involves drawing money from one bank account that does not have sufficient funds to cover the check and depositing in a second bank account. Before the check is submitted to the first bank for payment, the kiter deposits a check written off the second bank account, which also has insufficient funds. The kiter illegally collects interest on the two accounts.

chemical restraints Antipsychotic drugs such as Haldol, Stelazine, Prolixin, and Risperdal, which help control levels of neurotransmitters (such as serotonin/dopamine), that are used to treat violence-prone people; also called chemical straightjackets.

chemical straightjackets Another term for chemical restraints; antipsychotic drugs used to treat violence-prone people.

Chicago School Group of urban sociologists who studied the relationship between environmental conditions and crime.

child abuse Any physical, emotional, or sexual trauma to a child for which no reasonable explanation, such as an accident, can be found. Child abuse can also be a function of neglecting to give proper care and attention to a young child.

chiseling Crimes that involve using illegal means to cheat an organization, its consumers, or both, on a regular basis.

chivalry hypothesis The idea that low female crime and delinquency rates are a reflection of the leniency with which police treat female offenders.

chronic offenders According to Wolfgang, delinquent offenders who are arrested five or more times before they are 18 and who stand a good chance of becoming adult criminals; such offenders are responsible for more than half of all serious crimes.

chronic victimization Those who have been crime victims maintain a significantly higher chance of future victimization than people who have remained nonvictims. Most repeat victimizations occur soon after a previous crime has occurred, suggesting that repeat victims share some personal characteristic that makes them a magnet for predators.

churning A white-collar crime in which a stockbroker makes repeated trades to fraudulently increase commissions.

classical criminology The theoretical perspective suggesting that (1) people have free will to choose criminal or conventional behaviors; (2) people choose to commit crime for reasons of greed or personal need; and (3) crime can be controlled only by the fear of criminal sanctions.

cleared crimes Crimes are cleared in two ways: when at least one person is arrested, charged, and turned over to the court for prosecution; or by exceptional means, when some element beyond police control precludes the physical arrest of an offender (for example, the offender leaves the country).

closure A term used by Lemert to describe people from a middle-class background

who have little identification with a criminal subculture but cash bad checks because of a financial crisis that demands an immediate resolution.

Code of Hammurabi The first written criminal code developed in Babylonia around 4,000 years ago.

cognitive theory The study of the perception of reality and of the mental processes required to understand the world in which we live.

cohort A sample of subjects whose behavior is followed over a period of time.

collective efficacy Social control exerted by cohesive communities, based on mutual trust, including intervention in the supervision of children and maintenance of public order.

college boy A disadvantaged youth who embraces the cultural and social values of the middle class and actively strives to be successful by those standards. This type of youth is embarking on an almost hopeless path, because he is ill-equipped academically, socially, and linguistically to achieve the rewards of middle-class life.

commitment to conformity A strong personal investment in conventional institutions, individuals, and processes that prevents people from engaging in behavior that might jeopardize their reputation and achievements.

common law Early English law, developed by judges, that incorporated Anglo-Saxon tribal custom, feudal rules and practices, and the everyday rules of behavior of local villages. Common law became the standardized law of the land in England and eventually formed the basis of the criminal law in the United States.

communist manifesto In this document, Marx focused his attention on the economic conditions perpetuated by the capitalist system. He stated that its development had turned workers into a dehumanized mass who lived an existence that was at the mercy of their capitalist employers.

compurgation In early English law, a process whereby an accused person swore an oath of innocence while being backed up by a group of twelve to twenty-five "oathhelpers," who would attest to his character and claims of innocence.

computer virus A program that disrupts or destroys existing programs and networks, causing them to perform the task for which the virus was designed.

computer worm A program that attacks computer networks (or the Internet) by self-replicating and "sending" itself to other users, generally via e-mail without the aid of the operator.

conduct disorder (CD) A psychological condition marked by repeated and severe episodes of antisocial behaviors.

conduct norms Behaviors expected of social group members. If group norms conflict with those of the general culture, members of the group may find themselves described as outcasts or criminals.

confidence game A swindle, usually involving a get-rich-quick scheme, often with illegal overtones, so that the victim will be afraid or embarrassed to call the police.

conflict view The view that human behavior is shaped by interpersonal conflict and that those who maintain social power will use it to further their own needs.

conscience One of two parts of the superego; it distinguishes between what is right and wrong.

consensus view The belief that the majority of citizens in a society share common ideals and work toward a common good and that crimes are acts that are outlawed because they conflict with the rules of the majority and are harmful to society.

consent In prosecuting rape cases, it is essential to prove that the attack was forced and that the victim did not give voluntary consent to her attacker. In a sense, the burden of proof is on the victim to show that her character is beyond question and that she in no way encouraged, enticed, or misled the accused rapist. Proving victim dissent is not a requirement in any other violent crime.

constructive possession In the crime of larceny, willingly giving up temporary physical possession of property but retaining legal ownership.

contagion effect Genetic predispositions and early experiences make some people, including twins, susceptible to deviant behavior, which is transmitted by the presence of antisocial siblings in the household.

containment theory The idea that a strong self-image insulates a youth from the pressures and pulls of crimogenic influences in the environment.

contextual discrimination A practice in which African Americans receive harsher punishments in some instances (as when they victimize whites) but not in others (as when they victimize other blacks).

continuity of crime The view that crime begins early in life and continues throughout the life course. Thus, the best predictor of future criminality is past criminality.

Control Balance Theory According to Tittle, a developmental theory that attributes deviant and criminal behaviors to imbalances between the amount of control that the individual has over others and that others have over him or her.

corner boy According to Cohen, a role in the lower-class culture in which young men remain in their birth neighborhood, acquire families and menial jobs, and adjust to the demands of their environment.

corporate crime White-collar crime involving a legal violation by a corporate entity, such as price fixing, restraint of trade, or hazardous waste dumping.

covert pathway A path to a criminal career that begins with minor underhanded behavior and progresses to fire starting and theft.

crackdowns The concentration of police resources on particular problem areas, such as street-level drug dealing, to eradicate or displace criminal activity.

crime A violation of societal rules of behavior as interpreted and expressed by a criminal legal code created by people holding social and political power. Individuals who violate these rules are subject to sanctions by state authority, social stigma, and loss of status.

crime discouragers Discouragers can be grouped into three categories: guardians, who monitor targets (such as store security guards); handlers, who monitor potential offenders (such as parole officers and parents); and managers, who monitor places (such as homeowners and doorway attendants).

crime displacement An effect of crime prevention efforts in which efforts to control crime in one area shift illegal activities to another.

crime mapping A research technique that employs computerized crime maps and other graphic representations of crime data patterns.

crime typology The study of criminal behavior involving research on the links between different types of crime and criminals. Because people often disagree about types of crimes and criminal motivation, no standard exists within the field. Some typologies focus on the criminal, suggesting the existence of offender groups, such as professional criminals, psychotic criminals, occasional criminals, and so on. Others focus on the crimes, clustering them into categories such as property crimes, sex crimes, and so on.

criminal anthropology Early efforts to discover a biological basis of crime through measurement of physical and mental processes.

criminal justice system The agencies of government—police, courts, and corrections—responsible for apprehending, adjudicating, sanctioning, and treating criminal offenders.

criminality A personal trait of the individual as distinct from a "crime," which is an event.

criminological enterprise The areas of study and research that taken together make up the field of criminology. Criminologists typically specialize in one of the subareas of criminology, such as victimology or the sociology of law.

criminologists Researchers who use scientific methods to study the nature, extent, cause, and control of criminal behavior.

criminology The scientific study of the nature, extent, cause, and control of criminal behavior.

crisis intervention Emergency counseling for crime victims.

critical criminologists Researchers who view crime as a function of the capitalist mode of production and not the social conflict that might occur in any society regardless of its economic system.

critical criminology The view that capitalism produces haves and have-nots, each engaging in a particular branch of criminality. The mode of production shapes social life. Because economic competitiveness is the essence of capitalism, conflict increases and eventually destabilizes social institutions and the individuals within them.

critical feminist Scholars, both male and female, who focus on the effects of gender inequality and the unequal power of men and women in a capitalist society.

cross-sectional survey Uses survey data derived from all age, race, gender, and income segments of the population measured simultaneously. Because people from every age group are represented, age-specific crime rates can be determined. Proponents believe this is a sufficient substitute for the more expensive longitudinal approach that follows a group of subjects over time to measure crime rate changes.

crusted over Children who have been victims of or witnesses to violence and do not let people inside, nor do they express their feelings. They exploit others and in turn are exploited by those older and stronger; as a result, they develop a sense of hopelessness.

cultural deviance theory Branch of social structure theory that sees strain and social disorganization together resulting in a unique lower-class culture that conflicts with conventional social norms.

cultural transmission The concept that conduct norms are passed down from one generation to the next so that they become stable within the boundaries of a culture. Cultural transmission guarantees that group lifestyle and behavior are stable and predictable.

culture conflict According to Sellin, a condition brought about when the rules and norms of an individual's subcultural affiliation conflict with the role demands of conventional society.

culture of poverty The view that people in the lower class of society form a separate culture with its own values and norms that are in conflict with conventional society; the culture is self-maintaining and ongoing.

cyber crime A criminal enterprise that involves the theft and/or destruction of information, resources, or funds utilizing computers, computer networks, and the Internet.

cyber spying Illegally using the Internet to gather information from a victim that is considered private and confidential and that compromises the victim's privacy.

cyber stalking Using the Internet, e-mail, or other electronic communication devices to stalk or harass another person.

cyber terrorism Politically motivated attacks designed to compromise the electronic infrastructure of enemies and to disrupt their economy.

cyber theft The use of computer networks for criminal profits. Illegal copyright infringement, identity theft, and Internet securities fraud are examples of cyber theft.

cyber vandalism Malicious attacks aimed at disrupting, defacing, and destroying technology.

cycle of violence The idea that victims of crime, especially childhood abuse, are more likely to commit crimes themselves.

data mining Using sophisticated computer software to conduct analysis of behavior patterns in an effort to identify crime patterns and link them to suspects.

date rape Forcible sex during a courting relationship.

death squads Government troops used to destroy political opposition parties.

deconstructionist An approach that focuses on the use of language by those in power to define crime based on their own values and biases; also called postmodernist.

decriminalized Reducing the penalty for a criminal act but not actually legalizing it.

defective intelligence Traits such as feeble-mindedness, epilepsy, insanity, and defective social instinct, which Goring

believed had a significant relationship to criminal behavior.

defensible space The principle that crime prevention can be achieved through modifying the physical environment to reduce the opportunity individuals have to commit crime.

deliberation Planning a homicide after careful thought, however brief, rather than acting on sudden impulse.

delinquent boy A youth who adopts a set of norms and principles in direct opposition to middle-class values, engaging in short-run hedonism, living for today and letting tomorrow take care of itself.

demystify To unmask the true purpose of law, justice, or other social institutions.

denial of service attack Extorting money from an Internet service user by threatening to prevent the user from having access to the service.

Department of Homeland Security (DHS) An agency of the federal government charged with preventing terrorist attacks within the United States, reducing America's vulnerability to terrorism, and minimizing the damage and aiding recovery from attacks that do occur.

desist To spontaneously stop committing crime.

deterrence theory The view that if the probability of arrest, conviction, and sanctioning increases, crime rates should decline.

developmental theory A branch of criminology that examines change in a criminal career over the life course. Developmental factors include biological, social, and psychological change. Among the topics of developmental criminology are desistance, resistance, escalation, and specialization.

deviant behavior Behavior that departs from the social norm.

deviant place theory People become victims because they reside in socially disorganized, high-crime areas where they have the greatest risk of coming into contact with criminal offenders.

dialectic method For every idea, or thesis, there exists an opposing argument, or antithesis. Because neither position can ever be truly accepted, the result is a merger of the two ideas, a synthesis. Marx adapted this analytic method for his study of class struggle.

Differential Association Theory According to Sutherland, the principle that criminal acts are related to a person's exposure to an excess amount of antisocial attitudes and values.

differential opportunity The view that lower-class youths, whose legitimate opportunities are limited, join gangs and pursue criminal careers as alternative means to achieve universal success goals.

differential reinforcement Behavior is reinforced by being either rewarded or punished while interacting with others; also called direct conditioning.

Differential Reinforcement Theory An attempt to explain crime as a type of learned behavior. First proposed by Akers in collaboration with Burgess in 1966, it is a version of the social learning view that employs differential association concepts as well as elements of psychological learning theory.

differential social control A process of labeling that may produce a reevaluation of the self, which reflects actual or perceived appraisals made by others.

Differential Social Support and Coercion Theory (DSSCT) According to Colvin, a theory that holds that perceptions of coercion become ingrained and guide reactions to adverse situations that arise in both family and nonfamily settings.

diffusion An effect that occurs when an effort to control one type of crime has the unexpected benefit of reducing the incidence of another.

direct conditioning Behavior is reinforced by being either rewarded or punished while interacting with others; also called differential reinforcement.

discouragement An effect that occurs when an effort to eliminate one type of crime also controls others, because it reduces the value of criminal activity by limiting access to desirable targets.

disorders Psychological problems (formerly labeled neuroses or psychoses), such as anxiety disorders, mood disorders, and conduct disorders.

disputatiousness A cultural norm that considers violence an appropriate response to a conflict situation.

diversion programs Programs of rehabilitation that remove offenders from the normal channels of the criminal justice system, thus avoiding the stigma of a criminal label.

division of markets Firms divide a region into territories, and each firm agrees not to compete in the others' territories.

dramatization of evil As the negative feedback of law enforcement agencies, parents, friends, teachers, and other figures amplifies the force of the original label, stigmatized offenders may begin to reevaluate their own identities. The person becomes the thing he is described as being.

drift According to Matza, the view that youths move in and out of delinquency and that their lifestyles can embrace both conventional and deviant values.

early onset A term that refers to the assumption that a criminal career begins early in life and that people who are deviant at a very young age are the ones most likely to persist in crime.

ecological view A belief that social forces operating in urban areas create criminal interactions; some neighborhoods become natural areas for crime.

economic crime An act in violation of the criminal law that is designed to bring financial gain to the offender.

edgework The excitement or exhilaration of successfully executing illegal activities in dangerous situations.

egalitarian families Families in which spouses share similar positions of power at home and in the workplace.

ego The part of the personality, developed in early childhood, that helps control the id and keep people's actions within the boundaries of social convention.

ego ideal Part of superego; directs the individual into morally acceptable and responsible behaviors, which may not be pleasurable.

elder abuse A disturbing form of domestic violence by children and other relatives with whom elderly people live.

eldercide The murder of a senior citizen.

Electra complex A stage of development when girls begin to have sexual feelings for their fathers.

electroencephalograph (EEG) A device that can record the electronic impulses given off by the brain, commonly called brain waves.

embezzlement A type of larceny that involves taking the possessions of another (fraudulent conversion) that have been placed in the thief's lawful possession for safekeeping, such as a bank teller misappropriating deposits or a stockbroker making off with a customer's account.

enterprise crime The use of illegal tactics to gain profit in the marketplace. Enterprise crimes can involve both the violation of law in the course of an otherwise legitimate occupation or the sale and distribution of illegal commodities.

enterprise theory of investigation (ETI) A standard investigation tool of the FBI that focuses on criminal enterprise and investigation attacks on the structure of the criminal enterprise rather than on criminal acts viewed as isolated incidents.

equipotentiality View that all individuals are equal at birth and are thereafter influenced by their environment.

eros The instinct to preserve and create life; eros is expressed sexually.

e-tailing fraud Using the Internet to illegally buy or sell merchandise.

exploitation (of criminals) Using others to commit crimes: for example, as contract killers or drug runners.

exploitation (of victims) Forcing victims to pay for services to which they have a clear right.

expressive crimes Crimes that have no purpose except to accomplish the behavior at hand, such as shooting someone.

expressive violence Violence that is designed not for profit or gain but to vent rage, anger, or frustration.

extinction The phenomenon in which a crime prevention effort has an immediate impact that then dissipates as criminals adjust to new conditions.

false pretenses Illegally obtaining money, goods, or merchandise from another by fraud or misrepresentation.

familicide Killing of one's family.

felony A serious offense that carries a penalty of incarceration in a state prison, usually for one year or more. People convicted of felony offenses lose the right to vote, hold elective office, or maintain certain licenses.

felony murder A homicide in the context of another felony, such as robbery or rape; legally defined as first-degree murder.

fence A buyer and seller of stolen merchandise.

feticide Endangering or killing an unborn fetus.

filicide Murder of children.

first-degree murder The killing of another person after premeditation and deliberation.

fixated An adult that exhibits behavior traits characteristic of those encountered during infantile sexual development.

flash houses Public meeting places in England, often taverns, that served as headquarters for gangs.

flashover An effect in a fire when heat and gas at the ceiling of a room reach 2,000 degrees, and clothes and furniture burst into flame, duplicating the effects of arsonists' gasoline or explosives. It is possible that many suspected arsons are actually the result of flashover.

focal concerns According to Miller, the value orientations of lower-class cultures; features include the needs for excitement,

trouble, smartness, fate, and personal autonomy.

fraud Taking the possessions of another through deception or cheating, such as selling a person a desk that is represented as an antique but is known to be a copy.

front running A form of stockbroker chiseling in which brokers place personal orders ahead of a large order from a customer to profit from the market effects of the trade.

gang rape Forcible sex involving multiple attackers.

gateway model An explanation of drug abuse that posits that users begin with a more benign drug (alcohol or marijuana) and progress to ever-more potent drugs.

gay bashing Violent hate crimes directed toward people because of their sexual orientation.

general deterrence A crime control policy that depends on the fear of criminal penalties. General deterrence measures, such as long prison sentences for violent crimes, are aimed at convincing the potential law violator that the pains associated with crime outweigh its benefits.

General Strain Theory (GST) According to Agnew, the view that multiple sources of strain interact with an individual's emotional traits and responses to produce criminality.

General Theory of Crime (GTC) According to Gottfredson and Hirschi, a developmental theory that modifies social control theory by integrating concepts from biosocial, psychological, routine activities, and rational choice theories.

gentrification A residential renewal stage in which obsolete housing is replaced and upgraded; areas undergoing such change seem to experience an increase in their crime rates.

globalization The process of creating transnational markets, politics, and legal systems in an effort to form and sustain a global economy.

good burglar Professional burglars use this title to characterize colleagues who have distinguished themselves as burglars. Characteristics of the good burglar include technical competence, maintenance of personal integrity, specialization in burglary, financial success, and the ability to avoid prison sentences.

grand larceny Theft of money or property of substantial value, punished as a felony.

group boycott A company's refusal to do business with retail stores that do not comply with its rules or desires.

guerilla The term means "little war" and developed out of the Spanish rebellion against French troops after Napoleon's 1808 invasion of the Iberian Peninsula. Today the term is used interchangeably with the term *terrorist*.

hate crimes Acts of violence or intimidation designed to terrorize or frighten people considered undesirable because of their race, religion, ethnic origin, or sexual orientation.

heels Professional shoplifters who steal with the intention of reselling stolen merchandise to pawnshops or fences, usually at half the original price.

homophobia Extremely negative overreaction to homosexuals.

homosexuality Erotic interest in members of one's own sex.

humanistic psychology A branch of psychology that stresses self-awareness and "getting in touch with feelings."

human nature theory A belief that personal traits, such as genetic makeup, intelligence, and body build, may outweigh the importance of social variables as predictors of criminal activity.

hypoglycemia A condition that occurs when glucose (sugar) levels in the blood fall below the necessary level for normal and efficient brain functioning.

id The primitive part of people's mental makeup, present at birth, that represents unconscious biological drives for food, sex, and other life-sustaining necessities. The id seeks instant gratification without concern for the rights of others.

identity crisis A psychological state, identified by Erikson, in which youth face inner turmoil and uncertainty about life roles.

identity theft Using the Internet to steal someone's identity and/or impersonate the victim in order to conduct illicit transactions such as committing fraud using the victim's name and identity.

inchoate offenses Incomplete or contemplated crimes such as criminal solicitation or criminal attempts.

incivilities Rude and uncivil behavior; behavior that indicates little caring for the feelings of others.

index crimes The eight crimes that, because of their seriousness and frequency, the FBI reports the incidence of in the annual Uniform Crime Report. Index crimes include murder, rape, assault, robbery, burglary, arson, larceny, and motor vehicle theft.

infanticide The murder of a very young child.

inferiority complex People who have feelings of inferiority and compensate for them with a drive for superiority.

influence peddling Using an institutional position to grant favors and sell information to which their co-conspirators are not entitled.

informal sanctions Disapproval, stigma, or anger directed toward an offender by significant others (parents, peers, neighbors, teachers), resulting in shame, embarrassment, and loss of respect.

information processing A branch of cognitive psychology that focuses on the way people process, store, encode, retrieve, and manipulate information to make decisions and solve problems.

information technology (IT) A term that connotes all forms of technology used to create, store, retrieve, and exchange data in all its various forms including electronic, voice, and still images.

inheritance school Advocates of this view trace the activities of several generations of families believed to have an especially large number of criminal members.

insider trading Illegal buying of stock in a company based on information provided by someone who has a fiduciary interest in the company, such as an employee or an attorney or accountant retained by the firm. Federal laws and the rules of the Securities and Exchange Commission require that all profits from such trading be returned and provide for both fines and a prison sentence.

institutional anomie theory The view that anomie pervades U.S. culture because the drive for material wealth dominates and undermines social and community values.

instrumental crimes Offenses designed to improve the financial or social position of the criminal.

instrumental critical theory The view that criminal law and the criminal justice system are capitalist instruments for controlling the lower class.

instrumental violence Violence used in an attempt to improve the financial or social position of the criminal.

integrated theories Models of crime causation that weave social and individual variables into a complex explanatory chain.

interactionist view The view that one's perception of reality is significantly influenced by one's interpretations of the reactions of others to similar events and stimuli.

interdisciplinary science Involving two or more academic fields.

international terrorism Terrorism involving citizens or the territory of more than one country.

involuntary manslaughter A homicide that occurs as a result of acts that are negligent

and without regard for the harm they may cause others, such as driving under the influence of alcohol or drugs.

La Cosa Nostra A national syndicate of twenty-five or so Italian-dominated crime families who control crime in distinct geographic areas.

labeling theory Theory that views society as creating deviance through a system of social control agencies that designate certain individuals as deviants. The stigmatized individual is made to feel unwanted in the normal social order. Eventually, the individual begins to believe that the label is accurate, assumes it as a personal identity, and enters into a deviant or criminal career.

larceny Taking for one's own use the property of another, by means other than force or threats on the victim or forcibly breaking into a person's home or workplace; theft.

latency A developmental stage that begins at age 6. During this period, feelings of sexuality are repressed until the genital stage begins at puberty; this marks the beginning of adult sexuality.

latent delinquency A psychological predisposition to commit antisocial acts because of an id-dominated personality that renders an individual incapable of controlling impulsive, pleasure-seeking drives.

latent trait A stable feature, characteristic, property, or condition, present at birth or soon after, that makes some people crime prone over the life course.

latent trait theories Theoretical views that criminal behavior is controlled by a master trait, present at birth or soon after, that remains stable and unchanging throughout a person's lifetime.

left realism An approach that views crime as a function of relative deprivation under capitalism and that favors pragmatic, community-based crime prevention and control.

legal code The specific laws that fall within the scope of criminal law.

liberal feminist theory Theory suggesting that the traditionally lower crime rate for women can be explained by their second-class economic and social position. As women's social roles have changed and their lifestyles have become more like those of men, it is believed that their crime rates will converge.

life course persister One of the small group of offenders whose criminal career continues well into adulthood.

life course theories Theoretical views studying changes in criminal offending patterns over a person's entire life. Are there conditions or events that occur later in life that influence the way people behave, or is behavior predetermined by social or personal conditions at birth?

lifestyle theory People may become crime victims because their lifestyle increases their exposure to criminal offenders.

logic bomb A delayed-action computer virus that waits for a particular signal such as a date to appear before launching itself and disrupting network applications.

lumpen proletariat The fringe members at the bottom of society who produce nothing and live, parasitically, off the work of others.

madam A woman who employs prostitutes, supervises their behavior, and receives a fee for her services.

Mafia A criminal society that originated in Sicily, Italy, and is believed to control racketeering in the United States.

mala in se crimes Acts that are outlawed because they violate basic moral values, such as rape, murder, assault, and robbery.

mala prohibitum crimes Acts that are outlawed because they clash with current norms and public opinion, such as tax, traffic, and drug laws.

malware A malicious software program.

manslaughter A homicide without malice.

marginal deterrence The concept that a penalty for a crime may prompt commission of a marginally more severe crime because that crime receives the same magnitude of punishment as the original one.

marginalization Displacement of workers, pushing them outside the economic and social mainstream.

marital exemption The practice in some states of prohibiting the prosecution of husbands for the rape of their wives.

marital rape Forcible sex between people who are legally married to each other.

mark The target of a con man or woman.

Marxist criminologists Criminologists who view crime as a product of the capitalist system.

Marxist criminology The view that crime is a product of the capitalist system; also known as critical criminology or radical criminology.

Marxist feminism The approach that explains both victimization and criminality among women in terms of gender inequality, patriarchy, and the exploitation of women under capitalism.

masculinity hypothesis The view that women who commit crimes have biological and psychological traits similar to those of men.

mass murder The killing of a large number of people in a single incident by an offender who typically does not seek concealment or escape.

mechanical solidarity A characteristic of a pre-industrial society, which is held together by traditions, shared values, and unquestioned beliefs.

mens rea "Guilty mind." The mental element of a crime or the intent to commit a criminal act.

meta-analysis A research technique that uses the grouped data from several different studies.

middle-class measuring rods According to Cohen, the standards by which teachers and other representatives of state authority evaluate lower-class youths. Because they cannot live up to middle-class standards, lower-class youths are bound for failure, which gives rise to frustration and anger at conventional society.

Minnesota Multiphasic Personality Inventory (MMPI) A widely used psychological test that has subscales designed to measure many different personality traits, including psychopathic deviation (Pd scale), schizophrenia (Sc scale), and hypomania (Ma scale).

mission hate crimes Violent crimes committed by disturbed individuals who see it as their duty to rid the world of evil.

moral crusaders Rule creators who engage in activities to rid the world of behavior they consider wrong and depraved. Typically, moral crusaders are directed at public order crimes, such as drug abuse or pornography, although they are also interested in policy issues such as teaching evolution.

moral development The way people morally represent and reason about the world.

moral entrepreneurs Interest groups that attempt to control social life and the legal order in such a way as to promote their own personal set of moral values. People who use their influence to shape the legal process in ways they see fit.

Mosaic Code The laws of the ancient Israelites, found in the Old Testament of the Judeo-Christian Bible.

motivated offenders The potential offenders in a population. According to rational choice theory, crime rates will vary according to the number of motivated offenders.

Multidimensional Personality Questionnaire (MPQ) A test that allows researchers to assess such personality traits as control, aggression, alienation, and well-being.

Evaluations using this scale indicate that adolescent offenders who are crime prone maintain negative emotionality, a tendency to experience aversive affective states such as anger, anxiety, and irritability.

murder The unlawful killing of a human being (homicide) with malicious intent.

naive check forgers Amateurs who cash bad checks because of some financial crisis but have little identification with a criminal subculture.

narcissistic personality disorder A condition marked by a persistent pattern of self-importance, need for admiration, lack of empathy, and preoccupation with fantasies of unlimited success, power, brilliance, beauty, or ideal love.

National Crime Victimization Survey (NCVS) The ongoing victimization study conducted jointly by the Justice Department and the U.S. Census Bureau that surveys victims about their experiences with law violation.

National Incident-Based Reporting System (NIBRS) A relatively new program that requires local police agencies to provide a brief account of each incident and arrest within twenty-two crime patterns, including incident, victim, and offender information.

nature theory The view that intelligence is largely determined genetically and that low intelligence is linked to criminal behavior.

negative affective states According to Agnew, the anger, depression, disappointment, fear, and other adverse emotions that derive from strain.

negative reinforcement Using either negative stimuli (punishment) or loss of reward (negative punishment) to curtail unwanted behaviors.

neglect Not providing a child with the care and shelter to which he or she is entitled.

negligent manslaughter A homicide that occurs as a result of acts that are negligent and without regard for the harm they may cause others, such as driving under the influence of alcohol or drugs; also called involuntary manslaughter.

neocortex A part of the human brain; the left side of the neocortex controls sympathetic feelings toward others.

neuroallergies Allergies that affect the nervous system and cause the allergic person to produce enzymes that attack wholesome foods as if they were dangerous to the body. They may also cause swelling of the brain and produce sensitivity in the central nervous system—conditions that are linked to mental, emotional, and behavioral problems.

neurophysiology The study of brain activity.

neutralization theory Neutralization theory holds that offenders adhere to conventional values while "drifting" into periods of illegal behavior. In order to drift, people must first overcome (neutralize) legal and moral values.

nonnegligent manslaughter A homicide committed in the heat of passion or during a sudden quarrel; although intent may be present, malice is not; also called voluntary manslaughter.

normative groups Groups, such as the high school in-crowd, that conform to the social rules of society.

nurture theory The view that intelligence is not inherited but is largely a product of environment. Low IQ scores do not cause crime but may result from the same environmental factors.

obscenity According to current legal theory, sexually explicit material that lacks a serious purpose and appeals solely to the prurient interest of the viewer. While nudity per se is not usually considered obscene, open sexual behavior, masturbation, and exhibition of the genitals is banned in most communities.

obsessive-compulsive disorder An extreme preoccupation with certain thoughts and compulsive performance of certain behaviors.

occasional criminals Offenders who do not define themselves by a criminal role or view themselves as committed career criminals.

Oedipus complex A stage of development when males begin to have sexual feelings for their mothers.

offender-specific crime The idea that offenders evaluate their skills, motives, needs, and fears before deciding to commit crime.

offense-specific crime The idea that offenders react selectively to the characteristics of particular crimes.

oral stage In Freud's schema, the first year of life, when a child attains pleasure by sucking and biting.

ordeal Based on the principle of divine intervention and the then-prevalent belief that divine forces would not allow an innocent person to be harmed, this was a way of determining guilt involving such measures as having the accused place his or her hand in boiling water or hold a hot iron to see if God would intervene and heal the wounds. If the wound healed, the person was found not guilty; conversely, if the wound did not heal, the accused was deemed guilty of the crime for which he or she was being punished.

organic solidarity Postindustrial social systems, which are highly developed and dependent upon the division of labor; people are connected by their interdependent needs for one another's services and production.

organizational crime Crime that involves large corporations and their efforts to control the marketplace and earn huge profits through unlawful bidding, unfair advertising, monopolistic practices, or other illegal means.

organized crime Illegal activities of people and organizations whose acknowledged purpose is profit through illegitimate business enterprise.

overt pathway Pathway to a criminal career that begins with minor aggression, leads to physical fighting, and eventually escalates to violent crime.

paranoid schizophrenics Individuals who suffer complex behavior delusions involving wrongdoing or persecution—they think everyone is out to get them.

paraphilias Bizarre or abnormal sexual practices that may involve recurrent sexual urges focused on objects, humiliation, or children.

Part I crimes Another term for index crimes; eight categories of serious, frequent crimes.

Part II crimes All crimes other than index and minor traffic offenses. The FBI records annual arrest information for Part II offenses.

passive precipitation The view that some people become victims because of personal and social characteristics that make them attractive targets for predatory criminals.

paternalistic families Traditional family model in which fathers assume the role of breadwinners, while mothers tend to have menial jobs or remain at home to supervise domestic matters.

patriarchy A society in which men dominate public, social, economic, and political affairs.

peacemaking An approach that considers punitive crime control strategies to be counterproductive and favors the use of humanistic conflict resolution to prevent and control crime.

pedophiles Sexual offenders who target children.

penology An aspect of criminology that overlaps with criminal justice; penology involves the correction and control of known criminal offenders.

permeable neighborhood Areas with a greater than usual number of access streets from traffic arteries into the neighborhood.

persistence The idea that those who started their delinquent careers early and who committed serious violent crimes throughout adolescence were the most likely to persist as adults.

personality The reasonably stable patterns of behavior, including thoughts and emotions, that distinguish one person from another.

petit (petty) larceny Theft of a small amount of money or property, punished as a misdemeanor.

phallic stage In Freud's schema, the third year, when children focus their attention on their genitals.

phishing (carding and spoofing) Illegally acquiring personal information, such as bank passwords and credit card numbers, by masquerading as a trustworthy person or business in what appears to be an official electronic communication, such as an e-mail or an instant message. The term *phishing* comes from the lures used to "fish" for financial information and passwords.

phrenologist A scientist who studied the shape of the skull and bumps on the head to determine whether these physical attributes are linked to criminal behavior; phrenologists believed that external cranial characteristics dictate which areas of the brain control physical activity.

physiognomist A scientist who studied the facial features of criminals to determine whether the shape of ears, nose, and eyes and the distance between them are associated with antisocial behavior.

pigeon drop A con game in which a package or wallet containing money is "found" by a con man or woman. A passing victim is stopped and asked for advice about what to do, and soon another "stranger," who is part of the con, approaches and enters the discussion. The three decide to split the money; but first, one of the swindlers goes off to consult a lawyer. The lawyer claims the money can be split up, but each party must prove he or she has the means to reimburse the original owner, should one show up. The victim then is asked to give some good-faith money for the lawyer to hold. When the victim goes to the lawyer's office to pick up a share of the loot, he or she finds the address bogus and the money gone. In the new millennium, the pigeon drop has been appropriated by corrupt telemarketers, who contact typically elderly victims over the phone to bilk them out of their savings.

pilferage Theft by employees through stealth or deception.

pleasure principle According to Freud, a theory in which id-dominated people are driven to increase their personal pleasure without regard to consequences.

poachers Early English thieves who typically lived in the country and supplemented their diet and income with game that belonged to a landlord.

population All people who share a particular personal characteristic, such as all high school students or all police officers.

pornography Sexually explicit books, magazines, films, or tapes intended to provide sexual titillation and excitement for paying customers.

positivism The branch of social science that uses the scientific method of the natural sciences and suggests that human behavior is a product of social, biological, psychological, or economic forces.

postmodernist Approach that focuses on the use of language by those in power to define crime based on their own values and biases; also called deconstructionist.

posttraumatic stress disorder (PTSD) Psychological reaction to a highly stressful event; symptoms may include depression, anxiety, flashbacks, and recurring nightmares.

power The ability of people and groups to control the behavior of others, to shape public opinion, and to define deviance.

power–control theory The view that gender differences in crime are a function of economic power (class position, one-versus two-earner families) and parental control (paternalistic versus egalitarian families).

precedent A rule derived from previous judicial decisions and applied to future cases; the basis of common law.

preemptive deterrence An approach in which community organizations strive to eliminate or reduce crime before police involvement becomes necessary.

premeditation Consideration of a homicide before it occurs.

premenstrual syndrome (PMS) The stereotype that several days prior to and during menstruation females are beset by irritability and poor judgment as a result of hormonal changes.

price fixing A conspiracy to set and control the price of a necessary commodity.

primary deviance According to Lemert, deviant acts that do not help redefine the self-image and public image of the offender.

primary prevention programs Treatment programs that seek to correct or remedy personal problems before they manifest themselves as crime.

problem behavior syndrome (PBS) A cluster of antisocial behaviors that may include family dysfunction, substance abuse, smoking, precocious sexuality and early pregnancy, educational underachievement, suicide attempts, sensation seeking, and unemployment, as well as crime.

productive forces Technology, energy sources, and material resources.

productive relations The relationships that exist among the people producing goods and services.

professional criminals Offenders who make a signficant portion of their income from crime.

professional fence An individual who earns his or her living solely by buying and re-selling stolen merchandise.

proletariat A term used by Marx to refer to the working class members of society who produce goods and services but who do not own the means of production.

prosocial bonds Socialized attachment to conventional institutions, activities, and beliefs.

prostitution The granting of nonmarital sexual access for remuneration.

psychoanalytic (psychodynamic) perspective Branch of psychology holding that the human personality is controlled by unconscious mental processes developed early in childhood.

psychopathic personality A personality characterized by a lack of warmth and feeling, inappropriate behavior responses, and an inability to learn from experience. Some psychologists view psychopathy as a result of childhood trauma; others see it as a result of biological abnormality.

psychosis A mental state in which the perception of reality is distorted. People experiencing psychosis hallucinate, have paranoid or delusional beliefs, change personality, exhibit disorganized thinking, and engage in unusual or bizarre behavior.

public order crimes Acts that are considered illegal because they threaten the general well-being of society and challenge its accepted moral principles. Prostitution, drug use, and the sale of pornography are considered public order crimes.

racial profiling Selecting suspects on the basis of their ethnic or racial background.

Racketeer Influenced and Corrupt Organizations (RICO) Act Federal legislation that enables prosecutors to bring additional criminal or civil charges against people whose multiple criminal acts constitute a conspiracy. RICO features monetary penalties that allow the government to confiscate all profits derived from criminal activities. Originally intended to be used against organized criminals, RICO has also been used against white-collar criminals.

radical criminologists Criminologists who view crime as a product of the capitalist system.

radical criminology The view that crime is a product of the capitalist system; also known as Marxist criminology or critical criminology.

rape Unlawful sexual intercourse with a female without her consent.

rational choice The view that crime is a function of a decision-making process in which the potential offender weighs the potential costs and benefits of an illegal act.

reaction formation According to Cohen, rejecting goals and standards that seem impossible to achieve. Because a boy cannot hope to get into college, for example, he considers higher education a waste of time.

reactive (defensive) hate crimes Perpetrators believe they are taking a defensive stand against outsiders who they believe threaten their community or way of life.

reality principle According to Freud, the ability to learn about the consequences of one's actions through experience.

reasoning criminal According to the rational choice approach, law-violating behavior occurs when an offender decides to risk breaking the law after considering both personal factors (such as the need for money, revenge, thrills, and entertainment) and situational factors (how well a target is protected and the efficiency of the local police force).

reciprocal altruism According to sociobiology, acts that are outwardly designed to help others but that have at their core benefits to the self.

reflective role taking According to Matsueda and Heimer, the phenomenon that occurs when youths who view themselves as delinquents give an inner voice to their perceptions of how significant others feel about them.

reintegrative shaming A method of correction that encourages offenders to confront their misdeeds, experience shame because of the harm they caused, and then be reincluded in society.

relative deprivation The condition that exists when people of wealth and poverty live in close proximity to one another.

Some criminologists attribute crime rate differentials to relative deprivation.

restitution agreements A condition of probation in which the offender repays society or the victim of crime for the trouble the offender caused. Monetary restitution involves a direct payment to the victim as a form of compensation. Community service restitution may be used in victimless crimes and involves work in the community in lieu of more severe criminal penalties.

restorative justice Using humanistic, non-punitive strategies to right wrongs and restore social harmony.

restorative justice model View that emphasizes the promotion of a peaceful, just society through reconciliation and reintegration of the offender into society.

retaliatory hate crimes A hate crime motivated by revenge for another hate crime, either real or imaginary, which may spark further retaliation.

retrospective cohort study A study that uses an intact cohort of known offenders and looks back into their early life experiences by checking their educational, family, police, and hospital records.

retrospective reading The reassessment of a person's past to fit a current generalized label.

road rage A term used to describe motorists who assault each other.

robbery Taking or attempting to take something of value by force or threat of force and/or by putting the victim in fear.

role exit behaviors In order to escape from a stifling life in male-dominated families, girls may try to break away by running away and or even attempting suicide.

routine activities theory The view that the volume and distribution of predatory crime is closely related to the interaction of suitable targets, motivated offenders, and capable guardians.

sampling Selecting a limited number of people for study as representative of a larger group.

schizophrenia A type of psychosis often marked by bizarre behavior, hallucinations, loss of thought control, and inappropriate emotional responses. Schizophrenic types include catatonic, which characteristically involves impairment of motor activity; paranoid, which is characterized by delusions of persecution; and hebephrenic, which is characterized by immature behavior and giddiness.

scientific method A systematic means of investigation involving observation to test scientific hypotheses that can then be used to construct valid theories.

secondary deviance According to Lemert, accepting deviant labels as a personal identity. Acts become secondary when they form a basis for self-concept, as when a drug experimenter becomes an addict.

secondary prevention programs Treatment programs aimed at helping offenders after they have been identified.

second-degree murder A homicide with malice but not premeditation or deliberation, as when a desire to inflict serious bodily harm and a wanton disregard for life result in the victim's death.

selective incapacitation The policy of creating enhanced prison sentences for the relatively small group of dangerous chronic offenders.

self-control A strong moral sense that renders a person incapable of hurting others or violating social norms.

self-control theory According to Gottfredson and Hirschi, the view that the cause of delinquent behavior is an impulsive personality. Kids who are impulsive may find that their bond to society is weak.

self-report surveys A research approach that requires subjects to reveal their own participation in delinquent or criminal acts.

semiotics The use of language elements as signs or symbols beyond their literal meaning.

sentencing circle A peacemaking technique in which offenders, victims, and other community members are brought together in an effort to formulate a sanction that addresses the needs of all.

serial killer Someone who kills a large number of people over time and who seeks to escape detection.

serial rape Multiple rapes committed by one person over time.

sexual abuse Exploitation of a child through rape, incest, or molestation by a parent or other adult.

Sherman Antitrust Act Law that subjects to criminal or civil sanctions any person "who shall make any contract or engage in any combination or conspiracy" in restraint of interstate commerce.

shield laws Laws designed to protect rape victims by prohibiting the defense attorney from inquiring about their previous sexual relationships.

shoplifting The taking of goods from retail stores.

siblicide Sibling homicide. The median age of sibling homicide offenders is 23, and the median age of their victims is 25. The vast majority of sibling homicide offenders are males (87 percent), and they are most likely to kill their brothers. When lethal violence by brothers against their sisters occurs, it is more likely in juvenile sibling relationships rather than adult sibling relationships (31 percent versus 14 percent). Sisters killing their brothers or sisters are relatively rare events.

siege mentality Residents who become so suspicious of authority that they consider the outside world to be the enemy out to destroy the neighborhood.

situational crime prevention A method of crime prevention that stresses tactics and strategies to eliminate or reduce particular crimes in narrow settings, such as reducing burglaries in a housing project by increasing lighting and installing security alarms.

situational inducement Short-term influence on a person's behavior, such as financial problems or peer pressure, that increases risk taking.

skeezers Prostitutes who trade sex for drugs, usually crack.

skilled thieves Thieves who typically work in the larger cities, such as London and Paris. This group includes pickpockets, forgers, and counterfeiters, who operated freely.

smugglers Thieves who move freely in sparsely populated areas and transport goods, such as spirits, gems, gold, and spices, without bothering to pay tax or duty.

snitches Amateur shoplifters who do not self-identify as thieves but who systematically steal merchandise for personal use.

social bond Ties a person has to the institutions and processes of society. According to Hirschi, elements of the social bond include commitment, attachment, involvement, and belief.

social capital Positive relations with individuals and institutions that are life sustaining.

social conflict theory The view that crime is a function of class conflict and power relations. Laws are created and enforced by those in power to protect their own interests.

social control function The ability of society and its institutions to control, manage, restrain, or direct human behavior.

social control theory The view that people commit crime when the forces that bind them to society are weakened or broken.

social development model (SDM) A developmental theory that attributes criminal behavior patterns to childhood socialization and pro- or antisocial attachments over the life course.

social disorganization theory Branch of social structure theory that focuses on the breakdown of institutions such as the family, school, and employment in inner-city neighborhoods.

social ecologists Social scientists who believe that current social, political, environmental, and ecological trends impact and structure human behavior.

social ecology Environmental forces that have a direct influence on human behavior.

social harm A view that behaviors harmful to other people and society in general must be controlled. These acts are usually outlawed, but some acts that cause enormous amounts of social harm are perfectly legal, such as the consumption of tobacco and alcohol.

socialization Process of human development and enculturation. Socialization is influenced by key social processes and institutions.

socialization view One view is that people learn criminal attitudes from older, more experienced law violators. Another view is that crime occurs when children develop an inadequate self-image, which renders them incapable of controlling their own misbehavior. Both of these views link criminality to the failure of socialization, the interactions people have with the various individuals, organizations, institutions, and processes of society that help them mature and develop.

social learning theory The view that human behavior is modeled through observation of human social interactions, either directly from observing those who are close and from intimate contact, or indirectly through the media. Interactions that are rewarded are copied, while those that are punished are avoided.

social process theory The view that criminality is a function of people's interactions with various organizations, institutions, and processes in society.

social reaction theory The view that people become criminals when significant members of society label them as such and they accept those labels as a personal identity. Also known as labeling theory.

social reality of crime The view that the main purpose of criminology is to promote a peaceful, just society.

social structure theory The view that disadvantaged economic class position is a primary cause of crime.

sodomy Illegal sexual intercourse. Sodomy has no single definition, and acts included

within its scope are usually defined by state statute.

somatotype A system developed for categorizing people on the basis of their body build.

spam Mass e-mail that is commercial in nature, not requested by the recipients, and sent without a prior business or personal relationship.

specific deterrence A crime control policy suggesting that punishment be severe enough to convince convicted offenders never to repeat their criminal activity.

stalking A pattern of behavior directed at a specific person that includes repeated physical or visual proximity, unwanted communications, and/or threats sufficient to cause fear in a reasonable person.

status frustration A form of culture conflict experienced by lower-class youths because social conditions prevent them from achieving success as defined by the larger society.

statutory crimes Crimes defined by legislative bodies in response to changing social conditions, public opinion, and custom.

statutory rape Sexual relations between an underage individual and an adult; though not coerced, an underage partner is considered incapable of giving informed consent.

stigma An enduring label that taints a person's identity and changes him or her in the eyes of others.

stigmatized People who are labeled as outcasts or deviants because they have been accused of dishonorable conduct.

sting An undercover police operation in which police pose as criminals to trap law violators.

sting or swindle A white-collar crime in which people use their institutional or business position to trick others out of their money.

strain The emotional turmoil and conflict caused when people believe they cannot achieve their desires and goals through legitimate means. Members of the lower class might feel strain because they are denied access to adequate educational opportunities and social support.

strain theorists Criminologists who view crime as a direct result of lower-class frustration and anger.

strain theory Branch of social structure theory that sees crime as a function of the conflict between people's goals and the means available to obtain them.

stratified society Grouping according to social strata or levels. American society is considered stratified on the basis of economic class and wealth.

street crime Common theft-related offenses such as larcenies and burglaries, embezzlement, and theft by false pretenses.

strict liability crimes Illegal acts whose elements do not contain the need for intent, or *mens rea;* they are usually acts that endanger the public welfare, such as illegal dumping of toxic wastes.

structural critical theory The view that criminal law and the criminal justice system are means of defending and preserving the capitalist system.

subculture A group that is loosely part of the dominant culture but maintains a unique set of values, beliefs, and traditions.

subculture of violence Norms and customs that, in contrast to society's dominant value system, legitimize and expect the use of violence to resolve social conflicts.

subterranean values Morally tinged influences that have become entrenched in the culture but are publicly condemned. They exist side by side with conventional values and while condemned in public may be admired or practiced in private.

sufferance The aggrieved party does nothing to rectify a conflict situation; over time, the unresolved conflict may be compounded by other events that cause an eventual eruption.

suitable targets According to routine activities theory, targets for crime that are relatively valuable, easily transportable, and not capably guarded.

superego Incorporation within the personality of the moral standards and values of parents, community, and significant others.

surplus value The Marxist view that the laboring classes produce wealth that far exceeds their wages and goes to the capitalist class as profits.

symbolic interaction theory The sociological view that people communicate through symbols. People interpret symbolic communication and incorporate it within their personality. A person's view of reality, then, depends on his or her interpretation of symbolic gestures.

synthesis A merger of two opposing ideas.

systematic forgers Professionals who make a living by passing bad checks.

systematic review A research technique that involves collecting the findings from previously conducted studies, appraising and synthesizing the evidence, and using the collective evidence to address a particular scientific question.

target hardening strategies Making one's home or business crime proof through the use of locks, bars, alarms, and other devices.

target removal strategies Displaying dummy or disabled goods as a means of preventing shoplifting.

technocorrections The use of information technology to minimize security risks in secure correctional institutions.

temperance movement An effort to prohibit the sale of liquor in the United States that resulted in the passage of the Eighteenth Amendment to the Constitution in 1919, which prohibited the sale of alcoholic beverages.

terrorism The illegal use of force against innocent people to achieve a political objective.

terrorist group Any group practicing, or that has significant subgroups that practice, international terrorism.

tertiary prevention programs Treatment programs aimed at helping offenders that may be a requirement of a probation program, part of a diversionary sentence, or aftercare at the end of a prison sentence.

testosterone The principal male steroid hormone. Testosterone levels decline during the life cycle and may explain why violence rates diminish over time.

thanatos According to Freud, the instinctual drive toward aggression and violence.

theory of anomie A modified version of the concept of anomie developed by Merton to fit social, economic, and cultural conditions found in modern U.S. society. He found that two elements of culture interact to produce potentially anomic conditions: culturally defined goals and socially approved means for obtaining them.

thesis In the philosophy of Hegel, an original idea or thought.

three strikes Policies whereby people convicted of three felony offenses receive a mandatory life sentence.

thrill-seeking hate crimes Acts by hate-mongers who join forces to have fun by bashing minorities or destroying property; inflicting pain on others gives them a sadistic thrill.

trait theory The view that criminality is a product of abnormal biological and/or psychological traits.

transitional neighborhood An area undergoing a shift in population and structure, usually from middle-class residential to lower-class mixed use.

Trojan horse A malicious computer program that appears to be a benign application but contains illicit codes that can damage computer systems.

truly disadvantaged Wilson's term for the lowest level of the underclass; urban, inner-city, socially isolated people who occupy the bottom rung of the social ladder and are the victims of discrimination.

turning points According to Laub and Sampson, the life events that alter the development of a criminal career.

tying arrangement A corporation requires customers of one of its services to use other services it offers.

underclass The lowest social stratum in any country, whose members lack the education and skills needed to function successfully in modern society.

Uniform Crime Report (UCR) Large database, compiled by the Federal Bureau of Investigation, of crimes reported and arrests made each year throughout the United States.

USA Patriot Act (USAPA) Legislation giving U.S. law enforcement agencies a freer hand to investigate and apprehend suspected terrorists.

utilitarianism The view that people's behavior is motivated by the pursuit of pleasure and the avoidance of pain.

victim compensation The victim ordinarily receives compensation from the state to pay for damages associated with the crime. Rarely are two compensation schemes alike, however, and many state programs suffer from lack of both adequate funding and proper organization within the criminal justice system. Compensation may be made for medical bills, loss of wages, loss of future earnings, and counseling. In the case of death, the victim's survivors can receive burial expenses and aid for loss of support.

victimization (by the justice system) While the crime is still fresh in their minds, victims may find that the police interrogation following the crime is handled callously, with innuendos or insinuations that they were somehow at fault. Victims have difficulty learning what is going on in the case; property is often kept for a long time as evidence and may never be returned. Some rape victims report that the treatment they receive from legal, medical, and mental health services is so destructive that they cannot help but feel "re-raped."

victimization survey A statistical survey (such as the NCVS) that measures the amount, nature, and patterns of victimization in the population.

victimless crimes Crimes that violate the moral order but in which there is no actual victim or target. In these crimes, which include drug abuse and sex offenses, it is society as a whole and not an individual who is considered the victim.

victimologist A person who studies the victim's role in criminal transactions.

victim precipitation theory The idea that the victim's behavior was the spark that ignited the subsequent offense, as when the victim abused the offender verbally or physically.

victim-witness assistance programs Government programs that help crime victims and witnesses; may include compensation, court services, and/or crisis intervention.

vigilantes Individuals who go on moral crusades without any authorization from legal authorities. The assumption is that it is okay to take matters into your own hands if the cause is right and the target is immoral.

virility mystique The belief that males must separate their sexual feelings from needs for love, respect, and affection.

voluntary manslaughter A homicide committed in the heat of passion or during a sudden quarrel; although intent may be present, malice is not.

warez Refers to efforts of organized groups to download and sell copyrighted software in violation of its license.

web defacement Occurs when a computer hacker intrudes on another person's website by inserting or substituting codes that expose site visitors to misleading or provocative information.

Wechsler Adult Intelligence Scale One of the standard IQ tests.

Wernicke-Korsakoff disease A deadly neurological disorder.

white-collar crime Illegal acts that capitalize on a person's status in the marketplace. White-collar crimes can involve theft, embezzlement, fraud, market manipulation, restraint of trade, and false advertising.

workplace violence Irate employees or former employees attack coworkers or sabotage machinery and production lines; now considered the third leading cause of occupational injury or death.

CASE INDEX

Dodge, Kenneth, 172 *n*.219; 209 *n*.97; 244 *n*.15; 313 *n*.43
Dohrenwend, Bruce, 248 *n*.160
Dominick, Joseph, 497 *n*.40
Dong, Jie, 474
Donker, Andrea, 313 *n*.49
Donnelly, Patrick, 90 *n*.76
Donnerstein, Edward, 361 *n*.118; 461 *nn*.97, 98
Donohue, John J., III, 40–42
Donovan, John, 311 *n*.17; 463 *n*.168
Doran, Michael Scott, 352–353
Doraz, Walter, 166 *n*.28
Dornfeld, Maude, 312 *n*.27
Douglas, William O., 426
Dove, Alan, 486
Downey, Douglas, 207 *n*.20
Downey, Robert, Jr., 102
Downs, William, 88 *n*.13; 249 *n*.195
Doyle, Daniel, 359 *n*.44
Drake, Christina, 48–50
Drake, Francis, 350
Drake, J. J. P., 167 *n*.59
Drass, Kriss, 14–15; 210 *n*.129; 362 *n*.152
Dressler, Joshua, 22–23
Drew, Christopher, 363 *n*.187
Driver, Edwin, 171 *n*.180
Drugge, Jeffe, 361 *n*.114
Dugdale, Richard, 166 *n*.4
Duhart, Detis, 364 *n*.256
Dulmus, Catherine, 245 *n*.39
Dunaway, Faye, 368
Dunaway, R. Gregory, 62 *nn*.66, 71; 63 *n*.94; 246 *n*.74; 248 *n*.148; 303
Duncan, David, 402
Duncan, Greg J., 207 *nn*.11–14, 17; 208 *n*.80
Duncan, Joseph E., III, 130
Duncan, Susan C., 188
Duncan, Terry E., 188
Dunford, Franklyn, 116–117
D'Unger, Amy, 65 *n*.149; 313 *n*.45
Dunlop, Eloise, 314 *n*.77
Dupey, Thaddeus, 296
Durkheim, Émile, 9; 10, 11; 26 *nn*.20, 21; 144; 191
Durose, Matthew, 464 *n*.216
Durrant, Lynne, 315 *n*.135
Duwe, Grant, 337; 363 *n*.184
Dwiggins, Donna, 63 *n*.94
Dworkin, Andrea, 426; 459 *n*.3; 461 *n*.85
Dyson, Laronistine, 89 *n*.20

Earls, Felton, 65 *n*.147; 209 *n*.95; 210 *n*.118; 323; 359 *nn*.39, 40
Earnest, Terri, 208 *n*.59

Earp, Wyatt, 325
East, Rebecca, 284
Eaves, Lindon, 170 *nn*. 142, 143
Ebbers, Bernie, 403
Eccles, Jacquelynne, 167 *n*.42
Echouafni, Jay R., 471
Eck, John, 126 *nn*.92, 93
Edelhertz, Herbert, 422 *nn*.77, 86
Edwards, Edwin, 399
Egger, Steven, 363 *n*.182
Eggleston, Carolyn, 63 *n*.94
Egley, Arlen, Jr., 206 *nn*.1, 2
Ehrlich, Isaac, 128 *n*.170
Eichenwald, Kurt, 402–403; 422 *n*.58
Einstein, Stanley, 423 *n*.118
Eisen, Seth, 170 *n*.143
Eitzen, D. Stanley, 422 *n*.93
Elder, Glen, 248 *n*.138; 314 *n*.76; 315 *n*.117
Eley, Thalia, 170 *n*.154
Elizabeth I, England, 350
Elkind, Peter, 402–403
Ellingworth, Dan, 89 *n*.34
Elliott, Amanda, 209 *n*.115
Elliott, Delbert, 62 *nn*.67, 68; 63 *n*.108; 116–117; 125 *n*.86; 208 *n*.57; 209 *n*.115; 210 *n*.120; 245 *n*.48; 249 *n*.193; 315 *n*.112
Ellis, Lee, 166 *nn*.7, 9, 11–13, 15; 167 *nn*.48–50; 169 *nn*.112, 113, 116; 170 *n*.146; 171 *nn*.166, 172; 246 *n*.75; 314 *nn*.80, 88; 329; 361 *nn*. 106, 107
Ellisor, David Lee, 366
Elstein, Sharon, 361 *n*.104
Emerson, Robert M., 364 *n*.259
Engel, Robin Shepard, 64 *n*.113; 172 *n*.204
Engels, Friedrich, 26 *n*. 23; 253; 255; 277 *nn*.3, 7
Ennett, Susan, 64 *n*.131
Enos, V. Pualani, 83
Enrich, David, 460 *n*.53
Epstein, Gil, 125 *n*.50
Epstein, Joel, 422 *n*.87
Erez, Edna, 91 *n*.93
Erickson, Kai, 234; 248 *n*.164
Erickson, Maynard, 127 *n*.138
Erickson, Rosemary, 26 *n*.25
Erikson, Erik, 150
Erlanger, Howard, 360 *n*.63
Ernst, Frederick, 358 *n*.4
Eron, L., 172 *n*.224
Erwin, Brigette, 89 *n*.27
Esagian, Gkaro, 358 *n*.4
Esbensen, Finn-Aage, 63 *n*.101; 208 *n*.79; 211 *n*.193; 315 *n*.118

Esmail, Aneez, 362 *n*.173
Espelage, Dorothy, 63 *n*.97; 171 *n*.193
Espirito Santo, Maria Eugenia Do, 460 *n*.70
Estes, Richard J., 88 *n*.3; 435; 460 *n*.75
Estrich, Susan, 89 *n*.44; 361 *n*.131
Etheredge, Gina, 460 *n*.70
Evans, Gary, 207 *n*.15
Evans, Jeff, 167 *n*.68
Evans, Rhonda, 422 *n*.82
Evans, T. David, 62 *n*.66; 63 *n*.94; 210 *n*.150; 246 *n*.74; 248 *n*.148; 303
Eve, Raymond, 63 *n*.99
Evers, Tag, 274–275
Eves, Anita, 136–137
Ewing, Charles Patrick, 359 *n*.31; 364 *n*.230
Eysenck, Hans, 158; 173 *nn*.236, 238
Eysenck, M . W., 173 *n*.238
Ezell, Michael, 65 *n*.149

Fabelo, Tony, 498 *n*.103
Factor-Litvak, Pamela, 168 *n*.72
Fader, James, 64 *n*.142
Faga, Jeffrey, 207 *n*.32
Fagan, Abigail, 169 *n*.135
Fagan, Jeffrey A., 116–117; 207 *n*.40; 211 *n*.176; 227; 247 *n*.111
Fairweather, David, 361 *n*.114
Falck, Russel, 463 *n*.188
Fallon, Rebecca, 302
Falwell, Jerry, 428
Famularo, Richard, 171 *n*.194; 245 *n*.26
Fantaye, Dawit Kiors, 392 *n*.65
Faraon, Stephen, 170 *n*.143
Farley, Chris, 102
Farley, Reynolds, 64 *n*.135
Farnworth, Margaret, 62 *n*.63; 246 *n*.69; 292
Farr, Kathryn Ann, 465 *n*.236
Farrall, Stephen, 312 *n*.38; 313 *n*.54
Farrell, Graham, 89 *nn*.35, 36, 38; 386; 392 *n*.82
Farrell, Michael, 462 *n*.150
Farrington, David P., 38; 61 *nn*.29, 34, 39; 64 *n*.140; 79; 89 *nn*.35, 36, 52; 90 *n*.73; 109; 143; 169 *nn*.125, 127, 128, 132–134; 249 *n*.206; 300–301; 307–308; 311 *nn*.15, 20; 312 *nn*.25, 34; 359 *nn*.38, 58; 391 *n*.30
Farrooque, Rokeya, 358 *n*.4
Fass, Simon, 391 *n*.18

Faupel, Charles, 463 nn.185–187
Fazel, Seena, 358 n.19
Fein, Robert, 362 n.168
Feinberg, Joel, 459 n.7
Feinberg, Seth, 211 n.168
Feingold, Alan, 314 n.107
Fejes-Mendoza, Kathy, 63 n.94
Feldman, Shirley, 161
Fell, James, 127 n.125
Felman, James, 365 n.283
Felson, Marcus, 78–79, 81; 80; 90 nn.63, 75; 106, 107; 108; 125 nn.73, 84; 126 n.92; 376
Felson, Richard, 60 n.4; 90 n.69; 125 n.63; 211 n.175; 343; 359 n.47; 361 n.121; 362 nn.156, 157; 363 nn.218–220
Fendrich, Michael, 61 n.25; 460 n.64; 462 n.141
Fenton, Terence, 171 n.194
Ferguson, H. Bruce, 166 n.30
Fergusson, David, 40–42; 219; 312 n.28; 313 n.43
Ferracuti, Franco, 26 n. 24; 323; 359 n.43
Ferrell, Jeff, 125 n.78
Ferri, Enrico, 132; 166 n.3
Ferris, Kerry O., 364 n.259
Feucht, Thomas, 362 n.167
Feyerherm, William, 249 n.186
Fienberg, Stephen, 167 n.70
Figert, Anne E., 167 n.54
Figlio, Robert, 57; 63 n.109; 64 nn.136–138, 143; 125 n.49; 311 n.5
Figuerdo, Aurelio, 171 nn.167, 168
Finckenauer, James O., 416–417
Finkelhor, David, 74; 89 n.37; 360 n.99; 363 nn.201, 203, 204; 460 n.74
Finkelstein, Claire, 8
Finn, Peter, 88 n.11; 90 n.84; 91 nn.112, 113
Firestone, David, 421 n.16
Fischer, Mariellen, 168 n.100
Fishbein, Diana, 139; 166 n.33; 167 nn.57, 58; 168 n.80
Fisher, Bonnie, 76–77; 89–90 n.53; 348; 360 n.96; 364 n.262
Fisher, Gene, 40–42
Flaherty, Austin, 91 n.98
Flaherty, Sara, 91 n.98
Flanagan, Timothy, 60 n.20
Flannery, Daniel, 63 nn.94, 99; 314 n.81
Flay, Brian, 125 n.60; 462 n.160
Fletcher, Kenneth, 168 n.100
Flewelling, Robert, 61 n.27; 64 n.131; 359 n.59; 454

Flint, Anthony, 461 nn.113, 118
Flynn, Kevin, 363 n.190
Flynt, Larry, 338
Foch, Terryl, 169 n.118
Fogel, C. A., 168 n.75
Foglia, Wanda, 127 nn.132, 147; 128 n.148
Fong, Grace, 168 n.87
Ford, C. S., 459 n.25
Forde, David, 314 n.92
Formby, John P., 178
Formby, William, 126 nn.105, 108
Forney, Matthew, 497 n.48
Forster, Bruce, 160–161
Forsythe, Lubica, 392 n.77
Foster, Hilliard, 172 n.204
Foster, Holly, 280 n.99; 311 n.12
Foster, Jodie, 154; 330
Foster, Raymond E., 486
Fox, Ben, 125 n.62
Fox, James Alan, 44; 61 n.44; 336; 337; 362 nn.147, 174, 179; 363 n.183; 364 nn.250, 254; 461 n.99
Fox, Stephen, 372
Fraga-Vallejo, Miguel, 460 n.71
Francis, Janice, 391 n.18
Frank, Nancy, 420 n.6; 422 n.65
Frank, Steven, 498 n.77
Franklin, J. M., 173 n.261
Franklin, Joseph Paul, 338
Franks, John, 459 n.11
Franz Ferdinand, Archduke, 350
Frauenheim, Ed, 496 n.3
Frazee, Sharon Glave, 125 n.67
Freedman, Jonathan, 154–156
Freeman-Gallant, Adrienne, 169 n.129
Freemon, Melinda, 60 n.19
Freisthler, Bridget, 208 n.78
Frendrich, Michael, 463 n.174
Frenken, J., 360 n.85
Freud, Sigmund, 8; 149–150; 321; 358 n.9
Frey, William, 64 n.135
Fricker-Elhai, Adrienne, 462 n.153
Friedlander, Robert, 364 nn.268, 2712
Friedman, Andrea, 429; 459 n.21
Friedman, Daniel, 90 n.77
Friedrichs, David, 260–261; 278 n.41; 420 n.3
Friedrichs, Jessica, 260–261; 278 n.41
Fritsch, Eric, 126 n.89; 127 n.122
Fromm-Auch, Delee, 173 n.259
Frone, Michael, 360 n.80
Frost, Laurie, 160–161
Frye, Terry, 370

Frye, Victoria, 341
Fuchs, Siegmund Fred, 360 n.71
Fuentes, Angel Ilarraza, 364 n.260
Fuentes, Thomas V., 423 n.115
Fukurai, Hiroshi, 249 n.179
Fulkerson, Andrew, 125 n.87
Fulton, Betsy, 281 n.144
Furr, L. Allen, 48–50
Fyfe, James, 40–42; 126 n.116

Gabrielli, William, 170 n.159; 173 n.258
Gacy, Wayne, 336
Gaffney, Michael, 209 n.91
Gagnon, C., 65 n.146
Gagnon, John, 361 n.113
Gainey, Randy, 209 n.104
Galaway, Burt, 91 n.95
Gale, Nathan, 125 n.49
Gall, Franz Joseph, 8
Galvin, Jim, 249 n.171
Galway, Roberta, 378
Gans, Dian, 166 n.32
Gant, Charles, 169 n.102
Garcia, Luis, 364 n.247
Gardner, Carol Brooks, 364 n.259
Garfinkle, Harold, 235; 249 n.174
Garner, Connie Chenoweth, 247 n.128; 248 n.133
Garner, Joel H., 116–117
Garnier, Helen, 248 n.131
Garofalo, James, 90 n.56; 91 n.111; 364 nn.227, 239
Garofalo, Raffaele, 132; 166 n.2
Garry, Eileen M., 388
Gartin, Patrick, 116–117; 128 n.166
Gartner, Rosemary, 89 n.47; 114–115
Gary, Faye, 341
Gasca, Johnny Ray, 94, 96; 472
Gastil, Raymond, 324; 360 n.62
Gates, Bill, 193
Gebhard, Paul, 361 n.113
Geis, Gilbert, 60 n.6; 391 n.11; 420 n.13; 421 n.54
Geller, Susan Rose, 315 n.134
Gelles, Richard, 245 n.26; 363 n.198; 363 nn.202, 213
Gembrowski, Susan, 392 n.61
George, David, 168 n.87
Georges-Abeyie, Daniel, 64 n.114; 364 nn.269, 270
Gerber, Jurg, 464 n.209
Gerdes, D., 167 n.40
Gere, Richard, 433
Gerstein, Dean, 244 n.22; 312 n.26
Gertz, Marc, 47; 48–50; 62 n.59; 125 n.65; 208 nn.69, 70, 72
Gesch, C. Bernard, 136–137

Giambi, Jason, 424
Giancola, Peter, 462 n.151
Gibbons, Donald, 391 n.45
Gibbs, David, 116–117
Gibbs, Jack, 127 n.138; 249 n.202;
    279 n.62; 364 n.267
Gibbs, John, 63 n.94; 124 n.44; 125
    n.69; 303
Gibbs, Natalie, 125 n.75; 360 n.87
Gibson, Chris, 209 n.91
Gibson, Evelyn, 342
Giever, Dennis, 303; 314 n.95
Gifford, Robert, 392 n.79
Giglio, Greg, 42; 202
Gilchrist, Lewayne, 313 n.44
Gilliard, Darrell, 464 n.202
Gillis, A. R., 280 n.98
Gillis, Roy, 364 n.238
Ginzburg, Eli, 62 n.75; 311 n.18;
    312 n.23; 464 nn.204, 227
Giordano, Peggy, 61 n.23; 210 n.138;
    245 n.47; 248 n.146; 249
    n.188; 290–291; 311 n.11;
    315 nn.114, 132; 391 n.44
Giordano, Philip, 66
Giroux, Bruce, 312 n.30
Gjeruldsen, Susanne Rogne, 358
    n.19
Glass, Nancy, 341
Glazer, Daniel, 166 n.16; 461 n.125
Gleason, Walter, 89 n.18
Glennerster, Howard, 177
Glueck, Eleanor, 158; 173 n.235;
    244 n.4; 284; 311 nn.1–3
Glueck, Sheldon, 158; 173 n.235;
    244 n.4; 284; 311 nn.1–3
Goddard, Henry, 159, 160; 173
    n.247
Goetting, Ann, 244 n.5
Gold, Martin, 63 n.99
Goldberg, Jack, 170 n.143
Goldkamp, John, 40–42; 126 n.116;
    464 n.224
Goldman, David, 169 n.111
Goldman, M. S., 463 n.169
Goldstein, Michael, 461 n.96
Goldstein, Paul, 358 n.14; 358 n.20;
    460 nn.60, 62, 64; 463 n.174;
    464 n.204
Golub, Andrew, 463 nn.176, 177
Gondolf, Edward, 116–117
Gooch, Erik, 362 n.176
Gooch, Teresa, 61 n.40
Goodman, Robert, 171 n.190
Goodman, Sam, 373
Goodridge, Hillary, 20
Goodridge, Julie, 20
Goodstein, Laurie, 248 n.167
Goodwill, Alasdair, 362 n.170

Goodwin, Bill, 498 n.78
Goodwin, D. W., 462 n.158
Gootman, Elissa, 363 n.185
Gordon, Jill, 116–117
Gordon, Leslie, 314 n.76; 359 n.28
Gordon, Rachel, 359 n.58
Gordon, Robert, 173 n.253; 247
    n.107
Goring, Charles, 148–149; 171 n.179
Gorr, Wilpen, 127 n.120
Gossop, Michael, 464 n.226
Gottfredson, Denise, 89 n.50; 209
    n.102
Gottfredson, Gary, 89 n.50; 209
    n.102
Gottfredson, Michael, 51, 52; 60
    n.16; 62 nn.80, 83; 90 n.56;
    124 n.23; 230; 297–305; 312
    n.24; 314 nn.85, 86, 89, 90,
    93, 94, 97, 98, 102; 315
    n.109; 410; 422 nn.84, 85;
    464 n.224
Gottfredson, Stephen, 124 n.48
Gottman, John Mordechai, 341
Gottschalk, Earl, 421 n.21
Gould, Arthur, 461 n.86
Gould, Leroy, 54; 63 n.106
Gove, Walter, 125 n.77; 167 n.39;
    169 n.114; 249 n.173
Goyer, P. F., 168 n.85
Grandison, Terry, 89 n.20
Granic, Isabela, 245 n.46
Grann, Martin, 358 n.19
Grasmick, Harold, 126 n.109; 127
    nn.133, 139–141; 208 n.83;
    209 nn.105, 114; 210 n.122;
    305; 314 nn.98, 107; 315
    nn.116, 121
Gray, Gregory, 166 n.30
Gray, Nate, 400
Gray, Thomas, 462 n.140
Gray-Ray, Phyllis, 248 n.162
Graziano, Joseph, 168 n.72
Green, Donald, 127 n.138
Green, Lorraine, 110; 126 nn.i97, 98
Green, Rebecca, 497 nn.34, 35; 498
    n.72
Green, William, 360 nn.68, 74
Greenberg, David, 128 n.175; 128
    nn. 171, 172; 278 nn.15, 29;
    279 nn.56, 60
Greenberg, Stephanie, 208 n.61
Greene, Michael, 359 n.41
Greenfeld, Lawrence, 89 n.39; 128
    n.157; 464 n.202
Greenhouse, Joel, 167 n.70
Greening, Leilani, 172 n.229
Greenwood, Peter, 119; 128 n.181;
    464 n.225

Gregory, Alice, 170 n.154
Gregory, Carol, 63 n.105
Grierson, Jeffrey, 460 n.47
Griffin, Christine, 409
Griffith, Roberta, 498 n.95
Griswold, David, 247 n.127; 248
    nn.151, 158
Groene, Brenda, 130
Groene, Dylan, 130
Groene, Shasta, 130
Groene, Slade, 130
Groff, Elizabeth, 392 n.68
Groff, M., 173 nn.253, 258
Gros, Jean-Germain, 261; 278 n.42
Gross, Michael Joseph, 459 n.35
Gross, Samuel, 13; 26 n.28
Groth, A. Nicholas, 327; 330; 360
    n.84; 361 n.101
Grove, H., 421 n.54
Groves, W. Byron, 26 n. 23; 209
    n.102; 210 n.123; 277 nn.2, 3;
    278 nn.18, 52; 279 n.68
Grow, Brian, 496 n.16
Grubstein, Lori, 64 n.142
Gruenewald, Paul, 208 n.78
Grus, Catherine, 88 n.12
Gu, Joanne, 364 n.247
Guerry, Andre-Michel, 9
Guijarro, Margarita, 312 n.24
Gumz, Edward, 281 n.134
Gundry, Gwen, 169 n.134
Gupta, Sanjeev, 352–353; 497 n.52
Gusfield, Joseph, 427; 459 n.10; 462
    n.131
Gutierrez, Francisco, 464 n.213
Gwlasda, Victoria, 89 n.22

Haack, D., 167 n.40
Hackler, James, 388
Hackman, Gene, 368
Hagan, John, 207 n.25; 210 n.140;
    249 n.177; 266; 278 n.50; 280
    nn.97–99; 311 n.12
Hagedorn, John M., 42; 202; 245
    n.49
Hagin, Daniel, 313 n.44
Haikkanen, Helina, 393 n.88
Hakim, Simon, 91 n.103; 124 n.47;
    125 n.49; 392 n.74, 75
Halbfinger, David M., 421 n.42
Hale, Benjamin, 499 n.106
Hale, Chris, 63 n.102
Hale, Matthew, 329
Hall, Jerome, 392 n.62
Hall, Joseph S., 422 n.67
Hallam, J., 461 n.98
Halleck, Seymour, 171 n.187
Haller, Mark, 420 n.5
Hallet, Amanda, 312 n.24

Morash, Merry, 207 *n*.40
Morenoff, Jeffrey, 207 *n*.47; 209 *n*.95; 210 *n*.118
Morgan, Patricia, 99; 124 *nn*.30, 31
Moriarty, Laura, 116–117; 498 *n*.82
Morris, Jodi Eileen, 209 *n*.103
Morris, Norval, 124 *n*.16; 166 *n*.16; 168 *n*.74; 278 *n*.34; 311 *n*.6; 392 *n*.54
Morrison, Steve, 498 *n*.103
Morrissey, Carlo, 89 *n*.27
Morse, Barbara, 125 *n*.86; 173 *n*.261
Morse, Edward, 312 *n*.25
Morselli, Carlo, 124 *n*.26
Morton, Danielle, 464 *n*.202
Morton, James, 461 *n*.88
Moses, 18
Moy, Ernest, 358 *n*.5
Mrug, Sylvie, 246 *n*.56; 359 *n*.55
Mucci, Lorelei, 363 *n*.215
Mugford, Jane, 280 *nn*.124, 126
Mugford, Stephen, 280 *nn*.124, 126
Muhammad, John Allen, 338
Mullen, P., 172 *n*.200
Mullings, Janet, 128 *n*.177
Mullins, Christopher, 384
Mulvey, Edward, 61 *n*.28; 62 *n*.86
Muncer, Steven, 63 *n*.103; 171 *n*.169
Muris, Peter, 168 *n*.98; 315 *n*.122
Murphy, Eddie, 368
Murphy, Fred, 60 *n*.17
Murray, Charles, 23; 97; 124 *n*.9; 128 *n*.166; 162; 173 *n*.263
Murray, Ellen, 247 *n*.120
Mustaine, Elizabeth, 125 *n*.52; 463 *n*.183
Mustard, David, 48–50
Muth, Stephen, 460 *n*.67
Myers, Jane, 312 *n*.41
Myers, Wade, 362 *n*.176
Myrdal, Gunnar, 178; 207 *n*.19
Myrvang, Bjorn, 358 *n*.19

Nachshon, Israel, 166 *n*.12; 171 *n*.175
Nadelmann, Ethan, 456; 465 *n*.233
Nagin, Daniel, 126 *n*.103; 126 *nn*.106, 110; 127 *nn*.127, 145; 303; 313 *nn*.43, 45, 58
Najman, Jake, 169 *n*.135
Nanjundappa, G., 462 *n*.164
Nansel, Tonja, 217; 245 *n*.40; 362 *n*.163
Nation, Carrie, 441
Navarro, Mireya, 460 *n*.63
Neal, David, 60 *n*.19
Neapolitan, Jerome, 64 *n*.111; 360 *nn*.65, 66
Nee, C., 392 *n*.79

Needleman, Herbert, 139; 167 *n*.70
Negrey, Cynthia, 48–50
Negroponte, John, 356
Neilson, Kathleen, 244 *n*.10
Neilson, Martin, 145
Neisser, Ulric, 166 *n*.20; 167 *n*.71; 173 *n*.262
Nelken, David, 420 *n*.2
Neller, Daniel, 359 *n*.56
Ness, Elliot, 441
Ness, Roberta, 167 *n*.70
Nevid, Jeffrey, 160–161
Newman, Elana, 89 *n*.27
Newman, Graeme, 14–15; 278 *n*.18; 341
Newman, Oscar, 105; 125 *n*.80
Neziroglu, F., 167 *n*.36
Nicewander, W. Alan, 296; 314 *n*.79
Nicholas, Thomas Ian, 229
Nickles, Laura, 116–117
Nielsen, Arnie, 358 *n*.11
Niemann, Albert, 442
Nieuwbeerta, Paul, 89 *n*.33; 90 *n*.66
Nieves, Evelyn, 361 *n*.141
Nilsson, L.-L., 172 *n*.210
Nisbet, Robert, 26 *n*.17
Nobiling, Tracy, 64 *n*.121; 278 *n*.26
Noek, Robert, 333
Nolte, Nick, 368
Novak, Kenneth, 126 *n*.118
Novak, Scott, 454
Nurco, David, 312 *n*.33
Nye, F. Ivan, 47; 62 *nn*.62, 63; 277 *n*.13

Oakes, Jeannie, 245 *n*.35
O'Boyle, Michael, 219
O'Brien, Mary, 460 *n*.47
O'Brien, Robert, 40–42; 60 *n*.12
O'Callaghan, Mark, 173 *n*.265
Odem, Mary, 266; 280 *n*.95
Odiah, Chuk, 358 *n*.8
O'Faolain, Julia, 363 *n*.209
Ogle, Robbin, 211 *n*.166
Ogloff, James, 160–161
O'Grady, Bill, 216
O'Hara, Terence, 421 *n*.47
Ohlin, Lloyd, 61 *n*.34; 202–203, 204; 211 *nn*.186–192
Okut, Hayrettin, 188
O'Leary, Cecilia, 278 *n*.32
O'Leary, K. Daniel, 89 *n*.19
O'Leary, Susan, 363 *n*.214
Olivares, Kathleen, 303
Oliveira, Andrew, 422 *n*.76
Olsen, Virgil, 62 *n*.63
Olson, James, 124 *nn*.42, 43, 46; 125 *n*.56; 385–386; 391 *n*.20; 392 *n*.78

Olson, Lynn, 89 *n*.22
O'Malley, Patrick, 60 *nn*.20, 21; 246 *n*.65; 462 *nn*.135, 136
Onunwor, Emmanuel, 400
Opjordsmoen, Stein, 358 *n*.19
Opler, Mark, 168 *n*.72
Orbuch, Terri, 313 *n*.56; 314 *n*.73
O'Reilly-Fleming, Thomas, 363 *n*.182
Ornstein, Miriam, 61 *n*.27
Osborn, Denise, 89 *n*.34
Osgood, D. Wayne, 60 *n*.21; 63 *n*.93; 144; 167 *nn*.40, 44; 170 *n*.144; 246 *n*.65; 296; 314 *n*.79; 315 *n*.115
Osman, Susan, 361 *n*.108
Ostresh, Erick, 247 *n*.130
Ostrow, Miriam, 464 *n*.227
Ott, John, 167 *n*.65
Ouellet, Lawrence, 460 *n*.64
Ouimet, Marc, 314 *n*.98
Ouimette, Paige Crosby, 171 *n*.185
Ousey, Graham, 315 *n*.113
Overpeck, Mary, 245 *n*.40; 362 *n*.163

Pacino, Al, 368
Padina, Robert, 245 *n*.48
Pagulayan, O., 166 *n*.18
Paige, Karen, 167 *n*.58
Pallone, Nathaniel, 140; 168 *nn*.85, 89
Palmeiro, Rafael, 424
Palmer, S., 172 *n*.200
Papillo, Angela Romano, 248 *n*.141
Paradis, Emily, 88 *n*.16
Parent, Sophie, 303
Parham, Carrie, 48–50
Park, Robert Ezra, 9; 26 *n*.22; 176; 182; 207 *nn*.4, 5
Parker, Bonnie, 368
Parker, Faith Lamb, 241
Parker, Jocelyn, 365 *n*.274
Parker, Karen, 64 *n*.128; 208 *nn*.49, 50; 209 *n*.88; 296; 314 *n*.74
Parker, Robert Nash, 62 *n*.60; 358 *n*.2
Parra, Gilbert, 462 *n*.159
Parrot, A., 360 *n*.99
Parsons, Deborah, 281 *n*.137
Paschall, Mallie, 61 *n*.27; 64 *n*.131
Passas, Nikos, 420 *n*.2; 421 *nn*.18, 19
Pastore, Ann, 211 *n*.198
Pate, R. Hewitt, 412–413
Pate, Tony, 126 *n*.115
Paternoster, Raymond, 114; 126 *n*.111; 127 *nn*.138, 145, 14; 128 *n*.151; 211 *n*.158; 238; 249 *n*.207; 279 *n*.78; 303; 311

n.16; 313 nn.50, 58, 60; 315 n.119

Patil, Sujata, 26 n.28

Patterson, G. R., 312 n.40

Patterson, Gerald, 311 nn.13, 19; 358 n.23

Patterson, James, 246 n.75

Patterson, Thomas, 460 n.71

Pattillo, Mary E., 42

Paulozzi, Len, 362 n.167

Payne, Brian, 127 n.128

Payne, Gary, 210 n.150; 248 n.148

Payne, Monique, 207 n.25

Pazniokas, Mark, 88 n.1

Pearson-Nelson, Benjamin, 358 n.13

Pease, Ken, 89 n.38; 126 n.100; 386; 392 n.82

Pease, Susan, 173 n.264

Peay, Lenore, 241

Peete, Thomas, 127 n.142

Pelham, Molina, Jr., 168 n.98

Penrod, Steven, 361 n.118; 461 n.97

Pepinsky, Harold, 269; 280 n.117

Peras, Hanno, 312 n.36

Perea, Ignacio, 332–333

Perez, Cynthia, 62 n.75; 311 nn.7, 18; 312 n.23; 464 n.204

Perez-Melara, Carlos Enrique, 477

Pérez-Peña, Richard, 421 n.23

Perkins, Elizabeth, 392 n.81

Perry, T. B., 245 n.45

Perusse, Daniel, 170 n.149

Petchesky, Rosalind, 279 n.61

Petechuk, David, 245 n.50

Peter, Katharin, 245 n.41; 362 n.162

Petersilia, Joan, 249 n.172

Peterson, David, 248 n.140

Peterson, Ruth D., 62 n.72; 207 n.22; 209 nn.107, 109; 210 n.124; 249 n.177

Petraitis, John, 125 n.60; 462 n.160

Petricone, Michael, 471

Petrocelli, Matthew, 279 nn.66, 67

Petrosino, Anthony, 280 n.123

Petrosino, Carolyn, 280 n.123

Pettit, Gregory, 209 n.97; 244 n.15; 313 n.43

Pezzin, Liliana, 124 n.27

Philaretou, Andreas, 496 n.9

Philip, Michael, 64 n.115

Phillips, Coretta, 89 n.38; 386; 392 n.82

Phillips, David, 153; 172 n.213

Phillips, Julie A., 64 n.133; 207 n.27

Phillips, Lloyd, 124 nn.21, 22

Phillips, Monte, 168 n.87

Phillips-Plummer, Lynanne, 460 n.67

Piaget, Jean, 153–154; 172 n.214

Pickering, Lloyd, 314 n.99

Pickett, Kate, 210 n.142

Pickles, Andrew, 170 n.142

Pietz, Christina, 359 n.56

Pihl, Robert, 168 n.77; 169 n.130

Piliavin, Irving, 228–229; 247 nn.115, 118

Pilla, Ramani, 245 n.40; 362 n.163

Pinel, Philippe, 8; 149

Piorkowski, Chaya, 241

Piquero, Alex R., 128 nn.149, 164; 162; 167 n.423; 171 n.193; 173 n.255; 210 nn.149, 151; 279 nn.66, 67; 296; 303; 311 n.16; 312 n.32; 313 nn.46, 50; 314 nn.74, 75, 91, 104, 105; 315 nn.124, 125, 127

Pittman, David, 461 n.125

Pitts, Marian, 460 n.47

Planty, Mike, 245 n.41; 362 n.162

Platt, Anthony, 207 n.34; 259; 278 n.32; 279 n.69

Platt, Brenda, 433

Platt, Jerome J., 462 n.155; 464 n.229

Pliant, Lois, 498 n.78

Ploeger, Matthew, 63 n.96; 246 nn.82, 91

Plomin, Robert, 170 n.154

Plumridge, Libby, 460 n.55

Podio, Fernando L., 498 n.87

Podolsky, E., 166 n.35

Pogarsky, Greg, 112; 126 nn.103, 106, 110; 127 nn.127, 129, 138; 128 n.164; 303

Pogrebin, Mark, 247 n.113

Polk, Kenneth, 211 n.197

Pollack, Otto, 63 n.91

Pollitt, Mark, 497 n.50

Pomeroy, Wardell, 361 n.113

Ponder, Michael, 258–259; 278 n.22

Pontell, Henry, 420 n.4; 497 n.66

Poole, Eric, 247 nn.108, 113

Pope, Carl, 249 n.186

Popkin, Susan, 89 n.22

Porche, Dianne, 422 n.82

Port, Otis, 499 n.107

Porter, David, 498 n.67

Porter, James, 430

Porter, Rebecca, 423 n.133

Porter, Stephen, 361 n.114

Porterfield, A. L., 60 n.17

Post, Jerrold M., 354; 365 n.280

Potter, Gary, 423 n.125

Potter, Lloyd, 362 n.167

Potterat, John, 460 n.67

Potterton, Dave, 497 n.63

Pottieger, Anne, 447; 463 nn.172, 173

Poussin, Nicolas, 326

Powell, Andrea, 207 n.44

Powers, Edward, 126 n.91

Powers, Ronald, 364 n.228

Pranis, Kay, 272; 280 n.132

Prasad, Monica, 431; 460 n.48

Pratt, Travis, 172 n.221; 278 n.20

Presser, Lois, 281 n.143

Preston, Julia, 103

Pribesh, Shana, 208 n.75

Price, Jamie, 208 n.55

Price, Virginia, 460 n.54

Pring-Wilson, Alexander, 104

Prins, Herschel, 388

Prinz, Ronald, 166 nn.27, 29; 312 n.37

Priyadarsini, S., 246 n.87

Proffitt, Fiona, 365 n.275

Proulx, Jean, 312 n.34

Pruitt, B. E., 172 nn.228, 232; 173 n.267

Pruitt, Matthew, 208 n.49

Przybylski, Roger, 463 n.182

Puckett, Janice, 126 n.117

Pugh, Meredith, 61 n.23; 62 n.74

Pyle, D. J., 345

Qin, Ping, 170 n.147

Quetelet, L. A. J., 9, 11; 26 nn.18, 19

Quigley, Brian, 341

Quinet, Kenna Davis, 89 n.33; 362 nn.174, 182

Quinney, Richard, , 257; 259; 269; 278 nn.17, 48, 49; 280 nn.117, 118; 420 n.14; 421 n.25

Quiñones, Alan, 103

Quinsey, Vernon, 392 n.87

Quisenberry, Neil, 208 n.60

Raab, Selwyn, 423 nn.131, 132

Rada, Richard, 361 n.113

Rader, Dennis, 336

Radosevich, Marcia, 63 n.106; 247 n.95

Radosh, Polly, 280 n.129

Raffalovich, Lawrence, 40–42; 90 n.74; 208 n.52

Rafter, Nicole, 26 nn.10,11,15–16

Raghaven, Chitra, 462 n.148

Raine, Adrian, 160–161; 168 n.78, 86, 88, 93; 169 n.117; 171 n.176; 172 n.220; 313 n.51; 358 n.24

Raj, Anita, 363 n.215

Raja, Sheela, 88 n.10

Raley, R. Kelly, 64 n.132

Ramirez, G. B., 166 n.18

Ramsey, Elizabeth, 311 n.13

Stone, Karen, 245 *n.*26
Stone, Laurence, 363 *n.*210
Storr, C. L., 208 *n.*62
Stotland, E., 421 *n.*54
Stout, Ronnie, 358 *n.*4
Stouthamer-Loeber, Magda, 89 *n.*52;
   173 *nn.*245, 254; 245 *n.*53;
   311 *n.*15, 17; 312 *nn.*25, 27,
   30; 313 *nn.*51, 53; 359 *nn.*38,
   58
Strang, John, 464 *n.*226
Stratton, Howard, 315 *n.*136
Straus, Murray, 169 *n.*134; 245
   *nn.*30, 31; 321; 340; 359
   *nn.*27, 34; 363 *nn.*213, 307
Streifel, Cathy, 62 *n.*81
Stretesky, Paul, 139; 167 *n.*67; 207
   *n.*46; 422 *n.*92
Streuning, Elmer, 248 *n.*160
Strodtbeck, Fred, 247 *n.*107
Strom, Kevin J., 364 *n.*237
Strycker, Lisa A., 188
Stuart, Gregory, 358 *n.*7
Stumbo, Phyllis, 166 *n.*31
Styfco, Sally, 241
Su, S. Susan, 211 *n.*163; 244 *n.*22;
   312 *n.*26
Sudermann, Marlies, 91 *n.*90
Sullivan, Dennis, 259; 268–269; 278
   *n.*31; 280 *nn.*113–116
Sun, Ivan, 209 *n.*104
Sundance Kid, 325
Surratt, Hilary, 434; 460 *n.*57
Susser, Ezra S., 168 *n.*72
Sutherland, Edwin H., 4; 10; 13; 16;
   26 *n.*1; 160–161; 173 *nn.*247,
   251; 222–224; 246 *nn.* 77–79;
   371; 385; 391 *nn.*10, 12–14;
   396; 405; 410; 420 *nn.*7, 8;
   422 *n.*66
Swaggi, Vincent, 372–373
Swahn, Monica, 358 *n.*18
Swain-Campbel, Nicola, 219
Swango, Michael, 336
Swanson, Christopher B., 245 *n.*36
Swartz, Bruce, 498 *n.*74
Swartz, Marc, 402
Swartz, Marvin, 172 *n.*211
Sykes, Gresham, 226–228; 247
   *n.*102, 104–106; 278 *n.*44
Symons, Donald, 361 *n.*105

Ta, Myduc, 364 *n.*258
Tagliabue, John, 423 *n.*123
Tait, David, 90 *n.*71; 361 *n.*109
Tajima, Emiko, 358 *n.*21
Takagi, Paul, 259; 279 *n.*61
Tannenbaum, Frank, 236; 249 *n.*182
Tanner, Julian, 216

Tanskanen, Antti, 136–137
Tarde, Gabriel, 171 *n.*181
Tardiff, Kenneth, 208 *n.*53; 359 *n.*50
Targe, Gabriel, 149
Tatchell, Renny, 315 *n.*135
Tatchell, Thomas, 315 *n.*135
Taylor, Alan, 170 *n.*138
Taylor, Bruce, 60 *n.*11; 89 *n.*24
Taylor, Dawn, 171 *n.*197
Taylor, Ian, 259; 264; 278 *n.*30; 279
   *nn.*73, 74
Taylor, Jeannette, 170 *n.*148
Taylor, John, 393 *n.*89
Taylor, K., 160–161
Taylor, M., 392 *n.*79
Taylor, Mark Lewis, 271
Taylor, Natalie, 420 *n.*12
Taylor, Ralph, 124 *n.*48; 208 *n.*68;
   209 *nn.*84, 98; 210 *n.*129
Taylor, Robert, 126 *n.*89; 127 *n.*122;
   207 *n.*45
Teevan, James, 303
Teilmann Van Duesen, Katherine,
   170 *n.*159
Terrill, William, 208 *n.*77
Terry, Robert, 245 *n.*54
Tesoriero, James, 125 *n.*70
Testa, Maria, 360 *nn.*80, 82, 95
Tewksbury, Richard, 125 *n.*52; 463
   *n.*183
Thatcher, Robert, 168 *n.*80
Theerathorn, Pochara, 125 *n.*82
Theriot, Matthew, 245 *n.*39
Thistlethwaite, Amy, 116–117
Thomas, Charles C., 464 *n.*219
Thomas, John M., 422 *n.*94
Thomas, Melvin, 64 *n.*130
Thomas, Stephen, 40–42
Thomas, Suzie Dod, 279 *n.*89
Thomasson, Paul, 430
Thomas W. I., 17
Thomlinson, R. Paul, 359 *n.*56
Thompson, Carol, 422 *n.*89
Thompson, Kevin, 280 *nn.*104, 105;
   315 *n.*129
Thompson, Melissa, 99; 124 *nn.*18,
   25
Thorlindsson, Thorolfur, 80; 90 *n.*70
Thornberry, Terence, 61 *n.*24; 62
   *nn.*63, 79; 63 *n.*109; 125 *n.*70;
   169 *n.*129; 211 *n.*154; 244
   *n.*2; 245 *nn.*28, 37, 39; 246
   *nn.*55, 64, 69, 90; 249 *n.*200;
   292; 293; 312 *n.*24; 359 *n.*33;
   462 *n.*149
Thornburgh, Nathan, 497 *n.*48
Thorne, Ian, 393 *n.*89
Thrasher, Frederick, 176; 207 *n.*7
Tibbets, Stephen, 314 *n.*91

Tice, Peter, 312 *n.*27
Tifft, Larry, 61 *n.*26; 259; 268–269;
   278 *n.*31; 280 *nn.*113, 114,
   116
Tippetts, Scott, 127 *n.*125
Tita, George, 89 *n.*52
Titchener, Edward, 153
Tittle, Charles R., 47, 50; 62 *nn.*64,
   65; 126 *n.*107; 127 *n.*134; 207
   *n.*29; 211 *n.*195; 237; 244 *n.*3;
   249 *nn.*198, 199, 205; 301;
   305; 314 *n.*98; 314 *n.*107; 315
   *nn.*116, 121
Tjaden, Patricia, 364 *nn.*259, 261
Tobias, Aurelio, 311 *n.*17
Tobias, J. J., 391 *nn.*4,5
Tobin, Kimberly, 125 *n.*71
Tobin, Michael, 167 *n.*70
Tobler, Nancy, 315 *n.*136
Toby, Jackson, 279 *n.*63
Toch, Hans, 172 *n.*212
Tolmunen, Tommi, 136–137
Tomas, Joseph, 311 *n.*17
Tomaszewski, E. Andreas, 331
Tonry, Michael, 79; 89 *nn.*35, 36; 90
   *n.*73; 124 *nn.*13, 16, 48; 166
   *n.*16; 168 *n.*74; 208 *nn.*54, 64;
   209 *nn.*85, 86; 245 *n.*34; 278
   *n.*34; 298–299; 311 *n.*6; 362
   *n.*182; 392 *n.*54
Tontodonato, Pamela, 91 *n.*93
Toomey, Rosemary, 170 *n.*143
Topalli, Volkan, 392 *n.*52
Torrance, Mark, 409
Torres, Jose, 42; 202
Tosouni, Anastasia, 497 *n.*66
Townsley, Michael, 386; 392 *n.*83
Towns-Miranda, Luz, 392 *n.*86
Tracy, Paul, 57–58; 63 *n.*109; 64
   *nn.*138, 144; 65 *n.*145; 128
   *n.*156
Trapani, Catherine, 63 *n.*94
Traxler, Mary Pat, 244 *n.*14
Trebach, Arnold, 461 *n.*123
Tremblay, Pierre, 124 *n.*26
Tremblay, Richard, 65 *n.*146; 168
   *n.*77; 170 *n.*149; 245 *n.*50;
   303; 313 *n.*43; 314 *n.*98
Trendle, Giles, 496 *n.*4
Treno, Andrew, 208 *n.*78
Trickett, Alan, 89 *n.*34
Triplett, Ruth, 209 *n.*104; 249 *n.*191
Trumbetta, Susan, 125 *n.*75; 360
   *n.*87
Trump, Donald, 193
Tseng, Li-Jung, 244 *n.*23; 462 *n.*161
Tsuang, Ming, 170 *n.*143
Tuch, Steven, 64 *n.*126; 258; 278
   *n.*21

SUBJECT INDEX

gender differences, 384
international rates, 15
nature of, 382–383
as Part I crime, 31
professional burglars, 385
repeat burglary, 386
residential burglary, 383
stages of careers in, 385–386
Burning as punishment, 6, 18
Burroughs Corporation, 400–401
Businesses. *See also* White-collar crime
  drug-testing programs, 453
  enterprise crime, 396
  influence peddling in, 400–401
Business Software Alliance (BSA), 480
B vitamins, 136

Calcium, 135
California Personality Inventory (CPI), 159
Caller ID, 108
Call girls, 434
Call houses, 434
Cambridge Study in Delinquent Development (CSDD), 143–144
Campus rape, 76–77
  date rape, 78–79, 328–329
Canadian/Netherlands lottery, 473
Cannabis. *See* Marijuana
Capitalism
  Bonger, Willem on, 256
  and critical criminology, 260–261, 262
  and critical feminist theory, 264–265
  and instrumental critical theory, 261
  and Marx, 253–255
  and patriarchy, 267
  structural critical theory, 261
Capitalism, Patriarchy, and Crime (Messerschmidt), 265
Capitalist bourgeoisie, 253
Capital punishment, 112
  as deterrence, 114–115
  ethical problems, 98
  public policy and, 120
  studies on, 13
Carbohydrates, 136–138
Carding, 473–474
Career criminals. *See* Chronic offenders
Carjacking, 380
Cartographic school of criminology, 9
Catholic clergy scandal, 430–431
Cause-based terrorism, 351

Causes of Delinquency (Hirschi), 229
Center for Restorative Justice and Peacemaking, 271
Center for Strategic and International Studies, 479
Central nervous system (CNS) diseases, 142
Cerebral allergies, 139
Cerebral arteriosclerosis, 142
Certainty of punishment, 110
CERT Coordination Center (CERT/CC), 471
Cheater theory, 147
Cheating schemes, 381
Chechen terrorists, 351
Check fraud, 376–377
Check kiting, 377, 404, 405
Chemical influences, 135
Chemical restraints/straitjackets, 142
Chicago Area Project, 204
Chicago School, 9–10, 176
  and social disorganization theory, 182
Child abuse, 339–340. *See also* Sexual abuse
  crime and, 216
  cycle of violence and, 71
  international rates, 15
  self-report surveys on, 34
  violence and, 322
Child Online Protection Act, 482
Child Pornography Prevention Act (CPPA), 439–440, 482
Child protective services (CPS), 339
Children. *See also* Adolescents; Peers; Sexual abuse; Socialization; Teenage crime
  arson by, 387, 388
  exposure to violence, 323
  failure to act, 22
  Head Start program, 239, 240–241
  murder of, 333
  pedophiles, 20
  pornography and, 66, 437
  poverty and, 177–178
  prostitution and, 66
Children of the Corn, 132
Children's Internet Protection Act of 2000, 470
Child Sexual Abuse Prevention Act, 436
Child's Play 1-5, 132
China
  critical criminology and, 260
  terrorism in, 351
Chiseling, 398–399
  securities fraud, 399
Chivalry hypesthesias, 52

Choice theories, 10–11, 95–129
  attraction of crime, 104–105
  classical theory of crime, 96–97
  concepts of, 98–101
  crime, structuring, 100–101
  criminality, structuring, 99–100
  development of, 98
  eliminating crime, 105–120
  emergence of, 97–98
  just desert policy, 120–121
  offense/offender-specific crimes, 98–99
  public policy implications, 120–121
  rationality of crime, 102–105
  and substance abuse, 446–447
  targets, choosing, 101
  time and place of crime, 101
Chromosomal structure, 143
Chronic offenders, 56–58. *See also* Developmental theories
  drug use and, 449
  and General Strain Theory (GST), 197
  information processing and, 157
  intelligence of, 162
  labeling and, 237
  life course persisters, 2912
  persistent juvenile offenders, 57–58
  psychopathy and, 161
  and social disorganization theory, 183
  and strain theory, 191
  trait theory and, 134
Chronic victimization, 74
Churches. *See* Religion
Churning, 399
Circuit Court Automation Program (CCAP), 490
Circuit travelers, 434
Cities. *See* Urban areas
Civil liberties and information technology, 492–493
Civil rights
  critical criminology and, 260
  Patriot Act and, 355
Clarissa (Richardson), 326
Class. *See* Social class
Class and Class Conflict in Industrial Society (Dahrendorf), 256–257
Classes of criminals, 304
Classical criminology, 7
Classical theory of crime, 96–97
Classroom mode, Communities In Schools program, 218
Clean Air Act, 411
Clean Water Act, 411

Identical twins, 144
Identity crisis, 150
Identity theft, 473–474, 480
Identity Theft and Assumption Deterrence Act of 1998, 474
Ignorance defense, 23
I Know What You Did Last Summer, 132
Imaging, computer, 484
Immediate gratification, 142
Immigration, 262–263
Immigration and Customs Enforcement (ICE), 486–487
Impact statements by victims, 83
Imperatively coordinated associations, 256–257
Impulsivity, 143, 158
   and General Theory of Crime (GTC), 298–299
   types of, 305
Incapacitation, 118–120. *See also* Prisons
   of chronic offenders, 58
   logic of, 119
   and reduction of crime, 118
   selective incapacitation, 119–120
Incarceration. *See* Incapacitation; Prisons
Inchoate offenses, 19
Incivilities, 185
Index crimes, 30–31
   clearing, percentage for, 32
   trends in, 38–39
India, bride burning, 14
Individual strain, 191
Industrialization, 9
   patriarchy and, 267
Infanticide, 334
Inferiority complex, 150
Infidelity and homicide, 146
Influence peddling, 400–401
Informal sanctions, 113
Information processing, 153, 156, 488–489
Information technology (IT)
   automated fingerprint identification systems (AFIS), 484–485
   biometrics, 485–487
   civil liberties and, 492–493
   and communications, 487
   and corrections, 491–492
   in courts, 489–491
   and cyber crime, 482–492
   defined, 468
   and law enforcement, 482–489
   and pornography, 439–440
   pornography and, 469–470
Inheritance school, 132
Innovation, 192

The Inquisition, 6
Insanity defense, 23
Insider trading, 399, 408
INS (Immigration and Naturalization Service), 486–487
Instinct, 135
Institutional anomie theory, 193–194
Institutional involvement, 220
Instrumental crimes, 47
Instrumental critical theory, 261, 269
Instrumental violence, 320
Insurance, arson fraud and, 387
Integrated cognitive antisocial potential (ICAP) theory, 300, 306
Integrated theories, 293
Intelligence
   chronic offenders and, 57
   and crime, 159–160
   cross-national studies, 162
   defective intelligence, 149
   diet and, 137
   and Head Start program, 240–241
   human nature theory, 297
   and latent trait theories, 297
   lead ingestion, 139
   nature theory, 159
   nurture theory, 159–160
   reexamination of crime and, 161–162
Intent and *mens rea,* 22–23
Interactional theory, 17, 292
Interagency Telemarketing and Internet Fraud Working Group, 482
Interdisciplinary science, 44
Intergenerational deviance, 143–144
Internal Macedonian Revolutionary Organization, 350
International Crime Victims Survey (ICVS), 14
International terrorism, 349
Internet. *See also* Cyber crime
   child pornography on, 437
   correctional departments using, 491
   court records on, 490–491
   and pornography, 439–440
   prostitution on, 435
Internet False Identification Prevention Act of 2000, 482
Internet Fraud Complaint Center, 482
INTERPOL, 14
Interracial rape, 331
Interstate and Foreign Travel Act, 416
Interview research, 37–38

Intoxication defense, 23
Involuntary manslaughter, 333
Involvement, 230, 231
iPods and crime, 42, 43
IQ. *See* Intelligence
Ireland, restorative justice in, 275
ISPs (Internet service providers), 355

J. P. Morgan, 399
Jails. *See* Prisons
Jemaah Islamiyah, 350
J-Net, 490–491
Job Corps, 204
Jobs. *See* Employment
Joyriding, 378–379
Judges, 18
Junk foods, 135–136
Justice Department
   Violent Criminal Apprehension Program (VICAP), 337
   on white-collar crime, 411
Justice Studies Association (JSA), 274
Justice system
   reintegrative shaming, 269–270
   women in, 266
Justice Technology Information Network (JUSTNET), j488
Justifiable homicides, 324
Justification defense, 23
Juvenile violence. *See* Teenage crime

Kaiser Foundation, 154
Kids Count, 177
Kill Bill, 37
Knapp Commission, 400
Knowledge and criminality, 99–100
Known group method, 35
Kohlberg's stages of development, 156
Ku Klux Klan (KKK), 346, 347, 351

Labeling. *See also* Social reaction theory
   critical feminist theory and, 266
Lack of concern, 158
La Cosa Nostra, 413, 414–415
Larceny, 19, 374–382. *See also* Shoplifting; Vehicle theft
   check fraud, 376–377
   confidence games, 381–382
   credit card theft, 377
   embezzlement, 382
   false pretenses, 380–381
   as Part I crime, 31
   varieties of, 375
Latency, 150
Latent delinquency, 150
Latent trait theories, 285, 296–305, 306

Moral development theory, 153, 156–157
Moral entrepreneurs, 17, 234
Moral guardianship, 79
Morality
  crusaders for, 5–6, 428–429
  culture and, 427–428
  debate on, 426–427
  and General Theory of Crime (GTC), 304
  public order crimes and, 426–429
  social harm and, 428
The Moral Sense (Wilson), 138
Morgan Stanley, 399
Morphine, 142
Mosaic Code, 18
Motivation, 158
  for arson, 388
  and differential association theory, 223–224
  in routine activities theory, 79
  strain and, 190–191
  for terrorism, 353–354
  for white-collar crime, 408
MS Blaster worm, 475
Multidimensional Personality Questionnaire (MPQ), 159
Murder, 332–338. *See also* Hate crimes
  data on, 333–334
  degrees of, 333
  feticide, 333
  first-degree murder, 19
  mass murder, 337–338
  mental illness and, 151
  nature of, 333–334
  personal relations and, 334–335
  proving, 332–333
  rationality of killers, 104
  relationships, murderous, 334–336
  serial murder, 336–337
  social ecology of, 72
  spousal relations and, 334
  spree killers, 338
  stranger killings, 335
  student relations and, 335–336
  trends in, 39
MZ twins, 144

Naive check forgers, 376
Narcissism, 158
Narcissistic personality disorder, 330
Narcotic Control Act of 1956, 451
Narcotics, 443
  legal definition, 450–451
  source control, 451–452
Narcotics Anonymous (NA), 453, 455

NASA, 478
National Center for Policy Analysis, 111–112
National Center on Addiction and Substance Abuse (CASA) Survey, 444, 445, 456
National Center on Elder Abuse, 73
National Child Abuse and Neglect Data System (NCANDS), 339
National Counterterrorism Center (NCTC), 356
National Crime Victimization Survey (NCVS), 35–36
  assault data, 339
  burglary data, 382–383
  carjacking data, 380
  evaluation of, 36
  on patterns of victimization, 71–72
  problems of victims, 68
  rape data, 327
  robbery data, 341
  trends in data, 43
  validity of, 36
National Deviancy Conference (NDC), 259
National Food Service Security Council, 401
National Incident-Based Reporting System (NIBRS), 33
National Information Infrastructure Protection Act (NIIPA), 481–482
National Institute of Justice, 21
National Insurance Crime Bureau (NICB), 379
Nationalist terrorism, 351
National Mental Health Association (NMHA), 151
National Organization for Victim Assistance, 83
National Security Agency, 478
National Security Council, 356
National Stolen Property Act, 482
National Strategy for Homeland Security, 355–356
National Survey on Drug Use and Health (NSDUH), 442, 445
National values and violence, 324
National Whistleblower Center, 401
National White-Collar Crime Center, 482
Native Americans
  adolescent victims and, 70
  labeling and, 236–237
  sentencing circle, 272
Nature theory, 159
Naxalone treatment, 455
Need, general deterrence and, 113
Negative affective states, 195

Negative life events, 286
Negative reinforcement, 225
Negative stimuli, 195
Neglect of children, 339
Negligence and *mens rea,* 23
Negligent manslaughter, 333
Neighborhood associations, 188–189
Neighborhood hustlers, 373
Neighborhood Legal Services, 204
Neighborhoods. *See* Communities
Neocortex, 138
Neuroallergies, 139
Neurological disorders, 160–161
Neurophysiological conditions, 140–142, 148
Neuroticism, 143
Neurotransmitters, 138, 142
Neutralization theory, 226–228, 239
  testing, 227–228
  of white-collar crime, 408–409
Never Talk to Strangers, 132
The New Criminology (Taylor, Walton & Young), 259
New York Electronic Crimes Task Force (NYECTF), 482
Nigerian 491 scam, 473
NIMH (National Institute of Mental Health), 21
Nineteenth-century America, violence in, 325
Nonnegligent manslaughter, 333
Norepinephrine, 142
Norman conquest, 18
Normative groups, 229
NSF (National Science Foundation), 21
Nuclear Terrorism (Allison), 354
Nurture theory, 159–160
Nutrasweet, 137
Nutrition, effects of, 135

Objectivity of research, 21–22
Obscene phone calls, 108
Obscenity, 426–427, 437
  and law, 438–439
Observational research, 37–38
Obsessive-compulsive disorder, 69
Occasional criminals, 369–370
Occupational Safety and Health Administration (OSHA), 407
Ocean's 11/Ocean's 12, 358
Oedipus complex, 150
Offender accountability, 273
Offender-specific crimes, 98–99
Offense-specific crimes, 98–99
Office for Victims of Crime (OVC), 82
Office of Juvenile Justice and Delinquency Prevention, 21

adolescent victims and, 70
victimization and, 69
Potassium, 135
Poverty, 176
  child poverty, 177–178
  in cultural deviance theory, 199
  culture of poverty, 178
  deviant place theory, 77–78
  and differential enforcement, 234
  Head Start program, 239,
      240–241
  labeling and, 236–237
  minority group poverty, 178–179
  problem behavior syndrome (PBS)
      and, 287
  and prostitution, 435
  rates, 177
  sexual violence and, 331
  and social disorganization theory,
      183
  and social ecology theory,
      184–190
  social process theories and, 10,
      214
  and strain theory, 191
Power, 258
Power-control theory, 266–268, 269
  evaluating, 268
Powerlessness, 265
Power rape, 327
Preemptive deterrence, 264
Prefrontal dysfunction, 140
Premeditated murder, 333
Price fixing, 17, 258, 406. *See also*
      Corporate crime
Primary deviance, 236
Primary prevention programs, 162
Princess Diaries, 37
Princeton University Survey Re-
      search Center (SRC), 34
Principles of Criminology (Sutherland),
      222
Prisons
  costs of, 119
  critical criminology and, 259–260
  information technology in,
      491–492
  logic of, 119
  private prisons, 22
  security, information technology
      and, 491–492
  Privacy and information technology,
      492–493
Private prisons, 22
Probation, 163
Problem behavior syndrome (PBS),
      287
  substance abuse and, 446
Problem-solving, 157

Productive forces, 253–254
Productive relations, 253–254
Professional burglars, 385
Professional chiseling, 398–399
Professional criminals, 370–373
Professional robbers, 342
The Professional Thief (Sutherland),
      371
Profit killers, 337
Progesterone, 138
Prohibition, 441
Project on Human Development in
      Chicago Neighborhoods, 323
Proletariat, 10, 253
Prolixin, 142
Property crime. *See also* Theft
  declining rates, 72
  trends in, 39, 42
Property crimes, 19. *See also* Arson;
      Burglary; Larceny
  clearing, 31
  gender and, 54
Prostitution, 54, 431–437
  children and, 66
  controlling, 436
  and critical feminist theory, 265
  history of, 431
  incidence of, 432
  international trafficking in,
      432–433
  John lists, publishing, 108
  legalization issue, 436–437
  morality and, 426
  reasons for, 435
  social harm issue, 428
  types of prostitutes, 433–435
Pro Tech Monitoring Inc., 491
Protect Act, 436
Psychiatry, 8
Psycho, 132
Psychoanalytic perspective, 149
Psychodynamic theory, 149–150,
      158
Psychological trait theories, 148–163
  psychodynamic theory, 149–150
Psychopathia Sexualis (Krafft-Ebing),
      431
Psychopathic killers, 336
Psychopathy, 8, 143, 159, 160–161,
      320
Psychosexual stages, 149–150
Psychosis, 151
Psychosurgery, 163
Public Access to Court Electronic
      Records (PACER) system,
      491
Public education programs for vic-
      tims, 83
Public opinion/morality, 20

Public order crimes, 426. *See also*
      Pornography; Prostitution;
      Substance abuse
  morality and, 426–429
Public policy
  choice theories and, 120–121
  and developmental theory,
      308–309
  and social conflict theory,
      269–274
  and social process theories,
      238–242
  and social structure theory, 204
  and trait theories, 163
Pulp Fiction, 17
*Punishing Hate: Bias Crimes under
      American Law* (Lawrence),
      346–347
Punishment. *See also* Deterrence;
      Tipping point
  in classical theory of crime, 96–97
  criminal law and, 20
  as drug control strategy, 452
  just desert theory, 120–121
  media representations and, 97
  racial minorities and, 259
  severity, certainty and speed the-
      ory, 110
  severity of, 111–112
Pure Food and Drug Act, 450
Pyramid schemes, 381
  on Internet, 473

Quakerism, 268
Quality of life crimes
  trends in crime and, 42
  in Washington D.C. subways, 106
Quasi-experimental design, 37
Quorum Health Group, 404

Race, Evolution and Behavior (Rush-
      ton), 147
Racial minorities. *See also* African
      Americans; Latinos
  adolescent victims, 70
  convergence in crime rates, 56
  crime rate and, 40, 54–56
  and differential enforcement, 234
  family dissolution and, 56
  fear, race-based, 187
  and General Theory of Crime
      (GTC), 304
  inequality and, 181
  labeling and, 236–237
  marginalization of, 258–259
  and poverty, 178–179
  Rushton's theory of race and evolu-
      tion, 147
  self-reporting surveys and, 35

in cultural deviance theory, 198–199

delinquent subcultures theory, 199–202

gangs and, 202–203

of violence, 323–324

Substance abuse, 440–456. *See also* Alcohol use; Drug use

adolescent victims and, 70

causes of, 446–449

children of substance abusers, 216

extent of, 441–445

genetic factors, 446

problem behavior syndrome (PBS), 287

psychological view, 446

rational choice and, 446–447

social learning and, 446

subcultural view, 446

victimization and, 75–76

violence and, 321

Substance Abuse and Mental Health Services Administration (SAMHSA), 442, 445

Substantive criminal law, 16

Subterranean values, 226

Suburbia, social structure and, 79–81

Subway crime, 42

Sufferance, 348

Sugar and crime, 136–138

Suicide

brain chemistry and, 142

inmates, monitoring, 492

problem behavior syndrome (PBS) and, 287

as role exit behavior, 266

teenage suicide, 196

Summer, crime in, 45

Superconducting interference device (SQUID), 140

Superego, 149

Surplus value, 254–255

Surveillance, technology and, 487–488

Survey research, 33–35

Monitoring the Future (MTF) study, 34–35

self-report surveys, 34–35

Suspicion, 158

Sweden, prostitution in, 436

Swindles, 397–398

Symantec Corp., 480–481

Symbolic interaction theory, 232–233

Synthesis, 255

System abuse, 68

Systematic forgers, 376

Systematic review, 38

Target-hardening concept, 85

for shoplifting, 376

in situational crime prevention, 106

Target removal strategies, 376

Targets

choosing crime targets, 101

hardening of target, 85

for place of crime, 101

and repeat victimization, 74

in routine activities theory, 79

Task Force on Victims of Crime, 1982, 81

Tattoos, 132

Tax evasion, 404–405

Taxi Driver, 154

Technology. *See* Information technology (IT)

Technology Systems International, 492

Teenage crime. *See also* Peers

adolescent-limited offenders, 290–291

chronicity and, 57–58

economic loss and, 68

high school seniors, criminal activity of, 44

peak age for, 51

rational choice and, 114

trends in, 38–39, 40, 44

Telemarketing Associates, 407

Television

behavior modeling and, 152–153

closed-circuit television (CCTV) surveillance, 109

trends in crime and, 41

violence and, 154–156

The Temp, 132

Temperance movement, 441

Temperature and crime, 45–46

Temper tantrums, 140

Terrorism, 349–356

cause-based terrorism, 351

communications for combating, 487

criminal terrorism, 352–353

cyber terrorism, 468, 478–480

environmental terrorism, 351

groups, 349

history of, 349–350

justice responses, 355–356

legal responses, 354–355

motivation for, 353–354

nationalist terrorism, 351

political terrorists, 350–351

responses to, 354–356

revolutionary terrorists, 350

state-sponsored terrorism, 351–352

transnational terrorism, 352–353

Terrorist killers, 337

Tertiary prevention programs, 162

Testosterone, 138

Thanatos, 149–150

Theft. *See also* Fences; Vehicle theft

employee theft, 401

history of, 368–369

identity theft, 473–474

as instrumental crime, 47

occasional criminals, 369–370

as Part I crime, 31

professional criminals, 370–373

rationality of, 102

safecrackers, 372

train robbers, 372

Theory construction, 12–13

Theses, 255

Thinking About Crime (Wilson), 97

Three strikes policies, 58, 119–120

stranger killings and, 335

Thrill killers, 336

Thrill-seeking hate crimes, 345

Ticeteros, 434

Time

choosing time of crime, 101

violent crime, commission of, 72

Tipping point, 110

and capital punishment, 115

Titan Rain, 478

TOEFL (Test of English as a Foreign Language), 381

Torture, 6

female genital mutilation as, 427

Toughness as focal concern, 200

Touting, 473–474

Track systems, 216

Traffic violations, 31

Train robbers, 372

Trait theories, 130–173, 152–153. *See also* Genetics

arousal theory, 142–143

biosocial trait theories, 134–148

and chronic offenders, 134

cognitive theory, 153, 156–157

evaluation of, 147–148

evolutionary theory, 146–147

foundations of, 132–134

latent trait theories, 285

moral development theory, 156–157

psychological trait theories, 148–157

public policy implications, 163

Tranquilizers, 442

Transitional neighborhoods, 182

Transmitter wristbands, 492

Transnational corporations, 260

Transportation and crime, 101

and brain, 140–142
brutalization process, 322–323
causes of, 320–324
child abuse and, 216, 322
and evolution, 146
evolutionary factors, 321
exposure to, 323
and gangs, 324, 325
and General Strain Theory (GST),
197
hate crimes, 343–347
hormones and, 138–139
hypoglycemia and, 138
media and, 154–156
national values and, 324
in nineteenth-century America,
325
peer group influences, 324
perception-shaping and, 157
pornography and, 438
rationality of, 102–104
regional values, 324
and schools, 216–217
socialization and, 321–323
social learning and, 152–153
stalking, 348–349
subculture of, 323–324
substance abuse and, 321
and trait theories, 133
workplace violence, 347–348
The Violence of Hate (Levin), 346
Violent Crime Control and Law Enforcement Act of 1994, 354,
436
Violent Criminal Apprehension Program (VICAP), 337
Virility mystique, 330
Viruses, 475–476
VISA/MasterCard scams, 473
Vision Oil Company, 397–398
VISTA, 204
Visual perception problems, 140
Visual-spatial skills, 53
Vitamin C, 136
Vitamin deficiencies, 135–136
Volatile liquids, 442
Volstead Act, 441

Voluntary manslaughter, 19
Vory v zakone criminals, 416
Voyeurism, 431

Walden House, San Francisco, 455
War and rape, 326
Warez, 471
War on Poverty, 204, 240
Washington, D.C.
sniper, 48
subway system, 105–106
Wealth
and critical criminology, 260
power and, 258
Weapons
back-scatter imaging system for,
492
in carjackings, 380
defensive gun use, 49
in EU (European Union), 14
gun control issue, 48–50
patterns of crime and, 47
in schools, 217
trends in crime and, 41
victims carrying, 77, 86
Web defacement, 476–477
Website Billing.com, 377
Wechsler Adult Intelligence Scale,
162
Welfare, 204
cheater theory and, 147
Wernicke-Korsakoff syndrome, 135,
142
West Virginia Statewide Addressing
and Mapping Board, 485
*What Is to Be Done About Law and Or-
der?* (Lea & Young), 264
Wheels, theft of, 375
When Work Disappears (Wilson), 180
White-collar crime, 13, 396–413.
See also Corporate crime
bribery, 400–401
in Britain, 409
causes of, 408
chiseling, 398–399
client fraud, 404–405
compliance strategies, 411–412

components of, 397–407
in conflict view, 16–17
controlling, 411–412
corporate culture view, 410
deterrence strategies, 412
embezzlement, 401
enforcement systems, 410–413
exploitation of institutional position, 399–400
influence peddling, 400–401
power and, 258
rationalization/neutralization view,
408–409
redefining, 396–397
self-control theory, 410
social learning theory and, 222
WHO (World Health Organization)
assault in home, 339
global violence surveys, 14–15
Witchcraft, 6
Women. *See also* Gender
crime rate, 52–54
female genital mutilation,
427–428
liberal feminist theory, 54
and victimization risk, 72
Women's Temperance Union, 441
Worker safety crimes, 407
Workplace violence, 347–348
World Bank, 478
WorldCom scandal, 403, 406
World War II
rape during, 326
terrorism in, 350
World Wealth Report, 176
Worms, 475–476
WTO (World Trade Organization),
260

Yugoslavia, rape in, 326

Zealots, 349
Zen, 268
*Zero to Six: Electronic Media in the
Lives of Infants, Toddlers, and
Preschoolers,* 154

PHOTO CREDITS

Part Openers. 1, 93, 317: © Margaret Carsello/Images.com

Chapter 1. 2: Ed Andrieski/EPA/Landov; 6: T. H. Matteson, © The Trial of George Jacobs, August 5, 1692. Oil on canvas 39 x 53 inches. #1.246 Peabody Essex Museum, Salem, MA; 7: © The Image Works; 12: © Getty Images; 16: © Getty Images; 20: © Jesse Rinaldi/Reuters/Corbis

Chapter 2. 28: © Reuters/Landov; 30: © Axel Koester/Corbis; 43: © Simon Taplin/Corbis; 44: © AP/Louis Lazane/Wide World Photos; 53: © Alex Hofford/EPA/Landov; 55: © AP/Wide World Photos

Chapter 3. 66: © AP/Steve Miller/Wide World Images; 69: © Getty Images; 73: © AP/Wide World Photos; 75: © Chuck Savage/Corbis; 82: © AP/Mike Wintrath/Wide World Photos; 86: © David Young-Wolff/PhotoEdit Inc.– All rights reserved

Chapter 4. 94: © Getty Images; 98: © AP/Wide World Photos; 101: © Reuters/Corbis; 104: © Getty Images; 108: © AP/Wide World Photos; 112: © Michael Newman/PhotoEdit Inc. – All rights reserved; 118: © AP/Wide World Photos

Chapter 5. 110: © Reuters/Landov; 135: © Tom Boyle/Getty Images; 141: Dr Alan Zametkin/Clinical Brain Imaging; 151: © AP/Wide World Photos; 153: © Mary Kate Denny/PhotoEdit Inc. – All rights reserved;

162: © AP/Daily Press/Joe Fudge/Wide World Photos

Chapter 6. 174: © Keith Dannemiller/Corbis; 178: © William F. Campbell/Time Life Pictures/Getty Images; 185: © Catherine Karnow/Corbis; 190: © San Francisco Chronicle; 194: © Barbara Davidson/Dallas Morning News/Corbis; 202: © Spencer Platt/Getty Images

Chapter 7. 212: © AP Photo/Corpus Christi Caller-Times, David Pellerin/Wide World Photos; 215: © Tom McCarthy/PhotoEdit Inc. – All rights reserved; 217: © Lawrence Manning/Corbis; 229: Universal/The Kobal Collection/Zink, Vivian; 235: © AP/John Miller/Wide World Photos; 239: © Mario Villafuerte/Getty Images

Chapter 8. 250: © Getty Images; 254: © Rudi Von Briel/PhotoEdit Inc. – All rights reserved; 258: © Nancy Wegard/Getty Images; 262: © Spencer Platt/Getty Images; 265: © A. Ramey/PhotoEdit Inc. – All rights reserved; 268: © AP/Wide World Photos; 272: © Courtesy of Howard Zehr

Chapter 9. 282: © AP Photo/Doug Dreyer/Wide World Photos; 286: Republished with permission of Globe Newspaper Company, Inc.; 289: © Getty Images; 295: © Amy Etra/PhotoEdit, Inc. – All rights reserved; 302: © Richard Patterson/The New York Times

Chapter 10. 318: © Nelson "Speedy" Andrad/EPA/Landov; 322: © Les Stone/Corbis Sygma; 328: © Getty Images; 338: © Getty Images; 343: © AP/Wide World Photos; 350: © AFP/Getty Images; 354: © Fred Greaves/Reuters/Landov

Chapter 11. 366: Provided by the FBI; 368: © Roy 20 Cvii d. 41v. British Library/The Bridgeman Art Library; 370: © Marc Serota/Reuters/Corbis; 379: © Getty Images; 387: © Getty Images

Chapter 12. 394: © Chip East/Reuters/Landov; 398: © AP/Wide World Photos; 400: © Getty Images; 406: © Reuters/Corbis; 413: © Desmond Boylan/Reuters/Landov

Chapter 13. 424: © AP Photo/Bill Krostroun/Wide World Photos; 427: © Alinari/Art Resource, New York; 436: © Getty Images; 440: © AP/Wide World Photos; 448: © AP/Wide World Photos; 455: © AP/Wide World Photos

Chapter 14. 466: © Digital Vision; 470: © Ezio Petersen/UPI/Landov; 471: © Dennis Brack/Bloomberg News/Landov; 477: © Jarad Lazarus/Miami Herald/Pool/EPA/Landov; 479: © Getty Images; 484: © Digital Art/Corbis; 490: © Royalty-Free/Corbis

Time Line of Criminological Theories

	1775	1800	1825	1850	1875	1900	1925	1939

ORIGIN
Classical Theory

Beccaria *On Crimes and Punishment* (1764) — Kant *Philosophy of Law* (1887) — Brockway *The American Reformatory* (1910) — Mabbott *Punishment* (1939)

CONTEMPORARY THEORY
(Rational) Choice Theory (p.98)

Bentham *Moral Calculus* (1789) — Bentham *The Rationale of Punishment* (1830)

ORIGIN
Positivist Theory

Gall *Cranioscopy/Phrenology* (1800) — Lombroso *Criminal Man* (1863) — Garofalo *Criminology* (1885) — Kretschmer *Physique and Character* (1921) — Hooton *American Criminal* (1939)

CONTEMPORARY THEORY
Biosocial Trait Theory (p.134)

Dugdale *The Jukes* (1877) — Ferri *Criminal Sociology* (1884) — Goring *The English Convict* (1913)

ORIGIN
Positivist Theory

Maudsley *Pathology of Mind* (1867) — Tarde *Penal Philosophy* (1912) — Freud *General Introduction to Psychoanalysis* (1920)

CONTEMPORARY THEORY
Psychological Trait Theory (p.148)

Pinel *Treatise on Insanity* (1800) — Healy *The Individual Deliquent* (1915)

ORIGIN
Marxist Theory

Marx *Communist Manifesto* (1848) — Bonger *Criminality and Economic Conditions* (1916) — Rusche & Kircheimer *Punishment and Social Structure* (1939)

CONTEMPORARY THEORY
(Social) Conflict Theory (p.257)

ORIGIN
Sociological Theory

Quetelet *The Propensity of Crime* (1831) — Durkheim *The Division of Labor in Society* (1893) — Park, Burgess, & McKenzie *The City* (1925) Shaw et al. (1925) *Delinquency Areas* — Merton *Social Structure and Anomi* (1938)

CONTEMPORARY THEORY
Social Structure Theory (p.179)

Thrasher *The Gang* (1926) — Sellin *Culture, Conflict and Crime* (1938)

ORIGIN
Sociological Theory

Mead *The Psychology of Punitive Justice* (1917) — Sutherland *Principles of Criminology* (1939)

CONTEMPORARY THEORY
Social Process Theory (p.214)

Sutherland *Criminology* (1924) — Sutherland *The Professional Thief* (1937)

ORIGIN
Multifactor Theory

Glueck & Glueck *500 Criminal Careers* (1930)

CONTEMPORARY THEORY
Life Course Theory (p.292)

ORIGIN
Multifactor Theory

CONTEMPORARY THEORY
Latent Trait Theory (p.296)

Andenaes
General Preventive Effects of Punishment (1966)

Martinson
What Works (1974)

Cohen & Felson
Routine Activities (1979)

Clarke
Situational Crime Prevention (1992)

Packer
The Limits of Criminal Sanction (1968)

Newman
Defensible Space (1973)

J. Q. Wilson
Thinking About Crime (1975)

Katz
Seductions of Crime (1988)

Montagu
Man and Aggression (1968)

Jeffery
Crime Prevention (1971)

E. O. Wilson
Sociobiology (1975)

Mednick & Volavka
Biology and Crime (1980)

Rowe
The Limits of Family Influence (1995)

Sheldon
Varieties of Delinquent Youth (1949)

Dalton
The Premenstrual Syndrome (1971)

Ellis
Evolutionary Sociobiology (1989)

Friedlander
Psychoanalytic Approach to Delinquency (1947)

Eysenck
Crime and Personality (1964)

Bandura
Aggression (1973)

Hirschi & Hindelang
Intelligence and Delinquency (1977)

Henggeler
Delinquency in Adolescence (1989)

Moffitt
Neuropsychology of Crime (1992)

Wilson & Daly
Evolutionary Psychology (1997)

Murray & Herrnstein
The Bell Curve (1994)

Vold
Theoretical Criminology (1958)

Chambliss & Seidman
Law, Order and Power (1971)

Lea & Young
Left Realism (1984)

Hagan
Structural Criminology (1989)

Dahrendorf
Class and Class Conflict in Industrial Society (1959)

Taylor, Walton, & Young
The New Criminology (1973)

Daly & Chesney-Lind
Feminist Theory (1988)

Quinney & Pepinsky
Criminology as Peacemaking (1991)

Cloward & Ohlin
Delinquency and Opportunity (1960)

Kornhauser
Social Sources of Delinquency (1978)

Wilson
The Truly Disadvantaged (1987)

Agnew
General Strain Theory (1992)

Courtwright
Violent Land (1996)

Lewis
The Culture of Poverty (1966)

Blau & Blau
The Cost of Inequality (1982)

Messner & Rosenfeld
Crime and the American Dream (1994)

Lemert
Social Pathology (1951)

Hirschi
Causes of Delinquency (1969)

Schur
Labeling Deviant Behavior (1972)

Akers
Deviant Behavior (1977)

Kaplan
General Theory of Deviance (1992)

Becker
Outsiders (1963)

Heimer & Matsueda
Differential Social Control (1994)

Glueck & Glueck
Unraveling Juvenile Delinquency (1950)

West & Farrington
Delinquent Way of Life (1977)

Thornberry
Interactional Theory (1987)

Sampson & Laub
Crime in the Making (1993)

Weis
Social Development Theory (1981)

Moffitt
Adolescence-Limited and Life-Course Persistent Antisocial Behavior (1995)

Hathaway & Monachesi
Analyzing and Predicting Juvenile Delinquency with the MMPI (1953)

Wolfgang, Figlio, & Sellin
Delinquency in Birth Cohorts (1972)

Wilson & Herrnstein
Crime and Human Nature (1985)

Tittle
Control Balance: Toward a General Theory of Deviance (1995)

Eysenck
Crime and Personality (1964)

Gottfredson & Hirschi
General Theory of Crime (1990)

| 1947 | 1969 | 1975 | 1980 | 1991 | 1995 | 1997 |